THE WRESTLING OBSERVER YEARBOOK 2014

Online: F4Wonline.com

Twitter: @davemeltzerWON

Twitter: @WONF4W

Email: dave@wrestlingobserver.com

THE WRESTLING OBSERVER YEARBOOK 2014

THE YEAR OF
THE YES MOVEMENT

Dave Meltzer

TITAN INSIDER PRESS

Published by Titan Insider Press

This book is set in Garamond

10 9 8 7 6 5 4 3 2 1

This book was printed and bound in the United Kingdom

ISBN: 9798575151494

CONTENTS

CHAPTER ONE

HORRIFIC ANDERSON SILVA LEG INJURY

JANUARY 6

Anderson Silva, perhaps the greatest MMA fighter of all-time, was carried from the Octagon on a stretcher after suffering a compound fracture of his lower leg in losing via second round stoppage for the second time to Chris Weidman.

Silva, 38, had publicly hinted of retirement before the match, and had privately told his camp before the fight that should he beat Weidman and regain the title, that he would retire.

The injury was one of the two most visibly ghastly injuries in UFC history, as it appeared Silva's leg from just above the ankle was severed in two. Corey Hill suffered a similar injury in UFC competition, and did return to fight 13 months later, but was never the same. The injury brought up comparisons to Joe Theismann and Sid Vicious, who both made mention on Twitter and Facebook of it. Theismann never played again. Vicious did wrestle again, but not for several years, and was very limited in what he could do.

Silva suffered both a broken tibia and fibula slightly above the ankle when Weidman checked a low kick, essentially using his knee to block the kick. While some would call this a freak accident and say Weidman once again didn't prove to be better than Silva, that may have been accurate in the first fight. That wasn't the case here.

The move that ended the fight was something Weidman and trainer Ray Longo had been practicing constantly since the first fight. In that bout, the only thing Silva did that caused Weidman problems was using low kicks to open up Weidman for punches. While Silva has great reflexes, in straight boxing he is not that good without the threat of the low kick in place.

In the first round, Weidman knocked Silva down with a punch and was pounding him into the ground. It appeared Silva was knocked out briefly, but a second Weidman punch woke him up. Silva was in trouble, and in a lesser fight, it could have been stopped, but he regained his bearings quickly and was able to tie Weidman up. Still, Weidman remained on top, trying can opener necklocks, landing elbows and hard punches and working for a forearm choke.

Silva's left leg appeared injured, and those in his camp believed that he may have broken his leg originally when Weidman checked a kick in the first round, before it snapped in two early in the second round, and he collapsed on the mat.

Silva was stabilized in the ring, and taken out on a stretcher. Backstage, he was screaming in terrible pain. He was taken to the hospital in an ambulance and they did surgery that night, inserting a titanium rod into his left tibia, with a screw inserted just below the knee joint, and two screws just above the ankle to keep the rod in place.

Dr. Steven Sanders, who did the one hour surgery, said that Silva's age would be of no bearing when it comes to the bone healing process, which he estimated at three to six months. After that, there would also be soft tissue healing that would be needed, and he would have to begin rehab. Sanders estimated that it would be six to nine months before Silva could start training. He also noted that it was extremely close to being something far worse. It was a clean break with no bone fragments, meaning easier clean-up. If the bone had stuck through the skin, the possibility for infection would have been higher. If there had been damage to arteries in the break, there would have been a chance an amputation would have been necessary. Silva was in tremendous pain after surgery, but was released from the hospital a few days later. He has made no statements about whether he would consider fighting again, but given the injury and his age, there is a good chance his career is over. If not, he's highly unlikely to get another championship fight for a long time.

"Anderson is deeply touched by the outpouring of support from his fans and the entire MMA community," wrote UFC officials. "There has been no immediate decision about his future, and he would kindly ask for privacy at this time as he deals with his injury and prepare to return home to recover."

The injury was a very somber ending to what otherwise was a home run from both an atmospheric, fight quality and business aspect. UFC 168 on 12/28 at the MGM Grand Garden Arena from all accounts appears to have been one of the biggest shows in company history.

But it also means that UFC starts 2014 for the first year in history with absolutely nothing on the horizon that would appear to be a huge fight. If 2013 is any indication, there will be plenty of good fights. But huge fights, like Georges St-Pierre vs. Nick Diaz or Johny Hendricks, Anderson Silva vs. Chris Weidman, Ronda Rousey vs. Miesha Tate, or Jon Jones vs. Chael Sonnen, there is nothing there right now. The company's two biggest draws, St-Pierre and Silva are both gone for a while, and in Silva's case, likely all year if he even decides to come back. The idea of the big superfight at a stadium is gone with Silva out of commission, since he was the key guy for either Jon Jones or St-Pierre. Even Jones vs. Cain Velasquez is almost surely not happening until 2015, since Velasquez will be out of action until late in the year after shoulder surgery.

The closest thing to a big fight is Jones vs. Alexander Gustafsson, and that is contingent on Jones beating Glover Teixeira and Gustafsson beating Jimi Manuwa. And even a best case scenario has that fight in the late summer. And it's also a fight that only did 310,000 buys the first time around.

As improbable as this would have sounded a year ago, UFC enters 2014 with Rousey as clearly its biggest star. But she also doesn't have the right opponent. Even before beating Tate in the semifinal, Rousey was asked and agreed to defend her women's bantamweight title against Sara McMann on 2/22 in Las Vegas.

That's a quick turnaround. But, that show needed a main event. McMann won the silver medal in wrestling at the 2004 Olympics in the 139 pound weight class and is now 7-0 as a pro. With Rousey having won a bronze medal at 154 pounds in judo in 2008, this would be UFC's first fight, male or female, matching up two Olympic medalists. The fight, at the Mandalay Bay Events Center, would come right at the end of the Winter Olympics, which is a good hook for it garnering mainstream media and attention. That show will also feature Daniel Cormier vs. Rashad Evans. A match with Gilbert Melendez vs. Khabib Nurmagomedov was on a UFC poster for the event and confirmed by UFC on 12/28, only to have Dana White tweet a few days later that it wasn't a done deal.

Weidman's next title defense will be against Vitor Belfort, in a battle of the two leading candidates for in-cage fighter of the year. During 2013, Weidman finished Silva twice. Belfort went 3-0, with three head kick knockouts against tough guys. He was the second person ever to finish Luke Rockhold, the second to ever finish Michael Bisping, and the first to ever knock out Dan Henderson.

That fight opens up a hornets nest of issues, because Belfort, fighting in Brazil, has been approved for testosterone replacement therapy, which appears to have played a hand in an incredible career turnaround. Belfort went 2-5 between the ages of 27 and 29, when one would normally hit their peak. And the two wins were against former pro wrestler Yoshiki Takahashi, who by that time was long past his fighting prime, and unknown British fighter Anthony Rea.

Now, at 36, with 18 years of mileage on his body, he's destroying top ten guys like they were nothing. If the fight is earmarked for Brazil, there will be a lot of controversy at UFC with the idea they are protecting Belfort from commissions that may not allow his testosterone use based on testing positive for steroids in the past. If it's booked for the U.S., there will be tremendous pressure on commissions to balance fairness, criticism and the obvious financial benefit to their state of having the fight.

No PPV numbers are available at the moment, but early signs are they will be big. Because of the holidays, nobody had anything close to concrete numbers, but the DirecTV numbers were big enough that UFC officials were said to be thrilled. One cable system in the U.S. I got numbers from indicated that they more than doubled their numbers from UFC 167, the GSP vs. Hendricks fight that ended up doing about 630,000 buys. A Canadian source indicated numbers only slightly below UFC 167.

The weigh-in on FS 1 did 275,000 viewers at 7 p.m. Eastern. It was the all-time record for most viewers of a UFC weigh-in since leaving Spike. However, that's misleading, because weigh-ins are usually on FS 2 and often in the afternoon. The number for GSP vs. Nick Diaz on 3/15, which was 215,000 viewers, was far more impressive since it was at 4 p.m. on a station in less than half as many homes.

While it would be impossible to get statistics on this, the belief was that the attendance at sports bars was the largest in recent memory. We received reports from around the country from people noting places were packed hours before the PPV started and lines were out the door. One person in Los Angeles told us he went from place to place all over town, all packed, before giving up and ordering it at home. At Buffalo Wild Wings, the event was the prime event at almost all locations, which doesn't sound significant, except it went head-to-head with the Buffalo Wild Wings Bowl.

The show drew a sellout 15,650 fans at the MGM Grand Garden Arena, a record for a UFC event in its home arena, and a $6.2 million gate, the latter being the third largest in company history, trailing only UFC 129 at Rogers Centre in Toronto, and UFC 148, also at the MGM Grand Garden Arena, which was the second Silva vs. Chael Sonnen fight. That number doesn't include closed circuit locations in Las Vegas for the overflow.

The prelims on FS 1 did 1,554,000 viewers, making it the fifth most watched show since the launch of the station in August, and second biggest UFC number, trailing only the Sonnen vs. Shogun Rua debut show on the network on 8/17. For a comparison, the prelims for UFC 167, the GSP vs. Hendricks fight, did 998,000 viewers. The prelims for UFC 166, the Cain Velasquez vs. Junior Dos Santos fight, did 628,000 viewers. The TV main event, pitting Chris Leben in what is likely his final UFC appearance losing to Uriah Hall, did 1,869,000 viewers.

The post-fight show did 313,000 viewers, a record. The UFC Flashback special at 7:30 p.m., an incredible production built around the first Weidman vs. Silva fight, did 412,000 viewers, making it the highest rated replay of a UFC television show since moving to FS 1. That's impressive since the original airing did 156,000 viewers on 12/22, and the Christmas Eve replay did 168,000 viewers.

In Brazil, a one hour special airing Rousey vs. Tate and Weidman vs. Silva drew 10 million viewers on Globo, airing on tape delay starting at 2:40 a.m. Saturday night. UFC big shows featuring Silva and other Brazilian stars like Jose Aldo or Junior Dos Santos on Globo, airing four times per year, averaged more than 20 million viewers in 2011, 13 million in 2012 but were down to 6.5 million this year. Globo had heavily promoted the show, calling it the most important fight of the year with a lot of commercials airing during their prime time programming. When they do the shows, Globo never advertises a starting time, meaning you have to tune in around 2 a.m. and wait for it to start. Because of that, the usual late night programming on UFC nights that precede UFC usually doubles in ratings. Globo is the dominant station in Brazil the way nothing in the U.S. or Canada is, and is the second largest television network in the world when it comes to revenue.

Google searches, which are usually spot on when it comes to predicting PPV numbers (as in usually within 25,000 of the final number), were through the roof. Because Silva's broken leg and the graphic nature of it became such a major story, this would be the exception to that rule.

There were more than 5 million searches for UFC related topics on Saturday night. At least 2 million specifically mentioned Silva's broken leg. However, throwing out Silva related mentions, the number was still more than double that of UFC 167, and the numbers were way above the usual show even while the show was in progress, exploding right after the finish of the Rousey vs. Tate match, which would not be related to injury, or the main event.

Few UFC shows hit 500,000 searches and most are around 200,000. 5 million was identical to Floyd Mayweather vs. Canelo Alvarez, and the highest sports total of the year for 2013, the Super Bowl, was 10 million. While after the show, Silva was clearly the story, but before the fight, even though Weidman and Silva were all over the late advertising, there was more interest in Rousey and Tate. As far as who drew the house, it was Silva. As far as who drew the PPV and packed the locations, it was a combination of both fights, but reports from every place were that the people were there for the women more than the men. All indicators showed more interest in the women's fight than the men's with Rousey and Tate almost even, Silva slightly behind and Weidman trailing the other three greatly. By Monday, due to the injury, Silva was the person people were most interested in, but Rousey's name was far stronger than Tate coming out of the fight, and Weidman was still behind Tate even after being Silva twice.

In addition, UFC web site traffic leading into the show was at all-time record levels.

In Brazil, Silva's injury was gigantic news. Silva has been the "commercial darling" in the country in recent years. He's all over billboards and television commercials. While his stardom did decline after losing the championship, he was still behind only the biggest soccer stars and old-time soccer legends when it comes to star power in the country.

JANUARY 13

Anderson Silva's manager, Jorge Guimares, told TMZ that Silva is not retiring, saying that there was no nerve damage stemming from his broken leg. Dana White was also on ESPN, saying that he is under the impression Silva is going to fight again. It's going to be a long slow road for him at 39. I don't see him as the kind of a guy who is going to fight at a diminished level because he loves fighting. So until he starts hard training, which is probably nine months away, the only thing I take from this is mentally what he's telling people is he's not decided to walk away without a try. Guimares and Ed Soares, another rep for Silva, have been throwing out the idea of, when Silva is ready, which would likely not be until 2015, of having his return fight be against GSP. If Silva wants to fight, and GSP wants to fight by then, that could be the monster fight, depending on GSP's outlook. GSP, because of his record of never losing the title, and as a draw, probably could and should be able to come back and if he wanted a title shot his first fight back, get it, or get one tune-up before a title shot.

JANUARY 20

Anderson Silva was on one of Globo's biggest talk shows on 1/12, and made it clear that he wants to fight again. He met with Dana White and Lorenzo Fertitta this week and told them the same thing. But until he starts training, and that's probably a good nine months away, nobody knows how well he can recover from the broken leg at 39. He said on the show that he didn't believe he lost to Chris Weidman. "I believe that if you pay attention to these technical details, you will see that (the checking the kick) was instinct, not something that he trained to do." He said that he doesn't think Weidman should take credit for it as a win, saying the finish was an accident and that he's pretty sure he would have won the fight if his leg didn't break. He said that he's rewatched the tape and saw the technical mistakes he made. He said the night of the fight and surgery, he was scared that he would never be able to walk again. But he said that now that he's seen the improvement, he's confident he'll fight again, and he has made the decision he doesn't want to go out the way he did and does want to come back, although that won't be anytime soon. He just started his rehab on 1/14. He was in excruciating pain the night of the fight. He was screaming in pain after the fight was over and that sometimes he asks his wife to go for a drive so he can scream and cry he's in so much pain so his kids don't have to see it. He said he's still in so much pain that he can't sleep.

An update on Anderson Silva is that he's able to ride a stationary bicycle, and expects to be off crutches in two or three weeks. He believes he will be able to do some training by June. On Arsenio Hall, Dana White said Silva would be fighting before the end of the year.

Silva said he wants to box Roy Jones Jr. before he does another MMA fight. His contract wouldn't allow it unless UFC gives its approval, and from a UFC standpoint, I just don't see the point. White said it made no sense to him, but the way he said it was that it wasn't like he was going to say no way, but they'd have to talk about it and work out the details. There was a time when an MMA champ vs. boxer would have done huge business, and perhaps with the right guys it still would. But Jones Jr. today isn't that guy, and I think today's audience is more sophisticated than five or six years ago and unless it's special circumstances, the lure of that kind of fight's ship has sailed.

CHAPTER TWO

THE DANIEL BRYAN SAGA

JANUARY 6

In a move that seemed to come out of nowhere, Daniel Bryan seemingly turned heel at the end of the final Raw episode of 2013.

Bryan was being beaten down by The Wyatt Family after facing all three of them in successive singles matches. He had been given a clothesline by Luke Harper and a double choke slam. Bray Wyatt then began singing, and said, "This is where our story ends. It could have been different and this is your fault. I'm going to punish you. I want you to open your eyes."

Out of nowhere, Bryan said, "You're right." At first, the fans in Richmond, VA, were so surprised that they didn't even react. Then they started chanting, "No, No, No." It wasn't until the third time Bryan made it clear he was joining the group that the fans finally reacted and booed.

"You were always right," Bryan said. "No matter how many matches I won. No matter how loud these people cheered for me. You were always right. The machine would never let me win, no matter how loud you people chanted. You've chanted, `Yes, Yes, Yes,' in this very building I've been to, and they don't care."

He then said to Wyatt, "I'm yours. Let me join the family." Bryan asked for a hand, but Wyatt instead pulled away and gave him Sister Abigail, almost leading one to believe this was a double-cross. But then he put Bryan's hand on his heart and said, "This is forever."

Fans were chanting "No" and chanting his name but he left with them.

It was an interesting move in taking the wrestler who for the last several months had gotten the loudest fan reaction in the building most nights and turning him. Even with that reaction, it was clear that John Cena was and will always be top babyface, and C.M. Punk was positioned as No. 2, as the headliner on the other brand. It's not the same thing as when Steve Austin turned heel in 2001, since he brought a generation of fans to the table. The business has also changed to where it's not like doing this is risking business as it often did when the wrong guy was turned at the wrong time.

It's not even clear what the direction is, except apparently as a way to make Wyatt into a star capable of working with Cena at WrestleMania, as is the plan. Where Bryan fits into the show is unknown. It is said that Undertaker asked to work with him at Mania this year, and such a match would at least have the turn make sense.

But as of press time, the top four planned Mania matches are still Cena vs. Wyatt, Undertaker vs. Brock Lesnar, HHH vs. C.M. Punk and Randy Orton vs. Batista.

It would seemingly end the idea of a Bryan vs. Shawn Michaels match, although friends of Michaels have said that was never a consideration. And it's not like the turn closes any door completely, since Michaels could do the match as a face if he wanted to.

Since there should be a major Wyatt Family vs. Shield match before The Shield finally breaks up, having Bryan with Harper & Rowan vs. The Shield would make sense, but we've heard no hints in that direction.

Even though Bryan was not the top babyface when it came to positioning, he had the most fervent supporters. Fans voted him Superstar of the Year, even though he never even held one of the major singles titles except for a two minute and 22 hour tease. But this is one that it's hard to comment on until one sees the direction it's going. But as long as he stays in the group, he'll be the No. 2 guy behind Wyatt, particularly if Wyatt is the Cena opponent.

JANUARY 13

The Daniel Bryan thing is really confusing. It's also clear they don't have a complete battle plan on what they are doing. At the weekend house shows, he was introduced as Daniel Wyatt for his matches with Bray Wyatt. But on Raw, he was back to being Daniel Bryan, although he kept the same look, basically dressed exactly the same as Rowan, except for no sheep mask and he probably takes a much smaller size garbage carrier jump suit. If you think about it, if his name means anything on the marquee, changing to Daniel Wyatt will only confuse ticket buyers, so keeping him as Daniel Bryan was a good thing. Plus, it's clear he is going to end up back as a babyface at some point because Michael Cole didn't even treat his turn like a heel turn. The idea is he wants to hang around with them to become a monster. I think the idea is they want to give him a dangerous edge, with the idea people think he's a great wrestler but he's not dangerous. It's not a turn because in week one they already teased problems with the Wyatts on Raw and Michael Cole, under orders from Vince McMahon, did not act like he turned on friends or fans or anyone, and was taking about him the way you would talk about a babyface. At the same time, the crowd, which was behind him, was taken down a ton and he didn't get anywhere close to the reactions he used to. I think the only thing you can do is sit and wait. It absolutely could be something, like the burying of ECW, to get rid of unwanted chants after the crowd hijacked the show in Seattle. I don't want to say that's the case but it's possible. It could be a long-term story that will help him, although I'm not sure how. The idea is the fans will badly want him to leave the Wyatt family and he'll be more over because of the struggle to get back. Of course, that was the same mentality with Show being bullied by HHH and Stephanie, which did lead to a big pop when he punched HHH, but now with that angle done, with hindsight Show is roughly in the same spot he was in, his match with Orton didn't draw, his match with HHH never happened, and his storyline about HHH buying his house and him being broke, etc. went nowhere. In 2001, once they realized that the Steve Austin heel turn was a big mistake, they would do these teases to where people knew he was going back face but they didn't turn him for a while. In the end, when they did turn Austin back, he was never quite as over as he had been before and anyone in the company with access to numbers will tell you in hindsight what a bad decision that ended up being.

They picked the absolute worst time for all this. Travis Jackson of Michigan State's football team started doing the "Yes" chants himself during a game in November, and again after they scored a touchdown in the Rose Bowl last week when they beat Stanford. And then on 1/7, at the Michigan State vs. Ohio State basketball game, Jackson was leading the chants from the stands during halftime and it got picked and played up big on Sports Center. Sports Center and all media directly credited it to Daniel Bryan. As much as the chant seemed over at WWE shows, it was way more impressive visually at the basketball game because everyone was doing it, and also because it was taken as something significant as a sports story. But this is the time you take advantage of real life and you should be having a change of plans, shooting the guy through the roof as a babyface and getting him on talk shows as the originator (well, Diego Sanchez is the originator but except for Bryan and very few other people, nobody knows that, including UFC fans). Quite frankly, UFC should see if they can capitalize on this, but they don't have much claim because all the media has pushed it as Bryan and I'm guessing Jackson has no clue it came from Sanchez.

JANUARY 20

After a week where the "Yes" chants, at Michigan State basketball games were highlighting Sports Center, and attributed to Bryan, who was in an angle where he turned heel and was no longer doing them, he was turned back on the 1/13 Raw. Earlier in the show, after he and Wyatt lost via DQ to the Usos, Wyatt was blaming him and the crowd badly wanted him to stand up to Wyatt, but he bowed down to him and got on his knees. Wyatt gave him Sister Abigail and Bryan did nothing about it. Later, when they had the same match brought back in a cage as the main event, Bryan fell off the cage, hit Wyatt on the top rope, who crotched himself, allowing the Usos to climb out to win. The same scenario happened, but this time Bryan pulled away from the Sister Abigail. Wyatt dared Bryan to attack him, and Bryan wouldn't, until Wyatt called him a coward. Bryan then attacked Wyatt, pulled off his garbage man Erick Rowan outfit, revealing his red Daniel Bryan tights and he kicked the hell out of Wyatt. The whole place, which was dead for most of the match and really, the last 90 minutes of the show, was going crazy with the "Yes" chants, replicating the scene at the Michigan State basketball game. Bryan laid Wyatt out with the Busaiku knee. Timing wise, the turn made little sense with the fan base as behind him as they were. The plan was always to turn him back as evidenced by Vince McMahon making it clear to Michael Cole on commentary to never get on Bryan or portray him as a heel. The plan largely was in the long-term, as much as long-term there is, how it was originally going to play out. There wasn't any kind of great debate or big decision making regarding turning him back this week.

Now that he's back as a face, WWE really needs to get that footage from the Michigan State games and the ESPN coverage where they attributed it to Bryan and make him look like a big star. Regarding the "Yes" chants, the actual origins of the chants came from Tony Robbins book "Unlimited Power." When Diego Sanchez debuted doing the "Yes" chant on June 20, 2009, in Las Vegas, for his fight with Clay Guida (one of the greatest fights in UFC history by the way), announcer Mike Goldberg brought up how Sanchez was a big Robbins fan. Bryan Danielson has said in a number of interviews that he got the idea from watching Sanchez in UFC.

The bad news is that in the cage match, Bryan suffered a concussion. WWE officials confirmed the reports earlier in the day, including performers who said he was not able to remember a lot of the match and it seemed to be a serious concussion on Monday night. Nothing was confirmed at press time past the point it was a concussion, which means he won't be allowed to wrestle until he can pass imPACT testing. Bryan has had numerous prior concussions during his wrestling career, making him more susceptible. While WWE has a track record of stopping pushes of some guys after concussions (Ziggler, Fandango), Bryan is now top tier and I can't see that happening with him.

JANUARY 27

Bryan was on WGRD radio in Grand Rapids to promote Smackdown, and said that WWE has never seen any money in him, and was outspoken about the WWE's direction of his character. He said to this day, even with the loud fan reactions, he still doesn't think the company sees money in him, and he said this is very frustrating for him. He said this isn't an objective business like football. He noted that the company thinks he's getting a great crowd reaction but don't think he's selling tickets or getting people buying PPVs, and he said that's really about what it's about? He said sometimes it is frustrating dealing with the politics because he's not a political person. He said he's easy going, and as far as being successful in WWE, that's his biggest doubtful. He said he doesn't know why he connects with the crowd at the level it is, he said there are guys as good as him who don't connect, he couldn't teach it and he can't explain it. He said he got popular without what guys like Hogan and Austin got, where they almost never lost. He said the day after WrestleMania he lost to Langston in three minutes, and before he main evented SummerSlam he lost to Sandow in four minutes on TV. He noted he's never been the guy who the company has ever wanted to be the guy, and he said you can get crowd reactions like that for only so long but it won't endure if you aren't protected in booking. He compared himself to Clay Guida, who he said at one time was everyone's favorite UFC fighter, and at one point everyone was rooting for him, but he kept losing, people still like him, even love him but nobody buys PPV to see him. He said for long-term success as a main event star like Hogan, Austin or Cena, you have to be proteced in booking and that's never happened with him. He said he doesn't get frustrated easily and sometimes the crowd forces the company's hands to do things they really don't want to do. Bryan did say the company has gotten behind an idea from the Bella Twins that will be marketed called "The Yes Movement." He talked about being in Seattle and how the fans hijacked the main event segment, and he thought it was awesome because it was for him.

FEBRUARY 3

Based on the Royal Rumble, the stock price and all the other major stories, we are entering a period where it is going to be easier for WWE to make far more money with less actual popularity than any time in pro wrestling history.

Creative, the driving force behind most wrestling companies historically, is now in both a no lose and a no win situation. No lose because unless you become WCW bad, and that actually takes a level of talent that nobody in the company has (or doesn't have, depending on how you view it), you're bullet proof. Bad creative and house shows are going to do well because they are relatively rare. TV money is a cushion at the level nobody has had. And PPV, good or bad, is going to be relatively the same each month, because with six month contracts, the success of the impulse buys that used to fuel that aspect of the business will largely be gone.

Bad, because there are shows like the Royal Rumble, where the crowd wants what they want and are going to take down or even kill the impact of key parts of the show if they're mad.

Catering to the largest part of your audience to draw the most people is going to be replaced to having to cater and pacify, especially at the big shows, the hardest of the hardcore fans who come from all over the world and may be different from the actual masses that watch the television or even those who buy the merchandise and attend the matches all the other nights of the week.

Fans who pay their money have every right to find a way to entertain themselves. They can cheer or boo whoever they want. If I was a writer, I'd be frustrated if I was writing a good long program and it gets caught or ruined in the crossfire of an audience that has other ideas. But that's just part of the new job description and you've got to deal with it.

At the Royal Rumble, the idea going in is that the big items on the show were to kick off the build for the key WrestleMania matches. Brock Lesnar would destroy Big Show bad to set him up for Undertaker. There are little tweaks I'd have done different, but the basic framework of a two minute match and clean win is what I feared they wouldn't do, but is exactly what they did.

If Bray Wyatt was being groomed for John Cena, he had to beat Daniel Bryan in basic booking theory. I actually thought they might go with the idea that Bryan could beat Wyatt because Wyatt would screw Cena later and that would make up for it. Wyatt did screw Cena out of his title rematch, and Randy Orton won to retain. With Orton as champion, the title challenger, Batista, would then win the Rumble.

The sellout crowd of just over 12,000 (announced as 15,715) on 1/26 at the Consol Energy Center in Pittsburgh came in knowing the story as well. The story they knew was the flip side. That in a Royal Rumble filled with surprises, Daniel Bryan would come in as the big surprise, win and headline WrestleMania. The reasoning is because he's the cool thing and he gets the biggest reactions.

Bryan was never advertised for the Rumble, and that was actually to be part of a longer term storyline, that down the line it would play into his being held down when he finally does rise to a presumed real-life title run. What they didn't count on was the Bryan fans turning on the show when Bryan lost to Wyatt, outwardly attempting to kill the Orton vs. Cena title match as their interpretation of what they are being force-fed, and hate Batista, who they deep down knew was the only guy except Bryan who could actually in the Rumble. Orton was very upset after the match which was filled with chants of "Daniel Bryan," "We Want Refunds," "Boring," "We Want Divas," Yes," "We Want Angle" (who is from Pittsburgh), "Randy Savage" (Orton actually laughed at that one), "Y2J," "End this match," "This is awful."

It made for one of the more interesting nights in history. In a sense, it felt like the audience turned on the company. On the surface, that's terrible, except the people who hated the show did so with so much passion that instead of ditching following it, they seemed as interested as ever. The seasonal interest in wrestling is just as strong, and that's coming off a period from late August until now that creative has generally been pretty bad, and the PPVs have been on one of the worst streaks in a long time.

Bryan's tweets about being held down are storyline. The irony is hilarious. He's the point man for a revolution against creative, but in a sense (although the process looks to be sped up), it's creative scripting the revolution against them. It's borderline brilliant, except the Rumble show, the second biggest of the year, was kind of a casualty in its wake.

"Sorry guys, the machine wanted me nowhere near the Royal Rumble match," he wrote on Twitter. "But I thank everyone for their support. They try to keep US down and away from the top spots, but they can't ignore the reactions forever. Keep voicing your opinions."

He also pushed the phrase, The Yes Movement, to describe the revolution of the fans against the people who were scripting it, a moniker created by his future wife and sister-in-law, the Bella Twins.

This story actually got picked up by the BBC. A news organization that never covers pro wrestling, is seemingly above it, is reporting on a wrestling angle as if it's a news story.

But as noted, in trying to play this new audience, it also backfired. Batista, expected to be a babyface that would be the big return in going for the title at WrestleMania in one of the biggest matches on the show, after being gone for four years, was in the wrong place at the wrong time. Worse, the Rumble, one of the company's biggest matches of the year, went down in flames over the last ten minutes.

Everyone had figured it out. Bryan shows up at No. 30 to win. Out at No. 30 came Rey Mysterio, and the crowd turned on him. They booed the last ten minutes of the match in protest, and in particular Batista, thought of as the management chosen one. Hey, that ending would have been great. With the benefit of hindsight, of all people, Tommy Dreamer's idea of having Bryan come out in a Mysterio costume at No. 30, do a move or two and unmask was pretty brilliant. Although really, even that is over thinking because the basic idea of what everyone wanted, straight forward, was going to work. It's just that's not the direction they had planned.

Sheamus vs. Bryan had been added to the current plans for Mania, which, going into Monday, were still headlined by Undertaker vs. Lesnar, HHH vs. Punk, Cena vs. Wyatt and Orton vs. Batista. With Punk out of the picture, HHH vs. Bryan makes sense given the idea that Bryan is leading the movement of fans against the oppressive authority. Still, I'd book Orton vs. Batista vs. Bryan. In front of a larger version of the same crowd that comes from all over the world, there is a good chance the world title match, which should be the biggest world title match of the year, would be crapped on badly. With Bryan, it would probably rank with Undertaker vs. Lesnar as the show's biggest spectacle. Plus, Bryan does have to win the title some time in the next several months. There's nowhere better to kick off a good title reign than WrestleMania. More people will watch the title win. It'll feel like a bigger deal. He'll have more momentum to start as champion and the win will be more memorable and be more remembered for the rest of his career. However, that would leave HHH out of a WrestleMania program, so unless Punk comes back and his leaving was an angle, Bryan vs. HHH would appear to be the more likely alternative, which could lead to Bryan vs. Orton or Batista at Extreme Rules in Seattle.

Mick Foley, whose WWE contract is about to expire, claimed he was furious, and went over-the-top on social media to the point many in the company thought he had to have been told to play the angle (he has claimed that isn't the case), writing:

"As I mentioned on Twitter, I've never felt so disgusted at the conclusion of a WWE (or any) PPV. Like many of you out there, I just don't get it. The Daniel Bryan thing is a phenomenon. You get it. I get it. The fans in Pittsburgh (yes, I was thinking of writing "RIGHT TH...but I'm just not in a cheap pop mood) got it. But tonight, for the first time, I had to admit to myself that the powers that be are just not going to get it. And that makes me sad. I'm just honestly sad, just flat out fucking sad. Yes, I dropped an F-bomb there to emphasize how Fucking sad I am for the guys who bust their butts night in and night out--Ziggler, Punk, Bryan, etc. with no hope of getting their shot at this year's Mania.

You know who else I'm sad for? Me. In my two years as an official WWE Ambassador, I never once had to lie about my enthusiasm for the company or the product. Now, although I am no longer officially an Ambassador for WWE (believe it or not, my only official role in WWE is as GM for Saturday Morning Slam, a contract that ends in one month), I was still looking forward to being part of the biggest event of the year. I'll probably end up going anyway. but I'm about 1/6th as excited about it as I was just a few hours ago. I wanted so badly to hear 75,000 WWE fans chanting "Yes," and seeing fans walk away absolutely ecstatic about the outcome of a PPV for the first time in a while...a long while. But when given the chance to make it happen (unless they've got something MAJOR up their sleeve), WWE's answer right now was a resounding "NO, NO, NO."

One talent said that if Foley had voiced his opinion previously, it would be one thing, but he buried us (really he didn't bury any talent) only when his contract was expiring, but then said he's going to WrestleMania. The funny part is that same person noted that everyone actually agrees with what he said.

His son, Dewey, now an adult, made famous in the "cane Dewey promo" in ECW when he was a young child, got involved, writing

"Sorry people who know much about wrestling, but this company right now is in some serious shit. This is really bad for their company because one or two individuals truly believe that their opinions reign much higher over the millions and millions of people who watch their shows religiously on a weekly basis. It's such a horrible feeling obviously because it hits close to home. You have these guys who work their asses off 320 plus days a year, who barely see their loved ones, and they get completely disrespected and disregarded because Triple Fucking H thinks they're too small or not star material. My dad made your ass, and people told my dad all his life that he would amount to nothing. So HHH should know from experience that the people that work their asses off and that are told that they are worthless are the ones that make the company the best it can be. Without my dad, HHH is just a mid-carder. My dad went out of his way to make sure that he turned HHH into the intimidating, scary cerebral assassin, son of a bitch that he has become. So it's about time that people who deserve to be the best are given the opportunity to show it. WWE is a fucking dictatorship, and it is just truly a shame."

FEBRUARY 3

Within the company, the belief is still that Bryan is a guy who is a great wrestler who people chant for and is a star, but doesn't draw money in a major way, at least at the No. 1 star in the company level. Even Bryan himself in an interview last week said that you can't prove anything, but that the company does need to judge based on what sells tickets and PPVs as to who goes in the top position. You can look at tickets in the sense there are two tours, and the Cena vs. Orton tour charges higher ticket prices (because of Cena) and consistently outdraws the Punk and Bryan tour. We can argue forever regarding his build, and his build to be a main eventer sucked royally, yet if you watched the TV, you got the feeling there was great momentum. But of his four main events, only Hell in a Cell did even average numbers based on the show. SummerSlam was way down and Night of Champions and Battleground did poor numbers. Survivor Series also did poor numbers with Orton vs. Show, and Show was pushed super strong leading into that card. And the finishes didn't help in the sense they constantly screwed people on them. We didn't get numbers officially yet for TLC, which was the return to Cena vs. Orton, but preliminary indications were that show beat the prior year by a huge amount. To me, if it hadn't with the build of the first unified champion in 50 or 100 years or whatever they claimed that week, given the build, it should be a huge disappointment. None of that says with the right push he can't be the top guy. It only says the chants that make it appear in the buildings that he's far and away the most over guy do not reflect any measurable metric to the degree of a top guy. Even in the overrun two weeks ago when he did the turn back, his TV moving numbers were behind Cena (to his credit, he was in second place and not a distant second either), and last week he was behind Batista (the novelty factor, and it does appear it was more novelty factor than anything) as well as Cena, Orton, Punk, Lesnar/Heyman and HHH, but still well ahead of everyone else. Nothing is a perfect science, but every metric they usually use to figure who are money players, or who are on the verge, he does the level of a toip tier babyface, but not near Cena or Punk, as opposed to a guy over achieving his push, which is the perception you'd get from TV as him being a guy who the most over guy there's been in years. Again, with the right marketing, the "Yes Movement," fighting oppressive authority, it could click huge and I'd have made him champion last October, and I'd build to making him champion now. So that makes it easier to justify not going all the way with him or thinking the chants are a very vocal hardcore that doesn't represent the big picture if you are predisposed to believe he can't be a top guy based on the usual looks category. But I can't see them not giving him a title run over the next six months. The question then comes does he get the Batista style booked title run or the Punk style booked or the Mysterio style booked title run, because you can self fulfill prophesies of success even after giving someone the belt. On the flip side, there is momentum there with the "Yes" chant going mainstream and I'd sure push him really hard right now to take advantage of it. Plus, when you throw in the psychology that those running the company feel they do understand the business and have the belief that fans that make noise really don't, there is a natural push back against it. It's just an inevitable part of psychology. This is both the hardest and easiest time in history when it comes to the top national promotion. Because of all the new revenue streams, it is the easiest time ever to be profitable. If rights fees for the level of ratings were what they are, even a company as incompetent as WCW at the time would have a fighting chance to break even. A company as well run as WWE is on the verge of going through the most successful financial period of any wrestling company in history. On the flip side, it's harder because there is a fan base that is the most hardcore, most vocal, etc., that represents a viewpoint that may not be the best route for business nor represent the masses, which is funny because that's where the whole "Best for Business" storyline used to get heat comes from. They want certain things, and it can be a Zack Ryder push a few years back, or Bryan being the world champion and top star in the company. And the thing is, the nature of the company today is that the actual booking isn't life or death as historically it was. The company can do what they want because ratings aren't going to vary too much if Cena is the top guy or Bryan is, and attendance will vary some based on the top star, but it's still the brand that draws for the most part. It doesn't matter who holds the title, only who the top star on the show is. Yet at the same time, you want to make the fans happy, but also have to figure what most of the fans, and not the most vocal fans want. That's an impossible task to do 100%, but there are a number of metrics that you can look at. The problem is that to a degree, they are self-fulfilling prophesies in the sense the guys you don't beat very often and focus on are generally going to do better in those metrics. And some guys, like Mysterio, who look great in metrics (merchandise, hero to very important Spanish demo, used to be very significant when it came to moving ratings, especially with Hispanics) aren't going to be pushed past a certain level because they are seen as being big stars at shows but not who you can build around as a top guy because of size concerns. Plus, with him today, there's the age and injury concerns and they aren't going to push him a lot now. Yet at the same time, you'll have Batista, who is older and has also piled up injuries, but because he fits the prototype, is going to be pushed harder. And right now, since he's new, that isn't wrong, but compare the respective pushes for each man's return. But Batista was pushed as the bigger star in the past, was gone longer and his return was going to mean more all things being equal. The hardcore fans do have the ability to make a star, because the truth is, Punk and Bryan both never would have gotten anywhere based on what the company perceives a top star to be, but they were both more than good enough to be great TV characters, and a lot of that is because they talk so well, plus people know they work their asses off and have great matches. And Punk was for a long time very legitimately No. 2 of the full-timers. Still, Mysterio, Eddy Guerrero and Jeff Hardy all come to mind as people who were not booked strongly, but still moved ratings and merchandise. It led to Guerrero and Hardy going from mid-card to main event and Mysterio having runs at the top that he otherwise wouldn't have, although his upward mobility was still limited by his size in their eyes. But this conflict between the decision makers and most vocal fans is going to be a huge part of the business going forward. And I have to believe Bryan is going to get that title win, at best because they know his fan base is an important core to business and it's really not that important today who has the belt. The only reason not to give it to him would be stubbornness or having fun thumbing their nose at fans. But winning the belt itself means nothing. Whether he can be a long-term face of the company and take the spot Cena has is a very different story.

FEBRUARY 10

The White House's web site, which is a site that allows people to contact the Obama Administration to take action on important issues that people sign petitions for, saw nearly 100,000 people sign a petition that would demand Bryan be put in the WWE title match at WrestleMania. The petition was taken down as this was supposed to be limited to important national issues and apparently they didn't feel it qualified. Then wrestling fans tried to get a petition going involving Punk, but the web site dumped that one instantly.

MARCH 17

The only logical scenario for the WWE championship match at WrestleMania was put together on the 3/10 Raw in Memphis, where Daniel Bryan was both granted his match with HHH, and the stipulation that if he wins, he's added to the title match with champion Randy Orton and Batista.

The match, would be considered likely to go on last, and one doesn't have to over think the obvious in that the show at the Mercedes Benz Superdome in New Orleans should end with upwards of 70,000 fans chanting "Yes," as Bryan captures the title. If it doesn't happen that way, they are risking missing the timing in a business where making a breakout star involves timing as one of the key ingredients.

The scenario was put together in a creative fashion. Bryan brought out several dozens of supposed fans, a few of which actually were fans but most were people who were in various backstage roles in WWE on TV nights, all wearing his T-shirt and all chanting "Yes." The group refused to leave the ring and allow the show to continue unless Bryan was granted his match with HHH. Eventually, because they were holding up the show and for some reason, they had no security, to keep the show going HHH had to grant Bryan his match. Bryan then said that wasn't all he wanted, and said he also wanted a title shot if he wins.

Exactly when this storyline was finalized is unknown. Bryan was originally going to be booked with Sheamus down the card for the show. But when C.M. Punk left the promotion, Bryan was moved up and into the HHH program. As far as being added to the title match, that decision likely came at the exact moment the promotion decided to turn Batista heel, as an admission that the people weren't cheering him like a top babyface. It had to be at least considered coming off the Royal Rumble, but based on the way television was put together, it doesn't appear that it was finalized until Batista was booed in Minneapolis at Elimination Chamber against Alberto Del Rio. In hindsight, you could see the pieces come together from that point, although almost everyone figured it had to be done even before then.

Batista's not getting over as a face was more an example of wrong place, wrong time, as he was heavily booed by hardcore fans who resented his being booked to win the Rumble and get a title shot at WrestleMania ahead of either Bryan or Punk. It became natural to add a babyface into that match, and the only viable candidates would have been Cena, Bryan and Punk, and after the reaction to the Cena vs. Orton match at the Royal Rumble, even that would risk major fan rejection of the match. With Cena locked in with Bray Wyatt in a high-profile situation, that led to Punk or Bryan. Punk made that decision easy by leaving the promotion.

Bryan being booked in both matches seems to shut the door on Punk being in a major match at WrestleMania. It also seems to put the finishing touches on the top of the card, now all announced, with Undertaker vs. Brock Lesnar and Cena vs. Wyatt along with the two matches with Bryan as the card's top four bouts.

APRIL 14

For whatever happened over the past two years with Daniel Bryan as a small guy doing comedy routines about how funny it was that he thought he could beat big guys, somewhere something connected with the audience.

And it saved a WrestleMania that would have been lackluster without it. Bryan had the two best matches, a strong main event style match to open where he beat HHH, and then he beat champion Randy Orton and Batista, making Batista submit to the Yes lock, in 23:19, to become WWE world champion.

But with it, it was among the best WrestleManias in history, ending with Bryan overcoming the odds amidst a sea of "Yes" chants.

Daniel Bryan pinned HHH in 25:57 of a classic match. HHH was ridiculously big for a 44-year-old guy. Stephanie was in his corner acting as a valet with short shorts. Bryan's left shoulder was all taped up. HHH wanted to shake hands, but Bryan kicked him in the hand and went for a schoolboy. Bryan came off apron with a DDT on HHH on the floor. He did a flip dive off top rope that didn't hit solid, crashing somewhat into the barricade. It was almost a miss. Bryan was on the top rope, HHH fell on the ropes and Bryan crotched himself on top. HHH knocked him off the apron. HHH started working on the shoulder. HHH missed a tackle and flew over the top rope. Bryan went for a tope, but in coming through the ropes, HHH punched him in the face. HHH gave him a back suplex on the apron and Bryan teased a count out before beating the ten count. He used a chicken wing crossface on Bryan, who made the ropes. HHH continued to work the left shoulder. Bryan used two German suplexes for near falls. HHH used a Tiger suplex for what may have been the first time in his life. HHH went for a superplex, but Bryan came back with punches and a sunset flip power bomb off top rope. Bryan did two running dropkicks, and on his third attempt, ran into a clothesline. HHH went for a pedigree, but it was blocked and turned into a jackknife cradle. HHH used a crossface and had him in the move for a long time. Bryan reversed into a crossface of his own. HHH made the ropes. Bryan then hit two topes and a missile dropkick. Bryan was throwing kicks to the chest and one to the head as fans chanted "Yes." He went for the Busaiku knee, but HHH countered with a spinebuster. HHH hit the pedigree and Bryan kicked out. HHH used knees to the temple. He tried another pedigree, but Bryan got out, kicked him in the head and pinned him with the Busaiku knee. With the exception of Bret Hart vs. Owen Hart, this was probably the best PPV opening match in WrestleMania history. Stephanie was slapping the hell out of Bryan after the match and HHH nailed him from behind. He put his left shoulder next to the post and slammed a chair onto it. So the idea is HHH hurt him going into the main event. It was a basic storyline and also exactly what they should have done. ****1/4

Daniel Bryan won the WWE title in a three way over champion Randy Orton and Batista in 23:19. Rev Theory, who recorded Orton's entrance song, was there live performing the song for his arrival. Batista threw Orton's shoulder into the steps and Orton back suplexed Batista on the steps and back suplexed Bryan on the barricade. He did the same to Batista. Bryan came back with a missile dropkick on both. At one point Bryan did five running dropkicks, back-and-forth, on Orton and Batista who were in opposite corners. Bryan did a Frankensteiner off the top on Orton for a near fall. Batista suplexed Bryan over the top to the floor. Orton superplexed Batista. Bryan got Orton in the Yes lock. Stephanie McMahon and HHH came out and pulled the ref out of the ring so he couldn't call for the submission. They called out Scott Armstrong to ref. Batista used a Batista bomb on Bryan, who kicked out. HHH and Stephanie yelled at Armstrong. The crowd was going crazy. Bryan kicked Scott Armstrong in the head and they noted that three-ways in WWE are no DQ. Bryan did a tope onto HHH, Scott Armstrong and Stephanie. Really it was onto HHH and Armstrong. Stephanie was never hit but still took a bump. HHH then pulled out his sledge hammer. Bryan kicked HHH and got the sledge hammer and nailed him in the head. Stephanie selling her ankle and HHH were helped to the back. Orton tore the tape off Bryan's shoulder and started working on it again. Orton threw the steps on Bryan's shoulder. Orton and Batista cleaned out all three (English, Spanish and French) announcers tables. There was a loud C.M. Punk chant. They did a combination Batista bomb and RKO on Bryan, putting him through the table. Bryan sold like he was dead. Orton's lower back was all cut up from a monitor. Batista attacked Orton. They put Bryan on a stretcher and were taking him out, when he got up off the stretcher to continue. Batista threw Orton into the post. Orton did a draping DDT on Batista on the floor. Bryan got back in. He escaped an RKO attempt. Bryan put the Yes lock on Orton and Batista saved. He put the Yes lock on Batista and Orton saved. Orton tried an RKO on Batista, but it was blocked. Batista went for the spear on Orton, who leap frogged him and he nailed Bryan. That was a great spot. Bryan was taken out, and Orton hit the RKO on Batista, who kicked out for a good near fall. Bryan used the Busaiku knee on Orton, but Batista threw him out of the ring and made the cover, but Orton kicked out for a great near fall. Batista hit the Batista bomb on Orton, and didn't split his pants. When Batista got up, Bryan hit him with the Busaiku knee and then put Batista in the Yes lock and Batista tapped out. They did the big confetti celebration with Bryan in the ring as the new champion as the crowd, at least in the lower section of the arena, was going crazy. I was told it wasn't 70,000 people chanting Yes, as in the upper deck, it wasn't as big a moment as you'd think. But it was still an awesome spectacle, and the right thing to do on the right date for the next chapter in the story. ****1/2

MAY 19

WWE champion Daniel Bryan is expected out of action six to eight weeks, if not less, as he's scheduled for minimally invasive neck surgery on 5/15.

Bryan announced the need for the surgery, and portrayed it as a potential career ender, although vowing to return, giving the audience the impression he would be gone for a while.

Most of the details surrounding the surgery have been kept quiet. For the company's champion and one of its two biggest stars, there has been nothing in the way of mainstream publicity and official company sources are saying nothing.

What is known is that Bryan was examined during the past week for neck problems that were believed to be the result of wear and tear of 15 years of hard hitting and high flying pro wrestling and told to have minor surgery before it gets worse. Few knew until he got to television on 5/12 in Greenville, SC, and that afternoon, the television show had to be completely rewritten.

Bryan will be off the company's next major event, Payback, on 6/1 in Chicago. The plan was for him to face Kane in the main event in a Buried Alive match for the title, but it had not been officially announced. The match was scheduled to be announced on Raw this past week.

The 5/19 Raw show from London, England, is being advertised around the announcement of the decision as far as what to do about the championship. At this point, Bryan is only expected right now to miss one major show. It's not a lock that he could return for the 6/29 Money in the Bank show in Boston, but the expectation is he will be able to perform by then. While six to eight weeks has been used as the timetable, we're told that time frame right now is considered a worst-case scenario and he could be back in just a few weeks. A lot more would be known once he has the surgery.

My own feeling is that unless Bryan is going to be out three months or longer, taking the title from him is a very bad move. It's hard to tell this early for sure regarding the affect on popularity, but the portrayal of his character since winning the title at WrestleMania, and particularly in the past two weeks, has been questionable at best, and while I hate to overreact to one city's crowd reactions of clearly a minority of fans, the difference in Bryan's reaction coming out this past week with the last several months was hard to miss.

It was the first week after a really bad skit, where, as a main event babyface, in the attempt to make Kane into a monster challenger, he was positioned more like a low card face whipping boy set-up guy as opposed to the final conflict face. The next night, in Greensboro, he wasn't there for television, but when he was shown on the screen, he didn't get the reaction that one of the top stars in the promotion would get, but again, it's too early to necessarily read anything into that, because in the rapidly moving world, really been creative is usually forgotten within a few weeks anyway. But if it's part of a long-term direction, then it can do damage.

Plus, aligning him so closely with his wife, Brie Bella, in almost every scene he's in on Raw, hasn't helped him. You don't see John Cena in every scene with Nikki Bella, nor Natalya with Tyson Kidd or Jimmy Uso with Naomi. It's not a secret they are married, and there's nothing wrong with acknowledging it since it's a central theme on a different show and the actual wedding episode of Total Divas is expected to be heavily promoted and draw good numbers. Him doing one angle at some point where that's a major focus of it would work. But her always being there, and this specific angle the way he's been portrayed, has not helped him.

But later in the show, when Stephanie McMahon came out and seemed to tease she was going to ask him to vacate the title, before that happened, Kane dragged an unconscious Bryan out on the ramp. This portrayal was more along the lines of the prelim babyface that the top heel bully was being fed before he gets to the top star. One or two bad weeks of booking aren't death, but this hasn't helped him. If he loses the title this quickly after such a long chase, it cheapens the title win, going from the beginning of a new era to just being another transitional guy. He'll be viewed as someone who got there and couldn't hang. If it's a long time out, there is no choice. If he's out a long time, his return can to built up huge. But if he does this big farewell scene, and he's back on TV in four to six weeks without the title, unless he's booked strong as hell on his return, it will hurt him.

One of the positives is that without having PPVs that rely on people individually having to decide to specifically spend money for, it's now a network thing and the entire dynamic is different. The network subscribers are paid for through September or October. How many people were really going to add the network to see a Daniel Bryan vs. Kane match on a "B" PPV who for the most part had already decided WrestleMania's card wasn't strong enough for them to make the call? And for those who didn't get it for fear of technical issues, losing a weak marquee title match on a "B" show isn't going to change their purchasing decisions.

While doing a major show without a world title match isn't the best thing, it's also not the end of the world. In fact, there are almost no financial repercussions to it. Chicago is selling out either way. Yeah, there will be perhaps a small amount of money down on PPV outside of the U.S., and a little in the U.S. But this would have had far more repercussions six months ago. It's also the reason they have far less financial pressure and more leeway to go a little bit of time without the champion.

My gut says that Payback without Bryan and the title on the card would have done a pretty bad PPV number. But I'm not sure it would have done much better even with him. Both Evolution vs. The Shield and John Cena vs. Bray Wyatt are repeat matches, the latter being the third meeting. Every true money player currently on the roster and available on that date with Bryan out would be in those two matches. Doing a title tournament that doesn't include Cena, Orton, any members of The Shield, Batista or Wyatt would be a joke of a tournament. Plus, when Bryan does return, the way his exit was put together, it has to be against Kane. That means that if Kane doesn't win the tournament, Bryan won't come back in the title picture. So what are the alternatives, Wyatt winning and Cena chasing?

Ultimately, not making a move until Monday makes sense because they'll know a lot more, and there are ways to work around it, including doing a tournament on television if need be. But the best case scenario is to sit tight and bring Bryan back as champion, because a second chase will be old news and won't work well with a guy who had the moment of capture, but nothing changed. The capture a second time won't mean anything because people already saw what happened after that point.

Bryan was pulled from all advertising going forward, since the idea given on television is he'll be out for a long time.

Bryan made the announcement on Raw, saying that he knew winning the title would be an uphill battle, but the hill ended up steeper than he thought. When Bryan came out, it was a good reaction, but nothing at the level he'd been getting, and there were "No" chants and very light boos. He tried to joke and say, "So that's what it's like to be John Cena," so it was enough for him to acknowledge.

He attributed the injury to storyline reasons, the three tombstone piledrivers from Kane gave him a few weeks ago on television. He said that even after getting out of a neck brace, he beat Kane, but that his ring style comes with a price.

He noted that he believes the reason the people cheer for him and chant for him is because he's paid that price with his body, but unfortunately, he has to really pay the price this week with neck surgery. He said he wasn't happy about it, and how being WWE champion was his dream since he was a little kid. He then went back to storyline, saying what is frustrating is that people will be happy about it, noting Stephanie McMahon, HHH and Kane, saying they seem to be thrilled at the prospect that it seems like his career could be over. There were "No" chants at that.

"There's a chance it could be, but it won't be," he said. "When will I come back? I have no idea. Will I come back? Yes."

Bryan's injury does put him out for the company's traditional biggest money tour of the year, the post-Mania European swing. It's again no hit financially. The tour draws based on WWE coming, and the tickets are sold well in advance anyway. Fans in the cities Bryan was billed as the headliner won't be happy, but the tickets have already been purchased.

For a variety of reasons, mostly NBA playoff related, ratings are already at a low level. Smackdown has done its two worst ratings in the last 11 months over the last two weeks. Raw did its lowest rating not against football since July. Even though Bryan is champion, ever since he won the title, The Shield vs. Evolution has been portrayed as the key conflict. Next week's number may be helped with the idea of the situation with the world title being addressed. It'll be a real test of the value of the title. As far as Bryan's not being there and any affect it may have, the 5/26 show is one to watch.

It also focuses on the fact while the company has plenty of good wrestlers, it is terribly weak in depth when it comes to singles headliners, a lot attributable to a booking style that in most cases cuts people off before they can get to the top.

When Punk left, the company was one injury away from a problem, because they only had Cena and Bryan as headliners, and were running two tours. Sheamus had been groomed for some time to be in that slot, but never reached that level, and the U.S. title is more a hindrance than a help if a renewed push will get him there. At one point, Randy Orton in the plans for turning back, but that hasn't happened. Roman Reigns, Cesaro and Bray Wyatt may be given shots in the future, but Cesaro has just started the heel run to get him there, and I'm not sure his mic work will allow him to hang in the main event babyface spot. Reigns is clearly being groomed for the Cena spot, but it's also clear they aren't rushing it, which in his case is a good thing.

With Bryan's situation short-term, it's not really that big of an issue today. But it does bring to the forefront that they are one Cena or Bryan serious injury away from a problem.

MAY 26

Bryan Danielson, WWE's current heavyweight champion Daniel Bryan, underwent surgery for a nerve problem in his neck on 5/15 in Pittsburgh, under WWE Head of Medical Dr. Joseph Maroon.

Maroon had done neck surgeries on several WWE wrestlers in the past including John Cena and Edge.

The reports of Danielson suffering a broken neck were told to us to be untrue, and that it was a significant nerve issue that required a minimally invasive surgery.

Danielson has had neck problems for a significant period of time, but they worsened to the point he needed the operation, even though this was just about the worst time possible.

Danielson's surgery, according to the WWE, was a procedure called a cervical foraminotomy, which is to decompress the nerve root.

According to sources within the company, plans before the surgery were for Bryan to return on the 6/29 Money in the Bank PPV in Boston. The latest word is that he may not make that deadline and they are booking a new card if they are without him as a contingency plan.

The PPV after Money in the Bank would be three weeks later, Battleground, on 7/20 in Tampa. The belief is if he's not able to make it back for Money in the Bank, that would probably be the return, with SummerSlam four weeks later considered a worst case scenario.

Exactly what the company is going to do regarding the title is unclear. They had, on Smackdown, teased the idea Bryan would be on Raw in London, saying he would be on the show or they would update his condition in pushing the show on Smackdown. The WWE's web site said that he would be on raw. They also promoted the show around the idea that what would happen with the title would be decided.

After surgery, we were told he wasn't going to be in London, but he may appear on a taped interview. As it turned out, they did update his situation, but no promo of him appeared on the show.

On Raw, Stephanie McMahon came out to Bryan's music, getting the easy heat for mocking him. She teased the idea of taking the title from him, but ultimately nothing substantial was said and instead built it up for next week. The question about what happens to the title may be one of the biggest hooks the show has right now for ratings. It made sense to prolong it, because the 5/26 show, over Memorial Day, could struggle in the ratings. The tease was that he would appear on the show in Knoxville, and would be stripped of the title there. Generally, with a tease like that, it means they are probably going to do something different.

Stephanie McMahon stated that Bryan himself knows that you need an active champion, so she called on him to do the right thing and relinquish the title next week. She teased the idea of giving the belt to Kane, Bad News Barrett (which got a huge face reaction in London, which saw her come back with making fun of the crowd for how predictable they were), Batista or HHH. She said she was demanding Bryan show up in Knoxville and do the right thing, and give up the title, because that's what is best for business.

There are a lot of ways they could go. Given the 6/1 show is already advertising matches, and stipulation matches at that, and continued all the hype for those bouts, involving every top active guy, doing a tournament for the title that wouldn't include any of the top guys will greatly weaken the belt. What they could do is on 6/29, put the top guys like The Shield, Kane, John Cena, Bray Wyatt, Randy Orton and others in the Money in the Bank ladder match, and instead of it being for the guaranteed title shot, make it for the title itself.

If Bryan is not going to be back for Money in the Bank, a compromise, and I have no idea how you logically do this, but logic isn't always necessary, is find a way to take one of the two belts away, and do the interim title deal that boxing and MMA do. That way, you have a title to win at Money in the Bank, and there's a physical belt. But, Bryan is not stripped of the title either, because after that long chase, the idea of Bryan coming back and going back into a chase is going to make him come across as a failed champion. If he'd been booked stronger as champion, you could take it away from him based on injury and fans could get into the chase. But that didn't happen. He was champion, but was booked weak, so what's the great chase of the title when you figure if he gets it, he's still not being booked like a superstar.

For Bryan, with his style of wrestling, this neck operation may be the beginning of long-term problems. A number of the biggest names in wrestling history, who are following his situation, noted to me that he needs to start toning down his style.

Some have suggested giving up moves. The missile dropkick, because of the way he lands while doing it, the diving head-butt and the topes, because he often crashes into the barricade, were the three moves mentioned the most. But that's a tough deal. I know that with Chris Benoit, who had a more serious neck surgery, the idea of giving up the diving head-butts was suggested to him, he continued to use that and said that when he could no longer do the move, that's when he would probably want to retire. Harley Race, who pioneered the move in the U.S. in the 70s, has stated on many occasions the unnatural way of landing is brutal on the neck, and even though it was his trademark, recommended people not do it. Race did more of a falling off the top rope version and not a soaring version like Benoit, Dynamite Kid and Bryan are known for. Just a few weeks ago, Bryan did the move off a forklift two-thirds of the way across the ring in an angle with Kane on Raw.

Another way this could be handled is to not drop the moves completely, but save them for only big singles matches, so the long-term wear-and-tear won't be as bad, and he would still do what he wants in the big matches that he'll be most remembered for.

Bryan's "Yes" chant spread this past week to the San Francisco Giants baseball team. Every time a player on the team hits a home run, they do the chant in the dugout with the pointing to the sky. It hasn't been acknowledged yet by their regular announcers, but some local radio guys have picked up the significance of it.

JUNE 2

The WWE title situation is theoretically still on hold after the 5/26 Raw in Knoxville, where the second storyline of Daniel Bryan being asked to vacate the title led to no resolution and a teased end on the 6/1 Payback PPV from Chicago.

It also begins to explain the new purpose of WWE wrestling.

I thought it was clever to take the title situation and milk it for extra weeks to build ratings. But there becomes a point where people start seeing through it, and I'm not sure week three wasn't the deadline. Still, I can understand the situation. The PPV needs help with no world title match, so you sell that the title situation is resolved. Whether new people will purchase the network for it (the main goal now of an angle), who knows? But Payback is a weak show, with the only other real hook being Evolution vs. The Shield in an elimination match.

So going into the PPV, the situation is that either Bryan vacates his title, or Stephanie McMahon fires Brie Bella for putting her hands on her boss (when Brie shoved her several weeks ago on Raw), and the choice was up to him after he refused to vacate the title.

They tried to do an explanation regarding Stephanie not stripping Bryan by saying that if she did so, it would make him a martyr and the fans are cheering him enough as it is. She pushed it that the audience needs an active champion and unforgettable title matches, and he physically can't provide that right now.

Bryan essentially said he understood those points, but would not vacate the title because giving the belt back would negate everything that he and the crowd did this year, and would give Stephanie satisfaction.

Bryan, as part of the segment, said his neck injury was worse than anticipated, and blamed the added damage on Kane, clearly pushing Kane as his return opponent.

While we don't know exactly how the angle plays out, we do know that advertising is out for Bryan to wrestle on the 6/24 Smackdown tapings in Pittsburgh (dark match eight man tag, Bryan & The Shield vs. Randy Orton & The Wyatt Family) and on the biggest U.S. house show of the summer on 7/12 in Madison Square Garden, where Bryan vs. HHH in a street fight for the title started being advertised as the main event several days after Bryan's surgery. It should be noted that those in WWE were not aware of the ramifications of Pittsburgh and whether the TV ad was something created before the injury and fell through the cracks before it aired (company officials believed that to be the case but couldn't confirm it at press time, one area fan noted that specific match has been advertised for that date before Bryan's injury so it does look likely that they forgot to get the ads pulled) or was a new ad created in the past few days. Either way, I was directly told that Bryan wrestling in a match on 6/24 is more likely not to be happening, since 6/29 is right now his targeted return if all goes well. But he would probably be on television fairly regularly over the next several weeks since they have to build his match.

The WWE at press time internally was not listing Bryan for the Pittsburgh date, but he was listed as wrestling at the Madison Square Garden house show. The WWE web site was also listing Bryan for MSG but not Pittsburgh.

As of the plans being talked about at TV this week, Bryan vs. Kane in a Buried Alive match for the title was the going plan for the 6/29 Money in the Bank PPV main event in Boston. But right now it is up in the air whether Bryan will be ready. What was being said is that if he is not ready, then the Buried Alive match would take place on the following PPV show, Battleground, on 7/20 in Tampa. The expectation is Bryan would be ready for that date.

JUNE 2

Bryan was on Chris Jericho's podcast this past week. One thing notable was talking about when he was fired and his reaction. He said he was told he was fired and didn't sell it big at all. In fact, he told John Laurinaitis that it was fine because now that he's fired, he'll make more money than he ever has made in his career due to being gone from WWE. He noted that people think you make a lot of money just by signing with WWE, but during his period in WWE before he started getting a push, it was costing him money to be there because his road expenses were more than what he was getting paid due to the nature of his contract. He said that he made more money from 2006 to 2009 working indies and Japan than he made in 2010 with WWE, and he figured when he was fired, that he'd finally have his first big money year on the indie scene. Bryan was fired for spitting on Cena and choking Justin Roberts with his tie in the original Nexus angle after the first season of NXT ended. He noted that he was legitimately fired. He was out for three months before returning at SummerSlam as a babyface on Cena's team. He said WWE called him one month before SummerSlam to hire him back and told him to keep it quiet. He noted that when they first contacted him by e-mail, he ignored them because he was negotiating to return to New Japan. But then they called and pushed him to come back. One of the things that's really notable about Bryan, and I think this is a huge reason for his success, is that nearly everyone whose popularity skyrockets in sports and entertainment has a hard time keeping a perspective. He's the opposite. He came across as the same guy, and totally realizes that while he's a great wrestler, so much of his success has been a series of unique instances and they were all fan based as opposed to long-term planned. He noted that his first getting over as a face came from the idea of Sheamus beating him in 18 seconds at WrestleMania, which was to springboard Sheamus to the top as a babyface and there were no real plans for him. Yet, Sheamus didn't get over, the fans hated it because they wanted to see the match and the big reaction to Bryan was like a protest vote. Similarly, last fall, his role was to get Orton over for the Batista chase at WrestleMania, but it didn't get Orton over, and then nobody set up the Rumble to be his launch point. He noted that his role on the Rumble was to put over Wyatt, for Cena, and was never scheduled in the match. But he came across as such a nice guy on the show, as well as on Total Divas. The thing is, every guy who gets a push is going to have resentment and if it's someone who doesn't fit the mold, it's worse and people will look for faults. I'm not saying it didn't happen here, but even if there were people who were skeptical of Bryan as the top star with the promotion, everyone wants to see him succeed. The negative on him is he made it clear he knows nothing about his booking until he gets to the building. There are guys who are active about what plans are for them long-term, and he shows up and does whatever is scripted. But, there are times you have to speak up, as we've seen. He also said he believes he was, in 2011, going to be the first Money in the Bank winner to lose their title match. He said he thought he was going to lose to Mark Henry, who was world champion, but Henry was injured and they gave him the title. He said the only reason he thought he even won the briefcase was because Alberto Del Rio won one, and he was a strong heel at the time, so he figured the company wanted a face winning the other. Bryan was a face but was turned into a heel as champion. He noted that WWE had administered an ambition and personality test earlier this year. He said that the woman who administered the best said that he had the lowest ambition score of anyone they had ever tested. He said what upsets him the most are short matches on TV. He also said that he thinks every developmental wrestler should be shipped off for six months to Europe and six months to Japan to learn a variety of styles. He said Regal came up with the name Daniel Bryan. He noted the name he came up with was Buddy (his Dad was nicknamed Buddy) Peacock.

JUNE 9

Seth Rollins' heel turn ended up being the most talked about news of the week, taking the spotlight away from the world title situation, which ended up just plain weird.

On Sunday's Payback show, they promised resolution. Daniel Bryan was threatened by Stephanie McMahon to either vacate the title or Brie Bella, his wife, would get fired.

In a great segment, Brie Bella quit, and slapped Stephanie in the face. So the resolution was Bryan would remain the champion.

The next day, after all that, there was an about-face. Stephanie announced that the main event for Money in the Bank, the next PPV, on 6/29 from the TD Garden in Boston, would be Bryan vs. Kane in a stretcher match. The original idea, a Buried Alive match, has more finality and doesn't lend itself to potential rematches.

However, if Bryan doesn't wrestle, she said the winner of Money in the Bank would become the new champion.

The original angle was designed with the idea that Bryan would have the title confrontation with Stephanie on 6/1, to lead to Kane's match on Bryan's return on 6/29. That all went as planned.

One person close to the situation said that Vince McMahon, who was making all the decisions regarding this angle, took the same approach that he's done many times when main eventers are injured. The situation was compared with the 2012 Hell in a Cell show where McMahon presumed John Cena would be ready to face C.M. Punk, didn't have anything planned in case Cena's recovery wasn't record breaking. This led to the Ryback vs. Punk Hell in a Cell match where Punk had to win and end Ryback's streak. While the show itself ended up a far bigger success than if Cena was healthy, Ryback was never the same as a babyface because it wasn't the time for him to lose, and Ryback was never close to the same again. It was similar at the end of 2012 when Punk was injured and they had nothing ready for the TLC match other than do the Punk vs. Ryback ladder match on television as soon as Punk was back.

The problem is that Bryan's rehabilitation of his right arm is going slower than anticipated. One person said that not only is he not makings gains, but he's actually losing strength in the arm while doing rehab, which is concerning. Bryan was in Indianapolis for Raw and backstage, his situation was the most talked about thing among those in power. He was sent back to Pittsburgh to see Dr. Joseph Maroon, who did his neck surgery, to see what was wrong. Bryan will return on the 6/9 Raw for another confrontation with Stephanie.

Because of that, there was no certainty and they created the Money in the Bank backup plan because they didn't want to do a PPV without the world title at stake. The idea is Payback had it at stake in the angle.

Nothing is definite. There is a feeling, knowing Bryan's wanting to be in the thick of things and mental toughness, that even if it's not the right thing for him, that he'll wrestle on 6/29. There is tremendous real life pressure being put on him right now to be ready, whether direct or just implied.

As of right now, if Bryan doesn't work, they will do a ladder match for the title. They are considering a second ladder match where the winner would have the briefcase, but right now they are going with the idea Bryan vs. Kane will headline.

JUNE 16

The Daniel Bryan recovery from his recent neck surgery took a turn for the worst this past week as WWE officials found out on either 6/5 or 6/6 (most key people found out the latter day, although it's possible the top people knew a day earlier) that Bryan would not be able to wrestle on the 6/29 Money in the Bank PPV show at the TD Garden in Boston.

At that point, the decision was made to strip him of the WWE title and put the title up in a ladder match on the Money in the Bank show, which had been a back-up plan talked about on the 6/2 Raw show.

Based on the graphic on Raw, the match would have seven participants. At press time, winning matches to get into the match were Alberto Del Rio, Sheamus, Cesaro and Bray Wyatt. Randy Orton was also announced as being in the match. Company sources indicated John Cena would also be in the match, but that would not be official until next week. That would leave one spot remaining. Kane was not used this week on television, but he was planned for the title match with Bryan before Bryan was injured, and is the guy in storyline who injured Bryan and should face Bryan in his first match back. From that standpoint, he would make sense in this match.

The plan as of 6/9 was to go with two ladder matches on the show, one for the title, and the other for the briefcase that could be cashed in for one year as is usual for the show. With two Raw TV shows left until the PPV, there was no announcement made of such a second match. Given that Cesaro was originally one of the favorites to win the briefcase, and he's instead in the title match, his being in the key match is interesting. What's also notable is that my pick to win would have been Seth Rollins. It shoots the rocket for him after his turn, and he's filled with obvious contenders in Cena, Roman Reigns, Dean Ambrose, as well as Bryan. Rollins getting one of the final spots leaves Reigns and Ambrose with nothing for the PPV, since whether it's a ladder match or some other type of match, the very obvious direction as the hottest program for the PPV would be Rollins vs. Reigns & Ambrose. With Orton in the ladder match, that could lead to Rollins & HHH as a team, but all of this is speculation.

With the exception of the Usos vs. Luke Harper & Erick Rowan tag title match, there is no real clear direction of any serious programs right now, and with two ladder matches and something with The Shield, that would pretty much take in every key guy getting a decent push on the roster.

Little is known about Bryan's situation other than the bad news from last week that his right arm was actually getting weaker and not stronger since surgery, which was a bad sign.

This has led to a ton of speculation within wrestling as to his future. Bryan was also pulled from the only show he had been advertised on since the surgery, the 7/12 house show in Madison Square Garden where he was to face HHH in a street fight for the title.

The only thing we had heard was that they were still going with the idea that Bryan vs. Brock Lesnar would take place at SummerSlam in Los Angeles on 8/18. But that may not indicate anything because a week ago the idea was still that Bryan be working 6/29, but they were concerned and did formulate the ladder match back-up plan. At this point nobody has given an estimate return date for Bryan and because of that, the speculation has been running crazy as to what that means.

The only thing WWE had advertised all week for Raw was Bryan returning to confront Stephanie McMahon. The decision was made not to use Bryan on television. The feeling must have been after the way the angle played out, that him showing up and having to physically give back the title or announce he couldn't return on time would make his character seem weak after his wife quit the company specifically so he wouldn't have to give up the title.

It's been a very awkward situation. After that big pop and apparent resolution of the issue, then, for legitimate medical reasons, they felt they had to take the title from him anyway. It rendered much of the company's key angle direction as making no sense. It is unfortunate that reality screwed up the storyline, but they were guilty of assuming a certain probability while ignoring a very real possibility.

It was never a sure thing that he would be ready after surgery by 6/29, even though at first they did think he would. The company has often at times, when somebody is hurt and it's not a lock how quick they would recover from an injury, booked things with the idea the guy will be ready. At times, booking with that idea, bites them in the ass because nobody can predict recovery time from surgery 100 percent of the time. If the decision was made, as it apparently was at first, that it would be bad after the long chase and the big Mania win, to have Bryan lose the title quickly, then they could have bit the bullet. They could have also created an interim champion so Bryan wouldn't be stripped and Bryan would have an opponent other than Kane to return for. For whatever reason, they decreed in their own heads that they could go one PPV without a champion, not two, and weren't going the interim route.

But they went with a three-week storyline where heel Stephanie would get her comeuppances at the end, only for reality to change the story on them.

As far as who wins, if Bryan is to be back in July, you could have really any heel you want win. It could be Orton as the longer tenured headliner, Cesaro to take him a step up, Sheamus to precipitate a turn since people half ass boo him much of the time, Wyatt or Rollins. If it's a win the belt and lose in July deal, it really doesn't matter. The mentality about what would draw better doesn't matter with the network situation. It's just a question of who fits the storyline.

If there's uncertainty and it's long-term, the choice becomes more important. It's such a weird time. Cena and Orton are the enduring stars, and the natural inclination is to go with them. The most vocal fans want something new. My gut still says Rollins, because he would work with so many different foes. But it doesn't look like he's even a candidate.

The only thing we know is this. They have picked the winner, and have plans for the winner and a direction for the championship. They were flying by their seat of their pants the past few weeks.

JUNE 30

WWE will crown a new champion on 6/29 in Boston at the Money in the Bank PPV at the TD Garden, with Daniel Bryan out after neck surgery.

They are clearly teasing that the winner will face Brock Lesnar for the WWE title at SummerSlam.

WWE actually sent out a fan survey asking the question that if Lesnar was to challenge for the WWE title, who would fans like to see him face?

The men listed were the guys in the ladder match, with the exception of late addition Kane. What's notable is that the battle plan for SummerSlam was for the champion to defend against Lesnar.

That's not necessarily the winner of the ladder match, as they could do a cash-in. I could see Rollins doing a cash in to screw Reigns if Reigns was to win, as that's the only way I could see Reigns winning is getting taste without screwing up Mania. And the idea of Rollins headlining SummerSlam against Lesnar doesn't sound like a good mix.

The ladder match winner would appear to be the probable opponent for Lesnar. To no surprise, Roman Reigns ran away with the vote, almost tripling the numbers of Cesaro, John Cena, Bray Wyatt and Randy Orton, with virtually nobody wanting to see Sheamus or Alberto Del Rio against Lesnar.

I don't think they are asking fans as a way to consider who is winning unless plans change, because from what I've been told, the winner was decided upon about two weeks ago. Cena and Reigns felt to me like the favorites with Wyatt as a dark horse.

If they change their minds based on a poll result, they are creatively out to lunch, because fans don't know things like who is ready for a title, who would or wouldn't be hurt by a short reign, or if they are grooming someone for a long reign or things like are there more good challengers who could work with which guy for a successful reign.

Reigns is clearly being positioned as the hottest babyface, and as the guy to replace Cena, whose body is starting to break down. This bypasses Bryan, who had been the most popular wrestler in the company until going down with neck surgery. I don't think they were ever sold on Bryan as a long-term top guy and more a fad that the fans were into that would soon pass. Reigns first title win should come after a chase angle, and not be rushed into this week.

The problem is, somebody has to win and nobody is ready. Cena is somewhat flat in the sense of being ready for a championship run. But he is Cena, the established top guy right now, and Cena vs. Lesnar is a very viable SummerSlam main event. The timing isn't right for Cena, but the timing isn't right for anyone. While Wyatt's days as a babyface are probably coming sooner than later, I'm not sure Lesnar vs. Wyatt for the title is the way to go in two months. A Cesaro win would elevate him as well. Whether they see him as a title winner, or just a guy who can help have a great match in the main event, we'll see. But the question becomes what heel do they get it on for Reigns to chase. Orton is the one they always go to but his title reign that just ended did generally bad business and he's colder now than he was a year ago. Lesnar would be the best pick, but the question becomes how many dates is he willing to work, and at his price, is he cost effective to put the title on from SummerSlam through WrestleMania. They did set a precedent with The Rock in 2013 as far as putting the title on someone who would only wrestle on PPV.

Kane was added on Raw as the final person in the match. I can't see him as champion, but I could see Bryan, if he can physically do something, or even cause a distraction, cost Kane the match as revenge since Bryan vs. Kane is likely for SummerSlam or whenever Bryan returns.

JULY 13

The update on Bryan is that he may now also require shoulder surgery, as a full exam has revealed a lot of different shoulder and neck issues. At this point, because of uncertainty as to whether he'll need surgery and what surgery it could be, he's out of plans and there is no estimate on when he'll return. The plan seemed to be the Roman Reigns ascension to being the top guy at WrestleMania 31 whether Bryan was hurt or not, but now the TV is built around Reigns as the major badass. Without the injury, and if Bryan was still champion and Cena was top guy, it would likely have been a slower burn. The idea was Reigns working with Orton and maybe a big PPV match with HHH all along coming out of the Evolution vs. Shield program and Shield split.

AUGUST 4

Bryan Danielson had the craziest day on 7/24. It started with being part of a panel discussion with Hulk Hogan, Sting and Paul Heyman, and ended with him apprehending a burglar.

And in between, he officially announced he was doing an autobiography and found out he was going to need another operation.

Danielson got a measure of national publicity, as he chased down one of two burglars who had broken into his new home in Phoenix, took him down and held him in a rear naked choke while neighbors called 911 and police arrived quickly.

But earlier that day, he found out he would be needing a second operation, which would probably keep him out of action for another five to six months, just as his career had taken off. Danielson was the hottest wrestler in the company, but has been seemingly forgotten in current storylines given uncertainty about his return, with the only references regarding his wife's return angle with Stephanie McMahon. The top two babyface positions are seemingly locked for the long-term by the venerable top star John Cena, and the current heir apparent, Roman Reigns, although Danielson would figure to return in a strong No. 3 position.

But when that return will occur is uncertain at this time. Those in the company are tentatively going with the idea he'll return around the time of Royal Rumble. Originally the hope when he had neck surgery would be a return by June, but his inability to regain strength in his right arm had been concerning, and then the storyline, where he was going to keep the title, was changed to him vacating the title and perhaps returning against Kane for SummerSlam. Now, SummerSlam is no longer an option and it could be as late as the Royal Rumble.

Danielson talked about his injuries at a press conference with Phoenix police on 7/25, talking about the burglary.

He said the original injury was a compression of the ulnar nerve between the C-6 and C-7 vertebrae, in his neck, as well as bone spurs in the spinal cord. He said what they didn't realize is the ulnar nerve was also compressed at the elbow, which has resulted in his right arm only having half the strength of his left arm. He is expected to undergo a second operation where the nerve will be moved and placed under the muscle. He noted that while he doesn't have his strength on the right side, the injury isn't aggravating in daily life.

The Danielsons (Bryan and Brianna aka Brie Bella) had only moved into their new house ten days ago. Brie had been home all day, but when Bryan was able to get an earlier flight than expected out of San Diego, she went to the airport to pick him up.

When they got home, the door to the carport opened and closed. Bryan said that he and his wife, were most concerned about their dog, Josie (Brie and Josie were at the press conference). Bryan saw both men running out the back door, the door the two had broken into the house through. One got away, but he was able to chase the other about 400 meters before taking him down and putting him in a rear naked choke. Bryan said that he didn't put any real pressure on the move, just enough to keep him grounded and subdued until the police took him away.

Bryan said it probably wasn't the smartest thing in the world, and wouldn't recommend it. The incident immediately brings to mind a 2003 incident involving world kickboxing champion Alex Gong, who chased down a man who had smashed his car into Gong's parked car in the parking lot of the Fairtex Gym in San Francisco. Gong, on foot, chased down the man, who then shot Gong at point bank range, killing him. Later that day, police tracked down the accused shooter, who, after a lengthy standoff, fatally shot himself in the head.

Bryan said that the guy had pretty much run out of gas after running hard for about 50 meters, noting the guy wasn't in shape, and taking him down and putting the choke on him really took no effort. He joked that it probably would have made a better story if he had put him in the Yes lock. He said he wasn't really thinking about anything except that the men may have taken their dog.

Brie noted that she was in the house looking for the dog, so Bryan didn't know if they had the dog or not. She found the dog scared to death, shivering in the bathroom and having gone to bathroom on herself.

Police identified the man Bryan Danielson apprehended as 22-year-old Cesar Sosa, who was booked into the Maricopa County Jail and charged with burglary. It was discovered that Sosa had an outstanding felony warrant for his arrest on charges of burglary and kidnapping. The other man, who Bryan said that he didn't get a good look at, but some neighbors did, was not apprehended.

Bryan was praising his neighbors, noting that four of them had called 911 and another had called police about two suspicious men in the area, so police were close by investigating, even before the Danielsons had arrived home from the airport.

"I'm borderline ashamed for what I did," Bryan said. "It probably wasn't the best thing to do."

He said he was thankful that nobody got hurt.

"He was very tired," said Bryan. "It took zero effort to take him down and put him in the choke. You don't know how tough anybody is. He could have had the boxing skills of Mike Tyson, but he was so tired, it didn't matter. I train with Neal Melansen, who is one of Randy Couture's cornermen, and he says fatigue makes cowards of us all. Anyone who has done martial arts knows there's always someone tougher than you. But he put up very little resistance."

He said when he put him in the choke, he started getting worried that he might end up getting sued, which is why he didn't try to hurt him. He thought about the irony that someone breaks into your home and how then you could get sued for apprehending him.

He said he thought to himself, "What do I have to do to keep him here but not get sued?"

Bryan said it appeared to him that the robber had no idea who he or his wife were.

He said that later in the night, the neighbors, who he met a few days earlier at a block party, said that when he and his wife are on the road, they will move their cars and park in their driveways to make it seem like someone is there.

Bryan also noted that they were actually scheduled to put in an alarm system on 7/23, the day before the burglary. He said the appointment was that morning, but between his physical therapy appointments and having to get ready to go to San Diego, he had called and rescheduled the appointment until a few days later.

The burglars fled without taking anything. Bryan noted that they are "minimalists," in the sense they didn't have a lot of expensive things at the house.

But he noted they did break into the watch box that Nicole (Nikki Bella) had given them as a present. He said they had grabbed some watches that weren't worth very much, but did take an item of great sentimental value: a bracelet that his father, who just passed away on 4/21, had recently given him that was inscribed, "To the man you've become and to the son you'll always be," but in running away, they dropped it on the floor. His father gave it to him at his wedding. His father, Buddy Danielson, passed away when he and Brie returned from their honeymoon. Bryan was very emotional when recounting that aspect of the foiled burglary attempt.

"That was the last memento of my Dad," he said.

AUGUST 18

Phoenix police arrested three people, 30-year-old Alexandra Oliviera, 20-year-old Edwards Johnson and 21-year-old Gilbert Gastelum, whom police found allegedly burglarizing a home on 8/6, and believe them to be others in the group that attempted to burglarize the Bryan & Brianna Danielson home. The three were spotted in their vehicle, which matched the description and license plate of the one in the attempted Danielson home robbery. All three were booked on charges of burglary and participating in a criminal syndicate. They were able to get information from the man arrested in the Danielson robbery that Danielson subdued, which helped them make this arrest. They believe the group was part of a ring that had broken into a number of homes in the area.

AUGUST 25

Bryan has been doing almost nothing but rehab on a daily basis. He joked and said that he actually feels fine, but his right arm has almost no strength, which is the troubling issue. He was going to undergo surgery on 8/19, near his elbow as they believe there's a nerve issue there which isn't allowing the arm to regain strength. But then this past week, they postponed it and wanted to do more testing and see if they can fix the problem without surgery. He's pretty frustrated because he wants to be wrestling. He's been told that after surgery, he would probably be able to return in three months, so maybe as early as the end of November. But by delaying the surgery, they delay the return. He goes to two different physical therapy sessions, as well as gets acupuncture treatment and goes to an Active Release Technique class. Bryan was actually told in 2013 that he was going to need neck surgery because of his wear and tear. It was not a question of if but when. He didn't tone down his style as best we can tell, particularly doing the missile dropkicks and diving head-butts. He was hoping to go as long as he could without needing the surgery and is now happy he made it through WrestleMania. He also said that he thinks Yuji Nagata is the best wrestler he was ever in the ring with, said one of the best matches of his career that was never taped was with Minoru Suzuki, and thinks Shinsuke Nakamura is the best wrestler in the world, and when he said this, was only through day one or two of the G-1 tournament. He also noted in an interview with us at how crazy it was that the band of thieves who broke into his house were caught last week, figuring that after the one guy he tackled was caught and they knew the police were after them after so many burglaries and you'd think they'd lay low for a few weeks.

Bryan also told IGN.com about the angle with him having an affair with his physical therapist: "Yeah, to me, it's groan-worthy (notable he would say that, whether he felt it or not because the company doesn't really like people who say stuff like that and writers have been known to get reprisals from top talent who criticize them publicly). Don't think it added anything to the story. It was just like, `Ugh.' But they do what they do, and you just gotta roll with the punches. It's funny, because I feel sometimes you just have to overcome these things more so than anything else. Like, Brie and Stephanie have to overcome that flaw. To me, that was a flaw in the story. The story was so good, and then here's this flaw in it. But its' whatever. It doesn't hurt my feelings or anything. It's entertainment, it's not real."

SEPTEMBER 15

Bryan was told last week that he won't be needing a second operation after all. The situation has gone back-and-forth. Brie Bella, in doing promotional work for Total Divas, said that he's doing rehab on the right arm and the strength is slowly coming back. She said that you don't know how quickly the body heals, but they are targeting about three months from now for his return, but said it could be sooner.

OCTOBER 20

Bryan's future is back in question as his right arm is not regaining strength. There was talk backstage this week of him needing Tommy John surgery, which is something that major league baseball pitchers get, which is a reconstruction of the ulnar ligament. Bryan has issues in both his neck and his elbow. It can be as long as a one year recovery period. Right now the hope of a return for the Royal Rumble isn't looking good.

NOVEMBER 3

In Houston on 10/28, at the Smackdown tapings, Big Show, in a segment not taped for television, and seemingly taped to cheer Bryan up, led the crowd chanting "Yes" and telling them that Bryan may need elbow surgery. We'd reported it was likely he would need surgery because his strength in his right arm still isn't coming back.

The situation is significant. Bryan made a public appearance on 10/28 in Santa Clara. According to what we were told, even though he was wearing a long sleeve shirt, it was described to us, and photos backed it up, that you could tell Bryan's left arm looked big and has retained its usual muscle (while not a big muscular guy by wrestler standards, by normal person on the street standards, he's thickly muscled) and his right arm looked much smaller. We were told there is no timetable for his return nor a guarantee he will return. There have been reports that he's going to get Tommy John surgery, an elbow procedure common among baseball pitchers, which has a long recovery time. WWE officially has been quiet about his situation publicly but wrestlers have talked about him needing major elbow surgery.

NOVEMBER 24

Bryan was in the Bay Area again for the WrestleMania party on 11/14 at Levi's Stadium. Regarding his health, there is really no update other than at this point he is not having surgery done, but it is still possible he will need surgery. There is still no timetable for his return. It is whenever his strength comes back in the right arm and hand due to a nerve issue. There are no plans for him in storylines and the writers have been told not to figure anything in for him until further notice. When asked about WrestleMania, he himself has said that he would be really disappointed if he's not on the show and he's hoping to be able to wrestle by January so he can have a full program build for the show.

CHAPTER THREE

WRESTLE KINGDOM AND THE HISTORY OF WRESTLING AT THE TOKYO DOME

JANUARY 6

When the former Soviet Union fell into an economic collapse, a decision was made to raise money by contracting some of their prized athletes out to professional sports organizations.

Before Russians started competing in the NHL, the first deal, which made significant worldwide news, was with New Japan Pro Wrestling in 1988. Masa Saito and Hiroshi Hase, two New Japan wrestlers who had backgrounds as Olympians, were put in charge of training a group of high-level athletes—who had never seen pro wrestling—to become wrestlers in a short period of time.

A year earlier, the Tokyo Dome, the first indoor stadium of its kind, opened. The Dome, with its unique air supported white roof, looked almost like a half egg; hence in its early years, the building was known as The Big Egg, and sometimes, the Egg Dome.

On 1/4, when New Japan runs its 23rd straight January 4th event at the Dome, with the double main event of Shinsuke Nakamura vs. Hiroshi Tanahashi for the IC title and Kazuchika Okada vs. Tetsuya Naito for the IWGP title, it will be the closest thing to the quarter-century anniversary of pro wrestling being held in a building that has housed a majority of the biggest crowds and greatest shows in the history of the genre.

In 1990, 1995, 2003, 2004, 2005 and 2012, shows at the Tokyo Dome won Best show of the year. There is a good chance 2013 will be added to that list. No other building has housed two cards of the year. It would be a joke to even suggest that the No. 1 arena for pro wrestling over the last quarter-century, when it comes to legendary shows and matches, could be anything but the Tokyo Dome.

The Dome was built at the Korakuen Mall, which included an amusement park, restaurants, and not far from Korakuen Stadium, which it replaced as the home of the most famous baseball team in Japan, the Yomiuri Giants. One of the most famous wrestling matches of all-time took place on October 7, 1957, at Korakuen Stadium, where Lou Thesz retained his NWA title going to a 60:00 draw with Rikidozan, in a match that drew an 87.0 rating, the highest rated television show in the history of the country. Literally, an entire nation stood still.

Almost next door to the Dome is Korakuen Hall, a small arena on the fourth floor of a building that is separated from the stadium by only a restaurant, the symbolic home of Japanese pro wrestling since the beginning of time.

After making the deal and training the Russians, New Japan Pro Wrestling announced their debut on the biggest show in the company's 17-year history, "Super Powers Clash," at the Tokyo Dome on April 24, 1989.

While pro wrestling was a popular sport on television that drew solid crowds, the belief was that it was an expensive ticket arena event, not a stadium event. There were a few stadium shows in the 60s, with the last truly big hit being a 1967 match with International champion Giant Baba going to a 66 minute draw with NWA champion Gene Kiniski before 25,720 in Osaka. A show the next year at the stadium with Baba vs. WWWF champion Bruno Sammartino only drew 13,000.

New Japan had a golden era in the early 80s, a period nostalgia so strong for to this day that independent shows featuring Riki Choshu, Tatsumi Fujinami and the Original Tiger Mask, three of the big four of the era (Inoki was the big star, even though younger fans and hardcore fans were more into the Choshu vs. Fujinami matches) are regularly held and do decently well. But a lot of problems affected the product over the next few years.

New Japan's home base for its biggest shows was the 11,066-seat Sumo Hall at Ryogoku, which had been a problem. A riot at a late 1987 show for the debut of Big Van Vader ended up with the company banned from the building for one year. Their first show back, in early 1989, a double main event of a singles battle between the company's two biggest stars, Inoki and Choshu, plus an IWGP title match with Tatsumi Fujinami vs. Sid Vicious, had only drawn 8,000 fans.

The idea of booking the Tokyo Dome for the debut of unknown Russians was not without risk. But they drew a healthy crowd of 43,800 fans and a gate of $2,781,000, the latter would be a short-lived pro wrestling record, for a 14-match show. It immediately established the giant show concept once a year, or more if the right circumstances fell into place, as opposed to the tradition of a big show at a major arena at the end of every tour, as what you peak for.

The first Dome show featured a one-night tournament for the IWGP heavyweight title, Russian powerhouse wrestler Salman Hashimikov vs. Bam Bam Bigelow, New Japan's star foreign attraction, and a main event where Inoki would face Shota Chochoshvili, a Russian who in 1972 had won an Olympic gold medal in judo. In a match with no ropes around the ring, during the fifth round, Chochoshvili used a series of judo throws, called uranages, and Inoki was knocked out cold. Chochoshvili's pro wrestling career was short-lived—Inoki got his revenge in a rematch a month later. But the main event finish, the uranage, turned out to be a signature worldwide finishing move. It was popularized by Hase in the 90s after being taught it by the Russians, and turned into similar moves called the Rock Bottom and Book End in U.S. pro wrestling.

After the match was over, 73-year-old Thesz, who was on the show as the referee for the IWGP tag team title match, went to Inoki to tell him how proud he was of him as a businessman. In refereeing his match, Thesz met Hase, who is now a Senator in Japan. Thesz raved about him from that point forward, feeling he had a great mind for pro wrestling, was a fantastic in-ring wrestler, but would go on to big things outside of the wrestling. Hashimikov pinned Bigelow in 2:26 and became an instant sensation, having a short run as IWGP champion. Another debuting Russian, Victor Zangiev, a world teenage champion in 1981 and World Cup champion in 1985, became the best performer of the inexperienced crew, and popular enough that he became the prototype of a famous video game character, Zangief, in Street Fighter II. The show also featured the debut of a new character aimed at kids. Keiichi Yamada, known as the Japanese Dynamite Kid, donned a comic book outfit combining the Lion and Tiger, to become Jushin "Thunder" Liger. The idea was to create a character in the mode of the Original Tiger Mask, but for a new generation of fans. Liger pinned Kuniaki Kobayashi, who was Tiger Mask's biggest Japanese rival. Liger, who worked third from the top, and Super Strong Machine, who teamed with George Takano to defend the tag titles, are the two wrestlers who were on the first pro wrestling event at the Tokyo Dome, and will both be on Saturday's show, working the opening veterans nostalgia match.

Another name on the show was Benny "The Jet" Urquidez, a karate fighter turned kickboxing legend and later a well-known actor.

A promotion called the UWF had caught fire at about that time. It appeared what drew fans to pro wrestling was the idea of realism in a world that was anything but. The UWF, a worked promotion that eschewed usual pro wrestling spots, and built around stiff kicks, slaps, suplexes and submissions, had become all the rage. Almost every show was selling out as soon as tickets were put on sale. On November 29, 1989, the Tokyo Dome sold out for the first time, three days after tickets were put on sale, 50,000 tickets sold for a group that didn't even have television, for a show called "U-Cosmos."

The success of the UWF changed Japanese pro wrestling over the next decade. In the 70s and 80s, the business was built around unbeatable superstars. When the top stars squared off, finishes were often double count outs, or disqualifications. The system seemed to be working, as the business was popular and fans were drawn to the larger than life superstars, even if the big match finishes didn't prove anything.

But with the huge demand for UWF tickets, a company promoting realism and clean finishes, the two main promotions at the time, All Japan and New Japan, were suddenly falling behind. Both companies made changes, including booking a more serious wrestling product, and booking clean finishes to almost every match. It worked out great, as All Japan soon began a string of sellouts in Tokyo that lasted many years. New Japan, within a few years, would become the strongest wrestling promotion in the world.

Akira Maeda, the promotion's biggest star, defeated a former European judo champion, Willie Wilhelm from Holland, via submission, in the main event. The show also featured Duane Koslowski of the wrestling Koslowski twins of South Dakota, a member of the 1988 U.S. Olympic team, losing to Nobuhiko Takada in one of Takada's biggest career wins. There were also three pro wrestler vs. kickboxer matches, one of which pitted two men that were going to have notable futures.

In the worked match, the WKA world kickboxing champion, Maurice Smith, who nearly eight years later would beat Mark Coleman in a historically noteworthy match to become the UFC heavyweight champion, knocked out future and current pro wrestling superstar Minoru Suzuki in the fourth round.

New Japan booked the Tokyo Dome for the second time on February 10, 1990, for an event billed as "Super Fight." The original idea for the main event was Ric Flair defending the NWA title against Keiji Muto. But all kinds of problems arose. Flair had an issue of not being paid above his WCW weekly pay for headlining such a big money event. Relations between WCW and New Japan fell apart. With the building booked and no main event, New Japan president Seiji Sakaguchi went to All Japan president Giant Baba and asked for a truce to be called in their long war. By pitting All Japan stars vs. New Japan stars for the first time in more than a decade, plus having the pro wrestling debut of Koji Kitao, the biggest star in sumo as Futuhaguro, the show became the hottest ticket in town. Even though it didn't get near the media publicity of Mike Tyson's fight with Buster Douglas the next night, the 53,900 fans who packed the Dome greatly outdistanced the 30,000 there the next day for one of the biggest and most famous upsets in sports history. While it was a loaded card, to most fans, the real main event saw All Japan's Genichiro Tenryu & Tiger Mask (Mitsuharu Misawa) beating New Japan's Riki Choshu & George Takano via count out. What was notable that for Sakaguchi to get the deal with Baba, in the three-match series between the two companies, the host company, New Japan, lost two and had one draw. The show became more famous later for a brutal IWGP title match with Vader defending against Stan Hansen–the match where Hansen knocked Vader's eye out of its socket, which became a shocking visual remembered by everyone who saw it. The battle of each company's foreign powerhouse was a big part of drawing the sellout, as was the Kitao debut. Bigelow, in this sense, played the same role in putting over Kitao as he did when putting over Hashimikov on the first Dome show. When the show aired on TV-Arashi on a several day tape delay, it drew a 23.2 rating.

The success of the two prior shows at the Dome led to something nearly unheard of—the three most powerful pro wrestling companies in the world at the time, WWF, New Japan, and All Japan, combined for a show on April 13, 1990. As one could imagine, when you had Giant Baba and Vince McMahon working together, there were all kinds of problems from people seeing things in different ways. The sides had all kinds of minor problems and cultural differences. When McMahon and Hulk Hogan showed up fashionably late for the press conference, Baba felt it was an insult.

WWF only had two demands when it came to finishes, that their two big stars, Hulk Hogan and Ultimate Warrior, be protected. Baba built the show around Hogan defending the WWF title against Terry Gordy. McMahon had Warrior beat Hogan at WrestleMania just 12 days before the event, and Baba was insulted that he wasn't informed ahead of time. New Japan after a while, decided it didn't even want to be involved, and eventually only stayed with the provision its wrestlers would only work with each other. Then, just before match-time, Gordy decided it wasn't in his best interest to do a job for Hogan. Gordy noted that his business was based in Japan, where he was a rising star. He was treated as a serious wrestler. Hogan's business wasn't based in Japan, and while popular in Japan where he was a national star before the U.S., Hogan was not considered a serious wrestler at the level of Gordy. WWF felt insulted that Baba couldn't get one of his top stars to do business as agreed upon. Stan Hansen, at the time a bigger star than Gordy, volunteered to put Hogan over. As it turned out, when the story of how things happened got out, Hansen ended up more popular for losing. The idea is he did the right thing for business even though he was considered a bigger star in Japan than Hogan, for the good of saving the show.

Still, it was notable that WWF coming to Japan for the first time, and the three big groups on the same show wasn't nearly as strong as New Japan's show a few months earlier, as this event did 43,700 fans and a 14.1 rating when aired on television a few days later.

One of the things notable about the show is two of the key wrestlers of the 90s, Bret Hart and Mitsuharu Misawa, wrestled for the first and only time in a 20:00 draw in a prelim match. Misawa was just two months away from getting his big break with his win over Tsuruta at Budokan Hall. Hart was more than a year from his singles break when he beat Mr. Perfect for the IC title at Madison Square Garden. Other dominant stars like Toshiaki Kawada, Kenta Kobashi and Liger all appeared in prelims.

In 1991, the American wrestling war spread to Japan, as New Japan and WCW booked a Dome show, "Starrcade in Tokyo Dome," headlined by Flair vs. Fujinami in a controversial battle of world champions, while new promotion Super World Sports teamed with WWF for a show nine days later with Hogan & Tenryu vs. The Road Warriors. New Japan announced a sellout, claiming to have 64,500 fans, the largest indoor sports crowd ever in Japan. The gate was 430 million yen ($3.16 million based on the dollar value at the time). While that record was legit, the real attendance was probably 10,000 less, but it was sold out. WWF and SWS came back and announced 64,618 fans for their show, even though the real number was about 35,000 for a two-thirds full arena. The Flair vs. Fujinami show was notable because it aired in the U.S. on a several week tape delay as a PPV. The show also featured the 1991 match of the year, where The Steiner Brothers, who held both the WCW world and U.S. tag team titles, beat Hase & Kensuke Sasaki, the IWGP tag team champions, in a match where all three titles were at stake.

Fujinami, the IWGP champion, pinned Flair, the NWA and WCW champion. Somehow the end result was that there was a Dusty finish and the first ref called a DQ, even though fans left the Tokyo Dome celebrating that Fujinami had become the first New Japan wrestler to win the NWA title. The show was on a Thursday, and it wasn't until Saturday's afternoon newspapers in Japan where any hint of controversy was revealed. The story was that Dusty Rhodes and Barry Windham, the WCW reps at the show, went to New Japan President Seiji Sakaguchi and said they considered the match a no contest and that Flair was still champion, because Fujinami threw Flair over the top ropes, illegal under WCW rules, before the pinfall, and referee Bill Alfonso (long before he became a character in ECW), the original ref, saw it. Sakaguchi claimed that the over-the-top-rope rule isn't a DQ in Japan, so shouldn't have been a factor, plus that under New Japan rules, if something happens to the first referee, the second ref becomes the man in charge, and Massao Hattori's three count should have counted. What made it funnier is that Tokyo Sports interviewed Alfonso after the show (the idea was to keep the fact they were giving the belt back to Flair a secret for a few days), and stuck under the circumstances when asked directly who had won in his mind, he said Fujinami. The story that was supposed to come out was Alfonso claimed Flair won via DQ and Hattori would say Fujinami won. In Japan, the story was that Fujinami was NWA champion (in Japan the more prestigious of the titles), Flair was WCW champion, and a rematch would be May 19 in St. Petersburg (which Flair won). In the U.S. they never acknowledged Fujinami having won the NWA title, or that the NWA and WCW title were different. The match aired on PPV, showing Fujinami pinning Flair and the celebration of the title win, but airing later backstage footage of Flair getting the belt back due to the over the top rope move before the pinfall that Alfonso saw.

The January 4th tradition began in 1992, for another joint show between New Japan and WCW, which sold the

Dome out. The main event saw Choshu pin Fujinami to win the IWGP title in the latest chapter of their decade-long rivalry. Other big matches included Lex Luger keeping the WCW title over Chono, Sting & Muta beating the Steiner Brothers and Inoki beating Hase. In the opening match on the show, rookie Hiroyoshi Yamamoto lost to Black Cat.

Yamamoto, as Hiroyoshi Tenzan, will be appearing on Saturday's Dome show.

The next show at the Tokyo Dome was produced by Pro Wrestling Fujiwara Gumi on October 4, 1992. PWFG was a pro wrestling group that pushed itself as legitimate, built around veteran shooter Yoshiaki Fujiwara, but the two big stars were the cocky Suzuki and Masakatsu Funaki. Suzuki outraged the traditional pro wrestling community when he beat Joe Malenko, Karl Gotch's best ever student, who had been a name wrestler with All Japan, and said he was able to do so because Malenko had gotten rusty because he hadn't had a real match in so many years.

The show, called "Stack of Arms," drew 25,000 fans and $1.5 million, not a blow away figure in the least, but impressive for a secondary promotion. The show was built around the house shooters facing a new group of Russians. Among them were 19-year-old giant Aleksei Medvedev, a 6-foot-8, 265-pounder from Belarus who did some matches for the group, and would be notable for being a guy who was a pro wrestler, who left pro wrestling and then won a silver medal in freestyle wrestling at the 1996 Olympics in Atlanta, who lost to Bart Vale. Vale marketed himself all the way into a Sports Illustrated story about being the world's toughest man, using credentials from winning worked matches in pro wrestling, most notably a win over Ken Shamrock. While not listed in his record, Shamrock had his first actual shoot, when he took down and submitted WKA world cruiserweight kickboxing champion Don Nakaya Neilsen in just 45 seconds. David Gobejshvili, the Russian who, along with Bruce Baumgarnter, had dominated international wrestling for a number of years, winning gold in 1988 and bronze in 1992, made his pro wrestling debut, losing via submission to Suzuki. The main event saw Funaki go to a draw with Maurice Smith.

New Japan continued the annual January 4 tradition with loaded shows. In 1993, a sellout of 53,500 came for a show headlined by Tenryu pinning Choshu, The Hell Raisers (Road Warrior Hawk & Sasaki) going to a double count out with the Steiners in the show stealing match, an IWGP champion vs. NWA champion dual title match were IWGP champ Muto became a double champion pinning Chono, and, at the time, the jr heavyweight dream match where Liger beat Ultimo Dragon to win the IWGP jr. title.

The 1994 version saw Tenryu beat Inoki in the main event, IWGP champion Hashimoto beat Chono, Hulk Hogan pinned Fujinami, the Steiners beat Muto & Hase, Hell Raisers beat Scott Norton & Hercules Hernandez to win the IWGP tag titles and Liger beat the latest version of Tiger Mask, this time being Koji Kanemoto.

Even though it didn't draw the biggest crowd, the most noteworthy Tokyo Dome show of that period, and by far the high point of women's pro wrestling, was on November 20, 1994. The 23-match marathon show started at 2 p.m. and ended at 12:30 a.m., and featured everything under the sun. The crowd of 32,500 fans saw an eight-woman tournament featuring the stars of every woman's promotion, the "Five Star tournament," which actually produced one five-star match in the first round with Aja Kong beating Manami Toyota. Akira Hokuto, now the wife of Sasaki, beat Kong in the finals of the most notable woman's pro wrestling tournament in history.

The show had interpromotional matches, legends matches (including bringing back Chigusa Nagayo, Lioness Asuka, Jaguar Yokota and Bison Kimura), a kick boxing match, a shoot boxing (takedowns and boxing, but no submissions) match and two amateur wrestling matches, and even two men's matches, a Lucha Libre style match from Michinoku Pro Wrestling, and a midgets handicap match.

Kyoko Hamaguchi, age 16, did her first and only pro wrestling match on the show. The daughter of Animal Hamaguchi, she was groomed from a young age to do bodybuilding and amateur wrestling. The idea was to win a world championship as an amateur, and then, with her family name and credentials, become the star of pro wrestling. The latter never happened due to women's pro wrestling in Japan collapsing on a big-time a few years later, and the introduction of women's wrestling to the Olympics, keeping her going in a quest to win a gold medal. Hamaguchi peaked before women's wrestling was an Olympic sport, capturing the world championship at 158 pounds in 1997, 1998, 1999 and 2003. She competed in three Olympics, 2004, 2008 and 2012, capturing bronze in the first two and not placing in the third. Hamaguchi lost to Doris Blind, a world class wrestler from France, in the four-match shoot portion of the show.

Winning in the shoot portion was, also in her only pro wrestling appearance, Miyu Yamamoto, beating Ana Gomes. Yamamoto was part of Japan's royal wrestling family as well as a model. At the show, even though she was an amateur wrestler on a pro show, the crowd took to both her and Hamaguchi as stars, more her because she was a world champion and Hamaguchi, who became far more famous in Japan from TV commercials and was a genuine celebrity, at that point was just a teenage daughter of a pro wrestler. Yamamoto's father wrestled in the 1972 Olympics and was later the Olympic team coach. Her sister was a world champion. Her brother is the famous Japanese MMA star Kid Yamamoto and she was at one time married to MMA star Enson Inoue. By the time of the show, she had already won two of her eventual three world championships.

The most unique of all the Tokyo Dome pro wrestling events took place on April 2, 1995. It was the same day as WrestleMania was taking place in Hartford, but there was no question what the big show that day was.

At the time, Weekly Pro Wrestling was the most powerful pro wrestling magazine in the world, selling 300,000 copies on an average week. They came up with an idea to get every promotion in Japan to send in one match and do a super show, with the idea that nobody would want to be outshone and the matches would be outstanding. With the exception of WAR, which was at war with the magazine over coverage, everyone participated. As you can imagine, match order became an issue. It took a huge guarantee to get All Japan to participate, but the decision was made to put New Japan, the biggest promotion, on last. The All Japan main event, Misawa & Kobashi & Hansen going to a 30:00 draw with Kawada & Akira Taue & Johnny Ace, stole the show. The crowd was electric for the match all night, with loud chants of "Misawa" before the match even started. New Japan's IWGP champion Hashimoto beat Chono in the main event, but there was nothing the company's two aces could do to get the crowd up after what they had seen.

In all, 14 Hall of Famers wrestled on this show, which may be an all-time record. I can recall going to the building that day and thinking that there would never be a day in my life that I would see so much elite talent on one stage. It was a great show, a great spectacle, with several incredible matches. But I would still not call it the best pro wrestling show I ever saw, even though it was among the most memorable. But if it wasn't for the All Japan match, everyone would have left the arena talking about how the women stole the show.

Ironically, that show was not even remembered as the biggest show of 1995 in Japan. To this day, the October 9, 1995, match with Keiji Muto vs. Nobuhiko Takada is considered one of the biggest matches in Japanese wrestling history.

It started years earlier, when Lou Thesz, who was with the UWFI, would go back to his youth as a shooter and challenge all the other world champions. UWFI even paid WCW champion Big Van Vader what at the time was an enormous contract, $35,000 per match, to come in and as champion, put Takada over clean in the middle with an armbar on a show that sold out the 46,000 seat Jingu Stadium in Tokyo. They were forever challenging the big world champions to face Takada. There were negotiations with New Japan about putting Takada vs. the IWGP champion, with both sides trying to spin the fact that matches never happened their own way.

However, UWFI fell into financial problems, and were headed for the iceberg. With nowhere else to turn, they went to New Japan, this time dealing from weakness. What took place, from a live event standpoint, was the biggest event up to that time in Japanese history. Not only was the Tokyo Dome sold out, but there was standing room everywhere. They announced 67,000 people, which was the usual exaggerated figure, but there was no papering at all and with jacked up ticket prices, they did $6.1 million, a figure far beyond what any pro wrestling show in history had ever done. It was a different vibe for the show of interpromotional matches.

Dealing from strength, Muto beat Takada via submission with the figure four leglock in the battle of each group's world champions. Make no mistake about it, this was revenge and not business. Takada was hugely over at the time and a run of him against New Japan's big stars would do record business, but he should have won the first one. Years later, New Japan pretty much acknowledged that when a similar situation took place with All Japan and Toshiaki Kawada, as Kawada won the first big match over New Japan's champion.

Still, many point to this as the high point of New Japan Pro Wrestling. Takada headlined the next three Tokyo Domes, drawing a sellout again on January 4, 1996, where he gained revenge and beat Muto to win the IWGP title. Takada sold out every arena title defense, until losing on April 29, 1996, before another overflow sellout crowd of 55,000, to Hashimoto. While Hashimoto had already been a Tokyo Dome headliner, it was this win that really cemented him as the tough guy of the promotion because Takada had that real aura to him.

The main event was not a great match, although it was good. But in hindsight, the match that today many talk about as the most interesting was the opener. Four prelim guys battled, as New Japan sent two of its national champion amateurs, Yuji Nagata & Tokimitsu Ishizawa (who later became Kendo Ka Shin) against UWFI's tough prelim guys, Kazushi Sakuraba & Hiromitsu Kanehara. The most heated action was Nagata vs. Sakuraba, and tapes of that were shown extensively this year. Nagata of course became New Japan's biggest star during a down period, and Sakuraba became a national hero in MMA.

An interesting note is that 13 of the 18 pro wrestlers on this show ended up fighting in MMA over the next several years, with various degrees of success.

Three months later, when the traditional Jan. 4 show came along, the company was blazing hot. Historically, "Wrestle War in Tokyo Dome" on January 4, 1996 not only continued New Japan vs. UWFI, but this show was historically significant because Eric Bischoff attended the show, and that's where the entire WCW vs. NWO feud idea came from, when he saw the incredible heat.

The show also featured a portend of things to come. Hiroyoshi Tenzan vs. Satoshi Kojima, who would later headline the Dome against each other in the IWGP champion vs. Triple Crown champion feud, were on second. Nagata and Sakuraba continued their prelim feud in the opener. The singles battle of the long-time top tag team, Hase vs. Sasaki took place. But perhaps the show stealer of all was Inoki's last sensational match, as just before his 53rd birthday he had a classic with Vader.

Business was so hot they were back to the Tokyo Dome on April 29, 1996, as Hashimoto pinned Takada to win the IWGP title before 55,000. It was a loaded show that included a legends dream match where Tenryu pinned Fujinami, an interpromotional match where Muta beat Michinoku Pro's Jinsei Shinzaki, a dream match with the Road Warriors & Power Warrior (Sasaki) teaming togther for the first time beating The Steiners & Norton, Chono over Lex Luger, Savage over Tenzan and Great Sasuke beating Liger for the IWGP jr. title. The lineup was so loaded that Choshu was in the second match of the show.

Choshu would come back to headline the January 4, 1997, show, having just won the G-1 tournament. At the age of 45, he had announced in August he would enter his last G-1, a tournament he had never won. His quest became a huge story, particularly when he beat Hashimoto in an incredible match early in the tournament. He won the tournament and was able to draw a sellout.

Some notable undercard matches were a battle of generations, as the mid-80s New Japan best babyface tag team of Fujinami & Kengo Kimura were put together for a nostalgia run, and they beat Chono & Tenzan to win the IWGP tag titles. Liger beat Ultimo Dragon to win eight different junior heavyweight titles from around the world. And Inoki returned, beating Willie Williams. On February 27, 1980, Inoki went to a 15 round draw in a legendary match against Williams, a world champion in Kyokushin karate. But by this point, Williams was long past his prime and the match was terrible, unlike the first match, which was considered a legendary match. The second match on the show saw the debut of Super Liger, a wrestler in a Liger costume that was going to be his big rival. Chris Jericho was given his career break, and flopped so bad in it that the match, where he beat Kanemoto, never saw the light of day, and Super Liger was done after one match. Jericho has joked about choking on what was the biggest stage up to that point of his career.

The April 12, 1997, show, which drew 50,500, was originally supposed to have Hashimoto beat UFC star Ken Shamrock, as part of a deal where Shamrock would then win the second meeting and become IWGP champion. However, Shamrock signed instead with WWF. Instead, Naoya Ogawa, the 1992 silver medalist in judo and a three-time world heavyweight champion in the sport, who was to make his debut on the card, was moved to the main event spot, and started one of Japan's most noteworthy feuds ever, with Hashimoto, beating him in a non-title match. While a nothing match, the show also brought back Satoru Sayama, the original Tiger Mask, who had left New Japan in 1983, to lose to Inoki. It was Sayama's public announcements in 1983 regarding Inoki's business dealings that led to New Japan nearly collapsing and Inoki being forced out of power.

The next Tokyo Dome event was October 11, 1997, which is now noteworthy because a new promotion was formed and the main event was Rickson Gracie vs. Takada. Fans had clamored for that match for years, ever since Gracie had beaten up Yoji Anjo in his dojo in a real street fight (Anjo started it and was dealt with harshly). In fact, the fall of UWFI was traced to this, because Takada was expected to avenge Anjo's defeat. But the match never happened, because they couldn't convince Gracie to work with Takada no matter how much money was offered. By this point, Takada had gone through dream matches. His deal with New Japan was over, and a deal with All Japan, which would have been huge, fell through. With no big money matches left, he was a lamb being led to slaughter for a big payoff.

Pride One paled in comparison to what Pride would turn out to be. Several undercard matches were worked, including a battle of giants where Kitao beat Nathan Jones, who years later would have a brief stint in WWF. The semifinal, a boring 30:00 draw with Dan Severn vs. Kimo, left Severn with a bad leg injury. Severn had actually booked a fight six days before he was scheduled to face Maurice Smith for the UFC heavyweight title, but due to the injury, had to pull out. UFC was furious, and Severn was never used again, except brought back as an emergency replacement years later under new ownership, to face Pedro Rizzo, where he got waxed. Gracie armbarred Takada in 4:47 before 37,000 fans. But what was most notable is that eight percent of the Japanese homes that had PPV, which were probably less than 1.5 million in the entire country, ordered the show. A rematch a year later to the day saw Takada last 9:30 before submitting again to Gracie.

The January 4, 1998, Dome show, "Power Hall in Tokyo Dome," drew a sellout of 55,000 fans, billed as Choshu's retirement show. It's notable that 16 years later, Choshu is still wrestling. But he was serious at the time. Choshu's theme song, "Power Hall," was among the most famous entrance music ever in Japan (it was even used by Japanese fighters a generation later on UFC shows). He was going to retire with five singles matches as the big draw on a show headlined by IWGP champion Sasaki beating Muto, and the Don Frye vs. Ogawa feud continuing with Frye winning via submission. Choshu scored wins over Kazuyuki Fujita, Yutaka Yoshie and Tatsuhito Takaiwa. Then he lost via submission to Iizuka with the idea this would make Iizuka a big star. But in his final career match, he pinned Liger.

But that paled in comparison to what was next. Inoki, one of the big three pro wrestling stars and ten biggest name sports stars of the century in Japan, had his retirement show on April 4, 1998. While Inoki has done a few exhibition matches with Fujinami and Renzo Gracie, he never did have an official coming out of retirement match. The show drew an overflow crowd of 57,000 fans and a gate of $7 million, a pro wrestling record that held up until the 2009 WrestleMania, and is still the fourth biggest ever.

The show, and the week, was all about Inoki. Those who attended as guests for "The Inoki Final," included Muhammad Ali (who faced Inoki in what was, on a worldwide basis, New Japan's biggest match in history), Bob Backlund (who Inoki faced several times for the WWF title), Bischoff, Jeff Blatnick (the UFC announcer who won a gold medal in wrestling at the 1984 Olympics after beating cancer), Choshu, Kokichi Endo (a sumo who was Rikidozan's tag team partner in the 50s), Animal Hamaguchi, Killer Khan, Maeda, Wilhelm Ruska (1972 gold medalist in judo who had Inoki's first famous mixed match in 1976), Sakaguchi, Tenryu and Michiaki Yoshimura (a major star from the 60s known at the time as Japan's best technical wrestler and an early tag team partner of Inoki when he got his first push).

Inoki had planned to put over Don Frye in the main event, feeling it was the right thing for business, to create a new superstar on what was clearly going to be among the biggest pro wrestling shows in history. But plans change and everyone convinced Inoki, of all things, that he needed to go out on top and end the show that way. Frye accidentally broke Inoki's ribs, and the planned 15:00 match ended at 4:09 with Inoki winning with the Octopus submission.

A tournament was held to determine who would face Inoki, where Ogawa beat Brian Johnston (a former UFC fighter) and Frye beat Igor Meindert (a 6-foot-8, 270-pound former Russian wrestling champion), and then Frye beat Ogawa with punches from the mount, when Satoru Sayama threw in the towel for Ogawa, to get the shot.

Other noteworthy matches included Fujinami setting a record with his fifth IWGP title win, pinning Sasaki in 21:18 with a German suplex; and Muto & Chono retaining the IWGP tag titles over Hashimoto & Osamu Nishimura in a match where, if they lost, Muto & Chono would have to leave the NWO.

As successful as All Japan was during the 90s, Giant Baba cautiously avoided booking the Tokyo Dome. His thought was that doing super spectaculars would make the usual big shows less meaningful. It was similar to the reason Sam Muchnick never booked a stadium show, noting that while some people may do bigger business than us for one night, we don't hotshot and will always do steady business while others have huge up and down swings. However, the Dome business for New Japan had gotten so big, enough to carry almost an entire year, that Baba realized his thinking was outdated.

Baba booked a Tokyo Dome show on May 1, 1998, with a double main event of Kawada beating Misawa in 28:15 to win the Triple Crown, the first time Kawada had beaten Misawa in a title match, and Kobashi & Ace beating Hansen & Vader. The show drew 48,300 fans.

K-1 was starting to establish its own Tokyo Dome tradition every December starting in 1997, with sellouts for the annual heavyweight Grand Prix tournament. K-1 ran the end of the year at the Dome until 2006, selling out every year until 2003.

The January 4, 1999, New Japan show drew another sellout of 52,500. Muto beating Norton via submission to keep the IWGP title was the main event, while Tenzan & Kojima won the tag titles from Tenryu & Shiro Koshinaka. But the big draw was the Hashimoto vs. Ogawa feud, a match that was technically a no contest, but Ogawa pretty much shot on Hashimoto and exposed he was not a real fighter. This ended up being among the most controversial moves in modern Japanese wrestling. It did pay dividends, as Hashimoto vs. Ogawa is remembered as one of the biggest Japanese wrestling feuds ever. Nothing in pro wrestling reached the level of mainstream interest as their final match, even Muto vs. Takada. But it also started New Japan in a direction of which, a decade later, there seemed to be no return from.

They sold out again on April 10, 1999, when Muto beat Frye via submission to keep the IWGP title and Sasaki & Koshinaka kept the tag titles over Tenryu & Fujinami. Ogawa vs. Hashimoto was so hot they booked a third Dome, on October 11, 1999, with Ogawa beating Hashimoto with Fujinami as ref, Muto beating Nakanishi to keep the IWGP title, Tenryu over Sasaki and Frye & Chono over Norton & Kojima, drawing 48,000.

All Japan's second Tokyo Dome show, on May 2, 1999, was the Baba Memorial show. Baba had passed away from cancer three months earlier at the age of 61. He was still wrestling on every show until less than two months before his death. He was well aware he had cancer and didn't have much longer to live. Misawa and Kawada had a Triple Crown title match that was one of the best of their matches, where Kawada worked most of the match with a broken arm he suffered early on. Baba was hospitalized at this point and didn't have much longer to go, but watched the bout on TV, and made a statement that he had just witnessed the greatest match he had ever seen. He died a few days later.

They booked a ceremonial retirement show, since Baba had passed away without having one. Baba was, along with Inoki and Rikidozan, one of the three biggest wrestling stars in Japanese history, and it's actually inconceivable anyone will ever eclipse those three in the culture. What isn't known is that New Japan felt this show would be the perfect place for a dream match, with Kawada vs. Hashimoto, thinking it was time to pull the trigger on the All Japan vs. New Japan feud. Even though NTV, the network that aired All Japan was all for it, Motoko Baba, the widow of Giant Baba, who now owned the company, turned it down, saying that the show was going to sellout without it.

Baba's boots were put in the ring in one corner. Referee Joe Higuchi, who many believe was the greatest pro wrestling referee ever, came to the ring. The Destroyer came out, and stood in the corner next to Baba's boots. Gene Kiniski and Bruno Sammartino came out in the other corner. Lord James Blears, the figurehead president of the Pacific Wrestling Federation, came out to read a proclamation, all treating it like a tag team match of legends was about to take place. The bell rang, and on the screen, they showed clips of Baba's matches with Sammartino, Kiniski, Destroyer, Hansen, Bobo Brazil, Jack Brisco and Abdullah the Butcher. It was Baba who sold out the Dome with more than 50,000 fans, and his main protege, Misawa, who regained the Triple Crown from Vader in the main event.

New Japan sold out again on January 4, 2000. Sasaki beating Tenryu to win the IWGP title was the main event, but the big heat was for a tag team match where Hashimoto & Iizuka beat Ogawa & Kazunari Murakami.

This set up yet another Ogawa vs. Hashimoto match on April 7, 2000, at the Dome. What was notable is the show drew about 40,000 fans (announced as 60,000), the smallest for a New Japan Dome show, for their fifth Tokyo Dome main event, a record. But general public interest was through the roof for the Hashimoto vs. Ogawa feud, as Hashimoto vowed to retire if Ogawa beat him one more time. They also pushed it as Inoki's protege, Ogawa, against Sakaguchi's protege, Hashimoto. The thought was each would second their guy, but instead both were at ringside just rooting them on.

This was the second double-cross on Hashimoto, as the first was the original angle, which saw Ogawa shoot on Hashimoto and elbow his spine and attempt to injure him. During the 90s, Hashimoto, even though fat, because of his hard kicks and fiery comebacks with chops, was, to the public, the toughest guy on the New Japan roster. While he had a submission background, he was not that in real life. Ogawa somewhat exposed that myth with a shoot situation where Hashimoto could do nothing with him, and blew up fast. But the dynamic of the shoot being the start of the worked angle made this one of the biggest mainstream feuds Japan has had in the past 25 years. There were 34 million viewers on TV-Asahi watching the match, more than double what the network was expecting, and largest for a Japanese pro wrestling match in 14 years, since the Antonio Inoki vs. Leon Spinks wrestler vs. boxer confrontation.

When the stipulation was announced, Hashimoto was going to win. The idea Hashimoto would retire if he lost was the main reason it was so big to the public, as at that point, the feeling was to believe the stipulation. Immediately after the match, Fujinami said that Hashimoto was too young to retire. Ogawa suffered a dislocated shoulder, but won via knockout via judo foot sweep n 15:09.

What could be argued was the biggest MMA match historically in Japan took place on May 1, 2000, at the Dome. The show featured the final eight in a World Grand Prix tournament that opened on January 30.

Four years earlier, Sakuraba was opening the Dome. On this night he became a hero. Before 38,000 fans, Sakuraba beat Royce Gracie in a non-title match, when, after 90 minutes of a no time limit must be a winner match, Sakuraba's constant leg kicks injured Gracie so badly that his corner threw in the towel. At the 87 minute mark, Rorion Gracie was about to throw in the towel, when Helio Gracie refused to let him. Royce Gracie refused to quit until the 90 minute mark, and then Helio allowed Rorion to throw in the towel and shook hands with Sakuraba.

After fighting for 90 minutes, starting out at 174 pounds, Sakuraba then advanced to face Igor Vovchanchyn, the top Russian in the sport at the time, who was more than 50 pounds heavier. Sakuraba was winning the first ten minutes of the fight, when his system just shut down. He survived five more minutes where he had nothing left, before Takada threw in the towel for him. Vovchanchyn lost in the finals to former UFC champion Mark Coleman, who won what was, up to that point in history, the biggest MMA tournament of all-time.

Only a few weeks later, on May 26, 2000, a crowd of 25,000 saw Rickson Gracie beat Masakatsu Funaki via choke in 12:49 at the Tokyo Dome.

For years promoters in Japan offered seven figures to Rickson Gracie to face Sakuraba. Gracie was 41 by this time, and the challenge was never accepted. Gracie never fought again. Funaki also retired to go into acting, but returned more than seven years later for a New Year's Eve fight at the Osaka Dome where he was submitted by Sakuraba.

The elusive All Japan vs. New Japan feud started as New Japan attempted to recreate the heat of the UWFI feud. A lot had happened over the past year in All Japan. Misawa and most of the talent, with the exception of Kawada, Taiyo Kea and Masa Fuchi, left to form Pro Wrestling NOAH. All Japan brought Tenryu back and for survival, did the one thing Giant Baba would never do, the full scale program.

Do Judge!!, drew a sellout of 54,000 fans as Kawada, the top star from All Japan, beat IWGP champion Sasaki in a fantastic match. It was really almost a one-match show, although they did try and recreate the Vader vs. Hansen era match by pitting Steve Williams of All Japan against Scott Norton. All Japan won both singles matches, a far cry from the UWFI feud which was more about revenge than business. The attempt to rebuild Hashimoto saw him beat Fujinami via submission. As good as Kawada was, he didn't have the drawing power or heat after the first match that Takada had.

Sasaki vacated the IWGP title with a loss to the All Japan top star, and vowed to win a tournament on January 4, 2001, to prove he was worthy to hold the belt. The one-night tournament was excellent. Sasaki first beat Kojima and Tenzan pinned Nagata. In the semifinals, Sasaki beat Chono via submission, and in probably the best match of the card, Kawada beat Tenzan. Sasaki pinned Kawada with a Northern Lights bomb in a super heated rematch. An example of going to the well too often was with Choshu coming out of retirement, he faced Hashimoto and they worked it stiff and the crowd went crazy, but it turned into something that looked like a street fight and wrestlers came in and broke it up for both men's safety. But fans were furious, having been taught that every big match has a clean finish. They were trying to do the angle as the exception, but the people didn't buy it, with loud "refund" chants.

All Japan had a Dome show on January 28, 2001, drawing 30,000 fans, built around the retirement of Hansen, 51, whose lower back was so bad by this point that he couldn't even do a retirement match. It was really a one-match show, with the idea of Kawada & Sasaki as a team after their two great battles, beating Tenryu & Hase when Kawada pinned Hase. With Sasaki as IWGP champion and Tenryu as Triple Crown champion, it was the first time the two world champions would be in the ring against each other in history.

New Japan returned on October 8, 2001, drawing 47,000 fans for a match where wrestlers from All Japan, New Japan and NOAH would be involved. Nagata (New Japan) & Jun Akiyama (NOAH) beat Hase (All Japan) & Muto (New Japan but about to become All Japan). The other advertising was two "Vale Tudo" matches, which was the term used that year for worked shoots, with Nakanishi beating Tadao Yasuda and Fujita beating Sasaki. They also had a legends match with Backlund & Fujinami beating Dory Funk Jr. & Terry Funk.

But the big Tokyo Dome event was a month later. After Sakuraba had beaten Royler, Royce, Renzo, Ryan Gracie, he was destroyed in short order by the bigger Wanderlei Silva. Sakuraba was 174 against Royce without weight cutting although he was light because he needed stamina for a no time limit match. But in shape he was 180 pounds at best. Silva was 225, cutting to make 203.6t. Sakuraba was so big that him going for revenge was going to be the biggest match in Pride's history. It had barely been a year since the Sakuraba vs. Royce match, but everything in Japan had changed. Sakuraba vs. Royce couldn't sell out the Tokyo Dome, nor could either Rickson vs. Takada match, both doing in the middle 30,000s with heavy papering.

But now, Pride was selling out everything with Sakuraba. Sakuraba was doing well in the match, even winning the first round until he was slammed on his shoulder and it dislocated, and the match ended up being stopped. One interesting name on the show was Matt Skelton, who former U.S. national team wrestler Tom Erikson beat in 1:11. Skelton, a mediocre kickboxer and even less than mediocre MMA fighter, at the age of 35, went into boxing, a sport he had never done. After going 21-1, at the age of 40, he was British and European heavyweight champion and got a shot at WBA champion Ruslan Chagaev in Germany, losing via 12 round decision.

At the time, in Japan, pro wrestling and MMA were covered as essentially the same thing, only one was a shoot and the other wasn't. When Antonio Rodrigo Nogueira beat Heath Herring to become Pride's first-ever world heavyweight champion, it was considered the first time in Japanese history that a shoot world heavyweight title existed.

New Japan sold out with 52,000 on January 4, 2002, a show built around GHC champion Akiyama coming to New Japan to face Nagata, and he retained his title. It was the last time New Japan sold out the Tokyo Dome.

On May 2, 2002, they ran their 30th anniversary show at the Tokyo Dome, and drew 47,000 fans. The 13-match show included the first woman's match on a New Japan Tokyo Dome show, as Momoe Nakanishi & Kaoru Ito beat Manami Toyota & Yumiko Hotta. Ogawa & Hashimoto were a tag team by this time beating Norton & Tenzan. Bas Rutten had been working New Japan big shows, and picked up pro wrestling quickly, beating Nakanishi. The Steiner Brothers beat Hiroshi Tanahashi & Sasaki in a match where Joanie Laurer (Chyna) was the special referee. IWGP champion Nagata beat Takayama in a title defense. But the real main event was the first and only singles match with Misawa vs. Chono, going to a 30:00 draw.

An October 14, 2002, show drew 38,000, with Nagata retaining the IWGP title beating Pride star Fujita, K-1 star Bob Sapp beat Nakanishi and in the first-ever man vs. woman match on a Tokyo Dome show, Chono beat Laurer. Among notable underneath matches, Nishimura and Rutten went to a 30:00 draw which got some votes by the Japanese press for match of the year, fighting under European rules with Tony St. Clair as referee. Koji Kanemoto kept the IWGP jr. title beating Heat (Minoru Tanaka). Bryan Danielson worked a prelim match, teaming with Rocky Romero & Ricky Reyes to lose to Liger & Kakihara & Tiger Mask.

Pride booked the Tokyo Dome for November 24, 2002. It was billed as Takada's retirement match, and drew 52,228 fans, as Takada's protege, Kiyoshi Tamura, knocked him out in the second round. The show also featured the debut of 1992 judo gold medalist Hidehiko Yoshida, who beat Frye via armbar. The result stunned so many people, since it was Yoshida's debut, that for years people would claim it to be fixed even though X-rays showed Frye's elbow being destroyed and he ended up getting surgery because he was Don Frye and wouldn't tap to the "fake" armbar.

New Japan had been having problems for years, but they still could draw at the Tokyo Dome. The sign that things were really bad was that, even with papering, the January 4, 2003, show, where IWGP champion Nagata faced Josh Barnett, drew 30,000 fans, the lowest they had ever done. Barnett had beaten Randy Couture for the UFC heavyweight title on March 22, 2002, in Las Vegas, but tested positive for steroids and was stripped of the title. Barnett at times blamed the UFC and instead signed with New Japan.

Two weeks later was probably the worst Tokyo Dome show ever. A new promotion called Wrestle-1 debuted on January 19, 2003. Hogan had received a huge offer to do a dream match, Hogan & Takayama vs. Muto & Bill Goldberg. After meeting with company officials, he saw that they had no idea what they were doing, and felt it would hurt him to take the money because he would be part of a failure. He tried to explain that four babyfaces thrown together in a tag match with no build-up and no concept of where it was going to go made no sense. Hogan instead suggested doing a singles match against either Takayama or Ogawa, saying he would lose to either, figuring he knew how to lose, put on the right face, and get over more than the winner, as he'd proven in the past with Rock and Ultimate Warrior. However, he was turned down. When Takayama found out Hogan offered to lose to him and the promotion turned it down, he wanted no part of the show. The promotion at the last minute tried to make deals with Sting, Lex Luger and Goldberg, finally getting Goldberg for $125,000 for one match. Sting and Luger both turned down $25,000 for one match, so instead they got Brian Adams and Bryan Clarke.

Then it got better. They advertised Sapp vs. Ernesto Hoost, who had two legendary kickboxing matches with each other, as the main event. Then they said Hoost backed out at the last minute because his trainer didn't want him to do pro wrestling. When Hoost came to Japan, he said he was going to the show, but didn't want to do pro wrestling. Then, the day of the show, too late for most newspapers (still the main source of info at the time), Hoost shot an angle with Sapp. About 20,000 fans attended, but few of them were paid. Hoost, the non-pro wrestler, pinned Sapp after hitting him with a chair in 5:50 on a show with such weird matches as Goldberg & Muto over Adams & Clarke, Hashimoto over Joe Son (now serving a life term in prison for a rape and a murder), Mark Coleman & Kevin Randleman over the Giant Convicts (Jan "The Giant" Nortje & Dalip "Great Khali" Singh), Hase & Kojima over Terry Funk & Heath Herring and Ultimo Dragon & Kaz Hayashi over CMLL's best tag team, Ultimo Guerrero & Rey Bucanero.

New Japan still managed to draw 49,000 fans on May 2, 2003, for the dream match where Kobashi beat Chono to keep the GHC title while NWF champ Takayama beat IWGP champ Nagata in the title unification match. The 11-match show had five legitimate shoot matches on it, and six worked matches. The opening match saw Tenzan pin Hiroshi Tanahashi. Shoot matches included then-New Japan contracted wrestler Lyoto (now Lyoto Machida of UFC fame) beating Pancrase's Kengo Watanabe (a rugby superstar that they tried to turn into a fighter), Tsuyoshi Kosaka beat Dolgorsuren Sumiyabazar (an Olympic wrestler from Mongolia, the brother of Asashoryu, a huge Japanese sumo celebrity at the time and who later became Mongolia's national pro wrestling hero), Shinsuke Nakamura made Jan "The Giant" Nortje submit, Barnett knocked out powerlifter Jimmy Ambriz and Fujita knocked out Nakanishi.

They drew 37,000 on October 13, 2003, for what turned out to be Hogan's last match in Japan, beating Chono. The show featured three shoot matches, including a world title shoot as Barnett retained the Pancrase Open weight title beating Yoshiki Takahashi (who once fought in UFC) via submission. The actual draws on the show were Bob Sapp, the return of Hogan, and perhaps more than anything else, Seiji Sakaguchi coming out of retirement for one last match.

The main event was an elimination match with Sakaguchi captaining the New Japan team against the outsider shooters led by Sapp. Takayama & Fujita & Minoru Suzuki & Nakamura (who was in New Japan but was doing MMA at the time) & Sapp beat Tenzan & Nagata & Nakanishi & Tanahashi & Sakaguchi). It came down to Sapp & Suzuki vs. Tanahashi (in his first high profile Dome role) & Nagata, with Sapp pinning Tanahashi first, and ending with Suzuki knocking out Nagata in 39:54.

The biggest Dome show was on November 9, 2003, a hugely successful PPV show called Final Conflict 2003, with the final four of a middleweight tournament with Rampage Jackson vs. UFC star Chuck Liddell, and Wanderlei Silva vs. Yoshida, leading to the Silva vs. Jackson was in the finals. Of the 14 fighters on the show, eight either were or ended up as pro wrestlers.

New Japan opened 2004, with the traditional January 4th show, "Wrestling World 2004," drawing 40,000 fans, largely for the match where Sapp & Muto (who by this time was the top star of All Japan) formed a tag team to beat Chono & Tenzan. The 17-match show also had a champion vs. champion match where IWGP champion Nakamura beat NWF champion Takayama via submission. The show featured the retirement ceremony for Fujinami, who is still wrestling now, ten years later. Nagata beat Sasaki and Nakanishi beat Tenryu. Tanahashi beat Yutaka Yoshie to retain the new Under-30 championship (meaning you had to be under the age of 30 to fight for it) and Liger beat Takashi Sugiura to win NOAH's GHC jr. heavyweight title.

A May 3, 2004, show drew 35,000 fans headlined by Sapp retaining the IWGP title over Nakamura after two Beast Bombs. The show was built around four New Japan vs. K-1 matches. The other three were Yutaka Yoshie beating Jan Nortje in a terrible match, Tanahashi beat Sean O'Haire (who after being fired by WWF signed with K-1) via submission, and Musashi of K-1 beat Katsuyori Shibata with a super stiff high kick knockout.

By this point, Pro Wrestling NOAH, on the back of Kobashi, easily the biggest star in Japanese wrestling, had surpassed New Japan. After Kobashi's GHC title reign led to a series of Budokan Hall sellouts and was the best world title positioning and match quality run of the last 15 years, they booked a July 10, 2004, date at the Tokyo Dome for their biggest match possible, Kobashi vs. Akiyama for the title. Kobashi retained the title in 35:34 in that year's Match of the Year. The show drew a near sellout of 50,000 fans with the other big hook being a tag match where Misawa and Muto would face off against each other for the first and only time. Misawa & Yoshinari Ogawa beat Muto & Taiyo Kea. Liger came in from New Japan to defend the GHC jr. title against Yoshinobu Kanemaru, with Kanemaru taking the title. Takayama & Minoru Suzuki coming from New Japan retained the IWGP tag titles against Takeshi Morishima & Takeshi Rikio.

On January 4, 2005, a crowd of 46,000 came for a weird show, overall terrible, but it was the first Tokyo Dome show headlined by Nakamura vs. Tanahashi, who will be headlining nine years later. Nakamura won this by submission to take the U-30 championship. The show featured what was billed as an Ultimate Royal tournament, essentially a series of worked shoot matches with guys who all had shoot backgrounds. Ron Waterman, who was getting a monster push as the new foreign star, beat Nagata in just 1:41 of the finals. Waterman beat Masayuki Naruse, Nakanishi and Nagata in a combined 5:18. The show also had Nagata beating his brother, Katsuhiko Nagata via points in what was billed as an amateur rules match. Katsuhiko Nagata, much smaller than Yuji, won a silver medal in Greco-roman wrestling in the 2000 Olympics. Yuji followed beating Blue Wolf and Dolgorsuren Sumiyabazar, both brothers of Asashoryu.

The bad show, and the worked shoot style more than running its course left things in a bad way. On May 14, 2005, when Kojima had become the first man to hold both the IWGP title and Triple Crown title at the same time, Kojima coming back to New Japan to put their belt on the line against long-time partner Tenzan, drew only 21,000 fans, even with Misawa on the show. Tenzan won the match and took the IWGP title, while Kojima remained Triple Crown champion. Misawa & Fujinami beat Chono & Liger in a legends match. Nakanishi &

Tanahashi were IWGP tag champions at this tie and beat Nakanishi & Ka Shin.

NOAH's biggest show ever was on July 18, 2005, with a double main event of the last Misawa vs. Kawada match and the first and only Kobashi vs. Sasaki bout. While Misawa vs. Kawada was the legendary rivalry from the 90s, the Kobashi and Sasaki match stole the show with the endless chop sequence. Notable on that show is that the challenger to new GHC champion Takeshi Rikio (who had ended Kobashi's two year reign in a failed attempt to create a new star), was Hiroshi Tanahashi.

The arrival of Brock Lesnar on October 8, 2005, only drew 16,000 for a three-way match for the IWGP title. Fujita, the champion, defended against Lesnar and Chono, with Lesnar beating Chono to take the title. Tanahashi & Nakamura beat Kawada & Anjo in the semi.

Lesnar beating Nakamura to keep the IWGP title headlined the January 4, 2006, show drawing 31,000, with little underneath.

January 4, 2007 drew 18,000, and heavily papered, a disaster for the biggest show of the year, with a New Japan vs. All Japan theme. It was the first year the show was billed as Wrestle Kingdom at the Tokyo Dome, which is now the show's annual name. The show drew poorly even with four top matches, Kawada beat Nakamura, Suzuki retained the Triple Crown beating Nagata, Tanahashi retained the IWGP title beating All Japan's Taiyo Kea and Muto & Chono beat Tenzan & Kojima.

On January 4, 2008, they drew 20,000, with Nakamura over Tanahashi to win the IWGP title, while Kurt Angle, who held the IGF's version of the IWGP title (Lesnar never lost the title as the promotion cut his money while he was champion so he quit the promotion instead of coming back to lose to Tanahashi), beat Nagata. New Japan was working with TNA at this point and Angle vs. Nagata, Giant Bernard (Tensai) & Travis Tomko keeping the IWGP tag titles over the Steiner Brothers, Team 3-D over Togi Makabe & Toru Yano, Jr. champ Wataru Inoue over Christopher Daniels and Christian Cage & A.J. Styles & Petey Williams over Milano Collection A.T. & Prince Devitt & Minoru were part of that deal. Several of the matches aired later on Spike TV.

The January 4, 2009 show, drawing 27,500 saw Tanahashi win the IWGP title from Muto in 30:22, while Nakanishi & Hirooki Goto beat Misawa & Sugiura of NOAH. There were several matches again with TNA talent, and the matches aired months later on Spike TV. Alex Shelley & Chris Sabin won the IWGP jr. tag titles from Yujiro (Takahashi) & Tetsuya Naito. Tiger Mask beat Low Ki to keep the IWGP jr. title. Choshu & Chono & Angle & Kevin Nash as the legends team beat Bernard & Iizuka & Tomohiro Ishii & Karl Anderson.

On January 4, 2010, before 20,000 fans, Nakamura beat Takayama to retain the IWGP title, Sugiura beat Goto to keep the GHC title, Tanahashi beat NOAH's Go Shiozaki, Naomichi Marufuji won the IWGP jr. heavyweight title from Tiger Mask, and Yujiro & Naito won the IWGP tag titles in a three-way over Team 3-D and Bernard & Anderson. There was also a legends match with Terry Funk & Choshu & Chono & Nakanishi over Abdullah the Butcher & Yano & Iizuka & Ishii.

On January 4, 2011, before 18,000, Tanahashi beat Kojima to win the IWGP title on top, plus Nakamura beat Shiozaki and TNA champ Jeff Hardy beat Naito. Bernard & Anderson kept the tag title in a three-way over Bobby Roode & James Storm and Nakanishi & Strongman. A match that is being rematched this year saw Prince Devitt retain the jr. title over Kota Ibushi. It was also the Tokyo Dome debut of Kazuchika Okada, who teamed with Goto, losing to Sugiura & Takayama.

On January 4, 2012, before 23,000, Tanahashi retained the IWGP title over Suzuki, and Muto beat Naito in the top two matches.

Last year's show drew 29,000 fans, but that has to be made clear for comparison purposes that it was a paid number, and the numbers all previous years are total in the building. As far as paid went, you would probably have to go back to 2005 for a show at the same level. And inside the ring, it was probably the best of any of them. The promotion is nowhere near it's heyday, but it appears going into its 42nd show at the Tokyo Dome, that things are starting to look up.

JANUARY 13

After a year in which the promotion will likely dominate the pro wrestling awards, New Japan Pro Wrestling, a 42-year-old company that increased revenues 45 percent over the past year, put on its biggest show and announced its most ambitious year since its comeback.

The promotion, which has struggled for years, has made a comeback on the back of a cast of veteran characters, and a few young ones, who all have their own unique role.

Hiroshi Tanahashi is the star, promoted as the best pro wrestler of the century, which as overplayed as that sounds, thus far may be a distinction he deserves. He's got the look, the charisma and the ability, and has been the key face who has brought the promotion to its new level as easily the No. 2 pro wrestling promotion in the world. But at 37, his back and knee problems mounting, the idea that he can be counted on for a match of the year contender at almost every PPV is dwindling.

Shinsuke Nakamura is his career rival. He's charismatic in a very different way, and has become an excellent worker. Through his work, the IWGP Intercontinental title has become a big show main event belt, something that will no doubt continue with Tanahashi's victory over him at the 1/4 Tokyo Dome show.

But the key going forward is Kazuchika Okada. It was only two years ago when Okada returned from a long period in TNA, where he was best known for wearing a Lone Ranger mask and being whipped by Pope D'Angelo Dinero in a backstage skit. Because of his height, look and athletic ability, the promotion chose him to be their breakout new star in 2012, and to beat Tanahashi to win the IWGP title in February of that year despite him not looking at all impressive in his Tokyo Dome return. Because of the quality of wrestlers he's in with, rarely do you see the glimpses of his weaknesses. He's green in some ways. He actually has limited natural charisma, but it's covered up well with elaborate ring entrances, poses, a series of trademark spots, and a manager who does a great job talking for him. But he is an awesome talent, with arguably the best dropkick in the business. And after two years, he's got the credibility with the fans due to his two runs with a championship title belt that is booked to mean a lot. Every title match has a winner and a loser, and rarely is there controversy when it's over. Even if Tanahashi is the bigger star today, Okada is the future as the natural evolution comes along, where Tanahashi ends up in the position Yuji Nagata has held for the last several years, the former top worker in the company who can be counted on when needed to give you a great match.

Everything else is covered. Tetsuya Naito is struggling in the role of the new Tanahashi, but Togi Makabe is the house brawler, Nakamura, Minoru Suzuki and Katsuyori Shibata are the shooters, but different kinds. Nakamura blends a legit rep from being a college wrestling star and some MMA events in his youth to working strong style pro wrestling. Shibata works a ridiculously stiff brawling style. Suzuki works a more cerebral style based around timing and the appearance he's a badass, who is uncooperative and an asshole, but instead, those around him rave about his working ability. Kota Ibushi is the high flyer, the junior heavyweight star who is being booked to where he can compete with the heavyweights. And Hirooki Goto is the perennial bridesmaid. He's Ron Garvin in the days of Jim Crockett Promotions, in that he can, whenever asked, give you a great world title challenge, but if he ever gets the title, it's going to be as a career achievement award and is probably not going to be a good idea.

In many ways, the current New Japan hierarchy is reminiscent of a late 80s Jim Crockett Promotions, which is both a compliment, but not one, since that group grew its business greatly on the back of a great talent mix, went with a pat hand too long, and eventually fell into grave problems.

New Japan in the ring peaked at the G-1 Climax tournament with some of the greatest pro wrestling shows ever seen. But the toll was large. The guys in their 20s and early 30s seem to have survived it just fine, but the key guys on the roster, who are mid-30s to early-40s, paid a price that is still being paid today. But there is a time lag between ones physical peak and their drawing power peak.

In 2014, it's doubtful New Japan will be able to live up to the in-ring standard of 2013. It would be almost impossible. But it can grow as a business while preparing for its future.

Opening day was the sign of that in many ways. The 1/4 event, Wrestle Kingdom at the Tokyo Dome, headlined by Tanahashi's IC title win over Nakamura and Okada's successful IWGP title defense over Naito, drew 35,000 paid. The way the company announces attendance is different than the past, so as far as paid attendance is concerned, it's likely the company's most successful event since May 2, 2003, when a GHC title match where Kenta Kobashi of NOAH beat Masahiro Chono in a once-in-history dream match, plus an IWGP title vs. NWF title unification match where NWF champ (at the time a pro wrestling belt built around shooters) Yoshihiro Takayama beat Nagata (that generation's version of Tanahashi) nearly sold the Dome out with 49,000 fans.

The spectacle was there. And by most normal standards, the show was very good. But the January 4, 2013, show was among the greatest wrestling events of all-time. A look at this year's lineup from the start indicated they wouldn't be able to match it. And while the crowd was bigger, they were a lot quieter. Nothing on this show got the crowd to the frenzied level that a number of last year's matches did. The first half of the show was not good, although both tag title matches were fine, and the Gracies match was kind of an atrocity.

The four key matches that looked on paper to be can't miss, all were, but in all four of the matches, the same performers had better matches against each other in the past. And the card, which began at 4:30 p.m. in Tokyo and ended at 10 p.m., was too long. It did hurt the heat in the key matches.

From a production standpoint, nobody since the heyday of Pride has done a show at this level. When it comes to things like ring entrances and match videos, it put WrestleMania to shame and made UFC 168 feel like nothing but a bunch of fights that were sent in the ring. There is far more WWE and UFC can learn about making a big show bigger than New Japan could learn from WWE and UFC.

In particular, both groups can learn from the long storytelling arcs in the videos building the main matches. With Goto vs. Shibata, they went back to 1995, when the two were best friends in high school, with photos of them as teenagers competing as amateurs, photos and clips of them breaking into pro wrestling, Shibata going into MMA, and their brutal feud of the past year. As a general rule, when two people have the kind of feud these two had, the idea of them making up and then becoming a tag team right away gets over like a UFC fighter after a grudge match telling people in the cage right after the completion of the match that the grudge was all about selling tickets. But in this case, after Goto won (a result I disagreed with but understood that since Shibata had won previously and Goto is the house fighter that the program would probably end this way), and they embraced, it was something the audience was led to, and the immediate reaction is you want the two as a tag team. And that's the next direction, although with Goto's win, he gets the next IWGP title match with Okada.

Okada vs. Naito showed clips from 2007, when Naito was a dark-haired prelim wrestler and the two were working undercard matches against each other.

The musical acts, in particular Marty Freidman, the former guitarist from Megadeth, were used far more effectively. Friedman, who has lived in Japan for years and is a celebrity there as a 90s worldwide rock icon who is now part of a well known Japanese band billed as the greatest guitarist in the world, played Tanahashi's theme while going to the ring with him before the match, as well as after the match. In a trivia note, Freidman played on "Born Of Anger" on Fozzy's "All That Remains" album.

UFC could and should copy the video package done before all the IWGP title matches, where they show head shots on the screen of every previous champion. It makes the title match seem so much bigger playing on the history of the names who have held it (and in some cases, tells the story of foolishness going on with some of the faces having held it). It takes less than a minute, but sets the mood for a title match perfectly.

The use of legends, in this case Harley Race and Stan Hansen, was also more effective. Race, who is usually confined to a wheelchair, was very unsteady on his feet and needed a cane, but still threw a short punch that heel manager Bruce Tharpe oversold to get an easy pop. It wasn't the best thing physically, but it was Harley Race before an NWA title match. Everyone knows this NWA title means nothing in comparison to the NWA title of the past, but having Race there added something to when Satoshi Kojima won it. And more, you simply can't fake the look on Kojima's face after the match when he posed with Race holding the belt.

Hansen came out to a giant pop right before the main event. He wasn't there for comedy, or for older fans to see their legends abused as a measure to get heat. Many of the fans remember Hansen as the top foreign superstar in Japan of their childhood, and nothing was done to tarnish that thought. He was there and sat at ringside while Tanahashi and Nakamura did their thing in the main event.

Besides Tanahashi's IC title win over Nakamura and Kojima's NWA title win over Rob Conway, there were three other title changes on the Dome show. Kota Ibushi won the IWGP jr. title from Prince Devitt, and Karl Anderson & Doc Gallows (Doc in TNA/Luke Gallows in WWE) won the IWGP tag team titles from the Killer Elite Squad, Lance Archer & Davey Boy Smith Jr.

Devitt was really sick with the flu the day before, shaking and throwing up. He was feeling a little better the day of the show, but not himself, and people were really impressed he went out there and had the match he did, as one of four straight **** or better matches that closed out the show.

CHAPTER FOUR

UFC LAUNCHES FIGHT PASS

JANUARY 6

The UFC made its official announcement at a press conference on 12/28, just before UFC 168, of its new digital subscription service, UFC Fight Pass, which is open for business now as part of a two month free trial period.

The service will open only through the Internet at www.ufc.tv/page/fightpass and be available in the U.S., Canada, Australia and New Zealand. Starting on 3/1, it will be priced at $9.99 per month.

There wasn't much in the way of surprises. The channel will be focused on live coverage of a number of events throughout the year that won't be airing on U.S. television. These will be international shows aimed primarily at the local markets, using fighters from that area and airing in prime time.

While there seems to be the feeling from many that the company is running too many events, which has forced people to skip shows, and once they do so, it makes it easier to continue to do so. But UFC is battling a number of different masters. One is that there is more demand overseas for live events than the number of shows they have. Second is they want to expose and develop local stars, and to do so, that means consistently having local shows in the different markets.

The feeling is that European growth has been slow because the UFC events air live in the middle of the night, and while hardcore fanatics may watch, you're not getting the general public to sample shows at that hour.

For shows that are televised in the U.S., the former "Facebook prelims" are being renamed "Fight Pass prelims."

There will also be international Ultimate Fighter episodes, plus old fights from Pride, WEC, Strikeforce, Affliction, WFA and more promotions.

At the press conference, Marshall Zelaznik, the UFC's Chief Content Officer, who is in charge of the project, noted that they are hopeful to clear Android, Xbox, Roku, Apple and other devices by March, as well as expand the service into Europe, hopefully at the time it becomes a pay service.

For the debut event, on 1/4 from Singapore, which starts at 6 a.m. Eastern time, there will be the availability to watch the show live, or join it in progress and viewing it from the start. Or you could pick which fights you want to see. After the event is over, it will be available on archives.

The ten fight card features mostly unknown fighters, with many making their UFC debut. The lineup has Russell Doane vs. Leandro Issa, Dustin Kimura vs. Jon Delos Reyes, Tae Hyun Bang vs. Mairbek Taisumov,

David Galera vs. Royston Wee, Quinn Mulhern vs. Katsunori Kikuno, Will Chope vs. Max Holloway, Kyung Ho Kang vs. Shunichi Shimizu, Kiichi Kunimoto vs. Luiz Dutra, Tatsuya Kawajiri vs. Sean Soriano and Tarec Saffiedine vs. Hyun Gyu Lim.

What is interesting is that even though Canada will have access to the show via the Internet, Sportsnet 360 will be airing the top four matches on television starting at 9 a.m., so there is duplication. It was noted that UFC's television contract in Canada and in other countries would allow them to do that, while the U.S. deal would not.

In Australia, all UFC events air on the Australian version of Fuel TV, a cable channel that focuses on UFC and also airs surfing, TNA wrestling and Motocross. They announced that the Singapore show would air live (with the time difference, it starts at 2 a.m. there).

There will also be two events in March exclusive in the U.S. to Fight Pass. One will be the 3/8 show in London headlined by Alexander Gustafsson vs. Jimi Manuwa. The second has not been announced, but the originally planned 3/1 show in Macau has yet to be talked about publicly. At the press conference, they talked about the 3/8 show being the second one on the service.

The major PPV shows will also be put on Fight Pass after a certain period of time. Right now, they've got a number of shows, including UFC 166 (Cain Velasquez vs. Junior Dos Santos III) and 167 (GSP vs. Johny Hendricks) already up. Future PPV shows will be put up after they first debut as a television product on FS 1.

JANUARY 13

Here's the situation with Fight Pass and the different shows. BT Sports in the U.K. will be airing the 3/8 show from London as part of their package. What UFC is doing now is cutting deals with their European providers, BT in particular, to pay rights fees specific for a regular series of prime time television shows. They are making the same deal in Asia. They already have a deal in place like that for Brazil. Brazil will likely not get Fight Pass soon because of the nature of their TV deal. Asia and the U.K. are expected to have it available by March. The European shows in Europe and the Asian shows in Asia will be blocked from Fight Pass because they don't want to hurt their TV providers who are buying the shows. However, for both Asia and Europe, there will be a number of shows that won't be available on television each year and those will be Fight Pass exclusive, similar to the U.S., where all U.S. shows will be on PPV, FOX, FS 1 or FS 2, but some of the international events will only be on Fight Pass.

CHAPTER FIVE

JEFF JARRETT LAUNCHES GLOBAL FORCE WRESTLING

JANUARY 13

Regarding Jeff Jarrett, there is a ton of speculation going around that he will be starting up his own promotion. As far as whether it will be with Toby Keith, who was looking to buy TNA, that I don't know. There was talk something would be announced this week, but from what I've been told, there is nothing to be announced at this point. Connecting the dots there is a lot of smoke coming from different places, but exactly what it is and what will transpire, anything I would say would be more educated speculation. Jarrett would only say he's got a lot of meetings over the next few weeks before anything substantial can be talked about. The talks of Keith buying TNA came very close, as noted months back, actually closer than anyone knows, but talk in that direction appears to be dead at this time. Given the landscape, you can't promote a national wrestling product today without a television deal, and really, without a TV deal that also pays you, and I don't know how easy that will be, although it's been noted Keith has extremely strong ties with CMT, and the Spike deal with TNA expires in the fall. The key to this game may be Spike's contract with TNA. Spike can be a king maker here based on who they want to carry, or they can make a play for WWE, which would hurt anyone's chances of running unless another station of similar level shows interest in a weekly wrestling show. WWE is shopping the idea of making Smackdown a live Tuesday night show, figuring that the ratings would be better on Tuesday than Friday. Plus, with the premium stations are paying for live sports, even though live vs. taped means nothing when it comes to wrestling viewing (the percentage of people who watch Raw on DVR which is live, is significantly higher than Smackdown, which is not live) habits because 98% of the pro wrestling audience in their minds views that the show is live, the feeling is they'll make far more new money going live than what would be the added expense. The funny thing is, of all the stations that may see it that way, Spike would be the one station, with its experience with TNA where live shows do the exact same ratings as taped shows, where live vs. tape wouldn't be as much of an issue.

Jim Ross was inundated with questions regarding this, because he and Keith had dinner together this past week, but that isn't unusual because they are friends who talk at almost every University of Oklahoma football game and run in the same social circles at games. Ross wrote, "I have not had any conversations with anyone about starting a `new' pro wrestling promotion. I have not spoken to Jeff Jarrett since he left WWE on a day that doesn't rank too high on my list of fun days at work. Some websites are irresponsibly running with the story that just because Toby Keith and I are friends and fellow Okies who both follow the Sooners that I'm about to do business with Toby and Jeff Jarrett, which isn't true. Toby and I had dinner at the Sugar Bowl, he's a wrestling fan from the old days and, a hell of a entrepreneur with deep pockets. Nonetheless, the reason that we were there was to support our Sooners vs. Alabama in the Sugar Bowl and not talk about wrestling. We did talk the wrestling biz some, but that's not unusual for me in any conversation after a 40-year career within the genre. We also talked country music, business investments, OU football and we spent the afternoon together with ESPN's Brad Nessler, who's another wrestling fan. Yes, TNA came up a time or two, but that was really a non-issue in our conversations. I am not motivated to re-engage in the wrestling business on a daily basis and it would take a mighty healthy offer to consider such. The politics and paranoia that go with today's rasslin business isn't healthy for me to be around on a full-time basis, especially at this stage of my life. Plus, I have a specific philosophy regarding how the business should be presented that doesn't seem to be in fashion these days. My name has been linked to doing some voice overs for a couple of international wrestling promotions who air their product, including PPVs and DVDs in North America, but that's not something that we've pursued just yet. We'll see what the future holds on that one. Sounds interesting, though." A few notes on what he said. The last time Ross and Jarrett talked based on that post would have been when Jarrett last worked for WWF and Ross headed up talent relations, in October, 1999. Jarrett was IC champion and his contract expired one day before the PPV where he was supposed to drop the title to Chyna. Jarrett demanded a significant amount of money, believed to be close to $200,000, to do the job, which he got. Ross took tremendous heat for not having signed him to a deal before this point. The sides were said to be far apart on money on a new deal and there was at least talk at the time that McMahon wasn't interested in Jarrett as a high dollar player. When WCW folded in early 2001, because of what happened, McMahon had no interest in acquiring Jarrett, who instead, along with Bob Ryder and his father Jerry, started TNA in 2002. I don't know whether Ross has a non-compete built into his severance package from WWE, but I'd expect that he does because the strong impression I had was that despite the fact WWE acts like TNA isn't competition (and it isn't), they strongly did not want Ross showing up on TNA television. While I don't see them socializing as any evidence of anything, since they probably talk all the time around the football games, that said, if Keith were to start a wrestling company, whether Jeff Jarrett is with him (all signs point to this and I've got zero direct confirmation of it past a lot of smoke) or not, one would logically think he would go to Ross. Even if Ross can't do it based on a non-compete, and my belief such a deal is in effect, such a thing wouldn't go on forever. The international stuff Ross talked about is that it is well known AAA would love to have Ross announce their product if and when they attempt to break into the U.S. market on El Rey television. There would be natural speculation regarding him doing New Japan if they want to have an American broadcaster, but I'm almost certain there have been no talks in that direction, nor has New Japan spoken with any of the most obvious candidates about doing English language broadcasts of their big shows. With AAA, there had been no talks I'm aware of past the idea that they'd want him if he could do it.

There's an obvious question if there is going to be a start-up, and that is where the main event talent is going to come from. There are plenty of wrestlers who can fill time out there who are working indies and even with some former WWE pedigree like Chris Mordetzsky (Masters), John Hennigan (Morrison), some of the New Japan Americans, A.J. Styles, and guys on the indies like Chris Hero, and there are plenty of undiscovered guys like Anthony Nese, Ricochet, Rich Swann who can also entertain. But as far as the main drivers go, WWE has everyone tied up long-term and TNA has most of its talent tied up long-term and TNA has never really made that star that we're talking about.

JANUARY 20

Regarding Jeff Jarrett, there is nothing new past the point that we're aware of some major meetings he has between now and the end of the month to attempt to finalize the deal regarding starting a new wrestling company with Toby Keith as the backer. There are meetings in different parts of the country over the next couple of weeks. Jarrett is also making calls all over the world asking about what kind of talent is out there and available. One thing for sure is that Jarrett is of the belief they are starting a new company and that all talks of

Keith buying TNA are dead because the negotiations hit a snag. However, TNA was trying to sell to Keith after Janice Carter wrote the letter and it was TNA that went to Norman, OK to sell to him, not him coming to Texas looking to buy, so Janice Carter's letter that she sent talent was not the case at all.

FEBRUARY 3

Don't expect anything too soon from Jeff Jarrett and the new promotion. You really can't start the kind of operation he and Toby Keith are looking at doing without a television deal in place. Most likely that wouldn't come until the fall season at the earliest, and a key may be Spike's contract with TNA, which expires in October and what decisions Spike makes at that time. The AAA stuff probably won't be on TV until the fall season on the El Rey network as well. At first, there was talk about debuting in December, and then March.

FEBRUARY 10

The proposed Toby Keith-Jeff Jarrett promotion, which is a long way from happening, stemmed almost exactly as you'd think. TNA was for sale and Jarrett through his connections with the Nashville music industry and Keith in particular, tried to put together a bid to buy the company. The deal was very close at one point. Bob Carter came to Keith to finalize the deal and the two sides were close on a price, although they were not quite there. The belief is they were going to hash it out, but Carter only had one request in selling, which was that Dixie Carter would remain with her title, have some power in the company and remain a television character. Keith said he wasn't going to buy the company with any creative limitations, so the deal actually fell apart because Bob Carter in the end was going to protect his daughter. Someone in TNA who was aware of how it went down noted to us that, "That's why we all are still here," noting if it was about business, TNA would have never survived after the last golden carrots (prime time TV and Hulk Hogan) failed to increase popularity or take the company from losing money. At that point, the feeling was from Keith and Jarrett that they didn't need to buy the company, as they could start their own company from scratch. The deal falling through would have been shortly before Jarrett quit TNA in December. The other thing noted is when this story got out inside of TNA, those who had tried to believe the Janice Carter memo and thought the idea was that the Carters wouldn't sell, and the talks were for just a minority investor, realized they'd been had.

Jeff Jarrett produced about a 15 second video for his new promotion just saying "We're coming." One person who has knowledge of the project described it as being in step one of a ten step project of launching, and that it would likely be late in the year at the earliest before it's off the ground. As noted, the kingmakers here are likely to be Spike TV.

FEBRUARY 24

Jeff Jarrett did a video where he hinted at starting a promotion without outright saying it. He said his family has been in wrestling for 70 years, and he feels a boom period coming due to the WWE Network, AAA coming to the U.S. with Mark Burnett at the helm and what he is planning. Although nobody is saying it publicly, privately Jeff and Karen Jarrett are very unhappy with Dixie Carter and how things went down in TNA.

MARCH 3

Regarding Jarrett's group, while Toby Keith is the main guy behind it, it will likely be a group of partners and not all Keith's money. Keith was, at last report, worth $500 million, which is considerably more than Vince McMahon was worth before the stock went through the roof. But when the group was looking at buying TNA, it was always described to me as Nashville music investors (Keith is from Oklahoma, but as a country superstar, is considered part of the Nashville music scene) with Keith as the driving force, but not a singular owner. The key to them is getting a television deal that pays, which is the name of the game for every pro wrestling and MMA company. That's going to be the be-all and end-all going forward, as TNA and Jarrett's group are not going to be able to go out and tour and make any significant money, do anything on PPV, and they aren't going to be able to get video game deals or big merchandise deals. The lessons of 2010 for TNA are that you can't bring in names, even if they are huge names, and expand your audience significantly. You can't tour television without it being a far greater expense that yields no extra viewership. And live vs. tape doesn't matter, as long as it's presented as if it's live.

MARCH 17

Jeff Jarrett did a video where he said he would be making a big announcement on 4/7, the day after WrestleMania. Both he and wife Karen were on the video, where he mentions he's been going to shows in the Midwest, Mexico and Canada and has found some unique talent. He said he's been impatient to make this announcement. Kevin Sullivan (not the former wrestler or author but the longtime production guy with WCW and TNA) produced the video so that would indicate he's part of the new promotion. The expectation is that Jarrett's group will use talent from AAA. Devin Driscoll, who was a former WWE developmental wrestler, has been telling people in the Knoxville area that he's working with Jeff Jarrett on his new promotion. For whatever it's worth, Jeff and Karen Jarrett both worked on his Next Level Wrestling show on 3/8.

MARCH 24

A lot of people in the company are outwardly rooting for Jeff Jarrett, and not just because of the belief it opens up more jobs in the business, but as a safety net. With every week that goes by without an announcement by Spike and TNA of a new deal (the current contract expires in the fall), concern grows. Morale was high about a month ago because of the great crowd response they got on the U.K. tour, and the feeling they were part of a major league promotion. But then when Lockdown, the company's second biggest show of the year, couldn't draw at all in Miami, the mood changed. For the most part, the faith in creative, Dixie Carter and John Gaburick is low right now. There's the belief that Vince Russo is involved, and that it's being kept a secret, which doesn't help morale and leaves people confused since Russo hasn't led to any success in wrestling since he left Vince McMahon nearly 15 years ago. Just the entire handling of The Wolves has been brought up, as they were brought in by David Lagana for a big push, and they've already had a storyline that made Richards look bad as a face, had a one week title run that came and went with no fanfare and only made the belts look unimportant. Regarding Jarrett, and this is just dressing room talk and belief of things going around since nothing will be announced until 4/7, and even those friends with Jarrett say they haven't been told much of anything. The belief is it will start in January and CMT would be the home, but we're told more than one station is being talked with and nothing is definitive just yet. The CMT rumors are because Toby Keith is involved and he's got close connections with that network, and that speculation with Keith involved led to CMT. It was always thought that CMT and Spike would be the most logical homes, but Spike is not in the picture. The rumors in TNA is that Kurt Angle could be the lead star of the new group, which makes sense. Angle and Jarrett, despite major obvious issues in the past, are on good terms now. Angle's contract expires in the fall. Given what happened with Styles, Sting and Hogan, who, along with Angle, were TNA's highest paid guys, when their deals were up, has to make Angle's staying at anything close to the his old deal as something very much uncertain. Perhaps TNA would keep Angle at his current rate to keep him from leaving. If anything, if they wanted to keep him, they should be negotiating a new deal now. There is a lot of bad blood with Angle from the WWE side. Granted, that was also eight years ago and since then, almost every major name has gone back that was a persona non grata in the past. Angle would also be 46 by the time the group would most likely launch, and if anything, physically with all his injuries, he's not a young 46 by any means. The idea is to introduce a lot of new faces to the U.S. national scene. Jarrett has been scouting talent, as he's working indie shows every weekend scouting, as well as looking at videos of people recommended to him, including international talent in Mexico and a lot of TNA people have sent word of being interested. Jarrett was also the one who put together the Wrestle-1 and TNA deal.

There is also talk that the promotion would open with a Jeff & Karen Jarrett reality show that would build to the launch of the TV show and promotion a few months later.

APRIL 14

The announcement of Jeff Jarrett's new wrestling promotion on 4/7 was little more than a confirmation of what has already been known, and a name being given–Global Force Wrestling.

A release complete with a photo of Jeff Jarrett, 46, in a business suit and no tie, and wife Karen, 41, in a short, low-cut party dress, wearing heels and reclining on a sofa, was sent out with no key details past more announcements would be made.

Jeff and Karen were the only names in the release, positioned as the people behind the promotion.

The release stated that they promise to be the most fan-interactive and immersive wrestling experience in history. Fan-interactive is cool, and I'm not knocking it a bit. But WWE said the same thing, as did TNA, and neither company has had any real popularity growth. At best WWE is more popular with an existing fan base than before, but hasn't been able to really grow the fan base. TNA has a falling fan base even with getting more aggressive on working with fans. The point being, you should promise that, but that's not going to differentiate the company from anything there, nor garner a new fan base.

"Because of new media, new technology and more 'in-tune' fans than we've ever had, wrestling is poised for another boom period like it experienced in the mid-1980s and late 1990s," said Jeff Jarrett. "What we've going to deliver is a multi-platform, innovative brand that will engage fans in ways they've never experienced. It will provide a fresh perspective inside the business that fans have been clamoring for."

Even if we are on the cusp of a boom period, and sometimes fan enthusiasm convinces me we may be, but the numbers then constantly knock you back to a reality, boom periods in the long run benefit No. 1, and sometimes No. 2, if No. 2 is really good and competitive.

If we credit WWF in 1984 with bringing in a boom period, it may have helped regionals through 1985, and I'm not even sure that was the case. But by 1986, everybody was down except two players, and No. 2 was falling by 1987 and 1988. If we credit WCW in 1996 with bringing in a new boom period, it had little effect on anyone but WCW and WWF. ECW did gain in popularity for a year or two as well, and then both WCW and ECW were collapsing by 1999. If WWE brings in a boom period now, for a new group to benefit, they have to be something different and better in some ways, have to have charismatic stars, and need the television platform. Even the ability to get a cult following (ECW) isn't enough to succeed. Jarrett may be able to keep costs down and use primarily new talent, but the revenue is still going to have to come largely from television and having something on TV that clicks big to where the licensing community gets interest, because the other streams will be tough. Directly fighting Vince was the way to go in 1996, but Vince is at a completely different level now. I'm sure that's not even the goal. The goal is to carve out a profitable niche. The key to that is low costs, a great TV deal, and then being a success on TV. What that means product-wise should be a form of different but better. What that entails revolves around how creative Jarrett can be. There is talent out there, but everyone from PWG to Dragon Gate USA has guys up and down the roster who have real talent. TNA has loads of good talent that never broke through.

Everything will come in time, but we still know nothing we didn't know before. Even AAA was able to announce Mark Burnett and the El Rey Network, as well as a fall time frame for a television debut.

The release stated that Jeff and Karen Jarrett have been searching the United States and international ranks in search of undiscovered talent, and claimed they have information on more than 400 performers from around the world in a talent database.

Jeff Jarrett along with at least one other person affiliated with him have been searching at indie shows and viewing tapes. He also was in charge of the Ring Ka King promotion in India where he used several independent wrestlers who TNA did not pick up. He has noted there is a lot of talent on the scene that have not had national exposure.

There is no question that are wrestlers who can perform good matches, and wrestlers who can even perform outstanding matches, that are undiscovered. But there will need to be some name wrestlers with recognition as a base. But as TNA showed, you can have the biggest stars in wrestling history, and they had some of them, and that doesn't guarantee success.

In the end, it's about having a television partner strongly behind you financially, and the ability to deliver ratings.

The only product hint came in the statement by Jeff Jarrett, "The reality is we want to build a brand in which fans are watching our wrestlers evolve from day one and are truly invested in the lives of our talent in and out of the ring."

I'm taking this statement to mean the idea of a worked reality show, perhaps done along with lines of Total Divas, which had been rumored to predate the start of the promotion. The latter show is a hit, but it is done with a production company with a long history at the top of reality TV. Ironically, AAA, working with Mark Burnett on their scheduled fall launch, does have that, but with the El Rey Network, doesn't have a platform on a station that reaches significant viewership.

The biggest name brand talent on the outside right now are people like Tommy Dreamer, Carlito, Chris Masters, A.J. Styles, Matt Hardy and Kevin Nash. Kurt Angle's contract expires this fall. Christopher Daniels and Frankie Kazarian's TNA contracts expire shortly. Still, TNA had most of those names at one time or another, along with plenty of bigger names, and that wasn't enough to move the needle past a certain level. Reports are that Jarrett reached out to The Samoan family to use both students from Afa's wrestling school and family members who aren't in WWE.

APRIL 21

Jeff Jarrett's Global Force Wrestling announced on 4/15 that Dave Broome's ("The Biggest Loser") 25/7 productions would be working with him on his new venture. Broome would be working with them on both producing a wrestling television show and the talked about reality show. What's notable is that in a story with the Hollywood Reporter it was stated for the first time that the new promotion started because Jarrett and Toby Keith's attempt to buy TNA Wrestling failed. It was the first time a major trade publication had published the Jarrett/Keith link as well as confirmed what we had reported for months about the sales talks. Representatives for Keith had been in the TNA offices months back, openly talking to major employees about working together and were doing their due diligence. Keith had told confidantes about acquiring TNA provided the price was fair. Even though denied to TNA employees in the letter by Janice Carter, Keith was expecting to purchase the company and Bob Carter had flown to Keith's home in Norman, OK, to hammer out the finishing touches on the deal. The sides were said to be not far apart on a price, but the stumbling block was Dixie Carter. Bob Carter wanted a guarantee that Dixie would have a position within the company. She did not have to remain as a decision maker, but as a face saving and transitional move, he wanted her to have a position within the company and to remain as a figurehead on the television show. That ended up being the deal-breaker. The Jarretts and Carter were not on good terms and the Jarretts didn't want to run a company with her. A Hollywood Reporter story stated that Jarrett is shopping around television rights (those in wrestling still seem to believe there is either a deal with CMT or strong talks with that network). "It just won't be a bunch of wrestling matches; we have exciting announcements to come," said Jarrett. "TNA or WWE right now is match-after-match-after-match. Global Force Wrestling is not going to do that. There will be matches, but there will be a lot more and a lot more variety placed into the actual events that will be really innovative and fresh." The Jarretts also made news over the weekend. They were doing their weekend scouting, at a Dream Wave Wrestling show on 4/12 in LaSalle, IL and then for IWA Mid South the next night. Promoter Jay Repsel of Dream Wave Wrestling said that stories were all blown out of proportion when it came to his show. He said there were no problems between he and the Jarretts, saying Jeff was super professional the whole night. He said that Karen's 8x10s were not, due to a miscommunication, put out at the merchandise table. Karen did ask for her pay and was paid in full and then they left, but there was no money owed and no issues when they were taken to the airport the next day. He said Internet stories of money issues weren't the case, and he's since sent clips of the Dream Wave talent that Jeff and Karen said they were interested in over to them. But he said there were no real problems and don't know where the stories came from. The promoter the second night, Ian Rotten, had a different story. Reporter Jerry Wiseman, a longtime area fan and correspondent, noted that Jeff got half his pay up front, as is the custom working on the indies, but Rotten didn't have the rest of his money. He promised to send it within a few days.

Wiseman reported that Jarrett was allegedly screaming and cursing about it in the locker room and either slapped, knocked the glasses off or took the glasses off the face of 17-year-old John Calvin, who is Rotten's son, before calming down, and Rotten claimed Jeff would get his money in a few days as "he can use it for a defense attorney because I will be going to the sheriff tomorrow (Monday) to swear out a warrant for assault on a minor," Rotten said. Attempts to reach Jarrett the past few days were unsuccessful for his side of this.

JUNE 30

Regarding Global Force Wrestling, Toby Keith is not believed to have any involvement in funding the company. When the idea started, Keith was to be the primary backer after Keith & Jeff Jarrett pulled out of negotiations to purchase TNA. Jarrett does have a backer through a connection with Hermie Sadler of NASCAR fame, which is why Sadler's name has been mentioned so much with the company. But we're about six months since Jarrett left TNA and it was clear he was starting a company. There have been no significant announcements past tie-ups with New Japan and AAA. There is definitely talent out there to have a great in-ring product, but whether there are the few key guys with established big names needed at the beginning is the question. But the biggest question is can they land a paying national TV deal, because ultimately, everything revolves around that question. The idea was that the promotion would start out as reality show with Jeff and Karen Jarrett building the company and on the road every week scouting for talent, and that would start building the roster to lead to the first show. But there has been no announcement of a reality show deal.

AUGUST 4

Jeff Jarrett's Global Force Wrestling, which has been quiet for some time, sent out a press release announcing a promotional alliance with Revolution Pro Wrestling in the U.K., New Generation Wrestling in the U.K., Premier British Wrestling in Scotland, Westside Xtreme Wrestling in Germany (wXw, which books major names from the U.S. and Japan regularly), and Emerald Wrestling Promotions in Ireland. They also made reference to former TNA star Doug Williams as helping GFW in Europe.

OCTOBER 6

Jeff Jarrett is headed to Japan shortly to put the finishing touches on the battle plan for the Tokyo Dome show. He'll be at the 10/13 Sumo Hall show. My impression is they will broadcast either New Japan promotional videos and/or current New Japan shows on the Global Force Wrestling web site to build the Dome show, since they don't have any television support. It would make sense for the site to host the iPPVs the next few months but I've heard nothing in that direction and there is still no word of any broadcasting of the 10/13 show. Nobody has been able to make PPV work without TV support in pro wrestling with the exception of the UWFI in 1993, and that was with a huge TV ad budget (they bought commercials all over sports programming leading into the show) and this show will have no budget of the type. And nobody has been able to this point to use streaming on the Internet alone to build enough of a fan base in this or any similar genre, although my feeling is everyone would consider 10,000 buys as a home run here. New Japan Tokyo Dome shows in the early 90s were doing 60,000 to 80,000 U.S. buys and that was for shows taped delayed by several months, but they were also promoted by WCW, which had a lot of TV, and it was a different era in the sense PPVs were rarer and almost everything did better. The show will be called Global Force Wrestling presents New Japan Wrestle Kingdom from the Tokyo Dome. From the cable distributors side they want a $24.95 price tag, but New Japan charged $35 last year for the Dome on iPPV, so the price, not yet finalized, will fall somewhere in that range. I expect the PPV deal to be announced at the Sumo Hall show. The plan is for both a live showing, which would be on Saturday night right after what looks to be UFC's biggest show of the year ends (Jon Jones vs. Daniel Cormier; Ronda Rousey vs. Cat Zingano double main event), and a replay at 8 p.m. on Sunday in the usual pro wrestling PPV time slot. It will be available on iPPV in both English and Japanese. It may be available in multiple languages on regular PPV as well. There's still nothing on the potential broadcasting of the 10/13 show, past that there have been talks involving Jim Ross, but no deal has been reached. Ross teased it in an article by Brian Fritz, saying,

"I'm very interested in doing special projects and that certainly would be on that list of a special project. And I think if they were serious about their marketing of their PPVs, and I guess their big show is January 4th, that if they were really serious about that event being a hit in the English-speaking countries, that I might be able to help them. I think their style is right down my alley. They're physical, they're intense, their wrestling is logical and I am a fan of it. But I wouldn't want to do it in a TV studio somewhere and doing it as a voice over. If I did it, I'd want to be in Tokyo. I want to feel it. I want to be a part of it. I don't want to be artificial. I want to be emotionally invested and I want to be physically there at ringside." Ross said he's had no talks with New Japan, which is accurate, but there have been talks with the GFW side. There is a potential issue which Ross outright said, having to do with Oklahoma Sooners football, and if they have a bowl game that same weekend.

With Jarrett at the show, and Jarrett having already done an angle with Hiroshi Tanahashi at the Seibu Dome show, I could see Jarrett costing Tanahashi the title match with A.J. Styles, and the Dome being Styles vs. Kazuchika Okada, Tanahashi vs. Jarrett, Shinsuke Nakamura vs. Katsuyori Shibata, the tag team tournament winners against Karl Anderson & Doc Gallows for the tag title, either a singles match with Kazushi Sakuraba vs. Minoru Suzuki or possibly a tag. Sakuraba did an interview where he teased himself teaming with Wanderlei Silva against Suzuki & a partner, but Silva is under a UFC contract where UFC would have to approve of him doing this. Usually UFC wouldn't allow it, but given they can't book Silva for a fight perhaps ever again, and certainly no time soon, there's no reason for UFC to not allow it. New Japan owner Takaaki Kidani is a huge fan of the Pride era, but there are also those in New Japan who don't like the crossover given it was that crossover that hurt the company badly for years and it's only in last few years they've started to dig themselves out of that hole.

NOVEMBER 3

We've mentioned this before, but Toby Keith is not aligned with the Jarrett group. He had interest in working with Jarrett to start things up early this year, but for reasons we don't know, his interest has greatly cooled as far as doing anything with wrestling, as his buying TNA move was because they already had the national platform and revenue streams in place. Jarrett is also looking at venues in Las Vegas with the idea of regularly taping out of the same building, similar to what GLOW did during its run at the Riviera and the AWA did in the 80s at The Showboat. Of course, he needs a television deal first.

NOVEMBER 3

Jeff Jarrett met with Joe Koff of ROH on 10/22 to discuss ironing out his promotion of the 1/4 Tokyo Dome show. At least three ROH talents, if not more, are scheduled for the Tokyo Dome including an ROH title match with whoever the champion is (betting line being Adam Cole although that's not definite) defending against someone from New Japan. The issue is that ROH talent is contractually not allowed to appear on iPPV or PPV shows that air in the U.S. ROH booked talent to the Seibu Dome and that was an iPPV but it was not an issue. But direct PPV when ROH is also doing PPV is an issue that had to be worked out. The second part of the equation is Jarrett trying to get an agreement for ROH to promote the New Japan show on its television, because nobody except UFC in the 90s has ever been able to successfully promote a PPV without television backing it up. The focus of ROH through 12/7 would be building its own Final Battle show in New York, but from 12/7, they have no events until January and probably no major events until well past that point. Obviously that becomes a question whether Koff wants to promote a rival promotion in the same PPV marketplace, and if he doesn't see it that way, there would have to be some kind of a deal, likely financial, worked out to use their TV to promote somebody else's show. The main thrust of the meeting was just Jarrett introducing himself to Koff and to have some kind of an affiliation together.

NOVEMBER 10

Jeff Jarrett and Global Force Wrestling officially announced what had been reported here for some time, that the 1/4 Tokyo Dome show will air on PPV in the U.S. and Canada.

"GFW Presents New Japan Pro Wrestling's Wrestle Kingdom 9" will air both live, at 2 a.m. Eastern and 11 p.m. Pacific time on 1/4, which is a late Saturday night/early Sunday morning time slot, starting one hour after the completion of UFC 182, the Jon Jones vs. Daniel Cormier show.

It will also be replayed in the traditional Sunday PPV time slot, but one hour earlier, from 7-11 p.m. Eastern time.

All major carriers in the U.S. and Canada have agreed to get the show. The price was not announced. Originally the price was to be $24.95, but there were negotiations going on where that could change.

At this point we don't have any information on how the show will be marketed, as nobody has ever been able to successfully do live PPV pro wrestling events without television backing since the early UFCs. Nobody is expecting big numbers and if they could get 10,000 buys, it would be considered a home run. The plan is not for one show, but to start doing this regularly, if the first show is any kind of success. Whether that would be the monthly PPVs, a big four of Invasion Attack, G-1 Climax finals, King of Pro Wrestling and Wrestle Kingdom, once a year, or never again, will depend on what type of interest this show gets.

There will be announcing in both English and Japanese, the latter to alleviate the super hardcore fan who prefers it in its authentic form.

The negative is the four-hour window. As anyone who watches New Japan shows knows, their big shows are usually four-and-a-half hours and Tokyo Domes closer to five hours. Given all the talent in the promotion, plus the pageantry with the long and elaborate entrances, they will have to cut back on match time to hit four hours, causing them to rush through prelims. Another question would be if they will break Japan tradition and run a show with no intermission, which at least would give them about 20 more minutes to work with, which they'll need.

There is also a lot of political stuff going on regarding the ROH talent and the Tokyo Dome show. Everyone has a different story on what is going on. Jeff Jarrett and Scott D'Amore met with Joe Koff, the ROH CEO, in Baltimore last week. It was described to me in the end as more of an introduction and shake hands meeting with nothing decided. No deal was reached regarding ROH helping promote the show on its TV in the weeks after Final Battle, which will be ROH's second live PPV show.

Even more confusing right now is the plight of ROH talent on the Tokyo Dome show. Nothing is for sure, but we do know that Kyle O'Reilly, Bobby Fish and the ROH champion at the time were all earmarked for the show, which was to include both ROH and NWA title defenses, besides those of the Japanese belts.

The talent expected to be on the show from ROH was told that as things stood, they would still be on the show but their match would not air on PPV into the U.S., meaning the matches (believed to be two bouts although nothing is confirmed at press time for any ROH talent on the show) would be dark matches. That's both good and bad. The ROH matches will probably be good matches, plus, with Fish & O'Reilly winning the Super Junior tag team tournament on 11/3 in Gifu over The Young Bucks, they were supposed to be involved in the IWGP jr. tag team title match at the Tokyo Dome coming off their title shot at the 11/8 Power Struggle show with Alex Shelley & Kushida.

Fish & O'Reilly winning the tournament would indicate New Japan booker Gedo was going with the idea they would be on the Dome show. If they weren't, the Young Bucks could have gone over instead.

One ROH source said that everything is in flux but at the end of the day, everything will work out. Another person involved in the situation said that they believe, by the show time, it will all work out as well, but right now there is an issue in the sense Sinclair doesn't really understand wrestling. The feeling is it will hopefully be worked out.

To a wrestling fan, it's a no-brainer to have ROH talent appearing on the second biggest pro wrestling event of the year, and nothing looks more major league than tearing down the house before 35,000 or more people on an international stage to make you look like legitimate stars as opposed to guys working for a distant No. 3 U.S. promotion.

But from a businessman point of few, it's very different. This is ROH contracted talent that is not supposed to appear on iPPV or PPVs for any other company. They've let it slide with the New Japan shows in the past since it was only iPPV and a very small audience outside Japan watching.

But it can be looked at that ROH is in the PPV business and New Japan is in the PPV business working with Global Force Wrestling. The show is "GFW" branded, and if GFW gets off the ground, they will be competitors to ROH vying for the No. 2 or No. 3 slot in the North American market. Plus, it appears GFW will have the leg up on ROH when it comes to working with New Japan if GFW gets a television deal and starts up as a promotion. While one can argue it can be best for all concerned for GFW, ROH and TNA to all be cooperative with each other rather than adversarial, alliances like that in wrestling historically end up being short-lived, and that's when they aren't promoting in the same area. With all three groups promoting nationally, an alliance, while good on paper, will be difficult to maintain because of the competitive situation they are all put in. Plus, GFW and New Japan together, and ROH, are both trying to run regular PPVs.

With the two shows four weeks apart, the New Japan show on PPV can be construed as competition for Final Battle. But more in 2015, if GFW gets off the ground, or New Japan's show is successful, they and ROH will be competing for the same very small hardcore fan base.

Joe Koff of ROH told us that he doesn't see it as a story at this point because nobody from ROH is officially booked on the Tokyo Dome show at this time and there's nothing to talk about until that deal is made.

Two other sources said airfare for some ROH talent has already been purchased by New Japan, which makes things awkward.

ROH talent affected by this, which includes Fish, O'Reilly and Cole are said to be privately very down about all this, as one could imagine. Not just appearing at the Dome before the largest crowd and biggest show they've ever been on, but the ability to have it also air in the U.S. and try and have a great match could be career highlights for them.

The one thing is that if it does work out that the ROH talent can't be on the American PPV, which would mean they would likely be in pre-show dark matches from the U.S. standpoint, the four-hour window for the show will mean there would be less time constraints. Even at five hours they are likely to have to rush the undercard matches through because of how loaded the show is expected to be.

But New Japan has already pushed a 4 p.m. start time in Tokyo, which is 2 a.m. Eastern. So for this to happen, it would mean New Japan would have to change the start time of its show, plus work with time constraints on its biggest show of the year that they've never had to worry about.

Still, there are always going to be issues if New Japan tries to break into foreign markets, particularly the U.S. market.

An interesting note is that the announcement of the Dome show on U.S. PPV got almost no coverage in Japan until New Japan owner Takaaki Kidani called a press conference with media.

The time slot will be an issue to all but the audience that already follows New Japan, which is very small in the U.S. There isn't a big audience that will purchase a PPV on tape when the results are already out there and there's a good chance the video will be able to be accessed in places before the Sunday night feed. The one thing with Bound for Glory, which based on very limited numbers, looks to have been down 40 percent this year from the prior year and 70 percent from two years ago (more because the show wasn't promoted as well), is that the footage wasn't available before it aired on delay, although the results were.

There are talks with Jim Ross and Mike Tenay continuing. With Ross, I'm thinking the deal will either be done or not within the next week or two, but with an offer said to be tied to buys because of the limited budget, that could be difficult. With Tenay, I just can't see him making a deal until TNA makes its television deal, and then starts making offers to the people no longer under contract. At this stage, Tenay is under contract for voice overs of shows through 11/19, which is the final first-run TNA show, until a new TV would go into place in January, if such a deal is signed.

With UStream no longer airing New Japan shows and the Niconico web site being far too difficult to navigate for a non-Japanese unless you are someone who just has to watch it, there is a potential niche business for Jarrett and New Japan. There are those in ROH frustrated because they had an existing promotion with television and could have cultivated the same thing, particularly coming off the success of the New York and Toronto joint-promotional shows earlier this year.

If it was me, I'd do a deal where the Korakuen Hall shows for the most part, or perhaps others if they see fit, that are already airing in Japan anyway, would broadcast live for free on the New Japan U.S. site or a GFW site, using English language commentary. The idea would be like traditional wrestling, and New Japan does a good job with that, with all the tags on those shows pushing the PPV matches. I'd broadcast all the PPVs once a month on the Internet for maybe $20 to $25. I'd also do a similar G-1 package and also PPV maybe the final show of Fantastica Mania, or when they do the big doubles (split the main matches into two shows in a month as they did a couple of times last year), maybe offer a package of both for $30 type of thing. That way, even if the economics don't work for 12 live PPVs a year, and that probably isn't a good idea, the free shows can hopefully cultivate a small audience that will buy the iPPVs, and also perhaps generate enough to where they can do a decent number of buys for the four big ones. It's still a risk, because TNA had two hours of prime time TV with 1.2 to 1.5 million viewers, with English promos and even people who were well known major stars, and wasn't able to maintain a traditional 12-show a year PPV business. And today, WWE has changed the fans' perception of the "value" of watching a major show.

NOVEMBER 24

ROH signed off on Bobby Fish & Kyle O'Reilly being allowed to be on the PPV portion of Wrestle Kingdom. That's good in the sense they will probably have a great match. It's bad in that it means the show will have to be rushed even worse. More on the four hours. From talking with people involved with the show, the four hour limit can't be changed and everyone on both sides are aware of it. Right now there are nine matches slotted and I don't see how they can add any unless they do them as pre-show matches, even though that leaves nothing for some major stars like Yuji Nagata, Manabu Nakanishi, Satoshi Kojima, Tiger Mask, Taichi, Hiroyoshi Tenzan and Jushin Liger past they can do an eight-man pre-show match. The ROH title singles title match is a casualty of this and neither Adam Cole nor Jay Briscoe will be on the card. Cole was on the original card whether he was champion or not, and Briscoe was to defend if he was champion on the original card. I don't know about the NWA title past it was going to be part of the show. Lance Archer & Davey Boy Smith Jr. are definitely booked, but they could be in a multiple person match before the PPV starts. Given they are looking at casual fans, guys like Liger, Kojima and Tenzan should have a spot on the show since they all have major history as longtime big stars. The first half of the show, which would include both jr. title matches, is going to have to be rushed. Hiroshi Tanahashi and Kazuchika Okada are total pros in the sense that when they go in the ring, they will know they have a time cue that they can't go. They are believed to be good enough to improvise at the last minute to make it work. New Japan gives everyone cues but the stress of ending the show perfectly like in WWE isn't there, but on this show, it will be. Whether the main event can get 33 minutes like they got two years ago is unlikely, and as noted, Okada has publicly stated he was going to do a match. That was so weird to me to have someone in the world title match in the main event promoting the show say "six-star match" as the goal.

The number everyone involved is looking at for the North American market is 10,000 as a solid success and maybe 7,000 to 8,000 as okay. Less than 5,000 would be disappointing. The first show will determine everything, because the mentality is that the value of Jim Ross being with them and it being the Tokyo Dome show is that whatever they are going to do numbers-wise, the first show will be the highest, unless they get television. Based on those numbers, they will either come to the conclusion the idea isn't viable, or that it is and then jump in with a battle plan for 2015. I don't sense they are looking at 12 PPV shows, but two (the second being the G-1 finals) or four would happen if the first show is a success. One of the reasons the number doesn't have to be that high is all the cost of doing the show itself past the cost of beaming to the U.S., hiring the announcers and travel and pay for whoever else is involved on the technical side of making it work in the U.S., are costs the show already had and New Japan would take care of since they are already on PPV and iPPV in their home market. Even Jeff Jarrett's expenses as far as travel are on the New Japan side since he's wrestling on the show.

They are pushing videos on YouTube put together by Kevin Sullivan with interviews done with Jim Ross, as well as with the American talent the night of the Osaka PPV. The Ross sit down piece was excellent. This is a real experiment regarding strong major league looking Viral videos and the push by talent of how big it is to have their match at the Dome called by Jim Ross. For people like A.J. Styles, Karl Anderson, and everyone in the IWGP jr. tag title match, where they've never had Ross call their match, it's a real big deal. The Young Bucks and Kyle O'Reilly have talked about how they consider this show, between appearing at the Dome with Ross announcing as a sign that all of their hard work for years has paid off and they have made it in wrestling.

CHAPTER SIX

THE WWE NETWORK

JANUARY 20

The entire economic future of World Wrestling Entertainment will change in 2014, with the development of the new digital network and television rights fees negotiations both domestically and abroad.

It's the former that is getting all the publicity this week, but it's the latter that is, certainly short-term, the key to the company financially. It's the rights fees that are the hedge in case the network doesn't meet projections.

The WWE had an elaborate announcement party to announce the launch of the network on 1/8 in Las Vegas, hosted by Michael Cole, with presentations from company executives Vince McMahon, Stephanie McMahon, Michelle Wilson, Paul Levesque and Perkins Miller along with talent Shawn Michaels, Steve Austin and John Cena, along with Major League Baseball's Bob Bowman.

The presentation, carried live on the company's web site, came from the Wynn Hotel in Las Vegas, and garnered the company tremendous publicity as part of the CES convention, with the idea that they are the company ahead of their time. In reality, both the NBA and Major League Baseball have already pioneered a streaming service, baseball going back a decade, and UFC just launched a less elaborate network less than two weeks earlier. WWE's is different in the sense a pioneer in that none of those services were as much of a gamble to the core business, and it is also programming the digital network as if it is a television station, with a 24 hour, seven day per week schedule. The rest produced programming and events that were televised elsewhere and also streamed for those who couldn't access them otherwise. WWE is actually putting a full-time television channel on the Internet.

The WWE Network, which debuts with a one week free trial on 2/24, will be a $9.99 monthly service, although the minimum subscription term is six months at $59.94, starting in March. There is no ordering the channel in April, getting WrestleMania, and then canceling. After the first six months, all subscriptions will remain for a six month minimum turn at $59.94 unless there is a price raise at that point. In comparison to UFC Fight Pass, announced in a far more low key way on 12/28, a few miles down the road at the MGM Grand Garden Arena's press room, a service that allows fans to see all the UFC events that are not on television or PPV, and which is believed to allow month-to-month purchases, that is essentially aimed at the fan who wants to see every event.

The WWE Network is aimed at every fan, both current and even those who no longer watch the product. And their optimistic projections for subscriptions show it.

The UFC Fight Pass is projecting 100,000 subscribers at $9.99 per month, worldwide by the end of 2014. The WWE Network is projecting between 1 million and 2 million subscribers in the United States (the 50 states and Puerto Rico, the only places it will be launched at first) by the end of 2014. They project in the U.S. alone, they will have 2 million to 3 million subscribers by the end of 2015.

Even at those lofty numbers, between the start-up costs and the cannibalization of PPV, a WWE SEC filing stated that the company was expecting profits to be lower this year than last year.

"We expect the network will reduce OIBDA and net income in 2014 as the initial ramp in subscribers and revenue is not likely to be sufficient to offset both the foregone pay-per-view revenue and the incremental, direct expenses associated with a network launch, such as programming, marketing, customer service and content delivery costs," wrote WWE's Chief Financial Officer George Barrios.

Long-term, based on the U.S. market, they project in 2015, when there are no longer the start-up costs, that the network would break even with 1 million subscribers, earn $50 million in OIBDA (pre-tax profits) with 2 million subscribers, and earn $150 million in OIBDA with 3 million subscribers.

They are projecting that the network will, in the U.S., cannibalize about $60 million annually in money that had previously been taken in, largely in PPV and DVD revenue. They expect another $15 million annually in cannibalization of those revenue streams for 2015 when the network expands internationally. The costs per year right now are budgeted at $65 million, of which about $20 million is earmarked for programming.

Essentially, for 2015, they need $140 million in revenue to the company to break even. While that would figure to be 1,167,000 on a worldwide basis, because of splits in revenues, depending on what percentage use outside streaming devices, it would really be a number somewhere between 1.17 million and 1.67 million worldwide subscribers

The plan is to launch the network outside the U.S., in the United Kingdom, Canada, Australia, New Zealand, Singapore, Hong Kong and the Nordic countries in Europe, either at the end of 2014 or early 2015.

After the initial launch, they are projecting with 250,000 subscribers outside the U.S., they can break even on international revenue. With 750,000 subscribers internationally, they can hit $25 million in new OIBDA and with 1,500,000 subscribers internationally, they can hit $85 million in new OIBDA.

Are those numbers viable? Many have jumped on the bandwagon to say, at $9.99 with all that content available, they'll hit the goals easily. Others who have studied the concept and marketplace, have projected not being able to come close to those numbers. The truth is, nobody will have a clue because this has always been a shot in the dark. The only comparison is with Major League Baseball's network. Given MLB.tv has 3 million worldwide subscribers, and baseball is far more popular than WWE, that would make the 3 million figure seem optimistic, but break-even numbers wouldn't appear to be out of reach. Others, using research that shows the number of people who watch Raw, the number of homes that have Internet, and the percentage which at this point have already shown the proclivity to pay for a streaming service, have estimated numbers nowhere close to the needed mark.

Even so, it's a shot that's worth taking because the potential rewards are worth the gamble. And with the expected increases in television rights fees that, if achieved, would kick in during the fall, it's a risk the company will be able to financially withstand. But it is not a sure-fire success. The claim is that it's the direction chosen because it's the best direction. In the long-run, it was, because there was no truly viable alternative for the network. Putting most of the PPVs for free was an interesting play, but the original plans called for leaving the big PPVs off the network. Later it was every show but WrestleMania. Then it was WrestleMania on this year but not next year. Based on everything said, the network will carry even WrestleMania every year going forward.

Attempts to launch it as a television station didn't garner as much interest as they had hoped for, nor was there the enthusiasm by the cable companies as far as adding a WWE network as a premium channel.

In the United States, there are 98 million homes that have cable. With football season over, now in wrestling's strongest television period of the year, this past week there were about 3 million homes that watched Raw for free, and 1.9 million that watched Smackdown for free, many of which are duplicated.

There are 88 million homes that have Internet, less than the number who have cable. In some of those homes, the quality of the Internet may not be good enough or reliable enough for streaming. The vast majority of those homes do not pay money for any streaming content. Netflix, with 30 million subscribers has grown enough and paved the way in opening up a large customer base, has shown at least one-third of those homes are not adverse to paying for streaming content. WWE officials admitted that a year ago they would not have even considered this approach, but the success of Netflix opened the doors for it.

On a percentage basis, Monday's Raw did a 3.11 rating among people willing to watch a show that has 20 plus years of being on Monday, for free. Are 1.1 percent of the people who have Internet in the United States willing to pay $9.99 to watch more pro wrestling when they already can see six hours of new WWE programming and two hours of TNA for free each week already? Relatively few even bother to watch TNA or Main Event. To hit two million, you would need more total sign-ups than homes that watch Smackdown for free, even though cable homes exceed Internet homes. To hit three million, you'd need the same amount of homes that watch Raw, even with a smaller total universe where people would have the devices necessary to view it.

Major League Baseball's streaming service reportedly has 3 million subscribers, at $18.50 to $19.99 per month. That's encouraging in the sense another sport has done it and shown there is absolutely potential already shown that you can get seven figures of homes with a service like this. Baseball is more popular than wrestling, but WWE is plenty popular, is charging half the price, and will market it like crazy. Hulu Plus has 5 million subscribers.

But WWE does have a significant loyal audience. There is the argument that if they can get 600,000 U.S. homes to purchase WrestleMania, the majority of those at $69.95, in theory, 1 million at $9.99 would seem easy. But 2 million? Nobody knows. And WrestleMania is a unique attraction. Aside from WrestleMania and Royal Rumble, WWE didn't have a PPV show in 2013 that attracted more than 180,000 homes purchasing in the United States, and Survivor Series in the U.S. looks to have done less than half that. The question becomes whether 20 to 30 times as many homes that ordered Survivor Series at mostly $54.95, would have paid $9.99 to see it. The question is also how many fans from the past are willing to subscribe to a service to be able to stream, at their convenience, PPV content from 1985 to the present.

WWE has wanted its own channel since 2000 when, at the peak of their mainstream popularity, they were turned down in an attempt to get the then-Sci Fi Channel rebranded as their own WWF Network. After popularity nosedived just five years later, the idea of the network came because of how limited the interest was in the television product from cable stations in 2005. After attempting to get a bidding war going with the major cable stations, they were forced to take a television deal with the USA Network far less lucrative in the big picture than their previous deal with Spike TV due to limited interest in the product.

Today, things are different. While ratings are down from 2005, the value of reliable programming that is DVR-proof, as both Raw and Smackdown largely are, is seen as far more valuable within television.

The network has strong momentum because if you are willing to pay for pro wrestling content, the value when it comes to cost is very strong if one is any kind of a significant wrestling fan.

There will be about 1,500 hours of content on the network at the start, a number that will grow over time.

The network will have two distinctive services. The first will be a streaming programmed 24 hour channel offering the current television shows, network exclusive programming, and archived footage from the company's library of 100,000 hours.

The key programming available besides the monthly big shows on Sundays that used to be PPV shows, will be 30 minute live pre-and-post-game shows before both Raw and Smackdown on Monday and Friday nights, along with NXT, Superstars as well as replays of that week's Raw (while never said, based on the contract with the USA Network, we were told it would be a 90 minute edited version of the show but that hasn't been made official), Smackdown and Main Event, as well as Total Divas during its season.

The first series exclusives will be Legends House, a show taped years ago where WWE stars from the past like Roddy Piper, Gene Okerlund, Pat Patterson, Howard Finkel, Jimmy Hart, Jim Duggan and others shared a house together. Based on the previews, this did not look promising. When the network got delayed for so many years, attempts to sell it to television never worked out. A second announced original series will be WrestleMania Rewind, where each WrestleMania will be covered featuring interviews with the stars talking about their feelings on the show, along with never-before-seen footage from the shows.

A third is WWE Countdown, a show where each week there will be a topic, like Best Talker, Best Match, Best

Entrance Music, Best whatever, and fans will vote on them.

A fourth is The Monday Night War, a continuing series with comments from the participants and airing footage of Raw and Nitro shows between late 1995 and early 2001.

Plans are also for a daily studio talk show, perhaps starting by the summer.

Another unique feature is you can push a button and pick your favorite program and you will get an automatic text sent to you just before the show is scheduled to air.

There will be roughly five to ten hours of archived television shows per week on the network, similar to Classics on Demand.

Numerous other ideas are being talked about since Legends House, the Countdown show and WrestleMania Rewind have limited numbers of shows they can produce. Other ideas include a "Where are they now?" type of show, as well as reviving Tough Enough.

Besides the live stream is a video-on-demand service which will feature all shows that appear on the regular stream, which you can watch when you want, start from the beginning, middle or whatever.

Also available on-demand will be every PPV show from WWF/E, WCW and ECW, which would be roughly 411 shows (279 from WWF/E if the 1999 Over the Edge show where Owen Hart passed away is included as that show has never been released after the original airing), 111 from WCW and 21 from ECW).

In addition, every DVD release will be available. There will also be rotating programming from the company's vast library, mostly television shows concentrating on old episodes of WWF/E, WCW and ECW programming, which they clearly from the presentation, believed to have the most value to the current audience, and to bring back fans in the late 90s when pro wrestling hit a peak of mainstream popularity.

The historical footage will air mostly uncut. Controversial characters that WWE shied away from putting on DVD releases like Chris Benoit or Mel Phillips will appear, although there will be warnings on shows involving Benoit, or on shows where some of the footage would appear to be controversial, whether due to extreme blood, violence or bad taste.

Commentary by Jesse Ventura, also edited out of a lot of DVD footage over royalty issues, will air as it first appeared, as well as ring announcements by Gary Michael Cappetta, which, for legal reasons, were also edited out of prior releases. Music is a more touchy issue. Perkins Miller of WWE told us it's a case-by-case basis, particularly when it comes to 80s pro wrestling when a lot of the hit music of the times was used as entrance music. There will be parental controls available for content that is not considered TV-PG.

For people who think you can have access to the entire library, that is not close to the case. Only about 1.5% of the library will be accessible, and very little of it will be old territorial footage. And while they will add new content weekly, they will also remove content.

The highlights of what will be offered are the monthly big shows, which up to this point have been called PPVs. The first show of this type offered will be WrestleMania. That's the real gamble. Last year WrestleMania on PPV in the United States alone generated approximately $20 million in company revenue and the audience showed it was willing to pay $69.95 for the most part for the show. There is no question that putting WrestleMania on the network is the big hook where you are almost guaranteed several hundred thousand subscribers by the 4/7 date of the show. In doing so, it's likely to be a huge loss leader. They would need a huge number, impossible to directly say but well over 2 million and perhaps as many as 3 million subscribers in the month of April, to offset the revenue they would lose if the show isn't on PPV in the United States.

Of course, that in and of itself is tricky. WWE plans to offer traditional PPV for WrestleMania, and every succeeding PPV, while readily acknowledging the numbers of orders will likely decline greatly as subscribers opt for the $9.99 per month charge instead of $44.95 for SD or $54.95 for HD for the standard monthly show, and $59.95 for SD and $69.95 for HD for WrestleMania.

The question is, will cable companies continue to carry WWE shows. On the surface, this seems like a no brainer. Obviously, there are going to be people who aren't comfortable with trusting a stream, that may want to order PPV the traditional way. Even with the $9.99 per month network, far more people will opt to order WWE PPV shows through traditional means, than TNA's live PPV shows, which is carried everywhere. A lot of people want to make projections on how many will still order PPV the traditional way vs. how many will stream it for the lower price. But it's all totally uncharted water. WWE has done extensive customer surveys. But historically, and we've learned this but so has every other company over time, doing surveys on a regular basis, that what people say they will buy in a survey and what they will actually do are often very different. When it comes to purchases of wrestling related events, surveys a very days apart will often yield completely different results.

But it's safe to say several hundred thousand homes in the U.S. would like to order WrestleMania this year by traditional PPV means if it was made available to them.

But this puts DirecTV, Dish and inDemand in a quandary. The contracts for PPV shows through traditional means don't allow the promotion to undercut the PPV price on the Internet. The promotion can put the show on Internet PPV, as WWE and UFC do every month, but it has to charge the same price as television. Obviously, a new deal will have to be signed with WWE, since they are very much undercutting the PPV price.

If they allow WWE, which is a distant third in the U.S. PPV market to undercut the price by that great a degree and still air the shows, what kind of leverage will it give UFC and boxing, which are far more valuable to the companies.

In 2013, WWE did a total of 2.1 million PPV buys in the United States. UFC did about 5 million. Boxing did roughly the same.

If they still broadcast WWE events, while WWE only charges $9.99 per month on the Internet for them, how can they possibly stop UFC or boxing from undercutting the price as well? Let's just say, in theory, that the UFC averaged $26 in revenue from a $44.95/$54.95 show (most UFC orders these days are HD orders, which again shows that the majority of viewers have no qualms about price because they have the option and most choose the most expensive option). Let's just say they decide to take the same show and offer it on their web site for $40. Well, of that $40, they keep most of the $40 instead of only getting half. The lower price encourages people to save money and order it on the Internet. The more people who switch, the more money UFC gets while the cable companies on those lower priced orders go from $26 average per order to $0 on the viewers who switched over. The same holds true for boxing.

Is it worth it to those companies to give up the power over the clients they make big money with to keep whatever buys are left from the distant No. 3 group whose numbers are going to dwindle this year, and eventually down to very little? But the argument may be that PPV through television is a dying industry and that in a few years, everyone will order directly from the promotion instead of the cable company. If that's the case, the cable companies need to understand that and just make all the money short-term they can before that revenue stream dries up.

Even though WWE's plans were written about here and in other trade journals for weeks, many in the cable industry had no idea that the PPVs were going to be put on the network. Many companies found out the day of launch. A few others found out about a week earlier when one of the other PPV producers informed them of the rumors that were going on in the wrestling business.

The day after the announcement, DirecTV released a statement saying, "Clearly we need to reevaluate the economics and viability of their business with us, as it now appears the WWE feels they do not need their PPV distributors."

This shot may have been aimed at WWE due to a quote from Michelle Wilson, the WWE's Chief Revenue and Marketing Officer, who said to the Associated Press, "I'm just not convinced the pay-per-view platform is in it for the long term. It's not the best consumer experience."

DirecTV stated that WWE's popularity on PPV, "has been steadily declining, and this new low-cost competitive offering will only accelerate this trend."

No other providers have given statements on the record, but reports were that Comcast, which owns NBC Universal, was not happy with the idea that the satellite and PPV companies will be out as much as $60 million in total revenue over the course of a year. Many suspected this would not help WWE get the rights increase at the same time they were pulling millions off the books of the company they are trying to get the increase from. However, if WWE can get other suitors, whether it be FOX or Viacom, interested in their television package, the price for the television package that is a ratings juggernaut is going to rise significantly just based on the laws of supply-and-demand. It was said that WWE pushed to them that a significant percentage of their television audience is over the age of 50, and a lot of them will continue to order PPVs the way they always have.

What is notable is that the lapsed fan they are hoping to re-engage by offering the older historical tapes will, in theory, be the most adverse to signing up because of age. But that's not the case with people who grew up watching the 1998-2001 boom period, which will be focused on strongly when it comes to archived offerings. They have pushed to the USA Network that they expect Raw and Smackdown ratings to increase with the idea the network will make the brand overall more popular, with the idea the network will bring older fans back to relive the wrestling of their youth, and in doing so, will be exposed to the modern product and regain interest. That's a wait-and-see, because there are far too many moving parts in place to even estimate that. With many people, wrestling was a phase in their lives that they are past, and are not interested in reliving it anymore than they would be interested in rewatching old NFL games from the late 90s. With others, changes in the product are the reason they no longer watch the modern product. Unlike baseball, football, or basketball, where the game itself looks largely the same as it did 40 years ago, the entire lure and presentation of modern pro wrestling is completely different from prior eras.

Major League Baseball Advanced Media will be the streaming partner. They work with, obviously, Major League Baseball as well as Sony, and have streamed 20,000 live events. They are considered the state-of-the-art when it comes to this service. Most people who have subscribed to their service have nothing but good things to say, but there are exceptions.

The content can be streamed though the WWE web site app on virtually every device possible, including Amazon's Kindle Fire devices, Android devices such as Samsung Galaxy, iOS mobile devices such as Apple iPad and iPhone, Roku streaming devices, Xbox 360, PS 3 and PS 4 and Roku boxes. It will also start this summer being available on Xbox 1 and some Smart TVs, as well as Apple TV.

The revenue split on working with those groups will be about 70/30 in WWE's favor instead of the 50/50 split with the cable companies. If people stream directly from WWE, there is no revenue split.

To avoid confusion in the marketplace, there will be no sign-ups allowed until 2/24 at 9 a.m, a Monday morning. This is largely to avoid problems because the Elimination Chamber PPV, held the night before, will not be offered on the network. The network will debut, for free, at 11:06 p.m. that night, for a one week tryout. Raw will be strongly pushing the network every week, but the 2/24 show is expected to have nothing but network promotion.

The first live special, held during the free tryout week, will be a Thursday night special on 2/27, an NXT show from Full Sail University in Winter Park, FL, where the show regularly tapes.

The top two matches will be Bo Dallas vs. Adrian Neville in a ladder match for the NXT title and Antonio Cesaro vs. Sami Zayn in a 2/3 fall match in a rematch of what may have been NXT's best match this year. The impression I was given was it would be a live show from 9-11 p.m., head-to-head with TNA, and produced like it was a PPV but using almost all developmental talent. They will either do a regular NXT TV taping for the weekly show either before the special or the next day. The time slot is at this point not official. If it goes well, the plan would be to do a second network exclusive live NXT special later in the year.

Like with free trials of Netflix, as well as the current free period of the UFC Fight Pass, it's expected one will have to register with their credit card for the free trial week, and then cancel or they will start getting billed the monthly fee for six months.

Other questions remain unanswered. The increase in TV rights and subscription fees, which are brand related, as opposed to PPV buys and live attendance, which are far more star related, reduces the leverage and power of the stars. One performer noted to us that if the network is successful, any attempts at collective bargaining are dead, although in reality they weren't going to happen anyway.

There will be some advertising on the network, but they are not counting on significant ad revenue and have stated they want as little ad clutter as possible.

If WrestleMania is not on PPV, and the top stars at Mania have in the past received hundreds of thousands of dollars based on PPV revenue, will this change things? Are there going to be royalties based on network numbers to replace the lost PPV bonuses and perhaps dwindling DVD commissions? That would add to break-even, but none of this had been addressed to talent at press time. A few would talk privately to us about it, but I was told at the TVs this week, nobody was bringing it up because the television portrayal of talent being afraid to cross authority is a shoot in real life. It's a very different marketplace where there is little in the way of alternatives and the value of stars is less than at any time in pro wrestling history.

Does this remove the incentive to promote PPVs as big because they are not going to be close to the revenue stream they were? Does this remove the incentive to pay big money for people like Dwayne Johnson or Brock Lesnar? In theory yes, but there are no answers because nobody knows how well this will do.

What if these projections don't hold up and they don't break even? Is there any turning back and being able to put 12 shows a year back on PPV after establishing their value at $9.99, and then getting people to go back to paying more than five times as much for it? The battles between creating an incredible bargain and devaluing the former monthly PPV shows will be something to look back on. TNA, in a sense, pioneered this inadvertently, in taking all but its big four events from the PPV stage to putting them on Spike TV for free. The reality is they had little value on the PPV market which is why the move was made, and they have even less value now. WWE's non big-three events, maybe big four including Elimination Chamber (calling Survivor Series big four is being years out of touch) still had considerable value. The others had in a sense been devalued by three hour Raws, and lack of creation of big stars who were true money draws and creating money drawing angles, all of which the current trends worked against. Really, moving them to this network wasn't exactly the same as the economically forced TNA move, but it wasn't that big a risk. The move of Mania was another story, taking the brand name built and sacrificing its economic potential to build this network. That's the risk play here, because they've taken the one day of the year with extreme value, and have greatly risked that value by underpricing it.

The key people watching this will be UFC and boxing. If WWE's network built largely around the PPV shows can generate more money than either of those genres generate from PPV, with big shows with far more consumer power, it would indicate they could learn from WWE's trial and error on both what to do and what not to do. When all is said and done, the WWE network will probably, like WWE itself, go through a series of phases and changes, whether successful at first or not. Their newer fan base isn't the slightest bit resistant to purchasing a streaming network.

All programming except the PPVs will only be offered in English. The PPVs will be offered in English or Spanish.

FEBRUARY 10

For the WWE Network, the company released a list of all the PPVs that will be available when the network goes live on 2/24. It's every WWE wrestling PPV (no WBF or joint promoted shows, nor the Hogan match at the No Holds Barred movie PPV), every WCW show (however none of the joint promoted shows either such as the AAA When World's Collide which was one of the best PPVs held in the U.S. of all-time, New Japan joint promoted shows from the Tokyo Dome, K-1 joint promoted shows or the New Japan Collision in Korea) and every ECW PPV. The WWE ECW shows are available. The Over the Edge show in 1999 that was never released before due to the death of Owen Hart is on the list. I don't know if they will edit out the announcement of Owen Hart's death or the ten minutes in the ring they were working on him. All Chris Benoit matches on those shows will remain intact. Some of the music may have to be changed, but since they aren't charging for a separate DVD, people like Gary Michael Cappetta, Michael Buffer and Jesse Ventura, who had been edited off DVD's, are expected to appear as they were. That's about 400 PPVs in total. The Royal Rumble will be on when it launches but Elimination Chamber won't be.

As of right now, when people have asked DirecTV about showing WWE PPVs, they say they have not made a decision. It appears that cable companies will be showing WrestleMania, which opens them up for some interesting potential negotiations when it comes to boxing and UFC.

FEBRUARY 24

The first domino in the battle between WWE and traditional PPV providers may have been dropped this past week when The Dish Network quietly pulled Elimination Chamber from its PPV offerings for this coming weekend.

The dropping wasn't publicized and both sides have avoided any public comment. Dish Network subscribers who heard about it and asked, were told a multitude of different things from it being a web site glitch that would be fixed, to they are in talks, to that they are not carrying the show and telling callers they could order the UFC event the night before or the TNA show two weeks later.

The battle was expected to take place at WrestleMania, and DirecTV, larger than Dish Network, had threatened to cease carrying WWE events because by putting the shows on the network at a $9.99 per month price, they believed they were undercutting their distribution partners who were charging $69.95 for HD of the same event.

WWE has been in battles with cable distributors before, usually fighting over percentages of total revenues. In those battles, the WWE always went public, attempting to mobilize its fan base, and went over the top with criticism of those they battled with claiming they were not allowing fans their right to see such shows. The complete quietness on Raw, to the point it was shockingly never brought up, would indicate negotiations aren't dead, and are very sensitive.

However, if a deal isn't reached, there are going to be some unhappy consumers. Only a tiny percentage of Dish Network viewers would be aware there is even an issue, and they likely won't find out until they want to push the button to order on 2/23, only to find out the show isn't being carried.

In the past, such as WWE's dispute more than a decade ago with DirecTV, which saw them not carry the Royal Rumble one year, there was plenty of publicity on WWE television about it. In that situation, even though DirecTV at the time represented 20 percent of the homes in the U.S. that had PPV capability, the Rumble actually did shockingly well, to the point that damage was minimal if any. In fact, it ended up being one of the most successful Rumbles in history, more because interest was high that year. But with notice, people with DirecTV were able to find friends who would order the show, because in almost any neighborhood, it's the local cable that's dominant, not a satellite company.

The same thing would apply here if people knew of the situation. The Dish Network was in 14,049,000 homes as of November, or about 14.2% of the total PPV addressable U.S. homes. Last year's Elimination Chamber did 181,000 buys in North America, but that was due to a C.M. Punk vs. The Rock main event boosting it above usual levels. The prior two years did 138,000 (2012) and 145,000 (2011), which would be more along the lines of what this year should be expected to do. Of those, about ten percent would be from Canada and Puerto Rico, so 125,000 U.S. buys would be a good estimate for this year. Of that, 14.5 percent would be 17,800 total buys, or a hit of something in the ballpark of $461,500 to WWE and an identical number to Dish. It would be impossible to even ballpark a WrestleMania financial impact, because we don't know how much the lower priced network will do to PPV buys overall.

If WWE was able to get publicity out in time that those 17,800 buyers would know, most would find other ways to watch the show. Even at the last minute, many still will, because one thing history has shown is that people who want to watch something will usually find a way to watch it. In reality, the financial losses will be higher for Dish than WWE. But they can more easily afford it. The Dish Network takes in more than $14 billion per year in revenue, as compared to WWE, which will take in closer to $500 million in revenue. The Dish Network's profits for the year top $1 billion. The WWE's will be announced later this week, but the company was at $10.7 million in total profits after the first nine months of 2013. In a game of financial chicken, this is a mismatch that makes WWE vs. TNA look like a seven-game NBA final.

But when it comes to WrestleMania, the numbers are a lot more serious. That's a game that every major PPV distributor will be looking at, because it's the most expansive show of the year, and the network will be established for five weeks before it takes place.

The surprise is that the game is being played before WrestleMania, the first PPV after the Network launch. There is no undercutting of Elimination Chamber live, and WWE is going to live up to the terms of the previous contract by not putting the show on the network until 3/25. However, this has not been explained to the fan base, which has only been told all PPVs will be on the network starting on 2/24, and that would lead people to believe Elimination Chamber could be viewed free the next day in HD as opposed to spending $54.95 to see it live. WWE did not make that clear thus far in any of the build-up for the Chamber show, that for this show, it would only be available by traditional PPV methods. In a sense, by advertising "every PPV starting with WrestleMania," that would seem to exclude Elimination Chamber, but not in a way that most fans understood.

Another option is with the WWE essentially putting the market value of its PPV shows at $9.99, that the cable industry would insist that they drop the price on PPV as to not be undercut. But this would make them an even more distant third revenue producer behind Boxing and UFC. As it is, WWE is expected to lose a great deal of cable and satellite commercials for WrestleMania, with the inventory expected to heavily go to the UFC 172 show in Baltimore and the TNA Sacrifice show the next day.

FEBRUARY 24

Regarding the network, while the first week is free, similar to UFC and other start-ups when they give a free sample, people have to still sign up with credit card information and a subscription will automatically renew until canceled. The hope, and gimmick, like with all Internet subscription sites, is that people sign up for free, and then just forget or don't hassle with canceling, and become regular subscribers. There continues to be the talk of a cliffhanger ending on Raw on 2/24, to encourage sign-ups. What is notable is that because of the West Coast, where Raw airs three hours later, they will have to replay the post-game show. The pre-game show, if it's going to work for the West Coast, would have to be replayed while the live Raw is finishing up. The plan right now is for the post-game show on Raw to be shot backstage, since it would be going on at the same time as the main event dark match if it was done from a spot inside the arena.

MARCH 3

The WWE Network launched on 2/24 to two days filled with technical issues , confusion and complaints.

The idea that working with Major League Baseball Advanced Media would make things smooth sailing ended up not being the case. There were problems the first day in signing up, due to high volume demand. Some people who signed up couldn't get anything to play. The most common problem was, and this remained until press time, is many were able to get the live stream to work, but not the archived content. Some were able to get some content, not others, had issues with the system crashing, an error message, or heavy buffering issues. It seemed to depend which device someone was streaming content through. Many were upset that they believed they were getting a free week, only to find their accounts charged $9.99. Stories of customer service calls that have been told by multiple people were almost mind-boggling, like they were straight out of a sit-com.

It raises questions regarding streaming of a PPV event, where a far larger number of people than usual will be logging in, almost all at the same time.

For all the heat Ring of Honor took with their misfires, WWE itself was shut down in trying to stream WrestleMania in 2012 for two hours, and many people had problems with the 2013 Royal Rumble, and a few pre-game shows. The demand was far higher, because prior PPVs ranged from 3,000 and 20,000 viewers, and had problems. But going forward, there could be 1 million or more people watching a major PPV this year, and if their estimates are correct, three million in 2015, and not being able to handle the volume of far less than that is concerning.

After blaming the first day problems on MLBAM being overwhelmed by the number of orders, and second day problems stating they themselves were fixing bugs that affected 20 percent of subscribers looking to access archived material, the company said they hoped things would be going smoothly by the evening of 2/25. Still, we had gotten constant feedback from people from launch and through press time, both via e-mail and Twitter, saying they couldn't access content. People who actually surveyed a lot of people said the number had to be far greater than 20 percent, noting very few when asked individually said everything was running smoothly.

MLBAM stated that the initial demand at 9 a.m. Eastern "exceeded anything the company had ever seen in its history and overloaded the company's e-commerce processing system," for the earliest problems, but claimed all ordering issues were resolved by mid-afternoon. We had numerous people contact us after that statement was released saying it wasn't the case.

It was pushed in WWE Network publicity that it would only be available in the U.S., but on television, the WWE never once stated that. Fans in the U.K., Canada and the rest of the world were under the assumption they could get the network. The plan right now is for it to debut in Canada, the U.K., Australia, New Zealand, Hong Kong, Singapore, Norway, Sweden and Finland toward the end of 2014 or early 2015.

However, it was a relatively simple process to circumvent the system from outside the U.S. and order, and it appears a huge percentage of first day orders were from those countries.

In Canada, Apple TV had an icon to watch the network on Monday, meaning those in Canada believed they could get it, only to have it taken down the next day.

David Bixenspan, Ian Hamilton and Chris Harrington were able to track, because from the start, order numbers were given sequentially, total orders from about 8 a.m. to 4 p.m. Eastern time. At that point WWE evidently found out the numbers were being tracked and stopped giving out numbers. During that eight-hour period, there were more than 130,000 sign-ups. Whether that's good or bad is hard to determine, but it's not a number so overwhelming that they shouldn't have been ready for it and able to process it.

The number wouldn't include people who signed up after work ended on the East Coast, before Raw started, or ordered based on the hype going on during the Raw show. It would also have tracked a period from 5 a.m. to 1 p.m. on the West Coast.

Of the people who sent their numbers to Bixenspan, 17% appeared to be from Europe. A poll that we conducted independently, had, as of press time, indicated of those who had signed up, only 69.8% came from the U.S., with 9.3% from the U.K., 8.3% from Canada, and 8.3% from the rest of Europe. The 17.6% from Europe figure is remarkably close enough to the Bixenspan number that it almost has to be in that ballpark.

WWE itself had projected more than 80% of subscribers when it was all up and running a year plus from now, would be from the United States. Given that, it appears that most who want the network, ordered it quickly and figured out how to do it even though they weren't supposed to do so.

Our skew, based on the sample group, would likely skew domestic higher, not lower than the average. Given that fact, the expected early 2015 bump when those outside the U.S. will officially be able to order may not bring in the 250,000 to 750,000 new orders that they are expecting.

We did a poll on our site regarding the network. 20.4% said they had ordered the network, they've had some viewing problems, but overall said it was enjoyable. 13.1% said they ordered it, but have had significant viewing problems. 10.7% said they've ordered and had no problems. 7.0% said it was difficult getting an order through, but once it went through, there were no problems. 6.7% have not ordered, but are planning to order for WrestleMania. 4.5% are planning to order later in the year. 1.7% said they still haven't been able to order. 27.8% say they aren't planning to order.

The key to this is that if this is representative, and it's probably skewed toward people who will get it first because this is based on people who look for news on a wrestling web site so are more ardent and knowledgeable fans than most, that 84% of those who will order already have. So whatever number they've got now may be closer to max than believed. If they did 350,000 orders on day one, and nobody cancels before the pay period starts (and that's impossible to believe), that doesn't seem to indicate something in the ballpark of 1 million subscribers on the day of WrestleMania. That also would indicate there will still be several hundred thousand traditional PPV orders for WrestleMania. As far as after WrestleMania, both the domestic and overseas numbers would be expected to be lower, because those overseas who order the PPVs all the time, even the B shows, are the same people who are most likely to have already ordered the network.

It also indicates about an 11% bump from the current order levels for WrestleMania, and very few orders after that point. I strongly suspect that isn't completely representative and whatever the number is today is not 84% of what it will be a year from now. But it may be a large percentage. I do believe the day after WrestleMania number, which the WWE has said they will release publicly, will be very close to the number that ends up as the baseline going forward, at least for the U.S. market. Realistically, if they aren't close to 1 million then, it is unlikely they will be by the end of the year.

The company's first live event will be an NXT special, on 2/27, starting at 8 p.m., from Full Sail University, called NXT Arrival. While never said officially, those in the company believed the show, produced to be like a PPV, will be two hours in length, and feature guest appearances by John Cena, The New Age Outlaws and Sheamus. There will be a pre-game show at 7:30 p.m. with Bret Hart, Kevin Nash and Paul Heyman. The three main matches are Bo Dallas defending the NXT title against Adrian Neville in a ladder match, Antonio Cesaro vs. Sami Zayn 2/3 falls and Paige vs. Emma for the NXT women's title. The hope is if the show goes well, that they similar quarterly live specials like this on the network.

Most of the content advertised at the start was there, although many of the first-run television shows advertised haven't debuted yet. Many of the shows were produced years ago, such as Legends House being two years old. It was eerie seeing the debut of a feature on the first WrestleMania, the debut of the "WrestleMania Rewind" show, featuring Pat Summerall as the lead voice, since he passed away in April.

At its launch, also available was:

The expectation that all the current television shows would be up isn't the case. Superstars and NXT will be debuting first on the network, with NXT in a Thursday night 9 p.m. time slot, head-to-head with Impact starting on 3/6. NXT will remain on Hulu, but debut there on Friday nights instead of Wednesday night as in the past. The replays of Raw and Smackdown will remain on Hulu Plus the day after the show, with Raw edited to 90 minutes. But they will not appear on the network until 30 days after their television debut. Episodes of Raw and Smackdown for 2012, 2013, and the first three weeks of January 2014 were up the first day.

Superstars will air weekly on Thursdays at 10 p.m.

There were also 11 other episodes of Raw up, the first nine episodes in the show's history from 1993, and two episodes in 1998. For Smackdown, one episode, the first one from 1999, was up prior to 2012.

There were four ECW TV shows, two each from 1993 and 1994. Joey Styles had indicated once that the entire run of ECW TV shows would be available. The only pre-1990 territorial television show up was a November 2, 1982 episode of World Class Championship Wrestling.

There was also talk of every Madison Square Garden event that was taped being up, but in actuality, there were five shows, one each from 1975, 1977, 1981, 1984 and 1991.

There is also a Goldust mini bio, a "This is NXT" special," and three Legends Round Table shows that were originally on Classics on Demand. With the exception of the live stream, the PPV library, NXT and the current shows, the content is similar to the Classics on Demand 24/7 channel that was recently discontinued.

While not there in every case, the message that is supposed to appear before every show featuring Chris Benoit is to read:

"The following program is presented in its original form. It may contain some content that does not reflect WWE's corporate views and may not be suitable for all viewers. WWE characters are fictitious and do not reflect the personal lives of the actors portraying them. Viewer discretion is advised. You can block access to this program and others like it using the Parental Control feature in your WWE Network account settings,"

Before the Over the Edge PPV from 1999, the show Owen Hart died from falling from the ceiling, there were edits not showing certain aspects of the show, and opened with a message that read:"In Memory of Owen Hart (1965-1999), who accidentally passed away during the broadcast."

There are searches by wrestler, which have every wrestler they had records of appearing for the company. There are numerous names listed that nothing of that wrestler are actually on the network. The only name not in the search of mainline stars was Benoit.

Essentially, the technical reason some things did and didn't work, or didn't work on different devices was because for both video-on-demand and live streams, WWE and MLBAM are using a content distribution network of a number of caching services in various locations around the country. These servers bring content geographically closer to a user requesting it. But they only serve what is expected to be the most popular content. That's why the live stream has few problems, but some video-on-demand material that they didn't expect there would be much interest in, such as WCW and ECW PPVs, have had more problems. When a user requests content not part of the local cache, the cache has to request it, taking time and server resources.

What happened the first two days is too many users requested too much different content, and they don't have either the storage or bandwidth to retrieve it and serve it quickly enough.

The crashing of the ability to order it was because they were preparing for fewer orders than they received, which in a sense, is a good problem. That problem could occur again during WrestleMania week, so it would be encouraged that if you are ordering for WrestleMania, to order a week out when demand on the servers would be low.

In addition, at the launch presentation, they advertised that every DVD release will be available on the network. But at launch, only one, the Bret Hart vs. Shawn Michaels documentary was available.

Almost every WWE, WCW and ECW PPV show was available as advertised, with a few exceptions.

The key exceptions include:The December 12, 1989 No Holds Barred:The Movie/The Match show, the May 6, 2000, Insurrextion PPV (originally available on PPV in Europe only); July 10, 2002 Global Warning (originally available on PPV in Australia only); the 2014 Royal Rumble (which is likely to be available later this week when the 30 day window expires); the March 21, 1991 Starrcade in Tokyo Dome show; the July 14, 1991 Great American Bash (one of the worst PPVs ever, I was told it was available but in the big listing it wasn't there, but if you looked by the year it is); January 4, 1992 Starrcade 2002 in Tokyo Dome; January 4, 1993 Fantastic Story in Tokyo Dome; November 6, 1994 When World's Collide (one of the best PPVs ever); August 4, 1995 Collision in Korea (before the largest crowd in pro wrestling history); March 15, 1998 Uncensored (also likely an oversight and perhaps available but not in the big listing); and the February 12, 1999 ECW Crossing the Line show.

A few of those are likely oversights, a few, because they didn't air in the U.S., may have simply been forgotten, and a few, those working with other promotions, there may be a rights issue involved.

There are the expected music rights edits and the spot where Stacy Carter took off her top (which she did on her own for attention, thinking it would help break her out of the pack) and bared her breasts, was digitized as expected. A lot of profanity on old ECW shows was censored, specifically many interviews by Shane Douglas and double entendres promos by Joel Gertner. There were a lot of complaints by old ECW fans who believed that kind of stuff would be uncensored.

There are also some unexpected edits. Some WCW PPVs had matches missing or matches edited. It appeared in a few cases they used the version released on home video, cut to two hours, so some of the prelim matches were left off, and some of the matches had several minutes edited out. In those cases, the home video version is likely the only copy WCW had of those shows when they sold the library to WWF in 2001.

The network will be available only in English, aside from the PPV shows, where there is the option to get the Spanish language feed.

Regarding the lineup of major events, besides WrestleMania, they will air the entire Hall of Fame ceremony live at 9 p.m. on 4/5 (it will then be replayed on the USA Network two days later, edited down to about one hour), there is a Raw pre-show at 7:30 p.m. every Monday and post-show for 30 minutes after the show goes off the air. There are also Smackdown pre-and -post game shows at 7:30 p.m. and 10 p.m. every Friday.

WrestleMania Rewind will be a weekly series that airs Tuesdays at 9 p.m. WWE Countdown (fan voting to countdown the top 10 or 20 whatever in history) will be Tuesdays at 10 p.m. Legends House begins Thursdays at 8 p.m. This Is NXT is a one-hour one-time special already up. A show called Beyond The Ring, which will be the DVD documentaries of various major stars, will air Saturdays at 8 p.m. The Best of Raw will be a new show added each week on Thursdays at 4:30 p.m. The Best of Smackdown will be similar on Saturdays at 1 p.m. All of those shows will also be available on video-on-demand.

MARCH 3

It's still the calm before the storm, in the sense that whatever profits or losses WWE has this year will be chalked up to a transition period based on the new business era that really begins at the end of 2014.

At that point, it will be a business of two things: television rights fees and network revenue. The traditional economic model will be gone, and in theory, money and profits will skyrocket.

That's based on predictions of two to three million U.S. network subscribers and perhaps another 750,000 outside the U.S. Although they can do significantly less than those figures and still make money, with break-even once they get the network up internationally in late 2014 or early 2015 being somewhere between 1.25 million and 1.75 million worldwide subscribers, There's only a general range because of factors regarding who will watch via computer, and who will use streaming devices, in which case the general industry standard is the company that streams will get 30 percent of the $9.99 per month revenue.

The television rights fees are not going to be surprises. Once the new U.S. deal is signed, which Vince McMahon said would likely be by the end of April, it is almost surely going to be a long-term deal at a certain level. They have all but promised this will be at a substantial increase.

For total gross revenue, the company took in $508.0 million, the second largest year in company history, trailing 2008. The profits were $2.8 million. With the exception of 2002-03, which got hit badly by losses from The World Restaurant, the profits were the lowest since the 1996-97 dark ages.

And next year could be the same or worse, particularly until the new television deals go into place. The new U.S. deal, which hasn't been negotiated, goes into effect in October. The new U.K. deal, the largest non-U.S. deal, has been signed and will be triple the previous rates due to the competition between Sky and BT. But WWE won't be under the new terms until January 2015.

As a comparison, the 2012 numbers, the company took in $484 million but had $31.4 million in profits.

The drop was because of a $11.9 million decline in PPV profits (from $46.0 million to $34.1 million with gross revenue $83.6 million in 2012 and $82.5 million in 2011).

Even though PPV numbers were almost the same, the expense of high-priced talent, most notably Dwayne Johnson and Brock Lesnar, offset the increases in total buys, mostly on the front end of the year fueled by Johnson. Taking Johnson shows off the books, and PPV declined. Talent was also paid $2.2 million more which is likely based on increasing the head count in developmental, and the increased house show total grosses which talent is paid off.

There were also $11.7 million in movie division losses, mostly because of higher estimates on revenues than what was realized on films from 2010 to 2012, as well as losses from this year's movie "Dead Man Down." However, the company does expect to profit next year in the movie business based on yet to be garnered revenue from "The Call," the most successful movie the company has been involved in and perhaps the movie that saved that division.

The impression is that eventual profits from the movie business of titles released over the last 18 months would be about $3 million, over the lifetime of the movies, although at this point the division is still losing money each year. But even that number is largely due to "The Call," which was expected to turn about a $5 million profit for the company when all is said and done (the company has only received a percentage of that revenue as of the end of the year). Some of the straight-to-DVD movies may have broken even or made some, while others, like "Dead Man Down," were significant money losers. While they are talking about how this new strategy, the third movie strategy to date, is now turning the corner, that's only based on one successful movie that they purchased rights to and partnered on, as opposed to one they developed from scratch. But it has saved the division as Vince McMahon said they will invest another $20 million in a series of movies this year.

"We have a new business model," said Vince McMahon. "It is our third business model, actually. This one is working, and it is making money for us. We are a content company. We understand good storylines and an opportunity for our stars to appear in other forms of entertainment other than just in the ring, and we think, again, going forward, that this is going to be a considerable contributor to the bottom line."

The other difference is $5.2 million in compensation and benefits for new hires, largely to back up the network launch and a weaker performance in home video, where 51 percent of what was shipped by the latter part of the year was returned. A positive was house show business, which was up $7.8 million in gross revenue and $600,000 in merchandise sales for the year overall, based on a two percent increase in attendance and an increase in average ticket price based on increasing the high-end ringside ticket cost. However, that increase barely made up for increased cost of touring, as the bottom line saw only $600,000 total of that increase.

The profits came nowhere close to matching the dividend for the year, with $36 million paid out.

The company has $109.4 million in cash and short-term investments on the books as of the end of the year. That's down from $152.4 million at the end of 2012. The decline is a combination of two factors. The first is that the profits for the year were significantly less than the dividend. The other involves the payment of $11 million to senior executives based in bonuses based on profits achieved in 2012.

The company also has a revolving line of debt credit of $83 million. They used that line of credit to spend $30.9 million in a new company aircraft (that is not included in the profit/loss aspect of the year) and make other related improvements to the aircraft. Actual debt on the credit line at the end of the year was $29.6 million, from aircraft spending. So a realistic actual cash on hand figure dropped this year from $152.4 million to $79.8 million. The figure has dropped every year of late because the dividends are more than the profits, being $208.2 million in 2009. At its peak, in the early and mid-00s, the company had well over $300 million in cash-on-hand

That current business results are more negative than positive, but because of the potential for 2015, the stock has skyrocketed, peaking a few days back at $24.96 per share. It has declined to $23.71 at press time, the day after the launch of the network. That was bound to happen because Wall Street is big on the "buy on speculation, sell on results" axiom. The real test of the stock will come in April, or perhaps early May, when the network subscription figures will be announced and the U.S. TV contract is finalized. The market value of the company is now at $1.78 billion, the highest mid-week figure in more than a dozen years.

The story of the reaction, and the business itself going forward, is that everything is changing. Under normal circumstances, a major drop in profits even with increased revenues would cause what had been a stagnant stock to drop even lower. There would be concern over the falling divisions like merchandise and DVDs, and less profitable PPVs, as well as house shows for the most part being stagnant.

But the stock is skyrocketing because for the entire business going forward, if the right TV deal comes in, the usual major revenue streams become almost insignificant. It's all television deals and network success. And if TV revenue doubles, they can afford a network failure as nothing more than as a minor black eye while they continue to make more money than ever. And if they do get the TV deal they are hoping for, it will be a long-term deal most likely, and the numbers are guaranteed, barring a complete collapse which simply isn't going to happen.

The TV deal will be decided in negotiations over the next few months, and there will be an answer in the key U.S. market. The right answer, and the company is home free, at a different level than ever before. The stock is soaring because people are looking at that doubling or tripling television money, which would mean $140 to $280 million, in new revenue without any increase in costs, because it would be the same programming they are already doing. Add that to revenue, and much to the bottom line, and you can see the difference. Some people look at the NASCAR deal at $820 million a year, and WWE's package actually gets more eyeballs during the year, and think that's what WWE is now worth on the open market. If they get even half the deal NASCAR got in their new U.S. negotiations, the network can be a total failure and they're home free. If they only get a modest increase, then the network success becomes paramount.

CFO George Barrios noted that for the first three months of 2014, the projection would be losses of between $12 million and $15 million due to network start-up costs, in particular marketing and customer service costs and more staffing as well as management incentive compensation money. The company doesn't even want to offer any guidance as how next year will do financially, saying that they could provide a better picture in three months.

In three months, since the TV deal will be in place, and the network numbers will be out, everything will be clear. From now until the fall, the company will probably not have a strong bottom line. And as the stock market reaction to the news of a money losing quarter that just ended, and a far bigger money losing quarter that we were in the midst of was still strong, it is all about being viewed as having a strong future.

The key with these deals is for the most part, they will be storyline and booking proof, pretty much in both ways. Of course better creative and new stars that catch on will be a benefit. But even if it's lackluster and the actual product popularity declines, the TV money is going to be guaranteed for years. Plus, as history as shown with wrestling, even the worst creative, and that's simply not going to happen here, will do fine when it comes to ratings when it's the No. 1 company in the market. It is impossible for anyone to challenge WWE for that position, as shown by TNA's inability to gain ground in 2010, even after getting Jeff Hardy, who was actually WWE's hottest performer the previous year, Hulk Hogan, the most famous name in American wrestling history, and Ric Flair, an enduring legend with a long history of being a ratings mover.

The WWE's stated belief is that they will have 1 million network subscribers by the end of the year, a figure they will be happy with, and that it will grow to 2-3 million by the end of 2015. It's completely uncharted water. But my belief is there are two audiences regarding the network.

Ultimately, the driving force of the network is WrestleMania. The nostalgia programming will have some appeal, particularly with the price tag. The other PPVs at so much cheaper of a price than ever before will also have some appeal. I could be wrong, but my belief is the driving force is seeing WrestleMania at a low price, and that guarantees hundreds of thousands of subscribers, maybe a million.

The secondary subscribers are those who, unfamiliar with the technology, aren't ready. That will include people who will buy computers for their home (the number of homes with computers is still lower than those with cable, as shocking as that is to believe), but more, those who have it who get it, and are willing to spend money for it like they would for a PPV or an HBO.

My feeling is WrestleMania at $9.99 will encourage most of that audience to "speed up." If they have 1 million subscribers on WrestleMania Sunday, it would appear they are ahead of projections. But if they do, are there really one or two million more people who will be on the sidelines not getting it who will then order it until an expected increase comes for next year's WrestleMania? It could be a rush to order based on the hype, which I expect, peaking at Mania. From there, I really don't expect a drop. Because of the nature of six-month agreements, most people will come due either around 9/1 (the first group or those who order) or 10/8 (those who order at the time of Mania). At that point, there are no major shows until the Rumble. Do people cancel, or is the price low enough that they continue? My feeling is most won't cancel. But, from that point on, how many new people are you getting? You are getting people who are either new fans, or people with less aversion to buying something of this type. Is that another 1-2 million homes? The reality is it's a changing way of watching TV, that is going to happen, and a new service.

If Major League Baseball already has three million subscribers, and keep in mind that number will also increase over the next few years as its fan base makes those same mental changes, it tells you this gamble is more than worth taking.

Both the WWE Network and UFC Fight Pass become a paying service two days apart, with UFC Fight Pass on 3/1 after a two month free period, and WWE Network on 3/3, after a seven day free period. However, UFC Fight Pass will allow seven days free for anyone signing up to try it out the first time after the paid period begins. WWE's free period is over on Monday.

While UFC has not released numbers, depending on cancellations from those who have already signed up, they may beat their 100,000 goal by the time of their first major full event on 3/8 from London.

WWE has advertised its service far harder, has more of a cultural history of events, has far more of a weekly loyal television audience and has plugged it to its audience far harder. Plus, it is a better value in the sense that UFC is offering prelims that were formerly free, new live events that are the level of those that were formerly on television, and little in the way of first-run television shows yet, past foreign seasons of Ultimate Fighter, but they are expected to produce network exclusive shows going forward.

WWE is offering its entire PPV slate, has a far greater library that dates back more than 40 years in some cases, with substantial offerings from a 1997-2001 and a 1983-88 boom period for the industry, as well as a number of first run television shows. In addition, the barely three million U.S. home number that watches Raw each week in the U.S. is not the real limit now because of how easy it really is to subscribe from Canada and overseas, which in theory, were supposed to be blocked until an international launch in late 2014 or early 2015. WWE is also currently more popular in the U.S., so by that standard, the WWE's goals for this year don't appear to be out of line. Both companies are charging $9.99 per month, so price in both cases is not an obstacle.

That also means the late 2014 or early 2015 secondary international launch may not have the success level predicted because the hardcore audience, the base for the network, will figure out how to subscribe long before the end of the year and be listed in the U.S. category.

The network has dominated the talk the past few months because it's something new. It does have game changer potential far beyond WWE, since both boxing and UFC will be on the sidelines monitoring and adjusting their own future business based on it. But the TV negotiations are a more stable revenue stream and if they are the subject of any kind of serious bidding war in the U.S., will be a more important story.

Another thing is, if they can show a significant increase in U.S. TV rights fees, there's not even one iota of a risk to hurt the company if the network doesn't come in as expected. And if the network hits the way they project and the TV deal doesn't, they are still way ahead. The only way this company isn't booming in one year is if both fail.

Regarding the network, WWE announced that on 4/7, the day after WrestleMania, they would release their first subscription numbers.

Regarding the other big news of the week, which was Dish Network dropping WWE on PPV, McMahon stated that they have agreements for 85 percent of the PPV universe to carry WrestleMania. Since the Dish Network is 14 percent, that would indicate they are the only holdouts. It makes no sense to be an individual holdout, at least for WrestleMania because it only encourages people to seek it elsewhere.'

The key here is that would mean DirecTV is at least on board for WrestleMania. But it was also stated that from that point forward, who will be carrying the shows is on a month-to-month basis, meaning a lot of people aren't committing past WrestleMania. I think they'll weigh the percentage drop in buys and also weigh how much solidarity there is in the ranks about not carrying the shows going forward.

MARCH 10

Regarding things that are on the network that have been edited, for whatever reason, these are some of the things. The 1997 U.K. One Night Only PPV (which didn't air in the U.S.) is the home video version and not the PPV version, a three hour show edited to two hours. The Bret Hart vs. Undertaker WWE title match, which was one of the two main events (Davey Boy Smith as the local hero losing to Shawn Michaels in the match Smith dedicated to his sister with cancer where the finish was changed at the last minute) was edited off the WWE Network version, even though it is listed in the description of the show. What's notable is the three hour version aired in the past on Classics on Demand. Most, but not all, of New Jack's matches on ECW PPVs are out (his 1999 match with Mustafa at Living Dangerously 1999 is in) and his run-in on the Dudleys at Heat Wave 1999 was edited out, but other run-ins on other shows are there. The 1986 Hogan vs. Orndorff Toronto Exhibition Stadium show, King of the Ring 1993-97, SummerSlam 1995-97 and several In Your Houses are the home video release and not the actual PPV. WCW Bash at the Beach 1996 is the home video release. WCW Halloween Havoc 1990 is the home video release with the three hour show cut to two hours. Most of Jimmy Hart's WCW theme music is there, but not the DDP or Shane Douglas themes. That was weird because all of Jimmy Hart's WCW music was on Classics on Demand. On SummerSlam 1991, the song "Together," written by Hart and Jim Johnston during the Randy Savage & Elizabeth video before their wedding was replaced by different music, even though it was a WWE written song.

The talent in NXT was told at the TV tapings that the NXT product would be pushed more significantly now that the network is up. They were told that the company wants to get behind NXT as this pure wrestling product within the WWE. While some people may be brought up, like Emma, it's going to be slow and for everyone to be patient with the idea that with the network, they'll all be getting lots of exposure even without a call up. They are going to start marketing T-shirts for some of the NXT talent.

MARCH 17

On TV this week, they were back pushing one week free on the network, something that they originally stated would end on 3/3. They had continued to advertise a week free on the web site even after the free week period ended. As far as why they were pushing the free aspect this week instead of the network and its low price point to begin with is something you can only speculate on. They obviously get far more sign-ups when the first week is free, and most retain it. But I'd be very surprised if this continues through Mania, because the people who only bought the network knowing they could get Mania plus all the added content will be unhappy if they found out they could have timed things better and gotten Mania for free.

Based on our polls, 91% of the people who got the network free trial remained on it (that's probably above the average but it's also likely a very high percentage of those who get it free kept it since the percentage for other streaming services retaining free orders has been very high). Regarding how much can be expected as far as foreign gain, of those who ordered it, 13% based on our poll are from outside the U.S. (Many who were outside the U.S. ended up kicked off because it was found out). Based on our polling, there should be a 29.1% increase next year for foreign orders from people who say that they will order but can't due to not being in the U.S., which is slightly ahead of the 25% that WWE projected to gain at that time. So that contradicts the idea the international gain won't be as much as projected.

In what is probably very good news for this network, the UFC Fight Pass is already way ahead of projections, and that's with less hype, and more of an ancillary service for hardcore fans to have a chance to see everything, including prelim matches and some international shows not televised, as well as the library. UFC doesn't have anywhere near the WWE's library (although it has most of its library up while WWE has about 1.5% of its library up, UFC is claiming to have 5,000 hours of content up right now although I don't see how that's possible, but it's not like I've counted. WWE has up right now just under 1,300 hours of content up). But if the UFC numbers are way ahead of projections, the WWE numbers should at the very least have a ton of subscribers already, granted there is a huge difference in the break/even between the two services.

MARCH 24

The Dish Network has sent out a form letter to subscribers who ask about WrestleMania, saying they aren't carrying it and saying: "Please note that WWE is not willing to adjust PPV costs to satellite/cable companies, which is unfair to their customers. DISH needs to re-focus efforts to support partners that better serve DISH customers and other satellite/cable companies, including DirecTV, have also expressed they may no longer provide WWE PPV events in the future." DirecTV is carrying WrestleMania, but a number of companies are believed to be at least considering dropping WWE on PPV after Mania. WWE even said as much, that they expect 85% of the PPV universe to carry Mania (everyone but Dish), but after that, everything is on a month-by-month basis.

The WWE Network free trial period will end on 3/22. Everyone figured they would be ending it before WrestleMania. My gut says it's two weeks before instead of a week before because they want to give it enough time so there is no confusion or belief you can just wait to get a free work and get Mania. WWE has insisted in media reports that it has the capacity to handle the Internet demand for the show, after the recent high profile collapses of Internet broadcasts of television shows from major networks the past few weeks.

Still, there isn't a day that goes by where we don't get several complaints about the network, although of late it's been Xbox 360 users and some Roku 3 users who are unable to access certain events.

WWE released this statement regarding media questions on if they would be able to handle the volume of viewers of WrestleMania on the network, after the problems the Oscars and other recent streams that garnered mainstream interest had with crashing: At least some had problems with the post-game show after Raw on 3/17 . "Notwithstanding the overwhelmingly positive response to WWE Network, we want to ensure subscribers have the highest-quality experience watching WrestleMania 30 and all our programming, and thus have put in place significant quality assurances. These steps include increased capacity to handle high volumes of transactions, logins, and concurrent live streams, daily `stress' testing of all systems over an extended period, and the addition of technology experts to review our plan and procedure. We're confident that we'll be ready on Sunday, April 6." WWE has had no problems with the Tuesday night live Main Event shows, after about a five minute or so problem on the first NXT live special. There were some complaints about an issue with one of the live shows since then. The network problems now are more people being unable to access certain content, but not the stream crashing.

MARCH 31

WrestleMania will be carried by every major cable provider at the $59.95 and $69.95 (HD) prices, as well as part of the $9.99 per month WWE Network package.

The only holdout, The Dish Network, made a decision this past week to air the show. The Dish Network didn't carry Elimination Chamber and had made a decision to be done with WWE as a PPV provider. However, even though The Dish Network covers roughly 15 percent of the U.S. homes that have PPV capability, the Elimination Chamber showed something very interesting.

The Chamber show did 156,000 North American buys, at the top level of any "B" show in years with the exception of last year's show, but that number was drawn by a Rock vs. C.M. Punk match, and this had nothing close to that for mainstream appeal. What's clear, and the same thing happened more than a decade ago when DirecTV didn't carry the Royal Rumble and at the time everyone figured buys would be down 20 percent, but they actually did a record number of buys that year. Then, when WWE and DirecTV settled their issue (it was a dispute over which side got five percent of the revenue as WWE was seeking 50 percent and DirecTV was, at the time, getting 55 percent–the standard number at the time in the industry was 45 percent to the promoter, five percent to the people who operated the PPV channel, and 50 percent to the carrier), the actual percentage of homes available that purchased WrestleMania that year was almost the same as the Royal Rumble.

What happened then, and here, is simple. Everyone that wants to see a show is going to see it. The Dish Network subscribers, in almost all cases, found a friend with cable and watched it at their house. The 156,000 figure would be surprisingly high with 100 percent penetration, the idea it hit that figure with 85 percent, and was down far less domestically year-over-year than the Royal Rumble, showing Dish going dark cost WWE, on a statistical level, no buys at all.

It's not even that the product is significantly hotter. Raw ratings are down as compared to both a year and two years ago (Smackdown ratings aren't) and house shows are down eight percent so far this year, and also below 2012 levels. Domestic Royal Rumble numbers were down from the past two years as well, so it's not like PPV is any different.

In other words, if it had been the entire cable industry, that would be a different story. WWE still may have gotten buys through its web site, but the number of Americans who have purchased a PPV on the Internet is shockingly low. If all the cable companies and dish networks didn't air a show, yes, they would kill its viability. But to do so in any specific area, it would have to be both the local cable company and the dish companies. Any other stand just results in the cable company, or in this case The Dish Network, losing about $600,000 in revenue on this show, but WWE still getting the revenue because everyone who would have bought, still did, just from someone else.

How the economics affect WrestleMania is impossible to predict. We don't know how badly the network and its low price will cannibalize PPV. WrestleMania, being a special show, probably won't really tell us that much. Extreme Rules will be the real answer on how much the network costs the cable industry, and what the economics are.

The statement from the Dish Network is that after WrestleMania, they will evaluate carrying events on a show-by-show basis. Almost all cable companies are in the same boat.

While the PPV numbers for Royal Rumble and Elimination Chamber don't look strong at first glance, it's largely because of an international decline and whatever thoughts there were that people would skip the shows since PPV was going from a $54.95 to a $9.99 price tag with the network ended up not even being an issue.

Preliminary reports on the Royal Rumble are 285,000 North American buys and 160,000 international buys for 445,000 total. The numbers internationally are down from recent years, but the domestic number is closer in line, even though it was down 21.7% from last year domestic and 25.6% internationally. Besides the Rumble, this year's show featured Randy Orton vs. John Cena in what was being pushed as the biggest title rematch of all-time, even though nobody bought that line. It also had Big Show vs. Brock Lesnar and Daniel Bryan vs. Bray Wyatt. The Rumble was also the advertised wrestling match return of Batista. Even though he didn't get over in winning, his initial TV quarter hour rating was through the roof eight days earlier for his first appearance.

But it's really unfair to compare to last year. Last year's show featured The Rock challenging C.M. Punk for the WWE title, which was pushed far more than the Rumble. It was the most successful Rumble since 2008, when Jeff Hardy was on fire as a challenger for Randy Orton. That show did 364,000 North American buys and 215,000 worldwide. It also featured Alberto Del Rio vs. Big Show in a last man standing match for the world title.

A more apt comparison would be the 2012 totals, which were 299,000 in North America and 184,000 international. That show had the Rumble, Daniel Bryan defending the world title against Show and Mark Henry in a cage match, Punk vs. Dolph Ziggler for the WWE title and Cena vs. Kane, which was pushed as the biggest non-Rumble match on the show.

The North American numbers are likely to wind up ahead of the 2012 totals. With Lesnar on this year, but not last year, and Dwayne Johnson not on this year, the expenses were probably not that far different. They may have been a little higher last year, but one would figure last year to end up more profitable, and that show was less profitable than the not as well performing shows of the past several years because those shows had lower talent expenses.

Early estimates for Elimination Chamber are 156,000 North American buys and 47,000 overseas, for 203,000 total. This year's Chamber show had the Elimination Chamber match with Orton defending against Cena, Bryan, Sheamus, Christian and Cesaro, plus The Shield vs. The Wyatt Family and Batista vs. Del Rio.

That's down only 13.8% domestic for a show that featured The Rock, and there was no similar outsider on this year's Chamber show. It was down 21.7% internationally, so even with 15 percent less available homes in North America, the drop from last year domestic was less than international. Besides Rock defending against Punk, last year's show also had The Shield vs. Cena & Sheamus & Ryback, The Chamber match for a title shot with Jack Swagger vs. Bryan vs. Orton vs. Kane vs. Henry vs. Chris Jericho, and Del Rio vs. Show for the world title.

As compared with the non-Rock version in 2012, it's way up, as that year did 138,000 in North Amerca and 56,000 overseas. So what you can see is international PPV is down while North America was up. That show had two Chamber matches, with the WWE title with Punk vs. Jericho vs. Ziggler vs. Kofi Kingston vs. R-Truth vs. The Miz, and the World title with Bryan vs. Cody Rhodes vs. Santino Marella vs. Show vs. Great Khali vs. Wade Barrett, and the pushed main event of Cena vs. Kane in an ambulance match.

If there is a key to this, it's that it appears two Chamber matches are not superior as a draw to one Chamber match.

These are the final two shows where any kind of direct comparisons with previous PPVs can be made, given the network. It's clear PPV buys will be way down for WrestleMania, and overall viewership will be way up. How that balances out for revenue is anyone's guess.

APRIL 14

As of 4/7, the day after WrestleMania, the WWE Network had 667,287 subscribers. As noted in last week's story, that number would be the low end of expectations. It is by no means a failure, but it was a major disappointment to both Wall Street and to those in the company and most of those following the company.

The WWE sent out a press release stating that they were "on track to 1 million subscribers," which was the figure they had publicly stated they were expecting by the end of this year. Some reported it as a success, in the sense the company was touting that figure as break even. However, company investors and others familiar with the business of revenue splits noted that real break even would be somewhere between 1.25 million and 1.75 million, but that's also for 2015 when you add in the costs of international distribution and marketing, as well revenue in international markets.

The reality is this is still uncharted water, past the point that we have information that isn't speculation. Wall

Street analysts were predicting anywhere from 800,000 to 1 million to be the figure announced, which led to massive stock selling. The stock opened on 4/7 at $28.02 per share, fell to $23.90 at the end of the day, and fell again to $22.21 on 4/8, meaning the company lost 21% of its market worth over two days, and its on paper worth fell to $1.67 billion.

Some of that was going to happen even with what was considered a good announcement, because the WWE stock rise was built on hype, and the saying is, "buy on hype, sell on results." Better results wouldn't have hurt it that bad. Great results would have propped it up even more.

But like the first day estimates, it's hard to know what that means. Some were saying that after only six weeks, they were already two-thirds of the way toward their year-end goal. But they were those not really understanding the pro wrestling business. The single biggest lure of the network until the end of the year, by far, is WrestleMania for $9.99. While there will be trickling in new subscribers between now and the end of the year, and if you are a serious fan, the service is easily worth the money, at least at first, are there 333,000 people who did not feel WrestleMania for $9.99 is worth it that are going to think the network is? There is no answer for sure until the end of the year.

Those we spoke with internally groaned when the number came out, and it was widely considered a disappointment even though it can't be publicly spun that way. In the end, the network is going to be a success. In time, there will be enough people who will buy new television sets better equipped for this, and there are things they can tweak. Given the supposed U.S. number of $9.99 per month orders is only slightly larger than the orders of last year's WrestleMania on regular PPV (662,000 was the total North American number, but that includes roughly ten percent Canadian so the U.S. & Puerto Rico figure would be about 600,000), the question is asked how many new people out there, having turned it down for Mania, are now going to get it?

Another part of the situation is how many of the 667,282 subscribers are actually from the U.S. There were two first-day surveys that came up identical, one that we did, which came up that 17% of the first day orders came from outside the U.S. Some of them were shut down, but many were not. Another survey we did the day after Mania showed only 63% of subscribers to the WWE Network came from the U.S., (of the rest, 17% were from Canada and 12% from the United Kingdom), but that number sounds very low to the point I trust it only slightly more than the WWE's own survey about how half the homes in the U.S. have a pro wrestling fan. But even if we say that 15% of the number is not from the U.S., and that may be a conservative estimate, that leaves a 567,000 U.S. figure, which is very bad if it's close to the mark. When the numbers were first estimated, the belief was they would only draw this year from the U.S. market, leading to major international growth in 2015.

That would also indicate that the growth next year from international may be far less than expected because the super hardcore WWE fans around the world have already figured out how to get it.

Still, in time, people will be less reluctant to purchase services like this. There will be people who will drop after six months, particularly since that will be September or October and the next big event, Royal Rumble, doesn't come until late January. Plus, it's football season, and a solid percentage of casual wrestling fans lose interest that time of the year, but who knows what percentage of those casual fans even purchased the network. There will be others who trickle in and others who may get it and just figure that they don't have the time to watch all the programming. Eventually the number will be steady, and in the long run, who knows, as 24/7 Classics on Demand reached a certain level and then slowly declined from there, even as it expanded into new cable companies and international. If it is slow to hit break-even, or even if it is break-even, there are things that can be done to help turn a profit, such as increase the price (there have already been surveys aimed at the Canadian market for next year asking about an $11.99 price), or do the original idea, which is all PPVs except the big four, or all PPVs except WrestleMania, going forward, which may slightly lower network revenue but they'll pick it up with the $70 buys for WrestleMania.

But the WWE Network was not sold to Wall Street, or anyone, as this idea to break even. It was to be a financial game changer, the first of its kind. As it turns out, Major League Baseball, with 3 million orders already, was the game changer. Nobody was watching more closely than UFC. As noted, if they came out and did huge numbers based on putting Mania on PPV, UFC would have been fools to ignore the message. The message, loud and clear, is that, at least now, and probably in the foreseeable future, they would be fools to put their PPVs on their own version of the network, Fight Pass. The idea that by pricing shows so much cheaper, they open up so many more people to buy, appears to be a fallacy. In 2014, WWE had the same, if not less people watching WrestleMania for $9.99 coming with months of programming, than they did the year before at six to seven times that price. More likely, that won't be the case next year. Some people, probably few, didn't order figuring the show would crash, which in the majority of cases, didn't happen. Some double-dipped, buying the network and the PPV, but the stream not crashing is likely to lead to that not happening for future PPV shows.

Internally, WWE has budgeted that they will receive $78.6 million in network revenue this year. According to one person with access to figures, out of the $9.99, with splits to carriers that can get 30% of the orders (those ordering directly through the WWE web site have no such splits), the estimate is WWE is getting about $8.75 per month off the average buy. That's total revenue, not profit. Given that the service will be a paid service for nine months this year, it means they were expecting to average 1 million orders per month over the course of the year to meet budget. That is not going to happen. And with start-up costs, even if they got that average, the expectation was the profit from the entire company for the year would only be $9 million.

They were also budgeting that the pay-per-view business would be down to $47.1 million this year. In layman's terms, they are projecting a 40% drop in PPV revenue. Given they are expecting no drop internationally, the projection is they would maintain 47 percent of the North American PPV business, meaning WrestleMania, if projections are accurate and would have hit 630,000 domestic and 420,000 international buys this year for a non-Rock show based on the Mania name, that you'd keep the 420,000 internationals (which is unlikely because a lot more international than expected have the network) but have 295,000 domestic buys. In other words, WWE is budgeting 715,000 worldwide buys for WrestleMania this year from traditional means.

Conversely, for other shows you would expect domestic PPV numbers to be between 40,000 and 70,000 for the B shows, and about 97,000 for SummerSlam. If the numbers end up higher, cannibalization is lower than expectations. If they are lower, then cannibalization for this year is higher.

For 2015, the network is budgeted for $154.9 million in gross revenue. This is for a network available worldwide. To hit that figure, they have to average 1.5 million worldwide subscribers per month, so the idea is they will start the year at 1 million and end it at 2 million. At that point, they are expecting the PPV's internationally to fall off greatly, and 70% total cannibalization in all the PPV markets.

Given the first numbers, how realistic this is remains a question. What it looks like is when it all is said and done, the network will break even or be profitable, but the idea the network brings in $50 million to $150 million profit per year based on 2-4 million domestic and a 250,000 to 750,000 worldwide subscribers doesn't at this point seem realistic, let alone analysts who were talking 6 million as the eventual leveling off number. The stock price was built on the idea that it would do the numbers projected next year, and the idea that the television rights fees will double, triple or be similar to NASCAR numbers (about eight times what WWE currently earns). That's a discussion for the end of this month or early next month when the new deal is expected to be announced.

Based on a study of those who have the network, 84% are happy and say they will keep it, so if that's accurate, of the 667,000, there are 560,000 who believe they have it for life. 8.5% say they may drop it after the six months, but expect to pick it up a few months later for WrestleMania. 7.1% expect to drop it after the six months. But as far as growth goes, you could expect a 7.6% increase next year during Mania season, a 10.8% increase between now and the end of the year, 3.8% and another 3.2% increase from people who expect to get it at some point in 2015. That would indicate between those coming and going, very little growth between now and the end of the year and maybe even a decline, but an increase from this number during the Mania season. But leveling off U.S. numbers don't look to be appreciably larger than they are right now.

APRIL 21

The WWE made the announcement that WrestleMania is estimated at doing nearly 400,000 domestic PPV buys, and claiming that a record 1 million U.S. households watched the show.

With the network, it should have been a lock that more U.S. homes would watch the show than any previous show.

The first thing that should be noted is that "nearly 400,000" number in the sense WWE's original announcements have traditionally been optimistic. The last two years' first announcements at this point in time were 1.3 million and 1.2 million, because PPV buy estimates are an inexact science. This is not the idea of making up numbers, because it's a public company, and I believe the estimates were what they expected to end up with when they made them. As silly as this sounds in 2014, even the best estimates, weeks after the show, can be off by quite a bit when you already have actual numbers in hand. The actual final numbers were 1,219,000 and 1,104,000 worldwide respectively. That's not to say this year's eventual number will be higher or lower than the first announcement, just the past two years have ended up each being nearly 100,000 lower.

Still, the PPV number is great as the WWE had budgeted approximately 295,000 buys between the U.S. and Canada on PPV.

The idea that the 667,000 network subscribers and "nearly 400,000" domestic breaks one million isn't necessarily the case. It's virtually impossible it is the case, because of overlapping and also questions as to how many network subscribers are really from the U.S.

WWE pushed that more homes saw WrestleMania in the U.S. than any time in history. That should have been the case with the low price and new technology. There's also a better than even chance it's not true, based on how many of those 667,287 network subscribers aren't from the U.S., as well as the percentage of network subscribers who ordered the show on traditional PPV because of all the streaming problems the network had up to that point in time.

According to those in WWE, the "nearly 400,000" domestic figure does not include Canada, meaning just as the show didn't do what the company estimated as far as network buys, it did considerably better on the PPV front.

With a projection of 295,000 PPV buys between U.S. and Canada on PPV, that would really only figure to be 235,000 or so in the U.S., since one would expect 60,000 of the buys from Canada if one assumes Canadians for the most part don't get the network (which could be a faulty assumption).

But if you assume a lot of Canadians did get the network, that would also assume as well as U.K. residents did, and a strong number of other foreign residents did, the 667,000 number is not a U.S. number. And for sure it's not. Our own polling indicated 63 percent of the network subscribers were from the U.S. (420,000). I believe that is faulty on the low side, but with no evidence of that past a hunch. But it does indicate the U.S. subscribers are also probably not even near 667,000. There are also people who subscribe to the network that didn't watch Mania either live, later, or on PPV. I know of many people who ordered the network for the historical content that no longer watch the product, and didn't watch Mania. Our own polling indicated just under 70 percent of those in the U.S. with the network watched WrestleMania live, with 13 percent not having watched it yet, 11 percent watching it on PPV instead and six percent watching it after the fact. If anything, we would be skewed significantly on the high side there, not the low side. So that would indicate WrestleMania viewers both live and delayed on the network at 447,000 total, and again, you have to figure what the legitimate percentage of those viewing the network from outside the U.S. is. Given our polling, it comes to 282,000, but again, I think that's a low figure, but the real figure would be between those numbers. But no matter which of the two figures (282,000 and 447,000) is closer to the mark, the number is far lower than anyone could have expected, just as the PPV number is far higher.

The combined figure would be more than last year's Mania in the U.S. even under a worst case scenario, but is likely in the ballpark of the 2012 Mania for total U.S. viewership and is probably below the 1989, 2001 and 2007 versions. If you throw in closed-circuit viewers, it would be behind 1987 as well. By all rights, it should have been the most-watched WrestleMania ever in the U.S. Given a best case scenario on numbers, it could be close, but it probably wasn't.

Just being on the safe side given the overestimates in years past and saying the nearly 400,000 turns out to be 350,000, that's 58 percent of last year in the U.S. and probably 62 percent in North America of what the show did in comparison to last year had everything been equal in interest. And most would have expected, even up, for this year's show to do worse overall than last year if it was a stand-alone PPV. So the network cannibalization this early of PPV, while significant, is not as much as would have been expected or even projected from a WWE standpoint. That also would make the "break-even" for the network roughly 50,000 subscribers per month lower than original estimates. However, that number could change drastically if PPV is dropped by the regular carriers over the rest of the year.

The key thing to take out of all this is that reports of the demise of PPV are even more greatly exaggerated than beforehand, far more than WWE internally estimated and speaks that a major event pricing is very much price inelastic. All history has shown this, from periods of greatly raising ticket prices to wrestling and other major sports and then comparing live attendance numbers with lower pricing vs. higher pricing and generally there is little or no difference, and looking at price increases on PPVs and buy figures before and after.

Given the choice of spending $70 for WrestleMania, or spending $60 to get Mania, five other PPV shows and access to 1,300 plus hours of content on a network, somewhere between 58 (at 350,000) and 67 percent (at 400,000) of Americans who last year bought Mania still chose to still buy the PPV. That makes no sense, but it tells quite the story about people not embracing new technology. This may be a sign that there is more growth potential down the line with the network, or that hundreds of thousands of WWE fans don't care about network content, or PPVs, but will still buy WrestleMania every year.

The question becomes whether it's worth it to UFC or boxing to go for the cheaper price and volume vs. higher price and lower volume. The answer, right now, is that it's clearly not the time to consider the move. Even with adding a $10 bottom price to the $60 to $70 figure from one year ago, the homes went from about 600,000 U.S. last year to a minimum of 632,000 to a maximum of 847,000 this year. I would have predicted with a $10 bottom that WrestleMania was going to easily top 1 million homes this year, so my thoughts on the mass viewer gains from price cutting were greatly inflated. That may not be the answer two years from now and it is still very possible it is more cost effective for the smaller PPV shows, but all evidence on the big shows is strongly in the other camp.

But it also indicates lowering the price for a PPV is not going to greatly increase viewers. From a UFC standpoint, the idea of offering a $35 price for a PPV instead of $55 as a bonus for those who order the network, keeping a higher company price margin, may be the way to go, but even then, I see it as more switching viewers from PPV to the network, and there would be very little addition of new viewers at $35 that didn't buy at $55. That way, you get the best of both worlds. The one thing WrestleMania has shown is most people are willing to spend the high price, and such a high price point is not a factor if it's a show they want to see. You incentivize network purchasers and value by giving you a substantial PPV price break, while not costing you anything in the way of money, and at the same time, don't make the WWE mistake of undercutting the value of the big shows and underpricing them.

The news led to a stock rebound on 4/15, as it closed at $20.75 per share (opening at $19.99 per share) giving the company a closing marketing capitalization of $1.56 billion, which is still way down from the inflated number just before WrestleMania and the network announcement number.

It also could be that people who ordered the network purchased the show on PPV. I fit into that category and know a lot of people who did, based on having a lot of people over and not trusting the stream. Estimates have that figure at around 11 percent (50,000 to 80,000 depending on how many actual U.S. buys there are for the network). But that leaves 270,000 to 350,000 homes in the U.S. who turned down purchasing the network and purchased WrestleMania at full price.

Going forward, I would expect far less double dipping, and that figure should be closer to zero within a year. So the PPV drop from last year should be well above 38 percent going forward, and WWE has budgeted the PPV revenue to be cut in half for shows in 2015 as compared to 2014. The company had gone in budgeting the PPV drop for this year as being 53 percent in North America going forward, so nobody expects things to hold up at this level.

With Canadian buys in theory staying even, a B show with 100,000 domestic buys from last year would be expected to maintain about 10,000 Canadian, but if the Mania numbers holds up, could maintain 52,000 in the U.S., or about 62 percent of what it did last year. That probably won't be the case because the number of people with the network ordering the show separately on PPV would figure to drop going forward on a percentage basis, because it's not Mania, and the system held up.

That's way above what the company budgeted. But they also budgeted based on 1 million network homes for an average month this year (not the 1 million by the end of the year figure they had announced), so in that sense, here is how the figures should work from the U.S. for Mania.

At 350,000 U.S. buys going with the average of $33 per head, that's $11.55 million. At 667,287 network subscribers at $8.50 per head, that's $5.67 million or $17.22 million total. At 600,000 U.S. viewers on PPV buys, with no network, at $33 a head, that's $19.80 million in company revenue with considerably less expenses. However, the $2.6 million that Mania is down is far less than the amount every other month will be up. But there's also the cost of the network itself, so a true evaluation, the actual profit margin for the show itself will be way down from the prior year.

A true evaluation of all this can't be made until late in the year, when we factor in PPV declines, DVD declines, and real revenues and costs of the network. But a lot more answers will come in late May, when WWE releases an actual domestic and international number. If the international PPV buy numbers remain consistent with last year, then that means there probably weren't a ton of international buyers in that 667,287 figure. If the number of international buys is significantly less than 420,000 for Mania, that would indicate a very significant number of the current network subscriptions are from outside North America. A lot of how good, or not good, that network number really is, will be a lot more easy to analyze in five to six weeks, but any real analysis really should be made closer to the end of the year when we see the DVD sales numbers for the Mania and other shows.

But in late May, we'll have a lot more of a clue clues as to how well WrestleMania really did, the levels of international vs. domestic that 667,287 figure really is, and what that means for how much growth to expect next year, and the overall viability of high cost PPV vs. low cost network packaging.

If we go with company projections made before Mania, the 295,000 domestic PPV number and take out Canada and it's 235,000 at $33, that's $7.76 million, plus the expectation of 1 million subscribers, or about$8.5 million U.S. for network purchases that would be $15.76 million total. So the total income for Mania, because of the strong PPV number, looks to be around $1.56 million ahead of projections if the PPV number holds up to even close of what the company announced.

WWE released these numbers for WrestleMania week. The Hall of Fame attendance at the Smoothie King Center in New Orleans was 10,885. They claimed 13,299 for Raw in New Orleans, also at the Smoothie King Center. It's weird that the company itself would release the real building total when they went on television and announced the show a few days earlier as having drawn 15,401 (for TV for whatever reason the rule is to increase the paid number by 3,000 to 3,500 it seems). The paid attendance was just over 12,000. Axxess drew a total of 29,215 fans over seven sessions at the Convention Center, or a little over 4,000 per session.

APRIL 21

DirecTV made the decision this past week to no longer offer WWE PPV shows, effective immediately.

While DirecTV represents more than 20 percent of U.S. homes that have PPV capability (more than 20 million homes), as we saw with The Dish Network not carrying Elimination Chamber, it ends up making almost no difference, because people who want to see the show are going to find a way to see the show.

However, if The Dish Network, which at first wasn't going to carry WrestleMania, also follows suit, along with inDemand (which services the major cable companies), then it changes the dynamic completely. At press time, The Dish Network (which services another 14 million homes) is not listing Extreme Rules on its schedule, so it would appear they have followed suit. If inDemand follows suit, then it's a huge story because WWE is out of the PPV business in the U.S., the country it does most of its business in.

Losing both Dish and DirecTV could hurt in rural places that have no cable, but it's not going to be a killer unless inDemand follows suit. If that happens, that's a huge blow for this year and a blow for next year. WWE did expect the PPV business to be going away pretty much within a few years, so in a few years, it's not as big a deal, but it's very significant short-term.

At that point, U.S. homes would only be able to get the monthly shows, renamed Special Events instead of PPVs, through either individual event purchases on the Internet, which have historically been only a few thousand per show except for Mania, or through the WWE Network. As long as inDemand carries the show, there will be minimal damage from losing the dish companies because most who would have ordered it that way could find a friend with cable in their neighborhood and watch it that way, so you're really only losing singular viewers with no friends who like wrestling or viewers in the sticks. There was a precedent for a Royal Rumble that DirecTV didn't carry, which ended up being the most successful Rumble of all-time even without DirecTV, again showing that a singular satellite company pulling out isn't going to hurt WWE.

However, DirecTV has its reasons for making a stand, particularly at this time.

DirecTV had threatened to pull WWE PPVs as soon as the WWE Network was announced. They waited until after WrestleMania, thereby carrying Royal Rumble and Mania, the two biggest shows of the year. However, WrestleMania held up far better than expected on PPV, and they made the announcement after they had received their internal Mania numbers, which if they hold up like the rest of the industry, were somewhere between 58 and 67 percent of what they did last year.

A complete dropping of WWE shows by cable and dish carriers would drive those viewers to the network, but for those who were purchasing shows monthly, it's significantly less revenue per buyer so they have to make up with considerably more volume. This also would greatly increase the PPV cannibalization that it appeared from WrestleMania was less than expected.

This also changes break-even on the network in the U.S. If you remove the budgeted PPV revenue from 2015 and it goes to nothing if inDemand follows suit, then the Network needs to pick up that much revenue. Breaking even will at that point move from a 1.25 million to 1.7 million number range worldwide (depending on how many sign-ups go through streaming devices where revenue is shared at the 30% cut to the manufacturers of the device) to a 1.45 million to 1.95 million range. The thing is, if there is no other way but the network to get WWE PPV shows, at that point people will get the network. Those 100,000 or 125,000 people in the U.S. who want to see Extreme Rules are going to watch it, but if 58 to 67 percent of them would rather pay $55 than $10 to see it, switching from one service to another is a financial loss to the company, although one they did project to a great degree. But they did not project U.S. PPV falling to nothing or even a DirecTV and Dish Network drop when they made their projections. In other words, if people can't get the big shows on PPV, it will get WWE to 1 million subscribers, but now they may need considerably more than 1 million to make it worth it.

With the exception of SummerSlam, most WWE PPVs going forward this year would probably do between 75,000 and 140,000 U.S. buys. Maintaining 60 percent, which may be a little high, means 45,000 to 85,000, and DirecTV would probably figure into getting revenue on 25 or more percent of that number and Dish on 15 to 20 percent, since the proportion of people with dishes that buy PPVs is higher than those with cable. With them out of the picture, inDemand is suddenly being boosted because they become the only way to get the shows besides the network, so for short term money, it does give them the incentive to continue to carry. But whether that's worth it to risk a power play by UFC next becomes a different question, because any power play WWE pulls off, UFC, with its big shows more valuable, has far more leverage to follow in however way it sees fit, and Mayweather and Arum have more leverage than anyone to do what they want.

But a WWE PPV show today, to a provider, compared to a UFC or boxing show, is going to get far less outside promotional help, As far as orders go, it's probably not a ton more than a TNA Lockdown or Bound for Glory would do. DirecTV isn't risking this big financial hit, which they would have had they opted out of carrying WrestleMania. And it's a public showing that they aren't backing down to WWE, which is important regarding boxing or UFC going forward and the potential of them trying to undercut cable and dish providers down the line. Although inevitably, this does appear in some form to be a battle the providers at some point will lose, and it's just a question of when, not if.

The WWE made a heavy push this week to build up numbers by offering yet another free week to the network.

What's notable is not so much offering a free week, since a lot of services of the type do so, but the heavy promotion of a free week after two specific campaigns telling viewers that there were no more free weeks. At the end of February, WWE had promoted that the free week trial period was going to end the first week of March. A few weeks later, they started promoting free weeks and made it clear that was going to end two weeks before Mania. Then, only a week after Mania, they were pushing the free week as opposed to the low price, and perhaps harder than ever. All talent was told to Tweet about the network free week.

Doing another free week and making it a marketing campaign so soon has to tell the message that they are not getting new subscribers at a fast enough clip unless they offer it for free. It's a promotion that has diminishing returns when you go back to the same "free" card too often. Historically, the retention rate for those who sign up for free is high because people simply fail to go through the hassle of canceling. But promoting "free" too often has its shelf limits. That's why HBO and Showtime do free weekends on occasion, and other services offer a week free or a weekend free, but don't constantly promote it around a week free with three different promotional periods built around the word free over a seven week period.

WWE is pushing its offerings this week as Warrior Week, with new shows airing Wednesday through Friday at 10 p.m. relating to Warrior. There are several new series' starting this week on the WWE Network. There are a series of Roundtable shows on Ultimate Warrior, a documentary on Warrior's return, and a four-part series on the fallout of WrestleMania as well as the heavily promoted Legends House.

The belief is also that with the death of Ultimate Warrior, and WWE pushing programming related to him, such as constant airing of WrestleMania VI, and doing a Warrior documentary and other shows devoted to him, that this is an unexpected time that they can boost viewers. Obviously they need that based on the stock dropping due to Wall Street for the most part being disappointed with the first announced figure.

APRIL 28

The official word on Dish Network on WWE PPVs from Danielle Johnson of DISH corporate communications is:"Dish continues to evaluate all WWE pay-per-view on an event-by-event basis. We will announce whether WWE's Extreme Rules will be available closer to its air date." As noted, Dish is not advertising that the show is available at this time. Dish didn't carry Elimination Chamber, said it wouldn't carry WrestleMania, but relented on that show at a late hour. There are no hints regarding inDemand. past the point they haven't made any noise up to this point about not carrying WWE events going forward.

MAY 5

The Dish Network officially announced they weren't carrying Extreme Rules, and it's thought that both they and DirecTV are done doing business with WWE. That represents roughly one-third of the homes that have PPV capability in the U.S. WWE acknowledged in on Raw, but pushed hard signing up for the network or contacting your cable provider. As noted before, the 100,000 or so U.S. homes that want to watch the show are going to find a way to watch it, whether they have DirecTV or Dish, because Dish dropped Elimination Chamber and the number came in well above what would have been expected with full carriage. In addition, the 2002 Royal Rumble wasn't carried by DirecTV, but it was still the most successful Rumble in history even without 20 percent of the homes having the ability to get it. Both cases showed that people who wanted to see it, are going to find a way to see it. inDemand at this point is advertising both June PPV shows so at this point they don't seem to have any plans of dropping WWE. As long as they are in the game, WWE is still in the PPV game. InDemand dropping it would lead to those viewers to the network, as the people who want to see the shows are going to do so. In the long run, that's where they expect everyone to wind up, but this will speed up the process.

The WWE is now targeting late 2014 for the network roll-out in the rest of the world. Previous statements were it would be late 2014 or early 2015.

MAY 12

The WWE's quarterly investment conferences right now has less importance because we are in a transitional period of a changing business.

It's not about making money now. The company readily admits it won't be making any money short-term, not even in the WrestleMania quarter, which is usually the best of the year. In fact, in guidance, the company estimated they will lose between $15 million and $18 million due largely to network start-up costs, as well as expectation of lower licensing revenues (largely revenue declines from the video game) and lower home video sales.

It's all about 2015 and the new company, with bigger profits than ever due to new television deals and the growth of the network. And largely that's true, but until the big questions are answered regarding where the network ends up as far as subscribers go, and the new domestic television deal gets signed and announced, everything now is just biding time.

The old metrics—PPV, live gates, merchandise and licensing—may be up a little or down a little, but ultimately they don't matter much in the big picture. Live attendance has been steady for years. Based on creative and new characters, there can be some rises and falls, the same with merchandise. Licensing seems to be dropping due to market conditions, as things like video games and DVD sales are down, although WWE isn't doing badly on either account. PPV is a self fulfilling prophesy. When it comes to pro wrestling, WWE has made it yesterday's news. This is the last quarter where the numbers and comparisons are even relevant.

And while WrestleMania PPV numbers were above most expectations in the U.S., three years from now WWE concedes PPV revenue will be minimal if anything, and the even bigger decline is expected for Extreme Rules.

There are so many moving targets that nobody can really predict much. WWE is still sticking with the idea it'll have one million subscribers by the end of the year. DirecTV and Dish network are both helping them along by not offering the PPVs. That should both speed up the transition of those viewers to the network, as it decreases PPV numbers. Until the year is over, there are just too many moving parts. The key is if the profit margin of the network is greater than the profit margin of PPV, combined with declines from the elimination of 24/7 Classics on Demand, or decrease in DVD sales. There are also network costs of creating new reality shows without the usual rights fees from television to offset them. Even with what E! pays for Total Divas, it was noted on the call that the show is not particularly profitable. They make a little on it, but it's not a loser and it's content they can use forever. There is also the quiet loss of Main Event's domestic rights fees after the show wasn't renewed by Ion. Whether Ion made the call independently, feeling it wasn't worth what they were paying, or it was in response to the network in some form is unknown.

In future conferences, there will be one key number. The company said every three months at the conferences going forward, they will announce the number of network subscriptions.

On the call, CFO George Barrios said that they expected the network to end up at between two million and three million domestic subscribers and 500,000 to 750,000 outside the U.S. Those numbers are in the ballpark, but perhaps a little lower, than originally budgeted, so no matter what is said the launch was at the low end of okay, not the high end. Whether those numbers are viable when the number of total U.S. homes watching Raw for free the past two weeks were 2.90 million and 3.19 million is questionable. Some analysts, Laura Martin in particular who was talking about how the stock should be a buy and pointed to much higher subscriber projections, took umbrage with the numbers Barrios said, having publicly said she thinks the network will get six to eight million subscribers. Vince McMahon responded and said that they were making conservative estimates.

Part of the reason some analysts were so bullish on the network is both the idea that everything over-the-top is the wave of the future, and the other is the crazy stats that has been repeated. WWE claimed on the call that their TV worldwide reached 240 million homes. They claimed that in 120 million of those homes worldwide that there was at least one WWE fan, and that 80 million homes of them were fans of the current product. They claimed there were a total of 160 million current WWE fans, and that 40 million homes have former fans who aren't currently watching the product. The idea is that because the network airs so much old programming, it is their chance to bring back the old fans.

But those numbers are ludicrous, given that the biggest show in the history of the company only had 1,250,000 homes worldwide willing to spend money to see it. And that was in 2007, although they did come close to reaching that number in 2012. But you take out Donald Trump or Dwayne Johnson from the mix and the ceiling is lower.

Overall, even with adding $4.4 million in revenue from the network, and it being the quarter that revenues from "The Call" were finally reported, meaning the film business was a positive, the company took in $125,572,000 in revenue and lost $8,036,000 between 1/1 and 3/31. For the same quarter last year, even with the higher than usual costs of Royal Rumble and Elimination Chamber, they took in $124,001,000 and ended the quarter with $3,034,000 in profits.

The dividend payout at the end of the quarter was another $9,016,440. Overall cash on hand is $87,266,000, down from $109,387,000 three months earlier and $152.4 million at the end of 2012.

The difference in cash on hand and money spent or paid out more than revenues brought in the last 15 months is actually more than the $65.1 million indicated because there was another $31,568,000 spent in opening a line of credit for purchase of a new company jet. They have paid some of that money back in payments, but including that, the company has actually either spent or is in line through credit to have spent $89,977,000 more than they took in as far as cash flow is concerned since the end of 2012.

Still, the quarter was better than projected, because three months ago, they estimated first quarter losses would be between $12 million and $15 million.

Right now, analysts are projecting that the losing quarters will be over after the next one. WWE is projecting that the first six months of 2014 will end up with $23 million to $26 million in losses.

The consensus of stock analysts is that they will start making money from that point, and end the year with $12 million in losses, which means profits of $11 million to $14 million over the last six months of the year. A key is that the new U.S. TV contract, whatever it is, would cover the final quarter of the year.

There was more said about the network itself. They noted that they will be bringing Tough Enough back as a network show, as well as producing a second season of WWE Countdown and producing The Monday Night War series that had been advertised back in January, but had yet to start.

The only thing we were told about Tough Enough is that the new version will be different from the past. It's also the only new reality show that at this point is scheduled for the network between now and the end of the year.

What we do know about Tough Enough is that they are starting on plans for it. The show will be filmed at the Performance Center in Orlando, with a season filmed over 30 to 40 days. We don't have a date for it, but it is believed filming will start in June, if all goes according to current plans. An idea batted around is for it to have all "Andy Leavine's." The last Tough Enough had two "ringers," so to speak, Christina Crawford and Leavine, who were already under contract, and the rest came from tryouts. There is talk to limit it to talent already under contract. The idea would be that it would be talent getting ready to appear on NXT that they expect to eventually make the main roster, with the idea if you follow Tough Enough, you'll see them first, as the concept, perhaps even throwing in some name indie guys who haven't started on TV yet.

The current plans for 2015 are to have four or more reality shows, another Legends House, another Tough Enough and two other shows yet to be announced. I don't know if he's been asked, but there has been talk of using Ric Flair to headline the second season of Legends House.

Still, there clearly are some major problems with the network that aren't being talked about.

Matthew Singerman, who WWE hired in November as its Executive Vice President of Programming, the guy in charge of the network, was fired this past week. The company stated that they were going to be hiring a new head of programming. Reports are sketchy regarding this, with little past him being the first scapegoat for the network performing below expectations, and that this was major news internally.

Singerman was responsible for development of content, including both original unscripted and scripted shows on the network, the scheduling of programming and operations of all programming across all channels, both the network and other digital and television properties, and worked directly under Vince McMahon.

He had worked as a consultant on a number of start-ups, including the NFL Network, Nuvo, Pivot and Back9, as well as Senior Vice President of Programming for Reelz, and before that, the TV Guide Network.

They noted that on 3/30, the network had 495,000 subscribers, which means the growth to 667,282 meant roughly 172,000 subscribed the week of WrestleMania. I'm not sure what that means, but we'll go with the idea that the vast majority of those 495,000 probably subscribed in the first week. That means most subscriptions will run out the first week of September, and another 172,000 will run out the first week of October. To me, that seems to mean it's time to change the PPV schedule.

Besides Mania and Rumble, the No. 3 show of the year should be in October, roughly six months and a few days after WrestleMania every year. That will take some getting used to, as far as educating the audience as to the importance of shows.

For years Rumble, WrestleMania and SummerSlam had been the big ones, to the point that SummerSlam does roughly double a normal show, Rumble does triple and Mania does an even bigger multiple. And it doesn't matter what they put on the other shows, whether it's Punk vs. Cena after Money in the Bank, Lesnar's return, the biggest match in the history of wrestling (as they tried to promote the December Cena vs. Orton title unification match), the ceiling looks to be 160,000 domestic buys, which is not much interest.

Last year, when pushing the title unification match with John Cena vs. Randy Orton as the single biggest match in company history, and putting it on the TLC PPV, while the show did nearly double the North American buys from the prior year, it still only hit 146,000, or about the same as Chamber, since Chamber is traditionally a bigger show. But that shows how hard it is to change traditional buying patterns for PPVs. Even with the seasonal difference, it would make sense to do SummerSlam every year in mid-October, which I grant you, is no longer summertime. But changing the name and expecting people to buy the show in big numbers, or think it's a big deal, may be impossible, since loaded shows or big main events without the big three names don't come anywhere near big three level interest.

The company took in $4.4 million in network revenue, so they were getting $8.89 per buy. When asked if that's the revenue per buy per month that can be expected going forward, they said things could change, but they would expect $8 to $9 per buy per month. That number is after splits with XBox, Apple TV and whoever else they have to split revenue with. The splits vary based on the different contracts. That doesn't include the money paid, which we understand is a very significant amount, to Major League Baseball Advanced Media on their contract.

But based on that figure, if they are to average 760,000 buys over the next quarter (a number they would need to hit as the average to be on the path to hit 1 million at the end of the year), the first where the network is available for the entire quarter, that's roughly $18.24 million to $20.52 million in revenue. That's less than Mania alone on PPV, but far more than any other show. They lost perhaps $11.2 million in Mania PPV income (and gained $5.92 million in network income but if you include costs that would be well over $4 million), if we go with the impression that nobody outside the U.S. got the network. If they did, then the level of cannibalization would have been higher. We also have to figure on the decrease in revenue of the next three PPV shows, and that's unknown because we don't know how many of those buyers will watch on the network, nor do we know what the effect of the shows not being offered by dish providers will be.

But at 760,000 buys for the month of May, we'll estimate that at $6.5 million in revenue and $4 million in costs of revenue, or $2.5 million ahead. Last year, Extreme Rules grossed in the range of $4.9 million in revenue. I don't think this year's show would have done as well. Last year had Brock Lesnar as an outside attraction, and this year's show has a weaker world title match. To come out ahead, they'll need in theory 120,000 PPV buys worldwide (in reality it would be closer to 140,000 since international will make up a higher percentage and they need less per buy). Last year did 108,000 international buys, so, unless a sizeable percentage of the network viewers are the hardcores internationally who were buying PPV, it shouldn't, in theory, be that hard to get 32,000 domestic buys and be even. In reality, well, we'll have to wait and find out.

Fixed network costs are about $40 million per year, but that doesn't include production of new programming, costs of doing PPV shows (which now should fall under this umbrella) as well as you have to make up lost revenues and profits from PPV and perhaps revenues and profits from other sectors, most notably home video and the old 24/7 Classics on Demand service that was shut down. They also noted marketing costs will increase when they officially launch in a number of other countries in late 2014 or early 2015.

An interesting question was asked if WWE would be willing to sell a minority stake in its network to a major conglomerate such as Viacom, with the idea that the promotional muscle could drive revenues. They indicated it was nothing being talked about but said they didn't reject any viable business deal out of hand.

However, the way WWE has produced PPVs, there won't be another major show until the end of January's Royal Rumble. When it comes to subscription services of the type, the usual renewal rates, for services like HBO, Showtime, Hulu and Netflix, ranges around 80 percent. The WWE network will likely be higher because it appeals to a more hardcore and niche audience. The UFC comparison, which is closer to 85 percent renewals (UFC's first group of short-term subscribers expired the first week of April so they've already compiled those stats), may be a similar metric to expect here.

If we go with the idea they'll be at 872,000 to 910,000 at the end of August at the peak before the drop, they would be expected to have a drop of about 75,000 to 100,000 in early September (we're going to be nice and say 75,000 plus the newcomers would put it at 835,000 to 885,000 on 10/1, which would be the November announcement.

The November call won't factor in the losing of the Mania-week or Warrior week buyers. I expect the Warrior week buys, however significant they are, to decline at a far greater than the 15% I'm expecting across the board, but am factoring the same 15%. The Mania week buys may also decline more than the original buyers, since many of them got the network specifically for the show, and there's not another equivalent show until next year's Mania. I think that the decline among the original 495,000 subscribers will be the lowest, because that's the group the most excited about the service, as opposed to people who bought for a specific thing that is no longer a reason to renew. My own history of increases with this publication after deaths is that most of those increases are almost completely gone at the point renewals come up, and are not an indication of long-term brand strengthening.

Essentially, we need 41,000 to 50,000 natural growth per month between now and the end of the year to hit the 1 million mark, factoring in expected leakage off the bottom.

But still, the November call, giving information through September, will still give us probably the best look at where things really stand, and exactly where they will fall in relation to 1 million by the end of the year. The Warrior growth numbers we don't know, but the Mania growth numbers we do. The November number, provided the number is around 925,000, would be touch and go for 1 million. At 847,000 subscribers on 10/1 and going with 710,000 as of right now, would mean 212,000 new subscribers needed between now and 10/1 (137,000 plus estimating the 75,000 loss in September), or 42,000 gain per month naturally. We'd need to expect a number of 836,000 at the investment call in August. A number higher would indicate they should top 1 million. A lower number would indicate it will be a struggle. However, I'm guessing analysts would look at 836,000 as well on the way to more than 1 million, as pure growth continuing from 667,000, not factoring in this number won't account for any inevitable monthly leakage from the bottom. Instead it'll be lump sum leakage between 9/2 and 10/7, over a five week period.

If we get the 41,000 per month average (and I'm factoring in a Warrior growth at the same level as the Wrestling Observer Newsletter "Warrior growth" as being separate), that's 836,000 on 7/1 (August call), that would put us at 904,000 on 10/1 (November call), 904,000 on 11/1 and 949,000 on 12/1 and 984,000 at the end of the year. But at that figure, they are very unlikely to hit 1.5 million domestic at the end of 2015.

At 50,000, we're at 860,000 on 7/1 (August call number), 960,000 on 9/1, 935,000 on 10/1, 946,000 on 11/1, 989,000 on 12/1 and 1,032,000 at the end of the year.

The next number will be reported in roughly three months, so we'd want it 836,000 to 860,000 to be on track to 1 million.

Now, even with those figures and ending the year at 1 million, if we keep the same level of growth in 2015 as 2014, which is not going to happen, at a 41,000 per month average of new subscribers and being nice to a 100,000 gain in April for Mania, and 15% of new subscribes not sticking, you're at 1.5 million at the end of 2015, which would be way short of the 2.5 million projection they had for the end of 2015. At 50,000 with a nice Mania ramp up, you can get to 1.6 million. And this is being as optimistic as you possibly could be.

Essentially, to hit the 2.5 million projection at the end of 2015, you need to average 109,000 new subscribers monthly (figuring a consistent 85 percent retention rate, which may be higher than it turns out since that's above the industry average). Given that WrestleMania only gave you 172,000, the idea you can average that for a typical month, plus if anything, growth is going to slow, not gain, in time, that seems extremely unlikely. But to be on target for their projections, a projection which would mean the business change and turnaround is going to be huge, the August call has to hit a minimum of 960,000 subscribers and November would have to hit 1.2 million. Even with that, one would have believe the rate of growth will continue at the same monthly pace, which is not going to happen. Realistically, that's bare minimum with complete optimism growth rates remain stable for the next 19 months.

WWE has been constantly hot shotting in its approach, which is scary this early in the game. That tells me they feel it's imperative to get subscribers now, in time for the next call. It could also be that believe their retention rate will be high and they have confidence that at $9.99, people who they can get to try it, will stick with it. But still, they pushed on TV that the free period would end first on 3/2, then extended it to two weeks before Mania, and that's it, only to advertise it again on Raw two weeks after Mania. Then, on 5/5, they sent out an e-mail to every subscriber stating that they can get up to $250 by referring friends to the network. That was a well known promotion that many companies have used, but to do is so quickly after a free promotion and immediately after firing the head of the network seems to speak volumes.

The actual offer is not cash, but that if a network subscriber can convince a friend to subscribe, they can get $25 in free merchandise, plus WWE is also giving away $25 in free merchandise through the WWEshop.com web site to everyone who subscribes between now and 5/31. While it sounds like they are essentially paying $50 for every new $60 subscription, it isn't quite that bad. To fill a $50 order on the WWEshop.com, site, between costs of materials, shipping, and all aspects of fulfilling the order it costs WWE $41.56 and not $50. Plus, not every new subscriber will actually order the merchandise, and some that will, will order more than the $50 amount so they come off better.

A network subscriber can get a maximum of $250 in free merchandise by referring up to ten new subscribers. All subscribers and new subscribers also have to have a U.S. mailing address, so this won't work with referring to or referrals by those getting the network outside the U.S.

Another decision this week to try to build up subscriptions was to keep John Cena off Raw on 5/5 (Cena was in the building and worked a dark match) and push that his interview after his loss to Bray Wyatt would instead be on Main Event on the network the next day.

At the end of the day, the network will make money because there are ways to change things, from raising the price to eliminating WrestleMania from the package (but they may now be blocked from that, given the reaction from Dish Network and DirecTV of late, which was a reaction they were not counting on). WWE really wasn't profiting that much from the non-Mania domestic shows to where the network won't be cost-effective.

If the August call announces under 836,000, most likely this will make money, but it's not a major change for business and TV rights are really the key going forward. If they announce 1 million, the network is on the verge of making considerable money, but even then based on assumptions of growth staying at the same level (again, not going to happen), they won't reach projections. But if they announce more than 1.1 million, the network in this form would be a gigantic success, although with these hotshots to get new people early, that may slow down growth from this level as time goes on. That's not bad, it's just that the numbers I'm citing are best expectations possible based on the number announced, and the reality is the growth numbers will be lower, and probably significantly so.

For the Laura Martins of the world, they would have to hit 1.2 million on the next call, and that's assuming they retain the same level of growth, and that's using Martin's idea that nobody outside the U.S. gets the network, and that instead of 20% of the subscribers are outside the U.S. as WWE projects that it will end up as 50%. I believe 20% is extremely low. I think it'll be 35% minimum (36% of the Royal Rumble buys were outside North America, but that's including Canada, the U.S. alone did 58% of total buys for Rumble and there is no reason to believe the network percentage of viewers would be all that much different). But I also believe right now of that 667,000, the true U.S. number is 415,000 to 530,000, essentially numbers that would fit into the alarming low level, since 650,000 was really the bottom level of decent. And that's a key that the entire market and every analyst may be way off on.

We'll have a very good idea of that in three to four weeks, when the international buys from WrestleMania come in, of how many international buyers are in the 667,000 number.

That's the key number that right now, nobody knows. Well, WWE should have a good idea right now, but haven't given any indication. Last year's Mania did 502,000 buys outside the U.S. If we go with the impression that the U.S. number is 390,000 (one person very close to the top people gave me that number, WWE has only said "almost 400,000," but that number can't be verified), then the total announced buys for Mania should be 892,000 if almost all network buyers were from the U.S.

If total WrestleMania buys are 690,000, that would indicate the same percentage of overseas buyers as domestic buyers already get the network. Figures between 690,000 and 890,000, which is where it should fit in, will tell you if it's closer to one end than the other.

With UFC, the split is 65 percent U.S. and 35 percent outside, but they aren't banning anyone from subscribing. But it's also not available, and won't be, in Brazil, the company's top foreign market due to conflicts with existing television deals. Because WWE started really expanding internationally in the 80s and UFC didn't really expand until about 2007.

Since WWE is projecting an 80/20 split between U.S. and the rest of the world, they are very likely under projecting foreign, as theoretically because of the outrageous characters and simplicity, and bigger TV audiences, WWE exports better than UFC in most countries and the U.S. split doesn't include Brazil, a market where the opposite would be the case. However, an Observer poll on the WWE Network ended up with a percentage very similar to UFC already, which questions if international growth will really ramp up at that great a level.

They see the nearly 400,000 Americans who purchased the show on PPV as potential new customers between now and the end of the year, with the idea that will get them to one million. Vince McMahon pushed that 1 million domestic homes saw WrestleMania this year. That's likely not true, because some of the network homes weren't domestic and there is an overlap between the two numbers that people within the company noted–both people who have the network but ordered it on PPV. Also, not everyone who had the network watched WrestleMania on it, although the vast majority did. Some watched it on PPV, and someone in the company, when noting it was significantly less than 667,000 people watching Mania, said if there was a PPV party of 12 people, let's say, and five of them are network subscribers, they weren't watching Mania on the network. That said, I would guess that of those 400,000, the vast majority were not going to buy another WWE PPV show until next year's Rumble or Mania under normal circumstances so the value of the network decreases greatly to them until mid-January.

They were directly asked about talent payoffs, whether talent would be paid based on PPV buys or a 1 million figure plus international (in theory 1.3 million homes to 1.6 million), and if talent would share in the network revenue. The answer was the company wouldn't comment publicly on that question.

Right now there is a lot of grumbling about payoffs from the video game in particular, as well as house shows and the first two PPVs of the year, because all are down. The Mania payoffs, which should be expected to be sent out in early July, are going to tell a story. They will have to create a new formula because if they are only paying talent off the PPV, and not the network, payoffs will be way down coming on the heels of payoffs being down from every other aspect of business.

As noted by Mick Foley, the video game royalty checks this year were way down and a lot of talent was unhappy about it, but none would complain publicly. Another top tier star noted to us that he earned more than six times more two years ago from video game royalties than this year. Last year's royalties off the video game were way down because of the bankruptcy and everyone expected that. But the expectation was this year would be back to normal levels, and instead it was a small percentage or what it used to be. With the exception of the super merchandise movers like Cena and Punk, the video game royalties are the biggest supplemental income the performers have. Since Foley publicly said what he did, we got notes from three major names (these are not the Cena tier, but pretty close to it), and their video game checks were in the $10,000 to $15,000 range, and two years ago they were $70,000 to more than $100,000.

The general rule of thumb is that if you are in the video game, you get a royalty check for about $75,000 in the first quarter of the year. The check that the vast majority of performers got was $11,900. That's when people started freaking out, because the checks for Rumble and Elimination Chamber were both down. Now, both of those shows did less business, but the profit margin should have been up because the expense of Dwayne Johnson was $3.3 million (that's not just his pay, but all expenses related to him and special performers) but first quarter PPV revenue only dropped $1.3 million. In addition, pay for house shows decreased even though the houses themselves were up, but the expenses of building rental, advertising and promotions were up to the point profits were down.

The theory espoused across the board among wrestlers for the most part is that WWE is making up for business losses and network losses by underpaying everyone on both royalties and discretionary income (which is the house show and PPV revenue where there is a formula used, but nobody knows the formula. The guys see that they are getting paid less on similar houses, not realizing expense differences, and aren't happy. Plus, Sean Cleary stopped doing payoffs and Paul Levesque took over, and management has always wanted the buffer person handling pay (Jim Ross, John Laurinaitis, Jane Geddes, Cleary, J.J. Dillon, etc.) to take the heat.

Realistically, on a publicly traded company, I don't see royalty pays (merchandise and video games) being cut back on to fund the network. House show and PPV percentages, which have varied greatly as shown in the past, yes, there could be something to some of that. But again, if they are paying based on profits, the same houses were doing significantly less profit than any other year.

Regarding the video game payoffs, WWE, when it cut its deal with 2K Sports, reportedly 2K Sports didn't want to do the game right away, preferring to launch late 2014. After not making much money off the video game in 2013 due to the THQ bankruptcy, WWE didn't want to go without video game money for the 2014 books because that's tens of millions and it would look really bad for Wall Street, and give an illusion of a company falling in its licensing. So in cutting the deal, the report we got is the first dollars that come in, WWE was getting royalties at a substantially lower rate. They will start to make significantly more money once sales reach a certain level. Reportedly they have reached that level, but hadn't by 3/31, when the quarter ended and the check came in. Supposedly the money will even out and a far bigger than usual second quarter check will be coming to make up the difference, both to the company, and to talent.

About $8.0 million of the decline had to do with the settlement of the THQ deal and closing that deal up. But there were also lower revenues not only from video games, but also toys, clothing and novelties than the year before.

MAY 19

The reason a lot of WCW theme music is now being used on the network instead of dubbed over is settling some deals as well as the settlement of a lawsuit by Jimmy Papa, who had produced music for both WCW and World Class. Papa had sued WWE in 2012, claiming the company had used WCW theme music, as well as his most popular song, "Badstreet USA," that he had written with Michael Hayes. He sued WWE, Hayes and Jim Johnston for copyright violation and for claiming Johnston had written the songs. The case was settled with the terms sealed, past the point WWE is now allowed to use the music.

JUNE 2

An interesting note which is one of the stats the company has used regarding their thoughts on the network. In 2013, there were about 850,000 U.S. homes that ordered at least two PPVs. Keep in mind that WrestleMania in the U.S. did about 600,000 homes. That means most people who ordered Mania probably ordered at least one more show during the year. The second most ordered was Royal Rumble, which probably did in the 325,000 range (it did 364,000 in North America, but that includes Canada and Puerto Rico, although WWE for its own stats considers Puerto Rico as the U.S.) It also means that a lot of households, probably well over 250,000, ordered two PPVs this year and didn't order Mania. A lot of that has to do with groups and different homes for the group. Around 2008 (I could have the year of the study wrong by one year, but 2008 was when I knew about it), UFC did a big study on its PPV viewership. They found that even though there were fairly consistent baseline numbers (I think baseline was about 300,000 then), somewhat surprisingly, baseline shows were not ordered in the same homes. Further studying showed that groups ordered the shows but often switched whose home in the group they were watching in. They had an audience that watched every show, but not in their home. I don't know if this relates to wrestling, but they also found that even though it was groups watching, people didn't chip in to pay generally, and that the guy whose home would pay, but often the others would bring food and beverages. The other thing they found is that in groups of five to ten, usually only one or two people in the group were avid fans and the rest were families or friends, and that they watched far more for entertainment than sports. But WWE used that 850,000 homes that spent $100 or more on PPV to see two shows as the absolute minimum that would for sure get the network at $120 for all 12 PPVs and all the other content. Even though the deal where if you referred a friend to order a six-month sub for the network and you would get $25 in a merchandise voucher as would your friend, is good until 5/31, the WWE made the decision to stop promoting it two weeks ago. It was originally to be a three-week promotion. There are plans to upload a lot of new content in late August to go along with loading up the September PPV to get people to renew the network.

JUNE 9

When it comes to the WWE Network, we had noted that the next indication of how things are going would come with the release of the worldwide WrestleMania buys.

The key is, that number would indicate whether network subscribers were almost exclusively from the U.S., or spread around the world. If the 667,287 subscribers were all from the U.S., as it was purported, perhaps the 1 million U.S. number was viable at the end of the year. While even then, it would not be a good number, it would be soft and at the low end of acceptable, and you'd expect big growth internationally.

But if the number of foreign subscribers in that number was significant, that would indicate U.S. numbers are worse, and that foreign growth may be less than expected. Nobody, not WWE, nor anyone, knows the foreign vs. domestic breakdown because at this point the foreign subscribers have gotten it through a U.S. address. What we do know is UFC Fight Pass numbers have shown more foreign interest than expected. UFC had projected 75 to 80 percent U.S. subscribers going in, but the number was 65 percent, and that's not including Brazil (where it's not available), their best international market. WWE is also stronger than UFC on the international stage. WWE projected 80 percent of its subscribers by 2015, when it would be available around the world in all of their key markets, to be American. Even now, when it's supposed to be only American, we can question if it hit 80 percent.

The key was the WrestleMania PPV figures. WWE released 690,000 worldwide buys for WrestleMania. If you recall, they had announced a few weeks after WrestleMania that the show did "almost" 400,000 U.S. PPV buys, a figure far higher than even the most optimistic expectation.

Another item released cryptically by the company would have been WrestleMania paid attendance. Based on figures for house shows for the month of April both including and not including WrestleMania, the paid attendance for the show would have been roughly 59,500. Based on those figures, the absolute lowest the paid attendance could have been was 57,981 and the absolute most was 61,019. What's notable is that 55,000 of those tickets had been sold by early January, and there were plenty of tickets available the week of the show. What that would appear to indicate is that the travelers who arrange the trip ahead of time without knowing the card itself made up the majority of ticket buyers. The hope from January was to sell to the local community, not just in New Orleans but other cities in the area, and it appears that interest level was far smaller than expected. The total attendance at the Mercedes Benz Superdome when it came to ticket holders was 65,000. The company announced 75,167, so it was the usual low five figure "mark-up."

It should be noted that the three week later figure WWE releases is more enthusiastic than its figure a month plus later, which is a real number figure. The first number they figure is about where they expect to end up, and in almost every year, they have fallen short of that first announced figure.

We were told by someone in the company that the "almost" 400,000 figure was actually 390,000. WWE officially stated that the number was only U.S. buys, not even including Canada. Let's also go with the benefit of the doubt and say that 390,000 figure projects 12 percent above the real number, so we'll estimate 340,000 U.S. buys as the estimate of those 690,000

So here's a chart to ponder next:

Year	U.S. buys (approx)	Canada & intl &*(approx)Intl
2014	340	350*
2013	600	500
2012	640	580
2011	615	520

Figures giving WWE the benefit of the doubt on international, based on their original statement the split would be closer to 390 U.S. and 300 outside

Now, we are giving the international segment the benefit of the idea that the U.S. buys released were an estimated final number that could be way off and not a number similar to what the first reports have. Even in giving out of U.S. that edge, it dropped 30 percent from last year, which is very significant. If that isn't the case, foreign dropped 40 percent from last year, or more than U.S. and that would indicate foreign subscriptions are as close to what they would be with everyone who wanted to buy already getting the network, which I don't buy at this point.

This is where it gets tricky. If this year's Mania was on PPV this year, it was not going to match the 1,104,000 buys that last year's show did, because Dwayne Johnson, the big draw the past three years, did not wrestle on the card. It's impossible to measure what that means, so it's also impossible to measure what this means. The total buys and subscriptions on the day of Mania are 1,357,000. Of course it's 1,357,000 with a bottom price of $9.99 per month as opposed to 1,104,000 ranging at various different bottom prices, but far more than that and as much as $59.99 bottom price in the U.S. In theory, this should indicate that the network should easily get 1,357,000 worldwide buys. But that would indicate no duplication in numbers. Nobody knows how many people with the network bought the PPV because of PPV parties and not trusting the technology. I know the number is significant, but like the real number of foreign subscribers, exactly how significant is something nobody knows.

An issue is that international has also been falling faster than domestic. Rumble dropped 24% foreign without the network. Mania dropped 30% minimum foreign, perhaps 40%, in theory with the network not offered foreign but those stats right there tell you how significant foreign consumption of the network was. U.S. fell between 35% and 43% with the network, and those drops are not that different, meaning network penetration and purchasing by WrestleMania customers outside the U.S. may be as much as similar, although probably less.

Rumble dropped 17% domestic, and it had Rock last year and not this year. So if we say that 600,000 this year would have been 498,000 with no network (keep in mind there will be confusion about U.S. numbers, because usually domestic constitutes U.S. and Canada and the 600,000 and 498,000 exclude Canada), the network itself caused an additional drop of 26%. Based on that, if all the people who you would expect would have purchased the network had it been available by Mania, you would expect the Canada and international number to be about 280,000. It greatly exceeded that, meaning that's not the case. But the international number is 10 percent down from what we'd expect if you figure a 24 percent decrease (a number I'd consider high as Mania this year wasn't gong to decrease at the level Rumble did, but again all these stats are as beneficial to WWE as possible).

If we assume the 340,000 U.S. is really 390,000, then international falls to 300,000, barely over that 280,000 mark.

Essentially, we would expect the network had the whole world been getting the network, to do 280,000 buys, and without the network being available at all, closer to 380,000 buys.

At 350,000 out of U.S. buys, it means out of 100% max network subscribers outside the U.S. at this time, about 30% (30,000) already have it. At 300,000 out of U.S. buys, that puts the number at 80,000, or 80% of people who would have bought it by Mania already did. That doesn't mean it's 30,000 or 80,000 out of 667,287. It means at full capacity, and moving Canada to the international instead of domestic as usual, we're looking at a 54/46 split in favor of U.S. Instead it was 49/51.

I'm assuming 340,000 as the U.S. number based on the 690,000 based on previous year WWE reporting. But if they are reporting numbers as they have them and not as projected, things are much worse. Because that would indicate 80% of international fans who would have purchased the network by Mania found a way to get it already, meaning the overseas growth expected for next year won't be much.

If we go with the idea that 500,000 is the real U.S. number and 167,000 is the foreign number, we project 840,000 total viewers domestic and 520,000 foreign, or 62%. The split for Rumble was 65%. Using that, a 533,000 and 134,000 split would get us 880,000 domestic 480,000 foreign total purchasers between network and PPV, at that same 65% split. So our best guess estimate is that about 20% of the subscribers are already from outside the U.S. and the U.S. total on the day of Mania was 533,000.

The idea that the 533,000 will rise to 1 million in the U.S. is a lot lower odds than anyone has figured on. Still, even though the WWE Network likely being about 80 percent U.S. subscribers, now, the figure they expected to be once introduced to the new countries is not that they've hit the new countries capacity, but they undershot, or maybe overshot the U.S.

If we say they hit 1 million before the international launch, that would be 800,000 in the U.S. and 200,000 outside. If Rumble was a 65/35 split, the last major show with full worldwide distribution, our end of the year capacity if this was available worldwide would be about 420,000.

So with everything being figured, if the number is 1 million at year's end, getting to 1.22 million with foreign promotion, legal availability and push should come relatively quickly. But the 1 million number at year's end is not guaranteed.

For WWE business to break even in 2015, our current 533,000 in the U.S. has to hit 878,000 by next summer, which doesn't seem unreasonable. But the idea that a company that was making $50 million per year in profits when coming up with the network would be happy as a break-even company with a fully functional network after a year of record losses shows that is hardly the goal.

To hit the 1.9 million mark for the network to bring the company's overall profits to the level they were before there was a network, probably has to hit 1,235,000 by July 2015. If we say that they aren't going to get back to normal, that the consumer resistance to the new technology is still slow and it will take until 2016, then the 1,235,000 U.S. target (my target considering I'm giving them 35% foreign whereas they claim it'll be 20%), well above double the current total, has to be there by July of 2016.

In August, we'll have a great idea of how viable hitting these numbers are. If they aren't going to reach those levels, they can still raise the price because there are probably enough people willing to spend $15 per month that they can make this work in the end. The company may not have as many fans willing to spend money on the product as they believed they did, but they've got a very ardent hardcore fan base that, for the most part, isn't going anywhere, and to them, the network is a great deal.

JUNE 30

With the advent of the WWE Network, evaluating PPV numbers has become a tricky science.

The U.S. numbers would be expected to fall. In theory, international numbers should stay the same, but that hasn't been the case.

With WrestleMania, it appeared buys outside of the U.S. decreased about 30 percent from the prior year based on first reports from WWE. That's an estimated figure based on the idea that there were 340,000 U.S. buys for WrestleMania (the company announced "almost 400,000," but the original announcement is always based on a projection of final numbers based on early numbers and expected growth. The reported numbers a few weeks later by the company to stockholders are more solid, and based on actual reported figures up to that time).

WWE reported 690,000 total PPV buys for Mania, which is now estimated at 689,000.

Based on those figures, because the international decline, which in theory shouldn't have been affected by the network, but obviously was, told us a pretty significant portion of the network's original subscriber base of 667,287 came from outside the U.S.

We now have more figures. But without two key figures, one which WWE knows and one which nobody really knows, it's still hard to evaluate what it all means.

Extreme Rules on 5/4 in East Rutherford, NJ, built around The Shield vs. Evolution, Daniel Bryan vs. Kane for the WWE title and John Cena vs. Bray Wyatt in a cage match did 107,000 worldwide buys. That was broken down into 40,000 in North America and 67,000 internationally.

As a comparison, the 2013 version of the show did 137,000 buys in North America and 108,000 internationally. The 2012 version, which featured Cena vs. Brock Lesnar, did 159,000 buys in North America and 112,000 buys internationally.

Without Lesnar, there should have been expected to be a decline, although Lesnar on this run has been far stronger in North America than overseas because his 2008 to 2010 UFC run was when UFC was strongest in the U.S. and Canadian markets. The last Extreme Rules show pre-Lesnar, three years ago, did 108,000 buys both in North America and internationally.

So if we go strictly on head-to-head, the international number was down 38 percent from both last year and also the pre-Lesnar 2011 show, when Extreme Rules wasn't that big of a deal. That would, even more so than WrestleMania, indicate the international current network subscription numbers are significant. Another factor in that drop is that Germany, due to the greater penetration of WWE on television, was up from last year, meaning the decline in the rest of the markets would have actually been more than 38 percent.

From WrestleMania, we estimated 533,000 U.S. and 134,000 outside the U.S. based on the idea of a 30 percent foreign drop. A 38 percent foreign drop would indicate an even higher percentage of subscribers as of 5/4 were outside the U.S. WWE would know what the 5/4 subscription number is, but we won't be able to figure it until the number is released in about five weeks. If the overall subscribers has increased significantly from 667,000, and with different promotional offers and heavy advertising, it should, it would appear the foreign percentage of the increase would be the same or larger than our originally estimated 20 percent. That would again mean that the expected level of increases when the service is officially available internationally will not be as high as projected since so many of the expected subscribers in that growth phase already have it.

What the 40,000 number means is harder to determine. If WrestleMania did 340,000 buys in the U.S., which is lower than WWE's original announcement, that would be down 43 percent from last year, which was actually far less of a decline than expected by almost everyone. That either indicated a lot of people hadn't signed up for the network and just bought Mania as a one-off, or double-dipped, in the sense they didn't trust the stream, or maybe had Mania parties, and ordered Mania on PPV even though they had the network.

The fact WrestleMania did well on PPV and that there would be less Extreme Rules parties, the double-dipping, while not eliminated, would be expected to decline greatly. The Extreme Rules number indicated that to be correct.

The 40,000 figure includes Canada, which would be expected to do 10,000 to 15,000 buys for a show like Extreme Rules. Now, if a lot of Canadians that would have purchased the show have the network, that would also decline. Let's give Canada the same 38 percent decline as international, so of the 40,000, Canada would probably be somewhere between 6,200 and 9,300 total buys, leaving U.S. (and Puerto Rico) as doing 31,000 to 34,000 total buys. U.S. buys last year would have been about 125,000, so it's down 73% to 75%, a far greater percentage than Mania. It also should be noted that neither DirecTV nor Dish Network offered Extreme Rules. But Dish didn't offer Elimination Chamber, and it had no effect at all, as the domestic number is now estimated at 155,000, down from 181,000 the prior year, but that had Rock vs. C.M. Punk as the main event so it would have been down significantly no matter what, since every Rock PPV was well above usual levels. The non-Rock 2012 show did 138,000, so even without Dish, they were above the expected level.

If that increases in U.S. decline indicates a lot of new buyers for the network, that's good. If the network numbers didn't increase greatly from Mania to Extreme Rules, that would indicate substantial double-dipping and a very misleading number when WWE touted the idea that 1.36 million people purchased Mania.

But what we can say is the network killed traditional PPV in the U.S. already. It was inevitable it would happen, and the only question was how soon, and the answer was the second show. And ultimately, it has hurt it in foreign markets this year and will kill it by early next year. WWE in negotiations this year in foreign markets about PPV were up front about the idea that PPV would be a short-term business that would decline greatly early next year.

JULY 21

The announcement of the WWE network subscriptions will be on 7/31. This could lead to either a significant increase or decrease in stock price depending on the number announced. The 825,000 to 900,000 range would be considered okay I believe as far as the stock goes, but I could be wrong and it really isn't. To me, anything under 915,000 would be bad given all the hotshotting and promotions and that you are likely to lose 10-15% under the best of circumstances in September and October. A number about 910,000 to 925,000 would indicate hitting 1 million by the end of the year because of the loss of 70,000 to 100,000 at best in September and October (most services of this type lost 15 percent, UFC Fight Pass, the closest equivalent, usually maintains closer to 90 percent at the time of renewal). I don't know that Wall Street will understand that aspect, forget that with the six-month commitment almost nobody has canceled and nobody has had to renew yet, and will just have the idea of a 42,000 increase per month as on the way to 1 million, and based on that, 833,000 would be the goal to hit 1 million. And that's not taking into account 1 million is figured as a domestic number in their goal, and a very significant percentage of subscribers are outside the U.S. Anything below 800,000 I'd consider a disaster with all the hotshotting promotions, international buys and strong big events. Even hitting 1 million on 12/31, hardly guarantees continual growth to 1.4 million by July (although with full international promotion that is not unreasonable) and 2 million at the end of 2015 (a lot more difficult). The one thing I'm certain of is that WWE greatly underestimated its foreign projections. I believe they overestimated domestic projections but that we'll have a lot better idea of in a few weeks. While it is possible to cancel by simply not paying, the number of people who have done that is minuscule to the point it's not significant. The first cancellation point won't be until September, which is why the September Night of Champions PPV is going to be made into a special card. In September, about 495,000 people will be making a decision to renew. They need to do the same in October show, because that's when the 172,000 people who signed up the week of WrestleMania will all come due. For those who signed up for the free week, they got an e-mail blast saying if they signed up for six months by 7/19, they get a $25 off merchandise card from WWEshop.com, which, if they order merchandise, essentially means they can get six months for $35. This isn't the first time this offer has been made, as WWE a few months back had an offer that if someone had the network and referred to a friend who would sign up for six months at $60, they would get a $25 off merchandise card and the person signing up would also get a $25 off merchandise card. What's key here is that in the network breakdown, the accounting would show $60 in revenue to the network and profits (or less losses) on the network side, but the WWEshop would bear the cost of the expense and shipping of the merchandise with no revenue figured in. So that's something to look for in the next quarter business analysis is the profit margin on WWEshop as compared to usual levels to see if a significant number of people signed up for these incentives. When the announcement is made, WWE will have had three PPV shows since Mania, Warrior week, the $50 in merchandise deal for a $60 order, and countless other gimmicks. It's hard to believe they wouldn't reach 800,000. If they don't, it really tells me the only growth periods going forward will be January through April each year. In fact, with all the incentive orders, this quarter really came across as a hotshot to get numbers up by the reporting date to keep the stock price up. Every time you do a marketing gimmick, it loses its effectiveness for something similar in the future. HBO and Showtime will do free weekends from time-to-time, but you don't see them doing free weeks several times a quarter or offering nearly the full price of a six month subscription back if you order to jack up numbers now. But there is a difference as WWE is trying to get people to try out a new technology for free (Netflix gives you a month free and the UFC Network gives you a free tryout period at any time; WWE doesn't do that because of the PPVs as they don't want people watching a PPV for free; the one-week free trial with you not needing a credit card and only an e-mail address was something Hulu originated in 2011 and seemed to work in adding new subscribers). The reason the numbers aren't bigger is as much an aversion to this technology as providing a product not enough people are interested in. On Raw, they pushed that they were having the C.M. Punk documentary run on the network on Tuesday.

AUGUST 11

It was a monumental week in WWE, as despite far lower than expected WWE Network numbers, the announcement of cost cutting and a revised earnings report led company stock to rebound over the next five days.

The stock, hovering between $11 and $12.50 per share since the disappointing U.S. rights fees announcement, finished at press time at $13.97 per share, increasing the company's market capitalization to $1.05 billion.

The cost cutting, roughly $10 million this year and between $30 to $40 million in 2015, changed the financial outlook to where, if business stays at its current relatively steady level in most of its revenue streams, the company would need only 750,000 worldwide network subscribers on average next year for the company to break even, down from previous projections of needing to average 1.4 million subscribers. In addition, because the network will be on television and not the Internet, in Canada, the numbers should end up significantly better in that market than originally projected. In addition, the network's international roll-out is being rushed, with more than 170 countries and territories getting access to it this coming week, some five months earlier than first announced.

That's positive news, because the network news itself couldn't have been worse. On 6/30, the WWE network had 699,750 subscribers, and company sources have said that number dropped to about 690,000 by the end of July. That's only a slight increase from the 667,287 figure on 4/7, the day after WrestleMania. During that nearly three months, with all kinds of hotshot promotions involving friend referrals where the company would give away $50 in free merchandise ($25 for signing up and $25 for someone who refers someone to sign up), free merchandise at arenas for signing up, and included ability to watch the replay of Mania, and gimmicks like Warrior week, the company picked up 161,000 new subscribers, but 128,000 people canceled. In addition, during the month of July, the number that canceled was roughly 10,000 greater than the number that signed up.

Based on assuming a 90% retention rate of subscribers, we had figured the company needed to be in the range of 936,000 subscribers on 6/30, because of the expected September/October drop, to be able to hit the projected 1 million target by the end of the year.

Well, that 1 million domestic figure, which they have no chance of achieving, has been changed from a conservative year-end estimate to something different.

"Well, what we've always said... is that if we had 1 million by year end, we'd absolutely be thrilled," said Chief Strategy and Financial Officer George Barrios. "That would be incredible, and we would feel the same way."

Based on the rate of PPV dropping domestic vs. international, it would indicate the 700,000 current subscribers would be somewhere between 420,000 and 480,000 from the U.S., and 220,000 to 280,000 outside the U.S. While the network is not available in theory outside the U.S., it is relatively easy to get it and the hardcore fans that want it, which are seemingly the majority who get the network, are already on board.

WWE had projected 80 percent U.S. and 20 percent outside U.S. as its steady subscribers in 2015 when the network was available in an official capacity worldwide. Obviously those numbers will be nowhere close when international, without anyone supposed to be having access, would be between 30 and 40 percent already. My feeling is it will be a lot closer to 50/50 by next year. Because of moving the international distribution date up from early 2015, it's impossible to fully project what is viable, because of the Canadian market experiment of having the network as a TV station, and how much growth will come from international markets where it will now be advertised in, and accessing it will be easier.

The type of people who purchase the WWE Network will be similar to the PPV buyers. When shows were available in the U.K., the PPV split was generally 50 to 60 percent North America (of which five to seven percent would be Canadian). The UFC Fight Pass is at 62 percent in the U.S., and WWE has far more international presence and appeal than UFC. And keep in mind that Fight Pass is not offered in Brazil, the country that UFC is the most popular in, because it already has a broadcast channel, Combate, that airs all shows live. Similarly, Fight Pass is not available in Mexican, Central and South America (outside of Brazil) because UFC has a television subscription channel, working with Televisa, that carries all UFC events live.

Because PPV is only available in certain countries, if anything, if you would include the fan base in countries without PPV, plus flip Canada over from the domestic to foreign, and there is no reason the WWE Network shouldn't have a minimum of 50 percent of its subscribers outside the U.S. If we go with 450,000 as the U.S. figure, that would indicate a potential of 900,000 by the end of the year, and perhaps Canada would boost it past that level. That's more than enough to make 2015 profitable, although not close to enough to make the network decision cost effective.

The one statistic that was shocking is the number of people who ordered a subscription and canceled, which is a total contradiction of WWE's claim of 90 percent consumer satisfaction.

Between the network launch on 3/2 and 6/30, there were 828,000 homes that ordered the network at the $9.99 per month price tag with a six month commitment. That figure was along the lines of what I figured the 6/30 number announcement would be.

However, of those, 128,000 stopped paying, whether through a Paypal account, closing their credit card or not having money in their account, which is 15 percent right there, and that's before the original six month commitment starts running out for the bulk of subscribers between 9/2 and 10/7.

One of the problems, which was the Emperor's New Clothes that nobody talks about, is streaming and technical problems. While most report limited problems, usually minor annoyances at best, after every PPV show, we get a number of people who claim they weren't able to watch the show with any enjoyment. A lot seems to depend on the Internet connection, but the people who contact us the maddest with the network are those who try and sit down and watch the PPV and have nothing but problems. From my own experience, between regular watching of Ustream, the WWE Network and Fight Pass, that I get freezes and get kicked off far more with the WWE Network, which usually happens on Tuesdays when watching Main Event. But there are issues at times with everything. The 8/6 New Japan G-1 show from Takamatsu, according to several who watched it live and e-mailed us, was a technological disaster with the stream not working at all for a long period of time. On 7/29, in particular, I got bounced five times in the first 20 minutes of the show, on a daily where I, on the same computer, both before and after, watched Fight Pass and Ustream from Japan with no issues. Still, they were minor glitches I was able to see the entire show. In addition, it feels like there has been cost cutting because the picture quality, at least on Main Event, seems to have declined noticeably. The problems don't exist for me when watching shows on archives.

The key is that nobody was supposed to be able to cancel based on the commitment until September. Considering that more people canceled in July than signed up, leading to a 10,000 net loss, the retention rate is far lower than Netflix (95 percent) or even UFC Fight Pass (90 percent). And that's before technically not one person's subscription has expired.

The idea that 15% canceled before the end of their subscription is unheard of. Other similar services have told us that it is extremely rare that people cancel before their commitment is up. But the difference also is that most services of this type allow month-to-month subscriptions. In my own business, going on 32 years, people who cancel during the time frame of their subscription is almost unheard of. We may have five people a year do that, and three or four of them would be families who contact us that their family member who subscribed had passed away. Others with streaming services reported it is very rare for someone to cancel before their originally signed up commitment, citing it's almost always based on the subscriber death and being contacted by the family.

Within the streaming video industry, that number blew people away.

The difference is WWE didn't allow month-to-month subscriptions, although they are changing now. But enough of its fan base went out of their way to stop subscribing. WWE has not tried to collect from those who signed up for the commitment and stopped paying, because it would lead to bad publicity.

"We don't currently have a penalty policy on failed payments," said a WWE source. "However, we are continually evaluating this as well as various payment options and pricing plans."

Vince McMahon indicated changing the types of payments accepted to guard against people subscribing and then not paying.

"We are working on some things at this point, but we haven't implemented them yet," said McMahon.

The company has no policy currently on how it will handle those who stop paying and stop subscribing, if those people later sign up next year during WrestleMania season. Another question regards how to guard against them signing up for $9.99 and then stopping payment again after WrestleMania.

The question now becomes, Is that are those who was dissatisfied all canceling early? Will there is actually be no major September/October dropping period when subs run out? Or are they going to face a major drop in that period, meaning dissatisfaction with the product is far higher than they anticipated?

Among the key items this past week include:

- The network will be officially rolled out in 170 countries and territories on 8/12. The key countries are Australia, New Zealand, Hong Kong, Singapore, Mexico, Spain, Norway, Sweden and Finland. Other countries include Argentina, Aruba, The Bahamas, Belgium, Bermuda, Bolivia, Bosnia, Brazil, Cayman Islands, Chile, Colombia, Congo, Croatia, Cyprus, The Czech Republic, Denmark, Dominican Republic, Ecuador, El Salvador, France, Georgia, Greece, Guam, Guatemala, Hong Kong, Hungary, Iceland, Indonesia, Israel, Jamaica, Kenya, Lithuania, Luxembourg, Macao, the Netherlands, Panama, Peru, Poland, Singapore, South Africa, South Korea, Taiwan, Tonga, Turkey, Trinidad and Venezuela. The roll-out will be the same English language version with no differences with the current network. If there are foreign countries that speak a different language that start doing big numbers (like has already unofficially been the case in Germany), they will begin to work on a network version in those languages. The reason these international roll-outs are coming quicker is the original idea was to provide multiple feeds tailored for markets, with the correct language, or just minor changes. By just doing one feed and having everything identical, the costs are less and they can roll it out quicker, but they aren't in home languages in many of their markets and there is no tailoring for the market.

- The company signed a ten-year partnership with Rogers Communications in Canada, which would include television, digital rights, and the network. The network will debut as a regular television station, similar to HBO, starting on 8/12. The belief is that there will be one free week of viewing and then it will be offered for $11.99 per month, which will be awkward in that country because WWE is pushing $9.99 so hard on television. The offerings will be the same live stream as on the American network, and it will have some archives, but not nearly as much as on the streaming service. There will be a streaming version of the network available in Canada at some point, currently scheduled for a 2015 launch by Rogers. What is key here is that consumers are far more likely to subscribe to a television station than a streaming service, at least today. If Canada does well, it could lead to major changes, because Canada is a good test market for the U.S., but with less risk in experimentation than in the U.S. There are also two other notes. When the WWE announces the network numbers, it will include all television subscribers in Canada. In addition, with the significant new contract, which Vince McMahon said, "It's basically an offer that we couldn't turn down." Not only does it help the company bottom line, it has its repercussions on the UFC side. The UFC's contract with Rogers is coming due and after spending big on the NHL and WWE, it will be interesting to see how that affects the price they offer.

- The Network will be on Rogers Cable on Ch. 512, an HD-only channel, so it appears it will not be able to be accessed by customers who don't have HD. Rogers will be making its own deal with the various other Canadian cable providers to have access to the WWE network. A key is that if someone only has HD on one television in their home, that would be the only TV they could watch the network on.

- Regarding whether moving to television, like in Canada, will be done elsewhere, Vince McMahon said:"Canadians, they tend to look at things a little differently and it's an overall mix. I don't know that we're going to have that anywhere else. We know we might when someone combines our core television rights with network revenue. It's interesting, though, that we have the flexibility to be able to do that as it relates to the network, but I don't know that's necessarily going to happen anywhere else in the world. It could when you combine the two."

- The Canadian television deal is for Raw, Smackdown and Main Event on Sportsnet 360. So that would mean Main Event would either air first on the network and later on television, or simultaneously if moved to a Tuesday night time slot. NXT had been on television in Canada, but is not involved in the new television deal, likely being a network exclusive.

- The company is heavily advertising the network over the next two weeks, building toward SummerSlam, hoping that show leads to an influx of new subscribers, like WrestleMania did. They are also offering two changes from the previous six months at $9.99 per month plan. They will both offer a $19.99 plan for month-by-month subscriptions. This blows me away because it's going to flop, as not only will people not order at that price (except perhaps for WrestleMania and Royal Rumble), but will feel ripped off just at the suggestion of it. First, they have established $9.99 as the price point hard on television, so nobody is going to feel the value today is $19.99 per month, even those who would have originally gladly paid that amount at the start. Second, we've seen that those who only want to order for one month, will simply stop paying, although WWE is working on closing the loopholes that allow that. WWE will also offer an up-front one-time payment option, where you can pay $59.94 at first as opposed to having $9.99 drawn from your credit card each month. The idea of it is it would protect WWE, at least in those cases, because those people couldn't bail on their six-month commitment.

- The network will go live with the U.S. version on 10/1 in both the U.K. and Ireland. The U.K./Ireland is expected to be the second biggest market for the network, as it has been on PPV. As noted before, Germany, which has created a new audience because of more visible television from the recently completed deal, has been an unexpected surprise.

- There is still no set date for launch in Italy, The United Arab Emirates, Germany, Japan, India, China, Thailand. Austria, Costa Rica, Egypt, Iraq, Morocco, The Philippines, Qatar, Saudi Arabia, Switzerland, Thailand or Malaysia, past the point the company estimates the network being available in 2015 or 2016.

- Two new television series that will be added to the network shortly are The Monday Night War and WWE Rivalries. With the Monday Night War documentary series being released, they will start putting episodes of Nitro up, within the next six weeks.

- The battle plan is to start adding Nitros and Raws from the Monday Night War period around October, as an enticement for people to renew. The plan is to add a lot more other WCW television content (the PPVs and Clashes are already up), such as other TV shows in January. The plan as of right now is to start adding new World Class and ECW shows in September, right around the renewal time for original subscribers. It's interesting that WWE basically believes those are the promotions the current audience would be interested in, as there is no talk regarding Mid South, which was the best show of its period, or more AWA, Smoky Mountain Wrestling, Stampede, or any other the other libraries owned. Stampede may start getting featured along with other tapes of Canadian indies based on trying to get regional subscribers from Quebec, Alberta and British Columbia to the television station.

- The network will soon be available on several smart TVs and Blu-Ray players within two weeks.

- They also plan on delivering a new "resume play" feature by the end of the year.

- There seems to be a good chance that Smackdown will be moving back to Thursday night on Syfy. This past week at television, there were WWE production trucks with the giant talent photos for Smackdown listing it as airing on Syfy on Thursday at 8 p.m. Eastern and 7 p.m. Central. These were new trucks with the new WWE logo that will be debuting in a few weeks.

In response to the question, a WWE spokesperson told us, "A move has been contemplated, but no decision has been made. Someone was overzealous in updating our production trucks. The trucks are being fixed to reflect the current and accurate information of Fridays at 8 p.m."

A change would put the show head-to-head with NXT on the network (which WWE should and would likely move) and against the first hour of TNA or whatever wrestling property Spike would air if Spike would continue to air wrestling on Thursdays. Given the track record of TNA ratings when opposed by WWE programming, this move would not be good, and would no doubt play a part in any talks regarding TNA staying at a lower price on Spike. This is good news for WWE, as Smackdown ratings dropped about 20 percent immediately and never recovered when it was moved from Thursday to Friday. Television viewership is far higher on Thursday, meaning Smackdown should be expected to have a significant increase in ratings. For Syfy, keeping its highest rated show on the second worst night for ratings never seemed to make sense.

While losses for the second quarter were less than projected, the disappointing network numbers could lead to larger money losses this year overall than projected, even factoring in the cost-cutting.

The average number of subscribers between April and June was 650,000. While we know that international subscribers make up a great percentage, that doesn't mean all international potential subscribers figured out how to get it, or wanted to go through those methods.

If we figure on international gains getting the number to 900,000 by the end of the year and an average number of 750,000 for the ten months of the year that it was available, the projections would be company losses of between $59 million to $69 million for 2014. That means they have a solid shot at breaking the 2000 WCW record of most money lost in a calendar year in history by a pro wrestling company of $62 million.

So unless international gains are far more than expected, they look to be surpassing the original projected losses of $45 million to $52 million when they were projecting 1 million U.S. subscribers by 12/31, and that's even with throwing in the $10 million in cuts this year.

For 2015, the network needs to average roughly 750,000 subscribers for the company to break even, down from 1.4 million needed before the Canadian deal and the cost cutting. To cover the quarterly dividend and not lose actual company funds for 2015, the average would need to be about 1.1 million. To get to the level of profitability the company was at before there was a network, the number has to be steady at 1.3 million. To make the network cost effective given the costs of starting, they need be able to maintain a 1.5 million subscriber average at the point things balance out, when originally for the network to have paid off, the number would have had to have been 1.9 million. One of the reasons the stock has shown an increase is that these figures don't look insurmountable. It would be almost impossible to fathom the network not averaging 750,000 subscribers next year with easily availability worldwide plus Canadian television. Then again, having so many cancel over three months was also impossible to fathom. It doesn't appear to be a longshot, even with the disappointing numbers, that by 2016, and perhaps as early as 2015, that WWE will be more profitable than at any time in the history of the company, even with the record losses this year. In addition, they would be able to maintain that level of profitability going forward.

What got Wall Street excited is the idea that if the network gets to two million subscribers at a steady state, WWE's annual profits would be estimated at being around $137 million per year, the highest in company history. Even with the real numbers being major disappointments, some are chalking that up to a culture slow in adapting to the new technology, and not that there is a lower than expected number of people who are fans than believed based on ridiculous surveys the company quoted, and the current number represents close to the percentage of those who are willing to pay extra monthly for more content. Some analysts are still throwing around four to five million in expected subscribers in a few years, completely turning the company's financials around.

Additionally, we've been told that the network viewership is not strong for anything these days except the PPV shows, which are clearly the only real catalyst for sign-ups. The old shows don't do well, and because of that, archives have been slow to have been updated, particularly of older territorial footage. Many have described it as a new toy, in that people searched the archives when they first got the network, but after a while it's used for PPVs mostly, and some for things like Legends House, PPV and WrestleMania replays, and shows like NXT, Superstars and Main Event.

Viewer data showed that 91 percent of network subscribers watch one per week, and that the average subscriber has their network on 2.5 devices. The average number of subscribers per day during the three month period was 647,000. Prior to WrestleMania, in March. If that figure is maintained as the average over the final six months of the year (and with the international rollout, it should be much larger), the annual losses for the year would be estimated at between $73 million and $83 million. This would assume either no international growth because most who would want it already have it, or tons more cancellations in September and October when subscriptions become due that offsets international growth. That would be what I'd call a worst case situation.

The pre-and-post game shows are being phased out. They are cutting back on expenses such as delaying new shows. Obvious ideas like a daily news talk show isn't even being talked about.

Among the cost cutting measures were to fire approximately 55 employees (seven percent of the work force) on 7/31. The firings cut across all departments. Several in creative were let go, including Eddie Feldmann, the Senior Vice President of Creative.

Other ideas to save money have included doing more "Supershow" tapings, which would be Raw and Smackdown on the same night. That's difficult because it requires a live audience to sit through five plus hours. Another idea is to run less expensive arenas.

Another cut is the magazine division. The magazine itself had been largely break-even, or at times very slightly profitable, with consistently declining sales. The gross magazine revenue this quarter was down $500,000 from that of one year ago. The era of wrestling magazines worldwide is largely over. The dropping of the WWE publications leaves Pro Wrestling Illustrated, which has very little distribution, as the last remaining U.S.-based pro wrestling magazine.

The company laid off the magazine staff on 7/31, and on 8/5, contacted all subscribers to tell them that they are ceasing magazine publication. The final issues released will be an issue of WWE Kids dated in September, out shortly, and the final issue of WWE Magazine, which will dated October and be released on 9/16. The letter stated that for people who would still be owed issues on their subscription, that WWE will contact them in early September about how that will be handled.

There is a chance some form of WWE magazine publication could continue, as WWE is willing to license the name to a publishing company if they want to pick up the title either domestically or overseas.

Due to the layoffs, there will be additional losses of $4.5 million taken in the third quarter from severance packages and other money spent based on termination of employees.

The company also made a $2 million investment in preferred stock of a software appliance developer on 3/14.

For the WrestleMania quarter, traditionally the company's biggest of the year, WWE took in $156,310,000, and registered $14,497,000 in losses. That was actually considered good news because the company had projected $15 million to $18 million in losses.

For the same quarter last year, the company took in $152,282,000, but finished with $5,182,000 in profits. The big difference was the network.

The quarterly dividend, not figured into the profits and losses, was another $9,017,760.

The start-up of the network has done a number on the company's actual cash on hand. On June 30, 2013, the company had $119.9 million on its balance sheets, with no debt. As of the start of 2014, that figure was $109,387,000. On 6/30, the number had fallen to $78,903,000 in assets, not including $28.1 million in debt (for the new corporate jet). If the company loses another $44 million this year, which would be the best estimate right now, plus has two more dividends at $18 million, that would actually make the company's debt greater than its cash on hand. That's not really significant in and of itself, because many companies operate that way. But it would be a huge change from the WWE that carried in excess of $300 million in cash on hand years back.

Still, the stock price is up about $3 per share from this period one year ago.

Even with having four PPV shows this quarter instead of three, and with Mania, there has been a complete turnaround in profitability compared to last year, and even more, the year before (Rock vs. Cena I), when that WrestleMania was the largest grossing pro wrestling event of all-time.

Network subscriptions brought in $19.4 million. Keep in mind that WWE counts the entire $9.99 in revenue, and costs to various parties who they have to split with is not factored in are put in as revenue and then taken out as expenses. While in PPV revenue, WWE only figures in the revenue it receives after all the splits, so comparisons of actual revenue without factoring in profitability of network vs. PPV are very misleading.

Among the network expenses for the quarter included $7.1 million in programming costs, $3.6 million in advertising costs and $5.8 million in costs of customer service.

PPV revenue only fell 36% although that's because it's comparing four shows for the quarter against three, with Money in the Bank in late June instead of July.

Here's the updated PPV charts for this year, with buys in the thousands. W represents the total number of worldwide buys. D represents the total of domestic buys, which is the U.S., Canada and Puerto Rico. Keep in mind by adding the network, in theory there should be a major difference in North American numbers starting with Mania, but the international numbers should be identical.

	14W	14D	13W	13D	12W	12D
Rumble 517	337	579	364	483	299	
Chamber	203	159	241	181	194	138
Mania	690	424	1104	662	1219	715
Ex Rules	108	45	245	137	271	159
Payback 67	29	198	108	200	110	
MITB	122	53	223	169	206	114

The key thing to look at here is the domestic vs. international drop for a clue as to how much network penetration there is outside the U.S. The other thing to note is how well the Rumble did. The Rumble number really contradicts the idea PPV is inherently a dying business. It's softer for "B" shows to be sure, but when you have something people want to see, it will do as good as ever. Rumble was down from 2013, but that show had Rock vs. C.M. Punk. But this year's version beat the Rumbles dating back several years before that.

For WrestleMania, the domestic decline was 36.0%. The international decline was 39.8%. That would seem to say network penetration was greater outside the U.S. than in, but it's probably because there may have been an international drop greater than domestic for other reasons as well.

For Extreme Rules, the domestic drop was 67.2%, which tells you that a lot of people didn't trust the stream for Mania, but after Mania came off okay, people started giving up on PPV. It also should be noted that both DirecTV and Dish Network did not carry Extreme Rules, and did carry Mania. International fell 41.7%. In theory, international shouldn't have dropped at all. In this case, it indicates the adaptation level internationally was not at the level of the U.S., but was pretty darn significant given the PPV drop.

By Payback, the U.S. drop was 73.1%, while international fell 57.8%. This again points out international network viewership had to be significantly high.

For Money in the Bank, the U.S. drop was 68.6%, while international was up 27.8%. That's because Money in the Bank this year was on Sky Box Office PPV in the U.K., which is the company's second biggest PPV market behind the U.S. Last year it was a free show on Sky.

Another key with comparisons is how well Money in the Bank did and how poorly Payback did compared to the other "B" shows during that time period.

Payback was the show without the WWE title at stake since Daniel Bryan was injured. So it had The Shield vs. Evolution in an elimination match and John Cena vs. Bray Wyatt in a last man standing match.

Money in the Bank was the show that decided who the champion would be with the ladder match for the vacant title with Cena, Randy Orton, Sheamus, Kane, Roman Reigns, Alberto Del Rio, Cesaro (yes he was in a very successful main event only five weeks ago) and Wyatt, plus the Money in the Bank match with Seth Rollins winning over Dean Ambrose, Rob Van Dam, Jack Swagger, Dolph Ziggler and Kofi Kingston.

AUGUST 18

In a smart move, the WWE has dropped the one-month price for the network from the planned $19.99 to $12.99. That's key, because I can see a lot of people doing one-month orders for WrestleMania, Royal Rumble and SummerSlam at that price. $19.99 wouldn't have been too high, but when they established $9.99 as the price, at that point it looks like a rip-off, but $12.99 would be acceptable. In other similar businesses, the mentality behind the $19.99 would be to give a one month price but make it so high that people just say screw it, and order six months for the better deal. But at $12.99, the mentality is that they are going encourage the people who only get it for the big PPVs to order it a few months out of the year. The WWE's marketing has shown that the average network viewer uses it twice a week, as opposed to just for the PPV, so the feeling is that viewer will stick with it year-around. The network is also now available on Sony Internet connected TVs, Blu-Ray disc players, Blu-Ray home theater systems, and Samsung Smart TV devices, Blu-Ray players and Home Theater systems.

AUGUST 25

As far as the network in Canada goes, on Rogers cable as a TV product, you can order it by the month, meaning if you've got that system, a TV PPV is $12.99 a show, not to mention that all they hear on TV is $9.99 and they have to pay more. Funny thing is, the TV version is already far more successful than the streaming version, even with only about 40 hours of archived content compared to 2,000 hours for the streaming version. What's also notable there is in Canada a lot of movie theaters air WWE PPVs for $18 each, and the picture and sound are better in the theater, but one ticket for $18 vs. whole family at $12.99 looks to make it tough on the theater business when the rollout goes national. As it turned out, even before it went national, Cineplex, the chain that has broadcasted all WWE PPVs for years, has just dropped every show for the rest of the year throughout Canada, except for Survivor Series. This hurts most provinces who are not yet getting the network, although those parts of Canada can still order the show as a PPV until Rogers makes deals with the other cable companies to broadcast the network as a television channel. No deals are yet in place but they are working hard to close them. These orders the day of SummerSlam on Rogers will count as network subscribers and not as Canadian PPV buyers.

 The Canadian television experiment at this point looks to have been a huge success. SummerSlam buys at $12.99 in Canada were said to be far above projections. There is some question as to how many people will maintain the service, but it also may be an experiment about the viability of the network today. While we had tons of complaints about people having streaming issues for SummerSlam, Canadians who watched it on television had no issues at all. Given how ROH did roughly six times as many buys for a weaker show through television PPV vs. Internet PPV for far stronger lineups, the issue may not be the price as much as people not yet ready to make the move to purchase PPV's on the Internet. My feeling is that's a mentality that will change, and probably in just a few years and that ultimately the WWE Network will be successful. But for 2014, in the U.S. market, it may be time to investigate the viability of a television version. Rogers' projection for WWE Network orders for the first month was topped two days after the service was introduced.

AUGUST 25

One of our readers who subscribed to the network, and then his credit card expired, called customer service to renew. He was told to just start up a new subscription as his old subscription was closed after the card expired and he didn't respond to e-mails letting him know. When asked about the four months left, he was told, "Don't worry bout that. When people cancel or stop paying, we just close their account and don't charge them anything." He questioned that, saying he didn't want to get a surprise bill after subscribing. He was told the company policy at this point was not to enforce the six month agreement (not wanting to get a negative reaction from consumers on the network most likely) but they "just hoped people didn't know they could cancel at anytime."

SEPTEMBER 8

In PPV comparisons, it's pretty much impossible to get a read on what the numbers mean, because of the change in the way the business is. The 7/20 Battleground show ended up doing 31,000 domestic buys and 68,000 international buys, to finish at 99,000.

There's nothing to really compare that with, and even figuring international buys is hard to determine what it means because of the already existing international subscribers. Last year's July show was Money in the Bank, which has turned into one of the bigger shows of the year, doing 169,000 domestic and 54,000 international. But last year's Money in the Bank aired free in the U.K., the company's No. 2 PPV market, while Battleground was a PPV show. The 2013 version of Battleground, which took place in October, was also a free show in the U.K.

As far as comparisons go, on the domestic side, it beat Payback (29,000) but was far short of Money in the Bank (53,000). Essentially what we can say is that Money in the Bank was a strong performance by the new standards.

Keep in mind these domestic numbers are for the U.S., Canada and Puerto Rico, but the network technically isn't available in Canada.

Payback was built around The Shield vs. Evolution in an elimination match and didn't have a world title match since that was when they weren't certain about when Daniel Bryan would return.

Money in the Bank featured the ladder match for the vacant title, which figured to do strongly, and, since 2011, Money in the Bank has become one of the bigger "B" shows. Battleground was really a one-match show with John Cena vs. Kane vs. Roman Reigns vs. Randy Orton for the title. Since the network subscriber numbers in June and July didn't vary much, what we can do is compare domestic numbers and learn that not having a title match probably hurt and the four-way for the title with no undercard (the next two bouts down were the Dean Ambrose vs. Seth Rollins match that didn't take place and a Battle Royal for the IC title) overall wasn't strong as an attraction, based on how much stronger Money in the Bank, still a "B" show, did, in comparison.

The SummerSlam number will really be nothing that can be evaluated since the key is the network growth. But with the opening up of the international markets during this quarter, in particular the Rogers deal for a televised network in Canada which we know did well above expectations, even if the PPV number is, say 50,000 domestic, it still could be a big hit. But when we get the next set of network numbers, which will be in early November, that will include an international jump that theoretically should shoot the number up.

There will be comparisons that can be made, but they are going to be by quarters, and year vs. year won't be truly comparable until the final quarter of 2015.

SEPTEMBER 8

Evidently the hard and fast rule about not allowing network subscriptions to people with addresses on paypal that are not allowed is off the books. One reader, who was knocked off subscribing because he lived in the U.K., where the service isn't offered (even though he used a U.S. address to get the network, he was using a paypal account that gave his U.K. address), got an e-mail a few days later asking for him to re-subscribe. He joked that WWE was the one who canceled his subscription, not the other way around.

SEPTEMBER 22

In the WWE's new economic direction, this month was the most important since WrestleMania, because it's when about 495,000 or so of the first batch of network customers subscriptions expired.

The idea of SummerSlam with the one-sided Brock Lesnar title win over John Cena was to build to something more important. Night of Champions seemingly had to be a big PPV, because if a lot of people didn't renew, it would be a short-term disaster. And if that was the case, and the numbers don't show considerable overseas growth and maintenance of the U.S. numbers, the stock price will take a hit coming November. It's impossible to tell how things are going past that the Canadian numbers for a very different version of the product got off to a big start.

Another key aspect in the network business is that everyone involved in this venture and similar venture has had issues with credit card rejections. I'm told that not just with WWE, but with everyone, the amount of credit card cancellations and failures on month-to-month billing is so much farther beyond budgetary expectations that it shocked people. That is probably a big part of the huge numbers of early cancellations.

As far as Night of Champions, on 9/21 in Nashville, being a must-see show, with all the television shot, this show's success is built entirely on the main event. The idea of Cena taking a one-sided beating, coming back with a changed mentality, and going for revenge all made sense. The problem is he was good as new a week later, and while he did change in the ring in one match, it was forgotten after the match. As the match approaches, it feels more like just another Cena title match, just with a more appealing than usual champion he's chasing. As PPVs go, without the big name of the show, or the great build, it feels a little above average but far from the can't miss that should have been the goal.

And as for the rest of the show, it will probably provide an entertaining show because WWE hits more than it misses on the big stage, but it's just a usual show.

The result of Cena vs. Lesnar is important, because it probably determines the WrestleMania direction. Lesnar retaining should all but guarantee Lesnar vs. Roman Reigns at WrestleMania, providing they don't get cold feet on that direction. Cena winning should still lead to the ascension of Reigns, but with a different dynamic, and probably wind up with Seth Rollins as champion at some point. It would free Lesnar for a match that could be as important, or more, than the title match, whether it would be with Undertaker, Rock or even a Steve Austin, since he feels like the best opponent for any of the three should they work the show. There are no special stipulations, or better than usual builds underneath. If anything, the go-home Raw didn't help any of the matches except the main event, and perhaps Mark Henry vs. Rusev. Reigns vs. Seth Rollins was hurt by having a match on television that the crowd really didn't get much into, and having Reigns win clean. It felt like there was no longer a reason for this match other than it's a PPV and both don't have another opponent. Dean Ambrose is expected to return here, or at TV the next night. Randy Orton vs. Chris Jericho is Jericho's farewell for now.

As far as the title matches go, Sheamus vs. Cesaro for the U.S. title saw challenger Cesaro lose in a trios match on TV on the go-home show, which only makes sense if Cesaro is winning here. Dolph Ziggler vs. Miz for the IC title is a comedy feud, and comedy is fine in undercard. R-Truth, as R-Ziggler, and Damien Sandow, as Damien Mizdow, should both be at ringside interfering. The Usos vs. Goldust & Stardust for the TV title is just a tag title match with nothing special to it. And the Divas title, with Paige vs. Nikki Bella vs. A.J. Lee, should somehow have Brie Bella involved in some form given they are going hard with her program with Nikki.

They also announced a one-hour pregame show that will feature Christian doing a Peep Show interviewing Jericho.

The key focus of this show should be to have one wild match, whether it be Cena vs. Lesnar, or Rollins vs. Ambrose, or perhaps Reigns vs. Orton, set up for a Hell in a Cell, which is the gimmick for the follow-up show on 10/26 in Dallas.

SEPTEMBER 29

There is a lot of talk about how, only one week away, there has been so little publicity about the launch of the network in the U.K., which by all rights should be the network's No. 2 market (it won't be No. 2 at first most likely because the Canadian TV version is doing far better than the streaming version), since it's second behind the U.S. in just about everything. People who have called Sky to ask about it are told they don't know anything about it. There are Internet ads for WWE Network UK, which takes you to a generic network link. The link doesn't tell you about signing up on 10/1, only pushing that Night of Champions was available on the network on Sky Box Office. However, in the U.K., it's not even on Sky Box Office but on Sky Sports 3.

OCTOBER 6

The SummerSlam PPV numbers tell a story, and it's a confusing one. The show, headlined by John Cena vs. Brock Lesnar for the WWE title, did 63,000 domestic buys and 116,000 overseas buys. For domestic buys, it's more than double what Battleground did and the most for any show since WrestleMania. Being SummerSlam, it should have done the most. Money in the Bank did 53,000, so on a percentage basis, it was up 19% from Money in the Bank domestic. Last year SummerSlam was up 22% domestic from Money in the Bank. But the difference could be more people switching to the WWE Network.

The 116,000 overseas buys is shocking, because the WWE Network debuted in more than 170 countries, but not the big ones, including the U.K., and much of Canada. But it did include Australia, New Zealand and Mexico. The 116,000 compared to 125,000 the year before with no network for the John Cena vs. Daniel Bryan main event, and 96,000 (I believe this didn't include the U.K.) the year before on a show with Lesnar vs. HHH.

Given that the percentage drop of domestic and foreign hasn't been that much different, and here it's remarkably different, (domestic down 69.6%; overseas down 7.8%) on the first PPV AFTER the network was available in 170 countries is hard to read. At first, it would seem that new network buyers in those 170 new countries would be negligible, which would be a terrible sign, but we won't know that until November and even then I don't know that WWE will break down the network numbers on a per country basis and we already know there is some increase because of the success of the Canadian launch as a television station.

Without knowing network numbers, it's impossible to tell what the domestic number means, because it being the biggest since WrestleMania should have been a given.

But under any circumstances, the international number is outstanding, but if it coincides with no international network growth after being legally available in so many new countries, then it's a mixed bag in some ways, but still more positive. If there is even a decent amount of network penetration outside the U.S. and Canada from the launch on 8/12 in the new countries, and the show did 116,000 overseas buys, that would be tremendous.

What is also notable is that in the past, Lesnar has been far more of a domestic draw than an international draw, because UFC was so much bigger in his heyday in the U.S. and Canada than it was in most of the key foreign markets.

The top matches this year were Cena vs. Lesnar, Roman Reigns vs. Randy Orton, Stephanie McMahon vs. Brie Bella, Chris Jericho vs. Bray Wyatt, Seth Rollins vs. Dean Ambrose in a lumberjack match and Rusev vs. Jack Swagger in a flag match.

Last year was Cena vs. Bryan, Lesnar vs. C.M. Punk and Alberto Del Rio vs. Christian for the world title, so this year was clearly the better show. Last year's numbers were considered bad for the show, particularly with the added expense of Lesnar.

OCTOBER 6

The WWE Network scheduled debut in the U.K. on 10/1 has been pushed back to an undetermined date. WWE stated "The launch of the WWE Network in the U.K. will be delayed given discussions with potential partners. A launch date will be announced by 11/1." Given they already have the network going and have no partners in the network anywhere but Canada (where it is a TV station rather than over-the-top), this sounds like they are moving to a TV model rather than over the top, because that would be the only reason they'd want partners. That would seem to mean the test marketing of doing it on TV in Canada was more of a success than the over the top version in the U.S. However, Brian Elliott of Fighting Spirit Magazine reported that Sky said they were not going to launch any kind of a WWE channel, at least as of two weeks ago. One thing that also could be an issue in the U.K. launch is the Sky TV deal, which includes PPVs. Sky paid WWE a huge increase in rights fees this year, largely because of a bidding war for sports content (and luckily for WWE, in the U.K., the key sports stations consider pro wrestling as sport, unlike in the U.S., which hurts their rate). NXT still airs on Sky, as do the PPVs. The NFL's deal with Sky prevents them from airing the games that Sky airs for 24 hours after completion on their similar Gamepass service. The delay used to be one week, which was a major topic among Gamepass subscribers. Another issue concerns the company's DVD and Blu Ray deal with Freemantle, because Cinedigm was looking to dump the WWE video license partially feeling the network undercut their business deal.

The WWE sent in an application to the Canadian Radio TV Commission this past week looking for approval for the WWE Network as a TV station. In its letter to the CRTC, it said that the network (Canadian TV version), "will include every past WWE, WCW and ECW." That is the sentence. I don't know if that means every TV show, which I can't even imagine, or just every PPV at some point, like the streaming network offers. The key argument is that for a non-Canadian station to be allowed to broadcast into Canada, they must not compete with an existing licensed Canadian specialty or pay TV station. The four factors used are genre, program overlap, target audience and contribution to diversity. They claim the product distributed is unique and not currently offered by any Canadian pay or specialty service. Actually the PPVs are offered by all Canadian PPV carriers which are the main lure of the network, but any cable system that gets the network on television will have okayed it to compete with its own PPVs so that shouldn't be germane. They noted no TV station in Canada dedicates a significant portion of its schedule to WWE. They claimed WWE is a sports brand (their words, not mine) that is "easily distinguished fro mother types of wrestling programming." It also stated it is not comparable to other in-ring sports programming such as MMA, boxing or college wrestling. They note that TSN and The Fight Network air MMA and boxing, but those products are different from WWE. They also claim entertainment and showmanship are heavily emphasized in WWE, but not in MMA, boxing or college wrestling. It's interesting that while WWE's television shows strong numbers in almost every age group from young to old, they claimed that the WWE network is a highly niche audience aiming at Canadian wrestling fans, "mostly young males." They say their network is not targeted at general sports viewers. They noted that the NFL Network, Golf Channel and MLB Network have been approved and they compared the service to them, and like them, they are not targeting the average sports fan, but the avid fan of a single sport.

OCTOBER 20

The WWE Network announced on 10/13 it was starting to air commercials. The 30 second commercials would only take place around the top of the hour, between shows, and they would also play if you watch something on VOD, before the beginning of the show. They lined up Pepsi, Kmart and Mattell as their first sponsors, although they have partnerships with all of them already.

OCTOBER 27

In many ways, 10/30 is the most important day for the WWE since WrestleMania, and one can argue it is the most important day of the year for the company going forward.

That's the day that the network numbers are released. Unlike the original number releases, which were important, this will be the key in getting a real gauge of the long-term. It will give a handle of international interest level, as well as some handle on renewal rates of the original 495,000 subscribers.

As of 9/30, the date the number will cover, the network was available legally and promoted to some degree in 170 countries, instead of one, as well as on television to Rogers Cable subscribers in Canada. The number announced will include whatever drop off domestically from the first wave of original subscribers, but not include any losses from the 172,000 who subscribed WrestleMania week.

The company needs to average 1.1 million subscribers during 2015 just to maintain equal cash flow (take in the amount of money that is going out), and probably closer to 1.4 million to get profitability up to pre-network days. A number announced of less than 900,000 would not be good, because even with expected January through March growth, this is, minus the U.K. and some of Canada, pretty much close to the full-fledged number that's going to be at steady state. There may be a trickled upturn in numbers with more people signing in than checking out, minus the post-Mania drop, but it'll likely be slow. If the number is less than 900,000, it shows that the international growth isn't there like expected (in the sense maybe the people internationally who wanted it in large numbers already got it) and the Canadian TV numbers on their own weren't that big. If it's 1 million or more, that says things are moving along at a solid rate and the company should be able to make a profit in 2015 with the expected more growth from some upticking and opening up the U.K. and the rest of Canada.

There seemed to be the beginnings of a stock run-up, with the usual buy on speculation, sell on results. However, the momentum lasted exactly one day, when Nathaniel August, the founder of the hedge fund Mangrove Partners, went on CNBC and noted the company at current levels (the 6/30 number was 699,750, a number they had better be, and almost surely will be, far ahead of) can not make money, and needs to double that number to make the network financially worth it (basically, to get the company back to where it was before they had this idea). He said he believed that will never happen. Analysts are thinking with HBO and others coming out with similar services that have more appeal, that in homes allocating money for such things, the WWE Network will come up short. I'm not sure if I buy that, in the sense that if WWE promotes a product people want to see and the pay-per-views have enough appeal along with other programming, the cost is low enough, and it's a worldwide product. Whether they can get the product itself and the company hot enough is more the determining point.

The stock price at press time of $13.82 per share is still in the same range it has been in since the big drop after the NBC Universal deal was announced.

On the creative end there are a lot of questions. Business has been well below par in recent weeks. They are going into Hell in a Cell with a PPV that not only doesn't include the WWE champion, but the major angle on the go-home show, involving Randy Orton in a babyface turn with Seth Rollins, has nothing to do with Orton vs. John Cena and Rollins vs. Dean Ambrose Hell in a Cell matches. Shooting the big angle on the go-home show, and not leading to a change to the match people would now want to see more and that the go-home show was totally geared around makes no sense. It would have been better to have shot the angle on the PPV after the matches they have this week play out, or on Raw the next day.

Orton vs. Cena was announced with the winner getting a shot at Brock Lesnar's WWE title.

The rushing the Orton babyface turn may be with the idea that the Orton house shows have drawn poorly with him as a heel and Dean Ambrose as the top face. An Orton turn moves Ambrose down to the No. 3 face spot at a time when they need to create a strong 1-A face and not switch Orton back. Perhaps they want to take advantage of the RKO craze, if that's not overstating things, but the storyline leading to Orton turning has gone back weeks before that started and was accelerated after Roman Reigns went down with groin surgery.

The company is also even weaker on the heel side, because with Lesnar working sparingly, if Orton turns, it's Rollins in the No. 1 spot on one show and Kane on the other. That's a disaster unless the repackaging of the Wyatts leads to at least two of them with strong singles heel pushes.

Still, this is the perfect time to push Ambrose, simply because he's got a clear field to get over. Once Reigns comes back, the spot becomes Reigns' to lose. And there's still the situation with Daniel Bryan, whenever he comes back.

As of the weekend, Lesnar was scheduled to start back on 12/8, which would be the show where they start building his title defense at the Royal Rumble, which was originally planned for Cena. The 12/8 show is the Raw episode from Greenville, SC. It's also the new date for the Slammy Awards, and they may have ideas for that show that require Lesnar to be there. It's the go-home show for TLC.

As of the weekend, Lesnar was not scheduled for either Survivor Series or TLC. WWE is in discussions regarding dates on Lesnar as far as which TV's he's working to build up Rumble. But as anyone who works for them will tell you, they could call Thursday and want him back Monday to build for Survivor Series, because they are always changing directions.

For hits, Orton did give Paul Heyman an RKO on Raw, and essentially did a babyface turn when Rollins curb stomped him. He also laid out Cena and Ambrose with RKO's in the main event. That can be viewed, especially since it involves Cena, that if he laid Cena out on TV, that the plans going forward would be a Cena win, particularly since usual WWE booking is that a guy about to make a big turn will lose his last match in his old role. Plus, based on what Rollins did by laying out Orton, that should set up Orton vs. Rollins and not Orton vs. Lesnar, for November. But by bringing Lesnar's name into the mix, if Cena wins, it's clumsy for him to win his title shot this week if they are going two more PPV shows before the match. It would only emphasize for the next two shows that there is no title match. And Orton could beat Cena and Rollins and be, at least in the eyes of creative, "new" after the turn, and the Heyman RKO could lead to a Lesnar match. If the Lesnar return is at the Rumble, the opponent isn't as important since the Rumble concept in most years is the main selling point of the show.

The rest of the Hell in a Cell lineup is Big Show vs. Rusev, Dolph Ziggler vs. Cesaro in a 2/3 fall match for the

IC title, Sheamus vs. The Miz for the U.S. title, Goldust & Stardust vs. Usos for the tag team title, Nikki Bella vs. Brie Bella in a match that was first announced that the loser would have to be the winner's "bitch" for 30 days. But on television the word "bitch" was replaced by the term "personal assistant" (probably the correct pro wrestling terminology would be servant, slave or valet) and A.J. Lee vs. Paige for the Divas title.

There was no pre-show match announced, and the pre-show was advertised around seeing the panel, which will include Heyman.

OCTOBER 27

In a letter to the Canadian Radio Television Telecommunications Commission, Rogers Cable wrote that it was WWE, and not them, who decided to put the Network on in Canada as a television station as opposed to an OTT service (it's splitting hairs, both made the decision after reaching a financial agreement). They noted that they would also be doing an OTT service in Canada that would offer the same things the service in the U.S. does as far as archived footage.

NOVEMBER 10

In many ways, 10/30 was the most important day of the year for the WWE business, because so many questions would be answered about the WWE Network, which the company essentially banked so much of its future around.

Generally, the news was bad, but not as bad at first glance, although the reaction which came across almost like a panic, may have accentuated the feeling it was bad.

The company announced that as of 9/30, they had 731,359 network subscribers, 702,883 in the United States and 28,476 in the rest of the world.

Considering that the network launched on 8/12, roughly seven weeks before this reporting period ended, in 170 countries, the 28,476 subscribers outside the U.S., which includes Canadian television subscribers through Rogers, is a number that would be beyond disastrous. And that's because it's not the real number.

If anything, that made clear, as has the decline in PPV buys outside the U.S. when the network supposedly wasn't available in all those countries, that a large percentage of the so-called U.S. audience included much of the hardcore international fan base. One person with inside knowledge of the project told us months ago that it would become clear how much of the international fan base was already getting it after the launch (at the time scheduled for later this year or early next year) would end up netting very little increase. There are key markets, most notably the U.K., as well as much of Canada, which are the WWE's No. 2 and No. 3 markets, where the network is not officially available. However, the decline in international PPVs, Night of Champions doing only 18,000 buys outside North America, despite the network not being available in numerous PPV countries, tells us that most people all over the world who want it already have it.

Besides SummerSlam, the three month period also was a period where the first two years of the Monday Night Wars and a lot of other Raws were uploaded, and that didn't have a significant effect on garnering new subscribers. Part of the issue is the company strategy of not to take down old footage on YouTube. The idea is fans discovering old footage would then be more apt to get the network, because they'll want to see more from that era. At the same time, people may feel there is enough old footage out on YouTube that it's not worth spending money to see more.

The quality of the series like Monday Night War, with the predictable spin that anyone who lived in the era would see is beyond shallow and often not close to accurate, probably made no difference. But it's not like anyone is raving about the shows either, and there's no word of mouth in the public about missing good things.

There is now about 2,500 hours of footage up, compared to 1,500 hours at launch.

WWE had projected 1 million U.S subscribers at the end of the year, and another 250,000 upon immediate launch outside the U.S. in early 2015. Obviously at this point neither goal is attainable in the originally expected time frame. If we figure a similar state of growth going forward, about 750,000 subscribers at the end of the year is where they'll be, and the big growth spurt of 2015 isn't going to happen.

Aside from a WrestleMania and Royal Rumble boost that will almost surely be temporary, it's doubtful the numbers will be significantly higher at the end of 2015.

Keep in mind that UFC, which has less interest than WWE outside the U.S., had a 62% to 38% split when it comes to Fight Pass subscribers, and Fight Pass isn't available in Mexico, Central and South America, including Brazil, the company's biggest overseas market, because they have paid television subscription services in all of those countries that are superior to the network in that they duplicate the content, plus include all the live events from start-to-finish, including PPVs. Fight Pass doesn't include television shows that air in the countries available nor does it include PPVs until months after they take place.

WWE's PPV split was 55% to 45% on shows that were PPVs everywhere including the U.K., but throwing in Canada it's 50/50 It would be reasonable to assume that when the network was released worldwide it would be 50/50, or even more than 50% outside the U.S. because there are so many countries that don't even have PPV that have a WWE fan base. Instead, it's a 96% to 4% split.

Because of the lack of U.K. and much of Canada, as well as places like Japan, Italy, Germany, India, The UAE, Thailand, Malaysia and China (and as the almost non-growth from adding 170 countries has shown, the vast majority of people in all countries who wanted the network figured out how to get it long before the official launch in their markets), it should not be quite 50/50 right now. But at very minimum it should be 65/35, meaning a real split in the neighborhood of 475,000 and 256,000, and that's, if anything, being optimistic on the U.S. end. The countries listed are all expected to officially get the network in 2015.

So they are actually way behind on the U.S. and already ahead on foreign, which I thought from day one they were selling short. But maybe they were ahead of the game, knew going in that their hardcore base internationally would order at first and pretend to be from the U.S., and thus the split would turn out closer to 80/20, based on the expectation of inflated early numbers being attributed to the U.S.

The U.K. was scheduled to launch on 11/3 on the web, iPhone, iPad and Android devices. Less than an hour before the launch, the WWE sent out word, "The launch of WWE Network in the U.K. has been delayed until further notice." As of press time, WWE has not commented past that point, but it is simple to get the network in the U.K. if people want it, they just can't sign up as being from the U.K. WWE has not commented past that point. It was also announced as scheduled to be available on 11/18 on Xbox One, Xbox 360, Amazon Fire TV, Apple Tv, Roku boxes and some Smart TVs, and will become a pay service for $9.99 U.S. starting 12/1.

The timing of this was embarrassing, given people were able to sign up from the U.K. as it was no longer geoblocked, hours before the time they were scheduled to. But the geoblocking was put back on shortly before the scheduled launch time.

The delay was due to the same reasons the 10/1 originally scheduled U.K. launch didn't happen, which was negotiations with BSkyB, even though Sky had steadfastly denied them, and WWE had first made it clear they would not be commenting on the subject. But with the U.K. tour starting on 11/5 in London, WWE released a 40 second video of Vince McMahon apologizing for the delay, and saying it was because they are still negotiating with potential partners.

The negotiations include BskyB doing a linear channel, similar to what Rogers has done in Canada. Negotiating for a linear channel would seem to be a private admittance, since none of this has been said publicly regarding what talks were about, that the Canada model was working better. With the experience of testing out the two different models, one in its biggest market and the other in its third biggest market, that gave WWE a lot of knowledge about doing it the right way for the launch in its second biggest market.

The two sides also had to work out the Survivor Series issues. BSkyB had been advertising Survivor Series in the U.K. as a PPV for 14.95 pounds ($23.92) and with the network being free for the month, they are not just undercutting the price as in the U.S., but making the event free. That would lead to the hassle of some people who have already ordered it looking for a refund. Given the long partnership between the two sides, as well as the lengthy new contract which WWE got a major increase in rights fees, they have to work out a deal on that account. BSkyB was aware when they signed the contract about the PPVs eventually moving to the network, so that wasn't an issue. Making a show they have been advertising for a PPV free is a different animal. Plus when the contract was signed, the idea was BSkyB would be getting all the PPVs this year as exclusives since the network launch in the U.K. wasn't originally to be until 2015. These may not be the only reasons for the delay, but we've been able to confirm that they are two of the key reasons.

We also know that in Germany, the deal was done similarly, which may be why Germany doesn't officially get the network yet. The idea was they would get PPVs for a period of time, with the idea they should promote it hard and for the short-term rather than long-term, because in 2015, the German PPV business would be going away.

Sky's made two different comments were in different forms of social media. The first, because they were getting hammered by WWE fans who blamed them for the delay, wrote, "Please be advised that the delay on the WWE Network is in no way related to Sky. As previously advised, this is an independent service which Sky will not be providing."

While it's true the delay was ultimately a call by WWE, to say it is in no way related to Sky just isn't accurate.

On Twitter, after similar complaints, they wrote: "We understand that the WWE Network release date has been delayed and this isn't a decision that we have made and instead it was made by the WWE. You can get some confirmation on this here on our Community Forum. I appreciate that the delay is frustrating and would suggest directing any questions about it to the WWE themselves."

Besides adding more archival content, they are also planning on rolling out a resume play and watch list feature by the end of the year.

What appears to have happened is the Canadian launch going strong made it appear television was more successful and Canada was a good test market considering they made the over-the-top choice in the U.S. and it would be hard to change. But in time, the Canadian market's percentage of buyers at a higher price of $12.99 for television, with a far weaker service since it had the live stream but very little archival programming, was about the same per capita as the U.S. at $9.99, so they say. There is a chance they used math with the idea that 700,000 U.S. subscribers and available 20 percent of Canada would equal 14,000, so per caps are equal. If they are doing that, that's not the case because while they claim 700,000, the real number is nowhere close to that because so many internationals are listed as American. Plus, there are Canadians in Rogers market who get the better service already.

And even if not, using 700,000 as the American number, it still shows current superiority of a TV version, because you're doing the same with a weaker product (very little archived content, mostly just the live stream) and a higher price. But even with that, the difference may not mean going in with a partner makes sense, because with a partner, there becomes a revenue split. The U.K. launch was to be the exact same service as the U.S., including the same undercutting of the existing market PPV price.

But what isn't as bad is that the 702,883 U.S. was up from 697,752 three month earlier. This was during a period where, in theory, 495,000 subscribers had come due. I had anticipated a significantly lower U.S. number out of quarter three and significantly higher international numbers, which again also could actually be correct. But the fact is that 168,000 people had already dropped it by 6/30, long before the six-month commitment, so both the growth was less than expected and the big projected drop after six months didn't happen because that drop had already happened intermittently over the prior period.

Over the months of July through September, there were 286,000 new orders and 255,000 people who either canceled or didn't renew. There were 34,000 orders between 8/12 and 9/30 who officially claimed to be out of the U.S., and of those, 6,000 canceled after one month.

The net number of new orders listed for the U.S. (252,000 new orders, 249,000 cancellations) was 3,131. On the surface, that you could argue the number of new orders was really impressive because it's more new orders than during Mania season, but the number of cancellations is also alarming. But some of that is misleading because there were probably close to 137,000 homes listed as new orders that had previously ordered the network during that period, likely for SummerSlam. Many of them also likely canceled so are counted in both categories.

The number of people not renewing indicates that the 90 percent satisfaction survey is flawed. The company was very vague on what people were watching. Unlike months ago when they'd list the top ten shows viewed each week on their television shows, when investors asked what people were watching most on the network, past the vague and obvious answer of live events more than anything, they declined to answer the question. They said 90 percent of the subscribers will tune into the network at least once a week and 99 percent will do so once a month.

There have been 971,000 different homes who have tried out the service. That number is actually high, because it probably figures in twice people who ordered the service, canceled it at one point, and then reordered from a new e-mail address figuring that they needed to do so since they bailed on the six month commitment. It is 971,000 different e-mail addresses used to order, but how many different actual homes is less, maybe not by a lot, but nobody knows for sure.

There have been 423,000 individual cancellations or non-renewals so far. That's 44 percent of the different e-mail orders that have canceled. That percentage isn't perfect. In some cases, it is one person canceling twice with different e-mails. In others, it is somebody counted twice as different subscribers who canceled once. But that is close to what a source close to WWE who also told us about the large number of foreign subscribers early on also noted to us a few weeks back was a 40 percent cancellation rate. It also means that 183,000 homes that canceled at one point (19 percent, give or take the above variables), later renewed. So it means there are 240,000 who totally dropped without coming back, and another 183,000 of the current 731,000, who are picking and choosing months already, a percentage likely to increase. There are 548,000 who have ordered since the inception of the product and have never canceled. I'd call that a 56 percent satisfaction rate and another 19 percent somewhat satisfaction rate.

For that reason, even though the 172,000 who ordered the week of WrestleMania were not due and not figured into the 703,000 U.S. number (which is a one month old number being reported now), there may not be a significant drop from them at all. Those who weren't going to renew, for the most part, had stopped paying already. So there is no reason to expect a decline from this number in the fourth quarter, except....

The response to the bad numbers accentuated how bad they were. The first was to eliminate the six-month commitment, so you can order month-by-month at $9.99, with no discount for long-term purchases.

That somewhat changes the dynamics because the PPV shows are now more important, because the key reason to order are the PPV shows. Before, you only in theory needed a key show every six months to drive people in and they'd pay nearly $60, slightly more than the PPV price (except for WrestleMania). The concept is that people will find it a bargain to get so many PPVs at a low price, thinking the price point was why PPV business was struggling. Plus, with so many people only ordering two a year, the idea is you'd get them to pay about the same for the year, they'd get 12 instead of two, and without splitting it with the cable companies, the company takes in more revenue from the shows. And even now, they are taking in more revenue from every show except WrestleMania. But that doesn't figure into network expenses. That's why the company is losing money this year after being very profitable on the wrestling end itself annually before the network started, dating back to the turnaround of business in 1997.

With a month-to-month commitment, the PPVs still have to sell you on paying for them individually, like before, although the price is far less and you also get all the network content, so it's a better deal. Orders should be way, way up. For example, the WrestleMania bump, some starting in late January, others starting in late March, should be much bigger this year as everyone will see it as a $9.99 purchase. Before, many saw it that way, and knew ahead of time they were canceling. Others saw it believing it was really a six-month commitment that really costs $59.94. The post-WrestleMania decline in late April, that didn't happen this year, should also be very large next year.

This move had to be done. It looks like a backward step for WWE, but the consumers, by their actions and response to the network, forced it on them.

Vince McMahon, who said less during this conference call than any in recent memory, leaving it almost all to CFO and Chief Strategy Officer George Barrios, tried to spin the network numbers positively, using junk stats, such as SummerSlam ranking No. 1 in Twitter ratings and on social media that day.

"The Network as well has achieved a high level of audience engagement, 90 percent of our subscribers access the network at least once a week and it's just extraordinary in terms of engagement. By the way, in terms of that engagement and having gone through the revenue reverse periods, in our approval rating we feel that's why we've come up with the $9.99 per month, no commitment, cancel anytime, that's obviously like Netflix.

"So again, based on the renewal periods we've gone through and the engagement and the approval rating, we are really certain that that's just definitely the way to go."

WWE had instituted a $12.99 monthly price, but only 23,000 of the 286,000 new orders came at that price. People were already smart to the system that they didn't have to live up to the commitment and were ordering at $9.99 and then canceling. Because of that, this change only reflects the reality of a large percentage of the consumers.

The other change is that WWE will be offering the entire month of November for free. Anyone who signs up will get the service free, and start being billed on 12/1, although obviously they can cancel at the end of the free period. Occasional free weekends or weeks, or periods free for new consumers to try out the product are part of most subscription models. HBO and Showtime do free weekends a few times a year. The UFC Fight Pass offers a free month, although doesn't push it hard (and UFC doesn't push its price as much as push its content, while WWE pushes price first). The general rule for all these services is that a large percentage of those who order the free month become subscribers, so it's not a bad move. WWE has already done free periods numerous times this year, but always coincided the period to not include a live PPV.

The free-of-charge offer does not include those with Rogers Cable in Canada, which was a terrible P.R. move because Canadians saw the same episodes of Smackdown and Raw promoting it as free. It's already inundated with $9.99 plus even though it's also $11.99 in Canada. In the U.K., it will be free through 11/30, and in all cases, it is not a free month but just a free period through that date. For those in the rest of Canada who don't have what I'd call legal access to the network, as well as people in other countries, I hope the announcers don't go on the show early on making fun of people for actually paying for the show when they could be seeing it for free, even though they aren't supposed to be able to. Those who are current subscribers that unsubscribe, are able to then sign up for the free month, so it is not just for those who have never sampled it, or those who sampled it and previously gave it up. It's free for anyone who wants it to be free, except the Canadian TV subscribers.

The announcement was made on television on 10/31 during Smackdown in a taped piece with Vince McMahon. In the video they aired footage of the crowd wildly chanting, "Yes," which was supposed to be enthusiasm toward his announcement. In actuality, the chant was taped at the 10/28 Smackdown tapings in Houston, when Big Show announced that Daniel Bryan may need surgery, and asked the crowd to chant "Yes" in unison together which they would send to him as a way to boost his spirits. Between that and using the Ultimate Warrior promo the day before he died as a selling point in network commercials which focus heavily on wrestlers who have passed away young, this has not been the classiest period for the promotion.

Going free explains the weak Survivor Series main event, because the lure of Survivor Series now is "free Survivor Series," not "let's put on a compelling series of matches that people will pay extra to see or a strong title match to get new paid subscribers this month." The goal is to get a big audience watching, obviously produce a good show without giving away a money match, and they should shoot a major angle for TLC in particular, or Royal Rumble, to convince viewers to now spend money the next month.

However, some of that changed on Raw on 11/3. The main event with Team Cena vs. Team Authority was decreed by Vince McMahon that should Team Authority lose, they would no longer be The Authority. It's as heavy a stipulation as they could put on that match, but it's also a stipulation done a few years back in a John Laurinaitis match. As far as a PPV went, that stipulation didn't move numbers that much.

Currently there are 11,000 tickets out and 4,000 unsold for Survivor Series in St. Louis. They are doing local four-tickets-for-the-price-of-three family pack discounts on the unsold inventory. That's not unusual for a WWE house show, but to my knowledge it's rare for a PPV.

Raw was also changed because John Cena wasn't on the show. The original advertising for the show was that Cena was going to put together his team, but with him not at Raw, nothing like that happened. Cena was believed to be shooting scenes for one of the movies he's working on, but WWE has not said officially what the story was. But he was in Syracuse, NY, flew to Los Angeles to work on Monday, and then flew to London for a house show on Wednesday. I'm not sure how far in advance they knew. They did no backstage pre-taping the week before so he could at least have a presence on the show in some form and they could advance him putting together the team had they known in advance.

In Buffalo, when the show started, they just announced that Cena was unable to be there and offered refunds for the first 20 minutes of the show. There are two Raw shows left and not one match was announced on TV for Survivor Series, but it's not that big a deal anymore since it's a free show.

With Randy Orton starting to film "The Condemned 2" on 11/11, which explains the injury angle done on Raw where Seth Rollins laid him out with a curb stomp off the announcers table onto the ring steps, with Orton bleeding heavily (hard way juice), he is expected to be off television for a while and miss Survivor Series, which is in his home city. Orton had already been removed from the first week of the European tour where he had to be the headliner on one of the tours. He was also removed from the advertising in St. Louis for Survivor Series as soon as the movie dates were finalized. Orton had only been scheduled for the first week of the European tour, with Chris Jericho coming in for the shows Orton wasn't originally scheduled to be on. Somebody tweeted to Orton that they didn't want him turning face because he's better as a heel, and he wrote back, "Amen to that."

Right now, Orton is listed as being back for the post-Christmas house show tour, but those WWE listings are often inaccurate. He was removed from advertising for the Madison Square Garden show on 12/26 as far as the lineup went, but they can't very well advertise him for house matches until he does his "surprise" return after shooting a long-term injury angle.

While no matches were finalized, the Rusev U.S. title win over Sheamus that was put on the WWE Network as a special bonus on 11/3 after Raw was originally supposed to be on the PPV. Dean Ambrose vs. Bray Wyatt in a singles match was also scheduled and released by WWE, although not mentioned for Survivor Series on Raw. The A.J. Lee vs. Nikki Bella Divas title match was pushed, but only said to be coming soon, so even though that was also scheduled for Survivor Series, it's not a definite until it's announced (and even then it can change). It appeared they were building some sort of a tag team situation with either a four-team match with Goldust & Stardust, The Miz & Damien Mizdow, The Usos and Los Matadores, or a Survivor Series elimination involving those teams.

The main event is still open, but it was announced as a five-on-five elimination match for the power. Big Show asked to be on the team, so he's a likely third person with Cena & Dolph Ziggler. The Authority team will have Seth Rollins & Kane. If Show is on Cena's team, Mark Henry would likely be on the HHH team. They were teasing the idea of Rusev on The HHH team, which would probably put Sheamus on the Cena team. That leaves one spot left for each side. They showed The Authority scouting Ryback, who has been given his old push back, although Ryback has been positioned as a face, which makes him more likely on Team Cena. On Smackdown, Kane tried to recruit Ryback for the team, and Ryback walked out on him. HHH also could wrestle on his team.

What was also notable was the return of Vince McMahon and the tease that they were building an issue with HHH & Stephanie vs. Vince. That was the original plan for last year's WrestleMania, with the original plan to be HHH vs. Steve Austin, with the idea that either HHH & Stephanie or Vince getting control of the company Vince built, and Vince, to save his company, would go to his most hated enemy and biggest rival, Austin, to save the WWE. The Rock was the second choice if Austin wouldn't do it. Even after being advertised, Vince never returned and they dropped the idea.

We are already hearing from subscribers who canceled upon hearing the announcement this past week of the free month, then got a new e-mail address, and signed up, getting it free, although I doubt that will be widespread. Another aspect of this is what will be the reaction of the cable companies that still carry the show after DirecTV and Dish Network have dropped it. It was already negative with the idea WWE was undercutting them with the lower price, but now making the show free while they are charging $54.95 for HD is going to speed up the decline of PPV for good. One of the reasons losses weren't as great is because the PPV numbers in the U.S. held up better than expected, even with the announcers essentially insulting the audience for overpaying.

In the U.K., they are already pushing Survivor Series as a PPV event, while it is likely to also be offered for free, unless they hold the launch off until after that show. But in the U.S., the PPVs on inDemand are still bringing in $750,000 per month in revenue and SummerSlam brought in double that. I'm guessing most of those people won't get the network because they live in a part of the country that doesn't have reliable service or they don't have a computer. Even if half buy the network, that's only adding $120,000, so it's a sizeable monthly net loss.

It also now makes sense why Brock Lesnar isn't on Survivor Series, and isn't scheduled for a match until Rumble. But it doesn't make sense why the match for the shot at Lesnar was held in October when he's not back until late January. In fact, the free show should have been the match for the title shot with a hot angle involving Lesnar (using this show without him wrestling in lieu of one of his contracted TV dates) on the tail end.

But Lesnar himself is now a real question. Battleground, in July, the previous "B" show, without Lesnar, did 31,000 North American buys and 68,000 international buys on PPV. It featured John Cena retaining the WWE title in a four-way over Roman Reigns, Kane and Randy Orton.

Night of Champions, the last reported PPV, in September, with the Lesnar vs. Cena rematch from SummerSlam, did 30,000 North American buys and 18,000 international buys, while at the same time network numbers were almost identical. There should have been a 2,000 drop naturally because the Rogers 20% of Canada would figure to be about 2,000 PPV buys in July that wouldn't be there in September, so essentially the domestic is flat.

The 50,000 drop internationally is partially due to Night of Champions airing on Sky Sports (part of the Sky subscription package) as opposed to being on Sky Box Office (a PPV that would be counted). The difference wouldn't be 50,000, but it could be half of that. The rest of the drop could be Mexico, which didn't officially get the WWE Network in July, but did in September, but the total international new orders would say that would be minuscule.

Short form, worldwide, new orders two months later for a show with Lesnar were less than a show without Lesnar. Lesnar clearly had value on some of his PPV matches, particularly the first two. This year's SummerSlam, which really had nothing but Lesnar vs. Cena, held up far better than it should have on the PPV side. But after the squash finish, coming immediately back to a rematch without good storytelling didn't work. You could argue the match story at SummerSlam was the wrong story to build an immediate rematch (my gut strongly told me that from the start). You could argue that Lesnar was needed in September or the U.S. decline would have been worse, but if he made a difference, it would also show up in the PPV numbers, like it did at SummerSlam. The rematch was too quick, or the SummerSlam match was the wrong match for an immediate rematch, or both. But that's water under the bridge.

We now have a very different economy and Lesnar's contract expires at WrestleMania. While he's open to doing more than two more matches, the economics now seem to show that his contract is too high to make sense for anything but Rumble and Mania.

The idea for WrestleMania had been for Lesnar to lose the title to Roman Reigns, with the idea of making Reigns the new face of the company with Lesnar as the best possible guy to win it from.

But will that match have the same impact if it's known it is Lesnar's last match ahead of time? Before, the expectation was that Lesnar would be signed to a new deal, and probably have a babyface run. That still could happen. But can they afford that price tag? Would he be interested in wrestling with a lower price tag? Plus, he is going to play UFC against WWE because it's a lock he can get a good UFC deal.

The funny thing is, I think the UFC audience is smaller and those still there are far more understanding that fighting is a skill and a guy who is big and strong can't walk in and dominate based on size, super athletic ability and an NCAA championship wrestling pedigree. Lesnar did just that six years ago to a degree, but he's six years older and UFC is six years more advanced. Lesnar brought a ton of casuals to PPV and his fights became major events, and UFC is missing that. But I don't know if that'll be the case coming back.

He'll be 38, and while heavyweights can last longer, it's usually the hard striking heavyweights, not the wrestling or submission heavyweights (although Randy Couture was the exception, but Couture was a unique person and Lesnar has not devoted the time Couture had to the sport, and Couture is still the exception to every rule). Yes, I can already see the idea that the old Lesnar did what he did with Diverticulitis and he's cured, but that cured of diverticulitis card was somewhat played with the Alistair Overeem fight, which was three years ago. At, 38, he won't be as fast, or as strong, or as good an athlete. He doesn't have the skill and experience or one punch knockout power and skill to land it to make up for those declines, like a Mark Hunt, still a top contender at 40.

But with UFC looking for an answer, he may still draw a big number for a curiosity buy for his return.

The argument then becomes should Lesnar lose to Cena, which makes all these PPV shows without him seem silly. The whole idea was to protect Lesnar so the Reigns win is the most impressive it can be over a monster. Lesnar already did one lame duck WrestleMania match in 2004 with Bill Goldberg, and it wasn't pretty, because of the crowd reaction, and if Reigns beats Lesnar with the same kind of crowd reaction, it will kill his inauguration as the top star.

I don't think that will happen, but it already has happened and you can't overlook that it could.

But some of that was that Goldberg was also leaving so the crowd turned on both of them.

But the only other alternative is a Cena win, and Reigns beating Cena, or getting the title on Seth Rollins and Reigns beating Rollins. The latter will be a weak inauguration and unless they have some super strong other matches, it's not a WrestleMania main event, and the whole idea of the Reigns inauguration was for it to be a huge WrestleMania main event.

Perhaps Cena can also work as the symbolic passing of the torch, but that would have been better maybe at SummerSlam or the 2016 WrestleMania with the idea of Cena as the challenger, and the dream match that people have never seen. No matter what, a key component of Reigns being a success as the new star has to be a couple of killer fresh opponents for him to work with. Lesnar could fit one role. Perhaps Rusev, if he's protected, could be another, and Cena would be a third. Rollins can be an opponent, but he can't be the guy they are counting on to get Reigns to the level the top star in the company should be at, nor is Randy Orton, Kane, or Bray Wyatt.

As far as the economics of a special guest, like a Lesnar, Dwayne Johnson, or a Floyd Mayweather, let's just set the cost at $1.5 million (and keep in mind simply what they pay the talent for the show is only part of the costs, because they have to pay them for television appearances, costs of flights in, lodging and all kinds of perks which runs true costs up). For a non-Mania show, that would need 75,000 worldwide buys. For Mania at the higher price, that would need closer to 50,000 worldwide buys, which the top talent on a show like that is probably worth. But today, whether it's Mania or any show, they are going to have to be worth 188,000 extra purchasers individually of the network that weren't going to order without them. Is that viable? We are too early in the game to answer that question, but subscriber numbers didn't move and he was in two main events during the quarter. Would they have dropped if he wasn't on those shows? Maybe, may not, but it's hard to believe they'd have dropped 188,000 from what they did for both months, even though this year's SummerSlam did not feel like a SummerSlam caliber show past the main event. Then the question becomes, how much do you spend on Mania. Is it still Mania with no big money guest stars and at a $9.99 price tag? Mania payoffs and revenue would be the biggest of the year by far because they are still going to do something in the range of a $9 million or more at a live gate, and subs will be up that month. But the Mania profitability has been down the past two years, after the most successful show ever in company history when it came to pure profits for the first Rock vs. Cena match.

These announced network numbers would be a financial disaster for the company, except they aren't. The company has made cuts of another $15 million to $20 million per year in expenses, to add to the $20 million to $25 million in cuts talked about in July.

That's the reason the stock price didn't nosedive, even though revenue was far lower than analysts expected, and the network numbers had a shocking lack of growth based on most expectations. In fact, the stock, at $13.39 per share at press time, rebounding early in the week after a drop when the financials first came out, is close to where it was before the announcement, leaving the company with a $1.01 billion market capitalization.

The Wall Street consensus was revenues for the quarter would be $133.2 million, and they ended up being $120,183,000, partially because of higher network expectations. But Wall Street wasn't aware of the latest round of cost cutting. Company losses of $5,921,000 for the quarter were less than the $12.8 million projected even with the higher revenue projections.

Another reason is that the television situation doesn't look so bad after competing new deals in Canada and India. The total value of the seven key deals (U.S., Canada, Mexico, Germany, U.K., India and I believe The Philippines) was $130 million in 2013 and is contractually listed to escalate to $235 million in 2018. It's not quite the level promised, but these are numbers that are contractually guaranteed no matter how hot the product is or isn't, and is a backbone to keep them in the black even if the network never ends up close to projections.

For the first nine months of the year, WWE has lost $28,454,000. If they are to average 750,000 subscribers in quarter four, figuring an increase from the U.K. to some degree will be coming, the company's own projections (and keep in mind their internal projections have been skewed of late to the side where things look worse, not better, one of the reasons they "over performed" this quarter) is they will lose another $11.7 million and finish the year with $40.2 million in losses. Part of the reason losses will be heavier than this quarter as projected is because they are budgeting $5 million to $7 million in the upcoming quarter to produce both new episodes of Total Divas and unnamed new network programming, although Total Divas does turn a profit per episode based on the rights fees paid by E! The annual losses are down from the $45 million to $52 million in losses guidance when they had projected 1 million subscribers at the end of the year domestic alone with no international roll out.

For 2015, the current projection is that they can break even at about 750,000 subscribers on a daily average for the year. Unlike previously, where the feeling was still would be a steadily increasing number, right now it is more likely to be a big number in January and March, and then start falling off in April. To break even and pay for the current dividend over the course of the year, that will right now require about 1,150,000 subscribers, on average, for the course of the year. While that seemed feasible three months ago, it doesn't seem so today, so unless the dividend is cut again, it really can't be justified paying out $36.2 million per year, most of which goes to the McMahon family.

To get the company back to the $50 million to $55 million in profits it was doing before spending on the network started, they would need to average 1,250,000 subscribers for the year. To show how much the cuts have meant, that figure was closer to 1,900,000 subscribers to reach the prior level of profitability and 1,300,000 to break even when it was first budgeted. The 1,250,000 figure still may be possible in time, but it won't be any time soon. People cancelling the six month commitment and essentially forcing them to do the month-by-month deal the way they did because the public was already choosing to do so on their own and forced their hand, greatly changed the game.

There are questions regarding far more market competition with competitors in other entertainment forms getting into the game that have more widespread interest, whether it is major league sports or HBO or Showtime. While Netflix was just recently the hot thing, and it was the success of Netflix that led to WWE doing this in this manner in the first place, Netflix stock has gone down hard. But that's because there was optimism that Netflix would be in 60 to 90 million homes. They are in 36 million now and growth the last quarter was less than one million, but that's still growth, they are wildly profitable, and their stock still got hit hard.

There are other key questions regarding the network. Some feel that pro wrestling isn't hot right now, and there are already five hours of free television on the air with matches pitting top stars against top stars and endless angles. Frequently, key PPV matches are rematched on Raw and the Raw result negated the value of the PPV result. With the network, that's not as big a thing because it's a $9.99 purchase instead of a $54.95 purchase. But there are only so many hours in a day, and most people's lives don't revolve around wrestling, particularly when the average fan watching on television is a male 39 or 40 years old. And if you go to the local house shows, those fans aren't even going. The TV tapings attract a younger male crowd and the house shows attract kids with their parents along with a lesser amount of the younger male crowd. So the bulk of their viewing audience doesn't even attend the rare live events in the market.

Raw of late has been viewed in about 2.62 million homes live in the U.S., and maybe another 260,000 via DVR each week. Those numbers will probably go up about ten percent in January when football ends. Perhaps 475,000 to 500,000 is the number of homes willing to pay extra for more wrestling. It's not like any of those viewers don't know about the network. It's hammered to death to them. They probably know the network price better than they know the next PPV main event, or for that matter, who holds any of the titles including the heavyweight title. It's not a lack of promotion, and it's certainly not overpriced. You could move those numbers with a more compelling product, and more compelling PPVs. No doubt. They are still slow in rolling out new stars and getting them to the top. The Shield and Bray Wyatt debuted a long time ago now, and Wyatt has just gotten a reboot, The Shield has broken up and are the top guys in the promotion with the exception of John Cena and Randy Orton. There is great talent in NXT that can come to the main roster and contribute right now. Whether that talent will be money talent is a different question. What I can almost guarantee, because I'd be right unless they have a Rock or Steve Austin level star who can overcome slow booking and get over on their own demeanor, or a super worker that everyone likes like Daniel Bryan who becomes a cause, is that nobody in NXT will be a money player if they aren't booked like a money player. The company did do that with The Shield and Wyatt, and they were key parts of business at least stabilizing. The funny thing is the PPV business was ticking slightly upward when they made the call to kill it.

When it comes to the network, virtually all the archival footage and documentaries that were being pushed, aside from pushing things with people like C.M. Punk, Jeff Hardy and Ultimate Warrior, for different reasons, has been the late 1995 to 2001 period of time. That does make sense to focus on. It was the most popular that pro wrestling has been in this country with the possible exception of the early 50s, a period that is simply too far back.

They should have a set weekly schedule as opposed to what I call mish-mash programming past we know when Main Event, NXT and Superstars air.

Due to cost cutting, no original programming, like a second Legends House or another Tough Enough, has been filmed. The usage of historical footage has been disappointing. The talk of related non-wrestling programming seems to have been dropped, and I'm not sure it'll work. UFC is currently thinking out of the box, doing live events with Invicta and with other groups, and there is talk of adding kickboxing footage, boxing footage and footage of other combat sports. I'm not sure what would be complimentary footage for wrestling. There is also the threatening part. UFC could sign up Invicta, or another MMA group, or even one of the groups that air on AXS for live Friday night specials since UFC rarely runs Fridays. They air Nevada Athletic Commission hearings. WWE has done no thinking outside the box. The equivalent, a live Friday night ROH special, or a weekly or monthly New Japan, Dragon Gate or NOAH show would be something never considered. Why be enemies with foreign companies that aren't ever going to be real competition and if New Japan you perceive can be a threat in some markets, then go with PWG, Dragon Gate and ROH, which never will be. UFC this past week paid Invicta enough money to run a show and stay in business. Invicta got exposure. The fighters got a little name recognition. And the ones who stand out, at some point, are probably going to end up in UFC someday. Do you think if WWE had the same policy with a PWG to air its shows every few months, and paid them similar to what UFC pays Invicta, that PWG is turning down guaranteed money and their talent isn't thrilled to be performing before hardcore fans worldwide instead of just 400 people?

If you ask why, it's because that's how people in pro wrestling think and have always thought. But UFC is the same business model and they are doing exactly that. Now is that turning around their network business, not at all, and this wouldn't either. But there's no reason not to do that. The worst is it may create interest at a small level on some guys who they can then bring in. And perhaps no promotion will want to work with them.

Perhaps these ideas will be nixed based on cost cutting to begin with. They've cut back on pre-and-post game shows, and what one would consider an obvious idea, a daily or weekly news and talk show (like UFC does with UFC Tonight which has been steadily increasing its audience as a "go to" show because they always break news on it) has either never been considered even though that was one of those ideas that myself, and many in the company, thought was an obvious no brainer for the network. Again, shows like that do cost money and right now spending more money is not the ideas they are looking for.

I don't know if there is anything that can make a major change. But you can also program the old footage in the way it aired in the first place, weekly episodic television. Whether it's Mid South, AWA, Stampede, World Class,

WCW, WWF TV or old house shows, you could have a specific night for a promotion and release the shows. Some, like Mid South, were written to be compelling and viewed on a weekly basis. Most others that really isn't as much of the case. Again, the heyday of most of that is the 80s, and the reality is, most fans of that era have moved on and aren't going to relive it, and only a small percentage of modern fans will want to understand things that happened before they were fans or even born. And the reality is also that the live stream isn't that important, because with the exception of live events, consumers are mostly watching what they want, when they want. An idea like putting old WCW Saturday shows on Saturday at 6:05 p.m., and follow with a Saturday night WWF house show from the 70s, 80s or 90s, is not a bad idea at all. But in this day and age when it comes to the old programming, people will watch when they want, but the knowledge of when it's coming regularly will encourage and have it in their minds to think about watching. There has been no attempt to even try anything like that. They already own this footage so it's no significant added cost like producing Tough Enough would be.

The funny thing is, everything in the last paragraph was what I would have expected from the network when it was launched. The other ideas would have been things I wouldn't have thought possible when the network started, not that they were bad ideas, but there is a weird mentality about wrestling that doesn't exist in many other businesses, with the idea of presenting yourself as the only thing that exists, which came from the mentality from promotional wars. But this is not a competitive warring wrestling environment anymore. That day is over. There is a major league and nothing is going to change that they are the major league and nobody can challenge them as the major league unless they just go completely off the rudder. As much as people complain about the current product, which is lacking spark right now, it is still okay, the negatives aren't strong negatives and the big shows usually deliver. It's just stale on the personalities side and antiseptic on the delivery side, it's not real, but it needs to feel more real and less scripted and the 50/50 game needs to be tweaked. Really, there needs to be a much larger roster for television with more guys in the 90/10 category, some in the 10/90 category and less in the 50/50 category, at least on television. Unlike in other eras where top guys were booked as top guys, what we have now is a very talented roster of midcard workers and fewer true main eventers, which is not about the talent but the presentation.

The day of pretending nobody else exists has been broken to a degree, as WWE's web site will mention other promotions (usually not TNA), and it's a silly mindset that is completely antiquated to begin with. All companies should be in the business with the mindset of not insulting the intelligence of their consumer base, because they have easy access to info and it serves no purpose. It's just a holdover mentality from a different era.

Part of the problem is few associated with the network knows or understands the wrestling product worldwide. The ideas I've outlined will not make a significant difference in business. They are just ideas that may create some buzz programming that will lead to the network being viewed in a more cool manner by some (with the current international groups), or in a cool nostalgic manner for others (an older audience that watches the TV and I'm betting has been slow to embrace the network). There is nothing cool about the network past that you can watch NXT if you're so inclined, the quarterly NXT big show, and the PPV's for $9.99. The old stuff is put on with zero context. Imagine a TV station looking for soap opera nostalgia and then putting on individual episodes at no particular time and in no particular order? The documentaries feature dated interviews and are, in today's context, woefully slanted, which you'd expect, but the whole point is, the fact you'd expect it is one of the reasons they mean nothing. Wrestling presented as it was, in weekly episodic form would inherently get people up to date on storylines and in many cases, get them a little interested in what happens next. It is dated, but there is all kinds of stuff from the 80s on television today that has an audience. If they were presented out of order, with no promotion, or time slot (even if just to DVR and watch at your convenience), with no schedule, I can pretty much guarantee the interest and audience for those shows would be minuscule in comparison to what it is now and those TV stations that present those shows would be doing far worse.

Actual revenue from the network, PPV and other video-on-demand services was $26,119,000 in the quarter. Of that, $22,468,000 million came from the network, as on the average day during the quarter there were 723,174 subscribers, so they average $10.36 in revenue (whatever splits they have are counted as revenue to the company, whereas on PPV, the only revenue listed is after splits) per subscriber because of the $12.99 orders in

Canada or those who ordered single months at the higher price point. The other $3,651,000 came from PPV.

NOVEMBER 24

WWE CFO George Barrios was at the Wells Fargo Conference on 11/12 talking the WWE Network and future business. There wasn't much of note said past what at this point seems like the ridiculous notion that the network at a steady state would end up at between 2 million and 4 million subscribers. He did say that their research has shown shorter events like "Slam City" are being watched more on mobile devices, while longer events like the PPV shows are being watched more on television sets. He said they are looking at adding more short-form content to the network. When asked about the most-watched programming, he said PPV events by far are watched the most, and said the next tier down is Main Event, the NXT quarterly specials (specials and not the weekly TV show) and the Raw pre-show. Next is Legends House and Monday Night War, and the least watched is the old territorial footage and old PPV events. Barrios said that HBO and CBS adding over the top services will only benefit them because consumers will be more familiar with the technology. Regarding the issue of password sharing and asked how do you stop it, he said, "You don't." He said if the company saw rampant abuse, they may take action but they are not shutting down accounts over that reason. The UFC Fight Pass only allows a certain number of devices logging in from a single password at any time, as does Netflix. Some have theorized that's one of the reasons WWE numbers aren't moving.

DECEMBER 29

As much as they try to kill it, PPV isn't dying as fast as people expected. The 2014 Survivor Series on 11/23 in St. Louis, a show offered for free on the WWE Network as opposed to even being part of the monthly $9.99 package, still did 103,000 worldwide buys.

The number was broken down as 33,000 in North America and 70,000 overseas. This wasn't the undercutting of PPV but actually giving the show away in the United States, as well as much of the world.

Of that 33,000, one would expect between 10,000 and 15,000 came from Canada, where much of the country from a legal standpoint can't get the WWE Network (it is only available to those with Rogers Cable, and it should be noted that it's at a higher price than in the U.S., and it was not offered for free in November). The vast majority of the foreign purchases came from the U.K., where the network also is not available.

The number was an increase over the 21,000 North American buys and 35,000 international buys for Hell in a Cell on 10/26 in Dallas. But a direct North American comparison is that it was $9.99 on the WWE Network and still had the long-term commitment attached to that price. So in theory, the number of WWE network users should have skyrocketed with the free month, yet PPV buys increased 57% over the prior month. The idea that Survivor Series is bigger than Hell in a Cell is not the case. In 2011, Survivor Series was bigger because Dwayne Johnson worked Survivor Series. But in 2012, Hell in a Cell did 157,000 domestic buys to 125,000 for Survivor Series, and last year Hell in a Cell did 135,000 domestic buys to 98,000 for Survivor Series.

The number is only a surprise given one would think the free aspect would have held down the number. There are people who simply won't order the WWE Network because of an aversion to things like that, and others who don't get good enough service or had a bad experience with the network on earlier shows. For whatever reason, perhaps because far more log in at the same time, my problems with the WWE Network as far as freezing up as umpteen times greater than with Fight Pass (which sometimes has problems that get rectified usually within seconds) and New Japan World (where I've yet to have a problem, even for live events). Also keep in mind when comparing numbers to last year, that in the U.S., only inDemand still carries WWE on PPV, with both the Dish Network and DirecTV dropping it, although there are rumors they will carry WrestleMania in 2015 because of how well it did last year.

But if we look at the domestic numbers this year, they are 45,000 for Extreme Rules, 29,000 for Payback, 53,000 for Money in the Bank, 31,000 for Battleground, 63,000 for SummerSlam, 30,000 for Night of Champions and 21,000 for Hell in a Cell. The network numbers during that entire period were largely stagnant, so it's not like the numbers would vary based on anything except interest in the shows. So it's more that this year's Hell in a Cell was not that interesting as much as PPV was dying, because the 33,000 here was in the same ballpark as Payback, Battleground and Night of Champions. The stips of The Authority having to leave, and perhaps the late tease of Sting being there (although I doubt Sting meant anything major to that number unless it was replay buys, because there was no walk up at all for the live event so when it came to general public, either not enough people knew to have made a difference, or they did but it wasn't something that got people on the fence to want to see it once that story got out). It was a strong stipulation, but whatever it was, it was really a stronger international number than all the other shows but SummerSlam.

The 70,000 international would have been the second largest since WrestleMania, trailing only the 82,000 international for SummerSlam. The network was also free in most international markets, roughly 170 countries in total, although not the key markets. But still, network usage on those key markets is substantial, and one country where the network isn't technically available and it's not the U.K., is known to have been hovering between 65,000 and 85,000 subscribers depending on the month.

The real key is actually TLC, a show that would have likely done poorly had it been a PPV, and was no longer part of the free network month. The two variables are: 1) How many new subscribers did the free month bring in who didn't cancel; and 2) If that number grew, how did that affect PPV purchases.

CHAPTER SEVEN

AAA TELEVISION DEAL

JANUARY 20

The official announcement of AAA's attempt to break into the U.S. market and a television deal with the new El Rey Network came over the weekend, when Scott Sassa, El Rey Network's vice chairman, made the announcement on 1/12 at a press tour.

Sassa worked for Turner Broadcasting from 1982 to 1996. In his last four years there, he headed operations and programming for both TBS and TNT, when wrestling was a staple of both stations' programming. He left to become President of NBC Television Stations in 1997, and has gone through several jobs since being hired for the launch of El Rey.

Sassa announced that Mark Burnett, 53, best known for shows like Survivor, The Apprentice, The Contender and The Voice, would form a partnership with well-known film director Robert Rodriguez, who is part owner of the El Rey Network, along with Lucha Libre AAA, headed by Joaquin and Dorian Roldan, and Alex Garcia's AG Studios, to produce a weekly one-hour television show that would debut in the second half of this year.

"I'm at the point in my career where I could probably try anything," said Burnett at the announcement. "I've earned that right. This is building a bona fide sport within America. Clearly the Hispanic culture is really growing. Why wouldn't you bring Mexico's No. 2 sport to America? This is a long-term, big play for us."

They said that besides the weekly television show, there would be a variety of major wrestling TV specials on the station, as well as storylines building to PPV shows. They would also be opening up merchandising and licensing opportunities.

What is known is this product will not be traditional Lucha Libre, as the people who are going to be involved in the decision making want to create a new version of the product. Exactly what that will entail is unknown, but it is believed they don't think American fans will accept storylines building to hair vs. hair and mask vs. mask matches like in traditional Lucha Libre.

The television show will be built around a storyline where they will introduce five babyface stars to build the American brand around. The idea is the wrestlers will have discovered that there is a plot to destroy Lucha Libre and somehow because they know too much, the powers that be have exiled them to the United States.

The news comes at the same time that AAA's television situation in Mexico looks shaky, as the show did not air on Univision, the dominant network in Mexico, this past week, nor is it on the schedule for next week. CMLL has also been dropped by the network.

While AAA was tremendously popular in Mexico in the 1992-94 period, and again during a wrestling boom in the mid-00s, the Mexican brand of wrestling took a major popularity hit when WWE got Raw and Smackdown on major broadcast television in the country. Like what happened in other cultures, an extension of the territorial fall that happened domestically in the 80s and then went to other parts of the world, the same thing happened in Mexico. Ratings and the popularity of the traditional CMLL and AAA promotions fell greatly and both are struggling. AAA, which used to tape in arenas that held 5,000 to 20,000 people, similar to Raw, now usually is in 2,500-seat buildings.

AAA had a strong run in the United States during the boom period for the promotion, particularly in Los Angeles and San Jose, where it outdrew both WWF and WCW in both markets. On August 28, 1993, AAA drew what at the time was the largest indoor crowd in the state's history for a Konnan vs. Cien Caras vs. Jake Roberts three-way match that sold out the Los Angeles Sports Arena with an overflow crowd of 17,500 fans (breaking the Ray Stevens vs. Pepper Gomez record of 17,130 set on February 23, 1963, at the Cow Palace in San Francisco). The show turned away 8,000 at the door, according to police estimates. That number that would have been larger had there not been such a traffic jam in the area, with people showing up at the last minute looking for tickets that never even got to the arena to be turned away. Had the show been booked next door at the Los Angeles Coliseum, it would have set a state attendance record that would still be in existence today. They also ran a November 6, 1994, PPV, called "When World's Collide," which was among the best PPV events ever in the U.S, headlined by a double mask vs. double hair match with El Hijo del Santo & Octagon vs. Love Machine & Eddy Guerrero and a cage match with Konnan vs. Perro Aguayo Sr.

However, issues with disorganization on the AAA front and issues with WCW, which co-promoted the PPV, and Ron Skoler, who promoted the live shows under the IWC banner, saw things fall apart after that point. Very shortly after the show, the devaluation of the peso by close to 90 percent destroyed Mexico's economy, and the entire wrestling industry there suffered. AAA has run in the U.S. numerous times since then, mostly in Texas and California, but never had close to the same level of success.

The wrestling environment in the U.S. is also vastly different than 20 years ago. In that era, there were tons of pro wrestling fans, particularly Hispanic. While WWF was the dominant U.S. brand, among those from Mexico who came to the U.S., people like Konnan, Octagon, Santo, Blue Panther and particularly Perro Aguayo were as big and in many cases bigger than anyone in WWF at the time. Aguayo was closer to Bruno Sammartino, but still at the tail end of his career, than anyone on the U.S. scene. Today, the Mexican superstars to Hispanic fans are Rey Mysterio and Eddy Guerrero. Konnan, Octagon and Santo are like Sting, Ric Flair and Hulk Hogan, in the sense the Hispanic fans who came from Mexico know their names, but they'll get the nostalgia reaction. The modern stars like Aguayo Jr. (who is really the biggest star and most popular wrestler in AAA), Cibernetico, etc. aren't at that level.

The El Rey Network is currently only available on Time Warner, Comcast and DirecTV, so it doesn't have the national penetration, and even if it did, it's not like anyone watches the station. On DirecTV, it is not part of the basic package, but is part of another subscription tier. And it's coming at a time when there is too much wrestling on television, even though this is a different version of wrestling. But in the 90s, you put any decent wrestling on television, and viewership would be high for it. Today, nobody watches wrestling on television unless it's WWE brand, or, to a much lesser extent, TNA and ROH. But for an example, when AAA was on local TV in Los Angeles during the boom period, it was doing 6 and 7 ratings, as compared to what TNA and ROH do these days, which are 1s or less.

I would expect at least negotiations, if not a strong attempt at a relationship between AAA and the proposed Jeff Jarrett/Toby Keith promotion, if that deal gets put into play. Jarrett was in Los Angeles this past week for a meeting with Dorian Roldan regarding the two companies working together in the U.S. market. There has been American talent approached, mostly the top indie names, with the idea of mixing both Latin stars and good working American stars.

CHAPTER EIGHT

MAE YOUNG
PASSES AWAY

JANUARY 20

Johnnie Mae Young, a women's wrestling pioneer who gained far more fame as a comedy figure in her late 70s working for the WWF, passed away on 1/14 at the age of 90.

Young was in hospice care as she was going through kidney failure after a hospital visit more than a week earlier and was not expected to last the week.

Young was celebrated for having wrestled professionally in nine different decades, from the 30s to the 10s, something nobody else in history could claim. While that will likely remain a wrestling truism passed down forever and one of her calling cards, most serious historians have disputed the claim.

But Young was a pioneer, with claims she was part of the first group of women's wrestlers ever to work in Canada, in 1941, and was known in Japan for being the rival of Mildred Burke on the first women's pro wrestling show ever in that country in 1954.

She was amazingly tough and resilient, as when she wrestled well into her 70s, she wanted her male opponents to lay the clotheslines in, and took a well protected power bomb off the stage from Bubba Ray Dudley in a skit that, while Dudley did a great job of protecting her in, is probably something that WWE today would probably shudder at the thought they did it because of what could have happened had it gone wrong.

While in her mid-80s, in a WWE ring, in a match where the other women made sure to take care of her, she got light headed and fell down. She fell near the ropes without breaking her fall and everyone realized that she came very close to the ropes, and the way she fell, she could have broken her neck. At that point she was never put in the ring to wrestle again.

To compete in her supposed ninth decade, she was brought out on November 15, 2010, on Old School Raw, in what was billed as a falls count anywhere match against Layla and Michelle McCool. She was basically held onto by the babyface wrestlers on the stage to make sure she didn't fall, and carefully placed over a fallen heel wrestler that had been knocked out. It really would be an injustice to call it a pro wrestling match from that standard, as she got nowhere close to a ring.

In reality, Young is believed to have competed in seven decades, matching the record held by Lou Thesz, who debuted in the 30s and had his final match in 1990 in Japan at the age of 74 against Masahiro Chono. You really couldn't call the 2010 match anything resembling a pro wrestling match, even giving as much leeway as possible.

While she always claimed to have started in 1939, at 16, historians researching have been unable to find any records of her wrestling prior to 1941, when she turned 18 and went on tour with Billy Wolfe's troupe.

For years she had stated that her goal was, on her 100th birthday, on March 12, 2023, that she would wrestle a match against Stephanie McMahon.

"There will never be another Mae Young," said Vince McMahon at the time of her death. Her longevity in sports entertainment may never be matched and I will forever be grateful for all of her contributions to the industry. On behalf of WWE, I extend our sincerest condolences to her family and friends."

Young had been called to appear on the 1/6 "Old School Raw" in Baltimore, when company officials found out she had been hospitalized and would be unable to attend. Reports on 1/8 were that she was not expected to live much longer. Her death was actually reported on 1/9, first in the Charleston Post-Courier, which got the information from someone in the home she was in, that she had passed away at 1 a.m. that day. As it turned out, there was great confusion within the house and she was still alive, although still in grave condition, and lasted five more days.

It was actually her second career that is what made her a wrestling legend. Both she and the Fabulous Moolah were brought in as comedy figures as the old women in their 70s, and then their 80s, who would be brought to television for a variety of skits. The most famous was the idea that she had a relationship with Mark Henry, who got her pregnant, and she gave birth to a hand in one of those skits that many loved and many others hated.

It was that career that got her into both the WWE Hall of Fame and the Pro Wrestling Hall of Fame, and created the image of she and the Fabulous Moolah as the grand old ladies and respected pioneers of women's wrestling. During her career, Young was a name woman wrestler during the 40s and 50s early heyday of that genre. She retired a few times, but came back at different times into her 40s. She lived in California, and wrestled on occasion on Las Vegas shows for Moolah's LIWA annual promotion into her 60s and early 70s where she would amaze people with how much she could still do. Even after moving to the Carolinas, when Moolah invited her to live with her after she had lost family, in 1991, she would work Carolina indies as "The Great Mae Young," where on posters, they would put photos of her dolled up taken nearly 50 years earlier when she was a very pretty young woman, on the posters.

During her prime, she was never ranked as one of the elite stars on the level of Moolah, Mildred Burke, June Byers, Nell Stewart, Penny Banner, or even later like a Betty Niccoli, Toni Rose or Vivian Vachon. But she was sometimes regarded as among the top ten women wrestlers in the country.

She did have a reputation for toughness. Legend had it that she grew up in Sand Springs, OK, and wrestled against the boys in high school, and she was also a star softball player. She claimed that when she was in high school, she attended a show in Tulsa, not knowing wrestling was worked, and challenged Burke, the world champion with the noted round biceps that she'd flex in tons of publicity photos. Burke was a major attraction at the time, as she and promoter Wolfe, her husband, had largely built up women's wrestling to what was its mainstream peak of popularity during the 1940s and early 1950s.

The women's championships and top spots in those days revolved around women who married or slept with the promoters. Burke was married to Wolfe. After they divorced, he married Stewart. Byers married Wolfe's son. Moolah and husband Buddy Lee became the power brokers of women's wrestling after Wolfe's business went down, although after Moolah and Lee split up, it was Moolah who ran the business.

Young claimed that she went to a show, either in 1937 or 1939. Given that the former date was when she was 14, and by her own accounts she didn't take up wrestling in high school until 15, the 1939 date if this story is accurate would seem the most plausible). She said she challenged Burke, but instead was put in a shoot match with Gladys "Killem" Gillem, and pinned her in seconds. Historians have been unable to verify this ever happened.

At 18, she was a regular in Wolfe's troupe. She always claimed she could have beaten Burke but was never given the opportunity. She claimed in the book "Queen of the Ring," about Burke, that in seeing the Burke vs. Byers shoot match for the world title, that she didn't think either of them, who had the reputation of being the two best actual wrestlers of the women's troupe, were really good wrestlers and would have beaten either. But years earlier, when Frank Deford did a story on Burke, Young was adamant in claiming that in her prime that no woman of the era could have beaten Burke. Burke was 39 when she had the shoot match for the title, on August 25, 1954 where he lost the only fall when her knee dislocated in a two out of three fall match that was stopped as a boring stalemate by the Atlanta Athletic Commission after 47 minutes. Byers, who also outweighed her significantly, was 32.

But she was a very real street fighter. There are stories of Young beating up men for real, and not all of them nice stories, particularly in her youth, but even a story in a Texas dressing room from the 60s where she beat up Dr. Ken Ramey, the skinny manager of The Masked Interns, who was arguably the most underrated manager of all-time. There is little doubt she was among the toughest of any of the women wrestlers who were in the so-called golden age in the 40s and early 50s, when Wolfe had a huge stable of women wrestlers all over North America getting full-time work.

Her peers who were still alive were highly critical of Young and Moolah appearing as comedy figures in WWF, saying it demeaned all of them as wrestlers. Young claimed that any one of them would have taken the job had it been offered, which is likely true in most situations.

When the movie "Lipstick and Dynamite" came out in 2005, there was more bitterness. Most of the wrestlers were very negative about Moolah in particular, for her always keeping the world title for decades, never allowing younger talent to get to the top. Young was, of course, the lone voice always defensive of Moolah. The bitterness increased over business dealings and later when the movie was released, and all the women were brought in to do media, and because of their fame in WWF, Moolah and Young were treated as the stars and the rest as secondary characters.

CHAPTER NINE

THE LIFE AND DEATH OF THE ULTIMATE WARRIOR

JANUARY 20

The former Jim Hellwig (whose real name is now Warrior), the former Ultimate Warrior, was announced as the main event induction for this year's WWE Hall of Fame. According to those with knowledge of the deal, it was finalized a week before Christmas. It was a bridge put together largely when 2K Sports put together a deal with Warrior on his own to be part of this year's video game. Vince McMahon did have to approve it but there were reasons why he didn't turn it down. When Warrior was brought to New York for the announcement, people in WWE met with him. They wanted him in the Hall of Fame and his big hurdle was the "The Self Destruction of the Ultimate Warrior" tape from many years ago. He wanted Vince to apologize for it. Since Vince hasn't done so, it looks like the closest thing he's getting is a new DVD on him released in conjunction with Mania that will have a very different tone to it. Jim Hellwig, 54, was a competitive bodybuilder who won the 1984 Mr. Georgia contest and then placed fifth in his height class in the 1985 Jr. Mr. USA contest. When he was training in Southern California, he was discovered by Rick Bassman, who was recruiting good looking bodybuilders to become pro wrestlers, some of whom made it and some of whom didn't, and organized them to be trained by Red Bastien and Billy Anderson. Hellwig and Steve Borden, who became Sting, left the class after only a few weeks of training, sent photos and resumes to all the wrestling promoters, and Jerry Jarrett was the only one who saw the photos and decided to hire them. They lasted only a short time in his territory because they were so green, but Borden was always thankful Jarrett gave him his first job. After being fired, Bill Watts hired both of them. Watts wanted both to get off steroids and learn to work. Sting stayed and Warrior got a job with World Class Championship Wrestling, where he became good friends with Kerry Von Erich. In 1987, New Japan Pro Wrestling contacted him to play a futuristic character named Big Van Vader, who was going to get a gigantic push, and be managed by Japan's version of Johnny Carson (a talk show host in the Jay Leno/David Letterman role but more famous), however he signed with WWF and the role went to Leon White, who probably did a lot better with it long-term. Warrior became a huge star in his 1987-91 run in WWF, at one point being second to only Hulk Hogan. Vince McMahon in 1990 made the call to have Warrior replace Hogan as WWF champion, with the idea Hogan would become Bruno Sammartino, the former champion who didn't need the belt. Hogan put Warrior over, but stole the spotlight from him. Warrior drew very disappointing numbers as champion and within a few months, the plans were dropped and the decision was made to have Sgt. Slaughter beat him for the title and put the belt back on Hogan. Warrior himself was mad because Hogan earned more money than he did. In the summer of 1991, he told McMahon that he would leave unless he was paid the same as Hogan and was guaranteed to be equal to the highest paid guy on every PPV show he appeared on. McMahon agreed to the terms, signed off on it. He already had tons of advertising out for SummerSlam with Warrior & Hogan teaming in the main event and in those days he was far more of a stickler for planning far ahead and delivering exactly what was advertised on PPV. Obviously he didn't really in his mind agree to it even though he did sign off on it. Warrior was not the level of star Hogan was and paying him equal to Hogan didn't make sense. If Hogan found out, he'd be furious and the deal was if he gave Hogan a raise for PPVs, Warrior would have to get an equal raise. Warrior also asked for an easier road schedule but Hogan-like money on the road. After SummerSlam in 1991, McMahon announced Warrior was suspended, although everyone figured he was fired. He was brought back at WrestleMania in 1992 when Hogan was under the gun in a steroid scandal and McMahon felt he should take a year off so the heat would go away, and brought in Warrior to bridge the gap. Warrior was fired eight months later, allegedly because of GH related issues when McMahon went through his phase on legitimately wanting to crack down on PEDs. Warrior was brought back next in 1996, and to the live crowd in Anaheim that night, Warrior's return was way bigger than the Bret Hart vs. Shawn Michaels main event. But that again only lasted a few months. He was let go after no-showing a few house shows after demanding Vince buy a certain number of his comic books to sell at the matches. The demand occurred before the house shows. As it turned out, Warrior's father, who he was not close with, died that weekend, and when he missed the shows, claimed it was due to mourning his father's death. But McMahon didn't want to use him after that point. He came back for a short period of time in 1998 for WCW (when McMahon found out, he tried to make another deal with him to keep him from going to WCW), drawing a phenomenal first quarter hour for his return, but within a few weeks, nobody really cared and by the time he actually faced Hulk Hogan in the 1990 WrestleMania rematch eight years later, I was absolutely shocked how little it meant. WCW stopped using him even though they had signed him to a long contract. Warrior didn't wrestle after that, until one match in 2008 against Orlando Jordan in Barcelona. There had been attempts in the past to bring him back for the Hall of Fame, but he always turned them down, citing the idea there was a contradiction, that if what they put in the video was true, how could they put him in the Hall of Fame. He had also been critical of Bret Hart and others who had gone back to WWF. People seem to think Hogan will induct him. Given everything Warrior has said about Hogan, even to the point of claiming Hogan tried to get him to have sex with wife Linda, even in the phony world of pro wrestling, that would be too rich. Hogan immediately gave the public olive branch to this, saying to TMZ that Warrior was a good man and is happy for the guy. Just the idea Warrior is doing business with WWE after all he said is somewhat rich. But WWE has tried to bury the hatchet with everyone. It was inevitable this would happen at some point. It had been apparent it would happen this year for some time.

JANUARY 27

The chronology of the Warrior deal went like this. HHH met with Warrior in July on the same day as the 2K Sports press event when they brought Warrior into the game. It was the first official meeting between a WWE executive and Warrior since 1996. Vince and Warrior had a meeting in Los Angeles in August at SummerSlam weekend. They were scheduled to meet for 30 minutes, but it went a couple of hours as they worked everything out and at that point they started to try and work out a deal with him. The deal was completed in December. WWE is already selling Warrior merchandise.

APRIL 14

"Every man's heart one day beats its final beat. His lungs breathe its final breath. And if what that man did in his life makes the blood pulse through the bodies of others; If it makes them believe deeper in something larger than life; than his essence, his spirit, will be immortalized by the storytellers, by the loyalty, by the memory of those who honor him and make the running the man did live forever."

    —Ultimate Warrior on Monday Night Raw, April 7, 2014, 24 hours before his death

It had been 18 years since the Ultimate Warrior, the character played by Jim Hellwig, had appeared on a WWE broadcast.

In the past few days, he appeared on three. On Tuesday morning, he and his wife got on his plane from New Orleans to Dallas, and then connected to Phoenix, and first went to the Gainy Suites Hotel in Scottsdale.

"On April 8 at 5:50 p.m., 54-year-old Warrior James B. Hellwig collapsed while walking with his wife to their car at the Gainy Suites Hotel in Scottsdale, AZ," said Sgt. Mark Clark of the Scottsdale Police Department. "The Scottsdale Fire Department transported him to a local hospital where he was pronounced dead soon after arrival. At this point in the investigation, it appears as though a catastrophic medical condition caused his death."

A TMZ report stated that when he collapsed, he was clutching his chest according to witnesses. An autopsy will be performed, but the initial speculation is he suffered a massive heart attack.

The timing was spooky, and the vision of him as the main eventer at the WWE Hall of Fame, coming out with his two young daughters, talking to his wife and mother in the front row and telling them how much he loved them. He was introduced at WrestleMania the next day. One day later, he delivered what will always be remembered as his farewell interview on Raw.

He was limping badly, and when he went to shake the ropes, blew up right away, which may have been a sign. Whether he was aware of anything, because you could certainly go back with a different perspective and listen to his interviews Saturday and Monday and come to that conclusion, also could be purely coincidental. One person who knew him better than most noted the same thing that we did, that the interviews are exactly what he would have said and you could read something into almost anything. He shot down the idea he was aware of a serious medical issue and that anything could be read into a lot of his comments for years that could be viewed in hindsight like he was delivering his own eulogy.

What he said and how he said it was not unusual for him. The limp was also nothing new. It's not known how long he had been limping badly, but people who had meetings with him as far back as in 2012 noted he had the same limp.

However, he did have a premonition about dying young. People who dealt with him said he spoke openly about what he did and the chemicals he used to become the Ultimate Warrior. He matter of factly said in recent months that he believed he would die young. His father and grandfather died in their 50s, and he would outright say that the drugs he took would probably take years off his life. He also succinctly said without prompting that he didn't regret doing what he did, because without doing it, there would not have been an Ultimate Warrior.

James Brian Hellwig was one of the memorable characters in the wrestling industry. He got in by accident. He was a wrestler who, in many ways, along with Hulk Hogan, was characteristic of his time. He was a big, muscular competition bodybuilder whose physique was his calling card and his reason for being a success. Obviously he had more than just a physique, because there is a world full of big bodybuilders who would love to be able to do pro wrestling and make the money he did. He had a crowd appeal even when he didn't know what he was doing, once he grew his hair long and became the Dingo Warrior.

As Blade Runner Rock, with shorter hair, he was as big and muscular as anyone in pro wrestling, but there were no signs of this appeal. In Mid South, the Blade Runners were not well thought of, particularly when Bill Watts fired Kelly Kiniski (who was wrestling as Masked Superstar #2) to make room for them. Kiniski, the son of Gene Kiniski, was a nice guy, quiet, caused no problems, was technically very good, but had no charisma at all. He was a former football player at West Texas State who almost everyone on the circuit, including the locker room leaders like Ted DiBiase, Dick Murdoch and Jim Duggan, all liked. Murdoch, in particular, was furious that Watts fired a good kid like Kiniski to make room for two green bodybuilders with a few weeks of training, a few weeks in the ring, who, charitably at the time, were totally awful. Watts countered that the guys didn't understand business, because the look of the Blade Runners was unique. Rock was 280 pounds, and still cut at that weight. Kiniski had no potential to headline. The Blade Runners were a long way from being ready, but they did have a potential Kiniski didn't. The argument led to more problems, which resulted in Murdoch soon leaving the company.

Blade Runner Rock didn't fit in well, nor did the Blade Runners connect with the fans yet. He had issues in Mid South, being green to the business. Watts, who was 47 at the time, came out of retirement and worked some as a babyface against them and they were told by the other wrestlers that when the boss hits you, you have to go flying. Warrior couldn't comprehend why an old guy who was somewhat fat, although even bigger than he was, was booked to beat him like that. The reality is, Watts was the area legend at the time. There were other issues. He and Sting didn't get along well at the time. The feeling was Sting had a great attitude, and he didn't. He had already garnered a bad reputation after a short time in the business and quit. It was very possible his career was going to be over.

But the Dallas promotion was wanting new talent, plus, they had built their company around good looking guys to attract a female audience. The territory was past its peak, but Kevin & Kerry Von Erich were still there, teaming with the fake cousin, Lance Von Erich, a bodybuilder who looked like a model but couldn't work a lick. Physically, Jim Hellwig was similar to Kerry Von Erich, the company's biggest star. Like Lance Von Erich, when he came out, women took to him immediately and he was over. He wasn't over like the top guy in the company, but there was a connection with the fans there for the first time in his career. His interviews needed work.

At the time, Bruiser Brody was the booker. I can recall, almost as comedy, that when it came time to interviews on Monday nights in Fort Worth, Brody would cut his promos and talk about his matches. Then the Dingo Warrior would come out and do what would be beginning Ultimate Warrior interviews. Brody, instead of leaving, would be standing there in the background. When Warrior's interviews were over, Brody would say, "Marc (TV announcer Marc Lowrance), what Dingo was trying to say is....."

Gary Hart managed him when he first came in as a heel, before his inevitable babyface turn. Hart saw first-hand his issues with steroid use and problems with his first wife. Dingo Warrior was Hart's brainchild, the term Dingo being from Australia, where Hart worked in the 60s and 70s. While he used face paint before, his Dingo Warrior face paint which became the genesis of the Ultimate Warrior face paint was from aboriginal tribal war paint in Australia.

He wasn't making much money, but he was clearly turning a corner and was going to make it. The only question was where. He was tailor-made for WWF at the time, just needed a few more years to improve his ring work.

Officials from New Japan Pro Wrestling, at the time the No. 2 promotion in the world, were looking at creating a new top foreign star, Big Van Vader. They were looking at a comic book bodybuilder, who would wear a mask, and come out to great special effects. They had made a deal with one of the biggest celebrities in the country, the "Johnny Carson of Japan" (today that would be the Jay Leno or David Letterman, only times five) to manage Vader. He was going to come in and beat Inoki in two minutes, something that never happened before.

Hellwig was the original Big Van Vader, but he instead opted to go to WWF a few months before his debut, leaving Leon White, the second choice, for the role. Things probably worked out better, because Hellwig's look and the Inoki win would have gotten him over early in Japan, but it's hard to say if he'd have had any staying power. He only worked one match in Japan his entire career, in 1990, as champion, against Ted DiBiase, and the fans at the Tokyo Dome pretty well mocked him on that night. White went on to be an all-time great and Hall of Famer with the gimmick.

He was brought into WWF in 1987 as a project. The company saw promise in him and he worked as the Dingo Warrior, his name in Texas, working house shows. The idea was to keep him off television until he improved his wrestling. But at every house show, he got over like crazy. Fans were educated that big muscles makes you a tough guy, and he had big muscles and a great look. It was an immediate reaction that he got from people who had no idea who he was, and had nothing to do with his unique and often-mocked interview style, since nobody in the crowd had even heard one.

The reaction at the arenas led to them debuting him on television much quicker than originally planned. His name went from Dingo Warrior, to Dingo, The Ultimate Warrior, and finally just Ultimate Warrior. Once he was put on television, and given the name Ultimate Warrior, much to the chagrin of Badnews Allen, he was on fire. He always won. He was the company's hottest new star, and was booked that way, winning his TV squash matches quickly with a limited act of running to the ring, shaking the ropes, doing a few moves, and a splash for the pin.

He garnered even more momentum when he beat the Honky Tonk Man in 27 seconds as a surprise opponent at the first SummerSlam on August 29, 1988. Hulk Hogan was clearly the top star, and he was more and more being seen as the heir apparent. He was six years younger, had a better body, was better looking and had better hair. Very quickly, he and Randy Savage were battling over the No. 2 position. During his rise, he only lost once, an IC title loss to Rick Rude, at WrestleMania V in 1989, due to interference from Bobby Heenan, which was done to lengthen their program. In a sense they had to be careful booking him. Only the best wrestlers would be able to bring out good matches in him, and nobody clicked with him in the ring better than Rude. Eventually after gimmicks like a bodybuilding match, Warrior regained the title and headed for Hogan.

Still, even during his ascension, he wasn't always happy. Perhaps his best friend in WWF during his early period there, before Kerry Von Erich came in, was Owen Hart. Both came to the company at the same time. Hart was put under a mask as the Blue Blazer. Both, with no television, would tear down the house for their matches, Warrior with his ring entrance, physique and quick squashes, and Blue Blazer, with his unique moves. But the company made the decision that the Blue Blazer was too small to compete with the stars, limited his moves, and he was stuck in prelims.

Given that Owen Hart was among the most talented wrestlers in the world, and Warrior wasn't, and Warrior was the one in main events, one would think there would be resentment. But the two got along well.

Hart would note that everyone's time clocks were screwed up. The schedule was a killer in those days. They'd really do almost 300 dates a year, criss-crossing the country, changing time zones, taking early morning flights. Warrior was incredibly dedicated to training and eating right, because his body was his gimmick. Obviously he was taking every physique aid known to mankind to maintain that look while being on the road. He would be so wired he couldn't sleep. Hart would joke about Warrior at 2:30 a.m. doing his laundry because he was so hopped up. Hart wasn't happy there, feeling his talent was squandered and decided to quit and go to work in Japan. Warrior, also not happy even though he was on top, wanted to come with him.

Hart, in the nicest way possible, convinced him otherwise, just saying, "Japan isn't for everyone."

Until this weekend, Warrior's legacy was WrestleMania 6 at the Sky Dome in Toronto. The Ultimate Challenge, Hogan vs. Warrior, an unheard of battle of babyfaces, with the WWF champion vs. Intercontinental champion, was supposed to be the changing of the guard and the beginning of the new era of pro wrestling. Hogan put Warrior over in 22:51, when Hogan missed his legdrop and Warrior hit him with a splash, essentially the same finish Hogan would call when it was his time to put over The Rock.

It was Hogan's master performance. The match, heavily choreographed because, as their WCW match years later showed, there was great risk otherwise, ended up being a shockingly good match. In some ways, with the exception of Hogan vs. Andre, because of the stage, and that Hogan lost, it was probably the second most remembered match of the era.

The show sold out the Sky Dome in Toronto with 64,287 fans (the announced number that year was worked). As far as a real legitimate figure, it was the second largest of the time in North America, slightly beating a Hogan vs. Paul Orndorff match in Toronto, and behind Hogan vs. Andre at the Pontiac Silverdome. The gate of $3,490,857 U.S. (And it was more than $4.1 million in Canadian dollars at the time) was the all-time record for pro wrestling, more than doubling the North American record set the prior year by Hogan vs. Savage. It also beat the $2 million plus world record set 14 years earlier by Muhammad Ali vs. Antonio Inoki. The PPV numbers were under 500,000, which was a little disappointing compared to the previous few years numbers. In that era the babyface vs. babyface dynamic didn't work as well as babyface vs. heel that they had with Hogan and Savage the year before. Closed circuit attendance, a dying business by that time, was 53,000.

The story was supposed to be the finish, the shocking moment where the ref counted three. When Hogan returned to WWF at the end of 1983, after leaving the AWA, he would never suffer a pinfall loss. In fact, during his entire AWA run, which started in 1981, he never did. He suffered a few to Inoki in Japan and a tournament loss to tag team partner Stan Hansen once in Japan, but after 1981 or 1982, he no longer did any jobs. His lone loss, to Andre, was a crooked referee count. Hogan losing cleanly was momentous.

Hogan's work was masterful. The story was supposed to be Warrior winning to set him up to be the new champion. Instead, the story was Hogan losing, as he had the sad look on his face, put the belt around Warrior's waist, and left to a thunderous reaction while Warrior stayed in the ring, clearly No. 2.

He was never the same after his biggest win. In the build to the match, he was the new fresh thing and fans at every arena cheered his name and booed Hogan's when the match was being promoted. But on that night in Toronto, even though he lost, Hogan was clearly the star. People say it was a split crowd, but it was clear even during the match, the cheering for Hogan was louder, although it was not a crowd that booed either man. Fans watching went from wanting to see Warrior end Hogan's title reign, to seeing him as, instead of the heir apparent, the place holder for when the real top star returned.

Warrior's title run was devoid of fresh heel challengers, as Rude was someone he had already won a previous feud with, and Mr. Perfect was someone that Hogan had already beaten over-and-over. Business fell and a scenario was created where Sgt. Slaughter would come in as an Iraqi sympathizer when there was bad feelings in the U.S. against that country, just before what ended up being the Persian Gulf War. Slaughter would beat Warrior, and then drop the title to Hogan at the next WrestleMania.

Warrior worked with his other best opponent, Randy Savage, in a career vs. career match at that WrestleMania. He had his business issues with Vince McMahon in the summer of 1991, demanding the same schedule, same pay percentage, and equal money on all PPVs as Hogan. McMahon agreed to all the terms. Then, after the first show, SummerSlam of that year in Madison Square Garden, as soon as the match was over, McMahon suspended him, although it was really a firing.

Over the next 15 years were a couple of comebacks, both short-lived, three lawsuits and Hellwig berating McMahon every chance he could. McMahon, when asked, would refer to Hellwig as a nut case. Yet, for whatever reason, he would want to bring him back, time after time. Once, when asked about why, he said that he must be a glutton for punishment.

Still, a lot of the current wrestlers knew nothing about the behind-the-scenes, or what the guys who worked with him thought, and saw him as their childhood cartoon hero, whose ripping on the company for years wasn't known, and that he was an historical figure, who left, came back, was nice to everyone and clearly loved his family.

"Heartbroken," wrote Bryan Danielson. "My sincerest condolences go out to The Warrior's family. Seeing how much he loved his daughters and his wife this weekend makes it all the more heartbreaking. The Ultimate Warrior was my favorite as a kid, and getting to speak to him was one of my favorite moments. He was so nice to me."

There was a controversial side to Warrior. He had a short career as a college speaker that ended with anti-Homosexual remarks, which he later clarified to say that what he meant was if the entire world was homosexual, the species wouldn't be able to carry on. He was critical of a number of wrestlers who he said were weak-willed because they returned to WWF and McMahon, and mocked self-destructive wrestlers for their early deaths.

Some of his speeches will be looked at and examined as if he knew he had a health issue and knew ahead of time that this was his final act, both repairing his relationship with McMahon, who gave him the opportunity to be a big star and paying back receipts at the same time. Warrior had just signed a contract as a brand ambassador for WWE, as he mentioned in his Hall of Fame speech, the position Foley had until they decided against renewing Foley's contract.

James Brian Hellwig was born June 16, 1959, in Crawfordsville, IN. His father walked out when he was 12 and he was raised by his mother.

He attended Fountain Central High School in Veedersburg, IN, being a skinny 135 pounder, but he idolized Robbie Robinson, one of the top bodybuilders of that era, when growing up. He ran the middle distances on the track team. He went out for football one year, but quit before the season started. He was 6-foot-1 and 160 pounds when he graduated high school, and he had already been lifting weights for two straight years at the time. He had a good physique, but he was not naturally a guy whose body exploded when he started weight training.

He was solidly built as a college freshman at Indiana State University, but he looked nothing like a competition bodybuilder. He would look at photos of the bodybuilders of the time in magazines and tell people at the time, "I can't wait until I get that big."

He quit college after a year, and wound up in Georgia. By that time, he was huge. He was competing as a bodybuilder in Georgia, and studying to be a chiropractor. Once after he'd had a seven figure year as a pro wrestler, it came out that he had defaulted on his student loans to Life Chiropractic College in Marietta, GA. He won Mr. Georgia in 1984, and placed fifth in his class at the Junior Mr. USA contest in 1985. He was in Southern California training for his next contest when Rick Bassman spotted him in the gym and recruited him to join his concept of Power Team USA, with Steve Borden (who later became Sting), Steve DiSalvo, Dave Sheldon, who wrestled as the Angel of Death and passed away young, and a few other bodybuilders. He and Borden quit the camp after only a few weeks and were hired by Jerry Jarrett, first as The Freedom Fighters, Jim "Justice" Hellwig and Steve "Flash" Borden, doing essentially the gimmick that Bassman came up with. Then they were turned heel, managed by Dutch Mantell, and called The Blade Runners. Hellwig was Blade Runner Rock, and Borden was Blade Runner Sting.

Because they started together in camp, and on the road, and then one became the rising star in WCW while the other was the rising star in WWF at the same time, there was always the idea that he and Borden were friends. But both over the years said that they were not friends, especially when they parted ways.

Hellwig had issues in Mid South Wrestling with Bill Watts, and quit the company and wound up in Dallas where he became Dingo Warrior. Blade Runner Sting became Sting, with Eddie Gilbert's Hot Stuff Inc., and Gilbert saw him as a future superstar as soon as he turned him babyface against him.

Because he came and went so often, there was always a lot of curiosity about him. Whenever he would return, there would be tremendous interest. When he was gone, people always talked about him. Once, when he came back at about 235 pounds in 1992, there were rumors that he had died because his heart exploded, and was replaced by another Ultimate Warrior. Once, when they tried and failed to bring him into WCW, they created a clone of him called Renegade who they tried to push, and it led to Steve Austin temporarily shutting down a WCW taping when he refused to put Renegade over.

In 1998, after what appeared to be his final split with WWF two years earlier, Eric Bischoff brought him into WCW, essentially for Hogan to get his win back from eight years earlier. Even after all the problems, McMahon panicked at the idea that Warrior would work for the opposition and made another play to get him, failing this time. Warrior's debut on Nitro was memorable. He drew a quarter hour that was incredible for its time and blew the roof off the place. But his long interview saw viewers start tuning out. In week two, he meant nothing for ratings and in other appearances, people tuned out. His match with Hogan was not good, and that's being kind. Really, it was a disaster. It did above average pay-per-view numbers, about 300,000 buys, but hardly what one would have expected for the first match eight years in the making of one of the most famous matches of all-time. The more Warrior was on television, and the more bad angles they saddled him with, the less he meant. If WCW had just announced Hogan vs. Warrior, and never even put him on television or done an angle, business would have been significantly larger. But Hogan got his win back. Warrior wasn't used after losing, even though he was on a highly paid contract that had a long time left.

Aside from a 2008 show for Nu Wrestling Revolution in Barcelona, Spain, against Orlando Jordan, he retired from wrestling shortly after the WCW stint, and never appeared on national pro wrestling show again.

He had legally changed his name to Warrior in 1993. It wasn't because he was crazy, but because of legal issues with WWE. WWE tried to prevent him from using the Ultimate Warrior name in personal marketing. He tried to claim use of the character and name, since he was Dingo Warrior in Texas doing pretty much the same act. The actual name Ultimate Warrior came from Badnews Allen Coage, who wrestled as Badnews Brown in WWF, a former Olympic bronze medalist in judo and badass who referred to himself as The Ultimate Warrior in the 80s on promos. The WWF couldn't stop him from using his real and legal name in marketing. Still, they fought Ultimate Warrior, but once he changed his name to Warrior, he was able to market himself using that moniker.

Warrior married Shari Tyree, a highly paid stripper, before getting into wrestling, as a bodybuilder in 1982. During his big run, while still married but with his marriage on the rocks, he traveled with the woman who would a few years later become Melanie Pillman, Brian's wife. A model and stripper, Pillman saw her photo in a magazine and set out to find her, having no idea she had any connection with pro wrestling. Before he even met her, he said he was going to marry her. During the marriage, Hellwig had called her at Pillman's home and tried to get her to come back to him. Brian Pillman hated Jim Hellwig.

He married his current wife, Dana, who took his name. Since 2000, her name was Dana Warrior. The couple had two daughters who came out with him at the Hall of Fame ceremony, Indiana, known as Indy Warrior, who is 13, and Mattigan, known as Matty Warrior, who is 11.

Over the years he garnered a reputation of being difficult to do business with, although people who ended up close to both him and McMahon remarked to me that the reason for their constant love/hate relationship is the two were two sides of the same coin. Warrior was the bodybuilder Vince always wanted to be. Vince was the business success Warrior always wanted to be. Both saw things from their own perspective and neither was good at people questioning their ideas.

When Warrior tore his biceps a few years back and needed surgery, he was given a rehab program by his doctors, and noted he threw it away, and began doing curls with light weights right after surgery, squeezing at the top like he always did, exactly what his surgeon told him not to do. He remarked that doctors don't know what they were talking about.

The mentality comes from the steroid bodybuilder world he lived in before and during his wrestling career. When he was growing up, like all athletes, they heard the American Medical Association say that steroids do not aid in building muscle, and whatever weight gains were bloat from water retention. Anyone who had spent any time in a gym and seen the results on real human beings knew that was a crock, so began questioning anything and everything doctors said.

After Chris Benoit killed his wife, son and himself, Warrior made appearances on Fox News talk shows, and when the subject of steroids came up, tried to explain how steroids were actually good for you and doctors don't know what they are talking about. On the surface that sounds silly, having been around pro wrestling and the crazy death rate of his generation, but there were always excuses and other drugs that could be blamed. And in most cases of the drug deaths, they were guys who did a lot of different things for a long time so you couldn't single out any specific thing.

Warrior joked on Saturday night about blowing up during his interview. On Monday, he came out to shake the ropes. He got very tired doing little and he wasn't moving well.

If you look at the history of pro wrestlers from the period where Warrior was a superstar, premature deaths were hardly the exception. But the timing was crazy. Had it not been for something very unique, almost a fluke regarding 2K Sports and the most recent video game, nobody would have even thought of Warrior for this year's game. Once they did, and Vince, perhaps grudgingly, approved of him being in the game, that opened the door to business meetings which led to him headlining the Hall of Fame.

But it was Paul Levesque who put the deal together to get him in the Hall of Fame and bring him back into the company. Warrior had nothing but good things to say about Levesque this go-around, even though he still got his dig in at him for comments made on the DVD in the Hall of Fame speech. Realistically, his return was brokered by 2K, which had people working almost full-time jobs for months on end to keep him happy and from backing out of the deal. But in WWE, it was pretty much all Levesque. It was the spot produced for his return by the Looking4Larry Agency, run by Paul Heyman and Mitchell Stuart, that led to the press conference in New York where the ball really started rolling.

Just before his death, Warrior posted a photo of himself hugging Vince McMahon online, after nearly two decades of the two being at constant odds.

As a pro wrestler, Warrior, like other notables from Danno O'Mahoney to Bill Goldberg, was a shooting star. They got over in record time and became the biggest stars of their era. But for different reasons, their careers were short. I always thought that Warrior would forever be known for squashing Honky Tonk Man and pinning Hulk Hogan.

Instead, while those memories will remain, he will be the guy who was a big star, was off television for 16 years, came back as a much smarter and more reflective human being, and you could see so obviously that he lived for his kids. Whether the Hall of Fame is real depends on the viewpoint of the person involved. Warrior had decried it as fake for years, but there is no doubt he was in his glory getting things off his chest, treading thinly on some and settling debts with others. If it wasn't a big moment for him at the time, he wouldn't have brought his girls on stage.

The family had two homes, one near Scottsdale, AZ, and the other in Santa Fe, NM, where the family now lives. His daughters were home schooled. He loved to take his family to DisneyLand or DisneyWorld. When he wasn't home, he was constantly calling home. But he was always trying to rekindle his stardom.

He had tried and failed to get a number of television projects off the ground. One idea was "The Warrior Project," a semi-scripted inspirational reality show where he's try to save celebrities and musical acts caught up in the world of sex and drugs and have them focus on living a clean life, but there was little interest.

He also worked with ex-WWE writer Court Bauer on a 2012 project for The Cartoon Network called "Parts Unknown," an animated series based off the Clone Wars series. A number of people working at the network grew up during the height of his popularity, and key decision makers were interested. They had scripts, came up with licensing ideas, and the network was ready to give them a green light. Then, he made all kinds of unrealistic demands at the last minute which killed the project dead.

Bauer noted that he did a three hour interview with Warrior, where he felt Warrior came off great in it. Then he demanded it never see the light of day, threatening to sue if he was to ever air it.

He was a big fan of Steve Austin, and he was flattered that C.M. Punk put him over on Twitter and liked Punk's bluntness.

He made it clear that he didn't want to play the Ultimate Warrior character anymore. He didn't shy away form it, but he didn't want to be like Hulk Hogan, whose never escaped from his character, feeling he had more to offer not playing a raving maniac. He thought it was pathetic that guys in wrestling who were no longer active would continue to do their gimmick.

Even before the 2K Sports deal brokered his return, he was open to doing business with WWE, saying the past was the past, but it would have to be on his terms, and he wanted a public apology for the DVD. In the end, he never got that apology.

Like children of so many pro wrestlers from that era, his girls, who were born after his wrestling career ended, were still young when their father was gone. I have no doubt he wanted those girls to be proud of who he was and have this great memory of his last stand in a business they never experienced, since his wrestling career ended before either were born.

Instead, it is going to be tied in with the worst memories of their lives. Jim Hellwig grew up without a father from the age of 12. He did not want his daughters to do the same. And that is the real tragedy.

By Frankie Kazarian:
> *Like anyone reading this, I absolutely loved wrestling as a kid. Still do. Always will. Early, I loved the great athletes...the Ricky Steamboats, Tito Santanas, Bret Harts and the British Bulldogs. Then all of a sudden, HE hit the scene. This guy who looked like something off the cover of the heavy metal albums I was just getting into at the time. A warrior. A real life warrior. An Ultimate Warrior!*

The hair. The colorful face paint. The streamers. Jim Johnston's iconic heavy chugging riff that propelled him to the ring. I was hooked! I had a new favorite, and so did my dad. My mother and father are and have always been my biggest supporters. They took me to as many WWF shows as they could afford at the L.A. Sports Arena. Every time, my dad would paint mine and my friends faces like the Ultimate Warrior. Without fail. Each time with a different color scheme of course, as to keep up and not get redundant.

Fathers and sons bond over many things. I am blessed enough to share many interests as my dad. But one thing we both loved was the Ultimate Warrior. So much so that when my sister got married, it was on April 1st 1990.... yep, the day the Warrior beat Hogan at WrestleMania 6. She got married in Vegas, 3 hours away! What were we gonna do? This was the first PPV we had to have recorded. A family friend had to come to our house, order the PPV, put a VHS tape in the VCR, hit record, watch the whole thing then hit stop at the end. Upon returning home, the first thing we did was watch the recorded show. Then the moment came. Hogan missed the leg drop. Warrior splashed. Warrior won!!! He had the IC and heavyweight champion!! My dad who had gotten the flu earlier that day immediately pepped up stating that the win had made him feel better.

Fast forward to 1996. Warrior was coming back to the WWF! Returning at WrestleMania 12 here in SoCal at the Pond of Anaheim. Guess who was there live in Attendance? Me and my dad. When I was extensively researching wrestling schools, which was the first I reached out to? Yep, you guessed it, the Warriors academy of wrestling. See a theme here?

I do not mean to sound sappy or ramble on about my childhood memories. I just wanted to share with you a little bit of what makes me the wrestler, and the man I am today. A boy who bonded with his father over a shared devotion over this amazing character known as the Ultimate Warrior. I watched him this past Saturday, Sunday and Monday with a huge smile on my face, recollecting on the many hours of happiness he brought me. An hour ago I read that the Ultimate Warrior had passed away. I was stunned. Speechless. Heartbroken. Confused. This couldn't be real. As I sat in my car, I picked up my phone...and called my dad. As expected he was devastated to hear this terrible news. Just as bummed as I was. But I'm certain he, like me, will now cherish those face painting, tv screaming at memories just a little bit more. Thank you Warrior. You helped sculpt at least one, if not thousands of young kids into warriors who can only hope to have a career that will live in the immortal shadow that you have cast.

APRIL 21

The death of the Ultimate Warrior, born James Brian Hellwig and legally known as both James Brian Warrior and just plain Warrior, was due to a massive heart attack.

The nature of the death was expected, as Warrior collapsed, clutching his chest, on 4/8, at about 5:50 p.m., while walking with his wife, Dana, to their car, in the parking lot at the Gainy Suites Hotel in Scottsdale, AZ.

The Maricopa County Medical Examiner's office listed the cause of death as Atherosclerotic and Arteriosclerotic Cardiovascular disease, after a preliminary autopsy that was concluded on 4/10. The cause of death was similar to a large number of pro wrestling deaths from the heavy drug-era of pro wrestling when Warrior was a headliner.

The office is proceeding with a death investigation, attempting to find medical history by speaking with his doctors, as well as investigating what would have caused the heart attack, including obtaining toxicology reports. It could be as long as three months before the investigation is complete.

Warrior, who was 54, was not shy about noting his use of anabolic steroids, which based on different interviews he had done, started either from the age of 11 or the age of 15.

That 155 pounds after years of lifting is shocking, because most people are going to make the majority of their gains in their first two or three years of hard training. It is not known when he started using steroids, but he was competing in bodybuilding contests starting in 1982, so it would likely be before that time.

He competed in the Collegiate Mr. America contest in 1983 at 209 pounds. By 1984, his competition weight was 259 pounds (he weighed 279, not far from contest shape, two weeks prior to competition and felt he lost too much weight for his final contest, meaning his best ripped weight would be in the 260s, a gain of 51 or more pounds in less than two years). As a pro wrestler, he weighed 285 pounds when he broke into the business in late 1985. He ranged from 262 to 275 pounds on what was a killer WWE road schedule during his 1988 to 1991 heyday, where, for the gimmick, he had to remain cut virtually year-around.

While TMZ reported his death as natural causes as to mean neither drugs nor alcohol were directly involved, Cari Gerchick, the Communications Director for the Maricopa County Medical Examiner's Office stated that the initial ruling of natural causes was to mean the death was from a homicide, suicide or natural causes, and both homicide and suicide had been ruled out. Toxicology reports will not come back for several weeks, if not longer. It is not believed any more information will be released publicly until the completion of the investigation.

"We will continue to do a medical death investigation until we get to the point where we scientifically understand how he got to that point (where he suffered the heart attack), said Gerchick.

"All of the information will be in the final autopsy report," she said. "The medical examiners don't speak beyond the autopsy report."

From a media standpoint, the results are likely to not garner significant news no matter what they are. In the 2005 death of Eddy Guerrero, from virtually identical initial causes, when the cause of his fatal heart attack was linked to long-time usage of steroids and narcotics, because the media had moved on, that got virtually no play and outside of the most hardcore of wrestling fans, that aspect of the reasons for his death never got publicized. Some of that was also because, likely due to the steroid implications and the company being so sensitive on that subject, Guerrero's death certificate ended up being sealed a few days later per the wishes of his wife. The toxicology reports on Chris Benoit, showing a copious amount of steroids in his system, including five to ten times the usual amount of serum testosterone and a 59-to-1 T:E ratio. That did garner some media attention, but because it also came out a couple of months after his death, and because the media coverage of that story had burned the public out, that also didn't get nearly the coverage as the speculation had gotten in the period after his death.

The office is less concerned about the heart attack aspect of the death, and more of the key question, which is what led to the heart attack.

Warrior's father and grandfather both died in their 50s, and he had spoken about not expecting to live a long life. He had been up front in noting that the steroids he used to become the Ultimate Warrior would likely take years off his life, and had told friends of that over the past year.

APRIL 28

On the heels of what is still almost the surreal death of the Ultimate Warrior one day after his first appearances on WWE television in 18 years, the company produced a moving documentary on its network that aired on 4/17.

It was a remarkable production, perhaps the best thing the company has ever produced, particularly when you factor in it was only nine days after his death that it was released. The documentary was built around footage and comments, mostly from Warrior as well as talking head interviews with Steve Borden (Sting), who started his career with Warrior, Paul Levesque (HHH) who put the deal together to bring him back, Vince McMahon, in a way he's never been seen before, and Stephanie McMahon.

The show has been largely praised in wrestling, almost universally for the production, quick turnaround and story telling, although some in wrestling were also privately critical, given it's not the time or place to say anything negative on the subject.

The whole Warrior story is hard to come to grips with, because of the timing. An obviously moved Vince

McMahon noted a photo that his daughter took, with Warrior, that he posted before he left the building at Raw, as Vince wondered if it was the final photo ever taken of him before he died, and "certainly the last one with me." While probably not the case, since many fans saw him at the airports in both New Orleans and Dallas the day of his death, the timing of everything was so spooky it almost felt scripted.

"The first time you heard it, it's surreal, and at first you don't believe it," said Vince McMahon. "It's difficult to accept the news. It's unbelievable that it would occur and unbelievable about the timing of it, almost as if it were destined to happen that way."

The star of the piece was Warrior, the former James Brian Hellwig, the bodybuilder-turned pro wrestling star who Vince McMahon saw as the heir apparent to Hulk Hogan.

The reality is the relationship between Hellwig and McMahon was contentious for much of the last 22 plus years, with explosions, brief reconciliations, three lawsuits, and more explosions, and a final reconciliation right before his death.

It has left people with far more questions than answers. The big question regards the health of Warrior. It's very easy to read into the timing of this, and his speech on Raw in particular, and come to the idea that he knew his health was bad. It's easy to the come to the conclusion that to secure money for his family's future through a merchandise deal and to secure the legacy of his wrestling character, or his own personal wanting to make things right, things happened the way they did. He made things right. His young daughters for one weekend got to see who their father was when he was a celebrity, years before they were born.

The reality is, they could have been told about it for years, but unless they experienced it live, they would have never fully understood it.

Except much of that couldn't be true.

Few know just how much of a fluke it was that the pieces all fell into place. The documentary didn't go near it, and those who knew aren't talking. Suffice to say that WWE would not have reached out to Warrior any time soon, and had considered it a loss cause after he turned them down in 2010. And he was not going to take the first step either.

It was a 2K Sports deal that was a complete fluke that it even happened, that opened the door for discussions to be even broached. Even then, it was a very difficult negotiation period to get him in the video game. It was only during those negotiations that he said he would be willing to talk to McMahon, and the Warrior/Levesque discussions weren't easy either.

The problem is, he wanted a public apology for the Self Destruction of the Ultimate Warrior DVD. He never got that public apology. Even late last year, he questioned the logic of the idea that the company that made that DVD saying how bad he was, how unprofessional he was, could possibly consider him Hall of Fame worthy. It made no sense to him. If it was any world except pro wrestling, it would have made no sense. But ultimately, he realized, that in making no sense, him standing there giving the speech in the main event position thus became his vindication.

Perhaps the story of the documentary is that there is a thin line between love and hate. People who knew most of the parties in the DVD everyone except Warrior well, were noting how, "All those people saying all those things about him hated him," and for the most part, that was true of many, at least of the 2013. They had said it for years. From all appearances, that really did change in recent months. In the world of wrestling, how much the appearance is reality is subject to question. But it's a world where the last impression counts, and whether they truly liked him during much of the last quarter century, the last few days were pleasant and the timing of the death under any circumstances was no less shocking.

The Warrior who went to the WWE offices for the first time in 18 years on 3/19 was an enthusiastic, likeable guy as he talked with the merchandising people on new designs, as they were going to remake the character this year. The company had planned to push legends merchandise with the idea the network would create a nostalgia interest in the product, around a big four of Hogan, Undertaker, Warrior and Steve Austin.

Among the most moving parts of the documentary was interaction between Warrior and McMahon. McMahon was portrayed as like a father to Warrior, since Warrior's real father left him when he was young and never supported the family. He had no relationship after that point with him, before his father passed away in 1996. It's mind-boggling given all the things he said about McMahon over the years. Indeed, in going back for the Hall of Fame and to be on television, it was everything he had criticized everyone else for doing.

Warrior brought a copy of the book "The Little Engine That Could," based on a story McMahon had told him years ago about how he saw the rise of the WWF as a company, after his own series of business failures early in life. Warrior brought McMahon that children's book, signed it and gave it to him. There was a shot of McMahon, during one of the weekend shows, looking at the book.

Some of the past problems between McMahon and Warrior were talked about. Others weren't. Memories weren't perfect. Some things were confused. Some things just weren't right. Others were strange with the benefit of hindsight.

There was a conversation with Hulk Hogan, who Levesque told to stay away from Warrior at all costs all weekend until at least the Hall of Fame ceremony was over, coming to Warrior the next day to apologize. Clearly, no matter what the deal, Levesque knew it was fragile until it was over and done with, and even at the last hour, Hogan could be a snag. Warrior had a longstanding resentment of Hogan, his favorite target besides McMahon, when talking about the phony world he had left behind. He didn't specify what he was apologizing for, but in Hogan's new thing of not wanting enemies because life is too short. Hogan was willing to take whatever blame there was against a guy who in 2011 claimed that Hogan had asked, back in their heyday, for him to have sex with his then-wife Linda and also called Hogan a cocaine abusing dope-head.

But the biggest questions revolved around what Warrior was best known for, the physique that got him into wrestling and made him a shooting star. Warrior was a fanatic about what he ate, to the extreme, and training. Still, age is reality. It's hard to believe anybody naturally was going to look like Warrior did a few years back when he was doing training videos and at some public appearances. People who saw him last year at the WrestleCon convention, or late last year in public situations, remarked how huge he was. Warrior, when he was going to make an appearance a few months back, did say that he needed enough time to get ready for the shoot.

But backstage, he never took off his long sleeve dress shirt. It was shocking how you could see how small his arms looked even in a dress shirt. That isn't bad. Perhaps it was a sign that he had grown up, in the sense he had young daughters and had told people in the last year that he was well aware what he had done was going to take years off his life. It also could be injuries. He had torn both his biceps, the right in 1996 and the left in 2012. He had surgery on his left biceps in 2012, and ignored everything his surgeon and rehab people had told him, and even, in a video, laughed at them when telling him to take his time and only lift extremely light. He noted he was told to keep his arm in a sling and immobilized for nine days. He took off the sling on the drive home from the hospital and was doing curls with elastic bands immediately, and with weight soon after. He was told nothing heavier than five to ten pound dumbbells, and not even that for six weeks after surgery, and no using his normal weights for six months. Instead, he was using weights within days and using 35 pound dumbbells for 12 strict reps with a squeeze at the top four weeks after surgery. Perhaps you could say some athletes heal faster than normal. But he was 52 years old at the time.

In the last year, he had more problems with his biceps and his shoulder. He had been limping for years. Those who had been around him over the past year noted the limp had gotten a lot worse even in the last couple of months.

Even before his death, people had noted to me that he was seemingly out of breath and sweating profusely at times over the weekend, including during his speech. But he was seemingly out of breath and sweating profusely months ago at appearances as well. Warrior out of breath dated back to his wrestling career when that was part of his calling card with the idea his opponents would have to cover for him. He even joked about it in his Hall of Fame speech.

He was not one to listen to doctors, or go to them most of the time. It was ordered to shoot him to try and not let people see how badly he was limping on Raw, although it was evident, and there was no hiding how out of breath he was just by shaking the ropes. It's one thing for an old man who no longer trains to be like that, but he was someone who was a stickler for training.

Did he change his training or approach to training? Was he hurt and couldn't train? Did he have a health issue he was aware of? Obviously one or more of those things were true.

Borden, who only traveled with him a short period of time and didn't know him for very long before they started their careers together, was shaken up. They were the same age. They started in the business together. Because of that and the fact each man's early career had striking similarities, he was always associated in some form in people's eyes with him.

Warrior's photos as a competition bodybuilder were shown. He noted while he was going to chiropractic school in Atlanta, that he was more into training than school. He won Mr. Georgia in 1984, and went to California to prepare for higher level national competition. He wanted to be a pro bodybuilder, but living in Georgia, was aware of the top wrestlers like Ric Flair and Dusty Rhodes, and since they were considered big TV stars at the time, figured they were pulling in big money. While Warrior was physically larger than a lot of pro bodybuilders and in 1985, at nearly 300 pounds, was so big people did a double-take when they would see him, even when he was in Gold's Gym that was populated by bodybuilding dreamers and bodybuilding royalty. He didn't have the right genetics, and that was not due to a lack of effort, to compete favorably on the professional stage and never placed top five in any national competition. But as far as being a bodybuilder who would look good in a professional wrestling ring, the late 80s Ultimate Warrior was as close to perfect for his time, and that was an era that fans and promoters judged talent and toughness very much by what someone's size and body looked like. There was no UFC to give a reality check to what happens to big stiff guys in fights. The fans who had even the beginning ability to dissect who was really doing what to make a match were the minority. It was a giant fantasy world of fantasy people, and he was the closest thing to a comic book character. A lot of older wrestling fans saw through him. But for kids growing up at the time, they saw him as something and maybe with nostalgia, remembered him as something a lot better than when they saw him. It was time and place. While he was certainly popular in his comebacks in 1992 and 1996, after the brief initial honeymoon reactions, he never got over like he did the first time. In WCW in 1998, his first day saw curiosity of his return be gigantic. Even Ric Flair's return after a lawsuit settlement, while more memorable, didn't draw the ratings of Warrior's return. But the honeymoon ended sometime late in his first 18 minute promo. The more he was on TV, the less he was over. His ratings drawing power was gone by the third week in. He was booed in many cities and it was clear they had no idea what to do with him, past make sure he got in the ring and Hogan got his win back from 1990.

Through Ed Connors, who ran Gold's Gym at the time and was a guy who seemingly knew everyone, he was put in touch with Rick Bassman.

Bassman had an idea of training the biggest and best looking bodybuilders, and using that as his entree to get into pro wrestling. Bassman had seen, in particular, how big the Road Warriors were in 1985 as heels, and wanted to find All-American looking guys who could be babyfaces to oppose them, with the concept of Power Team USA.

Hellwig and Borden ditched Bassman quickly after he set up their training at a racquetball gym. They sent all the promoters photos. Only one even responded back. Jerry Jarrett saw the photos and gave them a start date. While Jarrett got them their foot in the door and Borden was always indebted to Jarrett, they actually didn't last long before he let them go. Bill Watts brought them in as a project, and it was a controversial call because his was a working based company and they were as green as they could. Watts and Hellwig had conflicting egos and if you think about it, the versions of each man in 1986 couldn't have possibly got along and they didn't. Hellwig and Borden didn't get along and Borden stayed and Hellwig left.

Warrior said that Borden was a guy who didn't want to think for himself and wanted everyone to think for him. He wanted to think for himself. Borden categorized Hellwig as a guy who wasn't shy about stating his opinion, on every single subject.

The documentary went through videos shot of him in Mid South, where both he and Borden looked much larger than they would when they each became stars. It followed him through Dallas, where he came in as a heel, but the girls liked him so he turned to team with the Von Erichs. They went to early clips from WWF, his television debut as Ultimate Warrior against Terry Gibbs in 1987, his match with Honky Tonk Man where he won the IC title in 1988, his title win over Hogan at WrestleMania VI in 1990, and his title loss to Sgt. Slaughter in early 1991 to set up his WrestleMania II career vs. career match win over Randy Savage.

Slaughter said that Vince McMahon had told him on the day of the 1991 SummerSlam show in Madison Square Garden, that Warrior had just held him up for $500,000 in cash the day of the show. He said that McMahon told Slaughter he was going to give him the money and then fire him after the match. Back at that time, everyone in wrestling was under the assumption Warrior made demands on McMahon right before the match, McMahon agreed, got the match in the ring, and as soon as the match ended, fired him.

It was a theme of the "Self Destruction tape," told in detail by Hogan, who claimed he told Vince they should handle it old school, with the idea guys would get Warrior in a room backstage and do a number on him, and perhaps break his leg and end his career.

Even though he distinctly told the story in 2005, in his 2009 deposition for one of Warrior's lawsuits, Hogan claimed to not recall ever saying it. When the tape was shown of him saying it, he couldn't recall who told him Warrior held up Vince, nor did he know if Warrior held up Vince.

For whatever reason, that story has been told so many times it's become truth, like Andre the Giant being 7-foot-4. Even after his death, it was portrayed that way in the documentary.

In reality, Warrior and McMahon had an issue that started when the general manager of a TV station, in the days when local syndication was the life blood of wrestling, told WWE's syndicator, Joe Perkins, that he was going to pull the show from his station because he asked Warrior for an autograph for his son and Warrior blew him off. He was mad Warrior embarrassed him in front of his son. Vince ordered Warrior to videotape an apology, which Warrior was furious about, and would never admit to blowing off the autograph request, even though that was his reputation at the time.

On July 10, 1991, Warrior demanded a release on $550,000 the company had allotted him to buy his home in Arizona, which, even though he felt it was too small because he thought it was less than Hogan got, he would accept that figure as his payoff for his WrestleMania VII match with Randy Savage. But from that point forward, he wanted it in writing that he would get equal pay as Hogan for every PPV show, major event, as well as the same percentage as Hogan for house shows (five percent of the after-tax gross in small markets, four percent in major markets), merchandise and the 900 line. Three days later, McMahon agreed to all terms. Still, a few weeks later, Warrior no-showed two TV tapings and several house shows three weeks later. So the story of it being the day of the show as has been told, is inaccurate as the show wasn't until August 26, 1991. Warrior did not receive $500,000 or $550,000 for working that SummerSlam show. He got $75,000. Even McMahon signed a deal that he and Hogan would be paid the same, both got $75,000 checks for that show, but McMahon also gave Hogan a $15,000 bonus. In Warrior's Hall of Fame speech, he smiled as he pulled out a check out that he had in his suit jacket and said something about it being his SummerSlam 1991 payoff. While never fully explained, the belief was it was his $15,000 bonus from the match 23 years earlier, so he was finally paid the same as Hogan.

McMahon's explanation for agreeing to terms that he later said he had no intention of delivering was that he already had advertising and weeks of promotion out for SummerSlam with Hogan & Warrior vs. Slaughter & General Adnan & Col. Mustafa (Iron Sheik) as the main event. As soon as the match ended, McMahon suspended him, and wrote him a nasty letter noting that he had paid him $1.3 million over the previous year in total, and that he would not pay him the same as Hogan, even though McMahon had agreed to that deal in writing. He said Hogan was a bigger star, a bigger draw, had a better reputation in and out of wrestling, stating the line that Warrior remembered for years, when McMahon wrote, "You have become a legend in your own mind."

Warrior noted that line in his Hall of Fame speech in saying that his being there in the main event position at the 30th WrestleMania Hall of Fame and the crowd reacting the way it did was proof the Ultimate Warrior character was a legend.

He returned in 1992 at WrestleMania. What happened there is that in the summer of 1991, Hogan went on the Arsenio Hall show, right after the trial of Dr. George Zahorian, a commission doctor at WWE events who supplied about 70 percent of the company's wrestlers, including Hogan, McMahon, Roddy Piper, Rick Martel and others with steroids. Hogan claimed he wasn't a steroid user, and had only used steroids three times in his life, all for injury rehabilitation. Wrestlers came out of the woodwork saying Hogan had lied, leading to a ton of media coverage. At first the hope was they would survive the storm, particularly since Hogan was still drawing well, even though the Hulk Hogan vitamin company almost immediately went out of business and other endorsements dried up and his reputation to the public at large took a temporary hit.

But in early 1992, McMahon changed his tune, as the media firestorm wasn't going away, and he saw Hogan as the lightning rod. So he made Hogan the sacrificial lamb. The idea was to take Hogan from the "Say your prayers and eat your vitamins," guy who was in reality getting his huge muscularity from steroids, to the sympathetic older icon. The idea was to garner sympathy for Hogan by teasing that WrestleMania VIII could be his retirement match.

He made the decision to send Hogan on a hiatus after WrestleMania. WrestleMania that year was built around the idea that Hogan would possibly announce his retirement. In fact, nothing of the sort happened. But Hogan was gone, and didn't come back until early the next year. To take his spot as the top guy, Vince didn't have any confidence in his own roster of stars to give anyone that position. So he called back Warrior.

The plan at the time, since McMahon had wanted Randy Savage to beat Ric Flair for the WWF title, was for Flair to regain the title a few months later, get into a program with Warrior, who would win the title at a major show in late 1992.

In the summer of 1991, before Warrior left, McMahon, in response to several mainstream media stories coming off the Zahorian trial, said that he would steroid test his wrestlers. He also claimed he would steroid test his bodybuilders, none of who seemed to believe such a thing was possible at the level they were at. It was months later when he had his first test, and half the people in his wrestling promotion tested positive for steroids. McMahon said that everyone who tested positive had to get off, which would be shown by lowering their levels in subsequent tests. No other drug program in sports had that type of thing built into it. Other drug testers said to accurately determine level lowering was not even possible, and a guy was either a positive, and should be disciplined, or a negative.

Still, Warrior was brought back, and tested positive for steroids in every test upon his return. He was never suspended on the grounds his levels were said to be lower in every test. One test showed a new steroid in his system, so that couldn't possibly be levels lowered. Warrior claimed he got it from a tainted supplement, so he wasn't suspended there either when Dr. Mauro DiPasquale, the head of the program, believed his explanation. That steroid never showed up on a subsequent test.

However, McMahon found out, apparently when Warrior told him, complaining about how his shipment from the U.K. for Growth Hormone for he and Davey Boy Smith, sent to the home of his chauffeur, Wendell Robinson, was seized and all he got was an empty package. McMahon made the call to put the title on Bret Hart, out of nowhere, in a dark match at a television taping in Saskatoon, Saskatchewan, feeling he needed to make an instant top babyface. It was government officials confiscating that package that was the reason McMahon, having his back against the wall and needing a new top babyface, gave Hart his first title run.

This situation was really strange for several reasons. First, and this was Hellwig's claim, Growth Hormone was not on the company's banned drug list in 1992.

McMahon on the documentary claimed Warrior and Smith were experimenting with Growth Hormone, which he said was new in those days and nobody knew anything about it. McMahon said that Warrior was offended that McMahon got rid of him over it and it caused a rift between them. He also said that Jim was missing dates which was another reason he got rid of him. McMahon evidently confused his missing the dates in the summer of 1991, or the dates he missed in 1996 which caused him to be fired that year, because on this run, that never happened.

What's curious to me is that in early 1992, before Warrior had even returned, both McMahon and DiPasquale had claimed that they were instituting the first test for Growth Hormone. The funny story was USA Today ran a story where McMahon talked about how they had a new test for GH on the same day the same paper ran a story about how GH was being used in track and there was no test. In one story, the best drug scientists in the world had no test, but Vince McMahon did. McMahon and I during this period had talked about Growth Hormone on a number of occasions, with McMahon also claiming they could test for it because unlike sports leagues, there was no union so he could have things tested for from his talent other sports couldn't, and claimed there was no way anyone could get away with using it in his company. Yet, his actual program evidently didn't ban it, and here we are 23 years later, and it's only been a few years since a test has actually existed, and it doesn't work very well nor catch almost anyone, and many major sports, including WWE, still don't test for it. And in all drug tested sports, the belief by athletes is it can be used with impunity.

Warrior noted that after his 1996 departure from WWF, that Hogan called a few times trying to get him to come to WCW.

Also not in the documentary, but only a month or so after the 1997 Survivor Series, when McMahon wasn't certain about the future of his company which actually started to explode only a month after with Mike Tyson's angle with Steve Austin on Raw, he offered Warrior a $750,000 per year five year contract. Warrior turned the deal down to take a more lucrative WCW deal.

But after he signed with WCW, they brought him in, had him lose to Hulk Hogan, and after one last Nitro appearance after the match, never used him again. They showed a clip of the Hogan-Warrior match, which was supposed to end with Hogan throwing a fireball at Warrior's face. But fireball never lit and he threw nothing in Warrior's eyes. Warrior sold it anyway. Then they had to improvise, which Warrior wasn't good at. The match was horrible even before the fireball. Hogan called it one of the ten worst matches of his career, but said all the blame should be placed on himself. It was implied, which was true, even though Eric Bischoff has denied it, that they threw all that money at Warrior for a few months to build up one match just so Hogan could get his win back from 1990. By the time the match took place, most of the interest was gone, since Warrior was the wrong fit in the wrong place at the time and the more he was on TV, the more worse off he was.

Warrior noted he was asked to do the Hall of Fame in 2010, but turned it down. A lawsuit filed by Warrior, his third, regarding the DVD, had been settled out of court in 2009. When McMahon went to shake his hand upon the agreement they would both drop their legal claims, Warrior refused.

"The most powerful thing I've ever done was not shaking his hand," he said.

Hogan was deposed by Warrior in the lawsuit, where he called Warrior a flash in the pan and said on a scale of one-to-ten, where would he rank Warrior's wrestling ability, and he said "Zero."

WrestleMania week saw Slaughter jokingly hand him a potato, in reference to Slaughter potatoing him during their 1991 run of cage matches, Hogan apologizing, calling him a great man and asking if he could start over. Warrior accepted his apology.

The footage of McMahon, with bloodshot eyes, talking about Warrior giving him the children's book, and in tears was moving.

But the most powerful footage was Warrior with his two daughters, amazed at seeing the crowd and telling him he did a good speech at Raw. The youngest was in awe that so many people remembered him from a time years before she was even born.

Cameras were around him constantly, including when he finally left. During the entire weekend, in every shot, he had a huge smile. For someone who decried everyone who had come back after differences with McMahon as being weak-willed, it was clear this provided him with some closure. As he left the arena after Raw, he talked about this as the beginning of the future of something great.

MAY 5

An article at the fivethirtyeight.com web site, an ESPN-based site, looked at the question of wrestler deaths, brought up once again by the highly publicized death of Ultimate Warrior.

Author Benjamin Morris noted growing up during the time of WrestleMania VI, and the number of performers on that show who have passed away.

He ran numbers on all major WWF stars who performed on PPV between 1985, the time of the first WrestleMania, and 2002, so what was considered a previous era and not a current era. It's early to know how the many changes between scheduling, lifestyle and drug testing put into place in 2005 (although it was also in place from 1992 to 1995) will change things going forward. In addition, until the current performers reach 50 and we look back and compare, we won't have a good reading on how much changes have been positive. The feeling is that things are a lot better than they were, but it's too early to tell how much better.

I don't suspect the problems will be nearly so bad for a number of reasons. The key is the recreational drug usage, while not gone, is nothing like the prior generation. Similarly, the steroid and GH usage isn't gone, but the out of control usage of huge amounts is probably not there. For example, if there is talent using low dosages of testosterone and GH that can fall under the radar of the current testing, that's low dosages, and you don't have guys who were 155 pounds as high school seniors running around at 275. The current look is an in-shape athletic look, and granted, that's not easy to achieve and maintain for a lot of people and you are still judged by your body, but in-ring performance and verbal skills are far more important. Still, a "bad" body even today is a huge detriment.

The guys with the big problems, as a general rule, were the heavy users, who were the blown-up huge bodybuilder types who combined that use with recreational drugs or heavy pain killer usage. There may still be heavy users of GH, but nobody still knows what the long-term issues are with that drug (they don't really know with steroids either as few studies have been done, and the ones that have been, like in Germany, yielded results so scary that everyone ignores them since they were foreign).

Before going further, I want to make a few points regarding WWE. While WWE has always promoted bodies as more of an indicator of star power than any other promotion, every promotion gave preferential treatment in almost every era based on physiques to some degree. And fans reacted to the physiques as well. Guys thought people with big muscles or ripped bodies meant they were tougher and better fighters. Women were attracted to them. Until the steroid era, where a good physique ended up in a large percentage of cases constituting bad health instead of good health, there wasn't any negativity in the portrayal. Even a "real wrestler" like Lou Thesz noted in his era he felt a main eventer shouldn't look like a guy in the stands.

You don't have to be the Ultimate Warrior, and in fact, I'd believe they'd prefer you weren't. Mason Ryan, the closest equivalent to Warrior–although more compared to a larger version of Batista, had a brief run on the main roster but now is in developmental and not even heavily featured. I was there when Jim Ross directly told John Cena when he was starting out to shed 20 pounds when he was a ripped up bodybuilder looking guy in his early 20s so he'd be more agile and have more stamina. But they emphasize weight training and correct dieting, as they should. But everyone is genetically different. With the program they have in place, a good percentage of people should be able to get a pretty presentable body without drugs and some genetically gifted should be able to get a very good body. Given that one of the things they look for in signing talent is their body, the idea is, as a general rule, you're getting people at the high end of the genetic scale to begin with. But that means people are going to look for an edge. I don't care what sport it is, or in Hollywood, use is there, because the lure is too big to stay in the spotlight, particularly as one ages, whether it's to tack on a few lucrative seasons at the end of the career, or be able to get lead parts as you age. But one would think low dosages aren't as dangerous as crazy dosages. But how much significant use over decades corresponds to long-term mortality rates is an unknown question.

Still, there are going to be guys who are talented in some form, whether they are great wrestlers in the ring or who can talk, or both, that may have problems getting the right kind of physique. And there are always going to be the Alexander Rusev types who are going to stand out because of their look. And in theory, it's a business based on extremes and uniqueness, that's where the PEDs come in, because they are an aid to get to where you are going.

In 2007, I did extensive research into the subject. The problem was very clearly not a WWE problem. It was an American pro wrestling problem. While there were young deaths in Japan and Mexico, on a percentage basis, it was not close to that of the U.S.

Of the companies involved, as far as the late 90s went, it was ECW, with the heavy drug culture, that had the highest percentage of early deaths. ECW had less emphasis on physiques at the time than the other two companies. WCW was second, and WWF was third. However, all three were fairly close. The point being that the heavy drug use away from steroids is probably a more significant part of the death rate than the steroids, which get talked about more. I did recently look at a summer 1992 issue of the Observer where I did full roster directories for WWF and WCW, and 25.4% of the WWE active roster at that point have passed away while 19.6% of the WCW roster has passed away.

The other research I found was that wrestlers from the prior generation, which would be categorized as the 1970s, did not have anywhere close to the same problems. Those wrestlers were wilder and more undisciplined, made less money and worked very hard schedules for the most part. They drank far more, they ate far worse. Steroids were around from the 60s, but use exploded circa 1984 when you really started seeing the difference in the bodies as a whole. Before that era, you had a few guys with the bodybuilder physiques. Post 1984, the guys who were pushed, with the usual exceptions since no rule in wrestling is hard and fast, they made up the highest earners and it became the look you needed to be a star. Cocaine was strong in the 80s and 90s. Pain killers were always a part of wrestling, but the drug of choice was more alcohol and marijuana in the 70s, with some heavy users, particularly of the alcohol. From that era, guys did die young at a rate more than Major League Baseball players, but nowhere close to the post-1985 generation, even with far more drinking, far more eating, and far more guys being way overweight.

Morris' tables covered WWF talent based on those who would have already turned 60 by April 1, 2014, and using Social Security Administration tables of the public at large. Keep in mind, that if anything, because this table was of people who made their mark in WWF (only stars, not enhancement talent was figured in—as it was figured based on people who had performed on at least 20 PPV shows), these are people who made good or great money during those years. They earned, on average, multiple times more than the average person being compared with, and thus, could afford better care. They also, if they developed drug issues, had a company that would provide free rehab, which the general public doesn't have, and followed up closely with those in the program, giving an emotional support staff. In addition, there is, due to the problems of the past, an emphasis on keeping the talent healthy that wasn't there with the prior generation to anywhere near the same extent. And as a general rule, due to their professional needs, wrestlers train much harder, particularly when it comes to cardio these days. The cardio requirements are higher than the past with the faster-paced style and generally lighter roster. Wrestlers also eat far better than the public at large.

Granted, the travel was very difficult and it is a very physical business, but other very physical sports where the career spans are shorter also have nowhere near the level of early death issues.

Age (as of 4/1/14)	Those in public passed away	Those in WWF
Born 1974-79	1.9%	10.0%
Born 1969-74	3.0%	16.0%
Born 1964-69	5.1%	10.0%
Born 1959-64	7.5%	20.0%
Born 1954-59	10.4%	17.9%

One thing notable is that the sample size in the individual age groups is relatively small, when you consider they are WWF performers who were only major stars (203 wrestlers in all) during a time frame. Looking at all major pro wrestling stars from that era, not limited to the biggest of the WWE stars would probably normalize things such as more deaths of those born 1969-74 than 1964-69.

On a percentage basis, between the ages of 35 and 40, a WWF wrestler from that era was 5.3 times more likely to pass away than someone in the general public. Between 40 and 45, a wrestler is also 5.3 times as likely to pass away. Between 45 and 50, a wrestler is 1.9 times as likely to pass away.

Looking at that, the ages of 35 to 45 is when a wrestlers career is coming to a close. At 45, the majority were out of the business, or hanging on working weekends but more part of the general public. Those with the real problems at the extreme end (and obviously some at the extreme end survived and some who weren't were unlucky, I'm speaking very generally) in many cases were already gone by 45. From 50 to 55, it jumps back up to 2.7 times the death rate, so this may be a case where the abuses from the past that may no longer be there start taking their toll the most, although it also could be with a larger sample the numbers would be closer. From 55 to 60, it is 1.7 times as likely.

If you look at modern generation WWE talent, the numbers thus far are different. The only death of a modern WWE wrestler born between 1974 and 1979 thus far is Andrew Martin (Test), which was the typical wrestler death of someone who had pain killer issues from serious injuries as well as was a steroid user. Lance Cade was born in 1981 so his death is actually too early to count on these lists.

Of those born between 1969 and 1974, you have Eddie Fatu (Umaga—pain killer issues and lost his job in WWE over refusing to go to rehab, and was in the 2007 investigation that had a number of WWE wrestlers getting steroids and GH from Internet-based Signature Pharmacy), Chris Candito (heavy pain killer and steroid use), Mike Lockwood (Crash Holly—suicide) and Nelson Frazier (Big Daddy V, who wrestled most of his career at more than 400 pounds). That's still almost triple by percentage what you would expect, but less than half of the prior generation. Of those, really, only Frazier and Fatu were in the post-Guerrero death generation when changes started to be made. Louis Spicolli, born in 1971, wouldn't make the list because of the cutoff of not fitting into the category of a top level WWF star.

With what little information we have, it does appear things are better. Logic based on all the changes in the business, including a more sane road schedule, drug testing, and a selection process where drug usage is considered when it really wasn't in the past is that it would be the case. But I'd really want to hesitate saying that directly until 2022, which is a long time from now, when a 30 year old WWE modern generation wrestler in 2007, at the time of the Benoit situation, hits his 50th birthday.

Of those born 1964 to 1969 the deaths are Chris Benoit (suicide, although it later came out he had significant heart issues at the time of his death), Owen Hart (falling from the top of an arena doing a stunt), Eddy Guerrero (heart attack with long-term steroid and narcotic use linked) and Rodney Anoa'i (Yokozuna—who was 600 pounds at the time of his death and at times was more than 700 pounds), which, by percentage is 2.4 times the general public. Once you get to those birthdays, almost all would be considered prior generation. Hart's death was an aberration, Yokozuna was a star in the 90s, and Benoit and Guerrero's death were the major catalysts of the change. Anyone older would be more prior generation. With the benefit of hindsight, the one thing that can be said is that most, if not all of the wrestling deaths prior to 2005 were to a degree in vain, other than the large number combined being a factor with the Guerrero death, which saw WWE start to take serious action. The Benoit death, even though it was not at the time from what had become the far-too-often pattern of wrestler deaths, the heart problems that were related to drug issues, ended up leading to major industry changes both as it pertained to drugs and concussions.

It should be noted that research using different standards of what a star is does even out those born 1954 to 1959 and 1959 to 1964, so the weirdness of the poll above just had to do with the sample used. According to research by Chris Harrington, overall, it's actually 20% of the wrestlers born 1959 to 1964 who were WWE stars have already passed away, which is nearly triple the general public. Of those born between 1954 to 1959, including modern names, it's 21%, or double that of the general public.

AUGUST 26

Dana Warrior, the wife of the late Ultimate Warrior, was mad at Hogan this past week. Hogan did a Grantland podcast promoting SummerSlam and told a story that he and Warrior traveled together in the WCW days for several days because Warrior didn't want to go home. That story doesn't sound right because Hogan and Warrior weren't on good terms in the WCW days (their real problems came during the deposition in Warrior's lawsuit against WWF for the "Rise and Fall of the Ultimate Warrior" DVD when Hogan called Warrior a flash in the pan as far as being a star and was critical of his working ability). Dana was already with him by that point and took it like Hogan was saying he was hanging with him and avoiding going home to her. If the story was true, it may have been in the WWF days, when the two were closer. She wrote, "I've been really quiet since the passing of my husband and the father of my girls. Someone sent me what Mr. Bollea had to say in a video interview with Grantland yesterday and I would just like to ask him to stop. He is the only person in the WWE Universe who did not give a call or send a card. My girls asked why he didn't check on us like everyone else and I explained simply there isn't a camera at our mailbox or in the house when we receive our calls. I would ask respectfully, Mr. Bollea, for you to understand my girls hurt and just let some time pass before you say anything more."

CHAPTER TEN

GEORGE SCOTT PASSES AWAY

JANUARY 27

George Scott, the booker who built Mid Atlantic Championship Wrestling into being a national powerhouse in the 1970s, and later booked the national expansion of the WWF in the 80s, passed away due to lung cancer at 11:30 p.m. on 1/20 at the age of 84.

Scott's health had been failing over the past month. He had been in hospice care since October. His weight had dropped from a very fit for his age 220 pounds down to just 140 pounds, and every day, he'd tell his wife of 27 years, Jean, "Am I going to die today?" Scott, whose lung cancer was likely due to his long-time smoking habit, was diagnosed with cancer more than two years ago. He had been living in Indian Rocks Beach, FL, since retiring from wrestling, with his second wife, who had been very active in local politics, including serving as City Commissioner.

Scott had two major careers in pro wrestling. The first was as part of the tag team of The Flying Scott Brothers, with younger brother Sandy (real name Angus Scott). Born in Scotland, George grew up in Hamilton, Ontario. He participated in a number of sports growing up, starting wrestling at the age of 12 and then weightlifting. At the time, Hamilton was a hotbed for producing top wrestlers, with Mike & Ben Sharpe predating the Scott Brothers, and many others, including John & Chris Tolos. He debuted at the age of 17, in 1948, and brought his brother into the business in 1953.

The Scott Brothers were one of the top babyface tag teams in the world over the next 15 years. They spent their early years mostly working for Stu Hart in Western Canada. The brothers were famous for being magic in the ring, but not getting along at all outside the ring. George, as the older brother, always wanted Sandy to do things his way. Then, when Sandy who passed away in 2010, didn't come to their mother's funeral, George never spoke to him again, even though they did have one last run as a tag team in the Carolinas in the 70s. The Scott Brothers held world tag team titles for Jim Barnett's massive promotion in the late 50s and early 60s, as well as the Southern tag team titles for Jim Crockett Sr., and had five runs as International tag team champions and three as Canadian tag team champions in Western Canada. They were also three-time world tag team champions for World Championship Wrestling, Barnett's national promotion in Australia, during the 60s.

George Scott, wrestling as The Great Scott, also had a run as U.S. tag team champions for Vince McMahon Sr.'s Capital Wrestling in 1963. On March 7, 1963, at the TV tapings in Washington, DC, Buddy Rogers & Johnny Barend were defending the tag titles against Scott, who was debuting with the promotion, and Pete Sanchez, a regular prelim wrestler. Rogers won the first fall over Sanchez with the figure four leglock, injuring him and he was unable to continue. "Killer" Buddy Austin, a regular pushed heel, came out and asked to replace Sanchez as Scott's partner, telling announcer Ray Morgan that they could beat Rogers & Barend, even with the handicap of being down a fall. This turned Austin face immediately, since Rogers & Barend were the two top heels. The commissioner in attendance at the show approved the substitution and it was announced the titles were at stake.

In the second fall, Rogers was disqualified for an illegal kneedrop coming off the top rope. Even though fans had been told forever that the titles don't change hands if there is a DQ win in any of the falls, this ruling was ignored. In the third fall, Barend held Austin in a full nelson for Rogers to dropkick him. Austin moved, Rogers dropkicked Barend and Austin pinned Barend to win the titles. Barend and Rogers then went at it after the match, with Barend also turning face to feud with Rogers over the WWWF title.

Scott & Austin lost the belts on May 16, 1963, also at the TV tapings in Washington, DC, to Brute Bernard & Skull Murphy. The tapings were the day before the May 17, 1963, Madison Square Garden show where Bruno Sammartino beat Rogers to win the WWWF title. In a title rematch, Scott & Austin split up with Austin going back heel, and Scott left the territory soon after.

George suffered a serious neck injury in 1972, and retired the next year. But his biggest claim to fame was from 1973 to 1981 as the booker of Mid Atlantic Championship Wrestling. He was hired by John Ringley, who took over the promotion after the death of Jim Crockett Sr. Ringley, the husband of Frances Crockett, was put in charge of the company, but after a nasty divorce, was kicked out of the company, and Jim Crockett Jr. took over. Crockett Jr. kept Scott as booker.

Scott changed the face of the promotion, which was known as a tag team territory. The Carolinas were a steady promotion, running multiple shows per night with dozens of towns weekly. The main events were revolving feuds in different markets with the top teams such as Rip Hawk & Swede Hansen, The Anderson Brothers, Johnny Weaver & George Becker (and later Weaver & Art Neilson), The Scott Brothers, Paul Jones & Nelson Royal, Brute Bernard & Skull Murphy, and others, year-after-year, mixing and matching for years on end. Unlike most promotions which had a few local homesteaders, but most of the roster would be talent coming in for six months to a year, and then leave, Crockett Sr.'s wrestlers made a nice living and could raise their families in an area although the travel and schedule were difficult.

Scott changed that and turned the style more physical, bringing in Johnny Valentine to be the top star. At first, the fans didn't like the slower paced harder hitting matches and crowds went down, but eventually Valentine's matches with Wahoo McDaniel started clicking. Valentine's run in the territory was short, but influential, as the main event singles matches became long and hard hitting. Valentine's career ended in the famous 1975 plane crash, where Ric Flair broke his back. But when Flair returned months later, taking over the top spot in the promotion, Jim Crockett Promotions was arguably the best wrestling territory in North America, even though its key cities like Greensboro, Charlotte, Norfolk, Raleigh and Richmond were tiny in population compared to most wrestling hotbeds.

In particular, Scott gave the first major push to a number of young wrestlers. Flair was a prelim wrestler in the AWA, recommended to Scott by McDaniel in 1974. Scott had him bleach his hair, introduced him as the nephew of established star Hawk, and told him to study tapes and pattern himself after Buddy Rogers. Instead, Flair wanted to be a copy of his two heroes, Dusty Rhodes on the mic, and Ray Stevens in the ring, but he eventually became the biggest star ever in that part of the country.

When Ricky Steamboat came to the territory from Georgia (Sammy Steamboat had been a major star in the 60s in the area), he had been a prelim babyface who hadn't gotten a break. Flair immediately wanted to work with him and did a series of angles with him, and he became one of the most popular wrestlers in the area's history. Greg Valentine, Johnny's son, became Flair's tag team partner, and at other times, Flair's biggest rival. Bill Eadie, who came over when the rival IWA went down as Bolo Mongol, had a mask put on him and became a big star as The Masked Superstar. Blackjack Mulligan, John Studd, the Iron Sheik, Roddy Piper, Jay Youngblood, Jimmy Snuka, Paul Orndorff and many others became headliners under Scott. The promotion expanded into cities like Buffalo, Cincinnati and Toronto. He and Crockett purchased 33% of Maple Leaf Wrestling from the late Frank Tunney, and the company, which had been struggling after The Sheik's predictability had killed business, revived behind the younger Carolinas stars like Flair and Steamboat.

"He was a good man to me," said Steamboat. "He played an important part in starting my career in the Carolinas against Ric Flair."

His reputation as a booker grew to where, when Eddie Einhorn put together the IWA, and was paying big money to start an attempt at a national promotion, his choice was Scott to be his booker. Scott claimed he was offered $250,000 a year, gigantic money in 1975, along with points in the promotion, but turned down the offer to stay with Crockett.

His run ended in 1981, when he quit after a series of disputes with Crockett and moved to Oklahoma to try and revive Leroy McGuirk's dying promotion. That failed, but in 1983, Vince McMahon hired Scott as his booker when he went national. The early booking was very strong, but Scott had philosophical differences with the changes in direction. He believed in a more serious wrestling presentation. He was also concerned with the rampant drug use that was taking over the business at the time, a byproduct of wrestlers being able to earn more money, and a far more grueling national travel schedule. While a lot of people claim credit for coming up with the name WrestleMania (WWE history gives the credit to Howard Finkel, but I've had people dispute that) but Scott claimed that he was the one talked Vince McMahon into naming the show WrestleMania instead of the Colossal Tussle. Scott had issues with Dick Ebersol over the content of the original Saturday Night's Main Event shows, hating the skits and wanting to make it a more serious wrestling product, and was against anything that he thought exposed the business, of which much of what WWF was doing at that time would fit into the category. Scott had been a stickler as a detail man in the Carolinas, to the point that if there were two shows being taped on the same day, if a wrestler was doing an interview on the first show, and wrestling on the second, he had to wear his street clothes for his interview on the first show because why would he be in his trunks when he's not wrestling. In particular, he was strict on guarding anything that would "expose the business," and felt the comedy skits being brought into wrestling fit into that category. He also had personal differences with Hulk Hogan, who had become a huge star by that time and wanted to do things his way. Scott was gone before the end of 1985, which led to Pat Patterson getting the position.

George saved a lot of his records, including the pay sheet for the first WrestleMania (no matter what he may claim publicly today, which is multiples of this figure, Hulk Hogan got $150,000 for the match and Mr. T ran up $22,000 in expenses the week of the show, which in those days must have thrilled WWE to no end). He even saved a letter written before WrestleMania from Vince and Linda McMahon, which talked about the procedures they were planning on going through to sign over the WWF when there appeared to be a good chance of the first WrestleMania failing and they would have to declare bankruptcy and lose the company.

He booked Dallas for Fritz Von Erich, but that promotion was past its peak and this was where it was clear time was starting to pass him by. Most notably, he turned Bam Bam Bigelow into a Russian, Crusher Yurkov.

He was later hired by Turner Broadcasting to replace Dusty Rhodes as booker of World Championship Wrestling in 1989. That run only lasted a few months. Scott's big move was to bring Steamboat out of retirement to challenge and finally win the world title from Flair, in Chicago. But wrestling had changed.

Scott was still in the mindset of rebuilding the house show business. At the February 20, 1989, Chi-town Rumble PPV, where Steamboat beat Flair in a classic match, he followed the title change by putting prelim wrestlers Kendall Windham and Steve Casey out for a long match, with the PPV ending with the wrestlers still in the ring. He did so with the idea of teaching fans that you had to come to the live event to see the entire show.

The company's next major show was the Steamboat vs. Flair rematch in New Orleans, on April 2, 1989, a free TV special going head-to-head with WrestleMania V. Scott's idea was to have a classic 60 minute draw on television with Steamboat retaining the title. But, because all the house shows were also being headlined by Steamboat vs. Flair, Scott, when he laid out television, did almost no promotion of the card for fear that if people knew Flair and Steamboat were wrestling for free on television, it would hurt the house shows.

"I worked with he and Sandy in the ring, but we also worked together in the Crockett office," said Les Thatcher. "He was the reason I was offered an office job in WWF in 1985 to handle the promos. Talented tag team, as good as they came, and as a booker, he was solid. I hate hearing it said that he lost touch, not so much as the people outside of wrestling tried to change it when they got involved and George was fighting them."

WWF had Hulk Hogan vs. Randy Savage that night after a one-year build in one of the hottest matches in their history, which set a domestic PPV record (767,000 buys) which even today has probably only been topped a few times in history even with the expanding universe. Flair vs. Steamboat did a 4.3 rating for one of the greatest television matches of the last 30 years. Scott was fired by Turner Broadcasting shortly before the show after management was in shock that their special was barely mentioned on television while WWF was hyping its head-to-head big show to death. With a booking committee, led by Flair, put into place, the first thing Flair did was change the finish of the match, scheduled as a two out of three fall 60 minute match that would be tied with one fall each after going the distance. Flair changed it to having Steamboat win a controversial pin at the 55 minute mark where Flair would have his legs under the ropes. The prior year, a Flair vs. Sting 45 minute title match head-to-head with WrestleMania had done a 5.8 overall rating and the main event peaked at a 7.8.

Scott's final booking job was with South Atlantic Pro Wrestling, an attempt to revive Carolinas territorial wrestling. Steamboat worked the shows for far less than he could have earned elsewhere, showing loyalty to the booker who gave him his first chance. South Atlantic was also where people like Dean Malenko and Ken Shamrock got their first breaks. Scott named Shamrock "Vince Torelli," as an Italian pretty boy type, and often had him team with Shamrock groomed to be the Steamboat of 15 years earlier. But the days of territories were over and the promotion shut down in 1994.

CHAPTER ELEVEN

CM PUNK
QUITS WWE

FEBRUARY 3

The status of C.M. Punk has become a major talking point in WWE, as he told Vince McMahon about 30 minutes before the start of Raw on 1/27 in Cleveland that he was flying home, and did.

He wasn't on the show and didn't appear at the Smackdown tapings the next night. WWE has since pulled him off all shows, although at press time he was still being advertised for Elimination Chamber on 2/23 in Minneapolis. We're told that he will eventually be pulled off that show as well.

It's sketchy what happened. Over the last week, ever since Punk's interview with Ariel Helwani before the Chicago UFC show where he openly brought up that his contract was up in July and didn't want to say what he was going to do next, several people who know him had noted not to be surprised if he leaves. Two different people said that he was "as good as gone" in July, and one said that they didn't expect him to even last until July.

There were frustrations with creative and with money, even though he has made great money the last several years. This was not a spur of the moment thing as much as something that had been building. The way we were told was that he couldn't take it any longer and told McMahon that he was going home. McMahon had been tied up all day since they were rewriting the show, based on what happened the prior night at the Royal Rumble to figure out a way to keep the show under control and not have the audience hijack it again. Punk had been scheduled for an interview on the show to presumably build up a match with Kane on the PPV, which would lead to his planned WrestleMania match with HHH.

Because McMahon was so busy, Punk didn't see him until 7:30 p.m., when he told him he was leaving. The reason the Kofi Kingston vs. Alberto Del Rio match on Raw went so long is because it came during the period laid out for Punk's interview and had to go a second segment to cover the time, so the key "money" segments would be in their correct time slots.

The working assumption internally has been for several weeks that Punk was leaving in July and not going to sign a new deal. The belief was that he is not a spender, has saved his money and doesn't have to work. It was a weird dynamic because he's one of the few guys on the roster that the company and Vince McMahon knew believed he didn't need them, and financially, really doesn't. So they can't deal with him from the same level as all the other guys who are scared to lose their jobs and spots.

Within the company, the reason was that he came to the realization that he would never be positioned higher than he was. His goal was to main event WrestleMania, as in be in the real main event. He felt that because he didn't fit the mold of what they think the top star in the company should look like, he would never be the guy and the centerpiece.

It's not known at press time what caused the situation to get to where it did and what was the straw that broke the camel's back.

Another person close to the situation who was aware it was coming, just didn't know when, said it was a classic case of being burned out, and noted the dichotomy that he's never had a job where he's made anywhere close to the same amount of money, nor ever been as famous, and gotten more out of wrestling than this one. But, he has been miserable at the job for some time, and he was a guy who loved working in pro wrestling when he made nothing or very little. It was noted that he never had the personal connection with Vince McMahon that most of the big stars had, and always knew he was not their kind of guy, didn't have the look they thought a star should have, and felt he got over in spite of how he was used and not because of how he was used. The feeling was that there was a communication issue and lingering unresolved issues that dated back some time, probably most of the last year, combined with frustration regarding creative going forward and of late.

Sheamus will be replacing Punk at all the Smackdown tapings where he was largely advertised as the main star. It is a brave new world and you can never rule out the possibility it's a work, and you won't know for sure unless Mania comes and goes without a return. Daniel Bryan will be advertised as the main star on Smackdown going forward since John Cena is not booked often on the Tuesday tapings.

Punk was at the Wizard World Comic Con in Portland, OR, on 1/25, as he flew form Chicago to Portland, then back to Chicago for UFC that night, and then to Pittsburgh for Rumble before leaving from Cleveland. During the Q&A, he seemed very lackluster about WWE. He basically said that he used to argue the creative but now he just shows up and does what he's told. He pushed the idea that he felt this was Daniel Bryan's year and knocked the short-term booking and planning several times. In many ways, this was similar to when Steve Austin left in 2002, when he publicly started complaining about creative, and a week later he was gone (of course that was precipitated by them wanting him to job to Lesnar clean with no build-up on Raw as opposed to Lesnar going through everyone to set up their first match on a major PPV).

Punk did a long interview with MMAFighting.com reporter Ariel Helwani from his home, since UFC was in Chicago. He said at the time that his contract was up in July and said there's no point in saying anything about it. He said if he doesn't sign, he wouldn't say so now, and if he says he is looking at not signing, and then he does, people will think he was working an angle. Plus, he said in 2011, when he started that angle where he was leaving, he was in his mind, 100%, out the door at that time.

The circumstances that ended up taking place led to him signing a three-year deal. He's always said that he won't be around as long as people think. Many in WWE have noted to us that Punk has not been happy with his creative.

At the same time, of the full-timers with the company, Punk, Batista, John Cena, Daniel Bryan and Randy Orton are the top tier. Batista is scheduled full-time but he is 45 and has had a lot of injuries in the past, although to his credit his body held up for an MMA camp, which is more intense than a wrestling schedule. The difference is the MMA camp is two months and a wrestling schedule never ends. While WWE doesn't "need" anyone, even Cena, Punk does have significant value given the lack of depth on top and injury rate.

You can also see with Batista and others that if you do really leave for a while, your value can increase greatly by not being there if you want to rest for a few years and then come back. There's the legends role of a few big shows a year, the Jericho role of half the year or so full-time (although as we've seen with Jericho and RVD, that role does limit greatly how much they'll push you), or leave, rest up injuries and come back full-time, waiting long enough for a Batista level return.

The one thing with Punk is he is a big enough star that if he does leave for several years, his return would be a big deal. Still, very few walk away at 35. Batista and Jericho left, but they both did so for other entertainment ventures. Punk hasn't seemed like he's interested in that direction.

He said some days he's hurting really bad and other days he's not, noting he's taken very little time off over the last ten years. He said when he took the two months off last year, that he probably should have taken more time. He wasn't fully healed but came back because the Payback PPV was in Chicago and he worked with Chris Jericho, starting a babyface turn.

As noted many times, the reason he turned heel when he was a hot babyface, was recognizing that he could be the top heel in the company, but would always at best be the No. 2 babyface. But after the heel run, he was turned back. Still, he was always in top programs, was beating The Shield in 1 vs. 3 matches consistently and was being groomed for a match with HHH at WrestleMania, which while not the main event, was guaranteed to be pushed as one of the key things on the show.

Vince McMahon does like a challenge in the sense if a guy looks like he wants out, like Punk did the last time, he may be able to cut a better deal than the guy who the company knows isn't going anywhere and is so glad to be there and afraid of losing their job that they'll take anything.

It's an interesting game because he is valuable, maybe second or third most valuable guy in the company, at a time when value of the individual means less than it ever has.

He was also asked about doing MMA. He talked about it like he'd like to do it, and noted that he knows people think he can't do it and looks at that as a challenge. He noted that people thought he couldn't do what he did in wrestling and he loves proving people wrong.

Bellator has already expressed at least preliminary interest in him. He would be free and clear of any WWE contractual obligations in July.

He thought some people who wanted him to fail would tune in to see him get beat up, but he gets punched in the face four times a week anyway.

I get the impression a part of him would like to do it the same way Batista did it as a bucket list thing. With Batista, it seemed on the surface to be a real bad risk, but in the end, he did it and wasn't hurt at all. With Punk, on the surface, it would seem the same thing. A theoretical big risk.

There was a time when a giant name pro wrestler doing MMA would have been huge, as noted by Brock Lesnar's UFC debut. But I don't see UFC using an 0-0 guy for the same reason they never used Herschel Walker, and at least with Lesnar and Kurt Angle (who they made a strong pitch for), they had the high-level wrestling credentials to make them real. Bellator should take him, but that limits the upside and PPV money.

The key is he's 35 and his body is beaten up from years of pro wrestling. While he does train in fighting disciplines, he doesn't have the competition background at a high level in any fighting sport. That is very old to start out in unless you want to compete at the beginners level. It's also hard to say if he goes against someone legit and loses, how it would affect him for a WWE return, either with the fans, or with management. And I'm not sure exactly what kind of challenge he'd be up for. Herschel Walker was up for the challenge, got a lot of publicity, but was put in with guys below his level that he was going to have no trouble beating. But he's also one of the great athletes of modern times.

Alberto Del Rio's previous MMA means nothing good or bad for him because most fans don't know of it. But Punk is such a big star people would know. Batista did one fight and few saw it and it meant nothing one way or the other, but he also didn't lose. Had he got knocked out, would it have made a difference? I'm leaning toward no from a fan standpoint because wrestling fans know the difference and if you are a star to wrestling fans, no matter your personal life shortcomings or screw-ups, in the end, you are still a star to them.

Punk also said he's told Vince McMahon (via text) that he'd like to induct Ultimate Warrior into the Hall of Fame, although one would think his leaving may nix that, and there probably was never a chance of it to begin with.

He said he's never met Warrior, but Warrior texts him inspirational messages before PPVs and they have a connection. He noted that Hulk Hogan, who is rumored to be the one who inducted Warrior, hates Warrior.

He tried to downplay the Michelle Beadle/A.J. Lee thing. His description of what happened with he and Beadle was exactly what we heard, well with one added thing. She was with a few of her girlfriends and walked past him and said, "Hey, fuckface" and then high-fived them. I heard everything but the high-five to her friends, which I guess would explain why he wasn't too happy about it. She had claimed it was a greeting of endearment (the two dated at one time briefly), and later went on Twitter and made a comment about girlfriends ruining guys' friendships with girls. His description of what happened with A.J. Lee (whose name he never mentioned, only saying "my girlfriend") was very different, trying to low-key it and play down that anything happened.

He said the connection with HHH and Rener Gracie is that HHH and Stephanie brought Rener and Eve Torres (the former WWE star who now is involved in teaching Jiu Jitsu to women) to teach their kids Jiu Jitsu and he put over how great both of them are at teaching kids.

When asked about the network, he said as a fan in 1997 he'd have loved if such a thing existed. As a wrestler, he doesn't know, because nobody knows how it'll affect PPV bonuses and none of the wrestles have been told much of anything. Across the board, among the wrestlers, there is a lot of curiosity regarding WrestleMania paychecks. The one thing is, with all the new money coming in, all the wrestlers should make far more because the revenue will be way higher presumably come October when the new TV deals are in place. However, wrestlers have never been paid a cut of the TV deals in the past, and the bulk of their income is either their downside guarantee if they are hurt or not used well, or a formula based on the house show revenue, the PPV revenue, how their merchandise does and a fee from the video game. The network won't hurt house show revenue significantly or at all. It may hurt PPV revenue a lot, and may hurt revenue on DVDs somewhat.

So that's a situation to look at. But if PPV and DVD business goes down with the network, but the company gets as much or more revenue based on network subscribers, what cut of the network will the wrestlers be getting is a real issue. In a sense, with more revenue coming in presumably, wrestlers should be paid better. Yet at the same time, with so much of that income more guaranteed rather than generated based on individuals, when it comes to the key guys and big moneymakers, how will their value be measured?

He said he has no problem with Batista coming back in a Mania main event spot, but he did have a problem with Dwayne Johnson because he doesn't think you should be in the business part-time and take a WrestleMania spot from someone who deserves it, but since Batista is around the long haul he has no problem. I hope he doesn't really mean that because it would tell me he doesn't understand the concept of a drawing card, since the three Mania shows Johnson came back for were the three biggest grossing events of all-time because of that fact. I really don't think Batista will make anywhere close to the same difference this year that Johnson made the last three years, not that he may not help.

The subject of Bryan came up and he said that Bryan gets the biggest crowd reactions at the shows, but he doesn't know if it's Bryan that is popular or the most popular wrestler, or that people just like screaming "Yes, Yes, Yes."

An interesting note is a few days later at a Q&A at a comic con he did, he said he thought this was Bryan's year and he'd like to see Bryan in the main event at Mania instead of Batista, said Batista was his friend, he's glad he was back. He said he had no problem with Batista in the main event because he's back full-time. He said his belief Bryan should be in the main event was meant as no slight toward Batista.

It's a weird deal because things are self fulfilling in many ways. The Bryan & Punk shows haven't done the kind of business the Cena & Orton shows do, and that would indicate the "Yes" chants aren't selling tickets like Cena, but the biggest draw in most cases is going to be the guy pushed as the biggest star.

He said he was happy for Bryan because he knew where he came from. Helwani asked about Bryan stealing the chant from Diego Sanchez but never acknowledging it (Bryan has acknowledged it in a few interviews I've heard) and Punk said something about how today people know while in the past people didn't know Superstar Billy Graham stole everything from Muhammad Ali and that Ali stole from Gorgeous George.

Graham did take a lot from Ali, but tailored it for his own thing and created a lot of new stuff. Dusty Rhodes took a ton from Graham, as he was in the AWA with Dick Murdoch when Graham was in his AWA heyday, and then used the same interviews when he went to Florida as a heel after the AWA, but also tailored it and created his own stuff.

FEBRUARY 10

The departure of C.M. Punk (Phil Brooks, 35) after eight-and-a-half years under a WWE contract remained the most talked about thing in pro wrestling this past week, with chants for Punk at most of the arenas the company held shows in.

Not a lot has changed in the past week. Punk walked out on 1/27 in Cleveland, about 30 minutes before the Raw television show was going to go on the air. There have been a lot of claims as to why, including reports claiming he was mad Dave Bautista returned and was getting the WrestleMania title match at Randy Orton (which would contradict what he said in an interview with Ariel Helwani a few days earlier, where he said he was fine with that).

Those close to the situation say that people looking for a singular reason or a simple reason are missing the point. Nearly everyone who knew him reasonably well said that they knew he was going to leave. At one point, Orton vs. Punk for the title was planned for WrestleMania, but that changed some time back. Some had noted to us that they didn't believe he'd last through July, when the three-year contract he signed in 2011 would expire.

From those within the company, the talk is that Vince McMahon wants him back, because he is the company's second biggest merchandise seller, behind John Cena, and one of its key performers, plus was figured into a key WrestleMania match with HHH. McMahon is said to be the one who is going to handle this situation even though HHH, or Paul Levesque, as he's really known by most who aren't wrestlers, runs talent relations. Some have said that Levesque felt that Brooks walking out was unprofessional, and that the company didn't need him or anyone. Others have noted that he can't express that feeling and it's best for him to stay quiet. Even though a guy walking out of a television shoot as a headliner and with no notice would be considered unprofessional, for him to express strong feelings would have people say he's putting his personal wrestling angle ahead of business. A key is that Punk made it clear that a match with HHH was not a match he was interested in at WrestleMania. This is in a sense is a slap in the face of HHH as a performer.

The reality is that a match with HHH, because of his power and long-time stardom, is guaranteed to be one of the key pushed matches on the show. On the flip side, if Punk was going to leave in July, which was his plans, it really wouldn't make sense for Punk to beat HHH, who is going to stay, and who, while not a full-time wrestler, will remain a key performer with the company for years to come. And even if HHH doesn't want to win, he's very well versed in both promos and matches at not really putting people over, even if he does get pinned in the end. And the reality is, if Punk is leaving, there is no reason for HHH to put him over past pacifying fans for the moment while not building the next step, unless it's to build for a return where HHH does go over.

WWE has made no public statements. Punk has, however, been removed from all advertising going forward. His name was never mentioned on Raw and the chants for him were not acknowledged in any form. Some expected a big burial like the company did in 2002 when Steve Austin walked out under somewhat similar circumstances, but the company probably learned to have the foresight to avoid that.

Still, they are clearly not confident he's coming back. He was removed from the open of the show and replaced with a shot of Kane. He was removed from a graphic on the app and replaced by Cena. On 2/4, a licensee was given the instructions to remove all graphics on merchandise going forward that was to have Punk and replace them with Randy Orton. The latter move, in particular, is a long-term move and wouldn't have been called for unless they were pretty sure he wasn't coming back soon.

Those who have spoken with him and told us to expect him to leave have noted his being unhappy about money and creative, that there were things he had been told would happen that didn't pan out. It wasn't any one thing, although his WrestleMania payoff for the Undertaker match was said to be one of many things. But it was made clear to me not to look so simply at one specific thing, past he had lost his enthusiasm and wanted out. Because he didn't live high on the hog, and can afford to go home and with the way he lives, he'll have no money worries for the rest of his life.

There was the continual frustration that he felt, correctly, that he didn't have the look that they believe a top guy should have and it was keeping him from that position. There were also a lot of injuries to be considered. He had a few MRIs done over the past two months regarding various injuries, and underwent ImPact testing for a possible concussion (he tested negative) the night before.

The general feeling in the company was that a lot of people were tired of his negativity and from an office standpoint, many were glad he was gone. Unlike a lot of fans, there was a mood that because of the way he left that they should move on rather than have him come back for a few months to a relationship neither wants, even though he sells a lot of merchandise.

Mick Foley, in particular, noted that he would watch him and cringe when he would go to the top rope for the Randy Savage elbow drop, noting he knew how much it hurt him to do it and suggested Punk to take that move out of his repertoire. He noted Punk was going to do everything he could to have the best match possible until he left.

Austin noted that, whether he agreed or not with the creative as it was in 2002 that led him to leave, he regrets doing so the way he did, because he left a lot of money on the table, as Punk is doing.

A key thing Austin brought up is that when he left, he, like Punk, would have been in breach of contract. They can't force him back to work if he doesn't want to work. However, when Austin left in 2002, because of the breach, they cut off all money, meaning he didn't get any merchandising checks from items that bore his name and likeness, or from DVD's sold featuring him, video game royalties, or any royalties. If he were to complete his contract, he would continue to get merchandise checks after leaving the company, which in his case, would be a significant amount of money.

McMahon did learn from the Austin situation, and situations with so many others who left on bad terms, that it's not smart business to bury a major star after an abrupt departure, because it only leaves bad feelings if he does come back. There is nothing that has said they have called him in breach and are holding up all future payments, only that they do have the right to do so.

Punk would not be able to work in pro wrestling, or MMA, until his contract expires in July, but he would be free and clear from that point forward to go anywhere or do anything.

WWE had talked of changing up the planned WrestleMania show based not just on Punk leaving, but the crowd reactions at the Royal Rumble. At this point, we are not aware of any major changes. The belief is Daniel Bryan vs. HHH will take the place of Punk vs. HHH, and the Cena vs. Bray Wyatt, Undertaker vs. Brock Lesnar and Randy Orton vs. Batista WWE title matches will go as first scheduled. From TV, it did appear Orton vs. Batista is still a direction. Lesnar, Paul Heyman and Cena all didn't work TV this week. Lesnar was pulled last week from the Raw show in Los Angeles. Cena will be back on that show and there is no word at this point if Heyman is booked on TV in Los Angeles and/or Ontario, CA.

Foley, who described himself as someone who knew Punk pretty well and had talked with him at length over his situation, said on one hand his leaving was shocking, but on the other hand, he wasn't surprised. Foley, who has also left the company a few times, frustrated with working there for different reasons, said he, like many, were aware of how frustrated Punk had been and said he had tried to convince Punk to look at the glass as being half full instead of half empty. But he said that someone who fancies himself on being the best in the world is not going to be able to do that.

"Punk is a really honest guy," Foley said in a video talking about the situation. "He rubbed people the wrong way. A lot of people personally don't like him, but if you were to ask the guy to change, you'd eliminate who he is. You'd take away his drive."

Foley noted Punk was undersized and didn't have the look that WWE wants, but in spite of that, he had become one of the top stars in the business.

"The sky should have been the limit, and it hasn't quite been. There have been some decisions made as far as his direction that I didn't agree with. I knew he was thinking of leaving. I knew he was looking forward to leaving for a while."

Foley said he would tell Punk to just take time off and let his injuries heal and comeback refreshed.

"He would say to me, `I'm not you. Once I'm done, I'm done.'"

He said that he expects to talk to Punk and will tell him to work out his contract, then take time off and heal up.

"If you still love the business, go back to the indies. Do it on your own terms. I have to believe he no longer needs the money but I think he's going to love the wrestling business for a long time to come."

Foley said he was glad Punk stood up for what he believed in, but felt it was an opportunity lost for both the WWE and Punk. He, like Austin, encouraged Punk to come back and at least work out his contract. Foley said he felt Punk's promos had been lacking for the past several months. Punk, in interviews days before quitting, said that he had gotten tired of fighting and was just accepting things.

Foley said he would encourage WWE that if he does come back, to not script his interviews at all and let him say what he wants. Foley noted that when they worked together, Punk refused to do scripted lines that made fun of Foley's weight. He said that a build for a Punk vs. HHH match would be a great buildup and almost guarantee a great match because both are good big game players.

A grandstand challenge to Punk for a fight that will likely never happen, was issued by Jason David Frank, the former Green Ranger of the "Power Rangers" and the World Series of Fighting. Their matchmaker and Executive Vice President, Ali Abded-Aziz confirmed to Ariel Helwani of MMAFighting.com that Frank's manager contacted them about such a match and said they would be interested in promoting it. He also said they were interested in having Punk fight if he'd like to. Bellator has also expressed interest in Punk. UFC President Dana White said he thought Punk, who he's met at several shows, including on 1/26 in Chicago, was a cool guy, but said Punk made no hints at wanting to fight in UFC when they talked last week. He said he didn't know if Punk could fight so didn't give a definite answer when asked if they would be interested in using him. Punk had told Helwani that there's a chance he'd fight, but he also says he's thinking of fighting so he can entertain himself reading people talk shit about him on message boards. Frank, who is 40, fought three times as an amateur and once as a pro, as a heavyweight, but hasn't fought in more than three years. If Punk were to fight, and the odds are against it because of the risk/reward aspect, based on his frame, he'd more likely fight at middleweight. But he has the same risk/reward as Dave Bautista, and is younger, and few really expected Bautista to fight, but it was something on his bucket list and he did it. Bill Goldberg, a big MMA fan who trained in the sport, had also entertained doing an MMA fight after WCW closed down, but in the end, decided against it.

FEBRUARY 10

Austin was on Arsenio Hall on 1/30 and talked about Punk leaving the company. Austin and Brock Lesnar are probably the two guys who can most understand the situation, since both did the same thing, although Lesnar did give notice and work through WrestleMania. Austin walked out in 2002 over creative reasons. He had been critical of creative in an interview, and then showed up on TV the next week and was asked to put over Lesnar on Raw. Based on logic as things were at the time, that made no sense, as Lesnar was on the way up and Austin was the top guy in the company, so their first meeting should have been a title match down the line on PPV. Lesnar hadn't even won the title yet. Austin has since said that he made a mistake in how he handled the situation. The company buried Austin like nobody's business the next week on TV, which was even more of a mistake, and claimed he'd never be allowed back. Anyone who followed wrestling one iota knew it was inevitable he'd be back and that they would regret the portrayal of their kickass babyface as the guy who ran away from a fight, which is how it was portrayed. Eventually, Jim Ross contacted Austin and got he and McMahon back together, and they made a deal for Austin to return, although it was relatively short-lived because neck problems let to Austin retiring after his match with Rock at WrestleMania 19 in Seattle in 2003. He was still a huge star, but he was not the same as far as being able to draw on his return as all those speeches burying him in 2002 took the edge off him. K-1 did the same thing to Bob Sapp, who had a business dispute over money and they portrayed him as a coward who was afraid to fight when he walked out, and the same thing happened. Of course, they made up, but Sapp's drawing power wasn't the same after all he propaganda of being a coward, which is the most negative thing a company can say about talent. Austin said his decision cost him a lot of money and that Punk doing so during WrestleMania season is missing out on a good payday. He figured either Vince McMahon would work Jedi mind tricks to get him back, or Punk will decide to return. Austin said Punk was under a lot of stress but believes it will all work out at the end. History tells us that same thing. When it was brought up that Dana White called Vince McMahon a "maniac" (he did so on the 1/27 Hall show), Austin agreed that McMahon was crazy as hell, but said it was in a good way.

FEBRUARY 17

After a week where the C.M. Punk news started dying down, people both in and out of the company are now looking at the 3/3 Raw, since it's from Chicago.

Either Punk will be back on that show and they'll get an incredible reaction for it, or there is a lot of concern how that show will play out. My gut says that if Hulk Hogan and Undertaker are brought to that show (both are scheduled to be brought back to TV at the 2/24 Raw in Green Bay), as they should be, plus Brock Lesnar, that while the Punk chants will probably be there, having Hogan there may serve as a counter. If Hogan was around too long, it would be one thing, but on week two and in Chicago, where he was a star dating back to around 1981, they aren't going to "turn" on him.

There was less concern this past week because while there were Punk chants at several house shows, they didn't pick up strongly nor last long. The feeling is that with nothing significant on that front happening with a Los Angeles television crowd, that it's a pretty much done situation with the possible exception of Chicago.

At the house show I went to in Oakland, it sounded like maybe four people who were clearly aware of the situation (since Punk was never booked for that show to begin with) started the chant. It picked up somewhat, but it was mostly little kids just parroting a chant, and not any kind of a protest akin to the nearly two years of "We Want Flair" chants at WCW shows from the summer of 1991, to early 1993 after he left the company for WWF.

At the Raw show in Los Angeles on 2/10, the company feared given they were in a major market, that fans could hijack the show and ruin the John Cena vs. Randy Orton TV main event, like happened with their match at the Rumble. So the idea was to bring Daniel Bryan out twice, including right before the main event, have him go over strong and get the chants out of the way.

For Punk, what happened, whether by design or an audible (and I'd be shocked if this was an audible because can you imagine the heat Rollins would have gotten had it backfired and he did it without prompting?), is that during the Dean Ambrose vs. Mark Henry U.S. title match, in the third hour, Rollins got on the mic as soon as they cut to a commercial at home, and said "C.M. Who? How about showing some respect for Dean Ambrose, the greatest champion in this company," which started the Punk chants (one person said the Punk chants started right before and Rollins said that in response).

The idea seemed to be that long before the three minute break was up, people would get it out of their system and at home, nobody would hear it. That seemed to work to a point. When they came back from the break, there were remnants and there was a woman right in front of the camera holding up a Punk sign, but it was barely audible and the chants never came back.

During that commercial break, Lawler made a remark about them going to die out soon, Cole on the headset said, How about "Go away, Go away," like they should chant that instead, while people were doing the chant. Layfield laughed and said there wasn't much determination in them (the ones chanting as it quickly died down).

During the videos they showed during commercial breaks on the show, there was a lot of Hogan and Sting, but everything with Punk was edited out. They even played the ad for the "Best of the Money in the Bank" DVD and everything with Punk was edited off the ad.

But they were not confiscating signs when you came through the door. There were a few Punk signs, and as noted, one was right in front of the camera shown during the Henry vs. Ambrose match, but that was about it.

The next night in Ontario, there was one small chant but one can argue the people who start those chants are smart enough to know it's not making it to television on a taped show. The crowd was said to have responded there pretty much the way one would program them to respond.

There is a mixed feeling within the company. Virtually nobody sides with him when it comes to walking out 30 minutes before a live TV shoot unless it's an elaborate angle (which on 3/3 we'll likely find out 100%, although those in the company certainly don't believe it's a work). Many have sympathy for some of his points about being promised things, or the heads of the company being so steadfast into believing that if you don't have the right kind of size and physique you can't be the top star. But they argue Punk very legitimately was No. 2 for a while. I guess the idea is that he really wasn't No. 2 because Cena was always around, and Dwayne Johnson was clearly ahead of him, and Lesnar was ahead of him, and now Batista was being positioned ahead of him.

While most conceded he was very popular, the belief was that he was not a ticket seller to live shows, and only on occasion was he a difference maker in PPV (clearly he was a few times).

On the flip side, he was the No. 2 merchandise seller, and his T-shirts in particular are a hot item so he is a strong revenue generator.

One person noted to us that he saw with his own eyes Staples Center security telling fans not to chant for Punk, and that security pulled two people aside and threatened to kick them out if they kept chanting it as they tried to get a chant going while they were on the air.

Regarding Punk, I don't know who he's in contact with, but it doesn't seem like he's in communication with many. The story is that those who have worked with him and know him that have tried to contact him haven't heard back, just like a TNA storyline about not returning phone calls, texts or e-mails in between shows.

It is notable that he really did come close to leaving in 2011 and when the angle started, he was gone. I think the moment it changed is when he was going through that period on Raw where he quietly lost every week, until all of a sudden things changed.

Jim Ross, who had been in communication with Punk in recent months, said he thought C.M. Punk would make a great MMA announcer.

"He's glib. He's intelligent. He's well-spoken. He understands infinitely the product and he knows how to entertain. He has everything that an MMA company would desire. And I think he would just be phenomenal."

During one of the periods where Punk was injured and he worked as an announcer on Raw he was praised for his instinctual timing in the role.

Mick Foley, another friend of Punk's, was on Live Audio Wrestling this past weekend talking about him.

"The last time I touched base with him was after the Rumble and I don't want to discuss what he said exactly. I'll just say I wasn't shocked when he decided to leave because he and I, there is a deep, mutual respect there and we like each other. I would say to him after I watched him at a house show and I would say, `Geez, you don't have to work that hard every night.' And he would say to me, `If I didn't, I wouldn't be here.' And I respect the work ethic and I understand if you're hurt and you're not enjoying yourself that it's not the place to be. I would hate to see C.M. Punk turn into what I did where my philosophy became, `Good enough is going to have to be good enough.' And it wasn't that philosophy that helped me succeed, to get me into the WWE Hall of Fame and I kind of regret going through a few years where things had to be that way. I don't think Punk wants anyone to see him at anything less than his best and I know he'd been frustrated for a while.

"He's a pretty outspoken guy, and in the end, he'll make the decision that's best for him. What I said, and I'll repeat for you guys, if he can reconsider one thing, it's not to let whether or not he's officially the main event dictate how good his match is. If he had a big match coming up at WrestleMania, I would encourage him to at least think about taking advantage of that. In 2006, in no way, shape or form were Edge and I the main event at WrestleMania, but we had a great match. I didn't walk away from that WrestleMania thinking it was any less special because we weren't the feature, so that's the only piece of advice I'd give him, not to let those words, main event, dictate how important the match is, but if your heart's not in it, it's not in it."

FEBRUARY 24

It's been really strange how silent everything is on the C.M. Punk story. However the story started, it would appear D-Day, at least for now, is the 3/3 Raw show in Chicago.

What I thought was strange last week was when the clip of Michael Cole, Jerry Lawler and John Layfield before Raw (it was incorrectly reported this took place during the commercial break in the Mark Henry vs. Dean Ambrose match) making fun of the fans for not being able to get a strong chant going for Punk, and it wound up on the Internet, that WWE didn't get it taken down. Usually something like that would be down within a few hours. That, and the fact that there is no way Seth Rollins was going to bring up Punk during a commercial break on Raw and get on the mic and incite the crowd to chant his name on his own, seemed ominous.

Given the Chicago show would be the first Monday where people have to pay to order the network and get the post-game show, a cliffhanger ending involving him showing up would be one of the best things they could do to get subscribers. Of course, if he's really done, then it's just fantasy booking.

Punk went AWOL on 1/27, right before Raw went on the air. WWE has never done an angle of this type, where it's not acknowledged at all on television. But it does fit into Punk's M.O. Still, the idea he'd tell so many people he was unhappy to make it believable he'd walk out and work the boys is not how WWE traditionally does business.

But never acknowledging his leaving as a storyline is also not how they've handled a top guy leaving in the past. Usually there is a quick burial and move on. It's also a weird time because of the hijacking the show issue. If WWE were to suspend him (firing him makes no sense because unless they paid him, he'd be able to the next day start negotiating and appearing on somebody else's television) and acknowledged it, even though it would be the "correct" decision, the live audience would make him a cause and could ruin live Raw shows.

Will Vince McMahon be able to, or has he already, pulled what Steve Austin and Chris Jericho called his Jedi mind tricks? Or has Punk already decided to be a puppeteer, as opposed to someone who realizes his body is breaking down and doesn't want to be out there at a standard lower than he's been willing to accept of himself? Or has he simply felt he's not happy there and doesn't want or need it anymore?

And if he's not there, how will the Chicago crowd react? This makes that night the most intriguing Raw episode of the year. Because it could be the most positive episode of the year. And it could be the most negative. But if it's the latter, it will be a one-week thing, because the build to WrestleMania will take over and carry the promotion from there.

MARCH 10

Ever since C.M. Punk walked out of the dressing room in Cleveland on 1/27, he has been the most talked about personality in the business.

For the last month plus, there have been all kinds of questions, and no real answers. Some people thought it was an angle from the start. If it was anyone but Punk, there would have been less thought in that direction. But he worked an angle in ROH when he was leaving for WWE developmental, making people think he was losing his title and leaving when he was still staying a few months longer, which some called the first Summer of Punk.

To a larger audience, his 2011 stint, which he still insists was not planned out at the start to turn out how it did, a similar scenario, telling people in advance his contract was up and he was leaving because of problems in the promotion, ended up making him the most talked about wrestler on a national basis and saw him surpass everyone but John Cena when it came to being a star.

It garnered him a win over Cena to take the title, in one of the more memorable matches of the last decade after he had convinced people he was leaving and that show was his last night with the company.

The idea that he would leave when his three-year contract was up in July was something he had talked about extensively with a number of friends in the industry. The idea he was going to leave wasn't a surprise. Many had told us he was as good as gone in July. A few were not surprised he left the day after the Royal Rumble. Still, the vast majority of those in the industry, no matter what the long-term was, believed he and Vince McMahon would come to an agreement to come back for WrestleMania. From his standpoint, there was a ton of money at stake. From the company's standpoint, he was one of their biggest commodities and they were embarking on not only the biggest show of the year, but perhaps the most important next few months since the end of the Monday Night Wars.

What was notable about this departure, unlike the others, was the complete silence. In 2011, while the title win over Cena was kept quiet, as was his agreeing to stay until he pinned Cena, his walkout with the belt and pipe bomb promo were very obviously clever storylines.

This year, it could have been the same thing. Raw on 3/3 in Chicago was going to tell the tale, in most people's thoughts. Many expected him back. Nobody knew. Even backstage, the response we got the day of the show is that he wasn't there, he wasn't scripted into the show, but nobody figured he would do anything but show up at the end, and noted that the show was scheduled to go unusually long. The expectation wasn't because of anything said, but just figuring out what would make sense for all concerned. There were the obvious mixed weekly signs. The company still had never made an announcement that he was suspended, even though he hadn't come back to work for more than a month. But Daniel Bryan was moved into Punk's planned spot at WrestleMania against HHH, and Christian moved into Bryan's spot, against Sheamus. Still, the Randy Orton vs. Batista world title match wasn't clicking to start with. Then Batista went heel in a promo that seemed to beg for Bryan to be moved into the title match. Without Bryan or Punk inserted into that match, it risked becoming the perfect ten year anniversary of the Bill Goldberg vs. Brock Lesnar match at WrestleMania 20.

It didn't take a booking rocket scientist to see that the way to end WrestleMania would be for Bryan to be in the match with Orton and Batista, and win at the end, before 70,000 fans and probably the largest audience ever to view a WrestleMania because of new technology, and to see how far Bryan could go when being given the real chance. And there were hints given all week between the nature of Batista's promos, and Batista helping lay out Bryan, that Batista vs. Bryan is a direction they are building to. More than ever before, the TV has been centered around Bryan as the top babyface, with Cena as the established star in a support role, which is a recent flip-flop. In addition, Stephanie McMahon did a backstage pass interview with her key line being that Bryan would never be a WrestleMania main eventer, which the way it was delivered, as a heel, would seem to indicate he would be.

Bryan being booked with HHH even if Punk was on the Mania card felt like a major missed opportunity, although there are very easy ways around that, booking that if Bryan wins over HHH, he's added to the title match.

As for Punk, the nuclear silence continued. For an angle, this would have been the best quality control I can ever think of. But if not an angle, he'd have been suspended long ago and while he may have been threatened with a contract breach for not talking, that wouldn't have prevented WWE from putting finality on his tenure, even if it was a short few sentence release.

The feeling was 3/3 would be the date that would tell the story, because Raw was in Chicago. That day came and went, with no Punk. Yet, Punk was the most talked about thing on the show, despite a title change and one of the company's best matches in a long time. The company encouraged chants for Punk early, with Paul Heyman holding up the mic, and later, John Cena encouraged them as well during his promo. Yes, in hindsight, it seems like they wanted people to get it out of their system since it was a given the chants would come and go the entire show.

The show was as much a wrestling show as a battle for control of the show. Upset fans vowed to hijack the show. Normally that means nothing, because the number of times you see planned fan revolts in sports usually end up embarrassing because of how poorly they work.

But WWE was clearly concerned, based on several things on the show. Bryan came out for a promo and his first words were how the company doesn't listen to its audience, the fans are making themselves heard and actually using the term, said we're going to hijack the show. The fans cheered, with the irony being they were rebelling against management by doing exactly what they were told to do in a promo scripted by management.

The show opened with "Cult of Personality," and a Paul Heyman promo. Fans were chanting for C.M. Punk. The announcers brought up Punk's name and talked about him. It was entirely different from the WWE's history in this sort of situation, when somebody was gone. It's one thing to learn from the mistakes made in burying Steve Austin in 2002 when he left under similar circumstances. But this was the opposite. When Heyman talked about Punk, it was in completely sympathetic terms, egging the fans on to support him saying that Punk was a guy who was never truly wanted in WWE, a guy they thought was too small to main event WrestleMania, didn't have the right look, and was the guy who would rebel against the system and the first family (McMahons). He said they didn't want him from day one and they don't want him now.

Obviously the idea was to encourage fans to chant for Punk as loud as they could, tell the fans he wasn't there, and get it out of their system. And it was also a way to get them riled up and then use that to garner a heel reaction for Brock Lesnar, which worked like a charm. The fans still chanted for Punk throughout the show. If anything, that promo was designed to make the fans stick around for the rest of the show (the loss of viewers from the start-to-finish on Raw was the lowest number since 12/9). Raw was also booked to be the longest show in recent memory, with the idea everyone would expect that return in the overrun, so they made it far longer than usual, with the idea of building up the most viewers. You could sense the Bryan vs. Batista main event was being built for a heel beat down on Bryan, since Randy Orton was out at ringside from the start, and HHH, Stephanie and Kane followed. The beat down happened. The whole crowd was chanting for Punk to make the save. The company knew full well the beat down on Bryan had to elicit that reaction.

One segment scripted into the show at one point was that Bad News Barrett was going to deliver the bad news that Punk wasn't there.

So the questions continue. If Punk isn't returning, why is everyone so quiet on the subject? If he is, why wasn't it in Chicago?

You would ask why would Batista vs. Orton still be seemingly on the books. They could announce that as late as the night of the show of a change, because from both the inside and outside, the idea of the show ending with Bryan as champion as the big Mania moment seems almost too easy given the current situation. On Raw, Bryan was in the ring at the end with both Batista and Orton out, and laid out by both Batista and HHH. The company is at this point playing the role of heels to their audience, with the idea that they are so arrogant they are giving them a title match they clearly don't want and a top of the WrestleMania card that could be easily tweaked to be better.

Is that a work to set up a big angle, since there are still four Raw's until WrestleMania? Or, because the entire business has changed, is it actually the feeling that they can do as they want. The draw of WrestleMania is still more WrestleMania itself. With the network and the low price, this year, the idea of the show more than anything on the show being the draw would be more than ever before. The lineup is now just the gravy on top and not the main course.

Key people in wrestling who have been in similar situations, Steve Austin, and Chris Jericho, who had all come and gone, were all expecting Punk to come back. Austin publicly said his walking out the way he did, very similar to how Punk did, was the biggest mistake of his career, and predicted a return before the show. Jim Ross thought there was too much money on the table for the sides to not work things out, and at least do WrestleMania. Jericho, who was the strongest of all, when asked on Twitter if Punk would be on the show, responded, "Absolutely."

For what it was worth, I saw so many mixed signs, which is good, because it was keeping people guessing. I was told by a major figure in the game, not their speculation, but they had been told it was 100% that Punk would be at the show. I was then told right after that they had been lied to. Aside from that, it's a subject that everyone is asking questions about because of the silence on the issue.

There are people in the company who were guessing, and they don't know, that Punk might be there next week in Memphis, with the idea now people actually do accept he's not coming back. Part of that is the unwavering belief that Vince McMahon is the master manipulator. But that's again because in wrestling, there is also the need to think everything is a work, especially when something garners this level of interest. The essential thought process is that Vince McMahon is too smart to make Batista vs. Orton a title match at WrestleMania, and that he'd be able to use his "Jedi mind tricks" to talk Punk into coming back to help with the Mania show. It was actually clever because most figured if Punk wasn't in Chicago, he's not coming back. And that very well could be the case. But they sure encouraged the chanting of his name and strengthened the talk about him for another week.

But it also could be that he quit and he's done. You could say coming back in Chicago was too easy. Chicago would have been fun, but timing-wise, he's got plenty of weeks left, and the longer it goes, the better it is. But now we're getting to the point of over thinking. Still, there is a precedent for that. In 2007, they did a long build-up for Chris Jericho's return, which was to be at the No Mercy PPV, in Chicago. Because word had gotten out so strongly, Vince McMahon actually delayed the return, which, in hindsight, missed the peak given how rabid the Chicago fans were that night to see Jericho, not that it made any great difference in the long run.

Or Punk isn't laughing at all, and all this attention is for something going nowhere.

As for WrestleMania itself, the undercard looks to be taking shape with Sheamus vs. Christian and Jack Swagger vs. Cesaro being angles teased for potential undercard matches. It also could be a three-way with those two, and Big E, involving the IC title. The Shield is imploding in some fashion, but with Wyatt and the family linked with Cena, a Shield battle amongst themselves could be in the cards. A.J. Lee submitted to Natalya at the Smackdown tapings in a tag match, which was the first tease of a Divas title direction.

MARCH 31

There has been no communication of late between Punk and WWE. What is still weird to me is that Punk has been completely out of communication with people who he's been friends with in the past. It's just surprising the level of nuclear silence on this one. In last week's issue, when noting the rise in the ratings for Talking Dead over the previous few weeks, and we noted Punk likely added a few hundred thousand new viewers, it was noted to us that Walking Dead had a very controversial last 15 minutes and that may have caused more viewers than usual to stick around for the discussion show. So it's probably a combination of the end of Walking Dead and some wrestling fans wanting to see what he was up to that led to the ratings increase.

MAY 19

Regarding Punk, from a source very close to the situation, he's had no contact with WWE in some time. He was frustrated with booking and with payoffs and basically said that he's happy now being home and wasn't happy on the road. His contract expires in July. Even before he left, a number of people close to him and said they didn't expect him to renew and some thought he wouldn't last until July, others thought, incorrectly, he'd last until July but probably leave at that point. Whether he will be free to do other things at that time isn't clear, because WWE has the right to claim that he still owes them six more months because he failed to perform the final six months of his deal. It's such a different wrestling world in the sense that for a guy like him, I'm not sure where there even is to go if it's not WWE. In WWE, it was noted that a year ago before he left he was champion and working on top as champion, and headlined big drawing PPVs with Dwayne Johnson, and while still strong and he was No. 2 to Cena on the road and as a draw when he left, he wasn't champion and the programs weren't as strong. But that can't be the key reason, because he left months before he'd have gotten his Rumble PPV payoff (PPV payoff come three months after the show, he left the day after the Rumble), which would have been the one theoretically well down from the prior year if that's the case.

MAY 26

Punk made a public appearance, using the C.M. Punk name and not Phil Brooks, on 5/17. He sang, "Take Me Out to the Ball game" during a Chicago Cubs game at Wrigley Field. He also appeared in the broadcast booth during the game, and mentioned that he would be getting married next month. They then panned to A.J. Lee, wearing glasses, beaming. Lee was advertised for some of the European house show dates, the ones coming up after TV, but the impression we have is she'll be returning after the wedding. At least as of a few weeks ago, the plan was for her to be back either late this month or in June.

JULY 21

Punk's WWE contract has officially expired and he's now a free agent, and with prior usage before coming to WWE, should have the rights to his name for any entertainment ventures. Punk has returned to Twitter and started making deals now that his WWE contract expires this week, wrote "Starting a band, a podcast and a fire. One of these is true (Okay, two)."

JULY 28

Punk, while doing a red carpet gig at the AP Music Awards on 7/21, when asked if he would ever wrestle again, said, "No, never ever ever ever." When asked what had happened over the last six months, he just that he had forgotten (there are apparently legal issues involved and he's staying quiet). He joked it was because of concussions and staph infections, noting that he can't claim drug use for not remembering the last six months because he doesn't do drugs. He also showed his wedding ring and said he was off the market.

SEPTEMBER 8

Attorneys for C.M. Punk sent a 22 page letter to WWE over royalties (I believe WWE stopped sending Punk royalty money over their claim of a breach of contract) and use of his likeness, particularly him being featured in the video game (the roster of the game was put together before he quit the promotion even though it was just announced two weeks ago).

SEPTEMBER 15

Whether this is coincidence or not, after WWE got Punk's legal letter regarding merchandise royalties, the WWE slashed all prices for Punk merchandise, including selling his DVD for $3 and any other Punk related merchandise is now selling for less than $3. Essentially, they are trying to get rid of inventory as quickly as possible and not worrying about profit. The Blu Ray was going for $3 but it sold out at that price quickly and at press time, was no longer available on the company's web site, although Amazon.com still carries it.

SEPTEMBER 22

WWE has now deleted all C.M. Punk merchandise from its WWE Shop web site, to the point that if you look for it, you get the impression that C.M. Punk never existed.

OCTOBER 13

For whatever this is worth, TNA, through an intermediary who is friends with C.M. Punk, made a play for him just like they did for Alberto Del Rio several weeks back. The idea pitched was a huge deal to be the top star of the company and money similar to Hogan, with the idea he could be their flagship guy and if he signed now, could help them broker a stronger television deal. Whether Punk would mean something at that level to a TV station that Hogan wouldn't I guess would depend on the product knowledge of the station doing the talking. That's where I thought the loss of Hogan was going to hurt, not so much in the bottom line, but if you have Hogan under contract to your company, perhaps the name would help in those talks. I'd think more than Punk, but again, Punk was the No. 2 guy in WWE for a while and has in some ways become a bigger star by disappearing. Punk expressed no interest in working in wrestling again. Punk did attend his first pro wrestling show, at least that we know of, on 10/4 in Louisville. He was backstage at the OVW Saturday Night Special show and it was said he only spoke with Cliff Compton (who he may have attended to see him win the OVW title), and his old coaches Rip Rogers and Trailer Park Trash. The wrestlers were all told to let him be and he wasn't there to be talked with. He and Compton left the show. Fans weren't told he was there and he never appeared in front of them.

OCTOBER 20

On the C.M. Punk at the OVW show last week story we had in last week's issue, OVW has said that none of the wrestlers were told not to talk to Punk.

NOVEMBER 17

C.M. Punk, a huge comic book fan, has officially reached a deal with Marvel Comics to debut as a comic writer in the upcoming Thor Annual #1, writing a story about a young Thor, which will be released in February. "The only thing said to me (by Jason Aaron) was, `I need a story about young Thor. Tell me what you think,'" said Punk. Punk said he pitched an idea and Aaron loved it, which was of young Thor as a brash, bratty teenager, with the idea that he's resentful that his dad won't yet give him the hammer, based on the idea of a father who won't let his son drive the expensive car. Punk said his plan is to become a full-time Marvel Comics writer. He had approached Marvel in 2011 about writing a story about Punisher. He said he'll also be doing stories on all kinds of other characters. Punk also filmed a segment with Rener (the really charismatic husband of Eve Torres) and Ryron Gracie talking about the Luke Rockhold vs. Michael Bisping finish. They showed Punk rolling with Rener and tapping him out several times. Even though it was training and who knows how much Rener was resisting, Punk showed really smooth ground technique. They teased the idea Punk would fight on a Metamoris show. I'd be very surprised if that happened.

DECEMBER 8

C.M. Punk (Phil Brooks), who had refused to talk about WWE since leaving the promotion on 1/27 in Cleveland, opened up on Colt Cabana's Art of Wrestling Podcast on 11/26, with a two-hour interview going in-depth on his issues with the promotion.

A lot of what he said was somewhat well known. He was banged up, burned out, and didn't like the way he'd been used. He didn't like being booked with HHH at WrestleMania, and was leaving when his contract was up anyway. And he had enough money not to care.

But there were a few much stronger revelations, including Punk blaming the WWE medical staff for incompetence in the treatment of what turned out to be a serious staph infection, which he claimed could have been fatal. He revealed he had legally kicked the ass of the company in an out-of-court settlement without even filing a lawsuit over withheld royalties and the non-compete clause, saying, "I got everything I wanted and then some." This settlement apparently included all royalties owed, a full release with the WWE's attempt at a one-year non-compete clause dropped, an additional financial settlement from WWE plus a nice check from 2K Sports for putting him in the new video game when he was no longer under contract to the company.

If you understand that WWE does not like settlements in lawsuits, and aggressively will defend itself, and if the company is on the wrong end, will drag a case out as long as possible to make the adversary spend money, the fact that they were quick with a settlement says that Punk had a super strong case, they knew it, and that they couldn't even bluff him and drag it out for a long time. The idea that he got his settlement without signing a non-disparagement clause, and that the only thing he agreed to keep confidential is the amount settled for, is almost unheard of in a case like this with a major company. But that does give him leverage for the future. Even though he can't legally sue over the issues they settled over, if they say anything negative about him, he can come after them by doing media interviews, and for a publicly traded company, the portrayal of the owner as old and out-of-touch and the Head of Talent Relations as ego-driven and incompetent is not something that would be good. That's why I can't see any kind of a strong retaliation, even though I'm sure all involved would want it, nor any attempts to publicly humiliate his wife, coming out of this.

In listening to the podcast, I got the feeling he wanted his story out, but didn't want to be the guy spending his life with the vendetta against WWE. Time will tell, but I don't see him making the media rounds unless provoked. If provoked, I expect it and then some.

He also claimed that Vince McMahon did not tell the truth to stockholders, which could be a very serious charge, when asked about the status of Punk. On the company's February investment call, when McMahon was asked about what the status of Punk was, he said that Punk was on a sabbatical from the company. In reality, the company had officially suspended him. Companies have to tell the truth on those calls. WWE already has several lawsuits out against them regarding the idea they misled investors with the kind of television rights fees they were going to get in the latest U.S. negotiations, and this could potentially be added.

The medical stuff was the most serious, although it didn't get the most attention. But it was the only thing WWE responded to at press time.

"WWE takes the health and wellness of its talent very seriously and has a comprehensive Talent Wellness Program that is led by one of the most well-respected physicians in the country, Dr. Joseph Maroon," said a company source to Yahoo.com.

Maroon was never mentioned once by Punk. In fact, in his complaints about his medical treatment, Maroon had nothing to do with any of that treatment.

What seemed to get the most headlines was that Punk was fired, through a Federal Express letter, which came on 6/13, the day of his wedding. While the timing certainly made WWE look bad, and given that his wife worked for the company and had asked for the time off for her wedding and honeymoon from the very department that would have sent the letter, they can't claim ignorance of what day it was. Nor can they, given Punk said he had told HHH two days earlier about the wedding. Now, this letter would have been sent on firing day, as WWE released Evan Bourne, JTG, Curt Hawkins, Teddy Long, Yoshi Tatsu, Brodus Clay, Camacho, Aksana, Drew McIntyre, Jinder Mahal and ref Marc Harris the day before.

What's notable is that all of those names were announced publicly, and that was the all-inclusive list of those let go that was given publicly, as well as on the company's web site. The company kept secret Punk was released, and it was just figured he was done when his contract expired a few weeks later. The fact he was fired just a few weeks before his contract was expiring clearly meant they felt a need to get in a last word, and thus, the timing would have to have been either the work of a department with no communications, a head of the department with no memory, or a decision to hit a guy hours before his wedding day with news of not only his firing but of withholding royalties and a one-year non-compete clause, that included UFC and all pro wrestling groups. Had his contract just expired, he would have been free to work anywhere he wanted.

Paul Levesque had called him two days earlier and he noted getting married in two days and Punk said he'd talk to him at length, if needed, when he got back from his honeymoon. It would be Levesque's department that would send out the notice.

Vince McMahon, when asked about Punk on the Steve Austin interview on the network on 12/1, clearly didn't want to go into detail on the subject. He just pushed that they would like Punk to come back and hoped some day it would happen. He then apologized for the termination letter coming the day of the wedding, claiming that was only a coincidence.

"I would like to apologize," McMahon said. "In a big corporation, the legal people don't know what the talent relations people do. He got his severance papers on the day he got married, and that was a coincidence. I want to personally apologize."

McMahon said that over time, a lot of people working for the company had said a lot of things, but later came back.

"I'm not going to wash the dirty laundry in public," McMahon said. "There are a lot of things he may regret some day looking back and I hope one day we could get together. You (Austin) and I did, Hogan, oh brother, Ultimate Warrior, I try to give the audience what they want, what's best for business."

There was also a conversation Punk described regarding "12 Rounds 2," the movie, where he was offered the lead, and then the next day, he read on the Internet that Randy Orton had gotten the part. In that conversation Punk said, when offered the part, that it was filming in November, which coincided with the European tour, and he was champion and didn't think they'd let him off the tour. He noted he would have been thrilled to avoid the tour and get a break from house shows.

He said Levesque (who he called HHH) didn't know the dates of the European tour, and then, after it was brought up, denied it was in November. Given that it's always in November, this portrayed Levesque as being, well, I don't know what exactly, but if the story as he described it was true the way he said it, it doesn't make Levesque look like someone who should be in the position he's in. This is a key part of the story. Levesque is being groomed to take over the wrestling end of the company. Wall Street has a lot of skepticism that anyone other than Vince McMahon can run this company, and even more, someone without a business pedigree. One of the key things is that Vince McMahon and the company have to protect Levesque's reputation or anything that would make it seem like he's either over his head or the wrong person for the future.

I'll just say something doesn't compute. Either the conversation didn't happen that way, Levesque forgot about the tour, which he should have immediately realized if Punk brought it up (even that makes no sense, they've been doing the same November European tour for years and it is the same thing as not remembering SummerSlam is in August or the Royal Rumble is in January), or he knew about the tour but is so stubborn that he had to deny it when it was brought up. And that makes no sense either. I have no idea which of the above is correct, but I don't believe the latter. But anything but the first one reflects upon him badly in that position.

The wedding story getting out as the major headline made the company look beyond petty. It is possible

Levesque was calling to tell him he was being let go two days earlier and he blew it off. That could be the coincidence, the day they were making the calls, he blew off the call saying he didn't have time to talk, and they then sent the notice to him via Fed Ex. Usually on termination day, a phone call comes from someone in talent relations, not letters from legal (which come later), so McMahon's version doesn't hold up. Plus, the fact WWE never announced his being released, ever, as they do for everyone, even for Alberto Del Rio. This gives the vindictive period theory more ammunition.

But sending him a notice that he was going to get a few hours before he was getting married, as if to throw him off or put a downer on one of the bigger days of his life, would be vindictive at worse or, since they knew about the wedding day, incompetent at best, since talent relations knew of the wedding since Lee had asked for the time off some time back and Punk had told Levesque directly two days before.

The reality is, the firing itself was a formality. The two sides were at an impasse, and Punk's three-year contract was ending a month later anyway. But what was the surprise, was the letter was not just a firing that he would have expected at any time, but a letter claiming he was being terminated for breaching his contract. They claimed, like with Alberto Rodriguez (Del Rio), that they had the right to withhold merchandise revenue due to the breach. Even that would be expected. But it's doubtful he would have expected WWE's claim that they owed him no merchandise money going forward due to the breach (including a large check that they had issued him a year before that he forgot to cash and he asked weeks earlier they re-issue it and the company had refused to do so and had ignored his frequent phone calls asking about it), nor expected the one-year non-compete clause worldwide. The clause was not just for pro wrestling, but specifically mentioned UFC and MMA. This was sprung on him hours before his wedding.

I don't know of the exact wording, but I do know that Brock Lesnar, who in 2004 had actually signed a worldwide non-compete until 2010 to get his release to try and play football, a term that didn't have a prayer of holding up if it ever went to court, was so broadly written that it could have been interpreted that Lesnar couldn't even do a movie where he played a wrestler or a fighter.

Rodriguez had the similar clause in his deal. Punk pointed this out to say it's clearly a contradiction when WWE always insists publicly they are not in competition with UFC, when UFC was specifically listed as a competitor in many non-compete agreements. McMahon told Austin that everything on television and entertainment is their competition, yet MMA, which competes for some of the same talent (besides Lesnar, and perhaps Punk, that would also include competing in recruiting All-American college wrestlers into their respective entertainment genres), much of the same PPV and live arena audience (a given when you look at how WWE live show numbers declined significantly for years when UFC would run in the same arena shortly before; and WWE PPVs one or eight days after a big UFC show declined below expected levels), is not competition.

It should be noted that when Jim Ross was given a non-compete as an announcer, UFC was not listed, nor was MMA. Ross' lengthy severance package and non-compete (something like ten months) was largely because of fear he would go to TNA, and they expressed no such fear of UFC. So by their actions, they do, or at least as of late 2013, considered TNA their key competition.

There have been plenty of rumors of late regarding Punk and MMA. A few weeks ago, he did a video rolling around with Rener Gracie, which asked if Punk would be interested in doing Metamoris. MMA insider Frontrow Brian had talked about UFC negotiations with Punk, and from all accounts, there is smoke to that fire. I can tell you factually that Bellator has significant interest in him as well. Right now every company knows the game in MMA right now is to attempt to get the casual fan that left back. To do that, you need people who come in with names. You have to also be able to make new names, but with Brock Lesnar and lately Bobby Lashley, it has been proven that pro wrestling fans, a sizeable television audience, will watch MMA events if someone they feel they know and are interested in will participate. But it has to be with a high profile group, because Dave Bautista with a smaller group didn't garner a lot of interest. For the same reason, there is currently interest in MMA in Alberto Rodriguez (Del Rio).

The interview pleased a lot of people and riled up many others. Virtually everyone in WWE kept quiet publicly on the subject, with the exception of Ryan Reeves (Ryback) and Brian James (a producer and the former wrestler known as Road Dogg). Punk portrayed Reeves, who he called "steroid guy," as a dangerous guy who took 20 years off his life, and listed a slew of injuries he blamed Ryback for. James just took a measured approach when dealing with people on Twitter, saying there are two sides to every story and he's only heard one side.

We were told most, but certainly not all, of the WWE talent loved some of what he said. Many were not happy about him complaining about his booking when he was booked better than all but a few guys over the past three years. The feeling of guys that while he complained about putting over Rock, Undertaker and Brock Lesnar in 2013, that most of them would have loved to have been in the position to work twice with Rock, and then do Mania against Undertaker and SummerSlam with Lesnar regardless of the outcome. One major name, while seeing Punk's side on the medical issue and some other issues , felt most of the interview was "sour grapes."

Many felt he came off badly about complaining that he was booked against HHH at WrestleMania, noting he'd be in one of the top matches and would get ample time to promote it. McMahon in the Austin podcast said that WrestleMania wasn't about one main event these days, although Punk's argument to that is that the guys in the one real main event get paid far better than just about anyone else on the show. Several felt he made himself look bad in complaining about having to put over Rock, Undertaker and Lesnar. The "two sides of every story" saying was said by others, but there was also a consensus that what he said about his experience in WWE was the same as many would say, with the difference that he made more money than all but a few, and they admired his balls to say it publicly.

Another person who knows several major WWE talents said, discounting the few that will parrot whatever Punk said, his experience is that there was a feeling that Punk's comments on Ryback were unprofessional and cheap, and that nobody bought Ryback kicked Punk as hard as he could or intentionally broke his ribs. However, there was the feeling Punk is a genius, particularly for how he handled the situation. There was a lot of hate for Colt Cabana (I really don't see why) according to one person. Some said they felt Punk was bitter. Almost nobody had any sympathy for his injury situation, noting that every top guy on the roster that works a full schedule has a litany of injuries.

Most agreed Punk not being allowed to walk Chael Sonnen to the ring on FOX and HHH walking Floyd Mayweather to the ring was a double standard and completely ridiculous (when that happened in May 2013, I heard that from a number of people). Nobody has even suggested this may be a work.

Most felt the idea of a three-way with Rock, Cena and Punk as he lobbied for as the main event at WrestleMania 29 would have been a bad idea. The consensus also was that Punk did not deserve, based on how over he was, to main event this year's WrestleMania. Regarding Orton vs. Batista, Batista is very well liked (Batista is cool, I'll just say that, and was in the wrong place at the wrong time with fans as far as a vocal part of the fan base thought they could force Bryan into the main event, saw Batista as the obstacle, and in the end they ended up doing so). The feeling was that the creative team totally misread the situation when it came to Batista and everything else at the time.

But the reaction was also that Punk's ideas were not the best thing for the company for Mania this year either, only the best thing for Punk. Those in the office were totally behind Paul Levesque for the most part. Aside from one person very close to Punk who parroted almost everything he said, nobody agreed with everything Punk said 100 percent.

But all were fully aware even a hint of saying anything publicly in any agreement with him would be career suicide unless it was done by an untouchable guy, and there are only a few of them.

In the Punk conversation with Cabana, Vince McMahon came off as out-of-touch, particularly when Punk recounted a conversation about UFC. Punk buried Levesque for beating him for no reason in 2011 when Punk was on the biggest run of his career. While Punk complained to a degree about losing to The Rock, Undertaker and Lesnar, and in particular, never getting a main event at WrestleMania, his losing to HHH seemed to bother him the most. It is the one loss he seemed to have the hardest time with, probably because it's the one loss that's very difficult to logically explain. It was clearly the wrong call at the time, and with hindsight, it still looks wrong.

He said that when his contract expired in July, 2011, he was "out the door and I wasn't going to resign." In describing his change of heart and signing a new three-year deal, he said it was at a meeting with Vince

McMahon.

"I wouldn't say he convinced me to re-sign. I'll say I talked myself into it."

"It's okay to be bitter at stuff. You have to eventually work and get through it. There are a few bright spots (during his WWE career), a few things that still get to me to this day."

"I didn't (listen to the podcast)," McMahon said. "I understand he used a lot of expletives. I heard there were a number of things he said. It's his point of view. There's two sides to any story."

Austin noted that after he left, it was Jim Ross who brokered the deal to get him talking to McMahon again that led to his returning. He noted that perhaps one of the problems is Vince doesn't have Jim Ross anymore.

"I know I wasn't the easiest guy to deal with and I wasn't the nicest guy to deal with. I was miserable. I was unhappy. Fuck, it, I made myself happy. I left. It wasn't an easy decision to make but it was a long time coming."

"Punk has a degree of lack of communication skills," said McMahon. "He's something of a loner. Had their been a JR (Jim Ross), I think we could have worked things out, but it didn't work things out. Anytime you get attorneys involved, it's going to go to hell in a handbasket."

Punk brought up what he said were the rumored reasons he left, that he was unhappy with the storylines, that he was physically banged up, that he was mad he wasn't going to be in the main event at the 2014 WrestleMania, that he was mad that he was being booked against HHH (Levesque).

"There's an element of truth in all of those things but I can't say there was one big thing that led to my decision. The big thing that led to my decision was my health."

He said he's grown to despise the term "pipe bomb," which he created and popularized in wrestling, after his 2011 promo in Las Vegas that was probably the most talked about thing of his career and easily the most talked about wrestling promo in years. He said maybe he should embrace it but now it sounds all douchey.

"Everyone wanted to interview me, GQ Magazine, the cover of USA Today, I had legitimate companies that wanted to give me money to sponsor me. The UFC was all the rage. People got paid a ridiculous amount of money to promote these companies. I had pretty big money deals on the table."

He said that in his return to WWE, besides the obvious, that McMahon purchase the rights to use "Cult of Personality," the entrance music he used on the independent level, he said he wanted to come back with a new hairstyle, and a new look, wanted to wear MMA fighting shorts, and have sponsors.

"I felt I deserved it," he said. "I got new eyes on the product."

He said Vince turned down that request, saying that the companies that sponsor Raw would get mad. Keep in mind that while probably true when it came to Raw sponsors, what Punk was proposing had been part of the MMA scene since its debut on televison, and was parts of a number of other mainstream sports, most notably NASCAR. He also said that the other wrestlers would get mad.

"It wasn't my hill to die on and I let it go."

A year later, Lesnar came to WWE, in fight shorts and with sponsors. Punk noted he didn't begrudge Lesnar at all, and said Lesnar probably came in with those sponsors that he'd signed a long-term deal with when he was in UFC. Punk said he thought his idea would open up a new revenue stream for talent.

"I was still in that mentality. I wanted to help everyone out. Then Brock gets it, without an explanation from Vince. I went to Vince. He just tries to blow smoke up your ass."

He brought up that nobody since 2011 has outsold Cena for merchandise, but he did. Punk's merchandise did outsell Cena's for a short period of time in 2011. Nobody else has done that in a long time. Punk remained the company's No. 2 merchandise seller for the rest of his run (during the periods he was a babyface, his numbers fell off greatly as a heel), and a strong No. 2, in the sense the gap between No. 2 and No. 3 was canyon-sized. When Punk quit, the reaction of a lot of people internally was that he was a pain to deal with, that he was not really a ticket seller, but that he was valuable because he sold a ton of T-shirts.

The next story is very interesting because it was something very much talked about at the time. Chael Sonnen had asked Punk to walk to the cage with him for his January 26, 2012, fight in Chicago, on FOX, with Michael Bisping. The show was the night before the Royal Rumble, a PPV show built around Punk defending and losing the WWE title to The Rock. Punk accepted the offer. Then Vince McMahon told Punk he couldn't do it, and also didn't want him even being at the show, although he did go to the show anyway.

Punk said that he felt, that whether Sonnen won or lost that fight, all people would be talking about is that Punk was in his corner, he'd be on national TV, it was the night before the Rumble, and it may sell some late PPV buys. He said since it was in Chicago, he'd get an enormous pop.

He'd have gotten a reaction. UFC fans, like boxing fans, may recognize guys in the corner, but the reaction to people like that is usually minimal. Perhaps this would have been the exception.

Punk's claim was that McMahon wouldn't let him, and that in the conversation, McMahon blasted UFC, saying it was barbaric and somebody was going to die. Punk claimed he shot back with Owen Hart's name. The reality is there have been far more people die in wrestling rings and boxing rings, and there have been far more serious injuries than there have ever been in UFC, and probably will ever be. UFC may some day have a death, odds are with enough time it will happen, perhaps the odds are as much from a dangerous weight cut than from an injury from a fight, although it has not in 21 years and deaths are very rare in MMA. WWE may some day have another death, but UFC's health issues are knees, backs, shoulders and elbows, more than deaths.

Punk said he reminded Vince how people think his product is horrible and barbaric, and he said Vince said "Did you know they are going to have women fight?" and Punk said, "Yeah, it's the coolest thing in the world, you'll see." He said Vince was out of touch.

"It's more promotion (for the Rumble), more eyes on the product, my home town people will be going crazy. Then the next week (it was actually more than three months later, the May 5, 2012, fight in Las Vegas against Miguel Cotto) HHH walks Mayweather to the ring."

There is one huge flaw in this subject. First, Vince had so much of a problem with UFC being barbaric that he was in talks to buy Pride and had paid people to research him starting his own MMA promotion years ago. At one point, they at least entertained the idea of buying UFC itself. When he decided against starting his own promotion (his idea was an all-heavyweight promotion built around Bob Sapp, with the idea Sapp would also become a major outsider draw as a pro wrestler on major shows), it was never about barbaric. His complaint was being unable to protect investments, i.e., the most charismatic guys may lose at the wrong time. It was the same thing he said in 2007 when UFC was gaining in popularity and outdistancing WWE in many demos, that the UFC business model couldn't survive because you would spend all kinds of money behind marketing someone, and then if they lose, all that money is wasted. Where Vince missed the boat is that, unlike with boxing, in UFC, because the fan base was more a pro wrestling fan oriented base, one loss doesn't kill ones marketability.

When this all went down, I was told Vince's reason was he didn't want his world champion on UFC's FOX show and not being identified, or treated like somebody who wasn't a big star. Keep in mind that I'd say 80% or better Punk would have been identified had he been in Sonnen's corner. He was identified on UFC television many times later that year when he attended live shows. But Vince didn't know that.

More than anything else, these comments Punk attributed to Vince made him appear to be the old man who is now out of touch. It was one of the most talked about things from Punk's entire rundown. However, something doesn't appear to make sense on the surface.

In January 2012, how would Vince McMahon have known UFC was about to have women fighters? Dana White and Lorenzo Fertitta were asked about that subject constantly, and the answer was always the same. "There will never be women fighting in the UFC."

The stories about women fighting in UFC and Ronda Rousey in UFC didn't even break until mid-November, nearly 11 months after this conversation. Now granted, I always thought it was an inevitability while White and Fertitta were publicly denying this. In addition, the Showtime/UFC contract didn't allow UFC to take anyone from Strikeforce, and Rousey, the entire reason they opened their eyes to women, was in Strikeforce.

They actually had to not renew their TV deal with Showtime to be able to bring Rousey, and the women's division, into the UFC. But this all happened months after the conversation.

It's one thing if someone was paying close attention after early March, more than a month after the conversation, the week of the first Rousey vs. Miesha Tate fight in Columbus, OH. Some have said McMahon probably meant that fight and didn't know the difference between UFC and Strikeforce, and they were owned by the same people, but that would only make sense a month later. The Rousey vs. Tate promotion wasn't done until the week of the fight, and the odds that a guy who really knows nothing about MMA and doesn't even know anything about any sports would know about such a fight is minuscule, even the week of, let alone close to two months out. It's even lower the idea he'd know about that fight when he had no idea who Rousey was until around SummerSlam 2014, because when Rousey was pitched for SummerSlam this past year, according to one person familiar with the pitch, neither McMahon nor Levesque knew who she was. Obviously, they all would today since Rousey did the ice bucket challenge with Stephanie and was given the run of backstage, and introduced on the show.

Again, the Vince McMahon who is so out of touch he thinks UFC is barbaric and people will die, has figured out women are fighting in UFC nearly two months before White sees his fight that opened his eyes to the subject, sees the potential, but even then keeps it quiet from almost everyone. The idea that maybe McMahon heard about Rousey and assumed she was in UFC doesn't add up. Rousey's first real big mainstream was being on the cover of the annual ESPN Body Magazine, and that was still months away.

The fact that HHH did walk Mayweather to the ring, and then got completely ignored by the HBO broadcast team, which was a given he would be if you know how HBO treats fighters and celebrities (they fawned all over the real celebrities like Justin Beiber who was there, but never mention pro wrestlers in fighters' entrances, and HHH was not the first, although I'd bet if it was Dwayne Johnson or Hulk Hogan it would be different), it was a lock to make him look on the broadcast like HHH was a nobody, and it did. But he did it anyway.

In fact, that very thing was laughed at by the few people who knew about what McMahon had told Punk at the time.

Punk said he would get outside offers, and then when he tried to get permission to do them, would get turned down. Then he said two weeks later Cena was doing the same exact same thing he was offered. He noted that everyone did charity work and visited Make-a-Wish kids, and claimed he saw as many kids as Cena, but Cena was the only one who would get the credit and when the media covered WWE stars doing make-a-wish, it was always Cena.

He then talked about the movie, claiming he was offered the lead role in "12 Rounds 2: Reloaded." He claimed when Levesque offered it to him, he wanted to do it. Cabana, who is one of the few people Punk confides in, said he told Punk not to do it. Punk said he told Levesque "They're lame as fuck" about WWE movies. But he said he'd get a credit and it's a new experience, plus it would get him off for a month and his body was hurting. He said it could be good long-term in case he wants to pursue acting after wrestling. He said one of his knees was torn up at the time and the other was twisted from doing the Mutalock on Cena. Plus he said, he'd get off house shows and still get paid. But he noted the filming was in November.

Punk said the next day, on the Internet, he read about Orton getting the role. He said Levesque could have called him to tell him.

"You couldn't have told me, so I wouldn't have to read that first on the Internet? But that's how they are."

He said when asked what happened, he was told Levesque had since found out the filming coincided with the European tour and they didn't want the world champion off the tour.

He made fun of fans who knocked him for leaving the company on twitter. He mentioned some of the comments like fans claiming they were the ones who paid for his house and that he owed them.

"WWE didn't make me. WWE was a fucking pit stop and I won't be defined by what I do for a living."

He said the problem is half the people who work in WWE grew up as fans and then have to eat a lot of shit because they have no other options.

"Pro wrestling is just the weirdest fucking business. Wrestling was awesome when it was me and you and (Dave) Prazak, and we drove to Ian's (IWA Mid South promoter Ian Rotten) shows."

"It's the most bipolar business in the world. They want you to be this character 24/7, but if you're caught being mean to people on Twitter, they'll admonish you."

He said they use their power because everyone is so afraid for their jobs and use it as a bizarre mindfuck. He said they weren't paying him enough to put up with it. He admitted making millions but said he should have been making $10 million.

He said for months after the network launch, he was asking how they would get paid for PPVs. Vince would laugh and tell him they haven't figured it out yet. He said he felt like he was the only one even asking. He said Randy Orton would be asking him.

He then started on the subject of concussions. He said the company's public reaction to concussions isn't about taking care of the talent, but protecting the company from a lawsuit like what happened with the NFL.

He said on January 26, 2014, he got a concussion early in the Royal Rumble.

"I knew it, and everyone knew it."

He said the testing WWE does for concussions is bullshit, noting that he passed the concussion test with flying colors. The Impact testing, a program put together by Maroon, has been heavily criticized in football with the idea you can dumb yourself down, thus lowering your baseline, and then beat the test later while still suffering from a concussion. You can also take Ritalin and then beat the test, although evidently Punk did neither. But he said they wanted him to run the ropes just to check on his motor skills. He refused.

Going back to 2012, he said he was beaten up and needed knee surgery, but as champion he needed to keep going. He told them he was getting surgery after dropping the title to Rock. But he said he was also complaining it wasn't the right thing for him to lose the title to a part-timer, and suggested that he, Rock and Cena should do a three-way at Mania, where he said they could eliminate him first in five minutes. But he said at least he would get his WrestleMania main event, figuring he'd been champion all year and did the company a favor turning heel, which cut his income in half since his merchandise money dropped way down due to the turn.

He said on the European tour, his elbow locked up every day on a 45 degree angle and he could only bend it about three inches.

So he finally got time off for elbow surgery. Since he figured he would have down time, he also got laser eye surgery done. He said Vince called him a day or two later saying he was needed at Raw to cut promos. He said one day he was at TV and Michael Hayes told him he was in a match. He said he hadn't gotten cleared. He said Hayes told him he was cleared. He said Dr. Chris Amann cleared him. He said he hadn't even been examined in Birmingham by Dr. James Andrews, who did his elbow surgery.

He said he came back and one of the guys in the original Nexus angle poked him in the eye that wasn't healed from the laser surgery. He said he couldn't tell the guys to stay away from his eye because they hid the angle from most of the guys, who didn't really know until they were all in the ring doing a beatdown. He said they tried to hide the angle, even from him, although he did say he had a vibe something was coming.

"As champion, I worked my ass off every show. I have a lot of fond memories of working with a lot of guys, Alberto Del Rio, Daniel Bryan, I like to think I'm an old school guy. You get hurt, you tape it up. How long was I on TV with my arm in a sling? I had my arm in a sling all day except two hours in the morning and two hours in the evening when I was doing rehab."

He said they never have long-term plans for anyone and Vince only cares about what the long-term plan for Cena is.

He said he never wanted the heel turn, but was told Rock was coming back and asked to work with a strong heel when he won the title. He was told that he could either turn heel, or he'd drop the title to Bryan, who then would have stayed heel to drop the title to Rock at that year's Royal Rumble.

He said he knew the turn would kill his merchandise money but Vince said he'd owe him. He noted a bunch of other times Vince said he owed him. He said when he was asked to go heel, he was told Rock vs. Cena would be the main event. He said they told him Undertaker needed somebody.

He then claimed credit for The Shield. He said the original idea when he went heel was to have a group with him to do his dirty work. He said the plan was for it to be Show, Bryan and Seth Rollins. He said he loved Show and Bryan. He said Show had been around too long and Bryan should be kept as far away from him as much as possible, saying he and Bryan should be this generation's Michaels and Hart.

He suggested three guys from FCW and Vince asked who, and he said Rollins, Ambrose and Chris Hero. Levesque shot down Hero and suggested Leakee (who is now Roman Reigns). "It wasn't my hill to die on. He's the pretty guy, but that's good, he can learn under me. They were supposed to be my group. Then things changed. They take others' ideas and then it became Hunter's idea."

He said the story has changed and he's never gotten credit, but he's the one who pitched for it, and they're all doing fantastic.

"Ryback took 20 years off my life."

He said he was beaten up and was told that Ryback wasn't ready, but that he should be able to carry him. The Ryback program was a last minute thing. Cena had an injury and was missing the PPV match, where he and Punk were supposed to wrestle in a Hell in a Cell match. Ryback was on fire doing squashes, and had a lot of momentum. Putting Ryback with Punk and having him lose, even with ref Brad Maddox giving him a low blow, killed Ryback's momentum.

"I'm already beaten up and I have to wrestle steroid guy," he said. "He's real hurty, sometimes deliberate."

He claimed Ryback kicked him in the stomach as hard as he could and broke his ribs. He said Ryback was a real piece of work.

After a rematch, the night The Shield was introduced, a third meeting was scheduled for the TLC PPV. But he underwent knee surgery. He was just getting out of surgery when he was told he was wrestling Ryback on the TLC PPV. He said he was told he'd be out four weeks and the PPV was in two or three weeks. He said they wanted him to do a horribly dangerous match with a horribly dangerous opponent. But he was told they had to do the match quickly because Rock was coming back, so they needed to get the Ryback program completed. Punk's surgery on December 5, 2012, was for a partially torn meniscus, so his TLC title match with Ryback was moved from the TLC PPV show (which with no world champion on the show, going with a Cena vs. Dolph Ziggler main event, bombed, doing 75,000 domestic buys) to the January 7, 2013 episode of Raw, so it was actually five weeks, not two-and-a-half weeks before he wrestled. The PPV was 11 days after his surgery and there was no way he was going to be doing that match.

He said he told Vince again that when he drops the title he'll need time off. Vince told him, "No, I need you for the rematch with The Rock."

He said that Rock beat him and then left, and Undertaker beat him and then left. He said he'd stolen the show at Mania but this time he should have gone on last. He said he knew he'd have a better match with Undertaker than Lesnar with HHH and Rock with Cena. He said this time they were telling him he should have gone on last so he said that he thought if they said that, they should pay him like he did.

"If you pay me like I did (main event the show), I have no problem. They didn't pay me like it."

He said by the time Mania was over, he had two bad knees, including a strained ACL, torn PCL, torn MCL, torn meniscus and bruise patella. He was then gone for two months.

He said he rediscovered life, he went to Black Hawks games, looked at his bank account and came to the realization that this was ridiculous.

"I don't need this anymore. I can work at Starbucks, and they may even give me insurance. It wasn't fun."

He said he got a tattoo of the Stanley Cup next to it where the words, "My summer vacation," because he never had a summer vacation in his life.

He said he was testing his knee doing Jiu Jitsu with Rener Gracie at a camp in Destin, FL, which he said was really an excuse to ride jet skis. He said he went to FCW in Tampa to see how he felt in the ring, and Vince called and wanted him back for the June 2013 PPV to face Chris Jericho, saying Chicago isn't sold out, but if he's on the show, he knows it will be. Then he asked him to face Brock Lesnar. He asked Vince who was going over, and Vince said Lesnar. He asked if he would get a rematch at the next PPV, and Vince said No, Lesnar wasn't wrestling until Royal Rumble. So he said he put over Rock, who was gone, Undertaker, who was gone and Lesnar, who was gone, and that his stock was dropping to the casual fan, because wins and losses matter as far as who they care about. He said he told Vince that he should tell Lesnar to work the house shows.

He said his goal was to do stuff feuding with Heyman, it got him excited and that there was no way they could deny him the WrestleMania main event. He was then asked to face Ryback as Heyman's guy. He said Ryback hurt him before and he'd rather work with Curtis Axel, since he said (sarcastically) that HHH did such a great job of getting Axel over. He noted that Ryback was supposed to press slam him through a table, and dropped him, missing the table, and he was hurting for weeks.

He said he confronted Ryback and said to him, that either he's dumb as fuck and he sucks, or that he did it on purpose. He claimed Ryback said, "I'm dumb as fuck."

Ryan Reeves (Ryback) claimed that he was never confronted by Punk and that this entire conversation was fabricated.

"For the record, if I quit for being fragile and insecure, I would make up excuses too," he wrote on Twitter. "Things didn't go my way for a long time and I kept going day in and out. Slander is a powerful thing and to state complete made up nonsense for no reason shows his insecurities. I will continue to bust my ass, study matches every chance I get, cut promos when driving and push myself for hours on end, even when hurt. Thank you."

Reeves later took down the posts.

Punk said he was feeling the worst he ever had. He said he then suffered a concussion in a match with Luke Harper. Even so, he went on the November 2013 tour of Europe. He said that was his own fault. He said he was either throwing up or dry heaving after every match, saying he was lucky he was in tag matches.

He said at this point he had no appetite, couldn't train, which he noted isn't good because you're supposed to look a certain way. He said the doctor gave him a Z-pac (antibiotics). He said he took so many Z-pacs that he shit his pants on Smackdown. He said he joked about in on Twitter and was told to take it down, so he wrote, "This poop ain't fun anymore," and for his own amusement, then blocked the WWE.

"I don't know what is up and down. I can't sleep. I can't train."

He said he was getting two MRIs a week, for his neck, his head, his chest, CATscan. Then he said his paychecks got smaller. He complained about his Mania payoff.

He said he was in the best match at Mania, and noted that he knows "best match doesn't mean shit, it's what draws," but he said he was in the match with Undertaker.

"I shouldn't get any less than Taker, Rock, HHH, Cena and Rock. I know I got paid less than all of them, and they couldn't lace my boots on that day."

"WrestleMania is the draw, not The Rock, that's how I feel."

The reality is it's a combination of both. With Vince McMahon vs. Bret Hart and Shawn Michaels vs. Undertaker, WrestleMania in 2010 did 885,000 buys (495,000 domestic). The next three years, with Rock as the main event, the numbers were 1,124,000 (679,000 domestic), 1,219,000 (715,000 domestic) and 1,104,000 (662,000 domestic). The 2011 show, with a Cena vs. Miz main event, would not have done well without Rock, and 2012 set records because of the year-build for Rock vs. Cena. It was the highest grossing overall event in the history of pro wrestling.

The 2013 show didn't do as well. Rock vs. Cena alone as that match meant less the second time. They also had Lesnar vs. HHH and Undertaker vs. Punk. But it was still the highest grossing live event in pro wrestling history. It's far more debatable about what the key people's value was for 2013 because it didn't have the killer Rock-Cena dynamic the first two years had.

The 2014 show had a different situation with the network. Revenue was way down, but it would have been no matter who was on the show. While Rock was on the show, his segment was not advertised and it would be fair to say he had nothing to do with the numbers, although it was notable that on the NBC special that aired later, the guy the show was built around, Daniel Bryan, had neither of his matches air or even had clips shown. Another point is that even though the company claimed record viewership by adding up worldwide PPVs (690,000) and network subscribers (667,000) and getting 1,357,000, there were actually fewer people watching, even with the lower price, than two years earlier at full price. We don't have figures but there were far less than 667,000 homes actually watching WrestleMania on the network and one person who did know said that there were more homes, and probably a lot more people, watching in 2012. First off, there were the network subscribers who attended live who would have been counted in 2014 figures whereas in other years they wouldn't be counted (although in fairness, many of them attending live may have ordered the replay in 2012). You also have the network subscribers who still ordered on PPV, not trusting the technology or they didn't have the technology to watch it on their TVs and had friends over, so those homes are also counted twice in 2014. Even if that wasn't the case, when you decrease the price point that much, even if the number was the highest, it's not a fair comparison. You can debate the value of Rock on Survivor Series and Elimination Chamber, but you'll lose that debate on WrestleMania. And Punk himself drew the biggest Rumble number since 2008 when paired with Rock.

He talked about his TLC match, on a show without Cena, and it doing so well, while he said the Rock & Cena vs. Miz & R-Truth match the month before did an awful buy rate, which was then blamed on Miz & R-Truth. "They twist the narrative."

The numbers don't back this up, and he came off badly saying that if he got $1 less than any of the names listed above, even Rock, that he would be outraged.

The 2011 TLC match, without Cena (Punk vs. Miz vs. Del Rio title match on top), did 98,000 domestic buys, down from 101,000 the year before. The worldwide drop was from 195,000 to 179,000.

The Survivor Series a few weeks earlier, with Rock's first match back, did 179,000 domestic buys, up from domestic 127,000 the year before. The worldwide increase was from 244,000 to 312,000.

The Survivor Series number was considered bad only because expectations were that Rock's first match back would do bigger numbers, but we were past the point when B shows were going to do well. For all the disappointment of Rock's first show number, and it was very much one, the only B show since that time that beat it domestically was the 2013 Elimination Chamber, which was headlined by the Rock vs. Punk rematch. And worldwide, nothing has come close, with the best being Lesnar's debut at the 2012 Extreme Rules that did 271,000 buys. That Survivor Series had two big problems. The draw was Rock's first match, but he was teaming with the one guy nobody wanted to see him team with, and the storyline of putting them together was weak. Plus, Miz & R-Truth at that point were extremely weak heels to headline, even though they had gone over Punk to get them ready for being in the main event.

He said PPV was dying and that was the reason they started the network. Actually, WWE PPV numbers had stabilized in recent years. PPV was doing slightly better once UFC's numbers started falling, just as WWE PPV was hitting the skids just as UFC's popularity increased. But he reiterated he was mad that nobody would tell him how they would be compensating talent with the switch to the network. He felt the lack of an answer to the question was unacceptable. He also seemed to have a chip on his shoulder that he was asking the obvious question and thought nobody else was asking.

Next was the single most damning thing said, because it was a direct attack at WWE medical.

He said he had a lump on his back, went to the doctor, who said it was a fatty deposit and asked him if it hurt. He said it didn't. He said there was a longstanding locker room tradition where if guys have growths, the doctor cuts it out in front of everyone and the boys film it. He said the doctor was lazy. He mentioned Dr. Amman during the podcast, but never mentioned Dr. Michael Sampson (the doctor who saved Jerry Lawler's life), who are the two touring doctors.

He said they didn't cut it out, but gave him stronger antibiotics. He said he was feeling even worse, and had diarrhea for three weeks, and spent the entire time nervous he was going to shit himself again in the ring.

He said he already knew Randy Orton vs. Batista was the scheduled WrestleMania main event. But he decided he was going to have an awesome Royal Rumble and change their minds, noting he knew in 2000 that Vince McMahon changed his mind and put Mick Foley in the main event. The thing there is Foley was put in because of the decision to have four McMahons in the corner, so they needed four guys. Foley did have great matches in January and February on PPV, but the addition wasn't so much his matches or that he earned his way in, but that they needed a fourth guy, and at the time, Foley was a far bigger star than Chris Jericho (the other choice had he not done it), so McMahon called Foley and asked him to renege on his retirement stip. After just billing a Foley retirement match, everyone looked bad by bringing him right back, but in the end, McMahon felt they needed a stronger fourth guy than what they had, and Foley, after some soul searching, felt the WrestleMania main event payoff and being in a WrestleMania main event meant more than honoring his advertised word and stipulation.

He said he was going to change their mind, plus he figured Orton vs. Batista would be a stinker of a main event, which almost everyone thought could be a bad idea. But he said Vince told him that Orton vs. Batista would end up being the biggest main event in WrestleMania history.

Once the Rumble was over, the sentiment was stronger that Orton vs. Batista would be a mistake. Punk was scheduled to start the Rumble and go 49-50 minutes, being eliminated in the final four.

Punk said when Kofi Kingston entered the Rumble, he hit him with a clothesline and gave him a concussion. He said he was out of it and motioned to the doctor and the doctor said, "What do you want me to do?" And Punk claimed he said, "You are the most useless fucking doctor in the whole world." He said the doctor asked, "Do you want me to tell someone?" Then he said the ref told him that Kane was coming out to eliminate him.

First a note about this. Kane was actually in the match fifth and almost immediately eliminated by Punk. Kingston came in several minutes later as the eighth guy in. Kane was scheduled to come back and eliminate Punk at the 49-50 minute mark. Apparently they called for Kane to come out and eliminate him early, and he said that if Kane did that, he'd quit. I don't recall Kane coming out then, but he did at the end.

Here's a huge problem. If Punk suffered a concussion, in this day and age, they should have a ruling and he should be out. Granted, it screws with the match, goes against everything wrestlers are taught about finishing the match when hurt, and goes against everything fans expect when they watch pro wrestling, that things like concussions and injuries don't prevent the match from going to the planned emotionally satisfying conclusion. But everyone needs to be re-taught, and the sooner the better. If NFL players with millions at stake in championship games get a concussion, they are not allowed back in the game. If a fighter gets a concussion, the fight is over, even though we've all seen situations where fighters have come back from concussions to win and that used to be what legends are made of. With Levesque on the Sports Legacy Institute board, that should put WWE in the position to be first to the dance, not last as it is now. And I know this absolutely hurts it from a fan point of view, and being a main event wrestler is about performing in constant pain and with a multitude of injuries.

But we know that if you have a concussion, you are susceptible to a second one. When Punk talked about this concussion, Cabana noted this was No. 12 or No. 13, and that's a scary number already. Granted, Punk threatened to quit the company if they changed things in the match and threw him out, and most wrestlers have the mentality that you work the match. The same thing happened to Undertaker against Lesnar at WrestleMania, where Undertaker got the concussion, worked the match blank, and then after losing, they took him to the hospital.

This is not a WWE issue, in the sense that if it's Mexico, Japan, TNA, or whatever, guys are going to work their match to its scheduled conclusion and worry about the concussion when the match is over. That's how you are taught. But the idea that you have the same standards as the NFL or NHL is not the case, because in those leagues, you're out of the game at that moment and not put back in.

Punk went to the back and wanted the growth cut out, saying he looks green and now has had a fever for weeks. Amann still wouldn't do it.

He said that night, he couldn't sleep, he looked over at his girlfriend (A.J. Lee) and thought, "I know I'm marrying this woman (he hadn't asked her yet but said he already knew he was going to), what am I doing with my life? I had a big moment of clarity."

He went to Cleveland for Raw the next night. They wanted him to take the concussion test. He passed the test.

They wanted him to run the ropes to check for balance and other signs of a concussion. He refused. Then they told him he had to take a drug test. He blew up, complaining that they just amended the drug test to remove strikes from guys who they otherwise would have to fire with one more positive. What's notable is that if he had refused the test, and he gave the indication he didn't take the test, that, by policy, should be a 30-day suspension. But WWE based on stories that have come out, whether it was Bob Holly's book, or other things, guys have refused to take tests and not been suspended. When Wanderlei Silva did the same thing, his career was over. He said that night, he was told he was working, then told he wasn't. He said his ribs were broken, both knees were a mess and he was sick.

He told Vince, "I don't love this anymore. I'm hurt. I'm sick. I'm confused. As a business, I don't know what we're doing anymore. Every day you tell me this is a team effort, but every day it's an individual effort for me. It's not fun. I have no passion for this. I'm sick and hurt and all you care about is my segment and when I'm going to pee in a fucking cup and I'm not going to do this anymore. How do you not see that bringing back Batista as a babyface is a bad idea."

He said Levesque then told him that Batista had just taken the same drug test, and he said he asked Levesque, "Did you." Levesque didn't respond.

He noted that when it came to Batista as a babyface against Orton at Mania, he had nothing against Batista, saying Batista himself said the same thing. He said he told them he sold shirts at the same rate as Cena until they turned him, he worked with dangerous guys, and all he wanted was the main event of Mania (that would be the greatest story of all-time given the timing of all this if this ends up with him in the main event at Mania this year). He said that he said they should fire him if they don't think he can main event Mania, because he'll go somewhere else and get over because he knows he can. He also claimed he said he couldn't believe Daniel Bryan wasn't in their plans for Mania (at the time he was scheduled to face Sheamus in an undercard match) because this is his year. "Two years ago it was my fucking year and I was white fucking hot and you fed me to this guy (HHH)." Vince said that you are in a main event at Mania, wrestling HHH.

He claimed he told Levesque: "With all due respect, I do not need to wrestle you. You need to wrestle me. I seriously resent you for not putting me over two years ago but you had to fuck with me, that should have been best for business but you had to come in and squash it, and I had to lose to Truth and Miz (to set them up for Rock).

He said that even though he was told he was going to beat HHH at Mania, he told Vince, "I don't want to give him the fucking privilege."

"I said a lot of shit in there. Hunter was gritting his teeth. He never liked me. You always hear the stories in the dirt sheets, but me and him in the room together, never good vibes. He always looked sideways at me."

Levesque brought up Punk was in the best match at Mania and that was the main event, and Punk said, "The last match is the main event. There is only one (main event) and I deserved it. I still deserve it, and now Daniel Bryan deserves it, and you're going to give it to Batista and Randy. How many active wrestlers have been in the main event (Rock, HHH, Big Show, Chris Jericho, Lesnar, Undertaker, Orton and Miz)? How are they going to get better? I needed that so I could learn so I could further become an asset to the product."

He asked Levesque to tell him he got paid the same as the other guys on top at Mania last year (Undertaker, Rock, Cena, Lesnar and HHH). Levesque said nothing. Punk then said he said, "I'm outta here." Vince had tears in his eyes and went for a hug and Punk said he patted him on the back, and he shook Levesque's hand and left.

He said a week later he got a text from Vince asking if he was ready to come back, and texted back, "No."

He still couldn't sleep. A.J. Lee told him to see her doctor in Tampa. He showed the doctor his lump and the doctor said it was an MRSA staph infection (one of the worst kind because it's resistant to many antibiotics). He got the lump cut out and had to go to the hospital and get an IV drip. He said of all his injuries and tattoos in painful places, and all the matches with Ryback, and the problems with his ribs, this was the worst pain he ever had. The doctor told asked him how long he'd had it. He said a few months. The doctor said, "You could be dead. You could have died."

This is a far worse deal than the attention it has gotten. MRSA is contagious and gone untreated, he not only put himself, but put those he worked with in danger, and anyone who came into contacted with surfaces that the infection touched like the ring or his ring gear. WWE could potentially be putting themselves at a huge exposure financially if any talent got infected, or if it spread in the buildings. I know of gyms where staph, and less contagious staph that MRSA ended up passed around. Granted, guys working with staph infections was also part and parcel of 80s wrestling, particularly with the Crockett promotions. One EMT told us that the EMS companies that work at arenas would be furious that they worked WWE events where a performer had untreated MRSA.

That brings up a similar story told by Bob Holly in his book, "The Hardcore Truth."

In late 2005, on the day Eddy Guerrero passed away, he discovered a bump in his underarm. He got to Minneapolis, where they were taping TV, and felt sick. Dr. Ferdinand Rios, the WWE's doctor at the time, diagnosed him with a staph infection that had spread to his forearm. He told John Laurinaitis that he was really sick and needed to go to the hospital. Laurinaitis told him they needed him for the European tour, which they were leaving for immediately after the Minneapolis show, so the hospital would have to wait. He said that he had a rep for not complaining, but felt so bad he told Laurinaitis, "I'm sick as hell." He said he felt if he went to the hospital instead of going on the flight, he'd be fired.

On the tour, his forearm swelled up to twice its normal size. Rios tried to drain the infection, but the infection had spread to the bone and Holly was hospitalized with MRSA. Surgery didn't clear it up. They put him on Vancomycin, which is the last resort antibiotic, which luckily worked, because they told him had it not worked, they would have to amputate the arm at the shoulder.

Holly noted that the company went against Rios' prognosis so would have been open to a major lawsuit, and were kissing his ass the whole time he was recuperating.

After that escapade was over, he was able to sleep. He slept for a long time. Then he was told he was suspended for two months, from 2/7 to 4/7, the day after Mania. After two months, he never heard from anyone.

"I had to listen to Vince on the investors call to hear I'm on a sabbatical. Why wouldn't he announce to the investors I'm suspended."

He got one royalty check after being gone but didn't get the next one. He also found a royalty check from 2013 that he forgot to cash and needed it re-issued. He called, saying he needed them to both re-issue his 2013 royalty check and send his new royalty check. Nobody contacted him after the phone call. Every day he called WWE and nobody ever picked up and nobody ever got back to him. He said he even gave up on the checks. He said it was a ton of money left on the table, as much as some people make in a lifetime.

He said he really didn't care, because they weren't slinging mud at him and he wasn't at them. He said he called Mark Carrano and Jane Geddes, and Geddes said she'd call him back, but never did. Nobody is telling him they aren't going to send his checks.

He said he was thinking more about his honeymoon and the Black Hawks march to the Stanley Cup. On 6/11, two days before his wedding, he got a text from Levesque. He said they hadn't had any communication since Cleveland. He said Levesque asked if they had time to talk.

"I'm a reasonable guy," he said he told Levesque. "I've always had time to talk. I've always been a phone call away. I'm getting married in two days and going on my honeymoon. How about we talk the day I get home. In the meantime, reissue that check and send me my royalties for two months. That's reasonable."

Punk said Levesque didn't respond.

The afternoon of his wedding, he got the Fed Ex letter saying he was fired, with all the stipulations attached such as not getting royalties and them claiming a non-compete for one year.

He said he had a staph infection they refused to treat and diagnose, had a concussion, needed time off, and then he said he had a non-compete right there naming UFC, saying he did get a kick out of WWE always saying UFC isn't competition, but for him and Del Rio, they are specified by the name of the organization in the non-compete.

He said he called up a vicious Jewish lawyer in Los Angeles, who called him back and said, "Let's get those motherfuckers."

"We got them. The only thing I can't talk about is the terms of the settlement. I got everything I wanted and then some."

He got all his merchandise money, he allowed them to sell whatever merchandise they had of his (this explains the merchandise back on sale) and he gets a cut, he's allowed full use of his name (which is why he's been on TV as C.M. Punk and not Phil Brooks). He talked about how dumb it was for them to have 2K advertise him for the video game, and he got a big check from them as well. He also got an undisclosed settlement check.

They asked to do a joint statement together saying they were going their separate ways (to try and stop the Punk chants at TV every week). They also wanted a non-disparagement clause put in the settlement, which Del Rio had recently agreed to. He refused. He told them that they called him a quitter in his home town on television, so if they want to go on television in his home town and apologize, he'll consider it. He said he has no plans to go on an anti-WWE tirade. He said the WWE lawyers kept telling his lawyer that they know he's going to TNA and his lawyer kept saying he's not going to TNA.

He said he has no desire to continue wrestling and will never wrestle again. He said he's letting them sell the merchandise they have in stock but there is no relationship and there never will be. He said the firing on his wedding day ended any chance of that. He said that for ten years, he was illegally listed as an independent contractor and they're scared about that one. He said he'd like to see a union for the guys and girls. He joked again about them saying UFC isn't competition but you can't work there for a year after we fired you on your wedding day.

"I failed at wrestling. I failed at my goal of the main event at WrestleMania, but I've come to terms with it. But that fucking match with Undertaker was the best match on the show, everyone from Vince to Kevin Dunn has said it was the best match and it should have gone on last."

"For all the people who will say I'm a quitter (he actually used the word quieter, noting that people who criticize him on Twitter often can't spell and said they'll say things they'd never say to his face because they know they won't get punched) you took your ball and went home, I didn't quit, I got fired."

It was pretty clear that the twitter criticism gets to him, more than it should. He even remarked, when talking about how Batista did an MMA fight, that if he did a fight, and won, people on twitter would still talk crap about him. Some people will talk crap about anything, but life's far too short to worry about people like that.

Some people will interpret this as WWE = bad, others as Punk is an egomaniac, some of his facts weren't correct, and use that to absolve WWE of anything negative. The reality is somewhere in the middle.

But on the egomaniac thing, or Punk has too high an opinion of himself, this is a fact of life that people who say these things about main event talent don't understand. They are all like that or they wouldn't be main event talent. If you don't have the confidence that you are the best, you wouldn't be main event talent. It amuses me when people read books by top stars or listen to interviews and go, "This guy is full of himself." If they are a top guy, either they are being honest with you and are, to a degree, full of themselves, or they are putting on fake performance. Privately, there isn't one of them who doesn't think they are the best, some are more subtle about it than others. And as time goes on, the ones who are comfortable with it, hold back on the fakeness a lot less. Punk was not the greatest natural athlete. He did not have a look that would have gotten him a push in another era. He had tons of great matches because he was in good enough shape to do so, worked hard enough to do so, and was smart enough to understand how to do so. His promo ability is top tier on the all-time list, which is something that is a combination of hard work, practice, and ego.

If you knock him for thinking he should have had a WrestleMania main event, just remember if he wasn't thinking that way, he'd be just a guy in prelims who would have never gotten higher than those in charge pegged him to get at first. And if that person had complained, nobody would give a rats ass what he said, true or not. Everyone has different goals. From the outside, the idea that someone believes they succeeded or failed as a pro wrestler based on whether they got a WrestleMania main event sounds like somebody with a major problem. While there is some realness to it, it's also in other ways a fake honor chosen largely by one guy. It's a guy who has a great track record historically at building his company, but also has greatly lessened the overall popularity of the industry at the same time, and whose track record at knowing what top talent is in this day and age and being ahead of the curve on it is spotty at best. The reality is this is a company that wanted to fire Punk years ago, that fired Daniel Bryan twice, and would have totally botched this year's Mania had Punk not quit. They even came close to cutting Cena, whose charisma was obvious in his first week of training school to anyone with an eye for talent. And it was a company determined to put Orton vs. Batista as last year's Mania main event. Worrying about their judgment to define how you look at your career is ridiculous.

Punk has pitched a reality show idea to Chael Sonnen with a payoff of them fighting at the end. But Sonnen still has a promotional agreement with UFC and would have to get their permission to do it, and he doesn't think they'll allow him to do a reality show. Plus, Sonnen is suspended from fighting for two years and considers Punk a friend and doesn't want to fight a friend.

He then took a dig at Jericho. Jericho, on his podcast, said in response to a question about Punk, said Punk hadn't talked with anyone since he left. Punk hadn't returned messages to a ton of people, including some names a lot bigger than Jericho. I know of others who he had been in contact with for years who he also cut off cold. I also know of some people who he has talked with, but they never wanted that they talked with him or what they talked about to become public. Suffice to say he's been a sympathetic ear for people with similar frustrations with the company. He said he doesn't talk to guys who have an agenda, who can report that they talked with him on their podcast. I'm not sure why he chose to take the dig at Jericho, since it was largely just an answer to a question he had been asked. But Punk is a different type of person. Even Cabana, probably his best friend in wrestling, has noted that he can be an asshole to people.

There's probably a lot to this. He's expected to do a fan Q&A through Cabana on one more podcast. I'm guessing what media he'll do will be very limited, probably to promote his comics, or maybe to talk with Ariel Helwani about MMA.

"If I stopped talking to you, you have an agenda and you wanted to use our private conversation to grab web hits."

It's possible this was related to Jericho's new book, "The Best in the World," even though Jericho praised Punk highly in it, including saying he was looking forward to his Mania match with Punk because he felt Punk was good enough that they could have a Savage-Steamboat caliber match. He also said he felt the two were a lot alike in that some people thought they were egomaniacs, arrogant and hard to deal with because both had a lot of confidence in their abilities and ideas.

But he brought up an incident from a 2010 show in Amarillo where there was a house show on the same day as the Olympic gold medal hockey game between the U.S. and Canada. The match was scheduled as Jericho & Punk vs. Edge & John Morrison, and Jericho and Edge both wanted to watch the hockey game rather than talk over the match, figuring they've all worked together enough that they could call it in the ring. Jericho and Edge were in a crew bus watching the game.

The game went into overtime, with the goal being scored just as Jericho's music was playing. Punk started the match, and never tagged Jericho in. The finish was Morrison pinning Punk. Jericho then asked Punk what his problem was, and Punk said that Jericho and Edge were both unprofessional for watching a hockey game instead of putting the match together. Jericho said he exploded back by saying "You can't call a match in the ring?" and that Punk was the one unprofessional because if even one person bought a ticket to the show to see him wrestle, they were deprived of it by Punk never tagging him in. Jericho wrote that he disagreed with Punk, but he said Punk has balls and that's one of the reasons he requested to work with him.

Jericho responded to this saying that he considers Punk a good friend, but had not talked with him since the early part of the year. He said that he never asked Punk to be on his podcast after Punk left the company. I don't know that Punk said Jericho asked him to be on his podcast past the idea he thought Jericho was trying to get in touch with him so he could talk about the situation, or say he talked with him. Jericho said that Punk was scheduled for a podcast show that they were going to tape on December 18, 2013, but then a few days before, canceled, saying he didn't want to go on because he had nothing good to say about wrestling. Jericho said he told him they could just do the podcast and talk comic books or something else but Punk didn't want to do it. Jericho said in January, when he was submitting names to WWE for interviews (he's not allowed to ask talent to be on his shows, he has to submit names to the office and then they will line things up, it's very interesting how this works as WWE heavily promotes Austin's show, allows guests on Jericho's show but doesn't promote it, and won't allow guests on Jim Ross' show), he did put Punk's name on the list, but Punk was still with the company at the time. He said he texted Punk a few times after he left the company, but never asked him to do his show and was just asking how he was doing, and Punk never answered back.

DECEMBER 15

CM Punk has spent his entire adult life proving critics wrong who felt he could never make it to the top in pro wrestling. Now, he's bucking even longer odds in starting from scratch in MMA, without a high-level background in any combat sport.

There is an irony here. His role in UFC, an outsider with a name expected to bring in an audience that usually doesn't buy the pay-per-views or watch the product regularly, is exactly the role Johnson played in wrestling, and that he complained about publicly. But there's a major difference. Johnson, before becoming a movie star, had a proven track record in wrestling. And in pro wrestling, the promoters have control to make sure the most marketable talent is always protected in the scripts.

Punk, in the UFC, comes in with no track record past he was a superstar in pro wrestling.

His description of his life is that he was a teenager in Chicago, and a big fan of both the UFC and pro wrestling. He wanted to do both. There was a fork in the road, and went to pro wrestling. But he felt, no matter how big of a success he was in pro wrestling, he would have regrets if he never tried MMA.

"People who know me know how long I've talked about doing this," he said Saturday night. "This isn't so much about the UFC. It's about me, and what I want to show about me. It's something I've thought about for a very long time, and once the opportunity presented itself, I'd have been a fool not to take it."

It probably didn't hurt that he and WWE management had a big blowup in January. He was beat up and banged up. His paycheck was going down after a long run as champion.

He had money. He was leaving. And if he didn't try MMA now, he probably never would.

He said he was going to fight either way. But he mentioned it to Dana White casually, and then, after his legal issues with WWE were settled on 10/26, White and Lorenzo Fertitta came to Chicago to close the deal. They largely agreed, but finalization slowed in the hands of lawyers, but he signed his deal roughly a week before it was announced during UFC 181, as the company all day had promised a major announcement. UFC's track record on promising major announcements usually wasn't so good. This one garnered a ton of reaction, as expected, both positive and negative.

Given the timeline, it's pretty clear that when UFC said they had a major announcement on 11/17, it was both the Reebok deal and the C.M. Punk deal was what they were hoping to announce, but couldn't finalize either in time.

The initial comparison that many tried to make was with Brock Lesnar, a guy who was a big star in pro wrestling and then went into UFC, and ended up being a gigantic drawing card and had a run as heavyweight champion.

But really, this is the opposite. Lesnar was a freak athlete, who had a combination of speed, strength, size and an NCAA championship's pedigree. When he was in pro wrestling, people always speculated how he'd do in MMA.

Lots of pro wrestlers who had various levels of success in MMA, from Sylvester Terkay, Dan Severn, Ken Shamrock, Kazushi Sakuraba to Bobby Lashley to one-and-dones like Bam Bam Bigelow, brought with them strong amateur wrestling backgrounds. Others, like the late Sean O'Haire, brought reputations into MMA as street fighters, which ended up meaning nothing against trained professionals. The number of pro wrestlers who have done MMA is well over 100, but not one has had any meaningful success who didn't have a background in competitive wrestling before pro wrestling.

Even Dave Bautista, who was a wrestling star on the level of Punk, who did one MMA fight at 43 years old, but in a smaller promotion, did some wrestling and bouncing before doing an MMA training camp and fight in 2012 as a bucket list kind of thing. Bautista's situation was similar, he was on top in wrestling making seven figures, but burned out, but he left more to be an actor who wanted to dabble in MMA. For Punk, he signed a multi-fight deal and is looking to transition into the sport.

He started immersing himself in training three weeks ago. When he agreed to terms, he said he weighed 215 pounds. He was down to 200 after three weeks of training. He said he was going to do a test cut, and would fight at either 185, or possibly 170.

The plan is to go to a major fight camp and if it means moving he and his wife into a condo in a new city, that's what he'll do. Daniel Cormier, the team captain of AKA and a big wrestling fan, has already invited him to San Jose. Robbie Lawler has invited him to come to South Florida and train with the American Top Team.

As noted last week, he had already approached Chael Sonnen about doing a reality show to lead into a fight. But Sonnen is suspended for two years, says he's retired, and according to those close to him, doesn't want to fight a guy he considers a friend.

It's hard to say what his long-term plan is. It's obviously not about winning championships or being ranked in the top ten. Perhaps it's a bucket list thing. He's got money and can train wherever he wants and dedicate himself as long as he wants. He doesn't want to fight until he's ready, and suggested that would be about six months from now.

It could be as simple as wanting to do a few fights, for the experience of learning the skills, learning the training, and having the experience, to further his knowledge, and eventually transition into a commentator role, something he clearly has excellent potential for.

Dana White said that this is not a Lesnar deal, as Lesnar only wanted to fight against top guys. White suggested that Punk would start out against a guy with a similar level of experience, which means an 0-0 guy. So this is closer to a Herschel Walker situation. Walker fought guys that those close to the situation knew he would probably beat. They had actually fought before, but they were not top fighters.

Punk is different from all the aforementioned names. He was never considered one of the toughest guy in pro wrestling. He was never a star high school or college wrestler. He's a lot younger than Walker, but he's far from being once one of the greatest athletes of the 20th century. There are no famous street fight stories like the old-time wrestlers or like the guys from another era who used to relish beating up people up who called them fake.

In wrestling, about the only fighting story Punk is known for was about a decade ago. As the story goes, it was outside a Waffle House in Nashville, where he got into it with Teddy Hart, the nephew of Bret Hart, who had trained in boxing. By most accounts, he didn't fare very well in that one.

He's a guy who has made a lot of money, lives a relatively frugal lifestyle, wasn't happy with life as a pro wrestler and decided it was now or never to chase his other dream.

"It was actually a really easy decision to make," he said. "Time will tell how wise a decision it was. I finally feel there's something I can put 100 percent of myself into and I'll get 100 percent back, not 30 percent back."

And he's well known enough that UFC felt it was the right business move to sign him. If they didn't, Bellator would have done so in a heartbeat. While promoters love to backbite each other, there isn't one MMA promoter around who has publicly criticized the idea, and every one who has contacted us said they'd have done it in a heartbeat. But the idea they signed him to keep him from Bellator would be inaccurate, since it was UFC that pushed for the deal before the Bellator experiment of 11/15 proved successful. Most UFC signings involve Joe Silva or Sean Shelby calling or e-mailing a manager and making an offer, and you either accept or you don't. This was White and Fertitta both flying to Chicago and taking a fighter to dinner and high-level negotiations over the course of a month.

They are banking on the idea his name value is strong enough that a lot of people who aren't regular UFC viewers will be interested to see if he can fight. It is a line UFC has never crossed. White was heavily critical of Strikeforce signing Walker. Whenever Shaquille O'Neal approached White with a similar proposition in the past, it fell on deaf ears, and O'Neal was another freak athlete. What Punk has going for him that Walker doesn't is that he's current. What he has going for him that O'Neal doesn't is a different question. Perhaps management feels Punk will immerse himself in the sport and take it seriously and O'Neal wouldn't. Perhaps it's just a different time and place with an ever-changing fan base and maybe it was nothing more than timing. Perhaps Punk sold himself better, or they thought a pro wrestler fighting would bring in more outside business than an NBA giant fighting.

How that translates into fighting is a different issue. He is clearly mentally tough, which is a good trait for fighting, and has money to have the best trainers. He has some proficiency in Jiu Jitsu and moves well on the ground.

"I definitely do think it's a win-win for myself and the UFC," said Punk in a Rolling Stone article on his signing.

Those at UFC said they've been inundated already with press requests for Punk. If he was looking to up his name, interest in Punk this past week was the highest it has ever been, with the interest level this past week 15% ahead of what it was in 2011 coming off his famous promo on Raw in Las Vegas.

Nobody knows if Punk can fight. Realistically, given his age and injuries from a career of pro wrestling, and lack of competitive background in any combat sport, the odds are greatly against him. This is a Kimbo Slice play, and even Slice had experience in actually fighting people, which isn't MMA, but it is something. UFC isn't going to make the Elite XC Kimbo Slice mistake. They aren't going to build the company around him or promote that he's a great stinker when he isn't. He'll likely be what Walker was, an attraction on the main card.

Punk will probably have more eyes and more talk on him than Walker had for his debut, which says something about the visibility of pro wrestlers and the changing of eras.

But Punk is a guy who always had the odds against him, and has spent a dozen years proving people wrong. This could be where his detractors finally get the last laugh. The odds are they will. But the odds have always been strongly with his detractors. And they've been proven wrong every step of the way.

"I would have started somewhere if Dana and Lorenzo told me to pound the sand," he said. "It's not about UFC. It's not about money. I enjoy being paid. This is about the journey of the first fight and showing what's inside of me."

Is this good for the sport? It is, and it isn't. It is, because it will bring attention to UFC and garner curiosity. It isn't, because if the idea that UFC is the major league and you have to earn your way in, well, he walked in, sight unseen, and didn't have the competitive background whether in amateur wrestling, kickboxing or Jiu Jitsu, to justify it.

Sonnen, on his podcast, said that he knew who Punk would face and it would be a real fighter who would be heavily favored against him. The name Sonnen was referring to without saying was Michael Bisping. Those close to Punk said the story isn't untrue, but also recognized there would be virtually no way such a match could happen. I can't see UFC booking that kind of match, even though from a promotional standpoint, it's two smart guys and an easy sell, but it's far too much of a mismatch. And no athletic commission should ever sanction it. Cathal Pendred, an Irish fighter with a 15-3 record, claimed on Twitter that he was going to be Punk's first opponent and that he had "won the lottery." That would likely be a terrible idea as well.

Still, UFC promoted Randy Couture, the only five-time world champion in history, against 0-0 James Toney, in a fight that was a complete mismatch and got sanctioned. And yes, Toney was a skilled pro boxer, but his style of boxing and stance made him a sitting duck for any decent wrestler. However, it did draw, and the Couture vs. Toney match was among the hottest UFC matches of all-time when it came to the crowd response, particularly for Couture's win. I don't want to say it was great for the sport, but it wasn't bad either. But, a steady diet of matches like that would be bad. The smart promoter is the one who knows how to make a match like that work, and also knows when to stop doing it because they can recognize it won't keep working.

UFC has booked 0-0 fighters in the past. But this isn't B.J. Penn, who got a huge contract for his time as a Jiu Jitsu prodigy when he was signed with zero fights. It isn't Lesnar. It's not even Matt Mitrione, who was a very good college football player who managed to land a spot on The Ultimate Fighter reality show and got in that way, or Matt Riddle, who came into UFC with zero pro fights but was a very good high school wrestler and wrestled in college. Still, there were no loud complaints about Angela Hill being put in a world title tournament this year with exactly one career fight and a couple of months experience, because she wasn't a celebrity nor a pro wrestler. But for a man, this is very different from any fighter this version of UFC has ever hired.

But boxing survived the recent Mickey Rourke travesty, and far worse. Archie Moore, one of the greatest boxers of all-time, had several matches against pro wrestlers who had never boxed. Muhammad Ali had agreed to face Wilt Chamberlain in what would have been one of the biggest spectacles of all-time, although Chamberlain after the fight was announced, ended up quietly backing out. And boxing today would be in the exact same position today if that fight had taken place. Until Ronda Rousey came along, the biggest woman's combat sport fight of the modern era involved a non-woman boxer, putting on the gloves, whose claim to fame was being the daughter of Joe Frazier. Jose Canseco was older than Punk, and had less training, when he did MMA. Sure, he was a great baseball player many years earlier and baseball is real, but when it comes to real abilities that transfer over, I'll take the dedication and pain threshold of a pro wrestler above that of a long since retired baseball player. Ken Kaneko was a famous Japanese actor and Bobby Ologun was a comedian in Japan, Amanda Lewis got MMA main events because her father created Star Wars and Yukio Sakaguchi got featured on MMA cards because his father was a pro wrestler. Akebono drew because he was a famous sumo, and while that is a real sport, it is as far away from kickboxing is as humanly possible, and his fights led to the highest popularity peak of kickboxing that there was.

Not only did none of this kill Japanese MMA or kickboxing, but Akebono, Kaneko and Ologun both helped to make it far more popular. And while some will note there is no Japanese major league MMA today, and try to tie that in, Japanese MMA died not because of one single freak show guy, but because of a combination of the organized crime connections that made TV stations steer clear, and the public losing interest because there were not enough Japanese superstars that appealed to the public able to win the big fights. Also, the freak show card, like every gimmick, is limiting. Done sparingly, a smart gimmick works. Done frequently, like anything, it loses its effectiveness. The early ones were a plus. In the long run, they beat the gimmick to death and people lost interest.

Punk himself is a student of the MMA game, and probably knows this. The idea of Punk debuting on a smaller stage would have hurt UFC's interest. They knew the biggest money was in the first fight. They told him that directly. People who don't understand that and suggested UFC should have had him fight a few times first, well, they don't understand.

But there is no guarantee this will work. Lesnar was a scary man. Punk is a cerebral man. Scary works better in getting people to buy the fight. Cerebral can work as well in selling the fight. But Lesnar has a physical charisma that translated well. With Punk, it's all a very big question. In Japan, some celebrities drew. Others bombed. But nobody ever reached the top that didn't have some kind of a legitimate athletic background.

As far as credibility goes, the credibility is the revenue, and that's based on what the fans want. So many people who follow MMA and think they know what's best, will ignore all evidence of what the fans show they respond to. This isn't to say they want Punk. But every major promoter in the sport would have made the same choice White and Fertitta made.

If credible sport was what the fans would want, it would be obvious to the promoters. I guarantee you most promoters, and without question those running the UFC, would rather do it the way the fans who are complaining about this say it should be done. But there are planes to catch and bills to pay, and if what you're doing doesn't appeal to enough fans, the next thing you know you've gone away.

If credible sport is what they wanted, a lot of fights that didn't draw should have, and a whole lot of fights that did draw shouldn't have. That isn't to say this will work. This is a completely different thing than UFC has ever done, and for that matter anything any major MMA promotion has done. There has never been someone as well known with no competitive sports or really any fighting experience at this age starting out with such a spotlight on him. There is zero track record on Punk as a fighter. Yes, we know it will draw a lot of talk and interest, but talk doesn't always translate to money drawn. How many things in wrestling have gotten a lot of talk using celebrities? Some have worked and some didn't draw at all, and the success or failure is based largely on the nature of the celebrity and the scenario.

UFC has never had a guy as famous come in who was as smart when it comes to promoting fights. They've also never had a guy, who at least on paper, doesn't appear to belong and the odds are strong that he'll never belong. It is an experiment.

At the end of the day, the people who talk about the credibility of the sport don't realize that the masses who have left are the ones who cared the least when UFC was presenting credible fights with the most skilled fighters this sport has ever seen, came back on 11/15 to see Stephan Bonnar and Tito Ortiz re-enacting the Jerry Lawler vs. Bill Dundee 1983 television show in Memphis with no matches. It's a sad fact of life. And that's what leads to these kind of decisions.

UFC has hundreds of millions of dollars in outstanding loans due in 2015, and to refinance that debt, it is very much to their advantage to get the best interest rates possible. Their bond rating has been devalued twice of late, and the people who do those ratings don't care that Demetrious Johnson is the most skilled fighter anyone has ever seen, they only know that PPV numbers this year are way down, and because of low PPV numbers, UFC's EBITDA is expected to decline 40 percent this year. And when PPV numbers were through the roof with Brock Lesnar, UFC didn't have people increasing their interest rates because they sullied the sport by headlining with a fake pro wrestler as many of the same people complaining here said when that was decreed as ruining the good name of UFC, nor did they have television stations cutting down on their rights fees because the record numbers were drawn by a fake pro wrestler or a gimmick non-fighter like Kimbo Slice. It's a promotion that was built on fights between people that insiders knew couldn't fight anymore at the top level, grudge matches played out on television, and larger than life personalities from pro wrestling. The promotions that didn't have those elements faded quickly, or never got off the ground.

Can Punk, admittedly banged up from years of wrestling, get through a training camp? Bautista was older, and likely more susceptible to injuries given his background, and he survived and fought. The issues of his concussions, with Colt Cabana hinting that there were 12 or 13 of them, then going into fighting is absolutely troublesome, especially for someone who readily admits striking is the weakest part of his game. One would think UFC would have subjected him to a physical before signing him and making this announcement, but we don't know that they did. What we do know is that White claimed they did such a thing with Kurt Angle years ago in 2008, Angle didn't pass, and he was never signed. Still, those concussions should be no less troubling if he was pro wrestling, given that's where he got them all from in the first place. If you have too many concussions to fight, you should stay the hell away from pro wrestling as well. I've still yet to meet the guy who has done a schedule like Punk in pro wrestling, and also done MMA, who didn't say pro wrestling is far more dangerous. Ken Shamrock was injured far more in wrestling. Don Frye was injured far more in wrestling. Frank Shamrock was a natural for pro wrestling and wouldn't even dream of doing it because he knew the level of damage those working full-time took. Brock Lesnar quit pro wrestling because he saw guys at 35 and how messed up they were, and when he realized that was him in eight years, and he was living on Vodka and pain pills to get through the punishment, he left, then went into fighting, and would only return on a limited schedule. Bas Rutten said pro wrestling was much tougher. King Mo and Rampage Jackson couldn't even believe how tough pro wrestling was on their bodies until they started training, and Mo was a world class wrestler. Jackson fought some of the most dangerous men of all-time, quit pro wrestling training almost immediately. That said, if he's getting knocked out taking a clothesline from a guy not trying to hurt him, one would question taking punches and head kicks from people who are trained at those moves and trying to hurt him.

Punk himself said that he feels pro wrestling is the more dangerous of the two, noting if he was a fighter and tore his knee ligaments, he would get surgery, but as a pro wrestler, he'd be pressured to keep going for fear of losing his spot. He noted if he got a concussion in a pro wrestling match, like he said he did at the Royal Rumble, you continue the match, in his case going 40 minutes of taking bumps on a fresh concussion. In a fight, they wave it off and you're not fighting again for 90 days.

MMA had zero damage from Walker or Bautista fighting. Boxing survived fixed fights with Mark Gastineau, systematic fight fixing at the lower level, and would have survived wrestler Brian Adams being in a PPV No. 2 bout (as Top rank scheduled years back, largely because Randy Savage promised to promote it), Wilt the Stilt, 62-year-old Mickey Rourke and if Big Show would have done a pro fight. The Kimbo thing was a unique part of MMA's history, but did it hurt it's growth? Well, he set ratings records, and eventually did kill a company based on a series of flukes. But what pulled the plug on MMA on CBS was people like the Diaz Brothers and Gilbert Melendez beating down Mayhem Miller in a cage on a live broadcast, ie. real fighters, not matches with gimmick fighters.

It's a sport, and a business. His fight will be real. And time will tell if it'll do business.

DECEMBER 15

Punk returned to Colt Cabana's "Art of Wrestling" podcast on 12/3, to answer any fan questions about his interview the week before, and to an extent, to address Vince McMahon's comments in the interview with Steve Austin two days earlier.

The situation was a little different from the first week, where Punk went into detail for almost two hours, laying out his history with WWE over the past three years and why he was no longer with the company.

The Punk on the second show was more about just joking with his friend, throwing in a few more stories as they came up, and saying that he didn't accept Vince McMahon's apology from two days earlier, calling it a television stunt and not legitimate.

"I don't want to hear it's a coincidence (that he got his termination letter and one-year non-compete that included UFC and MMA just hours before his wedding, as McMahon tried to claim)," he said. "I don't want to hear it was about lawyers (McMahon claiming it was an issue with the legal department sending the letter). I talked to HHH on the 11th (June 11, 2014, two days before his wedding). My wife had asked for that time off so she could be married on that day and I don't want to hear it's (the time the letter arrived) a coincidence. If that apology was sincere, you wouldn't have used it as a publicity stunt. You could have texted. You could have called. You could have showed up, I live ten minutes from the arena, and come to my house and apologize like a man. That's the fucking time line. I was sick and fucking hurt and I could walk because I'm an independent contractor and I was suspended. And nobody contacted me after the suspension. I got a phone call asking about coming back the day after elbow surgery. I got the phone call asking about coming back the day after knee surgery."

Punk also noted that the letter came on 6/13, and that meant if they were sorry and wanted to apologize, they could have done so for six months, but nobody from the company contacted him and they stopped returning his phone calls. Then McMahon apologized, claiming it was due to a miscommunication issue with the legal department, and that it was just a coincidence the letter arrived at the time it did. It was notable that even though the firing was hardly the most serious of Punk's charges (the misdiagnosis or lack of diagnosis of what turned out to be an MRSA staph infection being the most serious), it was the only one McMahon addressed and apologized for because it was the one that got the media attention, and was one that made the company look cold-hearted.

"He just waited until a TV camera was on so he could do damage control," he said.

And perhaps it was the most serious to Punk. Punk never said he was retired, and never said that he would never come back, but just talked about how much happier he was since being gone and that those who think they know his situation and say he'll be back don't know.

There is the matter of odds, in the sense that even Bruno Sammartino, Ultimate Warrior, Superstar Billy Graham, Jerry Lawler, Sable, Road Warrior Hawk, Ricky Steamboat, Brock Lesnar and Bret Hart eventually mended fences with WWE, and all had pretty strong and valid gripes with the company. The only ones who never did were Randy Savage, Chyna, Ole Anderson and Tom Zenk. Savage was a unique circumstance, and Chyna was a unique personal issue. Anderson was never a star in the company in the first place and they never tried to get him, and he certainly never called them. Zenk was never a star whose name meant anything for WWE to bring back. But all the other names would have said for years they would never be part of WWE.

"There are plenty of guys who think they know," said Punk. "Jericho is one of them. Jericho thinks I feel like he felt in 2005, when he left for two-and-a-half years. That's from his perspective. He felt in 2005 that he was never coming back, and sees me coming back, just wait three years and I'll come back. I can see his point of view, but they didn't fire you on your wedding day. They didn't purposely and maliciously try to ruin a day that's supposed to be special."

He also came back on McMahon's comments blaming lawyers for the problems between the two sides.

"Lawyers didn't jam anything up," he said. "They expedited the process. Look at Del Rio. He's already wrestling other places, because you can't put a non-compete on an independent contractor, period."

I don't know if that would hold up, but the WWE non-competes that didn't hold up to challenges, and in the case of Punk, Alberto Rodriguez (Del Rio) and Brock Lesnar, the company folded legally on them, is because no court was going to allow the excessive nature of them. For one, in all three cases, WWE tried to get a worldwide non-compete. In the case of Lesnar, he actually signed a contract stating he would not do any sports, or entertainment that related to his athletic endeavors (which could easily be construed to include movies or television shows where he did anything physical), with one exception, which was playing in the NFL, and agreed to a term of six years, through 2010.

After Lesnar opted out of pro football–he was a late cut by the Minnesota Vikings–very impressive considering he hadn't played football since his junior year of high school, which was 1995, and this was 2004–he declined trying to learn the game and playing in NFL Europe to develop his skills. In 2005, he started talks with New

Japan Pro Wrestling, and WWE was the one that initiated the legal action against him. Even though he had signed the papers, it was pretty clear the court would have never upheld something that would keep him from using his physical gifts to make a living for six years. What also likely hurt WWE is that when Lesnar then agreed to return to WWE based on the terms of his old contract, WWE turned it down and claimed he was no longer worth it anymore. In other words, they felt he wasn't worth a $1 million downside for a full schedule, but later paid him multiples of that for three matches a year.

The difference is Lesnar actually signed an agreement, but it was still likely to have been thrown out in court. For Punk and Del Rio, neither signed an agreement to be held to a one year non-compete so the argument would be whether a non-compete could be used as a disciplinary measure when firing someone for a term past the length of their existing contract while also claiming them to be independent contractors.

In the case of most WWE non-competes, the company pays the performer his regular downside for 90 days. The company does it because it doesn't want talent going directly from WWE television to either TNA or UFC in particular. In the case of Jim Ross, they paid him for roughly ten months, and in his case it was all about not wanting him to appear on TNA television as MMA was not listed in his non-compete.

With both Rodriguez and Punk, because they were fired for disciplinary reasons, the company felt it had the right to enforce a one-year non-compete against both, even though the company would not be paying them during that period. Both men's contracts with WWE were to expire before that one year period was out.

They also decreed, due to discipline violations, Rodriguez for slapping an employee, Punk for walking out, that they weren't entitled to any royalties even though the company would continue to sell products with their names and likeness.

However, in both cases, the wrestler had the goods on the promotion to force a quick settlement in their favor.

With Punk, while it seems like he's quite content with moving on with his life and just talking about comic books, television shows, pop culture and MMA, and doing whatever he wants, he is still a smoking gun. If he wasn't, WWE wouldn't have settled with him on such unfavorable terms, such as paying him whatever owed and then some, and signing off without even making him sign a non-disparagement agreement.

You'd have to be naive to believe the timing of the termination letter to be coincidental. There was no need for it to begin with, given his contract was expiring in a few more weeks and they weren't paying him anyway. The firing was clearly a paranoia shot of thinking they could get him back on his wedding day, and from a business standpoint, attempt to keep him from going to TNA for a year, because had they let the contract expire, he could have gone to TNA in July. Based on history, they didn't believe the retirement stories, because too many times in the past, wrestlers had told Vince McMahon they were burned out and leaving the business, only to sign with the opposition as soon as they were legally able.

He basically descried his appearances as cathartic for him and said that was it and he's moving on. He thanked fans who supported him and thanked those who purchased his merchandise. Whether it turns out to be that, he closed talking like this was his goodbye when it comes to talking pro wrestling. But I sense that he did so in a way to know he's got no vendetta and is moving on, but if the company were to go after him hard (and McMahon's apology showed just the opposite) or tried to screw with his wife's career, there is the underlying threat that he could make their lives miserable.

Punk said that the legal settlement came on his birthday (Punk turned 36 on October 26th).

"I got my signed settlement papers on my birthday and I gave back to the fans on Thanksgiving (when his first podcast with Cabana was put up). The only reason it didn't get done sooner is you were in Japan (Cabana competed in New Japan's Global League tournament that ended on 11/8) and I was in Los Angeles. I was harping on you the day I got those papers. I was really anxiety ridden and antsy so I could move on with the next chapter of my life. I didn't expect it to be this big thing. I didn't mean to bash the WWE. I just rolled with it."

Punk got plenty of publicity this week regarding UFC, since Dana White, when appearing on the Jim Rome show, teased the idea of talking with him about fighting and noting he was coming to UFC 181. Clearly there has been talk already in that direction. White said that this is different from Brock Lesnar, and that he doesn't know if Punk can fight. Lesnar came in and faced former UFC champion Frank Mir in his second pro fight (in his first, he quickly beat former Olympic silver medal winning judoka Kim Min-Soo). He said Punk would start out against a fighter with his same experience level, or essentially, a fighter with an 0-0 record.

"I have no interest in fucking going back," he said, but did note he meant at this time. "The difference in my appearance, in my mental stability between now and nine or ten months ago is so drastically different. He said that after he returned from his knee problems a few months after WrestleMania, he had "another year of bullshit, lies and miscommunication, and you get where I'm at right now."

He said he was told he would never have to work with Ryback again, and then got begged to work with him and got hurt again.

When talking about working with the Wyatt Family, he said that he was looking forward to it, thinking he could help teach them, have some fun, and also learn more at the same time.

"It's what this business is about," he said. "But it wasn't fun. I was so beat up, hell, somebody in the company has footage of those house shows. Watch me when I know Daniel Bryan is getting beat up, watch me crouch down in the corner because I know I have to take a hot tag, I'm dry heaving, and then I had to work with the Shield at the house shows. These three young hungry guys, and I'm thinking, What am I doing with my life?

He also brought up a story regarding the December 15, 2013, TLC PPV show. He said that one of his best friends was getting married on that day. He said at least six months, perhaps eight months, before, he told the office that he was not going to miss the wedding and not to book him. He was told it was a PPV date and he said, "I'm letting you know. You guys don't need me for this. It might have been less than eight months."

He said he told Vince McMahon, HHH and Michael Hayes that he was not working that show. He said he would call Mark Carrano up once a month to remind him to make sure everyone knew he was not available to work that show.

So a month before the show, he's told, "You're working The Shield, three-on-one, on pay-per-view.

"I told you guys, I've missed weddings, graduations, bar mitzvahs, I'm not missing my buddy's wedding."

He ended up working the show in Houston. That's why his match was the opener and A.J. Lee's title match with Natalya went on second. The two flew straight from Houston to Long Beach, got there just as the wedding ended, talked to a few people, he and his wife got a picture taken at "In And Out Burger" and flew back for Raw the next day.

He then did almost a comedy routine about how they wanted him to beat The Shield one-on-three, but one person after another all day came up to him to say, "You've got to make Roman look really strong."

"Every two minutes, somebody comes up to me and says, `You've got to make Roman look really strong.'" he said. "And I said, `You know what would make him look really strong? If he beat me. And they said, `But Vince wants to make you look really strong.'"

He also brought up how he brought the Wizard World deal to WWE as they wanted him first, and then suddenly, the office changes it to where a lot of people are doing the conventions. He said he wasn't mad about it, and that his wife has gotten dates on it as well. But he said he was scheduled for a signing in Nashville, and without anyone telling him, he somehow found out that Sheamus was scheduled for the signing and he was off. When he called his contact at Wizard World, they told him that the office pulled him from the signing. He noted that he was getting $20,000 for four hours of autograph signing.

He said he called Mark Carano, who told him that the advance for the tour in Mexico that weekend wasn't good and they needed him on the tour. Punk said he told him that was fine, but instead of four hours and not bumping for $20,000, now he's working four days in Mexico, so his paycheck for the weekend would have to be $20,000.

"Guess what my check was, and I probably had a full blown staph infection, four shows for five grand."

He said he brought the check to TV, put in on the cable and said "Fix this."

"I'm not a bad communicator," he said, in response to McMahon criticizing Punk's communication skills. "They just don't like the way I communicate."

He said he told Sean Cleary, who was the head of talent relations at that point, and told him to fix it, and also made a note that Jane Geddes and Cleary were not equipped for their jobs.

"I think he had a basketball background, he might have worked with the Celtics (Boston Celtics, Cleary was an assistant coach with a few college teams and the Celtics in the 90s). What does he know about how wrestlers who fall down should get paid and how it's structured? They probably talked bad behind my back and joked about it. I got $5,000 for doing hardcore street fight matches against Curtis Axel and Paul Heyman."

Punk said that he got a check for another $4,000 after his complaint, and he didn't say another word, saying it just added another notch in his frustration belt.

He said a few years ago, he was in negotiations for a Slim Jims endorsement deal ala Randy Savage. He said Slim Jims came to him, not the WWE and they negotiated the deal. But by terms of his contract, WWE had to approve of it after the deal was agreed to. He said the television commercials were already laid out. He would play a camp counselor at Slim Jims camp. He said he took the deal to WWE, and the next thing you know, Slim Jims campaign is with Rey Mysterio, Big Show and Eve Torres.

Then he told the story about how THQ wanted him on the cover of the 2011 video game. He noted that Paul Heyman (who works closely with the video game people) had first told him of that. Later, he said, he, through someone in the office, got sent the trail of e-mails where THQ kept asking for him to be on the cover and WWE kept saying they wanted Sheamus on the cover. He also told about when he had a friend, Dan Smith, who was with the TV show L.A. Ink, and they asked him if he'd get tattooed on the show. He said once again he went to the company with the deal, and the company sent Randy Orton to do the show.

DECEMBER 29

C.M. Punk did a ton of media this past week, doing the rounds at ESPN on 12/17 and then doing mostly New York media including Boomer & Carton on WFAN, Opie and Off the Record on TSN (UFC's new broadcast partner in Canada) on 12/18. The latter got contentious. It started when they played a comedy clip listing prospective opponents for him and put on Jose Canseco, Justin Bieber or Chef Boyardee (because Chef would have a grudge against him with the idea he's a vegetarian). Punk started shutting down the interview when Landsberg started asking wrestling questions, particularly when he brought up his wife working for the company. He just gave short answers and said he was here to talk about the UFC. When asked what Vince McMahon thinks about the UFC, he said Vince doesn't view them as competition, even though he himself brought up that they put UFC in his non-compete, which would appear to be a contradiction, something he pointed out himself in the first Colt Cabana interview. Landsberg asked Punk if he was pissed off at his questions, which was almost guaranteed to make things go from bad to worse. He said they are wrestling-centric questions and he wanted to talk about UFC. Landsberg then talked about how Punk hasn't had a fight and doesn't have an opponent. Then Punk said that he likes Landsberg's gimmick, and how he changes off camera to on camera (Cormier/Jones if you're paying attention) and how he tried to act like he's friend off camera and asked if Punk would big league him if they met at UFC 182 off camera, but then on camera, Punk said, "You try and act like the cool kid in school." I guess that referred to Landsberg asking the pretty obvious questions about A.J. Lee working for WWE and bringing up what he said about WWE's medical care on the Cabana podcast. Then Landsberg talked about it being disrespectful for Punk to be drinking coffee on camera while doing an interview, and that was pretty much it. Landsberg overreacted as Punk was making it clear he didn't want to be there. But Punk making it so obvious he didn't want to be there or talk wrestling came first. On the show, Punk said that Chael Sonnen made up the story about them doing a TV show together to lead to a fight. Punk said that Sonnen likes to twist things around, and that he called Sonnen up for an idea of doing a reality show based around Sonnen training him, but not leading to the two fighting. Sonnen couldn't fight Punk for a number of reasons, between the idea that nobody should sanction it, and even if they would, Sonnen is suspended for about 18 more months. While there is no target date for Punk's debut, the feeling right now is it will be in late 2015 and not on the July show as some had speculated.

CHAPTER TWELVE

WWE TELEVISION DEAL

FEBRUARY 3

The New York Post wrote about the WWE negotiations with NBC Universal to keep Raw on USA and Smackdown on Syfy. NBC Universal has an exclusive negotiating period that expires on 2/1. Those internally have said that WWE would prefer to stay on the two channels all things being equal. According to the story, NBC Universal was thinking about, as part of its offer, giving WWE space at Universal theme park in Orlando for a physical Hall of Fame. We had reported a long time ago that park sources had noted expectations that the WWE Hall of Fame would be there. The story reported that NBC Universal had not made a concrete offer, but have talked about adding the offer of space for a physical Hall of Fame as part of the deal. Within WWE is the belief they are staying on USA and Syfy and getting their Hall of Fame with the new deal. WWE is looking for $280 million from this deal, which would be close to triple the current deal, noting that NBC Universal paid $440 million per year to NASCAR, and WWE delivers similar ratings. The story mentioned Spike, Turner Broadcasting as potential partners. There is at least something to Spike. Turner had no interest in WWE in 2008, the last time the rights came up, and have shown no interest in pro wrestling in general since Jamie Kellner canceled what had been staple programming on TBS for three decades in 2001. Spike has said nothing public, nor should they. If they are interested and don't get it, they've pretty much told the world they were ready to dump TNA, which wouldn't be a healthy situation. At this point they are not allowed to make an offer until after 2/1. The split between Spike and WWE in 2005 wasn't the smoothest, but that's a long time ago. It's not a secret that WWE would like to stay with NBC Universal, but it's clear they are expecting a huge increase in rights fees over what they are currently getting. It's a key, because the increased stock price is based on the idea rights fees will at least double. The network doesn't have to make money the first year because they came in and told people they don't expect it to. If they don't hit 1 million subscribers by the end of the year, it could be a negative to stock price. But if they get a big rate increase from TV, a fixed income guaranteed for years, that will almost completely soften any blow, if the network isn't as big a success as they hope. So as far as the two, while the network will get most of the attention and is a huge story long-term because so many other entities will try and copy from the good and the bad, it's the TV negotiations that are probably the bigger financial story this year. Either way, the odds are very strong the company will be far stronger financially in 2015 than right now even if popularity stays the same or even decreases. Due to all this, the stock has gone through the roof, closing at press time at $21.96 per share, giving the company a market cap of $1.65 billion. Vince McMahon is very much a billionaire on paper today.

FEBRUARY 10

The first of the company's three major television contracts that was expected to be renewed with a major increase was signed this past week. The timing was almost too perfect for the U.K. contract. Newcomer BT Sports, which already got a key soccer contract from Sky and is also the home of UFC, was bidding for Sky content. Sky locked up a new five-year-deal with WWE, which goes through late 2019, reportedly tripling the previous contract. Sky will be airing roughly 12 hours of WWE programming per week, including Raw, Smackdown, NXT, Superstars and Main Event, as well as several recap shows and will have multiple replays. They've also changed their PPV deal. Before, in the U.K., there were several PPVs that aired as free TV specials but the major PPVs aired as PPV shows. Now, all 12 will air as PPVs, at a cost of $24.67 U.S., or about half the price in the U.S. WrestleMania will be more expensive. The contract included agreements and clauses related to the network. WWE has not publicly said anything about the network when it comes to the U.K. and what differences it will have. For UFC, in every country, there will be differences in Fight Pass based on the television deals in those countries, because you don't want to undercut your television partners who are paying for the rights. One difference I would think would be replays of Raw and Smackdown. Sky Sports airs Raw live and Smackdown before it airs in North America, but also airs multiple replays of both shows. I would think they wouldn't want the network to air the replays before they are done with their own replays. Sky Sports is a subscription service in the U.K. which costs the equivalent of $71 per month, and that doesn't include the price of the PPVs. For a wrestling fan who isn't a soccer fan or a fan of other channels, they could in theory get the network and dump Sky Sports, besides not buy the PPVs unless Sky got exclusivity on the TV shows for a few days at least.

WWE is trying to sell its broadcast partners on the idea that the network will raise the popularity of WWE so that, whether it's USA or Sky, ratings will be increasing this year. It's uncharted waters, so we'll have to see how that plays out. I don't anticipate it hurting ratings in the sense the key first-run television show and main weekly focus is going to be Raw, perhaps more than ever, and that's not on the network. If Raw is less of a focus, then ratings will drop, but I don't see that.

One of the things that benefitted WWE in this deal is that in the U.S., for decades, Vince McMahon ran away from the label of sports, while internationally the company hasn't done that. Gerritt Meier, the Executive VP of International for WWE, told the Hollywood Reporter , "Internationally, we have our anchor within broadcast much more on the sport side than domestically." The value of sports content on television is rising tremendously as compared to entertainment content, so WWE has been pushing that it is just like sports. The U.K. is WWE's second biggest market outside of the U.S., even ahead of Canada.

FEBRUARY 17

The New York Post ran a story intimating that negotiations between WWE and NBC Universal have hit a snag. NBC's Exclusive negotiating period ends this week and they are expected to be putting in a final bid on 2/14. What is fortuitous is that the USA Network's gap in being No. 1 in cable has been closing. While last year, if you took WWE out of the mix, USA would still have been No. 1 in prime time, this year that may not be the case and USA would badly want to keep that slot.

FEBRUARY 24

As was largely expected, the WWE television deal is now up for grabs, after the exclusive negotiating window with NBC Universal, which includes the USA Network (Raw), Syfy (Smackdown) and E! (Total Divas), expired on 2/15.

NBC Universal still has the right to match any outside offers, which for WWE, was the exact scenario they would have wanted. At the end of the day, they don't want to leave, but want outside suitors to drive up the price.

"While we were unable to reach an agreement with NBCU during this (exclusive negotiating) period, we have certainly appreciated our long and productive partnership," the WWE released in a statement to Variety. "With year-round live programming that is highly coveted by programmers, distributors and advertisers, we are extremely excited about our future. We look forward to engaging with potential partners who recognize the value of having the No. 1 show on cable and live content delivered 52 weeks a year."

The WWE could sign a deal with one conglomerate for product exclusivity and that conglomerate could put the shows on different stations, or they could sell all of the shows as individual entities to different conglomerates. It's hard to believe a major station would be willing to air pro wrestling in prime time four nights per week, since WWE is looking at next television season for a Sunday through Wednesday night prime time line-up of "Total Divas," (two seasons), Raw, live Smackdown and Main Event.

WWE Executive Vice President of Marketing Michelle Wilson noted this is the first time the Raw and Smackdown contracts expired at the same time, feeling that the timing gives WWE more power in brokering a deal.

In 2013, it was estimated that Raw, Smackdown, any specials, Total Divas and I believe this figure would also include Main Event on Ion, took in about $170 million in ad revenue. The WWE earned slightly more than $100 million in domestic rights fees, with the big increase being the addition of "Total Divas," which is believed to take in about $700,000 per episode, a similar number to both Raw and Smackdown.

Even though Raw is consistently among the highest rated shows on USA, it garners the lowest ad rates per viewer on the station.

The WWE was looking for $280 million or more in television revenue from the U.S. market. Thus, no matter what the ratings, under normal circumstances, it makes no economic sense for NBC Universal to go even to $170 million to keep the deal.

The reality is the stations could generate a solid percentage of that revenue in the same time slots even with shows with lower ratings. There are shows they can put on with minimal cost (and first run programming could be more expensive but would generate more revenue as well) where the profit margin would be higher than for wrestling.

Cable stations and satellite distributors pay stations for carriage rights and in most cases, that's far more important these days than ad revenue. The problem is, at NBCU, there is no belief that USA or Syfy would be cut back at all in carriage fees if they lose wrestling, since wrestling isn't seen as prestige programming by cable companies.

Another issue with wrestling is that with very few exceptions (MMA, Silk Stalkings in the 90s), wrestling fans are not station fans, just wrestling fans. They don't watch other programming on those stations.

Networks will spend far more than their ad revenue for football, baseball and basketball, especially the NFL, because history has shown the most valuable thing to build a network is to advertise your prime time shows during NFL broadcasts because it's a huge audience that will then watch other shows. The same tactic during wrestling seems to garner very little benefit for the station.

Even though Smackdown is Syfy's most popular show, it doesn't fit in with the station theme, but losing the show would hurt ratings overall.

For the week ending 2/9, USA was in a rare non-football season situation of being No. 3, on cable, at 2.01 million viewers on average, trailing The History Channel (Pawn Stars, American Pickers, Swamp People) at 2.23 million, and AMC (Walking Dead, Talking Dead) at 2.21 million. The latter had an usually big week with Walking Dead hitting an NFL-like 15.76 million viewers for its new airing.

Without Raw, USA would have fallen to sixth place, also trailing Disney, Fox News and TBS. However, that is not a normal week. For the entire year of 2013, USA Network without Raw would have still been No. 1 on cable, although its margin of victory would have been closer.

Syfy was No. 17 last week with 1.05 million viewers on average in prime time. Taking away Smackdown, which had its biggest audience in more than a year, it would fall to No. 24 at 820,000 viewers.

The value to USA is whatever financial and ego gain they get based on being No. 1 in prime time, because if nothing else, losing Raw would risk that position.

However, perhaps they'll pay more to keep a franchise they created and is still strong and based on history, will stay stronger than most cable competition for as long as forever is. Under normal circumstances, because it doesn't generate big ad rates, its value to most other stations wouldn't be that high.

When they do the comparison with what NASCAR brings as far as ratings go and what they bring, the difference is NASCAR commands far higher ad rates and has a higher caliber of sponsors.

Since the exclusive negotiating period with NBC Universal has come and gone without a deal, it's now a question as to whether there is interest from the outside.

Spike and FS 1 would make the most sense. The 2005 WWE split from Spike was acrimonious, but that was also nearly a decade ago. Spike also has its own wrestling franchise that, while it doesn't generate anywhere near the ratings, comes with a lot smaller price tag.

Plus, WWE also wants to place Superstars. I'm not sure what the thought process is on placing NXT on broadcast TV. The original idea was to place it starting this past September, but there was no interest, and now it's being advertised as a WWE Network exclusive show.

People at TBS and TNT have claimed that they will never get back into wrestling, and in 2008, showed no interest when WWE tried to get them to bid on Raw.

There are no rumors of ESPN having interest, and I can't see WWE not getting pre-empted often on ESPN, since WWE will never be one of the five biggest players on an ESPN. Going to ESPN 2, a secondary channel, is bad for WWE as it labels it secondary sports programming and WWE should do everything to avoid being labeled secondary anything.

Even if FOX has an interest in them, to help build FS 1, they would be an entity where it could make sense to pay for more than the ads bring in. It will help build a fledgling station that is still struggling to find an audience, and can help the station in a number of ways including potential carriage revenue, which for the station is unusually low.

But there are a couple of issues. The first is, while it would make sense for WWE to use FOX as leverage for a deal, in the end, do they really want to go on FS 1, risk the kind of ratings decline UFC got moving to that station, plus losing coverage in 10 million homes, or nine percent of the country?

In addition, how much WWE programming would a sports channel want to put on, and where would the rest of the WWE programming go in the Fox family?

As we've seen with UFC, with a sports station, the major sports are going to be a priority in the end, and if something huge in sports that they have rights to were to happen, would they, no matter the ratings, put wrestling as a priority over so-called major sports?

USA and Syfy don't preempt, while UFC is getting preempted and moved to FS 2 on its flagship Wednesday frequently. If FS 1 wants to carry wrestling (and I don't know if that's the case), that is a company that right now has to spend big to build a station and wrestling would raise the profile of the station. So they could overspend to get WWE to help build the station. But it's a risk for WWE, and one I don't think they'd want to take.

MARCH 17

An article in Bloomberg.com listed that the WWE had talks with AMC Networks Inc., Viacom Inc., Time Warner Inc., and 21st Century Fox regarding negotiations for domestic TV rights. Talks only mean something if an offer is made. AMC is an interested one. Due to "Walking Dead," AMC is now a top five station. Viacom would be for Spike, which confirms what I'd felt for a long time was a logical business move, and also explains why Spike hasn't renewed TNA's contract that is up at the same time the WWE deal is up with NBC Universal. Time Warner would be for TBS and TNT. For what it's worth, I'm aware of a wrestling proposal to that company very recently where they said that they had no interest in wrestling again. Still, that doesn't rule out WWE. Fox would of course be to help build FS 1, and put UFC and WWE on the same station. George Barrios, the CFO of WWE, said he expected the new deal to be announced at the end of April or early May.

MARCH 24

There has been a lot of talk this past week regarding suitors for the WWE TV package. The only major name that has come out besides those already talked about is WGN. One person following the situation closely noted that the key for WGN would be the belief adding WWE would help them expand the potential audience for the station (they are currently in about 73 million of the 99 million cable homes) and allow them to charge cable systems more for carriage, since they've got little strong programming. They are doing poor ratings but they've got money, as they are apparently the high Bidder for "Better Call Saul," a "Breaking Bad" spin-off, but didn't win out. They are currently getting less than 10 cents per home per month, but if they could increase to 90 million homes and get to 25 cents with WWE programming, that takes the station from $87.6 million in revenue from carries to $270 million. That, and ad revenue, could justify a bid well North of $250 million if they are willing to greatly overspend to build the station. It should be noted that WGN was the lone legitimate bidder in 2008 besides USA. The problem with WGN is the same as FS 1, but worse. WWE would love to get the word out they are in the game because it helps the price. But at the end of the day, do they really want to be on a station that nobody watches and that 26% of their current Raw audience doesn't get? George Barrios on 3/10 in giving a presentation at the annual ROTH Conference pegged early May at the latest to announce the home of Raw and Smackdown for the new year. He said a key point in the negotiations is WWE attempting to get a deal where they can get Raw and Smackdown replays on the network. Right now, the contract with NBC Universal doesn't allow them to put the shows on for 30 days, and they want to shorten that window. I'm not sure why Hulu gets them quicker, but Hulu also isn't allowed to show anything but an edited version of Raw. It was interesting that when asked about the ratings for the show Barrios indicated they were flatter than the company would like, but blamed it on external forces such as more competition. Regarding the AMC meeting, the web site Betaville claimed they had one exploratory talk and claimed the talks haven't gone anywhere. AMC was reportedly interested in WWE for merger talks, and it was merger rumors that helped fuel a stock price increase last week. From what we're told, besides WWE saying there are no merger talks, investors don't believe Vince McMahon will sell controlling interest in the company. However, there is concern over what happens if something happens to Vince McMahon. The feeling is Stephanie McMahon has taken a step back, that Paul Levesque is not someone who could be CEO of a public company (his actual management years of experience are only a few and he's never had anything resembling that kind of responsibility, and his expertise is in wrestling, not in things that a CEO would have although Vince has been training him), and that leaves Michelle Wilson and George Barrios. The question on Barrios is his knowledge of the modern media landscape and of the pro wrestling business, and Wilson's knowledge of the wrestling aspect is also a question. And both of them are the ones who are going to be responsible to a degree if the network fails or they don't at least double domestic TV revenues.

MAY 5

Rumors have it to not expect a television deal announcement until after 5/1. At the WWE shareholders meeting on 4/25, they indicated that the announcement of the new TV deal may be a little later than the late April/early May time frame they had first announced. WWE stock has been decreasing as people are wanting to get out and take gains with the feeling that if the deal announcement isn't good, the stock will decline at that point so it's less risk selling off now. At the meeting, they pushed how positive they are both short-term and long term on the network, how the 400,000 PPV buys surprised them and pushed the idea that this was the most-watched WrestleMania ever in the U.S. They pushed a 1.1 million number, and I have no doubt if you count those on the network and multiple viewership by the same homes you could probably get to that number. But live, there were nowhere close to 667,000 people watching, because a significant percentage of network subscribers didn't watch live, and a significant number of that 667,000 are really from outside the U.S.

MAY 19

There is nothing official on the new WWE contract but the word going around in the TV industry is the official announcement will be coming any day now. Some believe it'll be on 5/15 at the NBCU up fronts, and that WWE delayed the announcement to let NBCU announce that they are staying put. One thing that would seem to corroborate that is reports that E! has ordered ten more episodes of Total Divas, although they may have done that anyway since the show has been successful, and it's not like E! couldn't keep Total Divas if Raw or Smackdown went elsewhere. NBCU had the right to match any outside offer, and most expected WWE was going nowhere, with the only question being how much of an increase they'd be able to get, and whether Smackdown would move from Friday to a live Tuesday slot, which in time, would be expected to increase its ratings. Timing worked well for them, as in the U.K., the contract expired during a period that Sky and BT were in a bidding war for properties, and in the U.S., it came at a time when USA was no longer dominating at No. 1 to where it could afford to lose Raw and maintain the top spot. From the week ending 5/4, USA was a distant second to TNT by a 3.23 million to 1.95 million, although that's due to the NBA playoffs. However, if you take Raw out of the week, USA would fall all the way to 7th place, and a 22.6% decline in total viewers. Syfy, without Smackdown, would fall from 22nd place to 24th place, which isn't as big a deal , but it would still be an 18% decline in total viewers for the week. A year ago, USA could have lost Raw and still remained No. 1. Another positive sign, at least to me, is that on 5/12, Major League Soccer announced a new $90 million a year deal with ESPN, Fox Sports (for FS 1) and Univision for eight years. The key is that soccer does tiny ratings compared to wrestling or UFC for that matter (regular season games on ESPN and ESPN 2 this past season averaged 220,000 viewers and games on NBC Sports Net averaged 122,000). Even though it gets real sports coverage and promotion, the ESPN numbers dropped 29.3% last season, yet their rights fees went up five times from the previous $18 million contract. You look at that figure and compare audiences with WWE or UFC and it tells you how much the value of live sports has gone up. By all rights, WWE, even with its weaker audience profile, you are still talking about at doing 19 times the number of viewers as soccer every Monday night on USA as MLS does on ESPN. WWE's numbers are steady while soccer fell huge this past year. For another way of looking at it, the MLS for its new deal will get rights fees equal to about $6.77 per individual viewer per game. WWE, on its current deal for Raw and Smackdown, gets 23 cents per individual viewer per episode. Part of the reason the number was up is Major League Soccer signed an eight-year deal, and television is trying to lock up long-term deals. WWE's deal is coming up at a time when USA Network is struggling to maintain No. 1, so WWE's value to USA is significantly more now than one year ago. But it all comes down to bidders. MLS was able to get that increase because most likely every sports network around wanted them, and there's also a feeling, even with the declining ratings, that soccer is a sport on the rise with the World Cup coming.

MAY 26

After its new television deal came in well under expectations, questions persisted about the success of the network, and company projections showed money losses for this year far greater than expected, the WWE stock has taken a drubbing over the past few days.

The stock closed on 5/15, at $19.93 per share, up over a few days earlier based on the expectations of the announcement of a new U.S. television deal at the NBC Universal up-fronts that day. As expected, after the close of the market, WWE, represented by Paul Levesque, announced a multi-year deal with NBC Universal to continue carrying Raw, Smackdown and Total Divas. Total Divas had already been quietly renewed for a third season in the fall on E! The belief is that Raw will remain on Monday on the USA Network, and Smackdown will remain on Friday on Syfy, although the latter has been hinted at but not explicitly said.

When WWE and NBC Universal did their joint press release, Smackdown was referred to as "Friday Night Smackdown." When WWE was asked if that designation means the show will remain on Fridays, instead of moving to live on Tuesdays, since live sports programming is considered a premium for television networks, the only response was that the show currently airs on Friday.

And while WWE got a substantial increase in the new deal, it was well under the double or triple the previous numbers that they had hyped the possibility of. While they never explicitly gave an expected figure, Vince McMahon a few months back had all but said it would at least double, saying to Brad Safalow of PPA Research, LLC, that if they didn't get double, he'd let him put him in a hammerlock.

The company had continually noted that NASCAR, which it claimed as its closest TV equivalent, completed a new television deal for $820 million per year, and WWE's aggregate ratings over the course of a year were slightly higher.

What ended up being the bigger black eye came just a few days earlier, when Major League Soccer, which last year averaged 220,000 viewers on ESPN or ESPN 2, a drop of 29% over the prior year, and 122,000 viewers on NBC Sports Net, had increased its annual rights fees from $18 million per year to $90 million. For a comparison, in March of 2014, Raw averaged 4.32 million viewers live and Smackdown averaged 2.88 million.

The new deal was disappointing enough that WWE would not even publicly release the numbers, only talking in vague terms which would indicate the new deal averaging in the range of $142.5 million per year over the course of the deal. They said the deal has escalators clauses, meaning it would start at a lower number than that, reach that number in the middle of the deal, and end at a higher number.

The new deal works out that WWE is getting 38 cents per Raw and Smackdown live viewer (this is going with the idea a DVR viewer is worthless, throwing in DVR viewers and that figure decreases by close to ten percent) per two to three hour show. The Major League Soccer deal was worth $6.77 per viewer per game.

The first hint we got that the deal wasn't going to be good were after the soccer deal was announced when those who did know the deal were preparing for a bad week. We did get word at that time not to expect a huge television deal and as the week went on, the soccer deal became huge talk within the industry in the sense it was going to leave the company very embarrassed by week's end.

WWE wouldn't even answer the question as to the length of the new deal past that it was five years or less.

With early indications that the network was not going to be driving the kind of huge revenue increases touted in the near future, which had originally caused WWE stock to go through roof, it was the TV deal being looked at as the more important key to future growth.

But when the deal was announced, WWE's financial prospectus for 2015 listed network growth as the key in increasing to the profitable levels that led to the big stock run-up.

By the next morning the stock had fallen below $11, and ended up closing at $11.27. At press time, the stock was at $10.92 per share leaving the company with a market capitalization of $821.4 million. Over the three business days, roughly 59 million shares changed hands, an amazing figure when you consider there are only 75 million shares total and the vast majority are owned by the McMahon family, 40 million by Vince alone, and none of the McMahons sold any of their stock.

From its peak less than two months ago, before the first announcement of network subscribers, the stock and company value has fallen from $31.98 per share and $2.4 billion. The company has lost 66 percent of its value since that time. But it was greatly overtype by investors, some of who were pushing the idea that the network could get six to eight million subscribers, based on a clearly flawed study of how many wrestling fans there were in the U.S. and overseas, and that television rights should triple or more based on the NASCAR deal and the fact pro sports rights fees have gone through the roof in recent years.

In all, Vince McMahon has lost roughly $842 million of on paper worth since just before WrestleMania, with about $360 million of that in the last few days. It is paper money, he's still worth in the range of $700 million. One person with a long association with him noted to us that the actual losing of the stock money isn't going to bother him, but that all of the stories in so many of the major business publications and mainstream media that talked about $350 million in losses over one day, and that he's no longer a billionaire, would drive him crazy.

Virtually no explanation as to why WWE was unable to garner a better television deal was given. When Vince McMahon and CFO George Barrios were asked at a 5/19 call for investors about not getting the deal they expected, Barrios said that they projected correctly in three out of the four deals (meaning Thailand, India and the U.K.). The key is that nobody was willing to offer big money to get the wrestling franchise, even though it has a loyal and stable weekly television audience that is larger than most sports, and appears to be DVR proof.

Raw ranges right now between 88 and 92 percent of its viewership being live. Smackdown, somewhat surprisingly as the taped show on Friday, is usually viewed live by between 93 and 94 percent of its total viewers. Live sports usually are watched live by about 96 percent. Advertisers pay a premium for that type of programming because of the feeling those who watch on DVR are fast forwarding through the commercials, thus whatever audience isn't watching live may be worth little or nothing.

Very little had gotten out regarding interest past WWE having talks with Fox, Viacom, Turner, AMC and others. Almost no news came out of those meetings past Turner Broadcasting people telling those pitching wrestling projects that they had no interest in pro wrestling, and one company that did have interest said the money WWE was asking for was so ridiculously high that they lost interest immediately.

It is believed the total ad revenue that NBC Universal got from wrestling programming in 2013 was about $170 million, meaning if it gave away everything it earned in ads to get rights fees, that would be as high as it would go. NBC Universal was in the catbird seat, because they had the right to match any outside offer. Because no deal was done during their exclusive negotiation period, nor was one expected, the belief that the roughly $142.5 million average likely matched the best outside offer WWE was able to get.

Many sports are garnering far more than their ad revenue because sports networks like ESPN make their real money in carriage fees paid for by cable and satellite companies. The belief was that losing WWE wouldn't cost USA or Syfy any money in decreased carriage fees. Raw's big value is that the USA Network would likely not be No. 1 in cable in 2014, a position it has held for years, if Raw was pulled out of the mix. WWE had many times noted that, even though they were exaggerating its affect on USA ratings at the time they said it (ironically, what they said months back that wasn't accurate, actually is closer to accurate now), but the statements were repeated and led people to believe the kind of leverage to double or triple the previous deal, since USA Network profits exceed $1 billion annually so they can afford to spend to retain bragging rights to being No. 1 for the year in prime time cable. And perhaps they would have gone higher to do so, but WWE wasn't able to get an offer that would have forced that decision.

Thus, many analysts and stockholders were left feeling misled and unhappy with vague explanations and lack of any significant financial details past WWE projecting overall money losses at a rate nobody expected.

WWE's own internal projections are that in 2014, they will lose between $45 million and $52 million. From a financial standpoint, no pro wrestling company in history, with the exception of World Championship Wrestling in 2000 (which lost $62 million), has ever lost more money. While WWE had previously stated they would lose money over the first six months of the year, the belief had been loses would be $23 million to $26 million during that period, and the combination of the network and the new U.S. deal kicking in during October would lead to break even in quarter three, and substantial profits in quarter four, ending the year at close to break-even.

The belief was that would lead to record-breaking profits starting in 2015.

The realization is that it is a possibility that WWE will not even be profitable in 2015.

Until they get network subscriptions up to the 1.75 to 1.9 million range as a year-long average, not a final figure at the end of the year, the company's profits will end up below what it was doing from 2007 to 2010 before it started spending millions each year to start up the network.

At least two investigations for possible securities fraud were initiated. In addition, Lemelson Capital, a private equity firm that owns stock in the company called upon the Board of Directors to replace the current executive management team after all the money losses, execution issues and material misstatements by management.

Ademi & O'Reilly, LLP, released a statement saying:

"We are investigating possible securities fraud claims against World Wrestling Entertainment Inc., resulting from inaccurate statements WWE made regarding its business practices, financial statements and prospects.

Our investigation focuses on the extent to which WWE issued false and misleading statements regarding its business practices, financial statements, past and future business performances and prospects. Specifically, WWE's statements that it would double the value of its domestic contracts for its two most popular shows, Monday Night Raw and Friday Night Smackdown, and that the prospects for its recently launched streaming video network were strong were false and misleading."

Former Louisiana Attorney General Charles Foti Jr., a partner at Khan Swick & Foti, LLC, also announced a similar investigation.

"KSF's investigation is focusing on whether WWE and/or its officers and directors violated state or federal securities laws."

Lemelson Capital, who along with its clients are WWE stockholders, wrote about the huge projected losses in 2014 that, "This follows what we believe to be material misrepresentations by the company about both the performance and operating profit model of its WWE network, which the company has wrongly labeled a home run," said Emmanuel Lemelson, the Chief Investment Office at Lemelson Capital Management.

The company called on the WWE's Board of Directors to promptly replace the company's executive management team, or to explore selling the business, and that such changes would be a necessary component of successful strategy going forward.

"For example, promoting the WWE direct network's value to shareholders without a fair and accurate discussion of the implications to a traditional network revenue circumvented management's fiduciary responsibility as steward's of investor's capital, and is part of what has emerged as a pattern over recent years. Further, there are no pending operational developments in the pipeline to offset these significant losses."

What they were saying is that there were no business comparisons made between what the company could expect to have made had the network been a traditional television network, as opposed to being over the top.

During the conference call, there were no great revelations made, no real explanations given, nor were any management changes announced.

Vince McMahon did admit disappointment in the television deal, but offered no explanation as to how the deal went down and why the number ended up so much lower than expectations. When asked directly if the launch of the network caused NBC Universal to offer lower figures, he said he believed that starting the network did hurt them in the negotiations of the deal. He said that they could have waited until the new multi-year deal was signed to start the network, but that would have delayed the network launch for another year, stating the network had to launch right around the time of a WrestleMania.

That's notable, because just a few months ago, McMahon had stated that the launch of the network would boost company popularity overall, and that its television partners were aware of increased WWE popularity that would lead to higher ratings. While early in the game, there is no indication the network has led to any ratings increases. And the reaction within TV was not what McMahon indicated, given the price paid by NBC Universal and Ion not even renewing Main Event.

The company still was vague in answering all questions, including the departures of key management figures Perkins Miller (a key player in launching the network), Matt Singerman (the man hired to run the network) and Brian Maddox (Vice President of Global Digital Sales) all in recent weeks, saying they were not going to make comments on personnel decisions. When asked directly what the number of network subscribers is today, they stated they were going to release those numbers every quarter, meaning the new number will come out in early August.

This was caused for a lot of concern. The company was desperately needing good news to announce. Due to key promotional incentives going on, the post-WrestleMania talk on the show, and the interest and publicity stemming from the death of Ultimate Warrior, the increase in subscribers over the last six weeks since the last announcement should be well above usual levels. If anything, a figure released would represent faster subscriber growth than could be expected during a normal period, and thus would make the network seem, at the very worst, stronger at this point than it really was. Yet, nothing was said.

When asked about the low U.S. deal indicating that WWE has seen as having a low-rent audience, so to speak, Barrios said that didn't seem to have an impact in three of the four recent deals they have been negotiating. Of course, the U.S. deal, where it did, means far more than the other three deals combined.

WWE has been the main player in the pro wrestling industry, driving the business and its perception, for most of the past 30 years. This deal indicated loud and clear how the TV industry views WWE and wrestling in general. Even with the strong ratings, the feeling is that the television and those viewers had almost no value compared to most sports or entertainment. While wrestling had that perception long before Vince McMahon, it also shows than three decades under McMahon of attempting to clean up the image, publicize charity work, and repackage it as sports entertainment and putting smiles of faces of children and family viewership together have done little to change the real world's perception of the product.

The company's projections are that in 2015, unless they average a number in the range of 1.16 million network subscribers, the company, even with its TV rates increase, would lose money for the year, as opposed to previous projections of record profitability. That would be a worldwide number, and that number is probable it will be reached, but not guaranteed.

But the stock price was tied into hundreds of millions of dollars of profit per year, not a company that was formerly doing $50 million in annual profits a few years back, now breaking even.

Before spending to launch the network, which started in 2011, and has reached $75 million, the company was running steady annual profits between $45 million and $53 million. To reach the levels they were already at, they would need somewhere in the range of 1.75 million and 1.9 million subscribers for an average month in 2015, and that's not figuring in replacing any of the $75 million already spent the past four years for launch.

What investors didn't realize is that profits in most sectors of core business have been declining. The lower profits had been believed to be a result of network start-up costs while the core business was remaining steady, since ratings, pay-per-view numbers and attendance, the usual barometers, were stable.

But they had spent significantly more. They were using high priced non full-timers on television and pay-per-view on many of the shows that did the biggest business. They had spent more money on television. Touring had become more expensive, outpacing the small increases in gates. Merchandise production had become more expensive. They have greatly increased spending in developmental with the creation of the Performance Center. They are looking at opening new offices around the world. The movie business has had its problems, although it is doing better than before. So while revenues looked good, profit margins were down, combined with the network start-up spending and the bottom line was far worse than expected.

The 1.3 million to 1.4 million worldwide figure for subscribers needed to break even is based on the network itself hitting $40 million in profits, the figure PPV, the division being replaced, had been doing. Actual profits from the PPV division were $34.1 million in 2013, $46.0 million in 2012 and $40.7 million in 2011. But that's not figuring in losses in other sectors, most notably home video, that the launch of the network could cannibalize. With all PPV buyers forced to go to the network, that figure that doesn't unreasonable to be reached.

That figure was slightly higher than the 1.25 million they had stated worldwide, or the 1 million figure (a domestic number that had been used by the company and others publicly as the "break-even" mark) that most believed was the case for the network to be a success.

To reach $36 million in profits in 2015, and going forward, which would mean they would at least break-even with the current dividend payment and no longer be hemorrhaging cash on hand, they need to average between 1.5 million and 1.7 million network subscribers in 2015. To hit that average, if they open the year at 1 million, it means they need to end the year at between 2.0 million and 2.4 million. That figure to me is far from a lock. The big key is international growth, and there are so many variables in that model that it's impossible to predict accurately.

We don't know how many of the original 667,000 subscribers were international, so we really have no clue where the U.S. really is, and how much growth there can be fro m the international markets.

Cash on hand, which was once in the $300 million range with no debt, and as of 3/31 was $87,266,000 with nearly $30 million of debt. Going with projections of losses from 3/31 to 12/31, that figure would drop another $37 million to $44 million in losses over the remainder of the year, and $27 million more in dividend payments. In other words, actual cash will be down to between an estimated $16 million and $23 million, and if you throw in debt, the company would actually owe more money than it has in the balance books. That's not as bleak as it sounds, as many's companies like WWE rely on financing debt. UFC works that way, for example, with hundreds of millions in loans out that are financed. But WWE has never been in that position, perhaps since 1985.

And to get that out of more money going out than coming in during 2015, they either need to hit 1.5 million to 1.7 million subscribers by July, based on their projections, raise the price of the network that would lower the number of subscribers needed to break even, and/or cut the 12 cents per share stock dividend.

The company is still projecting that the network will end up making the company more profitable than at any time in its history.

Barrios said that in a steady state, a level they expect to reach in 2016, that they will have between 2.5 million and 3.8 million subscribers worldwide. There is no evidence at this point that they will get to that level, but a key point is the adaptation of consumers to over-the-top technology, and the growth of wrestling fans.

If they get to that level, the network will be the home run in the long-term that they have stated it would be.

Until August, it will be impossible to make any kind of an educated guess of patterns of gaining domestically. It won't be until November that we'll have a better handle on how many people are renewing as opposed to dropping when their first six-month subscription expires. But it really won't be until the second quarter of 2015, after the launch internationally, that any meaningful estimation will be able to be made regarding steady state business.

What scares me is the 2.5 million to 3.8 million projection is still based on a completely flawed study. The claim is that there will be about 98 million broadband homes in the U.S. in two years, which is reasonable, and that 52 million of those homes contain either current or former wrestling fans, which is ludicrous when you figure that only 2.68 million homes watched Raw this past week and 1.73 million watched Smackdown, both for free (March averages were 3.04 million homes watching Raw; 1.99 million homes watching Smackdown, many people use total viewers for their projections but number of homes would be the key for potential, because a family with three fans isnt ordering three subscriptions). So their projections are based on the idea that they only need four to six percent of those homes with current or former wrestling fans to subscribe and they are at two to three million.

They claim there are 58 million broadband homes outside the U.S. in the key international markets they are targeting, and that 25 million of those homes have wrestling fans. Using those numbers, if they get two to three percent of those homes subscribing, that will add another 500,000 to 800,000 subscribers.

At 2.5 million subscribers, the network would generate $60 million more in annual profit than the company was doing on PPV over an average of the past three years. At 3.8 million subscribers, that increases to $160 million annually above the prior PPV profit level.

If they open 2015 at 1 million subscribers, and end at 2 million, and I see that as being optimistic, the projected profit for next year will be $22 million to $35 million, meaning they will not even cover the dividend, and will be significantly below where they were before the profit margins started decreasing in 201,1 due to spending millions each year in getting the network started.

If we look further, at the $75 million in network spending before launch, and figure that into a five year plan to make it back that starts in 2016, and to have regular profit margins at the level of 2010, which, essentially means back to normal, they need to average a minimum of 2 million subscribers between 2016 and 2020. If they beat that figure, the network has led to new profits. If they don't, it means the network didn't pay off. There are too many factors involved to predict if that's a viable number.

A surprise in their projections is that they are expecting no money from PPV next year, and this comes shortly after signing a deal with Sky in the U.K. which moved several shows that had formerly aired on Sky as part of its regular subscription package, to individual stand-alone PPV. In the U.K., the major shows, and a few of the minor shows aired as PPVs, but several PPVs had previously aired on regular Sky channels. That was no longer the case with the new deal, which makes the belief there will be no PPV revenue almost contradictory to a new deal just signed.

This means the network would be the only legal source to watch the major events. Given that projection, that indicates there are no plans to take WrestleMania, or any PPV, off the network next year.

What the company did announce was that the combination of their deals in the U.S., U.K., Thailand, and what they expect out of a deal from India that is not yet completed, is the total from the four markets would be $200 million on average.

Keep in mind all of those deals have annual escalators, so $200 million is the average annual value, meaning that would be the expected number in the middle of the deal terms. If the new deals are for five years, that number would theoretically be reached in 2017. If the new deals are three years, then it would be 2016.

The U.K. deal is believed to be $30 million for the average length of the deal. The Thailand deal is believed to be $3.5 million. The India deal is being negotiated. If we go with $24 million (doubling the current $12 million which may be a conservative increase based on statements that have been made regarding the negotiations), that would leave the estimated $142.5 million for the U.S. deal for Raw and Smackdown, or barely half of what the company expectations were for, and less than half of what a number of analysts were expecting.

That figure does not include Total Divas.

It is believed Raw & Smackdown in the U.S. combined brought in $85 million to $87 million in 2013. But total company domestic revenue from television was $105.9 million, including Total Divas, several months of the since canceled Saturday Morning Slam, and a full year of the since canceled Main Event on Ion. Of that, Total Divas runs about $470,000 in per episode, and that number was also increased an undisclosed number in a new deal for a third season.

Using another vague number, the company stated the four new deals (U.K., Thailand, India and U.S.) would, on average, increase $90 million to $92 million over the prior deals. We know that the U.K. and Thailand combined increase is about $22.8 million. If we go with India's increase at another $12 million, and again, based on what they've said, if anything, that would be projecting low, that brings the figure to $34.8 million. That would leave $55.2 million to $57.2 million for a U.S. increase, bringing the average range of the new contract from $140 million to $144 million, so the $142.5 using those figures also appears to be on the money. However, if India's figures are higher, that makes the U.S. figures lower.

There were estimates based on the idea it was a three-year deal, which estimated the years for Raw and Smackdown combined at about $132 million in 2015, $142 million in 2016 and $152 million in 2017.

CHAPTER THIRTEEN

STING ARRIVES IN WWE

FEBRUARY 10

Sting had not signed a WWE contract as of the weekend. From the WWE side, they are saying the deal is super close. They are working on a merchandising deal. Right now the idea is not to use him at WrestleMania (which can all change), but maybe have him appear next year in Santa Clara.

FEBRUARY 17

Sting, while the deal had not been signed as of a few days ago, it's more the WWE side dragging its feet. As noted, Sting is not the priority in the company the way some of the other big-name deals have been. Even for me, I suppose he could do a face General Manager role but given the current storylines, why would The Authority hire a face G.M. that muddles their own power. I suppose they could build then to a Sting vs. HHH match for control of Raw, but does HHH really want that given whatever value Sting has is nostalgia, and nostalgia generally has a very short shelf life. Sting himself was hoping to get a match with Undertaker at this year's Mania, so I guess he bought into the Internet hype for himself since the company and Undertaker himself have had the Lesnar plan dating back to 2010. The one thing from the Sting standpoint is that since he lives in the Dallas area, he was willing to go with Undertaker and work out the match in private at Undertaker's gym, over and over, to get it right, which is what Undertaker's opponents the last several years have done. That's one of the reasons the matches have gone over so well. There was some question that Lesnar, who is in it because he makes huge money for limited work and only has a certain number of dates on his contract, of whether he would be willing spending several extra days working with Undertaker to get the entire match worked out.

MARCH 24

Sting was in London this week doing one of those talk shows. The report was someone there indicated they thought he had signed with WWE based on his answers. We still haven't gotten confirmation he signed. He said that he wanted to face Undertaker in his last match and had no interest in any other matches. He said he was on YouTube recently watching Undertaker vs. Shawn Michaels. That would be a good indication that he thinks that's happening because Sting doesn't pay any attention to wrestling. But his doing WrestleCon on 4/6 would indicate he hasn't actually signed his contract. If he was with WWE, he'd be involved somewhat in the Mania activities. If they were keeping him from Mania activities for a secret debut, they wouldn't want him in town working for somebody else. To me, Sting's late agreement to be at WrestleCon indicates he was expecting a deal before Mania and wouldn't commit until this week. He also said he has been purposely watching Raw the last few weeks but hasn't seen anything from TNA since he left. His three favorite matches were his 1988 Clash of the Champions match with Flair, his first NWA title win in 1990 against Flair and his Starrcade 97 match with Hogan. He said he was responsible for Bill Goldberg coming to WCW since he and Lex Luger met him in their gym and would talk with him about becoming a wrestler. He was asked about the Dangerous Alliance (his adversaries in the early 90s) and couldn't remember who they were. When asked what his favorite match to watch was, said he doesn't follow the product and couldn't give an answer.

MARCH 31

Regarding Sting, there is a working idea that he does one WWE match and then retires, which everyone presumes at this point will be with Undertaker at WrestleMania 31 in Santa Clara. Whether this is made clear at Mania itself, at Raw the next day, or at some point closer to the show is unclear. Right now the only thing confirmed is the idea is Sting will do one last match. The idea he's studying Undertaker tapes would lead one to believe it would be that match. The people who represent Sting in regard to his appearance at WrestleCon were saying he was not scheduled for either Mania or Raw the next day and the people at WrestleCon were paying for a round-trip ticket, with him going back home after the convention. Granted, that could change at any moment and Sting lives in Texas so it's not like he's flying across country to California and then back the next day, he could go home and come back for Monday. If WWE were to want to keep it a secret, they would make sure his people said that anyway, so it doesn't necessarily mean anything. The surprise is only that if he was working for WWE that weekend, why would he even bother with working with another group? Nobody has confirmed Sting signing, but it's also been considered inevitable for months, and has been talked about internally as this being the year it happens even before TNA was cutting all its higher paid talent loose.

APRIL 14

Sting has signed his deal with WWE. Not sure of the details regarding what role he will play but he is scheduled to be on television at some point, but not right away. It's seemed to be inevitable this deal would happen ever since TNA didn't renew his contract. The deal described to me as being close for a while, but now it's signed. Sting's assumption was he would work with Undertaker, which many expected. With Undertaker losing, and his future being in question, that would be up in the air. Years ago, Dwayne Johnson had said that there were a few guys he wished he could have one match with in a comeback, which at the time were Rey Mysterio, Randy Savage (which tells you many years back this was) and Sting. Whether he still feels that way, or in 2015, such a match would work on the WrestleMania stage, or be a good idea given the cost of a Johnson match, is the question. My feel is that it isn't right, and if Johnson was to wrestle next year, that coming off Mania, Lesnar would be the guy given Johnson vs. Lesnar was the original plan for this year. And I don't even know Johnson would wrestle next year past the point in interviews he has talked about it as a possibility. The Sting deal will include being on television, but whether that's as a regular character (he is obviously not going to wrestle full-time) or just to build for one match at next year's Mania, that isn't clear.

APRIL 21

Regarding Sting, WWE has made its offer which they had not done before Mania. It's pretty much agreed upon but he had not put pen to paper as of the weekend, but the ball was in his court. Those in WWE were aware of the contract being sent out and told me the deal was done, which it is thought in the company that it is. At least as of 4/14, Sting had not returned and signed the contract, but the belief is there are no significant snags in the negotiations.

APRIL 28

Nothing new on Sting past the thought that it's been a formality for weeks that he will be signing. I still haven't heard confirmation of the actual signature, but WWE is putting out a Sting DVD that he will be part of in the fall, and he was all over the Warrior documentary on the network.

MAY 19

Regarding Sting and rumors of him signing, from two sources very close to the situation, both said that for weeks the deal has been down to just dotting the i's so to speak, but it wasn't closed as of a few days ago. It could be at this point but we can't confirm it. It has been considered imminent since before WrestleMania. But Sting is scheduled for some projects as far as interviews go for the WWE Network. But that doesn't mean anything, because a lot of people who are interviewed for network specials aren't under contract, and Sting wasn't under contract when he did the interview for the Warrior documentary.

MAY 26

Since WrestleMania, and really even before, it's been believed that Sting signing was imminent. Now that it still hasn't happened, the feeling is that imminent is no longer the word. There was a deal a few years back in place where WWE believed Sting had agreed to come in for 100 dates–this was several years back, which would be the deal where Sting talked about them coming close once, but Sting ended up not taking the deal and took the TNA deal which probably guaranteed similar money for far fewer dates, since Sting only worked TVs and PPVs and no house shows with TNA, and didn't work all TVs or PPVs.

JUNE 9

As far as Sting goes, things were going very smoothly, but the deal ultimately offered ended up being similar to the standard $10,000 legends contract without any other guarantees. They are still in talks.

JUNE 16

On the Sting deal, they are offering him more than just the standard legends deal in the current negotiations. Our report that it was the legends deal was part of it, but there are more to the talks than just the legends deal. As of 6/9, he hadn't signed. A big rumor started that he had signed and would be at Raw on 6/16 because a casting web site in Los Angeles sent out some stuff. They are filming something on that day, but it's in Los Angeles, not for Raw which is in Cleveland. They were looking at hiring an orchestra for $700 a day plus 20% to the agency for a non-union appearance for someone to play a body double role for Sting. A company which is not WWE, but has a working business relationship with WWE, is looking at doing something with Sting. It would be for a business project related to WWE. They were looking for someone who was 6-foot-2 and 250 pounds and very muscular. They wanted someone with wrestling experience with long dark hair. They are looking for someone to shoot with Sting makeup, who from far away, would look like Sting, or could use Sting's head on a bodybuilder body. They are also hiring people who can play an orchestra at $650 per day. It's for musicians who can bring their own instruments. This deal would go through whether Sting signs with WWE or not, but obviously it would be better if he does. People weren't happy this made the Internet, particularly since Sting hadn't signed. The feeling is still they are close enough and a deal will be done inevitably.

JULY 6

Nothing is new on the Sting front, past the point that as of the weekend, he still wasn't signed. The company is working with the idea that it's imminent, but we've heard that for months. Ultimately, he wants in and they want him in, whether it's for a television personalty role, an ambassador, the Hall of Fame or doing a match or two is not clear. It all comes down to money because Sting doesn't have to sell himself short and he spent his entire career working with guaranteed money deals.

JULY 13

Regarding Sting, he posted "7.14.14" on his Twitter account, which people will take as a tease of something. That is the date of this coming week's Raw in Richmond, but the impression is this is something related to a different project, perhaps a video game. For a long time, there was no real impetus to get the Sting deal signed, since if he's going to be involved in next year's WrestleMania, that's a long time away, which may explain why the deal was so slow in being finalized.

JULY 21

The Sting orchestra commercial for the WWE 2K 15 video game aired on the 7/14 Raw show. They left the crowd mic'd during the commercial, expecting a big pop, particularly since Richmond is kind of considered more WCW country, although the heyday of Richmond as a major wrestling market was before Sting was a top star. The crowd popped big, but then booed when they realized it was a video game commercial and not a vignette for Sting coming to WWE. WWE also started selling Sting merchandise that night which made people think a deal has been done. We're told there is no deal at this point, not that there won't be because everyone has gone with the idea that it will eventually get done. The Sting marks for the characters they are merchandising was considered intellectual property of WCW, which WWF purchased in 2001, thus WWE believes they have the rights to merchandise it. The sides are still working toward a deal and given that HHH on his weekly interview with Michael Cole talked about the subject and strongly hinted Sting would be coming in says he has to belief the deal is happening. The playable characters are billed as two generations of Sting. They pushed the late 90s Sting in the commercial but the late 80s and early 90s Sting will also be a different character in the game. We were told the entire vignette came in at around a $200,000 cost. Sting himself did an interview with The Daily Mirror stating he'd like to do one last match at WrestleMania 31, and his goal would be with Undertaker. "Why now? It's a now or never thing," he said. "I've done so many things in the wrestling business, but the one thing I'd never done was wrestle or be a part of the WWE family. I didn't want to hang it up and retire, and disappear again without having done that in some capacity. I've made it clear I'd love to have one last hurrah, one last big match hopefully. And of course, I've been outspoken about Undertaker being the opponent." "I think, or at least I'm hoping, that Taker's still going to come back and that he's not done. If he's not done, and he would consider doing it, I'd love to work with him one time. I'd love to wrestle him one time before I call it quits." He said he always wanted to work with Rock, Cena and Orton as well. Years back, Sting was a guy Rock had talked about coming out of retirement to face, but that was roughly a decade back. Sting said that he's never personally met Vince McMahon. Sting didn't make the searching trends on Monday, nor did anything from Raw, and that when down to 20,000 that night.

JULY 28

Sting ended up being the 10th most searched for topic (20,000) on 7/14. There was a TMZ report this past week that said Sting had signed a PR contract but not a wrestling contract with WWE. According to those in WWE, that was a mistake by TMZ and that they confused a 2K contact (for the video game) with a WWE contract. Sting still has no deal, but they are trying to lock him in.

AUGUST 4

Sting appeared as part of the WWE panel for Mattel at the San Diego Comic Con on 7/24, along with Michael Cole, Bryan, Heyman and Hogan. That once again led to rumors about Sting having signed. He has a deal with Mattel, like with 2K, but not a wrestling deal with WWE at this point. He's still a free agent and in that sense, with all the recent publicity, he seems to have more value and momentum. The belief in WWE, even though he's not signed, is that there is more interest in Sting from the 2K announcement, possibly because he's more current and possibly because there is the feeling he could wrestle, than Warrior when they made the announcement last year. In Houston at Raw, when they aired the 2K commercial, there was a loud "We Want Sting," chant. Sting can still get big money for autograph shows on the outside. I can't see him wrestling on the indie scene. He talked openly about wanting to have a run in WWE, or at the least, a match at Mania this coming year, saying that at his age, it's now or never. HHH has brought up Sting possible matches and they've been negotiating for months. One source said they were hopeful of getting it done by SummerSlam, since Sting is coming to Los Angeles for the event, although at this point is not scheduled for the show itself. As Sting has noted, he has never in his life met Vince McMahon, so I guess he's going to personally meet him for the first time in less than three weeks. It's become a running gag now when people talk about Sting and his contract, basically that it's in the same place it's been since January when they started talking seriously. Sting at the panel talked about Cena, Undertaker, Orton and Rock as possible opponents and did say he was really against the idea of Undertaker's streak being broken. Cole was constantly pushing the WWE network, past the point of it being comedy, and he was very much in on the joke in the sense he was making fun of the fact he had to keep mentioning it. Hogan said that the backstage reaction when Lesnar beat Undertaker was like being at a funeral. Heyman pushed the idea that when Lesnar lost to Cena the first time that he wasn't 100 percent and was suffering from diverticulitis, but that it's a different story now and he's completely healthy. Heyman also put over Jimmy Hart (who was there since Hart travels with Hogan) as one of the greatest managers of all-time and said how Fred Blassie, Bobby Heenan, Lou Albano and Fred Blassie were better than he was, and that he can't touch their body of work so doesn't even try. He said he wasn't a manager, he's an advocate. He went from a sports agent to an advocate, Sting was introduced at the end, as a surprise. He was already booked for the Comic Con, but not as part of the WWE contingent. Cole put it over as Sting's first WWE appearance.

AUGUST 18

With Sting coming to Los Angeles for the 2K Sports panel discussion (the same one that got Jim Ross fired last year and removed Ric Flair from television and the company for months), he's expected to meet Vince McMahon for the first time in his life and I would think they'll probably talk seriously after finalizing a deal. Sting has deals with both 2K and Mattel and there is a merchandise deal in place regarding selling his T-shirts.

AUGUST 25

Sting and Hulk Hogan at the 2K launch were both pushing for matches at Mania. Hogan was pushing for something with Austin or Cena. He was pretty negative regarding his few matches in TNA due to how bad his back was doing. He said his back was better but he's now battling arthritis in his extremities that runs in the family. You always say never say never in wrestling, but Austin doesn't appear to want to do another match. Hogan brought up how much longer his main event run was but you could tell it was more trying to somehow build a match. Whether Hogan can pass a physical would be the question. He's Hogan and his first match in WWE in years will at a Mania will get over if it's carefully done. If Cena has nothing better going on , it can be pushed as a once in a lifetime dream match even at Hogan's age. I'm expecting Sting to work one match at Mania. He said if he could script it out, it would be one last match, with Undertaker at Mania. He's pushing this one hard and vocally and did so at a WWE panel so they can't be negative about it since Sting was in the office and talked plans with everyone. It probably depends on Undertaker's ability to do another match. Sting also talked about maybe facing Cena or HHH. Sting said that he was "very close" to signing, but was very confidently saying we'll see him again, but wouldn't say when, but he shouldn't wrestle until Mania. Sting was flown to Stamford, CT and met Vince McMahon maybe for the first time (he said that he might have met Vince at a NATPE convention for a brief second but he's not sure) face-to-face (they've talked on the phone in negotiations for years). He was shown around to tons of employees and shown how the operation works and they don't do that unless they are pretty sure they've got a deal.

SEPTEMBER 1

Sting would be the last major superstar of the last 25 years to have never had a WrestleMania match. The TNA guys haven't, but the TNA homegrown guys like A.J. Styles and Bobby Roode were never national stars anywhere near the level of Sting, who was a top guy for more than a decade with WCW when WCW was hot. Really, the only other one at that level who hadn't had a Mania match was Lawler, who finally got his match in 2011. To find truly major drawing cards in any year who never had a WrestleMania match, you'd have to go back to around 1986 with Magnum T.A., Nikita Koloff, The Rock & Roll Express and The Midnight Express, and before that, guys like Stan Hansen, Bruiser Brody, Abdullah the Butcher and Nick Bockwinkel.

DECEMBER 1

For years, there was an easy answer to the trivia question of the biggest name in post-1984 North American wrestling who had never stepped foot in a WWE ring.

That was Sting. At the 2014 Survivor Series, Sting, at the age of 55, took his name off the list. For years it was something that seemed like it would never happen. After how his contemporaries from WCW, Lex Luger, The Steiner Brothers and the Road Warriors went to WWF, and had little good to say, and all came back with negative stories, while Sting was always guaranteed one of the top spots in WCW and top money, it really made no sense to go. In 2001, when WCW folded, Sting, 42 at the time, figured his career was over. Things had come full circle. A decade earlier, Sting and Luger would talk about how Ric Flair was past 40 and should retire, and now he was the same age.

He did little wrestling for several years. He'd made his money, he had gotten heavily into religion and was raising his kids. He become Real Estate Steve at Gold's Gym in Southern California, where most of the semi-celebrity clientele didn't even know he used to be a famous pro wrestler. Then TNA and Spike TV called, offering him in the range of $500,000 for a one year contract where he'd work a limited schedule, television and PPVs when needed, hoping he could jump start the promotion.

It became a game. Every year was Sting's last year and he was going to retire at the end of the year. Every year, at the end of the year, Dixie Carter would offer him a new deal and convince him to come back for one last year. He would agree, thinking that this was the last year. His first last year was 2006. His last last year was 2013. Financially strapped, TNA could no longer afford him. He put over Magnus, letting Magnus beat him with the scorpion deathlock clean in the middle at Bound for Glory. While Magnus had a world title run in TNA, a year later, look at where he is. He also put over Ethan Carter III on the way out.

The fact Sting stepped into a WWE ring was not a shock. Those in WWE had talked for years, expecting it was inevitable. To much of the wrestling audience, TNA wasn't even on the radar. Absence makes one bigger, as shown by the response to Ultimate Warrior last year and the DVD sales for Bill Goldberg this year. But every year, Carter would offer a sweet deal and Vince McMahon wouldn't offer anything close. By last summer, the belief internally was that 2014 would be the year. The writing was on the wall. The lay of the land was that TNA was strapped financially, and would no longer be able to afford his deal. And Sting had negotiated with WWE for so many years that with no other option, they figured it was inevitable, the farewell run, the Hall of Fame, and this year's big get, like Bruno Sammartino and Warrior were the previous two years. The negotiations weren't easy, but since last summer, it had always been a question of not if, but at what terms, when, and against who.

Most likely, Sting will do one WWE match, at WrestleMania, probably against HHH. Dwayne Johnson, who teased a match with HHH recently, signed to do a movie in the spring. Sting had long said that he wanted to face Undertaker at WrestleMania, but if that's not possible, his choice would be HHH. A decade ago, Johnson wanted a match with Sting, figuring Sting and Randy Savage were his two dream matches left on the table, and then Savage passed away. If the match goes well, and there is clamor for more, he could always do another match. He should probably make sporadic appearances for the next few months, and be a regular weekly character down the home stretch.

The angle to set up such a match took place at Survivor Series. The card was a one match show, with a weak undercard and a main event that delivered all kinds of twists, turns and drama with Team Authority vs. Team Cena. If Team Cena lost, all members of the team except John Cena were to be fired. If Team Authority lost, then HHH & Stephanie McMahon would be removed from their roles as heel authority figures. The match came down to Dolph Ziggler and Seth Rollins. A couple of refs were knocked out and HHH gave Ziggler the pedigree and put Rollins, who had received a Zig Zag, on top. He then called for a referee, and it was Scott Armstrong, who hadn't been on television since the angle where he was let go as a referee. He counted to two, and stopped because music played. Sting came out. Both Rollins and Ziggler had to lay dead for three or four minutes. It wasn't logical, but the Sting debut overrode logical completely. Sting and HHH ended up staring down in the middle of the ring for a good three minutes before HHH took a swing, but Sting came back and laid him out with the scorpion death drop. Sting then put Ziggler on top, and left, and the recovered first referee counted to three, giving Team Cena the win.

It had been reported two days beforehand that Sting was to debut by PW Insider, later confirmed by those in WWE the next day. There was also talk of Randy Orton returning, based on Orton being spotted at the Albuquerque airport, where he was filming the movie, "The Condemned 2," flying to St. Louis. As we noted, Orton flying to St. Louis may not have meant anything storyline wise, since he lives there. As it turns out, Orton was not scheduled for the show, since he was scheduled to return in December. One source said he was never scheduled to return on the show, but it was the right time and place to bring him back, but the impact would not have been as large as Sting.

The reason they did the angle at Survivor Series was a decision by Vince McMahon. Aside from all other reasons, the primary reason is November was a big month for the WWE Network, with them for the first time offering a PPV show for free. The problem, the lineup was weak and nobody would have cared. McMahon felt it needed a heavy stipulation to garner interest, thus putting The Authority role in jeopardy and paying it off, with the idea a strong show would get as many people ordering for free to subscribe.

In addition, with Sting as a major character in the video game just being released, the timing was right for him to debut as a character on television. WWE also likes to tease something at Survivor Series to start the ball rolling for WrestleMania. There are few more rabbits they can pull out of their hat that would get the initial impact, perhaps only Goldberg (based on DVD sales), but Goldberg is much tougher than Sting to do business with and they never even came close last year even when Goldberg vs. Ryback seemed like a natural match-up based on organic fan interest.

At another time, the call may have been different. But the feeling was, with Survivor Series being a free show designed to sell people on maintaining network subscriptions, a logical build for an Orton vs. Rollins (or Orton vs. Rollins vs. Cena) match at the next PPV wasn't going to do that.

While Sting's return was kept secretive until a couple of days before the show, this was not a last minute call. Sting himself kept it quiet. He was on the road Monday though Wednesday doing promotion work on the 2K Sports video game, and never hinted it to anyone that he would be doing anything. But he had filmed footage for his entrance video and this plan had been in place for a few weeks.

Several others were also scheduled, with Daniel Bryan on television the next night, Roman Reigns in St. Louis doing an interview and saying he was about a month from returning, and Rey Mysterio is also to return soon. Reigns' appearance was kept low key, and the others, such as Mysterio and Orton, they could have done, but in both cases it would have gotten so overshadowed that the impact of it would have been minimized.

As far as The Authority role, that is clearly something that is not as well planned out. The original plan for Raw was that it would feature a segment with Vince McMahon and John Cena, which would lead to a period with no authority figure on the show. They ended the show going back to the mystery General Manager role, which came across so lame since that ran its course. There is some talk of a weekly General Manager of the night, which is the celebrity guest thing, which can help ratings when it's the right guy, and garner the company some mainstream buzz. But that kind of idea done weekly does run its course rather quickly.

With Sting stepping foot in a WWE ring, as far as wrestlers from the last 40 years, the biggest names never to do so that worked in North America would be Ole Anderson, Gary Hart (who was at a show and scheduled to start in the 80s, had a disagreement with agent Chief Jay Strongbow, and walked out), L.A. Park, Bobby Eaton, Jushin Liger, Love Machine, Kinji Shibuya, Pepper Gomez, Bob Armstrong, Great Muta, Dutch Savage, Blue Demon, Wilbur Snyder, Magnum T.A., Nikita Koloff, Gori Guerrero, El Santo, El Solitario, Danny Hodge, Abdullah the Butcher, Nick Bockwinkel (who technically did work in the ring, as he spent some time there as an agent as one of the guys breaking up fights but was never identified, even when Bobby Heenan was doing commentary, which was always awkward, but I don't believe he ever had a match with the company) and Fritz Von Erich. So as far as the biggest star of the last 40 years to never work WWF/E, you'd have to go with Fritz, Abdullah, Bockwinkel, Santo, Demon and Solitario.

CHAPTER FOURTEEN

TNA's Tumultuous Year

FEBRUARY 17

Regarding talk of Vince Russo in TNA, it was reported by Mike Johnson two weeks ago that Russo was CC'd some memos. A number of people in TNA all denied Russo had any involvement, including people regularly around the creative process who stated his name had never even been mentioned. A number of wrestlers said the same thing, that they had not even heard his name mentioned nor did they see any indication or fingerprints of his on the television. Russo has been in contact with at least a few people in the organization. Samoa Joe publicly on Twitter mentioned that he and Russo had just worked out their differences. Others close to Russo said that he has been following the product again and they believe that is something he would never do under normal circumstances. But the key was the thing noted last week when a rep from Wrestle-1 asked a TNA official directly if Russo was involved or coming back, because the future of the relationship between the companies depended on it, and they didn't get an answer. The TV that aired on 2/6 felt different from weeks past. It had different fingerprints on it, with the rushed wrestling, excessive backstage, more comedy in the verbiage (some of which was good dry humor) and the key thing was the Velvet Sky/Chris Sabin segment, because the humiliation of really pretty girls in the scripting is a Russo specialty. It really doesn't matter at this point. TNA has never been able to keep relationships with Japanese companies so this one was doomed to fail at some point. The ratings of Impact are going to be what they are. You could put the best product possible out there and it would take forever to move it because it's just secondary wrestling to people. You could put the worst product out there and it may drop slightly, but it's still wrestling on Thursday night on an easily accessible channel in a familiar time slot and there are enough die-hard fans to draw 1.2 million to 1.5 million, depending on the season since it's always in the same slot. The fact they lost Hogan, Styles, Sting and some people think they've lost Hardy and ratings are actually up (seasonal bump and stronger lead-in numbers) tells you aside from peaks from hot shot things like a Brooke Hogan wedding (and they don't have anything like that on the horizon) or climax of a long storyline, they'll do what they'll do. They look better and are higher now because of stronger lead-ins, but the pattern in recent weeks of starting big (like 1.4 or more every week) and then consistently dropping isn't good for any TV show, let alone wrestling that should naturally peak with the main event. But that happened long before any new fingerprints were there. Russo has not been at any shows, nor has any talent that we're aware of have any clue past the idea that rumors started getting out and some dismissed them and others thought there was something to them. The light on wrestling and rushed wrestling aspect could have also been because it was getting late and it was the second show taped in Glasgow, and they had three more days of TV yet to come. But that's probably not the reason. It's either a change in direction and focus that comes from the top or a new person with a different philosophy of show layout having input. The ratings are more-or-less going to be what they are under any circumstance. Russo's historical weakness, both here and in WCW (it wasn't in WWF because the guy calling the shots was Vince McMahon, who knew at the time where the money came from) was the ability to build programs that anyone wants to see. It doesn't matter as much now since they are largely out of the PPV business, and their programs don't build to house shows anyway. And it's not like the house shows could do much worse than they are doing now.

Unlike last week, where everyone we heard from said Russo's name had never been mentioned, at the weekend house shows, Russo's name was being talked about. But it's only people reacting to the stories out and not anything internal. Bully Ray and Abyss, who are pretty much both office and talent, both said to the wrestlers that if Russo was involved, they know nothing about it.

MAY 5

We've written this a few weeks ago but it's been mentioned to me by a couple of people in recent days who said that across the board there is a lot of concern about the TV situation. Management has told talent there is nothing to worry about, but those who follow the TV industry and see stations putting together fall schedules and nothing announced here are concerned. Unless Spike makes some huge bid for WWE, I don't see them canceling Impact. It's still above the station average and it's a somewhat compatible audience to promote Bellator and Glory. While you never say never and if there is the right bid, WWE has to do the right thing for its stockholders, but in 2005, the departure of WWE from Spike was acrimonious at best. At the time Spike was blamed for the big decline in company popularity between 2000 and 2005, but after nine years of constant station changes for Smackdown and Raw ratings not going up on USA, they probably have a more realistic view of those five years.

MAY 19

Those in production were significantly behind on pay, which is also happened around this time last year. The belief is that Janice Carter, who controls finances, earmarks a certain amount of new money (besides the revenue the company makes itself) to finance losing periods. Because they are taping so far ahead, and taping so many PPVs, which is what got them in trouble last year, they didn't have the money and when that's the case, people start getting paid late. It was reported that the production crew threatened to walk out this week, but Dixie Carter wrote everyone checks for what they were owed. What we were told is that many if not most in the crew hadn't been paid since early March. Not everyone threatened to walk at the start of the big week of tapings, but the majority did, and thus did get paid because it was at a time when TNA needed them. Unlike last year where tons of people including talent were way behind in being paid, for the most part talent is up to date. You may get your check mailed a few days or a week late, but it comes.

JUNE 2

At this point I'm really surprised we haven't had the announcement of a renewal. The WWE deal is with NBCU, and while wrestling isn't a star show on the station, there is something to be said for the station having wrestling, kickboxing and MMA and their ability to cross promote. They may have blown a good thing, with the creative for Rampage Jackson and Tito Ortiz last year, because we've seen very little crossover since, past showing Dixie Carter in the audience at the Bellator PPV show and the usual plugs that Spike asks them to do on the shows.

JUNE 9

As best we can ascertain, this is the situation with Spike and TNA. No contract has been signed, but most likely a deal will be in place before the contract expires in October, although the official word from Spike is there is no TNA update. For Spike, they do more than 1 million viewers a week, which is above the station average and they only have a few shows that beat it. Wrestling is also a good vehicle to promote the Bellator brand. Before PPVs or big shows they can run a preview show right after Impact and get 400,000 to 500,000 viewers watching, which is something UFC no longer gets for its PPV previews. They at this point still like the idea of a wrestling, MMA and kickboxing group all on their station. It doesn't matter to Spike that their conversion rate of viewers to customers is so low. I don't sense them as concerned about perceived quality issues. TNA business does concern them in the sense that the cash flow problems and late pay for a property on their station is an issue if the company has problems since the Carter family is not putting much money into the product so TNA has to be self- sufficient, and there only real strong revenue stream is the Spike money. Obviously Spike wouldn't want to sign with a group that could go out of business or have trouble delivering a new episode to them weekly. Spike has had other people in wrestling pitch to them, but not Jeff Jarrett, whose deal in exiting TNA included an agreement he wouldn't go on Spike. TNA does assure them of 1 million viewers per week and there's nobody else in wrestling where you could say with a guarantee that could do that other than WWE, which is obviously not an option. I'm not saying nobody else could do that, but it would be a risk to try.

JUNE 16

The morale was really bad on the road this weekend with two shows of the three drawing about 200 people outdoors in baseball stadiums. People noted that they had no idea what the PPV main event would be, because, as noted, the belief is no MVP and that was the talk. It's funny because they've now got long periods between shows and as of a few days before the show there were people who thought they were on the card but didn't know, nor know who they were facing, there were people who didn't know who weren't told who they were facing by the company until weeks after it had been written in the Observer, and fans aren't supposed to know the main event will be in a cage until the last and usually lowest rated segment of the show three days before the card. And as it turns out, that may not even be the main event. The wrestlers have seen so many guys let go, they know that the Carters are hardly putting any new money in and since wrestlers usually judge how things are going based on the crowds, there is a feeling of uneasiness about the future even more than ever before. The lack of the TV deal is part of it. Many have made calls of late to ROH. Some are hoping that Jeff Jarrett's new group will be their next move, but are concerned because so little has come out about Jarrett's group and it's getting around the time the fall programming is announced.

JUNE 30

TNA heads to New York this week to embark on the first of two three-day sets of tapings that is either an expensive Hail Mary or a continuation of the attempt to turn around its fortunes and change its direction.

The company, which got rid of most of its highest paid talent over the past year, with only Kurt Angle, Jeff Hardy and Bully Ray still around on reasonably big money deals, is going to survive based on two things, and they need both. The first, and most important, is to maintain their television deal with Spike. With most stations already setting up their fall season, and the apparent lack of interest in the television marketplace toward wrestling (WWE being unable to get Saturday Morning Slam, Superstars, NXT or Main Event on broadcast TV), TNA needs a Spike renewal which still hasn't happened. There doesn't seem to be anything that makes it seem like it won't happen and TNA is definitely preparing for things past October when it comes to future television, but Spike officials remain mum on the subject of TNA. Each week when no announcement is made continues to beget the obvious question as to why.

Morale is up from the good reactions to Dallas and television, but a lot of the talent is still scared about the future. There is the obvious concern among everyone whose contracts are coming due, given that they let A.J. Styles go after investing a year in a hard push to get him over, let Sting go, and let Christopher Daniels & Frankie Kazarian go, so the idea is that virtually anyone on the roster can be dropped, particularly if they've got a good deal. The mentality is that right now, all the checks clear and the last two weeks have been a positive.

Impact ratings remain above Spike's prime time average, which last week was 739,000 viewers. It's a good audience to promote its MMA and kickboxing programming off. The cost for 52 weeks a year of programming that has a pretty consistent audience is far less expensive than the costs of owning Bellator.

Since the Slammiversary show on 6/15, there has been a change in mood and morale, because they had a big responsive crowd in Dallas, even if it was a Von Erich nostalgia crowd, that made the promotion appear to be big-time.

They taped a month of TV in Bethlehem, PA, for shows airing through 7/10. They drew 1,000 fans both nights at the Sands Resort, but the crowd that was there was super enthusiastic and they were said to be some of the best TV's in a long time. The impression I had was they'd like to go back in the future, although there is so much going on now that nobody knows what the future is.

The 7/10 TV show in particular has some high quality matches, in particular a tag title match with the Wolves vs. Magnus & Bram (people in TNA are talking like Bram is the most underrated performer in the company and can't believe WWE gave up on both he and Ethan Carter III although in Bram's case it was more his getting arrested a few times, once for fighting a police offer, than a decision made regarding his talent), and the Austin Aries regaining the X title from Seiya Sanada.

There are changes being made, notably the end of MVP as a heel authority figure, being replaced by Angle, Bobby Lashley beating Eric Young to be TNA champion on the TV show taped on 6/19 in Bethlehem, PA, and Gail Kim beating Angelina Love to become Knockouts champion on 6/20 (air date 7/3) and Aries beating Seiya Sanada on 6/20 (air date 7/10).

Since Angle is the company's highest paid wrestler, putting him back on TV now that he's moving well, is at least making use of him. Plus, the heel authority figure angle is done to death on WWE right now so it makes TNA look bad to feature the same thing. It appears MVP will be a heel manager while his knee recovers, while Angle would feud with Dixie Carter. Tommy Dreamer was put on television, to join Bully Ray in a feud with Ethan Carter III and Rhino (who in theory was paid off by the Carters to turn on his former ECW friends) in a unique angle that Dreamer and Bully Ray created based on Bully missing the House of Hardcore show on 6/6 in Poughkeepsie.

TNA heads to the Manhattan Center from 6/25 to 6/27, which will tape all the television through 8/14 or 8/21. The second set of Manhattan Center tapings, from 8/5 to 8/7, should cover them through the end of the Spike contract which expires in late September or early October. There is talk now of making the Manhattan Center a regular venue for tapings, going about every six weeks from there, with tentative dates in October and December.

Granted, this is a very different era than 1993, but there's a reason WWF moved out of the Manhattan Center for Raw, which some older fans get nostalgic for because it was the original home venue. They were at least selling out at first, but it got to the point after repeated tapings that they weren't selling any tickets. TNA claimed it had sold out the smaller configuration on 6/27 based on Dixie Carter's Twitter, but tickets were still available for the other shows. We were contacted by fans saying that wasn't true. Hours later, we checked, and there were plenty of tickets in a number of price ranges still available for that show at press time. The idea here is that if they can put on big shows from New York and make it a cult thing, they'll get the hardcore audience, which is loud, on their side, which they once had to a degree but never completely, and for the most part lost in recent years.

New York has its huge advantages. Being an in-thing in New York and running as a regular New York property avails the company of far more media than being based in Florida or touring television nationally.

On 6/24, the company had several segments on Fox & Friends, the morning talk show on the Fox News Network, a level of mainstream exposure they rarely get, with multiple segments and appearances by Eric Young, Bobby Lashley, as well as appearances by Bully Ray, Velvet Sky and Gunner. The flip side is the costs of running in New York are enormous for a company that has had very public financial issues.

At the tapings, they will be returning to the six-sided ring that they used for years, until Hulk Hogan and Eric Bischoff came in and nixed it in early 2010. The ring gives them a unique identity, which is why I couldn't see dropping it at the time, but in reality, it makes no difference. They put it up to a fan vote, and even though babyface Austin Aries tried to campaign against it, as did a couple of others, the fans voted it in.

Most of the current wrestlers weren't happy about the change, which is funny, because in 2010, the TNA regulars weren't happy about the change to the four-sided ring with the idea the six sides had become a trademark.

TNA had probably the same percentage of good to great matches with six sides as four sides, if not more. But the complaints now are that the ropes are stiffer, footing is tougher, certain parts of the ring that you take bumps on are harder. A number of wrestlers who didn't complain publicly about it went to management about it, favoring the four-sided ring, but were told that the company is trying to look different.

There will be a press conference in New York on 6/25 involving Keiji Muto as Great Muta and probably some future affiliation with Wrestle-1.

For a company that has spent all year cutting corners, they are going in the opposite direction, running the most expensive market in the country, and bringing in some name talent. Given the 800-seat set-up, filling the building should be easy, but it hasn't been. I'd have thought the first night and third night, being a Saturday, in a market that size would have been instant sellouts since TNA has never done TV in that city, and that's before figuring in how much press they did in the market this past week.

The Young title run was an experiment that ultimately didn't work, although one could argue that with last week's show doing the best rating in four months, maybe it was starting to click. Still, the almost-weekly pattern of Young's title defense being the lowest rated part of the show told a story that they could either ignore, or react to. Granted, the problem is a lot less Young and more the overall product. And the idea that they had two world title matches and two tag title matches on the same show to garner the ratings increase is not something you can learn from or do weekly without burning it out.

Young is a reasonably good wrestler, who can talk, and who comes across to the viewer as a likeable babyface. He was hurt, badly, by years of being booked as a comedy prelim wrestler. Perhaps having this run will help him down the line and he'll be more established and ready if he gets a second chance, although a similar run was done last year by having a surprise underneath babyface go over in Chris Sabin, and after he was done as champion, instead of being pushed stronger, his contract wasn't even renewed.

Lashley isn't the answer as a heel, but since there are no answers, time will tell if he's better than Young. He's got the physique, does some cool athletic things, and MVP is a good mouthpiece. Watching the way Lashley has been booked climbing the ladder and winning the title, with clean wins, makes me feel the idea is for him to be a babyface down the line, but then he wouldn't have MVP to speak for him. Lashley has been put over strong since his return, beating Young three times and Samoa Joe once. The feeling seems to be that he looks the part is has the most legitimate credibility, but both of those things are less important now that at any time in pro wrestling history and fans don't care about bodies, and they don't care who is a legitimate wrestler. Even though the booking seems to make him feel like a big babyface run coming, he needs someone to talk for him if he makes that turn.

Lashley will defend the title on the 6/25 show against Jeff Hardy, who won a Battle Royal on 6/20 for the shot. The winner of that match theoretically defends against Aries on 6/26 as part of the Destination X show. With Aries cashing in the title to get his shot, then there will be some sort of a match, probably multi-person, to determine the new X champion. Among those returning on 6/26 include Muta, Low Ki, Homicide and Brian Cage. Matt & Jeff Hardy return as a team, probably working with Magnus & Bram. There also may be another Lashley vs. Young match taped on 6/27. When the two were on Fox and Friends, Young and Lashley had a confrontation where Young claimed Lashley needed help from MVP and Kenny King to win the title and that he would take it back in three days.

Even though the TNA name seems to actually keep people from buying tickets, because one would think an indie with those wrestlers would be able to sell 800 tickets in New York easily, the fans will respond to a wrestling-heavy show with the names they have and those they are bringing in, particularly since most on the roster can go. If the show has endless talking or bad angles, that could be a different story in New York, but given that Bully Ray is influential and Tommy Dreamer is on the staff, they have plenty of experience with how to get things over at the cult level in the New York market.

JUNE 30

Bully Ray did a lot of media to try and promote the New York tapings this week. You never know the difference in him between work and shoot, and quite frankly, that's fine if you go in understanding that. He tried to put over the Tommy Dreamer angle as not really being an angle ("Just because it plays out on TV doesn't mean it's a work"). From what I gathered, Dreamer (or Dreamer and Bully) came up with the idea as an explanation to his Poughkeepsie audience to explain Bully not being at the show as advertised. They took some leeway. Bully worked it into his feud with Dixie saying he wanted to do his best friend's show but Dixie forced him to attend the Spike Guys Choice Awards show and he could have been sued for breach if he hadn't, and how Dixie told Dreamer the night before, and said it was a scumbag move on her part. Let's be serious. When TNA and Spike were figuring out which TNA talent would be going to the show, there is no way the decision wasn't made or that Bully didn't know until the night before. That just makes no sense. Whether Bully could have said he had a prior booking and TNA could have sent someone else, I can't say with certainty. Bully had a choice of doing an indie for his friend, or being around Spike execs. But they worked out their angle, and obviously Dreamer didn't say what he did without Dixie knowing it was a work ahead of time, given that Dreamer works for TNA. When Bully was on Opie & Anthony, he tried to get them to come to one of the shows, saying he was putting Dixie through a table one of those nights. He said he would tell them which night off the air. My impression is Dixie is going through a table this week, and they aren't holding it off until Bound for Glory. They are taping through either 8/14 or 8/21 this week in New York. The second set of New York tapings will take them through the expiration of the Spike deal at the end of September. He also said that he really did date Brooke Hogan for a couple of months, but went back to his ex, and is now dating Velvet Sky. The Velvet Sky stuff is accurate. He talked to Opie & Anthony and told them how Hulk Hogan told him that Brooke always gets what she wants. I can't say for certain whether the Brooke stuff is legit or not although it was news to people in the company and Brooke had been dating the guy on the Cowboys that she ended up engaged with (before she broke it off shortly after announcing it which led to her being let go since she was doing an angle that she was married to Bully and it made mainstream news that she got engaged) the entire time she was doing the angle with Bully. On another show, he said his love life was "Velvety Smooth."

Bully seems to be the most influential guy in the promotion as far as someone without an official title in creative, but he's very aggressive on his agenda whether it be booking, television or whatever. That's not really anything new as he was the guy who got to work the program with Hogan, marry Hogan's daughter which was a great angle on paper which unfortunately Hulk was too beat up to give a payoff of, now feuding with Dixie and is really the lead face right now ahead of Hardy, who is pushed like a mid-carder, and Young, who was pushed in all the TV main events and given the title, but never fully overcame the years of being a comedy prelim guy. He should have a strong position because he's a good talker, knows how to do a match that will get over, and people still pop big for the table gimmick. The one thing about him as a face is he's not afraid to sell and put people over, since he's gone through table after table, put over EC 3 constantly, even though in the end he'll come out on top, which he should.

JULY 21

Even though everyone denied it, particularly Vince Russo to everyone who asked him for months, Russo is still working for TNA and has been for a long time, since months before it came out here. Russo accidentally CC'd Mike Johnson of the PWInsider web site into an e-mail with instructions to Mike Tenay and Taz, who were in Nashville this week doing a couple of weeks of voice overs of the New York shows, with instructions on what do to and how to handle certain situations. At first Russo went on Twitter in response saying, "Wow—just amazing to see that anybody will print anything as TRUTH without checking into it. Nice to see the SWERVE still works!!!" He then wrote, "Since an unreliable website has brought me so much free promotion—feel free to check out my web site." Then he wrote to Johnson, "Would you thank Dave (Scherer, Johnson's partner on the web site) for me for all the free promotion. If I knew it was going to be this easy, would have done long time ago!" Johnson wrote that the e-mail was legit, he checked into it and it was not an attempted swerve by Russo. Johnson wrote that he could publish the e-mail, and Russo was the one lying about the story. When Russo claimed it was a swerve on Johnson, he wrote, "Swerve? He's not that creative. More like trying to spin things.

The countdown begins Vince. It's all on you now." Russo eventually apologized to Johnson and wrote: "Recently, I accidentally sent an e-mail to a third party that was not meant for their eyes. The e-mail concerned my current involvement in TNA Wrestling. TNA rendered my services as a consultant to work with their announcing team of Mike Tenay and Taz. The condition from their side was that I kept it confidential between the two parties. As their employee, it was up to me to honor their wishes, so that's what I intended to do. My integrity means everything to me, so I just hope you can understand and forgive." Russo had been involved with creative long before he was working with the announce team. Months ago, their Japanese partners were upset and asked about Russo being involved and were at first never given a straight answer. However, John Gaburick later admitted to Keiji Muto that Russo was working there, but assured him that Russo was working underneath him, didn't have final say, and that he would be the one deciding on how the Japanese were portrayed and that what happened with Tetsuya Naito, Yujiro Takahashi and Kazuchika Okada would not happen with the Wrestle-1 talent. Wrestle-1 has been happy with how Seiya Sanada has been used. To me, it's just amazing that Russo could accidentally send Mike Johnson the e-mail with instructions to the announcers.

JULY 28

Here's some more on the Vince Russo situation from last week. The impression, which couldn't be confirmed, but is also the most logical is that Vince Russo didn't CC Mike Johnson accidentally, but when he sent the e-mail for announcers instructions on 7/15 to Taz & Mike Tenay, that he accidentally sent it to Mike Johnson instead of Tenay, as they were probably right next to each other in his address book. At least that's what a ton of people have speculated to me, and it makes more sense than anything else. TNA had been wanting to keep it a secret that Russo was working for the company, although we had already printed it months ago, as did PW Insider, and TNA had confirmed it to Keiji Muto of Wrestle-1. But for reasons I'm not completely clear, they had not let most of the talent know, which was weird, and there was talent who said it had been denied to them by the office when we wrote about it. I do know that Russo had denied it to everyone, including people who were his longtime friends. Russo had not been to any of the shows and had only worked with the people in creative and a few others. Some wrestlers knew but were never told, but figured it out. Others believed it to be a false rumor and were not happy about being, in their words, lied to. Spike TV officials were not fans of Russo, and the key to all this is TNA didn't want Spike finding out, more than fans or the other wrestlers, that they were still employing him and he still had at least a hand in creative. This goes back years with Spike. One person noted to us that years ago Spike told people in talks about doing creative with TNA that they made it clear they wanted nothing to do with Russo. Russo made the situation worse by claiming he had worked Mike Johnson into printing a false story and mocking him over it, when Johnson knew it to be false. I don't know that TNA had directly talked to Johnson to admit to it, but do know that they had ordered Russo to apologize to him, so the apology was not Russo insisting on coming clean, but being forced to do so by TNA. My impression is there was office contact with Johnson admitting it was the case going on at the same time Russo was trying to make fun of him and claiming to have swerved him, because every time Russo would write something about how he swerved them, Johnson would write back that we all know the truth and to come clean about it and there was no attempted swerve e-mail. However, Russo was legitimately told when he was brought back last year to not tell anyone. He noted that when he apologized, that he had kept it quiet because the people employing him told him to. For whatever reason, TNA didn't want the wrestlers, Spike TV or fans knowing Russo was working for them, even when it became clear when you could see his fingerprints on the television show with certain directions of storylines, certain types of matches, and certain Russo verbiage in interviews. As noted last week, his apology claimed he was working as a consultant to the announcers, but that's still not coming clean. The thing is, he had to admit to that much because the evidence was out there from the errant e-mail proving that, but the evidence Johnson had didn't prove he was part of creative, which he obviously has been for some time. I don't know how this impacts the negotiations with Spike over a renewal past the point Spike can't possibly be happy over this. At the end, they're going to make the right business decision in their minds. If they want wrestling, there is no alternative product to have. You could say ROH and if ROH got the level of money per week that TNA gets, they could afford to upgrade their production and sign better known talent, but I've heard zero indication there is any movement in that direction. Given Spike's interest in MMA and kickboxing, wrestling is a good show to have because it's an audience that is most likely to cross over and an audience the preview shows can air right after. So if anything, wrestling's value to the station increased once they purchased Bellator. But this story can't do much for anyone's trust in TNA.

AUGUST 4

TNA finds itself at a crossroads with its television contract with Spike TV set to expire in two months and not only is no deal in place, but at a meeting over the past two weeks, Dixie Carter was told that they are not interested in renewing the deal. The story was related by multiple sources, in a story reported in numerous places this past week, most notably TMZ.

One person with knowledge of the situation said Spike wanted to make things as amenable as possible. The tact is the opposite of what happened when Spike did the same thing with WWE in 2005, which left bitter feelings on the WWE side because it left them with no negotiating leverage and they had to take a much weaker deal with USA. It should be noted that Spike expected WWE to end up with USA in those 2005 talks, but they publicly canceled Raw and all the satellite shows, before the USA deal was completed. This left WWE with no negotiating leverage. WWE had to take a deal that gave them no satellite shows and took away the company's advertising revenue from its programming, or thus being worth significantly less than the deal they had with Spike.

Spike will not publicly talk about the deal nor make statements that would hurt TNA's leverage. The public story is that Viacom has a policy of not taking about ongoing negotiations. But if TNA can get a new television deal, it was said Spike was willing to work the transition as smoothly as possible. There is not a specific date where Spike would pull the programming even though the actual contract expires in two months.

Some are speculating that telling Carter they aren't renewing the deal is simply a hardball negotiating ploy, as was not making any deal this late in the game. With the contract expiring in two months and most major stations having already filled up their fall prime time programming schedules, TNA is down to very little negotiating leverage unless UTA, who was handling the negotiations, has a backup deal in place. Those in the television industry do not believe that to be the case.

The idea is that Spike is still willing to keep the show, but wants to cut down on the licensing fee number, or even the speculation that Spike wants to own its own wrestling promotion, is at this point nothing more than optimistic speculation, but neither is impossible.

Spike does own its MMA property, Bellator. The positive is that it eliminates these types of negotiations in the future. It guarantees Spike that if the promotion got hot that it would either risk losing them to a rival station or having to pay far more money to keep them. Spike is of the belief that they built UFC into a significant sports franchise and then lost what they built when networks with more money became interested, and thus doesn't want to go through that again. Owning allows Spike to avoid any issues if new content providers emerge either in or out of television, and guards against programming cost increases.

While there have been rumors of the latter within TNA for some time, the idea of Spike interested in controlling interest, there is nothing even to the extent of smoke that we can find in that direction past rumors within TNA. We have no knowledge of anyone in wrestling who would have been contacted by Spike if they were talking in that direction.

Right after the TMZ story came out, Dixie Carter contacted us in an e-mail saying that no deal was in place but negotiations were continuing. After the story came out, TNA sent out an e-mail to talent stating that no deal was in place but stating they hope to have good news announced shortly. Talent in TNA were given the impression that news would be announced at the New York tapings in early August, even before the story had come out, and were again told not to believe the story. A number of sources connected to both TNA and Spike were talking about this for days before the TMZ story.

In television, there is a lack of interest in wrestling due to the inability to get substantial revenue for advertising, no matter what ratings it delivers.

Talent and those in the TNA office had been constantly assured negotiations with Spike were going strongly due to the obvious nervousness of many due to no announcement being made.

Of course, TNA did a similar e-mail to talent when the stories of its sale negotiations last year broke, with Janice Carter stating that there were no talks and the stories weren't true. Those with knowledge of the talks called the e-mail an outright lie. It was well known representatives of Toby Keith were at the TNA offices talking with personnel about working with them, and talks got serious enough that Bob Carter flew to Keith's home in Norman, OK, to close the deal. The deal fell apart as the sides didn't come to a money agreement, although the figures were said to be very close and that wasn't the obstacle, but also because Carter insisted that Dixie Carter would have to be able to save face and be guaranteed a public position that would appear she was still in some form of control of the new company. That killed the deal. This led to Jeff Jarrett, who was to be one of the key people running the new group, starting Global Force Wrestling. Jarrett resigned from TNA late last year after the deal fell through, but has still not been able to sign a TV deal, and has publicly confirmed he and Keith were in talks to buy TNA and when they fell through, it led to his leaving and starting his own group.

In April, TNA inked a deal with UTA to represent them in television negotiations. That was the first sign that they were nervous about a new deal, because in the past they've been able to sign new deals without having to make a deal to give an outside company a significant cut as its negotiator.

According to various sources, there were two key reasons for Spike saying they wouldn't renew. The obvious one was that they didn't believe the product was cost effective for what they were paying for it, in that they could make more money in ad sales for programming that would be less expensive, even if it wouldn't draw as many viewers. People surprised that a station would drop a higher than its average rated prime time show miss the point that in both of the key methods of garnering revenue for a station, ads and carriage fees, wrestling programming at the TNA level is not all that valuable.

If this was the prime reason, it would keep the door open to a deal for less money. The value of programming is actually threefold, a combination of value in selling ads, carriage fees and boosting the network profile and average numbers. Wrestling has traditionally had a problem when it comes to selling ads, always having to sell as a far lower cost per viewer as most programming. If Spike were to cancel Impact, it would not make a difference in cable carriage fees. Impact did 1.42 million viewers on 7/24. Spike's prime time average for this past week was 822,000 viewers. That average would have dropped to 759,000 viewers without Impact, but either number would rank it No. 19 among cable stations. But it does have value in that regard.

The second was Spike was outright lied to about Vince Russo not working for the company. That's why TNA was in such a panic when Russo's e-mail accidentally was sent to Mike Johnson, because they had denied Russo was working there after Spike had made it clear a long time ago they didn't want him involved. TNA had evidently figured if they didn't tell anyone, that nobody would know. Even though people did know, there was no tangible proof until Russo's accident put TNA in a position where they couldn't deny it any longer. With negotiations already tenuous, this was a disaster. Why TNA continued to use Russo in creative when Spike made it clear they wanted no involvement with him is a question that nobody has come close to being able to answer.

On 7/30, Russo on Twitter claimed he was no longer with TNA.

"Officially done with TNA," he wrote. "Today they `suggested' a break. I declined. Finality was better for me." Hours earlier, Taz had written, "I unfollowed Russo earlier. He's annoying and all about his brand. #Go Away."

Those in the company thought that Bobby Lashley fighting in Bellator, a property owned by Spike, represented a positive in negotiations, since TNA would promote the Bellator show. But the fight is on 9/5, several weeks before the deal expires. Nothing has been said how that is impacted by the negotiations.

But even if they were to stay at a greatly reduced rate, that would be a major financial issue. Spike money was the company's biggest revenue stream, and the company has had serious financial issues including periods where people were paid months late, although everyone did eventually get paid. But costs have been cut greatly.

Recently, many of the production people, who were months behind in being paid, threatened to walk en masse on the first day of a multiple day taping, forcing Dixie Carter to write checks catching them all up. TNA has also been forced to either greatly cut back on new deals, or outright not sign talent, losing Hulk Hogan, Sting, A.J. Styles, Chris Sabin, Christopher Daniels and Frankie Kazarian in recent months.

Within TNA, it was noted to us that while many bought the e-mail, others, given he outright distrust on the Russo situation and those who were aware of the sale situation and how it was handled, didn't buy it at all. It was noted that the company should have told talent, whether true or not, that even if the TV deal doesn't get renewed, because at this late a date, that's obviously a possibility, that the company would continue because of international commitments. They said the lack of saying that was a red flag. In addition, the e-mail and statements, by not saying that, have only bought the company two weeks of reprieve before panic will set in. The assurances were made that something positive would be announced to everyone at the next set of tapings, so it's a time frame they need to have news by.

The Hogan loss, while not seeming as big at the time, is now significant.

One source with significant TV ties checked around with stations and said he found no real interest in the product among other stations. He stated that losing Hogan hurt a lot because he was the one guy that executives at stations who are in charge of negotiating these deals would have heard of. Having Hogan would at least get you in the door to make a pitch, and a video of Hogan or Hogan at a meeting could impress people. Hogan is not a deal maker himself, as shown by the lack of major outside licensing deals the company was able to make in Hogan's four years, but Hogan is a door opener.

Another bad sign for making an outside deal, particularly one that pays anything of note, is the plight of WWE over the past year.

During that period, WWE had two shows, Saturday Morning Slam and Main Event, canceled by CW and Ion respectively.

In both cases, ratings were above what the stations were doing in those time slots. Main Event was doing numbers slightly better on average than TNA. The two shows were generally both in the same range, but most weeks Main Event was viewed by more, although that's because Ion is in more homes than Spike. Main Event drew numbers above Ion's prime time average for a Wednesday night airing, particularly in the 18-49 demo. Slam, in an early Saturday Morning slot, was doing viewer numbers slightly lower than Impact. In both cases, when the shows were canceled, WWE, the No. 1 promotion in the world, was unable to get a new distributor.

In addition, WWE had planned to sell NXT in the U.S. market, but found no interest in the marketplace. And WWE was believed to have been getting less for Main Event, even factoring in that it's one hour vs. two hours, than TNA was getting for Impact. And given that Main Event (and Saturday Morning Slam) are far cheaper to produce, because the crew is already there to tape Smackdown, they could afford significantly less in licensing than TNA could to make it cost effective, and still couldn't make a deal. Similarly, WWE was already taping NXT to begin with for both international distribution and for talent experience, so any television deal would be added money since the costs of production are being spent either way, and they still couldn't get a deal.

Today, the only way a promotion can survive at anything past the grassroots level is to have significant television money coming in. One promoter noted to us that if you could draw 1,000 fans paid at every house show for a regular schedule and keep costs of talent low, you could make it, but "those days are long gone."

The key here is not if TNA can maintain television. They can always buy their way onto a station, like they did years back with Fox Sports Network. But history has shown that's a money-losing proposition, because in this day and age, a promotion, whether it be pro wrestling or MMA, can only make it on a national basis with significant television revenue. House shows are not going to draw enough, there are no significant licensing deals unless you are WWE, and PPV is dead for everyone but the top-tier boxers and UFC. TNA killed its PPV business and WWE undercut the value of the pro wrestling shows on PPV by moving to the network model.

TNA had pulled out of its paid programming deal with Fox Sports Network in 2005 because money losses were too high. At the time, the company had lost television except for a sports channel in Florida, and would not have survived, but timing was everything. When Spike and WWE had a falling out, Spike was interested in giving them a try, and TNA did strong enough numbers in the late Saturday night time slot that Spike was bullish on its potential for growth. But in recent years, after bringing in a number of the biggest stars, from the old stars of

WCW, to Angle and Sting, to Hogan, Ric Flair and Jeff Hardy, failed to move numbers significantly, the feelings of growth potential changed. Spike cut the replay airing of Impact, and also gave up on a third hour show that Eric Bischoff and Jason Hervey produced.

The problem is, you take a company struggling and remove its leading revenue stream, and they will either have to cut back significantly, or they are going to have to give up. Even a best case scenario looks to be losses of jobs in the industry. TNA had cut back greatly on talent, both numbers and cutting back to using lower paid talent, even before these negotiations started.

TNA had already stripped themselves of those stars, in particular Hulk Hogan, Sting, and to a lesser extent A.J. Styles. At press time, only two members of the current roster fit into that category of major names, Kurt Angle, whose contracts expires within weeks of the TNA deal expiring, making him a free agent at that point and he's made it clear he's looking elsewhere, and Jeff Hardy. A few others are believed to still have solid money contracts based on signing multi-year deals before the company started heavily cutting back on costs.

The loss, or even the survival with great cutbacks, of TNA, would be devastating to the industry. New Japan is already having trouble keeping the foreign crew it has working steadily. ROH has no openings for talent, although we have the impression that Samoa Joe and Eddie Edwards would likely get some dates, but in the case of Joe, he's used to making a lot more money. But those in ROH say they already have more talent than they can adequately use and for the most part, there are no openings. Few guys in TNA mean much on the independent scene. There will be a vacancy for a No. 2 group if TNA loses Spike and can't get a paying outlet, or even if they stay on with a greatly reduced budget.

It's clear Sinclair Broadcasting has little interest in ramping up ROH. So for the industry to not take a hit, it comes down to Global Force Wrestling getting off the ground with significant financing and a strong television deal, or the El Rey Network, with AAA scheduled to start as a weekly series in the fall, becoming a viable channel on the U.S. scene.

AUGUST 11

There was what was described to me as a panic on 8/6, the afternoon before the second night of tapings. It was a combination of the Observer web site report and all the other web sites reporting on the possibility of Smackdown moving to Thursday and what it means for TNA. This was combined with people expecting some kind of an announcement regarding the future or the TV, since many had been hinted to that big news would be given at the tapings, and there was no announcement made the first night, nor was anything said to anyone about any kind of a deal. It was incumbent that something be said to talent this week because they were told all along that there would be good news at the taping. They've all heard the story of Spike not renewing, and all were told it was a lie by management. Many are talking like they believe management, but others are more skeptical. But unless something is addressed in the next few days, the ones who believed management and had been told New York is when the good news would be announced, many are going be shocked into what may be reality. They didn't even have a meeting with the wrestlers, nor was anyone told at press time that any kind of meeting would happen on 8/7, the final day of the tapings. There wasn't even the minimal announcement that no matter what happens, we'll be continuing to tape television for international or the company will keep going, which, whether true or not, was something I was told needed to have been said to avoid the fear a lot of the roster had about their futures. But with nothing being said, and the knowledge that a Smackdown move to Thursday would be disastrous for ratings and hurt things with Spike if there was any chance of a new deal. Spike likely won't move Impact to Friday's due to Bellator, although Wednesday possibly could be done. But who knows if Spike has any interest going forward as those at Spike have said there is nothing new since our reports from last week. But if there are any negotiations with new stations, if the Smackdown move happens, it hurts Impact badly when it comes to negotiations with new stations.

AUGUST 11

Vince Russo, 53, was fired by John Gaburick on 7/30, although Russo at first categorized it like he was asked to take a sabbatical and he decided to quit. Later, he categorized it as being fired and indicated he believed he would never be working in a creative capacity in wrestling again, although he has said that many times in the past. Why he was hired in the first place remains a major mystery. Why they waited to fire him, knowing it would be an issue in tenuous negotiations with Spike, is another question. The reason everyone freaked out over the e-mail Russo accidentally sent to Mike Johnson, which linked him to writing the show, was because TNA was scared to death how Spike, in the middle of negotiations, would take it. I suppose you could argue the damage was done once the e-mail was out and firing him at that point wouldn't have made a difference, and quite frankly, at that point, people would have been just as likely to not believe it. But still, not pulling the trigger while negotiations were still going on was shocking if you think about it. Russo this past week, on his web site, where he's opened up somewhat on his role and doing a paid subscription service where he slowly reveals all, said that he was first hired back on October 24, 2013, by Gaburick, to critique the creative team of David Lagana and Matt Conway. He said that his role expanded. This confirms our reports that he was working there months before anyone had a clue. Gaburick expanded his role to dealing with and directly contributing to creative early this year. His expanded role in creative likely started as soon as you could see the Russo fingerprints with the pole matches, the Sabin-Velvet Sky feud and things like that. His claim, and this is accurate, is that he was originally hired just to critique shows. Eventually, Gaburick asked him to start consulting with Lagana and Conway on the scripts. Eventually, Russo was, in fact, at creative meetings with the two, even though this was still all kept from the talent and they would never let him attend the shows and work directly with the talent for fear of it getting out. I knew the first two parts but didn't know they actually brought him to meetings. If that's the case, then TNA was far, far dumber than I thought because, really, if nobody sees him and only a few people know about it, you can think you can keep a secret from Spike and his being caught by sending Mike Johnson an e-mail was something nobody could have ever predicted. If he's physically around people in the company or at meetings, that's a very different issue, although to their credit, until the e-mail, nobody had said he was physically around. He said that the job of helping produce and dealing with the announcers only started one month ago. He said that when Gaburick made the public statement that he was hired as a consultant to produce the announcers that it was a lie, and that he was hired as a creative consultant by Gaburick eight months earlier. Dear God, Gaburick never made a public statement. Gaburick, at the time Russo was on Twitter claiming he swerved Johnson, forced Russo to make a public statement, which Russo made on his own web site, saying he was hired to give advice to the announcers. The reason being that it was public knowledge he had from the e-mail to Johnson, and there was nothing in the e-mail that proved anything else, so they didn't have to admit to it. The statement was crafted so, with Spike, they could at least issue a deniability that Russo had anything to do with creative. When it came out, the company strategy for the public was to admit to only what they had to admit and deny everything else. But Russo evidently didn't remember or just felt he could swerve people on a recent story by claiming it was TNA that issued a public statement and not him. Russo also claimed that Gaburick told him some time back that he had told Scott Fishman (Spike's liaison with TNA) that Russo was back working there and it was not a secret from Spike. That contradicts the reason things happened the way they did when the e-mail was out, Spike a week later saying they weren't renewing the deal and multiple sources who knew of the meetings both with Spike and internally at TNA who pointed to being lied to about Russo as a key reason or the straw that broke the camel's back. The key reason was not Russo, and is simply business, that Spike either didn't want to work with TNA any longer, or simply felt that the price they had been paying for the show wasn't cost effective with its value to the station and was looking to get it cut down. However, Russo's time line of when he was hired and how his role expanded has not been contradicted by anyone, and based on how things all went down, feels accurate. Russo acknowledged being let go first on twitter, writing, "Officially done with TNA. Today they `suggested' a break. I declined. Finality was better for me." From those close to the situation, he was fired and anything else was just trying to put spin on it. Russo said that doing Jim Ross' podcast had something to do with his being fired by TNA. Well, given that he taped the podcast on 7/29 and he was fired on 7/30, it likely had more than something to do with it, even though the podcast hasn't played and I don't think anyone in TNA knows what was said. I'm not sure why that would be the case. Dixie Carter has been mad at things Ross has said regarding the company's creative and such. However, Kurt Angle did Ross' show just a few weeks ago. We never heard anything about Angle being in hot water for it. That show couldn't have thrilled Carter since Angle openly said he turned down their offer for a new deal with his contract expiring in late September and was looking elsewhere. A lot of people believed at first that the firing was a work, given how much deception has been involved with this entire situation. I can .tell you with certainty that it wasn't. But for people who don't believe it, there is nothing in how TNA has operated with this story that would make you want to believe anything and I was skeptical as well when I first heard it.

Russo wrote about the situation with Spike and theorized Spike saying they weren't renewing was a negotiations ploy to get the deal at a lower price, and also theorized that perhaps Spike would want to start its own wrestling company (exactly things we wrote about last week), but brought up Eric Bischoff heading that company. Bischoff was TNA's liaison with Spike for a couple of years when it came to the TV show, but that hasn't been the case for some time. It's all theoretical at this point. Bischoff was well thought of by Spike because he was viewed as the architect of the WCW boom from 1996-98 and creator of Nitro, which was a big television hit at one point. But Bischoff's TNA run, being in charge of the creative direction, was a huge disappointment. Times and the business have changed in the last decade plus. Additionally, Bischoff had a ton of people from Hogan to Kevin Sullivan to Zane Bresloff and many others who were feeding him ideas. While wrestling's popularity dropped bad in 1992, it had only been a few years and the country was filled with wrestling fans from the 80s boom that weren't far gone and could be brought back. Plus, there was an incredible amount of big name talent as virtually every 80s star was still around, and there were new stars being created all over the world with revolutionary styles that U.S. fans had never seen. Plus, the Nitro concept, going from the squash/interview format to a full-fledged entertainment show, was new, as even Raw and Antonio Pena's AAA tapings were only scratching the surface at the potential. Bischoff had a Hogan in his early to mid 40s who was a gigantic star to build around and understood his character to get over, but now he was late 50s and couldn't wrestle anymore and building around him as the big star as commissioner at that age no longer worked past the nostalgia phase. The idea for the big angle was Hogan vs. Sting, which worked great in its day, but that day was 15 years earlier. Bresloff passed away years ago, Sullivan is out of the picture and has been out of the business for more than a dozen years and things have changed incredibly over that period. Hogan's ideas to make him the star of the promotion, whether angles with his daughter or Sting, were no longer the way to go. Now, Bischoff no longer even has Hogan. And again, the idea of a Bischoff-led wrestling company on Spike is purely speculation at this point, but if you are looking from a TNA standpoint, I could see where you'd come up with that as a possible idea, given Spike did purchase Bellator and there are very viable reasons they'd want to run a wrestling franchise.

Russo claimed Spike never correctly promoted TNA. When TNA said it wasn't renewing the contract, several reports were that Dixie Carter said the same thing internally, blaming them for not promoting the product the way they promote Bellator (which they own). Russo also claimed that there is a 75% chance TNA signs a new deal with Spike at a reduced rate, a 50% chance TNA ends up on a new station and a 50% chance Spike starts up their own promotion. He then said that was all speculation. In doing the math on that, if you remember those hilarious Scott Steiner interviews that Russo was the one scripting, where he'd do these percentages that made no sense, well, at the time, I thought it was Russo's great sense of humor with the Steiner character, but given his percentages here, maybe the humor was unintentional.

Another thing that has to be brought up, which shows TNA knew they were in trouble in negotiations, is that back in April, they hired UTA to handle their television negotiations. UTA's deal in situations like this is working as an agent, which means they get a 15 percent cut. So unless they were able to negotiate a 15 percent raise from Spike, or a similar increase from another station, TNA would be coming out worse for wear.

AUGUST 18

On 8/7, Kevin Kay, the President of Spike TV was at the show and introduced himself to several of the wrestlers. Kay being there is interesting since Kay was the one who made the call not to renew the deal. As far as what that means is anyone's guess, but the sides are still talking. It is believed that all the shows that would air before the contract expires were taped this past week, which would mean the contract expires with the 9/25 show. It was noted to us that Spike could continue to air the shows without a new contract, although that wouldn't be a permanent thing. Even though, if a split takes place, and obviously these negotiations have been hard since no deal has been made, Spike is trying to be the best business partner at the end, exactly the opposite of how WWE viewed them in the 2005 split where Spike canceled WWE and undercut their leverage and WWE ended up signing a far worse deal with USA than they had with Spike. If TNA is able to secure a new TV deal but would need a short period of time before starting, Spike could continue to air them and not force them to go dark, which would be devastating for a wrestling company in theory, although every real sport goes dark and most TV shows are seasonal. Whether the talks regard a lower price or the rumored Spike wanting ownership are stories floating around but there is nothing that substantial that's out there.

According to those close to the situation, FS 1 has no interest in TNA. It's not a matter of real sports vs. fake sports as much as they don't have interest in spending money on TNA. FS 1 made no play for WWE, which could have turned station ratings around, so that indicated to me TNA was not an option.

AUGUST 25

Spike TV and TNA announced this week a move of Impact from Thursday to Wednesday night at 9 p.m. Eastern, starting with the 8/20 show.

The switch has to be considered a good sign for a company that is holding out any hope for good news, given that its contract with Spike expires at the end of September. The argument would seem to be: Why would they make a change with barely a month left in the contract if they aren't going to be keeping the programming?

While TV shows do change days and times while on the way down and on the verge of a cancellation, it's usually to a worse time slot. In theory, given how the lay of the land looks in the fall season, with CBS carrying NFL football in the fall on Thursday, and the strong possibility of Syfy moving Smackdown to Thursday, TNA may struggle with the move at first, but in the long run, it should be the better for it.

The move comes at a time when ratings, at least until this past week, were the best they've been on a consistent basis in more than a year, a turnaround from record lows earlier this year. The shows have been more wrestling-heavy shows, taped in New York farther in advance than ever before, showing the taped vs. live aspect means little to the TNA fan base. There has been a lot of ECW nostalgia. The shows have featured both dream matches from the past, like the Team 3-D vs. Hardys, reprising a famous WWE program, good working X division matches, strong tag title matches with The Wolves, and frequent TNA title matches with Bobby Lashley put over strong as champion. It was also building a several months storyline, which just paid off, of Bully Ray putting Dixie Carter through a table.

On 8/17, at a house show in Hagerstown, MD, Bully Ray (Mark LoMonaco, 43), told the locker room at this show that this may be goodbye. He noted that his contract expired before the next TNA house show (9/5) and didn't think a new deal would be signed. He said he wanted to say his goodbyes in case it is his last show. It is believed talks between the sides are continuing. Those within TNA are saying that the company right now is proceeding with the idea that he's finished as of now, although one key person said that they are not aware that he's done.

This was a big surprise because in the case of virtually every major player who wasn't renewed (Sting, Chris Sabin, Christopher Daniels, Frankie Kazarian, Hulk Hogan, A.J. Styles), their respective contract status was well known months ahead of time. Literally nobody, including people who are thought to be close to him, had any clue his contract was up, and obviously from him tied into television angles, nothing was done to close things out like was done with all the others. In addition, Bully Ray is not just a wrestler, but also is an agent, who helps talent lay out their matches. He is generally considered the company's best agent. Unlike Kurt Angle, he had been advertised on the U.K. tour, which indicated they, at least at that point, didn't think he was leaving. He was also announced to be inducted into the TNA Hall of Fame at Bound For Glory in October, and he was in the middle of a television program with Team 3-D vs. The Wolves vs. The Hardys.

Even though the writing off of Sting, Hogan and Styles was mind-boggling in hindsight, particularly the final appearances of the latter two, they were written out. Of course they weren't taping so far in advance, and while the company had issues at the time those stars left, it wasn't in nearly the uncertain state it is now.

LoMonaco was released by WWE in 2005 and even though he's still probably more well known as an ECW star or a WWE star, he spent nearly ten years in TNA, far longer than he spent in either other organization. In recent years, as a singles star, he's had the run of the place. He was TNA champion twice, lead heel for long periods in recent years, and even though he's been kept apart from Bobby Lashley, he's pretty much been pushed as top singles babyface since his turn at Lockdown. He largely books his own programs and is probably the most influential wrestler on the roster when it comes to creative.

He's also one of the few left (Kurt Angle, Jeff Hardy and Samoa Joe come to mind as other ones) who is believed to have a big money contract, and that's obviously an issue. He didn't tell anyone anything past his contract was up and he didn't think he was staying so he was saying goodbye. Interestingly, at the 8/6 tapings, when management wanted someone to tell talent not to believe the rumors about losing television, they used Bully Ray.

WWE had expressed no interest in him for years, and when Devon was available, never made a play for him. The negative is that he's got his detractors from his run before, notably Randy Orton, and his age is a factor. But he's better as a performer now than when he was younger. Much of the latitude he gets in his TNA matches he wouldn't have in WWE, and there are other factors as well. On the flip side, he's a great talker, plays his character better than just about anyone and has a unique character. The Bully character is far easier to make work in TNA because they have a lot of smaller wrestlers and the only thing near a giant is Abyss. WWE has a lot of talent bigger than he is. Even if they didn't want him as a wrestler due to style and age, he could still be valuable in a producer role or even a trainer role. But they also seem to have those positions filled and WWE is not in a hiring period.

Devon is working on a short-term contract that will expire in a couple of months. Team 3-D were really big in Japan years ago, but New Japan is overloaded with foreigners and the other groups don't have the kind of money to spend as compared to when Team 3-D were there after the WWE run ended.

As far as the TV move goes, the NFL Network Thursday games hurt Impact ratings in the past, but CBS, because of its greater availability and higher visibility, would be expected to draw bigger numbers and hurt TNA more.

Even worse than the NFL, is the possibility of Syfy moving Smackdown to Thursday. TNA has always gotten killed going head-to-head with WWE. Even after football season is over, if WWE makes the move, staying on Thursday could be disastrous.

The company announced a return to Bethlehem, PA, for TV tapings from 9/16 to 9/19, which in theory would be about five weeks worth of television as well as a One Night Only PPV for 2015. Originally they had booked the Manhattan Center for an early September run. Bethlehem would be far cheaper to run. The fact the company had not announced anything past 9/7 at this point last week was cause for concern, even though talent had been told of future house show dates that were not scheduled nor advertised. These two announcements would lead one to believe the company will remain on Spike TV, or at least the odds appear better from the outside. But there has been no deal announced. It is also known that those in TNA are under the impression there is a backup plan for another television deal, although the belief is that it is with a station far less visible than Spike.

What's awkward about the next tapings is that the first day and part of the second day, they would likely be taping the final two shows leading to Bound for Glory.

The rest of the tapings would air after. Given that TNA loads up its TV shows with title matches, they'd have to abandon the usual formula or they'd give away outcomes. Historically, TNA never taped Impact shows beore the PPV that would air afterward the PPV. Also, the post-Bound for Glory show or shows the two weeks after are usually among the company's highest rated of the year. But that's also because Bound for Glory usually had matches and angles that had been built for months and would usually end with a big angle and thus people would tune into see how things played out. The original plan was for Wrestle-1 to find an arena in Japan and to tape television the day or two after Bound for Glory, and at this point Wrestle-1 hasn't been told anything different. No arena has been booked for the second show, but Gifu and Osaka are under consideration for the city.

The move to Wednesday was clearly last minute. TNA had Mike Tenay and Taz in the studio doing voice over work two days before the 8/14 announcement. Nowhere in the commentary on the 8/14 show was there any talk of the day change. There was not even a late insert that could be done by either announcer from their home base, as often happens with inserting late Spike plugs for Bellator or Glory. I would expect there would be a number of audio edits on the 8/20 show. But that shows there wasn't a hint of a change two days earlier. There clearly wasn't at the recent TV tapings, since they taped a special show to commemorate 9/11 with references to it airing on that date, and the debut of war hero Christopher Melendez, for a show that will now air on 9/10. But there's plenty of time to make edits to that show

There is a question, given that the show has aired on Thursdays since April 2006 and fans are creatures of habit, how long it would take to get the audience to shift. For both WWE and TNA, when they stayed on their normal night but in each case moved the starting time up an hour, and promoted the change hard for weeks, it took the audience several weeks to fully tune in for the first hour. TNA fans had been loyal to Thursday, as during the period in 2010 when they went to Monday, they kept a Thursday replay, and most weeks the Thursday replay drew better numbers than the first-run Monday show.

On the 8/14 show, the only mentions of the move were three 15 second commercials mentioning Impact's new time starting next week of 9 p.m. that one would miss if not paying attention to commercials or if one DVR'd the show and skipped through (although 90% of TNA's audience watches when it airs) and one commercial right at the end of the show, that one would miss if they switched the channel when the announcers signed off.

TNA does have international commitments and contracts to provide programming. In addition as noted many times, Spike seemed amenable to keeping the show on the air if they needed some time to close a deal, either with Spike or with the new station. While TMZ has not followed up on the story, those at TMZ who broke the story said as late as this weekend that nothing has changed. Those at TNA are acting confident to partners that they have something ready to close and are not acting panicked.

During the heyday of Ultimate Fighter, when it aired with TNA on Thursdays as the lead-in, the move of that show was made to Wednesday because it was being hurt badly by NFL games.

On Wednesday, the show will go head-to-head in the fall with The Ultimate Fighter reality show. But that show wouldn't be significant competition for Impact at this point, given its ratings. A large percentage of people who watch TUF do so at their convenience because of its huge DVR numbers.

AUGUST 25

Vince Russo said that when he was first hired by TNA on October 24, 2013, that he was told that he could tell nobody he was with the company and that only three people were to know, he, Dixie Carter (who hired him) and John Gaburick. He said Carter told him that if anyone else found out, he would be fired, although obviously, in time, others found out and he even worked directly with creative and in recent weeks, with the announcers. Russo also said he was told months ago by John Gaburick that he told Scott Fishman, who is Spike's liaison to TNA, that Russo was with the company. Several sources indicated that the reason the company panicked when it was revealed that Johnson had proof Russo worked for the company was because they were in tenuous negotiations with Spike and Spike didn't want Russo there, and others said when the deal looked like it was falling apart, that was part of the reason. For what it's worth, Hulk Hogan said that he knows people close to Kevin Kay and that Kay was furious when he found out that "a writer they didn't like" was working there.

Russo gave the more details of his being let go, and this is basically true. He said he wasn't let go for sending the e-mail that may have cost the company its Spike deal. Russo pretty much said he's scapegoated on that, and there is truth to that, since there were people at Spike who months ago in conversations with non-wrestling people I know indicated they probably weren't renewing. If they were hot on renewing, the deal would have been cut before the Russo issue. However, it was an issue and it made TNA look awful. While there absolutely were people in the company who wanted him fired for that, Dixie Carter would not agree to it, as she's always been defensive of Russo. He said TNA sent him an e-mail telling him not to do Jim Ross' podcast. He ignored it and did it anyway, and was fired the morning after they taped. The story is that Carter always backed Russo, and even brought him back at a time when if it got out, it could risk her company, on the proviso nobody could tell anyone, but people found out and eventually the fingerprints were obvious on the TV show. She even backed him when he screwed up on the e-mail. But after all that, when he defied her by going on the Ross show, that apparently was one she couldn't take. Russo also said they were unhappy because he did an interview with Shannon Spruill (Daffney), who had sued TNA, on his podcast. Russo noted, correctly, that Ross had Bully Ray and Kurt Angle on in recent weeks and nobody from TNA threatened to fire either of them. Russo said that he also told Ross that if he'd do the show, he wouldn't talk about TNA anyway, similar to Eric Bischoff's stipulation in doing Steve Austin's show.

SEPTEMBER 1

Spike and TNA have announced Impact will continue through the end of the year. The good news is that it's not done when the contract expires (although we were told it wasn't going to be done at the end of September from the start), but the bad news is there's no announcement of a new deal. TNA is clearly not confident of anything past that point, because other than the U.K. tour, there is a freeze on almost all negotiations going on that have to do with the wrestling side of business. No new shows are being booked past that period and no new deals are being made. The way it was explained to us from the start was Spike would give TNA a reasonable amount of time to get a new deal, whether it was under Spike's terms or with someone else. They had actually offered the same deal to ECW in 2000, but ECW didn't take it because by that point Paul Heyman knew that no TV deal that he could keep a company going with was imminent once USA turned it down and Turner Broadcasting got out of wrestling.

There was a report that the Velocity channel was in talks with TNA about picking up Impact. What we can confirm is that there have been talks with Velocity and TNA, which started before any of the stories broke about Spike not renewing Impact. The only thing we know about now is that the belief is that talks aren't dead, but as far as how serious or how close they are, this is the TV business and nothing is done until the deal is signed and announced. Based on reports out there from a variety of places, they are only offering in the range of one-fourth of what TNA was making with Spike (or between $3 million and $4 million, and UTA would be getting a cut of that since they are handling negotiations). We can't confirm anything related to price past the point the number offered is far less than the company is getting on its current deal. Velocity is in between 48 and 52 million homes, or just over half of what Spike is in. It's on DirecTV Ch. 281 and Dish Ch. 246, as part of the Discovery Channel family. It's a male oriented station focusing on cars and sports and is carried on Cox, Comcast and Verizon cable stations. Even though it is aimed at men, it's not even in the top 50 stations on cable with the adult male demo. It's in less homes that Fox Sports Net was in when TNA had TV there for a few years.

They aren't the only station being talked with but at one point a few weeks ago were the most serious. As far as today, there is complete uncertainty as to where talks stand. The company would have to cut back greatly if this ends up as their destination, and they'd really be closer to ROH level as far as they wouldn't be able to afford hardly any big money contracts and there would be no chance for growth past that level.

SEPTEMBER 8

Whether this is true or not, the wrestlers were again told of late not to worry about television and that TV next year is all set in the sense there will be TV somewhere. As things stand right now, Bound for Glory is the only date on the schedule for the month of October and there are no future house shows scheduled. This has a lot of the talent which was working on a per-event deal kind of in a panic and worrying about their income being maybe half of what they expected it to be going forward unless they can get indie dates. The talent that worked the house shows regularly were making more than half their income from working house show dates. One thing that has changed is that the talent is allowed to appear on DVDs in the new contracts (or at least the contracts with a couple of people who relayed this info to us). They believe they are allowed to book themselves with any promotion that doesn't have national TV, or doesn't run on PPV, meaning the only companies they couldn't work out dates for are WWE, ROH and the El Rey promotion.

However, even if the talent works every TV, that's only 64 shows a year (52 weekly TVs, four PPVs and eight taped PPVs). Almost nobody works every show. The key spots will then be the ones who can get Japan, but that's with Wrestle-1, and Wrestle-1 is struggling and is only going to take maybe two to four guys each tour.

SEPTEMBER 15

Vince Russo made comments about Spike TV and why he felt they were horrible for TNA, that TNA would never grow on Spike, which led to Spike issuing a response noting that they went above and beyond what was in its contract to support and promote TNA over the years.

Russo, in an interview on the Pro Wrestling Report, said:

"I've been holding this back for years and I finally get to say this. I felt like Hannibal Lechter when he was strapped in and had his mouth wired shut. Spike TV is a horrible partner. Why TNA would ever want to partner with Spike is beyond me, unless there were no other options. If Spike TV were the only option to stay on television, then I would understand it. They are a horrible partner. They know nothing about the wrestling business. The way they advertised and marketed the program over the years was absolutely atrocious.

I can tell you this from a position where I worked with the USA Network, I worked directly with Bonnie Hammer. She was the female version of Vince McMahon. She knew what she was doing. When you had Bonnie Hammer at USA and Vince McMahon, the sky was the limit. If TNA signs another deal with Spike TV, great for them. It will move along for another two years and everyone will work, but the product will not grow on Spike TV. My hope for TNA is that a new network comes along and embraces TNA and gives them the time and investment to help grow the product. I can't say this enough. TNA on Spike TV will never grow."

Aside from the fact that WWE Raw moved in 2005 from Spike TV back to USA and its ratings never grew, and are today lower than they were on Spike, the reality is Spike TV saved TNA. They had already pulled out of the Fox Sports Net deal because the decision was made to no longer pay for television.

Fox Sports Net didn't care about the ratings TNA was getting, which were well above the station average. They were only interested in wrestling as a time buy, meaning the promotion buys the time, the same deal that had at the time with Real Pro Wrestling, which early on did similar ratings to TNA, although in TNA the RPW ratings didn't maintain and its funding ended and, unlike TNA, couldn't get a paying television deal and went under. TNA was on the verge of extinction, without a television partner, but when WWE left Spike to return to USA, Spike decided it wanted to keep wrestling, so they gave TNA a Saturday night show. Eventually in time, moved them to Thursdays, and tried Mondays in 2010, which didn't work. Most recently they moved them to Wednesdays in a relationship that ends at the close of 2014.

Spike was not happy with Russo's comments.

"I want to start by saying we enjoyed a great relationship, a very collaborative relationship with Dixie Carter and her team over the years," said David Schwarz, the Senior Vice President of Communications with Spike TV. "We took TNA from a late night spot on Saturday nights, doing 500,000 viewers, to a two-hour time slot that did two million viewers over time. Spike went out of its way, not in just adhering to its contract, but above and beyond the contract. We paid Hulk Hogan, we paid Eric Bischoff, with our money. We financed many shows. We financed U.K. shows. We helped promote. We gave TNA a prime time slot of Thursdays from 9-11 p.m. I think his comments are way off base. Clearly, he doesn't know what he's talking about. He's somebody who thinks more of himself than really exists. Vince Russo never meant anything to Spike TV. He had nothing to do with negotiations. Nobody cares about Vince Russo at Spike TV. Nobody cares or knows who he is. We have a great relationship with TNA. We went above and beyond for them, as they did for us. Dixie helped promote our shows. What Vince Russo is saying is complete nonsense."

Schwarz later told PWInsider that Russo "means less to Spike than gum that gets stuck on the bottom of a sneaker. What network would want to work with a guy who trashes other networks?"

SEPTEMBER 15

More people whose contracts have expired are just being given per-day agreements. Until a TV deal is completed, the company pretty much is doing a freeze on anything that has to do with commitments or guaranteed money. Not sure if Bully Ray, who maneuvered himself into being in the middle of things when his contract expired, will fit into this category. Bully Ray did not work the TV's this week, but he was not expected to nor advertised. They only taped PPVs, Xplosion and British Boot Camp and the next Impact taping isn't until 9/16 in Bethlehem, PA. If he's not there, that would seem to indicate they didn't reach a deal based on the idea that he was wanting a good deal at a time they are making no commitments, unless they felt he was valuable enough to make an exception. Besides being one of the company's best stars, he's generally considered the company's best agent, and has a hand in creative.

It is pretty much a lock, while nobody is saying it publicly, that TNA and Spike will part ways when this deal is up at the end of the year. As noted before, Spike was trying to be a good partner for TNA and give them until the end of the year to negotiate a new deal. While the public word is still both sides are in negotiations, the negotiations with Spike over a new deal ended several days before the TMZ story broke. While the Velocity channel has come up publicly, as has WGN America in some circles as far as a possible future destination, TNA is in talks with at least two others channels. There are at least four stations right now in play, and at least two of them would be more significant than either WGN or Velocity, and one is stronger than Spike but doesn't have the matching demographics of Spike. The report we got is the WGN America deal, if made, could include pre-emptions. The question is how much they can get when it comes to rights fees and until the deal is complete, they aren't making any new deals, or at least making very few, and it looks like they aren't doing much in the way of house shows, so those on a per-show deal are going to be earning a lot less at least until the end of the year. And there is, in TV, a big difference between talking and having meetings and inking a contract and right now, everything is up in the air regarding the future.

SEPTEMBER 22

The web site Grantland.com had an interesting story on TNA by Thomas Golianopoulos, questioning if this is the end of the company and will pro wrestling ever support two major promotions again.

Of course the reality is that pro wrestling hasn't supported two major promotions since WCW fell off a cliff in 1999 and 2000. Perhaps if TNA had a better battle plan, things would have been different. There were definitely times TNA showed signs of life. The company was profitable at one point, although never competitive. And no matter what, they were never able to turn the corner. For all the excuses people want to say, it may simply be nothing more than the reality of supply and demand. The casual audience, the masses, are only going to devote so many hours per week to pro wrestling. With WWE having four, five, up to seven hours per week, there's not a big market for something else. In the WCW days, you could say you had a similar dynamic and WCW flourished, but Smackdown wasn't around in those days. WCW also had a different fan base that had been run off.

Dixie Carter is someone who in person, is very charming, and always has an answer. The company is always profitable, even when they are behind on paying people and it's very clear they're not. TNA is always growing, slowly, but growing, even when the numbers indicate the opposite. And there's always the excuse. There's video games, or computers, or DVRs, or some reason why the audience was declining and people wouldn't buy tickets. It was never the product. Except, in the end, it largely was.

Even though the TNA office has been described as a skeleton crew, since so many people have left in recent months, Carter described it that they were overstaffed.

The story was largely good, well, except for the total lack of understanding the business with the description of Bruce Prichard, Eric Bischoff, Hulk Hogan and Vince Russo as all "men with historically successful track records."

Prichard had a couple of long runs as a key management figure in WWE, but he was never a guy steering the ship. Bischoff was, in the terms of being a wrestling promoter, the ultimate hotshot flash in the pan. He had three good years, 1996 to 1998, and it collapsed from there. Hogan absolutely had an incredible long-term track record as one of the biggest drawing stars in history, but his days as the guy who could count on the build around were over in 1998. As a special attraction who could come off the bench, sure, you could use him as long as his body held up. In theory, you could use him as a commissioner, except you couldn't. There are lessons about making top guys, and you can't make them easily when you've got the overriding personality there every week. If Bruno Sammartino was on TV regularly, Bob Backlund would have likely always been considered secondary, belt or not. Steve Austin would have had trouble as a top babyface with an incumbent Hogan still there all the time. John Cena would have never had a chance with Austin as a weekly character, even as a General Manager.

But the story had a number of quotes that need closer examination.

From Carter:"TMZ asked me, `Hey, is this story real, should we run with it?' I was watching a movie and didn't see it until some little wrestling site ran it. Then I gave TMZ a quote which said we're still negotiating. That never made it to print."

As it turned out, I've had a long discussion with the TMZ writer, at a party a few weeks later. I knew what I knew and I know what they knew. They knew. They had the story from the Spike side that it wasn't being renewed. I knew from the TNA side that Spike told Dixie Carter they weren't being renewed, that they'd probably be extended with a little breathing room to allow them to make a deal, and Carter had told people in the company that she didn't want to stay on the station anyway. Both sides, for the public, gave the "we're still negotiating," story, but they both knew the relationship was ending. Hey, even to this day, if you ask either side, they'll still give the same line publicly. But no, TMZ didn't ask Dixie if the story was real. I didn't either. I wrote her that night and said the story was going to break and did she have a comment. She did get back to me and her quote was put in the story.

The story all but said that TNA was losing its TV deal and said the industry was slumping. Actually, WWE is pretty stable as far as popularity goes. Business-wise, yeah, WWE is losing money like crazy, but that's due to changing the way it does its business. The jury is still out on if it'll pay off, but as far as popularity levels go, WWE is pretty much where it has been for the last several years. WWE has also had to make cuts, but if the network were to hit it big, WWE will be more profitable than it was during the Austin/Rock heyday.

Still, Carter admitted something she's never said before:

"We will die a slow death on the vine if we just stay as one two-hour show in the U.S. I have big decisions to make. I want this to be a big play. I don't want this to be a status quo play."

In a wrestling environment with so many hours of WWE television, is there a market for TNA adding a second show when the first show is declining and many weeks, people don't even stick with it through the main event.

Carter talked about her pep talk at the Manhattan Center in August, saying, "I may have let a cuss word or two slip. A couple of guys came up to me afterward and said, `We believe in you. We believe in this company.'"

One person there said that in fact, she didn't curse at the meeting, and the person said he didn't believe anyone went to her and said what she said. Aside from the producers or Bully Ray (who doubles as an agent), they didn't think anyone would talk to her at that level. That quote was the one talked about backstage at the tapings.

The biggest issue with the article is the description of Russo. Russo in his own mind believes hardcore fans only want to see four-star matches and the casual fan wants something else. He's right. It's all about storylines and dynamic personalities. It always has been. Great matches don't build business unless framed with great storylines. That's true of wrestling, boxing, MMA, or tennis for that matter. Russo's problem, and it's been the case for 15 years, is that his storylines don't resonate and his personalities don't connect.

"The Internet wrestling community thinks in-ring wrestling action should take up every minute of every show," said Russo. "That's what they believe the business is. That's what they are fans of. I mean, they rate fake wrestling matches on a star system. The matches are fake. They are not real."

Carter, on Russo, said, "He's a lighting rod. People hate him. But sometimes people love what he does but they don't realize he does it. He's a really talented guy."

I don't want to say nobody hates Russo. Some people do. But in reality that's a crutch. He's never been good with the big picture. The fan base doesn't care about Russo with very few exceptions. They just want to be entertained. Russo, and whoever was in charge of TNA creative, failed because they did not grow the television audience, and worse, could not convert that audience into being customers. Those are facts. Russo does have some talent for scripting certain characters, but certainly not women characters because his verbiage and stories have made them turnoffs when at one point they were the closest thing TNA had to ratings deliverers.

I hate to say this, but there are certain terms that whenever I read them, 95 times out of 100 they are going to follow with ignorance. Among those are Internet Wrestling Community, a laughable term which gives the impression there is some kind of a unanimity of opinion that is different from the masses. And in every entertainment form, the hardcore base is very different from what appeals to the masses. But there is always such a great divergence of opinion than any kind of blanket statement about an IWC is always going to lead you to a conclusion that puts you out to lunch. The job of the writers is to reach and grab the masses, and the numbers don't lie. It's right up there with people who use terms like mark and smark, when everyone gets it and everyone knows what it is, people just have divergent opinions of what they like. The key is, it doesn't matter what any one individual likes. Some people have good instincts about what will and won't work, but everyone is wrong a lot, and the numbers tell you the truth if you look at them objectively. The idea is to do what grows the business. There are certain principles and things that work that are somewhat timeless, and many others that change based on a varying and changing world, ones ability to sell their concepts to the public. Coming up with excuses as to why people are tuning out, nor not buying tickets or PPVs, is an attitude that will kill you, especially in a quickly changing world and industry where it's so easy to be left behind.

Seriously, who has ever insinuated that in-ring wrestling should take up every minute of a show. The idea that in-ring wrestling should even always be a certain percentage of a show is silly. It's all about entertainment and what the public wants and what you need to correctly tell your big stories. There have been one hour shows that featured one match that were great shows that people talked about for years and drew ratings. There have been very rare one hour shows that had no matches and all talking and were every bit if not more effective. But you can only do either of them on very rare occasions, and with two and three hour shows, you simply can't do either.

Right now, for WWE and TNA, matches generally do stronger in garnering an audience than talking, but you need both. But far more than match vs. talking is appealing personality and star quality, whether they are wrestling or talking, that is going to generally do better.

The key is you want good matches and good talking, as opposed to bad matches and good talking, or bad talking and good matches. The idea is that it all works together to build characters. Talking does better than wrestling at making you want to see a match. But unless you've got really awesome talkers, long talking segments burn people out, and too many talking segments on a show usually weaken the effectiveness of the talking segments you need people to remember when the show is over.

Perhaps there are people who believe that it should all be wrestling, but they'd be such a tiny percentage that even bringing it up is a strawman argument. And the silliness of the idea that it's weird to rate fake matches on a star system would only be valid if the same wasn't done for music, movies, plays, television shows and even food on a daily basis. Just as there is more to marketing movies than their star ratings, and more to marketing a restaurant than star ratings on food and the service, there is far more to producing wrestling than just good matches. But there is no victim card. If the creative is clicking, everyone will know because the numbers are there. When it's not, the answers are there as well.

WWF did turn around when Russo was on the creative team. Jim Cornette was there at the same time, and neither was really fully responsible for the turnaround, because when Cornette was gone, and Russo was gone, business continued to build. You could say Vince McMahon, and of course the buck stopped with him before they were there and long after they were gone, but Vince was in charge when the company was struggling and when it was kicking ass.

When it turned around, it was Steve Austin, The Rock, Mick Foley, DX, and to a degree Sable, and everyone else that made up the part of the show that carried things. It slowed down when Austin went heel, and eventually his body betrayed him, and Rock went Hollywood. Vince and the rest of the roster were still there.

Russo claimed the secrecy about hiring him wasn't about Spike TV. The panic about the Mike Johnson story getting out was completely about Spike TV, there would have been no panic in TNA otherwise. The word from Spike that they weren't renewing came days later. It wasn't the prime reason, but two people very close to the situation confirmed that it was a reason. But realistically, the reasons for the decision were about Spike wanting to add new original programming in prime time that they are developing, hoping that such programming could draw better ad dollars and more female viewers. If TNA was drawing what it used to be drawing, Russo or not, the likelihood is there would have been a renewal. The moving of Bellator to Friday also hurt, because TNA did help drive viewers to Bellator on Thursday and that was a great reason to keep the programming. On Friday, Bellator proved it could draw without TNA's lead-in. It doesn't draw as well as it did on Thursday, but with the NFL on Thursday, Bellator wasn't staying there.

The story also didn't understand the business as it was in 2002, saying TNA's business plan at the start was: "Instead of banking on cable rights fees, the largest revenue stream for most national wrestling promotions then and now, TNA sidestepped a television deal in favor of weekly PPVs."

While cable rights were TNA's main revenue stream, and are WWE's largest today, the largest revenue stream in 2002 was PPV revenue, by leaps and bounds. The TNA business model was to avoid the costs of producing television, and go right to PPV. It was completely flawed, because without television exposure, you can't draw people to your product to get them to buy your PPVs. Weekly PPV was a risk. Weekly PPV with no television was insanity. That version of TNA was about to go down, and land Jeff and Jerry Jarrett into bankruptcy, until Carter bailed them out and saved the company.

SEPTEMBER 29

At TV this past week, Dixie Carter told talent that she guarantees they will be on TV on January 7, 2015, the first Wednesday after the deal with Spike expires. Sources in the television world indicate that the belief is that TNA has not signed a deal (which multiple sources have confirmed is the case at press time), but is in very serious talks. The expectation is there will be a deal and the show will continue on Wednesday nights. The plan, if the deal goes through, is for the first TNA show after Bound for Glory to be a live television taping on 1/7 from the Manhattan Center.

As far as which of the four stations they were in talks with that they are supposed to be close with, that is unknown. Terms are unknown, and since television rights fees are a huge part of company revenue, the value of the deal, also unknown, will largely indicate whether they can afford to sign new talent and keep those whose contracts are expiring. At this point, nothing is being offered to wrestlers whose contracts have just expired or are expiring before January. Until the deal is signed, they simply can't afford to make any new deals.

For what it's worth, a number of people close to the situation appear to be confident the promotion will continue next year, but nobody has a read on who will be involved and at what level, if it'll be a bare-bones skeleton company, an ROH level company, or a company at the level, as far as budget goes, that TNA has been. As far as contracts go, everyone under a long-term deal is being figured in and talent that we're aware is being paid on schedule. Those with existing old deals are still getting a regular base check. But almost all the new contracts were with a small base pay, or none at all. They were largely based on the number of dates being worked, with no dates except Bound for Glory scheduled at this time through 1/7, that means three months with no TNA income.

The talent remaining under contract has been told they can take any indie dates they can get, and unlike in the past, they don't have to contact the office to approve the dates, or even let them know of the dates. The only thing they've been told is that they can't appear on television, PPV or iPPV.

The fact that nobody we're aware of, and this includes Bully Ray (whose final show is Bound for Glory at this point) and Samoa Joe, were offered new contracts of anything significant would indicate the 100% sure thing guarantee is not something the company is willing to bank on right now.

Television was taped this past week in Bethlehem, PA, for shows that will air through 11/19. They changed every championship, largely to make sure the titles were on people who have long-term deals.

They didn't want titles on anyone who may not be there if and when they open up.

The belief is that they will be continuing on Spike from 11/26 until the end of the year, and whether that means 12/17, or continuing with shows on Christmas Eve and New Year's Eve is uncertain. TNA and Spike both said it would be until the end of the year which would indicate the run would end on New Year's Eve.

The shows from 11/26 to 12/31 are believed to be archived "Best Of" shows or compilation shows with little if any new material. Going five weeks without new material and taping so far in advance does show how dire the financial situation is, because for those interested in the week-to-week storylines and characters, they will lose much of that fan base's interest over the five weeks.

That's not necessarily bad. All TV shows and most major sports have off-seasons, and there were promotions of the past who had off-seasons. But no major wrestling promotion has done this in probably three decades. Television wrestling has been produced almost everywhere as far back as anyone can remember as a year-around soap opera with no breaks.

Ironically, the new Lucha Underground group is doing television with a similar mentality, taping 39 episodes per year and having an off-season. The most famous example of this in the U.S. was Sam Muchnick's "Wrestling at the Chase," which for most of its existence, would not tape new television over the summer, and cut down on the live schedule. As funny as that sounds, part of the reason was Muchnick believing there should be a seasonal break, like other sports, and also because he was such a huge St. Louis Cardinals baseball fan that he didn't want to work so hard during the summer. They would use that off-season to air tapes from other NWA promotions. The idea is that it would expose its fans to different talent around the country, and those who looked the most impressive and garnered the most fan buzz would often to brought in as new stars when the fall TV season started.

TNA was talking with four stations, two of which were Velocity and WGN America. One of the other two was not a cable station. The belief is the other cable station is CMT, which currently airs Steve Austin's "Broken Skull Challenge."

They would have to do four TV's, which they could do in a two or three-day stint at the Manhattan Center, because the January tapings would have to cover them through 1/28. After that, they will be taping up to six weeks of new material, which could cover them into mid-March, on shows on 1/29 in Glasgow, Scotland at the Hydro; 1/30 in Manchester, U.K. at the Phones 4U Arena and 1/31 in London at Wembley Arena.

Because of these decisions, and timing, inherently, Bound for Glory has become a non-entity. The original idea of cutting from 12 PPVs to four was that it would make the four stronger. Instead, without doing long-term storylines leading to those shows, they've actually not gotten stronger at all, and Bound for Glory is likely to do less business than any "big" PPV in company history.

At the Bethlehem tapings this week, nothing was done as far as angles or interviews on shows that will air 10/1 and 10/8, for Bound for Glory. Not one match is announced publicly and the only thing we've been told is a lock is Great Muta & Tajiri vs. Great Sanada & James Storm.

At this point, the TNA wrestlers scheduled for Bound for Glory that are being advertised by TNA are Bobby Lashley, Team 3-D (who will be inducted into the TNA Hall of Fame in what may be both men's last appearance), MVP, Joe, James Storm, Great Sanada, Manik, Ethan Carter III, Abyss, Davey Richards, Eddie Edwards and Bram (who in a trivia note was the guy WWE originally picked to be the key guy in The Ascension, but he lost his job due to a few arrests in Florida). Ticket sales for the show are said to be good, although they are not sold out in 1,500-seat building.

Doing the show this way is part of the money saving deal that Jeff Jarrett originally put together when he was with the company. TNA will only be responsible for flying the talent to Japan, and paying the talent. Wrestle-1 will handle the production and do a television show for Japan, with the idea they are presenting TNA's flagship show of the year live. They will then transmit the tape of the show to Nashville, where the TNA announcers will voice over the show, that will air on a tape delayed basis in the usual 8 p.m. Eastern time slot.

However, Lashley and The Wolves are no longer scheduled for the show. Wrestle-1 had a press conference on 9/24 and claimed Richards had a leg injury (which he did have, but he was fully recovered and worked the tapings this past week) and that Team 3-D would replace them on the show. The actual reason is that because

The Wolves had lost the tag titles but it hadn't aired, TNA would have to present them as champions on the show for the timing of their television, but such a thing doesn't work in Japan where fans would react badly knowing The Wolves had already lost the titles. Edwards & Richards had no idea they were pulled from the show, even after it was announced in Japan.

Lashley is only listed on the TNA site but not being advertised in Japan. The mentality is that they can't jump their TV by showing the current champions with the belts at Bound for Glory to the U.S. audience before they win them on TV.

However, in Japan, the mentality is different.

There were already issues with the X title at the most recent joint show with Wrestle-1, where they taped Sanada losing the title, but since the match didn't air on television until after the Wrestle-1 event, the idea was for Sanada to go in as champion and score his big career win over Keiji Muto. But Japanese fans were well aware that Sanada had lost the title and Joe was champion. They were advertising a Sanada title defense. Fans called both the Wrestle-1 office and local media about the "fraud." Wrestle-1 felt it had to make the match non-title and admit Sanada had lost. TNA wasn't happy about that, because they didn't want a business partner to admit publicly that a title had changed hands before the match aired on television. So it led to this unique position.

That's why the decision was made not to use Lashley, Roode, The Wolves, Gail Kim or Taryn Terrell on the show. The original talk of Wolves vs. Team 3-D was changed to Wolves vs. a Japanese team, to no Wolves at all. The Wolves would be champions when Bound for Glory airs in the U.S. on 10/12 based on television, but in Japan, they can't come out with the belts or be called champions since they had lost the titles already to James Storm & Abyss. Even though Storm is a champion, he's not teaming with Abyss so they can get around that in Japan by simply not having him wear the belt to the ring, which doesn't matter since it's not a title match. Plus, the Japanese side doesn't want a lot of Wrestle-1 vs. TNA matches, as the gimmick for Japan is not a promotion vs. promotion rivalry like in prior shows, but in presenting a TNA major show that happens to have the top Wrestle-1 talent on it.

However, the plan is for Low Ki and Samoa Joe to be in an X Division match, with the belt not brought to Japan and, at least in Japan, neither will be acknowledged as champion.

This may be handled differently on the taped delayed U.S. broadcast, as one would expect Joe would be referred to as champion at Bound for Glory.

At press time, the Bound for Glory card was not completed.

What TNA is sacrificing, besides PPV buys for a show without title matches, nor the culmination of a big climactic angle like Bound for Glory has been built around in the past, is the usual big jump in the first show or two shows after Bound for Glory TV ratings.

At this point, these are the final scheduled appearances of Team 3-D and Joe. Joe has an injury, believed to be to his shoulder, and the belief is won't be 100 percent, but the belief is he'll be healthy enough to work by that date.

Even though Angle couldn't wrestle, his being in Japan would be a big deal, and he's not advertised for Japan or for the U.K. dates.

Bully Ray, Joe and Kim are all advertised for the U.K. tour, but that is also old advertising. At the time of the ads, even though they weren't under contract for next year, the belief was that they weren't in any danger of being gone. And come January, depending on the television deal, it's up in the air regarding what offers can or will be made.

Given the timing of the tapings, it was impossible to do important title matches at Bound for Glory. It would require not only not having any championship matches on TV through 11/19, but not even having the belts appear on television for six weeks or any interviews talking about title matches done before the public on shows that air after Bound for Glory. Since television for TNA is the priority over PPV, that is the master that had to be served during budget crunch time. With anything else, you give away who is on TV as champion after Bound for Glory, which makes the results obvious.

Every title changes hands on TV, but all the title changes are believed to air after Bound for Glory.

As for not having the post-Bound for Glory ratings increase, that's less important with a lame duck product on Spike.

Roode beat Lashley for the TNA title on the show that was taped on 9/18 at the Sands Casino in Bethlehem, PA, and probably airs on 10/15, if not 10/22.

The Wolves, Edwards & Richards, ended up winning the Full Metal Mayhem match, which was taped on 9/19 and probably airs on 10/8 or 10/15. The crazy thing about that, is that the night before the Full Metal Mayhem match was taped, they were taping a tag team tournament for the No. 1 contendership for the tag team titles before much of the same audience. The tournament probably airs on 10/22. Matt & Jeff Hardy won the tournament, which pretty well told fans there that for the Full Metal Mayhem match, which will air on TV before the tournament, that the Hardys couldn't win. And on that same show, Devon was forming a tag team with Tommy Dreamer, which kind of told fans that Team 3-D wasn't going to win either. Still, the three-way match was said to be fantastic, the best of the four matches the three teams have had, and will be the best thing presented on TV between now and the end of the Spike run.

Why the match was taped after the tournament and out of order is likely because they drew so poorly all week, between 200 and 350 fans (and the Thursday show was said to be heavily papered just to get in that range), and to push attendance on Friday night. It was felt that was the night they had the chance to draw the best, so they decided to push what they felt was the biggest match they could advertise. It was both pushed on the Internet and in the arena during the week that the Full Metal Mayhem match would be on Friday night.

Then, after that was taped, Abyss & Storm beat the Wolves later on 9/19 to win the titles. Storm had a contract for a tag title match in the Feast or Fired deal from the end of last year that nobody had ever called attention to in months. Abyss was a surprise partner as the new member of Storm's heel group.

The Knockouts title went from Kim to Havok on 9/16, and then to Terrell, winning a three-way over Kim and Havok on 9/18, which likely airs on 11/12. The original plan was for Havok to get a monster push as the new Kong as a heel champion. So they went with it for a few days of tapings and then put the title on Terrell since the feeling was that Havok wasn't getting over.

Joe suffered what was believed to be a shoulder injury either on 9/16 against Austin Aries ord on 9/17 against Gunner. Joe's contract is believed to expire after Bound for Glory, and if he was going to be offered a new deal, it wouldn't be until January and it wouldn't start until if and when the next show would take place. Given that he could get a new job, in wrestling or elsewhere, they needed to get the title off him.

Joe came out on 9/19 and said he wasn't medically cleared to wrestle and said he was giving up the title. Later that night, on the show taped for 11/19, Low Ki won a four-way over D.J. Zema Ion, Manik and Tigre Uno to become champion. Homicide was already injured so he was out of the picture.

The biggest contract of all, Angle's, is up on 9/27. Devon's deal expires at Bound for Glory. Austin Aries is another name not advertised for either the Japan show or the U.K. tour.

Aries certainly hinted on twitter that he was done, writing, "Much love to my entire Impact Wrestling family. We all busted our ass and put our bodies on the line with passion and pride. Thank you."

Angle has said he knows what his next destination is. If Global Force Wrestling has anything going, they would be able to pick up some good name talent right now. But we haven't heard anything regarding them offering name talent a deal, nor really anything past Jeff Jarrett having meetings. If Jarrett can get a television deal, and it is even possible he would be negotiating with some of the people TNA is, given there are not many stations around interested in pro wrestling, he could start out with a lot of the TNA stars.

OCTOBER 6

Because so few stations have any interest in wrestling, both TNA and Global Force Wrestling was largely in talks with the same stations. Since TNA is operational, has a history and has talent under contract, they have the edge over a start-up. So Spike not renewing TNA may have also changed the business landscape by making it more difficult for GFW to get a TV deal.

OCTOBER 6

A lot of the younger talent are feeling mentally checked out. With no shows planned (since few are on Bound for Glory) until 1/7 at the earliest, there's unhappiness. All are trying to get indie dates. With the exception of Eddie Edwards and maybe Samoa Joe, there doesn't appear to be much interest in anyone from the ROH front. A lot of talent has contacted Jarrett, but given it was December when Jarrett left and we're in October and really nothing has happened past some press releases, most don't take GFW as an option until they hear about signing of talent and a TV deal. There's the feeling that the ones who are under the new contracts are getting maybe $1,000 per month as a base if not booked and that's for a three month period minimum. While they can work wherever they want as long as it's not on PPV or iPPV, they are still under contract and can't make a deal with a Japan group, ROH or WWE during this period.

OCTOBER 13

One thing as far as the TV negotiations noted to us is that in the TV world, stations are leery on the product not just because it's pro wrestling, but because it has the stigma of something Spike dropped when ratings aren't that bad. It was above Spike's average almost every week, and they signed a new deal with Glory that has nowhere near the interest level. It was described that people are wondering what's the catch and why would Spike drop something that was doing 1 million to 1.4 million viewers each week (at the time the decision was made and before the move to Wednesday). The TV business word is that Spike dropped it because they didn't have confidence in the leadership being people who would get it to grow, and the numbers were on the decline, plus the Vince Russo issue came up again as a reason this week, in the sense Spike denies it publicly and privately it's not a secret that mess was a big part of finalizing the decision. As noted, TNA and Jeff Jarrett are in talks with many of the same stations, and TNA does have the edge because it's an existing product that has a history of doing 1 million viewers, which for a cable station outside the top 15 or so, is a good number.

OCTOBER 20

Dixie Carter told at least some talent to expect a major announcement very soon. There were claims of negotiating with someone who would "shock people" and have a new signing they expect that will help bring a buzz on the product. Nobody knows who those people would be, past Mick Foley denying it's him. The only thing that is news is talent has been told TNA will start back running on 1/7, although we'd reported that date for some time, but everything is still contingent on signing a TV deal.

At least some people whose deals are up or coming up have noted that nobody is getting back to them. I don't really expect any significant negotiations with people in that boat unless or until a new TV deal is signed.

One former wrestler noted that if something happens and TNA doesn't survive, that Dixie Carter could do everyone one favor at the end and sign over the names to the wrestlers so they could use them going forward in their careers. In particular people like Ethan Carter III, Angelina Love and Velvet Sky would then be allowed to continue using the names. If the company's intellectual property then ended up in the hands of WWE with the tape collection, as happened with ECW and the Dudleys, it would at least benefit them, given those wrestlers going by other names would have far less indie value.

NOVEMBER 3

A lot of uncertainty has picked up since we're now more than two weeks after Bound for Glory, and those in the company had been telling various wrestlers and other business contacts that the new TV deal would be announced the week after Bound for Glory, or at the latest, this past week. Every week with no announcement and delaying contract talks with those whose deals have run out becomes more concerning. However, there is talent that has been told the announcement is now imminent and we do know things related to closing the deal are happening in the next few days. As far as who the deal is with, there are no hints past the point that people from Spike were reported as being in Tokyo, which has created some obvious rumors.

NOVEMBER 10

John Gaburick went to New York this past week to try and finalize a television deal. No word as far as with who or what the deal is, but the company is operating like they are booking television taping dates and doing storylines for 2015 right now.

NOVEMBER 17

There is tremendous frustration at this point because no TV deal has been reached. At press time we received word that negotiations took place this past week between TNA and Destination America, which is a station in the Discovery Network family. Destination America is Ch. 286 on DirecTV and Ch. 194 on Dish, and available in 60 million homes, or about 52% of the country. Based on sources close to the deal on the Destination America side, they should know by the end of the week if a deal will or won't be reached, or at least that was what they were thinking as of mid-week. As best we can tell, everyone who has asked about a deal (it's possible Kurt Angle is the exception) has been told that they can't talk with them until a TV deal is made. There has been talent told Spike is still in the running and was the most likely place, which kept people from being negative, but the preemptions don't seem to be a good sign. Others have also been told differently regarding Spike.

Talent has been told since Bound for Glory that a deal is about a week away. We do know there was tremendous frustration it didn't happen last week. In recent days talent was told to expect a deal reached by 11/19, which is the date of the last first-run episode of Impact on Spike. But we did confirm talks are close. This was the first week that some of the veterans were privately saying they really aren't sure if the company is coming back. Al Snow, who is an agent, who only does rare indies because his regular job is working here, publicly said he was looking to fill up his calendar with dates starting next month.

Regarding the TV in Australia, there are more aspects to the situation. The station it is on is being rebranded. It was on Fuel, which has been rebranded in Australia as Fox Sports 5, which is actually a positive because it's getting a better spot on cable channel lineup. However, the station didn't air Impact this week. Impact used to air on Fuel on Saturday nights, and it aired on Saturday night, but only on the PPV channel rather than a TV channel. Foxtel said that they are doing nothing with TNA unless they sign an American television deal. If they get a TV deal, they'll probably wind up back on either Fox Sports 5 or Fox Sports 4.

NOVEMBER 24

TNA announced, first in a conference call to talent its new multi-year deal with Destination America, which is part of the Discovery Communications chain of stations.

The deal goes into effect in January with what is being termed the "World Premiere."

While a huge step down from Spike, the promotion told talent that it's a positive, claiming the Discovery Network is behind them and will be promoting them in a way the company has never been promoted before. The skeptical thought was if Discovery was behind them to a strong degree, they would have been put on The Discovery Network, which has full cable clearance, instead of a show in just over half the cable homes. While there is a claim that Destination America is available in approximately 52 million homes, on many systems it would be necessary to get an upgraded tier.

The time slot and date were not released. Those in the company were told that they believed it would be the same Wednesday night at 9 p.m. time slot, but that it wasn't confirmed, but that the show would start airing most likely the first week of January.

Originally TNA was going to do a live show on 1/7 from the Manhattan Center, but those plans are believed to have changed. The talent was told that they would hear within a few days when the next taping would be. The plan, which is not finalized, was to tape sometime in mid-to-late December. New York may still be the destination for the first set of tapings, but that was not confirmed.

The deal with Destination America will include far more program hours than Spike. There will be a replay of Impact that airs every week, plus specials and secondary TV series. One idea talked about was doing an American version of the British Boot Camp series.

TNA is expected to be flagship programming on the station. In addition, Discovery Communications was given international broadcasting rights to all programming in certain regions. The belief is that TNA will retain its rights in the markets it has already developed, like the U.K. and Australia, but in markets that TNA has no programming, Discovery will have the syndication rights.

The belief is that with the deal in place, John Gaburick will now be able to open up negotiations with talent whose contracts have expired or will expire before January. Among the names who fit into that category are Kurt Angle, Samoa Joe, Eddie Edwards, Bully Ray, Davey Richards, Gail Kim and Mike Tenay.

In its release announcing the deal, the flagship stars TNA was listing were Jeff Hardy, Bobby Roode, Angle, Bobby Lashley and Kim. Lashley becomes interesting because it was one thing for him to have the joint contract when both TNA and Bellator were on Spike, but it was another thing when they are different companies. A question becomes whether his MMA drawing power would decline if TNA was not promoting the shows and his appearances, which they wouldn't be any longer.

It is not known the rights fees which would be the key aspect of how much budget cutting would or wouldn't be needed and what kind of contracts could be offered. Clearly, things are going to be much tougher.

"Our partnership with TNA Wrestling will officially come to an end with our last telecast on 12/24," said Spike TV President Kevin Kay. "Dixie Carter and her team have been incredible partners to work with over the past nine years, delivering high-action entertainment and strong ratings. As Spike continues to evolve into a network reaching a broader audience, we continue to look across our schedule to find opportunities to add original scripted and no-scripted programming that appeals to a wider demographic. On behalf of everyone at Spike, we would like to with Dixie and TNA all the best and continued success."

While Spike made the call months ago to cancel, they attempted to be the best partners they could be on the way out. They kept TNA on the air for three extra months after the contract expired to give them time to broker a new deal. They also would not publicly claim that they had canceled the show, always using the term in public conversation that they were still in negotiations.

Privately, even though the ratings were above the station average, even with the move to Wednesday, and the show had a loyal audience, the ad rates they could charge were an issue. They also wanted programming that wouldn't be as heavily male-skewed, although wrestling's percentage of women viewers isn't all that much different than MMA or kickboxing. It was expressed to me that if TNA was doing the ratings it did a few years back, this call wouldn't have been made.

But it was a telling time for the industry that a show with a track record of one million viewers per week, a solid prime time number for all but the top tier of cable stations, couldn't get on a station with full national clearance.

As best we can tell, the most watched show in the history of the station was an April airing of the show Mountain Monsters, which did an 0.8 rating and 473,000 viewers. The station is in roughly half the homes that has Spike, so given that, if every Spike viewer who gets the station switched over, you're talking 500,000 viewers, and really it would be significantly less, because it's so much of a less viewed station so it's not like every person who watched it on Spike is going to move over.

The exposure for the product would likely be in the same ballpark as ROH and would probably stay ahead of Lucha Underground for now. Lucha Underground in a Saturday afternoon time slot wouldn't be in prime time like TNA will be, but Unimas has far more viewership than Destination America. TNA would have coverage in more places than ROH, but ROH would be on stronger local stations, including network affiliates, while Destination America is a station with minimal viewership.

Nothing was said regarding house shows. TNA no longer has a house show promoter and had let go the people who handled the merchandise. House shows will be more difficult with the smaller audience that would be watching the show, and many markets that TNA had run would have cable systems that don't get the channel.

The February tapings would be done out of the U.K. as that tour is still on. Right now there is nothing being said about house shows, since they got rid of their promoter, and the people who handle the merchandise, so that gives an indication they'll mostly just tape TV and try to farm out their talent.

Sources in Destination America were of the belief that the deal was agreed to on 11/12.

Destination America airs on Ch. 286 on DirecTV and Ch. 194 on the Dish Network in HD. It's also on Ch. 168 and 668 on Verizon FiOS, Ch. 315 on Sky Angel, Ch. 1465 (HD) and Ch. 465 (SD) on AT&T U-verse in most markets.

DECEMBER 1

TNA announced three nights of tapings from 1/7 to 1/9 back at the Manhattan Center in New York. As things stand right now, the plan is to do the first show either live, or on a one or two hour tape delay. That depends on Destination America confirming the Wednesday 9 p.m. time slot, which is expected but wasn't confirmed at press time. TNA had been working on several days of tapings on 12/15 with various locations being discussed, but the inability to do any finalization of dates until the Destination America deal was complete made it pretty much impossible to announce and put together such a series of shows on that little notice.

There were at least four different locations considered for the first taping. The others were believed to have been casino locations. The upside on the casino shows is that the deal usually is the casino buys the show and then is responsible for distributing and selling the tickets. The negative for a three-day run is it could be like Bethlehem where you only have a few hundred there and the show comes off badly. New York costs the most to advertise by far and the most to run. The upside is that whether they drw 500 or 1,000, those there will be super enthusiastic and they are easy to pop if they give them 90s nostalgia or tables, so it's really easy to book for that audience and have the show look hot. The negative is what that audience, will pop for, tables and 90s nostalgia, is going to do nothing to build your brand or make you look different on the new network. But they'll also be receptive to good matches. So they're in a situation where they are earning far less (the Destination America deal has TNA getting far less money but producing far more content than Spike), but spending more on the taping, but the flip side is they'll get the past crowd reactions. While nothing has been revealed about the deal past it is for "multi-years," we'll probably be able to gauge a lot of things by who TNA signs, what kind of money they are offering to people, and who they aggressively pursue as far as how much of a spending mode they are into at first. In the long run, once the drive to get people over to the station and change the product ends, guaranteed they'll have to tighten the budget badly.

From a visibility standpoint, they will probably be ahead of where they were in audience during the Fox Sports Net era (200,000 to 250,000 viewers), but nowhere close to Spike. There is an advantage over the Fox Sports Net era. On FSN, they were paying thousands weeekly to be on the air, and this deal pays them. Money losses were gigantic during the Fox Sports Net era to the point TNA dropped it even though they had almost no television (They got on one local market sports station in Florida) and the company was basically saved by the Spike deal coming through in late 2005. The funny thing is the PPV business in the Fox Sports Net era was actually strong (by modern standards at least, usually in the 30,000 to 40,000 buy range) because they had developed a reputation for putting on great shows.

The plan is for a reboot of sorts for the debut show, with new graphics and a new look. Josh Matthews will be replacing Mike Tenay as the lead announcer, working with Taz. The expectation is that Tenay will remain with the company in an on-air role. That change probably would have happened anyway, even if they weren't looking for a new look and changes on a new station. Part of the deal may be because they consider Jeff Jarrett Public Enemy No. 1 (they even did a video piece designed to mock Jarrett doing a Billionaire Ted-like skit on him) and signing Tenay would keep him from Jarrett, who wanted Tenay to be his lead announcer if he got TV. I had pretty much figured from the day Matthews was let go by WWE that TNA would bring him in because of the John Gaburick connection, and he was at a TNA show in New York immediately after being let go. He was signed right after his non-compete ended, and moved to Nashville some time ago. He was signed at the time to be an announcer, a job he hasn't started at yet. He's been working on the web site and other work for months. The only thing that may have changed the plans was Tenay's performance at Bound for Glory which some figured may have swayed the decision, similar to the fan reaction to Jim Ross in Chicago on the Hall of Fame induction swaying Vince McMahon and Kevin Dunn to cancel the plans of replacing him after the 2007 WrestleMania, which had been the plan. It probably would have only delayed the inevitable, because once the thought is in people's heads about age, it's just a matter of time before the decision is going to be made. With the doctrine of a complete new look for the product, changing the announcers in an easy cosmetic change.

With Destination America only available in the U.S., TNA now has to try and find a Canadian carrier. Dixie Carter on Twitter said they were negotiating for a new Canadian television outlet. Spike was available on cable in Canada.

While talent was expected to hear about the next taping date in December, nobody has heard anything and it's pretty much impossible at this late stage with no TV to promote a mid-December show as was planned. Right now I see late December as a rush job and early January being more likely. But no talent at this point has been given any future dates.

The 473,000 figure listed last week for the most-watched show on Destination America isn't correct as an episode of "Buying Alaska" two weeks ago did 535,000 viewers. The station averaged 214,000 viewers in a few weeks ago, which was its best week ever, but they are usually closer to 100,000 viewers most weeks in prime time and their biggest shows usually do closer to 200,000.

DECEMBER 15

Dixie Carter has been doing interviews talking about the move to Destination America, making it look like they were the ones wanting out of the deal, with the idea Spike wasn't going to give them more than two hours a week while Destination America will give them more air time with a replay and specials. She still praised Vince Russo, saying, "I'm a big Vince Russo fan. I think he's very talented. I think he gets a bad rap, but I feel like the way everything played itself out, when I'm negotiating a business deal and it's private, you have to keep certain things confidential, whether it's a new signing, or how your creative is going. All things are critical to the right element, and things were getting out concerning his involvement, and it was becoming a distraction. I think he's incredibly talented. I really do. But its like when you have a football player on your team, and that player is getting a certain amount of attention and distraction, he may be a very good player but you've got to ask yourself if it's the right thing for where you're at right now, and if you're trying to create a certain kind of locker room of peace, we were right in the middle of very important stuff, and we didn't need that. I'm a fan, but it wasn't the time to take it to another level. Vince has worked with us three different times and the one thing I've learned in wrestling is that you never say never and I'll never say never on Vince (coming back)." Don't ask me to explain any of that. A number of people were really surprised Carter would say that about Russo, particularly given the circumstances of his being gone, as Russo was told by Carter not to do Jim Ross' podcast, he didn't listen and did it anyway, and then John Gaburick fired him over that and the fact the way he handled the screwed up e-mail he accidentally sent to Mike Johnson (that he was supposed to send to Mike Tenay) by acting like he worked Johnson, not to mention that being one of the straws that broke the camel's back with Spike TV.

She said the goal for next year was to be unique and different and change things up.

Regarding the idea that WWE doesn't see TNA as competition, Carter said, "Well, I think it's ridiculous to say we're not competition. If we weren't competition, they wouldn't try to stop our growth at every turn. We're both wrestling companies and so competing for the same networks internationally and the same ticket sales globally and therefore you are competitors, but all we can do is focus on what we do best." Boy is that last sentence the opening for an easy joke. That said, WWE wouldn't need non-competes if TNA wasn't competition. They just aren't very strong competition.

DECEMBER 22

Destination America has decided in its infinite wisdom to move TNA to a Friday from 9-11 p.m. time slot. Given that Smackdown lost 20% of its audience moving to Friday and never got it back, it shows almost an incredible lack of understanding of wrestling history to make this move. For all the talk of Destination America wanting TNA as its flagship show, you don't put your flagship show on one of the two lowest viewing nights of the week. TNA will get a big push with a 12-hour marathon leading to the final Wednesday show on 1/7. The show is billed as being live, but will actually be on a two-hour delay, being taped at 7 p.m., but airing from 9-11 p.m. that night. Bobby Roode vs. Bobby Lashley for the TNA title will headline. The other names promoted for the debut show are Kurt Angle, Gail Kim, Jeff Hardy and Ethan Carter III. One would also expect a James Storm & Abyss vs. Hardy Boys match on the first set of tapings, since the Hardys won the tournament for a title shot in one of the last episodes on Spike. The move to Friday, from 9-11 p.m., comes in week two. The show will go head-to-head with Bellator, Glory and whatever other products Spike is offering as Spike's idea is weekly Friday night combat sports from a variety of promotions in that slot. It also goes head-to-head with New Japan on AXS as well. They will also replay the show immediately, from 11 p.m. to 1 a.m., and have a third show on Saturday morning airing from 10 a.m. to Noon (which is 7 a.m. on the West Coast). The Saturday show will be called "Impact Wrestling: Unlocked." It'll have the same matches as the Friday show, but some of the interview segments will be removed and there will be a feature segment where Mike Tenay does investigative stories. Tenay will be back to being "The Professor," and as noted before, will no longer be the lead announcer on Impact, with Josh Matthews in the spot. TNA wanted to keep Tenay. There will be backstage segments, personality profiles, as well as the top five ratings each week. The only thing we know is that Destination America made the decision to go with the Friday time slot and the Saturday morning for the replay show. There may be a second airing of Unlocked version of the show as well. Those in TNA were expecting the first-run Impact to remain on Wednesday. The only thing I can perhaps give as an explanation is that maybe they felt that there were two to three million wrestling fans used to watching wrestling on Friday nights, and, suddenly that's open with Smackdown moving to Thursday.

CHAPTER FIFTEEN

THE DEATH OF MABEL

FEBRUARY 24

Nelson Frazier Jr., a mammoth-sized man who wrestled around the world under names like King Mabel, King V, Big Daddy V, Big Daddy Voodoo, Big Vis and Viscera, passed away on 2/18 from a massive heart attack while in the shower, just four days after his 43rd birthday.

Both Frazier's agent, Eric Simms, and his early tag team partner Bobby Horne (Mo from Men on a Mission), confirmed the death late that evening. Reportedly, Frazier's wife, Cassandra Frazier, called up both Simms, and Frazier's close friend Chris Mordetzsky (Masters) that evening.

"Nelson was the most genuine guy I've ever met since entering this crazy business," wrote Mordetzsky.

At 6-foot-7, and at times as much at 500 pounds, Frazier Jr. was one of the largest pro wrestlers of the 90s. Born in Memphis, he broke into wrestling with Horne as The Harlem Knights, Nelson and Bobby, first working for George South's Pro Wrestling Federation in the Carolinas in 1992, and then moving to the USWA in 1993, Largely due to Frazier's size, the team was signed quickly by the WWF, and brought in as babyfaces Men on a Mission, with manager Oscar.

The team mostly did a dancing gimmick as undercard wrestlers with their rapping manager. They had a brief run as WWF tag team champions, beating The Quebecers (Jacques Rougeau Jr. & Carl "Pierre" Ouellet) on April 29, 1994 at a house show in London, England, before losing the titles back two days later in Sheffield, England.

In 1995, the team went heel, turning on their manager. It was the beginning of the end for Horne, since Frazier was clearly the star of the team. Frazier captured the King of the Ring tournament on June 25, 1995, at the Spectrum in Philadelphia in what was, up to that point in time, among the worst PPV shows the company ever put on. Mabel was given the tournament with wins over The Undertaker and Savio Vega, and christened King Mabel, as a way to get him ready for a championship program with Diesel (Kevin Nash), with the feeling with the size of the champion, a huge heel would make a good opponent.

The title match headlined SummerSlam, held on August 27, 1995, at the Pittsburgh Civic Arena, with Diesel retaining the title. That show, at the age of 24, would have been likely the highlight of his career.

He moved on to feud with Undertaker, which included legitimately fracturing Undertaker's orbital bone. The injury left Frazier with a reputation at the time for sloppiness, as he had hurt other wrestlers as well, so after

Undertaker, wearing a protective mask, defeated King Mabel in a casket match, he wasn't long for the promotion.

For the next two-and-a-half years he worked a number of territories, including having a short run as WWC Universal champion in a feud with Carlos Colon, and feuding with Jerry Lawler in the dying days of the USWA promotion, and made guest appearances in ECW and WWF, before returning full-time to the WWF in 1999 as Viscera, with white contact lenses and a bleached blond Mohawk. His biggest program was with Mark Henry, after giving a big splash to Mae Young, before being led go in August of 2000.

He wrestled sparingly the next few years, including two appearances when TNA was doing weekly Wednesday night PPV shows in 2003.

He returned to WWE in 2004 for another feud with Undertaker, a program that was quickly dropped. He was going nowhere until transferred into the Love Machine, Viscera, in an angle where he was in love with ring announcer Lilian Garcia. The angle ended when Garcia fell for him and proposed, only for Viscera to blow her off when The Godfather returned with ho's.

In 2007, he was moved to ECW, given the name Big Daddy V, a monster heel managed by Matt Striker. He even participated in an Elimination Chamber match in 2008, but was moved to Smackdown, and then never used for five months before being released in the summer.

He had done a few matches in Japan between WWF stints, but got a regular gig with All Japan Pro Wrestling in 2010 and 2011 as Big Daddy Voodoo, as part of the Voodoo Murderers heel group.

MARCH 3

Regarding the death of Nelson Frazier Jr. on 2/18, his wife, Cassandra, told TMZ that Frazier had lost 100 pounds over the past year, most in the last six months, which was why his suffering a massive heart attack was a surprise. Last year, he had been warned by doctors about his weight and high blood pressure. He was already suffering from diabetes and the blood pressure was making it worse. She said he had removed all salt and sugar from his diet, and that his blood pressure had dropped to where it was at a healthy level. The sad news is that he had no life insurance when he died and his original tag team partner, Bobby Horne, was trying to raise money for a funeral. It's always sad to hear that. Frazier Jr. didn't have that many years of making big money. He was on top in the mid-90s and would have made decent money, but that was the worst time in the industry. He should have had some decent money years in the Viscera run, but the Big Daddy V period in ECW was a time when a lot of the guys on that brand really weren't doing too well once you figure out expenses. And he had a lot of years in between at a time where he wasn't in places that would have paid consistently well. One good thing WWE is doing in Orlando are the financial planning seminars and pushing people to stay up on their taxes, don't acquire too much debt, and they really should push that if you are married and have a family, to take out life insurance. Things thankfully haven't been as bad in recent years, but pro wrestling is still a high-risk profession.

MARCH 10

There was some negativity toward WWE not acknowledging Nelson Frazier Jr's death on television on either the 2/21 Smackdown or the 2/24 Raw show, but they did have a graphic on the 2/28 Smackdown, especially since TNA got one up on 2/20.

Cassandra Frazier, Nelson's widow, was furious at WWE, likely for not even mentioning his name on the air or doing a graphic, but since apologized, citing the stress of the week. "I lost my best friend and the only man I ever loved, and I was very angry," she wrote. "Please forgive me and also to your fans, he was a good man, and he loved Vince, Stephanie and Triple H."

OCTOBER 20

Cassandra Frazier, the widow of the late Nelson Frazier (Mabel/Big Daddy V/Viscera) complained in an Examiner.com article that his longtime tag team partner Bobby Horne (Mo) had given her less than $100 from all of his fund raising efforts. Frazier passed away in February from a massive heart attack and had no insurance. His money was tight as he hadn't been working since he broke his arm a few weeks before his death, and the family didn't even have enough money to pay for a funeral. Horne had started fund raising. "I initially thought no one cared, no one remembered Nelson," Cassandra Frazier said. "I thought, `How can these people be so cruel, but then I found out they did care, and so many tried, to help, but I never received a dime that was sent to Bobby." She also said that Horne had told people the money he raised paid for Nelson Frazier's funeral, but she said that wasn't true. "If he paid for Nelson to be cremated and for his urn, then why did I have to sell almost everything in our house? I have almost nothing left. I have had to move so many times since Nelson passed, and you know if I would have gotten anything at all from Bobby, I might have been okay." She also said the only money she made from a Nelson Frazier benefit show was the money she made selling his photos. Horne said the money he raised went for the service, but Cassandra Frazier said the church where the service was held did the service for free, and she paid for the food at the service. "He's a liar, plain and simple," she said. "He was always asking people for money for his kidney transplant and his dialysis on Facebook, but hardly at all since Nelson died. He spent all that money on himself and his dialysis. He's a scumbag and I will tell that to his face." She also said she would take a lie detector test on her statements and asks if he would do the same. "Nelson didn't even like him. He didn't trust him. He didn't want him over the house, so why did I believe him when he said he would help me? I don't know."

Oscar, who managed Horne & Frazier early on in their WWE run, backed Horne, saying in an interview with Under the Mat radio that he was in constant communication with Cassandra Frazier, and said she was lying, saying Horne was broke before and is still broke. He said that once Horne asked people for donations, he got so much negativity that he shut it down and went on Facebook and said he was having trouble. He said Nelson Frazier had a few close friends who did donate, and Horne had proof he sent her the money.

CHAPTER SIXTEEN

BUCK ZUMHOFE CONVICTED

MARCH 17

Former 80s AWA star Eugene Otto Zumhofe (Buck "Rock'n'Roll" Zumhofe) was convicted on 3/5 in a Minnesota court, of one of the most heinous series of crimes in modern wrestling history.

Zumhofe was convicted on six counts of first degree sexual conduct and six counts of third degree sexual conduct, all involving his daughter starting from when she was 15. The convictions could put the 62-year-old former wrestler away for the rest of his natural life.

Zumhofe also now faces a 13th count of attempting to escape from custody was added after he attempted to flee after the verdict was read. Zumhofe reportedly attempted to run from the courthouse, but was tackled by security officers. He will be held without bond, pending sentencing, which is scheduled for 5/7.

Judge David Mennis heard arguments the next day from prosecutors attempting to garner a lengthy sentence, one that would put him away for the rest of his life. Kandiyohi County (Minnesota) Attorney Shane Baker said that there are factors which could double prison time, plus the judge can sentence him to consecutive terms for each individual charge. The prosecution brought up the particular cruelty of the sexual abuse as well as his pattern as a sex offender with underaged girls, including convictions of sex crimes in both 1986 and 1989, while he was working for the AWA.

The maximum penalty under normal circumstances for a first degree sexual conduct charge is 30 years in prison and a $40,000 fine.

Zumhofe's daughter testified against him, but Zumhofe in his testimony, denied all charges. His daughter also testified after the verdict, answering questions from Nathan Midolo, an assistant county attorney who was the prosecutor. She said that she wanted to remain a virgin for marriage and talked about injuries caused by Zumhofe's frequent sexual contact with her.

The daughter, now 29, was born on May 6, 1984, a date that Zumhofe, was wrestling on one of the biggest wrestling shows of the era, at Texas Stadium, the night of Kerry Von Erich's NWA championship win over Ric Flair. On that show, Zumhofe teamed with Iceman King Parsons, billed as the Rock & Soul Express, to win the American tag team titles from the masked Super Destroyers (brothers Scott & Bill Irwin).

The daughter had testified of sexual abuse starting in May 1999, just after her 15th birthday, until June 2011, when, at the age of 27, she stopped it. She estimated there were 1,800 separate acts of sexual abuse during the time period, including a time where she believed she was possibly impregnated by her father.

She testified that Zumhofe had sex with the victim's mother in Minnesota in 1983 when he was working for the AWA, in what was described as a one-night-stand. There was a paternity test after her birth to establish him as the father. Zumhofe had never met his daughter until 1998, when he contacted her at school when she was 13, and expressed a desire to meet her. She spent her spring break in 1993 at Zumhofe's home in Kandiyohi County.

A year later, she claimed Zumhofe contacted her again, saying he wanted to reunite with her family, both her and her mother. In April, he gave her a two-piece bathing suit on her 15th birthday, and encouraged her to sunbathe with it on and insisted on rubbing baby oil on her, including under her swimsuit bottom, claiming he wanted to make sure she didn't get funny tan lines.

She moved in with Zumhofe in June 1999, and her mother was to move in a few weeks later. She testified that the first night she was at the house this time, Zumhofe began touching her breasts, and took off her clothes and began touching her in intimate places. She claimed that within two weeks, it had escalated to oral sex and he also taught her to masturbate him, as well as asked her to dance in front of him in her underwear and watch pornography with her.

She claimed that escalated into intercourse within two weeks. The charges against Zumhofe were only related to the period between July 1, 1999, the date she claimed they first had sex, and May 5, 2001, the day before her 17th birthday. She claimed Zumhofe wanted to have sex with her two or three times daily, injuring her and never giving her time to heal. She claimed early on, it took eight weeks for the bleeding to stop because of the non-stop sexual abuse.

The victim's mother moved in, but upon finding out about the abuse, she moved out in September 1999 and wanted to take her daughter with her, call law enforcement officers and leave the state. She claimed that she stayed with her father because he threatened to kill himself.

She claimed for years, he continued to have sex with her multiple times a day in the early years, and two to three times a week in later years.

Starting in 2000, she was part of Zumhofe's independent pro wrestling troupe, called "Buck Zumhofe's Rock & Roll Wrestling," which ran shows in Minnesota, North and South Dakota, Iowa, Wisconsin and Illinois playing upon the fame he had from the AWA.

At the time of Zumhofe's arrest, Kandiyohi County attorney Jennifer Fischer noted to us that she was astounded that so many people within wrestling could see what was happening and that nobody ever came forward. One person from the promotion testified in the trial and sided with Zumhofe, and was bitterly attacked by those who supported the daughter that they would do such a thing.

She said during that period she was afraid to say anything for fear of reprisals from those in wrestling.

Another woman came forward, saying that in 2001, when she was 17 and his daughter was 15, and they were living in Cyrus, MN, said that Zumhofe wanted a threesome with her and his daughter and that she had witnessed Zumhofe inappropriately touching his daughter when she turned down the offer.

Other witnesses told authorities they had seen Zumhofe both french kissing his daughter and dirty dancing with her at a New London/Spice High School dance. Several witnesses told prosecutors that they knew Zumhofe shared a bed with his daughter.

The victim was married and moved away in June, 2011, and said Zumhofe became violent, threatening both her and her new husband, as well as once again threatening suicide.

Zumhofe spent 36 months at Stillwater Prison in Stillwater, MN, after being convicted on January 23, 1989, of fourth degree sexual assault with an unrelated underage girl. He was AWA light heavyweight champion when he was sent to prison, a championship Verne Gagne essentially created for him, since he was a very popular undercard wrestler, but considered too small to be a main eventer. He also had a 1999 conviction for violating a domestic violence order for protection in Kandiyohi County involving a previous girlfriend that he broke up with just before he talked his daughter into moving in with him. He had another conviction and served time in 1986.

During the 90s, he worked as a television enhancement talent for WWE, including losing matches to Undertaker and HHH.

Zumhofe was originally trained by Gagne, Billy Robinson and Khosrow Vaziri (The Iron Sheik) at Gagne's 1975 camp. The camp had a reputation for being physically brutal, with many top athletes not able to get through it without quitting. But it also had an incredible track record for success from those who did survive. Only four men were able to complete the camp, Zumhofe, Richard Blood (Ricky Steamboat), Jan Nelson (who only had a short career as a pro wrestler) and Scott Irwin.

He was sent on the road, working as a prelim wrestler for Roy Shire in Northern California, Don Owen in the Pacific Northwest, and Al Tomko in British Columbia.

His fame came in the AWA, when he wore a white jumpsuit and carried a big boom box to the ring. While he was supposed to be a modern character, the boom box usually played songs from when Gagne was younger from the likes of Elvis Presley and Chuck Berry. He was the second AWA wrestler to come out to entrance music (The Crusher, coming out to the Beer Barrel Polka, was the first).

It was really telling about the differences in times and the wrestling culture that Zumhofe, who was never a major headliner, continued to work regularly in the business after arrests and convictions. He was, at best, a popular prelim wrestler with better name recognition in his territory than almost any prelim wrestler in the early 80s. When the AWA starting coming to San Francisco and Oakland in 1981, even though Zumhofe almost always worked the first or second match and wasn't a good promo, and was okay as a wrestler but hardly a standout, the gimmick and name Rock'n'Roll Zumhofe had tremendous name recognition.

Early in the run, when getting off the plane, Verne Gagne would tell a story about how he was the AWA world champion and be going through the airport and girls would run past him and mob Zumhofe like he was a rock star. In that era, Zumhofe worked a seemingly endless program with Bobby Heenan, and they often had the best or second best matches on the shows. Every few years, Heenan, and after he left other heels, would break his boom box and he'd be out for revenge. Later, when he was perennial AWA world light heavyweight champion, they would do the gimmick where Heenan missed weight and would then beat him, but fail to get the title, setting up rematches.

The reality is that during the territorial era, sex with underage girls in different cities hit regularly was a staple of the pro wrestling environment. It was considered one of pro wrestling's fringe benefits that made up for the often bad pay. Part of the job of virtually any promotion of the era was cleaning up the mess if somehow the girls came forward, or their parents found out, which has continued even in the modern era. Still, Zumhofe, with his daughter, was a completely different level of deviant behavior.

MAY 19

Eugene "Buck" Zumhofe, 63, the 80s AWA star, was sentenced to 310 months in prison (25 years and ten months) on two first degree and two third degree counts of criminal sexual misconduct regarding his daughter between the ages of 15 and 17. He was sentenced to 115 months and 91 months for the first degree charges and 52 months individually for eacfh third degree charge, and the judge ordered the terms to be served consecutively. He was also sentenced to an additional ten years of conditional release, pay $200 in fines and register as a predatory sex offender. Zumhofe was convicted of the charges on 3/5, and attempted to flee from custody, while in the court house, but was tackled by security guards. Zumhofe now faces a charge of escape, which, under Minnesota law, could get him up to another five years in prison. The law requires any such sentence for escape to be served consecutive to his existing sentences, meaning whatever time he has to serve on that charge won't start until his sex crimes sentences end, either by early parole or after completing his 310 months. Assistant Kandiyohi County Attorney Aaron Welch asked Judge David Mennis to double the sentence to 620 months based on cruelty and the multiple forms of sexual contact with his daughter, noting that Zumhofe has shown no remorse for his actions, even after finally admitting (in a pre-sentence investigation) that they happened. Zumhofe's attorney, Carter Greiner, argued that Zumhofe should serve some prison time, but said he wants to submit to treatment and get help. Mennis turned down both requests regarding sentencing, but Zumhofe will be required to attend some form of sex offender therapy while incarcerated. The Kandiyohi County attorney's office wanted a sentence where essentially it would be a life term with no shot at parole. Zumhofe would be eligible for his first parole hearing at the age of 80, but even if he gets it, he would still have to start serving his term based on the escape charge.

CHAPTER SEVENTEEN

WrestleMania Matches that Almost Happened

The WWE web site this week had an article on ten WrestleMania matches that almost happened. Rather than go through all of them, I just wanted to give some thoughts on the ones I knew about.

WrestleMania 18 - Steve Austin vs. Hulk Hogan

"He was open to having a match, me not so much," Austin said on Jim Ross' podcast recently. "I thought the styles would clash. I didn't think it would be that great of a match."

"I guarantee you, if my head had been at a little different place, then by all rights a (match) should have happened. Physically and mentally where I was at, I could go. I think Hogan would have been a step or two behind that. That wasn't acceptable to me, and I didn't want to slow myself down. I say that with all due respect to Hulk Hogan, because he had a hellacious run. That was my thought process back in the day."

Austin instead wrestled Scott Hall in a forgettable match. The show ended up being stolen by Hogan, in his first WrestleMania match in nine years, working with The Rock in what was the main event, although not positioned as such.

When the deal was made to bring Hogan back, the idea was for Hogan against either Rock or Austin. There ended up being little discussion since Austin made it clear he didn't want the match, and Rock did.

A lot of things could have happened from there. The Toronto crowd wasn't going to boo Hogan, the heel, no matter what, and it wouldn't have mattered who the opponent was. With Rock, it wasn't much of an issue, and he even did another pseudo heel run a little down the line. It was a heel run, but he was always doing a wink about it. Austin had already done a heel run the year before, which was a huge mistake, in the sense he was never as popular as he was before the turn. History probably worked out better the way it did for all concerned. The crowd would have reacted to Hogan vs. Austin in a gigantic manner. They'd have reacted big that night to Hogan vs. anyone.

Austin felt at the time that Hogan couldn't work up to the level he was accustomed to and didn't want a bad match at WrestleMania. As it turned out, on that night, in that city, people were going to think Hogan's match was great no matter what the actual content was.

The match could have happened the next year, but that show was built around Hogan vs. Vince McMahon.

Austin's retirement match (which was kept a secret until after match time) was on the show against Rock, and he's never come back since.

WrestleMania 13 - Vader vs. Mankind
This was noted in Mick Foley's book, and there was a plan for this match at that show. The idea was to build around Vader as being the one who cost Foley his ear. I remember knowing that in advance, and there had been teases on television of that direction. It ended up being Mankind & Vader vs. Owen Hart & Davey Boy Smith.

Foley felt they intentionally nixed it, saying, "I think it was intentional, because I think the idea that me cutting an emotional interview about the loss of my ear would have overshadowed what was supposed to be on the top of the card."

I can't speak of a reason why, just know that there was a period leading up to the show that it was the direction, and plans changed to a match that had nowhere near the same level of potential interest.

WrestleMania 16: Kane vs. X-Pac
Sean Waltman said that he had an idea to do an explosive barbed wire match with Kane at the show in 2000, a match that had been made famous in Japan by Atsushi Onita in the 90s. He said that they tested out the idea one day of using explosives, and the idea was then nixed. Instead, the two ended up in a tag match with Kane & Rikishi vs. X-Pac & Road Dogg.

WrestleMania 19: John Cena vs. Jay Z & Fabulous in a Battle Rap
Yeah, that was made clear when John Cena did a rap at the show with a cardboard cutout of Fabulous. Jay Z was at first scheduled but then pulled out. They got Fabulous to rap with Cena as a sub, but he pulled out on the day of the show. Cena said Fabulous chose to take another booking at the last minute, which upset WWE to no end, so they buried him on the air.

WrestleMania 28: Big Show vs. Shaquille O'Neal
The WWE story noted that O'Neal said several times that he was going to face Show at Mania that year. What I can say about that is every time O'Neal said it, I heard from WWE that it simply wasn't true. And in the end, it didn't happen. So that's not really an almost happened. I don't know exactly what it was, to this day, whether O'Neal was just making it up, or whether negotiations fell apart over money. That is the type of specialty match Mania was built on, but given that they were paying big money for The Rock, once they locked him in, maybe the feeling was they were going to do record business and another high-priced outsider would have been overkill. Show instead wrestled Cody Rhodes that night for the IC title.

WrestleMania 12: Razor Ramon vs. Goldust in a Miami street fight
Dustin Runnels brought it up, that it was originally planned for the 1996 show and never happened. Runnels said the next day Scott Hall went to WCW, although that timing isn't correct, as he went about two months later and even worked the PPV after Mania. Both Hall and Kevin Nash had given notice long before the show. Hall actually opted out of the program as he didn't want to job on the way out to a guy who he thought was playing a somewhat gay character. So instead of giving him a new opponent, they pulled him from the card and finished him up by losing to Vader at the next month's In Your House show. Roddy Piper was contacted to do the show and while not filmed in Miami, they did a taped street fight edited into the show, as well as a live finish.

WrestleMania 17: Mike Tyson vs. HHH boxing match
HHH told the story about how such a match was talked about, but fell apart over money with Tyson with Mills Lane and Earl Hebner as referees (Mills Lane did referee at a WrestleMania a few years earlier). The bout never got into any kind of serious talks. What did happen as far as WrestleMania 17 went, is that HHH was first going to wrestle Michaels, but that fell apart due to uncertainty about Michaels at the time before the first TV to set up

it up. I don't recall if this was the year, but HHH was scheduled for a match with Ray Lewis, and Lewis canceled the day they were supposed to shoot the angle. The only years possible would have been 2001 or 2003, so I'm pretty sure it was 2001, because 2002 was always Chris Jericho and 2003 I remember being Booker T way ahead of time.

The weird one is HHH said there was also discussion about fighting "a big Japanese guy who was the Pride champion." He didn't know his name. There was never a big Japanese guy who was Pride champion. Kazushi Sakuraba, who is a pro wrestler, was sort of Pride champion but not really since they didn't recognize a 205 pound belt until Wanderlei Silva had already beaten him. The only Pride heavyweight champions in history were Antonio Rodrigo Nogueira and Fedor Emelianenko, neither of which were Japanese. The only Japanese Pride champion was Takanori Gomi, and given the size difference, I don't see that as possible. He could have meant Kazuyuki Fujita, who was a pro wrestler trained by New Japan who was a Pride star, or Bob Sapp, but that would have been years later since Sapp didn't hit it big until the next year.

WrestleMania 8: Ric Flair vs. Hulk Hogan

According to Hogan, which of course means don't believe a word of it, he claimed they had gone to Chicago, Minneapolis and Milwaukee with Hogan vs. Flair matches and broke all the old records. He said they could have doubled the ticket prices at WrestleMania and still sold out. He said then everything changed and he never knew why.

Whether Hogan vs. Flair was scheduled for the Hoosier Dome at any point is something that only Vince McMahon would know for sure. What we do know is that Sid Eudy (Sycho Sid/Sid Vicious), who had a valid contract with WCW, was offered the WrestleMania main event against Hulk Hogan in March or April of 1991. Why WCW didn't enforce its contract or go after WWF for tampering at that time is a question nobody could answer. Jim Herd, who was running WCW at the time, confirmed to me that Eudy was leaving because he was promised the WrestleMania main event. WCW upped its offer to him and at one point it was high enough that he indicated he was staying, but then changed his mind again. Again, he already had a valid contract and they were in a wrestling war, so there is an unanswered piece of this puzzle. And then, right after WrestleMania, when WWE went to suspend Eudy for failing a steroid test (a test that was before Mania), he quit and ended up back in WCW. The agreement was made that WCW would give Eudy his release provided he put over El Gigante in a stretcher match at SuperBrawl in May of that year. So then, he refused to go out on a stretcher and they still gave him his release. They had somebody else go out on a stretcher. But the point of all this was that in April of 1991, I was fully aware that Hogan vs. Sid was the main event for the next WrestleMania. Flair didn't have his falling out with WCW and Jim Herd over contract issues until the end of June.

Flair started with WWF in September and worked all the weekend house shows with Hogan starting on October 25, 1991. They drew well, but didn't set any records the first time in the market. Flair wanted to do 25 minute matches and Hogan wanted to do his usual 10, and they compromised at 11:35, with Hogan saying that we have to save the 25 minute match for Mania. I remember being told that in September and I thought it was weird since I knew what Sid was promised.

It really wasn't promoted to its most effectiveness. The best houses were early on, before Flair had more than one or two appearances on WWE television. The reality of that program in WWF is that the more they promoted it, in ineffective manner, the weaker it was. It was a gigantic match with 14,900 fans in Oakland based on the idea of Flair vs. Hogan with no angles and just the Flair from WCW was coming. The rematch on November 15 did 5,000.

Business really got worse after the Survivor Series build. The idea of Flair standing with three WWE wrestlers in promos hurt Flair vs. Hogan because the whole draw was Hogan vs. an outsider, not Hogan vs. the WWE version of Flair. After some bad houses, notably 4,500 at the Omni in Atlanta, Vince McMahon switched the booking of main events from Hogan vs. Flair to Hogan & Roddy Piper vs. Flair & Sid Vicious starting in February. Houses went up and there was no doubt the big heat was Hogan vs. Sid, not Hogan vs. Flair. This is from someone who was not a fan of Sid Vicious.

I don't know if that had anything to do with WrestleMania. I do know that a few weeks before Hogan vs. Flair was announced, I was told the angle was that Hogan vs. Flair would be announced, but it was Hogan vs. Sid and Flair vs. Savage and Hogan vs. Flair was just a one week or so thing to set up the Hogan-Sid angle. Hogan's recollection of course wasn't true, as Milwaukee (November 2, 1991) did 7,800 fans; Minneapolis did 9,000, and they never had a match in Chicago. They did good business, below Hogan's peak levels but better than Hogan had been doing for some time. But there were no major arena sellouts.

Anyway, I know for sure in January it was Hogan vs. Sid. And it may have been that way continuously from April. As far as what Hogan knew, I don't want to speculate, and the reality is, he may not remember at this point anyway.

WrestleMania 17: Vince McMahon vs. Mick Foley

Apparently Vince McMahon offered Foley this match, but he felt it was too early to do a comeback. Foley claimed he thought that the 2000 WrestleMania match, which came shortly after losing a retirement match, was going to be his last match. I can recall conversations with him after losing the retirement match where he did figure at some point he would come back, but was adamant it not be too early, figuring it would be a few years before he would dishonor the stipulation. He felt bad enough about doing the Mania match after he had vowed to everyone on TV that he wasn't doing a fake retirement like everybody else and coming back in two months. It also shows Vince McMahon's mind change. When Foley lost his retirement match, McMahon was calling him for a WrestleMania main event weeks later. When Ric Flair lost his, McMahon was adamant about him never wrestling again, to the point people in the company were upset he worked a tour in Australia even before doing matches with TNA. In all WWE stories to this day, they disregard history and state Flair's final match was against Shawn Michaels.

By 2004, when he did come back and have one of the best matches of his career against Randy Orton (a match Orton still considers his best match), it had been long enough and few complained he dishonored the stipulation.

He instead was a referee in the Vince McMahon vs. Shane McMahon match. The WWE.com story had Foley quoted as it being one of his three biggest regrets of his career not doing that match. The others were not attending the first Eddie Gilbert Memorial Show; and not writing the foreword to Lou Thesz's autobiography when asked. I guess that makes us related. Lou Thesz originally asked me to write his autobiography. At the time, with my schedule, it just wasn't possible. I actually set Thesz up with Kit Bauman, a reporter I knew from Texas, who I knew would do a great job with it and it turned out well, and the two became great friends.

CHAPTER EIGHTEEN

THE END OF
THE STREAK

APRIL 7

Virtually everyone involved in the Undertaker/Lesnar scenario believed that Lesnar should have been booked differently and more of a threat to Undertaker, since the only point Lesnar did anything was the go-home angle and that was still a sneak up from behind distraction with the announcers calling Lesnar a coward. In the original deal when this was first talked about in 2010, Undertaker had actually proposed that Lesnar beat him to end the streak (it was never seriously considered) thinking it would be the right thing for business, but that's years ago. Vince McMahon made the decision that in the build to this match that Undertaker never gets touched, although he was smart enough to read the tea leaves and change for the final week. It's funny how it seems that worked confrontation in front of Ariel Helwani in 2010 caused more talk than a month of buildup of TV shows drawing in excess of four million viewers when they have 100% carte blanche with no limits to script things for maximum build. In commentary, they've done nothing to establish Lesnar as a threat on the level of HHH or Michaels in years past, and its' not like they needed two physical confrontations where Undertaker got the better of him in seconds and made him seem like no threat going into the final week. Paul Heyman, when restrictions aren't as high, in media interviews, has pushed that Lesnar and Undertaker had three prior PPV matches and that Undertaker never won any of them (Lesnar won two, the other Lesnar was supposed to win but Undertaker refused to do a job that night, which wasn't necessarily the wrong move since it did build to a bigger rematch than trying to come back after a pin would have done and Undertaker did put him over in the Hell in a Cell rematch). Obviously he was not allowed to go in that direction on television.

APRIL 14

The big story at WrestleMania 30, as far as almost everyone knew as the show was going on, was the coronation on the big stage of Daniel Bryan as a somewhat unlikely WWE champion, in the sense when the plans for WrestleMania were put together late last year, nothing of the sort was supposed to happen. That did happen, but it wasn't the big story.

A crowd of around 70,000 at the Mercedes Benz Superdome, and the millions watching around the world were watching the closing moments on what really was a poor wrestling match that was getting little reaction, even though it was supposed to be a highlight event on the show.

The crowd was so cold, maybe because the match wasn't good, maybe because everyone knew the outcome, that when Brock Lesnar hit his first F-5, and The Undertaker kicked out, there was no reaction. Even when he did it a second time, there was very little reaction.

Then he did it a third time. Referee Chad Patton, who knew the same finish that everybody else thought they knew, hit the mat once, and then twice, and then didn't know what to do.

He was told Undertaker was winning, but the rule every referee is told is that if the guys doesn't kick out, you continue the count.

Undertaker wasn't kicking out. There was slight hesitation, which is why people were confused. Because he was confused. But he did his job.

It was at that point that time stood still, while Lesnar whispered in Undertaker's ear, "Thank you."

It was once in a lifetime. At least for this streak.

The most obvious pro wrestling comparison was January 18, 1971, at Madison Square Garden. Bruno Sammartino had been WWWF champion since May 17, 1963. There have been world title reigns as long, but it wasn't the same thing. Lou Thesz had people believing he was the greatest wrestler in the world. Perhaps some thought the same of Verne Gagne. But neither was Superman. Dory Funk Jr. drew for years based on the idea that he was beatable. So did Nick Bockwinkel. Perhaps Rikidozan losing to The Destroyer in 1963 had that effect, because he was a national hero that had never lost in Japan, but fans knew he could lose. He himself said that he could never beat Karl Gotch.

Bruno was mortal, but he was also Superman, and he connected in a way that few wrestlers ever had. He had lost matches via DQ, count out, blood stoppages, but he had never been pinned cleanly. Ivan Koloff went to the top rope that night and dropped a knee on his chest. The referee counted three. The place went quiet. Then women started crying.

Nobody knew it was happening. In real life, Sammartino was beaten up and tired of the never ending schedule and just wanted to rest. He asked out. In doing so, he took a young French Canadian who idolized him, and made him one of the three biggest heels in pro wrestling for nearly another decade.

I was live and saw Fedor's winning streak end in San Jose, and Anderson Silva's end in Las Vegas. Time absolutely stood still in the former. It wasn't that many seconds that Fabricio Werdum had Fedor in the triangle. The clock claims the fight only went 69 seconds. I could swear he was in the triangle for minutes because time stood still. And then he tapped. The place went bananas. That was a 28 fight unbeaten streak lasting nine years, and every one of those wins were not scripted.

Anderson Silva went 16-0 against tougher competition and was the greatest of all-time. Unlike Lesnar, and unlike Werdum, and certainly unlike Koloff, we all recognized that Chris Weidman had a chance to win that night. But the way it happened threw everyone for a loop. Time didn't stand still there at all. It was as in the time of a blink of the eye, a split second at most, to comprehend that the guy acting like he was wobbly to taunt the other guy and making fun that he couldn't touch him, actually was knocked him out. The place went crazy.

He went seven years unbeaten in the UFC, and nobody scripted those outcomes either.

There are conflicting reports and messages on how many people knew what was going to happen when Undertaker got in the ring, possibly for the last time.

It was reported here that a few years back, when Undertaker and Lesnar first talked about doing the angle for this match at WrestleMania 27, that Undertaker had said he would want to put Lesnar over. That was likely to build for a rematch. It wasn't set in stone. With knowledge of that, which we reported during the build-up, many figured it was Undertaker who made the call. That was not the case.

From the day the match was announced, until 3/31, at least, the finish everyone thought would happen was what was going to happen.

What happened after that was fuzzy. Only a few people knew before Sunday. If the ref himself wasn't told before the match, that tells you it was probably Vince McMahon, who made the call, Undertaker, who had to agree, Lesnar who had to know in advance, and Paul Heyman. I would presume Stephanie McMahon and HHH knew, but it ended with that. None of the agents knew. The actual script for the show did not have a finish listed, but for this show, that wasn't unusual, nor was it the only match like that, so there were no red flags.

Still, two major betting sites, had a late shift of money on Lesnar, so much that he went from a ridiculous 50-to-1 underdog, to an actual favorite.

As noted last week, McMahon had decreed that Undertaker would not get touched during the buildup. But the build to the match was weak and on the go-home show, Lesnar did leave Undertaker laying with an F-5.

With the benefit of hindsight, it wasn't that McMahon was so protective of his star against a guy who was in some fans' mind an outsider who became a star in WWE, but a superstar and super drawing card in UFC. Given McMahon's history, that wouldn't have been a stretch to assume that. It may have been simply McMahon knew Undertaker couldn't take the punishment.

The Undertaker character could not be put down at WrestleMania. He was a cartoon superman, who somehow had made his scripted matches into legitimate reality for people around the world. They had been told that the streak was bigger than the Dolphins going 17-0, or DiMaggio hitting in 56 straight games. The streak actually started out inauspiciously. It wasn't a long term plan. Many of the early matches were bad. Others were throwaways. Wins over Jake Roberts, King Kong Bundy and Jimmy Snuka on paper may look like nostalgia, but Snuka was a TV squash match and not pushed at all, the Roberts match was bad and Bundy had nothing left. The Giant Gonzalez match was worse. The Kane matches were hardly classics. But as match quality became more important in the post 2000 era, Undertaker rose to the occasion. Matches with Batista and Edge were strong WrestleMania headline matches. In the last five years, as his physical condition worsened and he was down to really doing only a few matches a year, and only one high profile one, the streak matches have been among the best matches of the year in pro wrestling. When put on the biggest stage, they become bigger and better.

Mark Calaway is a 49 year old man whose body turned on him more than a decade ago, but when he had his nights, like WrestleMania the previous several years, he simply denied the pain and became The Undertaker. I can recall having dinner with one of WWE's biggest names, telling me how badly Calaway was hurting and that he probably only had a year or two left. That was in the early fall of 1997.

People were remarking when he came back this year how much he aged. I remember a story a few years back when the idea was brought up to him about maybe retiring at Cowboys Stadium, with the idea they'd break the Pontiac Silverdome record and he'd be the main attraction. He said he wasn't going to last that long. The last three years, it was touch-and-go if he was going to come back, particularly last year. For some reason, this year it was always known he was coming back.

I had always figured it was a given that Undertaker would go into battle one last time, win, but this time nearly die in the process. The streak would be intact, and some kind of special effects would lead to a visual of him going to heaven, and we would never see the character again. Of course, being pro wrestling, two years later they'd try to figure out a way to bring him back. And it's not like they didn't already do that special effects deal with him before, and God knows how many times they killed Paul Bearer before he really died.

Lance Storm then wrote a piece. The short version of it was something that quite frankly, should have been said five years ago. It was a promo by an aging Undertaker confronting his own mortality, telling everyone that the streak would end, and he would retire when that happened. Such a thing would make the outcomes of his matches mean something. It would make WrestleMania mean something because instead of the common assumption that the guy would never lose, everyone knew he would at some point, just not when. The near falls would be bigger. People would probably have gasped and their hearts might have skipped a beat on that first and second F-5.

You could argue ending the streak was a bad idea. Or that even if it wasn't, Brock Lesnar, a 36-year-old part-timer wasn't the guy to do it with. And it wasn't for Paul Heyman's promo on Raw the next day, I'd agree with you.

Except, there was no choice. Whether Undertaker does another match or not, Vince McMahon was going on the assumption that this was his last hurrah, and he could either win, or lose. McMahon chose the idea that it was better to lose on your way out. That is the common wrestling mentality. Whether this should have been different, who knows? Lesnar happened to be the guy booked on the day McMahon came to this conclusion. Obviously, if Undertaker had told him that he was coming back next year, or argued, it may not have happened.

One person close to the situation said McMahon talked Undertaker into doing it. Another, who would also know, described it as McMahon making the call and Undertaker agreeing and that he wasn't talked into doing something he didn't want to do. It was not his original call, but he was in on it and never protested the call. And perhaps, like he thought in late 2010, if he was going to lose, maybe he thought this was the guy.

When it happened, fans were upset, but luckily they had the Daniel Bryan title win, which was really what everyone came to see since they all assumed Undertaker was winning and didn't care that much about the match. If it wasn't for that storyline, people would have probably been a lot more negative about the show. But they got a great show, and in the end, they saw two pieces of history in the same night.

At some point in the match, Mark Calaway suffered a severe concussion. The match wasn't very heated, and it was worse because he went blank and was having to be led through. Nobody knows the exact spot, because when it was over, Calaway didn't remember, or have any memory of most of the match. But he did know enough to not kick out at the key time.

At first, the announcers didn't know what to do. The graphic wasn't ready right away, nor was the music ready. The delay made fans think that maybe it was a mistake. The announcers were then given the cue by McMahon to talk about him as if this was the legendary gunfighter's last fight, and talk of it like we've seen Undertaker for the final time.

The spot he got hurt in may have been when Lesnar used a high single leg takedown outside the ring and Undertaker fell backwards on the floor, hitting the back of his head. But that's just speculation. The only thing for sure is it happened.

He also knew enough to stand there, and wait for the emotional outburst of the audience and the big standing ovation for the years of entertainment. Even if they didn't know that this was his last performance, and again, it's pro wrestling and it may not be, they knew that what he was best known for and what he will always be known for was over after 23 years.

The response was there. It wasn't what I'd have imagined. There's no way it could have been what Vince McMahon would have imagined.

Calaway legitimately was rushed to the hospital in an ambulance. Vince McMahon, even though there were two matches left in the show, including the main event, left with him to Ochshner Medical Center, where, after a CT scan, he was diagnosed with a severe concussion and kept overnight. The story that Paul Heyman told on Raw about coming close to a broken neck was just for drama, but the rest of what he said was legitimate. He was released Monday morning and was at Raw, but the decision was made not to use him. He was said to be limping bad and in rough shape.

There were many people in the company very unhappy about the call, but couldn't say so publicly. But McMahon thought, and was probably correct, that he had no more streak matches left. And he may not have really had this one left in his body. At that point, it's just a call. Do you end the storyline in a shocking way, or a predictable way? From a business standpoint, if he was never going to come back for a streak match, neither decision was better than the other.

The truth is, the story of every great streak includes the shock, awe, surprise and even sadness of when it ends. The most famous streaks in sports are most famous for the night they ended, or the match or game that ended it. And even in a scripted entertainment, this was no different.

STORY OF THE STREAK

3/24/91	Los Angeles	Undertaker b Jimmy Snuka (4:20)
4/5/92	Indianapolis	Undertaker b Jake Roberts (6:36)
4/4/93	Las Vegas	Undertaker b Giant Gonzalez via DQ (7:33)
4/2/95	Hartford	Undertaker b King Kong Bundy (6:36)
3/31/96	Anaheim	Undertaker b Diesel (16:46)

3/23/97	Chicago	Undertaker b Sycho Sid to win WWF title (21:29)
3/29/98	Boston	Undertaker b Kane (16:58)
3/28/99	Philadelphia	Undertaker b Big Bossman Hell in a Cell (9:46)
4/1/01	Houston	Undertaker b HHH (18:17)
3/17/02	Toronto	Undertaker b Ric Flair street fight (18:47)
3/30/03	Seattle	Undertaker b Big Show & A-Train (9:45)
3/14/04	MSG	Undertaker b Kane (7:45)
4/3/05	Los Angeles	Undertaker b Randy Orton (14:14)
4/2/06	Chicago	Undertaker b Mark Henry casket match (9:26)
4/1/07	Detroit	Undertaker b Batista to win world title(15:47)
3/30/08	Orlando	Undertaker b Edge to win world title (23:50)
4/5/09	Houston	Undertaker b Shawn Michaels (30:41)
3/28/10	Glendale, AZ	Undertaker b Shawn Michaels (23:59)
4/3/11	Atlanta	Undertaker b HHH No holds barred (29:22)
4/1/12	Miami	Undertaker b HHH/Hell in a Cell/Michaels ref (30:52)
4/7/13	East Rutherford, NJ	Undertaker b C.M. Punk (22:07)
4/6/14	New Orleans	Brock Lesnar b Undertaker (25:10)

APRIL 28

A major misconception, which we got into a few weeks ago, regarding the end of the streak is that it was Undertaker's call to end it. It is almost surely true that if he didn't want to have it ended, he could have put up a fight and it most likely would not have happened, so to an extent, that's true. Undertaker was scheduled to go over in the match until some point a few days before the match, when Vince McMahon changed his mind, based on Undertaker's physical condition and the feeling that there was a good chance this was his last match. At that point the decision was made. The mentality apparently was that if the streak was ever going to be broken and they were going to have that shock moment people will talk about forever, it's either now or never and he chose now. Lesnar just happened to be the opponent at the time, even though Undertaker apparently in 2010 had considered the idea of losing to Lesnar at Mania in 2011 to build for a longer program. But Lesnar in 2010, when that talk was going on, and Lesnar in 2014, are at very different cultural levels. As far as Undertaker's reaction when Vince suggested it, only he and McMahon know for sure. One friend of his said he was talked into it, but another person very close to the situation said that he didn't argue the decision.

MAY 5

The full story of the Undertaker loss will probably be public within a few weeks on a Jim Ross interview for his podcast with Michaels, which has already been taped. As reported here, the decision was one made by Vince McMahon, not Undertaker, and the result was planned for Undertaker to win until late in the game. I don't speak to everyone, but those who I do talk with say that privately, most think it was not the right call because they believe Undertaker is going to be back next year and one of the big attractions of Mania will be no more. But it's also said that nobody is about to say that publicly. It'll be interesting if Michaels does, because he's the closest thing to bullet proof outside of the family. To me, if he wasn't coming back, you had a call to make and either call was okay. If he's coming back at Mania, I'd have held off his loss until what would be agreed on would be the last match of his career. It should be noted that when Vince made the call, there were those who thought it could be his last match because of how bad his shoulder and hip was doing, and the concussion and going out in an ambulance legit doesn't help matters.

MAY 12

The Jim Ross interview with Michaels about the Undertaker's streak was notable more for what wasn't said. Michaels, who is friends with Undertaker and does know pretty much how everything went down, was so nervous, hemming and hawing and stammering when the subject was brought up, clearly not being comfortable discussing the subject and what he knew. He tried to play it down by saying he doesn't think about wrestling, let's the smart guys worry about things like that, and it wasn't his business. He did say the decision for Undertaker to lose went down about four hours before match time. I think it was a little earlier because I heard it was at 1 p.m. that afternoon when Undertaker was told by Vince that the finish was changing and nobody was supposed to know about it except for he and Lesnar and a handful of others who needed to know, but it would be correct to say the decision went down the day of the show in the afternoon. Michaels, who was watching in Gorilla, noted he was as surprised as anyone when the match ended. Vince felt it could be Undertaker's last match, and if he didn't lose now, there was no guarantee there would be another match. According to two people who know Undertaker, one said Undertaker had no real issue with it and was fine with it when Vince made the call. Another said Vince had to talk him into it, but either way the end result was the same.

JUNE 2

Undertaker is still pretty banged up from the Lesnar match. Right now there are people in the inner circle who believe Vince McMahon didn't make the decision for Undertaker to lose at the last minute, but simply waited until the last minute to let anyone know. There is still a lot of internal belief that it was the wrong call, basically I'm told that's the majority viewpoint but nobody can publicly say it, particularly since there is no indication Undertaker won't be back for next year's WrestleMania. My feeling is, if he is coming back, it was the wrong call. If he wasn't coming back, than it's probably the right call.

Mick Foley did a comedy shot in the Jacksonville area this past week. He brought up the Undertaker loss and everyone started booing. Foley then told the crowd that Lesnar was the perfect guy to beat Undertaker. The people in the crowd assumed it was because Lesnar was a former UFC champion and thus people see him as real. Foley said that wasn't it. Foley said it was because whoever beat Undertaker was going to wind up with heat on them but that wouldn't bother Lesnar because nobody cares less about what people in or out of the business think of him than Lesnar.

JUNE 9

Regarding Undertaker, when he has been asked if he's coming back for WrestleMania after the concussion from the PPV and all the other injuries he's had, he has said in the last week or two that it wasn't looking good. He is back training in the gym. I always believe he's coming back because it's usually negative until September, and then it becomes a maybe and he's been at every Mania for years.

CHAPTER NINETEEN

WWE HALL OF FAME

APRIL 14

The emotional highlight of the year, and for many long-time fans, the biggest event comes the night before WrestleMania with the WWE Hall of Fame ceremony.

The theme for this year's event at the Smoothie King Center, formerly known as the New Orleans Arena, was unpredictability.

But no matter who got the biggest pop and who your favorite induction was, the real star of the event was Diamond Dallas Page.

No, not for his speech, which was the typical induction speech where someone tries to put over how special their friend, rival, mentor, or whatever the connection is. But it was the fact that Roberts and Scott Hall were in good enough shape that WWE was willing to risk advertising them and putting them on stage.

Perhaps more than any major stars of the last few decades, Roberts and Hall were the biggest train wrecks, far beyond your classic stories of former stars that hit the bottle. Hall's health was so bad that there were times he was touch and go, and needed a pacemaker for his heart due to all the damage his excesses have caused. Roberts' troubles go back decades, including being bounced from both WWF and WCW when he was still a major attraction.

Multiple stints in rehab, paid for by WWE, didn't seem to help either guy. Page, a tireless promoter who refuses to get negative, publicly took in Roberts about 18 months ago with the idea of creating a documentary, where the end would be Roberts getting this huge pop as he came out for the 2014 Royal Rumble. It would promote DDP Yoga, credit it from taking a guy whose addictions to drugs and alcohol were well-known, and who has said he was clean, relapsed, and appeared to be beyond hope. Hall was even worse than Roberts, to the point his friends considered it hopeless as his health was failing and he was in-and-out of rehab. His story made an award winning documentary piece.

This is pro wrestling. And the real story of Page cleaning these two up is likely not as simple as Page would say. With Roberts, it's well known there have been relapses. But he did lose weight and at the Hall of Fame, like at the Cauliflower Alley Club, gave a speech that talked a great game. It's still Jake Roberts, in many ways an ultimate worker and performer, a guy who lives for manipulating emotions. Hall is certainly better than he's been. He, on the other hand, said few words, and it seemed his role was just to give fans a moment to pop with the staged reuniting of the Kliq on stage, Hall, Kevin Nash, Sean Waltman, Shawn Michaels and HHH.

The other story was the public return of The Ultimate Warrior. From being the rising star and apparent heir to the throne of Hulk Hogan in the late 90s, when wrestling was doing huge numbers on Saturday night's on NBC, there are few wrestlers of the last 30 years with his name recognition. A constant critic of Vince McMahon and of so many others, particularly those who had gone back to McMahon after problems, Warrior's return was precipitated by a video game deal put together by 2K Sports. They were looking for something special for this year's game, and virtually every star of the past had been brought back.

There is a story in and of itself in just getting Warrior, which is his real name, to sign the video game deal. And they also had to get Vince McMahon to approve it. This led to HHH, notable for calling Warrior an asshole in the "Self Destruction of the Ultimate Warrior" DVD, easily the most controversial the company ever put out, to make up with him and put this Hall of Fame deal together.

Warrior was clearly not scripted, and this night he viewed as his vindication. In a 40 minute speech, one that many thought was great, others thought was terrible, he rambled all over the place, constantly coming back to the DVD. His main point was that this company put out the single most negative DVD they ever had about a performer, but in the end, they were bringing him back to main event the Hall of Fame ceremony at the 30th WrestleMania.

The DVD has become an emotional subject, and there is an Observer issue when it came out devoted to both the fact and fiction of it. Warrior's defenders have been furious at the likes of Hulk Hogan, McMahon, Ted DiBiase, Bobby Heenan, HHH, Jim Ross or anyone else who had anything negative to say about him. What was weird is that there was accuracy in most accounts of how he was viewed. DiBiase, the guy Warrior has himself had years of negatives to say about and vice versa, gave what was the prevailing opinion of him at the time as a subpar worker who guys carried and made a star, and he didn't seem appreciative of it.

There are certain realities about Warrior. He got over instantly in an era where physiques were the most important thing about a performer. But it wouldn't be fair to say he was a physique and nothing else. Following the physical monster that was Hogan was going to be difficult, and given the mentality and direction of the business, the candidates seemed to be Warrior and Lex Luger, and perhaps Sting, who wasn't quite as big, but was a better performer and had more lasting charisma than Luger, and perhaps more importantly, was far more popular behind-the-scenes.

Warrior's popularity skyrocketed until the night McMahon picked him to beat Hulk Hogan at WrestleMania 6 and win the WWF championship at Sky Dome in Toronto in one of the more memorable pro wrestling matches ever. But he didn't click as champion, and lost the title quickly to Sgt. Slaughter. His returns were usually gigantic. And they didn't last.

The DVD ended up in a court case. What I thought was so weird about the DVD is that if they wanted to do a hit piece, and that was the goal (McMahon had targeted Bret Hart for a similar hit piece DVD, and filmed names like Hogan and others burying him, only to strike a DVD deal with Hart and do a 180 on the project that almost deified him), had they stuck to fair comments, they could have done it. But there were things in the DVD that were unfair and things portrayed, many that people now accept as fact, such as it being the day before the show that Warrior held McMahon up for money as opposed to more than a month earlier and the fact McMahon agreed in writing to his request. Others, such as gimmicking posters that never existed trying to show how he no-showed dates (and there were a few no-showed dates in 1996 on the weekend after he and McMahon had a blow-up, and the same weekend that Warrior's father passed away), made the DVD come across as a fraud itself.

The crowd of 10,000 fans was generally polite. WWE, the night before the show, had the arena e-mail all Hall of Fame ticket holders that they had e-mails for a short message:

"Please show the proper respect to the WWE Superstars and Hall of Fame inductees when they are on stage speaking. There will be no inappropriate behavior, cat calls or chants of any kind tolerated at all. Violation of this policy will result in immediate ejection from the Smoothie King Center without warning."

Part of this was in response to those in the company being embarrassed at the fan behavior, in particular, regarding Maria Menounos at last year's Hall of Fame, and to an extent, Donald Trump.

It may have been a general statement, but it also could have been fear of what could happen with Carlos Colon. I thought the odds were small of anything major happening. The crowd they get wasn't going to for the most part know about Bruiser Brody or have an attachment to him. But the Hall of Fame also has the mob mentality thing to where if something starts, it could snowball. As it was, there were people, not many, who did try and start a Brody chant, but it was barely audible and few would know what it meant.

The WWC, which Colon owns, was one of the hottest promotions in the world from the mid-70s through 1988, when booker Jose Gonzalez (who still wrestles as Invader I for the group), stabbed Brody, one of the biggest international stars in pro wrestling, in the chest and he died a few hours later in the hospital. There were witnesses in the babyface dressing room, but none testified in the trial where Gonzalez was acquitted on grounds of self defense. The knife used disappeared from the scene. It took place before the show started. The show continued and none of the wrestlers on the heel side, nor the fans, were aware of what happened. Gonzalez went home, changed out of his bloody clothes, came back, and worked his match later in the show. The Americans in the promotion went to the police, gave statements, and I believe all, if not almost all, left the island the next day.

The questions of what happened to the weapon, a knife that Gonzalez concealed under a towel that he went into the bathroom with when he called Brody (Frank Goodish) in for a discussion, were never answered.

After the incident but before the trial, Gonzalez, who was the No. 2 babyface in the promotion behind Colon for years, was portrayed as a sympathetic figure on the television. The wrestlers were told he was no longer with the promotion, but Bobby Jaggers, who worked as a television announcer, said that Gonzalez never left the promotion. After the acquittal, Gonzalez returned to the promotion and was soon booker once again.

WWC business went down after that incident, although there were comebacks. It never reached its prior level, but the reality is, that wasn't going to happen in a post-WWF expansion era, and while almost dying many times, and going through corporate reorganizations and name changes, it still exists.

There were people who blamed Colon, as the owner, given it was his booker. There were always wrestlers who would believe that the owner sent his booker to put out a hit to send a message to the dressing room, but I never bought that story. An owner would never have wanted that kind of publicity and the business was hurt by it. The reality is, it would have declined anyway once WWF was on TV, just like everywhere else, and after a few years, whatever effect there was from the incident was long gone. Chants of "murderer" at Gonzalez dissipated pretty quickly as he came back as a babyface. Today, as a heel, very few fans even know the story since it was nearly 26 years ago.

Jerry Lawler hosted the event, with almost all the WWE stars in attendance.

Warrior was clearly positioned as the main eventer. To most, it appeared they saw Roberts as the second biggest star, and he was put on early. Lita, the most current and youngest, got a good reaction as well. The reaction to Colon, the least well known to the fan base there, was polite and respectful. It was also clear that Mr. T's role and importance in the success of WrestleMania I has been forgotten in history. And his speech was something else, talking for 20 minutes about his mother, and never bringing up WrestleMania I, WrestleMania II, or his run-in during a Hulk Hogan vs. Roddy Piper match on MTV from Madison Square Garden which was the angle that set up the original WrestleMania.

As noted here before, the original WrestleMania was the most ambitious project in pro wrestling history, even more so than the Antonio Inoki vs. Muhammad Ali match in 1976 (which flopped from a business standpoint, even though Ali was probably the biggest sports star in the world at the time). If you took Mr. T, a huge television star on "The A-Team," who people believed was a real-life tough guy, and didn't have the T vs. Roddy Piper racial dynamic, it wouldn't have flown. Hulk Hogan was a big wrestling star and drawing great already, but he had no mainstream name nor was he big enough to open the doors to make the event be a major cultural event. Mr. T was more than big enough to do so, getting them on David Letterman and hosting "Saturday Night Live" the night before the show. Advances in most closed-circuit theaters were bad, and more than 65 locations were canceled a week out. Vince McMahon, running deeply in debt due to costs of expanding, gambled the promotion on a windfall here. George Scott, his booker, had a letter from Vince noting plans for George to revive the business should WrestleMania fail and the company be forced to declare bankruptcy. There's no way of knowing what would have happened had the show not succeeded, whether the company would have been forced to shut down, whether Vince would have to sell the company, or perhaps reorganize. But the show was a success, enough so that you really could trace winning the original wrestling war against the old school regional promoters, such as Jim Crockett and Verne Gagne, to that day.

It was very awkward, that in the middle of Mr. T reading a lengthy speech, that Kane's music played and he came out, to very publicly give him the hook. Mr. T later said that he was saddened the people couldn't hear the rest of his speech. He said that he was told that the fans wanted to hear their stories, and to take their time.

The show started with a video for Lita, real name Amy Dumas (pronounced Du-ma), with the other women in the audience putting her over as a pioneer for doing moves no woman before had ever done. The moonsaults and huracanranas were not done by the women in the U.S. in the previous generation, but were staples of women wrestlers internationally.

Dumas was 23 when she went to Mexico in 1998 to learn to wrestle. She had a brief run in 1999 in ECW, and was signed by WWF later that year. She remained with the company through 2006, most of that period affiliated with Matt and Jeff Hardy as Team Extreme.

TRISH STRATUS

Stratus noted the two were rivals, starting within a few weeks of each other with the company, and retiring within a few weeks as well. She noted Dumas was the godmother of her child.

"We shared many epic moments, one of the best was getting to main event Raw."

She spoke of her look, style of dress, with her thong showing, which Stratus called was "scandalous at the time," which is an exaggeration. It was different but it never garnered any type of significant negative reaction.

"She was relatable, girls saw something in Amy that they saw in themselves."

Stratus portrayed Lita's appeal as being someone you want to hang with, noted that were really tight, like peanut butter and jelly, or wrestlers and spray tans, and said she was her "bestie," and brought up her being a New York Times best selling author, and the only WWE wrestler listed in the Rolling Stone hot list.

AMY "LITA" DUMAS

The crowd chanted her name loudly. She did a 28 minute speech about her career in wrestling, which was a little on the long side. She first talked about going to Mexico to become a wrestler, knowing only the Spanish she'd learned in high school, flying to Mexico City and asking people, "Donde esta Lucha Libre," thinking it would get her to wherever she could train. She found Arena Mexico, and said she bought a ticket to a show, only to find out she went during the two weeks a year that the circus was in town (before the newer arenas were put up, they would move wrestling to Arena Coliseo at various times when major entertainment acts would book Arena Mexico). She went to Arena Coliseo. She met Ricky Santana, Miguel Perez, Dave Sierra (The Cuban Assassin) and Kevin Quinn, who were all working for CMLL at the time. She told a story about being there for a discussion between Rayo de Jalisco Jr., one of the big stars at the time, and El Steele, who later became Val Venis. She had some bags with her, and noted Rayo had left something behind and pulled out a Rayo de Jalisco Jr. mask, which most of the crowd, not familiar with the late 90s CMLL scene, didn't react to. She said her love for wrestling was due to admiring Rey Misterio Jr., who she saw as a combination rock star, athlete and super hero when she would watch WCW. Her car license plate at the time was "Rey Jr. #1." She went to see a show at the Macon Coliseum, and then found out the hotel the WCW crew was staying at to see him. She met Arn Anderson, who introduced her to Misterio Jr. She then pulled out two Miller Lite cans, one for Anderson and the other for Mysterio and she and Stratus drank a toast. She mentioned ending up in ECW, leading to an ECW chant, and on her first PPV, Heat Wave 99, got her first pro wrestling wedding proposal. Danny Doring proposed, but not with a ring, but with a condom. She mentioned her wrestling marriage to Edge and said she wore the most "sluttacular" dress in a wrestling wedding history. She mentioned the Kane wedding and that angle. She told a story about a girl, after the miscarriage angle, who had knitted her a baby blanket and she had to tell her she wasn't really pregnant. She said "Glenn" (Kane) was one of her favorite people to work with.

She then talked about suffering broken neck while filming the TV show "Dark Angel." She noted she was in such a wrestling bubble she had no idea who James Cameron (who directed Dark Angel) was or the movie

"Titanic." She said there was a stunt scene that went bad and she was dropped on her head, and was told her neck was broken in three places and she needed emergency surgery. Instead of listening to her doctor, she called Steve Austin (sitting in the front row), since she knew he had been through neck surgery. Austin set her up with Dr. Youngblood in San Antonio, and helped her through the ordeal. She thanked Danny McDevitt of Maryland Championship Wrestling, who helped her in training early along with Christian York & Joey Matthews (now Joey Mercury), as as people from Steel Dominion Wrestling and the Funking Dojo (Dory Funk Jr.). She brought up her cage match with Victoria, saying it was the first women's cage match in the company. She also praised Manami Toyota, who may have been the best woman wrestler of all-time, and if not, is on the short list of contenders, which got zero reaction. "I've never met her but she's blown my mind." She also thanked Luna Vachon, Terry Taylor, and said Jim Ross' announcing gave life to her matches and he also always gave her honest feedback. She praised Mickie James, who she worked with in her retirement match, and noted that Essa Rios (Mr. Aguila in CMLL), who she started as the sidekick of in WWE before being linked with the Hardys, was someone she actually had been a big fan of from Mexico before coming to WWF. She talked about being involved in the Hardys, Dudleys, and Edge & Christian program and their famous ladder matches, and also thanked Stratus. She then talked about growing up being part of the punk rock scene, saying that life taught her she could do what she wanted to do, and stood for things not popular in the mainstream. "My church was VFW Halls, dirty clubs and basements."

DIAMOND DALLAS PAGE

The fans were chanting his name. He said it was his 58th birthday, which led to loud "Happy Birthday" chants. He thanked HHH, and said without Dusty Rhodes, there is no DDP, noting Rhodes gave him every break he had in the beginning of his career. It's interesting he noted Dusty, but never mentioned Verne Gagne, since he started on national TV in the fading days of the AWA as the manager. He noted he had two mentors, Dusty and Jake Roberts, telling stories about living with Roberts in 1994. He said over the next few months, they would watch tapes together and Roberts would teach him ring psychology. He said what he did for Roberts was paying back that debt. He said Roberts wrote the book on ring psychology, his interviews were mesmerizing, his work was flawless, brought up Roberts' feuds with Ricky Steamboat, Rick Rude and Randy Savage. He talked about Jake moving in 18 months earlier and said their fantasy was to be on this stage on this very night. Well, they always said Rumble before WWE decided to do this instead.

JAKE ROBERTS

Roberts' voice was raspy. He mentioned Hiro Matsuda, Duke Keomuka, Fritz Von Erich and Bruno Sammartino as wrestling pioneers. He said he grew up and hated wrestling because his father wrestled, he never saw him, and he thought it was wrestling's fault. He said he later learned it was the guy, not wrestling, and he was hell bent on being a successful wrestler. He said how he hated wrestling for all those things, yet he did the exact same thing. He said he walked away from his family because he fell in love with wrestling. He said he should have spent his time more wisely. He didn't regret loving wrestling, because he loved to masturbate with people's emotions, talked about what a high it was and how addictive it was. He said he was 58 and he can't play the game anymore, but he was clearly positioning looking for a job as a coach or in creative noting his mind was still there. Fans chanted, "You still got it," and he said, "No, I don't. My heart and mind still want it, but it reaches a point where you can't do it justice. " He talked about drug and alcohol problems and all his mental pain, which he said was worse than the physical pain, and talked about the pain of lying to his children and his wife and not wanting to live.

"You don't want to carry on, your career is gone, all you have is shame and you can't do what your love anymore. What do you have left? Not much. You make some bad choices, I was jealous of my friends that are gone and I'd get angry with God, why not me, why not me?" He said, he didn't want to commit suicide and hurt his children. He said then Page stuck his hand out. "I was doing drugs every day, alcohol every day, I didn't want to live. You know what a stubborn SOB he is, the most positive person, he won't shut up. Dallas saved my life.

I know that, and I'm so grateful."

He brought up Page doing the Indiegogo account for the fans to chip in and pay for his shoulder surgery so he could train and how they donated $30,000 in one night, noting he had squandered all his money on drugs.

"I was given an innate amount of talent by God, you guys got a little of it but I wasted a lot of it, but I'm so happy tonight."

He brought up to the stage his 18 month old grandchild, saying that was his hero. He said he weighed 1.8 pounds and his twin sister weighed 1.1 pounds at birth. He went through ten surgeries and said at WrestleMania 50, this kid will be there. He said his family had given him a second chance and WWE did as well.

GENE OKERLUND

Okerlund, not Hulk Hogan, was the surprise inductor of Mr. T, although Hogan did do a skit with T at WrestleMania. This was more done as comedy, with Okerlund calling T a dear, close personal friend and then forgetting what his name was. Okerlund may seem a little old to put on regular TV, but he's underutilized by the company as he's got a classic style and I'd actually use him semi-regularly, although not as the lead interviewer since Renee Young is the best in that role for now.

MR. T

He got a lukewarm reaction. They pointed out he was inducted into the celebrity wing. I guess that makes sense, but he headlined two WrestleManias as a key participant. He started praising God, and this just wasn't the place for it. He talked about his mother, who raised 12 children as a single mom. That's quite the accomplishment, but he went on for 20 minutes on it. He never once mentioned either WrestleMania match, or even "The A Team," or anything past praising his children, his mother and God. The crowd was a lot better about it than a lot of crowds would have been, even chanting "Thank you mother." He noted his daughter wasn't there, as she was studying for her doctorate and his son has a Master's Degree. After 20 minutes, Kane's music played and he walked out. T realized he was getting the hook, and stopped right in the middle of his speech, saying, "I guess my time is up," shook hands with Kane and left.

KANE

Glenn Jacobs, as Kane, gave a very nice talk about his friend and former manager and traveling partner, Bill Moody, best known as Paul Bearer and Percy Pringle III. Moody was born in Mobile, and noted that no matter where he would live as a wrestler, to him, Mobile was always home. He noted he went to his first match at five, and was taking photos at the matches as a teenager. He noted that Moody grew up with Robert Gibson and Michael Hayes as fans, but didn't mention John Tatum. Moody went to the Air Force, stationed in Biloxi, and wrestled there. Then he worked as a funeral director, joking how Paul Bearer was a Mortician in real life. He noted he was Percy Pringle III and worked in Florida for Eddie Graham (there was a TV horror movie host character called Paul Bearer on Tampa television at the time who was well known, but the claim is Moody didn't know about him) and Texas for the Von Erichs before he came to WWF with Undertaker in 1990. Undertaker was actually around a few months, managed by Brother Love (Bruce Prichard), before Bearer came in. He noted he came in years later, and claimed the Undertaker vs. Kane feud was the best piece of storytelling WWE has ever done. Actually it was the most nonsensical in a lot of ways, but the original angle was good and effective as hell. He noted how easy and fun it was when he traveled with Bearer, because he made all the travel arrangements. He noted Moody loved Alabama football and country music, and how he grew to be a country music fan. He told a funny story about one day Moody told Jacobs he was sick and he couldn't drive, since Moody always did the driving. Jacobs said they were going to San Diego. So Jacobs, who had to wear a ski mask anytime he was near an arena because that's when he was a masked guy whose face was supposed to be scarred and burned up, was driving in with his ski mask on. As he got in the parking lot, driving a Cadillac, with all the fans waiting to see the wrestlers arrive, Moody suddenly got better, looked out the window and said, "It's a miracle. He can drive."

"I'm the one who owes him the most, if it hadn't been for Paul Bearer, there would have never been a Kane and I'm forever grateful."

He joked that after he was taken of the road as a manager, he'd be brought back from time-to-time and that "always ended in his demise." He mentioned Moody would still manage on the Gulf Coast scene, particularly Marcel Pringle. He didn't mention he was doing indies almost every weekend and a big part of Championship Wrestling from Hollywood. "The world lost a great entertainer, those of us close to us lost a great friend. Jacobs said that at Moody's funeral, he realized that Moody was what we all inspire to be, an international superstar.

Michael and Daniel Moody, his two sons, came out to accept. Daniel was carrying an urn with him, which presumably were Bill Moody's ashes. Michael Moody looked like a cross between Paul Heyman and Jeremy Botter.

The lights went out. Undertaker, appearing for the first time ever at a Hall of Fame ceremony, came out for his smoke filled entrance, in his character, got on his knees, also holding an urn and did a pose to a big photo of Paul Bearer on the screen.

KEVIN NASH
Nash quickly spoofed Mr. T's speech talking about the bible. He told about how he got a call from WWE and he had to decide if he wanted to leave behind the prestigious Vinnie Vegas gimmick to be Shawn Michaels' bodyguard. He said Michaels worked with Razor on a nightly basis and he got to watch two of the greatest of all-time. He said he had one biological brother, but through the business he's got four brothers. He said he didn't think anything would be more emotional than watching Shawn's induction, but that he was wrong.

SCOTT HALL
Hall was inducted as Razor Ramon. Nash never talked about anything past that first WWE run. Hall said he saw his first pro wrestling show at the age of eight and was in his early 20s when he had his first match. He then said he had the privilege of being guided by great talent and working with great talent. He said, "Bad times don't last but bad guys do." After everyone had gone so long, it was clear he was wanting to be in and out, and came off like it was a prelude for Michaels, Nash, Sean Waltman and HHH to come out on stage with him.

WADE BARRETT
The crowd was into his gimmick. He talked about the current group of WWE wrestlers and said, "I've got some bad news. This is the closest you pathetic wannabees will ever get to the WWE Hall of Fame." They showed Miz and Dolph Ziggler and a bunch of others. None of the guys knew this was coming and got a kick out of it. There was a "Randy Savage" chant.

CARLITO, EDDIE AND ORLANDO COLON
Lawler called them the Colon brothers, although Orlando (Fernando) is Carlos' nephew. Carlito got a big reaction. It was never acknowledged that Eddie and Orlando were Los Matadores and they never spoke about themselves. Carlito said little, but was the funniest guy of the night. "I'm used to Bingo Halls and high school gyms so thank you." He joked about the placement of his father's induction, saying that they were put after the Kliq reunion and before Ultimate Warrior. He joked it was like a PPV, people are going to be tired and need a rest, so send out the Colons. And, he joked, "Like usual, we got our time cut. It's like I never left." Then he switched and said, "This is about my Dad and I love him so much." He didn't say anything else, as it appeared Eddie and Orlando had worked with writers to deliver the speech.

Eddie (Primo/Diego) said Carlos Colon came from humble beginnings, born in Puerto Rico but raised in New York. He was raised by a single mother, who raised four children, including Orlando's father. He grew up watching WWWF, Bruno Sammartino, Argentina Rocca and wanted to be a pro wrestler. He started training at 14, but promised his mother he'd first graduate high school. Graduated on a Monday, on Tuesday he started wrestling. He spent six years as a journeyman, mentioning different promoters he worked for like Stu Hart. He mentioned Joe Blanchard in San Antonio, but he and Chicky Starr came there in the mid-80s after he was an established superstar in Puerto Rico, and he really didn't get over in San Antonio. He came to Puerto Rico in 1973. He founded Capital Sports, and they talked about him bringing in top talent like Andre the Giant, Yokozuna, Harley Race, The Funks, Roddy Piper and Dusty Rhodes. They said he was so big they couldn't make stadiums big enough, which was hyperbole. He noted that at the peak, the territory included Trinidad & Tobago, St. Thomas, St. Croix, and the Dominican Republic.

CARLOS COLON

Colon did a five minute speech, looking down and reading from a script. He noted he started wrestling 48 years ago and said in his wildest dreams he never thought he'd be standing there. It's just a weird Hall of Fame with it being part of deals in selling videotape collections. He thanked his wife, Nancy, who was Canadian and who he met early in his career in that country. He talked about wrestling Abdullah the Butcher, Race, Ric Flair, Dusty Rhodes, Tully Blanchard, Dutch Mantell, The Funks, The Briscos, the Samoans and many others. You can tell with both Colons how WWE wrote the speeches since the names mentioned were all WWE Hall of Famers (with the exception of Mantell, a current WWE character as Zeb Colter), even though Colon had many bigger rivals. He spoke mostly in Spanish. As noted, the Brody chants were light and didn't sustain, and I couldn't hear any other catcalls.

LINDA MCMAHON

Doing her first induction, noting that Warrior personally requested it, she talked about how he legally changed his name to Warrior. She explained that showed his passion or something. Given that the only other person I know of who did something quite like that was War Machine, who is perhaps the biggest nutcase in MMA, I'm not sure what that says. She said he was loner, committed to principles and passionate about his performance. She noted that when he came back for the last time in 1996, he asked that she be his direct office contact. She joked he would sometimes call and rant, and she would then put the phone on speaker, push the mute button and go to work until he was done with his rant. "During a rant, he called me mom, and I said, `You're behaving like a petulant child and I'm going to turn you over on my knee." She also said Warrior had a saying, "If your first thought is you can't, then you won't."

ULTIMATE WARRIOR

Editor's Note: This section was written before the death of Ultimate Warrior. I thought changing even one word or thought from this section would have been dishonest.

He came out at first with his two daughters. It's weird how at about 55, both he and Nash look a lot alike. Even though they had their go-around not too long ago, Nash was spared Warrior's wrath tonight. It was different because he went on-and-on about the DVD Vince McMahon commissioned, yet wouldn't say anything about McMahon. Warrior, with no modesty at all, said that this was, "The most anticipated speech in the history of sports entertainment." He said that people were squirming in their seats. He thanked his wife and his mom, who were both sitting there. He noted that his father walked out when he was 11 or 12 and never gave any financial support, but she provided for him and his brother and he learned hard work and self discipline from her. It was, by this point, really interesting about the theme of no father involved, with Mr. T, Colon, Jake and Warrior. He joked that he thought he was watching a DDP yoga infomercial and it's inspiring to see DDP yoga helping people fix their self destructive ways. And yes, Self Destructive was his first segue into the DVD that was the theme of this 40 minute speech. He talked about HHH putting this together, and then said, "I only met him for five minutes and he was an asshole," which was a line HHH said about meeting him for the first time to go over their 1996 WrestleMania 90 second squash, where HHH had all these ideas for a match and Warrior then told him it was going 90 seconds and he's getting squashed. "For spending only five minutes with this asshole, you sure learned a lot."

He said tonight shows after 18 years of exile you can come back and be the headliner for the Hall of fame at the 30th WrestleMania. A "One more match" chant started, which he shut down hard. "One more match isn't going to happen," he said. The fans didn't listen as he made that point, because they came back and did that same chant later. His first knock was against some veterans who tried to tell him what he was doing wrong. "I wanted to thank people even if it teaches me things that aren't going to work." His rep was being told things not to do, doing them anyway, and because he was the right act at the right time, he got over. He noted that he had a few hours of training from Red Bastien on a racquetball court with Steve Borden (Sting). He said Bastien and Billy Anderson enjoyed watching him and the other bodybuilders pound the crap out of each other. The story behind this was Rick Bassman was looking to get into wrestling with the idea that he could take good looking huge bodybuilders and make them pro wrestlers, to feud with people like The Road Warriors, who were one of the hottest acts in wrestling at the time. After maybe a few weeks of training, Borden and then Jim Hellwig quit the camp, sent out photos and resumes to all the promoters, and Jerry Jarrett hired them. He noted meeting Dutch Mantell, Jerry Lawler, Tommy Rogers and Bobby Fulton (he mixed up their names at first, but corrected himself), then went to work for Bill Watts where he met Ted DiBiase, and Dr. Death (Steve Williams). Next was the receipt headed for DiBiase, about learning how to throw a clothesline by copying him. He tried to make it as uncomfortable for DiBiase as possible, pausing to ask if DiBiase was in the audience. He said how DiBiase was trying to get him to leave the territory by giving him clotheslines so stiff his Adam's Apple was always hurting. Next was World Class Championship Wrestling, where he became Dingo Warrior, which he called the poor man's version of the Ultimate Warrior. He thanked David Manning, Rick Hazzard (two referees who worked in the office), The Von Erichs, Len Denton and Tim Brooks, who he noted were guys who worked because they loved wrestling. He also thanked Bruiser Brody and George Scott, who were the bookers when he was there, and also mentioned Bronko Lubich. He said he got signed by WWF when Scott recommended him to them, saying he was very raw and green but he could be something. When he mentioned "WWF," they actually sound edited the "F" on television. He must have gotten word to stop saying WWF, because he stopped in his tracks, and said he wanted the F back in. This led to "Yes" chants and him saying, "I can't believe Jerry McDevitt got his ass kicked by those wildlife people." He said he got a WWE (well F in those days) tryout in Tyler, TX. He said they brought him to New York where he wrestled Jose Estrada, a veteran job guy. In a pro wrestler exaggeration, he said Estrada called for him to press slam him 15 or 16 times to make him blow up. He joked he was already blown up by the time the match started. He also mentioned Steve Lombardi and Terry Gibbs as enhancement guys who helped him out at first. He went back to the DVD. He said how in the DVD it said that he wasn't welcome in the locker rooms (he usually dressed separate from everyone else in those days and often stayed in different hotels) because he wasn't one of the boys and was an asshole, "When I saw the DVD it made me angry and pissed me off and broke my heart."

He talked about the dressing rooms in those days where guys would have high security gear bags with locks, and somehow the British Bulldogs would still break into their bags and, "leave something in the bag that you don't want there."

He said he was a good guy and didn't deserve the things said about him. He said he wanted to thank the real superstars in WWE, talking about guys who work 25 years for the company to make the show happen, the people who put up the rings and drive from town to town on no sleep, and then after they're done, they come to the wrestlers and ask them if there's anything they can get for them. He said as part of the 30th WrestleMania, they should honor those people.

He said every year at the Hall of Fame they should have a Jimmy Miranda award. Miranda was one of the guys who ran the merchandise stands at the arenas when Warrior was there. He said the guy always had an awesome attitude and he wanted a Jimmy Miranda award created.

Then we were back to the DVD, saying it was filled with lies and mischaracterizations, and talked about how these people (without saying who, given it was the same Vince McMahon) "tried to program your minds against your fun memories." It was right then when I realized that the fans booing Batista and saying how they wished he never came back and wanted him gone now, are going to be chanting "One more match" at him in a few years and giving him standing ovations. Geez, plus the guy has a DVD coming out on Tuesday and all he's doing is promoting the one from eight years ago without mentioning the new one. But I do get where he's coming from, this was his day to gloat and boy did he do so.

And after all that, he talked about how Vince gave him the opportunity to use his imagination and use his creativity and go as far as he could. He then started putting Vince over, saying all the tough guys would go on the road and say when they got to TV or got to the Garden they were going to give Vince a piece of their mind. He said they'd go in all ramped and ready and come out like they were bobble heads. He said Badnews Brown (Allan Coage), who hated Vince and was a real-life tough guy, was so vehement that he thought it was going to happen and Vince was going to finally go down. He said that he had his meeting and he came out like he was a bobble head. He said the wrestlers learn psychology in the ring, but the psychology of Vince was at a whole different level. But he said Vince knew he was dedicated and didn't have to worry about him keeping up with his gimmick on the road.

He said wrestling allows people to play make-believe tough guys. He said that in the business there were only a few legitimate tough guys and the rest of us just play that role. Then he started praising John Cena for the Make-a-Wish stuff after bringing up how his fame allowed him to inspire children. He said that Cena doesn't even want people to know about the stuff he does. I know that's true, but it's not like they don't publicize it to death, so even though there is a part of him where you can say that and I will always praise Cena for his work outside the ring and he does a lot of stuff that doesn't get brought up, you can't over credit him because there are guys in the business who don't want the stuff they do to be known and it isn't. Cena may want to be one of those guys. He may do as much or more than those guys. But Cena's stuff is publicized to death.

Warrior said that he learned from Ed Connors (who at one time was the owner of the Gold's Gym chain) that Cena was an Ultimate Warrior mark, and said how Ray Lewis and The Rock were as well. He said that wrestlers don't put on hockey gear (well, Bill Irwin) or baseball gear (Steve Lombardi) or basketball gear, but all the other athletes put wrestling gimmicks on. He said that people always say he didn't appreciate or respect the business. He said the business was the gear bag he built his life after wrestling on.

Then he said how guys used to make fun of him for blowing up in the ring. He said that he was blowing up just giving this speech. But he said, he always continued the match. He would blow up doing his entrance but he continued the match. Then he would blow it out at the finish. He said he misses pushing his body to keep going, being on the road, and working on three hours sleep. He said you just will yourself to go.

He then said how everyone in wrestling on social media is just working their gimmick. But he said his gimmick was his. He said that nobody ever said anything to his face and he was always respectful to everyone in the business and the DVD was just wrong. He said the DVD made him angry and was hurtful. Then he said he was honored to be inducted with these other guys and the lady and said he had signed a contract to be an ambassador for WWE.

Then he talked about a letter when he was fired, He said Vince gave him a check, which he seemed to indicate was for that SummerSlam 1991 show. He brought up in a letter Vince wrote him. He said Vince wrote that he was a legend in his own mind. He said he was only 30 when he wrestled Hulk Hogan and he said he tried to be the best he could be but he didn't think he was a legend. But he said the Ultimate Warrior is a legend and will continue to be a legend to come.

We had another "One more match" chant which led to him saying no more matches. "It's hard for an athlete when you shouldn't be doing it anymore. But what this company needs is for the people who had their time there to step up and help the next generation come up. He told the wrestlers that their time will come, and it's not personal, but it will end and you need to use this opportunity to prepare yourself for all the wonderful things you can do in the arena of life.

CHAPTER TWENTY

RING OF HONOR STEPS INTO THE PPV ARENA

APRIL 28

After various tries to market big shows over the years, Ring of Honor takes the biggest step, with a live PPV show on 6/22, for "Best of the World 2014" from the Fairgrounds in Nashville.

No details of the show have been announced, but the names announced are Matt Hardy, Kevin Steen, Mark & Jay Briscoe, champion Adam Cole, Michael Elgin, Jay Lethal and Maria Kanellis. A.J. Styles is booked in Japan for the 6/21 New Japan PPV show at the Osaka Furitsu Gym so won't be available at this point. It is possible because of the time change to work on Osaka on one night and in Nashville the next, and when the big stars worked Japan in the past, it wasn't that unusual to do it. You can't do it the other way, in the sense work on 6/20 in the U.S. and 6/21 in Japan.

The show will air in the traditional Sunday at 8 p.m. time slot. It's a weekend with no major PPV competition, but in a loaded month as UFC runs 6/14, WWE runs 6/1 and 6/29 and TNA runs 6/15.

The show is expected to be carried by inDemand, Dish and DirecTV. It's well known that the cable industry was looking for a new partner in PPV and was offering a better deal than in the past, to make up for, depending on the system, expected declines or outright dropping of the WWE product. It is probable that at least two of the big three, if not all three, may not even carry the WWE events by that time.

Right now, it's a one-time experiment. Those close to the situation have said the expense of experimenting with one show is not a make-or-break situation. We don't know what break even will be, but Greg Gilliland, who put the deal together, is very conservative when it comes to these type of company deals. The belief is they will be fine if they can get 10,000 buys, which is not out of the realm of possibility, since years ago, ROH did that with some of its early PPV shows that were taped shows from two months earlier. The reason similar numbers don't work for other wrestling and MMA groups include more money earmarked for production and far higher talent and promotional costs.

If it works, they'll continue, and if not, then they won't. Nothing is for certain, but even if it does work, they wouldn't be doing another for a while, perhaps not until Final Battle in December.

ROH becomes one of three new products to attempt PPVs over the next few months, with Bellator on 5/17 and Glory on 6/21, the night before ROH, with a Saturday at 10 p.m. time slot (the UFC regular slot) from the Forum in Inglewood, CA for a show called "Last Man Standing" featuring an eight-man middleweight

(185 pound) tournament that would include Melvin Manhoef, a top star from the glory period of Japanese kickboxing and MMA.

It is expected that the ROH show will air both through Ustream as an iPPV as well as a regular PPV. That is depending on the success of Ustream broadcasts of ROH iPPV shows on 5/10 from Toronto and 5/17 from New York, major cards featuring the top stars of New Japan Pro Wrestling. There seemed to be significant interest in both shows with New York being sold out more than a month ahead of time at the 1,800 seat Hammerstein Ballroom and Toronto at this point being a given that it will sell out the 1,500 seat Ted Reeve Arena. Overall, ROH business has been up this year.

ROH was on PPV years ago, with taped shows airing on roughly a two month delay. The shows started with 10,000 buys, which for a promotion with no television at the time, was excellent. The number was strong enough to make money on a taped show, but would have been a loser at the time for a live show. That's why TNA cut back from 12 to four PPVs per year, because they weren't able to break even.

Numbers fell to 2,000 by the end of the run and it ended up being dropped, and the concept changed to live iPPVs. They started with about 700 buyers and had generally strong reviews for the shows, peaking at 2,300 buyers. But one misfire after another doomed them and they got out of the iPPV business because of all the problems and consumer complaints.

Next month will be their first go-around with Ustream, which has only had minimal technical issues broadcasting shows from New Japan, Wrestle-1 and Dragon Gate. However, Ustream did have issues on several occasions doing Invicta PPV shows, where the decision was made to take down the pay wall and refund consumers because of the problems.

MAY 19

Ring of Honor started its attempt to rebuild focus on major shows this past week with an iPPV on 5/10 from Toronto, which set up matches for a similar show on 5/17 in New York, building to a traditional PPV on 6/22 in Nashville.

The Toronto show, a combination event with New Japan Pro Wrestling, was an across-the-board success. The iPPV, with UStream, the same company that does New Japan, Dragon Gate, Wrestle-1 and Invicta (which did have numerous problems on a few of its shows, so the idea UStream is immune from the problems other companies have had isn't the case), went off live without a hitch. The picture quality was excellent.

While numbers were not released, the show did very well on iPPV (as in above most projections), above the other shows they've done since technical problems really killed that business after peaking at 2,300 buys a few years back. There is a legitimate chance they could break that record this week, particularly since they went against a live free UFC show (not a big show, but a show nonetheless), while this week goes against a Bellator PPV that just got killed losing its main event.

ROH also has far more television clearances than it did then, and it's going to take time and probably a series of successful broadcasts to rebuild that audience. But after several years, the reality is in the U.S., iPPV never took off to big numbers, which is why they are going back to PPV. It's also notable that even though New Japan big shows do very well on iPPV, where it has taken off, there weren't a ton of New Japan fans from Japan who bought this show.

The jury is still out regarding the effect of the WWE Network on iPPVs, in the sense, have they devalued the value of a big wrestling show, particularly with WWE producing so much available content and it being perceived as the major league? From those who are in the iPPV wrestling game, the feeling is it's too early to tell the effect, but right now numbers are running about the same as before.

The WWE effect is also there when it comes to PPV. The PPV providers are far more open to new products (Bellator, ROH and Glory all debut on PPV between now and 6/22) and are making more workable deals for small providers in an attempt to recoup some of the lost WWE revenue. They will also be pushing the big events harder. The timing didn't work out perfectly, because the New York show really should have been the first PPV. But if the first PPV does at least decent, there is the chance to peak for a few months to build Final Battle or whatever a second PPV show would be, and perhaps time it with the availability of some New Japan talent.

The live show sold out the Ted Reeve Arena with 1,500 fans, in advance, and they had to turn away about 100 at the door. New York (1,800 fans) at the Hammerstein Ballroom has been sold out even longer. Those who got in were perhaps the best big show wrestling crowd in recent memory. They were rabid, and enhanced every performer and every match. It's one thing to get into a **** match, but it's another to make a hit-and-miss comedy segment right after intermission get over like a million bucks. They reacted to the Japanese stars as superstars, but they were into the ROH talent every bit as much.

And the show itself was paced well. No match went too long. If anything, they left the customers both satisfied, but not exhausted, particularly important when they are running a bigger show in a week, which theoretically should be the one that does the bigger numbers. The show clocked in at three hours and two minutes, which included a 20 minute intermission, which felt to me like a good time length. My feeling is for ROH, a "super" show can go three hours and 30 minutes or a little longer, like a Final Battle. That may be impossible now because if PPV is successful, the biggest shows will be PPV as opposed to iPPV and that's a traditional three hour window. It was apparently stressed to the wrestlers not to go over their time cues, because this show and next week's show are both also training for 6/22, where they have to end the show in less than three hours.

The work was strong. There was nothing remotely resembling a bad match. The IWGP jr. heavyweight tag title match with the Young Bucks retaining over The Time Splitters (Alex Shelley & Kushida) and The Forever Hooligans (Rocky Romero & Alex Koslov) was the show stealer, a knock your socks off match that wasn't that far off match of the year consideration.

The fans were into the Japanese wrestlers, although more into Jushin Liger and Kazuchika Okada than the others. Liger was described as a freak, as the costume allows him to defy aging. Backstage, at 49, he looks old, bald and broken down. Once he puts the costume on, the body and head are hidden, and he can still be Jushin Liger, albeit without the flying moves that put him on the map in the 90s where he would be on the short list with Danny Hodge, Dynamite Kid, the Original Tiger Mask and Chris Benoit, as the greatest junior heavyweight wrestler of all-time.

The most over wrestler was Kevin Steen, which is no surprise, since being Canadian, he always is when ROH runs Toronto. After Steen lost clean in the main event to ROH champion Adam Cole, he gave a thank you speech that some took as a good-bye (this took place after the iPPV ended), and he had done the same thing at another indie show in recent weeks.

Steen is under contract to ROH through late July. He attended the most recent WWE tryout camp, and got rave reviews for his verbal ability. Nobody thus far has been contacted from that camp as far as being offered a deal, or having been turned down either, which is par for the course timing wise with other camps. The belief is those letters will be sent out within the next few weeks.

JUNE 2

While Sinclair Broadcasting doesn't look like it will release the iPPV number, the 5/17 War of the Worlds iPPV show did in the range of the biggest number the company has ever done, so it appears that most of the damage from all the misfires has dissipated. What we do know is it beat the Toronto number, which is a good sign coming seven days later, and also did strong replay numbers, which is based on positive word-of-mouth. There is no announcement of a next iPPV, as they'll probably be evaluating iPPV vs. PPV and doing a strategy after 6/22. They need significantly more PPV buys than iPPV buys to break even, but PPV is budgeted to where they can do fine with 10,000 buys or even a little less. After 6/22, the next major show would be the 8/15 date at Cyclones Stadium outdoors in Brooklyn. They got off to a fast advance, which is a positive sign, but that is by far the biggest venue they've played, and a stadium TNA did 5,500 fans in the first time they came in. Right now the plans are for it to be a loaded up show, and given advance deadlines, it's very unlikely to be a traditional PPV, but you don't need to clear dates far in advance when you do your own iPPV. Right now it isn't scheduled as such.

JUNE 23

At another time, Ring of Honor moving to a live PPV format would be a huge story and there would be talk of how important the first show is, and it being a potential game changer.

It actually feels there was more talk years ago when ROH went to PPV for the first time with shows taped two months earlier, which is not a reflection on ROH as much as it is a reflection on how much PPV has changed in recent years as well as how wrestling has changed.

Those in the company have referred to the 6/22 show from the Nashville Fairgrounds as a low-risk experiment. They are not in a situation, like ECW was years ago, where they were spending money that they didn't have, and needing a home run. But PPV for a secondary promotion doesn't have nearly the potential that it had when ECW made the move.

ROH doesn't have the killer lineup like they had on 5/10 and 5/17, when they returned to iPPV. They didn't set records, but they did appear to remove a lot of the negative stench from all the iPPV misfires that were a terrible embarrassment to the company over the past few years, even driving them out of that arena for a while. For the live event, the advance is said to be ahead of the company's January show in the venue (which drew 800 fans), but it's far from the advanced sellouts of New York and Toronto.

PPV is different, because people are far more familiar with it. Compared to its first foray on PPV, and ROH did 10,000 buys for its early shows on a two-month delay at first. But they didn't sustain those numbers and eventually the revenue dropped to where they got out of PPV even though costs of a taped show were minimal, but so was the revenue and they thought with the limited money, it was screwing up continuity and hurting DVD sales. At that time, that kind of a number for a live show would have been a money-loser, and with no television, the feeling was, and probably correctly so, that doing a live PPV couldn't make money and it was never tried.

Live PPV is great if you're UFC or major boxing. It was a huge game changer for ECW in the 90s, but even though the numbers they did would be considered remarkable for a No. 3 group today, it wasn't enough to sustain them after a few years. While Bellator's number was successful, whether it was profitable given the amount of money it took to get Tito Ortiz and Rampage Jackson, is questionable. Invicta tried PPV and hasn't run a show since December, which tells you how they did. TNA has cut back from 12 to four live PPV shows, which tells you how they were doing.

ROH becomes the third new promotion in the last five weeks to try live PPV. Bellator, did surprisingly well (an estimated 100,000 buys), but all the reasons it did so, a strong hype special repeated over and over on Spike, tons of advertising, and established PPV drawing cards like Jackson and Ortiz, don't apply at all to ROH. It also had the advantage of a live two hour show on Spike in prime time pushing late buys. The second new promotion, Glory, Spike's kickboxing franchise, debuts with a show on 6/21 from Los Angeles. They'll also do the same pattern with two hours of fights on prime time pushing people to get the PPV, which is a one-night middleweight championship tournament. But they don't have a Rampage vs. Mo special that between all its airings drew something like 2.7 million viewers to drive that number, which was a huge key to Bellator's success and unless you have a vehicle to duplicate that, you can't use the Bellator number as any kind of a benchmark.

What is significant is that in going to regular PPV, ROH has become more competition to TNA, or at least moves in the past few weeks make it seem that way. As noted, ROH can beat TNA's number, or even beat it handily. In another era with an even playing field, you could argue that would make them the No. 2 group. But today, they are still world's apart financially.

TNA has made some moves of late when it comes to contacting ROH talent. Names that have gotten out who were contacted have included Bobby Fish, Kyle O'Reilly and Jay Lethal. Lethal is under an ROH contract so couldn't appear, but a lot of ROH talent does not have contracts, most notably Roderick Strong, since he did the WWE camp.

Matt Hardy, who is a part-time ROH performer and an independent wrestler, returns to TNA days after Best in the World. Hardy will be appearing on the PPV, and may end up being a super heel in the building. Nothing is for sure after that, but the assumption would be he's not going to be working for ROH after this week.

TNA contacted Hardy for the New York tapings, and based on what Hardy told those in ROH, he turned down the offer. They came back with a second and much higher offer, well above his going rate on the indies, and a somewhat surprising amount of money considering how much they have cut on talent of late, and he accepted the second offer. The figure I was told would be in the range of double what he makes on the indie scene.

I have yet to see one television ad on the cable or satellite side for the ROH PPV, which to me, isn't a good sign, especially since cable and satellite companies if they wanted to push this as a new product should have used their own ad inventory on Impact, Raw and Smackdown to push it. One would think DirecTV as well as cable companies would have used its inventory to put an ad during Raw this week since in theory, it is in their best interest to have the new product kick off as strong as possible as a replacement for the PPV dollars lost when they dropped WWE. ROH, being an unknown factor with no track record hasn't led to partners helping it much. ROH doesn't have the budget to do so itself. It's relying on its own television shows and Internet buzz. There are no great expectations, nor does it seem like there are great fears.

It's tougher because what ROH was built on, having great matches, is something people get all the time on television now for free, and can click on the Internet to see more great matches than anyone has time for. What ROH had also at another time was hope, not that they don't now, but it was what ECW was sold on in the 90s. Fans believed they were on the ground floor with an alternative almost underground great wrestling product with the idea it would get bigger when more people discovered it, once they got television and then once they got PPV. But ROH is now a 12 year old product and as long as Sinclair Broadcasting is behind it, it is probably going to be around, but it's also not likely to get appreciably bigger. You can tell by the money put in. Sinclair hasn't given them the budget for a major league look on the television show, and the talent budget is limited as well.

It wouldn't surprise me to see ROH, given this is its first show on PPV, beat the numbers TNA does. At another point in time, that would be significant. But the economic differences, largely due to TNA's Spike and international TV deals, are still gigantic between the two. ROH's goal has to be slow, steady improvements, but more staying in business. They can't be No. 2 as long as TNA is on Spike no matter if they can sell more tickets to house shows and beat them on PPV. It's a game about television deals, and the funny part is ROH is owned by a major television conglomerate, but that's been the case for a while and the television and new ownership has not been a game changer past the point the company seems stable and surviving. It would not have survived without the deal because as a separate business, it couldn't make money on its own and Cary Silken had enough to save it for years, but not any longer than he did.

But can ROH do 10,000 buyers in the U.S. and Canada on a regular basis on PPV? Keep in mind WWE for its "B" shows ranged from 70,000 to 160,000 in the same market. When you consider the difference in organizational size, a 10,000 figure, which doesn't sound that great, all of a sudden takes on a different meaning. At another point in time, my belief is live ROH shows on PPV would do that and more. Today, it's so much harder to get viewers to buy anything but the "A" product because there is so much product put out by the "A" promotions, WWE and UFC.

The one thing that is almost a certainty is that the wrestlers themselves will deliver good action. The booking won't have the lame angles that TNA has too much of, the tired heel authority figures, and the product will be portrayed as serious. The lineup isn't over the top, as coming on the same weekend as a New Japan iPPV meant that a lot of key talent like A.J. Styles and The Young Bucks weren't available.

The bigger question is the production, look and how well the crowd comes across. Keep in mind this show is being done on a shoe-string budget, enabling a low break-even point, as compared to just about everyone else that does live PPV.

The PPV itself will have seven matches. The schedule live will include two dark matches, a tag match with Raymond Rowe & Hanson, and a singles match involving Adam Page.

The PPV match order is scheduled to start with a six-way where the winner gets a TV title shot, with ACH, Takaaki Watanabe, Caprice Coleman, Tadarius Thomas, B.J. Whitmer and Tommaso Ciampa. That should be a good action high spot oriented match, particularly with ACH as the standout.

From there, it's Jay Lethal defending the TV title against Matt Taven, with Truth Martini handcuffed to the post. Roderick Strong faces Cedric Alexander in a submission rules match. Mark & Jay Briscoe face Matt Hardy & Michael Bennett. Kevin Steen, in what is expected to be one of his last matches with the company, faces Silas Young, coming off the angle on the New York iPPV show. Bobby Fish & Kyle O'Reilly defend the tag titles against Christopher Daniels & Frankie Kazarian. And the main event has Adam Cole defending the ROH title against Michael Elgin.

The latter match has been booked to be a significant title match. At one point it was talked of Cole vs. Elgin as the climactic match of the year. Elgin has been booked strongly all year with him being the clearest and strongest groomed candidate for the title ever since Cole won it over him in the tournament final. This year, he's only had one loss, which was in the main event of the last iPPV when he did the job in the three-way IWGP title match that involved Styles and Kazuchika Okada. The big angle was done last week, where Cole tied Elgin up in the ropes and cut off his trademark hair mullet, and then put Elgin's wife, MsChif, in the figure four leglock. Today, a guy who usually performs well in big matches isn't enough to carry a promotion. Elgin does lack in verbal skills and facials, and doesn't have superstar charisma. But he does have a powerhouse believability to his style.

But if this experiment works, the ROH/New Japan relationship may be of benefit going forward. Timing future PPV shows when New Japan has weekends off gives the company access to a lot of talent that can really augment these shows to make them special, and also allow that talent to be worked into the television product.

JUNE 30

The first impression when Ring of Honor's first live PPV started was that it looked minor league.

No matter how good the action was, and it was, and whether you like or dislike the booking, for a casual fan in 2014, it's a perception killer. That said, this was PPV, and most of the audience buying the show were probably ROH fans, and most of those fans weren't buying it for high level production.

It's one of wrestling's great quandaries. ROH, with some of the best wrestling action in the world, is held back because of the look of the show. It makes it hard to really think you're watching big stars, plus since most of the talent is unknown, except to hardcores, there aren't the few big stars that people do know rub that can make other stars by working with them like ECW and TNA had. The look of the show was one thing when Cary Silkin owned the company.

But this is owned by a media company and the television airs on their own stations . It's pretty clear Sinclair Broadcasting bought the company and made the TV deal on the idea it was cheap programming. But one would think they'd still be after production values that don't stand out like a sore thumb in 2014, with hopes it can sell the tapes to overseas markets, which TNA makes money on.

ROH was the third of the new promotions to debut on PPV. Both Bellator and Glory may not have looked like Pride in its Japanese heyday, but the production was far superior. ROH was going to be compared with TNA, and even though ROH presented better wrestling for the most part, TNA's production the week before blew this away. The overall atmosphere with the larger crowd would have made it come across like it was the superior product to all but the built in ROH audience that already knows what it is.

It wasn't supposed to be that way.

ROH brought a lighting truss that every major league property that shoots in an arena setting would use, which would have been an upgrade from the usual ROH TV production. The funny part is that it's probably more important to have the increased production on television, because that's the vehicle for making new fans. But there's a reason that Glory, with virtually no U.S. popularity nor established name fighters on its PPV was advertised by DirecTV during World Cup games, and nobody seemed to see ROH ads almost anywhere.

The plans were changed a week in, due to a structural engineer refusing to allow ROH to use the truss because of the fear the Nashville Fairgrounds Arena couldn't handle the weight. So ROH had to rely on lighting trees. It was noted that the company paid for proper lighting, had it in their trucks but couldn't set them up. They also had to bring in an outside generator. Many remember the story of ECW's first PPV in 1997, where at Barely

Legal, the generator blew just seconds after the show had ended. If it had blown 15 minutes earlier, it would have been a disaster. There was fear the same would happen here. There were no problems, but apparently had they gone 20 to 30 minutes longer, things could have been bad. There won't be any decisions made regarding when to do a second PPV until the numbers for the first one come in. If the numbers are good enough, the second show would likely be Final Battle in December. The feeling is that would be at the Hammerstein Ballroom, so they would have the proper lighting and learn from the first show and have a backup generator. The feeling is to use better buildings for future PPV shows.

The show on 6/22 drew more than 1,000 fans, not sold out but fairly full with the set up they had. There are no early indications on the PPV but it'll probably be clear in a few weeks based on whether or not they start working on Final Battle as a PPV or an iPPV. There were no glitches or problems with PPV, but UStream had a problem in that on the night of the show, the replay was available without having to pay for several hours before it was fixed.

The show was built around hot action. It was the biggest night in the career of a large percentage of the locker room. The feeling is that PPV is bigger than iPPV. Even though more people, by far, watch on television, this was live and thus would be remembered. For a locker room that grew up with PPV as the big deal, this was their stage. Everyone delivered. While there were no matches of the year, every match on the show was good. The show was well paced. Nobody got shorted on time to where they couldn't have a good match. No matches dragged.

The main event saw Michael Elgin win the ROH title from Adam Cole. While Elgin was going to win the title at some point this year, since the year was built around it, the feeling seemed to be that they needed something big from a storyline standpoint for the first PPV. It's a balancing act. It was too early for Cole to lose, as he's really developed in the champion's role. But having something significant happen on the PPV took precedence. The change was a success because everyone from the fans, the announcers and the two wrestlers reacted in a way that this title was a major quest. They put over the names of the former champions who had left and gone elsewhere and become big stars like C.M. Punk, Bryan Danielson, Tyler Black (Seth Rollins), Samoa Joe, Austin Aries and others. They did a confetti celebration for the title change, and the fans did their part, throwing streamers at the finish when Elgin got the pin after a triple power bomb.

They had to rebuild the crowd heat because Elgin used his usual power bomb finish and Cole kicked out. For whatever reason, because it was so close on the kick out, fans started throwing streamers and celebrating. The visual was awesome but in clearing the ring and after the pop, it took a while to get the crowd back to the level the two wrestlers had built. But they were pretty much back by the end.

After the show, Adam Cole, Christopher Daniels and Roderick Strong were said to have given great speeches to what was described as a very emotional locker room.

One behind the scenes story is that Matt Korklan, the former Evan Bourne, was in Nashville and scheduled to make an appearance on the show as Matt Sydal. Based on what we were told, since the talent let go last week were given 90 day non-competes where they make their downside guarantees, WWE still has control over them through around 9/18. Korklan contacted Hunter Johnston, the ROH booker, as soon as he got released and said that he had been given the okay he could work for ROH. He was immediately booked for the show. ROH then contacted WWE to get it in writing, and after a few days, WWE told ROH that he would not be allowed to appear for ROH until the September date. Korklan was there and described as being on Cloud Nine, just happy to be there. He was scripted to come out for an interview before the title match and challenge the winner, saying he was coming after the title, but that had to be scrapped. He was there giving advice to the younger wrestlers after the matches as a way to justify the cost of his flight.

A few notes on the new talent introduced. Moose was introduced in an interview segment as the newest member of the roster and the company sent out a press release about him signing. He's 29-year-old Quinn Ojinnaka, who is 6-foot-5 legit and was a 295 pound offensive lineman who played 2006-2010 with the Atlanta Falcons, 2010 with the New England Patriots, 2011 with the Indianapolis Colts and 2012 with the St. Louis Rams. After his football career ended, he started training in Georgia under Curtis Hughes, and worked earlier this year as a bodyguard in Dragon Gate USA. He's in a tough position because a guy of his size isn't conducive to this style and he's green and most of the talent here is experienced and far ahead of him. Also, from his first promo, he didn't stand out. He's going to have to be protected. They are looking at him as a project.

Mandy Leon, who was the pretty girl host of the countdown show that aired on TV the night before, and did an interview segment, actually has been training at the ROH school to wrestle since April 2013 and had her first match two months ago.

Jay Diesel, who had a role in the Jay Lethal vs. Matt Taven match as a security guard, appeared to be introduced as talent. He's a former competitive bodybuilder and former boxer.

Nobody seems to know exactly what the future holds for Matt Hardy as far as any future dates here. Hardy stars in a few days with TNA. He worked his ass off on this show, doing much more than expected. He's still not under contract with either group.

JULY 13

Ustream, the company which handles the iPPV business of New Japan, Ring of Honor and Dragon Gate, and formerly handled the business for Invicta, has informed the promotions that it is getting out of the PPV business.

Exactly when this goes down is not certain, but at press time, they were still advertising carrying Dragon Gate's 7/20 Kobe Pro Wrestling festival show. At this point, there are no new listing for New Japan. Ustream carried the 6/29 show at Korakuen Hall, but didn't carry the 7/4 show with the Kota Ibushi vs. Kushida IWGP jr. heavyweight title change. They had not made an announcement regarding the G-1 Climax series, but on the 6/21 show in Osaka, they talked about iPPVs on 6/29 and 7/4, and pushed the opening day of G-1 from Sapporo on 7/21 with a loaded lineup. The 7/4 show did not air as an iPPV and the New Japan site at press time lists no new cards.

The impression we were given is there would be no further ROH shows on Ustream. ROH had nothing but problems doing iPPVs, and had pulled out of doing them because of one misfire after another. The company was leery, but were convinced to go with Ustream for 5/10 in Toronto and 5/17 in New York, because Ustream had been regularly delivering shows from Japan with no problems.

Sources at ROH were very disappointed because the success of the last three shows seemed to rebuild iPPV at nearly record levels, and the shows came across with no serious technical issues. The 6/22 show actually beat the New York show on iPPV, even though it was available on regular PPV. That was said to be a big surprise, since it was a less impressive lineup and the belief was iPPV buys would be minimal with the show on PPV. The best explanation is that consumer confidence gained from putting on two successful broadcasts and two such entertaining shows. Their May numbers probably weren't what they could have been given the lineup because a lot of the fans burned by all the problems may not have ordered.

We're told the various companies were informed by Ustream of this a few weeks ago, and it was considered a major disappointment for both ROH and New Japan. For New Japan, it's not that bad from their standpoint financially since they may do anywhere from a few hundred to around 1,500 orders (for the Tokyo Dome show) outside of Japan, so it's not a big business for them. But it has garnered them a regular hardcore fan base outside of Japan. But for those fans, which as it turn out, are in high numbers readers of this publication, it's a huge issue. While a lot of the smaller shows surface on the Internet pretty quickly, the major PPVs can take some time to do so. Also, it's far more convenient to know ahead of time what will be on and when, and unless they can get a new carrier, it would be the end for seeing major shows live. While the time zone difference makes that hard in the U.S., it's not as bad in Europe and some of the bigger shows that have afternoon starts can be viewed late night live on he West Coast.

The vast majority of New Japan's iPPV business, probably along the lines of 95 to 98 percent, which is by far the most successful of any company ever, is through their Japanese carrier.

The story that we've heard is that Ustream was only getting 10 to 15 percent of the revenue, far less than the 50/50 split that is common in the genre. But iPPV was never a major part of their business plan, just something they started doing.

They greatly over achieved their projections and were faced with the choice to spend more on resources for servers and customer support. The latter has been a problem during live shows. The shows themselves don't have lagging and buffering to nearly the degree most iPPVs end up having, which is probably a combination of both Ustream being the gold standard in this industry and New Japan's in-arena production. But there are issues at times with being able to see the show after ordering. It is not unusual to order the show watch it, but if you click off and try to go back, there are problems getting back on. It's not that unusual for people, if they don't watch it straight through, having to order a second time and ask for a refund later because of the lack of customer support. Last year, when we were at the Observer/Figure Four party, we were going to watch a New Japan show from that week, and there were technical issues after ordering that not only wouldn't allow the show to play, but because it had been ordered, wouldn't even allow you to order it a second time.

And while Ustream's reputation for New Japan shows was good, and they had no issues with ROH, there were problems with iPPVs when working with Invicta in the past, and last year's TripleMania completely misfired and ended up instead being offered for free. AAA is going with a different carrier this year.

The reports were that Ustream didn't like dealing with customer service on iPPV problems. Ustream did not respond to any questions regarding their future plans with iPPV.

JULY 13

Regarding the PPV number, it's hard to get it in the sense that early numbers can be off by a decent amount, and let's just say the early number estimate is 10,000 (which in fact, is the early estimate we got). That could be 3,000 and it could be 20,000, so what does it mean? There really won't be a closer number for about another month. The Glory show the night before is estimated at 6,000, which was a disaster because they spent money on production, ran from The Forum in Los Angeles, and had to pay fighters. For a UFC, a number after the first week is usually not too far off because of the volume (although it sometimes has been off considerably) and because the tracking is better. We'll know if and when Final Battle is announced as a PPV. If it is, then it did okay to good. If it's not, then it didn't.

The first show since the PPV takes place on 7/12 in Hopkins, MN, near Minneapolis, with Michael Elgin & Rowe & Hanson (the War Machine tag team that did a run-in during his match where he won the title vs. Adam Cole & Matt Hardy & Michael Bennett. Also announced is a Proving Ground (non-title) match with Jay Lethal vs. Takaaki Watanabe, Silas Young vs. Jimmy Jacobs vs. Matt Taven vs. ACH with the winner getting a title shot at Elgin on 8/22 in Milwaukee, B.J. Whitmer & Roderick Strong vs. Mark & Jay Briscoe, Kyle O'Reilly vs. Cedric Alexander plus Kevin Steen and Bobby Fish.

Unless things change, this will be Hardy's final show with the promotion. He had been booked on future dates but they weren't happy about him doing the TNA shows since the two companies are considered in competition with each other since TNA has been calling up key ROH talent (particularly those without a contract) and both are now PPV promotions. TNA is now hotly pursuing Bobby Fish & Kyle O'Reilly, whose contracts have expired, to come in for a program with Edwards & Richards. ROH is on a pretty strict budget from Sinclair, so getting into any kind of bidding for talent is something that hasn't happened yet and is unlikely to happen.

JULY 21

An intriguing story, coming right after Ustream made its decision to get out of the PPV business, is that Viewers Choice Canada, the main PPV provider in that country, will be shutting down on 9/30, ironically the same day as Ustream is currently planned to get out of the iPPV business.

The decision was made after Bell Media became the majority owner of Viewers Choice Canada in its purchase of Astral in 2013. Viewers Choice Canada provided the PPV channels for the major pro wrestling, MMA and boxing events for the past 23 years. But between the live sports events, the channels would be used for movies. Movies on PPV had turned into an in-demand, push a button and watch on your time, not on a PPV station's scheduled time slot.

Interestingly, Bell had dropped using Viewers Choice in favor of its own in-house channel, so that doesn't affect their subscribers. But Viewers Choice is still used for Rogers, Cogeco, Videtron, Bell Aliant and Eastlink.

The move may be because Rogers Sportsnet PPV is expected to change its name and carry both sports events and scripted programming. The other companies could strike a deal with either Bell or Rogers to carry their channels, so ultimately, this should not affect distribution of any of the events in Canada.

"While Viewer's Choice PPV will be shut down, there will be no disruption in PPV availability in Canada," said Steve Keogh of UFC's Canadian office. "With respect to UFC PPVs, we have 100 percent confidence that Viewer's Choice customers will be taken care of by affiliate partners of ours."

JULY 28

Ustream officially made a statement regarding iPPV, which strongly affects ROH, New Japan Pro Wrestling and Dragon Gate.

As reported here the past two weeks, they have now officially announced being out of the iPPV business.

The company's statement said:

"We are sad to tell you that we have decided to shut down our Pay-Per-view (PPV) feature on October 1st, 2014. It's always a tough decision to discontinue any feature, but we want to direct our resources to focus on other features and continue providing the best live streaming platform possible. Here's what you can expect:

- We will no longer allow scheduling of PPV events past September 30th.
- On September 14th, 2014, PPV event creation will be disabled.
- October 1st, 2014, we will shut down our PPV product, remove all PPV events and make all public PPV videos private videos.
- October 30th, 2014, all PayPal payments to broadcasters for ticket sales will be complete.

We encourage all users of Ustream PPV to continue using our Free Broadcasting platform, or to subscribe to our Pro Broadcasting service. Our Enterprise Pro Broadcasting plan includes the ability to hide your Ustream channel page and restrict where your content plays. Combined with your own e-commerce or payment gateway capabilities, this would allow you to build your own protected page and charge users to access it.

We are always eager to hear your feedback on this, or any other Ustream feature. Please email your feedback to feedback@ustream.tv"

The next to last paragraph seems to encourage companies to do a monthly subscription service, as long as the company itself handles the subscription end, and they will allow their platform to block access from non-subscribers. In a sense, this would be like a Fight Pass like service where the company could put content up, including the live events, but the access would be on a time frame subscription basis and not a per-event basis.

The change is due to the company wanting to get out of the business due to the technical support issue. Even though Ustream has the best reputation out there, there are still too many problems with this technology. We were flooded with problems both during the live show and the next day from people who had ordered the 7/21 G-1 Climax first night and couldn't access the content. We had two issues ourselves, one at the start of the Shelton Benjamin vs. Doc Gallows match, which cleared up in a minute, and a second, thankfully, during intermission, which cleared up before intermission ended, but lasted several minutes. Others reported problems during the Benjamin vs. Gallows match that didn't clear up live until well into the next match. A number of people also couldn't access a replay of the show even though they had ordered it, due to a glitch that was repaired by early afternoon. Like with the WWE Network's broadcasting of Battleground, many people had no issues and many had serious problems.

AUGUST 11

The company now looks to be continuing iPPVs through Ustream, with a new deal worked out where they will have to get a third party involved to process the orders, and that party will have to work with Ustream. It makes things more complicated and gives another avenue for a potential technical problem, but Ustream wants to get completely out of the e-commerce aspect of iPPVs. Ustream will continue to broadcast iPPVs for a fee provided someone else handles the e-commerce and customer service, aspects they wanted to remove themselves from. This is also an opening for both New Japan and Dragon Gate to continue, if they can get an e-commerce provider that would work with Ustream. The iPPVs will no longer stream from the Ustream site, but Ustream will handle back-end production. ROH will host them on their own site at ROHwrestling.com. So for New Japan to continue, they would have to make a deal with an English language company and likely host the shows from their own web site. If the technology works out between the commerce partner and Ustream, it's actually a plus because it gets the fans to the ROH site as the home of the shows.

CHAPTER TWENTY ONE

KENTA QUITS NOAH

MAY 5

Tokyo Sports reported on 4/30 that KENTA, the company's biggest star, is leaving the promotion with his final appearance being on the 5/17 show at Korakuen Hall.

The news was confirmed hours later at a press conference at the NOAH offices with KENTA, real name Kenta Kobayashi, and Naomichi Marufuji, the Vice President of the promotion.

"Thank you very much for all the fans who have supported me for the last 14 years. You only live life once and I'm taking a new challenge at 33 years old."

KENTA said that he can't reveal what he is doing next and would be making an announcement soon.

The belief is that he is headed to WWE. KENTA had a WWE tryout that started on 1/27, and lasted several days. After he got back, he claimed it wasn't a tryout and he was just there to see how they did things. There were wrestlers in NOAH who immediately contradicted that privately, noting he took a flight right out of Japan after a show directly to Orlando without any rest, and it was noted to us by various people he was there for a tryout. But nothing was said about it since.

Apparently the quietness was more because KENTA's contract didn't expire until 4/30, and was fulfilling those dates before making the announcement.

Those in Japan believe this will lead to a decline in the popularity of an already struggling promotion, that a decade ago was thriving, until losing its weekly network slot on NTV, and in recent years has suffered loss of major talent and significant economic problems, as well as the death of Mitsuharu Misawa and the end of the career of Kenta Kobashi.

KENTA will do two shows on per-show deals, the 5/3 NOAH show at Differ Ariake, and the 5/17 show, as his farewell, and in many ways, that show will be the end of an era for the promotion.

It's not confirmed it is WWE, although most believe that to be the case. There was New Japan speculation going on as well.

A former kickboxer, Kenta Kobayashi, born March 12, 1981, is only 5-foot-7 and about 180 pounds. For most of the past decade, he was considered one of the best pro wrestlers in the world. Both Daniel Bryan and C.M. Punk heavily took from his style which included hard kicks and submissions, and he popularized Punk's finisher, the GTS, which in Japan was called the Go 2 sleep. He had worked some U.S. dates with ROH. He wrestled Bryan in both singles and tag matches in Japan, including once winning the GHC jr. heavyweight title from him, with matches in both NOAH and ROH.

His style is based on hard kicks, as he did kickboxing as an amateur before starting pro wrestling in 2000, for All Japan Pro Wrestling. He left as part of the mass exodus that year when Misawa formed Pro Wrestling NOAH. Because his real name was so similar to Kenta Kobashi, who was also his mentor, he went by the name KENTA.

He talent was very quickly noted by fans an he became the most popular wrestler in the junior heavyweight division. It was a slow ascension to the actual top spot ion the promotion because in Japan, while smaller guys have been featured for decades, it was usually against other smaller guys. A major league promotion, like NOAH, wouldn't have a junior heavyweight beat the top heavyweights or hold the heavyweight title.

But in recent years, with the lack of new heavyweight stars and a changing fan base, the old rules were thrown out, although many felt they waited too long to establish KENTA as the group's top star.

MAY 12

There may be more to the KENTA leaving story than meets the eyes, as Akira Taue, the President of the company, has ordered a reorganization of the company. Within Japanese wrestling, the KENTA departure announcement was a huge shock. People connected on the inside had no inclination this was coming, and even the wrestlers and the NOAH front office had no idea, and were left stunned and shocked as they were given no advance word. A lot of people in the company were worried about not being told ahead of time, and also losing their signature star at a time when business is rocky at best. Katsuyori Shibata, who is friends with KENTA, noted that "It was his dream all the way" to go to WWE. WWE has not commented publicly on this, but the expectation is that is where he's headed. Daily Sports in Japan reported him going to WWE and those inside the Japanese scene are also under that impression, with the idea that at 33, he realized his body was feeling it from all those years working the tough style and if he was going to go, time is running out, plus NOAH isn't in line for any kind of a turnaround after losing so much key talent late last year.

MAY 26

There are probably a number of factors that led to KENTA making the decision to leave Pro Wrestling NOAH, but none of them are a good sign for the struggling company.

While undersized, at probably 180 pounds, for the big star of what is historically seen as one of the country's biggest groups, the 33-year-old had to have seen a combination of injuries starting to catch up with his body and the future of the promotion in making the call.

Takashi Sugiura said in Tokyo Sports that KENTA was leaving for WWE, which makes sense since he did a one-week tryout in late January and then didn't sign a new deal when his contract expired a few weeks ago. The reports from Japan right now are that WWE still has to get his visa work in order before he would actually sign a contract.

KENTA himself has been cryptic about his future, just saying that he can't yet say what his next move is, which make everyone pretty much sure it's WWE, because WWE doesn't like wrestlers to let it out that they've signed developmental deals. He joked that maybe he's going to open a restaurant, since a lot of Japanese pro wrestlers own restaurants after retirement.

Yahoo in Japan reported KENTA would start with WWE next month, and said KENTA dropped the GHC heavyweight title to Takeshi Morishima on 1/5 and also noted the death of his grandmother as catalysts for the move. He said after the death of his grandmother he recognized that it was time to move from Japan and make changes in his life.

His farewell show to NOAH, on 5/17 at Korakuen Hall, was the end of an era. While few remember it, Kenta Kobayashi, his real name, who was a kickboxer as a teenager (hence his heavy reliance on kicks and strikes) and protégé of Kenta Kobashi, actually debuted with All Japan Pro Wrestling on May 24, 2000. But almost immediately, he followed Kobashi and Mitsuharu Misawa in the formation of Pro Wrestling NOAH.

He was immediately noticed for how talented he was and within two years, was starting to get a small push, often as the junior member of a tag team with Kobashi. In 2003, KENTA & Naomichi Marufuji became a regular junior heavyweight tag team, given the push over the top when they defeated Jushin Liger & Takehiro

Murahama in the finals of a tournament to become the first GHC junior heavyweight champions on March 1, 2003, at Budokan Hall.

He and Marufuji later become rivals, starting in some highly-touted matches for the GHC junior heavyweight title, and then eventually bringing the feud to the heavyweight division and the GHC title. He became heavily copied, as some of his trademark spots, like the KENTA rush and Go 2 sleep were copied by C.M. Punk in WWE, and his Busaiku knee is the finisher of Daniel Bryan, who, as Bryan Danielson, he wrestled in both ROH and NOAH, including battling over the GHC jr. title.

Between the death of Mitsuharu Misawa, the retirement of Kobashi and the financial and exposure problems stemming from loss of network coverage on NTV, NOAH has fallen of late. If anything, that would put the pressure of KENTA to remain with the company, but he had talked often about wanting to test himself, and his window of opportunity was running low.

His final show with NOAH drew a sellout of 2,000 fans to Korakuen Hall, sold out well in advance. KENTA & Marufuji teamed together one last time, beating Katsuhiko Nakajima & Sugiura when KENTA pinned long-time rival Nakajima with the Go 2 Sleep in 28:31. The match was said to have been fantastic. He said nothing after the match, but waved good bye and bowed to all four corners as the crowd went crazy. He came out later in the show to do commentary in the Yuji Nagata GHC title defense against Mohammed Yone. After the show ended, after many fans had left and they were starting to take the ring down, those who stayed were chanting his name like crazy and he did get back in the ring and bowed to everyone, but never gave a farewell speech.

JULY 6

The WWE's Japan office officially announced that on the 7/12 show in Osaka, that a major Japanese superstar would be signing his WWE contract at 5 p.m. that day. It had already been reported that KENTA would be signing in Osaka but WWE hadn't confirmed it, although they inadvertently did. The ad for the Osaka show shows Hogan and a blacked out wrestler, but a code to see the ad lists it as "KENTA teaser."

JULY 13

The KENTA signing announcement takes place on 7/12 in Osaka. This is the Japan week with shows on 7/10 and 7/11 at Sumo Hall in Japan, as well as the Osaka show, as well as the 7/12 Madison Square Garden show. Charlotte debuts on the main roster on the domestic tour.

JULY 21

The signing of KENTA, in a ceremony with Hulk Hogan and Jimmy Hart on the 7/12 show in Osaka, marks a first, and something that probably could not have happened in a previous generation.

Kenta Kobayashi was the first genuine top star of a major Japanese wrestling promotion in history to leave his company to join an American promotion. Years ago, such as in the 90s when WWF had an interest in his near-namesake Kenta Kobashi, such a thing could not have happened. In Japan, the top stars were loyal to their companies, and the idea was the company would be loyal to them. They would headline as long as they were physically able, and then they'd keep their jobs and pay while working in the middle where they could tone down after their body was beaten up. If they couldn't wrestle, they would remain with an office position. While it was possible, particularly in the late 90s, to make more money in the U.S., it was considered short-term money, and short-sighted thinking. It was ingrained in the wrestlers that company loyalty came first.

In another era, KENTA never would have left Pro Wrestling NOAH, and WWE never would have considered a wrestler from Japan who was 5-foot-7 and 180 pounds, no matter what his talents. The fact they never made a play for Jushin Liger in his prime, not that they necessarily could have gotten him, but never made a play, tells you that.

But things changed. Pro Wrestling NOAH is a struggling promotion, closer these days to an independent, except for a few big shows a year, than a major league group. The idea it will be around forever, or even for several more years, is questionable, at best. Kenta Kobashi, its biggest star, was cut due to financial problems, and many of its biggest stars left for All Japan in the wake of his leaving. KENTA, almost by default, because the original picks like Takeshi Morishima and Takeshi Rikio didn't pan out on top, ended up being the surprise top star of the group. KENTA, at 33, was faced with a major fork in the road. He could continue beating up his body on a ship that is struggling to stay afloat, or he could roll the dice and try to make it on a worldwide stage.

For WWE, things also changed. The key is that the WWE Network will be expanding next year to Japan. For that reason, they wanted a top Japanese star. Yet, in so many ways, even though both sides had very good reasons to make this deal and to see it work, if the past is any indication, its chances of failure seem high.

It is very clear they are not bringing him in to fail, and that from an importance standpoint, there is more to this than meets the eye, and he's going in with his eyes wide open. The introduction of him was major. Hulk Hogan & Jimmy Hart were in the ring in Osaka and called him out, with Hogan calling him the future of wrestling. KENTA came out in a suit-and-tie and signed the contract with Hogan sitting there with him. The two then did the Hogan posing routine together. WWE immediately sent out press releases both in Japan and the U.S., announcing his signing.

A Tokyo press conference was held two days later at the Hard Rock Café in Tokyo, and another press conference is slated for his arrival this week in Orlando. The press release stated specifically he would be going to NXT first. On 7/14, it was announced that J Sports, a Japanese satellite channel, would be airing NXT due to KENTA being expected to be a regular on the shows.

At the press conference, KENTA said he was nervous being in the spotlight in the WWE ring with Hogan, and said he considered it a great honor and a special moment in his career. He said he's working on getting a place in Orlando and looking forward to training at the WWE Performance Center. He said it was a great facility with a lot of great equipment, and he has no trouble starting at the bottom if that's what they choose. He said learning English would be his biggest work in progress. In those sentences, you can see the attitude difference between KENTA, and Paul Levesque's first prized international superstar signing, Luis Urive, the famous Mistico who became Sin Cara.

When asked about his name, he said that was in the company's hands and he said it was up to them. He joked they he may be called Tanaka (the name of the biggest so-called Japanese star in WWWF history, Professor Toru Tanaka, and more in the news in the U.S. because of the former Japanese Pacific league superstar pitcher Masahiro Tanaka, who went 30-0 last season between the season and playoffs and then this year moved to the New York Yankees, perhaps his own hoped for vision of his own career path) or Toyota (the car name). He said that he knows he'll have to change his in-ring style but he'll work hard to do so.

He said it helps him because he personally knows Daniel Bryan and Cesaro from when they worked in NOAH, and both of his friends have top positions in WWE. He talked about how WWE superstars like John Cena and Rey Mysterio are known all over the world, but said he has little expectation of being as big a star as they were. He said he considers WWE the top organization in wrestling and it's been his dream to be in the WWE ring, even if it's just for a short period of time.

One could point out the last true superstar from another country who was also a smaller guy that WWE signed, Urive. He came in with great fanfare, and the company wanted him to succeed because they were looking for a new top Mexican babyface, plus he was Levesque's first highly-touted signing, so to an extent, Levesque's reputation as a talent judge could (although wasn't as it turned out) have been judged based on his signing and success. Given the company's U.S. demographics and product popularity in Mexico, there is far more apparent value in a top Mexican babyface than a top Japanese babyface.

There were a number of reasons for the failure that would not necessarily apply to KENTA. While the style KENTA worked in Japan is different from WWE style, it is not as different as the CMLL style. Really, aside from toning down the physicality and opening up to more comedy, slowing down a little and relying on more basic moves and some theatrical working, Japanese style can translate into the U.S. Plus, a lot of the match finish style that is now popular in WWE came from Japan in the 80s.

Involving Hogan in his signing and making a big deal about it, to where they even sent out a press release about his signing, seems to indicate a willingness, at least at first, to making him a star. They did a big press conference for Urive in Mexico and put it on television immediately. But as far as being a basic worker, KENTA is far superior and won't require opponents to adjust their styles to fit him. That's the one difference between the modern WWE with Urive and the LeBell organization in the late 60s when the Mil Mascaras-led Mexican invasion built business, as well as with promoters like Paul Boesch and Joe Blanchard in Texas.

With WWE, it's their style and you have to fit into that. When Mascaras, Rey Mendoza, Black Gordman, etc. came in the late 60s and were turning business around, the veterans in the territory worked with them. They learned their style and moves and to work the other side of the body. The mentality was that Mascaras and Mendoza were money and that they all make more money the better they make them look. That was different from the WWE mentality that he's a guy who may be a big deal in Mexico, but we're not in Mexico, his records and his stardom doesn't count, and he shouldn't be acting like he's a star until he is one here, and he has to learn to work like an American. Ditto when Mascaras went to Japan. Nobody ever told Mascaras what he couldn't do. Plus, Mistico did get over in New Japan Pro Wrestling outside of Mexico, nothing like Mascaras, but as good as someone of his type probably could have given the junior heavyweight positioning and time frame. But Sin Cara's not learning English worked against him. He lost respect of the locker room when he quit a match with Alberto Del Rio when he broke his finger, but the dye had been cast long before that.

There were plenty of Americans who hated Mascaras for the same reason Urive was hated, but he also ended up being just about the biggest drawing card of the 70s in key markets like Los Angeles, San Diego, Houston, San Antonio and Corpus Christi. Here in San Jose, an appearance by Mascaras would triple the gate, making him equal as an attraction at the time to Andre the Giant, and this isn't even a market that grew up with him. He was also a major star in Madison Square Garden.

He was the biggest draw to kids of anyone in Japan in his era and in that culture, remains a legend today. This had more to do with his costuming and flying moves, and the popularity of wrestling on television and because his style was different from everyone else in the promotion. If he had been put in the position to adapt to everyone else, or to change to a style that would more likely get him considered to be a great worker by the wrestlers or hardcore fans, he'd have never gotten out of the starting gate. Plus, in those days foreigners were supposed to be heels, and he was a babyface. He did his style, didn't sell a ton, and almost never put anyone over.

Second, while KENTA is a great worker and a proven headliner with a so-so level promotion, he is not as naturally cocky as Urive, who was a genuine celebrity and huge drawing card, closer to The Rock or John Cena in his culture. KENTA is a star to Japanese wrestling fans, but he is not a crossover celebrity nor a major drawing card, as a star, perhaps equivalent to A.J. Styles or a little above that level.

Urive hurt himself by not adapting to the style changes, and WWE accentuated it by putting him on the main roster without a transition period, and then when he did flashy moves that got over, the producers told him to change and tone them down. Without the flashy moves, he was just another smaller guy with agility. KENTA knows the style differences, is headed to NXT first, and probably knows he has to learn English, something Urive got major heat because he refused to study it.

Some will point to the success of Daniel Bryan, a rival of KENTA's back in his NOAH days and to an extent in ROH, and say it shows the former size mentality and size barrier for stardom is no longer there. And WWE performers who are talented can get away with being smaller than their predecessors because the fan base is more into action that slow powerhouses that don't do much these days.

But there is still a big problem: Promos. Yoshi Tatsu had a good look, could wrestle very well, and learned English. But because he didn't speak English like an American, he was portrayed as a child-like character, a role that limited him to prelims and eventually to nobody caring about him. He wasted the prime of his career and his best earning years making one-third of what he was already making when he left Japan. Unlike KENTA, he also had decent size.

You could always give him a manager to talk for him, but that requires him to be a heel, a tough role to be at his size past a prelim level. In addition, stylistically, he's more suited to be a babyface. He could be put into a tag team with someone with a better command of the language, like the Eddie Guerrero & Tajiri team in WWE from another era.

Also unlike Tatsu, and close to Urive, even if KENTA recognizes he's starting in NXT, and will almost surely have to work his way up from the bottom in WWE, he also thinks of himself as a headliner and it will be hard to accept something less if he's not there after a few years. Most WWE talents that don't make it to the top, while perhaps unhappy about some aspects and often filled with frustration, they are limited by the reality that there's nowhere else to go, and in most cases, they are unproven. KENTA in the same situation will have somewhere else to go, and as a headliner.

Another issue when he comes up is his key moves. His Go 2 sleep is a popular move in the U.S. associated with C.M. Punk. With Punk gone, whether they'll allow him to use the move because it will remind fans of Punk, something the company wouldn't want to do, is one question. Another is, at his size, can he do it safely with the really big guys that he could be in with. KENTA is considerably smaller than Punk. His Busaiku knee finisher was taken by Daniel Bryan. His Game Over was taken by Bryan and made into the LeBell lock, and it's now the Yes lock. His Tiger suplex would likely be banned because of the fear of neck issues because those types of moves aren't allowed in WWE.

So while all past indications and present indications based on what they push do not look good, this is a key situation. There were reasons WWE took little heat in the Sin Cara disappointment, even though there was blame and a lack of understanding that went to both sides. It's not like every problem in the Sin Cara situation wasn't talked about here ahead of time and it went off almost exactly as was predicted in a worst case scenario. But in this case, the personality traits are different and it's a very different caliber of performer. If this experiment fails, it's going to be clear that the WWE may sound good, but it's not the place to be if you're a top-tier Japanese wrestler.

SEPTEMBER 15

Both KENTA and Ric Flair will be appearing at the 9/11 NXT Takeover II show. On NXT this week, they heavily pushed the debut of KENTA as part of the show, but on Raw it was worded differently and made it sound like he would appear but not wrestle. WWE officials confirmed that KENTA will be appearing and making his WWE television debut, but he is not scheduled for a match on the show. J Sports announced this past week it would be airing the show live (it airs at 9 a.m. on Friday morning in Japan) on J Sports 4, because it would be KENTA's WWE debut. The way we had originally heard the story is that he would be introduced on the show and then have his first match at the TV tapings the next day, but the way he was pushed so hard on the NXT show would have given one the indication he was scheduled to wrestle on the show. Flair's appearance could be linked with KENTA. For a number of reasons pushing KENTA is a deal in WWE. The guy is one of the most talented wrestlers in the world and has been for the past decade. Granted, reputations like that actually can work against you in WWE. But he's also the first genuine top tier superstar in Japan they've had as a full-timer of more then just a short tour. Having a Japanese superstar should strengthen the Japanese market for merchandise and the network. There's a reason they brought Hulk Hogan out for his signing and there is talk they will link Flair with him on this special, and that shows this isn't the mentality of bringing in a foreign guy and having the mentality he doesn't know the language and thus can't get over or he's too small to get over in front of our audience.

In addition, because KENTA will be a regular on NXT going forward, NXT will start airing as a weekly show on J Sports 3 in a Friday from 5-6 p.m. time slot. J Sports isn't in a lot of homes in Japan and is probably best compared to something like AXS in the U.S., or if anything, not even at that level. But if you're a WWE fan, or a fan of certain sports properties that they carry, you probably get the station.

KENTA did an interview at the 9/6 show in Citrus Springs, FL. He spoke in English the entire way, so he's been doing his studying. That alone will help his cause because they see he's putting in the effort. Everyone was mad at Luis Urive (Myzteziz) because of the feeling he didn't even bother attempting to learn English and that gave them the idea he thought he was above it. With KENTA, he's playing the game and understanding there's more to WWE than just being a really good wrestler. He said that whoever wins the four-way on 9/11, he wanted to challenge them. The crowd was into him, but then again, when you draw 135 fans to a show and they are hardcore fans who go to see NXT, they probably will have an idea who KENTA is. The 9/11 show sold out in advance, but that's also a 400-seat setup.

CHAPTER TWENTY TWO

WWE ROSTER DIRECTORY 2014

WWE ROSTER DIRECTORY 2014

Name	Real Name	Age	Yrs Pro
Aksana	Zivile Raudoniene	32	5
Jason Albert	Matthew Bloom	41	17
Enzo Amore	Eric Arndt	27	2
Dean Ambrose	Jonathan Good	28	10
Curtis Axel	Joseph Hennig	34	7
Sasha Banks	Mercedes Kaestner-Varnado	21	4
Bad News Barrett	Stuart Bennett	33	10
Batista	David Bautista Jr.	45	14
Bayley	Pamela Martinez	24	5
Brie Bella	Brianna Danielson	30	7
Nikki Bella	Nicole Garcia Colace	30	7
Alexa Bliss	Alexis Kaufman	22	1
Evan Bourne	Matthew Korklan	31	14
Tyler Breeze	Mattias Clement	26	7
Daniel Bryan	Bryan Danielson	33	15
Carlos Cabrera	Carlos Cabrera	54	21
Camacho	Tevita Fifita	31	5
Cameron	Ariane Andrew	26	3
Sin Cara	Jorge Arias	36	15
Colin Cassady	William Morrisey	27	3
John Cena	John Cena Jr.	37	14
Cesaro	Claudio Castagnoli	33	14
Charlotte	Ashley Fliehr Latimer	28	2

Tony Chimel	Tony Chimel	52	23
Christian	William Jason Reso	40	19
Brodus Clay	George Murdoch	34	9
Michael Cole	Sean Coulthard	45	17
Zeb Colter	Wayne Keown	65	41
Baron Corbin	Thomas Pestock	29	1
Bo Dallas	Taylor Rotunda	24	6
Scott Dawson	David Charwood	29	8
Alberto Del Rio	Alberto Rodriguez	37	14
Diego	Edwin Colon	31	15
Tye Dillinger	Ronnie Arneill	33	12
Road Dogg	Brian James	45	23
Big E	Ettore Ewen	28	5
Emma	Tenille Dashwood	25	7
Aiden English	Matthew Rehwoldt	27	2
Fandango	Curtis Hussey	31	15
Fernando	Orlando Colon	32	9
Alicia Fox	Victoria Crawford	28	8
Sawyer Fulton	Jacob Southwick	24	1
Justin Gabriel	Paul Lloyd Jr.	33	17
Goldust	Dustin Runnels	45	26
Lilian Garcia	Lilian Garcia Jozeph	47	14
Corey Graves	Matt Polinsky	30	14
Vickie Guerrero	Vickie Lara Guerrero	46	8
Billy Gunn	Monty Sopp	50	25
Luke Harper	Jon Huber	34	11
Curt Hawkins	Brian Meyers	29	10
Mark Henry	Mark Henry	43	18
HHH	Paul Levesque	45	22
Paul Heyman	Paul Heyman	48	27
Hulk Hogan	Terry Bollea	60	37
Jo Jo	Joseann Offerman	20	1
Jason Jordan	Nathan Everhart	25	3
Hornswoggle	Dylan Postl	28	9
JTG	Jayson Paul	29	8
Kane	Glenn Jacobs	47	22
Great Khali	Dalip Singh-Rana	41	12
Tyson Kidd	Theodore Wilson	34	19
Kofi Kingston	Kofi Sardokie-Mensah	32	9
Konnor	Ryan Parmeter	34	13
Lana	Catherine Perry	29	1
Jerry Lawler	Jerry Lawler	64	44
John Layfield	John Layfield	47	22
Layla	Layla El	36	8
A.J. Lee	April Mendez	27	6
Sylvester Lefort	Tom La Ruffa	30	7
Brock Lesnar	Brock Lesnar	36	11
Teddy Long	Theodore Long	57	29

Brad Maddox	Tyler Kluttz	30	7
Jinder Mahal	Yrvaj Desi	27	10
Eva Marie	Natalie Nelson Coyle	28	1
Josh Matthews	Josh Lomberger	33	13
Santino Marella	Anthony Carellli	35	10
Drew McIntyre	Andrew Galloway	29	13
Stephanie McMahon	Stephanie McMahon Levesque	37	15
Vince McMahon	Vincent McMahon	68	44
Rosa Mendes	Melina Roucka	34	8
The Miz	Michael Mizanin	33	11
Rey Mysterio	Oscar Gutierrez	39	25
Naomi	Trinity McCray Fatu	26	5
Natalya	Natalie Neidhart Wilson	32	14
Titus O'Neil	Thaddeus Bullard	37	5
Adrian Neville	Benjamin Satterly	27	8
Randy Orton	Randy Orton	34	14
David Otunga	David Otunga	34	5
Paige	Saraya Jade Beavis	21	8
C.J. Parker	Joseph Robinson	25	5
C.M. Punk	Phillip Brooks	35	16
Summer Rae	Danielle Moinet	30	3
Mojo Rawley	Dean Muhtadi	27	1
William Regal	Darren Matthews	46	31
Roman Reigns	Leati "Joe" Anoa'i	28	4
Cody Rhodes	Cody Runnels	29	8
Alex Riley	Kevin Kiley Jr.	33	7
Justin Roberts	Justin Roberts	34	12
The Rock	Dwayne Johnson	42	13
Marcelo Rodriguez	Marcelo Rodriguez	44	14
Ricardo Rodriguez	Jose Rodriguez	28	8
Seth Rollins	Colby Lopez	28	9
Adam Rose	Ray Leppan	34	16
Erick Rowan	Joseph Ruud	32	10
Alexander Rusev	Miroslav Barnyashev	28	5
Ryback	Ryan Reeves	32	10
Zack Ryder	Matthew Cardona	29	10
Damien Sandow	Aaron Haddad	31	13
Byron Saxton	Bryan Kelly	32	6
Sheamus	Stephen Farrelly	36	12
Big Show	Paul Wight Jr.	42	19
Heath Slater	Heath Miller	31	10
Jack Swagger	Jacob Hager Jr.	32	8
Booker T	Robert Booker Tio Huffman	49	25
Tamina Snuka	Sarona Snuka	36	5
Richie Steamboat	Richard Blood Jr.	26	5
Yoshi Tatsu	Naofumi Yamamoto	36	12
Torito	Mario Mejia Jiminez	32	14
R-Truth	Ron Killings	42	17

Travis Tyler	Sam Udell	26	3
The Undertaker	Mark Calaway	49	30
Jey Uso	Joshua Fatu	29	5
Jimmy Uso	Jonathan Fatu	29	5
Rob Van Dam	Robert Szatkowski	43	24
Viktor	Eric Thompson	33	13
Xavier Woods	Austin Watson	27	9
Bray Wyatt	Windham Rotunda	27	6
Darren Young	Frederick Rosser	34	12
Renee Young	Renee Paquette	29	2
Sami Zayn	Rami Sebei	29	13
Dolph Ziggler	Nicholas Nemeth	34	10

BACKGROUNDS

MMA: Santino Marella (0-1 listed record), Alberto Del Rio (9-5 listed record), Brock Lesnar (former UFC heavyweight champion)

College Basketball: Kane (Northeast Missouri State/Truman State), Big Show (Wichita State), Undertaker (Angelina College), Colon Cassady (New York University)

Bodybuilding: John Cena, HHH (Mr. Teenage New Hampshire), Great Khali (Mr. India), Batista

Women's Bodybuilding: Aksana (2009 Arnold Classic winner), Alexa Bliss (14th place, 2013 Arnold Classic)

College Football: John Cena (Springfield College/Massachusetts, first team Division III All-American center 1998); Bray Wyatt (Troy University), Camacho (University of Texas); Kane (Northeast Missouri State/Truman State); Titus O'Neil (Florida); The Rock (University of Miami 1991 national championship team); Jack Swagger (Oklahoma); Jason Albert (University of Pittsburgh); Big E (University of Iowa); Roman Reigns (Georgia Tech, first team All-Atlantic Coast Conference defensive tackle 2006); Brodus Clay (Antelope Valley College; University of Nebraska-Kearney); Darren Young (Fairleigh Dickinson College); Jimmy Uso (West Alabama); Jey Uso (West Alabama), John Layfield (Abilene Christian, Lone Star Conference first team All-American offensive lineman 1988, 1989), Baron Corbin (Northwest Missouri State); Mojo Rawley (University of Maryland, 2008 Academic All-Atlantic Coast Conference)

Arena Football: Titus O'Neil (2003-2007 Utah Blaze, Tampa Bay Storm, Las Vegas Gladiators, Carolina Cobras)

Canadian Football: The Rock (Calgary Stampeders), Roman Reigns (Edmonton Eskimos)

World League of American Football: John Layfield, 1991 San Antonio Riders

National Football League: Mojo Rawley, 2009 Green Bay Packers, 2010 Arizona Cardinals (Injured reserve)

High School Football All-American: Titus O'Neil (1995 Parade Magazine All-American Swanee High School, Live Oak, FL); The Rock (1989 Parade Magazine All-American Freedom High School, Allentown, PA)

Amateur Wrestling: Bray Wyatt (Florida high school state heavyweight champion 2005); Kofi Kingston (placed in Massachusetts high school state meet); Alberto Del Rio (Multi-time Mexican national champion freestyle and

Greco-Roman and a number of age group championships, 1996 Greco-Roman bronze medalist, junior (teenage) world championships, 214 pounds; 1997 5th place, 214 at Pan American games); Richie Steamboat (youth age group championships); Randy Orton (youth age group championships); Cody Rhodes (2002 and 2003 Georgia high school state champion, 191 pounds); Jack Swagger (7th place, 2006 NCAA championships, heavyweight, Oklahoma); Dolph Ziggler (Mid American Conference champion at 165 pounds, 2001, 2002 and 2003, Kent State University); Brock Lesnar (1995 third place South Dakota high school state tournament, heavyweight; 1997 Junior College national tournament, 5th place, heavyweight Bismark Junior College; 1998 Junior College national champion, heavyweight, Bismark Junior College; 1999 NCAA championships 2nd place, heavyweight, Minnesota; 2000 NCAA champion, heavyweight, Minnesota); Bo Dallas (placed 5th in 2008 Florida high school state meet); Big E (2002 Florida state high school champion, heavyweight); Xavier Woods (placed in Georgia high school state meet), Jason Jordan (2005, 3rd place, Indiana state high school tournament, heavyweight; 2006, 6th place, Indiana state high school tournament, heavyweight; starting heavyweight at University of Indiana 2007-2010, went to NCAA tournament 2008, 2009, 2010); Sawyer Fulton (placed in Ohio state high school meet at heavyweight 2007 and 2008; Ashland College, 4th place NCAA Division II national championships, heavyweight, 2011; 3rd place NCAA Division II national championships, heavyweight, 2012); Travis Tyler (5th place, Colorado state high school championships, 215 pounds, 2006; Chadron State College 2007-2010)

College Baseball: Ryback (Community College of Southern Nevada)

Modeling: Alicia Fox, Justin Gabriel, Rosa Mendes, Brie Bella, Nikki Bella, Eva Marie, Lana

Lingerie Football: Summer Rae (2008 2011 Chicago Bliss defensive back, team captain, 2011 All-Star team)

Second/Third Generation: Justin Gabriel (Paul Lloyd Sr.); Bray Wyatt (Mike Rotunda/IRS, Blackjack Mulligan); Alberto Del Rio (Dos Caras, third generation as his grandfather was a pro wrestler); Curtis Axel (Curt Hennig/Larry Hennig); Natalya (Jim Neidhart/Stu Hart); Randy Orton (Bob Orton Jr./Bob Orton Sr.); Diego (Carlos Colon); Cody Rhodes (Dusty Rhodes); Goldust (Dusty Rhodes); Tamina Snuka (Jimmy Snuka); Jey Uso (Rikishi); Jimmy Uso (Rikishi); Bo Dallas (Mike "IRS" Rotunda/Blackjack Mulligan); Richie Steamboat (Ricky Steamboat); Roman Reigns (Sika of the Wild Samoans); Paige (Ricky Knight/Sweet Saraya Knight); Charlotte (Ric Flair); Road Dogg (Bob Armstrong)

Professional singing: Lilian Garcia, Lana

Cheerleaders: Vickie Guerrero (El Paso minor league baseball team); Layla (Miami Heat); Naomi (Orlando Magic)

College volleyball: Charlotte (Appalachian State University)

Beauty Pageant: Lilian Garcia (Miss South Carolina top ten place finisher)

Judo: Santino Marella (four-time Canadian age group champion)

Olympic weightlifting: Mark Henry (1991 teenage national champion, super heavyweight; 1991 6th place teenage world championship, super heavyweight; 1993 U.S. national champion, super heavyweight; 1994 U.S. national champion, super heavyweight; 1996 U.S national champion, super heavyweight; silver, gold and bronze medalist, 1995 Pan American games, super heavyweight; 1992 Olympics 10th place, super heavyweight; 1996 Olympics, 14th place, super heavyweight)

Powerlifting: Mark Henry (1988 Texas state teenage champion, super heavyweight; 1989 Texas state teenage champion, super heavyweight; 1990 U.S. national teenage champion, super heavyweight; 1990 U.S. high school national champion, super heavyweight; 1991 U.S. national teenage champion, super heavyweight; 1995 drug free world champion, super heavyweight; 1995 U.S. national champion, super heavyweight; 1997 U.S. national champion, super heavyweight; set state and national records in squat and dead lift in super heavyweight division); Big E (2011 USA Powerlifting national champion 275 pound weight class), Alexander Rusev

World's Strongest Man: Mark Henry (2002 Arnold World's strongest man contest winner)

Bare Knuckle boxing: Bad News Barrett

College Rodeo: Billy Gunn (Sam Houston State)

Professional Rodeo: Billy Gunn

Gymnastics: Alexa Bliss, Charlotte

CHAPTER TWENTY THREE

ANTONIO INOKI RETURNING TO NORTH KOREA

MAY 26

Antonio Inoki is apparently working on a deal for another show in North Korea this year similar to the World Wrestling Peace Festival in 1995 with Antonio Inoki vs. Ric Flair that drew 170,000 fans the second night and about 150,000 the first night (Shinya Hashimoto vs. Scott Norton main event), which are believed to be the two largest crowds in pro wrestling history. Every few years, these talks start and go nowhere, although it has made mainstream media in both Japan and North Korea, as well as the U.S. and the U.K., that the event would take place in August. The dates planned are 8/30 and 8/31 in Pyongyang, the city the original shows took place in. Instead of going back to May Day Stadium, they are going to run a 20,000-seat indoor arena with both martial arts and pro wrestling. It will be an IGF show with about 20 wrestlers brought in. The last time there was some trouble because Inoki purported it to be bringing in a sport, and he brought in New Japan, WCW and All Japan women wrestlers, and the North Koreans watching thought the matches may not be real. Even though it was the biggest two crowds in pro wrestling history, besides Kensuke Sasaki and Akira Hokuto, who met for the first time on that trip, went on a date, and were engaged by morning, almost everyone on that trip talks about it like it was a nightmare. Simon Inoki, who is looking at booking Americans, had already reached out to Jeff Jarrett and Global Force Wrestling.

JULY 13

Antonio Inoki was warned by political and governmental officials about running the shows this year in North Korea after North Korea test fired some scud missiles this past week. Inoki was urged to stay away from North Korea, which he's already gotten in trouble for visiting and trying to do business with in the past as a member of the Japanese Diet. So what do you think he did on 7/7? You go it. He held a press conference to announce a pro wrestling, Tae Kwon Do and MMA show at a 20,000-seat arena in Pyongyang, North Korea on 8/30 and 8/31. He said he would be bringing in 20 athletes from the U.S., Japan, The Netherlands and Asia and it would air worldwide on the Internet. He left for Korea for a one week trip on 7/9 and noted at his press conference that he would be missing the 7/13 IGF show in Fukuoka, but would do a live message from North Korea to the fans at the show. This story has gotten major mainstream publicity in Japan. Inoki was suspended from the Diet for 30 days last year for making an unauthorized trip to North Korea, although because Japan has revoked some of its sanctions against North Korea as part of negotiations going on, so Inoki is not expected to be punished for this trip or for putting on next month's show even though he's ruffling a lot of feathers in doing so. The event is a reprise of the 1995 show that Inoki, New Japan Pro Wrestling and WCW did that became the Collision in Korea PPV. As time has gone on and the legend of that show has increased, the attendance at the two shows was listed at 380,000 (up from about 311,500 for the two-days that was the real number) and it was claimed to have been the biggest PPV event in pro wrestling history (it did well below average on PPV for shows even during the dark days of pro wrestling in that era, but it was a show taped delayed by months without much in the way of hype). Even though that two-day affair would have been the two largest crowds, by far, in pro wrestling history, everyone that I know of that was on that trip speaks of it as a complete nightmare.

SEPTEMBER 1

Antonio Inoki's 8/30 and 8/31 shows in Pyongyang, North Korea, have gotten worldwide media attention over the past week because of the uniqueness of the event. It'll be an IGF pro wrestling show that will combine pro wrestling matches, aikido and taekwondo matches. Americans booked on the show are Bob Sapp, Bobby Lashley and Eric Hammer. Interesting that Lashley is flying to and from South Korea for pro wrestling just days before his fight in Bellator. That doesn't sound like the best idea, and hopefully he reconsiders. The guys who went to North Korea in 1995 for Inoki's shows, even though they performed before the two biggest crowds in pro wrestling history, most considered the experience a nightmare and will tell horror stories about the experience. Well, except Kensuke Sasaki and Akira Hokuto, who met, went out on a date, and were engaged by the morning, and 18 years later are still married and a well known celebrity couple in Japan. The two shows in 1995 drew 170,000 and 150,000 at the stadium, although very little of that was paid. The stadium is being refurbished so this week's shows are at the largest arena.

SEPTEMBER 8

Antonio Inoki's shows in Pyongyang, North Korea, on 8/30 and 8/31, got tons of press around the world including NBC coverage, noting they were the first pro wrestling shows in North Korea since the World Wrestling Peace Festival shows in 1995 and it was the first major sports event with foreign athletes since January when Dennis Rodman staged a basketball game. It started off badly as Jang Ling, a North Korean International Olympic Committee representative in his opening speech started attacking both the U.S. and South Korea, claiming that President Obama was using military exercises in South Korea as a prelude to a nuclear attack on North Korea. Three Americans worked the show, Bob Sapp (a lot of the press internationally and in Korea centered around Sapp because he briefly played in the NFL with the Vikings and Bears), Erik Hammer and Jon Andersen (who was Strongman in New Japan and CMLL for years). Bobby Lashley had been advertised but with his fight coming up on Friday, it would have been foolish to take that kind of a trip a week out. They brought in physical freaks with Sapp, Andersen (a huge muscular guy just coming off winning a national over-40 bodybuilding contest), Montanha Silva (a 6-foot-10 or so Brazilian who has done MMA) and Jerome LeBanner, an IGF regular who was a kickboxing superstar in the K-1 heyday. On the first night, Sapp & Andersen beat Atsushi Sawada & Shogun Okamoto when Sapp used the torture rack on Sawada. The main event saw Kazuyuki Fujita beat Hammer, a training partner of Josh Barnett. The second night saw Sapp beating Sawada in a singles match, Suzukawa beat Silva and Fujita beat LeBanner. Both shows drew legitimate sellouts, with 15,000 fans the first night and 15,500 the second night. But it's likely few if any actually paid and it was a government bought show where people were told to attend and most had no idea what they were seeing. Sapp said on the first night that it was a little eerie and scary at first, but once the match started, it went over well.

CHAPTER TWENTY FOUR

KURT ANGLE'S FUTURE

MAY 19

Kurt Angle may be almost done with the promotion. He just had another knee operation, this time a reconstructive surgery as opposed to the arthroscopic surgery that he was just coming back from. This will keep him out for five months, so he says, which is mid-October. His contract expires in September. That makes two surgeries in a row at the age of 45. TNA not advertising him for the U.K. tour this coming January makes me think there's a good chance he won't be around when this deal expires, similar to the other highly paid talent TNA didn't re-sign. He's talked about wanting to go back to WWE, but there's no way he could take the schedule. In the past, when his contracts have been expired, WWE didn't show interest in him. People talk about the idea of him being an instructor in NXT. I' m not sure they earmark the kind of money for that job as Angle is used to earning and if Jarrett has solid backers, even though the expectation is he'll go with mostly newer and lower priced guys, you do need a few established stars for early credibility. Things could al-ways be different now regarding WWE's views on him, but at best he should be doing a few matches a year. Those in TNA say not to read into this that he's 100 percent gone, however. The segment that aired on the 5/8 show was taped on 4/28, and he was still doing house shows last weekend, although he did very little on those shows. On TV, in the segment, he said he tore his ACL. I know that in one of his knees, he's been working without an ACL for years.

MAY 26

The deal with Kurt Angle and WWE, and this is why there was no response from WWE to him the last time his contract was due, is that after being scared in 2006, Vince McMahon made the call that no matter what, there was not going to be an Olympic gold medalist dying on WWE's watch. It perhaps was overblown when people said he was on death watch, but even before Benoit, and far more since, the issue has been, even if the chance was slim, this, at least a few years ago, was simply a risk McMahon wasn't willing to take. They were already starting to push Angle's comeback on Impact this week, saying it's a five month countdown which would be mid-October. That would be after his deal expires, so maybe they've made the call they'll keep him, figuring if they don't sign him he may end up with Jeff Jarrett. Then again, given how they pushed Hogan and Styles at the end and didn't sign them, especially Styles, what would be considered basic pro wrestling television logic doesn't exactly apply here.

JULY 21

Kurt Angle was on Jim Ross' podcast this past week and said that his contract expires on 9/21 and that TNA offered him a new deal but he hasn't signed it. He said that he believes the next wrestling contract he signs will be his last and he wants to keep his options open. That's all but outright saying he's hoping to go to WWE to finish his career. The last time Angle's contract was due, WWE wasn't interested. There's question whether Angle could pass a WWE physical, but even if he could, Vince McMahon in the past has been extremely negative about bringing Angle back, feeling the risk was too high if something had happened to an Olympic gold medalist while under their watch. Dana White said that Angle was asked to do The Ultimate Fighter season that Kimbo, Roy Nelson, Brendan Schaub and Matt Mitrione were on, and that's five years ago, and White said that Angle failed the physical. Angle claimed that wasn't the case, and he didn't do the season because he was called late and didn't have time to get into fighter shape. Ultimately, for Angle to get an offer, while that would usually be a Paul Levesque decision, in this case it's going to be a 100 percent a Vince decision. There are people in TNA who have speculated from day one that if Jeff Jarrett has significant money behind him, that Angle would be his pick as his company's flagship star. Even though there was nuclear heat between the two in the past, that is no longer the case, and Jarrett has told people many times over the years that he considers Angle the best worker he has ever been in the ring with, and considering the variety and number of people that entails, that speaks volumes about his thoughts on him as a performer.

Angle wrote on Twitter:"Rumors are the root of evil. The truth will endure. Here is the truth! I'm excited to say I'm coming up on my one year anniversary of being clean and sober. I'm very humbled. God has truly blessed me. It's been a difficult but exciting road to living alcohol/drug free. Then some heartless individuals want to create rumors of me `passed out' on a plane. Wow, I guess you can't take a nap on a plane when you're a recovering addict. But it only makes me want to stay clean even more!!!" There was a flight Angle was on recently that had several WWE writers on, going to a production meeting, and they saw Angle on the flight and they passed the word that he had serious issues. There was also a web site story on it, so that's what Angle was reacting to. Since Angle is clearly trying to get back to WWE, this did him no favors.

AUGUST 18

Angle is trying to pitch WWE on a deal that would be similar to the schedule Michaels did in his final years with the company, where he worked big shows and limited dates. As best we can tell, WWE hasn't shown much interest. As noted before, in the past, Vince McMahon was extremely negative on the idea of bringing Angle back.

AUGUST 25

Kurt Angle made inquiries recently about coming in and was pretty much blown off. Mark Madden reported, and we were able to confirm with a couple of sources, that Angle spoke to HHH and was pretty much blown off. Angle then called Vince McMahon, but McMahon, playing good cop/bad cop, said that HHH makes the talent decisions. Madden reported that HHH wasn't happy that Angle tried to go over his head. Angle pushed the idea of returning on a schedule similar to what Michaels worked his last several years, where he'd come in for specific shows and work very limited house show dates. Angle, 45 had told Madden that he felt he could do at most eight dates per month. Vince still seems pretty adamant about it not being worth the risk, saying in the past that absolutely nothing is worth putting the company in the position where an Olympic hero dies on their watch, because of the negative news stories that would follow. The fact Angle, whose contract expires in one month, is approaching WWE probably says something about the Jarrett promotion in the sense that with Angle's contract expiring with TNA, Angle would seem to make the most sense as the "foundation" star for Jarrett if he had something, and there's really no other foundation star out there. Angle has claimed TNA has offered him a new deal and he turned it down because he wanted to end his career in WWE and felt this next contract would be his last one. If Angle had a chance to come back, and there were no indications McMahon had changed his mind, they weren't helped by the reports from various WWE talent that were on a flight with him that he was passed out. Angle claimed he was just sleeping on the plane, and has claimed to be clean after going through rehab several months ago. But in the last year, between the rehab and two knee injuries, he's had a lot of down time.

SEPTEMBER 15

Kurt Angle did an interview this past week with Ring Rust Radio. He said that his recovery from knee surgery is going slower than expected. He noted that he didn't need this surgery, since he's been working for five years without an ACL (he wasn't aware of it for five years, but I believe learned it in the past year or so). But he said that his knee was starting to limit him as a performer and was shifting, so it got him nervous that it would blow out again so opted for the surgery. He said he was hoping to be in the ring in October, but that's not going to happen, and he's now hoping for December or January, and said that's even rushing it. He said that even though many would be surprised, he feels that he had more great matches during his TNA tenure than his WWE tenure, and felt he was more consistent in the ring in TNA. Regarding his future, given that his contract expires in two weeks, he said, "I am in the process of structuring a deal and I do have a company in mind. I haven't said yes because I want to make it a public thing with the company and myself. I can't really say who it is or where I'm going but I can tell you it's going to happen in the next two weeks, before my con-tract is even up. I won't be wrestling until January but there will be a signing in the next couple of weeks."

OCTOBER 6

Right now Kurt Angle, 45, on his future in an interview with AlternativeNation.net: "I can't really say who I'm going with yet or what company I'm going to sign with. I am going to sign, but I'm going to just sign for one year, and that's that. I think I'm pretty much done. I'm just going to have the best year I can have. Hopefully it'll be my best year, and I'm going to retire." He said he had a private meeting with Dixie Carter who told him what her plans were and said it was a positive meeting and she said the next TV deal they sign has to benefit TNA in every aspect. He said he was able to speak his piece with Vince McMahon, admitting to McMahon that he had a lot to do with the problems he had that caused the company to get rid of him. He said he spoke his piece to McMahon and he said as long as he and Vince McMahon don't have any issues, he's happy with that. "What I found out is that HHH is pretty much running the show now. I didn't know that. I really believed that Vince would always run the show until the day he died, but now they're in a position as a publicly traded company where you're not only answering to Vince and HHH, you're answering to shareholders." The story behind this is Angle was trying to get back with WWE and talked to HHH. He told HHH he wanted to come back to end his career there and told HHH how much he was making in TNA (which, at least based on what people who have been told of the conversation said, HHH was skeptical of the number) and HHH told him that he should take that TNA deal. Then he called up Vince and wanted to come back, and Vince told him that HHH is in charge now. Of course he's not completely in charge because Vince has final say-so, but this is just the usual good cop/bad cop game. He said that he won't be cleared to wrestle until January. Given that he shot an angle with MVP at the last tapings and they've been building it for some time, logic would say he's staying with TNA. But if you watched the last several months of A.J. Styles' booking in TNA, you'd know to avoid using logic based on television in this situation. He said that he's going to set up a press conference for his announcement in the next few weeks, when his contract should be signed, and he will start with the new promotion in January. This delay could be simply waiting for TNA to sign its TV deal, and then when they announce the TV deal, they can announce Angle is staying. But he said "I will not be at Bound for Glory due to contractual disputes." He wasn't there both because of the added cost of sending him when he couldn't wrestle, and also be-cause his contract expired on 9/27 and at best TNA would only offer him a per event deal in the sense even if he's staying with TNA, he's going to be like the others whose deals expire, in that he won't be getting paid for two months. He said for his last year, he wants no more than 40 dates. "The agreement has been made it's just that our attorneys have to complete all the bullcrap that goes with it. Both sides have agreed to it. We're just waiting for the attorneys to dot the I's and cross the T's." Regarding the TV deal, and this is from what Dixie Carter told Angle and it's what TNA has told the talent (although TNA insiders concede the situation is hardly like this), is that they have multiple offers and are choosing the best one. There are multiple negotiations and they will choose the best one who will have them, but it's not like there is a bidding war of stations to get TNA, since WWE couldn't even make that happen. "When it comes down to it, it is about money, and it is also about how you can get promoted on that network. I won't say that Spike did a bad job, but I will say that Spike could have done better. If it is going to be Spike, and I don't know, because Dixie really wouldn't say who it was, they're going to have to do a better job." When asked about Hogan and Bischoff, he had nothing bad to say about Hogan, but was clear he felt he could have been used better by Bischoff, saying they didn't put enough behind him and it led to him having an "I don't care" attitude and the mentality that he's just there to collect a paycheck. So he was political and said he thought Bischoff did a good job with the company, but not a good job with him and made him lose his passion, but then he took blame himself for losing the passion. He said John Gaburick made him care again and praised the Gaburick hire. He said he loved Vince Russo. He said there is no chance of him doing MMA. He claimed he had a match signed with Randy Couture for a promotion in California that Rico Chiapparelli was in charge of, and both had signed a non-disclosure agreement, but it never happened. If this is true, it would have been in that year that Couture was in a legal issue with UFC and Couture never would have been able to do it since he had an existing UFC contract. He said when Couture went back to UFC, that he asked Couture if he'd pitch the idea of Couture vs. Angle to Dana White, and Couture told him White wasn't interested. The story behind that was in 2006, when Angle left WWE, he and White negotiated and White thought they had come to an agreement and had contacted Daniel Puder to be his first opponent. During the meeting Angle would claim he was done with pro wrestling and pro wrestling ruined his life. Then Angle backed out and signed with TNA instead, so from that point on, White never took Angle's wanting to do MMA talk seriously. However, Angle was offered a spot in the Kimbo Slice, Roy Nelson, Matt Mitrione season of Ultimate Fighter. Angle claimed he turned it down because the offer came too late for him to get into shape to fight before filming would start. White claimed Angle failed the physical.

NOVEMBER 3

The expectation is that Angle has agreed to terms on a new TNA deal, which would be interesting if true, because it seemed like everyone else whose deal is coming due has been told that until the TV deal is signed, no new deals are being made.

CHAPTER TWENTY FIVE

SETH ROLLINS
TURNS HEEL

JUNE 9

In one of the bigger surprise major angles in a long time, Seth Rollins turned on fellow Shield members Roman Reigns and Dean Ambrose at the end of the 6/2 Raw in Indianapolis.

The move breaks up, at least temporarily, one of the most successful trios in the history of U.S. wrestling.

The Shield, who had been in WWE developmental for some time, but never as a unit, debuted on November 18, 2012, during the Survivor Series main event, a three-way with C.M. Punk vs. John Cena vs. Ryback.

Since that time, the group, in a long run as heels and more recently as faces, had been one of the most valuable acts in the company. They had good to great matches against virtually everyone they worked with, both on television and on PPV. They were a major key in the improvement in the match quality of the main event matches on both TV and PPV.

The group appeared to be at its zenith, having beaten Evolution in three straight falls of an elimination match at Payback the previous night in Chicago.

With Batista leaving to start promoting "Guardians of the Galaxy," it did appear Evolution vs. The Shield was done. Now it will continue with a new dynamic, with an association of Rollins & Randy Orton vs. Ambrose & Reigns at first.

The switch caused a lot of talk for a promotion that has been delivering great major shows of late, but its overall popularity is struggling. Raw had two of its lowest audiences outside of football season in the past two weeks. Smackdown has also fallen significantly. Some of that is seasonal, going against the NBA and NHL playoffs, but they are well below levels against that same programming in prior years.

The Shield were originally going to break up before WrestleMania, but their babyface turn took better than anticipated. The idea was to break Reigns off as a singles star and give him a slow ascension to where he would eventually replace John Cena as the company's biggest star.

But the feeling was that there was a lot of life and merchandise money in the group as faces with the three fist salutes. The dissension angle was dropped and the turn was canceled.

Last week's WWE Magazine had a short Q&A with Rollins where he talked about Reigns and Ambrose as his former partners. That would lead one to believe this turn was planned some time back. And in a sense, it was, but that was from the original turn. Those with knowledge of the situation said that the two key angles on Raw were both last minute decisions. Rollins' turn on Ambrose and Reigns was decided upon on Sunday afternoon. There was a brief tease in the post-game show after Payback, that wasn't subtle, but didn't exactly make people expect the turn either.

The decision surprised a lot of people, particularly since the figuring was if someone was going to turn, it would be Ambrose, who comes across the most diabolical. Some were questioning the Rollins turn noting that he's a spectacular flier, and stylistically, that lends itself more to a face role. At the same time, the heel turn and being associated with HHH and Randy Orton assures Rollins a continued main event level presence.

The turn itself came at the end of Raw. It appeared Evolution was done when Batista quit. But HHH vowed he had a plan and that he wouldn't stop until The Shield was no more.

At the end of the show, with The Shield in the ring, and Orton and HHH coming out for an Orton vs. Reigns main event, Rollins nailed Reigns with a chair shot. Rollins also hit Ambrose with a chair shot, and Rollins and Orton destroyed both guys with chair shots. Reigns had his Shield vest and shirt torn off and he was given one hard chair shot after another to his back, leaving him with all kinds of bruises and welts.

As far as why it was done, it was just to shake up the situation. There was more life left in The Shield, and there was a lot of advertising out as far as going back to The Shield vs. The Wyatts, a short-term program earlier this year that produced great matches and excitement. But things changed.

The turn reminded me somewhat of when Barry Windham joined the Four Horsemen and did his heel turn on Dusty Rhodes, although those two had nearly a full decade association as opposed to less than two years. The Freebirds, the group The Shield was most often compared with, never turned on each other in Mid South on the first run, but did in Georgia, and did again in Dallas. In the case of Georgia, booker Ole Anderson may not have considered them at the level they would be viewed at later. In Dallas, the turn came when they had been there for years, there was only a small number of headliners and it was done to freshen things up in a company that was already on the way down. But things were never as hot when they were apart as when they were together.

There are a lot of different ways they can go with this. Clearly, they will be deciding most of it on the fly. They could add a third member to The Shield, perhaps a newcomer from NXT like Sami Zayn who is a natural babyface who would benefit in positioning by debuting working with the top guys. That would allow HHH & Orton & Rollins to continue the program. There's also Batista and where he fits in when he returns. The timing was right for a shock angle. Whether this is the right shock angle is harder to say. There was plenty of life left in this Shield grouping as babyfaces for several more months. But the top of the card programs in WWE were not fresh at all.

JUNE 16

Regarding The Shield split and the magazine mention and the post-Payback thing, the deal is, in both cases, it was Dean Ambrose and not Seth Rollins being talked about. Ambrose was the one interviewed talking about his former partners in the WWE Magazine story. On the post-match of Payback, Reigns was commenting on thinking he had a torn triceps, and made a comment about it and Ambrose made a joke of it which led to Reigns giving Ambrose a nasty stare. The Rollins turn was a last minute decision, but we're told it wasn't an Ambrose turn changed into a Rollins turn either.

CHAPTER TWENTY SIX

THE CHANGING FACE
OF WOMEN'S WRESTLING

JUNE 9

WWE did the second of its planned quarterly NXT specials, NXT Takeover on 5/29 at Full Sail University in Winter Park, FL, before a turn away crowd in the 400-seat building.

The one thing about these shows is, you've got a lot of hungry talent who want to be on the main roster and who know they are being judged closely by the organization and fans on these shows. They also know they have more chance to create interest in their character than at any other show while they are in developmental. So whatever is lacking in experience in some is going to be made up in enthusiasm.

This show was a fun two hours. You had wrestlers who saw this show as a chance to prove themselves and a hot fan base in an intimate setting that is becoming the modern equivalent of the old ECW Arena. The two hours is a good length, because you have enough time for several big matches to get their due, but it's not so long that the show drags. The other thing about NXT is that it's not overbooked. Almost everything seems to have a direction. The interviews are usually about building to something. The characters are experiments and it's about learning what does and doesn't play.

The show seemed to hit every goal. The key was to produce an impressive live show with no glitches and have great wrestling along the way. They furthered storylines and left you wanting more, and to be excited about when they do it again. They set up the next title program with Adrian Neville and Tyler Breeze by giving both men strong wins in good matches over Tyson Kidd and Sami Zayn, respectively. And the losses continued storylines for Kidd and Zayn. The women's tournament final with Charlotte and Natalya came across as the epic women's match in modern WWE. It was presented differently than any women's match, almost like a world title match, was given time and it was the performance of a career of Natalya to insiders. But it also was the breakout performance of Charlotte, who came across like a future superstar if the women's division in its future changes from models doing short matches to women wrestlers doing serious pro wrestling. It was really a revelation, because it's so different from most main roster women matches, but is more along the lines of how women are treated in action movies and the rise of women stars in UFC and how in that world they've blown away the interest levels of women in WWE.

On this show were also a couple of main roster characters, most notably the husband-and-wife duo of Tyson

Kidd and Natalya. For Kidd, he's really got nothing to prove. Everyone knows he's got great wrestling talent. He's also been one of those guys that for whatever reason, he's never gotten any kind of a significant singles push. He's small, but that means less today than in any other era. He has a reasonably good body and a great tan, but his talking doesn't stand out in an era when that's as important as ever, if not more, for a top star who doesn't have spectacular physical gifts, and there are a lot of very good technical athletic wrestlers today.

Kidd was never in the right place at the right time. At 33, he may never get that break. He was here to provide Adrian Neville, the NXT champion, on the way up, with a win in a great match. And that's what happened.

On some shows, they'd have stolen it.

When the show was over, the show-stealing performance was from his wife. Many would say Natalya and Charlotte had one of the best women's matches in WWE history. From a pure technical wrestling standpoint, Natalya's match with A.J. Lee on Main Event, when the two were given ample time to put on a great match, was better. Even though both were presented in the same venue, the WWE Network, this one had more time, had the outside star power of Bret Hart and Ric Flair in the corners, and a storyline of two famous wrestling families. Because of that, this match was more memorable and emotionally, felt much more important, and was presented before it even started as far more significant.

One was a great television match. This was something far more. It was a statement. Natalya, who has wrestled at WrestleMania before 70,000 fans, said this match in front of 400 people was the best and most important match of her life. History will tell if that's the case or not, because the feeling when it was over was that it was different and far superior in presentation and execution to what had been the old women's division. You were left with the idea this match and its reaction were so good it could be a catalyst for changing the entire thought process of women in the promotion. Whether it will be is another story, and you also could do a mix of both. But the one thing is how the new women talent is learning to work in developmental, we're probably looking at a natural change just as the men's ring style over the last 15 years changed based on styles of newer talent.

The changing economics of wrestling is something we will probably talk about almost weekly for a couple of years, until it's gone from a transition and learning period of what it could be to where it's established in its new form.

Women's wrestling in the U.S. has gone through a number of different phases. Starting in the late 30s, and into the early 50s, it was a novelty that did business. Times were very different then. I wasn't there and can't tell you what the attraction was, whether it was fit young women in one-piece bathing suits who trained as athletes at a time when few women did, as a sexual titillation deal, pseudo athletics, or a little of both. Mildred Burke, the top star, was something of a celebrity who actually got votes some years in the AP's Female Athlete of the Year polls, so at least to a degree she was respect-ed athletically. She was a drawing card, and was presented as a big star. Young women who attended matches dreamed of being her.

Not too long ago, Mark James, who puts together wrestling anthology type books, sent me a book that had all the weekly programs in Nashville for 1951 and 1952. The most fascinating thing to me about it was that the women wrestlers were written up as serious athletes, and they regularly worked main events. When Burke came in, it was presented pretty close to the same as Lou Thesz (the touring world champion at the time) coming in. But it didn't have to be a world title match to headline. The way the business was done then, since the women were outsiders, meaning promoter Nick Gulas had to bring them in and pay a cut to Billy Wolfe, who ran the women's booking agency out of Columbus, OH, if the women weren't drawing houses significantly bigger than the local men, they would have never been around nearly as much. And they were on top a lot. But for whatever reason, a few years later that was no longer the case and never was again after that point.

Burke was the world champion, and a headliner, unlike the women in the era when I started watching. There were 150 full-time women wrestlers booked out of Wolfe's agency during that heyday. It wasn't until getting that book and under-standing the business of that era, when I realized that women wrestlers on top had to have regularly been outdrawing the men. The top names, whether it was Nell Stewart, June Byers, Burke, Cora Combs and several others, were always the main event.

Within a few years, women's wrestling in the U.S. collapsed. Wolfe and Burke had a marriage split, which both came out on the short end of. Buddy Lee and wife Lillian Ellison, better known as The Fabulous Moolah, started booking their own women out of Nashville. The popularity of women's wrestling declined greatly after maybe 1952 or 1953, and it never came back.

There were only a few full-time women wrestlers, who moved from territory to territory, mostly in groups of fours, working tag team matches as special attractions. Maybe they'd come in for a few weeks of the year, and would never head-line, although sometimes work second or third from the top.

Vince McMahon tried to revive women's wrestling on the back of Wendi Richter in 1984, but the huge push didn't take. Soon enough, Richter was gone, and almost forgotten. After that, McMahon for years had a women's champion and a regular opponent touring, but it was never pushed as anything big. He tried again to push Alundra Blayze (Debra "Madusa" Miceli, now a big star in the monster truck world) with the idea of a pretty but athletic female wrestler, mostly using her against Bull Nakano, one of the best working woman wrestling heels of all-time. It didn't get over the way he envisioned it, and when Blayze's contract expired, she wasn't renewed and women's wrestling was dropped by the promotion.

The most talented of that era's women, Sherri Russell (Sherri Martel) was far more of a star as a manager, even though she held women's championships. A few years later, Tammy Sytch and Rena Mero caught on as Sunny and Sable. This wasn't at all about wrestling. It was hot women with enhanced physiques in bikini posters. There were some trained wrestlers around, but they weren't even second fiddle. For the most part, women in wrestling ever since were bikini models trained to do bad wrestling matches, although a few pretty women who wanted to be wrestlers like Mickie James, Gail Kim and Lisa Marie Varon came along, and one of the models, Trish Stratus, grew into being very talented as well.

But no matter who came along, the women's match at the house show was a quick throwaway prelim match that was far more about pretty women in skimpy outfits than wrestling. While some of the women were reasonably good, that wasn't why they were there, and there were far better women working outside the main roster who never got a call. Some of them were very pretty in real world standards, but John Laurinaitis would tell people, "We're looking for 10s." Natalie Neidhart had been wrestling for years before she ever got a chance, and that's with being part of arguably the most famous wrestling family in North America. Sara Amato (Sara Del Rey), one of the best woman wrestlers in the country over the past 15 years, was hired by the company as a trainer, with the idea she didn't have the looks to be a main roster performer, without even testing it out by giving her a shot.

When Total Divas started, and that was less than one year ago, if you remember, one of the perversities of it was that Natalya was in the cast very much portrayed as the ugly duckling.

The problem is the models wrestling badly had long run its course. In 2013, the women segments on Raw led to more viewers tuning out than almost anyone on the roster. For more than a decade, people would joke about the crappy women's match put on before the main event on PPVs.

Hollywood and MMA left the WWE ideals passe. While WWE women were hemorrhaging viewers, Gina Carano was adding viewers for her TV fights at a rate that Steve Austin and The Rock would have been envious of. Natalya herself, in working a month on this match that she called the biggest of her career, specifically said she was looking at Ronda Rousey as the ideal.

WWE was taking models and training them to wrestle, yet Hollywood called Carano and Rousey for big budget movies.

The Charlotte vs. Natalya match story they were telling was the rookie who probably will be a superstar vs. veteran who may never get her due, proving that she's been overlooked and may always be, and the representatives of two famous families. In that sense, it was far closer to the Rousey vs. Miesha Tate dynamic that Natalya was using as her inspiration to emulate the emotion of, than the two minute long matches with often mistimed spots WWE has on television.

Putting Bret Hart, and especially a 24-hour a day showman like Ric Flair in the corners could have been a blessing or a curse. Ric Flair's rookie daughter couldn't possibly match the charisma and star power of her father, even at 65. Bret is more subdued and wasn't going to steal the spotlight, but he was still one of pro wrestling's all-time greats out there in front of 400 hardcore fans who go crazy whenever a "real star" shows up.

In a world racing ahead with no off-season and little time for change or reflection, I don't know if this match will be Rousey vs. Tate in Columbus, OH, which was a night that truly changed everything in MMA; or Samoa Joe vs. Kurt Angle in their famous TNA match that set business records, appealed to a new fan base, got a huge positive word-of-mouth buzz, and three days later was forgotten as if it never happened.

I don't know if a women's match can headline a WWE PPV today. But it's already been proven that the right woman with the right promotion can do big business on PPV. And WWE PPV's and business are very different. The stigma that women can't draw on top, which absolutely was true for 50 years, is no longer the case. And even if it isn't, the big shows are now more presentation of the show itself than creating that lure to make you hit a bottom and make an impulse purchase on a Saturday afternoon. Had that exact match with the same build, same elements and same time been put on a major PPV, they absolutely would have struggled with the bigger crowd earlier. And just as absolutely, they would have turned the corner and ended pretty close to the same destination.

We've already seen for more than three decades in Japan that women's matches can be as exciting, as technical, and as emotionally connecting as the best men's matches. People don't know them today, but for time, place and context, Manami Toyota and Akira Hokuto in no way should take a back seat to Shawn Michaels or Ric Flair, and in the ring, were as good if not better than any performers on today's WWE roster. We've already seen they can be as marketable, and even draw TV viewers, sell tickets and get people to pluck down money, although in Japan, where women wrestlers have been presented as athletes for decades, they've rarely headlined in a major promotion unless it's a women's promotion.

But in American pro wrestling, women have never been presented like that. And then this week they were. And they stole the show. And the Paul Heyman interaction with the losing Natalya, a break from the usual dull cookie-cutter pre and post shows that everybody does, did it a second time. The concept there is Natalya tried to proclaim that, in fact, because they put on a great show, that both were winners. And Heyman tried to take it back to the original roots, and that is serious pseudo sport and not performance art, noting that if she won, why did the other girl leave with the belt, and pushing that winning and losing is important. There was also another post-match deal where Kidd blew off Natalya.

In the case of Charlotte in particular, she's acknowledged as the daughter of Ric Flair. I get the idea of merchandising rights and all that and not wanting people to use real names. But Charlotte Flair is not her real name. The only argument for her to not have a last name when they constantly bring up she's Ric Flair's daughter is they don't want to portray her as serious competitor, which makes no sense since her athleticism is her main calling card and if she makes it, that'll be why, or they don't want women to have a star recognizable name, which is even sillier. If the idea was to hide her being Flair's daughter until she can live up to the name (like a lot of sons of famous wrestlers in Mexico do), I absolutely get not using the Flair name. But when it's flaunted, it just makes no sense.

CHAPTER TWENTY SEVEN

SHAKE-UP AT ALL-JAPAN PRO WRESTLING

JUNE 9

There is a major internal shakeup going on. I don't have all the details but the fallout is that Tokyo Sports reported on 6/4 is that all the wrestlers were planning on leaving the company and that Jun Akiyama would start up as the president of a new company on 7/1. All the wrestlers had only signed six month deals, which says something about owner Nobuo Shiraishi's commitment, so all contracts expired on 6/30 and the wrestlers are free to leave. As best we can tell, and this was all breaking at press time, is that all of the wrestlers are tired of Shiraishi and his decisions regarding running the company and the things he says in social media and they want out. They cite the decline in attendance to show that his direction isn't working. The attendance wasn't good at the start and the promotion was deep in red ink when Shiraishi bought the company after years of management by Keiji Muto. Muto and Shiraishi had problems from the start which led to Muto leaving and forming Wrestle-1, taking much of the talent with him, and business plunged even more. The wrestlers want to completely revamp the product. Akiyama would be the public face of the company as the biggest star but the guys who were handling the wrestling end were referee Kyohei Wada and veteran Masa Fuchi. Nobody wants to work for Shiraishi but right now they don't have access to any financial support. Akiyama has reportedly talked with Motoko Baba about getting back into pro wrestling as the owner. I can't see that at all, since she retired in 2002 and had no more interest at that point in her life to run the company or carry on the business without her husband, who passed away in 1999. Plus, almost all the wrestlers that were around in 2000, including Akiyama, quit All Japan largely because of her, to form Pro Wrestling NOAH. There is talk of them starting up and having to use a different name if Shiraishi doesn't sell or give up power. Other things said are that the first show of the new group would be 7/12 in Osaka and that they are talking with Baba about reviving the original three belts from the 70s, the old PWF, International and United National belts for the Triple Crown. Baba owned the belts themselves and spent years trying to get them back as Muto, when he was president, never returned them to her. Shiraishi created a new Triple Crown singular belt and returned the original belts to Baba.

JUNE 16

The fallout from the story last week is that, as expected, Nobuo Shiraishi is out of pro wrestling. It's being publicly portrayed that the wrestlers has all decided against renewing their deals, which all ended on 6/30.

They've formed a new company called All Japan Pro Wrestling and Motoko Baba, who handled much of the business of the original All Japan (1972-2002), her husband's company, publicly gave her blessing to this new incarnation. Jun Akiyama, the company's biggest public star, will be the face of the company as president, although Masa Fuchi and Kyohei Wada (famous referee) are going to be running the business end. They will run their schedule this month as planned and then start the new promotion on 7/12 in Osaka, with the first major show set for 8/30 in Nagoya. All of the wrestlers currently under contract will move to the new promotion, along with bringing back Tamon Honda, Akitoshi Saito, Masao Inoue and Kentaro Shiga as freelancers.

JULY 6

This was the last week of the promotion under the ownership of Nobuo Shiraishi. Jun Akiyama on 7/1 announced the formation of a new company called All Japan Pro Wrestling in English. The previous company that dates back to 1972 and Giant Baba was called Zen Nihon Pro Wrestling, which translated into English means All Japan Pro Wrestling, because Nobuo Shiraishi owns that company. Basically that company is dead, which would be a major news story, except all the wrestlers left were forming the new group, taking all the dates of the prior company and keeping all the belts and intellectual property. While nobody is saying it this way, it may be, given the dates and intellectual property and all the contracts expiring, that Shiraishi just decided to get out or seeing that the guys all agreed not to work for him, he left the business and allowed them a peaceful transition. The only real change is that they are no longer using the old offices, and will be running the promotion out of their gym, which they are maintaining.

  The Shiraishi run as owner has to be considered a total failure with the group at its weakest point in history. Shiraishi was a rich wrestling fan who bought the struggling promotion, made crazy statements about wanting to get rid of fake wrestling, and spent a lot of money early on advertising, which didn't pay off. He did land Akiyama, Go Shiozaki, Yoshinobu Kanemaru, Kotaro Suzuki and Atsushi Aoki from NOAH when NOAH was falling apart financially. But he then had problems with Keiji Muto (who basically brought him in because Muto had got the company in such debt they needed new ownership), who left and took much of the talent with him to form Wrestle-1.

JULY 13

The revival of the company under Jun Akiyama has gotten major curiosity buzz as every show from 7/12 to 7/27 is already sold out, as is the next major show on 8/30 in Nagoya at the Aiichi Gym, which is a major arena. Fans are treating this with the idea that the old All Japan that they all fondly remember is returning with Akiyama, the last remaining superstars of that era, as the president and top star. There's also a big movement pushing Akiyama as a Hall of Famer. This comes on the heels of news that Cable TV Yamagata is going to be the new financial backer of the company. They announced the formation of All Japan Innovation and All Japan Pro Wrestling. As noted last week, the old company, which folded at the end of June, was called Zen Nihon Pro Wrestling, which is the Japanese translation of the American term All Japan Pro Wrestling, although we're told that in Japan, everyone is still going to be calling it Zen Nihon Pro Wrestling. The president of Cable TV Yamagata, Kazufumi Yoshimura, is the new Chairman of the new All Japan company and they will own all television rights, merchandise rights and manage the company's fan club. The plan is to broadcast every show on either cable TV, satellite TV or the Internet. Miki Sasahara, the president of Iwate Cable TV, was announced as the Vice President. Motoko Baba, the widow of Shohei "Giant" Baba, was announced an a member of the board. That's more symbolic in the sense that the All Japan company is historically remembered as the Baba's company (Motoko Baba ran a lot of the business and played "bad cop" while her husband was the front man, top star, ran the wrestling end and was the "good cop"). The press conference was at the Tokyo Capital Tokyu Hotel, which was the hotel the Babas would always stay at in Tokyo, and Motoko Baba attended, which would be her first appearance at something related to pro wrestling since selling the company in 2002. It was said she booked the location of the press conference. The location was to be symbolic because it was Giant Baba's favorite hotel and Baba would hold press conferences there. Akiyama said that he had spoken with Nobuo

Shiraishi, the former owner, and he said he wouldn't fight them on ownership of the All Japan name since he's getting out of the wrestling business. Suwama was announced as the Managing Executive Director. Go Shiozaki was named the Fighter chairman. As time has gone on and the company has gone down, the nostalgia for Baba's version has gotten stronger. Having Motoko Baba, who sold the company to Keiji Muto in late 2002, and that's when it started on its financial slide, tied into the company is considered a positive in that the old Baba great promotion may come back. Motoko Baba had decided to close the company in 2002 because she wanted out at the time with the idea she had helped run it for 30 years and was independently wealthy. If not for Muto or someone else buying it, the company wouldn't be around in any form today, but Muto was not a business man, and pro wrestling interest in Japan declined greatly during the last dozen years, so the combination ran the company deeply into debt. But she probably isn't going to have much influence on the business past lending her name to it.

Chapter Twenty Eight

Chael Sonnen Retires

JUNE 23

Usually when a top fighter retires from the sport, the first reaction is to fondly look back at their successes, and talk of their failures as either character building or, if at the end of their careers, part of the inevitable circle of fighter life.

But as much as Chael Sonnen was a major figure in the MMA world from the night he took over the press conference after his upset win over Nate Marquardt more than four years ago which led him to challenging Anderson Silva for the middleweight title in one of the sport's most memorable fights in history, it doesn't feel like the time or place to do that.

I keep having this lingering thought in my head. One year from now, when UFC is running its 50-plus events a year with nowhere near enough drawing cards to fill the headline positions in the first place, a phone call or text is going to be made.

It'll either be Dana White calling West Linn, OR., after a main event injury to a light heavyweight or middleweight in a main event slot, or there's a major show and an open slot with nobody healthy with a name. Or, more likely, an injury will take place, Sonnen will see the opportunity, volunteer, as he's done so many times, to step in. There's the interview about not going out on his own terms the way he wanted to. And he's clearly going to remain in the public eye as a television presence for the company.

He may even believe today that he is retired. Or he may already be waiting for the problems to blow over. Sonnen may even remember the perfect interview from his childhood in the mid-80s cut by Stan "The Man" Stasiak, a former area pro wrestling headliner and at the time, a pretty much retired television announcer for Portland Wrestling, the show Sonnen grew up watching on Saturday nights. It was one of the classic promos of an era, about an old retired man coming back because he's still got a good fight left in him.

But there is a potential problem. It's the same problem that led to Sonnen's abrupt retirement on 6/11, one day after not even having a thought in his head that his career was going to abruptly end and that he would fail for banned substances.

There may be a health issue here. If Sonnen does need testosterone replacement therapy and can't function well without it, a very real possibility, his career could be over. When TRT was banned, Sonnen outright said that he was going to work with doctors and see what he could do, but it could mean he would have to retire. The stock answer to the question as to how his training was going came with the answer that he's doing well, but he reserves the right to say exactly the opposite a week or a month from now.

"Guys, I've had a great time," said Sonnen in his retirement announcement, which took place on 6/11 at the start of UFC Tonight, where, even in the middle of the controversy a day after his test result came out, he was used as a host. "I want to thank coaches Roy Pittman and Dave Sanville and I want to thank my coach, Clayton Hires. These guys taught me how to fight and they taught me how to set goals and work hard and persevere, and they stood by me. I want to thank FOX and the leadership at UFC. I want to thank Bill Brady, who gave me a second wind. He's a member of the Nevada State Athletic Commission, and he believed in me when I really needed someone to believe in me. And I owe the second wind in my career to him. And I want to thank the single most important opponent I've ever had. I couldn't have gotten where I am without the dance partner, Anderson Silva. Thanks you for the opportunity and the memories. Thank you for the invitation to the barbecue, even though I couldn't attend. I want to officially announce my retirement from competitive mixed martial arts."

Sonnen was taking three substances, HCG, Clomiphene and Anastrozole to get his body to start producing testosterone after it had been shut way down from the years of exogenous testosterone he was injecting into his system, as well as to suppress estrogen build up. Clomiphene is also used as a fertility drug and Sonnen had just gotten his wife pregnant, which isn't necessarily the easiest thing coming off years of exogenous testosterone injections.

It is possible, for health reasons, that Sonnen may be best served retiring. But the way it happened, while in the middle of training for a big fight on the year's biggest show, and then suddenly he retires a day after testing positive for two banned substances makes me feel this is hardly a thought out decision, and more a temporary changing of the narrative.

Sonnen was likely to be suspended by the Nevada Athletic Commission anyway, so he wasn't going to be fighting for several months. The majority of fighters when they say they are retiring, mean it at the moment they say it. But when reality sets in, if there's a big money fight that can have their name attached to it, the profession doesn't seem so bad. And in Sonnen's case, he's not leaving because he took a physical beating that made him question if it was worth it.

On 6/17, the commission had a meeting and placed Sonnen on a temporary suspension pending a hearing some time in the future.

The commission also discussed Wanderlei Silva's failure to take his test on 5/24. They heard testimony from the test collector who first went to Silva's home, but he wasn't there, and left a message at the door, and then went to Silva's gym, found him there eating, and requested a blood and urine sample. Silva said he would give it after eating, but then left the gym without telling the tester. When the tester was still at the gym, Silva's wife called the gym phone and told the tester that Wanderlei wasn't expecting to be tested and needed to take the test later. The test collector was in contact throughout the day with Bob Bennett, the Executive Director of the Nevada commission, who also contacted Marc Ratner and Silva's wife and told both that Silva needed to be tested immediately. His wife told Bennett that Silva would take the test, but she didn't know where he was. Silva himself never responded to phone calls or text messages from Bennett or the tester after that point. Bennett said that they made every attempt to have Silva submit to the test and he didn't.

At the hearing, Silva's high profile attorney, Ross Goodman, the son of longtime Las Vegas Mayor Oscar Goodman (who served three terms from 1999 to 2011) and Carolyn Goodman (the current mayor who ran and won after her husband wasn't allowed to run for a fourth term due to term limits laws in the state) stated that Silva had suffered a wrist injury in February which led to the fight being moved from its original 5/31 date to 7/5. Goodman stated Silva was taking anti-inflammatories, prescribed by a UFC doctor, as well as taking diuretics, which Goodman said was to avoid the water retention from the swelling. Goodman said Silva didn't take the test because he believed he would have tested positive for diuretics, and noted he had never been tested that far before a fight. Diuretics are banned because they can be used to dilute the urine and thus mask the presence of banned drugs in the system. Goodman said that Silva didn't dispute any of the details of what Bennett and the test collector said. Goodman said Silva realizes he should have taken the tests and apologized to the commission.

The commission ruled that they would file a complaint against Silva and later schedule a full hearing on the case.

Originally, Vitor Belfort's testing above allowable levels for testosterone while undergoing TRT on 2/7 was going to be discussed because Belfort was going to be applying for a license in Nevada to face Sonnen on 7/5.

After it was clear Sonnen would not be allowed to fight on 7/5, the UFC briefly attempted to get a substitute opponent for Belfort, but wasn't able to do so, and he was taken off the show.

With Belfort no longer fighting on that date, there was no reason for him to apply for a license. The reason he released his own drug test results publicly last week was to get ahead of the story before the commission meeting. Most likely if he knew how it would have gone down, he would not have released his results.

He's probably going to face the winner of Chris Weidman vs. Lyoto Machida, which would be expected to be on a late-year show. If that's the case, with his high test on 2/7 and the usual nine month suspension for a test failure, using the normal term limits of a suspension, he could be okayed for a license after 11/7 even if they take don't accept any issue with the test results. But there is a question regarding that, because it would be his second failure, having tested positive for an elevated testosterone ratio in 2007 from a fight he lost to Dan Henderson. Usually a second suspension carries harsher penalties than a first suspension.

The inability of doctors to agree whether the failed test proved he did anything and that his level of testosterone could be above the limits based on having taken a shot shortly before his test, and not from injecting more than he should have for TRT (which as of 2/7 was not banned), could mitigate the situation in regard to punishment.

When digesting the news over the last week, I keep coming back to a radio show I did with Sonnen several months ago when the subject of fighting while no longer on testosterone replacement therapy was brought up. Sonnen said that he was working with doctors on ways to boost his natural testosterone production, and that so far, he was feeling okay. He also said he would reserve the right to contradict that statement a few weeks or months down the road. He specifically brought up that if this didn't work, he may have to retire.

Translated from vague references into gym talk, I took that to mean he's on HCG to try and get his testicles back to hopefully produce enough testosterone that he could train hard enough and live a normal life without using testosterone. He never said it. I just figured it. HCG is a banned substance in most drug tested sports, including this one. There's a reason for that, but not one applicable in his case.

Unlike most in the media who celebrated the Nevada commission, and the UFC in general, banning TRT outfight in late February, my response was more measured. Yes, I wish it had never been approved in the first place. I was very skeptical of the real need by some of the fighters on it. And of those who I felt probably did need it, I assumed the legitimate medical reasons to need it because they had damaged their endocrine system through years of anabolic steroids. In other words, cheating, so if the damage from cheating weakens your body, c'est la vie.

But there were also exceptions, most notably Antonio "Bigfoot" Silva. Where Sonnen fell on that ledger, I can't responsibly speculate on. Many will likely offer their opinion based on things like if they find him entertaining, or hated his act, or just hate all drug use to where everyone on TRT was a cheater and love the idea that they got a big fish.

The idea that nobody in this sport would be approved for TRT was fine with me. Because of the ability to abuse the system the way it is now, they probably should be the rules today. The rare case of someone who needs it, I can accept as being akin to the 5-foot-6 super talented high school basketball player who wants to play Division I. Life isn't fair, and sometimes your physical limitations don't allow you to progress to the major leagues.

The problem was for the few, Sonnen, Dan Henderson, Silva, Vitor Belfort and whoever else had been using it consistently for years and were still headline players. Whether their reasons for initially needing TRT were legitimate years ago when they started or not, after many years straight taking exogenous testosterone, your body is not going to produce much testosterone on its own.

The commissions allowed and approved a situation that compromised the endocrine system in these fighters even more.

On that day when it was banned, the issue was, nobody thought of those few fighters. It was just an easy thing to do. Almost everyone in the media was happy. Even Dana White said he was glad the headache would go away. Nobody thought that there were really only a handful of fighters that this applied to, and that this was not a real substantial move to clean up the sport. But it looked like it was to the public. It was an easy response to a controversial and confusing issue.

Anything other than year-round constant unannounced drug testing of every fighter under contract is going to leave gaping loopholes for PED usage. And even that system, as cumbersome and as expensive as it would be, would have limited success in regard to the highest profile fighters. Those with money and celebrity to get the right connections to use substances and have the best advisers will usually be one step ahead of testing.

It was appalling that nobody in power considered that there could be significant health issues from having people who relied on TRT for years to just go cold turkey. There was no discussion with any doctors of how to handle those few. From a media perspective, the idea was that they were drug cheats so it doesn't matter would hold water if the regulatory bodies had not approved of what they were doing in the first place.

When the word came out that Sonnen had failed a drug test for Anastrozole and Clomiphene, my reaction was, well, once people realize getting off years straight of testosterone and the side effects, they would understand that it was kind of a given. But that didn't happen.

You absolutely can consider Sonnen a drug cheat regarding the positive test for the Anderson Silva fight, and he served a year in suspension time for it. I never expected him to be approved for TRT in Nevada, but when he applied that the Nevada commission doctor who examined him and his records, not Sonnen's personal physician or a quack at a Life Extension clinic, recommended it to the commission, at that point it was inherently not cheating unless his levels came in above the legal limits, which never happened. A different Nevada doctor last year in examining Sonnen's records did suggest that the original diagnosis years ago of hypogonadism and the testosterone shots as treatment from years ago could have been wrong and he could have been treated in other ways than testosterone. But that was a thought about years ago. Even that doctor said that by that time, after all the years of TRT, he did have medical need for it.

But the understanding of the circumstances and why the drugs were used didn't happen hardly anywhere. I didn't see one media story go past surface level that Sonnen cheated and got caught again. And I'm still mystified that Sonnen never contacted the athletic commission when he started using the drugs in question. I can almost understand why he didn't do so at the time he was given the surprise test, because he may have thought he would pass the test. But even that doesn't hold complete water because in one of his statements, he said that he didn't expect to test positive for what he did test positive for, but said he did expect to test positive for HCG. If he had volunteered that he was using the drugs and didn't test positive, he could have been suspended. If he had come forth with that information earlier than the test, it may have been taken differently. But it also may not have been approved. But he should have realized the possibility of the drugs showing up in his screen, and by saying nothing to the commission ahead of time, whatever explanation he had after the fact was far less likely to work.

"I absolutely take responsibility," said Sonnen. "When I spoke with Dana White yesterday (the day the positive test came out), and he was on Fox Sports 1, he was very clear to say that Chael needed to talk to the commission. I agree with that. This was out of competition testing. I'm only the third athlete to go through this. There are some moving parts and a little bit of a learning curve. In the meanwhile, my wife and I were having problems with fertility. This is a matter of health and being able to live in the next chapter of my life. At no point was there an attempt to slip around the system. I want to admit fault and accept full responsibility. Yesterday, when this came out, I was mad. I was a fighter and I went into defense mode. However, ultimately the rules are the rules and I'm a rules guy. I don't want to break the rules. And ultimately it comes down to the athlete to make sure he's in compliance."

He claimed he had taken a test of his own on 5/1 that showed him not testing positive and that his 50-day treatment plan using the specific drugs was over in April. He said he believes that the lab his 5/23 test was sent to had greater sensitivity toward detecting lower amounts.

There were the stories of how could Sonnen defend the use of drugs that are on the banned substance list and noting Dennis Siver got suspended for testing positive for HCG, the very drug Sonnen later admitted using of late.

The reason Anastrozole and Clomiphene are banned is the same reason masking agents and diuretics are banned. They are not anabolic agents or Growth Hormones.

Taking a masking agent doesn't make you bigger, stronger or faster. Anastrozole isn't going to help your bench press. What it is going to do is suppress your female sex characteristics from taking over after a male hormone crash from getting off testosterone. It's there to prevent the crash that can include development of gynocomastia, essentially swollen nipples that in worst cases can create small pockets that appear to be almost like small female breasts—bitch tits in laymen's terms. It's to prevent a crash that leads to depression, a lack of drive, losing muscle tone and getting a softer and more feminine aspect to the physique.

Why they are banned is because males generally are using those drugs to combat side effects of steroid use. Like with masking agents, the idea is, why would you need them unless you used steroids in the first place? So even if we didn't catch your steroid use because you are clever enough to time your cycle right or beat the system, we've got a second chance to get you by nabbing you for the drugs used after a cycle is completed.

Where this doesn't apply here is that men on TRT, which is essentially a low dose of steroids, are already known to have been on essentially a multi-year cycle. In other words, you're catching them for something you already know they did and they were approved to do.

When the commission banned TRT, they should have done so with a doctor who would recommend a treatment program for these athletes to avoid the crash and help get them back to as close to normal as possible. Had they done so, those drugs likely would have been part of the equation, and HCG surely would have.

For all the knocks on Dana White's appearance Tuesday on Fox Sports 1 in the media, he was one of the very few people talking about the subject that had a clue what he was talking about. Whether his number of five out of more than 500 was accurate depends on nitpicking. Far more than five UFC fighters have been approved for TRT in the last several years. Of those, some aren't fighting in the organization any longer, some have retired, and some have stopped using.

As best I can tell, on 2/27, when TRT was banned, that number this applied to was six active UFC fighters out of 500 on the roster–Sonnen, Belfort, Frank Mir, Antonio Silva, Ben Rothwell and Dan Henderson. Sonnen has now retired. Mir and Henderson probably don't have much time left. Silva, who is the one guy who does have a legitimate medical reason for needing it because someone with acromegaly and low testosterone has a significant chance of contracting diabetes, is currently suspended since a test done by UFC the day of his fight with Mark Hunt in December showed his testosterone level was too high. Rothwell is a journeyman fighter. Belfort is notable because he's active, a top contender, and he clearly has gotten off TRT because his testosterone level in recent tests sent to the Nevada Athletic Commission was at dangerously low levels.

Rampage Jackson and Joe Warren of Bellator have in the past been approved for TUE's.

Dr. Don Catlin, the best known doctor in the country when it comes to drug testing at the UCLA Lab, was on Inside MMA on 6/13. He's on an Olympic committee that rules on TRT exemptions and noted that people apply and virtually nobody is approved. However, he did say Sonnen was doing what he should have been doing to get off TRT, and this is the most well known and vigilant anti-drug doctor in the country.

That said, after all these years, it does feel like UFC and Bellator have relied too much on underfunded and often ill-informed athletic commissions on a major problems that plagues this sport, as it does any sport where speed, power and explosiveness are in demand.

And as for Sonnen, his attempt to deflect the issue on a discussion of in-competition and out-of-competition drug testing was ill-advised. His analogy is that if he broke his arm and used ibuprofen, and was tested and caught, it wouldn't count as a positive if it was out of competition. Similarly he could drink coffee and test positive for caffeine out of competition. But he knows he can't test positive for those compounds the week of the fight.

The analogy fell apart because the substances he tested positive for, because they are used to catch steroid users, are banned in or out of competition. Quite frankly, the day the commission announced the ban, they should have told those few fighters that they needed to be on those drugs for their own health as a recommendation, and not buried their head in the sand and just issued a ban without discussing with doctors the physical repercussions on those they had given prior exemptions.

JULY 6

When the news broke Saturday of Chael Sonnen failing another drug test, this one administered on 6/5, I was shocked, and it is likely many in the MMA community were stunned.

It wasn't that Sonnen failed a drug test, or the revelation that he, or any of a number of top athletes in the sport may have been using Human Growth Hormone (HGH) or Recombinant Human Erythropoietin (EPO). The fact that one was caught doing so, a first for the sport of MMA, and an extreme rarity in the sporting world, is major news in both MMA and on the drug testing front.

For all the talk of steroids, the belief by athletes is that certain drugs, HGH, EPO and Insulin, provide a strong performance enhancing stack and can be used with limited fear of detection. The standard urine tests don't pick up those drugs. Blood testing, which is expensive and not used with much regularity, has limitations in detecting those substances. There is a short window of detection for HGH and EPO, and because the body produces Insulin, is almost impossible to test for added use. Most sports don't test for those drugs with the feeling it's not effective. In the major sports, there are union issues that haven't been worked through involving regularly taking blood samples. In those that do, there have only been a handful of athletes who have ever been caught using HGH despite the knowledge within the sports world that use is rampant.

Three days later, UFC and FOX released a joint statement, each terminating Sonnen.

"The UFC and FOX Sports organizations announced today (6/30) the termination of their respective broadcasting services agreements with analyst Chael Sonnen. The decision comes in light of Sonnen failing a second test conducted by the Nevada Athletic Commission for banned substances in June. Sonnen was previously under temporary suspension by the Nevada Athletic Commission for failing an initial test conducted in May."

"You know, it's never easy making decisions like this," White said. "You know, Chael is a person I personally care about. I know a lot of people at FOX care about him too. The guy had four banned substances in his system, four banned substances in his system leading up to a fight here in Las Vegas. It's a tough one. It's one of those hard decisions you gotta make. It was definitely a hard one. It was something we had to do."

UFC had only once cut a fighter, Nate Marquardt, based on a drug test situation. Marquardt, on TRT, tested over the limit about two weeks before his fight and his level didn't return to acceptable by fight time, forcing them to have to scrap an advertised television main event at the last minute. Marquardt ended up being signed by Strikeforce and returned to UFC after Strikeforce was shut down, and actually won the main event of a show this past weekend. There had been cases of prelim fighters who lost fights and also failed their drug test that had been released in the past.

What killed Sonnen was not so much the failure, but the hypocrisy. He had just weeks earlier blasted rival Wanderlei Silva as being a fraud his entire career when Silva disappeared when ordered to take a surprise drug test. He had positioned himself after the ban on TRT as someone who always played by the rules that the governing body went with. When he came out so strong regarding the first drug test, noting he never took performance enhancing drugs, doing several interviews on FS 1 on the subject, the HGH and EPO failures made it seemingly impossible to do business with him right now.

Sonnen's failure may be breakthrough in itself, and an important message not just in MMA, but in all sports, that if testing is vigilant enough, perhaps the belief will change that you can use those substances with no fear of repercussions. But the circumstances really only lead one to open their eyes that the real message is more of a negative than a positive.

The circumstances of the detection methods, and if Sonnen is honest in addressing his time line of usage, at the scheduled 7/23 Nevada Athletic commission hearing, will reveal one of two things. Either Sonnen's failure was a fluke of timing, or it's a warning to athletes, as well as to the few top fighters who may be tested in the same manner he was before a scheduled major fight by the Nevada commission, that the game has the potential to change.

But there are scientific advances and there are costs involved. The fact is there have been tens of thousands of HGH tests administered in a variety of sports over the past six years since the first so-called legitimate test for HGH came out. The lack of failures led to widespread belief that the test was ineffective, and did virtually nothing to deter usage. The belief still remained in the heads of most athletes that HGH is banned, but you will almost never get caught using it. The combination of fast acting testosterone (there are some give a minor boost so you would never fail on the T:E ratio but you do get performance enhancing benefits when used in a stack with other drugs), HGH and Insulin (or in some cases Peptides) is a performance enhancing stack used regularly in drug tested sports.

HGH is used extensively in Hollywood, whether it be men or women, and in any profession where having a hard body is tied into marketability, particularly in older actors and actresses. The marked difference in TV star bodies from the prior generation and far more willingness to pose in skimpy swimsuit shots, even at older ages, for both men and women, is directly tied to the use.

When you watch WWE and ask how some of the people can look the way they do when the company is drug testing, there may be some very disciplined and very genetically gifted guys, but in a lot of cases, that is your answer. Because it would require great expense and catch nobody, WWE does not do blood testing. So even if Sonnen's failure is a breakthrough in that it shows testing detection has improved, that will mean little with most sports drug testing. Before, the odds were astronomically high that anyone would be caught by the far more expensive HGH testing. In Major League Baseball, the NFL, WWE or any major professional sport aside from Cycling and the Olympics, there is no worrying at all about doing exactly what Sonnen appears to have done regarding using HGH and EPO.

MMA would have been on that list last week, which may explain why Sonnen was so brazen about pushing that he had not taken performance enhancing drugs, and being critical of Wanderlei Silva when Silva ran out on a drug test and saying his career was a fraud.

Today, many people are saying that about Sonnen.

But in U.S. combat sports, it's going to take a few more Sonnen cases before a clear message is sent.

The belief has been that HGH, because it breaks down in the body so quickly, can only be detected in the relatively new tests for several hours after a shot is administered. Actual HGH disseminates throughout the body rapidly. After minutes, HGH in the blood stream is converted to a derivative form, which is why the original HGH testing caught almost nobody. The new and more sophisticated testing looks for an unnatural increase in IGF-1 or P3NP, that occurs shortly after an injection of HGH.

That remains in the blood stream for between four and ten hours, and can be active within cell receptors for up to three days. It's the ability to detect this form in the cell receptors that is what is said to have strengthened the detection methods of HGH.

A key part of this story is when Sonnen took his most recent HGH shot. Within the world of those who coach pro athletes to beat tests is to use low enough levels of testosterone to stay under 4-1 (Sonnen, Belfort and those coming off TRT, because they were being regularly tested for testosterone in their blood and perhaps if they were throwing in more expensive Carbon Isotope Ratio (CIR) testing which shows any artificial testosterone, would be nailed because CIR testing is rarely used in sports), and use HGH and insulin, or peptides with HGH, but HGH is the key. Steroids and HGH are different. Steroids enlarge muscle cells. HGH increases the number muscle cells and also thickens connective tissue and enlarges organs, which is why the steroid/HGH combo is effective and why bodybuilders of today look so much different from the heavy steroid users of a previous generation, because of the added muscle cells from the HGH are then enlarged from the steroids.

The belief, and this is where Sonnen's last shot comes in, is that the three day detection for HGH in current tests is believed to be propaganda and that the real detection time is two to four hours. Within that world, the belief is that Sonnen got caught for being stupid, because the idea is you inject HGH at 11 p.m., and no tester is coming to get you until 8 a.m., and thus, there is no fear of detection. The belief is they tested Sonnen within a few hours of his test and that he was not given smart advice about the late night shot. However, if it was more than four hours, this, which is major in the few sports that do test for HGH, that 11 p.m. shot doctrine may no longer be valid.

In theory, if somebody is cycling EPO and HGH, they could take a shot daily, so by that theory, even with the short detection span, catching people during their cycle shouldn't be anywhere near as rare as it is.

I don't know the exact number of HGH failures there have been over the last six years, but it's no less than five but I don't know that it's even hit ten yet.

Doctors have talked of being close to HGH tests dating back decades. In 1992, Vince McMahon and Dr. Mauro DiPasquale Jr., claimed to have come up with the first test that would catch HGH users, although nobody in the scientific community bought it and DiPasquale Jr.'s testing never caught anyone using it. There has been no legitimate test administered until recent years. The first actual positive test came in late 2009 of rugby player Terry Newton, widely believed to be a tip off because of awareness that he had just administered a shot. But with the belief HGH was rampant at the London Olympics, which were more heavily tested for HGH than any sports competition in history, there were only two failures.

With EPO, the belief is also that there is a short detection window, of roughly 19 hours, give or take a few. EPO is used to enhance endurance by increasing the red blood cell count. If Sonnen admits to having used the substances, and is honest in the hearing about when he last administered them, it will give more information that claims that modern science has improved in detection, or he tested positive because he was unlucky to have been tested right after administering a shot.

For those who believe PED's pervert this and other sports, a breakthrough like this is major because if athletes truly believe testing can detect the substances, and that they can be tested at any time, usage becomes a risk, which it wasn't before. The penalties of being caught, both reputation wise and financial, are huge. Stephan Bonnar lost his job as a FOX analyst over his second positive steroid test. He may have lost being given a lifetime job in UFC as a reward for the fight that put the company in the sporting consciousness. Sonnen could easily end up in the same boat. The problem is, as this case as well as recent publicized cases with both Wanderlei Silva and Vitor Belfort have shown, is the protocol of testing in this sport.

Belfort, who tested positive in February for a testosterone level being above allowable limits while under TRT therapy, this past week on Combate, the Brazilian fighting channel, gave an explanation. It was the Belfort positive and the idea doctors said that if he had just taken his normal dose, the potential was there for him to be temporarily over the limit, thus an explanation that, given what he was doing, he wasn't cheating. But his latest explanation changes that.

"I took a shot the day before (the test) in Las Vegas," he said. "I usually took the dosage throughout a week, but this day I took the whole weekly dosage. So, on that day, my levels were a little high, but nothing absurd. The limit was 1,100 and I was at 1,200."

There are different doctors and labs who will give a different opinion of what the high level of allowable normal is, usually between 1,100 and 1,200. Nevada, under Keith Kizer, wanted fighters to not just be below that limit, but by at the low to medium range of normal, more in the 500 to 600 range, with the idea the TRT gets them normal, not high normal. Belfort's actual test number in February was 1,472, well above any ceiling. Because he was not licensed in Nevada as a fighter, they legally couldn't suspend him, but if he applied for a license in Nevada, they could deny him the license based on the test result. Since Sonnen failed his test, Belfort had no opponent for 7/5, so UFC had him pull out of his 6/17 license hearing since there was no reason to get a license.

In all three cases, as well as that of Alistair Overeem in 2012, it was unannounced random testing done by Nevada that resulted in the failures, and not the standard urine tests done the night of the fight that fighters are expecting. All four fighters, had they not been star fighters in headline matches in Nevada, would have never been tested so stringently, and would have almost surely skated through, doing exactly what they had been doing for who knows how long, under normal circumstances. The idea they are the only ones is terribly naive. Based on talking with many fighters and trainers on this subject, the belief is that use is plentiful. Both Brian Stann and

Georges St-Pierre in recent months cited as one of the reasons, not the only reason, they chose to retire was the inadequate drug testing and proliferation of use. Michael Bisping's whole career changes when you take away the losses to people who were likely using PEDs when he fought them, and he's been vehement about the subject. However, the idea that some pro-drug guys propagate, that everyone is using and that you can't compete at the top level without it, is also not the case.

Fighting for 25 minutes in a championship fight takes unbelievable stamina, and EPO allows both harder and more intense training and develops more stamina in a fighter. If Sonnen was taking HGH while under TRT, the combination magnifies the effect, in other words, while his testosterone levels may have always been within normal levels, the affect of his added testosterone was multiplied if he was using HGH with it. Perhaps he will argue he only started on the drugs after getting off TRT, but unlike with Anastrozole, Clomiphene and HCG, these are performance enhancing drugs on the top of the banned list, and not drugs banned because the medical usage of them in athletes is coming off a steroid cycle and thus are used to catch people who may not test positive for steroids, but almost surely were doing them. In the case of Sonnen, the steroids, testosterone, were a given since the commission itself approved of the use.

If anything, this proves the need for year-around extensive testing throughout the UFC roster, not just for Nevada main eventers. But doing so looks to be cost prohibitive, so in the end, these failures only underscore there is a problem, and it's probably significant, and leave one frustrated about the lack of a viable solution. For every Chael Sonnen, are there 50, 150 or 250 others just like him on the UFC roster, only too low profile? Nobody knows. It's the same major league baseball argument regarding Ryan Braun, Alex Rodriguez or Barry Bonds. They absolutely were guilty, and like Sonnen, their respective attitudes publicly on the subject added to their troubles in the long run. But it was their success that is what cost them, as with the money at stake, plenty of mid-level players were likely doing similar things.

While no data is out, it would appear that the percentage of failures in the out of competition unannounced testing dwarfs those of the testing methods used in almost all states. If anything, the recent stories accentuate just how ineffective the testing procedures in MMA are unless one is scheduled for a high-profile fight in Nevada, or, like Jon Jones and Glover Teixeira, they agree to be randomly tested in a high profile championship fight and UFC agrees to foot the bill. And even in all those cases, most of the tests were done a couple of months before the fights and both fighters were fully aware they were going to be tested regularly during the short window.

Belfort knew he was going to be tested regularly and failed, but the unique situation of him not being licensed led to the commission not being allowed to suspend him.

Sonnen and Silva, since they were not in a title fight, did not know they would be tested. But in the case of Sonnen, it was naive to not think he would be tested, as a former TRT user. Still, after being tested on 5/24, he probably wasn't expecting another test on 6/5. It would be incumbent for the commission to at least urine test him and the HCG, Clomiphene and Anastrozole would show up. It is believed that all three of these drugs can be detected for at most ten days after most recent usage, although Sonnen did have legitimate medical need for all three drugs. And he's been around sports long enough to know that having a legitimate medical need for compounds that are on the banned list are banned.

Dana White at a press conference recently noted the cost of the enhanced testing that Jones asked for, for he and Teixeira, ran in excess of $40,000. That was only for a short period, basically testing throughout the training camp of two fighters. Multiply that by 500 fighters and for 12 months of the year instead of two months, and you get a figure of $60 million annually. UFC generates a lot money. Nobody in this sport generates enough money to come close to affording that bill. Granted, you don't have to do extensive blood and urine testing weekly on every fighter throughout the year to do enough testing to at least give fighters the fear a test could happen at any time.

There does need to be additional testing, enough that there is at least the fear of getting caught in the back of everyone's mind. One Olympic athlete in April spoke to me about being at the Olympic training center with two of the best known fighters in the UFC, and asking them about PEDs in their sport. The answer both men gave was that the lure to use them is strong, because careers are short, the differences in making money for different levels of success is huge, and the testing is totally inadequate.

Even though you can probably get a major group discount, and if UFC entered into an agreement with a major testing organization the bill would be nowhere near $60 million, nor would every fighter be tested constantly, there are still issues.

For years, White has given the line that UFC fighters have it tougher than anyone, except Olympic athletes, because they are tested by the government. On paper, that wasn't close to the case, because testing in most states, and when UFC does it themselves, is usually limited to a urine test on the day of the fight.

But today, there are two arguments that it is the case, given all sports, including UFC, by nature, are going to want to protect their top stars. There were allegations that baseball, as much as they wanted to clean up their image, that the few superstars were getting tipped ahead of time about a so-called random test. Years ago in the NFL, there was a news story regarding a number of starting quarterbacks that had tested positive, yet none of the names came out nor were there any suspensions. The story turned out to be accurate. Stories of multiple failed drug tests by Ultimate Warrior in 1992, at a time WWF was at its most vigilant on the issue, as it was far more of a priority than it appears to be today, although today's athletes are far more sophisticated than 20 years ago when it comes to what they can and can't do. Ironically, Sonnen fit into that category and it's so crazy he was the one caught, since nobody had talked more about following the rules of competition, and was more critical of rivals rumored to have built up impressive records while on the stuff.

Warrior was never suspended. It came out in one of his many court cases, with WWF allowing him to continue with the idea that his levels were lowered in tests so they claimed the positives were from prior use. But still, there was also another test failure for a new drug not in prior tests that again he wasn't suspended, with them accepting the tainted supplement defense. However, he was eventually fired when they flat out found out about a shipment of HGH from overseas that was intercepted by authorities.

Major Olympic doctors have written books mentioning positive test results in the Olympics that were covered up.

As far as Sonnen himself goes, the HCG and Anastrozole failures in the 6/5 test and the Clomiphene and Anastrozole failure in the 5/23 test, were almost surely still going to lead to a suspension. Sonnen, at the very least, needed to inform the commission ahead of time as to what he was using to attempt to get his testes to start functioning after years of TRT, which he didn't do. That doesn't apply to HGH and EPO, clear performance enhancing compounds.

As far as Sonnen's career goes, it is likely over now. He announced his retirement earlier this month. One could have argued some sympathy in punishment before. That argument can no longer be made.

Even if his suspension is over in a year, given his age, and questions as to how well his body can perform clean, as well as the controversy, make it a lot less likely he could come back and perform at near the top level, or that UFC would bring him back given the lightning rod of bad publicity.

Given what Sonnen failed for, he's now like the baseball players whose entire careers are called into question. He wasn't the only one using, but he's the one who got caught because of tests that had improved, or extreme bad luck of timing. But those drugs are an attempt to circumvent the system, break the rules with limited fear of repercussions. You can make an argument they could speed up his body being able to train at a certain level while going through the natural testosterone crash of cold turkey dropping TRT, there is no ambivalence as to whether HGH and EPO are banned or would be considered illegal to be used under any circumstances in this sport.

White was heavily criticized for defending Sonnen somewhat on the first test results, even though in that case White was more rational based on the evidence as was known at the time than many. With the new evidence, the situation is different.

I'm in the same boat, as I recognized there was a major problem in how the banning of TRT went down, even though it's best for almost all concerned for it to be eliminated from the sport and it would have been better if the can of worms was never opened a few years ago in the first place.

"We were made aware that a second random test, conducted earlier this month, resulted in a positive test for additional banned substances," said Dave Sholler, the UFC Senior Director of Public Relations, in reading a prepared statement to the media after the 6/28 UFC show, hours after the story broke. "Chael will have the opportunity to appear in front of the Nevada Athletic Commission next month, and through a statement released to the media tonight, he's pledged to cooperate. Our stance on the subject remains absolutely the same. We support the commission and we will continue to ensure that all UFC competitors compete on an even playing field, free of performance enhancing drugs and banned substances."

"I will cooperate with the commission and look forward to having a dialogue about how fighters who transition off TRT can avoid violating any rules," Sonnen said in a statement released to MMAFighting.com

Before, Sonnen had an easy transition after fighting, as he was FOX's golden boy announcer going forward. Sonnen had remained host of UFC Tonight and continued to serve in that role after the first test failure was announced, a decision that caused virtually no backlash. But a positive test for HGH and EPO changed his fate.

And it was a black eye for Fox Sports 1's UFC coverage on Saturday night, while covering a live event just as the news broke. During the live event itself, even though there was down time between fights, the Sonnen situation, which broke as the show was going on, was never mentioned. On the post-game show, it appeared it wasn't going to be mentioned either, until a simple reading of the UFC statement in response was read by Karyn Bryant at about 2 a.m., just before the show went off the air. That's almost as bad, if not worse, then ignoring it completely, because it only called attention to people who didn't know the story by that time just how badly they were burying it.

It can't be justified on what is supposed to be a news show on UFC to not mention a major drug test failure of a FOX co-host whose first failure weeks earlier was a lead item on one of their shows as well as a lead item on their UFC Tonight show where Sonnen explained his side of the story on the original test positives.

The fact his explanation on their network fell apart needed to be discussed, and was far more important and topical than the usual standard running through the results and highlights of a just-completed show.

Sonnen had potential as an endorsement pitchman because of his sales ability. He was even talked about within UFC as being the replacement as front man of the UFC itself should something happen to White. White had even brought that up before his test failures.

As bad as it looks for him, there's another reality of time. What happened with Sonnen, with the denial and then more evidence springing up making the denial look incredibly dishonest has happened with Lance Armstrong, who Sonnen himself once criticized, Marion Jones, a few baseball players who have some of the most impressive Hall of Fame credentials in history and are, in symbolism, not getting in at this point, and even Hulk Hogan, all of whom got far more mainstream coverage than Sonnen will. It disgraced all of them and did Hogan no favors short-term. Hogan did an almost complete recovery, in the sense two years later he was back to being big Hulk Hogan, and almost nobody even remembers today what happened. But Sonnen is not the cultural iconic figure Hogan is. And also, there is more of a stigma toward PEDs in a man-on-man fight because of the attempt to physically harm the opponent than in a performance situation, even though the competitive advantage aspect is there in both, and maybe as much in Hollywood and wrestling as in sports, because in sports if you can win with a bad body, you can be a champion. In Hollywood and wrestling, how you look is far more significant when it comes to your success.

The question regards what is next. WWE has had interest in Sonnen in the past, but Vince McMahon doesn't like using ex-MMA fighters on the belief that they won't be willing to do the schedule. In addition, his age would have worked against him, and I don't think even if those factors weren't there, that WWE would hire someone who had just tested positive for HGH. They did negotiate with Shawne Merriman, who failed an NFL steroid test, but that was years earlier and largely forgotten. Because of being 37, and the WWE being shy about signing people for training past the age of 30, and almost certainly 35, being a wrestler is unlikely.

Sonnen has spoken with Gerald Brisco at WWE to put together a meeting with Paul Levesque. According to those close to the situation, Sonnen was pretty much told he was too old to start wrestling training, but there could be interest in him as an announcer. But WWE would be leery right now given Sonnen's name being what it is right now, and WWE's being a publicly traded company and having to answer to stockholders who could ask questions.

As far as being a talker, he probably would excel, whether that's as a heel manager (a role that also takes training but the shelf life of the performer can be longer because age isn't as much a factor) or a television announcer. But I can't see anyone touching him for at least a few months, if not longer.

Plus, there are still commission states that regulate pro wrestling, although few do it seriously. But with Sonnen under a temporary Nevada suspension, and likely eventually for a longer one, he would technically not be allowed to wrestle in those states as long as the suspension is in effect.

TNA hired Pacman Jones, who crimes were a hell of a lot more significant than anything Sonnen did. But they may not be in the financial condition to do so, plus they creative when it came to Rampage Jackson, King Mo Lawal and Tito Ortiz was pretty much horrible. Sonnen, because of his talking, has more potential in pro wrestling, and for TNA, his age won't be as much of a factor. But as good as he can talk, he'd still be a novice in the ring and thus a manager or announcer role would fit. But in TNA, they have Taz in the spot and Taz is tight with John Gaburick, so there's no role except heel manager and right now there doesn't appear to be an opening.

Bellator under Bjorn Rebney would have probably hired him at some point because they jumped at UFC problem children like War Machine and Paul Daley. And for suspension reasons, he's not going to be able to fight again any time soon. Even if they offered big money for his return on PPV, it couldn't take place until after whatever suspension Nevada gives him expires. As far as Spike hiring him as some kind of a personality, it's a touchy situation. There's probably a part of them that would want to, but it's probably not happening now or any time soon. Also, Sonnen always felt to me like a Matt Hughes type who would always be loyal to the UFC brand, so the only way he'd make that move would be if he felt the doors to UFC were closed to him permanently.

At press time, Sonnen was still scheduled to compete in submission wrestling against Andre Galvao in The main event of the 8/9 Metamoris show in Los Angeles.

"Yes, he is on the card," said promoter Ralek Gracie to MMAFighting.com. "We will test his skills only."

That was a very tone deaf reaction.

Submission fighting is not governed by athletic commissions and thus his suspension in Nevada would not preclude his appearing. But he was using PED's and even if you aren't testing, it looks really bad as a sports competition to ignore the results of tests.

Even if this blows over in a couple of years, and time does heal a lot of wounds, over the short-term he may have to go silent for a while. And that may be the biggest punishment of all.

CHAPTER TWENTY NINE

WWE COST-CUTTING

JUNE 23

It's been seemingly years since WWE has sat down and cut a number of wrestlers. Part of the reason is that over the last year plus, the feeling was that once the network got started and the new television deal was in place, the company would be rolling in money, and there would be no economic need to cut people. A few people who weren't used weren't renewed when their contracts expired, but renewing people you've given up on would make no sense.

But the economic situation is entirely different than expected, with the company itself projecting to be $45 million to $52 million in the red this year. So the old rules no longer applied.

On 6/12, the company released 11 performers, most of which were expected since they had barely used them, like Evan Bourne, JTG, Curt Hawkins and Teddy Long, or Yoshi Tatsu, Brodus Clay and Camacho who had been used only in developmental of late. The only names who had been on television were referee Marc Harris, and minor surprise releases in Aksana, Drew McIntyre (the biggest surprise on the list) and Jinder Mahal.

There were expected to be more cutbacks made in different departments. The news was viewed positively by Wall Street, in the sense they are making changes that will help the bottom line. The price had been stagnant since the big crash when the TV deal was announced. But this week was a growth week, closing at press time on 6/17 at $12.13 per share, giving the company a market capitalization of $911.62 million.

Also cut on 6/11, the day after last week's Smackdown tapings in Green Bay, was Raw head writer Jay Gibson, although that move was not believed to have been budgetary, since people in that role in WWE often have short tenures. While Gibson's title may make it seem like this could cause a major change in the television direction, it's not as significant as it sounds. Gibson, who had been with the company for about five months, was more the head of an organizational chart than an actual writer. He would coordinate which writers handle which storylines as opposed to writing himself. He'd organize four writers and tell them to handle the John Cena storylines, four others to work on the Shield breakup, a few others to work on the HHH/Stephanie role type of thing. Gibson was said to have very little product knowledge itself, which was exposed when he would be asked opinions on things. But he had a very strong resume and excellent organizational skills, so he was very good at an aspect of what his job entailed. He was described as a professional in the writing field, and a nice guy, who ultimately was completely out of place working in WWE. Gibson, before coming to WWE, had worked from 2008 on the soap opera "The Young and the Restless," as a writer and eventually working his way up to Executive Producer. In 2011, he headed the team that won the Emmy Award for Outstanding Dramatic Series Writing Team. He also worked on a number of major movies including "Dead Poets Society," "Greencard,"

"Pretty Woman" and "The Thin Red Line."

The moves show Wall Street that they are cost cutting.

There were no major political agendas here. Aksana had been a Kevin Dunn favorite, but no longer was, and thus had little in the way of support. She was past 30, was not a good worker at all in the ring and she didn't have the look that she had when they first signed her years ago out of the bodybuilding world. With more women expected to be brought up soon, most notably Charlotte and Sasha Banks, a cut in the women's division wasn't a surprise. Aksana was only ahead of Rosa Mendes, but Mendes was saved when Bunim-Murray picked her to be in the cast of Total Divas.

McIntyre was the big surprise, because he came in as a major promotion favorite. At 6-foot-5 with a good physique and a good look, he was given a huge push from the start as Vince McMahon's chosen superstar. But he was pushed far too fast too soon and didn't live up to the hype. He ended up in the doghouse over incidents that involved then-wife Taryn Terrell, which resulted in him being buried and disappearing. When he resurfaced, it was part of 3MB, a comedy Job Squad group with Mahal and Heath Slater.

He improved, but had also been typecast. He did a great job of late in embracing his role, but when your role is to be a joke, doing a good job as a joke becomes a killer to future marketability. While Slater is still with the company, losing matches to minis on television is never a good thing for your career no matter how they spin it to you, since Chavo Guerrero Jr. was pretty well destroyed in a similar way.

It's a tough business right now, with TNA in bad financial shape, so it's not like they can add several new people. Plus, of the guys cut only Evan Bourne would probably fit in well with TNA. McIntyre is good, but has the stink of loser joke on him. Camacho, who has been off television for a long time, could be repackaged and TNA has done that with recent WWE cuts Michael Hutter as Ethan Carter III and Thomas Latimer as Bram. At another period in time, Japan would be an option. Years back, a number of WWE cuts got New Japan gigs, although most didn't last. But New Japan is overloaded with foreign talent and isn't giving enough work to those they have. Perhaps McIntyre could get a shot but most aren't going to have that option. Yoshi Tatsu, who started with New Japan, could possibly be brought back. His not being jobbed out on WWE television in recent years is a benefit in that case.

One person who knows the system politics as well as anyone said that Clay had a shot to be a star as a heel early, and had a shot a second time, but they gave up on him on his recent heel turn. The reality is, he'd been there for years, and while he's big, Vince McMahon and HHH want guys who have pleasing bodies and he doesn't have that. Plus, he was not good at all as a worker and hadn't improved past being noticeably not at the level of most everyone else on the main roster.

Mahal, who they tried to push as an Indian heel at the start, had nothing special going for him other than tall and in condition. His work was passable but nothing more, and his charisma wasn't there. Aksana was both not good in the ring, nor did her look stand out and she wasn't getting younger. Plus, the main people in charge of late had buried her for a long time, as they had with Hawkins and Bourne, who were never used.

JTG had a sense of humor about his departure, noting, "Damn. Why I pick up my phone!"

When the first list of those cut came out, he wasn't on it, because obviously they want to tell the talent first and they couldn't get ahold of him to tell him.

Most of the rest did a positive spin. Hawkins plugged deals he made immediately for shows with Jersey Championship Wrestling, Beyond Wrestling and Pro Wrestling Syndicate.

"Thanks for the good times WWE," wrote Bourne. "Sorry for not getting back on Raw after breaking my foot."

"I want to say thank you to WWE and the WWE Universe and Yoshi Army for these six years," said Tatsu. "It's been an amazing experience. In my last days, your huge `Yoshi Tatsu' chants at Full Sail were awesome. Please keep being cool. I love you guys."

"Thanks to WWE for the amazing opportunity," wrote Mahal. "Got a chance to see the world and do many amazing things. Excited to see what the future brings."

Clay wrote, "Is it better to be held down, held back, or let go?" I'm proud of all the obstacles I fought through and now greatness is on me. There is no sadness or bad feelings, only opportunity for me to break bread or play dad, so no sad tweets or messages."

Mahal and Hawkins immediately started pushing for indie bookings.

One person with a long involvement in the system noted to us there were some problems with the way the talent relations department is being run, in specific, with Bourne, noting that instead of having him sit home for so long, he either should have been brought to the Performance Center to work, or brought to television to get another shot. But it's a two-way street. Talent also has to push for spots, even though many have noted when they do and get shut down it lends to just keeping quiet.

Another noted there is a communications breakdown at the developmental level because talent doesn't know who to talk with if they have a problem. HHH is fine, but has so much going on he's not readily available and the people underneath, Canyon Ceman, Mark Carrano and Jane Geddes (when she was in the position before being moved to HHH's personal assistant) never wrestled. While Ceman and Geddes were both high-level athletes, actually significantly better than just about any of the wrestlers, it's a different dynamic. Ceman has the reputation for being a smart guy who understands business, but doesn't know the wrestling business and talent doesn't think he can relate to their issues but he's not disliked or anything. One person compared him to Jim Herd (it would be the reputation of Herd since the person in question never worked for Herd, in the sense he's a nice guy but simply didn't know wrestling or have a feel for it). Carrano has heat, although some of that is the natural heat since he's the bearer of the bad news. But one description of him is he carries himself like a big shot and acts like he's doing them favors when they get positive news. "With J.J. (Dillon), JR and (John) Laurinaitis, even if it was an illusion, talent at least felt they had someone who could comprehend their issues."

Regarding referee Marc Harris, he worked hard, but referee spots are very interchangeable and if you rubbed someone the wrong way, anyone can replace you. Harris was involved in a controversial situation on a TV months ago, made worse because he got into an argument with former referee Jimmy Korderas regarding how he handled the situation. It's not that he got let go for that, because that happened months ago. But it was felt he never should have done that in a public forum. So when the numbers game came up, it was his number that was called.

If Jeff Jarrett can get his new group off the ground, at least a few of these guys could help him, but I'd limit it to only a few because if a promotion is based on pushing guys who have the moniker of being job guys or failures in WWE, it kind of dooms them from getting anywhere. It's a funny deal because by a certain standard, whether it be size, the look, or polished ability, and certainly name recognition, these guys will have more than most of the indie talent. But if you push several to the top, you're in the same ballpark of so many promotions who have tried to build a lot around WWE castoffs, which has been a traditional blueprint for failure. It's the mistake that TNA made several times, particularly in 2010 with the Hogan invasion with the idea of bringing in "more famous" guys and having it backfire product-wise. But for Jarrett, it's ultimately not the talent decisions that are key, but the ability to get a television deal that pays him enough to survive, and then an ability to garner a good enough rating for the station that they don't lose interest in paying him. It's not easy, as we've seen with WGN, CW and Ion with WWE that even with WWE, stations quickly have lost interest in paying for WWE unless it's the highest rated Raw and Smackdown shows.

There is fear in WWE that if you lose your job it's the end of your career. And to an extent, it's a lot tougher without the guaranteed check. The indie scene right now isn't bad. A lot of promotions are doing decent houses using the bigger names. As Jarrett has noted, getting enough good talent to run strong shows is the least bit of an issue in starting a new group because there are a plethora of hungry and talented younger guys and veterans with name value who can still go. Guys like Matt Hardy, Tommy Dreamer, Carlito and Chris Masters are making a good living working weekend dates and on the indie scene, unlike in WWE and TNA, the promoter pays for your hotel and trans, and you can still your merchandise and get to keep the revenue.

A look at those individually:

AKSANA - Zivile Raudoniene, 32, she was a well known bodybuilder from Lithuania before John Laurinaitis signed her to be a wrestler. After winning the Arnold Classic in 2009 (the second biggest event of the year, behind Ms. Olympia), she signed with WWE. They used her in developmental in a number of roles, usually comedy to make fun of her foreign accent, like as a ring announcer who would botch things up. She also worked as a manager and started wrestling in early 2010. With only eight months wrestling experience, she was brought into NXT and immediately put into an angle where she was going to marry Goldust, until she turned heel at the wedding and slapped him. Eventually, on Smackdown, she did an angle where she pretended to have the hots for Teddy Long, using him to get a job, and then leaving him high-and-dry for her lover, Antonio Cesaro. That pairing was broken up and she worked as a wrestler for the last two years, but was not very good, and best known for accidentally dropping her knee on the eyeball of Naomi, fracturing her orbital bone. They had used her and Alicia Fox as a heel tag team to work with the Bella Twins, but with Brie Bella off and Fox being pushed as a single, and cuts being made and her having nobody going to bat for her, her number was called. She is coming off WWE television but I'm not sure how much demand there will be for her on the indie scene.

EVAN BOURNE - Matt Korklan, now 31, was one of the best high flyers in the business. Known as Matt Sydal in Ring of Honor, he signed with WWE in 2007, at the age of 24. He had started wrestling on St. Louis indies at 17, and stayed in ROH at 21 and in Dragon Gate at 23. He was brought to television with the ECW brand in 2008. He was good looking, had a good physique, but was very small by WWE standards which hurt him, probably about 170 pounds. He was usually used as enhancement talent, and was one of those guys who would every now and then, get a push, get over because he was the best high flyer in the company at the time, and then it would be dropped a few weeks later. He held the tag team title with Kofi Kingston in 2011. What pretty much killed him was a pair of drug test suspensions, one in November 2011, and the second in January 2012. Then he suffered a severe foot injury in an auto accident in March 2012. He was given up on really after the first drug test failure. In the past two years, he was only used very few times on developmental shows and never brought back to the main roster and had really been just sitting home collecting a check for his downside. If he can still do what he could do before, he could probably get regular work with ROH and Dragon Gate and be pushed well right now. Either TNA as a major X Division star or New Japan could also be options. He's very good friends with ROH booker Hunter Johnston. The feeling is that his main focus would be to try and get a Japan deal, and right now is taking indie bookings under his previous ring name, Matt Sydal. He's talented enough and even though he was never pushed to the top in WWE, he was always more popular than his push and he's not really tainted as a WWE failure like some of the guys in the sense fans see through his lack of push, and it's been so long since he's been on TV that people remember the shooting star press and the flying moves and have forgotten that most of the time he wasn't booked strong.

CAMACHO - Tevita Fifita, 31, the son of Ululi Fifita, who wrestled as Meng, Haku, Tama Tonga (the same name his brother who works for New Japan uses) and King Tonga. He played college football at the University of Texas at El Paso, and then trained under Bully Ray & Devon at the Team 3-D Academy. He had only trained for a few months when WWE signed him in February, 2009. At the end of 2011, he was brought to the main roster as the bodyguard for Hunico (Jorge Arias, the current Sin Cara), and the two later became a tag team. They weren't pushed at all. Hunico was injured, so he was sent back to NXT in 2012. He had a good look and seemed to have the basics down. He didn't really stand out in any way, but did seem to be improving. He never had a lot of serious exposure on WWE television to where I sense he'll be a major in demand guy on indies.

BRODUS CLAY - George Murdoch, 34, at 6-foot-7 and 375 pounds, had size going for him but never really improved enough in the ring. He was a high school football star and played some in college, and later worked as a bodyguard. He was a Rick Bassman guy in Southern California, and got a developmental deal in 2006. After about 18 months, the feeling was he hadn't progressed enough and was let go in early 2008. He was brought back in early 2010 and debuted late that year on the NXT show. At one point he looked like he was getting a big push as the heel bodyguard for Alberto Del Rio, but they broke that pairing up in less than two months. He was gone to do the movie "No One Lives," and they built up for months his re-debut. Due to disorganization, they scheduled his start a number of times and kept moving it back. He came back as a dancing babyface, The Funkasaurus, which got over big at first but was clearly a one-dimensional role with little upward mobility. In 2013, he was put into a team with Matt Bloom, then known as Tensai, called Tons of Funk. By November, he turned heel. Nobody cared about the Clay vs. Tensai matches and Tensai was taken off the roster and retrained to be an announcer. Clay hadn't been used much in the last several months past a few NXT matches against Adrian Neville. He'll get indie work but his best bet on that scene is to return to the dancing babyface character, because that was what he was best known for in WWE, and I believe he's going to use the name the Funky Dinosaur on the indies. Because that gimmick was memorable, he probably can do okay on the indie scene although it's hard to say how much legs it'll have.

CURT HAWKINS - Brian Myers, 29, trained with the current Zack Ryder after being trained together by Mikey Whipwreck. They were signed together in early 2006 as The Majors Brothers, with Myers and Brian and Ryder as Brett. They were brought up in 2007 as The Major Brothers, dropping the s, as part of a group headed by Edge as the Edge Heads. They were doing well until one day at a meeting, Vince McMahon found out that they weren't brothers, and, as crazy as this sounds, said that if they weren't brothers, why are we pretending they are. So they stopped being brothers and became Curt Hawkins & Zack Ryder. They did win the tag team title in 2008, but after losing, the team wasn't pushed and was broken up in 2009. From that point, the company stopped using him on the main roster. Months later he went to developmental as a three-man team called the Dude Busters with Trent Baretta and Caylen Croft. He was brought back to the main roster in 2010 to form a tag team with Vance Archer (now Lance Archer in New Japan). In 2011, he formed a tag team with Tyler Reks, but almost always lost, and were usually on the old NXT TV show. Reks quit the company in 2012 and Hawkins had major knee surgery and had been rarely used since. He had been used as Rock's training partner to help get him in ring shape for his matches the last few years. He also recently opened a wrestling school in New York on Long Island. He'll probably be doing regular work on the indie scene going forward since he's based in the Northeast where shows are plentiful. In fact, he was already working this past weekend, was aggressive in getting his booking e-mail contact info out and within a few days was booked solid through late August. He may start working under his real name.

JTG - Jayson Paul, 29, had started pro wrestling on the indie scene at 17 and was signed by WWE at 21. He was put together with Shad Gaspard as The Gang Stars, and then the two were brought up as Cryme Tyme, a mid-card babyface comedy team. The idea was they were thieves, but were portrayed as fun-loving babyface thieves. After problems in a match with Lance Cade & Trevor Murdoch, he and Gaspard were fired in 2007, but rehired six months later. They split up in April 2010, but the feud went nowhere and Gaspard was sent back to developmental and then fired. JTG had no push and was used either as a jobber or not at all until 2012, and rarely used in the last two years. Most people had forgotten he was even with the company. He had some charisma. He'll probably get some indie work, and the person who benefits the most from this is Shad Gaspard, because they can bring back Cryme Tyme for indie shows and autograph appearances. Gaspard is living in Los Angeles trying to make it as an actor, but has done some wrestling of late.

TEDDY LONG - Now 57, or 66, depending on what age you believe, Long hadn't been used since July 2013 when Vickie Guerrero became Smackdown General Manager and he was written off the show with a storyline firing. In his case, his contract had expired and since they weren't using him, there was no reason to renew him. This wasn't a surprise at all, as it was known he and Guerrero were both leaving shortly and Guerrero is just staying for her storyline departure to be written. In a company youth oriented, Long was lucky to be around as long as he was as a backstage authority figure. He had a long tenure in wrestling, starting as a copy who carried jackets to the back and then being hired as a referee for Jim Crockett Promotions in 1985. Because those in WCW management saw how good he was as a talker, they booked a heel ref segment that would transition him into becoming manager Theodore R. Long, most notably with Butch Reed & Ron Simmons as Doom. Long worked in the office for WCW, until being let go and being hired as a referee for WWF in 1998. He had been let go before and brought back by the company during that period, going to a heel manager before starting a long run as an authority figure. Right now, with no room for authority figures given the television role of HHH and Stephanie McMahon, there was no point in renewing him. Long was good in the face role because he was a great talker. Aside from autograph show appearances, I don't really see much left for him.

JINDER MAHAL - Born Vuvraj Singh Dhesi, he's now 27, and started at the age of 16 in his native Calgary as Tiger Raj Singh, often teaming with Gama Singh Jr. He was signed by WWE in early 2010. They liked him because he was tall and could speak both Hindi and Punjabi so he could be an Indian heel, like Tiger Jeet Singh. He got to the main roster in April, 2011, to feud with the Great Khali. That was a tough one because you can't have good matches with Khali, so it became a lame feud. A feud with Ted DiBiase didn't take because by that time they had given up on DiBiase. He had a program with Sheamus, but he was beaten like drum there. He was repackaged in 3MB in September, 2012, but that was a joke group. Mahal could be a lower tiered ex-WWE guy on the indies but it would be difficult for him to be a star anywhere.

DREW MCINTYRE - Born Andrew Galloway, he's now 29 but had not been seriously booked in years. He started training at 15 and had his first matches before his 16th birthday and was working pretty regularly by the age of 17 as Drew Galloway. He signed with WWE at the age of 21 after a tryout match with Sheamus where both were signed before a show in Manchester, England, in 2006. He was on TV at 22. He had a first brief run as the tag team partner of David Taylor, where Taylor was supposed to mentor him. But he was sent back to OVW in late 2007. After OVW, he was moved to FCW, and was brought back to WWE with a planned push to the top as "The Chosen One," the new superstar of the company in the summer of 2009. He had a six month long unbeaten streak and beat John Morrison for the IC title. He later won the tag team titles with Cody Rhodes and his serious push ended when they dropped the titles in October, 2010. At about this time, he and Terrell (known as Tiffany in those days) were in Los Angeles and went to a Playboy Club party without informing the company, which at the time didn't want talent attending things like that because of the image they were trying to protect. Nobody would have known, except at the hotel later that night, the two got into a loud argument that turned into a minor fight and the police were called. Company officials weren't happy about that, and that the arrest was out publicly before company officials knew any of the story. One person noted to us that Terrell killed McIntyre's push, describing it as the Sunny/Chris Candido situation, plus describing McIntyre as too nice and easy going, which did him no favors. He never recovered from it. The two were divorced after only a year. He did an angle where he tried to get together with Kelly Kelly (they booked this angle while he was still married to Terrell). But after being drafted to Raw in April of that year, he was never pushed again. He was brought back doing a losing streak gimmick, which most of the time is a kiss of death. The 3MB act started in September, 2012, but was a team that also never won. He's a guy who had real potential, but was pushed too fast, but has had far too much exposure as a joke that it would be difficult to overcome it on the TNA platform. Bret Hart was a huge supporter of McIntyre's feeling for years that WWE squandered his considerable potential. He could probably do reasonably well on the North American indie scene, and is planning on remaining in Tampa, where he still lives, and working as Drew Galloway. He would also likely be able to get U.K. bookings, particularly in Scotland, based on his heritage and WWE exposure. He's a guy who has the talent to be a star, but the WWE taint of the last year is really a negative on him for Jarrett, ROH or TNA.

YOSHI TATSU - Born Naomi Yamamoto, the name Yoshi Tatsu is in honor of his father, Yoshitatsu Yamamoto. He's almost 37 and was always a good wrestler, but pretty well wasted the prime of his career. Yamamoto had trained in boxing and Jiu Jitsu and passed a New Japan tryout in 2001 and started his career on October 12, 2002. He had the usual slow growth in New Japan, but made it to the 2006 G-1 Climax tournament and briefly formed a tag team with Hiroshi Tanahashi. He was destined to be a pushed star in New Japan, but he left the promotion and took a 67 percent pay cut and ignored a lot of advice to try out for WWE, where the feeling was they had never pushed a Japanese star well. He was brought to ECW in 2009 and had a lot of good matches, and got over as a babyface, but it was the stereotypical naive foreigner child-like role. When Syfy canceled ECW, he was around but never pushed. He was rarely used after early 2010, aside for the NXT TV show and in developmental or occasionally on Superstars, but hadn't had a television win in more than two years. He had a look, some charisma and was a good worker but the Japanese character held him back and he was never booked seriously. He was a favorite in NXT of late, but the feeling is that developmental isn't a place for someone who is 37 years old. Plus, he lost brownie points for wanting to move to Texas when the company wanted him in Orlando doing the rookie technique drills even though he had been technically proficient for a dozen years. Perhaps not fully understanding protocol, it was noted to us that he never got past anywhere because nobody ever went to bat for him, because he never kissed up to the key people. If he wants to move back to Japan, he may be able to get back with New Japan and he's a good enough wrestler where he could do okay there. He was very popular in Japan several years ago as the only Japanese wrestler on the WWE roster, and was allowed to have good matches in Tokyo when WWE toured. At press time, he had not heard anything from New Japan but had gotten offers from Wrestle-1 and All Japan. He believes he is more popular in the U.S. than Japan (I don't believe that to be the case) and he said he wants to stay here.

JULY 6

Vince McMahon has ordered major cutbacks, far beyond what has been done so far. The dollar figure going around is into the eight figures, so that the losses for this year aren't nearly as large as were being projected a month back. There is a lot of fear that there major cuts on the horizon besides the talent cuts and some production cuts that have already taken place. I can recall when the network first became obvious it would be a reality toward the latter part of last year that there was the fear that while the idea eventually would work, that there may be growing pains, but luckily with the new TV deal, the increase in rights fees expected would alleviate the network losses. When the TV deal was announced and the increase was far less than anticipated, the fallout of that deal is part of the reason things are happening the way they are.

JULY 21

Another financial cutback has to do with the production crew, which is a pretty big deal. They used to provide buses for the crew on Sunday to Monday on PPV weeks, and Monday and Tuesday every week. The gist was that after breaking down the set they would be done at about 1 a.m., get in the bus, sleep on the bus and be driven to the next arena where they'd get up in the early morning and set things up for the next night. Now, with no bus, they have to drive to the next city, which is often a few hours. So instead of sleeping, they may drive, get in at 4 a.m., and either set up with no sleep or get a hotel, and get almost no sleep. Plus, with the bus, after set up, they could go on the bus and get sleep before the show starts. The change is a lot more physically taxing and there is the feeling many are going to be looking elsewhere and be gone if they can get another gig.

CHAPTER THIRTY

SCOTT COKER TAKES OVER AT BELLATOR

JUNE 30

Scott Coker returned to the helm of a major promotion on 6/18 with his announced replacing of Bjorn Rebney as CEO of Bellator, the country's No. 2 MMA promotion.

Coker is familiar with that slot, having a run with Strikeforce which included a period of time as the No. 2 MMA promotion behind the dominant UFC.

But what has become evident is that the decision making by Spike TV and Viacom, through Spike President Kevin Kay, was more Rebney and Bellator President Tim Danaher were going to be out and then finding a replacement, as opposed to clamoring for Coker after his Zuffa contract and non-compete period ended in March.

It was very clear from Kay's opening statement at a press conference, which was anything but specific about changes or future direction of the company past ending the tournament format.

"As we move away from the tournament structure to a more traditional format, that's where Scott comes in," said Kay. "He's an incredibly forward thinking sports executive."

Rebney was not liked within the Bellator offices to the point that his firing reportedly led to people in the office singing, "Ding Dong The Witch is Dead."

Rebney was married to the tournament format, till death does them part. He had told me on several occasions that as long as he is there, they will be a tournament-based promotion.

Rebney was exiled from the promotion he created, and managed to get funding and keep alive until its future appeared secure when UFC left Spike, and Bellator was the only significant promotion for Spike to make a deal with. After feeling it was a huge part of the rise of UFC, it made sense from both sides to purchase the promotion.

For Bellator, it meant finances wouldn't be an issue. For Spike, it means that if they were successful building the brand, they would own it, thus couldn't lose it in a bidding war like they lost UFC, plus they'd be immune from the escalating rights fees sports programming was getting from television.

Long before there was MMA, Rebney, as a boxing fan and later a boxing promoter, would question why in every other sport there is a certain structure, a regular season and playoffs, tournaments, whatever, but boxing and kickboxing was done differently. He couldn't understand why there weren't specific tournaments to earn championship shots. When MMA got popular, it was done similarly. Title shots, like in boxing, were determined by the promoters based on a number of things, and marketability was one of them. The reality is that when your income is based on fan interest in your product, personalities and entertainment become a major factor.

That proved to be his undoing. A big issue was when Eddie Alvarez lost to Michael Chandler, Alvarez at the time was the promotion's top star. Based on the strict rules, he would have had to have gone into a tournament, which could have required three fights in about three months, and win them all, to get a rematch of the greatest fight in company history. The tournament structure in theory made sense. When you put a bunch of unknown fighters in a tournament, the ability to see someone win three times in three months in theory would give them enough exposure to make them a star. But in doing so many tournaments simultaneously, that didn't work out in reality. People just didn't care enough about the tournaments and winning them didn't resonate in most cases.

Instead, Bellator got its notice signing names like King Mo Lawal, Rampage Jackson and Tito Ortiz. Lawal was upset fighting unknown Emanuel Newton in a tournament. Jackson and Ortiz, at their age, weren't meant for fighting monthly although Jackson was put in a four-man tournament to set up his grudge match with Lawal on PPV. But even though that worked out, it was a risk in the sense either man could lose, or they could be put against each other in the first round of the tournament, but would then have to come back and be put in a match that may not click as big because it was the wrong opponent.

Coker gave almost no answers about any vision, past using the phrase Bellator 2.0, citing it being his first day on the job.

For now, things will go as scheduled. The company's next show on 7/25 in Temecula, CA, will go on as scheduled, and they will start a fall season of Friday night shows on 9/5, which is a head-to-head showdown with UFC, which will put on an FS 1 show ten minutes away from Bellator's Spike taping.

The plan, while not announced, would be weekly shows for a few weeks in the fall in arenas already booked, but not a full weekly season, and move to monthly major shows as soon as possible. The idea seems to be for a monthly Bellator and a monthly Glory show, and moving away from sold shows in small Native American casinos to running major arenas. The problem is, the Bellator name brand is going to be very difficult to sell tickets to. Even in Southhaven, MS, which was Rampage Jackson's first show in the Memphis market since he became a star, ticket sales for Bellator's loaded PPV were so bad that they didn't even announce any figures and the Mississippi commission wouldn't release the numbers.

Bellator had done better numbers on both MTV 2 and Spike for the monthly shows in the summer, even though summer is harder to draw ratings in. The Friday night shows had been averaging just under 700,000 viewers live, down from a little over 800,000 on Thursday.

The problem with monthly shows is that with the number of fighters under contract, the question becomes how do they fill their contracts. That was an issue with Strikeforce. While you hear now about how fighters liked Coker, and some did, there were a lot of complaints about an inability to communicate with him and being unable to get the fights on your contract and not getting any fights for nine months or longer which essentially starves people out. Still, Coker was much more liked than Rebney.

With what little Coker said, he did indicate that format, Rebney's idea, wasn't his future vision. He didn't seem to like the idea of weekly shows, nor of seasons, feeling MMA should be year-round. While there is something to be said about familiarity and patterned viewing, Bellator's history has shown that in the summer, when viewership should be lower, they would average more viewers doing monthly shows than weekly.

"To me, my vision is more continuity," he said. "Maybe not every week, but to build big superfights. The season, I think it should be a year-round sport. It shouldn't have a season, but that's something I have to sit down with Kevin and Bellator. I'll have a better understanding tomorrow."

Coker's approach is more traditional, to build big cards, similar to Strikeforce. Whether it would be a combination of major shows and minor shows, tiered that way, like he did with Strikeforce, there was no commitment. He had no answers about big shows on PPV vs. Spike. He was even vague when asked if he was going to promote women fights, something he a pioneer of in the past, but that Bellator dropped doing a few years back.

Rumors of Coker replacing Rebney had surfaced from almost the day Coker's UFC contract expired, and rumors of Rebney being replaced had started much earlier than that. Coker had signed a three-year deal in March after selling Strikeforce in 2011, to be the public face of the company. He had little to do with the real decision making after a while. Sean Shelby put the matches together and others at Zuffa ran the business end. Coker's role would be to remain the face of the company the week of the shows. The death of Strikeforce felt like an inevitability from the day of the sale. There was too much of a financial lure to move the marketable fighters to UFC. But there was a contractual relationship with Showtime. Showtime didn't want to have stars made on their network who would then leave for FOX and UFC, so insisted on a deal where everyone under contract to Strikeforce could not move to UFC, shortly after a deal was reached to move Nick Diaz, one of Strikeforce's biggest stars, to UFC with the idea Diaz vs. Georges St-Pierre would be big box office. This frustrated the top fighters, like Gilbert Melendez and Luke Rockhold, because they knew there were bigger fights for them on the outside, and they were stuck.

But inevitably, the relationship was doomed. Under the contract that Coker had signed with Showtime, they were in charge of the production. UFC had never given up those rights to its broadcast partners. This created awkward situations like Frank Shamrock, who White hated, being an announcer on a product his company owned because he had a Showtime deal. The relationship got worse. Strikeforce had a number of marketable heavyweights in a division UFC lacked depth in. While they fired Alistair Overeem, and then rehired him for UFC, that was a red flag for Showtime. When White saw the Ronda Rousey vs. Miesha Tate fight, and saw Rousey as a bona fide superstar, his hands were tied by the agreement in the sense he couldn't bring her to UFC. This all but guaranteed the end of the Zuffa/Showtime deal as soon as they could legally get out of it, which ended the Strikeforce name.

Coker did talk about working with other organizations. For the most part, Bellator only used its contracted fighters, past bringing in Shinya Aoki for a fight with Alvarez.

"If we can put a fight together that makes sense and drives the needle on Spike TV, we're going to do it," he said about working with other groups. "Some of the fighters we had in the past (in Strikeforce), we didn't have ownership of."

But the landscape is much different. In recent years, UFC has gone from 200 roster fighters to more than 500, meaning it has a far higher percentage of the top talent and marketable talent than even a few years ago. When Strikeforce was around, history showed that they had some of the best talent in the world. Strikeforce stars like Melendez, Josh Thomson, Luke Rockhold, Robbie Lawler, Nick Diaz, Tyron Woodley, Daniel Cormier and Fabricio Werdum went into UFC and did, if anything, better than many expected. Once Japan collapsed and UFC bought Strikeforce, they wound up with a monopoly on the best talent. While no doubt the best guys in Bellator in different weight classes are as good, if not better than the worst guys in UFC, aside from Alvarez and Chandler, I'd be hard pressed to come up with anyone on the Bellator roster that I'd expect would be hanging at the top level in any weight class in UFC.

And there are very few outsiders, perhaps limited to Yushin Okami and Ben Askren, and possibly Jake Shields, Marlon Moraes and Justin Gaethje who aren't in UFC today that I'd call possible threats to its top guys. The very size of the UFC roster doesn't leave many top contenders on the outside, and there are no obvious gimmicks that will work the way they would have five to eight years ago. The pro wrestlers doing MMA has been done. Herschel Walker is probably too old now, and that novelty has been done. Women are in UFC already, and virtually every top woman fighter is in UFC, Invicta or WSOF. The idea that they're talking with Kimbo Slice tells you that this is a company that is looking primarily to improve its television ratings as the singular goal.

UFC's big signing from Bellator, Hector Lombard, who destroyed everyone he faced as their middleweight champion, struggled at middleweight in UFC and had to reinvent himself as a welterweight to stay relevant.

According to Chael Sonnen's friend Frontrow Brian McMahon, Sonnen was contacted and asked to sign a confidentiality agreement to negotiate for the spot as Bellator CEO. That's notable only because Sonnen has no experience running a promotion, and his value would be as a front man promoting the fights, which he'd be very good at. It's not a secret, and hasn't been for a while, that Viacom was looking at getting rid of Rebney and it wasn't that they wanted Coker as much as they didn't want Rebney, with the fact they'd open talks with Sonnen telling you that much. He didn't sign the agreement and didn't negotiate for the spot. Kevin Kay told Josh Gross there was nothing to that story. Both FOX and UFC have plans for him for the future and he comes across as pretty loyal to UFC.

The landscape is also different from a fan standpoint. UFC has burned out the audience with so many shows, leaving interest in secondary promotions inherently lower than in the Strikeforce day when UFC hadn't so badly over saturated the market and Strikeforce was a different brand.

Bellator was averaging just under 700,000 viewers for weekly Friday night shows.

Changes in the night can be made. By accident, UFC established that Sunday may be a good night for MMA. With so many UFC events on Saturdays, which was the night Strikeforce ran its big events, that may be avoided with the idea it would limit the audience. Sunday night in the fall would be a terrible idea, but it would work for the rest of the year, as it avoids the direct competition from UFC and boxing. Bellator did better numbers on Thursday than Friday, but got complaints because, using TNA as a lead-in and starting at 10 p.m., main events were starting after midnight. Thursday in the fall is out because the one thing Spike learned from experience on with UFC is to avoid going against the NFL. Wednesday night would go against Ultimate Fighter during much of the year, but that should be seen as far less of a concern.

All the other questions are unanswered. Will Coker get Slice, at 40, who probably can deliver a one or two-time nostalgia pop? Rampage vs. Kimbo would almost be guaranteed to do big ratings, but it's a lot more questionable on PPV, although it could work if they were able to build animosity and have a strong hype special. The one thing Bellator has a huge advantage over UFC is that they can create hype specials and put it on television multiple times and get far more eyeballs than UFC can by putting similar shows on FS 1. But this is a marathon, not a sprint, and those hotshots aren't going to build anything unless you load up the undercard and promote a second match equally, not that it will help the draw, but try and use the eyeballs to focus on fighters that will be around for the long haul.

Within hours of Rebney being announced as gone, Jackson, the company's biggest star, who was the key in drawing 100,000 buys on PPV on 5/17, started taking retirement. That wasn't a surprise. Rampage made millions in UFC and they were never able to keep him happy, and everyone figured it wouldn't be long before his Honeymoon with Bellator would end.

Coker is not opposed to tournaments themselves. He saw them work in Japan, and copied it for a heavyweight tournament in 2011 that started out with a lot of interest, but lost momentum as the biggest stars fell out. But it wouldn't be the constant tournaments in multiple weight classes going on at the same time.

"We will do tournaments when the situation makes sense," he said. "I think a tournament makes sense, but the setting has to be right and the fighters have to be right."

The biggest questions are not so much Coker as Viacom, the key being whether they are willing to bid for top talent, like they did to get Jackson and attempted to get Melendez.

Coker assembled a strong roster at Strikeforce by paying his key talent considerably more than UFC was offering them. UFC was not happy when buying the promotion and seeing how high some of the deals were that they had to honor. But in doing so, the company was losing a lot of money, and the Fedor Emelianenko deal was a financial killer. His partners, the ownership group of the San Jose Sharks, wanted out, and UFC gave what they told me was the only real substantial offer. Coker, as part owner, made out like a bandit and was believed to be set for life.

He traveled the world and noted that his golf game really improved, but it was a learning experience and it almost seemed he was giving a message to some of the reporters he knew for years from the Strikeforce days.

"Retirement is overrated, and keep that in mind. I loved what I did. This is my 31st year in the business."

"There's a lot of fights out there, but I'll tell you what. When we started Strikeforce, you had Pride, the IFL, Affliction and Elite XC. There was a lot of product out there. I don't think that's a bad thing. It comes down to the fighters and athletes. We're going to develop world class fighters and put those fights on. We had a great platform with Showtime. The platform here (Spike) is in three or four times as many homes. This is a star building business. It's not just about the league. It's about building stars and making fights that you want to see, building fights that move the needle. Not all fighters move the needle and we'll do the best we can to move the needle for the network."

CHAPTER THIRTY ONE

EMMA ARRESTED

JULY 6

Tenille "Emma" Dashwood, 25, who lives in Winter Park, FL (the town where Full Sail University, where NXT is taped, is located) was arrested in a strange and highly embarrassing situation, charged with shoplifting a $21.14 iPad case from a Walmart in Hartford the afternoon of the 6/30 Raw.

Dashwood was arrested at 1 p.m. at the Walmart on 495 Flatbush Avenue and charged sixth degree larceny, a Class C misdemeanor, which is a theft of something valued at less than $250. She was released at 2:13 p.m. and returned to the XL Center in Hartford.

The maximum penalty is a $500 fine and three months in prison, but she is not in any danger at all of serving time on a first offense and her lawyer, Hubert Santos, said she was sentenced to a few hours of community service when she appeared in court the next day. She was told that upon completion of the community service and also completion of an on-line course that the charges will be dropped and she will have no record.

Santos claimed that she was using a self checkout machine and bought about $30 worth of items and simply forgot to scan in the iPad case.

They were preparing and shooting the backstage segment with Marella, Rose and the Rose buds starting at 3 p.m. Emma had already practiced doing the backward fall into the Rosebuds' arms in the skit at least six times.

At about 4 p.m., producer Brian James (Road Dogg) came into the room and told her, "You have to leave," and they shot the segment without her.

On television, Santino Marella acknowledged it as he was alone at the party with nothing but his cobra, and said he sent out invitations and even Emma didn't come to his party.

However, Dashwood was brought to a meet and greet with sponsors with several other performers in a luxury suite before Raw started, and she was still backstage at Raw hanging out during the show. Much of the talent had no idea of the story or why she was pulled from the segment. When the story got out regarding her explanation of simply forgetting to pay, the reaction we were told is that most were believing her story, just because nobody could understand the story when it first broke about why someone would shoplift something like that when she's earning a good income on the main roster.

WWE's statement after news of the arrest broke was, "WWE is aware that Tenille Dashwood (WWE Diva Emma) was arrested for shoplifting. Ms. Dashwood is ultimately responsible for her personal actions."

WWE had not taken any action at press time. WWE arrests for far more severe charges, such as a marijuana possession and speeding arrest by Jack Swagger, resulted in no punishment. Ariane Andrew (Cameron) had a DUI arrest and a charge at one point of attempting to bribe an officer (I believe the latter part of the charge was eventually dropped) a few years back, and she was suspended for 15 days. Tom Latimer, who is Bram in TNA now, who was originally part of The Ascension tag team in NXT, was fired after a fight with police officers after a second DUI charge.

Given those precedents, I don't sense any serious punishment coming from this from a WWE standpoint, perhaps something minor if anything, provided nothing like this happens again.

JULY 13

Tenille Dashwood (Emma) had a crazy day on 7/2, as she was fired in the morning, and rehired in the afternoon. The firing came as a shock to everyone, because it was so inconsistent with how the company has handled arrests of things far more serious. The reaction of the fan base was very negative. Really, she should thank Cameron and Jack Swagger, because without their recent examples of being arrested and not being let go, there wouldn't have been a recent precedent that made her firing for a shoplifting charge that is going to be dropped from her record after she does three hours of community service look so bad. She wasn't on Raw this week nor was her name brought up.

CHAPTER THIRTY TWO

SIX MONTH
BUSINESS ANALYSIS

<u>**JULY 13**</u>

As we finish the first six months of the year, you can't help but note what is going on right now with both WWE and UFC in regard to reaction in a changing business environment.

From a traditional business metric point of view, WWE has been pretty stable this year, throwing out the change in delivery of PPV and the implementation of the network. Its business has changed completely. But its popularity has stayed at relatively the same level. Television ratings are remarkably close to last year, down only slightly. Live attendance also remains steady. Live merchandise is down a little but web site merchandise is up.

WWE is also making talent changes with a very clear picture. For better or worse, the company is making a clear transition from John Cena to Roman Reigns as the face of the company, while keeping Cena in the superstar emeritus position in a role as "the greatest champion in WWE history." Other young talent is emerging, most notably Bray Wyatt, who may have the potential to be a Dusty Rhodes caliber babyface. The in-ring action is as good as it's ever been, and big shows have been consistently delivering for months.

If you look at UFC, you don't come to the same conclusion. PPV, long the company's most important revenue stream, is way down this year. Television viewership is also way down, but a lot of that is due to a change in station. They have nobody on the horizon that you can point to and say has a good chance to become a new major star. For 2015, it's still this year's stars, Jon Jones, Ronda Rousey and Cain Velasquez, with hoped for returns of Georges St-Pierre and Anderson Silva, and a hope that Chris Weidman or Anthony Pettis catch on, and hopes that a new champion may come from a foreign land to ignite business. Still, past Conor McGregor in Ireland, who is unproven against top competition, we don't have that guy anywhere.

Both companies are at their very core about developing stars. With WWE television being watched by millions, you have the vehicle to do so. For UFC, fewer viewers means what in 2010 may have been a star creating performance like what Matt Brown did with Erick Silva, may not have had much impact. In fact, that's where the 7/26 FOX show really comes into play, because if Brown gained something big, and he had the performance, attitude and unique charisma to be a cult star, it should show up in the FOX ratings.

Yes, while WWE is making cuts everywhere, UFC is making cuts nowhere, and Dana White is saying that people who think things aren't doing great don't understand a changing business. He's saying it is now an international sport with events around the globe and that things are stronger than ever.

Still, there is one point that is hard to get out of my mind. It's that anecdotal evidence people often use, but are often wrong, except when the big picture numbers back it up.

From 2006 to 2010, and still to a lesser extent through 2013, the night of a big UFC show was a big deal here. People would come over. They'd know the key matches and know most of the fighters. If I was away covering a show, we still often had a packed house, particularly if it was someone like Brock Lesnar or GSP on top. Those days are over. I may have a friend or two come over for UFC shows, and there are times nobody does. No biggie; almost nobody ever comes over for TNA and only a few show up for WWE these days, when it used to be packed during the heyday of WWE and WCW. But what I just said about UFC, evidence of nothing, is something that, if I say it to any MMA fan who used to watch with groups, they all say, "That's the same for me."

Obviously, running 50 shows is going to dilute viewership per show. It's like Major League Baseball or the NBA. Ratings for individual games are way down because so many more games air. It's not about big ratings for most regular events, it's about providing live sports programming that will deliver a core audience in a far more competitive sports environment. But those sports, while game ratings suffer, more than make up for it due to monster TV contracts.

UFC numbers on FS 1 are nothing like they were on Spike, and they are, with the exception of NASCAR or a major college football game, the highest rated programming on the station. The audience is down. The vehicle to promote shows, like Prime Times, without being on FX, is down to the point they no longer do series. Prime Times put in a position where a lot of viewers can see it are a strong catalyst in building monster PPVs. As much as people knock studying of Google trends, they are a tremendous tool to find out who people care about, who are stars, and rise and fall of popularity of stars, as well as on big events, who and what people most are interested in mainstream. What's been hurt in UFC is not the top tier stars, who were as big as ever last year, but the secondary stars dropped badly.

In the U.S., WWE and UFC were neck-and-neck in 2010. In 2013, WWE had a huge edge. In theory, more shows would mean more regular interest in UFC, but that hasn't been the case. With the lack of the big money matches this year, WWE's interest level is more than two-and-a-half times that of UFC, even if UFC as a company is said to be worth more than double WWE because of the value of a sports franchise due to the belief in skyrocketing TV rights. In Canada, where UFC had a gigantic edge for years, the loss of GSP had brought the two companies to being neck-and-neck so far this year after UFC was 53% ahead in 2013.

But, WWE, as a public company, there is no mistaking the financial problems caused by a lower than expected new television deal and the costs of the new network. The company is expected to finish the year deeply in the red. For all the positive product-wise, the WWE in 2014 is expected to end the year losing more money than any year in its history, and losing more money in a calendar year than any pro wrestling company in history with the exception of WCW in 2000.

UFC as a private company, little can be fully examined. Brazil, while also down from its peak as far as TV ratings and instantly selling out live events, still does huge ratings when on network television outside of prime time. The UFC strategy of live events in different parts of the world on prime time TV on good stations leads to gains in popularity in those markets makes sense. But even so, you at worst want to hold steady in your mature markets while building new ones. They are not holding steady in the U.S. and Canada, and in fact in a major popularity fall. But with a guaranteed TV contract, the effect of that fall may not be hurting them financially. That's the opposite of WCW, where the TV money was low and the decline in core business killed the company. But how much of a factor is the Spike to FX to FS 1 dynamic in that? But the deal also includes four shows on FOX that should have expanded the casual audience and made new fans.

As a sport and not WWE, are they able to garner big international television revenues? If a U.S. decline is offset by international growth, that would be an argument there is a big picture. But I don't know how a decline in U.S. and Canadian popularity could be part of a long-term growth plan, even if they are profitable and have a big safety net. Ticket sales for live events are still good, but with the absence of the big fights they are also way down. When we see merchandise sale numbers at UFC live events, they are excellent. Ratings can't be fairly compared and PPV is based on main events, and this year they haven't had strong ones.

Still, for the first six months of last year, the six PPV events generated $16.24 million in revenue, or $2,706,618 per show. For this year, through the end of June, that number is $10.99 million, or $1,831,475 per show, or a 32 percent drop. For PPV over the same six month period, they went from 2.78 million buys, or 463,000 per show, to 1.54 million, or 257,000 per show, or a 45 percent drop. Still, with the exception of just how bad the Demetrious Johnson vs. Ali Bagautinov fight did, none of this year's numbers were any lower than I'd have expected those same shows to have done in 2013, past had Ronda Rousey vs. Sara McMann taken place in early 2013 in February, it probably would have done the 100,000 more buys Rousey vs. Liz Carmouche did based on the novelty and huge amount of media publicity.

But Rousey on her own looks to be a 350,000 consistent player, partially because of limitations of challengers. Whether her quick finishes will help or hurt is hard to say. People used to say the first round knockouts were a disappointment in the Mike Tyson days because people paid so much money, but he drew huge for years. But a guy knockout artist with an aura where people are buying for devastation is not the same thing as a woman who they are buying because he's a star.

Jon Jones, the other big draw active this year, clearly declined after the canceled UFC event, past a big number with Chael Sonnen, and there's nobody who can duplicate Sonnen's ability to build a fight. With the exception of Cain Velasquez, who is injured, nobody else on the current roster is even at their level (the value of Chris Weidman will be better evaluated in a few weeks; as we've never seen him headline as champion without Anderson Silva, but even if UFC 175 does a big number, it's a combination of Weidman and Rousey and where Weidman stands going forward is still uncertain). Last year, all were well behind GSP and Silva.

For FOX, with only two shows, the sample size is too small. But this is significant because the big superstars don't fight on FOX, and it's the second tier stars. Last year's first two shows averaged a 2.31 rating and a $1.32 million average gate, which were main events of Demetrious Johnson vs. John Dodson (and Rampage Jackson had a lot to do with that one) and Benson Henderson vs. Gilbert Melendez, both title fights. This year's two shows averaged a 1.75 rating and $1.21 million average gate (helped by just how big Orlando's response to its first UFC was), with main events of Benson Henderson vs. Josh Thomson, not a title fight, and Fabricio Werdum vs. Travis Browne, also not a title fight. But it's a 24 percent drop in ratings. But they were also weaker shows with no Rampage this year nor any title fights.

Besides, the key is not live events in new markets as much as television exposure and events in new markets. Running once a year in New Zealand, for example, and drawing a $913,000 gate is all well and good if it leads to making new fans, but that's television exposure, not a live show that 8,089 people came to. The key to expanding the TV audience is well promoted shows in prime time on good outlets that people watch.

For example, the last London show, yes, it sold out, but they've sold out London for years. The key was it was on Ch. 5 in prime time, an over-the-air station that reaches tons more people than their BT Sports deal does. It gave them the ability to reach a new audience, and if they did well, they would have five slots a year on that station. On paper, all looked great. But the rating wasn't there, and they haven't been back on Ch. 5 since. But there are always going to be hits and misses.

Dana White is saying things have never been better. There are no indications like in WWE of cutbacks. In fact, White was talking this week about how the company is going to build a new office complex in Las Vegas, which would include studios, a workout gym, and the Ultimate Fighter gym will be part of the facility.

As far as long-term goes, UFC is dependent more on what kind of rights fees it can get from television. Ratings are important, as is the value and prestige of the brand and the economic situation from television at the time the deals comes due in 2017. White talked about their network as a game changer as well. But no matter what is said publicly, there has to be concern about the drop in popularity and a fan base that is having trouble keeping up with the names and number of shows.

As for WWE, unlike WCW, and other money losing companies who usually got that way due to failing to connect with their audience and rapid interest losses and fade away, there is no such issue with WWE. The losses are likely temporary, since they are due to the implementation and start-up of the network. The network is likely to grow economically in time, probably significantly. Will it reach the levels WWE predicted, or analysts predicted? That is too soon to say. But it will increase significantly from present levels as people accept new technology.

The cultural direction stemming from the lead of Netflix is that consumers are more willing to accept over-the-top services. The key to watch is if and when Netflix plateaus, because that would be the harbinger of the WWE network plateauing down the line. They are having a temporary rocky financial road. Long-term, as long as the fan base is stable, and it is, the machinery to create new stars is in order, which it also is, the prospects down the line are healthy.

WWE has worldwide popularity. It is still very conceivable that in 2016, when consumers will have less aversion to services like this, that it could be an overwhelming success even with the somewhat disappointing early returns. And there is still an international rollout for next year. No matter what percentage of current network viewers are from outside the U.S., and the number is clearly considerable, that is the hardcore audience that has learned to bypass geographically blocked services. The WWE hasn't even started a heavy marketing push in foreign markets, although there is an argument that the constant talk of the network on the television shows that air in every English language country does constitute a huge push.

But there is no mistaking that there are problems right now financially, with major cost cutting going on. The cutting of wrestlers a few weeks ago to help cut back on expected losses was just the tip of the iceberg.

A few different sources have pegged that Vince McMahon was ordering major cuts throughout the company. The number being bandied about is cuts that would total $20 million, so that the losses for 2014 are down significantly from the $45 million to $53 million projected.

Among the changes being looked at include some first class flyers flying coach, a new policy on international travel is being implemented, and there is talk of scaling back, but not eliminating, catering. In addition, there is a hiring slowdown as it regards original budgetary plans in the developmental sector.

While TV ratings and live show attendance are still important barometers of company popularity, from a financial standpoint, from this point forward, it lives and dies based on the network.

Essentially, the company will need, at a steady state, about 1.3 million to 1.4 million monthly subscribers worldwide to break even. Perhaps with the heavy cuts, that number may fall slightly. To get to previous levels of financial success, they need to get closer to 1.9 million subscribers. Once the number tops 2 million, unless unexpected costs arise (and there have been a lot of them with the network not expected going in), the company will be in its most financially healthy state it has ever been.

The business now, and going forward, is all about the subscriber numbers. PPV is going away quickly in the U.S., and the rest of the world follows suit next year. TV income is what it is for the next several years. Even in a period where sports rights fees have gone through the roof and entertainment rights fees have also gone up significantly, WWE did not get a major increase. Television is a strong revenue source, but the number is not going to escalate greatly. House shows, merchandise and licensing, categories the company had been built around for the past three decades, are now minor sectors. Popularity increases will help them, but the key is still today and for the foreseeable future, network subscriptions.

Raw on 7/7 made no bones about it. The entire television show felt like a commercial to get fans who haven't sampled the network, to try it out, for a free week, just by sending in an e-mail address. They noted that you don't even have to give a credit card number.

Raw pushed the free week, promoting not just the old PPVs, every WrestleMania including this year, the recent Money in the Bank show, as well as the prime time schedule for the week. This included debuting the first Monday Night War first episode. The series will become a regular weekly multi-episode show in a few weeks. This was a preview trying to use it to get new subscribers now by offering it in the free week.

They also uploaded a number of Saturday Night's Main Event, somewhat loading up on the Tuesday almost live Main Event show pushing a talk segment with Chris Jericho and Bret Hart, as well as pushing a replay of the great Warrior documentary. More episodes of SNME will be uploaded shortly, but after the free week. They pushed a 90 percent consumer satisfaction survey (which sounds believable because if you are a wrestling fan, it's a bargain). Obviously, the idea of making it as easy as possible for those who haven't tried to watch for free is a way to get paid subscriber numbers up starting next week from those who tried it out. The timing of now is to pump up the subscriber numbers since the second announcement will be made on or around 8/1, and a weak number will hurt the stock price. The timing if they get people buying the network on 7/14, when the trial ends, is that their subscriptions would run out on 1/14, or right before the Royal Rumble.

They need to have a number that at least indicates they will hit 1 million subscribers by the end of the year. One could come to the conclusion watching Raw that this hard sell was an indication they aren't on track and it's a desperation move to close the gap. But the marketing strategy was always to offer occasional free weeks, and pushing that you can watch it on your TV set and making it as simple for people to try it out should have been part of the marketing.

There is no question WWE has a loyal audience. The only question is, how many fans worldwide numbers are willing to pay for this service? Even if they hit 1 million by December, is the number of people interested and those who will break down the mental barrier to order in 2015 large enough to hit 2 million by July, the original projection? Maybe not. Can they hit 1.4 million by July of next year with expected early year international growth? That's plausible, but 1.4 million by July would only make 2015 into a break-even year. For a company hitting $50 million in profits annually, and paying out $36 million a year in dividends, a break-even year is not a success when the year was originally projected to be the single most profitable year in the history of the company. But if it's just a slower gain, and they get there in 2016, it's still a success. The next number will tell a story regarding short-term, but to make any kind of educated guess about long-term past thoughts about what percentage of homes that watch WWE television are willing to pay extra for more content, which is ultimately what will determine what the final number is. People who don't watch Raw are not going to get the network in any significant numbers.

For 2015 to be as profitable as the company was before they started spending on the network, they need to hit the 1.9 million figure as a full year average, meaning growing the first half of the year, hitting it by mid-year, and continuing to grow at the same rate until the end of the year. It seems unlikely but this is uncharted waters. While the service can always improve, the key question in the long run is not consumers being mentally willing to buy an over-the-top network. In time, and very quickly, that will happen. Baseball has already been successful at this. All sports will be doing so.

The question is whether WWE has enough fans around the world willing to pay $9.99 per month for extra programming, to hit and maintain the numbers in question. A 667,000 number after months of hard selling to get WrestleMania at a bargain price is an indication it won't be easy. An announcement of 850,000 subscribers isn't what I'd call great, since you need 1.4 million by next July just for the company to break-even. But it would be okay.

Given how hard the network has been pushed, the hotshot marketing, the quality of the PPV shows and the timing of the Ultimate Warrior death, a number at less than 850,000 would not be good.

But amidst all the hype are significant signs of cutting not just within the company, but on first-run programming for the network itself, which means second thoughts are being made as far as the value vs. cost of new first-run non-traditional wrestling programming.

The remake of Tough Enough was scheduled to start filming this week at the performance center in Orlando. We had heard last week that it was no longer a certainty it would be done, and if it was, the production budget was going to be greatly cut. Then, on around 7/3, the people working on the show were told filming was being postponed until October.

The idea had been for a second season of Legends House to go into production in October. There is some question whether there will be a second season. The first season was, except for PPVs, the most-watched thing most weeks on the network. One source in a country where Legends House aired on television noted that WWE sent them word that there would not be a second season of the show. Another WWE source said that there would be a second season, but filming would be delayed until after the completion of Tough Enough, probably not until early next year.

The reality shows are the most expensive things on the network. Legends House was done two years ago so its costs aren't even recognized on this year's books. But these are multi-million dollar shows. We know that Total Divas cost $400,000 per episode. So if you do a ten week shoot for a show like that, it's a $4 million cost over a ten week first run airing. A $4 million show over ten weeks, to be cost effective, would require such a show to bring in 200,000 new subscribers over the ten weeks to justify it. Granted, you then have the footage for all eternity and there is value in that. And if the show brings in 50,000 new subscribers and most of them stick around for a year, it's also a success. But for Total Divas, it's a lot better for the company to recoup the cost and make some profit by selling to E!, and then having rights to put it on its network six or nine months later, than spend the money for a first-run network launch. But year-old Total Divas episodes hardly have the value for the network that a first-run Tough Enough or Legends House would.

Dana White claimed that they were happy with the UFC 174 number and would have no problem going forward with putting Demetrious Johnson in a PPV main event. Kevin Iole reported the number at 125,000 buys. Our estimates have been between 95,000 and 115,000 buys.

"Demetrious is a guy who is getting better and better, and if he keeps finishing people and winning fights, sooner or later, he's going to break through," said White to Iole about UFC 174. "People are still getting familiar with him and with that division. We didn't go into that fight with the thought it would do a massive number. We know the market and our projection for what it would do was right on the money. This kind of **** is stuff I've heard for years and I'm just sick of listening to it, because it's so stupid and wrong. People are without any facts. We built this business in the U.S. and everyone kept telling us we couldn't. Then we built it in Canada and Brazil and now we're doing the same thing around the world. This is how you invest and build your business to make it strong for the long haul."

A bad PPV number, and this showed the baseline has gotten lower than ever before, is not a disaster if you are developing multiple new revenue streams. And it's a show that was going to do poorly. But you never want to lose overall popularity in any market.

The problem is that just plain putting on fights on television means nothing, just like pro wrestling matches. There are boxing matches constantly on free TV, and nobody watches and nobody breaks through as stars unless they appear on the highly rated HBO or Showtime cards. And even they are only known to boxing fans unless they are PPV headliners.

It's all about developing names and issues that people relate to. The less stars there are, the less interest there will be. With so many new faces on the roster due to so many new shows, there are more unknown newcomer vs. unknown newcomer fights with unrecognizable names. The less viewers see the new people coming up, the lower their ceiling as stars are and the lower their chances to breakthrough are. The more unknown fighters appearing on television, the less interest viewers have in those fights. One thing where boxing and MMA differ from wrestling is that when people watch wrestling, they are interested in the entire show, because they "know" almost everyone. With boxing and MMA, even if the TV set is on and people are in the room, if it's two fighters they don't know, people are having conversations and such. With UFC, there are more than 500 fighters, but the number of significant stars is less than when they had 200 fighters because they are on shows fewer people watch. For WWE, there are 65 to 70 regular roster performers, and almost everyone is recognizable and on TV almost every week.

CHAPTER THIRTY THREE

30 YEAR ANNIVERSARY OF BLACK SATURDAY

JULY 21

For the last few weeks, I've been trying to come up with a modern analogy for what happened 30 years ago this week. And the reality is there is no modern analogy that would fit. The closest would be if, in 2007 or 2008, when UFC was on the ascent and WWE was stagnant, when tuning into Raw on the USA Network, you would see the usual open of the show, but when it started, there would be an empty arena, and Josh Matthews, minus Michael Cole or Jerry Lawler, welcomed Dana White, who would be the closest equivalent, and he'd pitch to a bunch of taped fights that had already appeared on Spike. The idea is almost completely ridiculous. But on July 14, 1984, 30 year ago this week, that's almost exactly what happened. Shortly thereafter, Mike Rosen, an Observer cartoon writer from that period, dubbed it "Black Saturday," the name that has stuck with it for the next three decades.

The entire year of 1984 was one of weekly surprises for wrestling fans all over the country. In many markets, St. Louis and San Francisco among them, they already had their similar moment. Fans would tune into their weekly local wrestling show, in St. Louis it was the promotion Sam Muchnick had retired from nearly two years earlier that was one of the most successful in the country, only to see "Wrestling at the Chase" now being from the Arena in St. Louis, with the stars of the WWF. In San Francisco, "AWA All-Star Wrestling" was replaced by "WWF Superstars of Wrestling," on KTVU, the strongest independent station on the West Coast. The same held true in numerous markets around the country since WWF's battle plan for expansion was to go into existing markets, and buy the rights to put programming on the existing and established channel and time slot. In markets like St. Louis and San Francisco, which had been working on a barter system in that the promoter would provide the tape and in exchange, get some ad time to promote their house shows and the station could sell the rest of the time. McMahon came in, guaranteed the station $2,000 to $2,500 in markets of that size, less in smaller markets, more in larger markets, to air his shows. McMahon was not the first promoter to do so, as in the late 50s and early 60s, Jim Barnett pioneered that practice, much to the chagrin of NWA President Sam Muchnick, who felt such a practice in the long run would be bad for wrestling. In the 80s, the word got around and the cost of time slots escalated. Soon, in New York, stations were getting $8,000 to $10,000 per week. Ultimately, these costs were a key reason, in some cases the key reason, that Mid South Wrestling, Jim Crockett Promotions, ECW and Smoky Mountain Wrestling went out of business.

The change wasn't that big to fans in some markets, particularly in the AWA markets, because Gene Okerlund, the main voice of the product, Hulk Hogan, the top star, and David Shults, his big rival, all came over immediately. It was a flashier product with more stars, and business, at least in San Francisco, went way up. Of course, those in San Francisco never fully accepted the AWA as the local promotion as in local fans' eyes it never came close to matching the action and excitement of the Roy Shire promotion of the 60s and 70s. Those in St. Louis had seen the product and ratings decline badly in 1983 with the retirement of Muchnick on January 1, 1982, and the quitting of General Manager and booker Larry Matysik after the Ric Flair vs. Bruiser Brody record gate in early 1983. Matysik, who shared Muchnick's philosophy on how to run the market. That clearly appealed far more than the Bob Geigel/Harley Race philosophy that was in control the rest of the year, and produced television so bad that KPLR, the flagship station, wanted to get rid of their show and bring in a new promoter.

Each week, more major names from other promotions would show up on WWF television.

Pro wrestling's biggest national television shows at the time were World Championship Wrestling, a two-hour show produced by Georgia Championship Wrestling, Inc., taped every Saturday morning at the TBS studios on Techwood Drive, and airing from 6:05 p.m. to 8:05 p.m. Eastern on Saturday nights, and Best of World Championship Wrestling, a Sunday one-hour show at 6:05 p.m.

There was no staggered feed. On the West Coast, it was 3:05 p.m. to 5:05 p.m., absolutely the worst time, particularly in the summer. It was the big wrestling show to watch, and in the summer it was often frustrating, particularly if the Atlanta Braves baseball game would run long, as wrestling would be joined in progress, meaning key angles and matches never aired. The era was different. Wrestling fans were going to watch wrestling whenever it aired. And they were going to sit and wait for baseball games, whether they were in extra innings or long rain delays, to end.

Make no mistake about it, the shows were an institution. The time slot dated back to December 25, 1971, when booker Ray Gunkel moved the Atlanta TV wrestling show to Ted Turner's Ch. 17, WTCG (Turner had purchased the channel in 1970, changed the initials to WTCG, which in a promotional campaign, stood for "Watch This Channel Grow") in Atlanta. In 1972, when a promotional war started, because Ann Gunkel was so close with Turner, the station actually aired two different promotions. They taped back-to-back on Saturday mornings in the studio and that's where the two hour time slot came. In 1974, when Gunkel's All South lost the war, and Jim Barnett's Georgia Championship Wrestling bought her out, GCW got both hours.

In late 1976, Turner put his station up on satellite and it started airing on various cable channels. The idea appeared foolhardy. The idea is, if you were in San Antonio, why would you watch a UHF TV channel from Atlanta. Early WTCG shows featured ads for car dealers and furniture stores in Atlanta, as opposed to national advertising.

The reason people would watch were, they could see Atlanta sports teams, most notably the Braves, as well as reruns of The Andy Griffith Show. But it was Georgia Championship Wrestling that became the star on the station, the first show on cable television to be watched weekly in 1 million homes at a time when the station was only beamed into 15 million homes.

It was the weirdest thing. It was a two hour show, but from 1974 into the early 80s, it was treated like two one-hour shows. Gordon Solie would sign off after one hour. The musical intro would play to start the second show, and he would sign back on for a second hour like it was a completely different show. Often the same talent that worked the first hour matches would come back and wrestle again in the second hour.

In 1982, after Georgia Championship Wrestling had successfully expanded into Michigan and Ohio, it renamed itself World Championship Wrestling. The Georgia singles, TV and tag team titles in 1980 and 1981 became the National heavyweight (for a short period of time the Georgia and National titles were separate but they eventually merged), TV and tag team titles. When then babyface-delivering heel Kevin Sullivan was TV champion, he would say calmly to Solie that "I'm the best wrestler on national television," which Solie would disagree with, and Sullivan would claim the name of the belt says so.

The original success in Ohio and Michigan caused stockholders Jack and Gerald Brisco to push to Barnett to expand nationally to the markets where they were getting the most fan mail. Barnett refused to go into established markets saying the other promoters were his friends, while the Briscos argued that there were no friends.

But by 1984, Georgia Championship Wrestling had lost a lot of steam.

Three years earlier, the first run Saturday show averaged a 6.4 rating, and the Sunday show, featuring nothing but matches that had mostly aired the week before, and occasional matches from other territories, averaged a 6.6. It was the place to be. Besides the regulars, top stars from around the country would fly into Atlanta on Saturday morning for the national exposure. When fans tuned in on Saturday afternoon, you never knew if you'd see Ric Flair, Gino Hernandez, Kevin Von Erich, Mad Dog Vachon, Andre the Giant, Harley Race, Terry Funk, a former NFL star or boxing contender, a well known local politician, or even WWF champion Bob Backlund or AWA champion Nick Bockwinkel in studio. At the time, the announcing was being done by Solie and sidekick Roddy Piper, a dynamic that was revolutionary for its time.

But the promotion was having trouble financially. They fell deep into debt because of Jim Barnett, the controversial head of the promotion, using company money to pay for his lavish lifestyle, including $1,000 per month phone bills, a penthouse apartment, a private chef and a chauffeur. For years, Barnett living like a king off the GCW profits wasn't an issue, because in the state of Georgia alone, they were drawing about 800,000 to 1 million fans per year.

But things changed. Production costs increased. A huge change was that the Atlanta City Auditorium, the company's weekly building that held 5,300 fans, was shut down. During the 70s, they'd run every Friday night at the City Auditorium, and tape television the next morning. Every month or two, they'd load up the show, bringing in talent from other promotions like Ric Flair, Cowboy Bill Watts, Andre the Giant, or world champion Harley Race, and move it to the Omni, the 16,500-seat Arena, which would also house the holiday shows that drew the year's biggest crowds. Atlanta was the company's main profit center.

But when the auditorium shut down, Atlanta became a break-even proposition, or worse. They ran weekly at the Omni, which cost far more than the City Auditorium. They were still able at first to draw 5,000 fans most weeks, but the problem was, that was the number they needed to break even. Some weeks they lost money, some they made money. Going to the Omni itself was no longer a draw where the casual fan who wouldn't go weekly would hear that it's Omni week and that alone would swell the audience by a few thousand. The city that was the profit center was breaking even, and eventually, losing money most weeks. Suddenly, Barnett's lifestyle was a factor.

Ole Anderson, the booker and promo master, who Barnett had hired to handle the wrestling operations years ago and made him one of the higher paid talents in the business, thought things weren't right. He investigated the books. When he found out where the money was going, he threatened Barnett with embezzlement charges unless Barnett resigned immediately. Barnett, who was part of the cultural elite class in Georgia, hobnobbing with city leaders as this refined, very intelligent man, asked if he could retain at least a title in the company even if he would have no power and be taken off salary. Anderson offered no sympathy. The guy who led Georgia Championship Wrestling to winning a bitter promotional war over All-South Wrestling eight years earlier, the Treasurer of the National Wrestling Alliance, who booked the world champion for years, was completely out.

But not for long. Barnett was hired by Vincent Kennedy McMahon and before long was the Director of Operations for Titan Sports. At the 1983 National Wrestling Alliance meeting in Las Vegas, Vince McMahon, his father and Barnett all resigned from the alliance, which was step one in the "War of 84," which changed pro wrestling in North America forever.

Under Anderson, the mantra became cutting costs. The promotion formerly used the best talent in the country, but now became a second-tier regional group. Crowds were down, and pay for talent was down. Annual attendance for GCW in 1983 was down 60 percent. But with all the cost cutting, they were no longer bleeding money, and taking care of their debt.

At the time, Anderson was on a salary of $125,000 per year, huge money for a wrestler in 1983 and 1984. Georgia Championship Wrestling's profits for 1983 were $20,000. Several of the owners, used to big dividends each quarter, were making next to nothing with their stock, while mad that Anderson was making big money as booker and General Manager and were watching the attendance and ratings decline .

There were eight shareholders in GCW in early 1984. James Oates, a Chicago financier, who knew Barnett from college and was his money man in almost all his wrestling endeavors dating back three decades, owned 26 percent. Paul Jones, not the wrestler for the figurehead promoter from Atlanta, an ex-wrestling star in the area generations earlier, owned 22 percent.

Jack Brisco, Buddy Colt, Tim Woods and Bill Watts had been given stock under the recommendation of Eddie Graham in 1972 when ABC Bookings, the previous company, folded and Georgia Championship Wrestling, Inc. was formed, and the war with Gunkel started.

Watts came in as booker and Brisco and Colt were the top face and heel in Florida. Woods had been the biggest drawing card in Georgia a few years earlier as the white-masked Mr. Wrestling, but quit after setting a record gate with Gene Kiniski in a 1968 world title match in Atlanta, because he felt he wasn't getting a fair payoff from then-General Manager Ray Gunkel.

By 1972, Woods was one of the top stars in Florida. With Graham inserting himself in the role of making the big calls to get the new promotion going, he figured a big move would be to bring Mr. Wrestling back. This also led to the creation of Mr. Wrestling II, who became GCW's biggest star for most of the 70s, because Mr. Wrestling was still headlining in Florida so only worked major shows in Georgia, and he brought in his protégé who started headlining in the other markets. As a team, or as rivals, the two Mr. Wrestling's were the key players until the emergence of Dusty Rhodes as the top star in Atlanta, with his legendary rivalry with Ole Anderson.

When Jack Brisco was world champion, he moved from Tampa to Atlanta, meaning he worked Georgia all the time, a big factor in the wrestling war. Knowing he would need a manipulator who knew every dirty trick to keep the NWA in power since all the familiar stars went with Gunkel's All South group, Graham maneuvered Barnett to be General Manager and Watts to be booker. Later, when things had become successful, Graham brought Watts to Florida to book and Barnett brought in Jerry Jarrett as his booker.

Originally, Leo Garibaldi, the booker of the late 60s who built the territory around Mr. Wrestling, was brought in to replace Watts. The first thing Garibaldi did was have the guys Watts build lose to guys he brought in. Watts blew up, told Graham he needed to fire Garibaldi and "It can't wait," calling him a "dumb motherf***ker" a few times during the conversation. Watts came back to book a few more weeks before Barnett brought Jarrett in.

The idea is that if they were stockholders in Georgia, they would be more apt to work dates there since they'd not only get a payoff, usually a main event, but also get a percentage of the show's profits. It was felt that Brisco, Watts, Woods and Colt were all that important for the NWA side to win the bitter wrestling war when all the established stars from recent television went to the opposition.

The wrestling war in Georgia started on Thanksgiving morning of 1972. Ray Gunkel, who was running ABC Booking, had passed away after a match with Ox Baker. His widow, former model Ann Gunkel, now owning Ray's stock, wanted to act like an owner of the company. Not wanting a woman or someone they considered an outsider with an opinion around, the other owners folded the company, and restarted a new company without her. Ann Gunkel got financing and much to the chagrin of the NWA side, every single wrestler, office employee and referee, with the exception of mid-carder Bob Armstrong and prelim wrestler Darrell Cochran went with her. She promised better working conditions and pay. In the media, All-South, with all the local stars, was presented as the babyface promotion, with the idea Ann was the widow of Ray, the most beloved wrestler in the state, who the other partners tried to screw out of her husband's stock.

It was front page news, the biggest news story in the city that Thanksgiving morning that every wrestler in the promotion, except two, had quit to form a new promotion while the NWA had its traditional biggest show of the year that night.

The other Georgia owners turned to Eddie Graham, who ran Florida and was the powerful force in the Southeast that everyone listened to. Graham managed to get, at the last minute, several of his Florida stars, including Jack Brisco, as well as Watts, Mad Dog Vachon, Hiro Matsuda and others into Atlanta to put together an all-star card of matches that weren't promoted on television.

The NWA group retained the rights to the Atlanta City Auditorium, and with the NWA ties, was able to bring in all-star cards and the biggest names in wrestling while All South was limited in booking because wrestlers knew if they worked for Ann Gunkel, there was the threat of NWA blacklisting.

The corner was turned in 1973 when Mr. Wrestling drew big crowds in chasing Dory Funk Jr. for the world title. They built to a climactic match on June 1, 1973, at the Omni, where Mr. Wrestling announced he would unmask at the start of the match. There was a buzz in town, with the idea that the NWA would never allow a masked man to be world champion, and that by unmasking, Mr. Wrestling would be allowed to beat Funk Jr., or if they had a different mindset, would simply beat Funk Jr. since he had long been portrayed as the best technical wrestler in the business.

But one week earlier, Harley Race beat Funk Jr. in Kansas City to win the title. Mr. Wrestling unmasked at the start of the match as Tim Woods. He had already unmasked in Florida as Woods some time earlier which fans in South Georgia, which could get the Florida show off the Jacksonville station, knew about, but Atlanta fans except for the hardcores were unaware. The show drew a sellout of 16,500 fans, establishing the Omni as "The Madison Square Garden of the South," and GCW as a powerful promotion that the top talent came in for. The match ended in a 60 minute draw, with Race out from the sleeper hold when the bell rang.

Over the next decade, through buying others and selling to his brother, Jack Brisco owned 10 percent and Gerald Brisco also owned 9.5 percent, from buying Colt's five percent and buying five percent that his brother had purchased from Barnett to increase from his original ten percent.

The rest of the stock was owned by Columbus, GA promoter Fred Ward (15 percent), General Manager Alan "Ole Anderson" Rogowski (10 percent, who purchased his stock from Watts a few years after Watts formed Mid South Wrestling), Ward's son-in-law Ralph Freed, a partner in Columbus (5 percent) and Gene Anderson (2.5 percent, Ole's working brother whose real name was Gene Anderson, had purchased the stock Woods owned).

Both Briscos were frustrated that their dividends for owning Georgia was amounting to nothing, after also being frustrating that when the company was hot, Barnett didn't take advantage of the national following to expand.

In early 1984, even though the company had gotten itself out of the Barnett-incurred debt, Jack Brisco thought the direction of using the cheaper talent and attendance falling so drastically was in the long run a disaster.

At the time, the Briscos was wrestling in the Carolinas for Jim Crockett, working as heels and bounding the world tag team titles back-and-forth with Wahoo McDaniel & Mark Youngblood. Anderson was running Georgia, but his mother had died back in Minnesota, so he flew back for a week.

Jack heard that Roddy Piper, a good friend of his that he had feuded with in the Carolinas, had cut his hand. He called the WWF offices, and ended up talking to Vince McMahon. McMahon brought up the idea of buying their stock in GCW, and essentially doing a hostile takeover.

The Briscos were able to get the voting proxies from Jones and Oates to negotiate a deal. Jones was old and pretty much senile, so his wife really was making the decisions and the idea of getting $244,000 in cash and getting out of wrestling at that point appealed to her. Oates was willing to get out, as the only reason he had shares was because he acquired them for Barnett in a stock trade in 1974 where he got Georgia stock in exchange for selling the Australian territory when they got out. Suspicious minds would believe Barnett, one of the game's great manipulators, was behind this as revenge for Anderson kicking him out of the company he built. But from all accounts, Barnett had nothing to do with this and it was the Briscos as the point men.

When they went to meet with Vince McMahon, they controlled the rights to sell him 67.5 percent of the company, meaning he could take over.

After a conversation, McMahon sent Jack & Gerald Brisco tickets to LaGuardia Airport, and they met in the Delta VIP Lounge.

Keep in mind that Ward, Freed, Ole & Gene Anderson had no idea any of this was going on.

In getting Jones' proxy, the Briscos found out that Anderson was also trying to buy Jones' stock, as well as the stock of Ward and Freed, and with Gene, that would give him 54 percent, so he'd own the controlling interest and be able to make the moves he pleased without answering to the other stockholders.

What was amazing is that the conversation at LaGuardia Airport and verbal agreement to a deal took place in February or March 1984, but it took the WWF lawyers and the Briscos lawyers, until early April to finalize all aspects of the deal, but the principals involved had to keep it a secret.

Vince & Linda McMahon, their attorneys, the Briscos, Jones, Oates and their attorneys met at the offices of well-known Atlanta attorney John Taylor on April 9, 1984. After about 14 hours of final negotiations, Vince wrote a check for $750,000 to the various partners and owned 67.5 percent of the company, and for that moment, Vince and Ole Anderson were technically partners, although Ole didn't know it until a secretary called him while he was in Minnesota and told him that Vince McMahon had taken over the company, and figured that everyone would be out of a job.

Oates went along with the sale, but called the Briscos money-grubbers and felt they had double-crossed Barnett by not backing him when Anderson got Barnett kicked out of the company.

While everything had been secretive until that point, after that meeting, it was known in wrestling that Vince McMahon had bought the promotion and was going to take over TBS time slots. Anderson went to court to block the deal, stating bylaws that all owners had to agree on taking a new owner in, which didn't happen. There was a sleight of hand as before they sold the company, with their majority ownership, the owners there voted to rescind that part of company bylaws. In July, the judge ruled in favor of McMahon being able to take over the company, ruling he legally bought out the majority of stock. McMahon eventually paid Anderson $100,000 for his stock and paid Ward and Freed $150,000 and $50,000 each.

That may have been the reason McMahon ended up so far behind in paying bills for the next year. After the success of WrestleMania I, the $1 million buyout of the TBS contract by Jim Crockett Jr. and a major money booking agreement with New Japan Pro Wrestling, all in early 1985, made the WWF financially solvent and they started catching up on paying television and other bills.

While we were the only source that had reported the deal having gone down and a change being imminent, virtually all the fans tuning in on July 14, 1984, expected to see the usual studio wrestling show and the stars who worked in the area.

Instead, the show opened in the studio, but it was empty. Freddie Miller, the co-host of the show, who would introduce Solie and conduct interviews, instead introduced the new host, Vince McMahon, and welcomed the WWF to TBS. Miller was just about the only familiar face from the old show who appeared that night. McMahon then pitched to matches from different major arenas featuring his wrestlers.

McMahon had offered the GCW wrestlers jobs, and few took him up on the offer. He claimed publicly when criticized because of Solie's big following nationally at the time for not hiring him, said he had offered Solie a job. Solie always claimed that never happened. He told the existing champions, National champion the Don "The Spoiler" Jardine, NWA jr. heavyweight champion Les Thornton, TV champion Ron Garvin and tag team champions Garvin & Jerry Oates (who had a few days earlier beaten the Road Warriors, who were aware of the situation and figured Georgia was going down, so left to work for Verne Gagne) that they could come in as champions. Spoiler, who had the size McMahon liked, was 44 by that time and was on his careers last legs. He and Thornton, who was 50, actually were on WWF television with their belts and billed as champions for a few weeks, before it was completely forgotten and they ended up being essentially jobbers. The other key star who went with McMahon was Mr. Wrestling II, Georgia's biggest star. Wrestling II was always a headliner by that point, but at the age of 49, his best days were behind him. By WWF standards, Wrestling II was small, old and didn't have an impressive body, and was used as a job guy. Even after he left, the television exposure of II as a nobody pretty well killed his career marketability. The only guy working the Georgia territory at the time who ended up getting a push was Nikolai Volkoff, who was put into a tag team with the Iron Sheik and they became the company's top heel team, and is remembered as one of the company's more iconic characters of its expansion era. Volkoff had previously had runs as a mainline heel in WWWF.

TBS was besieged by so many angry phone calls that it became a national news story. The theme of the calls was that "We want our wrestling back with Gordon Solie." McMahon in the news stories talked about how fans would soon see the difference between what they had seen and his brand. He said that the ratings, which had dropped 35 percent from the peak of a few years earlier, would rebound to former levels. He also tried to claim that angry phone calls were not people acting on their own, but something his rival promoters had set up.

When the word got out the Briscos put the deal together, they were viewed negatively by many, particularly since Jack was a former NWA champion who had been a headliner in most of the NWA territories, and he and Gerald were NWA world tag team champions. Both of their wives were called and told stories about them having affairs on the road. Anderson threatened to send the Road Warriors to Tampa to break their legs. After word had gotten out about the sale, the Briscos dropped the NWA tag titles to McDaniel & Mark Youngblood on May 5, 1984, at the Greensboro Coliseum, and their last NWA match was a rematch the next day in Charlotte. In late September, they started as a team in WWF, feuding with Adrian Adonis & Dick Murdoch over the tag titles, but Jack retired in early 1985, never to come back, and Gerald, while he had a second run as a stooge for McMahon years later, ended his active career in early 1985 as well. But Gerald has been employed by WWE ever since, currently as a talent scout.

Ted Turner responded to the protests by working with Ole Anderson and giving him a one-hour show. Unfortunately, the only available time slot was 7 a.m. on Saturday mornings, and the short-lived Championship Wrestling from Georgia was formed, with Gordon Solie as announcer.

Because of the time slot, viewership was significantly lower and the new Georgia group struggled. Anderson's top attractions, the Road Warriors, left for the AWA, and most of his other major stars also went to different groups. While McMahon had put Spoiler as National champion on TV, Anderson's group, which used the National titles names and legacies of GCW, simply claimed Ted DiBiase had beaten Spoiler and was the National champion.

1984 was the key year in changing the pro wrestling business. For the next several months, the WWF had the key time slots on TBS, USA and by far the best national syndication package. Nobody could match them for television exposure and they outdistanced all rivals. It's hard to explain just how important this move was at the time. While several regional groups were doing great business in 1984, like the AWA, Mid South, World Class, Jarrett Promotions and Crockett Promotions, and the media was discovering wrestling because of the involvement of Cyndi Lauper, the only group that got covered was WWF. They were the group that was on both of the major national cable stations that carried wrestling, and they were the dominant group in New York, Los Angeles and Chicago.

Crockett eventually got the TBS slot a year later, and had a couple of big years, but he was always playing catch up, except in his home territory.

The TBS Saturday and Sunday ratings fell in 1984-85, despite McMahon claiming he would show the people a product that would be more popular than the one that preceded him.

In 1985, Turner and Watts reached a verbal agreement. Turner wanted to get into wrestling and Watts' television show was doing amazing ratings within his territory. In many of his markets, half the people watching television when Mid South Wrestling was on were watching his show. The agreement was that Turner would provide the time slot on TBS and finance a national expansion and Turner and Watts would follow Vince McMahon's lead and be his competition.

Put in an unfamiliar time slot on Saturdays, Watts' Mid South Wrestling did a 5.3 ratings average, making it the highest rated show on cable television, beating the WWF show in the familiar slots by 1.5 ratings points or more.

Knowing Turner was going to kick McMahon off the station between the falling ratings and not producing a show in his studios as per the contract, McMahon sold the time slot to Crockett, a deal brokered by Barnett.

When the deal was put together, Turner lost interest in Mid South and in promoting wrestling. He felt that for the good of the business, there should only be one promotion on the station, and it was Crockett. It was actually the deal that, until Solie was brought back years later by WCW, which ended the Solie run as the voice of wrestling on the SuperStation. Most figured Crockett would go with Solie when he got TBS, but instead, he went with the younger Tony Schiavone.

Crockett's business grew greatly in 1985 and 1986 while on TBS, drawing 1.9 million paying customers in 1986. Watts tried to make up for the loss of TBS by buying TV time around the country to have national exposure. But the bills put him deep in debt, and his home region stopped drawing, partially due to the oil business crash, that killed entertainment in his key cities like Houston and New Orleans.

In 1987, Watts, losing $50,000 per week because of the costs of his TV network and inability to draw at home, sold Mid South Sports to Crockett for $4.3 million, of which Watts actually only got $1.2 million. Crockett bought the company for its television network, but the cost of the time slots and overspending, plus being outmaneuvered by McMahon in the PPV world and stale top of the card booking led to him getting deeply in debt. Crockett Promotions sold to Turner Broadcasting in 1988 for $9 million.

CHAPTER THIRTY FOUR

JESSE VENTURA LAWSUITS

A slander and libel trial involving Jesse Ventura went to court this past week. This has gotten a good deal of national publicity over the years for a number of reasons. Ventura filed suit against Chris Kyle, a former Navy Seal who wrote a best selling book called "American Sniper." In the book, Kyle wrote about punching out someone talking negatively about the Seals and the military at a bar in Coronado, CA, in 2006. Kyle's book claimed that he attended a funeral of a former Seal and went to a bar where a celebrity, he called in the book Scruff Face, but in later interviews said was Ventura, who he said "most people seem to believe he was a Seal" (Ventura was on a Seal demolition team in Vietnam, although those who don't like Ventura have always claimed that isn't accurate). Kyle said he went to Ventura and introduced himself, and asked to say hi to someone who was injured in the Iraq war, but Scruff Face said he couldn't be bothered. He claimed the person started saying how the only reason we were in the war was because President Bush wanted to show up his father and how we were in the wrong in Iraq, murdering women and children. He said Scruff Face said he hates America and that's why he moved to Mexico (Ventura in fact did move to Mexico). He claimed guys were getting upset, Kyle told him to cool it and said his group was in mourning. Kyle claimed Scruff Face said, "You deserve to lose a few." and Kyle claimed they argued and Ventura threw a punch, and Kyle said he laid him out quickly. Ventura sued, saying the statements undermined future opportunities for him as a political candidate, speaker or media personality. Ventura's name was not mentioned in the book, but when he did his publicity tour, he claimed the person he punched out was Ventura, including on an interview with Bill O'Reilly. Ventura has always maintained that it never happened. Kyle passed away in the interim, killed in 2013 by a former marine he had befriended who was suffering from post traumatic stress disorder. Kyle was deposed before his murder and the deposition is expected to be part of the trial. Ventura continued his lawsuit against Kyle's widow, Taya Kyle, and the Kyle estate, even though many advised him to drop it at that point because of how it came across, suing the widow of a man who had been murdered. It's also considered a landmark case because the usual celebrity doctrine in a situation like this is the story will go away, and by filing a suit, it keeps the story going for years. It's also considered a landmark case because the standards for defamation are considered much higher for a public figure, that Ventura as a former Governor and TV show host and guest clearly is that. The Minneapolis Star-Tribune wrote a story about the first amendment implications of the case last week. For a celebrity, Ventura will have to prove that no such fight took place, but that his reputation was harmed by the story, and that there was clear malice in publishing and telling the story. Ventura can't win the case simply because the story wasn't true and if Ventura can prove it. Ventura would not agree to settlement offers, because he said he wanted it in a public forum that the brawl never happened and story was made up. "It was completely fabricated, that's why we are in court," Ventura said this past week. Ventura, represented by David B. Olsen (Brock Lesnar's attorney in his WWE lawsuit over the non-compete clause in his contract years back), claims he has several former Navy Seals who were at the bar the night in question who will testify that they heard Ventura saying nothing negative about the seals or the military, as Kyle claimed in his book and on his media tour, nor was there any confrontation, let alone a fight. Kyle was later killed. His book was No. 1 on the best seller list in early 2012, where Kyle claimed to have been the greatest sniper in U.S. military history, claiming 160 confirmed kills. A movie is being made based on the book although it is not known whether his version of the Ventura story would be in the movie. Ventura testified that he would never make a disparaging remark about the Seals, noting he was named co-Frogman of the Millennium in a magazine story and said it was the greatest honor of his life, bigger than being elected Governor. Ventura said he wasn't drinking that night because medications he takes forced him to give up alcohol in 2002. Ventura tried to claim the comments could have hurt his income, citing he earned nearly $11 million between 2002 and 2011, but only earned $190,378 the next year after the story came out. Lawyers for Kyle noted Ventura's income had been steadily declining, topping out at $3.8 million in 2003 when he was under contract to MSNBC for a show that never really went anywhere, and made $676,455 in 2011, before the book came out. Ventura tried to claim his income dropped in 2012 because TruTV canceled "Conspiracy Theory," which Ventura tried to claim was because of the publicity from the incident. But damaging testimony came on 7/14 and 7/15. Laura DeShazo of Salt Lake City, whose brother was a Seal, said she was at the bar that night, posed for a photo with Ventura and later saw a man, who she described identically to Kyle, punching Ventura. Laura's sister, Dr. Rosemary DeShazo, said she didn't see the fight but said she heard Ventura say that the slain Seal member, Michael Monsoor, "probably deserved it" and said "They did all the time." John Kelly, a current Seal, said he was at the bar, attending the wake of a slain Seal, and excited to meet Ventura and wanted to talk with him about the movie "Predator," that Ventura was in. Then he said Ventura started talking about his opposition to the war in Iraq, which he felt was the wrong time to be talking like that given it was Kelly's friends wake. He said he just walked away because he was losing his temper. Kelly said he later saw Ventura laying on the ground. When he asked what happened, he was told Kyle decked him. Kelly said his thought was that Ventura had it coming. Kelly said he never saw the punch, but did see Kyle leave the scene immediately, something Seals are trained to do if they get into a fight in town. Kelly also said Kyle told him later that night the story that Ventura had said they deserved to lose a few. Olson argued that it was a second-hand story and nothing more than gossip. Olson also argued Kelly was drunk, which Kelly admitted, noting he had 15 to 20 drinks and was hung over the next morning. But Kelly said he was both confident in his recollection and that he knows the story from being there. Andrew Paul, another Seal, who was Kyle's direct superior officer, was shown via videotaped deposition. He was not at the trial. He said he was at the bar, and also didn't see the punch itself, but he saw Ventura getting off the ground with a bloody lip and yelling at Kyle, "I'm going to f***** kill you." Paul said he also thought it was cool when he saw Ventura, one of the best known Seals ever, in the bar, and wanted to meet him, but soured on it hearing Ventura going off to anyone who would listen about the war and his 9/11 conspiracy theories (Ventura has always claimed he believed it was an inside job). Olson asked why, as Kyle's superior, that he didn't report what happened to the police or military authorities, and he said it wasn't that big of a deal if you're a Seal because you see a lot of things like that. Witnesses were not consistent in stories about where in the bar the fight took place. The Kyle family attorney argued Ventura lost his TV show gig and his income dropped because he continued to make outrageous and offensive statements on television and in books, and brought up a number of them. Kyle himself did a videotaped deposition before he was killed, saying Ventura was being offensive, that he talked with him, and punched Ventura because he believed Ventura was going to punch him first. It was noted that a petition was circulated to kick Ventura out of all Seal alumni groups because of his decision to sue Kyle's widow, saying it violates the Seal ethos to protect each other both on and off the battlefield.

JULY 21

Jesse Ventura's lawsuit against Taya Kyle, the widow of Chris Kyle continued this week, which led to Ventura being named the Fool of the Week by Eric Bolling on the Fox News Network. There was a video deposition from John Jones, a current Seal reservist who was in the bar the night of the alleged incident. He said he was a swimming buddy of Kyle, and the two became close friends. He said he never saw the punch, but did see Ventura on the ground and get up and was told that Kyle had punched him for talking shit. He said that he didn't see the punch, or hear anything Ventura said that was negative about the military, but also said he had been drinking too much that night. Jones said that he never tried to talk to Ventura that night, and had seen Ventura at other military events and never tried to talk with him. He said he's not much for meeting celebrities and said, "I had the observation that he talks a lot and doesn't listen."

AUGUST 4

The jurors in the Jesse Ventura defamation slander and libel case in St. Paul ruled on 7/29 in favor of the former Minnesota Governor and pro wrestling star, awarding him $1.8 million in damages from Taya Kyle, from the estate of the late Chris Kyle. The day before, the jury had told judge Richard Kyle (no relation to the defendant) that "We feel we will not come to a unanimous verdict. The jurors reportedly looked tired and depressed and Judge Kyle told them to give it one more try. The verdict came in after lawyers from both sides were confident that they had won, but there was a holdout. Both agreed that instead of it being unanimous, they would accept a verdict of eight out of ten jurors. The Kyle side lost the case due to that agreement. The jurors started deliberating on 7/22 on a case that onlookers believed Ventura would not win based on testimony from 11 different witnesses that were in the bar that night who had seem at least parts of what Chris Kyle had described in a television interview and in his best selling autobiography, of Ventura (whose name wasn't mentioned in the book but Kyle did say it was Ventura during an interview with Bill O'Reilly) allegedly saying negative thing about the military and being punched and knocked down by Chris Kyle in 2006. The judge noted that if the jury didn't reach a verdict, Ventura could ask for a retrial. The jury award was based on $1.3 million for unjust enrichment, with the idea that the "untrue" Ventura story helped sell that much in book revenue and another $500,000 for defamation due to the damage done to Ventura's reputation and earnings power from the story being told in public forums. Ventura had claimed he had never said what Kyle claimed, nor had he been punched in a bar in Coronado, CA, in 2006 when the incident allegedly took place. Judge Kyle had told the jurors that Ventura had to prove with clear and convincing evidence that Kyle knew what he wrote was untrue or that at least he would have had serious doubts about its truthfulness. Ventura's attorney, David Bradley Olsen, the same attorney Brock Lesnar used to get out of his WWE non-compete and wrestle in New Japan and fight in K-1 and UFC after Lesnar had signed a non-compete through 2010 when he left WWE in 2004 which was worldwide in scope where he had agreed he would not participate in any sport except pro football (the one thing WWE allowed in giving him his release), and that he wouldn't do pro wrestling or any form of entertainment related to physicality (the way the release was written, Lesnar in theory could have been barred from appearing in a play or movie if he did athletic things in it). Olson successfully argued that even though Lesnar had signed it, it was unreasonable due to the worldwide aspect and the six year time frame. Lesnar was sued by WWE on those grounds when he signed a contract with New Japan. The case was settled out of court, but Lesnar was able to work for New Japan and later fight. Olson claimed that the Kyle estate had earned more than $6 million from Chris Kyle's best-selling book and had asked for between $5 million and $15 million. Olson said it hurt Ventura that Kyle's comments made Ventura a pariah in the Seals community, a group he was very proud of being part of. Kyle's attorney, John Borger, noted that 11 witnesses all told a story that backed up Kyle's version. Richard Kyle said that the jury did not have to decide on whether they believed Ventura was decked in the bar, but whether Chris Kyle defamed him with the portrayal of him as saying that the Seals "deserved to lose a few" and claiming the U.S. military was killing innocent civilians in Iraq. Olson argued that the 11 witnesses had inconsistent testimony about what happened. The reality is, if there's a fight eight years ago in a bar and you bring in 11 people, there are likely to be inconsistencies. And there were people with Ventura who testified for him that no fight took place and that

Ventura would have never said that was attributed to him because he was never knock people who served in the military because of his own background and that of his parents. This was a big enough national news story that the single most searched for item in the U.S. on 7/29 was Ventura.

DECEMBER 22

Jesse Ventura filed suit against HarperCollins, which published the bestseller "American Sniper," which Ventura claimed defamed him with false statements. Ventura won a $1.8 million judgment against the estate of the late Chris Kyle in a lawsuit regarding Kyle claiming he decked Ventura in a California bar when Ventura made anti-Seals statements. Ventura claimed he neither made any such statements, nor was he decked by Kyle in a fight. The new suit came a week before the Christmas release of the movie, starring Bradley Cooper, based on Kyle's book. The belief is that the Ventura story, as alleged in the book (which never mentioned Ventura by name, but Kyle did say it was Ventura on some talk shows promoting the book), is not depicted in the movie. Kyle's widow is attempting to appeal the original verdict. The suit asks for $150,000. Representing Ventura in this case, as was in the original case, was attorney David Bradley Olson. Olson is best known in wrestling circles for being Brock Lesnar's attorney when he negotiated essentially the winning settlement against WWE, throwing out Lesnar's non-compete clause in his release, which allowed Lesnar to work eventually for groups such as K-1, IGF, New Japan and UFC.

CHAPTER THIRTY FIVE

LANA CONTROVERSY

WWE's streak of great PPV shows ended on 7/20 with a Battleground show that left more questions about the decision makers than anything else.

On a show where the matches didn't look as good on paper as most shows, the decision was made to eliminate the probable best match, Dean Ambrose vs. Seth Rollins, and instead shoot an angle with the idea of saving the match for SummerSlam. With the move, the show came across as them stalling out with features and longer out of the ring segments, and even then, the two ended eight to ten minutes earlier than usual.

Telling stories is all well and good, but if that the idea was to save the first match for SummerSlam, the match shouldn't have been advertised and an angle eliminating the match from the show should have first been done with the announcement the match was off on one of the television shows before the show took place.

Eliminating that match led to all kinds of stalling in the first 90 minutes, making the show drag. The crowd of 11,000 fans at the Tampa Bay Times Forum wasn't all that hot for most of the show, which didn't help matters. And aside from the opener, where the Usos retained the tag titles beating Luke Harper & Erick Rowan in two of three falls, nothing really stood out. One person noted to us that a lot of the crew was exhausted, with the crew that went to Japan still suffering the affects of the jet lag and the hard schedule, particularly John Cena and Bray Wyatt who had put themselves through the wringer over the previous ten days schedule-wise.

The main event had its moments, but it was really a throw away match, a four way where most expected Cena to win, and he did. There was tension teased and the match built to moments where Cena and Roman Reigns squared off, and later Kane and Randy Orton squared off, but neither confrontation got the kind of reaction expected.

The other case of questionable judgment, which shocked me if only because the company has been through this before, was Lana doing her pro-Russia interview before the Rusev vs. Jack Swagger match. She was out there forever, since they were clearly stretching out the non-wrestling segments. This would have been the week to tread carefully, given the Malaysian Airlines Flight MH17 tragedy, where 298 people died after a plane was shot down in The Ukraine. She came out mad and talked about the propaganda in the biased media during the week, never referencing the incident, but clearly it was in reference to everyone watching.

The references got far less heat than she had been getting, almost as if people could have fun booing the cartoonish Russia vs. USA throwback to another time period in wrestling, but once it had to do with real life today, it crossed the line into sleazy.

Newspapers and web sites around the world, including those in Europe, Australia, and in places like The Drudge Report, the New York Post and the Washington Post, wrote stories about the exploitation of the slain airline passengers in the promo, referring to Lana as "actress Catherine Jo Perry," and making fun of her Russian delivery.

While some would argue that's a win, getting that press for the angle, WWE history would teach the opposite.

"Last night's segment during WWE's Battleground event was in no way referring to the Malaysia Airlines tragedy," said WWE in a response to the media criticism. "The storyline with characters Rusev and Lana has been a part of WWE programming for more than three months. WWE apologizes to anyone who misunderstood last night's segment and was offended."

That was a unique choice of wording, given it was very plain what every single viewer would take Lana's statement about current events and media coverage to mean.

WWE had two similar high-profile incidents, although in both cases it involved main event angles with the company's biggest stars, as opposed to a mid-card deal.

In 1990, the company embarked to break its all-time attendance record, shooting for enough people at the Los Angeles Coliseum for the 1991 WrestleMania that they could claim a magic 100,000 plus, breaking their storyline number of 93,173 for the Hulk Hogan vs. Andre the Giant match at the Pontiac Silverdome.

The idea was to bring back Sgt. Slaughter, who played the Patriot American hero when he left the company in 1984 at a time he was the second or third most popular wrestler, due to a dispute with Vince McMahon over merchandising or alleged unionization talks. Slaughter had played that character in the AWA for years, and on indie shows, where he was the highest paid indie wrestler in the country. He was brought back to turn on his home land and side with Saddam Hussein, since there was tension with Iraq at the time.

A few years earlier, during the heyday of the Iron Sheik (who ended up changing his name to Col. Mustafa and going from being Iranian to Iraqi in the angle) & Nikolai Volkoff, when Vince McMahon was being interviewed by Larry King, he was asked about those type of angles. McMahon noted that you could do them after wars, as wrestling had done with evil Germans and Japanese from the 50s through the 70s, but he'd never do them during war.

A few months before WrestleMania, with the build up in place, suddenly, the U.S. was in a real-life with Iraq. Suddenly a typical wrestling xenophobic angle was exploiting a war. The idea wasn't there when it was started, but it was also known at the start there was a good chance a war could start. McMahon could have abandoned the angle, and picked it up later, or not. He chose not.

The result was a tremendous amount of negative press, a level that pro wrestling had never gotten in its history in the U.S. (although nothing compared to the level of 1999 after Owen Hart's death). WWE was written up as sleazy. One of its most-hyped celebrities at WrestleMania that year, Bob Costas, immediately pulled out over exploitation of the war.

Some thought all the negative publicity was good publicity. Since there was no precedent, nobody knew for sure. In the long run, there's little argument. Tickets for WrestleMania stalled. After a hard push, including a Hogan tour of military bases to promote the match, they had only 15,000 tickets sold for the Coliseum. McMahon created a story that due to security issues with running an outdoor venue, they had to move indoors to the Los Angeles Sports Arena, and they were even giving tickets away and failed to pack the 17,000-seat building for the biggest show of the year. PPV, which did about 767,000 buys in 1989 for Hogan vs. Randy Savage, and more than 500,000 for Hogan vs. Ultimate Warrior the next year, fell to about 400,000. A prime time Main Event on NBC featuring Slaughter vs. Jim Duggan and built around Hogan touring military bases to promote the match in late January, drew a record low rating that led to NBC canceling WWE. After one more show in April, NBC eliminated pro wrestling, leaving the company without its most-watched television show and the key to a great deal of mainstream exposure after a six-year run. While the loss of Saturday Night's Main Event was not a primary reason for this, WWE went into a huge business slump after the 1992 WrestleMania that continued until a 1997-98 comeback.

FOX picked up the series in 1992, doing a good rating for the first show, but a poor rating for the second, and

Saturday Night's Main Event left the airwaves until NBC revived it as part of a contract to get Raw from Spike in 2006.

A second similar incident took place in 2005, which was in bad taste on its own, but WWE was also the victim of timing of things out of their control.

Mark Copani, a muscular but otherwise forgettable wrestler in OVW, and real-life Iranian Shawn Daivari from Minnesota, were put together as a heel unit. The two claimed to be Arab Americans, and Daivari was authentic in that ethnicity, and could speak Persian. Daivari was a talented talker and decent worker, but considered too small to carry the role. They came in talking about how they were American, but because of their ancestry, they had to deal with prejudice after 9/11. The heat was supposed to be that they played themselves up as misunderstood martyrs, but would eventually out themselves as full-fledged heels.

This led to even working at WrestleMania where Hulk Hogan beat them down, and at Backlash that year, them teaming up against Hogan & Shawn Michaels.

On July 4, 2005, in an episode of Smackdown being taped for airing a few days later, in Sacramento, The Undertaker beat Daivari, and five men in ski masks came out with clubs and piano wire and choked Undertaker out. The incident was taken from the murder of a reporter and others who were choked out with piano wire during that time period.

On its own, it was among the most tasteless angles that company had done in years. However, that week, before the show aired, there was a terrorist bombing in London. Given the timing, the WWE made the decision to edit the angle off shows broadcast in Europe and Australia. They also made the decision not to do so in the United States, feeling since the incident didn't take place in the U.S., it was within the bounds of whatever level of taste they were operating under that year.

The angle was heavily criticized in a number of publications, including most major newspapers. UPN took as much, if not more heat than WWE, with the idea that most considered WWE as sleazy entertainment, but the TV station should have higher standards. UPN stated they would monitor the situation. The next week, UPN refused to air Hassan's promo. WWE decided to put it on its web site, where Hassan said that it was prejudice, that people assumed he was a terrorist (the five men in the attack were clearly portraying terrorists) only because of this ethnicity, and talked about the media coverage. In particular, he went after Don Kaplan of the New York Post.

McMahon had issues with the New York Post and in particular, sports columnist Phil Mushnick, in the early 90s, to the point McMahon filed a lawsuit against Mushnick and the newspaper, which was eventually dropped.

UPN would not allow Hassan on its station, hence he was banned from Smackdown, which was his brand in the days when WWE was running separate brands and separate PPV shows. WWE had someone playing a lawyer for Hassan claim he was refusing to appear on the show until the Great American Bash PPV, where he was to face Undertaker, due to his treatment by the American media.

Many had thought all the mainstream publicity would lead to big numbers, but the Bash bombed on PPV, doing the worst numbers the company had done for a PPV show in many years. Since UPN would no longer allow Copani on the air, the company blew off the character with Undertaker destroying him on the PPV. He ended up fired instead of being repackaged, and never wrestled again.

In this case, the coverage wasn't nearly as strong. But it was another example of WWE coming across as sleazy entertainment, which is one of the reasons their audience often looked down upon and the company's television negotiations went so poorly when you consider the ratings they deliver.

The next day, on Raw, Lana was interrupted before she could say anything. Lana & Rusev continued their angle, which was changed from Jack Swagger to Sheamus for Main Event, and then changed back the next day. She continued to praise Vladimir Putin and mock America, but there were no references to current events.

CHAPTER THIRTY SIX

WWE SUED BY STOCKHOLDERS

AUGUST 4

Robbins Arroyo LLP, a shareholders rights law firm, filed suit on 7/25 in U.S. District Court on Connecticut against the WWE on behalf of all people who purchased stock between 10/31 and 5/18. The lawsuit accuses WWE of making false and misleading statements concerning the company's ability to double its U.S. television rights. They certainly strongly hinted at it, forever citing the NASCAR television deal and comparisons of WWE ratings to NASCAR ratings, which were similar. Vince McMahon also told an investor at a conference when he suggested that the U.S. television rights could double, Vince said to Brad Safalow on a conference call that "If we don't double, I'll let you put me in a hammerlock." There were no guarantees stated, but based on how he said it, he was talking about far more than doubling, as if doubling would be well under expectations. The complaint alleges that during that period, WWE officers issued materially false and misleading statements in filings, press releases and conference calls regarding their ability to double their U.S. television licensing agreements. In 2013, WWE took in $106 million in U.S. television revenue, a number that also included Main Event (since canceled by Ion and put on the network) and several months of Saturday Morning Slam (canceled by CW), as well as Total Divas. The new deal is estimated at being at $132 million for the 2014-15 season for Raw & Smackdown. That doesn't include Total Divas, which, if two seasons air this year, would up the total by around $10 million. But there is no guarantee Total Divas will have two seasons in 2014-15, as shows like that usually don't have a long shelf life, even though Total Divas has done well in the ratings so far and appears to have some legs left. The lawsuit stated that WWE, when presenting ratings comparisons with NASCAR and the NBA, never mentioned advertisers pay far less for WWE television spots and thus, even with similar ratings, the value of the programming to stations isn't there. They also claimed WWE never told its stockholders that the launch of the WWE Network would hurt them in television negotiations. That is true, nobody ever said that beforehand that the launch could impact talks. I was surprised Vince McMahon outright said after the new deal came in and the stock price dropped so hard, that the launch of the network did hurt them in negotiations. People who purchased stock during that period have 60 days from 7/25 to join into the lawsuit. They also provided an 800-350-6003 number for such stockholders.

AUGUST 18

Brower Pivan, a powerhouse securities litigation firm from Stevenson, MD, is attempting to get in touch with WWE shareholders who lost in excess of $100,000 in stock value between 10/31 and 5/16, to discuss a possible lawsuit against the company. No suit has been filed and they are looking at getting potential clients through 9/23. Another firm, Levi Korsinsky out of New York, is also announcing it is investigating civil action and looking for clients who lost money. The premise behind these suits is WWE promised and led investors to believe it would greatly increase its TV rights, with statements indicating doubling would be a bare minimum, and they didn't end up closing to doubling.

SEPTEMBER 1

Yet another class action lawsuit was filed against the company on 8/26, by the law offices of Alfred G. Yates Jr., in Connecticut, again representing people who purchased stock between October 31, 2013, and May 16, 2014. The complaint, like the other few similar ones, allege the company issued materially false and misleading statements regarding the company's ability to negotiate a television contract price. During the period, the company issued releases showing its ratings being similar to NASCAR, with the idea that would be a barometer of what WWE could get for rights fees. However, WWE's new deal ended up being worth less than one-sixth of what NASCAR's television deal was.

That was the second lawsuit filed over the past week. The firm of Vincent Wong, Esq, out of New York, has filed a similar case, stating the company violated securities law by failing to disclose the company's true market value in television negotiations.

SEPTEMBER 8

Yet another lawsuit was filed against WWE based on the NBC deal coming in lower than stockholders expected. Curtis Swanson this past week filed a class action suit against WWE, Vince McMahon and CFO George Barrios, making at least the fourth lawsuit filed against the company in recent weeks. The lawsuit claimed WWE made false and misleading statements, engaged in a scheme to deceive the market and engaged in a course of conduct that artificially inflated the stock price and operated on a fraud to purchasers by misrepresenting the company's business prospects. Swanson said the company made false and misleading statements about their ability to transform the earnings through the next lucrative television deal. Swanson's suit said that WWE's ability to get a high price for its programming was undermined by the rollout of the network, which they never acknowledged, and that their ability to command the higher prices they talked of that pro sports were getting was undermined by the fact their ad rates are far below those of pro sports. It said that they made comparisons to the ratings of NASCAR and its $820 million per year television rights deals, noting they were like sports, the last major sports franchise that was not locked up for the long-term that was DVR-proof. Swanson is asking for damages plus interest for shareholders who purchased shares after the statements made by McMahon and Barrios and still held the stock when the NBC deal was announced and the price collapsed.

Brower Piven of Stevenson, MD, officially filed its lawsuit against WWE in District Court in Connecticut and is looking for clients who lost in excess of $100,000 when the stock lost its value. They are looking for clients who purchased stock between 10/31 and 5/16. The list of plaintiffs they will represent has to be completed by 9/23. The claim is violations of the Securities Exchange Act claiming the company failed to disclose its true ability to command rights fees for its television programming.

CHAPTER THIRTY SEVEN

JON JONES VS.
DANIEL CORMIER

AUGUST 11

A crazy incident, deplorable in many ways because it was real, has shot interest in the 9/27 Jon Jones vs. Daniel Cormier light heavyweight title fight through the roof.

The incident took place at a press conference in the lobby of the MGM Grand Hotel in Las Vegas on 8/4, where the fight will take place. Conor McGregor and Dustin Poirier, who are at this point scheduled as the No. 2 fight on the show, had just done an intense staredown and were leaving the stage, and security was close to the action more because they were concerned with McGregor and Poirier, since Jones and Cormier backstage had exchanged pleasantries and gave no indication of concern even though they've had Twitter and interview battles. While Cormier and Jones were mostly kept apart, they did get together, shake hands, and Cormier introduced Jones to his wife. On the other hand, McGregor and Poirier were intense backstage and had no contact with each other.

Jones and Cormier were brought up to the stage. Both walked forward. Jones pressed his head against Cormier's. It wasn't a head-butt, but Jones did put his head down to Cormier's as opposed to them walking forward chest-to-chest. Cormier responded with a hard shove, which Jones categorized as Cormier putting his hand on his throat. Cormier didn't shove him to the chest, but shoved him in the throat.

Jones started throwing lefts that didn't connect. Dave Sholler, the head of UFC public relations, jumped in and got thrown aside, and apparently hit his head on something. The backdrop on the stage collapsed. People were jumping in. Jones appeared to take Cormier down amidst all the madness, as they ended down the steps, off the stage, and on the floor of the lobby. Jones continually said that he took Cormier down easily, while others who have seem the tape claim it was more Joe Williams, the UFC head of security, in breaking it up and in them off balance coming off the stage that led to Cormier going down and he and falling off the stage was more the reason than Jones, although Cormier never denied Jones taking him down or offered an excuse past that what happened in a quick street fight has nothing to do with how the match would play out. Williams was the only casualty, reportedly ending up with broken ribs. Jones was on top, with both holding each other and trying to land punches, while security tried to pry them apart. The key aspect is that in all this, somebody, whether it be fighters, or security, could have gotten hurt. Well, at least one person did.

As security went to pull Jones off, Cormier was still doing up kicks trying to hit Jones. Footage also showed that Malki Kawa, Jones' manager, who said he was trying to break up the fight, looked like he was throwing a punch at Cormier when he was down. Cormier said he didn't know if Kawa hit him, but was told he didn't by UFC officials and Cormier said it all happened so fast. Jones said the arch of a punch was because Kawa was trying to get his hand free from someone holding it, but he never hit Cormier. Kawa said he was just trying to break up the fight.

After they were pulled apart, Cormier tried to throw his shoe at Jones (Jones claimed the shoe hit a female reporter, and others have said it was a Brazilian female reporter who is not making a thing of it, and Heidi Fang, a radio reporter for Fox Sports radio 670 AM in Las Vegas who hosts the MMA Fight Corner show was also grazed by the shoe. There was recognition that there were several children there and things could have been bad had one been hit) and Jones screamed like a pro wrestler doing the "roar" spot.

Someone from the UFC got Cormier's shoe and returned it to him. Jones' sunglasses went flying, and ended up being broken. But as everyone was rolling around, Cormier lost his cell phone. A fan picked it up, not knowing what it was. One of Cormier's people called the phone and when the fan picked it up, found out whose phone it was and returned it.

This led to tons of media, Twitter comments, a Jones Instagram message where he was laughing at Cormier, saying Cormier was an Olympic wrestler but it only took him six seconds to take him down and mocked him for being weak. Jones continued berating Cormier every chance he got, whether it be Twitter or elsewhere.

Most of the berating, since it started from day one, and really even before that, was more to build up the fight. Jones has learned the lesson of the difference in paycheck from a 300,000 buy PPV and a 700,000 buy show, and Cormier has followed pro wrestlers building matches and remained a fan of how it's done dating back to being a child in Lafayette, LA, watching Mid South Wrestling. Before the 2004 Olympics, he came to a TNA taping and had talked with them about possibly going into pro wrestling after the Olympics, but when he finished fourth and didn't medal, he decided to stay until 2008. By that time, MMA had exploded in popularity. But Cormier remains a big fan today, recently getting a huge thrill last week when he appeared on the MMA Hour together with C.M. Punk.

Cormier had been talking about facing Jones from the day the Strikeforce heavyweight division was brought into UFC. But this was no staged confrontation, since they'd have avoided the steps, and the injury risk. Plus, the babyface challenger (and the next day in Los Angeles, it was clear Cormier was the huge babyface) would not have been made to look bad, as the confrontation's psychology was completely backward in both logic and how UFC would promote a fight.

When UFC is promoting a fight, the rule of thumb is always to make the challenger and/or the underdog look like he is going to win, feeling the more questions fans have about the outcome, the more they become invested in the fight. Besides, both will end up being punished by the athletic commission over this in some form, and that doesn't happen for staged confrontations.

Both men appeared on Sports Center and Fox Sports Live over the next few hours, as well as TV sports shows all over the country. In both cases, they started apologetic. But they quickly got heated at each other, as each guaranteed victory. On Sports Center when Jones apologized, Cormier knocked him for being a phony and a fake.

On Fox Sports Live, Jones cut an amazingly biting promo. It was the type of promo that takes a viewer past the usual level, in the sense people seeing him, if they were behind him, would love him for it, and those who don't like him, would hate him and want to see him lose, badly. That much is planned, as Jones' new persona in an attempt to become the country's next Floyd Mayweather Jr. drawing card is not to be a heel, but to be a face to those who want to back him, but do so in a way that those who don't like him and won't like, will hate him and his words will make them want to pay to see the night he finally gets beat.

The incident clearly got the public's attention as Jones was the second most searched item on the Internet on 8/4.

There are two sides to this, in the sense that neither came off looking good, but the tension felt stronger than even Georges St-Pierre vs. Nick Diaz or Ronda Rousey vs. Miesha Tate (which one could tell the rivalry was real but at no point in the build did it come close to this level of physical danger even though the hatred came through at a higher level), and probably as strong as anything in UFC since Rampage Jackson vs. Rashad Evans. Jones came across totally unlikeable because he could have shoved Cormier back, but he was throwing punches immediately. While his worst behavior was seen by nobody, his Instagram post after the skirmish, which he later took down, did air on FS 1 on all their news reports and made him the ultimate heel. But Cormier was hurt as the babyface. His explanation for shoving Jones was weak. Plus, for better or worse, the public wants to get behind the badass, not the one they see as weaker. No matter that this skirmish may be completely different from a UFC fight where both start out knowing what to do, Cormier was taken down quickly and his throwing his shoe wasn't a babyface move.

I heard from a lot of people over the next day who are not UFC fans, but sports fans, who became well aware of this fight from the skirmish and it became a big event. But the reaction was not babyface Cormier vs. heel Jones, but two people who they both didn't like. So it's an edge, but without the strong babyface character, although when they calmed down and showed up in Los Angeles for another promotional day on 8/5, the crowd cheered Cormier and chanted his name. There are predictions in the industry that the brawl will increase PPV buys to the 650,000 to 700,000 range, roughly double what Jones has been doing of late. While UFC does not like that it happened, nor should they, they are also aware it will boost buys and interest significantly. It's two weeks after Floyd Mayweather Jr. vs. Marcos Maidana, but they just fought in May and did disappointing business the first time, so I don't see this as being the killer that Mayweather-Alvarez looks to have been for UFC on PPV last fall.

"I've never had another fighter put his hands on me by squeezing my throat," said Jones. "I reacted in self-defense by beating up Daniel."

As far as veracity goes, when setting up interviews for sportscasts around the country, but before being taped, the tension was the same as they were on Fox Sports Live, and Jones, in particular, was a completely different person.

Jones was talking to the people around him and Cormier was in a different studio. When someone mentioned that Cormier could hear him, he started calling Cormier names, including "bitch" and "pussy," and said, "I just whooped your ass." He also said, "They told me you were strong but you are weak. You are so weak."

When Cormier shot back, Jones started taunting him about money, saying how Cormier had to work as an announcer as a side job (he hosts UFC Tonight on FS 1), and said, "I am sitting on ten mill, what is in your bank account?"

Jones kept talking about how he took Cormier down and was on top while Cormier shot back at how all the security got in the way. Cormier said how this was nothing like a UFC fight because of all the people in between. Then both starting calling each other names like "pussy" and "bitch" until they were told they were going on ESPN in a few minutes.

When ESPN started, Jones was a different person, going from angry and taunting to mild and completely calm. It was at that point that Cormier immediately started laughing and talking about what a phony and a fake he was.

When the ESPN interview was over and they were no longer being taped, Jones asked if Cormier was still there and could hear him. Cormier said he was still there and Jones said, "You are such a bitch." Cormier said that he would have spit in Jones' face if he knew Jones was going to attack him like that and Jones said that if Cormier spit in his face, "I would kill you. There would not be a fight because I would kill you."

Cormier kept saying how much of a fake Jones was, and how lucky he was and how great his media people were to get him to change when the cameras were on and how he was able to hide what a jerk he was while he was doing media interviews and being in front of the public. Then the two started arguing back-and-forth with Cormier calling him a junior college dropout. At that point somebody told them that a satellite was still on and that it was possible sportscasters around the country may still be watching. Jones looked shocked and stopped talking immediately.

Jones on Fox Sports Live even noted that there was both good and bad, bad that the incident was ugly but good in that he recognized it helped sell the fight.

If you would have combined this incident with a Countdown series special, or even a single event Countdown show on a Spike or FX platform, it would probably lead to the show doing monster business. Unlike with Jones and Rashad Evans, who had heated incidents but never something like this, both seemed to get tired of the promotion because they started early and were shutting down as it came to the finish line. With Chael Sonnen, there was no true heat, and people saw it, plus nobody believed Sonnen had much of a chance to win.

"Daniel Cormier, being an Olympic level wrestler, I thought it would be a lot harder to get him to the floor," Jones said on Sports Center. "And sure enough, if you look at the videos, which I'm not very proud of, he was the one on his back and people were pulling me off him."

In watching the incidents, Jones came across extremely confident. Cormier guaranteed winning, was heated up, similar to the situation with Patrick Cummins a few months ago. Jones mocked Cormier's record, saying he has no idea what he's in for beating "almost 50-year-old" Dan Henderson, Cummins with four fights and Josh Barnett at the end of his career. Cormier shot back that he would have done the same thing to Jones' opponents that Jones did, and citing he beat martial artists like Shogun Rua that were very good, but it's only a 20-year-old sport, while he competed in the world's oldest sport (wrestling) at the highest level.

"This guy is such a fake human being," Cormier said. "He's a fake individual. I don't care to learn anything about Jon Jones that I don't know. I don't care about the incident. I care about Sept. 27, becoming the UFC light heavyweight champion. He's weak. He's a punk. He's a liar. He's dishonest. He's a whole bunch of things that he should not be proud of being."

Dana White was not present when the incident took place, as he and his family left that day for a vacation in Bora Bora.

"This is certainly not a proud moment for the UFC organization," said Kirk Hendrick, UFC's Chief Legal Officer. "We expect more from our athletes, especially these two gentlemen, who are very well-trained and highly educated professionals. Their actions were clearly a violation of the UFC's code of conduct."

The Nevada Athletic Commission requested the video to determine what action to take.

"We are going to reserve our right to penalize both fighters after the commission has made a decision," said Hendrick. "We expect more from our athletes and we are prepared to levy sanctions to reinforce the appropriate behavior.

"There are going to be ramifications," he said. "Whether you're the champion or this is your first fight in the UFC, there are going to be ramifications from the UFC for these actions."

It will be interesting to see how hard UFC promotes the fight both in commercials and video packages on upcoming television shows using the footage. The incident was replayed throughout the day on sports television channels and UFC did put up a feed, so it appears, while decrying it, they will also embrace it to promote the fight.

On Fox Sports Live, the two were insistent on being in separate studios but their long segment saw each get more agitated at the other the longer it went. When Cormier spoke at one point, Jones turned his chair so his back was to the screen. Later, when the segment ended, Jones got up, and while saying he stormed off would be a major exaggeration, he was clearly mad as he got up and left.

On radio interviews the next day, Jones talked about how it would be "easy money" beating Cormier, because he never has problems with wrestlers, and how he's talking so much to motivate himself to train harder.

The incident looks to shoot the UFC 178 show to where it'll be the most successful company event so far this year. They shot past any Gina Carano fight, even with Cris Cyborg or Gina Carano, when it comes to business potential, as well as the original Jones vs. Gustafsson rematch.

Exactly what that entails is anyone's guess but there are two strong personalities, both essentially undefeated (Jones has a loss on his record but that was a DQ in a fight he destroyed Matt Hamill in). They are two of the most talented fighters in the world. Jones has only lost three or four rounds in his career, while Cormier, who spent most of his career (13 of his 15 fights) as a heavyweight, has never even come close to losing a round.

The key differences are height, as Jones is about 6-4 ½ and Cormier is 5-10, and reach, with Jones having ridiculous 84.5 inch reach that has been impossible for any opponent except Alexander Gustafsson, who is his same size, to penetrate. Cormier's reach is 72.5 inches. Cormier is also 35 years old while Jones is 27, and it's not a secret Cormier has a bad knee that needs surgery. But Cormier has shown no signs of slipping, and, in fact, seems to look sharper every fight because he's new in the sport and his learning curve seems to be gaining significantly more than age has declined his physical abilities. Still, Jones has more experience and is younger and in his prime. Cormier has an edge in that he's training with Cain Velasquez, and as good as people in Jackson's camp are, there is no all-around fighter Jones can work with who can match Velasquez. Cormier's wrestling is still at a world class level, as on 7/5 in Las Vegas, he defeated Chris Pendleton, one of the country's best, in his wrestling retirement match.

While Jones did look vulnerable against Gustafsson last year, anyone who follows the inside of the sport knows that the Jones who faces Cormier is not going to be the same guy as the one who faced Gustafsson. Jones was living the life of a superstar and had no fear of Gustafsson, didn't train hard and it nearly cost him his title. It was a wake-up call, which is why he looked so much better against Glover Teixeira, almost untouchable, and scarily effective. With Cormier, the motivation would have been there since the two haven't liked each other for years, but this will take that to another level. Jones said that this has also given him even more motivation.

Cormier said that he's beating Jones twice, both in September, and then early next year, noting that when he wins, there will be an immediate rematch.

Jones said people will see it two ways, that some will find it entertaining, but others find it distasteful and he's apologizing to them.

"It's crazy, though, even though what happened wasn't acceptable, the fight is so much bigger than it was a couple of days ago," said Cormier. We've had some big fights. Anytime Georges St-Pierre fights, anytime Anderson Silva fights, it's a big deal. It's on that level now. It was on Good Morning America. That doesn't happen in MMA very often. Lorenzo called us and talked to us. He was pretty upset. But I don't now how upset he is going to be with the PPV numbers."

AUGUST 18

Knee and ankle injuries to Jon Jones has led to UFC's biggest event of the year now being scheduled for early next year.

Jones suffered a torn meniscus and sprained ankle while doing wrestling training on 8/11, and pulled out of his 9/27 bout with Daniel Cormier for the UFC light heavyweight title. Due to a brawl between the two seven days earlier, and the release of an except of the footage when neither man, at the time, were aware they were being filmed, that had been previously described in last week's Observer, interest in this was the biggest for any UFC fight in more than one year.

As things stand, the fight will now take place on 1/3, which leads to interesting bits of timing, since that date had been earmarked for Ronda Rousey vs. Gina Carano and possibly Johny Hendricks vs. Robbie Lawler. Clearly putting all three on the same show would be overkill, but Jones vs. Cormier and Rousey vs. Carano as a double main event should be one of the biggest PPV events in MMA history, and perhaps even one of the biggest events in PPV history.

UFC announced that the Demetrious Johnson vs. Chris Cariaso flyweight title match, originally set for 8/30 in Sacramento, would be moved to 9/27. They also announced that anyone who had already purchased tickets for Jones vs. Cormier could get a refund at the point of purchase through 8/22.

Johnson vs. Cariaso would be the weakest marquee PPV main event in modern company history. Cariaso as a challenger is weaker than Ali Bagautinov, who did a sub-125,000 buy PPV with Johnson in June. This does have the advantage of a stronger undercard, with Conor McGregor vs. Dustin Poirier, the return of Cat Zingano vs. Amanda Nunes, the return after three years of Dominick Cruz vs. Takeya Mizugaki, and Tim Kennedy vs. Yoel Romero. But while that is a good show as far as support for a Jones vs. Cormier fight, it's not stuff that will move the needle that much, unless McGregor and to a lesser extent, Cruz, are able to garner enough interest to make people want to spend money.

For Jones vs. Cormier, a few dynamics change. The first is that Cormier was going into the fight with a knee injury and delaying it three months gives him more time to heal the knee. He won't be getting his knee scoped, and even before being called to fight Jones at the last minute, had opted against having the knee surgery that he at first was planning for after his 7/5 wrestling match, saying he hates surgeries. In addition, Cormier was taking the original fight on shorter than usual notice as a late replacement for Alexander Gustafsson, but now he can rest and rehab his knee for two months and then start a full camp in October with three months to prepare. The other edge is that his main training partner, Cain Velasquez, will be in his home stretch of training at the same time.

While Cormier was at first critical of Jones for pulling out, given the Cormier tore his meniscus less than two weeks before his fight with Dan Henderson, and didn't pull out, the reality is Jones is not going to fight unless he's close to 100 percent. That's just how he is and there's nothing wrong with that. It also gives UFC time to at least consider a three week Prime Time build to get the footage already done on the air in front of eyeballs in the weeks leading to the fight, although to make that fully worth it would require FOX putting the build on general interest stations and not limit it to the low-rated core FS 1 audience. The injury also delays Gustafsson's title fight with the winner until the probably the late spring or early summer. And if Cormier wins, it would probably be longer since Jones would likely get an immediate rematch.

UFC is now in the position of having six to eight different championships, essentially everything but heavyweight and featherweight, ready for title defenses in December and January, the way injury recovers and other timing is working. Bouts that are announced include the light heavyweight (Jones vs. Cormier on 1/3), middleweight (Chris Weidman vs. Vitor Belfort which is scheduled for 12/6), welterweight (Johny Hendricks vs. Robbie Lawler which Hendricks has said he'd be ready in December or January), lightweight (Anthony Pettis vs. Gilbert Melendez which is expected for 12/6), bantamweight (the T.J. Dillashaw vs. Renan Barao winner on 8/30 should be ready to fight again during that period), flyweight (Demetrious Johnson or heavy underdog challenger Chris Cariaso should be ready by January), women's bantamweight (Ronda Rousey publicly said she wants to fight on 1/3, with either Gina Carano or the Cat Zingano vs. Amanda Nunes winner as the likely next opponent) and women's strawweight (the tournament final match takes place at some point in December on FS 1). Of course, injuries are likely to change at least a few of those timetables.

A double headliner of Jones vs. Cormier and Rousey vs. Carano would likely end up as among the biggest UFC PPVs in history, and could easily be the second biggest ever behind UFC 100. Not only is it a UFC 168 level marquee doubleheader, but it will merge two completely different audiences, much like the December show last year did. If Carano can get a deal that calls for a percentage, all of a sudden, that fight looks to have only increased her potential income if she can get it on that day. It's overkill to put Hendricks vs. Lawler there, but if it's not put there, that would likely move it to the Super Bowl show which already has Anderson Silva vs. Nate Diaz, so if you have that double headliner, that's a big one as well.

But it also puts UFC in a position where they aren't going to be doing even close to 250,000 buys on PPV until November, at which point they may, barring injuries, be in line to do a good show (Cain Velasquez vs. Fabricio Werdum on 11/15 in the debut in Mexico City) and three huge to monstrous shows in a row after that.

SEPTEMBER 29

Any questions regarding the legitimacy of the 8/4 brawl in the lobby of the MGM Grand Garden Arena between Jon Jones and Daniel Cormier were answered, under oath, at the 9/23 Nevada Athletic Commission hearing.

Both testified that nothing was set up, that they both greatly regret that it happened, and have each suffered, Jones financially, and Cormier emotionally, from the aftermath.

The commission fined Jones $50,000, which was ten percent of his $500,000 base purse for his next fight, as well as ordered him to complete 40 hours of community service work around Las Vegas. They felt the community service work would benefit people more than suspending Jones, whose recent knee surgery has already cost him a missed fight. Jones noted that his contract also included a cut of the PPV revenues for the next fight.

Cormier, who was ruled less at fault, but still somewhat at fault, was fined $9,000, which was ten percent of his $90,000 base pay for the 1/3 light heavyweight title fight in Las Vegas, and ordered to do 20 hours of community service work in his home city of San Jose. Cormier noted his contract for the fight calls for $90,000 guaranteed and a $90,000 win bonus. He said it was possible he would be bonused extra, depending on how the show does, but that would be a discretionary bonus on the UFC's part as he has no PPV bonus written into his deal for the fight.

Both appeared contrite and apologetic. Jones asked for leniency, noting that since the incident, that Nike dropped sponsoring him. While he nor his representatives would not say exactly how much it cost him, citing a confidentiality clause in his contract, they said it was greater than six figures annually. He also said he lost another six-figure endorsement deal that they had just about closed, because the company pulled out after the brawl.

Jones said he started throwing punches because Cormier grabbed his throat when he shoved him.

"I've gotten into many face-offs with a lot of real fighters," Jones said. "Me and Rashad (Evans) did it and me and Brandon Vera did it, but I've never had my throat grabbed. I've never had that happen, and I think that's where the unsportsmanlike conduct came into play. I definitely didn't have that happen. I saw Daniel Cormier pacing back and forth before. I could see that intensity, heightened senses. We walked together like magnets."

He said he had no clue anything like that happened and said he reacted in a terrible way.

"A lot of people loved that, but I understand it was disgraceful in a lot of ways, but the interest in the fight, it skyrocketed. It became a fight people wanted to see."

Jones was treated by the commission as the aggressor in two ways. The first was putting his head on Cormier's head and pressuring him, which resulted in Cormier shoving him. The second, and most important, was firing punches at Cormier in response to the shoving.

Jones readily admitted that everything said in the complaint about his actions were true, he didn't contest anything, and only asked for leniency.

Cormier and his lawyer argued that he should not be punished, claiming self defense. He noted that the two had a past history. He said when Jones put his head on his head he didn't want fans or Jones to think he was backing down or to gain a psychological edge. Jones said that same thing, saying he felt he had to respond to the shove or it would give Cormier a psychological edge and cause fans to think he backed down.

Cormier noted he didn't lose six-figure endorsement deals, but he also isn't in anywhere near the same economic bracket as Jones, who is believed to be worth eight figures. Cormier said that he runs a youth wrestling program in San Jose, which started with two kids and grew to 35 to 40 kids, but that parents of ten of the kids, including his best student, a two-time age group state champion, pulled out of his classes after the brawl. He noted that financially it wasn't a big hit, but emotionally it was.

"I didn't lose a Nike deal, I didn't have one," he said. "I had to go back to the kids I coach in wrestling, countless times I've had to apologize for my actions."

The commission seemed more unhappy that Cormier went on television later the night after the incident saying that if someone did that to him again, he'd respond the same way. Cormier said it was still the day of the fight and he was still fired up, but today he would give a different answer, saying now he would stand back. They were also mad at Cormier for publicly saying that even though what happened was not a good thing, it was probably a good thing for his pocketbook, noting that he expected the pay-per-view numbers to increase because of it.

Cormier blamed that incident, which aired on UFC Tonight on FS 1, on the fact the other hosts of UFC Tonight are his friends, and he often co-hosts that show. He said that he's an honest guy, and was talking the way he would among friends, but never should have done so on television.

During cross-examinations, Cormier was asked about the fight itself, and he said he had no problem giving away his strategy.

"I'm gonna go across the cage and take him down."

CHAPTER THIRTY EIGHT

ALBERTO DEL RIO FIRED

Alberto Rodriguez, who played Alberto Del Rio with WWE, was fired on 8/7 after an incident a few days earlier at television.

Rodriguez, 37, is a third generation wrestler. His father, Jose, who wrestled as Dos Caras, is generally considered the best working heavyweight wrestler ever to come out of Mexico. His uncle, Aaron, is a cultural legend, Mil Mascaras, without a doubt the most famous heavyweight wrestler ever in the country, as well as an international legend and movie star. Before becoming a pro wrestler, as Al Rodriguez, he was a world class Greco-Roman wrestler in the teenage division, and later placed fourth in the Pan American Games in the 211 pound weight class when he was only 20, and once beating Randy Couture as an amateur.

Rodriguez was fired for slapping Cody Barbierri, the WWE's Manager of Social Media Live Events, at television last week. According to several reports, the incident happened at catering. Someone made a remark to Barbierri about not cleaning off his plate, and as a joke, he said that was Del Rio's job. Rodriguez wasn't there at the time, but the joke, which he obviously took as a racial remark got back to him. He confronted Barbierri and said he didn't appreciate the remark and wanted an apology.

One performer noted that the story going around was Rodriguez slapped the shit out of him and Barbierri was on the floor, and that the firing wasn't so much that he slapped him, but how hard he slapped him.

The incident reportedly took place on 8/5 in Laredo, when much of the crew had already left for the Australia tour. According to those who have talked with Rodriguez, he was told after the incident, on the show that he strangely worked as a babyface against a heel Jack Swagger, that he was being suspended for a short period of time, until just past SummerSlam. The belief is that Barbierri threatened to sue the company, and at that point the feeling was for legal reasons, they had no choice but to let him go. Paul Levesque called him on 8/7 and let him go and he reportedly was furious.

A wrestler, particularly one with a legitimate fighting background, can't be attacking an employee in a publicly traded company, even given the remark. What Rodriguez did was how is probably how it may have been handled in Mexico, and in the old territory days, particularly with a top and an office worker if the office worker made a racial slur, but today you have to file an HR complaint.

However, many fans were furious for the obvious reason. Fans want wrestlers to be badass real-life alpha males who, like in the fantasy world on television, settle things. On a wrestling TV show, someone making a bad stereotype joke about one's heritage, would deserve to get slapped if that person found out. But real life is different.

What's notable next is the WWE Twitter, part of the department Barbierri is in one of the key people in charge of, likely in response to those sympathetic for that reason to the TV star Del Rio, made a quick response, writing, "Del Rio is responsible for his own actions. If you're angry at anyone, be angry at Alberto. There's no excuse for a pro athlete not to conduct themselves in a professional manner." Levesque also retweeted that on his HHH account.

The story of Del Rio being at TripleMania on 8/17 already broken as a legitimate mainstream news story in Mexico. The way the story played out, if AAA or he wants to go with it, could make him into a major babyface there, and he would be anyway.

Rodriguez was a trained MMA fighter, working under coach Marco Ruas. He posted a 9-5 record as a heavyweight, including high profile losses in Pride to Kazuhiro Nakamura and Mirko Cro Cop, the latter a famous match in 2003 where he fought with a mask. He used the name Dos Caras Jr. as an MMA fighter, and did most of his fights wearing a mask, although later in his MMA career he didn't wear a mask due to its limitations. He was more recruited into MMA in Japan because he was a pro wrestler and Mil Mascaras was one of the country's all-time wrestling legends, being offered big money for high profile matches, then him personally seeking out MMA.

Wrestlers, at least the ones we heard from, were sympathetic to Rodriguez. One said of Barbierri, that he was a jerkoff who was very arrogant, but said he was intelligent, but his attitude flew under the radar of management. Another noted that he had a few situations while on the road over the past year and had a reputation for talking down to wrestlers, but had the backing of Stephanie McMahon and was a key player in WWE's social media department that had been nominated for key awards.

Rodriguez worked most of his career under a mask as Dos Caras Jr., where he was a main eventer in CMLL and pushed as a star with New Japan Pro Wrestling. Because of his size and look, plus his background as being from a legendary family, he was highly coveted by WWE. He worked mostly Japan and AAA early in his career, but gained his greatest success in Mexico with CMLL.

As Dos Caras Jr., he won the CMLL world heavyweight title from Universo 2000 on July 8, 2007, and held it until dropping it to Ultimo Guerrero on December 22, 2008, by which time he was in talks with WWE.

John Laurinaitis had attempted to sign him for about two years, but there were hold-ups because they wanted him to work without a mask, which for many wrestlers in Mexico, particularly with famous names, is considered an issue of disrespect to family and heritage. But he signed in 2010 and was given a monster push with the idea he was a rich Mexican aristocrat.

The company's plans were to give him a main event heel run, and then turn him babyface, to give them the Latin American star who could replace Rey Mysterio. He was introduced with a strong series of vignettes and given one of the strongest debuting pushes of any wrestler in the last decade.

While he was very much a star, and headlined PPVs, he never got over to the level of his push, which was substantial. He'd drive into the arenas with a new expensive six-figure car every week, and have his own personal ring announcer, the just-released Jesus "Ricardo" Rodriguez (no relation). He did a natural feud with Mysterio, which he was put over in since he was to be the Latin star of the future, even though he was less than three years younger than Mysterio, who was often injured due to his style.

He was originally to win the world title on a number of occasions, which kept getting moved back, including an originally scheduled title win over Edge at the 2011 WrestleMania, set up by winning the 40 man Royal Rumble in January. He won that year's Money in the Bank. At SummerSlam, after C.M. Punk had beaten John Cena to win the WWE title, Del Rio cashed in his briefcase and won that title after Kevin Nash had softened up Punk in a post-match attack.

But even the push as being the only man ever to win the Royal Rumble, Money in the Bank and the WWE title in the same year never elevated him quite to the top. He dropped the title to John Cena at the next PPV on September 18, but regained it on October 2 in the Hell in a Cell three-way over Cena and Punk, and then retained on October 23 at Vengeance over Cena, in a Last Man Standing match due to interference from The Miz and R-Truth.

He then lost the title to Punk on November 20, at Survivor Series.

He had one of the most inexplicably botched babyface turns in history, which never fully took, starting in late 2012, then being dropped on a show. That was to be his big run, but it failed.

He won the World title from Big Show in a Last Man Standing match on January 8, 2013, in Miami. He lost it in one of pro wrestling's most memorable opponents in recent years, when heel Dolph Ziggler, getting one of the biggest babyface reactions ever in East Rutherford, NJ, cashed it in on April 8, on the Raw after WrestleMania. Ziggler, after winning, insulted crowds anyway, and Del Rio stayed face. However, the lukewarm reaction to Del Rio and cheers Ziggler got led to the company changing plans and doing a double-turn when Ziggler returned from a concussion and Del Rio used superkicks to win the title on June 16, 2013, in Chicago. This forced Del Rio to turn back heel, but as part of the turn, they had him turn on Ricardo Rodriguez, his ring announcer who was a key part of his act. The belief was that Rodriguez was so good and had gotten so popular that it would hurt Del Rio as a heel to still be associated with him. But the aura of the special ring announcer is what broke him from the pack. Without him, Del Rio was an athletic, but often light worker due to his original background in Mexico, whose smiling character and promos were very one-dimensional. Everything that made him a star, and even then, he never got over the way a top guy he was pushed at should have, the car, the ring announcer, the scarf, were dropped, with the heel turn, and he was no longer special. Del Rio lost the title to Cena, making a ridiculously quick return after triceps surgery, on October 27, 2013, in Miami.

For a number of reasons, mainly his just not being over at the level of his push and new acts being promoted to the top, he fell into the even-Steven mid-card level from that point and never had serious programs. He had made noise about leaving for some time, as he had publicly said he was looking at retiring young.

Like with Carlito, WWE didn't want to lose him because 20 percent of the television audience is Hispanic and Spanish speaking countries are a big part of future expansion plans, particularly in South and Central America. At major WWE press events, Del Rio was always featured along with Cena, Stephanie McMahon and Paul Levesque as the faces of the company, even ahead of far more pushed and more popular stars like Daniel Bryan, Randy Orton and C.M. Punk. But he had made it clear he was going to be leaving somewhat soon and one report was that he had told the company he was staying an extra year.

The talent overall was very sympathetic to him, because many didn't like Barbierri. It was also felt that Barbierri hadn't apologized after making a racial remark. However, at TV this week, we were told it was something nobody was talking about.

As far as the future goes, the biggest beneficiary looks to be the former Ricardo Rodriguez, as the two can do their act together on indie shows, although it'll likely be an expensive act.

Both AAA, for its U.S. expansion, and TNA, had immediate interest in Alberto. AAA had a policy in place or not using any ex-WWE talent for its new project, but exceptions would have always been made for Del Rio and Rey Mysterio. When Ricardo Rodriguez was let go, it was with a 90-day non-complete. Alberto's situation as far as the non-compete goes is unknown, but it is believed it'll be a 90-day non-compete, meaning he couldn't perform for TNA or AAA until 11/5, although Joaquin Roldan, the head of AAA, confirmed that he would be appearing on 8/17 at TripleMania, but only said he was a guest of the promotion. It was pushed as Alberto Del Rio being there, not Alberto Rodriguez or Dos Caras Jr., which is interesting. When Luis Urive came in, even though he claimed he had the rights to the name Sin Cara, and has been using the name on indie shows in Mexico, AAA would not let him use the name Mistico, since it was owned by CMLL, or Sin Cara, because it was a WWE name. Wrestlers do have the option of not taking the non-compete but almost all do because you get three weeks of contracted money without having the work. Ricardo Rodriguez confirmed taking his no-compete and thus couldn't be at TripleMania.

AAA had been interested in Del Rio even before he was let go, and there was talk within wrestling that when Del Rio would leave WWE, and he was expected to do so when his contract expired, he would probably work at least big show dates for AAA.

Guillermo Rodriguez, the brother of Del Rio, who had a brief stint in WWE developmental and now works in Mexico as El Hijo de Dos Caras, said that he, his brother and his father would be teaming up in trios matches pronto. Generally speaking, WWE will enforce the non-compete on televised promotions like TNA and AAA, but as far as working independent shows in Mexico or the Southwest, they are likely to be a little more lax.

AUGUST 25

The situation with Alberto Rodriguez's firing by WWE has led to a series of interesting repercussions, particularly the situation where WWE is insisting on a one-year non-compete within the United States and 90 days in the rest of the world.

From several accounts, Del Rio was furious at how everything went down. The incident took place at catering before the show on 8/5 at the Smackdown tapings in Laredo, when he gave a hard slap (think David Shults and John Stossel) to Cody Barbierri, WWE's Manager of Social Media Life Events, in response to Barbierri not apologizing for what Del Rio considered a racial slight. Del Rio was told by Vince McMahon that he was going to be fined $5,000 and suspended for two weeks, which would have been until after the TV's post-SummerSlam, but then either the next day or two days later (we've heard both said by different people, Del Rio has said it was the next day), he was told he was being released.

Based on interviews that he did with the media in Mexico City, this looks to be a situation where those in AAA are going to try and paint WWE as anti-Latino since AAA and WWE are competition with each other in Mexico.

In doing media, Del Rio, who said he will go from this point on under the name Alberto El Patron (El Patron was the nickname the WWE Spanish language announcers as well as Ricardo Rodriguez gave him that WWE never trademarked but everyone who watched WWE programming in Spanish knew him as), confirmed the basics of the story in last week's Observer, but said he didn't want to go into full details of his side of the story just yet.

However, we are told that Del Rio will be doing media in the U.S., going into more details as to what happened.

He described his situation as being banned from wrestling or doing MMA (WWE included MMA in the terms of his release since Del Rio fought in MMA regularly until joining WWE) in the U.S. for one year as part of the terms of his release. He said he was told that since he was fired for assaulting a company employee, he won't be receiving any severance pay for the year off.

WWE officials have confirmed that a letter was sent to Del Rio, real name Jose Alberto Rodriguez, although he's always gone as Alberto Rodriguez because his father, Dos Caras, was Jose Rodriguez, advising him his contract was being terminated for unprofessional conduct due to the incident on 8/5 in Laredo, TX.

All WWE contracts allow for termination based on certain listed breaches, and unprofessional behavior is one of them, which allow termination and up to a one year non-compete even though there would be no severance pay, no downside guarantee being paid during that period, nor would he been entitled to any future royalties on merchandise or DVDs. His specific contract and terms of his release banned him from doing any pro wrestling, sports entertainment, mixed martial arts or Ultimate fighting within the United States through August 5, 2015. He was also told he was prohibited from using the name Alberto Del Rio.

One lawyer reviewing this said that contracts that offer no compensation or consideration for enforced non-competes are frequently held by courts to be unenforceable. Also, the feeling is that if anyone challenged being withheld royalties after being fired in court, regardless of cause, they would have a case.

Del Rio said that he has been seeing a lawyer because when he got the terms of his release, he felt a one-year non-compete in the United States was excessive, particularly since he would not be getting paid by WWE for the year. He said he didn't know the laws in the U.S., but felt it wasn't fair that he couldn't work in the U.S. for one year as a wrestler or MMA fighter because he lives in the U.S. (San Antonio) and it's how he supports his family.

He is said to be financially well off. One vague question that wasn't addressed in his termination letter would be whether he could do autograph shows, but since that wasn't specifically prohibited, one would think he could do so. However, people representing Del Rio have contacted independent promoters in the U.S. and said that Del Rio would be taking both autograph signing bookings and wrestling bookings in the U.S. starting very soon, because he didn't believe a one-year non-compete where he wasn't getting paid at all could hold up. His asking price for outside bookings is said to be extremely high, described to me as "Bret Hart level."

He said that his contract expired in February 2015, and he was considering leaving WWE at that time before this happened. He said that he and his wife at first decided against suing to get his job back because he was going to leave anyway, but when he got the termination letter that included the one-year non-compete in both wrestling and MMA, that changed his position.

Those close to the situation said Paul Levesque told him when he was being let go to just keep his nose clean and when the heat died down, they would bring him back in six months. He said that he wasn't interested in coming back.

Del Rio appeared at TripleMania on 8/17, even though one could argue even that appearance violated his non-compete agreement, which he said was for 90 days outside the United States. After doing media all week, he came out at the start of the show and got a huge reaction.

Dressed in a black business suit, he came out with his father, Dos Caras, with his WWE theme music, which sources in WWE believe that they own the rights to.

He said that history would mark this as the day El Patron returned, but after the reaction, he feels like he never left. He said that seven years ago, he did what so many did, of chasing his dream and going to America, and through blood, sweat, tears, heart and passion, and being humble to God, you can make your dreams come true.

He said it was never easy, and his dream turned into a nightmare. He said that many of you can relate, or have family who can relate, who have gone to "the other side" looking for a better life for your family, but you encounter the monster known as racism. He said racism cuts through sex, race, religion, color whether you have money or you don't. He said his father taught him honesty and the ability to overcome adversity. He said that his father never backed down on his beliefs, and was successful and made it so I would never have to back down to anyone. He told his father that he loved him, kissed him, and said that in the U.S., they can take his job but they can't take his dignity and his pride, and he vowed that he swore to God he would never allow someone to disrespect the Mexican people. He said his leaving his job means he can't wrestle for the next 90 days, but he may come up with some surprises.

At this point, Konnan, Perro Aguayo Jr., Daga and El Hijo del Fantasma came out to confront him and his father. Konnan said that El Patron was just like the Mexican national soccer team, that he always choked in his important matches, and said something to the effect that Vince McMahon isn't the only one who doesn't like Mexicans, because he doesn't either. But the main confrontation was with Aguayo Jr., who said that in AAA, we fight for real and WWE is show. He said we don't run around chanting "Yes, Yes, Yes" or "You can't see me." He insulted and then shoved Dos Caras and it was on. Patron punched all of the heels, who took bumps, and all rolled out of the ring. Patron went to go after them but was held back by his father.

What's really notable is that even though he called himself Alberto el Patron, the chyron with his name listed it as Alberto Del Rio, the name WWE owns.

The main event at TripleMania was four-way for the TripleMania Cup, with Myzteziz (the original Sin Cara), Aguayo Jr., Dr. Wagner Jr. and Cibernetico. The finish saw Aguayo Jr. give Myzteziz a low blow and got the pin after a double foot stomp.

This brought out Alberto, Dos Caras, Rayo de Jalisco Jr. (who was there because AAA inducted his father into the AAA Hall of Fame earlier in the show) and AAA President Joaquin Roldan. Alberto got in Aguayo's face again over the insults Aguayo made about his father in the opening segment. Aguayo attacked but Alberto came back and took Aguayo out with the armbar, and ended the show waving a Mexican flag in the ring.

In one interview, he said he regretted slapping Barbierri, and told that to Vince McMahon. He said Vince McMahon said he understood where he was coming from, but slapping an employee is unacceptable, but that everything would be okay. He said the next day, Paul Levesque fired him.

Typically, WWE has 90-day non-competes when they release talent prior to the end of their contracts. As part of the non-competes, the WWE pays them their downside guarantee during that period. That's what keeps them from being able to work with other promotions. WWE often doesn't enforce the non-compete for non-television promotions, but it's a case-by-case basis. For example, Matt Korkland (Evan Bourne) was released, and wasn't allowed to appear on the first ROH PPV after first believing he could. Korkland was released on 6/12, so his 90 days are not up. But he has been approved to work, using his former ring name Matt Sydal, in Dragon Gate in Japan and just started with Evolve, which does iPPV events but has no television. Drew Galloway, Jesus Rodriguez (Ricardo Rodriguez) and George Murdoch (Brodus Clay), who are also part of the group released in mid-June, have also worked independent shows. None have appeared on television or PPV, although Galloway has also been on iPPV shows with Evolve.

Rarely is the non-compete longer, but Jim Ross' non-compete was approximately ten months because they badly didn't want him to work for TNA in particular. In his case, the non-compete was for any pro wrestling group, worldwide, but not MMA or boxing. He did one boxing show for Golden Boy, largely as a promotional gimmick for FS 1 and for him to show he could do real sports without being J.R. the wrestling announcer. During that show, he was never called J.R., nor did he wear his cowboy hat.

Del Rio said that he is now living in San Antonio (he had moved his family before he was let go from Miami to San Antonio, where he has several cousins living).

Things changed during the week. He said that at first he thought he had a 90 day non-compete in the U.S. and was free to work in Mexico, but later got the letter telling him the terms.

He appeared on "Primero Noticias," a major news program in Mexico for a lengthy interview. He said he'd like to tell the whole story, just saying there was an incident with a WWE employee, but it's a touchy legal situation and he doesn't want anything he says to be used against him in the U.S., saying they have a different kind of legal system than Mexico.

He said he was offended, and he believes he was the victim. He said WWE then said he displayed unprofessional conduct, and it's true, he did hit an employee. He said that they can take away his job, but not his dignity and his pride, nor will he let people offend Mexico. He said there were racist comments but that he reacted in an inappropriate manner and would not advise anyone to do what he did. He said he is completely embarrassed by his reaction, but he was mad because he demanded an apology and was laughed at.

He said exactly what happened will come out, saying that Jack Swagger was with him, as was one of the referees and others from the production crew all eating at catering.

Del Rio said it was not his first problem with Barbierri (who he never mentioned by name), saying that a while back, the person who offended him was pretending to read something on his laptop and said, he's reading that Del Rio is a "tal por cual," (which means a so-and-so, but can be used on women meaning a slut) and acted like it was just a joke and wanted to shake his hand. He said he told the person to get away from him. He said this happened seven or eight months ago. He said when the incident happened in Laredo and he demanded an apology, that the person smirked at him and wouldn't apologize. He said that he did lose his job and was embarrassed by his reaction, but he thinks WWE is the ones who have lost the most from the situation.

He said Levesque called him on 8/6 and fired him. He said Levesque told him that it hurts WWE more than him because they've invested so much time and money into him, but that they have no choice but to let him go. He said that as soon as the news got out, AAA contacted him, promotions in Japan contacted him (he worked for years with New Japan and several other Japanese wrestling and MMA promotions including Pride and Pancrase).

When asked if he was planning on suing WWE, he said he wasn't sure.

According to a few sources close to the situation, Del Rio was said to be mad that Barbierri wasn't fired, but publicly, for legal reasons, he has not said anything like that. At one point he considered speaking out publicly in the U.S. media but first opted against doing so. But at press time, the word was that his lawyers gave him the green light to talk in the U.S.

The situation, as those close to him believe, is that there is a lawsuit out against WWE and Big Show from a former guy in production who is suing Show for allegedly roughing him up during a filmed interview segment. WWE felt that having another incident like that, that if Del Rio wasn't fired, it would strengthen the case and strengthen a potential case by Barbierri that WWE provided an unsafe working environment. Those close to the situation have said that John Cena, Big Show and Randy Orton all told Del Rio they would push to get him his job back because most of the locker room was sympathetic to his position, but Del Rio made it clear that he doesn't want to come back. Del Rio has become a big-time hero in Mexico, where the basics of the story broke in mainstream news, although he would not confirm them.

As far as Rey Mysterio goes, the situation is still on hold, but it became news at TripleMania when, just as the iPPV and PPV broadcast ended, he showed up on the screen and then they cut away, with the idea it was a tease. For the live crowd, Mysterio stated on the video that he would like to be wrestling soon in AAA, saying he debuted in AAA 22 years ago and that he considers AAA as his home promotion. It was well known AAA wanted Mysterio on the show to make an appearance, but due to his being under contract with WWE, that was impossible. It's interesting they seemed to feel they could show the video to the live crowd, and show him as the show ending tease at the end of the PPV show. Mysterio's appearance was not cleared with WWE.

It would at least appear that the AAA U.S. project, would eventually feature Del Rio and Mysterio as its two biggest stars, and that in Mexico, they would have a strong threesome of Del Rio, Mysterio and Myzteziz, the original Mistico as its biggest stars at some point in 2015.

When his contract expired, the reports are that Mysterio told Levesque he wasn't interested in renewing and they had a handshake agreement that they were going their separate ways. He then was called by Mark Carrano, at the behest of Vince McMahon, saying they were renewing his contract for one more year based on his being injured for nearly two years of the period of his most recent deal. All WWE contracts have that clause, but it's not known if they have used it with anyone else. Mysterio was injured at the time. He has not worked for WWE since, with his last appearances being a brief return back in January. There was talk over the weekend, given that he lives in San Diego and SummerSlam was in Los Angeles, that he would come in for some media appearances, but that didn't happen, probably because the obvious questions would transpire.

Konnan has been Tweeting "Free Rey," of late. One could read the tea leaves and see the game here is that there is going to be a promotional war in Mexico with AAA and WWE, with AAA trying to portray WWE as the heel promotion that doesn't respect Mexico and screwed over Del Rio, who they'll try and push as a Mexican idol, and is keeping Mysterio from working in the U.S.

Another issue is Mysterio has not returned to fulfill that year as an active roster performer, so who knows if they'll claim the rights to keep him after the year is up. The company has not yet said anything publicly regarding Mysterio appearing on the AAA video.

SEPTEMBER 8

Alberto Del Rio and Ricardo Rodriguez are scheduled to team back up again for the WWC in Puerto Rico. On 8/30, the promotion did a show-long angle where Juan Manuel Ortega, the top heel manager, was going to the airport to pick somebody up. It turned out to be Rodriguez. The comedy in that is that they were shown driving in a car and Rodriguez was giving Ortega directions even though Ortega has lived in Puerto Rico his entire life and Rodriguez is the foreigner. At the end of the show, they wound up at an area golf course and Ray Gonzalez, the top babyface, was playing. Rodriguez went up to Gonzalez and told him that he knew who Gonzalez was. He asked Gonzalez if he knew who he was. Gonzalez said he knew of him and asked him what brought him to Puerto Rico. Rodriguez said that he came on behalf of El Patron, Alberto Del Rio, so they used that name on television. A key here with WWC is that WWC does have a working relationship with WWE, and promotes the local WWE shows, so WWE would more than likely allow Del Rio to use that name in Puerto Rico. Rodriguez said he was there to deliver a message from Del Rio, and spit in Gonzalez's face, so you can see Rodriguez vs. Del Rio will likely be the main event at the upcoming Aniversario show. The show ended at that point. Right now in Puerto Rico, Mexico vs. Puerto Rico in sports is a big deal. They also announced the return of Invader #1 on 9/6, so the sides have reconciled after all the mainstream news about Invader's home burning. He just said he was going to deliver a special message to the fans. The belief is it'll be something like him thanking the people of Puerto Rico for their support, which will lead to a heel coming out and setting up his return feud. Former Universal champion Gilbert is back, doing a version of Piper's Pit next week. Mason Ryan also debuts, as the babyface challenger for Universal champion Mighty Ursus.

NOVEMBER 3

Alberto Rodriguez has signed to do a Kayfabe Commentaries DVD, which is notable because of the nature of his firing. There had been talk he was going to do major media, which he didn't do, regarding his firing which lends me to believe there were negotiations with WWE to keep things quiet. This probably also explains him working in Mexico and in Japan this coming week when he's got a worldwide non-compete for one year. It's also notable that he hasn't yet worked the U.S., and a lot of indie groups wanted him, as well as him and Ricardo Rodriguez together. That tells me a lot is still in the negotiation phase regarding how his situation turns out. He did an interview with Fighting Spirit Magazine that will be out this week. Among the things he said was when wrestling in WWE they only want you to do their style and they have you in a box and you can't think outside the box. He said he doesn't blame WWE, because it works for them, but now he's going to mix American, European, Japanese and Mexican styles in his matches going forward. He said his father would have a big retirement event sometime in the first six months of 2015 that will have he, Mil Mascaras, his brother Guillermo Rodriguez (El Hijo de Dos Caras), stars from Japan and that Rey Mysterio wants to be there. He said there were constant racist jokes in WWE when he was there and he never liked them, but he never said anything because usually they were said by important people. He said they would joke not just about Latins but also African-Americans. He said if a nobody (like Cody Barbierri) said something, he'd say something but if important people said them, he wouldn't say anything. He said at first he was told he was going to be suspended after the incident with Barbierri, but then, when they realized there was a lawsuit out when Big Show slapped someone doing a vignette, they were afraid Barbierri would sue and there would be two lawsuits of talent slapping non-talent. They told him, "We need to let you go until things cool down." They gave him the impression they'd bring him back in a few months. He said he told them that if he wasn't hired back by the time he hung up the phone, he wasn't coming back and noted he's already made up his mind he was leaving the company when his contract expired anyway. He said that the person who called him, who he didn't name, to let him go, was a high up person who always made racial jokes and said because he does it everyone else thinks it's okay to do it and claimed he told him that. He noted he was going to leave because the money was down and he was only home 38-40 hours each week to see his family. Rodriguez claimed that Myzteziz is getting $5,000 per match in Mexico (that sounds high, although he and Perro Aguayo Jr. were making money only the biggest names in WWE were making during the boom period many years ago) and doing two or three matches per week. He said the new hot guys in the company these days in WWE are making $500 per match. He said one wrestler told him (the hint would be one of the Usos, because he made it clear the guy had a brother, but it could by Wyatt) that he did a match on Superstars, a long match on Raw, a promo on Raw and then a dark match at the end of the show and got $500 for it. He talked about wrestlers getting $2,000 for a four-show tour of Mexico. He noted that the young guys are not unhappy about it, but not completely happy either, but have no choice. He noted guys like he and Mysterio weren't happy and they had somewhere else to go to make money. He said he once complained to HHH about doing a tour and getting his check, and this was when he was champion, and claimed he used to make more money for a week of small town shows for CMLL. He said that was two years ago, but because he would stand up and fight over money, he was always paid well in the end, but he said he would complain to the head of talent relations (HHH or John Laurinaitis) every week. He said they would always fix his check when he complained. He claimed he got $10,000 per week in Japan as Dos Caras Jr. (that sounds way high to me because he was never a major headliner in Japan although will be now). He said Blue Demon Jr. and El Hijo del Santo, when he was in WWE talking with them about money, said he could make the same money in Mexico doing an easier scheduled and make his own rules. He said most guys in Mexico don't make big money, but Myzteziz does, he will and Mysterio will and he said when Mysterio comes to Mexico that business will pick up. He said AAA offered him far more than CMLL could have which is why he went there. He said he got the AAA offer, went to Paco Alonso (CMLL president) who he called his good friend, and Alonso said he couldn't match the offer because they didn't have a good television deal yet. He said that Drew Galloway was his really good friend, the best man at his wedding, and he was working on bringing him to Mexico in 2015.

NOVEMBER 17

A confidential legal settlement has been reached between Alberto Rodriguez, formerly Alberto Del Rio, and WWE, regarding his non-complete clause.

The belief is the sides agreed that Rodriguez, 37, would agree to make no more remarks publicly talking negatively about WWE, most notably the subject of racial jokes or implying insensitivity of top officers in the company, and in return he got a financial settlement that includes his non-compete clause being dropped.

Rodriguez on Twitter put out a joint statement with WWE stating, "Following my departure from WWE, an understanding was reached with regards to my future booking opportunities. We wish each other well in our respective future endeavors."

According to sources close to the situation, WWE was very conscious toward any potential public reaction tying them in with racism against Hispanics, given Hispanics make up about 20 percent of the U.S. audience and Mexico is one of the company's top international markets. At a press conference before the recent Mexico City show, it was said that the press conference was more them bringing out the new Sin Cara and have him talk about all the opportunities he was given and it came across like they were trying to push that they weren't racist more than promoting the shows or the new station they started with.

Another source close to the talks said that there was a last minute change. At one point, the joint settlement was expected to include a WWE apology for inappropriate remarks. The source said WWE agreed, but then in its written settlement agreement, took that out of the deal. The story is that Rodriguez had already agreed to the monetary settlement and complete freedom to work anywhere he wanted, so he didn't press the apology. There may have been some sympathy because the apology would have essentially been a public admission that higher-ups in WWE were making racially insensitive remarks, and that going public in 2014 could be bad for the company.

Rodriguez had done media interviews in Mexico, as well as the U.K., talking about racial jokes said by top executives. The original Sin Cara had said the same thing in Mexico, but noted that he didn't believe that had anything to do with his WWE run not being a success. Rey Mysterio had remained quiet through this period although it is well known WWE wanted him to return and speak for the company.

Those close to the situation said WWE had offered Rodriguez his job back. Part of the reason he was let go was a fear of a lawsuit by former Social Media manager Cody Barbierri, who Rodriguez allegedly slapped. Rodriguez has admitted the circumstances, that a social media manager made a racial remark (at catering, when someone told Barbierri he should clean off his plate, he said, "that's what Del Rio is here for"), he asked for an apology, the person smirked and didn't, and he slapped him. Barbierri has just left WWE and one would expect that all loose ends regarding potential legal action were taken care of before his departure. Part of the reason Rodriguez was let go rather than just fined was believed to be because of the potential for a lawsuit by Barbierri.

Rodriguez noted that he was told he would be brought back, but claimed he said when at the time of his being fired that he was not coming back if the situation wasn't straightened out at the end of his phone call (believed to be with Paul Levesque). Several of the top WWE wrestlers went to management about wanting him back, but he himself declined the future offer at the time.

Rodriguez was given a one-year, unpaid, non-compete term from the date of his firing. It was highly unlikely such a term, even with the slap being a contract breach, would have held up in court.

Rodriguez had wrestled for AAA and on independent shows in Mexico, as well as for Wrestle-One in Japan, even with the non-compete in effect, with the feeling it would be unenforceable outside the U.S.

It is believed the settlement includes an agreement he would not sue the company, that he would no longer publicly talk negatively about the company, and that the non-compete would be dropped. He was seeking a settlement amount as well, but it is unclear if he got that or not. Because WWE owns the name Alberto Del Rio, he will use the name El Patron Alberto going forward. The settlement would appear to open the door for Rodriguez to start with the Lucha Underground promotion with its second run of tapings that start on 1/17.

DECEMBER 22

Alberto El Patron will debut for ROH on 1/3 in Nashville at the TV tapings, facing Christopher Daniels. As noted last week, he has signed for multiple dates. It's interesting that ROH is using him because unless he's doing them a favor, he doesn't come cheap and ROH has a low budget. I'm not sure he's going to be a big needle mover either, because he was never the star the Hardys were nor does his style fit in with the product like A.J. Styles, even though he does seem like a hot commodity because of the nature of his firing and how he fought back against the WWE and won. Other dates he's signed for are 1/30 in Dearborn, MI (against ACH), 1/31 in Dayton and the 3/1 PPV show from Las Vegas. I believe A.J. Styles will also be on the 3/1 show. The connection is likely with Court Bauer, who works closely with Rodriguez on business and media and also works with ROH. Regarding Alberto and MMA, he just got a big money offer from Bellator and that's not his only big money offer, so it's really up to him if, at 37 (he'd be 38 by the time he fought), he wants to go back and do MMA. He can make far more in MMA right now than wrestling, but he can do really well in wrestling alone, between AAA, Lucha Underground, ROH and indies, or TNA as well. He was 9-5 as an MMA heavyweight from 2001 to 2010, but he never beat anyone of note and lost to people who weren't of note, with his most famous fight being, while under a mask as Dos Caras Jr., getting a fast head kick knockout loss to Mirko Cro Cop in his heyday on a Pride show. He lost to guys Bobby Lashley would destroy if you're looking for a comparison.

DECEMBER 22

TNA made another play for Alberto El Patron of late. It was said to be a very serious money offer (the number we heard was $400,000 for a one-year deal, and considering we don't even know if TNA will be running house shows or how many, and they tape in bunches, and who knows about PPV going forward, so that could be a couple of dates a month) but the impression I have is they will either have to up the money or drop asking for exclusivity (in regard to things like PPV and the like). Plus El Rey has offered a substantial guaranteed money deal and the expectation is he's going there. John Gaburick worked closely with him in WWE so that's why they are hot to get him. TNA is pushing the idea that he'll have more U.S. TV exposure than with anyone else, which may or may not be the case in comparison with ROH. It's not even a lock (but it is probable) that TNA will beat the Unimas numbers for Lucha Underground, but for the demo he'd be strongest with, Lucha Underground on Unimas would hit it far harder. The reason why every wrestling promotion wants him and MMA groups want him as well is that everyone is looking for a Latin superstar. The feeling is that Latinos carry boxing, and they should be stronger in MMA, but aside from Cain Velasquez, nobody has really mobilized them as a fan base and even Velasquez, because he doesn't work hard at promoting himself, hasn't pulled big numbers out of that demo past his fight with Brock Lesnar and his first fight with Junior Dos Santos that he lost. TNA has constantly looked to make a Latin star and Bellator and other groups are looking at things the same way.

CHAPTER THIRTY NINE

WAR MACHINE ARREST

AUGUST 18

This was the week for MMA fighters and accusations of heinous crimes.

War Machine, the former Jon Koppenhaver, 32, was accused of a horrific beating of one-time girlfriend, porn star Christy Mack, on 8/8.

Mack, 23, claimed that Machine, his legal name, attacked her at 2 a.m., leaving her with numerous serious injuries.

Even before her statement, but when the story broke later that day about him being wanted by the Las Vegas police after inflicting what police called "severe, but not life threatening injuries," to a man and a woman at their home, Bellator sent out a release stating he was fired.

"We have a zero tolerance policy here at Bellator when it relates to any form of domestic violence," said Bellator President Scott Coker. "And after learning of this latest incident involving Jon Koppenhaver, War Machine, Bellator is releasing him from his promotional contract with the organization."

Mack, who claimed Machine broke up with her in May and had moved from her home in Las Vegas to San Diego, showed up at the house late that night and without a single word spoken, started beating up on the other person in the house, Corey Thomas.

Machine, on Twitter, wrote about the incident saying, "I'm not a bad guy. I went to surprise my girlfriend, help her set up her show and to give her an engagement ring and ended up fighting for my life" and "I only wish that man hadn't been there and that Christy and I would be happily engaged. I don't know why I'm so cursed. One day truth will come out."

However, part of her story does fall apart regarding the breakup, because of both parties constant use of Twitter. Both had posted photos of them together, including one of them having sex, from just two weeks ago, so her May break-up story has holes in it already.

Machine is being charged by Las Vegas police with one count of battery resulting in substantial bodily harm, one count of battery by strangulation, two counts of battery with substantial bodily harm, one count of open and gross lewdness, one count of assault with a deadly weapon and one count of coercion and threat with force.

She claimed that he beat up her friend and ordered him to leave, made her undress and shower in front of him, and then started punching her in the face. She said the beating resulted in 18 broken bones around her eyes, her nose being broken in two places, teeth knocked out, other teeth broken, and that she can't chew or see out of her left eye and her speech is slurred from swelling and lack of teeth. She said she also received a fractured rip and a ruptured live from a kick and her leg was so badly injured that she can't walk. She said she also has lesions from a knife that Machine pushed into her hand, ear and head, and sawed off some of her hair with.

"I believed I was going to die," she said in a statement. "He has beaten me many times before, but never this badly. He took my phone and canceled all of my plans for the following week to make sure no one would worry about my whereabouts. He told me he was going to rape me, but was disappointed in himself when he could not get hard. After another hit or two, he left me on the floor, bleeding and shaking, holding my side from the pain of my rib."

She said he left and she thought he was looking for a sharper knife and she ran out the back door, hopped the fence to the golf course behind her house and ran to a neighbors house. She said she was naked and was running through the neighborhood, knocking on doors and finally one neighbor answered, who brought her to the hospital.

War Machine continued to tweet while being on the run from police. There was a $10,000 reward by Las Vegas police for information leading to his arrest. Publicly, Duane Chapman, better known as Dog the Bounty Hunter, said that he would find Machine and bring him to justice if Machine doesn't turn himself in.

As Jon "War Machine" Koppenhaver, he was on the sixth season of The Ultimate Fighter, where he had an incredible first match, winning a bloodbath over Jared Rollins in 2007. He was fired by UFC for comments he made about Evan Tanner after his death which got a lot of people furious, basically saying that he thought Tanner committed suicide because he knew his career was over and that he had no money for all his time in UFC. Even after Tanner's death was ruled to not be a suicide, he continued to talk like that. He also had an issue with matchmaker Joe Silva, and refused fights so was let go.

Bjorn Rebney at Bellator immediately signed him, but he was then fired after writing on Myspace that he hoped somebody would kill Barack Obama and every president to come. After that, in a fight scheduled for April 17, 2010 for Wild Bill's Fight Night in Duluth, GA, the day before, he left a message on Twitter saying he was going to no-show the event, and did.

Still, Bellator brought him back at the end of 2011. But before he could start, he was sentenced to one year in jail on an assault charge.

Among his arrests have included a 2007 case in Las Vegas where he was found guilty of punching a man and choking him unconscious in a parking lot fight, and given three years probation and 30 days community service. In 2008, he had a second assault charge based on fighting people who he said were catcalling him. In February, 2009, he was arrest for a fight the gay night club "Krave" where he was working as a topless bottle server. In November, 2009, he punched out a number of people at a birthday party for a porn star. In 2010, he was arrested in San Diego after pushing a bar owner and destroying several glasses. Later that year, he was again arrested in San Diego after an incident at the Pacific Beach bar. Koppenhaver, who starred in 12 porn movies, took War Machine as his legal name because he had gotten a legal letter from TNA regarding using "War Machine," as his nickname, claiming Terry Gerin (Rhino) owned that name. He then had his name legally changed to War Machine, since you can't be stopped from using and marketing your real name.

AUGUST 25

Former Bellator and UFC fighter War Machine was captured by U.S. Marshals and local police in Simi Valley, CA, on 8/15, and was scheduled to be extradited to Nevada, where he's facing a bevy of charges including a new attempted murder charge.

Machine aka Johnathan Koppenhaver, besides the new charge is also charged with several counts of battery, including by strangulation, assault with a deadly weapon (a knife), coercion by force and open and gross lewdness for allegedly giving a terrible beating to former girlfriend and porn star Christy Mack (real name Christine MacKinday), who suffered 18 broken bones in her face, and a ruptured liver along with numerous other injuries.

By the weekend more than $73,000 was raised in a GiveForward fund raiser for the various surgeries Mack will need on her face and other medical bills. In Las Vegas, ever since the attack, the police search for Machine had remined one of the lead stories, and often the lead story, in the news for nearly a week. It had become one of the biggest news stories in the country all week long, due to both the occupation of Machine as an MMA fighter, Mack being a well known porn star, and more the savage nature of the beating and Mack's posting of her injuries and photos of her in the hospital. According to one person in the adult video industry, even a week after the beating, she was still completely unrecognizable.

Police found Machine at the Extended Stay America Hotel in a city where he used to live. At the same time they found him, Duane Chapman, best known as Dog the Bounty Hunter, who garnered a lot of publicity this past week by vowing to bring him in, had staked out Machine's home in San Diego and found that his pet snakes had not been fed in some time.

Police came after a call from hotel guest Mary Casamento, who called saying a big dude was yelling at and pushing a small woman who was trying to calm him down. She told police she saw the man grab the woman by the hair.

I was in Southern California at WWE activities and the capture of War Machine was the lead story on every newscast.

Another hotel guest, Nicolle Blankenship, appeared on television, saying she was there when the marshals started banging on the door. They broke into the room and she said they yelled, "Gun," and then said authorities shot Machine with a taser, he went down and they handcuffed him. Police found a small amount of cash and some pizza in the room.

Corey Thomas, the unfortunate person in the home, and in bed with Mack when Machine came in, ended up with a broken nose and two black eyes from their confrontation after punches from Machine, and was also bitten by him. Thomas was a former reality show star on VH-1's "Megan Wants a Millionaire," who made a fortune in web design. The arrest warrant against Machine charged Machine with repeatedly punching Thomas in the face, causing substantial bodily harm, and also strangled (choked) him. It also charged listed him punching and kicking MacKinday, as well as licking his fingers and rubbing her genital area. It also accuses him of using a knife to her head and forcing her to take a shower. MacKinday said that Machine told her, "That's my pussy and I'm gonna take it back now."

There were reports that friends of War Machine saw Mack and Thomas out together at some area night spots and tweeted him, and that led to him going to her home where the confrontation started, with him allegedly first attacking Thomas and forcing him to leave.

What Mackinday told police about her relationship with Machine was different from what she said publicly. She said to police that Machine was her boyfriend at the time of the attack and they had been in an on-again, off-again dating relationship for the past 15 months. She said the two don't live together, but he has a key to her house and spends the nights there often, but lives in San Diego where he runs the Alpha Male Clothing Company.

She described Thomas as someone she has a non-sexual relationship with, although admitted to having sex with him in the past.

She said to police that Machine and Thomas fought for about ten minutes with Machine mostly holding him in a near naked choke before letting him go. She said Thomas was bleeding profusely from the beating and Machine had Thomas' blood all over him. She dialed 911 on her cell phone which she hid from Machine, but didn't say anything for fear he'd find out, but left the line open.

She said Machine told Thomas to get out of the house and said he would kill him if he called police. He said he was giving all of his friends Thomas' information and they would kill him if Thomas did something that led to anything happening to Machine.

She said Machine threatened to kill her, and took her cell phone so she couldn't call the police.

She told police that Machine would go through her instagram and twitter accounts and whenever he found something he didn't like, he would hit her in the face, either with an open hand or a closed fist.

However, when police talked to Thomas, he said that he was in bed with MacKinday, who he described as "his girlfriend," at her home when Machine came in and jumped on top of him and punched him in the face about 16 times and then put him in a choke, almost putting him unconscious. Thomas said he got out of the choke once, but Machine jumped back on him and punched him in the face. He said Machine let him go, and told him he would have his friends kill Thomas if he told anyone what happened. However, Thomas did then call police shortly after being let go, and was then transported to a local hospital trauma center to treat his injuries. He suffered a broken orbital bone and other bone fractures in his face, as well as multiple contusions.

OCTOBER 27

War Machine attempted suicide on 10/14 at the Clark County jail in Las Vegas. According to a report on TMZ.com, a guard saw Machine in his cell sitting on the ground with his feet on the bunk bed. When the officer said something to him, he was unresponsive. The officer went into the cell and found Machine with a piece of linen around his neck, which was tied to the leg of the bed, and his face was purple. The officer cut the linen and removed it, which appears to have saved his life. Machine's vital signs were pretty much gone and he was next to dead when the officer came into the cell. About 15 minutes later, they were able to revive him. He was taken to medical isolation on suicide watch where he remains at press time. Officers found several suicide notes in his cell. In one note, Machine quoted Nietzsche saying, "to die proudly when it is no longer possible to live proudly," and wrote that even though he's now dead, he experienced more in his short life than five average men combined. He also apologized to his family and friends. He wrote to Christy Mack that he forgives her for cheating on him and hopes she can forgive him for what he did, saying "I loved you more than freedom." He told his brother to make sure to keep Alpha Male shit alive. Regarding his case, he wrote, "They wanna charge me with battery and... Fine, do it, but don't railroad me with BS fantasy charges like rape, attempted murder, kidnapping and burglary. It's making it impossible for justice." He wrote that he knows Christy Mack will be pressured by "her scumbag agent" to testify against him for money, and said how today's society has killed men, and that he was never meant to live in this era. He also quoted Nietzsche again, saying, "I often laugh at the weaklings who think themselves good because they have no claws." He has an 11/14 court date facing 32 charges against him.

Machine's lawyer, Brandon Sua, said Machine was suffering from anxiety and depression in jail and he keeps saying that he doesn't believe he'll get a fair trial. Worse, he could get a fair trial. He was moved to the medical isolation cell and kept on suicide watch.

DECEMBER 1

War Machine on 11/20 pleaded not guilty to a variety of charges from an attack on former girlfriend Christy Mack and the man he caught her with, Corey Thomas. Machine faces 34 felony counts including sexual assault, kidnapping, strangulation and assault and battery.

CHAPTER FORTY

BROCK LESNAR
SQUASHES JOHN CENA

AUGUST 25

Brock Lesnar won the WWE title for the first time in more than ten years, in the most one-sided title change of any length in company history, beating John Cena at SummerSlam on 8/17 at the Staples Center in Los Angeles.

The match consisted of Lesnar destroying Cena from the opening bell, throwing him around at will, including delivering 15 different released German suplexes, a few of which saw Cena land badly on his already damaged neck. Lesnar laughed at the little offense Cena mustered, kicked out of his Attitude Adjustment, and finished the match by simply powering out of his STF, and getting on top for vicious ground and pound, and delivering an F-5 for the pin. Cena was kept off Raw the next day to sell the beating.

As far as one-sided savage beatings that a territory's top babyface would take, the only person I can think of who did that on occasion would have been Jerry Lawler in Memphis, who in trying to establish a new top heel to draw, would work a match similar to this (usually much shorter) in a first meeting. I can recall him doing so for the debuting Kimala and the original Lord Humongous (Mike Stark). In the case of Kimala, the Lawler vs. Kimala run was a big success. In the case of Humongous, I don't recall how successful it was, but guaranteed it did work and was more successful than had the first match been a traditional back-and-forth match where he put the big newcomer over clean. But as a weekly headliner, Lawler lost all the time so those were the rare extreme measures, done with a heel they were going to run with for weeks on end, and who was debuting on top and had no history with that gimmick (both Kimala and Humongous had worked the territory before, Stark without the mask had even had a run on top as a face with a heel Lawler years earlier). Since Lawler in both cases was winning out in the end, it did help business, got a longer run of singles matches than usual out of it, and Lawler wasn't hurt at all in the long run for it.

Of stars at the level of Cena, during their run as the top face, I can't think of any other modern examples. Dusty Rhodes never did it. Hulk Hogan never did it. Bill Goldberg never did it. HHH never did it. Shawn Michaels never did it. Bruno Sammartino never did it. Giant Baba never did it. Jumbo Tsuruta never did it. Mitsuharu Misawa or Kenta Kobashi never did it. No world champion tippy top star babyface in the history of the Capital Sports promotion ever put their heel opponent over in this way.

You could sort of say Shinya Hashimoto did it with Naoya Ogawa, but how much of that was Ogawa just taking it as opposed to it being worked out is a question, and that was one of the biggest modern programs that crossed over big mainstream, doing multiple Dome programs and 20+ ratings.

Antonio Inoki definitely did it on December 27, 1987, at Sumo Hall, in creating Big Van Vader. The idea was that they were going to create a new monster in one night, in the gimmicky Vader, with his spiked headpiece that blew steam was making his debut, managed by late night television host Takeshi Kitano, which garnered a ton of media attention at the time.

Inoki, a bigger star in Japan by far than Cena would be in the U.S. today, put Vader over clean in a one-sided squash in 2:49. But there were differences here. For one, it was a quick match. For another, Inoki just had a match with Riki Choshu right before, so he had that excuse. As far as success went, Vader became an instant sensation and one of the legendary characters in Japanese wrestling history. It also led to a riot at Sumo Hall, which saw New Japan banned for one year from what was at the time its flagship big show location.

From a WWE standpoint, there were the quick title changes like Sammartino over Buddy Rogers in 1963 and Diesel over Bob Backlund in 1994, but they were done in a minute. Some older fans compared it to the June 16, 1975, Madison Square Garden title match with Sammartino vs. Waldo Von Erich, but in this case, the one-sided destruction was the face winning and caused by unique circumstances. Sammartino had just suffered a broken arm in a match with Bobby Duncum, and had no business wrestling, but in that era, WWWF couldn't run MSG without him. So he came out and essentially just kicked the hell out of Von Erich and pinned him in just 4:12, a main event so shocking that everyone there remembers it to this day. But even that was over in one-fourth the time.

While it didn't have nearly the excitement of a usual WWE main event, the stiffness and the ability of the match to take one out of the "expected" pro wrestling zone was more reminiscent of a Japanese match, and because that never happens in WWE (Lesnar vs. Cena in 2012 was the closest to it), it made it one of the most memorable matches in recent memory. While not quite as brutal as their 2012 match, this was close to that level with Lesnar delivering hard knees to the body like one would in a real MMA fight.

The idea was to get Lesnar over as strong as possible as a monster, to make him break out of the pack. That was accomplished. The idea was also to get Cena over for not quitting in that situation and for taking the beating. In the Staples Center, it didn't work, as fans cheered Lesnar and even after, booed Cena and sang "Na na na na, good bye," thinking the beating meant he would be taking time off.

Cena didn't appear before the crowd the next night for Raw in Las Vegas. He didn't appear on television, but did appear before the live crowd at Smackdown in Phoenix the next night.

Surprisingly, given how the match was laid out, Lesnar vs. Cena for the title will headline Night of Champions, which this year is an event more important than SummerSlam, because the first six-month network subscriptions are expiring on 9/2.

The first big hook event for renewals of the most hardcore of fans, the first group of subscribers, is the PPV on 9/21 from Nashville. The problem is the lack of depth of true headliners, which is more a function of WWE's booking that mostly makes mid-carders, so when the headline situation needs something new, there are few options.

This leaves only four viable headliners who could have faced Lesnar. There is Dean Ambrose, who is in a different program and while he may have great potential and will probably be the next Punk, he's not ready in their eyes for that spot. And his movie shooting schedule may not allow it. There is Batista, who is supposed to return, and I don't think has ever worked a program with Lesnar on the big stage (they worked back in OVW), but Batista didn't get over as a singles headliner on his last run, although the circumstances are completely different now. But still, if they were to go to that, Batista needs to return, make a face turn (he sort of left as one with the blow up of HHH and his quitting, but it was more ambiguous) and build it, and this month would be too soon unless there was no other option. There is Roman Reigns, who most likely they are going to keep out of the title picture until he wins it at WrestleMania, since he is the chosen one and this is his period to rise. Having him lose a title match now would be counterproductive. And his winning this early, not at Mania, a month after Lesnar has won the title won't maximize the impact of his win.

The other opponent is Cena. But in theory, while the match was super compelling and much discussed when it was over because it was different, it also felt like the single worst layout of a match to build a rematch. This was a match where the loser has to disappear for a while and comeback with a make over, having a come to Jesus meeting or something to reinvent himself and explain why things will be different next time.

All of a sudden what seemed like a brilliant and gutsy scenario to get people talking now comes across as a shock for the sake of talk, but making no sense for the direction they are going in. If you use logic of building fights, which WWE is in control of, and apply it to boxing or MMA or kickboxing, or tennis, or football, or basketball or baseball and you are trying to build a big rating for a game the very next month or for a PPV, do you book a 35-34 game that comes down to the wire, or a 72-0 game where the home doesn't get a first down and the visitors laugh them off the field? Indeed, this is very close to the scenario Vince McMahon talked about as to why UFC would never have staying power, when he saw Rampage Jackson destroy Chuck Liddell, and felt all the work in building Liddell was then wasted because he was done as an attraction (Cena isn't done, and Liddell wasn't done either).

If you are UFC and you can control the outcome to build a rematch, do you book a close fight, or a one-sided slaughter where it's the most popular fighter who sells more merchandise than every other fighter in the company combined loses and gets finished, without winning a minute, let alone a round, and then you still try to draw with an immediate rematch?

So SummerSlam was a super effective build for Lesnar as a top heel star. But it was more like a build for Lesnar to be a super strong heel and needing a new babyface to be the one to chase. Without that person in the picture (well, that person is in theory Reigns but for it to work, Lesnar has to keep doing that to everyone until he faces Reigns), they don't have the follow-up for this month.

As far as the WrestleMania build, I see these viable choices.

Choice A, which seems the most logical, is Lesnar beats Cena again, with Cena being competitive and another heel screws him and Cena goes into a program with that heel, Lesnar beats another top face in January and then loses to Reigns at WrestleMania.

Choice B, is that Cena gets his win back with a slip on a banana peel finish in a match he gets completely destroyed in, but he's beaten so badly that Seth Rollins cashes in that night. Cena and Rollins can battle for a few shows, and eventually Reigns beats Rollins (or even Cena) at WrestleMania.

That way you don't have the situation where the championship is on hiatus, off house shows and television for a long period of time and on every PPV.

They could always negotiate with Lesnar and make him an offer to do one match per month. Lesnar isn't getting younger and socking away more money in his tenure in the business isn't something I can see him wildly protesting. The idea of him doing a full road schedule may not happen because his need for more money given the deal he has wouldn't be there. But once a month between now and Mania where he's guaranteed to headline every major show and have a career run as a monster hardly sounds like something he'd reject without thinking. Dwayne Johnson had a far busier schedule and when he agreed to the deal for the championship, he did appear on every PPV during that period. It would simply be a business decision, whether the two sides could come to a financial agreement.

CHAPTER FORTY ONE

SMACKDOWN
MOVING NIGHTS

SEPTEMBER 1

The expected move of Smackdown to Thursday was confirmed on 8/24, when Syfy's web site had a schedule listing showing that on Thursday, 10/2, Smackdown would be airing from 8-10 p.m.

Those in WWE had been of the belief the move would be with the 10/2 show, but nothing official had been stated.

The move returns Smackdown to its original Thursday night slot in the U.S. after nine years on Fridays. The move had been expected ever since fans has spotted one or more WWE production trucks at the 8/5 Smackdown tapings that were painted up listing the time slot as Thursday at 8 p.m. on Syfy.

In addition, Syfy had already announced the TV show "Haven" was moving from Friday to Thursday night at 10 p.m., and Syfy has scheduled the two shows together since Adam (Edge) Copeland, who was one of the big stars on Smackdown for years, has a recurring role in "Haven."

The move was one of the key reasons Spike moved TNA Impact to Wednesdays, doing so as soon as possible to establish the show in the new time slot before the fall season was to start.

Smackdown debuted on April 29, 1999, at the peak of WWF's popularity, in a Thursday time slot on UPN. At the time, it was presented as a one-time pilot. WWF was on fire at the time, and the show went weekly starting on August 26, 1999.

It was pushed as the return of pro wrestling to weekly network prime time television for the first time since the mid-50s, when the Dumont Network folded. UPN, without informing WWE ahead of time, announced a move to Fridays prior to the 2005-06 television season. While Smackdown never drew higher ratings than Raw, because UPN was in more homes than Spike, there were plenty of weeks where Smackdown had more viewers than Raw in the early years of the show. That ceased to be the case with the move to Friday. The move was made by UPN because they had programming that could command much higher ad rates, and Thursday was the most advertised night of the week due to movie opens. More often than not, Smackdown was UPN's highest rated show during its Thursday run, but it was also during much of that period the show that generated the lowest ad rates, or near the lowest ad rates, of any network show.

Ratings dropped 20 percent immediately with the Friday move. Numbers had ups and downs, but in recent years have been remarkably steady even as most television numbers have fallen.

When UPN merged with WB, to form CW, Smackdown remained one of the most popular shows on the network until it was canceled at the end of the 2007-08 season. WWE struck a deal with the fledgling MyNetworkTV, a smaller attempt at a broadcast network, which carried the show for two years at a lower rate, before canceling it over costs as the network itself was in bad financial state.

It moved to cable on Syfy for the 2010-11 season. Syfy had been airing Tuesday night wrestling with the ECW show starting in 2006.

On UPN and CW, it made sense for Smackdown to air on Fridays. It was able to garner strong numbers on a weak night, where its low ad rates didn't hurt as much as they would on Sunday through Thursday.

But when the move was made to MyNetwork, remaining on Friday made no sense because with both MyNetwork and Syfy, the show drew far bigger ratings than anything else on the station, and on Friday, the audience ceiling was lower.

Even though the show will be head-to-head with the NFL in the fall, the move from Friday to Thursday should increase audience more than the football bite. And even if it only holds steady during football season, it should still be far above Friday numbers from January through August. I've never understood why this move wasn't made four years earlier, because the key value for Syfy in having Smackdown is how it can increase the station's weekly average, and it would do so more significantly with a larger Thursday audience.

For WWE, it's only good news because Thursday nights in general carry more viewers, which should, in teory, lead to increases in other revenue streams.

While not announced, one would expect NXT and other key first-run WWE Network shows, Superstars or reality shows, would be moved to a new date, with internal speculation thinking it would be Wednesdays. It also somewhat changes the game for TNA, as it eliminates both Monday and Thursday as viable nights for them to draw an audience, no matter what station they wind up on in 2015.

No word has come from WWE regarding this move, nor how this affects the rest of the world. The belief is, Canada would switch back to Thursday with the U.S. In countries like Australia and the U.K., where, with the time difference, they had been getting Smackdown nearly a day before the U.S. Continuing that would require a crunch on deadlines.

SEPTEMBER 8

UFC, Bellator and WWE Smackdown will all be going head-to-head on television on 9/5.

For UFC and Bellator, this is an interesting competition because not only are they both running live TV shows on FS 1 and Spike, but they are also running only a few miles apart, with the UFC live show at the Foxwood Resorts Casino in Ledyard, CT, while Bellator runs at the Mohegan Sun Casino in Uncasville, CT.

However, Smackdown will not only win the fight, but most likely draw more viewers than both MMA shows combined. How the audience shakes out will be most interesting. Is Smackdown hurt at all? Will UFC and Bellator compete for the same audience, or will they compete for a split audience, and how will the audience split?

Smackdown has been ranging from about 2.4 million to 2.8 million viewers on Fridays. When Bellator was in season, it was averaging just under 700,000 viewers, but with a title match, plus King Mo, Cheick Kongo and Bobby Lashley, with no UFC, one would think the number would be in the low 800s. There is no history of UFC on Fridays. While few will compare the Smackdown number, and most see it at UFC vs. Bellator, Smackdown did load up on the show with a late addition of John Cena.

UFC will be running a ten-fight show, with the entire card on FS 1, from 7 p.m to midnight Eastern time. Bellator will only be running from 8-10:15 p.m. Eastern, and on the West Coast, because Spike does a staggered feed, part of the Bellator show will go unopposed and most of the UFC show will as well.

For those in Canada, due to Sportsnet airing the Toronto Blue Jays on one of its channels and Smackdown on the other, the UFC event will not be televised in Canada, which may be a first. It will be available live for Canadian Fight Pass subscribers.

Bellator usually runs from 9-11:15 p.m. on Spike, but because UFC goes on the air earlier, they've decided to go earlier as well. This will be the start of their final "season" of weekly fights, which will take place through November. In 2015, they move to a schedule of 16 shows per year, which generally will mean one show per month, plus one extra major show per quarter that will be the equivalent of a PPV, but not on PPV, as evidently the company's debut on PPV wasn't cost-effective.

What's notable is that not only should Bellator draw better, since they are in a 7,000-seat arena while UFC is in a 2,900-seat arena (which was virtually sold out two weeks ago), but they could do bigger TV numbers as well. Bellator has a show built around its biggest stars, and Spike is a far more powerful station than FS 1. In fact, the only edge UFC has is that it's UFC.

SEPTEMBER 15

In one of the strangest stories, the move of Smackdown back to Thursday is now off the books.

Syfy never made the announcement of the Thursday move, but put out its television schedule for the month of October a week earlier, which listed Smackdown at 8 p.m. and Haven at 10 p.m. on 10/2, 10/9, 10/16, 10/23 and 10/30, all on Thursdays. The TV show "Spartacus: Vengeance," was listed in the old Smackdown time slot most Fridays, although on 10/3 a theme of horror themed shows called "31 Days of Halloween" was to air from 7-9 p.m. and Spartacus: Vengeance from 9-10 p.m. In later weeks, there were two episodes, airing 8-10 p.m., on Fridays.

One person within WWE said that all the key people in the company had been aware of the change long before that, noting that it wasn't a coincidence several of the ring trucks had been repainted and stated Smackdown on Syfy is airing Thursday at 8 p.m. Officially, company officials told us at the time that the show could be moving to Thursday but nothing was definite, and that the ring trucks were painted prematurely. Others in the company said the move was all but official, but not quite official.

Even after WWE officials confirmed to us that the decision was made for Smackdown to remain on Fridays from 8-10 p.m., the Syfy web site still listed the show as having moved to Thursday for a day or two. The move back to Friday was then reflected in updated schedules.

The decision was made to change the Thursday prime time plans with Haven at 8 p.m. and Spartacus: Vengeance running two episodes from 9-11 p.m., and Smackdown staying put.

Haven has been Syfy's most successful series, partially because of airing after Smackdown, which is the station's highest rated show by a large margin, and in some weeks the highest rated show on cable on Friday night, something no other show on the station comes close to on any night. With most shows in rerun mode this time of year, Smackdown was, for the week ending 8/31, the 15th highest rated show on cable for the week, with 2.73 million viewers. Syfy was the 15th highest rated cable network for the week, averaging 998,000 viewers in prime time.

It was surprising to break up the combination because the same viewers who stay with the station to watch "Haven," which includes former WWE star Adam Copeland (Edge) as one of the stars, can be monetized for their full worth as a viewer on a regular television show, even though their value as a viewer is weak per person when they are watching wrestling.

Even though the decision means Smackdown avoids the NFL Thursday night game in the fall, this was not a WWE decision but a Syfy programming decision. But one would have expected, even during football season, significantly more people would have watched on Thursday than Friday. After football season, the difference would be even greater.

OCTOBER 20

The future of Smackdown on Friday night is back in question as Syfy made the announcement this past week of a new show, an adaptation of the 1995 movie "12 Monkeys," which they announced would debut on 1/16, a Friday, in the 9 p.m. time slot. People with "12 Monkeys" have since confirmed the 9 p.m. Friday slot will be their regular slot, so Smackdown is once again scheduled to move away from Friday, which had been the plan starting in October but things changed. No word if the move will be to Thursday, which was the original plan, or not. Also no word on how that will affect international Friday deals in Canada, the U.K. and Australia. Those at WWE have said nothing official has been announced yet.

NOVEMBER 17

Syfy and WWE announced this past week that starting 1/15, Smackdown will be moving back to its original Thursday night, in the 8-10 p.m. time slot.

Smackdown debuted in 1999 on UPN on Thursdays, and was moved by UPN to Fridays in 2005 because of the introduction of what the network believed would be new flagship programming. UPN folded and became CW, which canceled the show in 2008, where it moved to MyNetwork TV for two seasons, averaging 3.4 million viewers.

While Vince McMahon predicted with the move to Syfy in 2010 that viewership of the show would be nearly the same as Raw, it has been about two-thirds that of Raw, averaging 2.6 million viewers.

Reports of a move to Thursday surfaced in August, when WWE had some of its trucks painted listing Smackdown on Thursday at 8 p.m. on Syfy. At the time, the move was scheduled for the fall season, and Syfy even listed the new time slot on the scheduling grid, where Smackdown would lead-in to "Haven," a show that features Adam "Edge" Copeland as a regular character.

It was confirmed Smackdown would move a few weeks ago when Syfy introduced new programming on Friday nights. The move was expected for Thursday, but not confirmed, until this week.

There is no word on how this will affect most international deals. Currently, the U.K., Ireland, Australia, India, Singapore and The Philippines get the show well before the U.S. One would expect U.K. and Ireland to still get it before the U.S., since that would be Thursday prime time. For the other countries, which, due to the time difference, which were already getting the show on their Thursday night, it is not clear.

Australia had been the first country to get Smackdown, but it looks now like that will be Canada, which will get the show on Sportsnet 360 on Wednesdays from 8-10 p.m.

WWE is a major priority to Rogers, which paid a significant increase this year for both broadcast rights to WWE programming and the WWE Network as a linear channel, as well as eventual broadband rights to the channel in Canada. However, it is not in the league of the NHL as far as priority programming to Rogers, which spent $436 million for NHL rights in a 12-year deal earlier this year, and had committed to the NHL on Thursdays.

Smackdown had aired on Fridays in Canada before the move was made in the U.S. due to NHL games when Sportsnet 360 was known as The Score.

WWE also announced with the move that NXT will move from a Thursday at 8 p.m. time slot to Wednesday at 8 p.m. on the WWE Network. Actually the first airing of NXT had been moved to 4 p.m. on Thursday. This will put NXT head-to-head with Lucha Underground, and create a Wednesday night schedule that also includes Impact, which the company is planning for a Wednesday night time slot in 2015, but at this point doesn't have a television deal, and Ultimate Fighter. In Canada, NXT and Smackdown will be head-to-head.

The move was likely delayed until January because of NFL football on Thursdays, making it a less advantageous time of the year to make the switch.

I had never understood why Syfy and even MyNetwork TV kept the show on Fridays, given that in both cases, it was the most popular show on the station, but the total audience potential was held back being on a weaker night. With CW, it was understandable because they had programming that drew much higher ad rates and sometimes comparable numbers that they could put on Thursday.

The beneficiary of all this is Bellator, which now will have Friday to itself with its monthly specials, although it was only Bellator's first hour that went against Smackdown. Bellator did routinely gain audience after Smackdown ended, but it was probably more because people knew the higher profile fights were coming later in the show.

But it's eliminating a competitive show that skewed heavily male and drew strong numbers in the 18-49 demo that was going head-to-head every week.

Smackdown's audience decreased 20 percent in the 2005-06 television with the move. Thursday is a far better night for television and one would expect this to lead to a significant audience increase, perhaps as much as 20 percent.

TNA was moved to Wednesday, partially anticipating this move would take place in October.

CHAPTER FORTY TWO

LUCHA UNDERGROUND
DEBUTS

SEPTEMBER 8

The elusive major attempt to market Mexican wrestling in the U.S. to both the Hispanic and non-Hispanic audience, talked about for decades ever since a successful few year run in California faded away, is on the verge of becoming a reality.

It's been a running joke since the mid-90s, more from AAA than anywhere else, that "next year" we'll be running the U.S.

Well, somebody is coming. It's affiliated with AAA, was originally talked about as being AAA, but it's not in any way the AAA product that appears to be making a comeback in Mexico.

Lucha Underground, the latest name for the group, debuts with a TV taping on 9/6 in Boyle Heights, in Los Angeles, in a TV studio-like setting, for a weekly show on the El Rey Network from 8-9 p.m. Wednesday nights, which will debut on 10/8.

Aside from web site listings, some online tweets and posts and flyers on the cars who attended the PWG shows over the weekend in Reseda and some posted signs in the area, there doesn't seem to be much publicity for the weekend tapings.

There have already been a lot of comparisons made between this and Wrestle Society X, the MTV show which tried to present a different version of pro wrestling. This itself is expected to be yet another different version. Time will tell whether that's good or bad. The reality is it depends on the commitment from the distributors and producers, which include media heavyweights like Robert Rodriguez and Mark Burnett, and finding a vision that can create a loyal audience.

Enthusiasm had been high for the project, but that has dissipated as contracts were sent out, and literally at the 11th hour, there are scripts done and tapings set, but nobody knows what talent will or won't be there. Much of the talent offered contracts lost enthusiasm given aspects of the contracts that left people with bad tastes in their mouths,

The main issue is that El Rey is a station that has limited clearance and no viewership. Today, you need a network that can provide strong viewership to open a wrestling franchise up to make money in merchandising, licensing and doing live events, which is the ultimate goal this company has, with that starting around the fall of 2015.

AAA seems to be increasing in popularity in Mexico as attendances are bigger this year than in the past few years. With the potential of a superstar lineup that would include Alberto Del Rio, Rey Mysterio (next year) and Myzteziz, to go along with Perro Aguayo Jr., they may grow even bigger in 2015. If they can harness some of the "undiscovered" spectacular performers around the world and have the ability to make stars, there may be potential in the Mexican-American market, a market that is growing in the U.S. and supports pro wrestling at about double the rate of the rest of society.

But AAA is still far from the boom periods of the early 90s and mid-00s.

In the early 90s, when AAA had its run of success in the U.S., it was because it was on in a good time slot on a station that delivered huge ratings in Los Angeles, there were a lot of Lucha Libre fans, and they were loaded with both new style workers and legendary characters from the past.

This program isn't going with the legends (very notable that Myzteziz is not part of this roster, who seems to be the guy who has helped increase business in Mexico, nor Aguayo Jr., Cibernetico, La Parka and the other big names in the promotion). There is no Perro Aguayo or El Hijo del Santo or Cien Caras or a main event heel like a Jake Roberts or Mexican hot celebrities of the time like Konnan or Octagon like what AAA had in that era.

The idea doesn't seem to be to bring AAA to the U.S. like bringing in a major Mexican entertainment act to Hispanic cities. Instead, it looks to create something from scratch using some young wrestlers from AAA and mixing in some American names, a few who have had exposure with WWE and TNA, and others who are great working indie guys.

Another key aspect is that they are trying to do it with a minimal talent budget, and in this industry when your competition is WWE and TNA, that approach for a national product would make it difficult to get traction. For example, it would seem to be obvious where one would turn for an English language announcer in Jim Ross. While Ross may not want to be part of a start-up in pro wrestling, the key is that there were people with the project very interested in him a few months ago, yet he was never given a serious offer and was never personally approached at any point.

The expectation is there will be a second station carrying a Spanish language version of this, believed to be on UniMas, which used to be known as TeleFutura. UniMas is the third highest Spanish language network in the U.S., behind Univision and Telemundo. It averages 720,000 viewers in prime time, so it's roughly as popular as Spike, but with a different audience, and its strongest in Hispanic Males 18-34.

The reality is, between UniMas and El Rey, if they are in prime time on UniMas, and Spike drops TNA, this promotion will be No. 2 in the U.S. on television in 2015, even if it makes no breakthrough to the Anglo market. But if they are not in prime time on UniMas or able to get to that level of viewership if they are, at least at first, that is not going to make much of an impact. Plus, this is a very difficult time to create a new promotion from scratch, when the casual audience is lower and the fervent audience for the most part are fans of WWE, not pro wrestling.

The talent situation is very much up in the air right now, with only days until the first taping.

Konnan (as an on-screen performer most likely in a heel manager role), Ricky Reyes, Karlee Perez (Maxine for a brief run in WWE), Martin Casaus (who was in the last season of Tough Enough, the guy who looked like Donny Osmond, and was injured) and B-Boy have officially signed.

The biggest name floating around is Ricochet, but there is a hold-up since he has an existing contract with Gabe Sapolsky's Evolve/Dragon Gate USA group, and that doesn't take into account agreeing to a deal that many feel isn't worth signing for.

Other names that have been floated around include The Young Bucks (who have reportedly turned down the offer), Ryckon Stephens (Ezekiel Jackson), Angela Fong (a very athletic Oriental woman and former British Columbia Lions cheerleaders, who had the most potential of any woman in WWE developmental as a worker, but at the time they weren't all that concerned about athletic ability of the women, and she got dumped in the numbers game when Gail Kim was signed because, you know, they all look alike), Frankie Kazarian (also reported to have turned it down), Matt Cross, Scorpio Sky and Rocky Romero.

What is notable is that at first, the thought process was to not use ex-WWE talent, unless it was someone like Alberto Del Rio or Rey Mysterio, but now they ended up with interest in a ton of them. Del Rio may be appearing in the crowd at the shows taped this week, with the idea of him not wrestling to get around his non-compete.

It'll be impossible to get a read on what this is until it airs, and perhaps most importantly, until we see the time slot it airs in on UniMas and what kind of an audience it gets. It is going to draw a lot more fans on that station than on El Rey, even it will premiere first on El Rey.

There are a lot of complaints going around regarding the contracts offered. The wording of the contracts includes exclusivity for seven television seasons, which scares people regarding how long seven seasons could be, given it could be and probably means seven years. If this goes nowhere, but stays in existence, much of the talent doesn't want their careers paralyzed or to make a commitment that pretty well kills their dreams of going to the WWE for so many years.

Andre Verdun, a former wrestler out of San Diego, is representing a lot of the Southern California based talent. It's coming down to the wire because there is a publicity shoot scheduled for 9/4 and at press time, very few had actually signed.

On 8/29, the casting agent brought in a new group of talent and had them cut promos and read scripts to replace any of the wrestlers in the current scripts in case they don't sign.

The last impression we had is that they would do 39 first-run episodes per year, which will be shot over seven months, and air over nine months. The idea is to have an off-season in the summer, similar to the way Wrestling at the Chase in St. Louis was done during the 60s and 70s was done.

The people involved are looking at this, after one year of television, at becoming a wrestling franchise with the merchandising, perhaps recreating the Lucha Libre movie genre, and touring live events.

Another issue is that the contracts stipulated that the promotion would have to approve of all independent bookings. It also had a standard rate of pay with no raises built into the contracts, as well as a long non-compete period which offers no guarantee of pay during that period.

There was also a provision regarding publicity days, which the contracts don't pay for.

Verdun reportedly redlined a lot of the contracts and sent them back to the company. Verbally he was told they would agree to those changes, but when the new contracts were sent back, 90 percent of the changes he redlined were rejected and of the ones that were accepted, many were changed again. The promotion is telling the talent that all the issues are being worked out and that they will all be able to do independent dates, just as they have been doing, but the new contracts still aren't reflecting that. But a lot of those issues are minor.

We're told the two key issues are the length of the contracts, the lack of downside guarantees on pay, as performers were all given contracts that listed pay per appearance with no guarantees on appearances, but still have the insistence as far as the contract on exclusivity. The per match pay would be less in some cases than these same talents made for independent bookings. In fact, some of the best known talent from the list got contract offers of $200 per match to start, with an increase to $500 per match if you become "a regular." However, B-Boy and Ricky Reyes, who don't have nearly the names of some of the others, who have signed, both signed for more than $200 per match. The feeling from talent is that the producers see the talent as not significant, and view it more as casting a television series using unknown actors and not offering good deals, and that the talent is completely replaceable.

For obvious reasons, nobody with options was going to sign a seven-year exclusive deal with no downside guarantee in the contract.

On 8/29, a number of the wrestlers offered contracts were told that it was now a "take it or leave it" situation and told they had a deadline of 9/2 to sign, or their roles would be re-cast. As of 9/1, we don't know of anyone who had signed given that ultimatum, and rehearsals for the first tapings were supposed to start on 9/2, with publicity work and a photo shoot scheduled for the next day. On 9/2, a producer told a talent that hadn't signed that there wasn't such a deadline and that was only a rumor, but others noted there were emails fro m the legal department stating that specifically.

On 9/1, Verdun sent a list of changes that would have to be made from the latest contracts sent out on 8/29, before anyone would consider signing. As of last word, the reports were that contracts would make it clear to allow talent to work indie dates without getting approval, but that an El Rey taping date would always have to be first priority.

To me, I've always felt the biggest problem when it comes to Lucha Libre in the U.S. is the inability to accept what it is and nobody making an attempt to promote it to cater to its fan base, and instead try to change what it is and draw from outside its fan base.

The only viable Lucha Libre in the U.S. is to cater completely to the Hispanic audience with an authentic product, and hope the product itself is good enough and gets hot enough that you may get some fans out of the core demo interested. But that number will never be the key to the success.

The one time it was successful in the last 25 years was when you had a super hot product in Mexico, it had strong local television in Los Angeles airing the authentic product in good time slots, and had very good local promotion. The problem has always been that it can get off hot—the first major AAA show at the Los Angeles Sports Arena in 1993 drew 17,500 fans and turned away 8,000 at the door, at a time when nobody was doing business like that except for WrestleMania day. But while business remained good for a few years, it didn't sustain and faded away, from a combination of AAA losing popularity and losing the local television.

Yes, there is a history of Mil Mascaras, Chavo Guerrero and his brothers including Eddy, Rey Mysterio, Jose Lothario and others as Mexican talent that was able to successfully headline when pushed to the top with existing and established promotions, but calling something Lucha Libre and using a cast filled with Americans and attempting to cater to that audience would be something that hasn't worked in the past.

During the heyday of AAA in the U.S., in 1993 and 1994, you took the established hottest promotion in Mexico that was using its biggest shows and biggest matches on two and even three hour television shows weekly. Essentially, they were doing Nitro a few years before Nitro. They had a weekly soap opera, contemporary music, special effects years ahead of the U.S. Essentially, they were the trend-setters. But as far as breaking through into the U.S., they did great in Los Angeles and San Jose, not so good in San Diego or Oakland, and okay in Chicago and New York, but not great at all.

The television show was about presenting big matches with the top stars and building angles for big matches that would play out. The stars came across like superstars because we saw them with the big musical entrances and the catchy music performing before 5,000 to 15,000 fans, just like today's Raw, except with a far better quality of music, more creative costuming and talent with a wider variety of unique characters. The style of wrestling with the high flying was new and innovative, and ahead of its time. But even then, the audience was almost exclusively Hispanics. An attempt to merge audiences, like doing a joint show with ECW talent in Chicago, didn't draw hardly anyone but Mexican fans, and they only wanted to see the authentic product.

The amount of non-Hispanic interest, even at best, was tiny. When they did 17,500 fans in Los Angeles for La Revancha at the Sports Arena in 1993 (Konnan going for revenge against Jake Roberts and Cien Caras in a three-way, a show that turned away 8,000 at the door) in what may have been, to this day, the hottest wrestling show ever in the city, I doubt there were even 100 non-Hispanics in the crowd. This feels more like an attempt to take a storyline and a lot of Americans, have them feud with Mexicans and do a weekly TV shoot. Without the ability to make them larger-than-life (much harder now because of how the game has changed), and really, it not being WWE which has so many hours of TV, it's going to be tough. But the base audience of Mexican-Americans, to me the best thing to do is present the authentic Lucha Libre product, on TV, from Mexico, with the weekly storylines building up the major shows. The idea would be to work at drawing fans from the Hispanic demo primarily, and make this "your wrestling." The big difference today is to the Hispanic demo, "your wrestling," is WWE. Will Del Rio and Mysterio be, to the Hispanic community, what Jeff Hardy, Hulk Hogan, Sting and Ric Flair, were to the wrestling fan community in 2010 in TNA?

I've always felt when you remove multiple week build-up and major shows from the equation, a key element of wrestling that makes it work is gone That's the element that people who don't really know wrestling don't really understand.

The mentality here is that they are producing a television show, not a wrestling show, but to me, that's arguing sports entertainment vs. wrestling. They are the same thing. You want a great television show with the soap opera like elements of pro wrestling that brings the audience back weekly. It's a multi-pronged business that needs a variety of elements to sustain itself.

Konnan, the AAA booker, has an involvement in the project and his goal is to present a great in-ring product in conjunction with everything else. But he's not the booker here, and it's not being booked like a pro wrestling company. The head writer is Christopher DeJoseph, who had a long stint on the WWE writing team, and was also the performer Big Dick Johnson. There is a second writer who has no wrestling background that comes from the reality TV side, plus Matt Stollman and Chris Roach, who had worked in WWE creative in the past. But those close to the situation say DeJoseph is the only key player in production who has a clue about the business, and that the Burnett legal team has no clue.

It's going to be something different, but what "different" is, is still unknown, and very little may leak out because of the NDA's from the tapings. It probably won't be until October until we get the gist of it. But unless it catches on to where people sample it in big numbers come October, it doesn't matter if what it's presenting is good or bad if there isn't an audience watching to begin with.

In-ring, the idea is replicating PWG, with hot matches and fast and spectacular wrestling before a small enthusiastic crowd. But that's at best, a tiny part of the equation. It's good to have as part of the equation, but ROH has been around for a dozen years both with and without television, and it's largely treaded water. PWG has a few hundred fans and some loyal DVD buyers, and survives, but 99% of the pro wrestling fan base has no idea it exists.

Now, you can't beat WWE because the financials are so different. The audience is used to a certain level of major league production, so the barrier to entry as far as being major league wrestling, is far higher than it was in 1993. Plus, you have so few "wrestling" fans as opposed to WWE fans. Those fans can get more than their fill from WWE, and have the opinion they don't need to watch anything else, because if anyone was a real star, they'd be in WWE. And that was very different from the mentality 20 years ago, particularly among Hispanics, where it was part of their culture and they had cultural heroes.

SEPTEMBER 15

In a project that started with much fanfare, the first tapings of Lucha Underground took place this weekend in Boyle Heights, in Los Angeles, and already left people with the feeling of what could have been with a revitalized AAA product doing an Hispanic-geared project built around names like Alberto Del Rio, Rey Mysterio, Myzteziz, Perro Aguayo Jr. and Blue Demon Jr.

Instead, we got a show that was described as a cross between Wrestle Society X with Vince Russo style booking at the first taping on 9/6, with a heel owner (believed to be an actor) and his Authority like henchman, the Crenshaw Crew who were Cortez Castro (formerly Ricky Reyes, real name Rick Diaz), Cisco (formerly Lil Cholo) and Big Ryck (using that spelling, Rycklon Stephens, the former Ezekiel Jackson).

The first show was taped in a largely empty studio, with a few wrestling fans and most extras, maybe 100 people in all, who were mostly hired to be studio audiences at television shows, and were being paid $9 to act as fans, but in a building with no air conditioning and them having no emotional attachment, they just sat there for the most part. There weren't even enough to come close to filling the building. Aside from wrestling web sites and social media, the only word regarding tickets was flyers put on cars at the PWG Battle of Los Angeles shows the previous week. There were virtually no Hispanic fans at the first show, but Blue Demon Jr. and Dorian Roldan on twitter promoted the second night of tapings and gave the address, just telling fans to show up.

The second show on 9/7 had more wrestling fans and a hotter crowd. There were still several dozen extras.

All week long, the promotion urged the talent to keep everything under wraps after stories got out regarding contract negotiations. Fans had to sign non-disclosure letters about the results of the tapings, yet pretty much everything got out both nights anyway, not that in the long run it will make a bit of difference.

The shows are said to be the complete brainchild and vision of Mark Burnett, the reality show guru. The shows are completely scripted. Much of the talent on the original roster list didn't sign over the contract issues noted last week, including Joey Ryan, The Young Bucks, Candice LaRae, Frankie Kazarian, Matt Sydal and Scorpio Sky.

There were a few wrestlers who were considered stars and given good deals, which included Chavo Guerrero Jr., Konnan, the former John Morrison (whose name is Johnny Mundo, Mundo being Spanish for world–his original name in the script was Johnny World and that still may be what his name ends up being), the former Jackson, and the pairing of the masked Prince Puma and manager Konnan. Prince Puma is Trevor Mann, better known as Ricochet. A deal was worked out between Evolve and the promotion to get Mann. There were reports of the promotion spending big money to buy him out of his contract, but those close to Evolve denied that, just saying all three sides reached a deal that worked in all of their best interests. The idea is that the rest of the shows were scripted out and they believed that the talent and roles they had done scripts for could be filled by hiring new people.

Matt Striker and Vampiro will be the English language announcers for El Rey. No word on the Spanish crew for UniMas, nor has there been any announcement from UniMas on the show, when it starts, or the time slot. Vampiro was heavily criticized in his announcing debut as an English language announcer for TripleMania. The reports we got is that talk of Jim Ross as an announcer, which never even got to the point of negotiations, was nixed because they felt Ross was too connected in fans' eyes with WWE. The joke was that they then hired Striker, and hired Jackson and Morrison to be two of the top stars.

The shows are heavily interview oriented and backstage skit oriented, so the live crowd didn't see much of the product, mostly just the matches.

They ordered all fans to put away their phones as they were afraid of information getting out, but it still did. They ended up confiscating phones, but didn't ask anyone to leave because the building was so empty to begin with.

From fans, the complaints were long periods of down time. It appeared they had spent a lot of money on the set.

They only taped five matches the first night, and it appeared two of them were dark matches.

Famous B (Brian Winbush) pinned B-Boy (Benjamin Cuntapay), both using their Southern California indie names, so that may have been a dark match. A second match saw someone billed as Mil Muertas, a masked man that was AAA star Mesias (best known as Puerto Rican star Ricky Banderas, real name Gilbert Cosme), managed by a woman who was Karlee Perez, the former Maxine in WWE, beating Magnificent Martin, who was Martin Casaus, the Donny Osmond looking guy on the Steve Austin season of Tough Enough. Martin was seconded by Kitty Meow, who was Kitty in the old WOW promotion.

The next three matches were for what is likely the debut episode on 10/8, which means they are only taping one television show per night, which is decidedly not cost effective for a one hour television show.

The matches were described to me as WWE style television bouts. Chavo Guerrero Jr., as the agent, was telling people to do less and make it mean more. Konnan was pushing more of a PWG style. The point being, this was not a Lucha Libre show even though Lucha was in the title.

Before the first match, "the promoter" came out, who is a heel and announced that whoever impresses him the most tonight will get a $100,000 bonus. Blue Demon Jr. (Luis Robadan) pinned Chavo Guerrero Jr. Demon's knee went out during the match in catching Guerrero Jr. on a dive when he slipped on a ringside mat. They went to the finish twice but Demon's knee wouldn't hold up. Son of Havoc, who was Matt Capiccioni, better known as Matt Cross, also from the Austin season of Tough Enough, beat Sexy Star (Dulce Garcia) , the masked AAA woman wrestler, in what I believe was a two out of three fall match (either that or they taped multiple matches). Sexy Star is not someone who should be doing long singles matches. I was told this match didn't work at all. The last match was Johnny World (Morrison) pinning Prince Puma (Ricochet) in a good match, but not a great match. Konnan was not with Puma, although that could be because he just had his hip replaced and he'd have to be out there on crutches and they may not have wanted to debut him on television like that. The Crenshaw Crew then attacked both guys and were revealed as the heel owner's henchmen.

Of the five AAA wrestlers announced for the project, three, Fenix, Drago and Pentagon Jr., weren't there, with reports that it was due to working visas not being completed, which in and of itself sounds like a bad sign. In fact, the only person on either taping who is not a U.S. citizen is Sexy Star.

AAA was doing television tapings over the weekend in Mexico where most of its top stars were.

They've also announced that bands will be playing at the TV tapings. Whether that will be to entertain fans during the long breaks, or part of the series, is unknown, but from what I did hear, nobody spoke of bands playing as part of the finished product, only that it will be a show built heavily around backstage scripted segments.

Hernandez and Ivelisse Velez didn't appear before the audience the first night, but did the second night. Melissa Santos was the ring announcer. She had a background as part of a Women of Wrestling revival attempt by David McLane in recent years. The report we got is that she was cute, and she could correctly pronounce the names of cities in Mexico, but aside from that, she was terrible.

On 9/6, a show likely taped for 10/15, Hernandez pinned Ricky Mandell in a dark match. Hernandez won with the pounce. Mandell came off the top rope and Hernandez was supposed to catch him at one point but lost his balance and stumbled. The Crenshaw Crew cut a promo, but were attacked by Johnny Mundo and Prince Puma. Mundo went after Big Ryck. Cisco and Castro attacked Mundo until Puma made the save and a tag match was made. Mundo & Puma then beat Cisco & Castro using simultaneous 450 splashes on each guy. Puma did cool stuff and was the standout. Guerrero Jr. & Sexy Star beat Son of Havoc & Velez when Guerrero pinned Havoc after a frog splash. Guerrero Jr. & Sexy Star were the faces. Decent bout. Muertas beat Demon Jr. After the match, Guerrero Jr. teased making a save for Demon Jr., He chased Muertas off with a chair, but then did the swerve and hit Demon Jr. with a chair. Two refs jumped in, but Guerrero Jr. laid them out as well. B-Boy and Famous B, who will likely have different names, ran in, and both got taken out with a chair shot. Sexy Star (who teamed with Chavo in week one), came out, but Chavo hit her with a chair as well. Chavo continued to beat down Demon Jr. with a chair until apparently the show ended with Chavo sitting in the ring laughing while everyone all over the ring was laid out.

One person at the taping noted the show, which took 90 minutes to tape, felt like it was the Guerrero Jr. show. The idea of building around Guerrero Jr. as the top heel rival for Demon Jr., a guy who was booked in a Heath Slater-like role in WWE and didn't get over in TNA, and is now about to turn 44, made no sense. Even though Eddy Guerrero was a superstar to Mexican Americans and Chavo Sr. was a headliner in California in the 70s and Gori is a Mexican legend, Chavo Jr. was a prelim guy in the U.S. and never any kind of a star in Mexico, nor is he a Guerrero just breaking into the business.

The plan is to tape 39 episodes at the studio over the next seven months as the first season, and then next year try to break out with touring, major shows, PPV and merchandise.

One person said that it looked to be a about a $700,000 production, which is roughly what WWE spent for Raw in a major arena as recently as a year ago. So they nickeled and dimed talent and lost key people (although probably the biggest factor in losing out on the top talent was more the seven year exclusive contracts), but could save millions if they just taped two shows per night instead of one, or even taped three-ways and not have the long delays between matches by getting everything not match related done in pre-tapes. Considering they have a writing team that mostly worked for WWE, including head writer DeJoseph, clearly those ideas wouldn't be a secret.

SEPTEMBER 29

The debut of Lucha Underground on the El Rey Network has been moved back three weeks, as they are now scheduled to start on 10/29 with a two-hour special from 8-10 p.m., meaning the second hour goes head-to-head with Impact. The company sent out a press release with a cast for the show. The heel promoter goes by the name Dario Cueto (played by Luis Fernandez). Besides the names listed here before, also on the roster will be Angela Fong, at this point using her real name, and Holly Michelle. The company has responded to the criticism that there isn't enough Lucha by bringing in more wrestlers from Mexico and doing more Mexican vs. Mexican matches. Still, agent Chavo Guerrero Jr., who is the head agent, has been pushing the wrestlers to slow down, like any veteran would. But there have been complaints they are trying to push people into a WWE style and away from a Lucha Libre in-ring style. After the first two weeks of tapings, the reaction seems to be that Puma (Ricochet) and Johnny Mundo (Morrison) are the two guys to build around. Brian Cage is also in negotiations to be added to the roster. The fans who have attended have reacted the biggest during the Lucha style matches. There is talk of using Luis Urive, the original Mistico, in the project and Alberto Del Rio will be used as soon as they feel he can be legally cleared. Mascarita Sagrada is going to be using his real name. The idea is to have male vs. female matches as well as having the minis face both women and the larger guys in straight matches. They are looking at introducing a championship title toward the end of the year.

OCTOBER 6

To the surprise of nobody, they announced they are going to start doing four-hour tapings, with shows on 10/4 and 10/18, as opposed to taping one show per night as has been done. As of this weekend, they are taped through 11/26. They are trying to do a more Lucha oriented product after criticism of the early tapings not feeling like Lucha. The enthusiasm of those involved has taken a major positive turn with the tapings this past week because of the Lucha flavor, better matches and better crowd reactions.

NOVEMBER 10

Lucha Underground, the adaptation of pro wrestling put together by Mark Burnett and Robert Rodriguez for the El Rey Network, debuted on 10/29, as the freshest new version of the product seen in this country probably since Nitro was created in 1995.

The one-hour show, featuring an excellent main event with Johnny Mundo (John "Morrison" Hennigan) vs. Prince Puma (Trevor "Ricochet" Mann) was, unlike so many groups who are just trying to be WWE and do a bad job of it, this group is completely different, in look and feel, even if the heel owner being the focal point of the show is beyond overplayed.

The show was clearly expensive to produce, and unlike with WWE, there is no money coming in, not merchandise, live gates or anything. But the promotion is partially owned by Rodriguez, who also owns the network it's on. The show was created for flagship programming, with the idea pro wrestling is really popular in Mexico and the station is meant to appeal mainly to Hispanics who mostly speak English.

The El Rey Network is in limited homes, on some cable systems and DirecTV. It claims a universe of 40 million homes, but since it's on expanded instead of basic tiers on most systems, that figure is probably exaggerated. Even so, nothing it has draws any ratings to speak of.

The debut episode of the show did 8,000 viewers in the Male 18-49 demo, and we don't have overall numbers. But given that 50% of the viewers were above the age of 49, and there had to be some under 18 viewership, the total viewers, if nobody under the age of 18 watched the show, that would be 16,000 viewers. It's more likely closer to 20,000 viewers. The audience in syndication on UniMas, a network of UHF stations, would be considerably larger for the Spanish language version and it was always known that if this show was to garner any popularity, it would be the Spanish language version until El Rey gains a foothold of some sort.

It was the second most watched show of the week on the network, behind airing the movie "The Day of the Dead." El Rey also replays the show out of prime time. Still, given the stations it is on, the ceiling for this at this point is very low. However, El Rey was hoping that with the millions of wrestling fans in the U.S., that this would be the flagship show that would put the station on the map, with the idea of at least a percentage of the wrestling fans seeking it out, based on the idea that TNA still does 1 million viewers most weeks on Spike. Word of mouth on the show was very good, but people still have to have the station, hear about it, and find it. How things trend over the next two months is important, although the people involved have been told there is a multi-year commitment to the project, and the idea is to build toward touring and merchandise in season two next year. But the cost of production per viewer watching at first is a scary statistic.

The heel owner, Dario Ceuto, played by Luis Fernandez-Gil, an established actor, while playing something of a stereotypical role, can deliver a line like just about nobody in pro wrestling. In particular, his backstage scenes, because of the film being used giving it a different look, were far more gripping than the usual backstage fare. The story of the first episode, that he's the owner, and is bringing the best "fighters" (the word used, not wrestlers and certainly not sports entertainers) from all over the world to compete in his "The Temple," an underground Fight Club like hall, and would be giving $100,000 cash to the best performer on the show.

Ceuto is established as being from Spain, not Mexico, so he speaks the language, but he's not Mexican. He's like every stereotypical good-looking older and distinguished looking Mexican mob leader. Konnan did the best backstage scene with him. Konnan played the role of the retired legend who has no allegiance to anyone. He represents, endorses, and talks for Prince Puma, the young star of the promotion, and at the end has been through all the wars and in negotiations, talks his Mexican slang and is only in it for the green.

It was portrayed as if this was the debut of a new promotion, but linked itself to AAA in Mexico, with opening video clips of the legends of Mexico like El Santo, Blue Demon and Perro Aguayo, and showed brief big crowd clips from AAA events including the most recent TripleMania, labeled as such.

After the opening match, they are backstage in the office, and the scene is more like a movie scene than a backstage pro wrestling scene. If anything, right there, it was as if they were so far above what you see in WWE and TNA, both in verbiage and delivery, that they made both products seem like shlock. Konnan's Mexican slang may go over viewers heads, but he rolls out his lines like they are real, and he plays his character like it should be played, as opposed to WWE where guys are speaking in manners like are all wrong for their characters, or TNA, which just feels like a second-rate copy of WWE far too often.

At first glance, the location establishes the group as minor league. But they at least tried to play it to their advantage, with announcers Matt Striker and Vampiro describing it as a dirty, dingy, hot aggressive building, like a boiler room type of heat. Striker has the ability to come off as smug, even without trying, which is why he could have been an effective heel manager if given a shot in that role. He was far better here than in his last few years in WWE. At one point, he even seemed to want to show how he wasn't the announcer he was in WWE. He started talking about different wrestling styles, mentioning the World of Sport (European style from the pre-90s) style, and then following by encouraging viewers to look new styles up on the Internet, and brought up how he can talk about all these things here.

I can't say Vampiro brought anything major to the table, but he was fine in his role as a legend of Lucha Libre. It almost appeared his role was to build up a long-term feud with Konnan, because he took every chance he had to swipe at him. If this makes sense as the season goes on in storyline, and Vampiro does eventually transition past just being an announcer at one point, then we have to see how it plays out. But his role seemed to be to point out how great Puma was, but that in the long run, the Konnan influence will backfire on him. Vampiro did try hard in the main event, pushing just a few minutes in that it was a match of the year. After a series of hot moves by Puma, saying, "I'm getting up," as he joined the crowd for a standing ovation.

A big advantage is the show is one hour. Another even bigger advantage is the production and cinematography. It has the feeling of a movie. They got artsy with the shooting of the matches with completely different camera angles than any show. Those were hit and misses. Different is better, but they went to the ceiling camera far too often, switched more than they should have, and also shot to the announcers during matches far more than necessary.

The character introductions were excellent, but the booking was weird. The two characters introduced and pushed, AAA's Sexy Star and Puma, both lost.

Sexy Star was given a good introductory piece, trying to be a hero to women, talking about being lost in life, contemplating suicide and finding Lucha Libre, and that every woman is sexy and every woman can be a star. They gave her a special ring entrance and tried to make her essentially the Ronda Rousey of the promotion. Then, she had a match with a small male wrestler, Son of Havoc (whose mother is not on the TNA roster), played by former Tough Enough cast member, longtime independent wrestler and gymnast Matt Capiccioni, also known as Matt Cross. He was the only person on the show where nothing was done with his character development. He was a short guy in a mask with a long Wyatt family member beard growing out of it. He, in a voice that sounded like a Black Scorpion 1990 leftover, made fun of the idea of a woman facing a man. The announcers put it over that he, the male heel, was making a mistake in underestimating her. Then he beat her in 83 seconds after a backbreaker.

With the whole domestic violence feeling in the culture, a man vs. woman match has a double negative feel, past the athletic credibility issue. It's one thing to do a mixed match and have a woman do a few quick high spots with a man, or to have a gimmick match in some form after a program has been built up. But this was a match out of nowhere with the idea a heroic woman is facing an overconfident, arrogant man, who doesn't respect her. Then he beats her that quickly. That only made her come off like the proverbial fighter whose false hype has been exposed. Granted, this could play out and make sense in storyline form down the road, but the match ending, after the intro video, was the proverbial letting the air out of the tires.

Puma, a 26-year-old independent wrestler from Alton, IL, was the right choice to build as the new top star. As Ricochet, he's won the Open the Dream Gate title earlier this year as well as New Japan's Best of the Super Junior tournament. He's had incredible matches with the likes of Uhaa Nation and Kota Ibushi in Japan and is clearly something special. It's a risk to make him the top guy, because even next to Mundo, who everyone knows from WWE is not a large pro wrestler, he looked small.

He was first shown in a scene at an old-school ratted out movie boxing gym, with a ring, with Konnan in the role of his Mickey (old trainer from the Rocky series), sparring in the ring and showing all kinds of great moves and unique speed. They put over the mask as sacred, and it was really an incredible introduction piece.

With the mask on and his dark skin, he's billed as an Aztec native who grew up in Boyle Heights, a rough section of Los Angeles where The Temple is located. It does lead to problems down the line, because he'll never be able to do a live interview, past a few words. Of course, with Konnan with him, he can be protected, but it limits him with media, personal appearances and fan interactions if this thing does catch on.

He had a great match with Mundo, but then lost at the end. In his case it wasn't quite as bad. Sure, he was pushed as the face of the brand, and then immediately lost to a mid-card WWE guy who the announcers kept pushing had not been in the ring in three years (not true) and was suffering from ring rust. But the match had some incredible spots. Win or lose, Puma showed himself to be at a different level. Plus, he ends up winning their world title later in the season, so he does overcome this in time. But losing his first match when he was the unknown, made no sense.

After the match, as Ceuto refused to give Mundo the $100,000, both Mundo and Puma were attacked by two heels, while Ceuto explained he was bringing in talent from all over the world. The attackers, who will be known as Cortez Castro and Cisco, were independent wrestlers Ricky Reyes and Lil Cholo, although were portrayed as unknowns. A third attacker, Big Ryck, Rycklon Stephens, the former Ezekiel Jackson, choke slammed Mundo at the end of the show. Striker made it clear he knew who he was, so as not to insult the intelligence of a viewer who may have recognized Ryck and Jackson. It will be established that this is Ceuto's heel group, The Crenshaw Crew. That final scene did feel like every other pro wrestling heel beat down angle.

The editing was very good. The opener was pushed as members of two of the most legendary families in Lucha Libre history, Chavo Guerrero Jr., pushed as the grandson of Gori Guerrero, and Blue Demon Jr., pushed as the son (and once in commentary, the grandson) of Blue Demon. The match was said to have been pretty bad live, but edited from 13 minutes down to five minutes, all but one missed spot was edited out and it came across like a good match. Guerrero Jr. submitted, and later was shown in Ceuto's office. Ceuto browbeat Guerrero Jr., who looked terribly frustrated with himself. Ceuto emphasized that he tapped out, and what would your grandfather and uncles think of you? This sets up the Guerrero Jr. turn, and Ceuto said that he would be bringing in a monster to take out Demon Jr. Hopefully not Tony Hernandez.

We were told this gets better, particularly in upcoming weeks when more of the best AAA talent comes in. Although it'll be hard to top this main event.

But the show is on a station (the El Rey Network) few get and almost nobody watches, and that's a big disadvantage. Unless the station grows in both exposure and popularity, the ceiling is low for it's potential to reach all but the most hardcore fans. The Spanish version, on UniMas, also had no publicity. Both stations air the show multiple times during the week, with the Wednesday night prime time debut on El Rey. UniMas is a series of syndicated stations that is in most major markets, including New York, Los Angeles, Chicago, San Francisco, Philadelphia, Denver, Miami, Atlanta, Boston, San Antonio, Dallas, Houston, Miami, Tampa and Orlando, but in most of those markets is a very minor Spanish language station. So far this television season, UniMas averages 560,000 viewers in prime time, and this show doesn't even air in prime time. Among Spanish local stations, it is a distant third behind Univision, the monster, and Telefutura.

The weakness is that a key part of the lure of a wrestling television show is building toward the big match and big show. Promotions without that element have historically never survived over the long haul. In fact, there is no single example that contradicts this. Perhaps that element will exist down the line, but there was no hint of it in its first week, and no plans for live events until possibly the second season. I think the character developmental vignettes here, with stars created and better protected (particularly at first), but using authentic AAA wrestling with their angles leading to their big shows as the product introduction before larger audiences would be superior.

But this was a very strong debut because it felt completely different, and the one hour format where almost everything was good. There was enough wrestling in the hour to where it felt like the focus of the show, but the new characters were introduced with vignettes and backstage that was generally better than you usually see. It never dragged. I can't see people watching the first show, particularly the last match, and not being impressed by it, and the initial reaction we've gotten on the show has been positive.

But as far as the elements that hook you from the soap opera and match building side, that keep you coming back, they weren't there in week one. The one aspect of that tried, the beat down of the two babyfaces by the heel owner's crew, was the part of the show that was the least different and also the least impressive.

DECEMBER 15

I don't know what's going to happen here because the show is expensive to produce and the ratings aren't moving the way the station would like. It appears each shoot is costing hundreds of thousands of dollars, and national ads on the station during wrestling are going for between $150 and $300 for a 30 second spot. If you add that up, the show doesn't make sense. The cancellation of "El Matador," which was supposed to have a commitment for a second season, says that El Rey is not fully committed to its first-run programming if it doesn't catch on. The hope was that Lucha Underground, which has been heavily advertised on Raw and has gotten strong word-of-mouth, would be a show that would bring people to the station and start putting the station on the map.

CHAPTER FORTY THREE

SEAN O'HAIRE
PASSES AWAY

SEPTEMBER 15

Sean O'Haire, the 2000 Rookie of the Year, who ended up as one of the people whose career path changed when WCW died, passed away on either 9/8 or 9/9 at the age of 43.

It was reported at press time that O'Haire was found by his father at 8:30 a.m. on 9/9, in his bedroom at the family home in Spartanburg, SC, next to his bed, with a red rope tied around his neck that was connected to the bedpost.

The Spartanburg County Medical Examiner's Office at press time said that they had just gotten the body and was in the process of going through an investigation on a cause of death, but could only release that there did not appear to be evidence of foul play involved. They also said they were awaiting toxicology test results, and said that suicide was an option. A celebration of life was scheduled on 9/13 at the family home.

Born Sean Christopher Haire on February 25, 1971, sharing a birthday with Ric Flair, O'Haire was one of a group of big, muscular young wrestlers that a desperate WCW tried to build around when they were going down the tubes in 2000, as part of The Natural Born Thrillers.

He was big, muscular and agile and had a major supporter in Eric Bischoff, who had decided that when he took over the reigns of WCW in early 2001, that O'Haire would be one of his major projects. When he was first breaking in, and appeared on a Brian Pillman Memorial show, Les Thatcher saw him perform as a completely green newcomer and told me he hadn't seen someone that size who was so agile since the days of Don Leo Jonathan.

While nobody fooled themselves into thinking he would duplicate the unique success of Bill Goldberg, that was the model of what the attempt by Bischoff was going to be to push him after he rebooted the company in 2001.

Whether it would have worked or not to any degree is a different issue. But it never happened. Bischoff's bid to purchase WCW fell through when Time Warner canceled the television shows, and WCW was sold in a fire sale to WWE. O'Haire's pro wrestling career became a victim of timing.

In the end, he had a unique legacy as one of the few people ever to work for such diverse groups as the WWE, WCW, New Japan, Pride and K-1.

O'Haire & Chuck Palumbo were the final WCW tag team champions, and defeated Lance Storm & Mike Awesome on the final WCW show ever, the live Nitro on March 26, 2001, where the storyline had Shane McMahon scooping the purchase of WCW from Vince McMahon.

But they came into WCW with the black mark over their head. They came into WWF as the WCW tag champions, losing the titles to Undertaker & Kane that August. They were the victim of a half ass legit gang beating, with beating probably being too strong of a word, but hazing probably being too weak. Very quickly, because they were trained in the Power Plant with a faster-paced style and less time selling than WWE wanted, and with completely different styles and fundamentals of working, plus they were inexperienced, they got the reputation of not being able to work. A few weeks after losing the title, the 2001 Goldberg was toiling in Ohio Valley Wrestling.

He had a few more chances, most notable playing the role of the devil on your shoulder encouraging people to do all the wrong things, in an attempt to do something with him in 2003 with the Smackdown brand. A series of vignettes introduced him, getting over the catch phrase, "I'm not telling you anything you don't already know."

Quickly he became paired with Roddy Piper in what may have been Piper's last serious full-time run with the company. During this run, O'Haire scored wins over Hulk Hogan, via count out, as well as Chris Benoit and Eddie Guerrero, and even with his working limitations, seemed on the verge of the push that had been dropped for him two years earlier. But when a taped interview with Piper aired on HBO, talking about how so many wrestlers had passed away and how uncaring the business was, WWE fired Piper immediately. Without Piper there, O'Haire's push was dropped cold. He was later sent back to developmental, and cut in April, 2004.

O'Haire was something of a noted bar fighter, who got into trouble regularly while living in Hilton Head, SC. He was a name all the local police knew as a guy who was trouble.

In pro wrestling, he had the reputation of being a bad ass guy, who could more than handle himself with the guys with reputations as tough guys, and had a reputation for winning 17 Tough Man fights in South Carolina before he got into wrestling.

But being a street fighter in bars was very different from being a professional fighter, as he would soon find out.

After being cut by WWE, O'Haire got hooked up with Rick Bassman, who was booking foreign talent for pro wrestling, boxing and MMA into Japan. Bassman had booked pro wrestlers Sylvester Terkay (The Predator in Japan, who gained some fame there as a Bruiser Brody reincarnation), Tom Howard, Nathan Jones, Bart Gunn and Stefan Gamlin into both MMA and kickboxing. O'Haire then moved to Southern California to train with the Valor Fighting team.

O'Haire first went to work with New Japan Pro Wrestling, but was signed by K-1 since he was willing to fight for real. K-1 liked the idea of doing a WWE wrestler vs. K-1 fighter gimmick for television, and on the December 31, 2004, show, at the Osaka Dome before 35,000 fans in what was billed as K-1 vs. pro wrestling, O'Haire was knocked out in the second round by Musashi. O'Haire, with no experience as a kickboxer, faced a guy who had just taken second at the World Grand Prix tournament a few weeks earlier. O'Haire came out, swinging wildly, and going for broke. Musashi just laid back and waited for him to blow up, which happened two minutes into the first round. Musashi knocked him down with a left high kick at the end of the round, but he was tough enough to get up. In the second round, Musashi knocked him down two more times before it was stopped at :44 of the round.

While living in San Clemente, a beach town, O'Haire got into about a half dozen fights in his first few months in town.

Bassman questioned him, given Bassman was a small guy and had lived there for ten years and never encountered any trouble, while O'Haire was a jacked up 270-pounder.

"Rick, I have no idea. People just like to pick on me," he told Bassman.

He fought three more times as a kick boxer, all in Las Vegas on K-1 shows, losing to Gary Goodridge, Chalid Arrab and Justice Smith (who placed fourth in the 2004 Tough Enough that was won by Daniel Puder, where Miz took second and Ryback took third, and after not making it as a pro wrestler, became a star briefly with American Gladiators).

He also wrestled on UPW shows in Santa Ana at the Galaxy Theater, where he'd often team up with Palumbo. He married Joy Elizabeth, the sister of the wife of Tom Howard.

He also did some MMA, winning his first two fights in the first round.

"As he did in pro wrestling, Sean came out of the gate hard and fast in MMA," said Bassman in a Facebook article. "And as happened in pro wrestling, the potential went unrealized. For, as many of us do in these wacky worlds of pro wrestling and mixed martial arts, Sean had his share of demons, which stood in the way of what could have been, and should have been, huge success. But those same demons are the ones that make a person who they are."

In his third fight, he lost a high profile bout to Olympic silver medalist in judo, Kim Min-soo (the same South Korean that Brock Lesnar beat in his MMA debut), and had a 29 second knockout loss to Butterbean on a Pride show. He was listed at 4-2 in MMA, but he had a number of unrecorded wins and losses on small shows from 2006 to 2008 in the U.S.

O'Haire's fight with Butterbean took place on October 21, 2006, in Las Vegas. Butterbean vs. Mark Hunt was scheduled. There were visa issues with that fight, including Keith Kizer's questioning it being a fair match given Hunt was an experienced MMA fighter and Butterbean wasn't. Pride asked Bassman if he would get a colorful heavyweight ready, which likely meant a pro wrestler, and offered $3,000 and all expenses. Bassman picked O'Haire, who considered it a paid holiday in Las Vegas.

The day before the show, Hunt was out due to the visa issues, so Pride offered O'Haire $30,000 to take the fight, which he did. So O'Haire stopped drinking eight hours before the fight. Then, Nobuyuki Sakakibara, the President of Pride, came to Bassman and said that fans were expecting a stand-up heavyweight battle with Butterbean vs. Hunt, and feared, correctly, that O'Haire would try to keep the fight on the ground.

"It's immediately apparent that I'm being asked to make sure Sean keeps it standing up," said Bassman. "I mildly protest, saying that doing so will eliminate his only true hope."

A Pride booker, Yukino Kanda, then told Bassman they would give O'Haire a $5,000 bonus. Bassman responded back, asking for $10,000, since Pride had a reputation for being very liberal in spending money at the last minute to get what they desired.

Bassman went to O'Haire with the proposal.

"He's like a kid in a candy store, from $3,000 to $40,000, just like that. It's when his initial joy dies down that he says, `Fuck, I'm gonna get killed aren't I? Could you just ask Bean not to break my face?"

Bassman went to Butterbean. Butterbean agreed with one stipulation, saying that he loses his cool if he gets kicked in the face, so told Bassman to tell O'Haire not to kick him in the face.

So O'Haire went out and celebrated his big payday and that he wasn't getting punched in the face. He went to dinner before the fight and he and Bassman drank three bottles of wine.

The match started. O'Haire didn't try for a takedown, as promised. But the first thing he did was kick Butterbean in the face.

Butterbean closed the distance and knocked him out with seven punches, mostly to the side of the head but one or two to the face, in 29 seconds.

O'Haire had a number of arrests over the years, once for assaulting a woman in a bar in 2004, but was found not guilty when the woman recanted her story. He was in a much publicized bar fight in 2007 in Hilton Head Island, SC. In this one, police reports at the time said he was picking on someone, who ended up fighting him outside the bar. This time, O'Haire came out on the worst end, suffering several fractured bones in his face and skull, as well as a fractured orbital bone. He still fought MMA for another year or so, even though he ended up with vision damage in his left eye from the fight. In 2009, he was arrested in Georgia on charges of allegedly choking his girlfriend. He was also charged with both battery and criminal trespassing, but the charges were later dropped. In 2011, he was once again arrested in Georgia on a battery charge.

At the time of his death, he was working as a personal trainer at Exzel Fitness in Spartanburg. He had also worked in recent years as a hair dresser.

O'Haire debuted with WCW in the summer of 2000. The company was losing money at a record rate. WCW was attempting to relieve itself of most its high-priced veteran talent and replace them with cheaper, younger wrestlers that Paul Orndorff and DeWayne Bruce (also known as Sgt. Buddy Lee Parker) had trained at the Power Plant.

On his debut show, on Nitro, on June 26, 2000, O'Haire & Mark Jindrak (now Marco Corleone in CMLL) defeated Rey Misterio Jr. & Juventud Guerrera. Eventually, Mike Sanders was used as a mouthpiece for a group of muscular newcomers called The Natural Born Thrillers, which also included Shawn Stasiak, Johnny The bull, Reno and Palumbo.

O'Haire was billed as being 6-foot-6 and 270 pounds, and while he was really several inches shorter, he was very agile for his size and able to come off the top rope and use Jeff Hardy's swanton, which they called the "Sean-ton bomb," as his finisher in WCW.

Three months after their debut, O'Haire & Jindrak won the WCW tag titles in a Battle Royal on September 25, 2000, at the Nassau Coliseum. They dropped the titles and regained them on a taping of Thunder on October 9, 2000, in Sydney, Australia, to Lt. Loco (Chavo Guerrero Jr.) & Cpl. Cajun (Mark "Lash" Leroux), before losing them again on November 16, 2000, in Oberhausen, Germany, to Alex Wright & General Hugh G. Rection (Bill DeMott). The silly names and rapid fire title changes were a sign of just how out of control and going down the tubes WCW was at that point.

O'Haire & Palumbo won the titles on January 14, 2001, from Kevin Nash & Diamond Dallas Page, in Indianapolis. The title change came after Bischoff got control of the big picture booking when the deal was announced where Fusient Media had agreed in principle on a deal to purchase WCW from Turner Broadcasting. At that point, the booking got more stable as Bischoff wanted to relaunch the brand as soon as the deal was finalized, with the tag title being a jumping off point for making O'Haire the upcoming singles superstar.

But the deal fell through in March, when Turner Broadcasting canceled all WCW programming after Jamie Kellner, who felt pro wrestling was lowbrow, was put in charge of the entire Turner Broadcasting empire. Bischoff attempted, on an impossible deadline, to put together a television deal that would allow he and his partners to buy the company. But he was unable to do so, and Turner Broadcasting sold the company to Vince McMahon for only $2.5 million, with the promise to spend another $2 million on advertising on Turner stations.

There are all kinds of "what ifs" regarding the career of O'Haire, but in the end, nobody who had power saw him the way Bischoff did in 2001, and the opportunity never arose. He had the size and body that Vince McMahon coveted and he was immediately signed when WWE took over WCW, but the knock of not knowing how to work buried him quickly. He was fortunate in his later chance in WWF to be hooked with Piper, a legitimate legend, as his muscle, but the role fell through because of Piper being fired and with him being associated with Piper, they stopped pushing him.

SEPTEMBER 22

Another note regarding the death of Sean O'Haire. In 2001, the reason O'Haire lost his spot in WWF after the WCW buyout came because he allegedly showed up loaded at a house show, and because of it was careless and nearly hurt Crash Holly bad when he dropped him recklessly on a spot. He was sent to OVW shortly after that. WWE also tod TMZ that O'Haire had gone through six different rehab treatments, paid for by WWE, since 2008, including one earlier this year. In WWE sponsored rehab, they continue on a regular basis to have someone talk with the talent and see how they are doing with rehab. After O'Haire got out of rehab in 2014, he never returned their phone calls.

Another note is that we couldn't come up with anyone but O'Haire who performed in WCW, WWF, Pride and K-1. Of the big MMA and wrestling organizations of that era, WCW, WWF, Pride, K-1, UFC and New Japan, O'Haire performed in every one of them except UFC, which would also be more than anyone else, which is a unique trivia note. Ken Shamrock would have done all but WCW and K-1. Dan Severn also did all but WCW and K-1. Kimo did all but WCW and WWF. Bob Sapp did all but WWF and UFC, and he came very close to WWF on a few occasions even being promised the ECW title (the entire Bobby Lashley push as ECW champion from the date and nature of the title win was originally booked for Sapp, but Sapp and WWE couldn't come to terms). Plus, Sapp also did Strikeforce and Shamrock also did TNA.

One reader noted a real interesting comparison of Batista and O'Haire. Both were about the same age when they wanted to get into wrestling. Both were tall bodybuilder types who were tough guys on the bar fighting scene. Neither did a lot of sports growing up. Both went to the Power Plant at the same time. DeWayne Bruce drove Batista off but O'Haire stayed. O'Haire got on TV first and became a star, to a degree first. O'Haire had Bischoff behind him as a big supporter. Batista had HHH, Vince McMahon and even Jim Cornette from day one in developmental behind him. It is notable to think if Batista had stayed at the Power Plant and been trained the WCW way, what happened, and what a lucky break it was that they wanted to run off a big bodybuilder.

CHAPTER FORTY FOUR

MICHAEL ELGIN VS. RING OF HONOR

SEPTEMBER 15

Ring of Honor made a last minute change of its championship on All-Star Extravaganza iPPV from Toronto on 9/6, as Jay Briscoe became only the second two-time champion in company history (Austin Aries being the other) when he defeated Michael Elgin.

The decision to take the title off Elgin came on either 9/5 or 9/6, but appeared to be finalized just hours before the show. Originally, Elgin was to hold the title most likely through Final Battle, where Adam Cole was the odds-on-favorite to become the second two-time champion, win the title, and then possibly defend it at the Tokyo Dome show on 1/4. It was not believed to be 100 percent that Cole would win the title, but that was when it would change hands and Cole was the most likely candidate. Cole was expected to win the title at some point over the next year when he signed a new contract.

There was a number of issues with Elgin of late, including him booking himself on a several week our of the U.K. during August, even though under contract to ROH, which had several key dates including the ballpark show in Brooklyn where, as champion, he was needed. So he ended up cancelling that tour. Then he lost via pinfall to Trevor Lee on the PWG Battle of Los Angeles show last week. ROH officials weren't happy with that feeling their world champion shouldn't be losing on someone else's show, which is an old-school mentality that most major promotions still have today about protecting the value of the world title. In that same tournament, A.J. Styles, the IWGP champion, had to be eliminated with a DQ loss.

There was tremendous heat on him for an interview he did with Brian Fritz that was released the day before the show that said his goal for next year was to try out for Major League Baseball. Elgin, who is believed to be 26 or 27, would be old to try out as a prospect, particularly since it's doubtful he's played much baseball in years. He started as a pro wrestler at the age of 16, although he did play baseball in Ontario at the high school and college level. He said that he's hired a batting coach and has been doing baseball inspired workouts for conditioning rather than his former bodybuilding oriented weight training program for pro wrestling.

There have been a number of denials that the baseball comment had anything to do with the title change, and Elgin said it was something he was never told. Officially the company categorized the title change as a creative decision.

However, what actually happened showed it was, at the very least, the straw that broke the camel's back, among several reasons. Even though there was frustration on both sides, and the loss to Lee was last week, the plan was originally for Elgin to retain the title. When the Fritz interview ran, higher-ups were furious. While it felt like a throw away comment, the feeling was that he was booked to promote the company and the iPPV when doing the interview and instead acted like being world champion wasn't a big deal and wanted to play baseball. There were people in power who were furious at the interview. However, the only thing said within the company officially is that they had decided to change directions and no specific reason was given, but others have talked about the different reasons, which also included communications issues and the feeling that as champion, he was not as big a star as the Briscoes and Cole. Elgin thought he was going to have a long title reign, but people started realizing that the reign was likely to end at Final Battle. Elgin also said he was never told not to do a job while champion in the PWG tournament, while others have said that he should have known that a world champion with ROH shouldn't be doing jobs outside of ROH, let alone with non-ROH talent. It wasn't until after that interview that the sentiment changed toward taking the title from him the next day, which was then finalized by those above Hunter Johnston on 9/4, by the same people most upset about the interview

Elgin was given the advice to keep quiet and let everything blow over.

Briscoe's win, which came off as a big surprise to fans since nobody expected Elgin to lose the title in what is considered his home town, did not have the usual pageantry of an ROH title change. It didn't even end the show, as the decision was made well beforehand to end with the Kyle O'Reilly & Bobby Fish vs. Young Bucks two of three fall match with the feeling that nobody would be able to follow it.

The title run had been frustrating for Elgin. He wasn't strong with facial expressions or on promos, but could do a lot in the ring, in particular impressive power moves that always got over, and he always worked hard. He was not picked by New Japan for the Seibu Dome show when many of his peers were, even though he came in on his own dime to do a tryout. It appeared when he won the title that he was going to be booked for a major program with A.J. Styles, but with Styles winning the IWGP title, booking finishes for that program became an issue, as did the schedule of dates getting Styles, and it never materialized. He was following Cole as champion, and Cole carried himself better as champion. The change from Cole to Elgin was more because Cole had been champion and gone through most of the guys, and a title change would open up new title matches, as opposed to any negativity toward Cole.

Elgin also thought his reign as champion would go into next year, meaning he would go into the Tokyo Dome as ROH champion, and that would be another chance to prove himself to New Japan.

Whether the reasons for taking the title from him early were good or not, they ended up with the value of hindsight being unquestionably the right decision, and a lucky one.

After the show, Elgin was stopped trying to get across the border from Canada to the U.S. because he hadn't gotten his new visa paperwork finalized and the old visa had expired. Elgin, who lives in St. Louis, was headed to Cleveland, to work the next day for Absolute Intense Wrestling, where he held their championship. They were running three straight nights. Elgin had retained his AIW Absolute title on 9/4, doing a 60 minute draw with Josh Alexander and Tim Donst. He was to retain his title here, and then return to defend the title on 9/6. When he couldn't get across the border, it was announced at the AIW show that the title was vacated and Donst beat Alexander to win it.

Elgin was booked originally to lose the AIW title in a return three-way with Donst and Alexander on that show, likely with Donst pinning Alexander so Elgin didn't have to do the job.

To make things worse, Elgin brought a lot of stuff to Cleveland and kept it there since he was going to Toronto and coming back, and was unable to get his stuff out of Cleveland.

At press time, the belief is that he'll have to remain in Canada for 90 days, and live with family there. ROH is assisting Elgin in trying to get things sped up, but at this point he will be unavailable to work for the promotion until the Final Battle show in New York.

Elgin, real name Aaron Frobel, was aware of this, because he had, the prior week, canceled a 9/12 to 9/21 tour for Legend City Wrestling in Newfoundland and Labrador, telling the promotion that his paperwork was all tied up and if he did the tour, he may not be able to return to the U.S. In a letter to the promotion, he noted that he owned a home in the U.S., is married (to pro wrestler Rachel Collins Frobel, better known is MsChif) and told the promotion he had two dogs and was trying to start a family and couldn't risk not being allowed back.

The heat on Elgin from management was significant enough, after the interview and combined with the other factors, to where his future with the company was considered tenuous. The visa issue had nothing to do with the title change, as it was made before he was held up at the border, which happened after the show.

Elgin was given the advice to lay low, and those close to the situation said he probably wouldn't. He then wrote this on Facebook:

I want to start this by thanking friends that have reached out in this terrible time, but I want to rectify many claims that have been made. I am a very easy person to deal with. All I care about is things being done correctly. I'm in no shape or form saying that my way is correct or that I'm always right, but sometimes you need to find middle ground, which has obviously been an issue. Did I spent one minute of my time to say I wanted to try baseball? Yes. Was it intended to hurt ROH or show a lack of interest? Not at all. For 30 minutes prior I was speaking highly of ROH and the world title.

Like any interview, my main goal is to have people hear my beliefs of ROH, their history and their world title. I was never turning my back on wrestling, as it's been the only thing that's constant in my life since a very young age. I did play baseball in high school and college, so I wasn't just overhyped due to any situation. I have given my life and well being to wrestling so you can dislike me and jump on the `Let's Hate Elgin' bandwagon if you wish, but know the story. I wrestle hurt and risk my health because of my live and respect to wrestling and the men and women who came before me. I'm not going into more detail because then I'm whining.

Many issues have arose, and it could be easy to point fingers. I will say many things were a misunderstanding that led to recent happenings. If I'm at fault, I have no problem owning up and taking responsibility. But as for now, I will say claims, reports and opinions are very wrong and just rumors. I do hope that one day (sooner than later), things will be corrected and my name is restored.

I will admit I'm in Canada, very angry, disappointed and so many other feelings that I don't feel like going into detail about. I'm not asking for goodwill or handouts, but show some decency while you have no correct info.

All I know is, I am without my beautiful wife, our great pets and new house. We have two mortgages to pay and many other bills that my money is going toward. I have almost zero clothes and personal belongings. This is a more drastic situation than anyone could understand. To my family in St. Louis, I love and miss you. To Elgin supporters and haters alike, thank you for supporting wrestling because without you, I wouldn't be anywhere.

SEPTEMBER 22

Michael Elgin's situation has worsened. He's getting work on small indies in Ontario while he's stuck there. But the 90 day thing we were told for him to be able to return to the U.S. is now considered a best case scenario, but it's possible it could take longer. Elgin was really upset about it, being away from his wife, home, pets, etc. for three months. He's been added to some indie shows over this past weekend and the next few months in Canada.

OCTOBER 6

Michael Elgin is back in St. Louis. He managed to work things out and was able to return this past weekend, but he's not on any ROH bookings at this point and there are issues on both sides.

OCTOBER 13

What may have been Michael Elgin's first match back in the U.S. was on 10/4 in Alton, IL for St. Louis Anarchy Wrestling. His issues with ROH have been worked out at least to a degree, although there is an angle going on. He was being advertised on the 10/11 show in Kalamazoo. Then, hours later, he tweeted to ROH, "I said this on our call, thank you for getting me back home. But, an article doesn't fix lies and damage done. I QUIT." It is a angle, although a silly one given they just did a fake leaving the promotion and surprise return angle with Matt Taven. ROH then announced Elgin wasn't going to be there. What we can say is that when they announced he was, it wasn't working an angle at that moment. Elgin will instead be wrestling Jeremy Wyatt for Dynamo Pro

Wrestling in Glen Carbon, IL, on 10/11. When Elgin wasn't allowed to come back to the U.S. after the 9/6 show in Toronto due to visa issues, it was thought it would be 90 days minimum before he could return. ROH wrote on their web site that their legal counsel went to work on the problem and Elgin was able to return home this past week.

OCTOBER 20

Michael Elgin, who worked indies around his home in St. Louis this weekend rather than the ROH show, appeared before crowds of 68 on 10/11 and 45 on 10/12. It was described that he almost had a breakdown backstage on the second night in Belleville, IL, saying he deserved to have more people watching him.

NOVEMBER 3

Michael Elgin was in Lakeland, FL. They are doing an angle that is kind of similar to what TNA did with A.J. Styles in that in storyline they are working problems with the promotion, and in reality there are problems with the promotion. On the 11/1 TV show, Elgin comes out for an interview and ends up walking off. He doesn't appear to the best of my knowledge on the 11/8 show, and then on 11/15, he is scheduled for a match with Caprice Coleman. He refuses to wrestle, and then lays down to let Coleman beat him. Coleman didn't do so. Security then came out and eventually talked Elgin into leaving the ring. Elgin is not scheduled on the company's next two shows, 11/7 in Columbus, OH and 11/8 in Toledo. The angle is Elgin's idea and he's under contract for a few more months. At this point, he has no angle for Final Battle and he's not scheduled for a match on the show.

NOVEMBER 17

Even though Michael Elgin had tweeted about being left off the shows this past weekend, it was an angle as he did run-ins on both shows. He was positioned as a heel. In Toledo, he showed up during the main event, the Survival of the Fittest match to lead to the elimination of Tommaso Ciampa, so that's his likely direction. He'll likely continue in this role, not being advertised and showing up to heckle everyone and cost a babyface something. Elgin vs. Ciampa is talked about for Final Battle.

CHAPTER FORTY FIVE

UFC REHIRES THIAGO SILVA

SEPTEMBER 15

In perhaps the most shocking move the UFC has done in recent memory, Thiago Silva was brought back to the promotion on 9/5, one day after all charges against him in connection with a series of incidents from earlier this year were dropped.

Over the years, when it comes to business maneuvers, whether one would agree with UFC moves or not, I could always understand the rationale. But this one, I'm completely dumbfounded. MMA right now is reeling from bad publicity regarding two stories, the alleged domestic assaults by former UFC fighters War Machine, which was a major national news story, and Josh Grispi, which got significant regional coverage. So the timing of hiring back someone back whose past includes allegations, even if just dropped, that make it appear the company isn't completely against anything related to domestic abuse couldn't be worse, especially since the biggest story in sports right now involves Ray Rice knocking out his wife in an elevator.

In this case, UFC's decision was much like the deaths in pro wrestling, in the sense the company benefits by being largely below the major sports radar, and with the Rice case in the NFL and so much more extreme due to the visual being public, the initial coverage of the hiring of Silva was actually minimal, non-existent outside the MMA media and Deadspin. So the risk is more if another fighter has an issue and it becomes a story, then part of the story could be the UFC's decision here, or worse, if anything happens with Silva in any form.

Domestic violence is always a serious issue and when it goes to the level of police involvement, SWAT teams, and that night where innocent parties were scared to death in a gym, that's only making it worse.

But even throwing out the timing of Machine, Grispi and Rice, why anyone would think it's a good idea to hire Silva is something I can't comprehend. At best, it's a lightning rod for criticism by political enemies, as well as women's groups and others at a time the company doesn't need to give enemies any more fuel. At times UFC and White himself have been targeted based on statements and tweets from years back where they were probably ill-advised, and in cases with Tweets and interviews by fighters, bad judgment. They were things fighters were used to saying joking around with their friends, and not understanding you can't do that in social media. But while some statements were ill-advised, they were not inherently violent. The Rampage Jackson rape joke video was somebody's idea of comedy that wasn't funny in the real world. Not all jokes work. It was a really dumb thing, and UFC's enemies have used it to death on them. But in all cases when it came to talent, it was a situation where UFC wasn't aware of something until it hit. In some cases, the company took public action. In other cases, they took their lumps from enemies because the situations were overblown.

This is a completely different story. They know they have political enemies, who will pressure sponsors. They know the past, plus Silva has hardly had a sparkling track record with the company given two drug test failures and two previous lengthy suspensions during his tenure. They should know the current political environment. They are not the NFL, which is bullet proof. They are still a controversial second tier sport in the real world that doesn't have a tradition that will save them, and already have had past situations where they have either been threatened by sponsors or lost sponsors for incidents that could be argued pale in comparison to this.

This isn't Silva on their watch doing something and them having to react. This is Silva being fired, and then brought back, a decision they made, a few months later.

At worst, Silva does something else, and the company no longer has the excuse that they didn't know who he was or what he was, and nobody will accept the excuse that they had no idea about a certain person given the track record. It's one thing if this was a superstar the caliber of Jon Jones or Georges St-Pierre (or a better comparison perhaps is Floyd Mayweather Jr., or some would bring up Mike Tyson), because the rules for money players in all forms of sports or entertainment are different, and they will always get chance after chance.

It's not like Rampage Jackson, who in the latter case, they kept under circumstances that a lesser star may not have survived. And even in his case, whatever he did wasn't at this level either.

This is an above average fighter with no real name value, and you're guaranteeing some bad publicity due to timing and having enemies, and risking worse, with very little up side. And the company did get some bad publicity at first from the usual circles.

The UFC's argument is that the charges against Silva were dropped. The argument is if the system feels he is not a criminal, that UFC should allow him to earn a living fighting if he's a good enough fighter to compete at their level.

However, according to Broward County investigators, the reason the charges were dropped was because his wife, Thaysa, who now goes by the name Thaysa Kamiji (she went by the name Thaysa Kamiji Ramos da Silva, or shortened to Thaysa Silva earlier this year) was no longer cooperating with the investigators.

According to documents released by authorities, charges against Thiago Anderson Ramos de Silva for aggravated assault with a firearm, domestic battery, writing threats to kill or do bodily harm and resisting arrest without violence were dropped because the prosecutors stated that Thaysa officially divorced him in June, and moved back to Brazil on 7/4, thus was no longer cooperating with authorities to press charges. Without her in the picture testifying, a judge dropped all charges on 9/4.

Police were first called to the Oakland Park, FL, residence of Thiago and Thaysa Silva on 1/30, and described her as visibly shaken and sobbing uncontrollably when they arrived. Thaysa Silva, a highly ranked Brazilian Jiu Jitsu black belt who has competed at the world championship level, claimed that she and her husband had gotten into an argument. She claimed he accused her of having an affair with Pablo Popovitch, her Jiu Jitsu coach and the owner of Pablo Popovitch Mixed Marital Arts Academy in Oakland Park, near Fort Lauderdale. Popovitch, separated from his wife, later confirmed the two were romantically involved, but said Thiago and Thaysa had split up some time back and Thiago had already gotten a new girlfriend.

During the argument, Thaysa alleged that Thiago had picked up a silver colored revolver, pushed her onto the sofa, pointed it at her, and threatened to kill her.

She said she began screaming when he put his hand over her mouth, held her down and put the revolver inside of her mouth and threatened to pull the trigger. He didn't pull the trigger, however. She said that he then left the residence, and drove away. She told Broward County Sheriff's deputies that she was afraid he would kill her and filed for a protection order.

On 2/5, Thaysa Silva said she came home at 8:53 p.m. and Thiago was there. She told him to leave and told him she had a protective order against him. He told her that she was the one who needed to leave, but eventually, he left.

He then allegedly sent her a text message that stated, in Portuguese, "I am gonna fuck you up and you are going to die. I am going to hire someone to kill you and I am gonna move my girlfriend in."

According to the police report, on 2/6, at approximately 7:44 p.m., Thiago Silva showed up in his 2012 Dodge Charger in front of Popovitch's academy. Popovitch, Thaysa Silva and about two dozen other adult students were training in the gym at the time. He was honking his horn continuously, which led to Thaysa Silva going outside. She claimed she found him "extremely intoxicated."

She claimed he then pulled out a black pistol, pointed it at her, and told her that she had "ten seconds to bring Pablo outside, and if he doesn't come out, I will go in the gym and start shooting everyone."

Thaysa Silva signaled for Popovitch to come outside, while Thiago Silva continued to allegedly point the gun at his wife. Thiago Silva allegedly made death threats to Popovitch and Thaysa Silva. Both ran inside the academy, and he locked the front door and called police while Thiago Silva drove off.

Officers arrived at Thiago Silva's home. Silva allegedly gave them the middle finger and barricaded himself into the home. A SWAT team was called. After a lengthy standoff, they were able to convince him to come back outside. However, he did not listen to police commands, so a taser was used on Silva, claimed to be for officer safety reasons, and he was taken into custody at about 11:12 p.m. that night and booked into Broward County Jail.

Silva is a UFC quality fighter. Still, if we even compare UFC standards to those of WWE, there is not a chance that a similar level performer in WWE in the same situation gets hired back for a few years, if ever. They nearly fired someone, well did for a few hours, for petty shoplifting. Would TNA use that person then? Someone of that level of star, not a chance. So it's saying something when you're standards are lower than WWE and TNA.

"The truth is they didn't find no proof," said Silva on The MMA Hour. "I never pointed any gun at my ex-wife. I never tried to hurt (her). Everything she said was a lie. So that's the truth. The state, they couldn't prove another thing, so that's the truth. I'm just glad the truth came out. Trust me, they (UFC) knew I didn't do nothing, so they gave me my job back."

Silva claimed that he wanted a divorce and she wanted money from him that he didn't want to pay, so she lied and he claimed she set him up.

Silva spent 30 days in isolation while in jail because officers considered him dangerous to other inmates. He said he has had no contact with his ex-wife, and has no idea where she is.

Thiago Silva, 31, was a light heavyweight fighter in UFC with a 16-3 record with two no contests at the time of the incident. Both no contests were originally wins. The first was a January 1, 2001, win over Brandon Vera in Las Vegas, that was overturned when Silva attempted to use non-human urine in his sample after the fight. He later admitted using banned substances, claiming that he had suffered a severe back injury in training and was broke, and needed to use them to be able to get through camp and through the fight to get paid. The second was on November 10, 2012, when a quick submission win over Stanislav Nedkov in Macau, China, was overturned, when a UFC drug test came back positive for marijuana. In his last fight, on 10/9, in Barueri, Brazil, where he defeated Matt Hamill via decision, he missed weight by two pounds. At the time of his arrest, he was scheduled to face Ovince St. Preux at UFC 171, on 3/15 in Dallas.

Thaysa Silva spoke to the Brazilian web site UOL, who said that she had a good relationship with Thiago even after they broke up, but she believes cocaine was the reason for his change.

"We had a healthy relationship," she said. "We always talked, each one respected the other's space. He became (aggressive) over the past three weeks. I think that's the consequences of the use of cocaine."

But she said she had to deal with his aggression dating back years, saying she had never gone to the police because she feared his reaction. She said she decided to end her relationship because of his drug use.

"That's what ended the marriage. The problem was cocaine. He always thinks he's above the law. My neighbor knew that she should call the police if she ever heard me scream. He had the cocaine paranoia. He came to my house, tore my clothes and pointed a gun at my head. I already suffered some abuse. But I always withdrew because I was afraid."

Thiago Silva's lawyer, Scott Saul, who was with the fighter at his house when the SWAT team was there, told TMZ that the police went overboard.

"There was no allegation of harm against anyone," he said. "But they treated it like a terrorist threat."

Popovitch, on Facebook, wrote that he believed Thiago Silva was under the influence of alcohol or some kind of drug.

"Thaysa has been separated and living alone since December of 2012," he wrote. "Thiago has been charged with battery in the past and was seeing other girls and moving on with his own life. It's very unfortunate that this had to happen. The last thing I wanted was to see Thiago in this manner. I wish him all the best and hope this will soon be over."

At one point Silva was being charged with attempted murder, but that charge was thrown out because Silva never fired his gun at anyone at any point.

Thiago Silva grew up destitute in Sao Paulo, Brazil, running away from home due to an abusive father at 13, living in slums and drug trafficking hot spots. At 18, he began training in MMA. He debuted as a pro in 2005, winning eight straight fights in Brazil, seven via stoppage. Then, after knocking out Tatsuya Mizuno in a fight for Pancrase in Japan, he was signed by UFC, and debuted on May 26, 2007, with a win over James Irvin. His career started struggling due to painful back injuries that made it difficult to train.

He had increased his record to 13-0 when he was knocked out by Lyoto Machida on January 31, 2009, in Las Vegas, a fight moved back several months due to his injuries. He lost a decision to Rashad Evans on January 2, 2010, where his conditioning, being unable to follow up after hurting Evans at one point, played a factor, and he noted he had little training before the fight.

His troubles got worse. After needing a year off due to back injuries, he physically overpowered Vera for three rounds to take a decision on January 2, 2011. The win gave him a high-profile match with Quinton "Rampage" Jackson, but his urine sample came back from the Vera fight and showed no human hormones, meaning the sample was falsified.

Silva admitted before the Nevada State Athletic Commission of falsifying the sample, claiming his back went out 45 days before the fight, and he was broke because he hadn't fought for a year. He claimed he took injections of banned substances in his back and spine that allowed him to fight, and then used a product that he believed was a masking agent that would have prevented him from getting caught. He was suspended for one year, he was fined 25 percent of his purse. The result of the match was overturned to being a no contest.

Silva returned on March 6, 2012, losing a decision to Alexander Gustafsson in a main event in Stockholm, Sweden. He next submitted Nedkov on November 10, 2012, in Macao, China, but that decision was overturned because in a UFC drug test, he tested positive for marijuana, and he was suspended for six months. In 2013, he picked up a knockout win over Rafael Feijao and a one-sided decision win over Hamill, both in Brazil.

Thaysa Kamiji Silva, a black belt since 2007, was a gold medalist in 2012 in the Pan Am Jiu Jitsu No gi championships and a silver medalist in the World No gi championships that year in Los Angeles. Also from Sao Paulo, she met her husband while in college where she and some of her friends began training Jiu Jitsu.

At the time of the arrest, Dana White said, "This guy will never fight in the UFC again." In July, when Silva's name was brought up, White said again that he would never fight in UFC again.

"When this thing went down, I said he'd never fight in the UFC again," said White after bringing him back in an article on the UFC web site. "When I watched it unfold on TV and heard of the charges, it didn't look good for Thiago Silva. But he was acquitted of all charges. How do you not let the guy fight again?"

"He went through the legal process and came out of it untainted," said White. "He deserves to be able to make a living again. He's back under contract."

The problem is that if evidence had come out that exonerated him, it would be one thing. But charges were dropped, according to police, because his wife was gone. He was exonerated from a legal standpoint, but it's not like the incident at the gym never happened as there were two dozen witnesses, nor the SWAT team incident. But, it can be argued in his defense, all charges from those incidences were also dropped. But there is no up side in bringing him back, both from the potential of a public relations problem not only now, but even more, should any fighter under contract, let alone Silva himself, do something bad that garners publicity and part of the narrative is that this is a company that rehired Silva.

Silva is expected to fight again around January, or perhaps a little later, as he's currently doing rehab on his knee after tearing his ACL.

SEPTEMBER 29

It only took two weeks for Thiago Silva to make the UFC look bad in hiring him back. His ex-wife, Thaysa Kamiji, posted videos of Silva with a gun and other embarrassing videos, as well as made a statement that she left the country and moved to Abu Dhabi with new boyfriend Pablo Popovitch because she feared for her safety. The video came out the same day as Roger Goodell's speech and UFC couldn't afford to appear soft on domestic abuse so he was fired on 9/19. That same day they placed Anthony Johnson, who was one of the company's rising stars and one of the top four light heavyweights in the company, on an indefinite suspension. This came after Bloodyelbow.com reported that the mother of two of his children made a statement that Johnson had knocked out two of her teeth in 2012, but at the time she didn't press charges. The alleged victim went to the police again on 9/5, claiming she was scared of Johnson, who is the father of her children. She claimed Johnson went to her house and took her dog on 8/24. She also claimed she got phone calls and text messages from unknown males threatening her. She said those didn't come from Johnson, but she think it's from his friends. She said the 2012 alleged incident was captured on a security videotape, which she has in her possession, saying it took place at a supplement store that she was at the time working at. She said Johnson talked her out of pressing charges at the time. Johnson said that it sucked being accused of something that he didn't do, and in time, he'd be able to prove it. UFC said they were suspending Johnson pending completion of an investigation of the matter by a third party law firm. Johnson had a prior arrest in 2009 for domestic violence on another woman who he was dating, and pleaded no contest the next year to misdemeanor domestic violence and given three years probation. Johnson claimed on Facebook that the whole thing was a series of lies.

CHAPTER FORTY SIX

THE BIGGEST MATCH IN MEXICAN WRESTLING HISTORY

SEPTEMBER 15

After years of building, what is being pushed in some media circles in Mexico as the biggest match in the history of pro wrestling in Mexico, Atlantis vs. Ultimo Guerrero, in a mask vs. mask match, headlines the 81st anniversary of pro wrestling in Mexico on 9/19 at Arena Mexico.

This is the second year in a row that the two wrestlers will combine to headline the company's biggest show and perhaps set the company's all-time gate record. Last year, they did a swerve as they had spent all year building the match up. However, at the last minute, it was announced that the company's other hottest feud, that between La Sombra and Volador Jr., would be part of the equation. Last year's 80th anniversary show had Sombra & Volador Jr. facing Atlantis & Guerrero, and the winning team would get to headline the show and do the mask match. The 17,000 fans who paid $700,000, expected to see Atlantis vs. Guerrero. Instead, it was Sombra & Volador Jr., who won the match and had the mask match. It was a high flying spectacle of outrageous proportions, but the crowd was chanting "Fraud," for much of the second half of the show, because, even though it was a far superior match to what they would have gotten, this was not the main event they expected or wanted. The match left a bitter taste in fans' mouths. Whether that will hurt this year remains to be seen but there is talk that the advance at this point is not at the level the company had hoped it would be. Historically CMLL business is hurt when high ticket price outside shows come to town, and the UFC and WWE both have events on sale, and AAA just had a high ticket priced event also in the market. While UFC isn't until November, they sold 20,000 tickets in the market in recent weeks.

They probably needed to wait close to a year to give the match because of the bad taste left. Atlantis, 51, a Hall of Famer, has been one of the top names in Lucha Libre since breaking out as the top high flyer of his time in the late 1980s television boom period. Atlantis, Octagon, Konnan, Dandy and Rayo de Jalisco Jr., were the original group of superstars who endured because they were CMLL's biggest stars when wrestling returned to television in Mexico City after it was banned from TV since the 50s.

Atlantis remained a main eventer, but as he got older, he was just one of the masked men in the crowd. His career was revitalized in 2005, when he turned heel and formed Los Guerreros de la Atlantida, a tag team with Ultimo Guerrero. Atlantis turning was a complete shock since he was a white-masked babyface who it was figured, like Octagon, Mistico or El Hijo del Santo, would never turn. Unlike the other three, all of whom did turn and for the most part, the turns flopped about as bad as the times WCW tried to turn Sting, Atlantis had great success, having a long heel run, lasting six years. In 2011, he turned back and started feuding with Guerrero, and the two have been each other's key dance partner for more than three years.

The match will be basically the 30th anniversary of his coming out party, when 21-year-old Atlantis beat Talisman before 18,000 fans at the 1984 Anniversary show in a mask vs. mask match. Since 1984, he has retained his mask 16 times, including one of the biggest matches in the history of Lucha Libre in 2000 when he beat Villano III in a mask vs. mask match, the only match from Mexico ever to win the Observer's Match of the Year award. This is also Atlantis' 10th anniversary show main event, which is probably the equivalent of being in the true main event at WrestleMania or the Tokyo Dome on ten occasions. Only El Santo, with 12, has headlined more anniversary events.

Guerrero, 42, has an interesting story in getting here. In 1997, he was supposed to lose his mask while working for Promo Azteca, but quit the promotion to join CMLL. By never losing his mask, he's in the position to headline a huge match 17 years later with it at stake.

While some have talked of this as being the biggest match ever, in Mexico, the 1952 match where El Santo beat Black Shadow for his mask at Arena Coliseo is almost always considered the biggest match in Mexican wrestling history. Other matches considered at near that level were Rayo de Jalisco Jr. vs. Cien Caras mask vs. mask in 1990, Konnan's mask vs. Perro Aguayo's hair in 1991, Konnan vs. Caras retirement in 1993 (which sold out the 50,000-seat Plaza Mexico) and Atlantis vs. Villano III.

SEPTEMBER 29

In what in many ways was the single most historically significant moment at a wrestling show of the year, Atlantis defeated Ultimo Guerrero in their mask vs. mask match, drawing what was reported to be the largest gate ever for Lucha Libre.

More than 17,000 fans, a standing room only crowd, paid in excess of $1 million, for CMLL's 81st anniversary show at Arena Mexico in Mexico City. In doing so, CMLL has become only the second promotion ever to run in the North, South or Central America (WWE obviously being the other) to ever draw a $1 million gate. WCW fell short of that figure even for its biggest stadium shows in 1998.

Reports were that the most expensive seats were filled with older and more affluent fans who came back for nostalgia purposes to see what is likely the end of an era. Atlantis' mask is considered among the most valuable in history and he's been a headliner for the promotion for more than 30 years. He headlined the biggest show of the year for the first time on September 23, 1984, when he sold the arena out, defeating Talisman in a mask vs. mask match. His mask was also at stake as the key drawing point on Anniversary shows in 1989, 1993, 2010 and 2013.

The gate record broke the previous mark of $900,000, set at the 80th anniversary show on September 13, 2013. While the final match was La Sombra vs. Volador Jr. in a mask vs. mask match, it was Atlantis and Ultimo Guerrero who drew the house. The entire year was built up toward their mask vs. mask match, but at the anniversary show, it was announced there would be a tag match where the rivals, Atlantis & Guerrero and Sombra & Volador Jr., would meet in a tag match, with the winners being put in the main event with the mask at stake. Everyone came to see Atlantis vs. Guerrero. And even though Sombra vs. Volador Jr., ended up being one of the most spectacular high flying matches you'll ever see, the older crowd hated it, booing it and chanting "fraud," because it was not what they came to see.

Obviously the promotion knew it had one match that it could charge high ticket prices for and set a record with, so they worked out a way to get two gates in successive years out of it. This year, fans were told, over and over, that it was a singles match and somebody was losing their mask.

There were more people in the building than last year, even though it was raining heavily the afternoon and evening of the show. Lots of the CMLL wrestlers who weren't booked on the show, came anyway, because they wanted to see the main event.

Like last year, the impact of the match made it seem like, at least for one night, that CMLL was the hottest promotion in the world. But this was the end of the journey, not the beginning. Atlantis has been wrestling for the promotion consecutively since 1983. While Negro Casas is almost three years older and is still going strong, he was a star in the 80s for the rival UWA, and doesn't have a mask. Due to that tenure, which has included ten times as a headliner on the promotions's biggest show of the year (second in history behind El Santo, with 12 anniversary main events), his mask was the most valuable entity in the promotion. At this stage of the game, he is never going to have a rival like Guerrero, who he worked against for years, then teamed with from 2005 to 2011 as a heel. When Atlantis did his inevitable turn back, it was to culminate in a mask vs. mask match that had been built up for three years.

Jose Gutierrez Hernandez, his rival, started wrestling in 1990, and became Ultimo Guerrero in 1996. He was supposed to lose his mask in 1997 while wrestling for the Promo Azteca promotion, but quit the promotion before his big match to join CMLL. Ultimo Guerrero & Rey Bucanero became the promotion's top tag team for years, and are generally considered as one of the four greatest tag teams in Lucha Libre history, along with Rene Guajardo & Karloff Lagarde, El Santo & Gori Guerrero (the father of Eddy Guerrero) and Angel Blanco & Dr. Wagner.

The match more than served its purpose, which was one of those larger-than-life moments that wrestling rarely has but everyone in the building is well aware they are part of it. Before the first match, when the lineup was being announced, fans went crazy when the main event was announced.

The post-match, after Atlantis got the third fall submission with his Atlantida, better known as the torture rack or the Argentinean backbreaker, was the most emotional and most gripping moment in wrestling in years. Guerrero removed his mask, while the camera would shift to his family at ringside, crying rivers, and they weren't the only ones. He announced his name, said he was 42 years old, from Gomez Palacio in the state of Durango and had been wrestling for 26 years. His face, exposed for the first time, was covered in tears, which led to tears from most of the female fans, and some of the male fans in the crowd. Guerrero handed Atlantis his mask. Atlantis on the mic said that he defeated a great warrior, and of all his career victories, he would keep this mask in a special place. Guerrero's father came into the ring to hug him.

The closest thing to this scene would have been Undertaker losing to Brock Lesnar. That was more of a shock. Everyone expected Undertaker to win. Here, fans didn't know, and were split in expectations, with the older fans generally thinking Atlantis would win, since he always has in the big matches, while younger fans expected Guerrero to win, figuring he's younger, has more in the tank for the future, and Atlantis, a week before his 52nd birthday, had to be on the way out. That was more of a shock, but this was more emotional. As far as the post-match went, with the fans crying and the families of both men being shown, this felt much bigger, although it felt no bigger than in 2000, when Atlantis unmasked Villano III. That was the most recent match that would be a good comparison for this one.

The ring was showered with people throwing in money at the end. Even 30 minutes after the match had ended, there were still fans lined up to hand money to the wrestlers. Given the gate, the belief is that Guerrero would have received the largest one day payoff in the history of Lucha Libre.

The show got heavy mainstream media coverage in Mexico. It was not the lead story for the night in the sports newspapers, but it did make some covers. The media coverage was very respectful, stating that Lucha Libre may be a spectacle, but for one night, it was very serious sport.

But the feud must continue. Two nights later, at Arena Coliseo, which drew an above usual Sunday crowd of 3,300, at higher than usual ticket prices since it was the first show Guerrero would wrestle without his mask, Atlantis & Valiente & Volador Jr. headlined against Guerrero & Rey Escorpion & Mephisto. Guerrero tore up an Atlantis mask a fan was wearing at ringside. In the third fall, Guerrero gave Atlantis a low blow and pulled his mask off for a disqualification. Volador Jr. went to a fan at ringside to get an Atlantis mask so he could hide his identity, but Guerrero destroyed that mask. The faces got Atlantis another match, to protect his identity. Guerrero, left, furious that he couldn't expose his rivals' face. Still, the crowd was super behind Guerrero because of the sympathy of the unmasking and there was a vibe from the crowd that they would rather see them team than continue to feud. The only thing left in the feud would be Guerrero putting up his hair against Atlantis' mask, which would be a story, but also anti-climactic.

CHAPTER FORTY SEVEN

THE ROCK TEASES WRESTLEMANIA MATCH

OCTOBER 13

The Rock, in an interview taped backstage on 10/6 at Raw and airing on the Smackdown 15th anniversary show on 10/10, teased the idea of a WrestleMania match with HHH on 3/29 at Levi's Stadium in Santa Clara.

The match will be first teased at the start of Smackdown, when Stephanie McMahon, appearing live, talked about how Rock was the one who came up with the term "Smackdown," that became the name of the show, but how her husband, HHH had beaten The Rock before.

During Smackdown, a backstage vignette aired with Rock, HHH and Stephanie. They talked about the first episode of Smackdown (actually it was the second episode because the show debuted on April 29, 1999 with a single episode show before it became a regular series on UPN in the fall). But WWE history has forgotten that first episode so the second episode, main evented by Rock vs. HHH, has become the first-ever Smackdown main event. HHH beat Rock in that match, which HHH brought up. Rock brought up that he gave HHH a rock bottom through the table. They brought up different matches from their past, some of which Rock won and some of which HHH won. Rock then brought up that he would win if they wrestled in the main event at WrestleMania this year. WWE isn't going to tease something in that direction if it's not the planned direction.

Rock had said in the past that he didn't want to wrestle again unless it would be a record setting show, and as big or bigger than his two matches with John Cena. The first was the highest grossing PPV event in pro wrestling history and the second was the largest gate in history. Levi's Stadium is not going to be able to beat the MetLife Stadium gate unless they significantly increase ticket prices, because the East Rutherford, NJ, stadium has 14,000 more seats. But Rock appearing would theoretically be a strong boost for last week network sales.

Rock vs. HHH had been talked about for WrestleMania at the Superdome. The original idea for the Superdome show main event was Steve Austin vs. HHH, with Vince McMahon coming back as a babyface character feuding with Stephanie and HHH, in a match for control of the company. Before that, the idea was Rock vs. Brock Lesnar as one of the main events. The idea was that Vince would go to his all-time greatest rival and the man he considered the greatest wrestler in company history, Austin, to save the company for him. That never happened. Austin was never on board for that angle and Rock was the second choice. As it turned out, Rock opted out of doing WrestleMania, and the decision was made not to bring Vince back as a television character, so none of this happened.

HHH vs. Dave Batista had been talked about for Mania this year, in what would be Batista's retirement program. With the way the angle went on TV, that doesn't look like it's going to happen.

The segment included HHH saying if they were to wrestle again, that he'd win. Rock made fun of HHH's entrance music and said he'd win. They went back and forth, with HHH saying he whipped Rock's ass every time they wrestled. Rock said that would never happen this year. They went face-to-face, and then did comedy, but neither would back down. HHH said that Rock was setting him up for an "it doesn't matter" line. They ended up breaking the tension, but ending it with both vowing that if they were to wrestle, they would be the one winning.

Rock made a surprise appearance on Raw the night before in Brooklyn. It was kept a surprise from most. The script had a Big Show segment. The announcers, who were told that they were pitching to a segment with Big Show in sensitivity training. That segment was plugged earlier in the show. When Rock's music played, Lawler noted, not on the air, that he thought Show was coming out dressed like The Rock.

With nobody knowing about his return, although there were rumors that day since it was known he was in New York. The Raw rating (2.63) was the lowest non-holiday rating so far this year, and among the lowest in the last 17 years. In 2011, when Rock returned for his program with John Cena, which headlined three straight WrestleManias (two matches and once as referee for Cena's match), his debut was a surprise and didn't draw a good rating either. But week two, after the news had broke, was a 3.8. But it was made clear at the time he'd be back on week two. Rock isn't being advertised for Atlanta on 10/13 or for any shows.

Rock's return angle was interrupting a promo by Rusev, and eventually, being threatened by him, not backing down, throwing the first punch and knocking him out of the ring. On Smackdown, Lana did an interview and mentioned getting back at Rock, so in some form that doesn't appear to be a one-and-done situation.

The Fast & Furious 7, which The Rock is one of the stars in, will be released on 4/3, which is the weekend after Mania. It'll make the schedule tight in the sense he usually goes all over the world to promote his movie releases. But it's not something from a schedule standpoint he hasn't done before.

There may be a nostalgia factor besides the pure business factor for Rock returning for this year's show. He was born in 1972, in Hayward, about 29 miles from the new stadium. His first wrestling matches he attended, likely before he even has memories of them, were in places like the Cow Palace in San Francisco and the San Jose Civic Auditorium, where his father and grandfather often teamed up, many times with his mentor, Pat Patterson. If nothing else, even though it can't possibly come near the gross revenue of the 2012 or 2013 shows because the economics are different, it could and probably should be the most widely viewed Mania in North America of all-time because of the low network price point.

But it's a risk. Rock suffered a hamstring injury in his first match with Cena, and a series of injuries including a torn abdominal muscle in the second match, which required surgery, and forced the hold-up of filming of "Hercules." Studios that may want a project for him in the spring or summer can't be happy if he does do Mania, given the fear of injury.

Reports this week was that the company was starting to finalize its WrestleMania plans and that included two special stars, the other one likely to be Sting. Sting had wanted to face Undertaker. Undertaker lost this year with the idea it was probably his last match, and that was before suffering a concussion early in the match and ending up in the hospital. The last word he had told people, and this is months back, was that he didn't expect to be back. But that's often the word in the early fall, and it's been years since he's missed a Mania. Sting's second choice was HHH, who now looks taken. Hulk Hogan has pushed for a match with Cena. If he's willing, and can pass the physical, they could do a retirement match. Hogan hasn't wrestled at a WrestleMania since 2003 and will be almost 61 at match time, so if he can't do it this year, that should be it. Still, Sting has indicated that, while not putting a limitation on himself, he is looking at doing one last match, as he'll turn 56 the week of the show. Hogan and Sting retiring together could be a hook, but they would be better separately.

It is believed the other main event is still set up as Brock Lesnar vs. Roman Reigns for the WWE title. It's unclear if Rusev is being groomed for Cena, but that was also something that had been talked about. It's impossible to know right now how hot the Reigns chase will be, or if they'll change directions and go with Dean

Ambrose. It's also unclear how Daniel Bryan fits into this, which, like this past year, depends a lot more on the fans pushing his position.

Lesnar is scheduled back on TV in January to build for his next match, a title defense, likely against Cena, at the Rumble, which takes place on 1/25 in Philadelphia. If they are going with Cena vs. Rusev, or whatever direction they are taking Cena, the person he's going with would make sense as the guy to cost him the title. There is the element of predictability in all this, but historically, when it comes to Mania booking, they go with the straight forward, feeling that's the best thing for business, whether some fans can figure it out ahead of time or not.

OCTOBER 20

Regarding Dwayne Johnson and WrestleMania, he was walking around New York when the TMZ cameras showed up (funny how those things happen) and asked. He gave a clear tongue in cheek answer saying, "I don't think so. I might get hit in the mouth. I don't want that."

CHAPTER FORTY EIGHT

BILLY JACK HAYNES
SUES WWE

NOVEMBER 3

80s star Billy Jack Haynes (William Albert Haynes III), 61, filed a 42-page lawsuit on 10/23 in U.S. District Court in Portland, OR, citing egregious mistreatment of its wrestlers for its own benefit, as well as concealment and denial of medical research and evidence concerning traumatic brain injuries suffered by WWE wrestlers.

It's almost a lock that lawsuits like this will be filed in every sport with head blows, after the NFL's settlement with its players. The lawyers for Haynes are trying to make it a similar class action suit, asking for in excess of $5 million, and attempting to round up wrestlers to join in. They are asking for damages in an amount to be determined at trial, attorneys' fees, compensatory and punitive damages, complete costs of the lawsuit and pre- and post-judgment interest on any such awards.

In August, 2013, the NFL settled a lawsuit filed by more than 4,500 former players, representing 18,000 players, for $765 million. There were arguments that the NFL got off cheap. Awards would be capped at $5 million for those with Alzheimer's, $4 million for those diagnosed after their death with chronic traumatic encephalopathy (CTE), and $3 million for players with dementia. With WWE, it will be interesting to see if others join in.

A similar lawsuit was filed last November by ten former NHL players, claiming the league purposefully concealed the risks of brain injuries and exposed players to unnecessary dangers they could have avoided, and that the league refused to ban fighting.

The fact it is Haynes, whose credibility could prove to be a major issue because of outlandish statements he's made in the past, such as once claiming in an interview that Vince McMahon was the father of Chris Benoit's son David, hurts him bad in being the point man in this specific case.

One lawyer noted to us this may not be as bad as it sounds on the surface, noting if he was handling the case, he would use those outlandish statements as evidence his brain has been scrambled. He said the wacky statements could only be used to attack his credibilty if it can be proven he knew they were false whe he said them. The claim was that in deposition, if he truly believed his statements, then it can't be used against him at all in trial because it's irrelevant to the issue of the case. But it can be used against him if he knew they were false when he said it.

Still, Haynes being point man hurts in getting other wrestlers to join in. There is something already up on the Internet similar to the class action suit ads you see on television for other wrestlers who have suffered injuries or cognitive damage to join this suit as a plaintiff.

The case got immediate attention in Haynes' home area, with an article in the Portland Tribune and other media coverage. Billy Jack Haynes was probably the top babyface in the Oregon territory during the 80s, after the departure of Roddy Piper. He had a very checkered career, promoting against Don Owen, begging for his job back, and making frequent comebacks and leaving, as well as making some crazy claims about the business and people in the business after his career was over.

WWE's rep when it comes to these things is usually to fight and not settle, although at times, when necessary, there have been quiet settlements of lawsuits. But this may be a case where they take the former because a settlement with Haynes would open the floodgates for every wrestler who the company doesn't have under contract from the last 30 years.

The lawsuit claims that WWE has "subjected its wrestlers to extreme physical brutality that it knew, or should have known, caused long-term irreversible bodily damage including brain damage." It also states, "For most of its history, WWE has engaged in a campaign of misinformation and deception to prevent its wrestlers from understanding the true nature and consequences of the injuries they have sustained. WWE's representations, actions and inactions have caused its wrestlers to suffer from death, long-term debilitating injuries, lost profits, premature retirement, medical expenses, and other losses as alleged herein."

"Billy Jack Haynes performed for WWE from 1986-1988," said Brian Flinn, WWE's Senior Vice President of Marketing and Communications. "His filed lawsuit alleges that WWE concealed medical information and evidence on concussions during that time, which is impossible since the condition now called chronic traumatic encephalopathy (CTE) had not even been discovered. WWE was well ahead of sports organizations in implementing concussion management procedures and policies as a precautionary measure as the science and research on this issue emerged. Current WWE procedures include ImPACT testing for brain function, annual educational seminars and the strict prohibition of deliberate and direct shots to the head. Additionally, WWE has committed significant funding for concussion research conducted by the Sports Legacy Institute (SLI), leaders in concussion research, and WWE Executive Vice President Paul Levesque sits on SLI's Board."

The key to the NFL lawsuit was that there was evidence the league misrepresented medical information and outright denied any reasonable connection between the game and long-term health consequence. There was evidence that officials misled and misinformed players concerning already known health consequences of head trauma and there were top NFL officials on record saying there was no relationship.

WWE did at first fight and deny the evidence of the SLI after they had examined the brain of Chris Benoit, and Chris Nowinski was a strong critic of WWE, particularly after the death of Lance McNaught (Lance Cade). But in time, WWE ended up changing direction to the point they are economic supporters of the groups and Levesque is on their board.

The NFL case also had a major name like Mike Webster, who had passed away, to build around, as well as a current name like Junior Seau. As noted, Billy Jack Haynes is not the person as the front person and appears on the surface to be a weak link that has a good chance of causing this specific case to go nowhere.

The lawsuit notes that with the wrestlers labeled as independent contractors, they are not provided with health insurance, disability insurance or unemployment insurance. WWE today requires all of its wrestlers to have independent health insurance, and also covers costs for all injuries suffered in the ring and provides drug and alcohol rehabilitation for any wrestler who has ever been under contract to the promotion.

Haynes wrestled full-time from the summer of 1982 through early 1988, and irregularly through 1995, with a few shots here and there after that point.

A key aspect of the case is that Haynes only worked a relatively short period of time in his career with WWE, a two week period in 1984, where he came, got a big push, and quit, and as a regular from June 1986 to early February 1988. At that point he quit the promotion, and started promoting on his own against Don Owen. His promotion started in May 1988, but was done within a few months and he lost a lot of money on the venture. He was not popular with a lot of the Oregon wrestlers, both those who left Owen to work with him and he closed down quickly leaving them without work and it took a while before the bridge was repaired to return in most cases. Those who didn't felt Owen gave Haynes a break in making him the company's top star when he was only a few months into the business. He also turned on the Owen promotion to the athletic commission, leading to a lot of trouble for a promotion that was struggling to survive in the days of dying regionals.

It would be difficult, when it comes to his health issues, to specifically isolate WWF, since his matches, mostly in Oregon were bloodier and more violent. Although a lawyer looking at this also said that shouldn't matter if he can show evidence of concussions in his WWF tenure. Haynes also worked for a number of regional offices, starting his career with Stampede Wrestling, where he was first trained, and also working in Florida, World Class, Jarrett Promotions, WCW (as Black Blood), AAA and New Japan Pro Wrestling. He also did some boxing, had several street fights and other non-wrestling situations where he suffered significant physical punishment.

In early 2006, it was reported that Haynes was beaten up by two people with brass knuckles outside a body shop in Portland. Years later, Haynes claimed the attack was because he was skimming off the top while being a mule in what he thought was a marijuana smuggling ring. He skimmed, he claimed, because he thought he was being underpaid and lied to, when he found out he was smuggling cocaine and not marijuana. Haynes said he was attacked again in 2007 and an unknown perpetrator stabbed him in the face, breaking his orbital bone in his right eye, which now hangs.

Haynes was an outspoken critic of the WWE and Hulk Hogan in 1992, after being fairly close with Hogan and teaming with him many times during his WWF run. One of the reasons was an incident that he was furious with WWF is that he drove from Portland to San Antonio because he was told they were interested in bringing him back and he was getting a tryout to return. It should have sounded suspicious, in the sense Haynes was a well-known commodity with the physical presence that got over in that era, even though he was marginal inside the ring. When he got to San Antonio, there was no tryout and nobody knew what he was talking about. He felt humiliated and furious that the company would do that to him. Years later he claimed he found out it wasn't the WWF office that called him, but it was a practical joke set up by one of their wrestlers, Brian Adams.

That would be the case with almost any wrestler who would join in on the suit, as virtually nobody from that era worked their entire career in WWE. At the same time, that would also hold true for the NFL and NHL, as virtually every player on an NFL roster played football for years at the high school and college level, and in the NHL, at the junior and minor league level. It is impossible to pinpoint the time frame of damage, which probably includes everything before, during and after. In addition, CTE thus far can only be detected in people who pass away, although there are a number of older wrestlers who have had issues with dementia, scarily common really among older pro wrestlers that worked in the past, and I worry more about the future, because those wrestlers did not take the level of head jarring blows that the guys in the 90s were taking.

In the lawsuit, Haynes claimed he wrestled for WWF with little time off and no off-season. He claimed he suffered 15 concussions during his career, and a myriad of other injuries. He claimed he used drugs to manage to pain and contracted Hepatitis C from wrestling and took numerous blows to the head from chairs, chains and other weapons.

He stated that "as a result of the head trauma he sustained while wrestling in WWE, Haynes suffers from depression and exhibits symptoms of dementia."

In 2013, Haynes was hospitalized with an aortic aneurysm and liver and kidney issues.

Hayes asked the company to establish a trust fund to pay for medical monitoring of all wrestlers as frequently as determined to be medically necessary, and "to pay to develop and research other methods by which the risks of those affected can be reduced."

It also asks that the company provide information to treating physicians to aid them in detecting such injuries.

The lawsuit noted significant injuries suffered as a direct result of WWE matches and that during the course of a career, "WWE wrestlers sustain countless blows to their head, both concussive and sub-concussive. These blows alter wrestlers' brains. This, in turn, results in an array of side effects, including depression, cognitive deterioration and suicide. Though aspects of the disorders caused by repeated head trauma continue to come to light, the debilitating effects of receiving repeated blows to the head have long been known."

It also blamed WWE, and its doctors, for not stopping matches when wrestlers have sustained head injuries, and made claims they have negligently or purposely failed to diagnose concussions.

The lawsuit cited WWE performers using chair shots to the head (currently banned), including using a photo of Vince McMahon hitting someone with a chair to the head. It brought up the 1999 match with Dwayne Johnson vs. Mick Foley from the movie "Beyond the Mat," and the 2008 chair shots delivered by Michael Hickenbottom (Shawn Michaels) on Lance McNaught (Lance Cade), and the company auctioning off the chair, as well as a WWE web site article on memorable chair shot attacks, and that even though the company bans such moves, they still promote clips of chair shots to the head in a WWE Network promotion.

It said that WWE ignored mounting research and has continued to allow and even encourage repeated blows to the head with and without weapons. The problem with that point is in court, when jurors are told the blows are not meant to hurt anyone if former or current wrestlers testify for WWE, how will the jury take it? But a lawyer said one could cross examine wrestlers and ask that since the blows aren't meant to hurt people, that nobody ever gets hurt and the wrestler either says no, people do get hurt, or he says yes, they don't, and then a smart lawyer would shred his credibility with endless in-ring injury examples.

It noted that WWE did not test its wrestlers for blood transmitted diseases before allowing them to wrestle, even when WWE required wrestlers to cut themselves. While WWE has banned blood in matches since 2008 and has banned blading on-and-off, depending on the time period and Vince McMahon's feelings at the time, there were times when blood was used before WWE had the extensive medical program it now has.

They went after Stephanie McMahon's 2007 testimony before the U.S. House of Representatives Committee on Oversight and Governmental Reform where she claimed there was not one documented concussion in WWE history, which was one of the sillier things to say, noting she made this shortly after Candice Michelle was knocked out in a match and instead of the match being stopped, she was dragged to the center of the ring. That match, on live television, caused a change in protocol. They also brought up Undertaker suffering a concussion in a 2010 match with Rey Mysterio but the match continued until its scripted end. While not listed, the same could be said for this past year's WrestleMania match with Undertaker and Brock Lesnar, where Undertaker suffered a concussion early and the match continued until its planned finish. The question in both cases is that there was no diagnosis until after the match. We've never seen an incident where somebody has gotten knocked out in a match and it's called immediately, which, in theory, is the case in combat sports.

They also claimed that erasing Chris Benoit from history was to cover up the link between Benoit's death and brain damage suffered, although clearly that was not the reason. Vince McMahon decreed that Benoit would never be shown or talked about again on WWE television within days after his death, because of the belief that he had killed his wife and son, before any findings came out as to Benoit's history of concussions.

The claim that WWE knew or should have known about research on concussions that dated back decades and that dating back to 2001, neurological experts recommended that athletes who suffer concussions should sit it out and 2006 research that someone suffering a concussion should never return to the game. Here's the deal. It doesn't matter what year it was, whether it was 1972 or 1992, it was always well known that taking full force shots to the head with chairs was not a good thing. Different promotions had different standards regarding killer chair shots to the head. They were done infrequently in most places, perhaps frequently in some, and never in some, until the 90s, where they became a lot more common throughout wrestling, from the biggest major leagues to smallest indies.

The claim is the rampant steroid use in pro wrestling increases tolerance to pain and thus those on steroids are more likely to wrestle through head injuries, and WWE, by encouraging use, increased the likelihood its wrestlers will hurt themselves and each other. The claim is WWE concealed or failed to acknowledge research concerning the risks of head trauma, has down played the injuries suffered by wrestlers and denied that WWE wrestlers have suffered or are at risk of suffering concussions and long term brain damage. The concealed research was the point that forced the NFL settlement and was also where, in the past, companies such as UFC, WWE and other sports leagues felt they were not in danger of similar lawsuits because of the belief they never concealed the results of research.

The lawsuit claimed that in 2006, following the steroid-related death of a high profile wrestler (Eddy Guerrero), the WWE put its Wellness policy in place and when implemented, 40 percent of the wrestlers tested positive for steroids. I don't recall that, but do remember that it was just about 50 percent who tested positive the first time WWF did steroid testing in late 1991, and that was after months of wrestlers being given advance warning tests were coming.

It noted Haynes wrestled without an off-season or down time and on average had 26 or 27 matches a month and at one point he had matches on 97 days in a row. While there are not complete records available (although close to complete records are), based on incomplete records, there were maybe four months during his WWE run where he came close to that number and I'm very skeptical if at any point he worked 97 straight days. His toughest schedule was Christmas 1986 through WrestleMania 1987, and he worked a minimum of 67 matches in 95 days, and there are likely another dozen or so with no records during that time frame. But even then, he didn't work New Year's Eve, and there were no shows the few days before Mania, and they took time off before Christmas and before WrestleMania.

In another way of looking at it, if you look at the schedule, when he was when he had an off day, and noting at the time, the company flew you to your shows but didn't fly you home, it's not that much of a stretch. On his rare days off during that run, mostly on the East Coast, it made no sense to pay to fly to Portland, OR, for a day, and then fly back. Even then, the idea he wasn't home for 97 days (in which sense the 97 straight days on the road could be not as big of a stretch as it sounds even though there were days off) is a little much. But he very well could have not been home between leaving on December 24, 1986 for a Christmas show in Detroit and coming home March 18, 1987, after a show the night before at the Cow Palace in San Francisco. That's 85 days, and that will drive most people insane. But putting that 97 figure in the lawsuit when it wasn't even necessary and doesn't appear to be true doesn't help the case.

They said during his time with the promotion, Haynes was perpetually exhausted and thus more susceptible to injury and to injuring others. The claim was that Haynes was pressured by WWE to wrestle through head injuries and other injuries. Anyone who has been around knows that wrestlers are pressured to come back early from injuries, although today, not early from concussions where they have to be medically cleared before the company will consider putting them back in and do err on the side of caution. But that's a relatively recent change. He claimed WWE doctors downplayed the seriousness of his head injuries and discouraged him from seeking additional medical help, and Haynes said he was never encouraged by a WWE physician to see a neurologist. This is another issue where the overall credibility of Haynes will hurt, because whatever is or isn't true, a lawsuit is like a chain, and it's only as strong as its weakest link, and Haynes may be a weak link to this suit. Even if there are valid points, the invalid ones will hurt the credibility of the valid ones.

Another tough point is "Haynes was also forced and encouraged to take steroids and other illicit drugs. He did so at the behest of WWE. WWE intimated that he would be fired if he refused. He received steroids, along with various other illicit drugs, directly from WWE-affiliated physicians on a monthly basis. These drugs masked the pain stemming from his WWE matches, and caused him to wrestle through dangerous injuries, including injuries to his head."

There is no doubt that in the 80s, and long after that, there was a belief that the body was a huge part of the push, and it even is, to a lesser degree, part of the equation today. Drugs that make the body more presentable thus, you can argue, are encouraged whether it's in WWE, or in sports, or in Hollywood, for a number of reasons. Some of those drugs are very difficult to test for, and WWE doesn't test for some, and they exist today. It's nowhere near as prevalent as in another era, but does exist and it was widespread in different eras when no testing was taking place (through early 1992 and again from 1996 to 2006, and given the Signature Pharmacy debacle, it can't be argued that use wasn't very significant even with testing in 2007). I can see the word "encouraged," but "forced" is a tough one and I don't know that anyone was threatened with being fired if they didn't take steroids. Nobody had to force anyone to do anything. The guys who were picked to be part of the promotion, for the most part, already were doing it and it played a part in them being picked. Those who weren't doing it beforehand, because they were being compared nightly to a crew that mostly was, had that implicit pressure to also do so. But it's not like people were saying that you have to get on steroids or you will be fired, even if encouragement to increase size or tighten up was there in a business that had such a strong body image.

One well-known performer in a reaction to the suit said that the closest he ever saw or heard of someone in the office telling someone to take steroids was 2002 or 2003, when a guy getting a tryout was told by someone in developmental that they needed to do whatever it took to completely change his body "to look the way we want guys to look." He then specifically pointed out Charlie Haas as an example of a guy who had done just that and was on the main roster. Haas was extremely muscular at that time. Others have pointed out the bad example HHH set when he ridiculed Chris Masters on the air when he lost significant weight.

When Mike Bucci was working in the office, he did a seminar where he told aspiring wrestlers that they needed to do what they could do to get the right kind of body for WWE and get the contract, but at the time of the contract, they had to make sure they were able to pass the test. We don't know the exact wording he used, and if it was intimating or outright saying anything, but those attending took it that they were told they needed to get on steroids to get noticed, but after getting an offer, they had to make sure they could pass a test or they wouldn't get signed.

The performer also said the only person he ever spoke to that used steroids who made it clear he didn't want to was Lance McNaught (Lance Cade). McNaught evidently told this to a number of people, although when Nowinski said something similar, Trevor Murdoch, McNaught's longtime partner, lashed out at Nowinski claiming he was making it up and that Cade would have never told him that or been close enough to him. Linda McMahon also tried to deny any relationship with McNaught and Nowinski even though they were at times tag team partners.

The wrestler noted that McNaught had come to him saying that he didn't want to and was afraid to take steroids, but that people in the company kept telling him to get in better shape and he was doing everything he could as far as training. He said that everyone who was being called up from developmental was on the gas and most of them weren't nearly as talented as he was. McNaught did start taking steroids and got called up shortly after.

McNaught passed away on August 13, 2010, at the of 29. The autopsy reported that his death was an accidental death due to mixed drug intoxication combined with the effects of an enlarged heart. The medical examiner did not directly link steroids to the enlarged heart, but steroid use has been known to enlarge hearts and a number of pro wrestler deaths have included steroid users who suffered heart attacks and were found with enlarged hearts.

A WWE wrestler had turned an e-mail in to the company after McNaught's death where McNaught told them he had ordered some steroids in March of that year and was expecting to fail a drug test he had just been given. McNaught's death ended up as a political issue because it came when Linda McMahon was running for senate in 2010.

In particular, in the suit, there is a claim is that in Haynes' March 29, 1987, WrestleMania III match with Ray Fernandez (Hercules), that he got hard way juice when he was hit four times with a ten foot chain, and needed 20 stitches and suffered a severe concussion. I don't know if that was hard way juice, but in that era, hard way juice was rare as compared to self inflicted juice.

CHAPTER FORTY NINE

ECW EXPOSED

NOVEMBER 17

As part of WWE's attempt to build up the network during its free month, they announced ECW week, kicked off by Paul Heyman and Joey Styles doing a live "ECW Exposed" show on 11/10 immediately after Raw.

It was mainly Styles asking Heyman some questions, as well as taking fan questions, and then the show abruptly ending at midnight for regularly scheduled programming even though Heyman was in his element and clearly wanted to go on a lot longer.

There was a lot of talk about how ECW would have been the hot thing on social media had it existed in that day. They pushed the idea that the term "Extreme" in culture in the late 90s came from them and they were the forerunners of it. Heyman tried to also push they were ahead of the curve producing shows in a basement (Ron Buffone's house) because some of the biggest names today now have studios in their basement. Well, there is a difference in working out of a basement because they are so rich they can have the studio built for them, as opposed to not being able to afford it in any other way, and it's not like Heyman didn't say that as well.

Styles noted that there are parental warnings on the new ECW Hardcore television shows because of language. They went through the firing and hiring of Sabu, and how Sabu vs. Taz worked because in real life the two couldn't stand each other so it brought believability into their feud.

Styles pushed the idea that ECW was important in the big picture because it was where Steve Austin first cut his teeth doing his own promos. ECW was the first place where Austin's personality really shined, as in WCW, he was a very good worker with a good look, but didn't show the personality that made the difference between being a star and a big-time superstar. Still, even with that, his time in ECW was short, on the way to WWF, where whatever he showed in ECW was forgotten when he was given a new Ringmaster character. But the fire in his promos did come across when he came up with the badass character that made him the biggest short-term draw in wrestling history.

They also talked a lot about Brian Pillman appearing on ECW TV when he was under contract to WCW, with Heyman admitting that the entire time he was running ECW he was always in contact with Kevin Sullivan, and that he finalized the Pillman deal through Eric Bischoff.

At the time it happened, Heyman was always denying he was working with WCW, because he pushed that WWF (who he also had even closer relations to during that period) and WCW were the mortal enemies and they were the underground movement that through hard work could compete with more well-funded competitors. He always portrayed it as Pillman coming to them, which was true, since everything regarding Pillman in ECW was a collaborative effort of Heyman and Pillman, but Pillman was WCW talent, as much as everyone went to almost ridiculous lengths to show that wasn't the case.

WCW gave Pillman to ECW for free with the idea they thought it would convince their audience that Pillman had really been fired for being a loose cannon, doing and saying things on the air and behind the scenes that cost him his job. The idea was to fool everyone and eventually build for him to return.

This was actually all Pillman's idea and he convinced Sullivan and Bischoff of it, and told them to keep in between them and not let anyone else know. There were very few he kept abreast of what he was really doing, limited likely to Kim Wood, his father figure and assistant coach with the Cincinnati Bengals when he played on the team in 1984; and to a degree, Bruce Hart, who he started with in Calgary as his tag team partner; and Terry Funk, because of Funk's creativity when it came to out of the box angles.

Pillman's master stroke was working the people who thought they were the only ones working with him into giving him a legitimate release. The idea was if he had the full legal release, the word would get out from the WCW office and people would buy his firing as legitimate and not storyline. The funny thing is that it didn't actually make a difference. Most people in wrestling in time figured out what was up.

But for Pillman, the idea ended up being brilliant. Pillman, with his release, then started negotiating with WWF legitimately, double-crossing Bischoff and Sullivan on their agreed upon angle. For Sullivan and Bischoff, especially Bischoff, the idea of the angle was to fool everyone else. For Pillman, the idea was to get himself hot, become a free agent, play both sides against each other, and appear on ECW where he'd have the most leeway to do his thing and get over while he negotiated the two against each other. His goal was to get a Lex Luger level contract.

Pillman always resented that he believed he was so much more talented and creative than Luger, but Luger made so much more money and was pushed harder than he was. It wasn't any personal dislike for Luger, but of the system and mentality of those in charge in pro wrestling at the time.

In particular were times years earlier when Luger would laugh at him when he'd try to learn different styles of wrestling and study tapes to get better in the ring.

Heyman noted that Pillman became so hot during that period that WCW wanted him back quicker for the Triple Decker cage atrocity they were planning on a PPV. In actuality, Pillman thought returning to get leg dropped by Hogan (it was Hogan who asked for Pillman in the match because Pillman was getting so hot underground) was the last thing he wanted for his return match. So Pillman, who needed surgery from time-to-time because of polyps that continually returned in his throat, scheduled a surgery. In reality, and I'm pretty sure Sullivan knew this (Pillman at least thought that way), Pillman could have had the surgery at any time, but scheduled it to where he wouldn't be ready for that PPV, thus avoiding being leg dropped and pinned in what he thought would be (and was) one of the worst PPV main events in history.

Heyman noted that the original idea was for Pillman to wrestle one match in ECW, to lose to Shane Douglas, because Heyman needed to rehab Douglas after a failed stint in WWF. But that never transpired in 1996 because Pillman got in a humvee wreck that put him out of action for a long time.

That was 18 years ago, but the only thing not accurate was Heyman's time line, saying that Pillman signed with WWF, and WWF was going to allow Pillman to do the match with Douglas, and then he got in the humvee wreck. Actually, Pillman signed with WWF after the wreck.

Pillman never had any intention of going to WWF. The goal was always to stay in WCW, particularly since he thought by having Sullivan and Bischoff as the only ones in on his angle, that they'd take care of him thinking they all pulled something off together. But he did want to get the leverage high, feeling also, that if he got $450,000 a year (main event money at the time) that by getting that contract Sullivan and Bischoff would book him as a main eventer and not a mid-carder.

Even before the humvee wreck, Pillman's body was starting to fall apart. He had back problems and he was an undersized lineman who played football through college, where at a legitimate 5-8 3/4 and juiced up to 223 pounds (his actual wrestling weight was between 198 and 202 pounds in shape), he was a Division I-AA First Team All-American noseguard.

He felt the pressure to make big money for the next several years, figuring his career had a finite time left, and he was supporting five children.

If the truth were to be told, that was more of his motivation for coming up with all of his crazy ideas than anything else.

He went to WWF instead, because after the wreck, Bischoff would not give him a no-cut clause in his contract, I guess for fear of Pillman not being able to perform as well and being on the hook for years for a big-money deal. Pillman knew, after the wreck, that physically he was done, but told nobody of that (he even kept that from me until just before he died) for obvious reasons. To show the level of paranoia at that point, Sullivan thought Pillman worked the wreck at first and was really in the hospital to get facial reconstructive surgery so he would look exactly like Michaels, and that he was going to WWF to feud with Michaels. I had been pushing Pillman to go to WWF. He would always argue against it, feeling in the end, WCW would pay more than WWF. He felt once WCW paid him main event money they'd push him as a main eventer to justify the contract.

I felt WWF's main event side was far thinner. Michaels was their top guy, who at the time needed a fresh opponent, and that Pillman's size, which was the only thing that held him back from being a top guy, wouldn't be an issue against Michaels, but would be for the top of the WCW roster.

Plus an advantage was Jim Ross running talent relations, as they knew each other and were friends from WCW, and Ross liked hiring credentialed athletes. Ross and McMahon agreed to the no-cut clause on his contract and that's why he went, as Bischoff's guarantee was higher. I don't know if Bischoff was sincere about this, because it was at Pillman's funeral that he told me, but he said his biggest regret was not closing the deal on Pillman, maybe feeling that if things were different, maybe he'd have lived.

In 1997, when Heyman was planning that year's November to Remember, and by this time Pillman was wrestling regularly in WWF, Douglas pitched to Heyman about seeing if WWF would agree to let Pillman wrestle him at the November to Remember show that year. Heyman told Douglas that Pillman, whose drug issues had gotten bad (some of that was due to trying to wrestle in so much pain because of a destroyed ankle from the humvee wreck, but it's not as though there were no issues before the wreck), wouldn't be alive in November. He never told that part of the story on the air for obvious reasons.

Pillman died that October.

Styles asked Heyman who on today's roster, if they were transported back 18 years, would have done well in ECW. He mentioned Brock Lesnar first, as well as Dolph Ziggler (who he said reminded him of Douglas and Shawn Michaels), Cesaro (who he said was underutilized in WWE), Daniel Bryan (he noted that they used Michael Shane, a Michaels school graduate and had ECW continued probably would have used Bryan and thought Bryan may have attended an ECW show at the end with Shane), and that if ECW had continued a few more years, that C.M. Punk may have been its flagship star. He also put over John Cena, talking about his work ethic and longevity at the top, comparing his tenure as the top guy to people like Bruno Sammartino and Lou Thesz.

They aired videos of Eddie Guerrero and Dean Malenko talking about their time in ECW and their final match.

Heyman talked about his seven different lawsuits against WCW (which always ended up in settlements where WCW would let him use talent for big shows).

When asked what was ECW's biggest flaw, Heyman said not having an ad sales team.

Heyman defended using New Jack when asked about it, saying he was one of the most fascinating characters in pro wrestling history, and was worth it even with the lawsuits and legal fees, and talked about how he came off as legit.

When asked about money WWF gave ECW, Heyman said that the $1,000 per week was an agreement he and Vince made when Vince took Too Cold Scorpio away from ECW and it cost ECW $1,000 per week in a sponsorship deal with Tommy Boy Records. He said WWE agreed to pay the company that money to replace the lost sponsorship, but he was not himself on the WWE payroll. Those in WWF always described it at the time as Heyman being on salary as a consultant. He noted the $500,000 (give or take a little) loan in 2000 was an agreement to keep ECW from suing them since WWF was negotiating with TNN (now Spike) while ECW was on TNN. From the WWF side, I was told about the loan that they believed ECW was going out of business, wanted to avoid any legal complications since TNN was offering five times what USA was and WWF wanted to take the deal, plus they worked into the loan that they were a secure debtor which gave them the leg up if the company went bankrupt to own the intellectual property.

I was told at the time that they never expected to get their money back from Heyman when they loaned it to him. That was one of the best investments WWF ever made, because as a secured debtor, they ended up being able to buy all the ECW intellectual property for a ridiculously low amount in the big picture.

When people used to knock ECW as far as it being something that had a lot of talk but never made any money, the reality is, it made a huge profit in the end, but it wasn't Paul Heyman or those in business with him who made any profit. The person who made the most profits off ECW were WWF, in marketing DVDs and using the footage in other ways. They could have made tons more if they had marketed ECW merchandise, particularly in 2005 when ECW nostalgia went through the roof.

The last $88,000 loan Heyman said was because WWF knew ECW was about to die, and at the time WWF wanted to keep it alive because they were in talks of buying it and didn't want it closing. Shane McMahon wanted WWF to buy the company and for him to run it, and Shane McMahon always wanted to run a company by himself. I had never heard that, but the timing does sound accurate. I did know Shane wanted WWF to buy ECW and for he and Heyman to run it at one point. In the end, Vince wouldn't buy the company, which is the same thing that happened when Shane wanted Vince to buy UFC at about the same time, and in 2006 when Shane wanted Vince to buy Pride. Once Vince made that call, WWF let it die, and picked up its assets later in 2001 in bankruptcy court.

CHAPTER FIFTY

NEW JAPAN MAKES
MAJOR BUSINESS MOVES

DECEMBER 1

New Japan Pro Wrestling has signed its first-ever U.S. television deal, essentially a 13-week tryout on AXS TV that will debut on 1/16 in the 9-10 p.m. time slot.

The deal, which had been in negotiations for two years, was completed this past week between AXS TV and TV-Asahi, which owns the broadcast rights to the main television shows. New Japan was involved in the talks, however the talks were kept completely secret from everyone in U.S. pro wrestling. Nobody knew anything until the first television commercials aired on 11/21, even Jeff Jarrett, and pretty much everyone in wrestling was scrambling for information on 11/24 on what was going on.

The story behind the release was that they were set to make the announcement on 11/20, but all sides decided to hold off because TNA had just announced its television deal the night before. New Japan and TV Asahi at that point suggested 12/1 as the new release date, likely so they could announce it at their big press conference to announce their streaming service.

However, once the word leaked, AXS made the decision to release it on 11/24.

The 13 week show will feature major main events from matches held during 2013 and early 2014. The shows I believe will be the same one hour shows that airs in Japan, in Japanese, on the TV-Asahi satellite station BS Asahi, and also airs in Singapore.

The first show and possibly shows will have matches from the January 4, 2013, Tokyo Dome show, which was one of the best shows in company history. The very first show on 1/16 will be headlined by Hiroshi Tanahashi vs. Kazuchika Okada for the IWGP heavyweight title from that Tokyo Dome show. There may be more than one show covering that card, as I believe an early episode will also include the highlight Dome appearance of Ayumi Nakamura singing Kaze Ni Nare ("Become the Wind") to lead to the Minoru Suzuki vs. Yuji Nagata match. The series will include matches from the 2013 G-1 Climax tournament, and I believe the two most talked about matches from that year's G-1, Katsuyori Shibata vs. Tomohiro Ishii and Shinsuke Nakamura vs. Kota Ibushi, are both scheduled to air. The series will pretty much be headlined each week by a major PPV main event from that 17 month window, culminating with the A.J. Styles vs. Okada feud over the IWGP title, which will air on the final schedule episode on 4/10.

New Japan's idea for the show originally was to have the first six episodes cover the Tanahashi vs. Okada feud, trying to get it over as something big to American fans, airing all six singles matches in order, and then have the rest of the shows cover other wrestlers or programs.

The time slot is golden for AXS, because it's the lead-in to some of the station's most popular programming, the Friday night fights, which include a number of smaller MMA promotions including Legacy Fights, Resurrection Fighting Alliance, XFC, Maximum Fighting Championships, as well as Lion Fights (Muay Thai) and other kickboxing, MMA and boxing shows. It's the time slot formerly held by Inside MMA, the weekly talk show hosted by Kenny Rice and Bas Rutten, which is being moved to about 12:30 a.m., or whenever the live fights end.

Based on certain things in the deal, if the show is picked up after the test run, at this point it would be more building in the sense it would be in order, but would likely run about six months behind what is going on in Japan. Obviously if the show gets popular things can change. The weekly TV-Asahi network show in Japan is 30 minutes, and because there are more commercials in a Japanese broadcast, it wouldn't even fill a 30 minute slot. So they are going with the one hour show that airs in Japan and some foreign territories.

Mauro Ranallo, the host of Showtime Boxing and former Pride, Strikeforce and Stampede Wrestling announcer, will be doing the play-by-play with Josh Barnett as the analyst. Barnett worked for several years with New Japan before ending up with the IGF.

The voice over work is scheduled to be done for the season in about two weeks over a four or so day period in Los Angeles. The story behind Ranallo being picked was they had hoped for him, but with his high profile work in boxing, the original thought was he was out of reach. Then the feeling was that it wouldn't hurt to ask, and he was excited at coming in, because he is a fan of Japanese wrestling, and had done similar work for The Fight Network in doing voice overs for the Canadian market during the heyday of Pro Wrestling NOAH.

Barnett was chosen for two reasons. The first is that he used to work for the promotion, and also, they wanted an MMA tie-in with the idea that putting wrestling before MMA would help both the way wrestling helped Bellator's ratings originally on Spike, and figured a well-known MMA voice talking in MMA and wrestling context would be the right formula. There will be subtitles as the shows feature a lot of hype and interviews by the top Japanese wrestlers building up matches. The pageantry before and after the matches will be included in the series, as well as Japanese style interviews.

This is going to become a very interesting political situation because ROH talent like Kyle O'Reilly, Bobby Fish, The Young Bucks, Adam Cole, Matt Taven, Michael Bennett and at least a few others set to debut were all to get regular bookings next year. Now it wouldn't just be ROH wrestlers appearing on a PPV that would have limited viewership, but on television, and in many cases, putting people over. Even though ROH and New Japan had meetings recently involving setting up joint shows in 2015, nobody in ROH was aware they were in talks or close to a U.S. TV deal until it came out on the Observer web site.

The year is going to be interesting, because if this show is successful, you'll have ROH, TNA, New Japan and Lucha Underground all on smaller stations very close in footing and penetration.

ROH isn't cleared in the most homes and has no penetration on television in the major markets like New York, Chicago, Los Angeles, San Francisco, Toronto or Philadelphia (which is notable since New York, Chicago, Toronto and Philadelphia are seemingly their four most successful house show markets). While they would be in less homes than TNA, they are on far stronger stations, as in many markets they air on Saturday or Sunday nights on local network affiliate stations that people actually watch.

TNA is expected to retain its two hour Wednesday night time slot, plus get a weekend replay, on a low-rated Destination America network. Actual ratings for TNA and ROH were similar, but TNA was in more homes on Spike. There is a level of brand loyalty that they'll bring to their new home, but they are also going to lose a number of viewers both because they have no access to the station or because some are from the Spike base and they won't follow them to a new station. The viewership between ROH and TNA could be similar, and really, I'd expect ROH to have an edge.

New Japan is an unfamiliar product, but it's also got the highest television production values. It has the best wrestling, but it's also foreign wrestling. AXS is in about 43 million homes compared to 52 million for Destination

America. Wednesday is a better television night than Friday, and TNA also brings a base audience with it that New Japan won't have. However, New Japan is on a night with more compatible programming since it's already fight night on the station.

Lucha Underground is on a terribly low rated English station, but they are already up to 200,000 viewers in Spanish each week. They have some positives for growth. The first is they are strongly geared to the Hispanic audience, which is historically strong for wrestling, so they have a ethnic niche none of the other groups have. The other is the production of the show is such that they could get an upgrade. The big weakness is that even though all their advertising is geared toward a Wednesday night showing, about 90 percent of its audience is watching at 4 p.m. Saturday, a non prime time slot. The keys are if they are upgraded into prime time on Unimas, it is a lock they will have more viewers than the other three. The other is that Unimas is a secondary station to Univision. Univision hasn't had an interest in wrestling, but they've never been presented with a product with that level of production values. A move to Univision changes the game. Univision's prime time viewership is double that of USA and more than triple that of Spike and Syfy. That's not to say that if that move were to happen that more viewers would watch the show than Raw, because that will not be the case. But the potential is there to be, not necessarily competitive, but definitely having a niche audience and popularity in circles the same or greater than WWE, which last year seemed beyond impossible for anyone.

So the point being is that if there is a battle for No. 2 when it comes to television, it's wide open. The one that is going to be in last place will be Lucha Underground, but it is also the one that, by far, has the most potential.

The big advantage of New Japan is that the U.S. market is just ancillary income. Unlike ROH and TNA, they don't have to, nor do they expect to make their money here. With a strong home base, and having a television deal that pays, probably not a lot, but it's still added income and added exposure. If they don't draw ratings and fail, they are no worse off than they were last week. And while WWE may come after some of their talent when contracts come up, they can't strip them of talent nor does everyone in New Japan dream of WWE like almost everyone in ROH wants to be in WWE.

There is also potential for cohesive battle plan for the U.S. market using AXS television to its advantage by airing a weekly up to date television show with Korakuen Hall footage to build to PPVs, either on the Internet or regular PPV, could, in time, build a following and due to the lack of strong alternatives in wrestling today. The foreign aspect will be hard. Great wrestling has never been a factor in drawing great ratings. Wrestling is less hot than at any other period because there's a generation of people who didn't grow up as wrestling fans, nor the millions of casual fans as in other eras. Now once you get to the audience under 40, it's almost all people who grew up as WWE fans (the WCW fans are long gone and moved on) and not wrestling fans. The older audience, which is half the WWE's television audience, are less apt to sample an unfamiliar product. But on a small station, it's not like they need a million viewers a week to be a success.

DECEMBER 8

New Japan owner Takaaki Kidani, announcing his goals of surpassing WWE and UFC as the No. 1 sports entertainment group in the world, copied WWE with the announcement on 12/1 of New Japan World, a streaming video service at http://njpwworld.com that will air all of its major shows, even down to the monthly price of 999 yen.

The service launched immediately after the announcement of the press conference, and was accessible worldwide. The next day, Kidani, without giving any numbers, said they were blown away by the number of sign-ups outside of Japan.

Kidani stated the first year goal was 100,000 subscribers, figuring at the time that almost all subscriptions would come from Japan, and figured they could eventually do several hundred thousand subscribers with strong international growth, and in particular brought up eventually having English language announcers for major shows and English subtitles, similar to how the show on AXS television would be done. He's hopeful that the service, which will include all major shows as well as the weekly one hour television show World Pro Wrestling (although it appears they will run one month behind) will help international expansion, which is the group's current focus.

What's notable at the press conference is that they didn't push that for the first time ever, the company will have a regular television show in the U.S.

Kidani said that they right now are the No. 1 company in the world when it comes to the actual wrestling product, but they are behind WWE when it comes to business.

Like with WWE, they are undercutting their PPV price, and will be airing their version of WrestleMania, the Wrestle Kingdom 9 show on 1/4 at the Tokyo Dome, with a two-hour pre-game show and four hour main show, on New Japan World, both live and with archives put up immediately after the show.

The service is priced at essentially the same price as the WWE Network and UFC network are for monthly subscriptions. Unlike both, they are including all of their up-to-date content with the exception of the one hour television show, on the service. In that sense, it is like UFC's Latin America channel. Also different from the WWE service, this is no 24 hour live programming, and also different from both, the library is only New Japan content as opposed to purchased rights for footage from other companies. Also, unlike UFC, there is no price break for ordering multiple months, at least at first. Because the yen has fallen against the American dollar of late, the price at press time was $8.42 U.S., $9.54 Canadian and 5.36 British pounds, per month.

This undercuts Jeff Jarrett's English language produced PPVs on television throughout North America and on the Flipps App on the Internet worldwide outside of Japan, which was charging $34.95 for the show alone. Last year's Tokyo Dome was 3500 yen on either PPV or iPPV in Japan, and $35 for iPPV in the U.S. through Ustream. Essentially, like WWE has done with its PPV business, New Japan is killing its two-year-old iPPV business.

In this U.S., the mentality has been that it's easier to get people to order a PPV on television as opposed to through a streaming service, although WWE may have sped up the curve on changing that one. ROH was doing maybe 2,000 iPPV buys for big shows, and did six times that on traditional PPV with a weaker show, its first time out of the blocks. However, WWE moving from PPV to the network saw regular PPV drop down to 21,000 buys in North America for Hell in a Cell, and that includes Canada, where the WWE is theoretically not even available to be ordered in 80 percent of the homes, and it's a scaled down version.

But ultimately, the regular television PPV for New Japan is likely to have a short run. For the 1/4 show, while the super hardcores in the U.S. and Canada will order the network, a large part of the television audience won't likely even know there is a New Japan World service, and for most, the Japanese commentary is a deal breaker and Jim Ross is a positive. But in the long run, once New Japan World starts broadcasting in English, people will learn to stream it for the lower price, provided there are no technical issues like what badly damaged ROH for years. The idea of Jarrett being able to build a PPV franchise with New Japan, which was a longshot but not an impossibility, via the traditional PPV route, seems far more than a longshot today.

A big difference is that while WWE takes in the lion's share of its $9.99 per month, so there was some argument for doing it the way they did, New Japan and TV-Asahi are equal partners in this venture, since TV-Asahi owns the broadcast rights to the library. So they go from getting 50% of the Niconico higher priced sales from iPPVs to 50% of a much lower price point. Plus, for this year, the plans of doing doubles, which is two straight nights of PPV quality shows, means fans get both shows for the low price instead of having to order two shows individually. A usual New Japan PPV would be 2000 yen, so if there's a double, like in February, it goes from 4000 yen for someone wanting both shows, to 999 yen, and you throw in probably three or more house shows during that month as well. It's a super deal for the hardcore fan. The difference is, because of the television situation, New Japan is carried by the hardcore fan base. WWE is not, and the idea of the network was that the increase in casual fan buys by giving them far more content at a lower price makes up for getting far less money from the most ardent fan who buys everything. For New Japan, it's far more of a risk. In addition, WWE, being an American product, has been able to provably be successful exporting their product, while New Japan has never been able to do so.

For example, the service would also enable subscribers to stream the entire G-1 Climax series in August for 999 yen per month. In 2013, to stream G-1 it cost $150 and in 2014, it cost $110 if ordered in advance and $160 if ordered the days before the first show. They also talked about how next year they were looking at doing every show of the tag team tournament airing live.

Besides doing four live events in December and five in January, they also have archival footage of some of the most important historical matches in New Japan history, dating back to 1972.

The first major event that will air is the finals of the tag team tournament from Nagoya on 12/7. Perhaps because of existing deals, this show will not air live, but looks to air on an eight-hour tape delay, at 10 a.m. Eastern time and 7 a.m. Pacific time.

The other shows airing in December are a 12/15 hour show from Koga (5 a.m. Eastern time), and the 12/19 and 12/20 shows at Korakuen Hall (both starting at 4:30 a.m.). Lineups haven't been announced, but by tradition, the year-end Korakuen Hall shows usually have great main events. Last year they put the Tokyo Dome two main event matches together in a tag match.

The January lineup will be open with a 1/3 festival at Differ Ariake which airs in the U.S. on Jan. 2 at 10 p.m. Eastern time. I'm not sure if that will be matches with undercard guys or a fan fest.

The Tokyo Dome live broadcast will have a two-hour live pre-show at Noon Eastern on 1/3.

The Tokyo Dome show itself is likely to start at 1:45 a.m. Eastern time with one match, probably a multiple person match just to get people spots on the card, before the introduction of the main card at 2 a.m.

They will also air the "Raw after WrestleMania" show on 1/5 at Korakuen Hall, which starts at 4:30 a.m. Eastern time on Monday, the two major Fantastica Mania shows on 1/18 and 1/19 from Korakuen Hall, also with a 4:30 a.m. start time, plus the opening of the next tour, which will be 1/30 in Tokorozawa at 5 a.m., which starts the build for the two major New Beginnings shows in February.

Going forward, all Korakuen Hall shows are expected to be streamed live.

In Japan, most of these shows either aired as PPVs and iPPVs or they were live on Samurai! TV. It's not clear what that means for the relationship with Samurai! TV. What is known is that when local media tried to contact services that worked with New Japan, Samurai! TV, Gaora TV, G+ (all sports channels that rely on a lot of pro wrestling programming, all would be very minor channels by U.S. standards) and several local stations that air New Japan declined to comment.

The network also includes all the matches from the 67 commercially released Best of New Japan DVDs, featuring many of the biggest matches in company history, dating back to 1972. There are also documentaries that are to be added in time, including the 2014 G-1 Climax documentary on the tournament that aired in Japanese theaters. There is also every episode of the one hour World Pro Wrestling show from January 31, 2013 until the first week of November.

It also has every 1/4 show at the Tokyo Dome in its entirety from 1992 to 2014, as well as most of the other Tokyo Dome shows, as well as a complete collection of the major PPV shows starting with the 2011 Tokyo Dome show. Not all G-1 shows from the last four years are up, because some shows are owned by television stations other than TV-Asahi.

In comparison to WWE and UFC, there are positives and negatives. The positive is on day one, this service worked far better than WWE, which was filled with technical issues at launch. The navigation is far superior to the other two, with searches on the front page with the names of every wrestler with a match, and you can search based on wrestler name, based on year, based on arena, based on television announcer and based on championship belt of tournament.

For those who don't know Japanese, it's best used in Google chrome with translations, even though some of the names are screwy. Without the translations, it would be almost impossible to navigate for someone who doesn't read Japanese. However, it is inevitable an English version of the New Japan World web site is forthcoming and probably very soon. Riki Choshu is Choshu Force, Dynamite Kid is Thomas Billington (his real name), Jushin Liger is Beast God Thunder Liger, Vader is Big Bang Vader, Manabu Nakanishi is The Spiral Nakanishi, Shinsuke Nakamura is Eup True, Yuji Nagata is Hiroshi Nagata, Alex Shelley is Patrick Martin (his real name), Doc Gallows is Doc Gyarozu, Karl Anderson is Machine Gun Carl Anderson and Bad Luck Fale is Bad Rack Whare. But most everyone else is their usual ring name.

The negative is that WWE opened with 1,500 hours and now has more than 2,600 hours, and UFC has now increased its Fight Pass to 6,000 hours of footage. WWE has matches from numerous promotions, well in excess of 100,000 hours, but only a small percentage is up. UFC has virtually the complete libraries of UFC, Pride, Strikeforce, Elite XC, WEC, WFA, Invicta and other promotions, with almost all of what it has up. New Japan World only has New Japan, and has closer to around 350 hours of footage, nowhere close to its total library, but the quality, as far as main events and big names in the footage, is strong because everything before 2011 is either Tokyo Dome shows or either big name matches or significant historical matches.

The archives include most of the biggest matches in company history, but there are plenty missing. For example, the biggest match in New Japan history, Antonio Inoki vs. Muhammad Ali, isn't there. However, Inoki's mixed matches with Monster Man Eddie Everett, bodybuilder Mike Dayton, boxer Chuck Wepner and judo gold medalist Willem Ruska are there. At the press conference, they noted the Antonio Inoki & Seiji Sakaguchi vs. Lou Thesz & Karl Gotch match is up. Legendary matches like Andre the Giant vs. Stan Hansen, Inoki vs. Billy Robinson, Inoki vs. Hulk Hogan, Kensuke Sasaki vs. Toshiaki Kawada, Naoya Ogawa vs. Shinya Hashimoto and Keiji Muto vs. Nobuhiko Takada are all there.

The forwarding and reversing, at least on my computer, is the best of the three. WWE's tool bar on the bottom is poor, and at times a disaster, although apparently an improvement is forthcoming. UFC's works fine, but often there are issues in going away from full screen. The video and audio quality is excellent. From my experience thus far, the buffering has been non-existent, unlike WWE, which has constant issues and UFC, which has occasional ones, but that still has to be tested with a major live event.

The move is a big risk. Traditional televised PPV shows are not big in Japan for a number of reasons. Unlike in the U.S., where fans of wrestling were used to paying for tickets for major shows, and then the next generation was the big shows on PPV; while the boxing culture was closed-circuit tickets for the big fight and later PPV; the Japanese culture has always been about the biggest matches being available on free television.

While PPV did very well for Pride a decade ago, and the early New Japan PPV shows when it was first introduced also did well, it has lost popularity over time. Only a small percentage of the Japanese homes had the necessary equipment to even order PPVs. IPPV had pretty much rendered traditional PPV useless as last year's Tokyo Dome show only did 7,000 buys in Japan.

However, for the new generation, the iPPV concept, which started in late 2012, was a big hit, peaking with more than 100,000 orders of the last two Tokyo Dome shows. Like with WrestleMania and WWE, the company is undercutting the price and thus, the Dome show almost surely will gross significantly less money this year. Kidani is a big admirer of Vince McMahon as a businessman, and the mentality here may have been as simple as, well, this is what WWE does and they are the world leader, not realizing what a disaster, at least short-term, the WWE Network has been. And perhaps he sees it that WWE will turn it into a success and long-term is the game. The problem from New Japan is they have huge long-term issues because of the age of the roster and having not developed marketable new top talent in years.

The company is planning on cracking down on its content being uploaded to the Daily Motion web site, which is where the majority of international New Japan fans follow the shows. At press time, a ton of New Japan content was still up.

The plan is also for the service to be available soon on Smart TV, PS 3, PS 4, Xbox One, and Apple TV.

DECEMBER 29

After three weeks, New Japan World has 10,000 subscribers. That's a worldwide number. The key will be how it goes after 1/4, which is the first really major show broadcast live, but they did have a PPV show on 12/7 and have had three live events since then before this number was announced. But it is something that they offer a streaming service for a month at half the price of a PPV, and get less subscribers than they'd get for streaming just the PPV. The first time New Japan did a streaming PPV, and this was with just a few days notice in 2012, they had 25,000 orders and were topping 50,000 by the second or third show when they had time to promote it. TV Asahi, partners in the network, have publicly predicted 40,000 subscribers as of 1/4.

CHAPTER FIFTY ONE

VINCE MCMAHON ON STEVE AUSTIN PODCAST

DECEMBER 8

Vince McMahon spoke about a lot more than C.M. Punk on 12/1, in a one plus hour interview with Steve Austin that aired on the WWE Network.

It was probably the most fascinating program the network has aired. Austin is a very good interviewer in the sense he makes you like him, and thus, you open up more. This led to a funny sequence, where they were wrapping the show up at midnight to go to regular programing, but Vince still wanted to talk. He said that he owned this network and they were going another 15 minutes.

McMahon came off well in the sense he got you to like him. On the flip side, he was in some circles trying to be honest, and in others, trying to promote or defend the product. Austin never went on the attack, nor was he going to, but he brought up his key complaints, such as the lack of top tier stars, the overwriting of the shows, and the frustration that a talent like Cesaro is on a treadmill to nowhere.

After the show, a lot of current talent ended up frustrated when they realized, from his own mouth, that McMahon believed that nobody since John Cena has had the drive to want to be the top guy, with his hope that Roman Reigns, Dean Ambrose, Seth Rollins and Bray Wyatt will change that. He gave what I believe was his honest appraisal of Cesaro, but in doing so, frustrated a lot of people who don't share in the idea that Cesaro, past being physically talented as a wrestler, doesn't have it to be a star.

There may be a ceiling as far as subscriptions, based on the current popularity level of the product, but this was the kind of can't miss programming that gets people talking, and with a few exceptions (documentaries on Ultimate Warrior and The Shield), the network has been a disappointment in that regard. The Monday Night War show could have been a hit, but for some current fans, it's not the guys they know, and for the fans who lived through it, you can only go a few minutes before you realize how skewed the history is. And after a few weeks, it's the same story told over-and-over. It would be to the company's benefit to have Austin, or someone, and it would have to be someone who is no the outside but gets the business, talk to the leaders as a network exclusive. Maybe once every month or two would be the right time frame. Vince should be on maybe twice a year, because more than that, it'll burn out and also kill Vince's mystique. His charm and performing ability got him through this one, but if you really listened, you can't help but have some concern.

Austin brought up Punk, which due to timing, he had to. Austin had listened to the Punk podcast over the weekend, and had strong opinions of it, but never interjected those opinions, preferring to let McMahon talk. He also brought up subjects like the bloated writing staff, Randy Savage in the Hall of Fame, Shane McMahon and the WWE Network.

The first talk was of the network, and here McMahon was the predictable CEO.

"It's going great," he said. "We have a 90 percent satisfaction rate."

You can skew numbers all you want, but when you have a 56% renewal rate when subscriptions expire and 25% canceled early and never came back, that is not a 90% satisfaction rate. The two aren't the same thing, and people may not subscribe for economic reasons, but it's a $10 a month bill and if you're that satisfied, you don't go out of your way to cancel and never come back.

The U.K. launch was brought up, and McMahon said he hoped it would be settled soon, by the first of the year, but also said nothing is definite on that subject. He didn't address why they've announced several dates, and had to pull back each time, the most recent being a heavily promoted date they pulled out of 20 minutes before scheduled launch.

"I do have high expectations," he said. "It definitely will take a little time. It takes a lot of time to build up the content and give them exactly what they want."

When Austin used the term pro wrestling you got the first glimpse of the guy who is seemingly surrounded by people telling him the world is still flat.

"Pro wrestling is what my dad did," he said.

You can change the term all you want, but after 30 years, everyone still calls it pro wrestling. While the term sports entertainer is used more now than ten years ago, real people in the real world don't say John Cena is a star sports entertainer or Dwayne Johnson used to be a sports entertainer. And Vince wants to believe he's changed that world and he hasn't. Little kids who only know WWE still say they are wrestling fans, and nobody says, I watch sports entertainment every Monday, or "let's go to the sports entertainment show." I can call my oatmeal "steak" every morning, but when I do, people look at me funny, and I can't go, "oatmeal is what my dad called it" and think if I keep calling it steak that people will no longer think it's oatmeal.

Besides, pro wrestling and sports entertainment are the same thing. If anything, when you watch an old tape and see audience intensity, it's far more gripping theater when presented as if it means something as opposed to some light-hearted clown show. Vince runs from comparisons with actual sports entertainment. Pride, WWE, UFC, and the NFL are all sports entertainment. With the exception of WWE, and perhaps Pride, none of them were pro wrestling.

Austin asked Vince about the Raw show that night. Vince tried to put the show over. It was a boring show, but I don't think Vince can go out there and say that. But when he said he thought Bray Wyatt looked pretty damn good when he had a match with so little reaction you could hear crickets chirp, that was a tough one. He said the six-man at the end was really good, but if so, that's a very low standard for good.

Austin complained that sometimes the opening segment goes too long, and Vince said that two guys wrestling for wrestling's sake doesn't get it done, which is true.

McMahon said that today's locker room is not as ambitious as in the past, and that they don't want to reach for the brass ring, saying the last one that did was Cena. McMahon talked about how the Millenials have a different attitude, that they don't want to fail. He said that if you try and reach for the brass ring, you may fail and they have an insecurity if you fail at something, you're exposed.

He said that all he can do is give people the opportunity, and said how the current roster has resources that Austin never had, talking about how big social media is. There are two problems with that. The first is, social media does not turn people into money draws. And when it comes to pro wrestling stars, it often hurts people more than helps them, by making them too familiar and less elusive. The key to stars is that people want to pay for people who they feel are stars, not people like them, or people who say dumb things. Now, if you are on TV presented as a star, you can be an idiot on social media and still be a star. But if you're not presented as a star on television, social media isn't getting you over. If you are presented as a star on television, social media and being more familiar is a disadvantage to most, in getting over to the level of an Austin.

Austin flat out said they were weak on main event depth and McMahon agreed.

One top star noted to us that they saw it as Austin out there trying to be the voice of the wrestling fan in asking questions a fan would, and that McMahon, even though he wasn't feeling well at all that day, was still on his game enough to deflect well.

The feeling is that even when a smart person would sense he was either full of it or not getting it, an average person will see that it's Vince McMahon, he talks confidently and authoritatively, and he's Vince, so he must know what he's talking about.

The comment that got to a lot of people was saying about the current locker room, "They're not as ambitious, they're not trepidacious, they don't want to reach for the brass ring. The last one who did was John Cena. Dean Ambrose, Seth Rollins, Roman Reigns, Bray Wyatt, I think you've got some people chomping at the bit."

The problem is the environment. A guy who comes in with the swagger of a star, whether it's Sin Cara, or Conor McGregor, is going to be beat down so badly for it that they'll beat the star right out of him. Before, the whole idea was to constantly create new stars. Today, it's over managed where people come out with reasons this guy or that guy can't be a star. And when guys become a star, like Ryback in 2012, and they're limited, they shorten their run by putting them in positions they shouldn't be put in. There's a famous story about Bill Watts, Junkyard Dog and Ernie Ladd.

Watts decided he was going to go with JYD as his top guy. Ladd, the booker, had JYD go 20 minutes with Super Destroyer (Scott Irwin), a solid worker, and the match was terrible. Ladd called Bill up and said we have a problem. Our guy doesn't have it. Watts fired Ladd and told him he already knew he couldn't work, so we never put him in a position to expose that. Then Ladd told Watts that the only way to keep him over is never beat him in anything close to a fair manner. There have been plenty of guys who were very limited in certain key performing aspects that were still very successful when put in top positions. The key is to know their weaknesses and then hide those weakness from the fans, instead of saying, "well, they have a weakness, therefore they can't be on top."

Or with a C.M. Punk, they'll go so far and then decide that they didn't increase business so it's the Internet fans and the key to business is the masses. Daniel Bryan was the same way. And he's not wrong, but he is wrong. He's right in that some people on the outside who complain to them about why aren't you pushing "my favorite" have no clue what a main event guy is, and it's not musical pops and it's not chants. But where he's wrong is that if the audience goes strongly in a direction, you should listen and take it as far as it can go. It may fail. It may succeed. If you don't try, it won't succeed. The problem isn't that the talent isn't ambitious, or is too passive, but that management is not willing to take a risk of making a new star and going with him, and has a mindset of not noticing that there are qualities like likability, that mean more than look and while Yes, Yes, Yes means far less than some people think, given people chant it when Daniel Bryan isn't around just as loudly, that doesn't mean you never give a guy who tears the house town a fair shot for enough time to see if he can get the brass ring.

When Austin got his first main event run in late 1996, business didn't turn around, really, for about a year. If Vince had the wrong guy in his ear saying, "That guy is a good worker, but he's bald, and those promos only work on guys in one demo who want to hear swearing but those loud guys aren't the masses who want Sid Vicious," and Austin was then booked the way Punk or Bryan were booked, I'm not saying the wrestling war ends differently (WCW was self destructing either way), but Austin never comes close to the heights he reached.

Besides, nobody tried to take that brass ring more than Punk. Bryan didn't, because Bryan, by his own admission, lacks ambition more than just about any superstar in the modern business history. He's just happy to be a pro wrestler. He's really good at it, and has a likeable quality. But he himself sees the "Yes" chant and his success as fluke and timing and kind of marvels at it. Punk on the other hand, sees himself as a failure because as long as his title run was and no matter how far he got, he never got to be the guy and be in the real main event on the big show.

Austin said that the talent walks around like they are on egg shells, because there's nowhere else to go, noting TNA isn't competition. When he said they're afraid to do anything for fear of pissing anyone off, Vince said, So, they better not piss anyone off then."

One of the reasons top talent could be what they were is if they were good, they knew they had plenty of other options. Losing their job in WWF or WCW wasn't the end of the world. It isn't now either, but talent doesn't really believe it.

"He absolutely buried the entire locker room with the Cena was the last guy to reach for the brass ring comment," noted one star.

"He went out of his way to not get in a public war of words with Punk, but Punk clearly reached for the brass ring."

"Bryan is a little different. He's complacent and his gimmick so pushed him through the roof. Dolph has really busted his ass (to get to the top), but never understood how to combat HHH's perception of him and subsequent constant burials behind the scenes, or how Michael Hayes would bury him just to cozy up to HHH and show him, `I'll back you up in conversations with Vince.' But the comment was just such an indictment, and a terrible one, on the whole crew."

"I'm looking for someone with charisma, with a great deal of heart, innate skills, who wants to learn," said Vince McMahon. "We all learn every day. As a promoter you do. You want someone with those skills, verbal skills, physical skills, has the passion for the business. Then you give them those tools and there you continue to build and from there you've got yourself a star."

McMahon said the audience ultimately makes or breaks a star, and that is the case. But a great promoter leads his audience and a good promoter takes cues from his audience. They clearly didn't listen to their audience from SummerSlam 2013 to Royal Rumble 2014. Right now, it's hard to say if they are or aren't, because the audience most weeks comes across like the beatdown wrestlers, not getting behind anyone to a great degree because the rug has been pulled on them too many times.

The other controversial statement as far as talent was concerned was when Austin directly brought up Cesaro, a guy that was getting over on his own eight months ago to where he could have been a top face, and that the company was even behind (just before WrestleMania, Cesaro was on the company's internal list for its future to be a top babyface and wanted their licensees to be aware of it). Then, creatively, it fell apart, largely because he was booked into oblivion, losing all the time.

"He's not connecting yet," said McMahon. "We hope he will. He doesn't quite have the charisma, the verbal skills, those sort of things he's lacking. The audience needs to care about you. They need to feel your presence. He's got extraordinary physical talent."

Austin challenged him, saying he was breaking through and lost his momentum and asked what he needs.

"I'm not certain," he said. "I don't have the answer to everything. I listen to a lot of people, take a lot of people's advice, I'm not so sure he has the answer. He's a great in-ring talent, but there's something missing. I can't put my finger on it and say, `Now we're going to the dance.'"

Austin also challenged him on the bloated writing staff, noting that during the period the company was its most successful, it was Vince McMahon and Pat Patterson at the pool, and maybe Jim Ross, and later there were a few guys. McMahon responded that the company needed the huge writing staff because times have changed and you have to evolve. And that's true, but if the change is not for the better, in the sense the product isn't better with the changes, than the change devolves, not evolves.

Austin then asked about Shane McMahon. Vince said that Shane is happy, working in Japan. Shane McMahon heads a company trying to get pay-per-views of movies into the Chinese market. Vince confused Japan and China. The idea that Japan and China are the same thing has been common in WWE for decades, dating back to making racial comments in promos at Japanese wrestlers with names of Chinese food dishes. It's similar to their thinking Puerto Ricans and Mexicans are the same demo.

One person who knows Shane McMahon well noted that Vince saying the departure was mutual is just not the case, saying Shane took his 50 (million he had in WWE stock) "and got the f*** out of there."

Austin and Vince talked about the similarities of when he walked out over creative differences in 2002 and Punk walking out. Austin has many times felt it was the biggest mistake he made. While he didn't agree with the creative, he felt he was wrong in walking out and should have tried to work through it. Austin noted that after he agreed to come back, Vince said he had to fine him $650,000. Austin said that was a heavy number and Vince asked him, "What do you think is fair?" and Austin said, "$250,000." And they settled on that. Austin said that he's always wondered if he said the wrong thing, and asked Vince if he said $125,000, would Vince have accepted it. Vince never gave an answer.

This was the one awkward part of the show as one could see Vince wanted off that subject. When Austin brought up that Vince wanted to fine him $650,000, you could see a hand off screen, and Austin apologized for bringing it up and Vince looked uncomfortable.

Austin then brought up Brock Lesnar's win over Undertaker and how that went down. Vince went on a speech about how nobody wants to give back to the business more then Mark Calaway. He said that there comes a time to do that, and it was that time. Vince said over the last two years, there was nobody else who Undertaker could have worked with and given back to the business in the biggest way to make someone a bigger star. Vince said to look at the roster, and there was nobody on the talent roster, and it was a combination of timing and having the right person in Brock there to pull it off. McMahon talked of it like this was Calaway's decision and Austin flat called him on it, saying he didn't believe Undertaker made that call.

McMahon admitted he made the call.

"That's on me. Those decisions aren't easy to make, but you have to make difficult decisions some times. That's my job to do that. I think I made the right call at the right time. Coming into this year's WrestleMania, I don't think Brock Lesnar can be any hotter than reminding people that Brock Lesnar beat the Undertaker's streak."

Based on what he said, it leads me to believe there are only two options for Lesnar at Mania. The first is continue the original plan, which is Lesnar gets past Cena and loses to Reigns. The second is that Cena beats Lesnar due to distraction from Undertaker, and Undertaker faces Lesnar at Mania. Obviously the latter depends on Undertaker being healthy.

Austin then brought up Lesnar not being around very much, which is essentially questioning him about the contract he signed Lesnar to. McMahon said that he doesn't think you would want him on television every week, and he's better as a special attraction. Then he did a bad analogy of comparing Lesnar to Jake Roberts' snake, and how at first it was a big deal but after a while, people saw the snake so much it was just part of the show.

"Brock, per the contract we made with him only allows us x number of dates," he said. "It's not about the title that draws people into the arena, it's about the performer, his opponent, the story and how they're going to resolve that story. Does it (the title) help, sure it does, but it's not just about the title."

Austin asked about Randy Savage going into the Hall of Fame and McMahon said, "Absolutely, definitely." This has been a given since McMahon got Lanny Poffo to work with him on the DVD. Austin pressed him as to when and McMahon said, "Soon, not so sure if it'll be this year, but I'll say soon."

Austin brought up Sting, and McMahon did a double negative that ended with him saying the opposite of what I think he was trying to say. He said Sting is a character who it's better not to see a lot of. "I won't be surprised if he doesn't show up at WrestleMania."

Austin then brought up history and this is where it got pretty bad historically. He said he hated Ted Turner's philosophy which was to hurt the competition, while his philosophy was to help his own company. It is true that Eric Bischoff really wanted to be the guy who put Vince out of business, but if you think for a second it wasn't a two-way street, you're naive, and after all this time, bringing up Turner, a guy who probably spent five minutes a year thinking about pro wrestling, as his competition would be like Dana White saying that he's battling Sumner Redstone and how Sumner Redstone is trying to ruin him, and pretend it's not Kevin Kay or Scott Coker.

"I think we had a much better product. It was something new with Hogan and Scott Hall, it was new, the NWO, but it was just a matter of time before we beat them. We had a better product. We had more passion than they did."

Austin brought up Vince putting the territories out of business and Vince said he didn't, "They put themselves out of business."

That's not true. Cable television put everyone out of business except Jim Crockett. I knew territorial wrestling was dead in 1981, which was just a question of how many years it would take. How can a guy running Kansas

City, St. Joseph and Sedalia compete with a guy taking in money in major markets? Quite frankly, Crockett did an amazing job of staying in the game for years when his big markets were Charlotte, Greensboro, Norfolk, Richmond and Atlanta. But he made a number of bad business decisions, such as going with a pat talent hand for too long (the same mistake that killed WCW), did live events with bad finishes that convinced people not to return and he had to pay big money to keep his top talent from leaving, and couldn't make enough to cover his talent bill as his TV bill.

"I didn't have the money. All I had was creative skills, a really strong work ethic, a lot of luck, a set of grapefruits. Verne (Gagne) was a multimillionaire. I had nothing. The guys in Kansas City had money stashed away but they didn't put it in the business. I kept reinvesting in the product."

Gagne was a multi-millionaire, but McMahon took over a company that grossed far more money by running in larger markets. McMahon had a bigger company than anyone, from the day he took over in 1982, based on what his father had sold him. He had both the New York and Los Angeles markets to himself, meaning he was wrestling to the national media. The idea they didn't invest in the promotion isn't true, as Gagne and Crockett both went broke trying to save their businesses in a changing environment. Vince was better overall than Crockett and Gagne as a promoter, but if the roles were reversed, and it was Crockett's father running the Northeast when he passed away in 1975, and he gets on MSG and USA cable early on, and Vince's father is in Charlotte handing things off to him in 1982, as good as Vince was, he's losing that war whether he's smarter or the harder worker.

He put over Bill Watts, saying he was a street smart guy, which he was when it came to wrestling, but about Crockett, McMahon said, "He wasn't the brightest branch in the tree. I didn't think he understood the business."

Crockett made a lot of bad decisions, but he also took his territory from being just another regional territory, to within a few years, the strongest wrestling territory in the country, with the best talent. He, Watts and Jerry Jarrett had the best per capita business on the highest television ratings, but in those days, you made no money off television. Once McMahon established to TV programmers that the wrestling promoter pays you to get on the air, as opposed to a barter deal where you get the tape for free and he gets half the ad time and you keep the other half, the profit margins got thinner to the point Watts and Crockett started losing money. In the end, Watts couldn't have stayed in business unless his deal with Turner would have gone through. It would have been tough for Crockett, but in his case it wasn't a sure thing because he had good talent. The economic changes hurt, and Vince McMahon sabotaging his PPV business was also a big deal. The only time Vince was a legitimate underdog that he portrayed himself as was the late 90s, and he should not have won that battle. But he was lucky that Rock and Austin came along at the same time, and that Bischoff was totally clueless about what the wrestling audience wanted and produced such a horrible product. And then, after he was gone, they hired Vince Russo, who was maybe one-third as smart as Bischoff.

Austin then pushed McMahon on the subject of Jim Ross. He said he thought that McMahon and Ross were the two smartest guys in wrestling. And he brought up it was Ross who brought him and McMahon back together.

McMahon pushed the idea that Ross wanted out, and moved to Oklahoma. Ross has always privately claimed his issues with McMahon started because McMahon felt he abandoned him moving back to Oklahoma. But Ross worked as the head of talent relations from Oklahoma for years, and after McMahon replaced him in that role with John Laurinaitis, living in Oklahoma was immaterial to his job as an announcer, which they on several occasions dropped him from and then brought him back. Even the Laurinaitis situation was weird. Laurinaitis was brought in to learn under Ross and replace him at some point, with Ross watching out for him and cleaning up his mess until he got it all down.

It was not an issue of Laurinaitis replacing Ross, but a question of when. But McMahon, to have the power at the end, didn't wait for Ross to give his timetable, but made the call to put Laurinaitis in charge of Ross one day.

"There's no heat from my standpoint," he said. "There was an incident in Los Angeles that you were part of. You stated your opinion (Austin felt Ross should not have been fired). I'd rather not go into it. You just don't do that. It was very unprofessional, very unlike Jim. I like Jim as a human being, he's got a lot of institutional knowledge. I'm not sure we won't get back together."

Austin also brought up that McMahon didn't like blood in wrestling, yet in the most important match of Austin's career, with Bret Hart, blood was a key element in the match, and that match got the ball rolling for the guy who made McMahon more money than any wrestler in history ever did.

McMahon said that he probably was pissed off about the blood, "But it's not what I want. It's what the audience wants. I'm a pretty good listener. When your listening to the audience and they're going crazy and you've got color (blood), it's against policy, but listen to the audience, look at what's going on there. From a company standpoint, I was a little pissed off, but it was what the audience wanted."

Vince closed by denying age, and in particular, Punk's remark that he was old and out of touch.

"I work as many hours as I always have," he said. "I'm enjoying the business now more than I ever have, and I always have enjoyed it. I think I haven't lost a step. Physically I haven't. People think I'm out of touch. Most people who say that are the critics. You have to listen to the audience, not the critics."

DECEMBER 29

Morale in WWE, which wasn't good before, has been noticeably different according to several sources since the Austin/McMahon interview. The basic feeling is that McMahon crapped on just about everyone in the locker room except Rollins, Ambrose, Reigns and Wyatt, and made it clear those were the only ones he saw with top star potential. The obvious points about nobody for years being willing to reach for the brass ring hit home with the guys who have had stop-and-start pushes and never were booked in a manner that would have made them anything but mid-carders. The key points brought up were the burial of Cesaro, particularly since he looked to be a guy, and was even thought by management ten months ago as being a guy, who would be a top babyface. This fell apart when they turned him heel and booked him like a mid-carder, the brass ring comment, and the comment about how they didn't have anyone except Lesnar who could have beaten Undertaker.

After morale got bad because of that interview, HHH stepped in and gave a speech to the entire roster which was described as an attempt to do damage control that backfired. As a general rule, the guys in NXT love him, but on the main roster, whatever he said lost him a lot of credibility, particularly with those who have been there for some time. Admittedly, he was put in a bad position, trying to come up with a positive spin on what Vince said to a locker room that he buried and are frustrated because most were done in by the stop-and-start booking and a promo style that gets almost nobody over.

CHAPTER FIFTY TWO

UFC CLASS
ACTION LAWSUIT

DECEMBER 22

The class-action antitrust lawsuit filed on 12/16 in federal court in San Jose, seems to come down to a line of what constitutes building a strong business, and what constitutes attempting to crush opposition, which can be argued are at times one and the same thing.

The Ultimate Fighting Championship over the last eight years, with the fall of the Japanese-based rival Pride Fighting Championships, has emerged as the dominant force in the mixed martial arts business. While there have always been dozens, and now hundreds of promotions, including many that have national television exposure, UFC has in recent years has had a dominant market share, and controlled most of the sport's top fighters.

During that period, a number of companies attempted to be competition. Almost all failed, many of which then had their intellectual property, which included contracts and videotape libraries, purchased by Zuffa, LLC, the parent company of the UFC.

In doing so, there were less options for the elite level fighters. And in recent years, with the implement of the sponsor tax, fighters themselves had seen a onetime lucrative market dry up, both from the tax and from market conditions. Some companies found, over time, that it was not economically worthwhile to spend the level of money that they had in sponsoring fighters. And with more shows, and smaller audiences, the value of sponsoring a UFC fighter, unless it was a major champion, wasn't as strong as in what some would call the period of the sport's greatest mainstream popularity, from roughly 2006 through 2011.

The lawsuit, filed by current UFC fighter Cung Le, and former UFC fighters Nathan Quarry and Jon Fitch, is being handled on contingency by lawyers representing five major law firms.

Le said that while he is still under contract with the organization, he would not fight for the UFC again. But he said if given a release, he would be open to fighting for another organization.

This will likely be a slow process that the plaintiffs hope will change the structure of the sport. But at the press conference announcing the suit, nobody spoke in any specifics of what they wanted or expected the end result to be. The only thing said was about creating an environment where there was more competition for fighters services and likenesses for merchandising endeavors, thus increasing the revenue going to fighters.

Le, 42, who was one of the main stars of Strikeforce, has been a UFC headliner since Zuffa purchased Strikeforce in 2011. He had major recent issues with the promotion concerning an announced drug test failure and suspension for allegedly using Human Growth Hormone in a test taken at his 8/23 fight, in Macau, China, where he lost to Michael Bisping.

Due to irregularities in the testing procedure, the results were later ruled invalid and UFC rescinded his suspension. Le had publicly asked for an apology, which didn't happen. He then asked to be released from his contract, which also hasn't happened. This coincided with Scott Coker, the former head of Strikeforce, a promoter he had worked for from 1998 to 2010 as both a San Shou fighter and later an MMA fighter, taking the job as the head man of Bellator.

Le said his involvement in the suit had nothing to do with the bad publicity stemming from the drug test story.

"Not at all," he said. "My involvement is more for the fighters, past, present and the future. That's why I'm involved in this lawsuit."

"It's about how we were treated, how we're paid, and what we have to go through. If it wasn't for us, there would be no MMA, and there would be no UFC. What's fair is fair."

Quarry, also 42, is a retired fighter who was part of the cast of the first season of The Ultimate Fighter reality show in 2005. The show was a key building block of the modern success of UFC. While he didn't win the show, as he was injured during the competition, he was one of the most popular fighters in the cast. Later in 2005, Quarry had a shot at middleweight champion Rich Franklin, which he lost. He remained with the UFC, last fighting in 2010, due to back injuries, that resulted in spinal fusion surgery. He retired officially in 2012.

"I think, more than anything, it (taking part in the suit) was to see current, former and upcoming fighters recoup some reward for their hard work," said Quarry, who co-hosted the TV show MMA Uncensored on Spike TV, in 2012. "Now, it's such a monopoly that the fighters have no real options, and that's not the American way."

Quarry, who has always been very popular with his fellow fighters, said fighters who have known about the suit have been quietly behind him. He also noted that for fans who think this will hurt the sport, that historically in major sports when athletes filed suit for free agent rights, that the end result of the enhanced competition for the athletes is that it ended up benefitting both the athletes and the fans. They led to the sports becoming more lucrative for everyone.

"Competition is good for the sport, good for the fighters, and good for the fans," he said.

Fitch, 36, who just competed three days earlier for the World Series of Fighting, losing to Rousimar Palhares in a match for their welterweight title, was not at the press conference. While he was there via phone line, he never spoke during the proceedings. He fought for UFC from 2005 to 2013. For almost that entire period, he was considered one of the top ten welterweights in the sport.

In 2008, he faced Georges St-Pierre for the welterweight title, losing via decision.

He was released by UFC in what may have been the most controversial firing in company history, since he was still listed in the company's top ten contenders.

His career was hurt because he was viewed as not being an exciting fighter, which likely cost him a second shot at the title. He had come off one of the most exciting fights of his career in a win over Erick Silva, but then lost to Demian Maia in a lackluster showing, and was let go. Dana White cited Fitch's salary and that he felt at his age, he was declining as a fighter, as reasons for letting him go. Fitch has since gone 2-2 in the World Series of Fighting, although both fighters who beat him, Josh Burkman (who has since been signed by UFC) and Palhares (who was fired by UFC in 2013 because he had injured fighters by not breaking heel hooks after tap outs and ref stoppages, and also had failed a steroid test in 2012), were clearly UFC-level competitors.

Fitch's name came up in a dispute years back when Zuffa required its fighters to, with no compensation, assign their likenesses in perpetuity for video game usage when the company signed a deal with THQ, Inc. Fitch attempted to negotiate a fee for his likeness, as did other fighters under the management of DeWayne Zinkin. UFC President Dana White terminated Fitch, although that termination only lasted a few days.

For a time, White claimed any fighter who appeared in a competing video game produced by EA Sports (which years later acquired the UFC license when THQ had financial problems) would never be allowed in the UFC. However, when top fighters who were in the EA Sports game became available, that provision was quickly forgotten about.

Former UFC welterweight champion Carlos Newton, who is not a plaintiff, was also at the press conference expressing support for the fighters. According to Robert Maysey, a longtime MMA fan and writer, and one of the lawyers involved in the case, Newton had been a strong supporter from day one.

The legal team involved is a strong heavyweight panel.

Eric Cramer has been listed since 2011 as one of the country's top antitrust lawyers. Michael Dell'Angelo is one of the top lawyers at Berger & Montague. That firm won a $100 million cash settlement from JP Morgan Chase & Company, from the bank's role in the collapse of commodities broker MF Global, which forced MF Global to distribute about $1 billion to former commodities customers who Dell'Angelo represented in a class action suit.

He was also one of the lawyers involved in a $163.5 million settlement in the Titanium Dioxide antitrust litigation. Benjamin Brown is a leading class action antitrust attorney. Joseph Saveri has specialized in antitrust law and class action litigation for more than 25 years, and has been involved in cases in dozens of industries that involved monopolistic business practices. Joshua Davis of the Saveri Law Firm has more than 15 years experience in antitrust class action suits. Maysey is the MMA business expert on the panel, a name familiar to most MMA industry insiders from his writing about topics that this lawsuit encompasses for many years.

However, it was claimed unionization is not what this lawsuit is about.

There is little doubt that more competition is the best thing for the athletes. But the question is whether the UFC's domination of the MMA business comes from having the right name brand, getting on strong television first and them building an organization to a level that the others who tried to compete couldn't make it work profitably, or did UFC engage in anti-competitive practices that stifled competition and put rivals out of business?

A key aspect of the suit is that the competition for top fighters ceased when a number of organizations, including Pride, Affliction and Strikeforce were purchased by UFC. But in all three cases, the purchase was because the promotions were looking to get out of the business. Pride and Affliction were about to cease existence anyway. Strikeforce was losing money and its parent company wanted to divest itself of its MMA brand, Zuffa made the best offer. According to those with Silicon Valley Sports, the Zuffa offer was the only truly serious one made.

It wasn't a good thing for fighters at the time. But the FTC investigated UFC on antitrust charges on the Strikeforce purchase in 2011 and 2012, and found no unlawful activity had taken place and did not pursue the matter.

But since the Strikeforce purchase, Bellator was purchased by Viacom, a far stronger financial entity than had backed Strikeforce.

While nobody would argue that Bellator is equal to UFC, nor from a quality of fighters standpoint, even equal to Strikeforce at the time of the purchase, it appears to be very much a competitor. On 11/15, when the two companies went head-to-head, with Bellator on Spike TV and UFC on Fox Sports 1 and pay-per-view with its first show ever in Mexico, Bellator captured the lion's share of viewers and seemed to generate more public interest.

However, the lawsuit dismisses Bellator as competition, even though there were two very public examples, Gilbert Melendez and Eddie Alvarez, where the competition between the two sides led to each fighter getting far more lucrative and beneficial deals, including potential title shots specifically written into their deals. But those incidents are the exception rather than the rule.

"Another potential competitor, Bellator, is viewed within the MMA Industry--and by the UFC itself--as a minor league, a training ground for future UFC fighters, or as a place for former UFC fighters to compete after they have been released by the UFC," stated the lawsuit. "Bellator athletes lack significant public notoriety, in part because it is a `minor league,' and in part because UFC refuses to co-promote with any of Bellator's fighters regardless of talent or merit, leaving Bellator unable to promote MMA events of relative significance. Bellator's bout purses, gate revenues, attendance figures, merchandise sales, television licensing fees and ad rates are minimal compared to those obtained by the UFC."

The question becomes whether vigorous competition crossed over into anti-competitive practices. This is one of those struggles that is expected to take years to play out, and little in the way of details past the basics of what the key arguments will be, were talked about in the press conference.

The lawsuit addresses issues of exclusive fighter contracts, UFC decisions that they claim have restrained fighters from making as much as they could from both the sponsorship market and the merchandise and licensing market.

Dell'Angelo said that the domination of the market by UFC and ability to extend the contracts indefinitely, since the UFC has the rights to match outside offers when the contracts expire, prevents rival promotions from garnering the best talent and makes real competition in the marketplace virtually impossible.

"That gives UFC all the leverage to drive fighter compensation down and its own profit margins up," said Dell'Angelo.

There are fundamental issues here regarding what share of revenue the athletes deserve. While the major team sports' athletes can get 50 percent of total revenues, largely due to unions and collective bargaining, neither of which MMA has, nobody really knows exactly what the UFC percentage truly is. One of the things this lawsuit is likely to uncover in discovery is the real percentage. When ESPN did a story on this same subject, there were people claiming the percentage is less than ten percent, which would clearly not be the case because that would take the athletic commission payoff records as the real numbers and not figure in the PPV bonuses, which are substantial on a successful show, and locker room bonuses. Lorenzo Fertitta said on ESPN a few years back that the revenue going to the athletes isn't far from 50 percent. From a business standpoint, the closest comparison to the UFC business is not the boxing business, which at the secondary level pays terribly little and at the top level is propped up by HBO and Showtime where the few big stars receive the lion's share. Entry level fighters in UFC make far more than their boxing counterparts, and the biggest boxing draws make multiple times more than their UFC counterparts. But the people putting up the money for the big fights are HBO and Showtime, not the boxing promoters. With WWE, it's a similar business structure.

In fact, the fundamentals of this case when one looks at it, one company controlling the U.S. market share to a great degree, no true free agency because of the lack of a viable alternative even though there are others on television, that if this case ends up favorably for the plaintiffs, WWE would be sitting ducks for something similar.

WWE pays talent based on set salaries, as does UFC, that are artificially low compared to the revenues the sport generates. There is little negotiating power. While there are no champions clauses to maintain talent, nor rights of first refusal, there is also nobody out there for the most part willing to guarantee most of the talent anywhere close to what they earn in WWE, with the exception of if that talent already has a name in Mexico or can fight, in which case the true competition for those few talents are UFC, Bellator or another MMA group, and not TNA, Lucha Underground or even New Japan Pro Wrestling.

The big difference is WWE wrestlers get a cut of video game revenue and merchandise revenue. WWE wrestlers are not allowed to do outside deals without first clearing it with the office. UFC fighters have no such restrictions. For all the decrying of the Reebok deal and sponsorship taxes hurting outside revenue, in the major sports, while you can get outside endorsements, and in UFC you still can, you can't go on the playing field and be a billboard for non-league sponsors in the NHL, NFL, NBA or Major League Baseball. WWE talent can't be either, unless you're Brock Lesnar who has a special deal.

WWE performers were earning a base salary, but the highest number on the base, unless you are a specialty performer like Dwayne Johnson or Lesnar, is $1 million per year. But the biggest stars earn multiples of that, with the lion's share previously being PPV bonuses and merchandise revenue.

With the Reebok deal, UFC is attempting to set up a more structured situation when it comes to marketing apparel and fighters getting a percentage. Whether this will end up for the better or worse is too early to figure out because nobody knows who is getting what. But the champions, who were able to make individual deals, have mostly already signed up, although they did have little leverage in the sense they couldn't go to Under Armor or Nike and let the free market determine their worth.

Like UFC fighters, at least for the big names, the talent is also paid on revenue derived from 30 percent of the after-tax house show gates, and a similar percentage of company revenue from PPV. But WWE essentially, with no input of talent, talent reps, or a union process (which UFC also has), essentially killed PPV. However, to keep the top guys who would complain happy, they are being paid based on a percentage of more than what they would have gotten for pay-per-view given the decreases in the buy numbers. But that's only the top people.

But based on the key revenue stream, television revenue, web site revenue, network revenue, the talent doesn't share in that. In UFC, that is similar, in that talent is not paid a percentage of the very lucrative worldwide television deals, or any Fight Pass Revenue, or revenue from UFC's Latin American television network. They are not even paid a percentage of the live gates directly in their contract (although the same could be said for WWE as any money above the downside and merchandise side is listed as discretionary money determined by the company). There are pay-per-view bonuses, different for talent, which kick in at a certain point. Of those bonuses that we are aware of, many kick in at a higher number than most of the recent shows have done, and some kick in at about that level. But aside from those in UFC, nobody really knows what percentage of revenue is going to the fighters.

The UFC, from the late 90s through probably 2005 or 2006, was losing significant money on virtually every event. Zuffa went $44 million in the hole before starting to turn things around.

In its fiscal year that ended on September 30, 2013, Zuffa grossed $483 million and had EBITDA in the $110 million range. Of that revenue, roughly $256 million came from live events (live gates and pay-per-view revenue) and $227 million came from television, licensing, merchandise, sponsorships, advertising and digital revenues. For WWE, they took in $508 million during 2013, of which was $213.4 million from live events and $294.6 million from television, licensing, merchandise, sponsorships, advertising, digital revenue and movies.

The UFC's 2014 number, as least as far as EBITDA goes, is estimated at being down 40 percent due to all the injuries that have lead to weaker pay-per-view main events and a huge drop in buys from the previous years. But even during a year that was almost a disaster, devoid of any truly huge fights and some of the weakest marquee pay-per-view main events in company history, the company is still profitable. And, barring another catastrophic year of injuries, the company would be expected to be significantly more profitable in 2015.

The lawsuit states that the fighters are paid a fraction of what they would make in a competitive marketplace. One could argue that's the case if there was a competitive marketplace and there was a company like Affliction spending like crazy to bid for certain top talent, and then going out of business two shows later. But the reality of the marketplace is that right now, no company is generating the kind of revenue where they could lift the salary structure of the sport significantly to be the strong competition. And in the case of a Gilbert Melendez, he was a free agent, and did benefit from this. But an opening match fighter, who one could argue is either underpaid, based on the amount of training and expenses required to get ready for a UFC fight, and the punishment; or argue isn't because aside from the top tier names, most on the roster mean nothing when it comes to adding revenue to an event; it's not like in an open market there would be bidding wars to up the $8,000 and $8,000 guys (who not that many years back were $3,000 and $3,000 guys, so things have gotten significantly better and that's not with larger live gates or larger PPV revenues, but due to other aspects of the UFC business increasing) to where their market value would be appreciably higher. They are men and women filling out cards, in some cases future prospects, in some, people who were once stars, and in some, just guys.

Lawyers, and fighters, were generally vague on questions, stating they didn't want to get into details or that aspects, such as if other fighters have talked about joining in, or more specific complaints about UFC business practices. They either referred to the suit itself, or said the information would play itself out in the future. Lawyers involved noted this will likely be a lengthy process. Zuffa will likely respond in some form to the suit, and it will go into discovery. In the end, the case will likely be settled in some form, and the information will likely end up sealed. The lawyer's leverage in discovery is that how much the real percentage of revenues the fighters earn would be the first thing that would come out, as would payouts of headliners and more details of how the UFC business runs, which UFC wouldn't want out, because that's one of the reasons they haven't gone public.

A jury trial here would be a risk, because so much could be determined by sympathy and not logic. The plaintiffs could have that sympathy factor, the rich owners and fighters who comparatively, didn't make much. Quarry, who headlined a PPV against Rich Franklin in 2005, before the company made money, earned $10,000 on a 200,000 buy show. That was during the period when UFC was swimming in red ink. That would look sympathetic to a jury, but there are no modern examples of anything like that, because pay has increased greatly, as have revenues, since that time. Fitch earned about $162,000 for his title fight with St-Pierre in 2008, which was considerably more than what his contract indicated he should have been paid for that fight, but one could argue that it is still a low amount for the challenger in a high-profile title match on what Lorenzo Fertitta said was a 625,000 buy show. But one could argue the real main event on that show was Brock Lesnar vs. Heath Herring, and without question that PPV number was drawn by the combination of St-Pierre and Lesnar.

On the flip side, UFC paid for Quarry's back surgery late in his career, which they didn't have to, but to a jury, that could be considered something expected given his injuries occurred from competing in the sport. And today, UFC does offer insurance to its fighters, whether the injury took place in or out of the sport. WWE performers have their in-ring injuries taken care of by the promotion and are required to purchase health insurance.

Cramer detailed what is likely to happen next.

"Zuffa will be served formally, and they will have an opportunity to respond," he said. "They can either answer, or move to dismiss. We don't know what they will do. If they answer it, we begin a period of discovery. We expect it to move forward."

The end of the line, in the event there isn't a settlement, would be a jury trial in San Jose.

Maysey, who has attempted to unionize wrestlers in the past, although the lawyers here said that unionization was not one of the goals of this action, was emotional with the filing of the suit, seemingly the culmination of years or work.

He said the difference between this and the major sports leagues, which also control virtually all the top talent and have the stadium and television deals to where it would be a virtual impossibility to compete with them, is that the leagues have teams with individual owners, and the teams are in competition, plus the biggest leagues have players associations. Even in individual sports, like golf, he argued that each tournament is not owned by the same owner, even if the major league tournaments for the most part fit into the same organizational banner.

Newton, who said almost nothing, tried to differentiate this from boxing by saying that the championship belts in UFC are owned and controlled by the promotion, not by an outside sanctioning body. But as much as we like to think otherwise, the boxing of another generation with eight real world titles and all the promoters bid for the title matches isn't really the case. Boxing does have outside sanctioning bodies, but the belts these days are almost worthless, and the drawing power is the name value of the fighters and the fight. The Arena League and Canadian League champions in football, or the Mexican or Japanese League champions in baseball, really can't compete for the NFL or Major League baseball championships.

The lawyers said that they are not filing a lawsuit about the fairness or unfairness of the Zuffa contracts.

However, a point made in the suit mentions the exclusivity clause, which prohibits fighters from playing their trade with rival promotions, and UFC's decision to not co-promote events with other organizations. Again, it's hard for me to conceive of why UFC should legally have to promote an event with another organization. It also mentions the champion's clause, which allows the UFC the right to extend a fighter's contract as long as they hold a UFC championship. This blocks rival promotions from bidding for the person generally considered best in the world in their specific weight classes. They also bring up UFC's right to match any outside offer given to a fighter whose contract expires, making it difficult to sign up a fighter whose deal has ended.

They also note that UFC has the ability to merchandise fighters in perpetuity worldwide, which would lower the fighter's leverage to garner merchandising or video game deals for the fighters themselves after leaving the organization, since the company negotiating with them wouldn't even get exclusivity on the rights of the fighter they had signed in the marketplace. If I was to sign GSP or Rampage Jackson up for a video game deal, his value would be mitigated because UFC could still put him in their video game. If I wanted to produce Rampage Jackson action figures and cut a deal with him, the value of exclusivity wouldn't be there for him to sell, because

UFC could market a rival product with Jackson's likeness. They also note that if a fighter loses and is cut, the UFC still can merchandise the fighter when no longer with the organization, or even after retirement. It also notes a fighter can't even sit out the terms of his contract, because if a fighter refuses to fight, like Randy Couture did years back, the UFC can freeze the contract length. This is because the contract would also call for a certain number of fights to be fulfilled. A fighter doesn't have to fight to complete his contract. He can retire when he wants to. But he can't go elsewhere and fight without fulfilling his contractual dates unless it is UFC that didn't offer him fights. UFC has some power to starve guys out by not offering fights, but it is minimal because within the time terms of the contract UFC has to offer the number of fights on the contract.

But a fighter can't, in mid contract, like Couture attempted to do, announce he was retiring as champion, while still having fights remaining, and then try to take bidding as a free agent for an outside fight with Fedor Emelianenko, as Couture attempted to do.

They also note that UFC not allowing certain sponsors on its broadcasts cuts back on potential income for fighters. They note that sponsors not only have to pay sponsorship tax, but UFC bans a number of companies from sponsoring if they compete with companies UFC has existing deals with.

Also mentioned was that in or about January 2014, UFC had added in contracts a provision that allowed them to lower the pay of fighters during the contract period if they lose fights.

It claimed UFC had exclusive deals with key venues on the Las Vegas strip, which wouldn't allow rival promotions to run in those key arenas. I've had those within the industry suggest that in particular is not the case. Promotions have run shows at venues like The Hard Rock Hotel and Casino (on the strip) , The Orleans Arena (off the strip) and the Thomas & Mack Center (off the strip) in Las Vegas.

It also noted that Quinton "Rampage" Jackson had negotiated an action figure deal with Round 5 and a Reebok deal, but UFC blocked both deals and entered into deals of its own with both companies.

There was also a claim that UFC had threatened sponsors that if they work with rival promotions, the UFC would ban them from being part of UFC events or sponsoring UFC fighters. The suit mentioned in particular that Fedor Emelianenko, according to his manager, Vadim Finkelchstein, had a potential seven-figure one-year sponsorship deal with Tapout that fell through with Finkelchstein claiming Tapout was told to either dump Emelianenko or lose access to UFC events.

Mentioned also in the suit was a claim that UFC embarked on a campaign to monopolize or monopsonize the industry, claiming the purchase of WEC in 2006 was to block rivals from getting television on Versus (now NBC Sports). Versus at the time was negotiating with the IFL. UFC had an exclusive television deal with Spike, and did purchase WEC with the specific goal of getting onto Versus, and blocking IFL was part of the goal, perhaps a major part. But it also opened up new fighters and new weight classes. In the end, the IFL was able to get television on MyNetwork TV, which ended up being a stronger distribution platform than Versus. But the IFL's TV show ended up canceled due to declining ratings. The purchase of WFA was of a promotion that was essentially done, and UFC got the videotape rights and contracts with some key fighters, notably Jackson and Lyoto Machida, who eventually became UFC light heavyweight champions.

Pride was essentially done when UFC purchased it. Affliction had also lost millions of dollars and was looking for a way out when UFC made a deal with them, accepting them back as a sponsor, and they shut down operations and in the deal, UFC got the videotape library of their two events. They claimed UFC forced Mark Cuban to shut down HDNet Fights, but that was more a business decision with Cuban feeling it was more cost-effective to pay fees to broadcast shows other promoters did, and they have aired events regularly for years, first on HDNet, and to this day, after the name change to AXS TV.

The claim was that UFC regularly counter programmed against Strikeforce, claiming it as a means to prevent Strikeforce, due to UFC being the stronger company, from promoting successful events and pressured sponsors to withdraw from Strikeforce by threatening to ban them from UFC fighters and broadcasts if they didn't.

But counter programming has been part and parcel of competitive sports businesses since the beginning of time. Given most major shows are on Saturday nights, as UFC and Strikeforce each expanded their schedules, it was a given there would be Saturdays with both companies running.

In the end, Bellator's existence and its recent success, and the fact there has been bidding for certain talent, tells me this is not a monopoly. And even if UFC controlled an even higher market share in North America than it does, much of that has been because the other promotions were not able to economically make it work. Competing against the big dog, whether it's the NFL, NBA, NHL or WWE or UFC head-on, is extremely difficult (in fact, I'd say the one most susceptible to potential competition from that list would be the UFC) because of the economic differences. It is because those businesses have grown to the point that the fan base on those sports or entertainment forms for the most part aren't that interested in spending money to support rival versions over the long haul.

However, there are points, such as fighters not getting revenue for their likenesses being used in the video games that will have a good chance of not looking good to a jury. The champion's clause could also fit into this. But the reality of the champion's clause is that while it exists in contracts, UFC has not used it one in the modern era, and has always made sure to have a new deal with a champion signed before he went into his final fight of his contract as champion. So, even if that aspect of the contracts don't fare well under legal challenge, it will not appreciably change the UFC business.

But aside from points like that, what this case will come down to is the line between natural competition in an industry, and anti-competitive practices, and if it ever gets to a trial, how a jury will view those points.

CHAPTER FIFTY THREE

BITS & PIECES

JERRY LAWLER

(JANUARY 13) There was a scare with Lawler, who wasn't on Raw on 1/6. Lawler had complained over the weekend of chest pains. He was in Baltimore, and after lunch, got sick and threw up in the mall he and his girlfriend (who he took on the trip) were walking around in. With that, combined with the chest pains, he was rushed to the hospital and there was fear of another heart attack. But he checked out fine and they diagnosed him with a stomach virus. He didn't appear on the show, but did an interview backstage playing down the incident, dressed up in his old school ring costume and smiling a lot. He didn't mention the chest pains, just acting like he threw up his lunch and everyone overreacted since he had once had a heart attack. He was back in the arena at least an hour before the show started but the decision was made not to use him. Apparently talent was told no tweeting or talking about the incident, although it did get out and was reported on by a Memphis radio station and Memphis area web site. WWE wouldn't make any statements on it past providing a link to his interview once it played. I thought the way it was handled on TV came across pretty sleazy. They mentioned that Lawler was sick, but he didn't have a heart issue, and then told people to go on the app to get the full details. There's nothing wrong with pushing the app (obviously they do it too much but they have reasons that they do) to accentuate storylines (although it's a mistake to use it for primary storylines or key moments in a match or story), but to use "go to the app" for a health issue on a beloved star who everyone very clearly remembers had a heart attack in 2012 that was nearly fatal came across pretty badly.

HULK HOGAN

(JANUARY 13) Regarding Hulk Hogan and WrestleMania, Roddy Piper has pushed for an idea of Hogan & Cena vs. Piper & Punk. I can get the idea of Hogan vs. Piper 30 years later but don't like it. For one, it's a tag team babyface battle because Piper can't be a heel now and while you can argue Punk should have stayed a heel longer, he shouldn't be turning back this early. Whenever I've heard about Hogan, the feeling has always been that they can't count on him to pass a physical.

(JANUARY 20) Hogan also reached a verbal deal to return this past week although it's been pretty clear for several weeks that this was happening. Hogan won't be at a match at WrestleMania, at least as things stand now, no matter what Piper has been pushing for, because Hogan can't pass the physical, although no doubt he will be around that weekend and be part of the show. I don't know that an actual contract has been signed, but it's openly talked about that he's in. Hogan was talked about to be brought in for the network launch which would have been his return, but they decided to save his return for later. As noted here before, Roddy Piper was trying to push the idea of Piper & Punk (which is why he endorsed Punk last week on Raw) vs. Hogan & Cena. That would be weird because in that match, Cena would be booed like crazy, no way will they boo Hogan, Piper or Punk unless they go so far heelish and even then I'm not sure. Piper had contacted Punk to try and get him on board for the idea. Based on TV this week, it sure seems like the HHH vs. Punk deal at Mania is still on.

(JANUARY 27) As things stand right now, while Hulk Hogan will be returning, and making an appearance in some form at WrestleMania, after being examined, the company made the call to not only not put him in a match, but not book anything physical involving him. Hogan said that he was filming a Super Bowl commercial on 1/16. As far as when he comes back, it could be any time now. Perhaps they could tease it at the Rumble, and there's some talk of debuting him (as well as bringing back a lot of big names that weren't on Old School Raw) on the 2/24 Raw, the day the network launches when there will be a push to get the biggest audience possible and probably go off the air with something that you'll need to tune to the network to get more info on I'm guessing.

(AUGUST 11) For whatever this is worth, Hogan is claiming that he is going to wrestle one more match. Hogan was on the Matthew Aaron show this past week, and said, "Brother, my goal is to perform in the ring again. It's not if, it's when. I've been training like crazy. My back doesn't hurt at all. My back's perfect. Now I've finally got my back straightened out, and I'm really trying to get myself into shape because if you step inside that WWE ring, you better bring it, and the last time I brought it, they begged me to take it back." He also said, "If I get in there, I want to make sure I'm ready to go and I give them something to remember me by, so my goal in life is to perform again in that WWE ring." Hogan did say that there would be no more leg drops, and that he was foolish using the leg drop as his finisher, stating that was the reason he had so many back problems later in life. This is Hogan. Within WWE, the mentality is Hogan is a retired wrestler who has a guaranteed money public relations/brand ambassador type contract that calls for a certain amount of dates per month, and leaves him not exclusive to the company, meaning he can call his own shots on outside endeavors.

(NOVEMBER 17) Regarding Hogan and WrestleMania, the decision will largely depend on whether Hogan can pass a physical. This goes for everyone over the age of about 45 that is under consideration for being brought back on the show, including Sting. Since the situation with Lawler, WWE has instituted strict physicals for older talent before they'll let them do anything physical, which is why nobody has even been running into Hogan's fists on Raw.

DOLPH ZIGGLER

(JANUARY 13) Ziggler is out of action with his second concussion in less than a year. He was wrestling Ryback on the 1/6 Baltimore show in a match for Superstars and was knocked out after taking a stiff clothesline. After he took the clothesline, he became disoriented, and it almost looked like he fainted during the match. He then rolled out of the ring. He did get back in and continue, but you could tell he wasn't the same, and they went right to the shell shock finish. It seemed early since he hadn't even gotten a comeback spot in. He was in the ring for some time being worked on before going to the back. They put up the "X" sign and he didn't get up for a long time. They were changing the ring to get ready for Raw with him still laid out. Dr. Chris Amann said on the WWE web site, "We were able to evaluate him in the ring. He was having some confusion and disorientation. We took him to the back to the training room and confirmed a concussion. He's currently feeling better but we'll proceed with ImPACT testing and further evaluation to determine when we can get him back in the ring." We've heard Ziggler was being sent to Pittsburgh to be examined by Dr. Joseph Maroon (the WWE's head of medical), which is not a good sign. Ziggler, 33, was at the peak of his career, getting an amazing reaction on the night he won the world title from Del Rio in April at the Izod Center in East Rutherford, NJ. But he suffered a concussion a few weeks later, getting kicked in the face by Swagger. It was basically being in the wrong place at the wrong time as the kick landed too perfectly and Ziggler's head was in too perfect a spot. When he returned in June, they immediately took the title from him and the decision was made not to push him. The same decision was made regarding Fandango, who was being pushed to be a new major star, and when he got his concussion, his push was also stopped. There was a ton of dressing room heat on Ryback, who had a rep for being too stiff with people already. Even though a lot of people figured that Ziggler's crazy bumping style, reminiscent of Curt Hennig, could and probably would catch up to him (as it did Hennig when he turned 33), both of these injuries have had nothing to do with his bump style and in each case were because of the power of the blow his opponent gave to him. But getting a concussion makes you more likely to get another. If a top guy like Cena or Orton gets a concussion, it doesn't change their situation one iota, but if a guy who is being pushed gets one, they seem to get off his bandwagon with the idea maybe they are too susceptible to a future one and he's not a guy we are going to put major eggs in his basket. Although with Ziggler, his push being cut off was because they were mad at things he was saying in press interviews. But with Fandango, there was no issue like that at all, he just stopped getting pushed when he came back.

(JANUARY 20) Things thus far appear to be positive for Ziggler. He was in Pittsburgh being examined last week after Raw and given testing which seemed to indicate he's recovering well. Dr. Chris Amann on the WWE web site wrote, "Fortunately all of those tests appear to be equivocal to baseline and within normal limits. His symptoms have improved significantly since the injury on Monday, so our plan right now is to have him continue to rest, and when he is asymptomatic, have him start doing some light cardiovascular exercise, and if that goes OK, we will proceed with our exertional protocol."

JESSE SORENSEN

(JANUARY 20) Jesse Sorensen did an interview with Highspots.com, and while most of this has come out, among the things he said was that after the accident in the hospital, his mother was freaking out over the medical bills, and Dixie Carter assured her in front of everyone that she would not have to worry about money. She also said, "As long as I have this company, you'll always have a job." He said Dixie went so far as to tell his mom that she thought of Jesse like a son, and when Jesse's mom would use the phrase, "My son," Dixie would correct her and say, "You mean our son." I should note that obviously TNA financially was hit hard and Sorensen being let go couldn't have been an easy decision. A key point is that the key decisions as far as financial prudence were made by Janice Carter by that point. While Dixie was the president and running things, this may have been a decision out of her hands. Today, the reason John Gaburick was brought in was to handle the contract talks, since Gaburick had no emotional attachment to anyone in TNA because he knew nobody (well, maybe Taz since they knew each other from WWE since Gaburick worked on the TV side in WWE under Kevin Dunn as he was Dunn's life-long friend). Sorensen in response to criticism of him still wrestling said that wrestling makes him happy and you have to live life to the fullest. He noted that his mother's insurance maxed out at $10,000, and thus he had to pay for his MRIs, doctors' appointments, CT scans and had to rehab himself. He said his friends in WWE were stunned when they heard the situation because in WWE, if you get hurt, the company takes care of all the bills. He said the only way out from the huge bills was his mother filing for bankruptcy. TNA's response was to give him a job in production that he said paid decently, but he said it wasn't a lot of money compared to guys like Hogan (well, that's quite the comparison, because nobody was paid a lot compared to Hogan, as even Sting and Angle weren't close to being paid in the same league). He said that TNA seemed stunned by the massive negative reaction when he was fired and that after they were bombarded with negative reaction, Dixie called him and asked if they could release a joint statement saying the release was 100 percent amicable and he asked to be let go to pursue other things. He said he wouldn't agree to it and just told her she should let it blow over, and that his mother was furious at Dixie for even making the call and asking. Shannon Spruill once said that she had asked Sorensen to join in her lawsuit against TNA (which TNA settled out of court because the independent contractor aspect was going to be challenged in court) but he turned it down out of loyalty to Carter. The statute of limitations on Sorensen suing TNA regarding the injury, the same thing Spruill did, is believed to have expired.

(FEBRUARY 10) Jessy Sorensen did another interview on the Monster Factory radio show. He said how a debt collector called him one day saying that he owed $50,000 in medical bills when he was under the assumption that TNA was covering them since that's what Dixie Carter told him and his mother. He said he told the woman he called that TNA was paying the bills and she had no idea what he was talking about. He said that both Carter and Bruce Prichard told him to send the bills to the office and they'd take care of them, which he did, but they never took care of them. He said that his mother, who had to declare bankruptcy, lost her restaurant in the bankruptcy. He said the job that TNA talked about when he was let go about how highly paid he was, actually paid him about $30,000 a year which couldn't even cover his medical bills and that his checks were always arriving late. He said to cover bills, he had two other jobs, waiting tables at a Clearwater beach restaurant and managing at a gym. He said the restaurant was next door to Hogan's merchandise shop on the beach so wrestling fans were often coming into the restaurant, seeing him, and asking him why he was waiting tables. He said a lot of the TNA talent had second jobs and were making more from their other jobs. He said Dixie Carter would tell people that they are starting out. He said he didn't understand why people working for the No. 2 wrestling company had to have a second job to make it. He said he's now making at his other jobs about double what he made in TNA. He said when the firings started happening, he was in catering with Brian & Earl Hebner and worried he would be the next to go. They told him there's no way TNA would fire him because of all the bad publicity it would bring. He also said Zema Ion didn't call him for months after the accident and Ion later told him it was because he lost his number.

(MAY 5) Jessy Sorensen did an interview with Chinlock radio saying that he met with lawyers about suing TNA regarding paying for his injuries, and brought it up in a phone conversation with Bruce Prichard. Three days later he was on the phone with Prichard, Dixie Carter and Dean Broadbend (the CFO of TNA), and they offered him the production job. He said with the benefit of hindsight, he probably should have sued and chalked it up to being young and foolish. He said that he had friends in WWE who told him that TNA not paying his medical bills was bullshit.

(OCTOBER 13) Jessy Sorenson, 25, announced his retirement this past week. I hadn't seen his name around of late, so it appeared he'd lost interest. He wrote that his decision had noting to do with his injury, a broken neck that left him temporarily paralyzed, on February 12, 2012 when Zema Ion did a moonsault off the top to the floor that hit him on the top of his head. He did return to wrestle, although not for TNA, but he hadn't worked much, if any, for several months after suffering an ankle injury.

MATT HARDY

(FEBRUARY 3) Matt Hardy, 39, and wife Rebecca Reyes Hardy, 27 (pro wrestler Reby Sky) were both arrested on assault charges on 1/1. TMZ reported the incident after obtaining mug shots and a copy of a 911 call which led to the arrests. An employee of the Hampton Inn in Emporia, VA, called 911 at 5:45 a.m. on 1/1 saying that she had been told there was a man beating the hell out of his wife or girlfriend in one of the rooms. She said she was the only employee on staff and was scared to go in there. Police arrived at the room and found both Hardy and Reyes Hardy with marks on their faces and took them in. Both were arrested for assault and battery and each filed restraining orders against the other. They were each released on $3,500 bond. The two apparently made up since as Hardy uses social media often, has talked about his beautiful wife many times since the incident, and has posted photos of the two of them together. They've also continued to do wrestling shows together since that date. ROH, where Hardy is a semi-regular headliner, was completely blind-sided by this news.

(FEBRUARY 10) On the Matt Hardy/Rebecca Reyes Hardy fight that was reported last week, TMZ later reported that the fight was because Hardy was behaving in a way where she thought he was impaired on New Year's Eve, and got on his case about it, which led to the fight.

(FEBRUARY 24) CEO Joe Koff issued an apology after criticism of comments he made on the 2/16 edition of Live Audio Wrestling when asked about the alleged New Year's altercation between Matt Hardy and wife Rebecca Reyes Hardy (Reby Sky). When asked, Koff said, "You know, I gotta tell you John (interviewer John Pollock), there's really not a lot about it. I mean, I saw the stuff on TMZ and I saw a couple of Facebook comments about Matt wrestling in Philadelphia. I think it's really not a big deal. I don't have a position on that. I think that charges were dropped. You never want to get involved in domestic stuff, in domestic relationships and domestic disputes. But if the court of law or the judicial system could find no fault with it, I don't feel that's something we necessarily have to take a stance…I'm not shirking that. I'm just saying that it wasn't as a big as, I think the fact that C.M. Punk said that he wasn't gong to wrestle for WWE, or when that story came out around that same time, I think it kind of overshadowed it…I mean, had the outcome been different, from a judicial standpoint or a charge standpoint, I can accept that. But really it was just a domestic battle. You know, they're two wrestlers, they're probably very physical people." Even before the show aired, a lot of people were worried about how it would come off. Two days later, Koff wrote, "I want to take a moment to clarify my comments on the John Pollock radio show last week. When asked about the Matt Hardy domestic violence situation, I was probably not clear enough in stating my views. Both Sinclair Broadcasting Group and I totally abhor and condemn any form of domestic violence in any situation. That has always been my view and anyone who knows me knows my position on that. I am a husband, a father and a grandfather. I believe in the quality of family life. If my statements on the radio show appeared to be insensitive, I sincerely apologize. Domestic violence is a serious issue, and I do not condone it in any way." There wasn't any action taken regarding Hardy, who does appear on the shows this coming weekend. Hardy, who keeps a very high profile to the public, ignored the story and just posted photos of him and his wife after seeming like a happy couple.

JIMMY SNUKA

(FEBRUARY 3) After nearly 31 years, there will be a Grand Jury investigation of the death of Nancy Argentino, 23-year-old girlfriend/mistress of Jimmy Snuka, it was announced by Lehigh County District Attorney James Martin on 1/28. Argentino passed away on May 10, 1983, from blunt head trauma at the Lehigh Valley Hospital. She was found clinging to life at the George Washington Motor Lodge in Allentown, where the WWF wrestlers would regularly stay every three weeks in those days since Allentown's Ag Hall was the home of company television tapings. Snuka, in his book, claimed that in traveling to Allentown, that Argentino got off on the side of the road to go to the bathroom, slipped and hit her head. He said it didn't seem serious, but she wasn't feeling well enough the next day to attend the tapings, and when he went back to the hotel after, she was clinging to life. It was, at the time, ruled an accidental death. However, during the ordeal, Snuka, who at the time was the most popular wrestler in the WWF, in explaining what happened, gave contradictory stories to different people at the hospital. Vince McMahon came to Allentown to talk to the local authorities and the case concluded from there. Years later, her family hired a private investigator, and then with evidence, filed a wrongful death lawsuit against Snuka, winning a default judgment. Snuka, now 70, claiming he was destitute, never paid. Argentino's death was said to be consistent with a moving head striking a stationary object, and at the time of her death, had more than 24 cuts and bruises, on her head, ears, chin, arms, hands, back, butt, legs and feet. Forensic pathologist Isidore Mihalakis recommended at the time that it be investigated as a homicide until proven otherwise. The case had been dormant for decades, there were a couple of major news stories on it in 1992, including a piece by Irv Muchnick, which was later republished in a book that he wrote, and then wrote an e-book with Argentino's sisters updating the case last year after it had become a significant news story once again. Last year, on the 30th anniversary of the death, it got significant coverage in a number of newspapers, spurred on by the Argentino family, most notably Nancy's sisters, and Muchnick, the nephew of legendary promoter Sam Muchnick, who wrote a series of follow-up articles. Because the case was never closed. Police records were difficult to come by. But the case was revived when the Allentown Morning-Call ran a series of front page articles on the subject last year. They were able to garner new information, including a police report that said Snuka had told at least five people, including the responding officer, that he shoved Argentino, causing her to fall and hit her head. He later told police that he was misunderstood as Argentino had slipped and fallen, and hit her head, when they stopped on the side of the road for her to go to the bathroom.

(FEBRUARY 10) A correction from last week in the Nancy Argentino story. We wrote that the Argentino family hired a private investigator years later and got a default judgment against Jimmy Snuka in the wrongful death civil case. In actuality, they hired the private investigator very shortly after the Allentown police decided against going forward with the case against Snuka. The default judgment was in 1985, two years after Nancy Argentino's death. Irv Muchnick, who has covered the story for decades, actually was the first reporter to investigate it back in the early 90s, wrote a piece where he believes that the most likely charge if something is to come out of this would be involuntary manslaughter. And if that's the case, the statute of limitations on that charge expired a long time ago. There is no statute of limitations for first or second degree murder, or voluntary manslaughter.

SIN CARA

(FEBRUARY 3) Luis Urive, the first Sin Cara, appeared on TV show Tercera Caida this past week and claimed that he owned the rights to the Sin Cara name. He had already opened a Sin Cara Gym in Mexico City and now that his WWE contract has expired, he's taking dates using the Sin Cara name. That's notable since WWE is using Jorge Arias as Sin Cara at the same time. Urive can't use the Mistico name because CMLL owns it and has given it to a new wrestler. Urive said that his lawyers may be looking at WWE using the name for a new wrestler saying he's got proof he owns the name. I do remember that WWE wasn't able to register the name in Mexico, but I'm virtually certain they did for the U.S. He said that the reason it didn't work out in the U.S. was because WWE told him he couldn't wrestle the way he did in Mexico and said that psychologically screwed him up because he kept getting told what he couldn't do and felt limited in the ring. He said he couldn't understand it, because when they signed him, it was because he was a star wrestling a certain way, and then he was told he couldn't wrestle that way. Anyway, that one didn't work and it didn't work for all the reasons I said it wasn't going to work the day that they signed him. He admitted he looked awful on WWE television, but said since he left, he's spent a lot of time training and getting in better shape. He was frustrated he wasn't allowed to do what he does best. He said he would be working indies in Mexico and will work with Dr. Wagner Jr. and L.A. Park, the two biggest name indie wrestlers. He said he's now focused and can wrestle the way he wants to. He said he has no problems with either Jorge Arias (who took over Sin Cara in WWE) or Del Rio. He said he thinks Hunico is a good guy. While he was on the show, they aired highlights of the new Mistico vs. Mephisto match on the 1/18 Fantastica Mania show in Japan. He noted he has nothing against the new Mistico and that he helped him get a break when he was Dragon Lee and also helped his brother, Rush. He wished him well but said he's not at his level and he said that it does bother him that some promoters use his look as Mistico as opposed to the new Mistico on posters to sell tickets to see him. He said when he came to WWE, after his first match, the first thing he was told was not to do certain things, and that affected him mentally. You're always going to have problems when you take a guy who legitimately was one of the biggest superstars of the decade and a major draw, and then tell him not to do things that got him over in the first place. It was part of what I considered the inevitability about the relationship. Urive thought he was a major star. It would be like Steve Austin going to Japan or Mexico and the promoters telling him not to do all the things that got him over and mentally, how he'd handle that, particularly if he then struggled to get over. It's nobody's fault, but it was part of the almost inevitability of why the relationship was doomed from the start. Mysterio never had a run close to what Sin Cara had so he didn't have that cockiness to where him being told by HHH to tweak things didn't offend him in the least. But it also explains why CMLL guys will always do better with New Japan than WWE, because with New Japan, the promotion doesn't tell them what not to do, and the other wrestlers get a kick out of working their style and with them instead of the opposite. Again, you can argue both ways. They are just different mentalities although I obviously prefer the New Japan mentality of trying to make everyone the best they can be as opposed to everyone working within the same parameters. It's the mix of styles and styles of matches on a single show that make New Japan the best big event promotion in the world. But a big difference is also the fan base. Japanese fans watching an unfamiliar style react well often because it's different from what they usually see. In WWE, general fan reaction is biggest to things that are embedded in their heads by virtue of always seeing it. He said he's going to work indies in Mexico, with a date on 2/1 in Mexico City and 3/1 in Tijuana the only things he's booked for. He said he'd be open to work AAA, CMLL or Todos x Todos (El Hijo del Santo's promotion). He said Jorge Arias and him used to travel together and Arias, as the new Sin Cara, is only doing his job. He said the only problem they ever had was in the past when he started as Mistico and Arias, who used the name in Juarez, was mad somebody in Mexico City was using his ring name. He said the La Mistica finisher was a move that actually happened by mistake when he slipped trying to do a head scissors when training with his uncle, Tony Salazar, and to block falling flat on his face, he held onto the arm and landed in a Fujiwara armbar position. He said Arias is a good guy. He said that he didn't study English when with WWE (and this was a big issue with management). He said that they say WWE style is safer, but he got hurt more doing WWE style than he ever did working in Mexico. He noted that even though he didn't get a push, he was one of the best merchandise sellers in WWE. He also spoke highly of Mysterio, and said the most humble top stars in WWE were Mysterio and Dwayne Johnson. He said he's thankful to Paco Alonso for giving him his break, as that allowed him the chance to go all over the world and be with WWE, but was negative about CMLL booking. He said he owned the Sin Cara name and isn't afraid of WWE suing him. There were people who thought he was full of it on that.

CHAVO GUERRERO

(FEBRUARY 17) Chavo Guerrero Jr., 43, who seems to have disappeared from the scene since leaving TNA in the Feast or Fired angle (nixing his planned heel turn on Hernandez, who has also disappeared), was a guest on Chris Jericho's podcast this past week. He noted that he's got a small part in a movie "Fight to the Finish," where he plays an MMA trainer, and is working on doing some television shows with Rampage Jackson like a reality show (the two live near each other in Orange County and became friends when their sons played football together) and perhaps even promote MMA shows together. It was a really emotional interview because he talked in depth about the forbidden subject of Chris Benoit, who was also one of Jericho's best friends. Both talked about how hard it was emotionally to cope with what Benoit did. Jericho believes that it was the concussions and given what happened with several NFL players whose brains had issues, it's nothing you can rule out. Bob Holly, who was one of Benoit's best friends as well, has in his mind dismissed this. Chavo, who was the closest person to Benoit over the last year of his life besides his family (Chavo, Benoit and referee Scott Armstrong were regular traveling partners) said that he didn't notice any kind of a change in Benoit, although did joke about the Houdini thing with him. Benoit sometimes would disappear. He'd be sitting there talking to you, you buy him a beer and he's gone. Or he tells you to call him in five minutes, then you do, and he doesn't answer. Then again, that was the running joke about Paul Heyman for years as well. William Regal once mentioned how Benoit called him to come over (they both lived near each other in Peachtree City, GA) to watch some new tapes, he'd go over, and he knew Benoit was in the house but he wouldn't open the door when the bell rang. Both Jericho and Guerrero Jr. talked about how messed up they were mentally by what Benoit did because they both considered him a close friend and almost their role model for being a wrestler and Jericho said he had to question a lot of what he believed in to come to grips with it. Jericho noted that of all the brains that Chris Nowinski's group studied, that Benoit had the most damage and that was the only way he could rationalize what happened and come to a conclusion. When Guerrero Jr. was in TNA, besides wrestling, he was somewhat working as an agent on finishes and helping the younger guys lay out matches for the last several months until the deal ended.

JAKE ROBERTS

(MARCH 3) Jake Roberts, 58, told TMZ this past weekend that he was diagnosed with skin cancer. Roberts underwent surgery on 2/24 for what he said was a half dollar sized tumor behind his knee, which was growing into his muscle. He said he discovered the tumor about a month ago, and had a biopsy done. The results came in that it was cancerous on 2/21, and emergency surgery to remove it was scheduled. Roberts vowed he would be at his next booking, on 3/14 for Jersey Championship Wrestling, as well as at the WWE Hall of Fame ceremony three weeks later. Roberts said to TMZ:"If the devil can't defeat me, cancer doesn't stand a chance in Hell. Pray for sick children who face this horrible disease cause The Snake will be just fine." After surgery, he wrote, "Surgery went well and feeling good. Won't know if the growth is all removed, or spread until test come back. Doc optimistic and so am I." Cancer is cancer and it's nothing to play down, but a lot of wrestlers (from all the tanning) get it that you never heard about, and people get skin cancer and if caught early, it's not as bad as the usual C word that you never want to hear.

(MARCH 10) An update on Jake Roberts' surgery on 2/25 from an interview he did with Bill Apter the next day. Roberts went through five-and-a-half hours of surgery on his leg. The doctors won't know for a while if they got rid of all the cancer. They also don't know yet what kind of cancer it is, so it may not have been skin cancer. He also has two more small growths on his other leg that he's concerned about. The good news is that it was diagnosed early. The bad news is, there is a lot of waiting, and he admitted that for a guy like him, who is battling every day to stay sober, that kind of waiting and worrying isn't a good thing.

(SEPTEMBER 8) Jake Roberts was hospitalized this past week in Las Vegas and in an induced coma for several hours after complications from double pneumonia. Roberts, real name Aurelian Smith Jr., 59, hadn't been feeling well for at least a week, according to attorney, manager and roommate Kyle Magee. Diamond Dallas Page, who helped turn Roberts' life around a few years ago, said he was with Roberts a few days earlier, and he was complaining about being in pain, but didn't want to miss his booking for protégé Sinn Bohdi (Nick Cvjetkovich, 41), who was doing a birthday show in Las Vegas on 8/29. Roberts was in pain and having trouble breathing while on the flight on 8/27, and alerted the flight attendants. Upon landing, was rushed by ambulance from the plane to Desert Springs Hospital in Las Vegas, where he was put in an induced coma and given a battery of tests. He had pneumonia and fluid buildup in both lungs and spent a few days in the Intensive Care Unit. He regained consciousness but was in-and-out late on 8/28. By the next day, he was completely alert. Page joked that he was "stable, he's coherent, a little grumpy." Doctors discovered from numerous tests that he had a mass in his brain, which there is a belief may have come from the punishment he took while wrestling. The infection from the pneumonia also spread to other organs. He was transported to a new hospital in Las Vegas which was better equipped to evaluate him a few days later. He was still hospitalized as of press time, had just been removed from being hooked up to a ventilator on 9/3, which was earlier than expected, and doing breathing exercises. They are hopeful he doesn't have to go back on it. He also was able to talk. Sinn Bodhi wrote on Facebook that Roberts flipped off a nurse when she told him he couldn't have a donut, since he's not allowed to eat any food and all of his nutrients have to come from an IV.

(SEPTEMBER 15) Jake Roberts said during an interview at the 9/6 Future Stars of Wrestling show in Las Vegas that while undergoing tests, doctors found cancer in his chest. He said he wasn't scared and would be fighting it. He was released from the hospital on 9/5 but is remaining in Las Vegas for treatment for the time being. This would be his second battle with cancer over the last year, as he had cancer in his leg that was removed earlier in the year. His voice was weak, but he was at the merchandise table throughout the show that night.

(OCTOBER 6) Jake Roberts got positive test results as the tumor found on his lungs was benign. He still has an issue with his brain to deal with.

(DECEMBER 15) A documentary on the recent life of Jake Roberts, called "The Resurrection of Jake the Snake," directed by Steve Yu, will make its world premiere at the Slamdance Festival, which takes place in late January as an alternative to the Sundance Festival. The festival is for movies that are made by first-time directors and with budgets of less than $1 million. The description of the movie is that Roberts charts his personal and professional comeback while battling crippling addictions. Listed as the cast are Roberts, DDP, Chris Jericho,

Steve Austin and Adam Copeland.

LIONHEART

(MARCH 10) Adrian McCallum, 31, who wrestles in the U.K. as Lionheart, the top heel on the U.K. independent scene, suffered a broken neck in two places in his 2/28 match with A.J. Styles, which was the main event in Preston, England for Preston City Wrestling. Lionheart beat Styles, but after the match, Styles delivered a Styles clash. McCallum accidentally moved his head, to where Styles, in the normal execution of the move, landed with McCallum taking it on the top of his head. Roderick Strong did the same thing a few weeks ago and he was out of action for a short period of time. The McCallum injury is a lot worse, as he suffered a broken neck in two places but is not in need of surgery. He wasn't moving his arms or legs afterwards. It was the end of the show and they asked fans to leave the building as quickly as possible. While obviously the Styles Clash can be dangerous, Styles has been doing the move for years and it's always been a safe move. Hiroshi Tanahashi and others also do it without anyone being hurt. McCallum wrote:"To update, my neck is broken in two places. I have had an MRI and the positive spin is there is no immediate requirement for surgery, although that may change. I don't want to bore anyone or appear to fish for sympathy, as I will comment more in depth in time. All I want to say is that the outpouring of support, calls, messages, etc. has been truly overwhelming. Reading them all has reduced me to tears more times than I can count. I thank you and I love you. I know now what the future holds, and as emotional and drained as I am, I will fight back from this." The injury took place on a show that drew a sellout 1,300 fans.

LINDA MILES

(MARCH 17) How is this for a Where Are They Now? Linda Miles, 35, who was the winner of the second season of Tough Enough with Jackie Gayda (now fitness model Jackie Haas/wife of Charlie), was seen on TV a few weeks ago as a referee at a Division I women's college basketball game (University of Indiana). Miles was a starter at Rutgers, good enough to get a WNBA tryout, but not good enough to make a team. She then got into Tough Enough and getting a WWE contract out of it. She didn't exactly endear herself to people with her attitude in wrestling, and was cut after two years. She was brought up to the main roster as Shaniqua, the manager of the Basham Brothers tag team. After wrestling, she was trying to hook up a job as a sportscaster on television. Last we had heard she was a substitute school teacher in Cincinnati.

WWE MERCHANDISE SELLERS

(MARCH 17) The current biggest merchandise sellers at the arenas are, in order, Cena, Bryan, Punk (down on the list because he's been off TV and not at the arenas), Batista, Sheamus, Hogan, Orton and Lesnar. On the web site, the best sellers are Cena, Punk, Bryan, Hogan, The Shield, Austin, Lesnar, Undertaker and Orton. Most notable is no more Sin Cara on the list since the change in the person playing the role, and no Mysterio, who for years had been in the top tier. Amazing how if someone is booked to be nothing, their merchandise doesn't sell so well. They are going to make a big push for Hogan for merchandise and legends merchandise based on a big four of Hogan, Undertaker, Warrior and Austin. Notable Warrior ahead of Michaels and no Dwayne Johnson (whose deal is that he gets a much higher cut of his merchandise than others and who isn't expected around any time soon). They also want all four of the big four at WrestleMania. Austin had talked about not wanting to go just to be there, and being happy to watch it from home, that he wouldn't be going unless there was a good reason. We know that they want to find a storyline for him to be at Mania in a non-wrestling fashion and the idea of him being there has been thrown at him, but we haven't heard of any kind of a deal. If you remember back, the original main event idea for this year's Mania was Austin managed by Vince McMahon vs. HHH, but they gave up on that one a long time ago.

JIM ROSS

(MARCH 17) I've heard a lot from several people on a commentary thing from the 3/3 Raw. Before the Christian vs. Sheamus match, coming off a WWE Network commercial, Layfield started talking about how much he liked Vince McMahon as an announcer. Lawler then delivered the line asking how he would compare Vince McMahon as an announcer to Jim Ross. Layfield responded that Vince was better because he could speak English, and then used the line of saying it's like comparing horse manure to ice cream (the line Bobby Heenan used in 1991 when Ric Flair was coming in when he tried to compare Flair's "real world title" to Hogan's title). The genesis is that certain parties were very upset at Jim Ross for telling a story on Opie & Anthony's radio show that week about Vince McMahon sharting. The story was back from well over a decade ago when Vince was doing the heel Mr. McMahon character in the Austin era, and Gerald Brisco, who has a notoriously weak stomach, was working with him in the Gorilla position as the guy who timed the segments to make sure the show stayed on track and segments hit at the right time. So before going out, Vince went to fart in Brisco's face, but accidentally shit himself. He went to the ring for his segment, did it with no problem. The brown stain was visible in the back of his Khaki pants and the camera people were all aware but didn't dare shoot it. That's all the story he told. The way the story was told at the time is when he came back, he must have changed clothes, and was holding the loaded old pants. He tried to chase Brisco down with to make him vomit, and HHH grabbed Brisco to hold him in place so he couldn't get away, but Brisco used one of his old amateur moves and reversed and escaped. Anyway, that story ended up going from Opie & Anthony to TMZ and tons of other web sites, so that was the receipt. It was clearly set up, and Layfield is often the voice of Vince. The segment was clearly set up since Lawler fed Layfield the line (notable because Lawler and Ross are legitimately best friends), but whether Layfield laid the segment out on his own or Vince did, I couldn't say.

(MAY 19) Dixie Carter is evidently not happy with Jim Ross on his podcast talking about how bad TNA creative is. Somebody with a fake Jim Ross Twitter account wrote something about John Gaburick not knowing creative and complaining about the decision not to sign Chris Sabin and Dixie wrote, "It's official. You know as little as the real J.R." She then got hammered badly for the remark and deleted it. Apparently she was texting the real J.R. like crazy, being all apologetic and nobody could understand why she wrote it in the first place. I sense she was frustrated with Ross burying TNA creative, but not realizing how badly doing it would appear to backfire on her. TNA creative is a sad laughing stock. It's not pointing the finger at any specific person because it's the inability to change from a concept that hasn't worked in years that's the biggest problem right now. And they have good things about the product, but the constant turns, inability to understand how to create a top babyface and being a copy of WWE instead of trying to find a concept that is different from WWE have been issues of years, and it never changes. They've had to ax all of their well paid talent and are now playing the game of hoping the ratings don't fall too much, and luckily, they probably won't.

KANE

(MARCH 17) Kane has started up a new insurance company in Knoxville called The Jacobs Agency, with his wife. They offer auto, home, motorcycle, RV, boat, life and commercial insurance, as well as retirement planning. Kane has told people in the area that he's been planning to retire for some time now but it's hard to walk away from the money, so he's going to continue while he can still make the big money. The feeling locally in the political world is that at some point he would be interested in running for public office as a Libertarian party candidate.

WWE EXECUTIVES PAY

(MARCH 24) Some notes on WWE executive pay. Senior management consists of Vince McMahon (CEO and Chairman of the Board), George Barrios (CFO & Chief Strategy Officer), Michelle Wilson (Chief Revenue Officer and Chief Marketing Officer), Stephanie McMahon (Chief Branding Officer), Paul Levesque (Executive Vice President, Talent, Live Events and Creative), Kevin Dunn (Executive Producer), Casey Collins (Executive Vice President of Consumer Products), Michael Luisi (President, WWE Studios), Gerret Meier (Executive Vice President, International), Laura Brevetti (Senior Vice President, General Counsel) and Basil DeVito Jr. (Senior Advisor, Business Strategy). Levesque as COO is a television title and not his actual title. His role is to oversee talent, produce the live events (basically oversee the person who books those shows) and creative (working with Vince McMahon). The current base salaries are Vince McMahon at $1,184,500, Barrios at $700,000, Levesque at $550,000 (he also has a $1 million per year contract as talent), Dunn at $700,000 and Luisi at $600,000. Actual compensation , including stock grants, for the top people for 2013 ended up as $1,724,958 for Vince McMahon (Vince doesn't get additional stock grants since he owns so much stock to begin with, his earnings in 2012 were $2.456,359 and in 2011 were $1,111,395. The difference is no money from profit incentives in 2011. They lowered the level of profits needed for incentives to kick in for senior management in 2012, so he made $1.3 million that way, and profits were way down in 2013 but they still paid the execs some money because they had lowered expectations and don't figure network start up money against them); $1,378,197 for Barrios; $2,511,331 for Levesque (whose actual earnings as a wrestler between match payoffs, and merchandise and licensing money was $1,868,639; in 2012 Levesque made $2,912,231 which was $488,482 in salary as an executive, $305,000 in profit sharing incentive bonuses and $2,118,769 for being a wrestler which would be his mostly PPV payoffs and merch money; in 2011 Levesque made $336,538 in pay as an executive, $74,100 in stock grants, no profit sharing and $2,074,042 as a wrestler for $2,484,680 total), $1,744,184 for Dunn and $1,403,228 for Luisi. Keep in mind with the stock up significantly, the value of the stock is nearly double today of what is reported. With today's stock price, for example, Dunn would be closer to $2.3 million. Stephanie McMahon's total earnings for last year was $778,394, of which $325,000 was as television talent. As far as stock goes, the four biggest owners are Vince McMahon (39,272,641 shares, current value $1.21 billion), Linda McMahon (9,066,770 shares, current value $280.2 million), Stephanie McMahon (2,511,071 - so even with her big sell off over the last year , with the stock increase, she's now worth about $77.6 million just on her stock) while Paul Levesque owns 50,764 shares ($1.57 million) and Intrepid Capital is the largest non-McMahon stockholder at 2,847,474 shares. Levesque's $1,868,639 came from his role as an authority figure on TV, merchandise and five matches during the year, which were PPV matches at Mania with Lesnar and a cage rematch at Extreme Rules, and three Raw matches (two on the same night) with Axel. His $2,118,769 in wrestler pay in 2012 was a combination of his work as an authority figure and three matches, a Madison Square Garden trios house show match, and PPV matches with Undertaker (Mania) and Lesnar (SummerSlam). His $2,074,042 from wrestling in 2011 came from nine matches, which were four PPV matches (Mania vs. Taker, and B PPV matches with Punk, Kevin Nash and a tag with Punk vs. Miz & R-Truth, plus four dark matches at TV tapings, all tags or multiple person matches, and a singles street fight with Sheamus at MSG). His downside as a performer for all of those years was $1 million, so the over and above is based on PPV payoffs and merch. One year, Vickie Guerrero as G.M. of Raw earned around $80,000 in her role when she was white hot and that included Eddy Guerrero merchandise money.

CHAEL SONNEN / STEPHANIE MCMAHON

(MARCH 24) Chael Sonnen was on TSN's "Off the Record," ths past week, a Canadian sports talk show that he's been on several times in the past. While doing an interview, he attempted to give out Stephanie McMahon's private cell phone number, the one to reach her in emergencies such as her kids being sick at school. Sonnen was on the show to promote the current season of Ultimate Fighter Brazil, and it airing on Fight Pass. This is the behind the scenes of what happened. Host Michael Landsberg was told to ask Sonnen about whether C.M. Punk would be at WrestleMania. Sonnen and Punk are friends. So Landsberg asked the question, and Sonnen said he would answer if after the break. At the time they weren't scheduled to go to a break. Later, when asked again, Sonnen said he didn't know, but he knew someone that did, and held up a piece of paper with a phone number. On the air, it was digitized so you couldn't see the number, since he taped the interview on 3/10 but it aired on 3/11. Sonnen then said, "Tell Hunter I just played the game." After the interview ended, Landsberg, in a later cut away, noted that the interview had been taped and that they were not going to put the number on the air. He said they did call the number and confirmed it was Stephanie's private number. Sonnen has several friends in high places in the company and there are those in the company who would like for him to come in. But the reality is, given his age (he turns 37 in a few weeks) and WWE's emphasis now on a certain learned style of working, by the time he got that style down, he'd be pushing 40. Plus, Sonnen's future in his mind is as an announcer for FOX, not as a pro wrestler. He did attend the Power Plant for WCW about 15 years ago while attending college, they liked him and wanted to sign him, but he decided to return to college and try and win an NCAA title and then WCW folded and he went into MMA. Another weird deal is on the show, as a rib on Sonnen, they showed a photo of Sonnen from high school with an autograph from HHH, with the idea that he went to him for an autograph then. But the timing there pretty much says that didn't happen. Sonnen graduated high school in early 1995. Paul Levesque debuted with WWE on television in April of that year doing the Greenwich snob gimmick, but didn't go as HHH (how it was signed) until a few years later.

SHANE McMAHON

(APRIL 14) There was a huge story at www.buzzfeed.com on Shane McMahon and life after WWE. It noted the first time he quit the company was at 15, when he had a summer job working in the warehouse, and then got a construction job for triple the money and his father at the time was happy for him. Shane said that he quit the company in 2009 because, "There was always that one little question: Can I get it done outside of the company? My dad, although I learned so much, he casts a big shadow." It's well known that Shane's goal from childhood, when he was 12 years old, was to follow in the footsteps of his father. Well, he'd say the footsteps of his great-grandfather Jess, a boxing and wrestling promoter from the 30s to the 50s, grandfather Vincent James McMahon, who promoted from the 50s through selling in 1982, and his father. He would tell similar age kids of the top wrestlers how he would be running the company like his father and they would be stars in the company like their father. While the article tried to downplay the idea that wasn't going to happen because Stephanie and HHH had been chosen to take over, and he denied it, that was the lay of the land at the time. Over the years, Shane had tried to push the company to buy ECW, the UFC and they even had talks about buying Pride (although in this case I don't know how strongly Shane felt on that one). The idea was always that Shane would prove, under the company's umbrella, but on his own, that he could run a successful operation and be the heir apparent. But none of those deals went through. He was to be the face of WCW, but that was more for the public than reality, but his father changed his mind quickly on a separate WCW branch of the promotion. He's gotten involved in a number of businesses, most notably YOU on Demand, a video-on-demand company in China. When he started, there were a lot of skeptics, because China had no history, like the U.S., Australia or Europe, of people paying for individual television content, but the country does have 700 million smartphone users and 210 million cable TV subscribers, so those numbers would at least indicate gigantic potential if people start to think in that direction. The company has yet to break through and be profitable, but the upside is huge if and when it does. An issue is that pirate DVDs are an enormous business, to the point they are charging $1 to $3 per movie, with the idea you get a better quality and a legit quality by pushing a button as opposed to searching through channels on the street. He was CEO of the company, but is now Chairman, turning the reigns over to Weicheng Liu as CEO, who knows the language. The story noted the company's financial numbers are not pretty right now. He's serious enough about the gig that he loaned the company $7 million to keep it going. The company lost $8.19 million last year, down from $15.14 million in losses the year before, but stock has gone up based on potential. McMahon predicted it would break even by the end of this year or early next year. "The numbers are so big over there that it doesn't take much once you hit a little groove. This is a labor of love to create something from nothing. I like it when they say, `Oh, you can't do that. There's no way you can build something like that.' That's what fuels me, to pull off the impossible." It noted on the day of the WWE Network launch, with his father and sister on stage and his mother in the crowd, he was at a motorcycle shop in Brooklyn that he co-owns and didn't seem to really care about the breakthrough in the company he at one time was expected to run. He still thinks he could have played in the NFL, even though he never played in college. While he denied any sibling rivalry, he did say his father was tough to work for and felt he was held to a higher standard. Vince McMahon, interviewed for the story, admitted that he was harder on Shane than a non-family member, but also said that they are very close personally, just don't work together. He talked about when Calvin Darden Jr. attempted to swindle him into buying Maxim, and said, "Every time I asked the pertinent questions, there'd be no response and no answers. So I passed. Good thing I did." When asked if he'd come back to wrestling, he gave the never-say-never attitude. Historically, sons of people who started a major business and worked with their fathers who left, in the vast majority of cases, come back. When asked if he would like to run WWE, he said, "It's in my blood," but then gave a more measured corporate answer of, "If I feel it's the right time and I could make a significant difference, I would consider it." As for Vince, he said Shane was always welcome back if that's what he wants to do.

DAVID BENOIT

(MAY 5) David Benoit, the 21-year-old son of Chris, will make his pro wrestling debut on a Hart Legacy Wrestling show on 7/18 in Calgary, teaming with Chavo Guerrero Jr., who was one of Chris' best friends and his traveling partner at the time of his death. Benoit has been training for a while, some with Harry Smith.

(MAY 12) The pro wrestling debut of David Benoit, the son of Chris, scheduled for July in Calgary is now unlikely to happen. Benoit & Chavo Guerrero Jr. (As noted, probably Chris' closest friend at the time of his death) were supposed to team. David Benoit has flirted with the idea of wrestling but has never formally trained. Smith Hart, the oldest son of Stu, was trying to convince him to do the show thinking it would garner attention and help draw. After word got out, Chris Jericho, who has known David for years and I believe he and Harry Smith were among the few in wrestling to keep in contract with him over the last seven years, contacted the promotion and was furious about them advertising David in a match, saying he hadn't been sufficiently trained to do a match. Chavo then canceled his booking. It appears that David Benoit's booking has also been canceled. Smith Hart had told Chavo that David had experience wrestling and would be okay. Smith Hart then told Jericho that they were never planning on David wrestling, just doing an angle with him, although when we got the word, it was David & Chavo. Smith Hart then called David Benoit and said he wanted him in a match and tried to convince him he could get through with it without training and that it wasn't going to be that difficult. David Benoit had asked HHH and William Regal about becoming a wrestler years ago. They told him they wanted him to finish high school and also felt Lance Storm in Calgary was the best person in the area to train him. Benoit had enrolled in several training camps, but never showed up on the first day, so he was never trained. Apparently Chavo was first told by Smith Hart that David was fully trained and ready to debut, so Chavo agreed to team with him, until he found out that wasn't the case. Jericho, who has always tried to look out for David, was really mad and tried to get the match stopped. Dan Severn vs. Harry Smith was also to be on the show. The original idea was to get Kurt Angle to wrestle Harry Smith, but Kurt's body is banged up and he doesn't want to take any dates outside of TNA right now. Severn then canceled and it's possible Harry Smith won't be able to work because the show may be on the day he has to fly to Japan for the G-1 Climax tournament.

(MAY 19) Smith Hart contacted us about last week's story saying that his brother Bruce and he had spoken to David Benoit about training with them and Harry Smith prior to a match and if he wasn't prepared, they'd have pulled him from the show. Bob Johnson then said that Bruce and Ross Hart have nothing to do with Smith Hart's Hart Legacy group and never will, and they train wrestlers at the Hart Brothers University.

BATISTA

(MAY 12) The big story hovering around Extreme Rules this past week involved the direction to Payback, the WWE's next PPV show on 6/1 from Chicago. Batista was originally scheduled to finish up on the Chicago show, with the plan being that he would put over Daniel Bryan in the title match. However, he decided a few weeks back that he was going to take off after Extreme Rules, and had been pulled from all advertising of shows after 5/4. A number of different ideas were talked about, including him finishing up at Extreme Rules and losing the fall in the six-man that was the most anticipated match on the card. The plan was for Bryan to pin Kane, who was only supposed to be a "one-shot" challenger. Even as late as show time, the situation was still uncertain. The one thing changed was that after Bryan had pinned Kane, Kane sat up, a change in plans in case they would have to go to a rematch. Even after the show was over, Vince McMahon was still going with the idea of trying to talk Batista into doing the match with Bryan. There were stories going around that Batista didn't want to put Bryan over because of his size, but I don't know if that's the case, because that would contradict his feelings on the guy from the start. When Bryan was first in WWE and he was getting squashed by the top guys most of the time (not all the time), Batista was supposed to squash him on Raw, and insisted on giving Bryan a lot of the match and letting him look great. He refused to squash him because he saw the guy had talent. Everything Batista was scheduled for on his return largely changed. It's easy to blame creative, but in his case, creative only changed because the fans forced the change. There was an obvious direction to go this year at WrestleMania and it wasn't Batista over Randy Orton for the WWE title. Batista did put Bryan over via submission at WrestleMania. But it's evident he wasn't happy about doing it a second time. At one point Batista was going to finish up at TV this week, and at that point the plan was for Roman Reigns to pin him in a singles match. Eventually they got him to agree to stay through the next PPV, so creative changed to where he beat Seth Rollins via count out on Smackdown and didn't wrestle on Raw, but he also didn't have to put Bryan over for a second time. Batista's original booking was to have him win the title at WrestleMania for a short run, then lose it and leave for the summer to promotion "Guardians of the Galaxy." WWE liked the idea that they would have one of the stars of a hit summer movie in the promotion and once the promotional work was over, he'd return. Exactly what happens next is unclear, as he's not advertised for any shows going forward. After all that, the Payback top matches at press time are scheduled as Bryan vs. Kane in a Buried Alive match for the WWE title and a rematch with The Shield vs. Evolution. The other big match will involve John Cena and Bray Wyatt in some form, whether single, tag or handicap match. This could change, but everything was built in that direction at TV this week. Essentially it was viewed that Batista got his way.

AJ Styles

(May 12) A.J. Styles became only the seventh foreigner ever to win the IWGP heavyweight championship when he defeated Kazuchika Okada, thanks to Yujiro Takahashi turning on Okada, in the main event of Wrestling Dontaku on 5/3 at the Fukuoka International Center Arena. Styles joins only Hulk Hogan, Big Van Vader, Salman Hashimkov, Scott Norton, Bob Sapp and Brock Lesnar as non-Japanese to have held the title created in 1983 when Hogan beat Antonio Inoki in the finals of a tournament. The match was well worked, excellent in many ways, but was marred by a tough crowd that didn't really know Styles and get into his trademark moves. Styles did the right things at the right time, but the crowd didn't recognize his key stuff. Still, they were hot for the final several minutes of the match. With the win, Styles will defend the title on 5/17 in New York against Michael Elgin, with the winner headlining New Japan's No. 3 show of the year on 5/25 at the Yokohama Arena, where Okada gets his rematch. Bullet Club members The Young Bucks and Karl Anderson had interfered twice early on and were kicked out about eight minutes into the match. After Styles missed his spiral tap, Okada used a high dropkick to the back of Styles' head, followed by a tombstone piledriver. The Bucks and Anderson came back out, distracting the referee. Takahashi, a member of the Chaos group in New Japan with Okada, Shinsuke Nakamura, Gedo, Jado, Tomohiro Ishii and Yoshi-Hashi, went into the ring all covered up. Takahashi then showed his face, and clotheslined Okada. He took off his jacket and had a Bullet Club shirt on, and laid Okada out with his finisher, the Tokyo Pimps (dominator). Styles then followed with a brainbuster and Styles Clash to score the pin in 24:31. A lot of people didn't like the finish, given the IWGP title matches have been straight matches, with little in the way of interference in recent years. Even those that had interference never had it be the reason for the title change. To me, doing it once isn't a bad idea, as long as it is once and it doesn't turn into an American title where The Bullet Club are interfering and saving the title for Styles in every defense like a Four Horsemen or NWO style unit.

Scott Hall

(May 26) There is a lot of concern over Scott Hall, after he blew off a weekend appearances in Northern California this weekend. Hall, with son Cody, were scheduled to appear for Kirk White's Big Time Wrestling promotion at a convention and a show in Newark, CA, which included a number of big names including

Ric Flair, Ricky Morton, Robert Gibson, Chavo Guerrero Jr., The Godfather, Molly Holly, Ezekiel Jackson, Christopher Daniels and Frankie Kazarian. White has been promoting shows in this area for two decades and bringing in top talent and there's never been a money issue that we've heard of, and in this situation, even though it could cost him some late people on the fence, he immediately put the word out when finding out Hall wasn't coming. He had paid Hall's $1,600 advance (50% deposit that the top guys get), and on 5/16, when Hall and his son were scheduled to fly out of Atlanta to San Francisco, he texted White and told him he was in a bad place. His son tried to get him out of bed, and DDP, also tried to get him to get out of bed and make his booking, as did his agent, Bill Behrens. He simply refused to go. As far as what condition he's in, that's pure speculative but when he was asked some time back regarding rumors he'd been drinking, which go back months, and his answer was that he hadn't had a drink that day, and he had written something on Twitter months ago about how he'd drink if he wanted to. Jake Roberts, on Roddy Piper's podcast, said he was very concerned with Hall and said he was having problems with demons. Behrens wrote to White:"I regret that Scott Hall decided last minute he would not make the trip from Atlanta with his son Cody to Big Time Wrestling's Wrestlefest and wrestling event. His son, Cody Hall, Dallas page and myself all tried to change his mind but he could not get past the personal issues that had him unwilling to travel to California. Kirk, you are a true professional who goes out of his way to deliver what he promotes and promises. I hope the fans who attend WrestleFest and that evening's wrestling event do not feel shortchanged by Scott's decision. I am confident all who attend will have a great time. I believe it is Scott Hall's loss to have missed this opportunity to meet his many fans and to see his son Cody wrestle for the first time in California. I am sure in time he will come to regret his decision, if he has not already." Cody Hall (who isn't 6-foot-8, but it probably 6-foot-5 or so and agile for his size) came to fulfill his booking on his own and was at the convention and wrestled. On the company's web site, they told fans who had pre-ordered a Hall autograph or photo-op that they would be refunded directly via paypal or if they came to the event, would be refunded in cash at the event.

(JUNE 23) Don't expect Scott Hall to be used going forward by Northeast Wrestling. Promoter Mike O'Brien said, "Scott Hall was his old self (he worked for the group a week ago). Not his physical condition, but a real cocky asshole. You give everyone a shot. Safe to say you won't be seeing me book him or his dangerous, green son again." O'Brien ran shows 6/6 in Spring Valley, NY, before 1,021 fans, using Mick Foley, Jerry Lawler, Matt Hardy and Booker T as the top stars. Hardy beat Caleb Konley in the main event. Booker, who is 49, worked his first match in a long time in a trios match teaming with local wrestler Brian Anthony and Spring Valley High football coach Andrew Delva to beat The Platinum Exchange. Hall, Hardy and Christy Hemme were the stars on the 6/7 show in Ansonia, CT. Hall managed his son and Hemme was a referee.

(JULY 6) Another bad weekend report for Scott Hall at a New England Fan Fast. Hall, who got into town the previous day, was said to have been a mess and was 90 minutes late for his signing. All I can say is if you are a promoter and book him, it's at your own risk.

(AUGUST 4) This week's Scott Hall story revolved around an incident this past week, when many of the biggest names in the business, including Ric Flair, Bill Goldberg, Kevin Nash, Bret Hart and Edge, were in Phoenix for an autograph convention. They were asked to sign a giant birthday card for six-year-old Danny Nickerson of Boston, who is battling terminal was battling cancer and may not have much time left to live. Everyone there, and there were far more names than just the ones mentioned, including but not limited to Christy Hemme, Candice Michelle, Angelina Love, Lita, Sean Waltman, Maria Kanellis, Lisa Marie Varon, Taryn Terrell and Brooke Tessmacher, not only signed, but went on camera to give personalized wishes. Goldberg, in particular, who was clearly choked up, spoke at length to him and told him to call him at any time if he wanted to talk. Hall refused to sign the card. The reaction from a number of people in the last few days was not just how incomprehensible it was, but that in Hall's case, it's even worse because he made top dollar in wrestling during a boom period, blew his money on drugs, then got fans to pay for a number of surgeries including a hip replacement in a fund raiser, and then he pulled this. Goldberg had real problems with Hall to begin with, but if you know Goldberg when it comes to children battling health issues or having problems, I don't even want to think about how he'd feel about Hall now.

RODDY PIPER

(JUNE 2) The latest Roddy Piper podcast craziness is that he claimed he never worked for Bill Watts (I don't recall him ever working that territory) because he claimed when Watts ran the Superdome, he would only pay the main eventers, and gave everyone else a note in their pay envelope that read, "You should be honored just to get to work on a card like this" and wouldn't pay them. That's complete B.S., as in it never happened. Piper told this story before on a Legends of Wrestling roundtable. As it turned out, Jim Ross was on the panel that show and said it wasn't true. Not that it would preclude them working together again, because this is a regular thing that he says something they get mad at, and always work with him again, but WWE was very upset at Piper of late. It may be about his remarks on a DVD interview about Pat Patterson, or could be regarding something else having to do with Legends House promotion.

WWE COMMENTARY

(JUNE 2) Some people saw the live satellite feed of last week's Smackdown as it was being beamed back from London. Among things noted is that Kevin Dunn got mad at the announcers for using the term "making out," and made them do it again and change it. When Vince yelled at Layfield, he called him JR. Deadspin even wound up doing an article. One of the major differences is the fake crowd noise. It was noted how quiet the crowd was during the tapings, and how different it came across by the time it aired on Friday. Throughout the show you can hear on the original version both Layfield and Cole in discussions with Vince and with Kevin Dunn. At one point Cole actually went to Vince, who was ordering him to say something, saying, "Do you want me to say that every time, because I've said it a shitload of times tonight."

ABDULLAH THE BUTCHER VS. DEVON NICHOLSON

(JUNE 9) The three-year legal battle between pro wrestler Devon Nicholson, who wrestles as Hannibal, and Larry Shreve, best known as Abdullah the Butcher, came to a climax on 6/3 when Nicholson was awarded a $2.3 million judgment on his claim that he contracted Hepatitis C in a match with Shreve. Ontario Superior Court ruled after a one-week trial that Nicholson contracted the disease on May 26, 2007, in a match in Cochrane, Alberta, where video evidence of the match showed that Shreve used the same blade on himself and Nicholson. During the course of discovery, Shreve was ordered to take medical tests which concluded that he was also suffering from Hepatitis. Shreve has 30 days to appeal the ruling. Shreve did not take the stand in his defense. Whether Nicholson will get any money from Shreve, 73 (although some sources have him at 77), from the judgment is another issue. Nicholson had filed a $6.5 million lawsuit against Shreve in 2011. A key to the case was that Nicholson, in 2009, had a WWE tryout and was offered a three-year contract pending the results of his medical exams. When the exams showed he had Hepatitis C, the contract was rescinded. Based on this, WWE no longer offers contracts until after all medicals have been completed. Nicholson, 31, left pro wrestling but was allowed to compete in amateur wrestling while battling the disease. He placed second in Canada's trials for the 2012 Olympics in the super heavyweight division in Greco-Roman, and was its alternate. He had talked of trying for the 2016 Olympics, but had also at times felt that the amount of money, time and effort it took to train for wrestling at that level wasn't worth it. Nicholson has wrestled of late for Jacques Rougeau's promotion in Quebec and occasionally runs his own shows. Nicholson was a high school wrestling standout, who won the Junior (teenage) national championships in 2001 and a spot on the country's junior national team. But his goal was pro wrestling, so he gave him college offers to train under Bruce Hart. He mostly wrestled Canadian independents but had a few runs in Puerto Rico. He had WWE and TNA tryouts in 2009 and 2010, both of which went well but he wasn't hired because of Hepatitis C. He went through a series of experimental medical procedures in 2012 and 2013, and by the end of last year he claimed he was completely cured of the disease and would be starting back in pro wrestling. In July, 2011, he filed the suit against Shreve and another suit against WWE for $6 million. The lawsuit with WWE was settled out of court in 2012 with neither side commenting on terms. Nicholson, who said he was going to try out for ROH in an interview with Slam! Wrestling and was hopeful of a July tryout with WWE. Nicholson had gotten a ton of mainstream publicity over the past three years regarding the lawsuit and his documentary, "Don't Bleed on Me," which concerned the suit. He said he's also glad he stopped Butcher from wrestling and bleeding. The situation with Nicholson also brought forth to the public the dangers of double juice matches. While not gone completely, rampant blading and double juice matches are banned in most major promotions and done less frequently in the ones that don't outright ban them.

RICOCHET

(JUNE 16) Ricochet (Trevor Mann) joined a very select group this past week, of foreigners who have captured major New Japan Junior heavyweight tournaments. Ricochet followed in the footsteps of only Dynamite Kid, Wild Pegasus (Chris Benoit), the second Black Tiger (Eddy Guerrero) and Prince Devitt when he pinned Kushida on 6/8 at the Tokyo Yoyogi Gym to capture the 2014 Best of the Super Junior tournament. At 25, he was the youngest winner in tournament history. Dynamite Kid was a similar tournament but not names Best of the Super Juniors at 25 years and two months while Mann is 25 years and eight months. Ricochet defeated Bushi on 6/6 in Kyoto, to tie Kushida for first place in the A block with a 5-2 record, but Kushida got the actual first place position because he beat Ricochet in the tournament. On 6/8, he won a quick match over B block winner Ryusuke Taguchi in the semifinals and a long, outstanding match over Kushida in the finals, to add to a year where he became the first foreigner ever to win the Open the Dream Gate championship, the top belt in Dragon Gate, and also defeated Johnny Gargano to win the Open the Freedom Gate title, the top belt for Dragon Gate USA. The tournament win sets up Ricochet (or as the name is spelled in New Japan, Ricoche) getting his shot at the IWGP jr. title held by Kota Ibushi on the company's annual Dominion PPV on 6/21 from the Osaka Bodymaker Colosseum in what has the making of one of the best matches this year. Kushida had defeated Jushin Liger in Kyoto to win the A block, and defeated Taichi, who ended up going into the final four as an alternate. In the B block, Taguchi, Alex Shelley, Taichi and Kenny Omega all finished with 4-3 records. Based on how they fared against each other, the first tiebreaker, Shelley got the top spot, Taguchi the second spot, and Taichi the alternate spot. Shelley suffered a right shoulder injury early in his match with Tiger Mask in Kyoto. The two went right to the finish, only going 3:13, but Shelley's shoulder was injured to the point he couldn't continue on to the final four. The injury doesn't appear to be serious because he is scheduled on the Osaka PPV show. Ricochet represented Dragon Gate in the tournament, making him only the second non-New Japan wrestler to win it, with Ibushi, then under contract with DDT, winning it in 2011. New Japan is looking to bring in Ricochet as a regular in the role as a babyface top foreign junior heavyweight that Devitt had for many years. While a lot of the crowd didn't really know Ricochet from what I was told from those there live (it sounded good but I was told it was a small Dragon Gate contingent and most didn't react to him), aside from being one of the guys in the tournament the past two years, he is both a remarkably gifted wrestler but also has an ability to get over. As the match went on, the usually nationalistic fans cheered him louder than both Taguchi and Kushida.

(SEPTEMBER 8) Trevor Mann, as Ricochet, continued one of the biggest years any wrestler has ever had on the independent scene by winning a loaded Battle of Los Angeles tournament, coming on the heels of winning New Japan's Best of the Super Junior tournament, having a run as the Open the Dream Gate champion, and being the Open the Freedom Gate champion. Ricochet beat Chris Sabin, T.J. Perkins (Manik in TNA) and Kenny Omega to reach the finals, a three-way where he went over on Johnny Gargano and Roderick Strong in a tournament that featured 24 of the best wrestlers in the U.S. that are not signed with TNA or WWE. The three days, held at the 400-seat American Legion Post #308 in Reseda, CA, with tickets priced at $40 and $55 for each night, featured some of the best action in the country with a loaded line-up that included a number of the top ROH stars including champion Michael Elgin, tag champions Bobby Fish & Kyle O'Reilly, Strong, ACH, Tommaso Ciampa, Cedric Alexander and Adam Cole. Evolve regulars Biff Busick, Johnny Gargano, Ricochet, Rich Swann, Chris Hero and Drew Gulak were also involved, as were Southern California wrestlers Candice LaRae (the only woman), former TNA wrestler Sabin, current TNA wrestler Perkins, DDT's Kenny Omega (perhaps the world's most underrated talent), Pro Wrestling NOAH's Zack Sabre Jr., as well as Chris Hero, former WWE star Matt Sydal and current IWGP champion A.J. Styles. Styles had crazy weekend schedule, first flying in to beat Brian Myers (formerly Curt Hawkins) in the first round on 8/29, then flew to Hawkesbury, ONT, for an IWGP title defense there, and then flew back for the final night. Styles, as IWGP champion, was the only guy protected in the tournament, as he lost to Strong via DQ and was eliminated. The only other non-finish elimination was to PWG champion O'Reilly, who was attacked by Strong, and given a beatdown. The semifinals were scheduled as Strong vs. O'Reilly, Gargano vs. Trevor Lee (who upset Elgin in the quarterfinals so the ROH champion lost cleanly) and Ricochet vs. Omega. Strong advanced on a bye with the O'Reilly injury, likely to set up an O'Reilly vs. Strong PWG title program, as well as Ricochet being in the title mix. Gargano and Ricochet followed with wins to set up the final.

Day One

1. T.J. Perkins pinned Bobby Fish by reversing the fish hook into a pin.
2. Roderick Strong pinned Biff Busick with one of his versions of the backbreaker.
3. Trevor Lee pinned Cedric Alexander with Orange crush.
4. Joey Ryan & Candice LaRae, billed as The World's Cutest tag team, retained the PWG tag titles in a three-way over Christopher Daniels & Frankie Kazarian and Rich Swann & Ricochet when LaRae pinned Swann after a reverse huracanrana.
5. Michael Elgin pinned Tommaso Ciampa in a battle of ROH stars using the lariat.
6. A.J. Styles made Brian Myers submit to the Boston crab coming off a Styles clash.
7. Kyle O'Reilly made Drew Gulak submit to an armbar.
8. Kenny Omega & Zack Sabre Jr. (debuting in PWG) & Chuck Taylor beat Adam Cole & The Young Bucks when Taylor pinned Cole after the Awful waffle.

Day Two

1. Candice LaRae pinned Rich Swann for the second straight day, using an inside cradle.
2. Ricochet pinned Chris Sabin after a 630 splash.
3. ROH tag champions Bobby Fish & Kyle O'Reilly beat Drew Gulak & Biff Busick with the double-team Chasing the Dragon on gulak.
4. Matt Sydal (Evan Bourne) pinned Chris Hero using a shooting star press.
5. Zack Sabre Jr. pinned Adam Cole with a rolling reverse cradle.
6. Kenny Omega pinned ACH with Croyt's Wrath.
7. Matt & Nick Jackson beat Christopher Daniels & Frankie Kazarian using their double-team spike tombstone piledriver for the finish.

Day Three

1. Johnny Gargano pinned Candice LaRae.
2. Ricochet pinned T.J. Perkins after the Benadryller (a GTS, but ending with a kick instead of a knee).
3. Trevor Lee pinned Michael Elgin with a small package.
4. Kenny Omega pinned Matt Sydal when he had Sydal up on his shoulders, and took him off into a spike like move, called the Electric chair driver.
5. Roderick Strong beat A.J. Styles via DQ.
6. In a battle of submissions, Kyle O'Reilly beat Zack Sabre Jr. with a triangle. After this match, Strong attacked O'Reilly to knock him out of the tournament, which ended up putting Strong directly into the finals.

7. Young Bucks & Adam Cole beat ACH & Chris Sabin & Brian Myers when the Bucks used a springboard 450 double-team spike tombstone piledriver to pin ACH. The Bucks named the move the Meltzer driver. I saw it in a series of still shots and it was amazing. With the way the Bucks were put over here, one would think they'll be going to Ryan & LaRae vs. Bucks soon.

8. Gargano pinned Lee to advance to the finals.

9. Ricochet pinned Omega with the Benadryller to advance to the finals.

10. Joey Ryan & Rich Swann & Willie Mack (final PWG appearance before going to WWE) & Chris Hero beat Bobby Fish & Tommaso Ciampa & Cedric Alexander & Drew Gulak & Biff Busick when Swann pinned Fish after a splash off the top rope.

11. Ricochet beat Gargano and Strong in a three-way to win the tournament.

ROH vs. TNA

(JUNE 16) There may be something going on behind-the-scenes as it regards TNA, with the two companies running PPVs one week apart, and ROH's show being from Nashville, where TNA has its home offices. TNA has made some moves, including contacting some ROH talent. One report from ROH is that TNA has gone after several key ROH talents this past week, although those talents were all said to be under ROH contract. The story is that ROH is trying to make sure there are no issues with the contracts. This all was going down at press time. The only names that have somewhat gotten out that fall into this category is Bobby Fish & Kyle O'Reilly, and that Davey Richards was the conduit. No doubt he'd like to work with them in TNA since the tag team situation there is weak. Although Adam Cole's name is the only one that has come out, a number of ROH wrestlers are expected to get good paying shots in New Japan toward the latter part of the year, after G-1, since new Japan pretty much has all of its plans for foreigners booked through that period. Karl Anderson and Doc Gallows when they were at the ROH shows were really putting over how great it is to work New Japan, with the minimal stress and politics that most Americans talk about. To most in wrestling now, New Japan has replaced TNA as the No. 2 promotion as far as prestige goes, but that's not universal since TNA is still based in the U.S. and its shows air internationally. There was more money in TNA, although that may not be the case anywhere. But ROH working with New Japan allows it to work out dates and is a nice way to keep talent from going to TNA that would have considered it even six months ago. There is also the situation with The Wolves, who, even though they are tag team champions in TNA, there is the feeling they haven't been put over well, so it makes people leery about going. But even now, no matter how you slice it and TNA may beat ROH on PPV this month and may even draw better live, TNA is still the better paying and far bigger company. But another negative on TNA is the belief that if you go to TNA, it's very difficult to get to WWE, and for almost all wrestlers, that is the ultimate goal. Plus right now, the morale in TNA isn't good.

PAT PATTERSON

(JUNE 23) The final episode of Legends House which aired on 6/12 was built around the guys revealing their biggest secrets, with the big build of Pat Patterson saying that he was gay. Tony Atlas told the story about how his current wife met him when he was homeless in the late 80s, which was such a secret it was in his book and he's told the story many times. Jim Duggan talked about the car accident that killed his then-girlfriend Vickie while he was working for Mid South Wrestling (also in Duggan's autobiography), Gene Okerlund talked about his wife giving him her kidney to save his life, Hillbilly Jim mentioned that when he finally made money, he bought his single mom who raised him a house and a car before he ever bought himself one. Jimmy Hart talked about his daughter passing away. Patterson saying that he was gay and had been keeping it a secret for 50 years. This got some mainstream pub which was funny because Patterson being gay hadn't been a secret in wrestling for decades and it was clearly a scripted big ending of the show that had been in the can for years. Some people took this as a big deal or some important social statement by him wanting to relieve some burden. Time doesn't support that viewpoint. It was designed for ratings, and later to get people to subscribe to the network (it was originally done as a ratings ploy because Legends House was originally shot for a television network, and when that was slow in launching, they tried to sell it to a TV station but nobody picked it up). If it was to make a social statement or have him unburden himself, why was it hidden in the can for years after being filmed? If it was that important to him or such a big thing, it clearly wasn't important enough to put out for two years. The current fan base and media wasn't going to know it was public knowledge in mainstream media in the 90s and they didn't want to ruin their shocking season finale. In clips building it up they cut away to the other guys in the house being shocked, but on the show, given that everyone knew, they didn't have the other guys oversell it much. Aside from the big reveal being hardly some hidden secret or any kind of a big reveal, the last episode of the show was quite touching and the characters came off very sympathetic and likeable. There's a reason most of them were very successful in their era. It was funny that E! And TMZ and The Advocate did report on the Patterson thing like it was a current news story. Hopefully it was next to their stories on water being revealed to be a liquid. It got nowhere near the attention of Darren Young, who had more than 100,000 searches stemming from the TMZ report of his coming out. Patterson, when the show was taped, was originally going to be the Darren Young as the person they would push as the first pro wrestler to come out, but the timing of the show airing didn't allow that to happen. Patterson the day after got 6,000 searches in comparison, even though the same TMZ reported it and it was on the WWE Network and teased on Raw. Young's situation was never touched on during WWE programming. I got a ton of media questions regarding Young and the Patterson thing got almost nothing in that regard. A lot of that is also Patterson being from another generation and not having been on TV regularly since the Stooges era, even though he's a legitimate pro wrestling Hall of Famer. Almost every media outlet in 1992 that reported Patterson resigning from WWF noted that as part of it and Vince McMahon openly talked about Patterson being a victim of prejudice against gays. He tried to portray Patterson's resignation being out of loyalty to the company, and that he would never return, but tried to make him sympathetic. McMahon defended Patterson during that period while not defending Terry Garvin or Mel Phillips, who resigned at the same time. In a legal settlement with Tom Cole, a former ring crew boy in the Northeast who had gone public with the charge he was let go after refusing homosexual advances from Garvin, and alleged very inappropriate acts by Phillips, it was stated by WWF that neither Garvin nor Phillips would ever work for the company again. Patterson's name wasn't mentioned in the settlement so McMahon protected him in the settlement and Patterson returned to work for the company, and still does today. Patterson's name came up many times and it was very public that he was gay, it was openly joked about during commentary at times. As compared to Garvin and Phillips, where there were multiple accusations at the time, and people coming forward who then went quiet and disappeared, there was no strong direct evidence of any wrongdoing by Patterson. The main direct allegations against Patterson in 1992 was by a former announcer, Murray Hodgson, who tried to use a story that he turned down an advance by Patterson and was then fired. Time established that Hodgson was clearly a con man, a pathological liar (and he was actually a very convincing liar but the kind where the truth would always catch up to them) with no credibility who in my opinion was looking at a way to get a settlement from the company, and because it was openly known Patterson was gay, filed a suit claiming he was fired after turning down an advance. Patterson would also rib people or say things based on that knowledge, which Hodgson also saw while he was in WWF. Patterson joked around about being gay for decades, which is why this "coming out" thing felt so silly to me as a breaking news story, because he'd been open about it forever. There were open comedy remarks made on television about it dating back to 1965 and I was told this week by the reporter who wrote it that perhaps the first article about Patterson being gay came out in 1980. Dwayne Johnson, his protégé, openly talked about his mentor, Pat Patterson, being a gay man who kicked ass as a pro wrestler when Johnson played a gay character in the movie, "Be Cool." His long-time partner that he talked about on the show, the late Louie Dondero, who was around with him dating back to his days in San Francisco and who secured the backing and tried and failed to buy out Roy Shire in the 70s when Shire wouldn't sell (which, given the price and the benefit of hindsight, was a mistake Shire made). Dondero later at times worked for WWE. The other cast members didn't oversell it to a comical degree, but it did expose the show as a complete act when they were acting like it was a revelation to them, although Howard Finkel did make it clear he knew. Even more, in the clips this week building up the reunion special, Patterson talked about how he was happy he was no longer living a lie, and they once again teased an Atlas vs. Duggan fight, which both show how completely scripted those aspects of the show were. Patterson hasn't lived a lie for a minimum of nearly 50 years. If anything, the story of Patterson is that in an industry where plenty of owners were racist, most used characters that played stereotypical roles and plenty were way behind the times, that Patterson never had any trouble getting work or headlining. He was a top star for more than 20 years in-ring, and had an office role for the next three decades. On the flip side, for a gay man who was a performer and booker, Patterson played the typical pro wrestling gay stereotype character before he came to San Francisco and made his name as a money drawing headliner as part of his legendary tag team with Ray Stevens, as "Pretty Boy Pat Patterson," and later booked comedic gay bashing acts like with Adrian Adonis and other acts in WWF that encouraged fans to chant gay slurs loudly at the arenas. The story of Patterson as a wrestler in the 60s and 70s, when he was a main event caliber star everywhere he went is that if you knew how to perform and draw as a main eventer and could make a promoter money, in those days, you'd have a job in wrestling unless you were just so ridiculously unprofessional. And even then, if you could draw, you'd probably find regular work. In the 60s and 70s, Patterson was really a master inside the ring as far as working, stuff looking good, controlling of the crowd, and could do it equally well as a face and as a heel. In the history of the San Francisco territory, most would rank him second in importance and long-term drawing power only behind Ray Stevens. Patterson & Stevens were one of the greatest tag teams in wrestling history and almost surely the best of the 60s, in the sense they could go heel or face, work great in the ring and were main event draws. You can directly trace the decline of the territory to when Patterson and Shire had a falling out and he left. His being gay was no big secret even then. I don't know that most fans knew it, but pretty much all the regular ringsiders did and it never made one iota of difference and that was late 60s. When I was in high school, it's not like everyone in school knew it or even that everyone in school knew who Pat Patterson was, but plenty of people knew it in the sense it was not a secret to those who followed wrestling in the area. He was also such a big star to those who watched wrestling that it was rarely if ever talked about in any kind of a negative way, which is kind of amazing when you think about that era. If you think about all the wrestlers Bobby Heenan managed during his career, and he was at ringside watching as closely as anyone, he would always say the four best performers were Stevens, Patterson, Ric Flair and Curt Hennig, even ahead of Nick Bockwinkel who he always ranked as No. 5 on the list of the best guys he managed. Regarding singing "My Way," which was really a cool deal on the show, Patterson singing "My Way" at karaoke bars after shows also dates back regularly for decades and I would guess that most of those in the cast had been there for that numerous times when they worked there in the 80s.

(JUNE 30) A funny note about the coverage of Pat Patterson coming out in his home town of Montreal. TVA Sports and Le Journal, the leading French language newspaper, covered the story. What was funny is Le Journal ran a story on Darren Young last year and in the article they listed that Orlando Jordan, Chris Kanyon and Pat Patterson who were all pro wrestlers who had come out previously, so in their own newspaper they listed him as having come out and then ran a story on his coming out a year later.

TNA TELEVISION TITLE

(JULY 13) The TV title, which hasn't been talked about in a year, has been dropped. Abyss won the title on June 2, 2013, beating Devon, for a title that had rarely been in play since 2012. The title change made no sense since they were doing the Joseph Park angle and Abyss was a one-time thing at the time. He never defended it again and it was never talked about again. The storyline is that Kurt Angle as new Director of Wrestling Operations has officially dropped the forgotten title to clear up loose ends. In 2012 they had decreed that the title would be defended every week on television, which made sense for a TV title. They did that for a while and then forgot about it, and even still had the belt on Devon when his contract expired in September 2012. They did revive the belt with Samoa Joe and then Devon (when he was brought back) as champion, before Abyss beat Devon last year.

WWE Talent Pay

(JULY 13) A lot of talent unhappiness over money. That's always a concern, but there's a realization that nothing is going to be done or changed as the complaints are that guys in the same positions are making less money on the same houses, for reasons explained here weeks ago. The company announced a fining system in recent weeks which didn't help. They are back on the dress code kick, in the sense that if you were in public anywhere you are seen by fans, you have to dress in a professional manner. A failure to do so will result in a fine. It was also said that as far as arrival times at all arenas, if you are even one minute late arriving, a fine will be implemented. Then, this past week, the quarterly royalty checks were sent out. If you recall from the last quarter, the usual video game royalty check in the first quarter, the big one, has historically been around $70,000 if you are a star and in the game. Obviously if it's a bigger star, it's bigger, but that figure would be for people who would be considered major stars. Well, people at that level for the most part got around $11,700 for the first quarter of this year. Mick Foley went on a public rant about it. Lots of talents were privately very unhappy. One person who alerted us said that it was the nature of the sending of revenues from 2K Sports and the timing is different but some of it would be made up for during the next quarter. Well, the second quarter royalty checks came in and the number that most of the top level guys got was $1,555. I will say this much, there were guys in WWE who talked with UFC guys in Las Vegas and the subject came up. It was a pretty big deal this weekend. The WWE guys didn't feel so bad because almost none of the UFC guys get anything from the video game. I believe if you are on the cover or are used in the video game ad itself you make something, but just being in the game you don't. Don Frye refused to allow his likeness in the game the first year and I guess they felt it important enough that he got paid, but nowhere near what WWE people got. But that's probably the reason he's not in the new game. The big thing is that WrestleMania payoffs should be mailed out this week. Nobody has been told anything, but if the talent is getting paid only on the PPV revenue, that will be down significantly from last year and bonuses will be declining monthly from the other shows. But if they pay a percentage of the network revenue to talent, the gap may close for Mania and be the same or more for the rest of the shows. The feeling is no talent is going to do anything, because they all recognize there is nowhere else any of them can go and make even close to what they are making. But money concerns are not only the biggest issue from a management standpoint, now it's also the most concerning issue among the wrestlers.

(AUGUST 4) A funny question was when someone asked how the PPV bonuses work with the network, and Bryan said that nobody really knows. From what we understand, the WrestleMania checks were sent out this past week and pretty much everyone should have gotten them over the past few days. The only thing I heard is that people who expected to get screwed, given the unhappiness over the video game royalties, said that wasn't the case and the payoff was better than they feared and about what they expected. As far as a comparison of guys from equal spots on the card last year or this year and how it overall compares, right now I don't know anything about that. But it did do 689,000 buys or so on PPV at the highest price of the year, plus did a $10 million live gate, so payoffs, even if limited to the PPV, would be big even if nothing from the network is kicked in. Because we haven't gotten anything from anyone in the same spot both years for a comparison, it'll probably be a week or so before we know more unless it's spelled out on the SEC filings over the next week. Cole quickly changed the subject and did it so obviously and painfully that it was actually comedy that everyone there recognized. Bryan heavily put over KENTA, and said KENTA kicks hard and is a great wrestler and that a lot of WWE guys have that to look forward to. Cole then joked about how KENTA will soon be on NXT, exclusively on the WWE Network.

(SEPTEMBER 1) Regarding WrestleMania payoffs, we didn't hear any complaints, but then again, the show ended up doing 690,000 buys on PPV and while substantially less than pre-network numbers, it was still a big number. Batista was asked about Mania payoffs on The LAW when promoting the movie, and kind of dodged the subject saying it wasn't something he could answer and be politically correct. "From the talent's perspective, that's a tough question because I could put myself in a politically incorrect spot. As of this moment, with the WWE

Network losing money, I don't think the talent is benefitting the way they should." But it's the PPV shows going forward where the PPV numbers really fell hard. The key outsiders (Hogan, Rock and Austin), because they weren't advertised and pushed ahead of time and not in a match, were all given a flat fee as opposed to the usual percentage deal top guys are figured in for. Lesnar also has a guaranteed figure, and Undertaker has his big downside guarantee even though he only works a few shows a year, so it's kind of understood his big guarantee is his Mania payoff.

(OCTOBER 6) Given the payoffs for the first PPVs after WrestleMania with the new formula are in (Extreme Rules and King of the Ring), the payoffs were described to me as "really bad," which says that talent is getting paid based on PPV revenue and getting nothing extra from all the PPV revenue that has been eliminated based on starting the network. There are a few people who are being taken care of and a few who have deals in place that guard against this happening to them, but rank and file, that's not the case.

NATALYA

(JULY 13) There was an apparently crazy lawsuit filed against Natalie Neidhart (Natalya). Christopher Donnelly, who is currently in prison in Pennsylvania, filed a lawsuit on 6/27, representing himself, hand-written, asking for $250,000, claiming Neidhart was a dominatrix who had beaten him between the period of 2005 and 2009 when they were together at hotels throughout the U.S. and had forced him into extreme sexual abuse and even to prostitute himself. Neidhart has been mainly traveling with current husband T.J. Wilson (Tyson Kidd) for her entire WWE career. The suit was immediately thrown out of court due to no evidence being presented and apparent mental issues with the plaintiff.

MATT BLOOM

(AUGUST 18) Matt Bloom, 41, who is using the name Jason Albert these days when he announces on NXT broadcasts, announced his retirement this past week. He had been transferred from the ring to the Performance Center some time back. Bloom was an offensive lineman at the University of Pittsburgh, who was working as a school teacher when he got the idea he could make more money as a wrestler. He signed up for Killer Kowalski's school, and because of his size and the fact he could move, quickly got a WWE developmental deal and was working as Baldo in Memphis. The original idea for him was to be George Steele Jr., the son of the animal, because he had a hairy back. He worked from 1999 through 2004 on the main roster as Prince Albert, Albert and A-Train before being released. He had a strong run in Japan, first with All Japan in 2005 and 2006, given the name Giant Bernard, because a Japanese booker thought he reminded him of the 60s wrestler, Jim "Brute" Bernard. He had a strong run from 2006 to 2012 with New Japan, where he won the New Japan Cup in 2006 and for much of the period was New Japan's top full-time foreigner. He formed major tag teams with Travis Tomko and Karl Anderson. Bernard & Anderson were the 2011 Observer tag team of the year, becoming the first team to hold both the GHC (NOAH) and IWGP (New Japan) tag titles at the same time. He returned to WWE in 2013 after WrestleMania as Lord Tensai, with Sakamoto. The gimmick was that of an American who used to be in WWE that had become a superstar in Japan. He was given a big guarantee to leave New Japan and was supposed to be the top heel in the promotion, working with John Cena. To get him over, he scored TV wins over both Cena and C.M. Punk, but the character wasn't connecting. For one, his main trait was being able to work as a monster against super talented Japanese wrestlers like Yuji Nagata and Hiroshi Tanahashi, where his size and their movement around him made the matches. But not being the biggest guy in WWE, like he was in New Japan, took that gimmick away. He quickly just became Tensai, and became a lower card act, never getting the originally planned run since he didn't get over at that level. His most memorable run was when they turned him into a dancer, with Brodus Clay as a tag team, and Naomi & Cameron as dancing seconds. They made for an easy underneath act, but were never pushed to a serious level. Once they split the team up, it was a disaster for both Clay & Tensai. Tensai was quickly dropped from the main roster and started working as an announcer in NXT. Clay lasted longer, but was given little push before being cut. His biggest claims to fame besides the two IWGP tag title runs and his New Japan Cup win was a reign as IC champion in WWE, and winning the New Japan G-1 tag team tournament in 2007 with Tomko as a partner and in 2009 with Anderson as a partner.

WWE MAGAZINE

(SEPTEMBER 8) The WWE Magazine ceased production and its office was shut down this past week. The magazine had been a break-even proposition for years, never losing significant money nor making it, as cutbacks were being made to make up for declining readership. When the company went into the cost-cutting because of the losses that have incurred this year, to pacify Wall Street, the magazine, which evidently was losing money with the belief that it wasn't going to turn around, due to market conditions, was shut down. Some will categorize this move as another part of the company victimized by the high expectations of the network not being realized, and the timing of the decision itself appears to have been due to that. But it was really based on market conditions.

WWE TAPE LIBRARY

(SEPTEMBER 22) There was a lot of confusion during the week from a story by TheWrap.com that WWE was in negotiations to sell its complete 150,000 hour videotape library to Warner Brothers. Those close to the situation have told us the story was untrue, but another source with close knowledge of the situation said that it was a deal between Warner Brothers and Cinedigm for the home video distribution rights to the library, and talks are very serious between the sides. Cinedigm has been very negative about its relationship with WWE so them deciding to unload was not a surprise, because they believe the network decision has badly hurt their DVD and Blu Ray business. During their earnings call last month, Cinedigm COO Adam Mizel, said: "On the WWE renewal, that business over the last 24 months has declined significantly as they have shifted their business model accordingly. And so when we look at the expected revenues going forward and the expected return rates that go with that and ultimately the margin we'll earn and the cost in servicing that business, we made a proposal to them that we thought was profitable and made sense for us and should make sense for them. They didn't want to do that. They were looking for a deal that I think would have relied on us, at us losing money and we are not in the business of servicing customers while we lose money." So they wanted out. The deal has not been announced but one person with close knowledge of the talks said that it is close and more than likely to happen.

STEVE AUSTIN

(APRIL 28) Steve Austin said that he would be tempted to do a match with Brock Lesnar (the two have never wrestled) for a WrestleMania match. If Lesnar was kept super strong for a year, it would be a big deal as Austin's return should be equal to Rock's match with Cena two years ago, because I don't see Austin doing a match anywhere but Mania whereas Rock did the Survivor Series tag match first, probably because it was Madison Square Garden and his WWF debut was at the Survivor Series in 1996 in Madison Square Garden.

(SEPTEMBER 22) Regarding Austin at Mania, some people have taken the fact he's talking about training hard right now as a sign he's getting ready. The last we heard is that it's not out of the question for this year, but it comes down to the right creative and the right money.

(SEPTEMBER 29) The company has told its distributors to go into heavy production of Austin merchandise, so expect him to return to television in some form, or for at least a renewed push of his merchandise. On Raw, they promoted his podcast, which they haven't even done for Jericho, even when HHH was a guest. It's interesting that HHH was on Jericho's podcast and he has constant WWE guests, Austin has some, and WWE has not allowed any of its talent to do Jim Ross' show.

(OCTOBER 13) Austin has gotten a lot of people talking with a comment on a recent podcast that he's training for a comeback, but never went past that point. The only thing I know is that Austin was about 270 pounds recently, and wanted to get to 240. Those close to him, and he himself, have always downplayed it but also have the "never say never" line. Austin has since responded by claiming that his "comeback" was a comeback to Gold's gym in Venice. There's been more talk over the years of him coming back at Cowboys Stadium, which would be 2016. If Undertaker's body allows him to, he had talked about retiring at Cowboys Stadium. If Rock is coming back this year, I don't think Austin coming back makes sense, because the only opponent is Lesnar and it makes more sense to use Lesnar to make a younger star then have Austin beat him, and Austin shouldn't come back and lose. The idea is that the 2016 show will set the all-time attendance record, where they will claim a number of more than 93,000 to "set the record" and WWE will need something out of the box like Austin to sell the number of tickets they'll have available. Austin turns 50 in a few months and the fact he has turned down all requests for a comeback match since retiring at the 2003 WrestleMania says something, and he's had a number of injuries since retiring. Austin has said he'd need four months of straight hardcore training to get back in the ring because he wouldn't want to go in and give anything but a top performance. Austin is about to start filming a new season of Broken Skull Challenge. I've always had the impression he would never rule it out, but mentally, he's not looking at wrestling again. Jim Ross wrote about it and came to the same conclusion, that it's not out of the question but 2016 would be more likely. I was hanging around him at SummerSlam and he's a lot bigger than you'd think, as far as arms and shoulders go.

(OCTOBER 27) Austin said he's ruled out wrestling at this year's Mania. He said between deer hunting season, another season of his reality show, and a project scheduled for February that he isn't allowed to reveal at this time, he doesn't have time in his schedule to start training the way he needs to. He also said he doesn't have the desire to do it either. If Austin is to wrestle one last match, most figure it would be at the 2016 WrestleMania in Dallas, but people close to him have said the betting odds are that he isn't going to wrestle again. Because of people misconstruing any hint of possibly wrestling as thinking he's wrestling this year or next, he said on his podcast, "I'd consider anything if the perfect situation or opportunity arose and it would be more than a million dollar question. I don't want to sit here and promote a match, sell a match, or talk about making a comeback. The dirt sheets, or whatever you call them, and I talk to Dave Meltzer and Wade Keller all the time and they're nice guys and I would consider them friends, I see Dave at almost every MMA fight, but I don't want to stir any pots or hint or tease anything. People get their panties in a wad and say, `Stone Cold, either do it or not.' So, anything can happen, but I'm not going to endorse, promote, sell or tease anything in regards to a match." Immediately this led to a number of web sites, including the WWE web site, doing polls on who fans wanted to see him face at WrestleMania (Lesnar won on the WWE site).

UFC REEBOK DEAL

(DECEMBER 8) The UFC announced on 12/2 a six-year deal with Reebok as its exclusive merchandise partner for live events, a deal that Dana White called the company's biggest non-television network deal in its history. The deal is a major game changer in the MMA landscape, but whether that is good or bad remains to be seen. In talking with people on the ground floor, there is the expected trepidation. The deal was significant enough that it was covered by the New York Times and CNN. U.K. reporter Gareth Davies reported the deal as being worth $70 million total over the six years. This was the big announcement that White was going to originally make on 11/17, when he said, when asked about the promised major announcement, that they didn't get the deal done in time. The key component of the deal, which goes into effect in July, right before one of UFC's traditional biggest events of the year in Las Vegas, is that talent sponsorships at live events are gone, and in their place is a flat fee that Reebok will pay every performer every time they fight. Fighters will still be allowed to have sponsors, but they can not wear any sponsor gear during UFC publicity outings, or the week of the fight. The sponsor names and logos on ring outfits and the big banners with sponsors will be history once this deal goes into effect. All fighters will have to wear Reebok uniforms when they fight, but will be able to choose from a number of different designs for both men and women. UFC CEO Lorenzo Fertitta said that "the vast majority, if not all, of the revenues" will go to the fighters. From what we understand, if you are a champion in your weight class, Reebok will make individual sponsorship deals, but there is limited leverage because the champions can't go elsewhere. Then there will be a specific amount, the same for every show, no matter your position on the card, that a fighter will earn as sponsorship money for every fight. The money will be broken up into tiers, with a certain set fee for anyone ranked in the top five in the official UFC rankings, a set fee for anyone ranked No. 6 to No. 10, and another for No. 11 to No. 15. All fighters out of the top 15, which means the vast majority of the roster, will get the standard fee. If the figure of $11.67 million per year is accurate and UFC has 500 fights in a calendar year with two men or women in each fight, it would mean an average fighter would get about $11,667 per fight. But given the champions and top contenders will make far more, a bottom level fighter is probably not making a huge amount. But if it is more than they were previously making from sponsors, and the sponsorship market for fighters has dried up because most sponsors have found the cost of sponsoring is higher than the business increase one gets unless you're with a superstar-level performer, then it is still a good thing. There are obvious and inherent problems here, particularly because of the UFC rankings and who gets to vote. The rankings are a vote of media members, but a lot of the key media members (I'm in this category) do not vote (that's out of choice, I've been approached about if the rankings and who got to vote getting cleaned up if I'd be interested, as I'm sure would be other key members who don't vote). The issue with fringe media members is that access to talent for fringe media is limited, and this will encourage those who vote to have more access with the idea they'll rank the talent higher. Now, for managers, there is a major economic incentive in the ratings, and that leads to inherent problems. There is always skepticism whether the flat fee will be more or less than managers have been able to get for fighters. Joe Lauzon said it best, saying that until we see actual numbers of what this means, nobody should have an opinion, either positive or negative, on this. This does lessen the value of business managers who are strong at getting sponsors. The UFC said it's a good thing because fighters can concentrate on training and fighting and less on having to worry about getting sponsors. Plus, the interviews where fighters thank sponsors as opposed to trying to get their personalities over and build future fights were not a good thing, and they will also be a thing of the past. Reebok will also market merchandise for fighters. Quite frankly, it makes sense now to give fighters numbers to wear at the start of their careers, as silly as this sounds, like an NFL, NBA or baseball player, with their name, and market them at live events and at stores. Fighters will receive 20 percent of the sales of their merchandise. Previously, fighters could retain close to 100 percent, but they wouldn't have the power to merchandise things like uniforms, so it's essentially a new revenue source. A number of apparel and lifestyle brands, from Tapout to Punishment Athletics to Dethrone, who made their names from UFC fighters wearing their gear, are out of the picture. This will in turn, benefit Bellator, with no such restrictions. There will be a new influx of sponsorship money in that direction because it is now the leading place they can go as opposed to No. 2, and a highly visible Bellator fighter, like a Tito Ortiz, Bobby Lashley, Joe Warren or Will Brooks, will be a far better position for outside revenue. For someone like a Brock Lesnar or a C.M. Punk, it becomes a big part of a decision making situation. Lesnar, for example, if he comes back, would no longer be able to wear gear with his sponsors in UFC, and instead would get paid a flat fee depending where he's ranked. If he's No. 7, for example, he'll get the same sponsorship revenue as a Iuri Alcantara, Chris Cariaso or Myles Jury. But if he were to go to Bellator, for him, fighting on free television and expected to draw huge ratings, and as high profile as he is, he should make a killing in sponsorships. White said that he had spoken with "50" or so fighters ahead of time, which would be the top guys. I'm virtually certain Lesnar was one of them. On the flip side, while their money for being sponsored would be the same, a Lesnar would make far more than a Cariaso based on his cut of his name specific merchandise. Lorenzo Fertitta hinted at the idea of creating merchandise for retired fighters as well to get royalties from.

HEATH SLATER

(DECEMBER 8) A simple assault and battery warrant for Heath Miller (Heath Slater), 31, has been issued by Atlanta police stemming from an incident nearly four years ago late night after the WrestleMania show in 2011 at the Georgia Dome. Corinne Oliver, who was working as a security guard for the WrestleMania after party at the Hyatt Regency hotel in Atlanta on Peachtree Street, claimed that between 4 and 5 a.m., that Miller approached her and asked her to go to his room. She said no. She claimed that he tried to talk her into it, said she was pretty and then grabbed her in a choke hold, and dragged her, trying to get her onto the elevator to his room. She claimed she had to struggle to get his arm from around her neck. Oliver never filed a report at the time. Her attorney months later, when the story originally broke, claimed she contacted her supervisor at Allied Barton Security Services, but after months of inaction, she filed a police report in June of that year, three months later. She claimed she waited because her supervisors kept telling her that they are handling it and would get it resolved. The security firm did confirm at the time that Oliver had reported the incident to them that morning. In the police report, Oliver claimed that there were other wrestlers who witnessed the incident and didn't help. At the time the story first broke, it was reported that Miller denied the incident took place and that he was with his fiancé the night Oliver claimed this took place. Oliver has later claimed she suffered damage to five vertebrae in her back.

(DECEMBER 15) Slater responded to the charges against him as listed last week, saying, "The charges and civil suit brought against me are completely frivolous. I am innocent and these charges will be dismissed as soon as any judge hears the evidence. My attorney, Don Samuel, will handle this matter." That statement would seem to mean Slater was also sued over the alleged incident, where Corrine Oliver claimed damage to her neck vertebrae from a choke hold.

RANDY SAVAGE

(DECEMBER 22) Lanny Poffo did an interview with Interactive Radio ripping on everyone on the WWE DVD who told stories about Randy Savage and his treatment of Elizabeth backstage. "I would like to shout out to every main event jibroni that disgraced themselves on my brother's DVD by making fun of the way that Randy treated Elizabeth. You are all divorced. All of you. All of you are divorced. How are you questioning my brother. What did you want him to do? Let Elizabeth shower with Brian Knobbs? Is that what you wanted? I mention Brian Knobbs because he was always trying to earn his name of Nasty Boy. I would have wanted my own locker room. There were people putting Halcion in people's drinks There were people using people's suitcases as toilets. It was like National Lampoon's Animal House. My brother was just a no nonsense guy in a world full of nonsense. I would say he was a better husband than Chris Benoit, wouldn't you say?" A better husband than the guy who murdered his wife isn't exactly the toughest standard. On the Randy Savage Hall of Fame thing he gets asked about in every interview: "Okay, I'm bending and let me explain why. The day I turned 59, it finally hit me. I'm the older brother. There were a lot of times in my life, being the Macho Man's brother and Angelo's son, I didn't get my way. As the last man standing, I am now. So, I told my mother, I'm willing to allow the WWE to put Macho Man Randy Savage in the Hall of Fame by himself. I'm not going to have a blinking contest with Vince McMahon. He's got balls of steel and he's willing to cut off his nose to spite his face. I'm just not man enough to do that, fellas. I can stand up to a lot of people, but not him. He's got more guts and brains than anyone I've ever met. Even Randy would have told you that. What is the Hall of Fame anyway? It isn't for the Macho Man, it's for the Macho fan and they are the ones that made him great. I'm sorry Randy, I hope that you're not mad at me. Maybe we'll find out later." He also said nobody from WWE has called him on the subject, but he's come to the conclusion they won't induct the Poffo Family as a group, so he'll accept them inducting Randy on his own."

KEVIN NASH

(DECEMBER 29) Details are sketchy, but Kevin Nash, 55, on 12/24, late Tuesday night at 12:14 a.m. Eastern time, after Volusia County (FL) deputies had gotten word about an altercation between Nash and son Tristen, 18. The deputies arrived and arrested Nash, who was charged with battery. His mug shot taken showed cuts near the left eye and on the cheek. He was being held without bond at press time. After leaving the scene, police returned after getting a 911 call that Tristen, who is 6-foot-5 and 200 pounds, had attacked his mother, and he was also arrested for battery. The police report stated that Deputies were called at 12:07 a.m. to Nash's house in Daytona Beach Shores, FL, on a call regarding an alleged assault and battery, domestic violence charge on a parent (Kevin Nash), listing his son (Tristen Nash) as the victim. The report listed that the deputies believed it was not drug related, but it was alcohol related. According to a series of police reports, a Deputy arrived at the Nash home where he, his wife, and his son live. Kevin Nash told the officer that his son arrived home intoxicated, disrespectful and belligerent to both Kevin and his mother, Tamara Nash. Kevin told one story, but then deputies noted he then changed his story. His second story was that his son spit in his face and threw his shoulder and elbow into his face. He said at that point he took his son down. Nash had a scratch mark that was bleeding near his left eye, but he did not realize or know how he got scratched, but believed he must have been scratched when he was holding his son down on the ground. He said his son fell to the ground because he was intoxicated and his son was bleeding from the elbow from the fall. Kevin Nash refused medical treatment, refused to complete a written statement detailing the incident and refused to allow the deputy to take a photo of his injury, stating "Get a subpoena." Tristen Nash stated that he arrived home and an argument started between he and his father. He said his father got upset because he came home intoxicated. He said he was intoxicated due to a relationship issue with his girlfriend. He said his father grabbed him by the throat with one hand and grabbed his shoulder with the other hand and forced him to the ground. He said his father was holding him down putting pressure on his chest to the point he was unable to breathe. He said that when he was tackled down that he hit the back of his head on the ground and blacked out, and lost consciousness for a brief period of time, and his elbow also hit the ground and started bleeding. He said that he scratched his father's face while being held down due to trying to get his father to let him up because he couldn't breathe. The deputy saw the cut on Tristen Nash's left elbow and redness around his upper chest and lower neck, but there were no marks or swelling from the back of his head. Tristen Nash refused medical treatment and refused to complete a written statement, but did allow the deputy to take photos of him. Kevin Nash was determined by the deputy to be the primary aggressor in the incident and charged with domestic battery. Tamara Nash, after Kevin Nash was arrested, then changed her original story, and stated that Tristen attacked Kevin first, and she was in fear because of past physical altercations between she and her son. Kevin Nash, who was listed as 6-foot-10 and 277 pounds, was taken to the Volusia County jail. At the time of the arrest, Tamara Nash said she was afraid Tristen Nash would destroy the house and possibly become physically abusive to her and said she called her mother. She said her mother was coming to pick her up and take her to her mother's house. Officers remained in the house waiting for her mother to arrive. About 20 or 30 minutes later, Tamara Nash told the officers she had changed her mind, and instead had decided she was going to lock Tristen out of the house. She said she instead called her brother, Jerry McMichael, to come over and talk to Tristen. A second call came to the Sheriff's office at about 1:53 a.m. that an argument took place between Tristen Nash and McMichael. According to the police report, an agreement was made that Tristen Nash would be let in, would go into his bedroom and go to sleep, while McMichael would stay at the house. About six minutes later, there was a 911 call from the residence reporting a physical altercation in the kitchen involving all three. The officer on the 911 call reported he could hear a struggle over the phone and McMichael stated he was holding Tristen Nash down on the ground after Tristen Nash tried to punch him. Two officers went into the house. McMichael told the officers that Tristen Nash "slung his mother around the kitchen" and tried to punch him, and he then took Tristen Nash down and held him on the ground, and contacted deputies. Tamara made a comment stating, "You assholes" and went up the stairs and refused to talk to the officers. Tamara Nash then refused to cooperate with the deputies and left the area. Tristen Nash was taken into custody. Tamara Nash continued to refuse to cooperate with deputies. McMichael said he would cooperate and began writing a statement when Tamara Nash came outside the residence and started arguing with him in a loud voice. McMichael then acted frustrated with the situation, and at that point refused to cooperate with officers and drove away from the residence. Tristen Nash was then charged with simple battery and domestic violence and transported to jail.

CHAPTER FIFTY FOUR

INS & OUTS

EDDIE EDWARDS AND DAVEY RICHARDS

(JANUARY 6) WWE: Eddie Edwards & Davey Richards won't be back at the next NXT tapings and aren't going to be offered a contract. The basic gist of the situation was that HHH didn't want to sign them after the tryout camp because of their size. The feeling is they are loaded with guys who aren't big who can go so the mentality is that they are looking for guys who can headline WrestleMania in five or ten years out of these camps. A lot of people went to bat for both of them, feeling they should get a deal and several pushed that they should go directly to the main roster. So HHH agreed to give them a several month tryout period. The problem with that at first is that WWE also didn't want them on anyone else's TV past the commitments they already had with ROH until the end of the year. But after the first taping, HHH made the decision not to sign them. There were stories out that it was because in the match with The Ascension, there was a spot where Richards landed on his head, which was an accident. Essentially, when they were working on their match, Viktor picked Richards up without dipping down first. So when they did the match at the tapings, Richards went up, and this time, Viktor dipped and the end result was Viktor lost him and he landed on his head. The ref told them to go home under orders from HHH in the back. They did, but not right away. I don't know that had anything to do with the decision not to sign them because it would make little sense regarding Edwards who had nothing to do with the spot, and they were not there to be a team as WWE could have picked one and not the other. After seeing their tryout match, I'm at a loss because they are far better than almost everyone in NXT with the noted obvious exceptions like Sami Zayn and Adrian Neville. The other is that even in working as a jobber team, they got over bigger as far as building their match then just about everyone but Zayn has. I get the size and look issues, but to me the litmus test is do they connect and get over with the fans, and there wasn't even a question about it. I do recognize the issues with Richards but being dropped on his head wasn't his fault and Edwards isn't Richards and hasn't had any issues with any promotions he's worked for that I'm aware of. On 1/1, Richards, when talking about things he did in the past year, said that he signed a new wrestling contract. He didn't specify with who.

KAITLYN

(JANUARY 13) WWE: Kaitlyn (Celeste Bonin, 27), gave notice and finished up with the company on the 1/7 show in Philadelphia. Bonin, who was recruited from the bodybuilding world, was rushed to the main roster after winning a women's NXT competition based on the idea her personality connected with the fans. When she was chosen for the show, she had only a handful of matches and had her first pro wrestling lesson only two months earlier. She was a last minute addition to the show when another woman was cut by WWE when it was found out she had a porn past she hadn't informed the company about. She signed with WWE in the summer of 2010 and debuted on WWE television on September 7, 2010, and won the competition on November 30, 2010. She quickly became tag team partners with A.J., and later feuded with her for much of last year. She had only worked sparingly since August, and recently got engaged to bodybuilder/fitness entrepreneur P.J. Braun.

BATISTA

(JANUARY 13) WWE: Batista signed a two-year contract. That doesn't necessarily mean he'll be there for two years, given age, injury, and schedule, but that is the length of the contract and he is being booked as a full-time performer.

RICOCHET

(JANUARY 20) WWE: The decision was made to pass not only on Eddie Edwards & Davey Richards, but also on Ricochet (Trevor Mann). He did all kinds of spectacular stuff in his tryout, and Joey Mercury had told those in the company specifically to pay attention to him because he's really talented. But the decision was that he was too short and that they already have guys on their roster now and in developmental who can do all the spectacular flying and felt he was just like a lot of other guys, some of which they already have with Adrian Neville in particular.

(JUNE 2) WWE: Regarding Trevor Mann's (Ricochet) tryout several months back, apparently he was super in the ring but didn't get signed. Exactly why he wasn't signed is weird but one person familiar with the process said it was all psychological. Not that he didn't have psychology, but he was a victim of timing and circumstances. Usually when guys come in, even with indie reps, it's no big deal unless it was the KENTA deal, but WWE understood that. But with Mann, when he came in, there were a lot of younger wrestlers there who reacted to him like he was a big deal, but to the company, he's just a guy whose never done anything who they don't know who is getting a tryout for a developmental deal. Since management didn't know who he was, that was already a strike until Jamie Noble outright told people that this guy was something special. In the end, that didn't help, as even though he got high marks from the judges, the decision was that they already have too many guys of that size in developmental right now, and they've got more than their quota of high flyers.

MVP

(JANUARY 27) TNA: Talks with Hassan Assad (who was MVP in WWE and New Japan), 38, have gotten serious and he may be doing a surprise debut on one of the upcoming TV tapings in the U.K. He said that he has not signed a contract on Twitter after we reported they were in talks. The belief in TNA is that he is with them and about to start. I don't know that he's the mystery investor, but from a timing standpoint, it was right after he agreed to come in that they came up with the idea and a lot of other things lead me to believe he's the guy earmarked for the position, but that's not 100 percent. The babyface investor vs. Dixie Carter angle is supposed to carry television through October.

TOMMY DREAMER

(JANUARY 27) TNA: Tommy Dreamer returned as an agent at the 1/16 tapings in Huntsville. He was never shown beaten up on camera, as the other agents were. He was taking the spot of Jeff Jarrett, who quit the promotion. It was a John Gaburick move, since Gaburick would be well familiar with him from WWE.

CHRISTOPHER DANIELS AND FRANKIE KAZARIAN

(JANUARY 27) TNA: Daniels and Kazarian's deals are up in April and Daniels has one of the better remaining contracts still on the books. There is strong speculation he's going to be the next one to get the cost-cutting treatment. Pretty much everyone left who has a good deal is expecting things to change as soon as their deals are up.

(APRIL 14) TNA: The contracts of Christopher Daniels and Frankie Kazarian are coming due within the next few weeks. Neither had signed a new deal at press time. Daniels was one of the guys who had one of the company's better remaining contracts, and after A.J. Styles, Sting and Hulk Hogan were all dropped (they all had bigger contracts than he did, but his deal was good, and there were also the Mickie James and Chavo Guerrero types) the feeling was that he was the next major one to watch. He and Kazarian have not been used on television in several weeks, which I wouldn't consider a positive. My impression is TNA hasn't made either an offer at this point but it wouldn't be the first time TNA waited until the last minute on talent they wanted to keep. The biggest one coming due after that is Kurt Angle in August or September. Angle has certainly made noises and said all the right things as far as getting into WWE, but in the past, WWE has shown no interest in him.

(APRIL 28) TNA: It certainly appears that Christopher Daniels and Frankie Kazarian are leaving imminently. Bill Behrens, who represents both, pushed that both are available for more indie dates. In the case of Daniels, it was noted that he would be available to appear on television shows, iPPV shows and DVDs. Wrestlers under TNA contracts who work indies are banned from doing all three. Daniels' contract expires this week. This was not said for Kazarian. Daniels had one of the last good contracts left in the company so the feeling was strong, particularly when they stopped bringing him and Kazarian in for TV, that this would be how it would go down. Daniels & Kazarian did work the final day of television, doing a job for the Bro Mans on a match taped for an upcoming PPV show, but have been off Impact for weeks. Kazarian's deal expires next month. Daniels will be available for matches, seminars and other appearances, as will Curry Man, his masked Japanese alter ego. The company is going on the mentality it's on a youth movement (although Magnus in his latest FSM column seemed to take umbrage at the youth movement moniker thinking it was a creation of reporters who don't realize the new characters are in their late 20s and early 30s), which, translated into dollars and cents means replacing the guys on good contracts with guys who will agree to work for $300 to $500 per show.

(MAY 19) TNA: As expected, Kazarian's final shows with the promotion were this past weekend as TNA opted not to re-sign him. Christopher Daniels & Kazarian will be working indies both singles and as a team, and are expected to work as a team for at least some ROH dates. It was also clear if you looked at the booking that the decision on Kazarian (Frank Gerdelman, 35), was made along with Daniels. When The Wolves were first being talked of about coming in, there was at least talk of them doing a program with Bad Influence, but it changed to the Bro Mans, who started being pushed as the key heel team and Bad Influence was used sparingly of late. Kazarian started in TNA as a regular in 2003, left for WWE in 2005, returned in 2006 and has been there ever since, including a run as the Suicide character.

(AUGUST 4) TNA: Christopher Daniels & Frankie Kazarian were critical of the promotion in an RF Video interview, excerpts of which were released this past week. Daniels said, in hindsight, he thought it was mind-boggling that TNA got rid of them. Well, it's more an economic issue than pure stupidity. He said he couldn't understand why anyone thought it was a good business decision. He noted the company made the call to go with the Bro Mans ahead of them, and he praised the Bro Mans, and said Jessie Godderz has worked his ass off and improved greatly, but said that he and Kazarian were more entertaining and better wrestlers. When asked about checks coming late, Daniels said that last year in December they were three weeks behind and it ruined his holidays, noting he was down to a single digit in his savings account before the check came on 12/23. Regarding the Claire Lynch angle, which they noted was terrible and said the woman who played the role had no idea what she was doing, thought she wasn't that pretty and joked that originally Claire Lynch was going to be Dixie's niece, and felt the woman got picked because they didn't want to hire an actress better looking than Dixie. He said the angle was originally scheduled to end with a paternity test where it would be revealed that A.J. was not the father. When Daniels was asked about who he'd want booking TNA, he gave the names Scott D'Amore (who, with the benefit of hindsight, was the best booker TNA ever had, because unlike most of the others, he understood who would work the most optimum with who, something neither Eric Bischoff nor Vince Russo had any clue about, so the PPVs under D'Amore were often can't miss while they went downhill after he was out of power), Konnan, Raven, Tommy Dreamer, Bully Ray, Kevin Nash and Jeff Jarrett. He made it clear for any of those names that if they booked, they shouldn't be active performers. I can't say anything about Raven because I've never seen him in action when he had power. As for Dreamer, he can put together an entertaining house show with a good mixture of divergent talent, but the only booking I've ever seen from him in charge of a TV promotion was OVW when Jim Cornette was suspended, and it was bad. Bully Ray is clearly a smart guy, but I've never seen him in charge either. Nash was one of the worst bookers I ever saw, but that was also 1999 and people hopefully get smarter in 15 years, plus he was an active performer and it was clear when he booked it was to get he and his friends over and he didn't care about anything else. If you notice, every name suggested was a former wrestler, and he said that they need guys with a wrestling mentality and that TNA right now doesn't have anyone like that, because the guys in creative (John Gaburick, David Lagana, Vince Russo and Matt Conway) all had never been wrestlers.

MICK FOLEY

(JANUARY 27) WWE: Foley's WWE contract is set to expire and will not be renewed. The two sides will continue to work together on a case-by-case basis. He said the only real difference, besides not getting a regular paycheck from the company, is that he will work WWE dates around his own schedule of touring shows, rather than work his touring shows around WWE dates. WWE had no full-time role for him when Saturday Morning Slam was canceled by CW. He said he hoped WWE would work with him in the future on his live shows. "A WWE produced first-class multi-media one-man Mick Foley show has always been my long-term goal. As WWE showed with the roll-out of the new network, when they go into something, they go all in, and I'm crossing my fingers, hoping they'll go all in on a fall 2014 15th anniversary "Have a Nice Day" production, even if it's just for a limited run."

KENTA

(FEBRUARY 3) WWE: In what to me was a huge surprise, Pro Wrestling NOAH star KENTA (Kenta Kobayashi, who turns 33 in March) has been at the Performance Center since Sunday for a several day tryout. I'm not sure if he'll work this coming week's tapings or not. His last match in Japan was 1/25 and he flew out the next morning to Florida and started his tryout the next day. The KENTA thing has its ironies. KENTA was one of the hot young stars in Japan a decade ago, and Punk, in particular, copied a lot of his stuff, including the GTS finisher, and made it his own in the U.S. market. He was also one of Bryan's favorite wrestlers, and Bryan's Busaiku knee was KENTA's other finisher. Except for his really fast kick and chop routine that Punk used to do when he first came in and was either told not to or stopped on his own, almost all his big moves are already established by someone else here (who took them directly from him), which means he's going to have to drop his biggest spots. At the time, KENTA was a big star and Punk and Bryan were indie guys who studied tapes and looked up to him. Now, KENTA, even though he held the GHC title for a year and was second in the Japanese MVP voting to Okada by Tokyo Sports, because NOAH has fallen so badly, he's less of a star while Punk and Bryan are two of the biggest stars in the world. As a general rule, the cornerstone guys of the promotions in Japan have great loyalty to their companies and are lifers, so between his size (5-foot-7, 180ish) the hard striking style (which doesn't fit well with WWE) and language issues and WWE's usual treatment of Japanese talent (Yoshi Tatsu was a good worker and a bigger guy, who had a cool look, maybe could never be a superstar but could have been a good working underneath guy), it's not the right fit in some ways. Still, this may tell you just how bad things in NOAH are because you don't go to Orlando for a week as a tryout guy when you're a long-time main eventer unless you're looking to get out. He's also considered NOAH's biggest star to its limited audience, so it'll be a big blow to that group if he signs here. That also changes the dynamic of him in Japan. Daily Sports in Japan reported he was going to be offered a contract and NOAH would be doing a farewell show for him. That may be a premature story but I have little doubt he'd impress WWE officials since it's not like they see talent at his level walking into the Performance Center for first looks, and aside from having to tone down the physicality, and tweak a few things, his style will work against Americans a lot easier than the guys from Mexico.

(FEBRUARY 10) WWE: KENTA either didn't look for or didn't get offered a WWE contract after his stint at the Performance Center in Orlando. He was there all week. He didn't work at the NXT tapings. It was an individual tryout, and there were contingency plans to really push Naomichi Marufuji if he signed with WWE. His size worked against him because, as noted, HHH has said that they have too many small guys already in developmental. The idea now is they are looking to find guys with the potential to be WrestleMania headliners, and you know what that means in WWE. KENTA had in the past said that his goal was to go to WWE and wanted to give it a try. KENTA noted that there were guys bigger than him, and guys who were far better athletes than he was, and they haven't made it yet. He said it's not just about being a good pro wrestler. He said it was a good experience but said that it wasn't a tryout. If it wasn't, they wouldn't have had so many people scouting him.

RIC FLAIR

(FEBRUARY 17) WWE: Flair has signed a new contract with WWE. All his appearances and business deals have to be cleared by the office, which means he's not going to be able to take some things he's gotten in the past, and companies that don't like having to deal with WWE aren't going to be happy. He can be booked apart from WWE, but in every deal they insist on a clause that if WWE calls and needs him for anything (such as recently when he had a gig at an auto race in Georgia and got pulled by WWE at the last minute), then everything is off. That makes booking him risky, because it's a high dollar deal, $10,000 or more for an appearance, plus advertising, trans, hotels, and within the contract it can be pulled at the last minute by WWE.

ROB VAN DAM

(FEBRUARY 17) WWE: Van Dam was at the 2/10 Raw show backstage. He came for a meeting with HHH. He wrote on twitter that he's interested in coming back. Not sure how WWE views it. We know they weren't happy about him leaving, even though his deal he signed over the summer was a 90-day contract, he fulfilled it, didn't complain about being buried at the end, but WWE wasn't happy that he wouldn't sign a new deal at the time. WWE didn't bring back Jericho this year either. On the Jericho side, there was talk in 2013 of him coming back as usual for the first several months of 2014. The issues that kept them apart were more creative, as I didn't sense financial played into it.

(SEPTEMBER 1) WWE: RVD is either about to finish up his current run, or did finish it up at the Smackdown tapings on 8/26 with his loss on this week's show to Rollins being his being written out. RVD has a cyclical agreement where he'll go for a few months as opposed to having a long-term contract. When both sides are in agreement, he can be brought back for several more months. The deal pretty much guarantees he won't be pushed hard and his role will largely be putting over new talent.

(SEPTEMBER 8) WWE: When RVD was asked if he was done with WWE for good, he just responded, "For better or for worse." RVD's understanding with the company was that he would work full-time for short, agreed upon, periods of time, somewhat similar to Jericho's deal. The first time he came in, they wanted him to stay longer than agreed but he didn't. The run that ended last week ended his second cycle in.

KEVIN STEEN

(FEBRUARY 17) WWE: While it's not a lock, there has been talk seriously of both Kevin Steen and Michael Elgin being invited to a talent evaluation camp. Steen has known about this for some time and the feeling is that if he shows up out of shape, they'll look down on him a lot. A few years ago, when Takeshi Morishima worked a dark match, and with his flying around at 330 pounds, even though nobody knew him, his match got over pretty big. WWE, however, including Vince McMahon, felt it almost as a sign of disrespect that a guy would come to get a WWE tryout in the shape he was in. Those who have been at camps and noted that they start off testing conditioning making you do stuff designed to blow you up to see who can gut it out the longest, with the idea they can tell from that who wants it the most, feel Steen will need a miracle to get through that aspect of the process. I've also had guys question that process, noting that a lot of guys on the main roster, if they were put through that, could never pass it either and some have been solid money drawing stars. WCW did that to Dave Bautista before he ever signed with WWE, and he became one of the biggest stars of the last decade.

(AUGUST 18) WWE: The Kevin Steen signing announcement was made on 8/12, with the idea of timing it in conjunction with the launch of the WWE Network in Canada. At this point, only Rogers Cable homes have access to the network. Rogers is attempting to make deals with the other cable companies, but hadn't finalized them at the time of the launch. To me, that's a big mistake as they should have done the rollout nationally and not made it a rush job. This launch was said to be similar to the U.S. where they offered one week free on TV, but on 8/12, we got a ton of reports saying there was no free week after all. It's priced at $11.99 per month. What is weird is, Canada is getting the same $9.99 per month figure constantly pushed on television so that already has to lead to some resentment. Rogers is big in the Toronto area, but most of Eastern and Western Canada can't get the network on television and aren't supposed to get it streaming. Rogers services less than 20 percent of the country, although they are in talks with the other cable companies about providing the WWE Network to them. The launch of the streaming version in Canada is still some time off. It will be the live channel plus VOD content. There will be major complaints this week about the VOD content, because it's nothing but 12 old PPV events, SummerSlams from 1991, 1998, 2000, 2002 and 2003, WCW Great American Bash from 1989, WCW Bash at the Beach from 1994, 1996 and 1998, and ECW Heat Waves from 1998 and 1999, plus the first ECW One Night Stand show in 2005. Virtually everyone we've heard from in Canada that gets the network is sticking with the streaming version that they aren't supposed to have, but there are still questions regarding consumers buying a TV network vs. streaming service. One person who did switch said that the one advantage is that the picture quality is far superior on the Rogers channel that streaming. Even today, the ROH iPPVs from Toronto and New York, the company's two strongest shows of the year, did 1,500 to 2,200 or so buys, while the PPV from Nashville, a far weaker show, is estimated at 12,000, and that's the niche ROH audience, young males, that would that one would think would have no aversion to ordering a show on iPPV. Even factoring in the ROH problems on iPPV, the fact is they never topped 2,300 or so even before those problems, and had done two month old taped PPVs many years earlier before they even had TV that did 10,000 buys. But it's smart to use Canada as an experimental market for its television potential, but I'm surprised they'd go in with such a limited VOD component. The WWE Network is on Ch. 512 on Rogers in HD, Ch. 398 for non-HD and Ch. 397 for the VOD content. As part of the deal, NXT is being taken off television in Canada and is strictly on the network, which is notable because from a "legal" standpoint, that means 80 percent of the country just lost access to it. The 170 countries (not including Canada) that had the network available starting on 8/12 represented 2.79 billion people, but only 230 million of them have broadband access. Analyst Chris Harrington, who has been pretty close on his estimates thus far, estimates this launch should net 253,000 new subscribers, and that would push the total to just under 950,000 worldwide, and that does not include Canada, nor the U.K., which is expected to be the No. 2 market for the service and doesn't come onboard until October. Another person in the industry who has knowledge of VOD expansion into foreign markets predicted a number from this particular expansion of 70,000 subscriber growth, noting they are doing no advertising past their TV show in most of the markets, and these are almost all markets where people are not used to paying for programming, let alone paying for wrestling programming. The steady state 1.3 million figure, the number needed to put the company's profits at the same level they were before launching the project, is not unattainable. But thus far, they've fallen short of even the most pessimistic projections from the start of the venture. For those who have geoblocking services that allowed them to order the network outside the U.S. (And get around the geoblocking), I was told the official launch in the new countries saves them about $5 per month. The fact they made a specific announcement for Steen (and this was actually planned for last week, but the decision was made to hold it for the network launch, Steen actually signed months ago) tells you they are high on him. To show how high they are on him, reportedly Ambrose was told not to do Steen's running cannonball into the corner move any longer, as they want it to be a new move for when Steen comes to the main roster. Steen starts in Orlando on 8/25. On the WWE web site, in the Steen story, they listed him as both a former ROH and PWG champion, and that Pro Wrestling Illustrated ranked him No. 10 in their top 500 in 2013. Steen credited a chance airport meeting with Austin in 2005 to encourage him to work on running his mouth if he wanted to be a top guy that turned his career around, because no matter how good his in-ring may be, ultimately what was going to make him break out were his verbal skills. Dwayne Johnson is also a big fan of Steen's work.

PRINCE DEVITT

(FEBRUARY 24) WWE: Regarding Prince Devitt, even though he is booked for the New Japan Cup tournament, that is not a sign that he has signed his new contract. As of last week, he had not, and was considering the WWE offer. William Regal was the one who brought him to WWE's attention. He makes a very good living with New Japan, but not close to the level of someone with his same star power would in WWE. However, with New Japan, he's guaranteed a good spot, in fact he could be the top foreigner in the company this year if he was to sign. With WWE, he'd be starting off at almost 33 and have the handicap of being 187 pounds. Neither are a kiss of death, but both are a handicap, and he doesn't look old and has a great physique which helps out. But a small guy in WWE has to be tons better to even break even so to speak. At the same time, if he waits a few years, his window of opportunity will start closing and do you want to end your career having the regret that you never tried? There's also the advantage that working for New Japan, you don't have the kind of road expenses you have in WWE. There is potential to make more in WWE if you make it to a good level, but a guy like Sami Zayn or Adrian Neville is likely making a lot less and they are both very talented guys. Also, working for Japan, he can live in Ireland but working for WWE, he'd have to move to Florida. He will probably have to go to Orlando just because WWE now has the doctrine that everyone on the main roster has to go through there. But his time there would be short. A lot also depends on the offer. If they greatly beat his New Japan numbers on downside, and actually commit money to him from the start, that greatly encourages them to bring him to the main roster. They don't like paying people decent money who aren't contributing on the main roster.

(MAY 19) WWE: Not that this was a surprise, since it had been known by New Japan for a long time that Prince Devitt was leaving when he didn't sign a new deal in January (and wrestlers with the promotion were aware of it earlier than that), but he wrote on Twitter, "Thank you New Japan for the most wonderful eight years. I will never forget you." There is no official word he's WWE bound, but those who worked with him in Japan expected him to be WWE bound as early as last fall.

(AUGUST 4) WWE: The WWE officially announced the signing of Fergal "Prince" Devitt this week. He's starting imminently. This deal was inevitable when he didn't renew his New Japan contract in January. It was just the timing issue of getting a visa, doing medicals, etc. Devitt is 33, which is older than they like to start people, but he and KENTA are both special talents. He's from Ireland and has been wrestling for 14 years. His big break came in 2005 when he was invited to train at Antonio Inoki's old gym in Santa Monica, CA. He got his tryout as a young boy with New Japan in 2006. The Prince Devitt name came because he said the Japanese had a hard time pronouncing Fergal. He was so impressive that on some shows they put a mask on him and gave him the name the Pegasus Kid. The first Pegasus Kid was Chris Benoit, which tells you from the start how impressed they were to give him the name of someone who was so heavily respected. This was a year before Benoit killed his family and himself. He moved up from young boy to a pushed junior heavyweight over the next few years, first winning the IWGP jr. title with Minoru (Minoru Tanaka) as his partner on January 27, 2008, from Dick Togo & Taka Michinoku. His most famous tag team in Japan, Apollo 55, was with Ryusuke Taguchi from 2009 to the breakup in 2013 when Devitt went heel with the Bullet Club. On July 5, 2009, they beat Chris Sabin &

Alex Shelley to win the IWGP jr. tag titles and he went to the finals of the Super Junior tournament that year, losing to Koji Kanemoto. Four years later he turned on Taguchi and became the top star of The Bullet Club. He was in a great spot with New Japan, as the first foreign junior heavyweight (he's really about 185 pounds) who was getting a legit top push as a heavyweight, something that even people like Chris Benoit and Eddy Guerrero never got. In last year's G-1 Climax tournament, he scored wins over both Hiroshi Tanahashi and Kazuchika Okada. His New Japan run included three IWGP jr. titles, including a 14 month reign as champion that ended at the 1/4 Tokyo Dome show when he lost to Kota Ibushi, at which point they pretty much knew he was leaving. But he was professional staying with the company until 4/6 to tie up all loose ends, including putting over Taguchi to end their program. He left as a babyface, shaking hands with Taguchi and being turned on by The Bullet Club, with A.J. Styles replacing him in the role as the top singles star. He was actually signed months ago, but like all the signees, they are told to deny, and keep quiet. Other titles he held in recent years included the NWA middleweight title for CMLL, the IWGP jr. tag titles six times (twice with Minoru, four times with Taguchi, and he and Taguchi are generally considered the greatest junior heavyweight tag team of the modern era in New Japan. His six title reigns with the belt ties Jushin Liger for the most in history. He won both the 2010 and 2013 Best of the Super Juniors tournament and his 2010 match with Taguchi against Ibushi & Kenny Omega was voted match of the year that year by the Japanese press, which is an amazing accomplishment since that award usually favors dream matches and heavyweight matches.

(OCTOBER 6) WWE: Fergal "Prince" Devitt was given the ring name of Finn Balor. He debuted as the tag team partner of Hideo Itami (KENTA) at the NXT tapings on 9/25 in Winter Park, FL. He got a huge reaction. It's expected that Kevin Steen will be getting his name change shortly and then debuting.

SANTANA GARRETT

(FEBRUARY 24) TNA: Santana Garrett, 25, will be starting here soon. It was announced at a Shine show a few weeks ago that she was going to TNA. She had worked in TNA in 2010 briefly when Orlando Jordan was doing the bisexual gimmick and she was his girl. When that gimmick pretty much died, she was out, but did work one of their One Night Only PPVs last year. It's part of the new idea of trying to bring in newer and cheaper talent that is fresh on the national stage.

(DECEMBER 15) TNA: Santana Garrett (Brittany), 26, who was in the middle of the Samuel Shaw and Gunner storyline, was offered a one-year deal but turned it down and is likely going to work indies. She's looking at doing both modeling and more wrestling. She worked the Shine iPPV on 12/5, which she couldn't have done with TNA. However, the dialogue between the sides isn't dead and it's possible they could end up doing business before the next tapings and keep the storyline going.

REY MYSTERIO

(FEBRUARY 24) WWE: Mysterio's contract is the next major one to expire, in about two months or so. He has one of the highest downsides, and is also one of the biggest merchandise sellers. He's got all the knee issues and it's clear from his return that WWE has no plans to feature him. Usually at this point WWE would be aggressively trying to get him to sign a new deal and that hasn't really been the case. When there was talk of him not coming back some time ago, some of the company's business partners in Latin America freaked out because he's the most important guy it is believed in those markets. But it's long gone from the days when Smackdown was a top ten rated show in the Hispanic demo when he was there, and dropped greatly when he wasn't. With Mark Burnett's AAA project in the U.S., it would figure to be a lock that if he doesn't sign, he'd be the featured guy in that project.

(APRIL 7) WWE: Mysterio's contract expires later this month. He hasn't signed a new deal but they are looking at something where he'd wrestle limited dates and spend more time as a brand ambassador for Latin America, which is kind of what he's been doing of late anyway. He's been going to foreign Spanish language countries promoting the product and doing limited wrestling.

(MAY 12) WWE: Mysterio was in Stamford on 4/30 at the corporate offices. He was there to talk a new contract. Not sure what went down past the point we were given the impression the offer he'd get was to be an ambassador for the company, particularly in Spanish language markets, and wrestle part-time. The best way to describe it right now is that everything is up in the air. Vince McMahon wants him back.

(JUNE 2) WWE: On the Rey Mysterio front, his contract was to have expired a few weeks ago. He got word that Vince McMahon had renewed it for one year, even though there was no option period of that type in the contract. WWE contracts are allowed to be frozen in the event of injury. The WWE went with the idea that due to his missing so much time during the contract period due to injuries, that Mysterio owed them time and he was renewed through May of 2015 on that basis. He's got a very healthy downside, so he'll make good money, whether he's used well or not. But I don't know how he'll be used because I don't know how confident they are in his ability to hold up long enough to invest a lot in him to have hit at the top level at this stage, even though there are serious depth issues on house shows. Right now he is out of action with a hand injury.

(JUNE 9) WWE: There is more to the Rey Mysterio situation than he was simply renewed for another year. It's a potential legal situation that has yet to play out. Mysterio was looking at leaving with the expiration of his contract a month ago, before Vince McMahon renewed it for another year citing the time he had been out of action during the previous contract due to injuries. Right now he's officially still on the injury list and nothing is being talked about regarding when he would return.

(JUNE 16) WWE: Since a lot of people have asked about this related to Mysterio and last week's issue, all standard WWE contracts are written with the clause that the company can extend the contract based on the wrestlers not performing for an extended period of time due to an injury. So WWE doing the automatic renewal of his expiring contract is something specifically mentioned in his deal and in all standard deals. I haven't heard of it being used for anyone else. They could do that with Punk in July should they choose. The advantage is that they could keep him from working for anyone else. The disadvantage is if they did renew him, they'd have to pay him his downside, which right now, they wouldn't be paying him since he's refusing to work.

(JULY 28) WWE: There is nothing official new on Mysterio. As noted before, he is still under contract. There is no date set for a return, and there is some question if there will be a return. Reportedly he has stopped cashing any of the checks the company has sent him, which is usually a prelude to action being taken to get out of the deal. As noted, his contract expired months ago, but the company renewed it for another year based on the idea that he owed them a year from the previous contract based on time off due to injury. That is part of the standard wrestling contract everyone signs.

(AUGUST 18) WWE: Hugo Savinovich, the former WWE Spanish language announcer, who is now affiliated with AAA, outright said that Mysterio is coming to AAA as soon as he works out his WWE contract issues, when talking about Del Rio being at TripleMania. While widely expected that Mysterio would be in AAA as soon as he was legally able, Savinovich was the first person affiliated with the company to publicly say so.

(SEPTEMBER 1) WWE: Regarding fallout of Mysterio's taped appearance at TripleMania last week, there has been nothing, at least as of press time. Nobody from WWE had contacted Mysterio about anything since May. No phone calls, e-mails, letters (aside from his checks, which are coming regularly). Nobody asked why he did the show, threatened him for doing it, or anything. He also wasn't asked to appear at the house show in his home city of San Diego on 8/23. WWE legal didn't contact AAA either.

(OCTOBER 27) WWE: In something that somewhat confirms what everyone has hinted about or knows, Hugo Savinovich, who works for AAA as a liaison to Puerto Rico and U.S. business, told KGB Wrestling that Mysterio is done in WWE and will come back to AAA when his WWE deal expires. This is a very touchy subject for obvious reasons. Mysterio is under contract to WWE through April. They want him back. He obviously doesn't want to go back, but if he doesn't go back, they can extend his contract, like they did, because they also don't want him walking right into AAA or Lucha Underground. They weren't happy he was at the Lucha Underground tapings and photos came out, but he also is allowed to visit friends and go to shows as long as he doesn't appear on camera. It's a really weird deal because a video of him did play at TripleMania, which took a lot of balls by AAA. AAA also used Del Rio before he had gotten a release from WWE (which he hasn't gotten yet). I've never seen a promotion except WCW do this, and WCW ended up in a lot of trouble when they did. So it will be interesting how this plays out. But it was really telling to me that Mysterio did not appear, even doing just a guest appearance, for the Mexico shows, particularly since Flair ended up being pulled off those shows.

(NOVEMBER 17) WWE: Mysterio in Buffalo on 11/3 met with Vince McMahon and Paul Levesque. Nothing definitive came out of it other than Vince wanting him to return to action. For those who think Levesque is really the one running things, this was all very clearly a Vince meeting and Vince was running the show. At least from the WWE standpoint, the belief is that he'll be back shortly and working fairly regularly between now and WrestleMania. His contract expires in late April. The only thing we've heard is that they've asked him to do more dates than most think is prudent for him. I don't know if that's just not learning, since he will break down on a nearly full schedule. But the belief is they'll reach a compromise. Creative has been told to come up with some ideas for him.

TANDY O'DONOGHUE

(MARCH 3) WWE: Tandy O'Donoghue has been promoted to Executive Vice President of Strategy and Analytics starting 3/15, a newly created role, working under Chief Strategy and Finance Officer George Barrios. O'Donoghue will be responsible for overseeing corporate strategy, business development and data analytics. Her role will be to identify and execute cross-functional high-impact initiatives including the global rollout of the WWE Network, the development and execution of long-term strategy and global content monetization initiatives, as well as lead efforts to secure strategic equity investments and partnerships and will use advanced data analytics to support short and long-term decision making across the company. She was previously Senior Vice President of Affiliate Relations and business development, where she was responsible for the day-to-day management of the PPV business and the launching plans for the WWE Network.

AJ STYLES

(MARCH 10) NJPW: A.J. Styles is expected to start here, perhaps as early as April. It's not official but talks are going on and those in the promotion are expecting a deal. He should be a great addition because he's an American who can work with the top mix with all kinds of new matches.

(MARCH 17) NJPW: This is not official, but there is a good chance A.J. Styles will be debuting with New Japan Pro Wrestling on the Invasion Attack PPV, which is 4/6 at Sumo Hall. I was outright given that date from someone close to New Japan. Styles' booking schedule shows nothing for that weekend, yet Styles is booked every Saturday night for a few months. My impression is that it's either meant to be kept quiet until they announce the card, or he'll be appearing as a surprise like the Gracies did the first time to issue a challenge on that card and not announced ahead of time.

(MARCH 24) NJPW: It is believed A.J. Styles has signed a one-year deal here. Nothing can be officially confirmed because both Styles' side and New Japan want things a secret until they announce it, which is expected to be in conjunction with the Invasion Attack show.

(MARCH 31) NJPW: A.J. Styles has signed and is going to be given a major push as a singles headliner, to work with all the big guns, with a title shot at Kazuchika Okada coming sooner than later. In a sense, Styles position may be a replacement for Prince Devitt in some form, not as the leader of The Bullet Club necessarily, but Devitt did not sign a new contract for 2014, and given it's now March, the belief is he is WWE-bound as soon as that deal fully materializes. He's been a very different performer here the last several months, clearly not taking any risks as compared to before and just playing heel, although that dates back to his injuries last year. At least in Japan, between his history and the way he carries himself, he comes off with big star presence. Devitt was in talks to do shows for House of Hardcore, and he said he couldn't, saying it was because New Japan has an exclusive deal with ROH. A.J. Styles asking price on the U.S. indie scene is $2,500 per shot. He may have a different deal here since they have him for multiple dates. It would appear he made the right call not signing with TNA, as reports had his offer there in the $200,000 range. If you figure an average month that he'll get six indie dates, a week with New Japan (which will likely be at well over his U.S. money), plus he gets to keep all of his merchandise money and, on the indie scene, they pay for hotels and take care of the trans so you save on rental cars, the expenses are way down in comparison to working a TNA (or WWE) schedule. The question is how long he'll be able to pull down that kind of money, because historically, talent is most valuable coming right off TV and then their value on the indie market drops. But even if that's the case, a regular gig with New Japan should take up the slack.

(APRIL 7) Indies: Regarding A.J. Styles price on indies, while things vary based on promotion, how many dates booked, if it's someone he knows well, etc. but his asking price in the U.S. and Canada is $3,000 per shot. The $2,500 figure we had last week was for someone he knows well. The price for a show outside the U.S. and Canada is $5,000. I believe in Japan, it would be a contract situation, but he's booked solid every Saturday and a lot of Fridays, and as noted, he gets to keep his merchandise money and doesn't have the road expenses working indies since when you work for indies, the rule of thumb is that you are picked up and a hotel room comes with the package so no rental car and hotel room. The point remains, at this stage of the game, when he's fresh off television and his shows are generally drawing well, it looks to me like he'll do considerably better on the indie scene than he would have had he stayed with TNA this year. Usually in time, for guys coming out of a major promotion, the asking price drops over time, but name wrestlers can make a solid living on the indie scene. One of the issues with WWE guys as opposed to TNA guys, is when you're used to 3,000 to 15,000 fans every night, the indie scene can be a come-down, but Styles is working before generally as big or bigger crowds on indies than he did with TNA.

TOO COOL

(MARCH 10) WWE: Too Cool did an interview for the web site after the NXT show and said they were going to be back in WWE. That sounds strange to me. You have to figure given their ages, the idea of Brian Lawler with his track record, and now being 42, and the Too Cool gimmick doesn't work with someone that age, Plus they had The Ascension pretty much beat them and the match wasn't even any good. Plus, while Scott Garland looks like a 40 year old who eats right and goes to the gym, with his bald head, he doesn't exactly look like a WWE guy, even though the worm spot will still always work in a match. Logic would indicate they'd bring two guys from NXT up if they wanted to add people to touring. I guess we'll see. Garland had moved on and gotten a job as a firefighter.

DRAKE WUERTZ

(MARCH 10) WWE: Drake Wuertz, 29, better known as Drake Younger, signed a WWE developmental deal after being part of the December tryout. He stood out in a tryout that was described as overall having the least amount of talent as any in recent memory. He's been wrestling on the indie scene since he was a teenager in

Indiana, and had moved to California where he had become a regular for most of the local groups. His last match before leaving is scheduled for 3/15 for the remake of All Pro Wrestling at a show in Daly City down the street from the Cow Palace, against Adam Thornstowe.

(MAY 19) WWE: The former Drake Younger, under his real name of Drake Wuertz, was refereeing NXT house shows over the weekend, which seems to confirm rumors that he was going in to be a referee rather than a wrestler. We're told that when he heard back from his tryout, he was told that they weren't looking at anymore cruiserweight sized guys (there always going to be exceptions to every rule but that's the general rule right now) because they have enough in the system, which led to him making a deal to get in as a referee. Also at NXT this past week was Kazma Sakamoto, who had been working for Keiji Muto's Wrestle-1 promotion as one of its lead heels. Sakamoto had been the second of Tensai, before the character was dropped and he was released. So that makes he and Jody Kristofferson as guys who were cut last year and brought back this year.

OCTAGON

(MARCH 17) AAA: This had not been publicized, but Octagon is no longer with the promotion, which is a big deal. I think that means only referee Tropicasas has been with the promotion since its debut in 1992. Konnan was there at the start and is still there now, but he had a long period away. Octagon had never left. Octagon is back on indies and doing a program with Fuerza Guerrera, which started in 1990 in CMLL and was a major program in the early years of AAA, where they teased a blow-off mask match that never happened. Octagon said his tenure with AAA ended on 3/1. When asked if he'd return to CMLL, he said he felt his relationship with Paco Alonso was good enough to where he could do so, but has no plans right now to do so. For what it's worth, AAA owns the Octagon name, but is allowing him to use the name on indies.

RONDA ROUSEY

(MARCH 24) WWE: Rousey was asked about pro wrestling this past week. Rousey, Shayna Baszler and Jessamyn Duke all live together at Rousey's home in Venice Beach, along with Marina Shafir, who competed in judo with Rousey and now is an unbeaten amateur MMA fighter. Rousey was something of a fan in the past, and her Rowdy Ronda nickname was taken from Roddy Piper. Baszler is a huge fan and pretty avid historian, who has trained under Billy Robinson. When Baszler moved in, she couldn't miss Raw, and now all four of them, who do the Four Horsewomen gimmick, watch Raw every week. Baszler noted to us that shortly after Robinson passed away, that she was watching all kinds of stuff on him including his match with Antonio Inoki. The women all went out with C.M. Punk on 2/22 in Las Vegas after Rousey beat Sara McMann. "I think the first thing I said to him was, `I love you,' which was terrible and not smooth at all." You have no idea how many people, months ago, in WWE had predicted that A.J. Lee and Ronda Rousey were on a collision course. She said Punk was "super cool." This past week, Rousey and Baszler sent out an instagram of them practicing pro wrestling in a ring, including Rousey doing a flying armbar. The two are expecting to post more stuff and Rousey said she'd be happy to do something with WWE, although noted her schedule right now is tough. TMZ reported that she would be interested in doing WrestleMania 31. That would be dependent upon whether UFC would allow it. I know that Jon Jones had interest, or at least his management did, in having him do this year's Mania, but nothing transpired from the WWE side.

LE'D TAPA

(MARCH 31) TNA: The reason the Gail Kim vs. Le'D Tapa program was so rushed is because the decision was made to release her. Even though she wouldn't have been a highly paid performer, the new people in charge decided against going with the character any longer. She hardly had the chance to improve given her brief tenure and how few matches she worked, but she was really only there as a protection for the heel Knockouts champion. When the title was taken from Kim, the role didn't make as much sense, and they appear to have moved on from Kim being the focal point of the division. So, in the first match after the split, she put her career on the line and lost. Tapa, real name Seini Draughn, 31, is the niece of The Barbarian of Powers of Pain fame in the late 80s. She got her contract with TNA on February 28, 2013, when she and Ivelisse Velez did a Gut Check segment. The result was almost preposterous given that Velez, who had been cut from WWE after appearing on Tough Enough and being the most advanced woman in their developmental system (they claimed she had a bad attitude). The crowd loved Velez, and was furious when she was cut from the evaluation since she appeared ready for a spot and Tapa was really green. But Tapa had size and moved well. She was sent to OVW for a few months, and brought back in late September for her role as the bodyguard for Kim. The day after she was cut, she was back in class at OVW.

WWE TRYOUT CAMPS

(MARCH 31) WWE: Names we've seen listed for the WWE tryouts camp in Orlando from last week included ACH, Arya Daivari (the younger brother of former WWE wrestler Shawn Daivari), David Starr (who has worked for CZW), Kevin Steen, Michael Elgin, Rocky Romero, Roderick Strong, Ronny Reeves, Willie Mack and Zane Dawson. We've confirmed ACH, Steen, Strong and Dawson. Mack was someone that AAA had on its radar as far as promoting in the U.S. Apparently Steen and Strong did well, with Strong as the star of the camp, both from an athletic standpoint and they were impressed with his speaking ability. Keep in mind people there saying doing well doesn't necessarily equate to being signed, because in the end, it's about what HHH sees in you, particularly if you're a name from the outside, which can work against you, since their mentality is they'd rather develop guys from scratch, but they don't want to close their minds to people who are really talented either. The Romero name is interesting because he's been a regular with New Japan, and his partner, Alex Koslov, had a bad experience with WWE.

(MAY 26) WWE: Some of the wrestlers from the late March tryout camp got word the past few days regarding deals. Willie McClinton Jr. (Willie Mack of Pro Wrestling Guerrilla) was at least under the impression he'll be offered a deal contingent upon his passing medical testing, but he hasn't gotten an actual offer. As is pretty obvious from his speech at the ROH show, Kevin Steen must have an idea something is brewing, but officially he also has not gotten an offer at press time. Other names at that specific camp included ACH, Rocky Romero, Arya Daivari (younger brother of former WWE performer Shawn Daivari), David Starr, Roderick Strong, Ronny Reeves and Zane Dawson. We were told that Strong (who the coaches ironically listed as the best wrestler in the tryout), ACH and Romero were all told via e-mail that they would not be being offered a deal. Steen, 30, is one of the best-known wrestlers in the country who has never worked for a major promotion, and an interesting figure. He is one of the best talkers in the business and quick witted on his promos. He's a great worker, but his body is exactly the type that Vince McMahon hates. But he has dropped probably 35 pounds and if he goes to Orlando and dedicates himself to eating right and training, the feeling is he's a big boned guy and will be able to put on size and change his look. He's been wrestling for 14 years, starting on his 16th birthday after training under Jacques Rougeau Jr. By 2004, he was working in the U.S. with Combat Zone Wrestling, and in 2005 starting appearing in PWG, usually touring with El Generico (Sami Zayn). He was a top star as a heel in ROH for years, and was clearly the group's top star since coming back. Steen has always claimed problems with Jim Cornette when Cornette came in as the lead of creative. He lost a loser leaves town match with Generico at Final Battle of 2010. Steen said that he was paid every month while he was gone by Cary Silkin and Cornette told him he'd be back in a few months. There was heat because he dropped 40 pounds because Cornette wanted him in better shape, but then Cornette delayed his return until July, feeling that for credibility of the loser leaves town, he shouldn't come back for six months at least. By then Steen was up around 290 pounds. But upon his return, he was booked like Stone Cold Steve Austin, as the top guy in the promotion, the anti-authority heel, which ended up making him a huge babyface long before his official turn. He won the ROH title on May 12, 2012, and held it for 13 months, before losing to Jay Briscoe on April 5, 2013, and then turned official face. He was clearly the biggest regular star in the promotion to the ROH fans for the past three years. The update as of this week on McClinton Jr., 27, is that he has been spoken with since the camp. He's from Los Angeles and is a short, really heavy guy who is very agile and apparently did well in the cardio at the camp in March, which is a concern among heavy guys. He started wrestling in 2006 on Southern California indies, and moved to PWG in 2010. AAA was high on him and his name was mentioned to me several times as far as being on their radar when they get on television late this year and expand into the U.S. market. Another signee this past week was Noah Kekoa, a Hawaiian who was trained by Afa Anoa'i at his wrestling academy. Kekoa was Afa's WXW champion.

(SEPTEMBER 15) WWE: They had a tryout camp this past week in Orlando. Jeff Cobb, who represented Guam in the 2004 Olympics at 185 pounds in freestyle wrestling and has been one of the top indie workers in California, was among those attending. Cobb is very good in the ring and actually a super athlete who can do amazing things you don't see from amateur wrestlers like shooting stars and such. He has a unique double rotation powerslam move that he can do on really big guys. He's 5-foot-10, or at least that's what he was in 2004, but he's not tall and he's 32. But unlike most of the amateurs they sign, he's been doing indies for years and moved from Hawaii to California to train under Oliver John (a super underrated talent who fell through the gaps somehow) and works a full schedule of weekend indies in the area, so he knows what pro wrestling is and has made the sacrifices. His placed 21st in the Olympics in the weight class where Cael Sanderson won the gold medal and Yoel Romero (UFC) placed fourth. Romero beat him 10-0 via tech fall in 4:31 in the Olympics. Cobb was the Oceania wrestling champion in freestyle in 2001, 2004, 2005 and 2007, and the Greco-Roman champion in 2005 and 2007, all at 185. Other names that have come out are Rich Swann, who should be in a major promotion right now because of his charisma and unique athletic ability, and Nick Ruiz, who is another Northern California independent wrestler.

(NOVEMBER 3) WWE: A new group of wrestlers signed from a camp over the summer, who started out this week in Orlando, are headed by Sunny Dhinsa, who is something of a surprise. Dhinsa was the 2011, 2012 and 2013 Canadian national freestyle wrestling champion in the 264 pound weight class and placed third in the 20-and-under world championships last year. Dhinsa was attending Simon Fraser College in British Columbia as a freshman last year. As a teenager, he took second at the 2011 Pan American games but failed to qualify for Canada's Olympic team as an 18-year-old heavyweight. He was training for the 2016 Olympics, and really one would think his peak would be 2020. But he had said that he wanted to train for 2016 and go to WWE that year. But after an offer by WWE, he decided to give up amateur wrestling. Gerald Brisco had scouted him a few years back and had kept in touch with him ever since. There's a fine line here. It's the guy's choice, but I know amateur wrestling officials, and they tend not to like pro wrestling to begin with. Amateur wrestling people don't even like when guys like Ben Askren leave for MMA because of the feeling they are taking guys who still have medal potential out of the sport. Brisco generally works with college officials and doesn't sign people until their eligibility is up. But this was the exception. Except for Dhinsa, everyone else were all signed with an emphasis on their look. Also signed was Zahra Schreiber, a model from Saginaw, MI, who was training under Jimmy Jacobs at the House of Truth Wrestling school in Center Line, MI. She's a heavily tattooed up brunette. WWE usually frowns on women with large amounts of tattoos, but that does make her different from all the women on the roster and different is good. Another signee is Dustin Mueller, a 6-foot-6 bodybuilder from Chicago. The second new woman is Gionna Daddio, a blond Hooter's Waitress and model. The final newcomer is Josh Woods, a muscular heavyweight wrestler who looks a little like Josh Thomson, but bigger. Woods was 108-16 with 57 pins at the University of Central Florida, winning the NWCA championship as a freshman in 2011, placed second in 2012, fourth in 2013 and third in 2014, becoming the college's national champion since UFC fighter Tom Lawlor. He's trained with Lawlor, and is 2-0 in MMA. It is notable that guys like Dhinsa and Woods are choosing WWE, as for a period of time, those kind of guys were mostly MMA bound.

JONATHAN COACHMAN

(MARCH 31) WWE: WWE looks to be either close to or has just signed a new deal with Jonathan Coachman. What the two sides had been talking about of late was a part-time gig. He'd keep his ESPN job, but they'd like him to do in-studio wrap-arounds and an idea thrown out would be for him as the host of a WWE talk show that would air on the network. Coachman on Twitter on 3/25 talked about having a cool announcement for WWE fans in the next month or so regarding something happening in the summer.

(JUNE 30) WWE: Months ago, Jonathan Coachman hinted that he was going to come back and work in a limited role on the network. We'd heard about the deal shortly before the network launched and Coachman had teased that he would have an announcement coming soon regarding wrestling. Coachman was going to stay with ESPN, just do some network projects. Evidently it fell through since when Coachman was asked on Twitter by someone who said that everyone wanted to see him back, and he responded by writing, "Except WWE."

SIN CARA

(APRIL 7) WWE: The company announced that Luis Urive, the original Sin Cara, had been released from his contract. He's expected to go to AAA whenever his non-compete clause ends. Those in AAA are under the impression he's being paid for three more months by WWE as part of his non-compete, so would be available to be signed on or around 6/26. That's why he never came out in front of the people when he did that AAA appearance, because WWE claimed he was still under contract.

SEAN CLEARY

(APRIL 7) WWE: Sean Cleary, who had taken Jane Geddes role in talent relations, which included handling the payoffs, left his position and is back in Human Resources, which was where he came from a few months ago. The change happened about a month ago. Geddes had been moved last year from talent relations to being HHH's right-hand person as far as keeping track of his scheduling, when they got rid of HHH's assistants several months back. HHH is personally handling talent payroll now. The feeling is that won't last long and it's said he's trying to find someone for that position because of the time consuming nature of that role. Jim Ross did payroll forever, and then John Laurinaitis for a short period of time (Ross still did it long after officially being out of talent relations), followed by Geddes and then Cleary.

VICKIE GUERRERO

(APRIL 14) WWE: Vickie Guerrero, 45, finished up with the company this past week. There wasn't any drama to it. She just wanted to move into the regular world. She had been attending college in Houston studying Medical Administration. She had left once before and has been attending college for some time. She came into the company as a recurring character in 2005 as Eddy Guerrero's wife. She became a regular in 2006 after Eddy's death as an authority character on both Raw and Smackdown over the last eight years. She was the G.M. of Smackdown at the time she gave notice.

(APRIL 21) WWE: Vickie Guerrero isn't gone after all. After those in WWE confirmed a report of her departure came word later in the week that she's leaving but it's like the Eve Torres leaving (Torres gave notice but stayed a long time after doing so and still has a relationship with the company). A number of people had noted to us that she was leaving last week, but she said she wasn't leaving a week later. The official company word as of right now is she is with the company.

(JUNE 23) WWE: Vickie Guerrero is expected to be done next week after the angle with Stephanie McMahon this week. If not, it's imminent. As noted before, most were under the impression she was finishing at Mania, but she decided to stay until they had a way to write her out.

(JUNE 30) WWE: The angle on the 6/23 Raw show where Vickie Guerrero, 46, was fired was her long talked about farewell. She was talking about leaving over WrestleMania weekend, but the agreement was she would stay until she was properly written out of the storyline, which was the last two weeks. I believe she's going into the nursing industry, as she has been studying Medical Administration in online college courses the last few years. She was pretty much universally liked and respected as a performer for her ability to get nuclear heat. The farewell show, where Stephanie McMahon allowed Vickie to shove her into what was supposed to be runny shit, although obviously it wasn't, since the announcers kept talking about how much it smelled, showed how much respect they had for her because usually you aren't getting the top heel authority figures to sell for someone on their last show. She left to Eddie's music, and did Eddie's shimmy dance on the way out, also covered in whatever the brown stuff was. The announcers were pushing it as perhaps the last time a Guerrero is on WWE television. Vickie had appeared as Eddie's wife a few times on WWE television starting in the summer of 2005 in the storyline where he claimed the big secret that he was really the father of Rey Mysterio's son. That storyline led to gigantic spikes in quarter hours, particularly in Hispanic markets and led Smackdown to being the highest rated English language network show in Hispanic households. Vickie returned in 2006, after Eddy's death, first as the widow of the beloved Eddie, but then making her own name as a heel. In 2007, she started as an assistant to Teddy Long on Smackdown. She then became General Manager when they did a storyline heart attack angle putting Long out of action. The original idea was that Kristal Marshall and Guerrero found secret medical records of Long and conspired to give him the heart attack since Marshall (Bobby Lashley's girlfriend at the time) was marrying Long in storyline. The angle never came to fruition as WWE fired Marshall, which later played a hand in Lashley leaving. Vickie's biggest role was as the storyline wife of Edge with its twists and turns, as the two carried the Smackdown programming during that period. She left the company for the first time after that angle, but returned for a storyline romance with Eric Escobar, a character who never got over and an angle that didn't go anywhere. She had another more successful run with Ziggler, which led to a feud with A.J. Lee when Ziggler dumped her for Lee. She was so well regarded that she won Best Non-Wrestler in the Observer awards in both 2009 and 2010. There's also been talk of her in relation to the WWE Hall of Fame. They turned her babyface in her final show. "The ride has come to a halt," said Vickie Guerrero on Twitter after her final show. "I'm so grateful for the wonderful blessings in the last nine years, live, love and laugh. Heading home to begin a new chapter in my amazing life. Thank you, Jesus."

EZEKIEL JACKSON

(APRIL 14) WWE: Rycklon Stephens, who worked as Ezekiel Jackson, was the first post-WrestleMania cut. Stephens contract expired this past week and the company made the decision not to renew, which is hard to second guess since they gave up on him years ago. From the word going around, WWE isn't going to be doing a lot of cutting, outside of developmental and disciplinary reasons, but guys who aren't used that reach an age where they don't see future upside in them, may not get renewed. Stephens, who turns 36 in two weeks, was a bodybuilder from Guyana who was signed in 2007, and brought to the main roster in the summer of 2008 when Brian Kendrick picked him to be his bodyguard. He transitioned from there to being a babyface wrestler. Like so many huge bodybuilder types including Mason Ryan, Jackson Andrews, Bobby Lashley and others, he got a big push and then they soured on him. He is the answer to the trivia question as the final-ever ECW champion, as he beat Christian on the final ECW TV show on February 16, 2010. He also had a run as IC champion after breaking away from The Corre and Wade Barrett. It's been about two-and-a-half years since he had been used, between injuries and just being on the sidelines. It was actually surprising he was still on the roster since he had only a few matches in the last 30 months. He had an undisclosed surgery in January and had been out ever since.

SHAWNE MERRIMAN

(JUNE 2) WWE: Shawne Merriman, 29, has signed with WWE. The storyline idea is to make him this generation's version of Steve McMichael. Well, hopefully not exactly. Merriman was a legitimate NFL star with the San Diego Chargers, where he was a 6-foot-5, 270 pound linebacker from 2005 to 2007 after being the 12th pick in the draft that year, but recurring injuries ended his career a few years back. He did a tryout last year and didn't do all that well based on several reports we got, blew up early, etc. But he was interested. The idea right now is to train him as an announcer, like how McMichael started, to get him on TV while he's also training, and then transition to being a wrestler when he's good enough. He played at the University of Maryland with Mojo Rawley. He also had a steroid positive in the NFL some years back. People who saw him in New Orleans this weekend said he looked jacked as hell.

(SEPTEMBER 1) WWE: For those asking about former NFL star Shawne Merriman, who was training to be both a wrestler and an announcer, and had signed a deal around WrestleMania time, he is no longer under contract and has no affiliation with the company.

(SEPTEMBER 8) WWE: On the Shawne Merriman situation, Merriman never signed a contract with WWE. He appeared doing some network programming around Mania time. The categorization of it now is that he was making a guest appearance, although we were told at the time they were looking at him to be an announcer and he was going to do wrestling training.

CHRIS SABIN

(APRIL 21) TNA: Chris Sabin is expected to be gone from the company as his contract is expiring. It's pretty much confirmed because he's booking himself on indie dates with company's that don't book through TNA or use TNA talent. Christopher Daniels & Frankie Kazarian were again not used for the next three weeks on Impact but were brought in for the X-Travaganza PPV taping. Sabin also worked the X-Travaganza show and put over Low Ki.

(APRIL 28) TNA: Chris Sabin's contract officially expires in a couple of weeks, and as things stand right now, it looks like he won't be re-signed. He also hasn't been used on television either. I have the impression that decision was made some time back, at which point they started phasing him out of the X title picture. When Alex Shelley left to go to Japan, at that time, the feeling was that Sabin wouldn't renew his deal and would go to Japan when it was up. TNA gave Sabin a big push last year, all the way to the TNA title, but then after losing it, turned him heel and did a feud with Velvet Sky, leading to a storyline breakup, and he wasn't really used much since. He was brought back for the last night of TV last week to put over Low Ki for a taped PPV show.

(MAY 19) TNA: Chris Sabin, (Josh Harter, 32), had his contract expire this past week. He had been with the company for 11 years, holding the TNA title once, the tag title once with Alex Shelley, and the X title eight times. There was the feeling that he wasn't the same after having reconstructive knee surgery on both knees, the right knee in May 2011 and left knee in June 2012. In 2013, he was pushed all the way to the top, in a summer program where he beat Bully Ray to win the TNA title on July 18, 2013, in Louisville, as part of a long comeback story, but then he lost it back on August 15, 2013, at the Norfolk Impact. Then after being an unlikely top babyface, he dropped down quickly, turned heel to feud with Velvet Sky. Once that feud ended on the European tour, he wasn't used since they probably made the call not to renew him by that point since they had all the financial issues.

LOW KI

(APRIL 21) TNA: One would suspect Low Ki is coming in since he won an X Division tournament for a title match at the X-Travaganza show, even though that show won't air until toward the end of the year. The plan right now is for him to work some house shows and future TVs. MVP is a big proponent of his. It was a weird feeling on talent. A lot of them were happy to see new faces coming in, since so many top guys had left and few newcomers had come in. But that was a mixed bag, because at the X-Travaganza, the guys who do work for the company weren't happy about putting over guys who weren't with the company, feeling it made no sense.

(JUNE 9) TNA: The last we heard, Low Ki is scheduled to return here shortly. He had told promoters who tried to book him he was retiring a few months ago, but is now coming back. AAA is also trying to sign him for their

U.S. invasion that is scheduled at this point for the fall and he has told other promoters who have talked with him that he expects to be working for TNA. He recently filmed a One Night Only X Division show in Orlando for TNA. Taryn Terrell, who returned after giving birth also at the Orlando tapings for an all-women One Night Only show, is expected to be back at the Bethlehem, PA tapings.

STEVEN WALTERS
(APRIL 21) WWE: Southern indie wrestler Steven Walters of NWA Anarchy is starting soon in developmental. He had his last match with his home promotion over the weekend, losing to Corey Hollis and gave a post-show speech talking about heading to WWE developmental.

TOM LATIMER
(APRIL 28) TNA: Tom Latimer from England, who had a tryout at the last tapings, was either offered a deal or has been given the impression he will be getting one. He was Kenneth Cameron of The Ascension in Florida before being let go after getting into a fight with a police officer. Latimer is married to Ashley Fliehr (Charlotte/Ric's daughter) of WWE.

RICH BRENNAN
(APRIL 28) WWE: New NXT announcer Rich Brennan is Rich Bocchini, who had been the announcer for Booker T's Reality of Wrestling promotion in the Houston area. His background included announcing for the Rio Grande Valley Killer Bees of the Central Hockey League and the Houston Aeros of the American Hockey League as well as working as Communications Manager for Comcast Sports Houston.

TONY NELSON
(APRIL 28) WWE: Gerald Brisco's blue chip recruit this year is University of Minnesota heavyweight Tony Nelson, who won NCAA titles in 2012 and 2013, but lost in the finals this year. Nelson wrestled for J Robinson, who was Brisco's roommate in the late 60s when both wrestled at Oklahoma State. Nelson also has some NFL offers. Brisco said that Nelson could be in the main event at WrestleMania in four years. The quickest ever would be Lesnar, who started with WWE in developmental in the summer of 2000 and was in the sort-of main event at the 2003 Mania with Kurt Angle (it went on last but Vince vs. Hogan was the match promoted the hardest), so less than three years. Kurt did it in four-and-a-half years and Dwayne Johnson in three. They are putting the hard pressure on him since Brisco tweeted, without mentioning his name, saying that he told him he needed to know by Wednesday (4/23) because "the WWE waits for no one. Make the right decision."

PERKINS MILLER
(MAY 5) WWE: Perkins Miller, one of the company's highest ranked executives as Executive Vice President of Digital Media, one of the key people involved in the network launch, has left the company for the NFL, where he will be Chief Digital Officer of NFL Now. NFL Now, an online network that will feature highlights and allow fans to create their own channels based on favorite teams and players, will be launched this summer. Miller came to WWE in August 2012 as one of the key people hired to launch the network and was considered a major hire by the NFL. His leaving was a big surprise since he had just given a presentation to business partners talking about WWE's expansion plans for the network overseas three weeks ago. In 2008, before he was with WWE, Sports Business Journal ranked him as one of the 20 most influential people in digital sports, and he had been head of digital media for NBC for the Olympics and was a Senior Vice President at NBC Sports, where he was part of the team that launched the NBCSports.com site.

BILL GOLDBERG
(MAY 5) WWE: Bill Goldberg definitely has interest in doing WrestleMania 31 if the right deal can be made. That was also the deal last year and no deal was made, because he's not coming cheap. He's kept himself in

shape, training almost daily at his Muay Thai gym, although he'll be 48 by next year's Mania. It's just that there are no great attractions that you can bring back from the past and part of Mania is the superstar from the past that you haven't seen like Rock, Hogan and Warrior, and it's also part of the video game.

(JUNE 2) WWE: Bill Goldberg was on Ring Rust Radio talking about a possible match: "There have been a number of different publications that have run the story that Goldberg's back and he's begging to have another match again and he wants to get back in the ring. At the end of the day, I would definitely listen to that type of conversation but it's not something I wake up every morning and I pray to God to and hope I can lace up my boots one more time because I have to end on a nostalgic note. If the opportunity arose and it was a favorable condition for everybody involved, and I mean working condition, not necessarily the money, and opponent I would definitely cater the thought." He said he trains several days a week at Muay Thai gym so he's ion shape, although that's not pro wrestling shape. Goldberg being in the company's best selling DVD of last year besides Mania would indicate there is interest in him and it's been ten years since his last WWE match. There was bad blood from him regarding both Vince and HHH from his last run, but they've made up with just about everyone else. I just don't know if they feel it's worth huge money for a one shot with Goldberg for Mania because he's not wrestling cheap. Obviously it didn't happen this year. I could certainly see a Hall of Fame (although when they were in Atlanta HHH argued against it on a radio show when it was brought up saying he wasn't in the business long enough) for him, but I don't know if the circumstances will ever be right for both sides for a match.

(JUNE 16) WWE: Goldberg spoke to Jim Ross on Ross' podcast and seemed open to a WWE return, as we've noted before. He said that his son is now 7, and he'd love to have his son see him wrestle. He said they talked but they never get past the prelim stage. Those in WWE noted Goldberg's money price was high, but the fact Goldberg's DVD has outsold every DVD the company has released in the last nine months could be used as evidence there is interest in him. His DVD was ahead of the pace of the Warrior DVD even. Goldberg said he'd be interested in working with Lesnar, who he's friends with, HHH, who he's not, and Reigns, because they went to rival colleges and were both college football stars. He admitted that he never watches wrestling and only hears what people tell him on the Internet. He said when he played for the Falcons, that some of the players would hang around with the WCW wrestlers who were based in Atlanta, but he never wanted to be a wrestler. But he said he liked Sting and saw him as a credible athlete. Goldberg used to say that he had made money in football, and his accountant told him it was time to get a job after football was over. He trained at Sting & Lex Luger's Gym and they had talked with him about wrestling because of his size and look, so he took them up on the offer. Goldberg himself has a podcast but doesn't talk much wrestling and notes that he doesn't watch the shows on TV.

LEYVONNA ZAKARI SWAGGART
(MAY 5) WWE: A new developmental wrestler is Leyvonna Zakari Swaggart, 24, who did a women's tryout camp earlier this year. She started this week. She's from Oakland, but has lived for years in Southern California and worked as an actress on the reality TV show "Pageant vs. Playmate" where teams of pretty girls competed. She was on the Pageant team as she'd done beauty pageants in California when she was younger. She's of Samoan descent and is either friends or a relative with the Usos. She went through the same tryout camp as former TNA wrestler Sarita (Dark Angel in CMLL) went through and to this point wasn't signed from. Sarita has the look and experience, but the age could be a hindrance since she's already 35.

CHRIS JERICHO
(JULY 13) WWE: Jericho talked about his return on his podcast this past week. He said that there was discussion of him coming back to work with Bryan last year at Mania (this would be toward the latter part of 2013) but they didn't go in that direction. This would have been before the Bryan vs. Sheamus plan. He said at the time, he

brought up when the Bryan thing fell through, about working with Wyatt, but he was told at the time (this would have been late 2013) that they were earmarking Wyatt for Cena. He said that about a month ago, someone from creative brought up his working with Wyatt in a program over the summer. He noted that unlike past summers, he hadn't been able to put together an extensive tour for "Fozzy," so he had a few dates booked but that was it. I don't think he said this, but the impression I had was he was up for working with Wyatt but it took several weeks before Vince officially agreed to go in that direction. He said on 6/27, he and Paul Levesque negotiated for all of five minutes before reaching a deal. He was hidden out in a production bus until his segment, with the exception of working with The Wyatts and Miz in setting up the segment. I know that they wanted it to be a big surprise, but it did get out a couple of hours ahead of time. He had his first match back on the 7/6 house show in Toronto against Miz, the night before the Raw match. Jericho didn't say how long he had signed for, but as things stand right now he's staying through the 9/22 Raw in Memphis, which is the day after the Night of Champions PPV, which would be his final major show. He will be working a regular house show schedule through that point, although has some time off for Fozzy commitments. He has several dates with Fozzy during that period, including his record release on 7/24 in Los Angeles at The Whiskey and an 8/2 date in Syracuse, as well as three September dates while he' sunder his new WWE deal. He's got a regular Fozzy touring schedule from 9/23 to 10/11.

WWE Developmental Cuts

(May 12) WWE: There were a number of developmental cuts over the past week just as a number of people were coming in to get started. The five cuts were:1. Martin Harris, who wrestled under the name Danny Burch. He's 32, and was from London, England. He wrestled as Martin Stone in England. He'd been used strictly as enhancement talent on television and didn't have anything special when it came to size or look. His work was fine, but not spectacular and the emphasis in developmental is on youth. He had knee surgery and the feeling we got from someone there is they believe he was given up on at that point; 2. Joel Pettyfer, 27, from Exeter, England. His NXT name was Oliver Grey. He and Adrian Neville were the first NXT tag team champions. He tore his ACL right after he got the titles, and had just come back from reconstructive surgery and had been used since his return as an enhancement guy. You could tell once he came back from knee surgery, which was just recently, that they had long interest in him since he was just getting squashed; 3. Barri Griffiths, 32, from Wales, the huge bodybuilder known as Mason Ryan. This was the biggest surprise. He was on the main roster in 2011 and 2012, as part of C.M. Punk's New Nexus. He was rushed onto the main roster before he was ready because of how big he was, and then sent back to developmental. He'd dropped weight, although still huge, and gotten better, but I was told they felt he wasn't improving at a fast enough rate. His big problem is that his selling looked really bad and he'd been around long enough that he should have gotten past that. Vince loved the way he looked, so brought him up way too fast even though warned it was too soon and they were making the same mistake they've made over and over (we'll call it the Chris Masters mistake). The problem is he couldn't sell in a manner that worked. It was noted that it must have taken a lot to cut someone who looked like that, plus they liked the idea of having a superstar babyface from Wales. It really shows the difference in mentality as a guy who looked like that would have been promoted as a major star in the 80s. I was told he had a great attitude, always worked hard and tried hard to do whatever they asked. He had no ego, as I recall when he first arrived and they rushed the FCW title on him, he questioned it, noting that guys were so much more advanced than he was. The curse of being a huge bodybuilder like he is or Ezekiel Jackson or Bobby Lashley is that when the right people see you, they often rush you onto the main roster when you aren't ready, and then give you the super push. It usually doesn't work out, although in the case of Lashley there were many other issues involved. Then they consider you a guy they tried with but it didn't work. But he was still a very mechanical worker, and he had signed a five-year deal in 2009 and he wasn't anywhere close to being ready for the main roster, and the idea of developmental is not meant as a five-year program for 32-year-old guys. One person noted to me that it's not easy for them to send a guy who looks like that out the door; 4. Shaul Guerrero, 23, who used the name Raquel Diaz. They were high on her a few years back because she was such a good talker. She was not a good worker and was getting hurt often trying to work, as she bumped awkwardly. There was a saying that there's never been a Guerrero that couldn't work, but while that was accurate until she came along, it's no longer accurate. The company made the decision because of all her injuries to take her out of the ring. She still could have had something in a manager role. But she quit the company once and they never put her back on TV when she returned. She got hurt before and then when she got hurt when she came back, the decision was made not to have her in the ring due to the injury risk. However, the departure was a surprise since she had just started shooting promos (which hadn't aired), talking for Baron Corbin. There was also concern that she had too many tattoos added, and concerns about binge dieting. But because she could talk and who her mother is, her cut was a surprise to many; 5. Sarah Backman, 22, a Swedish blond world arm wrestling champion who was given the name Shara. She actually left more than a week ago and it was her own decision. She had been there just over one year and had yet to make it to television.

(SEPTEMBER 29) WWE: There were two developmental releases this past week. One, Kendra Smith, who used the name Kendall Skye, asked for her release. She was an actress from Los Angeles who Dusty Rhodes liked at the start because she did well in promo class and presentation. She took longer inside the ring, partially held back by a couple of injuries. She had been with the company since early 2013, and was wrestling on the house shows, and had been tried out as a ring announcer, but hadn't been used on television. Before coming to WWE, she was a stunt women who had trained as a kickboxer. She was working on the "Mad Max" film when signed by WWE and actually left the film to move to Tampa. In developmental, she had suffered two serious wrist injuries, and had done more ring announcing than wrestling, probably having less than two dozen matches. Her promo work was said to be outstanding from the start. Because of her promo work and kick-boxing skills, the original booking idea was to groom her to be WWE's Ronda Rousey, a role everyone seemed to be high on, but the idea was then dropped. She was also pitched for a female bodyguard role for A.J. Lee when she first got there, but the role was given to Tamina Snuka. The belief is she gave wrestling a try, and felt it was better for her to return to the entertainment industry. The other was Alexander Jones, who wrestled as Troy McClain. He was brought in after Cena recommended him. Jones was also discovered in Southern California, and had trained at Knokx Pro Wrestling, the school run by Rikishi, Gangrel and the Black Pearl. That's also where Rusev came from. The story is that he was attending the University of Southern California studying strength and conditioning, when he was at the USC gym, on a day Cena was in Los Angeles training at the same gym. He was not a wrestling fan growing up, but had become a fan in college and met Rikishi and Gangrel at a Fitness Expo in Los Angeles where they were trying to get new students for their school and he signed up. Cena liked his look, and then after a conversation, found out he was already training to be a wrestler. He got a tryout in the August 2012 camp and his conditioning was top of the class. He got high recommendations from both Gerald Brisco and Jim Ross. He was offered a three-year deal and started in Florida in January, 2013. Ross and Brisco both pushed that he had the potential to be the next guy, essentially the next Cena, that's how high they were on him from his conditioning drills. He was given a Tony Robbins motivational speaker gimmick, which he did a lot of tryout promos for and I believe he did it in front of the crowd at some NXT house shows. But it never went anywhere. He was originally from Amboy, IL, where he was a star high school football player. McClain had done some enhancement work on the NXT television show of late, usually losing in about a minute, as well as house shows. His release was a surprise to some, not that he had shown great potential or progressed at a rapid rate, but because being a Cena guy, many thought would have protected him.

BRIAN MADDOX

(MAY 12) WWE: Brian Maddox (no relation to Brad), who was Vice President of Global Digital Sales, has left the company for a job as Vice President of Advertising Sales for Silver Chalice Ventures, which creates video channels and new digital media for sports products.

HERNANDEZ

(MAY 19) TNA: With less fanfare, the contract of Shawn Hernandez, 41, also expired this past week. Hernandez had been with the company for more than a decade, starting in late 2003. He hadn't been used on TV since December. Last year they were building to a Hernandez vs. Chavo Guerrero Jr. split and feud, but the decision due to cost cutting was made to drop Guerrero Jr. and then they had nothing for Hernandez, who in 2006 with TNA, won Tag Team of the Year honors with Homicide as LAX. Dixie Carter loved Hernandez, and the goal was to make him the Latino superstar the company has been wanting and has tried numerous times to make. In 2010, they even sent him to AAA and paid him, with the idea of being a star in Mexico, and living there would improve his Spanish and his weak promos, so he could be brought back in 2011 with a big push. He was immediately brought back and made an anti-American heel with Anarquia as Mexican America. He was put together with Chavo in 2012 as a babyface team, with the idea Chavo could be the worker and had the Guerrero name. But they never got over since Chavo had been far too badly damaged credibility wise in his WWE run to be taken seriously as a pushed commodity. Hernandez was in the 2013 Bound for Glory series and only got one win, over Jay Bradley, and there really wouldn't have been any value in him going with Chavo since it would have been a prelim feud.

REBEL

(MAY 19) TNA: Some notes on Rebel, the new woman on the roster in the Managerie group. She is Tanea Brooks, 35, an actress and model who was a Dallas Cowboys cheerleader from 1998-2000, and was the cover girl on the Cowboys cheerleaders 2000 calendar. She was with Christy Hemme in an all-girl dance troupe called The Purrfect Angels at one point, so that was her connection that got her involved in wrestling. She also, as shown on TV, is known for doing fire tricks. She's done modeling, acting and dancing professionally. Like Hemme and Summer Rae, she also competed in Lingerie Football, with a team called the New York Euphoria about a decade ago, and was in a Trace Adkins video.

THE VON ERICHS

(JUNE 9) TNA: Ross & Marshall Von Erich, the sons of Kevin Von Erich, will debut with TNA on the 6/15 Slammiversary PPV show. Kevin will be at the show as well, held on Father's Day, which comes from Arlington, TX, near Dallas, where Kevin was a superstar during the early and mid-80s. Dixie grew up in the Dallas area and if you lived in the area in the 80s, even if you weren't a wrestling fan, you knew who the Von Erichs were, and she would have been a teenage girl, one of their strongest demos at the time, when the territory caught fire. They are pushing it as the first televised match of the new Von Erich tag team. Both have wrestled in the past with Pro Wrestling NOAH, mostly in prelims and almost exclusively as a tag team, but haven't wrestled there in a long time and there was a reason. The book on them in Japan is that they weren't bad kids, but they didn't think they had a future in the business. We're told it's just a one shot deal for the Dallas market. For the market, it's a good publicity hook because a lot of the key people in the local media would have grown up on the Von Erich family and Kevin as the last member of that wrestling family returning to Dallas (he's lived in Kauai, an island in Hawaii for years). Kevin hasn't been back in Dallas for years. Ross was a good high school football player and I actually figured he'd end up with at least a WWE developmental deal based on his look, as when Kevin came in for the WWE Hall of Fame, people were remarking at how much Ross looked like Kerry. But he doesn't resemble him much anymore. Due to back injuries from wrestling that flare up on long flights, Kevin has declined most offers to come to the U.S. Kevin was able to live somewhat in paradise in Hawaii because of being the last heir of Fritz Von Erich, who made a lot of money, as well as money he made in other business endeavors, including selling the World Class tape library to WWE. He said that his plan in life was to never leave Hawaii and never wear shoes again, although admits when he comes to the U.S. for this trip he probably will have to.

(JUNE 16) TNA: There was a jump in ticket sales with the publicity in the Dallas market last week that Kevin Von Erich would be appearing at Slammiversary with the area debut of sons Ross & Marshall Von Erich. As noted, we're told it's a one-shot deal for the brothers. It should have jumped ticket sales when you realize how big the Von Erichs were dating back to Fritz as the top star of the 60s and 70s, and then his sons in the 80s. While there is all the tragedy that actually killed Dallas as a big-time wrestling market until the rise of Steve Austin in the late 90s and the wrestling boom, nostalgia usually forgets the bad and remembers the good. It's been years since Kevin, the last remaining Von Erich, was at a show (he did a Raw many years ago in Dallas) in the area. The debut of his sons is a legit news story in the market. I hope they do well. They didn't knock them dead in NOAH where they were brought in as rookies to be trained but didn't last. I'll bet that the teams on the roster are hoping it's not them as the ones who have to carry them and put them over.

On TV at this point, there was no mention of the Von Erichs at all. Kevin Von Erich did cut some promos, which I believe were to be for local advertising in the Dallas market. I haven't heard from anyone who has seen them as of yet, although a number of people in the Dallas area noted that they were advertising around Kevin Von Erich being there.

(JUNE 23) TNA: With falling ratings, bad ratings patterns, losses of talent and depressing house show business, things had not been looking up for TNA this year. It's a shame that when the company put its best foot forward, so few saw it. Slammiversary on 6/15 was not promoted well on television, and going head-to-head with what ended up being the deciding game of the NBA Playoffs did them no favors. The TV was built around Eric Young vs. MVP for the TNA title, and that match fell apart due to MVP's knee injury. A telling sign about TNA is that it probably didn't matter anyway because the audience they have left is at this point the group they haven't yet driven away. The issues with TNA have never been about talent. They went into the Dallas market, got a lot of late media hype built around the local storyline of Kevin Von Erich returning on Father's Day for his sons U.S. television debut. It resulted in a healthy and enthusiastic crowd of 3,500 fans, which was not a papered crowd, at the College Park Center at the University of Texas-Arlington campus. By today's standards, seeing TNA with a crowd like that looked great, but you only have to go back two years ago, when they ran the same building for Slammiversary and did 5,000 fans at a time they had far more star power. TNA's production crew once again deserves credit because they made the crowd appear on television to be twice as large as it really was. There was a real change in morale coming off the house shows with so few fans to seeing a nice sized and super lively crowd. The show featured a moment, in some ways sad, in others nostalgic, that has nothing to do with TNA and clearly had a lot to do with the atmosphere and crowd size. The biggest long-term star in the history of pro wrestling in Dallas was Fritz Von Erich. Originally a heel, when he gained control of the promotion and the territory in the mid-60s, the former Nazi heel became the All-American local badass from nearby Lake Dallas. The biggest and baddest heels came to town, and Fritz knocked them off. More than any other promoter, he was able to groom his sons for superstardom. After Fritz retired as a regular wrestler in 1982, the television shows built around David, Kevin and Kerry Von Erich did gigantic television ratings. As far as local fame went, very few wrestlers in any part of the country had the name recognition and star power of the Von Erichs. But unlike Fritz, who ruled the roost for decades, his sons candles burned out long before their legends ever did. David was only 25 when he died. A younger brother, Mike, was brought in as a replacement. He had health issues, was not the athlete or wrestler that his brothers were, and was filled with inner turmoil and committed suicide. Several years later, Kerry, was for a brief period of time was one of the biggest stars and drawing cards in wrestling, but whose career had gone downhill due to major drug problems, followed suit. Yet another brother, Chris, who tried wrestling but was too small and physically fragile, also committed suicide. There was yet another brother, Jackie, the oldest, who died as a young child when he was electrocuted. In all, Kevin Von Erich would note that at one time he had five brothers, but by the time he was in his mid-30s, he had none. Fritz Von Erich passed away from cancer in 1997 at the age of 68. The problems with the Von Erichs, revelations about the drug use, and a number of other factors killed wrestling to the mainstream by the late 80s, and Dallas never really recovered as a wrestling market until the Monday Night Wars and the rise of Steve Austin in 1998. Kevin moved years ago to Hawaii, but his sons, Ross & Marshall, wanted to become pro wrestlers and were sent to train with Harley Race. Later, because of their name, and the fact Fritz was a gigantic star in Japan during the 60s (a 1966 match with Giant Baba vs. Fritz Von Erich was the first Budokan Hall sellout) for his iron claw finisher. Kevin was a spectacular performer when it came to flying, based on the standards of his time. Wrestlers hated to work with him because he was so stiff, as Taz even noted in code with the line "cemento," when discussing a match he had with Kevin early in his career. He had a lot of injuries, masked them with a lot of pain killers, and you could really see his heart in the ring start to falter even as early as 1984 when David died. It was Bob Ryder of TNA who was given credit for the idea of bringing in Ross & Marshall Von Erich, with Kevin, to the show. Now 57, Kevin is so racked with injuries that he rarely travels from Hawaii because the plane flights kill his back. It's been years since he's been in Dallas, although he did appear at a Raw in Dallas to a big reaction many years back. As a celebrity that anyone who lived in the area would know instantly, he opened a lot of media doors. Stating that his goal in life is not to wear shoes, Kevin, who wrestled bare foot during his career, perhaps from watching Jimmy Snuka in the area, was wearing flip flops while introduced and I believe took them off when he did his run-in. Even with a tremendous opener, and generally good work, the emotional moment of the show came when his sons were being beaten down after a DQ against foes Jessie Godderz & DJ Zema Ion (who deserve credit for carrying them to at least a decent short match) and Kevin hit the ring and cleaned house, and put Ion in the claw that his father made famous. Why they did a DQ finish instead of having the Von Erichs win was a head scratcher. I mean, I get the surface logic, they are newcomers against our regulars, but it's the Bro Mans "B" team who lose all the time anyway so you can't put over the Von Erichs in Dallas when the crowd came to see them? It was both nostalgic and sad at the same time, because it represented a finale. The reality is there is nowhere for Ross & Marshall to work in Dallas and gain the experience to carry on the name even though the local crowd really wanted to like them. The territorial era of wrestling ended a long time ago and very few wrestlers in any territory had the connection to the public and mainstream recognition that the Von Erichs had in the 80s, and those who did like Ric Flair or Jerry Lawler have never gone away to where a return to the market would be such a big deal. I'm not sure a moment like Kevin putting the claw, the family trademark move, on DJ Zema Ion to a national television audience can be replicated again. "That show was beautiful to me," said Kevin Von Erich on Facebook. "The response from the fans, awesome, and this first step by my sons is to be the fist step into a great new chapter in our lives. They didn't step away, they stepped up, and can only go onward and upward from here. For sure I just had the best Father's Day a man could ask for." What surprised me was how small Ross was. While not nearly as muscular, he was very short, and reminded me somewhat of Anthony Nese as far as being a good athlete. He didn't stand out at all past being crisp in basic moves, very green and having nice dropkick. Marshall is bigger. I thought he'd be David Von Erich's size but was nowhere close. He had some fire, and wrestled barefoot like Kevin. Past the one time nostalgia deal here, the family connection no longer means anything because the Von Erichs have been gone for 25 years and TNA isn't the place for guys to learn. I didn't feel either had the potential of even a Garett Bischoff, who started here green and was protected because of his father being a major force in creative. Bischoff had a look and swagger about him, but needed lots of ring time, and the current business on television isn't the place for that as fans typecast you based on early impressions.

JEFF COBB

(JUNE 2) WWE: Jeff Cobb, a former Olympic wrestler from Guam who is a super athlete who moved to Sacramento to train under Oliver John and is a Northern California regular, apparently got word that his age (31) may be an issue as they want guys starting out to be younger. Cobb physically reminds me of Brad Rheingans, an 80s wrestler who worked AWA and New Japan but would never make it today because he was incredibly bland. Cobb isn't that, but he's short and has freaky power like a Cesaro type, with great lower back strength that allows him to do some amazing moves with big guys and he can fly as well. I thought his height would be an issue more than age because he looks younger than he is.

(AUGUST 25) WWE: Jeff Cobb, who wrestled in the 2004 Olympics representing Guam, and is the best athlete of the Northern California independent wrestlers, has a WWE tryout scheduled at the next camp over the first week of September. From what people who know him say, he'll kill it at the athletic agility and conditioning drills and he can work. His negative is that he's probably 5-foot-9 and is past 30.

TNA INCOMINGS

(JULY 6) TNA: Lots of newcomers were brought back at TV this week. Besides the previously announced Tommy Dreamer, Matt Hardy, Low Ki, Homicide, Great Muta, Brian Cage and Rhino, they also used Gene Snisky (Snitsky), Rycklon Stephens (Ezekiel Jackson, but I doubt they can use that name so not sure what name they are going to use for him), King Mo, Al Snow with Head and Devon. The first taping built up a new Dixie Carter-led heel faction of Ethan Carter III, Rockstar Spud, Mo, Snisky and Stephens. I'm surprised to see Mo back since he's still active in Bellator and everyone but Mo tells me that you can't do both pro wrestling and MMA at the same time given the demands both require these days. But Mo was more of a bodyguard and didn't work any matches, and the issue with pro wrestling was more the nightly pounding. I know that the ECW reunions are good for an easy pop, and this worked live. They really loaded up on the show and to try and make this a hot product for the New York market and even with the weak attendance the first night, they did sell out the second and third nights and the TV was far better than what they've been doing. Stephens isn't that old but he's still got the WWE washout feel, but if they have an idea for him, that's one thing. But Snisky is 44 years old, hasn't worked much in years, and was never good when he did work. It did appear they were only in for two days because they were fired in storyline by Dixie Carter after the second night of tapings and didn't work the third night, and are not figured into anything going forward. Dreamer also isn't scheduled as talent for the next tapings but he will be back behind the scenes. Homicide, Devon and Low Ki are scheduled to be back for the next tapings.

JOSH MATTHEWS

(JULY 6) WWE: Josh Matthews (Josh Lomberger, 33), was released this past week after nearly 12 years as an announcer. As Josh Lomberger, he was discovered in the first season of Tough Enough in 2001. Lomberger, Chris Nowinski and Maven Huffman were the three men's finalists, with Huffman getting the nod. Lomberger was hired by Kevin Dunn to be a backstage interviewer, and moved to commentary in 2006 on a number of different shows including Raw, Smackdown, Heat, FCW, Main Event, Saturday Morning Slam, Superstars and ECW. In 2011, Matthews, Michael Cole and Booker T were the regular commentary trio on Smackdown and did some Raw announcing when Jerry Lawler was wrestling. Of late, he's been hosting the pre-and-post game shows before Raw, Smackdown and the PPVs. He had already filmed the pre-game show on cable for the Money in the Bank PPV, which tells you how little time in advance it was known that he would be let go before the decision was made. Lomberger was at the TNA tapings in New York right after he was let go and he does have a connection to John Gaburick, given Gaburick was one of the main people behind Tough Enough, and it wouldn't shock me that Gaburick may have even played a hand in Kevin Dunn pushing for Lomberger as an announcer. He was believed to be the latest victim of budget cutting. At about the same time, the shows Lomberger hosted were changed in a budget cutting measure. The pre-and-post-game shows before and after Raw were changed from being done at the arena to a studio setting. The shows before and after Smackdown were canceled. They also didn't have a post-show or press conference for Money in the Bank, as they went from the end of the PPV, and started airing a replay of the PPV at 11 p.m. Renee Young is now hosting the shows they are still doing.

(AUGUST 25) TNA: Josh Lomberger, better known as Josh Matthews, who was introduced around right after being let go from WWE at a taping, has his non-compete with WWE expire around 9/20. It wouldn't surprise me to see him in as an announcer, since John Gaburick has known of him since the original season of Tough Enough, but he could not use the Josh Matthews name.

(SEPTEMBER 29) TNA: TNA this past week put on its web site a story that Josh Matthews was at the company headquarters in Nashville. Then they took it down. The belief has been that Matthews was going to start as an announcer for the group if and when they start on a new station next year, or perhaps even be introduced earlier in a backstage segment on Spike. His non-compete is over. It's been expected he was coming in since he was introduced around at the TVs months back, right after WWE let him go. He and John Gaburick have a connection since Gaburick was a key player on Tough Enough season one, where Josh Lomberger (real name) was a cast member, and Kevin Dunn (Gaburick's main ally in WWE) hired him to be an announcer when they decision was made not to hire him as a wrestler.

MARK KOWAL

(JULY 6) WWE: Mark Kowal, the Senior Vice President and Corporate Controller was appointed the company's Principal Accounting Officer. Kowal, 38, has been with the company since 2001. He was named Vice President and Corporate Controller in 2004, and made a Senior Vice President in February.

LAUREEN ONG

(JULY 13) WWE: Laureen Ong, the former President of the Travel Channel, was elected to WWE's Board of Directors. She had spent three years with the channel, with her responsibilities being brand building strategy, program development and creating new business opportunities. She also was the former COO of the Hong Kong based STAR Group Limited, a TV channel which goes into 55 countries. She was also the first President of the National Geographic Channel when it launched and was once awarded the Woman of the Year award in Women in Cable Television. She has a long history in TV, as she was Vice President of Programming for the Chicago White Sox cable channel, Sportsvision, from 1979 to 1986.

RASHAD EVANS

(JULY 13) WWE: Add Rashad Evans to the list of UFC fighters who have recently inquired regarding going to WWE. Evans, who is almost 35, is recovering from major knee surgery and had talked about considering retirement even before that. Fighters who get to that point recognize that they need to plan for after fighting and WWE seems like a transition, but thus far we've never had anyone be successful at it in the U.S. except those who were pro wrestlers first (Lesnar and Ken Shamrock). We'd heard his name bandied about in the company of UFC guys thinking about WWE as a future destination for years. I don't know that he's directly spoken to WWE, but he was talking to people in the pro wrestling business this weekend about the idea. In recent years, people associated with Chael Sonnen, Shayna Baszler, Roy Nelson and Frank Mir have also tried to open up talks or we've heard very vague ideas suggested for Baszler at one point. In the case of Nelson and Mir, neither seemed to get anywhere. WWE and Vince McMahon in particular, are leery about using former MMA fighters, particularly big stars, since they are used to huge payoffs and he doesn't think they'd survive the schedule. Some of this comes from McMahon's failed negotiations with Bob Sapp, who he wanted badly, but the negotiations never got past a certain point due to money and schedule. Plus, McMahon knows virtually nothing about the modern UFC scene. With Evans, like Sonnen, age is also an issue. Sonnen's name is the only one with some smoke, in the sense there are people who throw ideas regarding him out there although the impression we've got is any interest would more be as an announcer, and that would likely not happen now because of the controversy associated with his name. WWE doesn't like the idea of signing novices who are in their mid-30s from other sports with the idea they come in with their bodies beaten up, and by the time they are trained, they may not have much time left.

JIM ROSS

(JULY 28) WWE: Jim Ross' severance package with WWE expires this week. He was let go on 9/11, so it was roughly a ten plus month non-compete package. He would now be free to do pro wrestling on TV or PPV which he would not have been able to do previously, or, in theory, work for a promotion. As noted before, the best fit, because I just don't see him in ROH as a possibility, and he's expressed negativity on TNA (but you never say never but I don't think he'd want that) would be New Japan. The problem is the cost-effective question because there are so few English language viewers, plus Ross would like to do the events live, and the cost of flying to Japan every month is significant. But after watching G-1, the style aspect is something he's tailor made for, and his familiarity with the audience and ability to promote removes a significant barrier to entry for a lot of English language fans. The package did allow him to do non-pro wrestling events on television, like the boxing show he did over Memorial Day weekend, and MMA events that he's in talks about doing.

BARRY MCMULLIN

(AUGUST 4) WWE: Barry McMullin was hired this past week as Senior Vice President of Sales & Partnership Marketing, to work underneath Michelle Wilson. His past includes working for the PBR, NBA and the Salt Lake City organizing committee for the 2002 winter Olympics. He held a similar role with the PBR and secured deals with Pabst Blue Ribbon beer, Monster Energy drink, Dr. Pepper and Tyson Foods.

WWE CUTS

(AUGUST 11) WWE: Jesus Rodriguez (Ricardo Rodriguez), Jody Kristofferson (Garrett Dylan), Sam Udell (Travis Tyler), Danielle Jackson (Dani Jax), Shaun Ricker (Slate Randall) and Will McNamee (Mac Miles) were all let go this past week. Most were the victim of budget cuts when the company is trying to get leaner. Rodriguez, 28, was the only main roster player. Those close to him say he was frustrated and that he wanted to be a wrestler and it wasn't happening and asked to be released. He shined in his role as the ring announcer for Del Rio, winning Best Non Wrestler in the 2011 Observer awards. He was actually the second choice for the role but the original person, also a wrestler, turned the spot down saying they had no interest in being a ring announcer. They did tryouts with Los Angeles based wrestlers who spoke Spanish, and Rodriguez was the best and was hired. The guy who turned it down in hindsight feels he made a terrible decision since WWE has never used him as an extra or given him a tryout since he turned down the role. Rodriguez started on the indies in Southern California in 2005, and was signed for the role in the summer of 2010. He and Del Rio spent three years together as heels and later a face run. But when Del Rio turned heel last summer, the decision was made that people like Rodriguez too much and it would hurt him as a heel, so they split them. That was the kiss of death for Rodriguez. They used him as a face feuding with Del Rio, as a second for Van Dam, but very much like Colter right now, the face position for a manager has a short life expectancy. In Rodriguez's case it was shorter than most as he and Van Dam had no chemistry. He was in developmental as El Local, working as a tag team with Kalisto, but was injured, and Sin Cara was given his spot to eventually do a Luchador tag team with Kalisto, but with Sin Cara having been buried for so long, that pretty much limits the upside of the team. There were also issues in that because of his physique not being up to their standard, even when his body was completely covered in his ring costume, they set a weight goal that they wanted him at and in the mind of the company, he was having trouble keeping to it. Rodriguez had both a talent contract and an announcers contract. He was cut this past week even though his two-year talent contract only had two more weeks on it. He was also doing the Spanish language announcing, but with budget cuts, a three man Spanish broadcast crew was one too many. Kristofferson, 29, was brought back earlier this year after being cut last summer, which was a personal issues deal with HHH promising him when he took care of things, he would be brought back, and kept that promise. He had been Captain Comic under a mask, often as one of the Rose Buds, as well as Garrett Dylan, with about two years in developmental. He's the son of famous actor and singer Kris Kristofferson, who has come to many of his matches both in California and Florida, but he never wanted to trade in on his father's name, although it did help him get signed. Udell was a high school and college wrestler from Colorado who had advanced only to the enhancement talent level in NXT. Jackson was an actress who had not made it to NXT television. Ricker, 31, was an 11-year pro trained by Les Thatcher who had been with Championship Wrestling from Hollywood and other Southwest indies. He was a participant on "The Hero," a TBS reality show that Dwayne Johnson hosted, and got a deal after that. One person said he had, by far, the most potential of those cut, but unlike the others which were the numbers game and being not what they wanted or not progressing, Ricker was a different issue.

One person said he had the charisma they wanted but there was an issue regarding sending an e-mail that got him buried. Another person noted that his Twitter account was not what the company wanted. McNamee had just started on shows in an enhancement role.

RICKY STEAMBOAT

(AUGUST 11) WWE: An update on Ricky Steamboat. Steamboat is no longer working full-time here. He wasn't cut, in the sense he still as a legends contract (those are usually $10,000 per year), but his regular job as a brand ambassador was eliminated. I'm somewhat surprised about this one just because Steamboat had all those health problems related to injuries in the Nexus angle years back, to the point it was life-or-death for a few days and I don't know if he ever fully recovered. I know as of a year later he was still having fairly serious problems stemming from bleeding on the brain.

RAFAEL MORFI

(AUGUST 18) TNA: Rafael Morfi, the Senior Director of Live Events, has given notice and will be leaving for a job with the New York Cosmos soccer team. That's a major departure. He came from WWE and had a great reputation there (he lost his position when HHH & Stephanie wanted to put their own people in those positions). Jayme Sharp, the Production Chief Engineer, is also leaving.

MARK YEATON

(AUGUST 18) WWE: One of the biggest surprise releases in years in WWE was Mark Yeaton, the perennial timekeeper, who was let go this past week. While this wasn't a big news story to the public, internally I heard far more comments about Yeaton being released than Del Rio, and for those who had been around for a long time, they were absolutely shocked when this came out. Yeaton, had a number of other functions including show producer and ringside director. He had been with the company since 1984 as the timekeeper who sat to the left of the announcers table on all television shows, as well as working with production. From anyone's accounts, he had never been any kind of a problem and was always considered a model employee who never missed work. He was best known for getting superkicked by Shawn Michaels in his 1996 WrestleMania main event with Bret Hart, and by some as the guy off camera who would throw all the cans of beer at Steve Austin that he'd catch and drink at the end of his promos. He must have been pretty great with the aim, because if the guy couldn't throw accurately, it could have made Austin look real bad, and he never did.

WWE CREATIVE TEAM

(AUGUST 18) WWE: Besides Eddie Feldman, the Senior Vice President of Creative being released, they also cut several other members of creative. From those who knew the situation, the creative staff had become bloated, with more than two dozen members. Feldman reported directly to Paul Levesque in creative, which is the position they run through like crazy, as it seems everyone put in that position lasts less than one year. Among the others let go were Paul Napoli and Kevin Eck. Eck was a reporter with the Baltimore Sun for years, including doing their pro wrestling column.

ODB

(SEPTEMBER 1) TNA: The latest contract to expire and not be renewed was ODB (Jessica Kresa, 36), who was the storyline wife of Eric Young. ODB, in a trivia note, tried out for the first season of Tough Enough (the one won by Maven Huffman and Nidia Guenard), but was cut, and then started training for pro wrestling. She appeared as ODB in some early TNA matches dating back to 2003. She was in WWE developmental in 2006 and 2007 and showed more personality than any of the women, but that was during the period where the WWE was "looking for 10s," so one woman after another far less over than her was getting shots and she couldn't even get a developmental deal. She was contacted by TNA just for a Battle Royal when they debuted the Knockouts division in 2007, but was impressive enough that she got a contract and was a regular through

2010. She was brought back in 2011, and eventually did the Young storyline. The TV wedding was April 12, 2012. She sometimes wrestled, sometimes just was around backstage and sometimes refereed. She hadn't done much on TV all year, and her last appearance was doing a match on Xplosion in April. During her tenure with the company she held the Knockouts title four times and was named TNA Knockout of the Year in 2009.

TNA OFFICE

(SEPTEMBER 1) TNA: Several office people were also let go this week due to budgetary reasons. The office was said to be a skeleton crew to begin with. Most were office people whose names people wouldn't know. Jimmy Jay, the protégé of Don West, heading the arena merchandise sales, was among the casualties. The other merchandise guy, Dewey Barnes (who also worked for a period of time as enhancement talent on television when Ethan Carter III was debuting), was also let go. With Rafael Morfi, the guy who was in charge of promoting house shows, leaving for the New York Cosmos, and no house shows on the schedule left (the remaining shows all became PPV tapings), one gets the feeling they are cutting back on house shows going forward.

ALAN REBHUN

(SEPTEMBER 8) WWE: Regarding Alan Rebhun, the Vice President of Venue Merchandising and Operations, who was let go, we have some more notes on WrestleMania weekend, including information that was inaccurate last week. The vending company he had hired at WrestleMania did not go bankrupt and while there was shortage of money, others contradict the claim it was huge, citing these figures and that because of it, last week's item was incorrect in that sense. Merchandise sales at WrestleMania 30 surpassed budget projections by $300,000 and was the second highest in the history of the company, being $100,000 less than WrestleMania 29 (the difference being WrestleMania 29 drew a larger attendance because it was a bigger stadium). The company that was contracted to handle concessions has licenses for a number of NBA, NFL, MLB and NHL teams. Rebhun brought a team of WWE employees to observe their working at the NBA All-Star game at the Superdome, the same facility. Their bid to handle the concessions was approved and signed by people above Rebhun. The shortage of money referred to last week was due to a theft at the superstore, which grossed $1.4 million in merchandise sales over four days. Also, a WWE staff accountant signed for a certain amount of cash, and then claimed he was $5,000 short when preparing the deposit. The contract with the concession company had a one percent shrinkage clause and the shorting was less than one percent (which would have been about $14,000). According to one person close to the situation, the WWE road staff was upset they weren't given the deal to run the concessions at the Superdome after issues at WrestleMania 28 in Miami where merchandise sales were split between two separate companies and neither would share inventory nor resources which resulted in poor performances. There were also negative reports from execs at Sun Life Stadium regarding the issues at that event. The Superdome also posed a lot of logistical challenges. There were issues with the local work force. Rebhun was not involved in the selection of people working the building but merchandise sales in the building was more than $800,000. There were also obstacles because you couldn't even walk through the hallways easily before and after the show due to overcrowding in the narrow hallways. Rebhun was told he was let go as a financial decision, not anything to do with any misconduct.

VERONICA LANE

(SEPTEMBER 8) WWE: Erika Hammond, 23, who was using the name Veronica Lane in developmental, has left the company. She was a model who placed second in the 2010 Miss Teen Texas contest and was one of the models signed off a camp for models in Los Angeles which included Catherine Jo Perry (Lana).

TIM WIESE

(SEPTEMBER 22) WWE: Tim Wiese, 32, a former German Bundesliga (first division essentially) soccer goalkeeper who played a few games with the national team, claims he has gotten an offer from WWE. He's a big enough star that this has gotten a ton of mainstream publicity in Europe over the past few days. He was let go by his last team, TSG Hoffenheim, in January. His contract was through the summer of 2016 at $1.3 million per year. Since January, he has almost completely changed his physique to where he's almost got a Batista "Drax the Destroyer" type body, which he attributes to getting heavily into bodybuilding because he wasn't playing soccer anymore. Almost every media outlet in Germany has covered the story and it's broken into several other countries as well. His quotes are that he "was willing to listen and not refuse it on principle." From sources close to the situation, the WWE did have people internationally who knew of him since he was a pretty outgoing personality who is known in Germany, and may have been his new physique, and contacted his agent, but this was a ways back. At that time they talked that if he was interested, they would give him a tryout, but no contract offer was made, and nothing was heard back. The belief is that it was a dead issue and it was described as if nobody from the WWE side expected any of the pub and there are no talks now, not that there couldn't be talks at some point in the future. Some stories also brought up that Stuart Tomlinson, a U.K. goalkeeper who was a far lesser known player, has been in WWE developmental for the past ten months. The positive for WWE is that he's got genuine name value in Germany, and he'd give WWE a level of press, particularly when they run the market, that they couldn't get otherwise. There's always the question of someone who gets a physique overhaul in just a few months and then goes into WWE, plus a genuine star athlete, used to making a certain level of money and being pampered, then starting from scratch in developmental. Some people who get what it is may make it, but others may find it far more physically grueling and frustrating. Plus, the age is a factor since he'll turn 33 in December. Those at WWE haven't commented officially on the story at press time. He said, "I have an official inquiry from the WWE. It's about working for them as a wrestler. I will listen. I don't shit my pants. Why should I immediately say `No?' Wrestling is very popular, especially in the States. I will go through the inquiry with my agent next week." Wiese played six games for the German national team and was on the 2010 World Cup team. Since retiring from soccer, he's concentrated on "bodybuilding" and is now 255 pounds.

(NOVEMBER 17) WWE: It's being reported in Germany that Tim Wiese, 32, a former a star soccer goalkeeper in Germany, would be appearing at the 11/15 show in Frankfurt, but he would not wrestle and his role in the show is unknown. Wiese, after leaving soccer, shocked fans when he showed photos of himself with a Ryback physique and said in September that he had a WWE offer. At the time, those in WWE said that months earlier, his agent and a brief conversation with them, but nothing further had transpired. Wiese played six games for the national team between 2008 and 2012 and was listed as the No. 3 goalkeeper for the national team for the 2010 World Cup.

MAHABALI SHERA

(SEPTEMBER 29) TNA: TNA announced the signing of 24-year-old Mahabali Shera from India, a business decision for the Indian market. Shera wrestled with the Ring Ka King promotion a few years back. He'll be used as the local star to promote the television by partner Sony Six in the market. TNA is a big part of the station, which airs two hours of wrestling Monday, Tuesday and Wednesday nights. Impact airs Monday, TNA's Greatest Matches airs Tuesday, and Xplosion and another hour of TNA's Greatest Matches airs on Wednesday.

ARDA OCAL

(OCTOBER 6) WWE: Arda Ocal, who covered pro wrestling for The Score and also for the Baltimore Sun web site, has been hired to work as a TV announcer and given the name Kyle Edwards. Ocal has been a major fan for years and also has announced MMA as well as pro wrestling.

KENNY OMEGA

(OCTOBER 13) NJPW: New Japan held a press conference on 10/3 and announced that Kenny Omega would be signing a contract and start here on 11/1 after his DDT contract expires at the end of this month. They also announced Kota Ibushi had signed a new one-year dual contract, in the sense he's under contract to DDT as a regular and to New Japan for the major shows. Omega's final DDT show will be 10/26 at Korakuen Hall, teaming with Ibushi against Danshoku Dino & Konosuke Takeshita (who they are grooming to be their next top guy).

EUGENE

(OCTOBER 13) WWE: WWE released both Nick Dinsmore and Matt Martlaro on 10/1. Dinsmore, 38, had been a coach for the past year. Martlaro had been a liaison with HHH's office and NXT and for developmental in general for a few years. Dinsmore was very popular with most people. There were a lot of people who were not unhappy he was let go, but people were shocked it happened. Dinsmore is now taking bookings for indie dates.

JUSTIN ROBERTS

(OCTOBER 20) WWE: A surprising cost cutting release was ring announcer Justin Roberts, 34. Roberts had been a ring announcer with the company, both for television and full-time on the road, since 2002. It was portrayed as simply a money issue. His contract expired and the two sides could not come to an agreement on a new deal. Those close to him have said he said it was strictly a business thing on both sides, but he later noted that it was a company decision and they told him they had decided to go in another direction. He was the Smackdown ring announcer much of the time between 2002 and 2009, and has been the ring announcer for Raw since the September 28, 2009, episode, where he took over for Lilian Garcia. The announcement of his departure came hours after the completion of the 10/13 Raw show where he was still on the job. The release was a surprise to almost everyone. He had been a fan since high school, and had always called ring announcing for wrestling his dream job. Originally from Chicago, he started ring announcing for the Pro Wrestling International promotion at the age of 16. He went to college in Arizona and continued to ring announce for the IZW promotion, as well as the Dale Gagne version of the AWA, before being hired by WWE out of college. His contract expired this week. No word on the replacement, although Lilian Garcia and Eden Stiles have both been ring announcing on the other shows and Tony Chimel, a longtime ring announcer, is also with the company. New hiree Arda Ocal, using the name Kyle Edwards, has experience ring announcing wrestling and MMA.

(OCTOBER 27) WWE: Not much more this past week on the story of Justin Roberts being let go. As noted last week, he's publicly told people he knows that they simply couldn't come to a financial agreement. One person close to the situation said that he had said he was willing to continue working based on his old deal while they worked on reaching a new deal, but the company opted not to do that. Lilian Garcia was back this week as the ring announcer on Raw, which is to be a permanent move, and Eden Stiles (Brandi Reed Runnels, the wife of Stardust Cody Runnels) has taken over as the ring announcer on Smackdown.

WILLIE MACK

(OCTOBER 20) WWE: Also let go this past week was William McClinton Jr., 27, better known as Willie Mack. He had agreed to a developmental deal. He was an agile fat guy at about 280 pounds. There was an issue that came up in his medical or physical testing that has not come out. He'd been on hold of late. He and Kevin Steen were both told at the same time that they were being brought in and there were delays in his start date. However, he was scheduled to arrive in Orlando on 11/1, but whatever came out that had delayed everything ended up leading to WWE making the decision not to use him. Konnan had tried to recruit him for Lucha Underground right at the time he agreed to the WWE deal, so it wouldn't surprise me to see him end up there.

LOU SCHWARTZ

(OCTOBER 20) WWE: Lou Schwartz was announced as the new Chief Digital Officer, taking the position formerly held by Perkins Miller, who left WWE for the NFL in April. Schwartz's job is to focus on expanding the company's digital and social media presence and manage the WWE Network, the WWE YouTube channel, WWE.com and the app. He will report directly to Vince McMahon.

THE GREAT KHALI

(NOVEMBER 24) WWE: Great Khali (Dalip Singh Rana, 42), is no longer with the company. His contract expired this past week and the decision was made not to renew him. Khali was trained in Hayward, CA in 2000 at the late Roland Alexander's All Pro Wrestling School. During training, he accidentally killed trainee Brian Ong in 2001. Ong had suffered a concussion but continued training and took some bumps from Khali and died. A lawsuit led to a $1.3 million judgment against All Pro Wrestling. He was signed in August, 2001, by New Japan Pro Wrestling, where he often teamed with Giant Silva. He didn't get over, and after splitting the team, he lost a singles match in August 2002 to Silva and his contract wasn't renewed. WWE signed him in 2006 and put him over huge, including having him pretty cleanly beat Undertaker in his first major PPV match. Undertaker beat him later and he also worked a WWE title program with Cena where he was pinned for the first time in 2007. Khali moved to Smackdown and won the world title in a Battle Royal that July. He held it for a few months before losing to Batista in a three-way that also involved Mysterio. He came and went, had numerous injuries and problems with his legs over the next seven years. He also had surgery in 2012 to remove the tumor on his pituitary gland that caused his acromegaly that led to his huge size and features. Realistically, they did about as much as they could with him. I never expected he'd be able to last seven years.

STUART TOMLINSON

(NOVEMBER 24) WWE: Hugo Knox, who just started doing matches on the road this weekend, is former U.K. soccer goalkeeper Stuart Tomlinson, who signed with the company in December. Tomlinson, 29, played 2003 to 2009 with Crewe Alexandra, and also played for Barrow, Port Vale and Burton Albion. He retired after the 2013 season due to injuries. Muscular for a soccer player, his nickname in that sport was "The Tank." He's also been a model and was on the cover of the U.K. version of Men's Health, so he's got the physique.

MIKE TENAY

(DECEMBER 15) TNA: Mike Tenay has agreed to his new deal where he will remain a television personality but no longer be the lead broadcaster on the show. Jim Ross called John Gaburick and I believe Dixie Carter up this past week pitching the idea of letting Tenay do the Tokyo Dome show with him. He pitched the idea that they would plug TNA during the broadcast in exchange. It was turned down. Tenay has agreed to terms on a one-year deal, which seems to tell me that Jeff Jarrett isn't close to a television deal, since if he was, he'd have made a play for Tenay as his lead announcer.

CHAPTER FIFTY FIVE

2014 BUSINESS YEAR IN REVIEW

BIGGEST EVENTS AND TOP DRAWS
Period covered based on our awards balloting year of December 1, 2013 to November 30, 2014

LARGEST ATTENDANCE
- 65,000* - 4/6 WWE WrestleMania New Orleans Mercedes Benz Superdome (Daniel Bryan vs. Randy Orton vs. Batista)
- 35,000 - 1/4 New Japan Wrestle Kingdom Tokyo Dome (Shinsuke Nakamura vs. Hiroshi Tanahashi)
- 21,000* - 8/24 AAA TripleMania Mexico City Arena Ciudad (Perro Aguayo Jr. vs. Dr. Wagner Jr. vs. Cibernetico vs. Myzteziz)
- 21,000* - 11/15 UFC 180 Mexico City Arena Ciudad (Fabricio Werdum vs. Mark Hunt)
- 19,234* - 3/15 UFC 171 Dallas American Airlines Center (Johny Hendricks vs. Robbie Lawler) All-time U.S. MMA at-tendance record
- 18,000 - 8/10 New Japan G-1 Finals Tokorazawa Seibu Dome (Shinsuke Nakamura vs. Kazuchika Okada)
- 17,000* - 9/19 CMLL 81st anniversary show (Atlantis vs. Ultimo Guerrero mask vs. mask) All-time CMLL gate record
- 17,000* - 4/19 UFC on Fox 11 Orlando Amway Center (Fabricio Werdum vs. Travis Browne)
- 17,000* - 5/2 ONE FC Manila, Philippines Bibiano Fernandes vs. Masakatsu Ueda
- 16,127* - 3/22 NCAA Division I tournament finals Oklahoma City Chesapeake Energy Center
- 15,996* - 12/8/13 NCAA wrestling State College, PA Bryce Jordan Center Penn State vs. Pitt All-time U.S. college dual meet record
- 15,500* - 8/31 IGF Peace Festival Pyongyang, North Korea Arena (Kazuyuki Fujita vs. Jerome LeBanner)
- 15,175 - 3/21 NCAA Division I tournament semifinals Oklahoma City Chesapeake Energy Arena
- 15,000* - 5/19 WWE Raw London O2 Arena John Cena vs. Luke Harper
- 15,000 - 8/8 WWE Sydney Allphones Arena - Roman Reigns vs. Kane Ric Flair referee
- 15,000* - 8/30 IGF Peace Festival Pyongyang, North Korea Arena (Kazuyuki Fujita vs. Erik Hammer)

*Denotes sellout crowd

MOST MAIN EVENTS DRAWING MORE THAN 10,000 FANS

- 32 - John Cena
- 17 - Randy Orton
- 11 - Seth Rollins
- 10 - Bray Wyatt, Kane
- 7 - Daniel Bryan, Batista, Luke Harper, Roman Reigns
- 5 - Dean Ambrose
- 4 - Erick Rowan, Big Show
- 3 - Negro Casas, Ronda Rousey, Cesaro, Ultimo Guerrero, Perro Aguayo Jr.

With so few promotions able to draw 10,000 fans to an event, this marks the seventh time, and the sixth straight year, that John Cena has finished first in this category. His other years as the top draw, based on headlining the most shows that did 10,000 fans, were 2007, 2009, 2010, 2011, 2012 and 2013. The only wrestlers who have been No. 1 in seven different years in history have been Jim Londos (13), Bruno Sammartino (8), Hulk Hogan (8), Bill Longson (7) and Lou Thesz (7). Cena was up from most recent years. His 2010 total was 38 shows that drew in excess of 10,000 paid, in 2011 he head-lined 33, in 2012 that number was 19 and in 2013 the number was 27. Cena's nine years in the top ten tie him with Gene Kiniski, The Sheik, Ray Stevens, and HHH. He still trails Jim Londos and Lou Thesz (who co-hold the record with 21 years as a top ten draw, a longevity record that Cena has almost no chance of ever reaching), Bruno Sammartino, Ed "Strangler" Lewis, Ric Flair, Hulk Hogan, Joe Stecher, Dick the Bruiser, Andre the Giant, Argentina Rocca, Killer Kowalski, Bill Longson, Buddy Rogers, Whipper Billy Watson, Yvon Robert and The Crusher. Cena would be the all-time 11th biggest drawing card in pro wrestling history, based on total longevity and domination of his era at the top, behind Londos, Sammartino, Thesz, Longson, Hogan, Lewis, Rocca, Flair, Rogers and Stecher. Orton moves to 34th place on the list. Orton would be the third highest ranker in history not to be in the Hall of Fame, behind only Mistico and Dick Shikat. Batista and Kane also move into the top 50 of all-time after this year.

ESTIMATED NORTH AMERICAN BUYS

- 1,025,000 - 12/28/13 UFC Chris Weidman vs. Anderson Silva; Ronda Rousey vs. Miesha Tate
- 925,000 - 9/13 Golden Boy/Mayweather/Showtime Floyd Mayweather Jr. vs. Marcos Maidana
- 900,000 - 5/3 Golden Boy/Mayweather/Showtime Floyd Mayweather Jr. vs. Marcos Maidana
- 750,000 - 5/12 Top Rank/HBO - Manny Pacquiao vs. Timothy Bradley
- 545,000 - 7/5 UFC Chris Weidman vs. Lyoto Machida; Ronda Rousey vs. Alexis Davis
- 420,000 - 4/6 WWE WrestleMania Daniel Bryan vs. Batista vs. Randy Orton
- 400,000 - 12/4/12 Top Rank/HBO Manny Pacquiao vs. Brandon Rios
- 350,000 - 4/26 UFC Jon Jones vs. Glover Teixeira
- 350,000 - 2/22 UFC Ronda Rousey vs. Sara McMann
- 350,000 - 3/8 Golden Boy/HBO Canelo Alvarez vs. Alfredo Angulo
- 337,000 - 1/26 WWE Royal Rumble Rumble/John Cena vs Randy Orton
- 300,000 - 3/15 UFC Johny Hendricks vs. Robbie Lawler
- 300,000 - 6/7 Top Rank Miguel Cotto vs. Sergio Martinez
- 300,000 - 7/13 Golden Boy/Showtime Canelo Alvarez vs. Erislandy Lara
- 300,000 - 11/22 Top Rank/HBO Manny Pacquiao vs. Chris Algieri
- 230,000 - 2/1 UFC Renan Barao vs. Urijah Faber; Jose Aldo vs. Ricardo Lamas
- 215,000 - 5/24 UFC Renan Barao vs. T.J. Dillashaw; Daniel Cormier vs. Dan Henderson
- 205,000 - 9/27 UFC Demetrious Johnson vs. Chris Cariaso; Conor McGregor vs. Dustin Poirier; Eddie Alvarez vs. Donald Cerrone
- 185,000 - 11/15 UFC Fabricio Werdum vs. Mark Hunt

- 180,000 - 10/25 UFC Jose Aldo vs. Chad Mendes
- 159,000 - 2/23 WWE Elimination Chamber Randy Orton vs. Daniel Bryan vs. John Cena vs. Sheamus vs. Christian vs. Cesaro
- 146,000 - 12/15/13 WWE TLC John Cena vs. Randy Orton
- 125,000 - 8/30 UFC T.J. Dillashaw vs. Joe Soto
- 115,000 - 6/14 UFC Demetrious Johnson vs. Ali Bagautinov
- 100,000 - 5/17 Bellator Quinton Jackson vs. King Mo Lawal
- 63,000 - 8/24 WWE SummerSlam John Cena vs. Brock Lesnar
- 53,000 - 6/29 WWE Money in the Bank John Cena vs. Bray Wyatt vs. Alberto Del Rio vs. Roman Reigns vs. Cesaro vs. Kane vs. Randy Orton vs. Sheamus
- 45,000 - 5/4 WWE Extreme Rules Daniel Bryan vs. Kane; The Shield vs. Evolution
- 33,000 - 11/23 WWE Survivor Series John Cena & Dolph Ziggler & Ryback & Big Show & Erick Rowan vs. Seth Rollins & Kane & Mark Henry & Luke Harper & Rusev
- 31,000 - 7/20 WWE Battleground John Cena vs. Randy Orton vs. Kane vs. Roman Reigns
- 30,000 - 9/21 WWE Night of Champions Brock Lesnar vs. John Cena
- 29,000 - 6/1 WWE Payback The Shield vs. Evolution
- 21,000 - 10/26 WWE Hell in a Cell John Cena vs. Randy Orton; Dean Ambrose vs. Seth Rollins

CROWDS OF MORE THAN 15,000

	2014	2013	2012	2011	2010
WWE	3	4	10	10	11
CMLL	1	2	0	1	2
AAA	1	1	1	0	1
UFC	3	4	12	5	8
New Japan	2	1	1	1	1

The chart shows the decline in major event attendance in WWE and UFC in particular. It should be noted that in 2009, WWE had 20 events that drew more than 15,000 fans.

UFC PPV BUYS (based on December to November)

	Shows	Buys	Average
2007	10	4,660,000	466,000
2008	13	6,885,000	530,000
2009	13	7,755,000	595,000
2010	15	8,970,000	598,000
2011	15	5,950,000	397,000
2012	13	6,025,000	463,000
2013	13	5,470,000	420,770
2014	12	3,825,000	318,800

The scary part is that the numbers are skewed in a sense, because the UFC 168 show, which took place in late January, is listed for this year. However, that's also misleading because the New Year's show is traditionally a big show, and the last New Year's show was at the end of 2013, and this year's would be in early 2015, so not including it would be some-what misleading. But you take that show out of it, and include the 12/6 show, UFC did 12 PPV events and approximately 3,180,000 total buys for a 265,000 average, which would be the lowest number for the promotion since 2005.

UFC AVERAGE GATE OF NORTH AMERICAN PPV SHOWS

	Shows	Total gate	Average
2007	10	$26,700,350	$2,670,035
2008	10	$32,857,231	$3,285,723
2009	11	$34,005,156	$3,091,378
2010	14	$40,841,459	$2,917,247
2011	14	$43,839,517	$3,131,394
2012	9	$31,125,774	$3,458,419
2013	12	$35,386,997	$2,948,916
2014	10	$24,416,991	$2,441,699

Even with much higher ticket prices for a lot of the shows, the gate average for the big shows was the lowest in many years. It actually would have been even lower (barely topping $2 million) if you didn't figure in UFC 168, which was the third largest live gate in UFC history, trailing only the Georges St-Pierre vs. Jake Shields show in Toronto and the second Anderson Silva vs. Chael Sonnen match in Las Vegas. It is understandable when almost every main event falls through.

LARGEST GATES IN NORTH AMERICA

- $9,800,000* - WWE WrestleMania 4/6 New Orleans Mercedes Benz Superdome, Daniel Bryan vs. Randy Orton vs. Batista
- $6,277,733** - 12/28/13 UFC 168 Las Vegas MGM Grand Garden Arena, Chris Weidman vs. Anderson Silva, Ronda Rousey vs. Miesha Tate
- $4,233,621* - 7/5 UFC 175 Las Vegas MGM Grand Garden Arena Chris Weidman vs. Lyoto Machida, Ronda Rousey vs. Alexis Davis
- $2,600,000 - 3/15 UFC 171 Dallas American Airlines Center Johny Hendricks vs. Robbie Lawler
- $2,300,000 - 4/26 UFC 172 Baltimore Arena Jon Jones vs. Glover Teixeira
- $2,262,675 - 9/27 UFC 177 Las Vegas MGM Grand Garden Arena Demetrious Johnson vs. Chris Cariaso, Donald Cer-rone vs. Eddie Alvarez
- $1,738,959 - 5/24 UFC 173 Las Vegas MGM Grand Garden Arena Renan Barao vs. T.J. Dillashaw
- $1,651,000 - 2/1 UFC 169 Newark, NJ Prudential Center Renan Barao vs. Urijah Faber; Jose Aldo vs. Ricardo Lamas
- $1,558,870*** - 2/22 UFC 170 Las Vegas Mandalay Bay Events Center Ronda Rousey vs. Sara McMann
- $1,553,738 - 4/19 UFC on FOX Orlando Amway Arena Fabricio Werdum vs. Travis Browne

*Denotes sellout. Announced as $10.9 million but WWE when announcing WrestleMania gates includes ticket service charges which nobody else includes in gates
**Denotes sellout and includes close circuit airings in city
***Denotes sellout, breaks the all-time gate record for a show headlined by a woman's match as the top bout, breaking the record of $1,350,191 set on February 23, 2013 for the Ronda Rousey vs. Liz Carmouche fight in Anaheim.

BIGGEST DRAWING CARDS BY THE YEAR

- 1916 - Joe Stecher
- 1917 - Joe Stecher
- 1918 - Joe Stecher, Ed "Strangler" Lewis, Wladek Zbyszko
- 1919 - Ed "Strangler" Lewis
- 1920 - Joe Stecher
- 1921 - Ed "Strangler" Lewis

- 1922 - Stanislaus Zbyszko
- 1923 - Ed "Strangler" Lewis
- 1924 - Ed "Strangler" Lewis and Jim Londos
- 1925 - Ed "Stranger" Lewis, Joe Stecher Wayne Munn and Stanislaus Zbyszko
- 1926 - Jim Londos
- 1927 - Jim Londos and John Pesek
- 1928 - Jim Londos
- 1929 - Gus Sonnenberg
- 1930 - Jim Londos and Dick Shikat
- 1931 - Jim Londos
- 1932 - Jim Londos
- 1933 - Jim Londos
- 1934 - Jim Londos
- 1935 - Danno O'Mahoney
- 1936 - Danno O'Mahoney
- 1937 - Jim Londos
- 1938 - Jim Londos and Steve Casey
- 1939 - Jim Londos, Vincent Lopez and Dave Levin
- 1940 - Jim Londos
- 1941 - Bill Longson
- 1942 - Bill Longson
- 1943 - Bill Longson
- 1944 - Bill Longson
- 1945 - Bill Longson
- 1946 - Bill Longson
- 1947 - Bill Longson
- 1948 - Gorgeous George
- 1949 - Gorgeous George and Whipper Billy Watson
- 1950 - Lou Thesz and Argentina Rocca
- 1951 - Lou Thesz
- 1952 - Lou Thesz
- 1953 - Lou Thesz and Blue Demon
- 1954 - Argentina Rocca
- 1955 - Lou Thesz
- 1956 - Argentina Rocca and Whipper Billy Watson
- 1957 - Lou Thesz
- 1958 - Argentina Rocca & Miguel Perez Sr.
- 1959 - Argentina Rocca & Miguel Perez Sr.
- 1960 - Buddy Rogers
- 1961 - Buddy Rogers
- 1962 - Buddy Rogers
- 1963 - Bruno Sammartino
- 1964 - Bruno Sammartino
- 1965 - Bruno Sammartino
- 1966 - Lou Thesz
- 1967 - Bruno Sammartino
- 1968 - Bruno Sammartino
- 1969 - The Sheik

- 1970 - The Sheik
- 1971 - The Sheik
- 1972 - The Sheik
- 1973 - The Sheik
- 1974 - Bruno Sammartino
- 1975 - Bruno Sammartino
- 1976 - Bruno Sammartino
- 1977 - Superstar Billy Graham
- 1978 - Superstar Billy Graham
- 1979 - Bob Backlund
- 1980 - Bob Backlund
- 1981 - Bob Backlund
- 1982 - Bob Backlund
- 1983 - Ric Flair
- 1984 - Hulk Hogan
- 1985 - Hulk Hogan
- 1986 - Hulk Hogan
- 1987 - Hulk Hogan
- 1988 - Hulk Hogan
- 1989 - Hulk Hogan
- 1990 - Hulk Hogan
- 1991 - Hulk Hogan
- 1992 - Ric Flair
- 1993 - Konnan
- 1994 - Konnan
- 1995 - Shinya Hashimoto
- 1996 - Nobuhiko Takada
- 1997 - Shinya Hashimoto
- 1998 - Steve Austin
- 1999 - The Rock
- 2000 - The Rock
- 2001 - Steve Austin
- 2002 - The Rock
- 2003 - Brock Lesnar
- 2004 - HHH
- 2005 - Kenta Kobashi
- 2006 - Mistico
- 2007 - John Cena
- 2008 - Mistico
- 2009 - John Cena
- 2010 - John Cena
- 2011 - John Cena
- 2012 - John Cena
- 2013 - John Cena
- 2014 - John Cena

CHAPTER FIFTY SIX

WRESTLING OBSERVER HALL OF FAME

NOVEMBER 24

Ricky Morton & Robert Gibson, the Rock & Roll Express, who have spent the last 32 years on-and-off as a tag team, from the major promotions to the smallest of indies, join Ray Fabiani, who promoted pro wrestling on-and-off for 48 years, as the newest inductees in the Wrestling Observer Newsletter Hall of Fame.

Morton & Gibson, facing being off the ballot after 15 years, garnered 64 percent of the vote, putting them over the top after being the second closest to making it, but not getting in last year. The team joins its biggest career rivals The Mid-night Express, who were elected in 2009.

The Rock & Roll Express didn't have the actual main event credentials to compare with most on the ballot, but were a key part of two strong periods, the high point of Mid South Wrestling in 1984-85, and the most successful period of Jim Crockett Promotions in 1985-86. They also anchored Smoky Mountain Wrestling in the 90s. Morton, in particular, was considered one of the best babyfaces at selling during the modern era. But as a team, Morton & Gibson had the most longevity together of any major tag team in pro wrestling history.

Their success spawned a number of imitations, although they themselves in a sense were spawned by the success of The Fabulous Ones, Stan Lane & Steve Keirn, in Memphis. After The Fabulous Ones became huge draws in Tennessee and Kentucky through use of music videos in the early 80s, Jerry Lawler put Morton & Gibson together. Both had been members of strong tag teams, Morton with Ken Lucas in Texas and Eddie Gilbert in Oklahoma, and Gibson with his half-brother Ricky for a number of years in different places.

The key to the act was that they could sell and work at a faster clip than most, upping the tempo of matches from their era, but also that women loved them, particularly young women. That was a combination of looks, the way Morton sold, and the way they were marketed with the music videos.

After the music video treatment preceded them, in the famous Watts/Jarrett talent trade in early 1984, Morton & Gibson exploded on the scene in Mid South Wrestling, being one of the keys to the best year in the history of the promotion, which went from having very few women at their house shows, to overflowing with them. What's notable is that the Rock & Roll Express' best city was Houston, and Morton had worked Houston years earlier. While he did well, once headlining in the city against AWA champion Nick Bockwinkel, he was nowhere near the level of star he became with Gibson. Similarly, Morton had worked in Oklahoma three years earlier for Leroy McGuirk, as part of a tag team with Gilbert, before McGuirk folded and Bill Watts brought Mid South

Wrestling in, and while they were a good babyface team, few in the territory even remember Morton before the Rock & Roll Express.

Morton was really the key to the act. Although he was already 26 when the team was formed in 1983, he could almost pass for a teenager. The minute the team looked 30, because of their gimmick, they were going to be dead as far as their original gimmick because of who the appeal was to.

But even though the last major promotion strong run of the team was in 1990 (they were in WWF in 1998 as part of an NWA angle that went nowhere), they became almost like a rock band from the 50s and 60s that could continue to successfully tour smaller buildings as a nostalgia act and play their familiar hit songs.

Still together today, even though they've had breaks, turns, feuds, and a period when they didn't team, for the most part, they've been together since 1983, and are believed to have had the most longevity of any major tag team in pro wrestling history.

They got over so strong in the Carolinas in particular that they still wrestle as a team there to this day. They are remembered more fondly than any tag team ever in that part of the country, even the ones like the Road Warriors who head-lined more shows in that area during the same time frame, the Midnight Express, the greatest tag team of that era (who were their career rivals) and Ricky Steamboat & Jay Youngblood, who headlined what is remembered as one of the two biggest shows in the history of Carolinas wrestling. What's amazing is their longevity was while doing an act that seemingly required them to at least look like they could pass for their 20s to be effective, and now Morton is 58, and Gibson being 56 and balding.

Balloting this year was the deepest in history, making it one of the toughest ballots ever. There were no slam dunks who became eligible, and nobody else came close to making it.

Brock Lesnar, the current WWE champion, came 13 ballots shy and finished in second place. Carlos Colon, who has been close for years, was six votes shy in his region, and Cien Caras was also six votes shy.

A new rule was instituted this year which is a 15-year rule. After being on the ballot for 15 years, a performer needs to at least get 50 percent of the vote or they are off the ballot.

Because of that new rule, somewhat patterned after the Major League Baseball Hall of Fame, dropped next year from the ballot are Gene & Ole Anderson, Gran Hamada, Owen Hart, Gorilla Monsoon, Fabulous Moolah, Pedro Morales, Dick Murdoch, Seiji Sakaguchi, Jimmy Snuka, Wilbur Snyder and Jesse Ventura.

In the case of Snyder and Gene Anderson, they are probably not going to be back on the ballot, unless a reason surfaces that would make it appear they would have a shot at getting in. In the case of Morales, because of the data in the re-search this year, which came out after most ballots had come in, he'll probably be put back on in two years for a last shot. The fact is that even though his numbers of big show successful main events and his Madison Square Garden record in particular are Hall of Fame level, and he held both the WWA and WWWF world titles, most of that was known, and he had never fared well in the balloting. But my thought it was everyone who had Hall of Fame numbers of a headliner in this year's research would get another ballot run. What has always hurt Morales was his post-1973 career was not that impressive, past his WWF return as the perennial babyface IC champion.

Ole Anderson (in 2020), Hamada (in 2032), Owen Hart (in 2029), Monsoon (in 2026 because Monsoon is on the ballot as a non-wrestler), Moolah (in 2017), Murdoch (in 2024), Sakaguchi (in 2020), Snuka (in 2022) and Ventura (in 2024 be-cause he's on the ballot as an announcer, not a wrestler) will eventually return for one last chance in the historical candidates category. Their returns to the ballot will be 30 years after their last year as a significant star and major player.

Anderson was already in that category as part of the Minnesota Wrecking Crew tag team, but in studying his career, really Ole Anderson individually is a stronger candidate than the Anderson Brothers team, as he was a successful singles star, and also formed championship tag teams with Ivan Koloff, Stan Hansen and Arn Anderson. But while the end of the original Minnesota Wrecking Crew was in 1982, meaning they were eligible for the historical candidates a few years ago, Ole Anderson's final major run, as part of the Four Horseman and with Arn Anderson, ended in 1990, meaning he would be eligible reappear on the ballot as a single in 2020.

For someone to be voted into the Hall of Fame, he or she needs to be named on 60 percent of the ballots from his or her region. There is also a time frame for North America, split up for modern and historical candidates. The modern category is for those who were still headliners with major groups after 1985. The historical category encompasses the years from 1948, when pro wrestling was first introduced on television, through1984. For those before 1948, there are additions made sparingly since most of the major players from that era are already in.

The other regions besides North America are Japan, Mexico, Europe and the rest of the world, which includes places like Australia, New Zealand, Hawaii, Puerto Rico, Singapore, India and South Africa.

Balloting is done by a large panel of historians, former and current wrestlers and major wrestling personalities, as well as reporters. All balloting is anonymous, although there is no rule preventing any balloters for releasing their own individual ballot, but we will not release any ballots nor any names of anyone involved in the process.

Wrestlers and wrestling personalities who get between 10% and 59.9% of the voting from their region will remain on the ballot next year. Those who get less than 10% of the votes from their region are dropped from the ballot. They can be put back on in two years provided either their careers have continued to move forward, or if voters feel there is new evidence or a reason they would garner more interest.

Wrestlers and wrestling personalities, provided they get at least 10% of the vote, can remain on the ballot up to 15 years, or longer if they can remain above 50%. At that point, if they are in the historical category or a non-North American, they will be not be brought back. In North America, they can get one year in the historical category and need to garner at least 50% to stay alive.

The Rock & Roll Express fared strongly in every category, finishing fifth among historians, fifth among active wrestlers, eighth among former wrestlers and third among reporters.

Lesnar was top 30 in every category, finishing second among historians, 21st among active wrestlers, 25th among for-mer wrestlers and first among reporters.

Colon finished eighth among historians, second among active wrestlers, didn't place in the top 30 among former wrestlers (it is always notable that Colon's peers in the ring have never voted for him, with the general explanation always being that those who worked with him felt he was not a Hall of Fame caliber performer, just someone who owned a territory and put themselves over and he never got over when in any other place he tried, but those younger who weren't about see him in a different light as the wrestling legend in his island), and second among reporters.

The difference in balloting in each group is significant. Billy Joyce, who was the top British heavyweight for a generation and long-time champion, and some say the greatest shooter out of Wigan ever, was a virtual unanimous pick among British historians for a Hall of Fame spot. But he got no support by almost anyone else.

Among active wrestlers, it was most interesting because the top five were Yuji Nagata, Colon, Gene & Ole Anderson, Volk Han and the Rock & Roll Express.

I've had it expressed to me by a number of wrestlers, including Bryan Danielson who has said so publicly on more than one occasion, that Nagata is the single best guy they had ever been in the ring with. In that sense, he was similar to Kurt Angle, as far as peers being high on him. While Nagata was the top star in New Japan and has had a very successful career, he was never the guy who was quite a Hall of Fame level star. But as a worker, was he a Hall of Famer? I've always thought so, but it's been very difficult for great workers to get in, unless they have gone all over the world and made it to the top of WWE like Chris Benoit, Eddy Guerrero, Kurt Angle or Rey Mysterio. It's not necessarily fair, but a guy like Kiyoshi Tamura, who is as good in the ring as anyone, and did come close in the past, flounders as people have forgotten his name because his style went extinct.

However, Colon and the Andersons have been taught to current wrestlers as being legendary, because Colon was on top for so long, and the Andersons had the reputation as the best heel team ever in the Carolinas, and Carolinas history survives better with wrestlers because it was the territory that really became WCW, so its history lasted until early 2001, while the other territories really died out in the 80s. To a degree, the Rock & Roll Express fit into that category, but most modern wrestlers who voted have seen them enough and they are the team studied by newer wrestlers when it comes to working as babyfaces in a tag team match, and had a classic feud with the Midnight Express that included a strong nostalgia run that lasted until health issues no longer allowed Bobby Eaton to perform.

Among former wrestlers, the top two were rivals and very similar in style, Dick Murdoch and Killer Karl Kox. Murdoch has always done incredible numbers among his peers, because Murdoch was as talented as any 275-pound wrestler of his era. As far as an all-around worker on his best day, Murdoch was as good as anyone of his size. But Murdoch wasn't always on his best day. Murdoch has never got enough support except from those who worked with him, and probably knew him best, even though he came very close to getting in for several years. He fell from the top of the pack as his supporters started getting older and dying off. In recent years he had no longer come close to getting in. Kox was the second biggest heel, behind Killer Kowalski, during the glory days of World Championship Wrestling in Australia and a solid territorial star in the 60s and 70s.

Lesnar, likely because of his historical importance and uniqueness of his abilities, finished first among reporters.

Volk Han went from a guy who has been on the ballot and gotten limited support to someone topping 50% this year, which could have been his last year on the ballot. Han is an interesting case. For his style, he is among the best of all-time. Having seen every one of his matches, and he didn't have that many matches or a long career, as far as ability in the ring, he was absolutely a Hall of Famer. And he did headline some successful shows, and was pretty famous in his own way in Japan. The question becomes if someone with so few matches should be a Hall of Famer, and the answer isn't as cut and dried. It is notable than Han does better each year, while Tamura, who was more complete because his submission game wasn't quite as good but it was still amazing for pro wrestling, and his striking was far better, went from being a strong candidate when he was still active to being forgotten.

Wrestlers are eligible for the ballot once they turn 35 years old and have at least ten years of pro experience, or after they've had 15 years of experience if they are under 35 and started young.

The highest finishing newcomers to the ballot were Los Misioneros de la Muerte, the trio of El Signo & El Texano & Ne-gro Navarro, who were the team that popularized trios wrestling in Mexico during the 80s and drew consistent huge houses around the country, particularly in the heyday of the UWA at El Toreo in Naucalpan. But even they got only 36%.

Next year's ballot should be easier in a sense, although not deeper. A number of strong candidates are dropping off, and as the years go by, there will be far more dropping off than be added on.

Daniel Bryan, Shinsuke Nakamura, Samoa Joe and Randy Orton will be eligible next year. There are very few new candidates that are strong after that, because with fewer places and fewer headliners, it's become a business where individual stars are less important than ever before. KENTA is eligible in 2016 and the original Mistico in 2017. Mistico's case is very interesting because he's got the drawing power past any point to get in, but was hurt greatly by his WWE run. KENTA didn't have the drawing power, but was among the best in-ring performers of the past decade, but his own future is WWE and it's not a good fit. Perro Aguayo Jr. has already been on and off and could be put back on at any time. But the number of additions going forward will be slim.

Joining them on next year's ballot will be Cowboy Bob Ellis and Rocky Johnson, because of how they fared in research on headliners done this year, A.J. Styles, who had been one-and-done but because several had asked for him to be put back on based on his New Japan run, Montreal promoter Eddie Quinn and former NWA President and long-time Central States star and promoter Bob Geigel.

Dropping off the ballot next year for failure to get ten percent of the vote this year are Ciclon Negro, Giant Haystacks, Ken Patera, Emil "King Kong" Czaya, John DaSilva and Jan Wilkens.

It's hard to say who will benefit from that. Lesnar is clearly a strong candidate, but also has a number of people who ab-solutely won't vote for him. His success financially puts his long-term run in WWE in question, and he will likely never go back full-time to pro wrestling. While he is booked like a super attraction of the past, the change in the way the business is makes such a thing less important. Colon is a situation, in the sense the group that "should" support him the most doesn't at all, which is actually a great example of reputation after the fact vs. reputation during the fact. Ivan Koloff made a big jump this year, but was still under 50%. He did reasonably well with every group, but was only 15th place among reporters and wasn't top five in any group.

Two other strong candidates, who hovered around 50%, were Karloff Lagarde, who was half of one of Mexico's most famous tag teams with Rene Guajardo in the 60s and also a major singles star, and The Assassins,

Jody Hamilton & Tom Renesto, who were considered behind only Ray Stevens & Pat Patterson as the top working heel tag team of the 60s, and who also drew very well in a number of territories.

The Assassins' strength was among their peers, placing fifth, as well as ninth among reporters, and they fared well with every group. Lagarde placed fifth among reporters, which was his strongest category.

Of newcomers to the ballot, only Los Misioneros topped 35 percent and nobody was a strong voting candidate. Jun Aki-yama, who had fallen below ten percent in the past, did better than before, but was still far from a contender. Austrian promoter/wrestler Otto Wanz, New Japan's Minoru Suzuki, Ultimate Warrior, C.M. Punk, George Scott, the tag team of Hiroyoshi Tenzan & Satoshi Kojima, Los Brazos, Larry Matysik, Junkyard Dog, Akira Taue and the tag team of Brute Bernard & Skull Murphy will all remain on the ballot.

Punk and Warrior make interesting candidates, because Punk peaked at being the second biggest star in the world, a level that would get in almost any time historically. Warrior was also a huge star, and one of the most well remembered figures of the last 25 years. But like Punk, his time on top was short, and he wasn't very good in the ring unless carried, and wasn't someone who was going to get Hall of Fame votes among his contemporaries.

Punk had the great matches going for him and a strong cult following, but his leaving hurt him and this era is harder for someone to be a strong candidate. With Punk being rejected, Dave Bautista falling off last year, and with John Cena and Hiroshi Tanahashi already in, there is nobody who is close to a sure thing going forward. Randy Orton has all the numbers going his way as far as headlining big shows for a number of years, but he was less successful as a top draw than Batista. Mistico has the numbers but also has the failed WWE run. Shinsuke Nakamura is interesting. He may be the best performer in the world in-ring in 2014, pretty much made a secondary title draw like the main title, and has longevity as a top guy. Daniel Bryan was a Hall of Fame worker without a doubt. So are a plethora of people on this ballot like Nagata, Hamada, Tamura, Edge, Saint and Bastien. And none of them even come lose this year. Bryan has great longevity as being one of the best in-ring performers, but so did a lot of people just mentioned. Bryan was also a long-time independent main eventer who headlined and carried a WrestleMania. That's the biggest show of the year, but Nagata head-lined Tokyo Domes and Ultimo Guerrero really drew the two largest houses in CMLL history and has been a top worker and main eventer, and even significant draw, on-and-off for well over a decade and still didn't come close. L.A. Park has four Wrestler of the Year awards in Mexico, but fell greatly.

The change in the business makes it very difficult for current wrestlers to get in. Nobody has ever gotten in based on independents. Unless things change, I can see it being next to impossible for anyone to get in unless they were with WWE, New Japan, or guys from CMLL's last big run, and even those guys that were the key building blocks (Guerrero and Dr. Wagner Jr.) didn't fare all that well this year.

Most others stayed about where they were. Koloff had a solid increase but was still a hefty 39 votes shy. Nagata also had a strong increase over last year, but part of it was the Japan ballot should have been easier this year with the elimination of Kensuke Sasaki and Hiroshi Tanahashi.

But a number had double-digit drops in percentages, including Mark Lewin, Kox, Blue Panther, Jackie Pallo, Park, Dr. Wagner Jr., Tamura, Domenic DeNucci, Hector Garza, Kendo Nagasaki, and John Tolos. Lewin, Kox and DeNucci were all candidates strongest out of Australia, and Panther, Park, Wagner Jr. and Garza were all from Mexico. The Australian ballot didn't change much, and even though Carlos Colon came close and drew a lot of voters that wouldn't vote for the Australians, the same was the case last year. With the Mexican ballot, Cien Caras moved up and Los Misioneros did well, plus Los Brazos were added (although they didn't do as well), so it was a tougher ballot. Villano III also dropped, but not by as much.

The Pallo and Nagasaki drops are due to more Americans voting for Big Daddy in the category, who actually fared poorly among those in the U.K., particularly from former wrestlers, but increased his number slightly due to votes from foreign countries. But that hurt others from that category.

Next year will also be interesting because of how well Koloff, Kinji Shibuya and Bob Ellis did in research on drawing on top in major market main events. Koloff did well this year and jumped, but Shibuya was a non-entity and Ellis was on the ballot in the past and got no support.

WRESTLING OBSERVER HALL OF FAME BALLOTING RESULTS

PERFORMER	VOTE	PCT	2013
ROCK & ROLL EXPRESS	212	64%	55%
Brock Lesnar	185	56%	47%
Carlos Colon	76	56%	59%
Cien Caras	53	54%	45%
Volk Han	52	51%	42%
Gene & Ole Anderson	119	49%	52%
Ivan Koloff	159	48%	34%
Karloff Lagarde	47	48%	52%
The Assassins	117	48%	53%
Mike & Ben Sharpe	47	46%	39%
Dick Murdoch	147	45%	46%
Jerry Jarrett	145	44%	38%
Jim Crockett Sr.	107	44%	44%
Big Daddy	46	43%	38%
Jesse Ventura	139	42%	39%
Bill Apter	138	42%	43%
Mark Lewin	51	38%	48%
Yuji Nagata	38	37%	26%
Los Misioneros de la Muerte	35	36%	----
Edge	117	36%	37%
Jimmy Hart	117	36%	34%
Gene Okerlund	117	36%	35%
Fabulous Moolah	114	35%	32%
Seiji Sakaguchi	35	34%	34%
Red Bastien	83	34%	41%
Sting	110	33%	33%
Gorilla Monsoon	110	33%	27%
Pedro Morales	81	33%	22%
Gary Hart	108	33%	34%
Villano III	32	33%	41%
Rollerball Mark Rocco	35	32%	39%
Killer Karl Kox	44	32%	50%
Stanley Weston	75	31%	39%
Don Owen	99	30%	29%
Jun Akiyama	30	29%	----
Gran Hamada	30	29%	30%
Howard Finkel	95	29%	30%
Johnny Saint	31	29%	32%
Wilbur Snyder	69	28%	24%
Blue Panther	27	28%	41%
Billy Joyce	29	27%	22%
Jackie Pallo	29	27%	46%
Huracan Ramirez	26	27%	19%
Enrique Torres	62	25%	34%
George Gordienko	26	25%	25%
Otto Wanz	26	25%	----

Tim "Mr. Wrestling" Woods	58	24%	32%
Ultimo Guerrero	23	24%	----
L.A. Park	23	24%	46%
Dr. Wagner Jr.	23	24%	35%
Masahiko Kimura	24	23%	16%
Kiyoshi Tamura	24	23%	44%
Horst Hoffman	25	23%	21%
Curt Hennig	76	23%	30%
Jim Crockett Jr.	75	23%	26%
Minoru Suzuki	23	22%	----
Sgt. Slaughter	71	22%	24%
Domenic DeNucci	29	21%	37%
Johnny "Wrestling II" Walker	52	21%	29%
Owen Hart	69	21%	21%
Ultimate Warrior	65	20%	----
C.M. Punk	63	19%	----
George Scott	63	19%	----
Jimmy Snuka	61	19%	20%
Kojima & Tenzan	17	17%	----
Los Brazos	16	16%	----
Larry Matysik	39	16%	---
Junkyard Dog	52	16%	----
Akira Taue	16	16%	----
Hector Garza	15	15%	32%
Kendo Nagasaki	16	15%	39%
Spyros Arion	20	15%	22%
June Byers	35	14%	20%
Kinji Shibuya	35	14%	15%
Jim Breaks	15	14%	16%
Dick Hutton	32	13%	11%
Dave Brown	43	13%	12%
John Tolos	31	13%	26%
Bernard & Murphy	16	12%	----
Vampiro	11	11%	16%
Mario Milano	15	11%	14%
Johnny Barend	14	10%	16%
Pepper Gomez	25	10%	16%
Von Brauners/Weingeroff	25	10%	19%

Votes needed for induction into the Hall of Fame: U.S. and Canada modern (198); U.S. and Canada historical (147); Japan (62); Mexico (59); Pacific Islands, Australia, New Zealand, Puerto Rico (82); Europe (65) Less than 10% of the votes from the region and dropped from next year's ballot: Ciclon Negro, Giant Hay-stacks, Ken Patera, Emil "King Kong" Czaya, John DaSilva, Jan Wilkens

Dropped from next year's ballot due to 15 year/50% rule: Gene & Ole Anderson, Gran Hamada, Owen Hart, Gorilla Monsoon, Fabulous Moolah, Pedro Morales, Dick Murdoch, Seiji Sakaguchi, Jimmy Snuka, Wilbur Snyder, Jesse Ventura.

Added to the ballot next year: Cima, Bryan Danielson, Cowboy Bob Ellis, Bob Geigel, Samoa Joe, Rocky Johnson, Shinsuke Nakamura, Randy Orton, Eddie Quinn, A.J. Styles

Will be dropped after next year if not inducted or 50%: Cien Caras, Carlos Colon, Villano III, Volk Han

TOP TEN AMONG DIFFERENT VOTING GROUPS

HISTORIANS	WRESTLERS	EX WRESTLERS	REPORTERS
1. Billy Joyce	1. Yuji Nagata	1. Dick Murdoch	1. Brock Lesnar
2. Brock Lesnar	2. Carlos Colon	2. Killer Karl Kox	2. Carlos Colon
3. Volk Han	3. The Andersons	3. Jerry Jarrett	3. Rock & Roll Express
4. Cien Caras	4. Volk Han	4. Seiji Sakaguchi	4. Cien Caras
5. Rock & Roll Express	5. Rock & Roll Express	5. The Assassins	5. Karloff Lagarde
6. George Gordienko	6. Misioneros de la Muerte	6. Fabulous Moolah	6. Big Daddy
7. Ivan Koloff	7. Jim Crockett Sr.	7. Rock & Roll Express	7. Ben & Mike Sharpe
8. Carlos Colon	8. Bill Apter	8. Masahiko Kimura	8. Jerry Jarrett
9. Mark Lewin	9. Ivan Koloff	9. Red Bastien	9. The Assassins
10. Dick Murdoch	10. Jesse Ventura	10. Jim Crockett Sr.	10. Gene Okerlund
11. Bill Apter	11. Ultimo Guerrero	11. Ivan Koloff	11. Rollerball Mark Rocco
12. Seiji Sakaguchi	12. Karloff Lagarde	12. Jesse Ventura	12. The Andersons
13. Killer Karl Kox	13. L.A. Park	13. Mark Lewin	13. Enrique Torres
14. Stanley Weston	14. The Assassins	14. The Andersons	14. Edge
15. Blue Panther	15. Gorilla Monsoon	15. Curt Hennig	15. Ivan Koloff
16. Jesse Ventura	16. Jun Akiyama	16. Gary Hart	16. Bill Apter
17. Johnny Saint	17. Big Daddy	17. Jackie Pallo	17. Jimmy Hart
18. The Amdersons	18. Edge	18. Kiyoshi Tamura	18. Jim Crockett Sr.
19. Assassins	19. Los Brazos	19. Owen Hart	19. Stanley Weston
20. Gary Hart	20. Cien Caras	20. Jimmy Hart	20. Howard Finkel
21. Red Bastien	21. Brock Lesnar	21. Gorilla Monsoon	21. Sting
22. Pedro Morales	22. Jerry Jarrett	22. Don Owen	22. Jesse Ventura
23. Wilbur Snyder	23. Fabulous Moolah	23. Wilbur Snyder	23. Pedro Morales
24. Jim Crockett Sr.	24. Rollerball Mark Rocco	24. Brock Lesnar	24. Los Misioneros de la Muerte
25. Gorilla Monsoon	25. Johnny Saint	25. Horst Hoffman	25. Blue Panther
26. Jimmy Snuka	26. Mike & Ben Sharpe	26. George Gordienko	26. Villano III
27. Sting	27. Dick Murdoch	27. Rollerball Mark Rocco	27. Jun Akiyama
28. Karloff Lagarde	28. Sting	28. Otto Wanz	28. Yuji Nagata
29. Huracan Ramirez	29. Gene Okerlund	29. Bill Apter	29. Dick Murdoch
30. Jerry Jarrett	30. Jimmy Hart	30. Pedro Morales	30. Don Owen

RAY FABIANI Ray Fabiani was called the "mat maestro," and in his case, it was more than just sportswriter alliteration. As a classical violinist and manager of opera houses, Fabiani walked comfortably at the highest levels of the fine arts. As a wrestling promoter, he tended to interests in Philadelphia, Los Angeles, New York, Chicago, Pittsburgh, Boston, Washington, D.C., and other cities for 47 years, successfully operating in as many large U.S. cities as anyone in the pre-national era.

He truly kept a foot in two different worlds; in March 1959, he supervised soprano Renata Tebaldi at the Academy of Music in Philadelphia, presented her with long-stemmed roses, and then hopped in his car to bail out two wrestling fans who'd been sent to jail for assaulting a referee at the Philadelphia Arena.

To Fabiani, advancing the cause of opera differed little from pitching wrestling, a business he entered in 1923 at the behest of Italian grappler Renato Gardini. "Actually, it wasn't all that odd. I've always had a flair for organizing, promoting, whatever you care to call it," he said in a 1958 interview. "Here was something new to tackle. I kept my hand in opera as well."

With Tom Packs of St. Louis, Jack Curley of New York, Paul Bowser of Boston and a few other promoters, Fabiani was at the helm of a boom period for wrestling in the late 1920s and early 1930s.

He derived much of his success from a close association with Jim Londos, whom he met while he still was in the music business in Chicago. Londos was a fixture in main events in Philadelphia starting in 1924, when

Fabiani promoted wrestling at the Philadelphia Philharmonic Auditorium.

Fabiani later promoted world title change matches between Londos and Dick Shikat in 1929 and 1930. Fabiani and Londos struck several non-wrestling business deals, including a skating rink and a midget race track, and the Greek idol wrestled in Philadelphia for Fabiani as late as 1953. Fabiani understood one thing that many of his fellow promoters did not: treat your top guys with respect.

"With me, he was a great guy. He always treated me great," Bruno Sammartino said in a 2012 interview with Greg Oliver.

Fabiani billed Sammartino as "The Great Bruno" on a Reading, Pa., show in November 1959, a month into the future champ's career. "He was the big opera impresario too. When the greatest opera stars came, he would have me come to the opera, meet these people. I got to know Franco Corelli—in my opinion, he was the greatest tenor I ever met—and many others."

Aurelio Fabiani was born in Naples, Italy, on April 28, 1891. He signed one government document fixing the date at 1895, but the 1891 date fits his time line. He emigrated with his family to the United States in December 1903, and attended South Philadelphia High School and the University of Pennsylvania. A slight man at 5-foot-11 and 150 pounds, he was more suited for a life in an orchestra pit than athletics. Fabiani trained in Brussels with Eugene Yaase, known as the "King of the Violin," and was first violinist with opera companies in Philadelphia, St. Louis and Chicago by the time he was 25.

In a 1937 interview, Fabiani said Londos, a classical music lover, approached him backstage after a concert in Chicago and brought him into the business. Londos might well have met him in Chicago, but numerous accounts suggest Gardini was the key player in Fabiani's professional turn from concert master to wrestling magnate.

In summer 1922, Fabiani was fired as first violinist with the Chicago Civic Opera company amid claims that he extorted money from a singer by promising her a job. Fabiani later sued the company manager for defamation. The matter was not settled publicly.

He promoted wrestling cards in Baltimore in 1922 and 1923, relying on Gardini to attract Italian ethnics, took an opera company to Cuba in 1923 and then moved to Philadelphia that year.

Though Philadelphia was the nation's third largest city, pro wrestling had been comatose for years. Initially, Fabiani didn't fare much better. His second show there produced only $400 in gate receipts, about half of what he owed headline wrestler Joe Parelli. But he paid his wrestlers in full "without a murmur," as Philly sportswriter Gordon Mackay put it, earning a reputation as a fair man in an unfair game and boosting the reputation of his promotion in the process.

"The signor completely deodorized a sport that has become so badly decomposed as it were that nobody would have anything to do with it," Mackay said.

His first big show in Philadelphia was a match between Gardini and Ed "Strangler" Lewis in May 1924. Regularly featuring Gardini and Londos, often against each other, he started to turn a profit.

"The big moment of my wrestling promotion career came one night when I eagerly phoned my wife with the information that the show that evening had been successful, and instead of going into the hole for several hundred dollars, we had just broken even on a $20,000 house," he said.

On June 10, 1926, Fabiani brought together Londos and world champion Joe Stecher for the inaugural athletic event at Municipal Stadium (later John F. Kennedy Stadium). Stecher retained his title in front of a crowd of between 10,000 and 15,000. In his first four years as a promoter, Fabiani put on at least eight world championship matches, depending on your definition of "world championship."

He continued to place Londos in top spots even without the belt, matching him with Pete Sauer (later Ray Steele) and John Pesek.

By this time, attendance at Fabiani's shows in Philadelphia was burying that of Madison Square Garden, which did well to draw 4,000 or 5,000 to irregular shows.

In June 1929, Shikat beat Londos for the heavyweight title before 25,000 at Municipal Stadium, with Fabiani reportedly guaranteeing a $35,000 purse. A year later, Londos won the rematch and started his long run as wrestling's greatest drawing card, with Fabiani firmly behind him. Fabiani extended his reach into Boston as matchmaker in 1931 and combined with Toots Mondt and Mike Jacobs to operate in New York after Jack Curley's death in 1937.

By casting his lot with Londos, Fabiani was sure to be on the winning side of the promotional wars that racked wrestling in the 1930s. A series of matches between Londos and Everette Marshall drew sellouts to Philadelphia in 1933 and 1934.

In 1935, saying he was fed up with wrestling cliques, Fabiani staged a major international tournament in Philadelphia to find a challenger to the heavyweight title held by Danno O'Mahoney. While some of that was promotional doublespeak, it worked well and elevated Fabiani in the wrestling world.

A drawing of names on November 15, 1935, attracted the lieutenant governor of Massachusetts, a state athletic com-missioner and representatives of the Chamber of Commerce. Fabiani-backed Dean Detton won the three-month tourney and later that year captured a version of the world title from Dave Levin in Philadelphia before 9,000 fans.

Fabiani also promoted the Nov. 18, 1938 match at the Philadelphia Convention Hall where Londos beat Bronko Nagurski to regain the heavyweight title.

With his resume and refined sensibilities, Fabiani was a perfect response to anyone who questioned wrestling's respecta-bility.

"A talk with Ray Fabiani, a sensitive man who gave up a brilliant career as a concert violinist to promote professional wrestling, leaves a warmer spot in one's heart for the groan and grunt boys," wrote Paul Mickelson of the Associated Press.

In time, Fabiani's clout extended beyond wrestling and music; he helped pack the convention hall in Philadelphia for the 1940 nomination of Republican presidential candidate Wendell Willkie.

Fabiani had his share of rocky paths with two of his wives. He was estranged from Mercedes Courtney when she died at 23 in June 1933 of an apparent overdose of sleeping pills; she was being treated for a nervous disorder. In December 1935, he married Helen Day, a blonde 20-year-old dancer and showgirl, and that was trouble from the start. They split in 1937 and engaged in a bitter, seven-year-long custody fight of their two children.

Among the lowlights: she won a court order that allowed her to bang ceaselessly on the door of his apartment. He con-tended she slugged the children's' nursemaid in Central Park in New York and was unfit to be a mother; the mess cost him his car and a lease on the Hippodrome in New York, where he had ran high-level cards in 1937 and 1938.

Little wonder, then, that Fabiani was receptive to a cross-country move. In October 1941, he left Philadelphia to take over the Los Angeles wrestling office from George Zaharias, the husband of Babe Didrickson Zaharias, the greatest fe-male athlete of her time, and some would say, of all-time.

Londos was on the West Coast and still a headliner, but attendance was down as World War II approached. In 1942, Paul Zimmerman of the Los Angeles Times said Fabiani "performed some sort of a miracle" by keeping wrestling alive at the Olympic Auditorium. The sluggish business caught up with Fabiani, though, forcing him to declare bankruptcy in 1949.

Though Fabiani professed to be an advocate of straight-up wrestling, without a lot of sideshows and gimmicks, he tried to woo baseball Hall of Famer Jimmie Foxx into the ring in 1934 during his holdout with the old Philadelphia A's and was more responsible than anyone for signing boxing great Joe Louis to a sad effort at grunt-and-groan in 1956.

From 1950 to 1952, Fabiani promoted the Rainbow Arena in Chicago with Leonard Schwartz and Londos. He broke with Mondt in 1954, when Mondt used his power in the National Wrestling Alliance to parcel out wrestlers based on his whims. Lacking star power, Fabiani shut down some of his venues and claimed Mondt cost him more than $14,000.

When the National Wrestling Alliance designated Mondt and Rudy Dusek as promoters for Philadelphia, Fabiani used his clout with the state athletic commission to seize control of all Pennsylvania rights and elbow out Mondt. Various accounts credit Fabiani with bringing in Vincent James McMahon to the New York office around that time, though he ran several programs in 1956 in Washington, D.C., directly against McMahon's troupe.

Fabiani's top draw was the debt-riddled Louis, whom he brought into wrestling at a figure reported to be $100,000. Fabiani later talked about competing against McMahon with the help of Buddy Rogers, but eventually became partners with him in the World Wide Wrestling Federation. In fact, Fabiani offered to sell the Philadelphia territory to Sammartino, who declined because he was buying the Tri-State promotion, based in Pittsburgh.

In 1962, he was elected general manager of the merged Philadelphia Lyric and Philadelphia Grand Opera Companies at $20,000 a year. Fabiani continued his pursuit of outside interests, trying unsuccessfully in 1962 to woo an expansion American Football League team to Philadelphia. He continued through the 1960s as general manager of the Philadelphia Lyric Opera and became first president of the American Opera Association, a six-city consortium, in 1965. He left wrestling in 1971, handing off Philadelphia to Phil Zacko when a stroke left him partially paralyzed. He continued as co-manager of the opera company until his death on April 26, 1973, two days short of his 82nd birthday.

—*Steven Johnson with Greg Oliver*

CHAPTER FIFTY SEVEN

WRESTLING OBSERVER NEWSLETTER AWARDS

CATEGORY A AWARDS

The following are the results of the 35th annual Wrestling Observer Newsletter readership awards, along with a listing of the previous winners in the various categories. On a worldwide basis, these are the most covered mainstream international pro wrestling awards. The awards are based on the time frame from December 1, 2013 through November 30, 2014. Readers are encouraged to send in their comments on the results. Winners determined by points voted on a 5-3-2 basis. First place votes in parenthesis.

WRESTLER OF THE YEAR

1.	SHINSUKE NAKAMURA (323):	2,262
2.	A.J. Styles (188):	1,739
3.	Hiroshi Tanahashi (145):	1,563
4.	Kazuchika Okada (92):	1,268
5.	Daniel Bryan (55):	481
6.	Rush (37):	423
7.	Ricochet (8):	261
8.	John Cena (21):	206
9.	Seth Rollins (13):	199
10.	Brock Lesnar (17):	180

HONORABLE MENTION
Negro Casas 107, Atlantis 90

Shinsuke Nakamura, 34, who placed seventh last year, ended the three-year streak of Hiroshi Tanahashi in a four-way battle that had no obvious winner. Daniel Bryan was the odds-on winner until getting hurt, putting him out of action from May through the rest of the year. This opened the door up. A.J. Styles seemed the favorite, combining being the champion in New Japan, being a top guy on the U.S. indie scene and having killer matches, but Tanahashi beat him for the IWGP title in October. Tanahashi swept the three major awards in Japan (Weekly Pro, Tokyo Sports and Nikkan Sports), but still finished be-hind two New Japan-based stars in the attempt to win it for the fourth year in a row, something only Ric Flair has done. Nakamura passed Styles with late voting. I think that had something to do with the star power he exuded at the Tokyo Dome, and being more familiar to American voters. While G-1 was a killer tournament for all of the top four, Nakamura scored the highest in match quality, and dominated the IC title for most of the year. After regaining the title from Tanahashi, Nakamura elevated the title. Nakamura vs. Tanahashi for the IC title was the main event at the Tokyo Dome show as well as the Invasion Attack and New Beginning show. Nakamura's as IC champion or challenging for the title main evented eight of the company's 13 major PPV shows and he and Tanahashi's program early in the year elevated the belt to being almost the equal to the IWGP belt. Nakamura also won the New Japan Cup, and further elevated the IC belt by issuing a challenge for that belt instead of the IWGP belt when he won the tournament. Nakamura also lost to Okada in the finals of the G-1 Climax tournament. Okada and Styles also held the IWGP title during the year, with both having high match quality. Okada also won G-1 and defended the briefcase into the Tokyo Dome. The top four finishes of New Japan stars set the pace in the voting across most categories this year.

PREVIOUS WINNERS
1980 - Harley Race; 1981 - Ric Flair; 1982 - Ric Flair; 1983 - Ric Flair; 1984 - Ric Flair; 1985 - Ric Flair; 1986 - Ric Flair; 1987 - Riki Choshu; 1988 - Akira Maeda; 1989 - Ric Flair; 1990 - Ric Flair; 1991 - Jumbo Tsuruta; 1992 - Ric Flair; 1993 - Vader; 1994 - Toshiaki Kawada; 1995 - Mitsuharu Misawa; 1996 - Kenta Kobashi; 1997 - Mitsuharu Misawa; 1998 - Steve Austin; 1999 - Mitsuharu Misawa; 2000 - HHH; 2001 - Keiji Muto; 2002 - Kurt Angle; 2003 - Kenta Kobashi; 2004 - Kenta Kobashi; 2005 - Kenta Kobashi; 2006 - Mistico; 2007 - John Cena; 2008 - Chris Jericho; 2009 - Chris Jericho; 2010 - John Cena; 2011 - Hiroshi Tanahashi; 2012 - Hiroshi Tanahashi; 2013 - Hiroshi Tanahashi

MIXED MARTIAL ARTS MOST VALUABLE
1. RONDA ROUSEY (551): 3,503
2. Chris Weidman (75): 1,693
3. Jon Jones (49): 1,164
4. Conor McGregor (5): 323
5. Robbie Lawler (23): 265
6. Anderson Silva (4): 146
7. Daniel Cormier : 145
8. Johny Hendricks (6): 113
9. Donald Cerrone (3): : 85
10 . Tito Ortiz (2): 73

Rousey, 27, became the first woman ever to win one of the big five awards in a year. During our awards period she went 3-0, with three finishes, two of which were in less than 66 seconds and the last two were via striking instead of an armbar. Rousey's business numbers blew away anything that any woman in combat sports has ever done. In her ten pro and three amateur MMA fights, 11 of them didn't get past the 90 second mark. The overall depth and talent level isn't at the level of the men, but it's a level of division dominance that no fighter in UFC history has ever approached. Weidman went 2-0 during the period, with his second knockout of Anderson Silva and a win over Lyoto Machida, and headlined over Rousey in two of her three fights. Jones was generally considered the best male fighter in the game, but only fought once during the calender year, a decision win over Glover Teixeira, so he really couldn't win the big categories this year. McGregor was the fastest rising star, but went 2-0, with wins over Diego Brando and Dustin Poirier. He was valuable in the sense he put the featherweight division on the map, but he has yet to headline a PPV.

PREVIOUS WINNERS
2007 - Randy Couture; 2008 - Brock Lesnar; 2009 - Brock Lesnar; 2010 - Brock Lesnar; 2011 - Georges St-Pierre; 2012 - Anderson Silva; 2013 - Georges St-Pierre

MOST OUTSTANDING WRESTLER
1. A.J. STYLES (220):   1,819
2. Tomohiro Ishii (247):   1,671
3. Shinsuke Nakamura (190):   1,639
4. Kazuchika Okada (46):   697
5. Hiroshi Tanahashi (34):   604
6. Ricochet (54):   466
7. Sami Zayn (12):   289
8. Katsuyori Shibata (11):   182
9. Negro Casas (8):   179
10. Seth Rollins (4):   171

HONORABLE MENTION
Daniel Bryan 122, Kyle O'Reilly 96, Adam Cole 91, Kota Ibushi 72, Tetsuya Naito 71

A close top three race saw Styles (37-year-old Allan Jones) place second in first place votes, but win based on the most overall votes. Once again this was a category of New Japan dominance, as the promotion had six of the top eight finishers, and a seventh, Ricochet, worked a number of big matches for the group during the year. It's all a matter of opinion here as any of the top five could have been deserving winners as all had the level of years that could win this thing. After having won in 2012 and 2013, Tanahashi fell to fifth this year.

PREVIOUS WINNERS
1986 - Ric Flair; 1987 - Ric Flair; 1988 - Tatsumi Fujinami; 1989 - Ric Flair; 1990 - Jushin Liger; 1991 - Jushin Liger; 1992 - Jushin Liger; 1993 - Kenta Kobashi; 1994 - Kenta Kobashi; 1995 - Manami Toyota; 1996 - Rey Misterio Jr.; 1997 - Mitsuharu Misawa; 1998 - Koji Kanemoto; 1999 - Mitsuharu Misawa; 2000 - Chris Benoit; 2001 - Kurt Angle; 2002 - Kurt Angle; 2003 - Kurt Angle; 2004 - Chris Benoit; 2005 - Samoa Joe; 2006 - Bryan Danielson; 2007 - Bryan Danielson; 2008 - Bryan Danielson; 2009 - Bryan Danielson; 2010 - Daniel Bryan (Bryan Danielson); 2011 - Davey Richards; 2012 - Hiroshi Tanahashi; 2013 - Hiroshi Tanahashi

MOST OUTSTANDING FIGHTER
1.   RONDA ROUSEY (259): 2,164
2.   Chris Weidman (193): 1,486
3.   Demetrious Johnson (63): 690
4.   Robbie Lawler (89): 605
5.   Donald Cerrone (51): 552
6.   T.J. Dillashaw (13): 492
7.   Jose Aldo (39): 404
8.   Jon Jones (15): 287
9.   Daniel Cormier (12): 134
10.   Conor McGregor (3): 97

HONORABLE MENTION
Fabricio Werdum 63

Rousey performed a rare double here. In the past decade, the only other person to win Most Valuable and Most Outstanding in the same year was Anderson Silva in 2012. Rousey's three wins with three stoppages, two in the first round, beats out Weidman two wins, although Weidman's two wins, were of the highest caliber of competition. Johnson retained the flyweight title all year, with three wins, a knockout over top contender Joseph Benavidez, a dominant decision over Ali Bagautinov and a submission over Chris Cariaso. Lawler went 3-1 during the period, with a close loss to Johny Hendricks, which he avenged later in the year to win the welterweight title, plus he scored wins over Jake Ellenberger and Matt Brown. Cerrone went 4-0 during the year, with three finishes, and having already gone 2-0, he's off to the strongest start of 2015. Dillashaw went 3-0, including winning the bantamweight title from Renan Barao in one of the biggest title win upsets in MMA history, as Barao came in with a nine-year unbeaten streak.

PREVIOUS WINNERS
1997 - Maurice Smith; 1998 - Frank Shamrock; 1999 - Frank Shamrock; 2000 - Kazushi Sakuraba; 2001 - Wanderlei Silva; 2002 - Antonio Rodrigo Nogueira; 2003 - Randy Couture; 2004 - Wanderlei Silva; 2005 - Fedor Emelianenko; 2006 - Mirko Cro Cop; 2007 - Quinton Jackson; 2008 - Georges St. Pierre; 2009 - Georges St. Pierre; 2010 - Georges St. Pierre; 2011 - Jon Jones; 2012 - Anderson Silva; 2013 - Cain Velasquez

BEST BOX OFFICE DRAW
1.   RONDA ROUSEY (286):   1,825
2.   John Cena (129):   910
3.   Hiroshi Tanahashi (46):   838
4.   Shinsuke Nakamura (63):   559
5.   Brock Lesnar (53):   507
6.   Daniel Bryan (13):   263
7.   Chris Weidman (2):   261
8.   Atlantis (13):   235
9.   Anderson Silva (19):   166
10.   Ultimo Guerrero :   145

HONORABLE MENTION
Jon Jones 118, Conor McGregor 109, Kazuchika Okada 99

Rousey had more than double the first place votes of John Cena in a year where nobody really stood out. The win here gave Rousey three of the big five awards, and all three that she was eligible for. Rousey and Jon Jones were UFC's biggest draws, but since Jones only fought once, he wasn't going to win. Cena remained WWE's biggest draw and pro wrestling's biggest draw for the sixth straight year, including headlining 32 shows that drew more than 10,000 fans, his best numbers since 2011. Really, there was no great standout this year. UFC's biggest draws, Anderson Silva and Georges St-Pierre, were out of action. Jon Jones only fought once, against a non-draw, although to be fair, two of Rousey's opponents had even less name value than Glover Teixeira. The WWE drawing power lessens as time goes by because of the network model taking away from PPV's interest level and the company's pressure to put on shows that will draw. New Japan had a successful year, and Tanahashi and Nakamura were its stars, but New Japan is still not at the level of any number of hot promotions of the past, or even New Japan during most of its existence. Almost everyone's placing here comes more by default than anything.

PREVIOUS WINNERS
1997 - Hulk Hogan; 1998 - Steve Austin; 1999 - Steve Austin; 2000 - The Rock; 2001 - Kazushi Sakuraba; 2002 - Bob Sapp; 2003 - Bob Sapp; 2004 - Kenta Kobashi; 2005 - Kenta Kobashi; 2006 - Mistico; 2007 - John Cena; 2008 - Brock Lesnar; 2009 - Brock Lesnar; 2010 - Brock Lesnar; 2011 - The Rock; 2012 - The Rock; 2013 - Georges St-Pierre

FEUD OF THE YEAR

1.	JON JONES VS. DANIEL CORMIER (256):	1,792
2.	Daniel Bryan vs. The Authority (199):	1,424
3.	Rush vs. Negro Casas (97):	738
4.	Atlantis vs. Ultimo Guerrero (35):	648
5.	Hiroshi Tanahashi vs. Katsuyori Shibata (70):	527
6.	Adrian Neville vs. Sami Zayn (54):	523
7.	Ronda Rousey vs. Miesha Tate (51):	449
8.	Hiroshi Tanahashi vs. Shinsuke Nakamura (26):	423
9.	The Shield vs. The Wyatt Family (27):	390
10.	Tomohiro Ishii vs. Tetsuya Naito (44):	349

HONORABLE MENTION
Dean Ambrose vs. Seth Rollins 298, Evolution vs. The Shield 240, Brock Lesnar vs. John Cena 159, A.J. Styles vs. Kazuchika Okada 150, Jay Briscoe vs. Adam Cole 128, Luke Rockhold vs. Michael Bisping 73

This is also a first, as Jones vs. Cormier won without having one match during the calendar year. Their match in January drew the most interest, topping 750,000 North American PPV buys while going head-to-head with the NFL playoffs. A press conference brawl followed by some of the year's best promos by Cormier, and some of the best footage during media appearances after the brawl, saw it win without a match. Bryan vs. The Authority was the obvious pro wrestling winner, a storyline that wasn't even planned at the start of the year. The Bryan program as far as being a top guys was considered a cult run in late 2013 and they were going to move on. But a combination of the crowd rejecting Dave Bautista as a top babyface and C.M. Punk's departure pretty well forced the company's hand. Bryan's quest saved what otherwise could have been a lackluster WrestleMania with two Match of the Year candidates and a storyline people sunk their teeth into. But its abrupt ending, and the program was getting worse after WrestleMania, left it in second place.

PREVIOUS WINNERS
1980 - Bruno Sammartino vs. Larry Zbyszko; 1981 - Andre the Giant vs. Killer Khan; 1982 - Ted DiBiase vs. Junkyard Dog; 1983 - Freebirds vs. Von Erichs; 1984 - Freebirds vs. Von Erichs; 1985 - Ted DiBiase vs. Jim Duggan; 1986 - Hulk Hogan vs. Paul Orndorff; 1987 - Jerry Lawler vs. Austin Idol & Tommy Rich; 1988 - Midnight Express vs. Fantastics; 1989 - Ric Flair vs. Terry Funk; 1990 - Jumbo Tsuruta vs. Mitsuharu Misawa; 1991 - Jumbo Tsuruta & company vs. Mitsuharu Misawa & company; 1992 - Moondogs vs. Jerry Lawler & Jeff Jarrett; 1993 - Bret Hart vs. Jerry Lawler; 1994 - Los Gringos Locos vs. Mexican AAA; 1995 - Dean Malenko vs. Eddie Guerrero; 1996 - WCW vs. NWO; 1997 - Steve Austin vs. Hart Foundation; 1998 - Steve Austin vs. Vince McMahon; 1999 - Steve Austin vs. Vince McMahon; 2000 - HHH vs. Mick Foley; 2001 - Kazushi Sakuraba vs. Wanderlei Silva; 2002 - Ken Shamrock vs. Tito Ortiz; 2003 - Brock Lesnar vs. Kurt Angle; 2004 - HHH vs. Shawn Michaels vs. Chris Benoit; 2005 - Batista vs. HHH; 2006 - Tito Ortiz vs. Ken Shamrock; 2007 - Undertaker vs. Batista ; 2008 - Chris Jericho vs. Shawn Michaels; 2009 - C.M. Punk vs. Jeff Hardy; 2010 - Kevin Steen vs. El Generico; 2011 - John Cena vs. C.M. Punk; 2012 - Hiroshi Tanahashi vs. Kazuchika Okada; 2013 - Hiroshi Tanahashi vs. Kazuchika Okada

TAG TEAM OF THE YEAR

1.	YOUNG BUCKS (509):	3,374
2.	Bobby Fish & Kyle O'Reilly (159):	2,042
3.	T-Hawk & Eita (158):	1,344
4.	Usos (36):	731
5.	Masato Tanaka & Takashi Sugiura (56):	561
6.	Alex Shelley & Kushida (8):	479
7.	Goldust & Stardust (3):	101
8.	Luke Harper & Erick Rowan (2):	99

=9.   Eddie Edwards & Davey Richards (14):   92
=9.   Jun Akiyama & Takao Omori (10):   92

HONORABLE MENTION

Karl Anderson & Doc Gallows 89, Matt & Jeff Hardy 66, Hirooki Goto & Katsuyori Shibata 63, Mark & Jay Briscoe 61

Matt Massie, 29, and brother Nick, 25, better known at Matt & Nick Jackson, The Young Bucks, ran away with the award with a combination of non-stop wrestling action and clever marketing. The duo held the IWGP jr. heavyweight tag team titles and the ROH tag team titles during the year, and had a series of matches in ROH and Japan with second place finishers Redragon, Bobby Fish & Kyle O'Reilly, who ended the year with both sets of belts. T-Hawk & Eita, who held the Open the Twin Gate titles on three occasions during the awards period, and had some of the year's best tag team matches, placed third. They had far less exposure worldwide than the other two teams. The Usos, who held the WWE tag titles twice during the year, and Masato Tanaka & Takashi Sugiura, holding the tag titles in Pro Wrestling NOAH and Zero-One at the same time, en route to winning the big three awards in Japan, rounded out the top five.

PREVIOUS WINNERS

1980 - Freebirds (Terry Gordy & Buddy Roberts); 1981 - Terry Gordy & Jimmy Snuka; 1982 - Stan Hansen & Ole Anderson; 1983 - Ricky Steamboat & Jay Youngblood; 1984 - Road Warriors; 1985 - British Bulldogs (Dynamite Kid & Davey Boy Smith); 1986 - Midnight Express (Dennis Condrey & Bobby Eaton); 1987 - Midnight Express (Bobby Eaton & Stan Lane); 1988 - Midnight Express (Bobby Eaton & Stan Lane); 1989 - The Rockers (Shawn Michaels & Marty Jannetty); 1990 - Rick & Scott Steiner; 1991 - Mitsuharu Misawa & Toshiaki Kawada; 1992 - Miracle Violence Combination (Steve Williams & Terry Gordy); 1993 - Hollywood Blondes (Brian Pillman & Steve Austin); 1994 - Los Gringos Locos (Love Machine Art Barr & Eddie Guerrero); 1995 - Mitsuharu Misawa & Kenta Kobashi; 1996 - Mitsuharu Misawa & Jun Akiyama; 1997 - Mitsuharu Misawa & Jun Akiyama; 1998 - Shinjiro Otani & Tatsuhito Takaiwa; 1999 - Kenta Kobashi & Jun Akiyama; 2000 - Edge & Christian; 2001 - TenKoji (Hiroyoshi Tenzan & Satoshi Kojima); 2002 - Eddie & Chavo Guerrero; 2003 - KENTA & Naomichi Marufuji; 2004 - KENTA & Naomichi Marufuji; 2005 - America's Most Wanted (Chris Harris & James Storm); 2006 - LAX (Homicide & Hernandez); 2007 - Mark & Jay Briscoe; 2008 - The Miz & John Morrison; 2009 - Eddie Edwards & Davey Richards; 2010 - Chris Hero & Claudio Castagnoli; 2011 - Giant Bernard (Tensai) & Karl Anderson; 2012 - Christopher Daniels & Frankie Kazarian; 2013 - Seth Rollins & Roman Reigns

MOST IMPROVED

1.	RUSEV (181):	1,372
2.	Charlotte (152):	1,281
3.	Sasha Banks (2):	383
4.	Erick Rowan (41):	313
5.	Luke Harper (15):	241
6.	Bobby Lashley (19):	205
7.	Tomoaki Honma (19):	182
8.	Cedric Alexander (22):	172
9.	Ethan Carter III (19):	154
10.	Tomohiro Ishii (18):	137

HONORABLE MENTION

Seth Rollins 127, Kyle O'Reilly 125, T-Hawk 199, Tyler Breeze 114, Daisuke Harada 99, Joe Doering 92, Ricochet 90, Nikki Bella 89, Jay Lethal 78, Hanson 74, Roman Reigns 70, Adam Cole 63

The WWE had the top five finishers in one of the closest awards race of all. Rusev (29-year-old Miroslav Barnyashev, who really was born in Bulgaria) went from a very limited performer to one of the company's hottest heel acts in combination with real-life girlfriend Catherine Jo Perry (Lana). Charlotte (28-year-old Ashley Fliehr-Latimer, the daughter of Ric Flair and husband of TNA's Thomas "Bram" Latimer) took a close second. The most accomplished athlete in the WWE's women's division, as a volleyball and gymnastics star growing up, Charlotte has the potential to bring women's wrestling up a notch in both popularity and respectability if handle correctly. Her leading rival right now in NXT, Sasha Banks, 22-year-old Mercedes Kaestner-Varnado, has the poise right now to where, like Charlotte, she should be a main roster star right now. Some of the other picks are a little more questionable. Tomoaki Honma and Tomohiro Ishii are in more of a spotlight role, but both have been great workers for years. Ditto Luke Harper, who has gotten more a chance to show his wares, but he's not significantly better than he's been for a long time. Similarly, Bobby Lashley has been pushed smarter than in the past with a long and dominant TNA title run, but it's more improved booking than an improved wrestler.

PREVIOUS WINNERS

1980 - Larry Zbyszko; 1981 - Adrian Adonis; 1982 - Jim Duggan; 1983 - Curt Hennig; 1984 - The Cobra (George Takano); 1985 - Steve Williams; 1986 - Rick Steiner; 1987 - Big Bubba Rogers (Ray Traylor); 1988 - Sting; 1989 - Lex Luger; 1990 - Kenta Kobashi;

1991 - Dustin Rhodes; 1992 - El Samurai; 1993 - Tracy Smothers; 1994 - Diesel (Kevin Nash); 1995 - Johnny B. Badd (Marc Mero); 1996 - Diamond Dallas Page; 1997 - Tatsuhito Takaiwa; 1998 - The Rock; 1999 - Vader; 2000 - Kurt Angle; 2001 - Keiji Muto; 2002 - Brock Lesnar; 2003 - Brock Lesnar; 2004 - Randy Orton; 2005 - Roderick Strong; 2006 - Takeshi Morishima; 2007 - MVP; 2008 - The Miz; 2009 - The Miz; 2010 - Sheamus; 2011 - Dolph Ziggler; 2012 - Kazuchika Okada; 2013 - Roman Reigns

BEST ON INTERVIEWS

1.	PAUL HEYMAN (411):	4,395
2.	Conor McGregor (169):	1,675
3.	Jay Briscoe (44):	582
4.	Michael Bisping (20):	452
5.	Stephanie McMahon (25):	417
6.	Daniel Cormier (3):	387
7.	Adam Cole (21):	277
8.	Dean Ambrose (11):	193
9.	Bray Wyatt (7):	139
10.	Lana (7):	131

HONORABLE MENTION
Bruce Tharpe 116, Sami Zayn 90, Daniel Bryan 74, Rush 71

Paul Heyman, 48, ran away with the category for the second straight year, after winning a close race last year over C.M. Punk. With Punk out, the strong No. 2 was Conor McGregor and nobody else was even strong in the running. Most notable here is John Cena, who has won the award in the past and finished 6th last year, got almost no votes. Cena, at his best, is right at the top in pro wrestling. He thinks well on his feet, but his scripted material got a lot worse as the year went on, particularly after Vince McMahon took over more complete control of Raw.

PREVIOUS WINNERS
1981 - Lou Albano and Roddy Piper (tied); 1982 - Roddy Piper; 1983 - Roddy Piper; 1984 - Jimmy Hart; 1985 - Jim Cornette; 1986 - Jim Cornette; 1987 - Jim Cornette; 1988 - Jim Cornette; 1989 - Terry Funk; 1990 - Arn Anderson; 1991 - Ric Flair; 1992 - Ric Flair; 1993 - Jim Cornette; 1994 - Ric Flair; 1995 - Cactus Jack (Mick Foley); 1996 - Steve Austin; 1997 - Steve Austin; 1998 - Steve Austin; 1999 - The Rock; 2000 - The Rock; 2001 - Steve Austin; 2002 - Kurt Angle; 2003 - Chris Jericho; 2004 - Mick Foley; 2005 - Eddie Guerrero; 2006 - Mick Foley; 2007 - John Cena; 2008 - Chris Jericho; 2009 - Chris Jericho; 2010 - Chael Sonnen; 2011 - C.M. Punk; 2012 - C.M. Punk; 2013 - Paul Heyman

MOST CHARISMATIC

1.	SHINSUKE NAKAMURA (421):	2,527
2.	Hiroshi Tanahashi (71):	1,015
3.	Conor McGregor (136):	993
4.	Daniel Bryan (73):	638
5.	John Cena (37):	532
6.	Sami Zayn (16):	437
7.	Dean Ambrose (17):	391
8.	Ronda Rousey (29):	363
9.	Brock Lesnar (28):	255
10.	Rush (19):	232

HONORABLE MENTION
Kazuchika Okada 217, Akira Tozawa 115, Negro Casas 91, Jay Briscoe 99, Tomoaki Honma 82

This was both one-sided and expected. Shinsuke Nakamura came from fifth place last year, behind Hiroshi Tanahashi, The Rock, John Cena and Daniel Bryan, to running away with things this year. Once again, this was a category Bryan had a shot at winning if he wasn't out of action for more than half the year. Even with Bryan back full-time and McGregor being higher profile, Nakamura is probably a big favorite to repeat here because it feels right now like he's that far ahead of the field.

PREVIOUS WINNERS
1980 - Ric Flair; 1981 - Michael Hayes; 1982 - Dusty Rhodes and Ric Flair (tied); 1983 - Ric Flair; 1984 - Ric Flair; 1985 - Hulk Hogan; 1986 - Hulk Hogan; 1987 - Hulk Hogan; 1988 - Sting; 1989 - Hulk Hogan; 1990 - Hulk Hogan; 1991 - Hulk Hogan; 1992 - Sting; 1993 - Ric Flair; 1994 - Atsushi Onita; 1995 - Shawn Michaels; 1996 - Shawn Michaels; 1997 - Steve Austin; 1998 - Steve Austin; 1999 - The Rock; 2000 - The Rock; 2001 - The Rock; 2002 - The Rock; 2003 - Bob Sapp; 2004 - Eddie Guerrero; 2005 - Eddie Guerrero;

2006 - John Cena; 2007 - John Cena; 2008 - John Cena; 2009 - John Cena; 2010 - John Cena; 2011 - The Rock; 2012 - The Rock; 2013 - Hiroshi Tanahashi

BEST TECHNICAL WRESTLER

1.	ZACK SABRE JR. (145):	1,221
2.	Kyle O'Reilly (78):	841
3.	A.J. Styles (58):	610
4.	Hiroshi Tanahashi (61):	588
5.	Daniel Bryan (62):	517
6.	Shinsuke Nakamura (75):	506
7.	Cesaro (34):	461
8.	Kazuchika Okada (55):	460
9.	Timothy Thatcher (64):	407
10.	Minoru Suzuki (46):	401

HONORABLE MENTION

Virus 350, Drew Gulak 289, Sami Zayn 203, Kushida 155, Katsuyori Shibata 117, Yuji Nagata 92, Cima 90

Daniel Bryan's neck injury ended his streak of taking this award at nine straight years. He may have won some on reputation, but it's one of the most dominant runs of any award in history. This was one of the most spread-out voting of any award, with the U.K. based Sabre, 27, moving up from 5th place last year, even though he was mostly a lower card wrestler with Pro Wrestling NOAH. Sabre finished well ahead of ROH and New Japan's Kyle O'Reilly, whose style is based on using legitimate moves in Jiu Jitsu and figuring out a way to make them work in a dramatic wrestling contest. The big names, Styles, Tanahashi, Bryan and Nakamura took the next four spots. Timothy Thatcher, a West Coast based independent wrestler, cracked the top ten.

PREVIOUS WINNERS

1980 - Bob Backlund; 1981 - Ted DiBiase; 1982 - Tiger Mask (Satoru Sayama); 1983 - Tiger Mask; 1984 - Dynamite Kid and Masa Saito (tied); 1985 - Tatsumi Fujinami; 1986 - Tatsumi Fujinami; 1987 - Nobuhiko Takada; 1988 - Tatsumi Fujinami; 1989 - Jushin Liger; 1990 - Jushin Liger; 1991 - Jushin Liger; 1992 - Jushin Liger; 1993 - Hiroshi Hase; 1994 - Chris Benoit; 1995 - Chris Benoit; 1996 - Dean Malenko; 1997 - Dean Malenko; 1998 - Kiyoshi Tamura; 1999 - Shinjiro Otani; 2000 - Chris Benoit; 2001 - Minoru Tanaka; 2002 - Kurt Angle; 2003 - Chris Benoit; 2004 - Chris Benoit; 2005 - Bryan Danielson; 2006 - Bryan Danielson; 2007 - Bryan Danielson; 2008 - Bryan Danielson; 2009 - Bryan Danielson; 2010 - Daniel Bryan; 2011 - Daniel Bryan; 2012 - Daniel Bryan; 2013 - Daniel Bryan

BRUISER BRODY MEMORIAL AWARD (BEST BRAWLER)

1.	TOMOHIRO ISHII (424):	2,785
2.	Katsuyori Shibata (181):	1,834
3.	Dean Ambrose (42):	781
4.	Kevin Steen (30):	532
5.	Jay Briscoe (48):	367
6.	Togi Makabe (28):	316
7.	Brock Lesnar (32):	278
8.	Luke Harper (8):	194
9.	Hirooki Goto (1):	154
10.	Minoru Suzuki (2):	128

HONORABLE MENTION

Takashi Sugiura 99, Bray Wyatt 75, Bully Ray 63

Ishii, 39, won the first major Observer award of his career after a year where he had some of the best matches, battling for match of the night in the world's deepest promotion. Ishii took second last year to this year's second place finisher, Katsuyori Shibata. Ishii is the ultimate example of a guy who was destined to just be a decent worker on the undercard, who garnered a cult following in Tokyo, which spread to the rest of the country and resulted in him getting a push. Still, as much as he seems to have a superhuman ability to take punishment, his knee and shoulder were both banged up this year, and he didn't miss a beat, being in the best brawls of the year virtually working with one arm. Of course, the lessons of Shinya Hashimoto in not taking time off for shoulder problems and not getting them taken care of is not a long-term wise decision. With his age and injuries, combined with his style, longevity is not likely to be his friend.

PREVIOUS WINNERS

1980 - Bruiser Brody; 1981 - Bruiser Brody; 1982 - Bruiser Brody; 1983 - Bruiser Brody; 1984 - Bruiser Brody; 1985 - Stan Hansen;

1986 - Terry Gordy; 1987 - Bruiser Brody; 1988 - Bruiser Brody; 1989 - Terry Funk; 1990 - Stan Hansen; 1991 - Cactus Jack (Mick Foley); 1992 - Cactus Jack; 1993 - Cactus Jack; 1994 - Cactus Jack; 1995 - Cactus Jack; 1996 - Mankind (Mick Foley); 1997 - Mankind; 1998 - Mankind; 1999 - Mick Foley; 2000 - Mick Foley; 2001 - Steve Austin; 2002 - Yoshihiro Takayama; 2003 - Brock Lesnar; 2004 - Chris Benoit; 2005 - Samoa Joe; 2006 - Samoa Joe; 2007 - Takeshi Morishima; 2008 - Necro Butcher; 2009 - Necro Butcher; 2010 - Kevin Steen; 2011 - Kevin Steen; 2012 - Kevin Steen; 2013 - Katsuyori Shibata

BEST FLYING WRESTLER

1.	RICOCHET (543):	3,365
2.	Kota Ibushi (142):	1,907
3.	Flamita (104):	1,182
4.	Adrian Neville (42):	909
5.	ACH (18):	371
6.	Fenix (9):	309
7.	Aero Star (2):	287
8.	Titan (35):	273
9.	Sami Zayn (19):	270
10.	Mascara Dorada (17):	199

HONORABLE MENTION
Kushida 100, Kalisto 72, T-Hawk 70

Ricochet, 26-year-old Trevor Mann, capped off his biggest career year to date, which got him in the top ten for Wrestler of the Year. He was the first non-Japanese wrestler to win the Open the Dream Gate title, the leading belt in Dragon Gate, as well as taking the Open the Freedom Gate title, the leading belt in Dragon Gate USA/Evolve, and winning Lucha Underground's title under a mask as Prince Puma and being one of that television show's most -pushed commodities. He also won this year's Best of the Super Junior tournament in New Japan, leading to an excellent junior heavyweight title challenge to second place finisher Kota Ibushi. Ricochet, who previously won the award in 2011, finished ahead of four-time previous winner Ibushi of DDT and New Japan Pro Wrestling. The two flip-flopped their top two positions last year, with Ibushi, now 32, winning by a wide margin last year. New to the top ten are Fenix and Titan, who were both Honorable Mentions in 2014, and newcomers Aero Star and Flamita.

PREVIOUS WINNERS
1981 - Jimmy Snuka; 1982 - Tiger Mask (Satoru Sayama); 1983 - Tiger Mask (Satoru Sayama); 1984 - Dynamite Kid; 1985 - Tiger Mask (Mitsuharu Misawa); 1986 - Tiger Mask (Mitsuharu Misawa); 1987 - Owen Hart; 1988 - Owen Hart; 1989 - Jushin Liger; 1990 - Jushin Liger; 1991 - Jushin Liger; 1992 - Jushin Liger; 1993 - Jushin Liger; 1994 - Great Sasuke; 1995 - Rey Misterio Jr.; 1996 - Rey Misterio Jr.; 1997 - Rey Misterio Jr.; 1998 - Juventud Guerrera; 1999 - Juventud Guerrera; 2000 - Jeff Hardy; 2001 - Dragon Kid; 2002 - Rey Mysterio; 2003 - Rey Mysterio; 2004 - Rey Mysterio; 2005 - A.J. Styles; 2006 - Mistico; 2007 - Mistico; 2008 - Evan Bourne; 2009 - Kota Ibushi; 2010 - Kota Ibushi; 2011 - Ricochet; 2012 - Kota Ibushi; 2013 - Kota Ibushi

MOST OVERRATED

1.	KANE (143):	1,117
2.	Roman Reigns (145):	1,113
3.	Randy Orton (5):	397
4.	Big Show (23):	357
5.	Ryback (18):	331
6.	Michael Elgin(49):	326
7.	Bray Wyatt (26):	225
8.	Yujiro Takahashi (27):	218
9.	John Cena (25):	197
10.	Batista (15):	166

HONORABLE MENTION
The Miz 105, HHH 99, Brock Lesnar 97, The Ascension 72, Bad Luck Fale 63

Glen Jacobs, a 47-year old veteran of 23 years after playing college football and basketball, won the only category that came down to the final ballot. Kane won the award in 2010. Second place Roman Reigns, 29-year-old Leati Joe Anoa'i, who WWE has been grooming to be its future flagship star made the list because he's probably not fully ready for the level he's being pushed. Randy Orton, last year's winner, placed a very distant third.

PREVIOUS WINNERS

1980 - Mr. Wrestling II (Johnny Walker); 1981 - Pedro Morales; 1982 - Pedro Morales; 1983 - Bob Backlund; 1984 - John Studd; 1985 - Hulk Hogan; 1986 - Hulk Hogan; 1987 - Dusty Rhodes; 1988 - Dusty Rhodes; 1989 - Ultimate Warrior; 1990 - Ultimate Warrior; 1991 - Ultimate Warrior; 1992 - Erik Watts; 1993 - Sid Vicious; 1994 - Hulk Hogan; 1995 - Hulk Hogan; 1996 - Hulk Hogan; 1997 - Hulk Hogan; 1998 - Hulk Hogan; 1999 - Kevin Nash; 2000 - Kevin Nash; 2001 - The Undertaker; 2002 - HHH; 2003 - HHH; 2004 - HHH; 2005 - Jeff Jarrett; 2006 - Batista; 2007 - Great Khali; 2008 - Vladimir Kozlov; 2009 - HHH; 2010 - Kane; 2011 - Crimson; 2012 - Ryback; 2013 - Randy Orton

MOST UNDERRATED

1.	CESARO (377):	2,275
2.	Tomoaki Honma (99):	1,189
3.	Tyson Kidd (29):	585
4.	Dolph Ziggler (35):	422
5.	Sami Zayn (16):	252
6.	Dean Ambrose (18):	175
7.	Yuji Nagata (1):	102
8.	Chris Hero (8):	70
9.	Katsuyori Shibata (10):	63
10.	Austin Aries (1):	58

Claudio Castagnoli, 34, won this by a wide margin for the second straight year. This year was more frustrating because he was on the verge of big things with fans getting behind what they expected would be a babyface turn. Before WrestleMania, WWE told people it did business with that Cesaro would be one of the top babyfaces for later in the year. Then it fell apart. They did a heel turn to put him with Paul Heyman, and apparently figured that enabled them to not give him wins at all since Heyman was with him. The idea that they'd beat him like a drum, but he'd stay over before his big babyface turn fell completely apart and the turn was forgotten about. Now there's a question if he'll ever get the green light, particularly since Vince McMahon openly stated he was missing a connection with the audience. Tomoaki Honma, 38, who was top ten last year, lucked into Kota Ibushi's injury spot in the G-1 Climax tournament. He lost every match, but had some of the best matches of the tournament and came off as a bigger star. In fact, he lost every major singles match he was in, and was always there to provide action and be the guy who gets the top guys over. Honma will probably never be pushed as a major star in New Japan, but looks like he'll retain his cult favorite level and have some of the better matches going forward. At best he can hope for is to go from a late replacement and sneaking into G-1, to being someone expected to be a key part of it this year. Tyson Kidd, who was sixth last year, moved up to third this year. A previous winner in 2012, his combination of being such a top level worker and someone who has a character but a cat-lover gimmick that gets him on the field but won't get him pushed past a certain level, and with his size, makes him someone who will be a career place winner here. Dolph Ziggler, the 2011 winner, is another. Ziggler has been the victim of as many stop-and-start pushes of anyone in history. The crowds always get behind him for the start, no matter how many false teases there are, and then a few weeks later, the company always takes him back down.

PREVIOUS WINNERS
1980 - Iron Sheik; 1981 - Buzz Sawyer; 1982 - Adrian Adonis; 1983 - Dynamite Kid; 1984 - Brian Blair; 1985 - Bobby Eaton; 1986 - Bobby Eaton; 1987 - Brad Armstrong; 1988 - Tiger Mask (Mitsuharu Misawa); 1989 - Dan Kroffat (Phil LaFon); 1990 - Bobby Eaton; 1991 - Terry Taylor; 1992 - Terry Taylor; 1993 - Bobby Eaton; 1994 - Brian Pillman; 1995 - Skip (Chris Candito); 1996 - Leif Cassidy (Al Snow); 1997 - Flash Funk (Too Cold Scorpio); 1998 - Chris Benoit; 1999 - Chris Jericho; 2000 - Chris Jericho; 2001 - Lance Storm; 2002 - Booker T; 2003 - Ultimo Dragon; 2004 - Paul London; 2005 - Shelton Benjamin; 2006 - Shelton Benjamin; 2007 - Shelton Benjamin; 2008 - MVP; 2009 - Evan Bourne; 2010 - Kaval (Low Ki); 2011 - Dolph Ziggler; 2012 - Tyson Kidd; 2013- Antonio Cesaro

BEST PROMOTION

1.	NEW JAPAN PRO WRESTLING (779):	4,064
2.	Ring of Honor (16):	1,038
3.	Dragon Gate (36):	884
4.	Ultimate Fighting Championships (23):	835
5.	CMLL (8):	504
6.	World Wrestling Entertainment (4):	392
7.	Pro Wrestling Guerrilla (8):	348
8.	AAA (3):	279
9.	Bellator MMA (3):	238
10.	DDT (1):	91

HONORABLE MENTION
This was as dominant a year as voting in this category has ever been. New Japan's big shows were at a different level, and they

increased business at a major level during the year, being well over double the level they were just two years ago. But they followed WWE's lead in creating New Japan World, and early numbers indicate that isn't knocking them dead at all. The difference is they went in with far lower expectations so they aren't going to be having to do the cuts WWE did this year. The two major groups had problems this past year, UFC with injuries devastating its main event picture, particularly on PPV, and running so many events that only a couple of shows seemed special. Still, their show quality was high as a general rule. WWE also produced some of the best PPV shows in its history over the past year and the work quality was better than most years. But their television was not good. ROH improved its business, with regular dates from A.J. Styles and Matt Hardy, until Hardy went with TNA, and the emergence of teams like Redragon, The Young Bucks and Christopher Daniels & Frankie Kazarian after they were part of TNA's budget purging. Adam Cole and Jay Briscoe both improved their games as singles headliners and the company slowly has expanded its domestic TV distribution. But while their TV audiences in 2015 will be at the same level as TNA, and they are in the house show and PPV businesses that TNA seems out of, they are still well behind in international distribution.

PREVIOUS WINNERS
1983 - Jim Crockett Promotions; 1984 - New Japan Pro Wrestling; 1985 - All Japan Pro Wrestling; 1986 - Mid South Wrestling; 1987 - New Japan Pro Wrestling; 1988 - New Japan Pro Wrestling; 1989 - Universal Wrestling Federation Japan; 1990 - All Japan Pro Wrestling; 1991 - All Japan Pro Wrestling; 1992 - New Japan Pro Wrestling; 1993 - All Japan Pro Wrestling; 1994 - AAA; 1995 - New Japan Pro Wrestling; 1996 - New Japan Pro Wrestling; 1997 - New Japan Pro Wrestling; 1998 - New Japan Pro Wrestling; 1999 - World Wrestling Federation; 2000 - World Wrestling Federation; 2001 - Pride Fighting Championships; 2002 - Pride Fighting Championships; 2003 - Pride Fighting Championships; 2004 - Pro Wrestling NOAH; 2005 - Pro Wrestling NOAH; 2006 - Ultimate Fighting Championships; 2007 - Ultimate Fighting Championships; 2008 - Ultimate Fighting Championships; 2009 - Ultimate Fighting Championships; 2010 - Ultimate Fighting Championships; 2011 - Ultimate Fighting Championships; 2012 - New Japan Pro Wrestling; 2013 - New Japan Pro Wrestling

BEST WEEKLY TELEVISION SHOW
1.	WWE NXT (416):	2,961
2.	Ring of Honor (175):	1,744
3.	Lucha Underground (106):	1,369
4.	Dragon Gate Infinity (100):	838
5.	Ultimate Fighter Season 20 (76):	796
6.	WWE Raw (2):	234
7.	NJPW World Pro Wrestling (28):	226
8.	TNA Impact (2):	110
9.	WWE Smackdown (9):	88
10.	WWE Main Event (2):	84

HONORABLE MENTION
CMLL 72

This is a funny one to me. There was no television show that to me was a winner, and perhaps Dragon Gate Infinity is really the best at serving all masters. NXT is a solid show. It's a throwback to a better than average old school territorial pro wrestling show where the job is to build up the big show and constantly create new characters, with a roster combining green guys on the way up and some very good working stars. The plus is they had some very good wrestlers this year, most notably Sami Zayn and Adrian Neville, to build around, the huge success with the women's division built around Charlotte. So it was like a small territory that had better wrestlers than usual and was hotter than usual, but was definitely not a major territory. ROH is similar in the sense it comes across as a different concept of old school. ROH has more emphasis on longer matches, but the goal is the same, to build the quarterly major shows. They have better overall talent, and far more depth, but have a much smaller production budget so the NXT show has a far better look. Lucha Underground is a different concept, as it feels like a television drama that happens to center around a wrestling promotion. Still, their in-ring as a general rule blows away NXT, as does its acting, and the production is different. They also have introduced new concepts to wrestling, some of which have been good, others haven't worked as well. But it lacks the destination. Having to do with distribution on a weak channel, its growth has been limited. But in comparing the top three shows on this list week-to-week, Lucha Underground has been the better show most weeks.

PREVIOUS WINNERS
1983 - New Japan World Pro Wrestling; 1984 - New Japan World Pro Wrestling; 1985 - Mid South Wrestling; 1986 - Universal Wrestling Federation (Mid South Wrestling: 1987 - CWA 90 Minute Memphis live show; 1988 - New Japan World Pro Wrestling; 1989 - All Japan Pro Wrestling; 1990 - All Japan Pro Wrestling; 1991 - All Japan Pro Wrestling; 1992 - All Japan Pro Wrestling; 1993 - All Japan Pro Wrestling; 1994 - Extreme Championship Wrestling; 1995 - Extreme Championship Wrestling; 1996 - Extreme Championship Wrestling; 1997 - New Japan World Pro Wrestling; 1998 - WWF Raw is War; 1999 - WWF Raw is War; 2000 - WWF Raw is War; 2001 - New Japan World Pro Wrestling; 2002 - WWE Smackdown; 2003 - Pro Wrestling NOAH; 2004 - WWE Raw;

2005 - UFC Ultimate Fighter; 2006 - UFC Ultimate Fighter; 2007 - UFC Ultimate Fighter; 2008 - UFC Ultimate Fighter; 2009 - WWE Smackdown; 2010 - Ring of Honor; 2011 - WWE Smackdown; 2012 - TNA Impact; 2013 WWE NXT

PRO WRESTLING MATCH OF THE YEAR

1.	A.J. STYLES VS. MINORU SUZUKI 8/1 TOKYO (298):	1,855
2.	Kazuchika Okada vs. Shinsuke Nakamura 8/10 Tokorozawa (143):	1,310
3.	Hiroshi Tanahashi vs. Katsuyori Shibata 9/21 Kobe (74):	524
4.	Atlantis vs. Ultimo Guerrero 9/19 Mexico City (49):	522
5.	Tomohiro Ishii vs. Hirooki Goto 11/8 Osaka (47):	471
6.	The Shield vs. The Wyatts 2/23 Minneapolis (37):	417
7.	Katsuyori Shibata vs. Tomoaki Honma 8/3 Osaka (10):	330
8.	Daniel Bryan vs. HHH 4/6 New Orleans (25):	287
9.	Tomohiro Ishii vs. Tetsuya Naito 2/11 Osaka (20):	226
10.	Tomohiro Ishii vs. Tomoaki Honma 7/26 Akita (19):	181

HONORABLE MENTION

Kazuchika Okada vs. Kota Ibushi 3/6 Tokyo 166, Brock Lesnar vs. John Cena 8/17 Los Angeles 136, Daniel Bryan vs. Batista vs. Randy Orton 4/6 New Orleans 132, Shinsuke Nakamura vs. Tomohiro Ishii 8/1 Tokyo 108, Hiroshi Tanahashi vs. Katsuyori Shibata 7/26 Akita 102, El Texano Jr. vs. Psycho Clown 8/18 Mexico City 75, Tomohiro Ishii vs. Kota Ibushi 5/25 Yokohama 72, Cesaro vs. Sami Zayn 2/27 Winter Park, FL 72, Yuji Nagata vs. Katsuyori Shibata 8/1 Tokyo 64, Ricochet vs. Kushida 6/8 Tokyo 63, Prince Puma vs. Johnny Mundo 10/29 Boyle Heights, CA 62

The dominance of New Japan is evident here, with eight of the top 11 coming from the promotion. And if anything, that's been a hindrance to New Japan, not a help. There were multiple matches in the G-1, and throughout the year on big shows that were better than the non-New Japan matches that placed or got honorable mention, but when you have a G-1 like this past year, great matches became so commonplace they were forgotten. Styles vs. Suzuki wasn't even the main event on the 8/1 Korakuen Hall show. Where it stood out was it was different from any of the others. The funny part is that both wrestlers, when it was over, knew they had done a good match, but it wasn't until they read feedback the next day, which surprised both, that they had any inclination it was a match of the year candidate, let alone a potential winner. Atlantis vs. Guerrero, which finished fourth, was a very good match, but it was more the post-match that made it. If you include the post-match, it was the best overall match presentation in many years. Perhaps Daniel Bryan's WrestleMania win was the only thing close in that realm. And I'm not even sure that was close.

PREVIOUS WINNERS

1980 - Bob Backlund vs. Ken Patera 5/19 New York Madison Square Garden; 1981 - Pat Patterson vs. Sgt. Slaughter 4/21 New York Madison Square Garden; 1982 - Tiger Mask (Satoru Sayama) vs. Dynamite Kid 8/5 Tokyo; 1983 - Ric Flair vs. Harley Race 11/24 Greensboro; 1984 - Freebirds vs. Von Erichs 7/4 Fort Worth; 1985 - Tiger Mask (Mitsuharu Misawa) vs. Kuniaki Kobayashi 6/12 Tokyo; 1986 - Ric Flair vs. Barry Windham 2/14 Orlando; 1987 - Ricky Steamboat vs. Randy Savage 3/29 Pontiac; 1988 - Ric Flair vs. Sting 3/27 Greensboro; 1989 - Ric Flair vs. Ricky Steamboat 4/2 New Orleans; 1990 - Jushin Liger vs. Naoki Sano (Takuma Sano) 1/31 Osaka; 1991 - Rick & Scott Steiner vs. Hiroshi Hase & Kensuke Sasaki 3/21 Tokyo; 1992 - Dan Kroffat & Doug Furnas vs. Kenta Kobashi & Tsuyoshi Kikuchi 5/25 Sendai; 1993 - Manami Toyota & Toshiyo Yamada vs. Dynamite Kansai & Mayumi Ozaki 4/21 Osaka; 1994 - Shawn Michaels vs. Razor Ramon (Scott Hall) 3/20 New York Madison Square Garden; 1995 - Manami Toyota vs. Kyoko Inoue 5/7 Tokyo; 1996 - Mitsuharu Misawa & Jun Akiyama vs. Steve Williams & Johnny Ace 6/7 Tokyo; 1997 - Bret Hart vs. Steve Austin 3/23 Chicago; 1998 - Mitsuharu Misawa vs. Kenta Kobashi 10/31 Tokyo; 1999 - Mitsuharu Misawa vs. Kenta Kobashi 6/11 Tokyo; 2000 - Atlantis vs. Villano III 3/17 Mexico City; 2001 - Keiji Muto vs. Genichiro Tenryu 6/8 Tokyo; 2002 - Chris Benoit & Kurt Angle vs. Edge & Rey Mysterio 10/20 Little Rock; 2003 - Mitsuharu Misawa vs. Kenta Kobashi 3/1 Tokyo; 2004 - Kenta Kobashi vs. Jun Akiyama 7/10 Tokyo Dome; 2005 - Kenta Kobashi vs. Samoa Joe 10/1 New York; 2006 - Dragon Kid & Ryo Saito & Genki Horiguchi vs. Cima & Naruki Doi & Masato Yoshino 3/31 Chicago; 2007 - Bryan Danielson vs. Takeshi Morishima 8/25 New York; 2008 - Shawn Michaels vs. Chris Jericho 10/5 Portland, OR; 2009 - Undertaker vs. Shawn Michaels 4/5 Houston; 2010 - Undertaker vs. Shawn Michaels 3/28 Phoenix; 2011 - John Cena vs. C.M. Punk 7/17 Chicago; 2012 - Hiroshi Tanahashi vs. Minoru Suzuki 10/8 Tokyo; 2013 - Hiroshi Tanahashi vs. Kazuchika Okada 4/7 Tokyo

MMA MATCH OF THE YEAR

1.	ROBBIE LAWLER VS. JOHNY HENDRICKS 3/15 DALLAS (225): 1,724	
2.	Matt Brown vs. Erick Silva 5/10 Cincinnati (113): 1,371	
3.	Mark Hunt vs. Antonio Silva 12/8/13 Sydney (217): 1,353	
4.	Chris Weidman vs. Lyoto Machida 7/5 Las Vegas (86): 982	
5.	Ronda Rousey vs. Miesha Tate 12/28/13 Las Vegas (97): 656	
6.	Jose Aldo vs. Chad Mendes 10/25 Rio de Janeiro (61): 569	
7.	Dan Henderson vs. Shogun Rua 3/23 Natal (2): 205	

8. Robbie Lawler vs. Matt Brown 7/26 San Jose : 122
9. Michael Chandler vs. Will Brooks 5/17 Memphis (21): 121
10. Jamie Varner vs. Abel Trujillo 2/1 Newark (2): 108

HONORABLE MENTION
T.J. Dillashaw vs. Renan Barao 5/24 Las Vegas 95

This was a list with UFC domination, as only one match, the Michael Chandler vs. Will Brooks PPV match from Bellator, cracked the top 11. Every match on the list was very good and it's all personal preference. In my opinion, timing of being last December greatly hurt Mark Hunt vs. Antonio Silva, which I think would have won or at least challenged for the top spot had it taken place a few months later. When I look at this list, to me the two best were Hunt vs. Silva and Aldo vs. Mendes. The surprise was Lawler vs. Brown, which I was at live and thought was a disappointment because Brown really never got his game going. Henderson vs. Rua had the great come-from-behind finish and was good, but I thought many bouts were better. Lawler vs. Hendricks was a fight I saw as a strong match of the year candidate. Brown vs. Erick Silva was more a blow-away fight with the Brown comeback from death and savage beating, but with Lawler-Hendricks it was a title fight with two guys putting on a great performance and the outcome was in doubt until late in the fifth round.

PREVIOUS WINNERS
1997 - Maurice Smith vs. Mark Coleman 7/27 Birmingham; 1998 - Jerry Bohlander vs. Kevin Jackson 3/13 New Orleans; 1999 - Frank Shamrock vs. Tito Ortiz 9/24 Lake Charles; 2000 - Kazushi Sakuraba vs. Royce Gracie 5/1 Tokyo Dome; 2001 - Randy Couture vs. Pedro Rizzo 5/4 Atlantic City; 2002 - Don Frye vs. Yoshihiro Takayama 6/23 Saitama; 2003 - Wanderlei Silva vs. Hidehiko Yoshida 11/9 Tokyo Dome; 2004 - Quinton Jackson vs. Wanderlei Silva 10/31 Saitama; 2005 - Forrest Griffin vs. Stephan Bonnar 4/9 Las Vegas; 2006 - Diego Sanchez vs. Karo Parisyan 8/17 Las Vegas; 2007 - Randy Couture vs. Tim Sylvia 3/3 Columbus; 2008 - Forrest Griffin vs. Quinton Jackson 7/5 Las Vegas; 2009 - Diego Sanchez vs. Clay Guida 6/20 Las Vegas; 2010 - Leonard Garcia vs. Chan Sung Jung 4/24 Sacramento; 2011 - Dan Henderson vs. Mauricio Shogun Rua 11/19 San Jose; 2012 - Chan Sung Jung vs. Dustin Poirier 5/15 Fairfax, VA; 2013 - Gilbert Melendez vs. Diego Sanchez 10/19 Houston

ROOKIE OF THE YEAR
1.	DRAGON LEE (190):	1,476
2.	Moose (142):	1,092
3.	Yuga Hayashi (145):	982
4.	Alexa Bliss (55):	927
5.	Cachorro (81):	910
6.	Australian Suicide (56):	550
7.	Ashley Remington (47):	396
8.	Black Panther (3):	378
9.	Chris Melendez (15):	152
10.	Naoya Nomura (2):	72

There were more good candidates, mostly out of Mexico, than most years. The second Dragon Lee was a solid winner, but Cachorro placing fifth was a complete miscarriage. At worst he should have been in the second spot. With his ability and being the son of Blue Panther, his future with his new name, The Panther, I see him as an almost sure-fire superstar for decades unless his ring style leads to early injuries that take him down.

PREVIOUS WINNERS
1981 - Brad Armstrong and Brad Rheingans (tied); 1982 - Steve Williams; 1983 - Road Warriors; 1984 - Tom Zenk and Keiichi Yamada (Jushin Liger) (tied); 1985 - Jack Victory; 1986 - Bam Bam Bigelow; 1987 - Brian Pillman; 1988 - Gary Albright; 1989 - Dustin Rhodes; 1990 - Steve Austin; 1991 - Johnny B. Badd (Marc Mero); 1992 - Rey Misterio Jr.; 1993 - Jun Akiyama; 1994 - Mikey Whipwreck; 1995 - Perro Aguayo Jr.; 1996 - The Giant (Paul "Big Show" Wight); 1997 - Mr. Aguila; 1998 - Bill Goldberg; 1999 - Blitzkrieg; 2000 - Sean O'Haire; 2001 - El Hombre sin Nombre (Rayman); 2002 - Bob Sapp; 2003 - Chris Sabin; 2004 - Petey Williams; 2005 - Shingo Takagi; 2006 - Atsushi Aoki; 2007 - Erick Stevens; 2008 - Kai; 2009 - Frightmare; 2010 - Adam Cole; 2011 - Daichi Hashimoto; 2012 - Dinastia; 2013 - Yohei Komatsu

BEST NON-WRESTLER
1.	PAUL HEYMAN (377):	2,336
2.	Stephanie McMahon (129):	1,103
3.	Lana (28):	987
4.	Bruce Tharpe (41):	524
5.	Dario Cueto (21):	334

6.	Konnan (9):	239
7.	Gedo (2):	163
8.	William Regal (1):	108
9.	Rockstar Spud (3):	105
10.	Maria Kanellis (2):	102

HONORABLE MENTION

Truth Martini 99, Zeb Colter 82, Veda Scott 70

Paul Heyman captured this category for the third straight year, and sixth time overall, although he probably won't be around long enough to tie Jim Cornette's 13 years winning between this and its previous manager of the year version. It was strong year for the category, with Stephanie McMahon and Lana being two of the best characters on WWE television, and the acting of Dario Cueto and Konnan on Lucha Underground being the best in the industry.

PREVIOUS WINNERS

1999 - Vince McMahon; 2000 - Vince McMahon; 2001 - Paul Heyman; 2002 - Paul Heyman; 2003 - Steve Austin; 2004 - Paul Heyman; 2005 - Eric Bischoff; 2006 - Jim Cornette; 2007 - Larry Sweeney; 2008 - Larry Sweeney; 2009 - Vickie Guerrero; 2010 - Vickie Guerrero; 2011 - Ricardo Rodriguez; 2012 - Paul Heyman; 2013 - Paul Heyman

BEST TELEVISION ANNOUNCER

1.	WILLIAM REGAL (192):	1,273
2.	Shimpei Nogami (170):	1,189
3.	Joe Rogan (109):	1,053
4.	Steve Corino (69):	745
5.	Brian Stann (127):	689
6.	Kevin Kelly (45):	608
7.	Mike Tenay (28):	316
8.	Matt Striker (8):	307
9.	Jimmy Smith (34):	261
10.	Mike Goldberg (7):	190

HONORABLE MENTION

Nigel McGuinness 161, Tom Phillips 145, Michael Schiavello 142, Jose Manuel Guillen 136, John Layfield 115, Renee Young 107, Hugo Savinovich 92, Michael Cole 86, Sean Wheelock 72, Jon Anik 71

This category is notable because there was no clear-cut winner, and the winner was someone taken off as an announcer months ago, and the guy who placed a close second was Japanese. Regal, born Darren Matthews, 46, was moved from the commentary booth to the figurehead commissioner role since the decision was made that NXT should be about grooming announcers for the future in WWE, and they simply don't think of Regal for that role. Given the state of WWE announcing, that's quite the debatable decision making, but it was the decision made. The other note is that if New Japan on AXS lasts more than 13 weeks, Mauro Ranallo, who got almost no votes here (he did some MMA, mostly Invicta, but his main work on television was boxing and kickboxing), may be the favorite for next year. And if Jim Ross continues to do New Japan big shows, he may also be a favorite. My own thought is Brian Stann should have finished higher, and Dan Hardy, due to a lack of television exposure, is underrated and the entire Fight Pass European team comes across like two guys you'd just like to sit and watch cool fights with, like they are your two buddies who know the sport, speak well, and you all learn together watching.

PREVIOUS WINNERS

1981 - Gordon Solie; 1982 - Gordon Solie; 1983 - Gordon Solie; 1984 - Lance Russell; 1985 - Lance Russell; 1986 - Lance Russell; 1987 - Lance Russell; 1988 - Jim Ross; 1989 - Jim Ross; 1990 - Jim Ross; 1991 - Jim Ross; 1992 - Jim Ross; 1993 - Jim Ross; 1994 - Joey Styles; 1995 - Joey Styles; 1996 - Joey Styles; 1997 - Mike Tenay; 1998 - Jim Ross; 1999 - Jim Ross; 2000 - Jim Ross; 2001 - Jim Ross; 2002 - Mike Tenay; 2003 - Mike Tenay; 2004 - Mike Tenay; 2005 - Mike Tenay; 2006 - Jim Ross; 2007 - Jim Ross; 2008 - Matt Striker; 2009 - Jim Ross; 2010 - Joe Rogan; 2011 - Joe Rogan; 2012 - Jim Ross; 2013 - William Regal

WORST TELEVISION ANNOUNCER

1.	JOHN LAYFIELD (165):	1,378
2.	Jerry Lawler (125):	1,287
3.	Michael Cole (146):	1,252
4.	Taz (36):	655
5.	Alex Riley (49):	399

6.	Vampiro (9):	288
7.	Matt Striker (33):	264
8.	Mike Tenay (4):	93
9.	Tom Phillips (8):	78
10.	Byron Saxton (4):	61

The theme here is that the three voices of Raw battled in a close race for worst, with John Layfield, 48, winning. This is more an indictment of the decision making as to what Raw announcing is supposed to be as much as the guys themselves. Lawler and Cole finished second and third last year behind Taz, who fell to a distant fourth, while Layfield moved from fifth to first. Layfield also placed third last year for best announcer, while falling out of the top ten this year. The problem was a combination of overexposure of himself for five hours a week, the job description from up top, and a very repetitive feeling product.

PREVIOUS WINNERS
1984 - Angelo Mosca; 1985 - Gorilla Monsoon; 1986 - David Crockett; 1987 - David Crockett; 1988 - David Crockett; 1989 - Ed Whalen; 1990 - Herb Abrams; 1991 - Gorilla Monsoon; 1992 - Gorilla Monsoon 1993 - Gorilla Monsoon; 1994 - Gorilla Monsoon; 1995 - Gorilla Monsoon; 1996 - Steve McMichael 1997 - Dusty Rhodes; 1998 - Lee Marshall; 1999 - Tony Schiavone; 2000 - Tony Schiavone; 2001 - Michael Cole; 2002 - Jerry Lawler; 2003 - Jonathan Coachman; 2004 - Todd Grisham; 2005 - Jonathan Coachman; 2006 - Todd Grisham; 2007 - Don West; 2008 - Mike Adamle; 2009 - Michael Cole; 2010 - Michael Cole; 2011 - Michael Cole; 2012 - Michael Cole; 2013 - Taz

BEST MAJOR WRESTLING SHOW
1.	NEW JAPAN G-1 8/1 TOKYO (313):	2,227
2.	New Japan G-1 8/3 Osaka (166):	1,297
3.	WWE WrestleMania 4/6 New Orleans (115):	920
4.	CMLL Anniversary show 9/19 Mexico City (49):	502
5.	New Japan G-1 7/26 Akita (8):	406
6.	New Japan G-1 finals 8/10 Tokorozawa (35):	402
7.	Dragon Gate Dead or Alive 5/5 Nagoya (23):	388
8.	UFC 168 12/28/13 Las Vegas (60):	347
9.	ROH 5/10 Toronto (16):	190
10.	WWE SummerSlam 8/17 Los Angeles (8):	166

HONORABLE MENTION:
ROH 5/17 New York 150, UFC Fight Night 7/19 Dublin 145, NXT Takeover 5/29 Winter Park, FL 117, New Japan Wrestle Kingdom 8 1/4 Tokyo Dome 106, UFC 175 7/5 Las Vegas 91, New Japan King of Pro Wrestling 10/13 Tokyo 85, New Japan G-1 Climax 7/21 Sapporo 82, UFC 178 9/27 Las Vegas 74

Like with Match of the Year, the dominance of New Japan almost worked against itself, as there were several PPV shows his year, as well as G-1 shows, that could have won this in other years, but got forgotten because of the number of great events. For all the negativity about wrestling, the number of great big shows, whether it be New Japan, WWE, NXT, AAA, CMLL, ROH or UFC is probably as much as anything ever. While wrestling styles change and differ, the production of shows as a general rule improves. While nothing touches the old Pride promotion in that regard, wrestling has evolved worldwide in presentation for the most part. Still, the G-1 shows that finished in four of the top six spots were just house shows with one phenomenal match after another. The 8/1 Korakuen Hall show was so great that four matches on the show would have had a shot at placing in match of the year if they had not been on such a loaded show. In all, there were five four-star or better matches with Hiroyoshi Tenzan vs. Hirooki Goto (****1/2), Tetsuya Naito vs. Togi Makabe (****1/4), A.J. Styles vs. Minoru Suzuki (****3/4 and the match of the year winner), Yuji Nagata vs. Katsuyori Shibata (****1/2) and Shinsuke Nakamura vs. Tomohiro Ishii (****3/4). Osaka was its closest competitor two days later, a show that included Ishii vs. Davey Boy Smith Jr. (****1/4), Goto vs. Naito (****14/), Suzuki vs. Makabe (****), Shibata vs. Honma (****3/4) and Tanahashi vs. Nakamura (****1/2). WrestleMania was the big show of the year which paid off with the Daniel Bryan storyline and his two matches were in the match of the year discussion. The CMLL anniversary show may have been better, because even though there were better matches in the ring, the start-to-finish presentation of Atlantis vs. Ultimo Guerrero was the pro wrestling highlight of 2014.

PREVIOUS WINNERS
1989 - WCW Great American Bash 7/23 Baltimore; 1990 - WWF/New Japan/All Japan U.S. and Japan Wrestling Summit 4/11 Tokyo; 1991 - WCW Wrestle War 2/24 Phoenix; 1992 - All Japan Women Wrestlemarinpiad 4/25 Yokohama; 1993 - All Japan Women Dream Slam I 4/2 Yokohama; 1994 - New Japan Super J Cup 4/16 Tokyo; 1995 - Weekly Pro Wrestling Multi-Promotional show 4/2 Tokyo; 1996 - WAR Super J Cup Second Stage 12/13/95 Tokyo; 1997 - WWF Canadian Stampede 7/16 Calgary; 1998 - ECW Heat Wave

8/2 Dayton; 1999 - ECW Anarchy Rulz 9/19 Chicago; 2000 - EMLL first PPV 3/17 Arena Mexico; 2001 - WWF WrestleMania X-7 4/1 Houston Astrodome; 2002 - WWE SummerSlam 8/25 New York Nassau Coliseum; 2003 - Pride Final Elimination 11/9 Tokyo Dome; 2004 - Pro Wrestling NOAH 7/10 Tokyo Dome; 2005 - Pro Wrestling NOAH Destiny 7/18 Tokyo Dome; 2006 - Ring of Honor Glory By Honor V 9/16 Manhattan Center; 2007 - ROH Man Up 9/15 Chicago; 2008 - WWE WrestleMania 25 3/30 Orlando; 2009 - Dragon Gate USA Open the Historical Gate 7/25 Philadelphia; 2010 - UFC 116 7/3 Las Vegas; 2011 - WWE Money in the Bank 7/17 Chicago; 2012 - New Japan Kings of Pro Wrestling 10/8 Tokyo; 2013 - New Japan G-1 Climax tournament 8/4 Osaka

CATEGORY B AWARDS

Winners determined by first placed votes.

WORST MAJOR WRESTLING SHOW

1.	WWE BATTLEGROUND 7/20 TAMPA :	275
2.	TNA Lockdown 3/9 Miami:	69
3.	WWE Royal Rumble 1/26 Pittsburgh:	42
4.	WWE Survivor Series 11/23 St. Louis:	40
5.	TNA Sacrifice 4/27 Orlando:	33
6.	WWE TLC 12/15/13 Houston:	26
7.	WWE Hell in a Cell 10/26 Dallas:	23
8.	UFC 177 8/30 Sacramento:	17
9.	WWE Night of Champions 9/21 Nashville:	12
10.	UFC 4/16 Quebec City:	9

PREVIOUS WINNERS

1989 - WrestleMania V 4/2 Atlantic City; 1990 - WCW Clash XII 11/20 Jacksonville; 1991 - WCW Great American Bash 7/14 Baltimore; 1992 - WCW Halloween Havoc 10/25 Philadelphia; 1993 - WCW Fall Brawl 9/19 Houston; 1994 - UWF Blackjack Brawl 9/25 Las Vegas; 1995 - WCW Uncensored 3/29 Tupelo; 1996 - WCW Uncensored 3/24 Tupelo; 1997 - WCW/NWO Souled Out 1/25 Cedar Rapids; 1998 - WCW Fall Brawl 9/13 Winston-Salem; 1999 - Heroes of Wrestling 10/10 Bay St. Louis; 2000 - WCW Halloween Havoc 10/29 Las Vegas; 2001 - WCW Unleashed 2/14 Los Angeles; 2002 - WWE King of the Ring 6/23 Columbus, OH; 2003 - WWE Backlash 4/27 Worcester; 2004 - WWE Great American Bash 7/27 Norfolk; 2005 - WWE Great American Bash 7/24 Buffalo; 2006 - UFC 61 7/8 Las Vegas; 2007 - WWE ECW December to Dismember 12/3/06 Augusta; 2008 - WWE Survivor Series 11/23 Boston; 2009 - TNA Victory Road 7/19 Orlando; 2010 - TNA Hardcore Justice 8/8 Orlando; 2011 - TNA Victory Road 3/13 Orlando; 2012 - UFC 149 7/21 Calgary; 2013 - WWE Battleground 10/6 Buffalo

BEST WRESTLING MANEUVER

1.	YOUNG BUCKS MELTZER DRIVER:	323
2.	Kazuchika Okada Rainmaker:	153
3.	Adrian Neville Red Arrow:	54
4.	Young Bucks More Bang for Your Buck:	46
5.	Sami Zayn tope into DDT:	19
=6.	Cavernario Barbaro splash off top to floor:	18
=6.	Seth Rollins curb stomp:	18
8.	Fish & O'Reilly Chasing the Dagon:	13

PREVIOUS WINNERS

1981 - Jimmy Snuka Superfly splash; 1982 - Super Destroyer (Scott Irwin) superplex; 1983 - Jimmy Snuka Superfly splash; 1984 - Davey Boy Smith power clean in combination with Dynamite Kid dropkick off the top rope; 1985 - Tiger Mask (Mitsuharu Misawa) tope con giro; 1986 - Chavo Guerrero Sr. moonsault block; 1987 - Jushin Liger shooting star press; 1988 - Jushin Liger shooting star press; 1989 - Scott Steiner Frankensteiner; 1990 - Scott Steiner Frankensteiner; 1991 - Masao Orihara moonsault off top rope to floor; 1992 - Too Cold Scorpio 450 splash; 1993 - Vader moonsault; 1994 - Great Sasuke Sasuke special; 1995 - Rey Misterio Jr. flip dive into Frankensteiner on floor; 1996 - Ultimo Dragon running Liger bomb; 1997 - Diamond Dallas Page diamond cutter; 1998 - Kenta Kobashi burning hammer; 1999 - Dragon Kid dragonrana; 2000 - Dragon Kid dragonrana; 2001 - Keiji Muto shining wizard; 2002 - Brock Lesnar F-5; 2003 - A.J. Styles clash; 2004 - Petey Williams Canadian Destroyer; 2005 - Petey Williams Canadian Destroyer; 2006 - KENTA Go 2 Sleep; 2007 - KENTA Go 2 Sleep; 2008 - Evan Bourne shooting star press; 2009 - Young Bucks More Bang for Your Buck; 2010 - Ricochet double rotation moonsault; 2011- Ricochet double rotation moonsault; 2012 - Kazuchika Okada rainmaker; 2013 - Kazuchika Okada rainmaker

MOST DISGUSTING PROMOTIONAL TACTIC

1.	WWE INSULTING FANS WHO PURCHASED PPVS:	65
2.	Dixie Carter tweeting a Storm is coming to Japan during a typhoon:	62

3.	TNA building TV for months around Dixie Carter table spot:	49
4.	WWE having Lana playoff of plane going down in The Ukraine	42
5.	WWE firing C.M. Punk on his wedding day:	33
6.	UFC hiring Thiago Silva and then having to fire him:	32
7.	WWE false advertising Rollins vs. Ambrose on PPV:	31
8.	CZW saying if Havok loses she has to give a blowjob to DJ Hyde:	28
9.	WWE botched U.K. network launch:	26
10.	WWE using Warrior's last Raw speech to promote network:	22

HONORABLE MENTION

WWE telling fans to chant "Yes" for a video for Daniel Bryan when it was really to splice it into a Vince McMahon speech on the network 21, WWE constant false advertising 18, WWE misleading stockholders on what they could get for network rights and what their fan base is 14, TNA lying to Spike TV on Vince Russo 13

PREVIOUS WINNERS

1981 - LeBelle promotions usage of The Monster claiming he was built in a laboratory; 1982 - Bob Backlund as WWF champion; 1983 - WWF pretending Eddie Gilbert had re-broken his neck after original legit injury in an auto accident; 1984 - Blackjack Mulligan fake heart attack by Championship Wrestling from Florida; 1985 - Usage of Mike Von Erich's near fatal illness to sell Cotton Bowl tickets by World Class; 1986 - Equating an angle of Chris Adams' blindness with the real death of Gino Hernandez; 1987 - World Class' handling of the death of Mike Von Erich; 1988 - Fritz Von Erich's fake brush with death; 1989 - Jose Gonzalez's babyface push by WWC; 1990 - Atsushi Onita stabbing angle with Jose Gonzalez; 1991 - WWF exploiting the Persian Gulf war; 1992 - WCW push of Erik Watts; 1993 - WCW Cactus Jack amnesia angle; 1994 - WCW retiring Ric Flair; 1995 - WCW Gene Okerlund 900 line come-ons and lies; 1996 - WWF teases and usage of fake Razor Ramon, Diesel and Double J; 1997 - WWF Melanie Pillman interview on Raw the day after Brian's death; 1998 - WCW exploiting Scott Hall's drinking problems for angles; 1999 - WWF continuing Over the Edge PPV after the death of Owen Hart; 2000 - WCW making David Arquette world champion; 2001 - Stephanie McMahon interview on 9/13 TV equating the bombing of the World Trade Center to her father's steroid trial; 2002 - WWE Katie Vick necrophilia angle; 2003 - McMahon family all over television; 2004 - Kane/Lita pregnancy/wedding/miscarriage angle; 2005 - WWE not editing off the show its terrorists angle the day of bombing in England; 2006 - WWE exploiting the death of Eddy Guerrero; 2007 - TNA signing Pacman Jones and having him do the Making it Rain on television when his doing that at a strip club led to the paralysis of a wrestler; 2008 - WWE teasing a Jeff Hardy drug overdose on the Internet to try and garner late interest in a PPV show; 2009 - WWE Piggy James angle making fun of Mickie James' weight; 2010 - Stand up for WWE campaign; 2011 - WWE Anti-bullying message when they preach on television exactly what they don't practice on television; 2012 - WWE presentation of C.M. Punk and Paul Heyman exploiting Jerry Lawler's heart attack, as well as airing clips of him being worked on and playing up footage of him near death; 2013 - WWE exploiting the death of Bill Moody

WORST TELEVISION SHOW

1.	WWE RAW:	283
2.	TNA Impact:	168
3.	WWE Smackdown:	77
4.	Championship Wrestling from Hollywood:	8

PREVIOUS WINNERS

1984 - WWF All-Star Wrestling; 1985 - Championship Wrestling from Florida; 1986 - California Championship Wrestling; 1987 - World Class Championship Wrestling; 1988 - AWA on ESPN; 1989 - ICW Wrestling; 1990 - AWA on ESPN; 1991 - Herb Abrams' UWF; 1992 - Global Wrestling Federation on ESPN; 1993 - Global Wrestling Federation on ESPN; 1994 - WCW Saturday Night; 1995 - WCW Saturday Night; 1996 - AWF Warriors of Wrestling; 1997 - USWA; 1998 - WCW Nitro; 1999 - WCW Thunder; 2000 - WCW Thunder; 2001 - WWF Excess; 2002 - WWE Raw; 2003 - WWE Raw; 2004 - WWE Smackdown; 2005 - WWE Smackdown; 2006 - WWE Raw; 2007 - TNA Impact; 2008 - TNA Impact; 2009 - TNA Impact; 2010 - TNA Impact; 2011 - TNA Impact; 2012 - WWE Raw; 2013 - TNA Impact

WORST MATCH OF THE YEAR

1.	JOHN CENA VS. BRAY WYATT 5/4 EXTREME RULES EAST RUTHERFORD, NJ:	122
2.	Sakuraba & Nagata vs. Gracies 1/4 Tokyo:	89
3.	Naomi vs. Cameron 9/15 Lafayette:	39
4.	Divas Survivor Series match 11/23 St. Louis:	34
5.	Eva Marie vs. Bayley 7/17 Winter Park, FL:	25
6.	Samuel Shaw vs. Ken Anderson 4/27 Orlando:	22
7.	A.J. Lee vs. Cameron 2/23 Minneapolis:	20
8.	Aksana vs. Naomi 2/3 Omaha:	19

9.	A.J. Lee vs. Nikki Bella 11/23 St. Louis:	16
10.	Layla vs. Summer Rae 6/29 Boston:	14

HONORABLE MENTION
Undertaker vs. Brock Lesnar 4/6 New Orleans 13, Batista vs. Alberto Del Rio 2/23 Minneapolis 11, Gracies vs. Takashi Iizuka & Toru Yano 4/6 Tokyo 11

PREVIOUS WINNERS
1984 - Fabulous Moolah vs. Wendi Richter 7/23 New York Madison Square Garden; 1985 - Fred Blassie vs. Lou Albano Nassau Coliseum; 1986 - Roddy Piper vs. Mr. T 4/2 Nassau Coliseum; 1987 - Hulk Hogan vs. Andre the Giant 3/29 Pontiac; 1988 - Hiroshi Wajima vs. Tom Magee 4/21 Kawasaki; 1989 - Andre the Giant vs. Ultimate Warrior 10/31 Topeka; 1990 - Sid Vicious vs. Night Stalker (Bryan Clark) 11/20 Jacksonville; 1991 - P.N. News & Bobby Eaton vs. Terry Taylor & Steve Austin scaffold match 7/14 - Baltimore; 1992 - Rick Rude vs. Masahiro Chono 10/25 Philadelphia; 1993 - Four Doinks (Bushwhackers & Men on a Mission) vs. Bam Bam Bigelow & Head Shrinkers & Bastion Booger (Mike Shaw); 1994 - Jerry Lawler & Queasy & Sleazy & Cheesy vs. Doink the Clown & Dink & Wink & Pink 11/23 San Antonio; 1995 - Sting vs. Tony Palmore 1/4 Tokyo Dome; 1996 - Hulk Hogan & Randy Savage vs. Ric Flair & Arn Anderson & Meng & Barbarian & Kevin Sullivan & Ze Gangsta (Tiny Lister) & Ultimate Solution (Jeep Swenson) & Lex Luger 3/24 Tupelo; 1997 - Hulk Hogan vs. Roddy Piper 10/26 Las Vegas; 1998 - Hulk Hogan vs. Warrior 10/24 Las Vegas; 1999 - Al Snow vs. Big Bossman Kennel from Hell 9/26 Charlotte; 2000 - Pat Patterson vs. Gerald Brisco evening gown match 6/25 Boston; 2001 - Undertaker & Kane vs. Kronik (Brian Adams & Bryan Clark) 9/23 Pittsburgh; 2002 - Bradshaw & Trish Stratus vs. Christopher Nowinski & Jackie Gayda 7/8 Philadelphia; 2003 - HHH vs. Scott Steiner 1/19 Boston; 2004 - Steven Richards vs. Tyson Tomko 9/12 Portland; 2005 - Eric Bischoff vs. Teddy Long 11/27 Detroit; 2006 - TNA Reverse Battle Royal 10/24 Orlando; 2007 - Chris Harris vs. James Storm 4/15 St. Charles, MO blindfold match; 2008 - HHH vs. Edge vs. Vladimir Kozlov 11/23 Boston; 2009 - Sharmell vs. Jenna Morasca 7/19 Orlando; 2010 - Kaitlyn vs. Maxine 10/19 Edmonton; 2011 - Sting vs. Jeff Hardy 3/13 Orlando; 2012 - John Cena vs. John Laurinaitis 5/20 Raleigh; 2013 - Natalya & Naomi & Cameron & Bella Twins & Jo Jo & Eva Marie vs. Alicia Fox & Aksana & A.J. Lee & Tamina Snuka & Rosa Mendes & Kaitlyn & Summer Rae 11/24 Boston

WORST FEUD OF THE YEAR

1.	NIKKI BELLA VS. BRIE BELLA:	299
2.	Minoru Suzuki vs. Toru Yano:	50
3.	John Cena vs. Bray Wyatt:	42
4.	Samuel Shaw vs. Ken Anderson:	38
5.	Daniel Bryan vs. Kane:	37
6.	Bully Ray vs. Dixie Carter:	26
=7.	Fandango vs. Summer Rae & Layla:	13
=7.	Adam Rose vs. The Bunny:	13
=9.	Mark Henry vs. Big Show:	12
=9.	Samuel Shaw vs. Gunner:	12

PREVIOUS WINNERS
1984 - Andre the Giant vs. John Studd; 1985 - Sgt. Slaughter vs. Boris Zhukov; 1986 - Machines (Andre the Giant & Bill Eadie) vs. King Kong Bundy & John Studd; 1987 - George Steele vs. Danny Davis; 1988 - Midnight Rider (Dusty Rhodes) vs. Tully Blanchard; 1989 - Andre the Giant vs. Ultimate Warrior; 1990 - Ric Flair vs. Junkyard Dog; 1991 - Hulk Hogan vs. Sgt. Slaughter; 1992 - Ultimate Warrior vs. Papa Shango; 1993 - Undertaker vs. Giant Gonzalez; 1994 - Jerry Lawler vs. Doink the Clown; 1995 - Hulk Hogan vs. Dungeon of Doom; 1996 - Big Bossman vs. John Tenta; 1997 - DOA vs. Los Boricuas; 1998 - Hulk Hogan vs. Warrior; 1999 - Big Bossman vs. Big Show; 2000 - Hulk Hogan vs. Billy Kidman; 2001 - WWF vs. The Alliance; 2002 - HHH vs. Kane; 2003 - Shane McMahon vs. Kane; 2004 - Kane vs. Lita & Matt Hardy; 2005 - McMahon Family vs. Jim Ross; 2006 - DX vs. McMahons; 2007 - Kane vs. Big Daddy V; 2008 - Rey Mysterio vs. Kane; 2009 - Chavo Guerrero vs. Hornswoggle; 2010 - Edge vs. Kane; 2011 - HHH vs. Kevin Nash; 2012 - John Cena vs. Kane; 2013 - Big Show vs. The Authority

WORST PROMOTION

1.	TOTAL NONSTOP ACTION:	438
2.	World Wrestling Entertainment:	125
3	CHIKARA Pro:	17

PREVIOUS WINNERS
1986 - AWA; 1987 - World Class Championship Wrestling; 1988 - AWA; 1989 - AWA; 1990 - AWA; 1991 - Herb Abrams UWF; 1992 - Global Wrestling Federation; 1993 - WCW; 1994 - WCW; 1995 - WCW; 1996 - AWF; 1997 - USWA; 1998 - WCW; 1999 - WCW; 2000 - WCW; 2001 - WCW; 2002 - XPW; 2003 - World Japan; 2004 - New Japan Pro Wrestling; 2005 - New Japan Pro Wrestling; 2006 - World Wrestling Entertainment; 2007 - Total Nonstop Action; 2008 - Total Nonstop Action; 2009 - Total Nonstop Action; 2010 -

Total Nonstop Action; 2011 - Total Nonstop Action; 2012 - Total Nonstop Action; 2013 - Total Nonstop Action

BEST BOOKER

1.	GEDO & JADO:	611
2.	Genki Horiguchi:	55
3.	Paul Levesque/Ryan Ward:	54
4.	Joe Silva:	53
5.	Hunter Johnston:	51

PREVIOUS WINNERS

1986 - Dusty Rhodes; 1987 - Vince McMahon; 1988 - Eddie Gilbert; 1989 - Shohei Baba; 1990 - Shohei Baba; 1991 - Shohei Baba; 1992 - Riki Choshu; 1993 - Jim Cornette; 1994 - Paul Heyman; 1995 - Paul Heyman; 1996 - Paul Heyman; 1997 - Paul Heyman; 1998 - Vince McMahon; 1999 - Vince McMahon; 2000 - Vince McMahon; 2001 - Jim Cornette; 2002 - Paul Heyman; 2003 - Jim Cornette; 2004 - Gabe Sapolsky; 2005 - Gabe Sapolsky; 2006 - Gabe Sapolsky; 2007 - Gabe Sapolsky; 2008 - Joe Silva; 2009 - Joe Silva; 2010 - Joe Silva; 2011 - Gedo & Jado; 2012 - Gedo & Jado; 2013 - Gedo & Jado

PROMOTER OF THE YEAR

1.	TAKAAKI KIDANI:	602
2.	Dana White:	190
3.	Scott Coker:	47
4.	Vince McMahon:	21
5.	Joe Koff:	12
=6.	Sanshiro Takagi:	11
=6.	Roldan Family:	11

PREVIOUS WINNERS

1988 - Vince McMahon; 1989 - Akira Maeda; 1990 - Shohei Baba; 1991 - Shohei Baba; 1992 - Shohei Baba; 1993 - Shohei Baba; 1994 - Shohei Baba; 1995 - Riki Choshu; 1996 - Riki Choshu; 1997 - Riki Choshu; 1998 - Vince McMahon; 1999 - Vince McMahon; 2000 - Vince McMahon; 2001 - Antonio Inoki; 2002 - Kazuyoshi Ishii; 2003 - Nobuyuki Sakakibara; 2004 - Nobuyuki Sakakibara; 2005 - Dana White; 2006 - Dana White; 2007 - Dana White; 2008 - Dana White; 2009 - Dana White; 2010 - Dana White; 2011 - Dana White; 2012 - Dana White; 2013 - Dana White

BEST GIMMICK

1.	RUSEV & LANA:	131
2.	The Bullet Club:	88
3.	Yosuke Santa Maria:	78
4.	Damien Mizdow:	72
5.	Shinsuke Nakamura:	68
6.	Dean Ambrose:	37
7.	Tyson Kidd:	33
8.	Rockstar Spud:	14
9.	Brock Lesnar:	13

PREVIOUS WINNERS

1986 - Exotic Adrian Street; 1987 - Ted DiBiase Million Dollar Man; 1988 - Rick Steiner Varsity Club; 1989 - Jushin Liger; 1990 - The Undertaker; 1991 - The Undertaker; 1992 - The Undertaker; 1993 - The Undertaker; 1994 - The Undertaker; 1995 - Disco Inferno; 1996 - NWO; 1997 - Stone Cold Steve Austin; 1998 - Stone Cold Steve Austin; 1999 - The Rock; 2000 - Kurt Angle; 2001 - Hurricane; 2002 - Mattitude; 2003 - John Cena as a rapper; 2004 - JBL; 2005 - Mr. Kennedy; 2006 - Latin American Exchange; 2007 - Santino Marella; 2008 - Santino Marella; 2009 - C.M. Punk Straight Edge Society; 2010 - Alberto Del Rio; 2011 - C.M. Punk; 2012 - Joseph Park; 2013 - The Wyatt Family

WORST GIMMICK

1.	ADAM ROSE:	140
2.	Samuel Shaw:	82
3.	The Bunny:	58
4.	Corporate Kane:	49
5.	Bray Wyatt:	40
6.	The Menagerie:	36

7.	The Authority:	33
8.	Dixie Carter as heel owner:	25
9.	C.J. Parker:	20
10.	New Day:	17

PREVIOUS WINNERS

1986 - Adorable Adrian Adonis; 1987 - Adorable Adrian Adonis; 1988 - Midnight Rider (Dusty Rhodes); 1989 - Ding Dongs; 1990 - Gobbledy Gooker; 1991 - Oz (Kevin Nash); 1992 - Papa Shango; 1993 - Shock Master (Fred Ottman); 1994 - Dave Sullivan; 1995 - Goldust; 1996 - New Razor Ramon, New Diesel and New Double J; 1997 - New Goldust; 1998 - Oddities; 1999 - Powers that Be; 2000 - Mike Awesome That 70s Guy; 2001 - Diamond Dallas Page Bob Patterson gimmick; 2002 - Richard & Rod Johnson as giant penises; 2003 - Rico; 2004 - Mordecai; 2005 - Jillian Hall as Mole Girl; 2006 - Vito as the toughest guy in a dress; 2007 - Black Reign; 2008 - Great Khali kiss cam; 2009 - Hornswoggle; 2010 - Orlando Jordan; 2011 - Michael Cole heel announcer; 2012 - Aces and 8s; 2013 - Aces and 8s

BEST PRO WRESTLING BOOK

1.	DEATH OF WCW BY BRYAN ALVAREZ & R.D. REYNOLDS:	257
2.	The Best in the World At What I have No Idea/Chris Jericho:	135
3.	Bluegrass Brawlers: The Story of Professional Wrestling in Louisville/John Cosper:	18
4.	Is this Legal/Art Davie/Sean Wheelock:	16
5.	Memphis Wrestling 1977/Mark James:	12

PREVIOUS WINNERS

2005 - Death of WCW by Bryan Alvarez and R.D. Reynolds; 2006 - Tangled Ropes by Superstar Billy Graham and Keith Greenberg; 2007 - Hitman by Bret Hart and Marcy Engelstein; 2008 - Gorgeous George by John Capouya; 2009 - Midnight Express 25th Anniversary Scrapbook by Jim Cornette; 2010 - Countdown to Lockdown by Mick Foley; 2011 - Undisputed by Chris Jericho; 2012 - Shooters by Jonathan Snowden; 2013 - Mad Dogs, Midgets and Screwjobs by Patric Laprade and Bertrand Hebert

BEST PRO WRESTLING DVD

1.	LADIES AND GENTLEMAN, MY NAME IS PAUL HEYMAN:	381
2.	Macho Man: The Randy Savage Story :	52
3.	Wrestling Road Diaries II:	9

PREVIOUS WINNERS

2005 - Rise and Fall of ECW; 2006 - The Bret Hart Story; 2007 - Ric Flair and the Four Horsemen; 2008 - Ric Flair Definitive Collection; 2009 - Macho Madness; 2010 - Chris Jericho Breaking the Code; 2011 - Bret Hart vs. Shawn Michaels; 2012 - C.M. Punk Best in the World; 2013 - Jim Crockett Promotions the Good Old Days